SECOND CENSUS OF THE UNITED STATES 1800

VERMONT

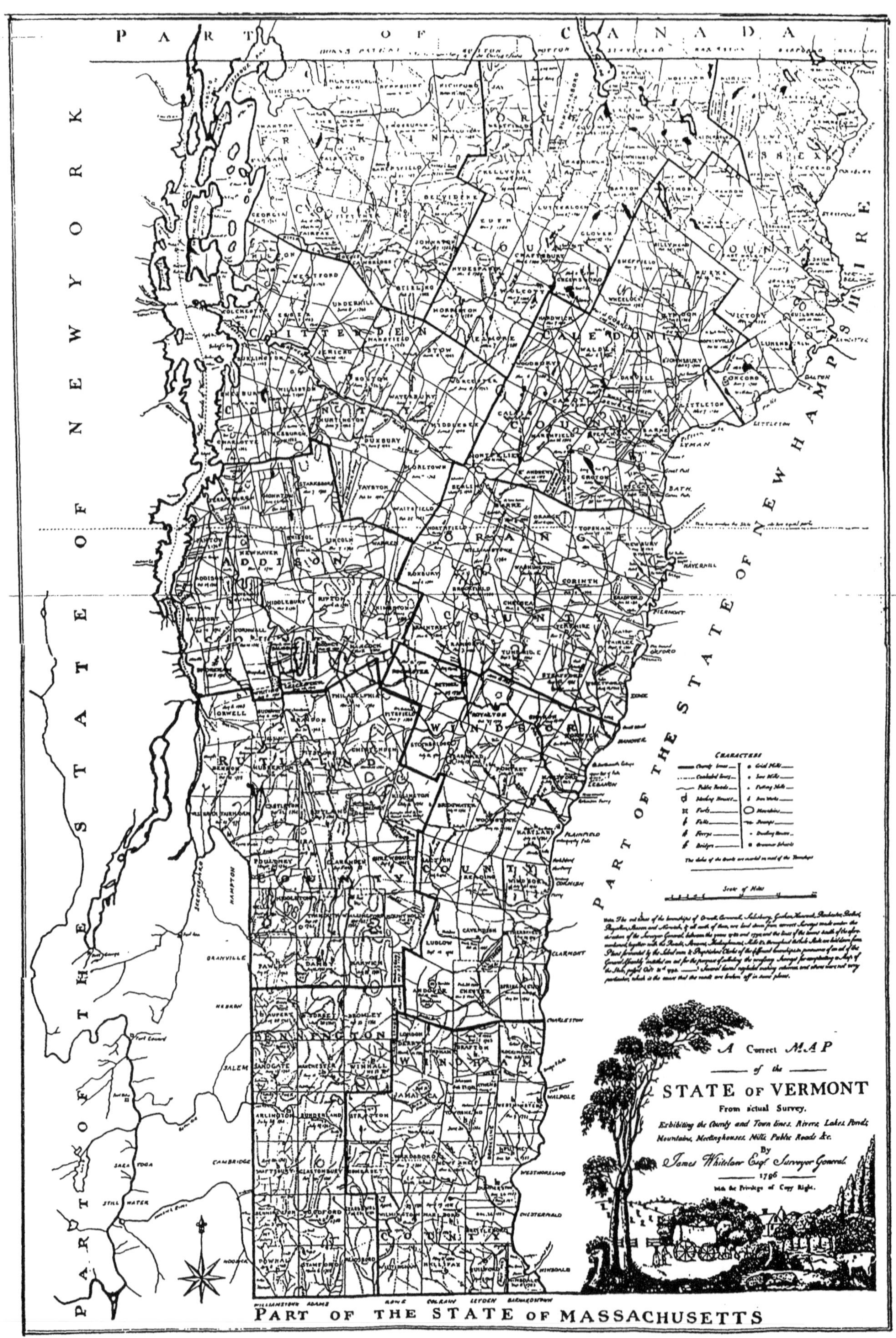
PART OF CANADA
PART OF THE STATE OF NEW YORK
PART OF THE STATE OF NEW HAMPSHIRE
PART OF THE STATE OF MASSACHUSETTS
A Correct MAP of the STATE OF VERMONT
From actual Survey.
Exhibiting the County and Town lines, Rivers, Lakes, Ponds, Mountains, Meetinghouses, Mills, Public Roads &c.
By
James Whitelaw Esqr. Surveyor General.
1796
With the Privilege of Copy Right.
CHARACTERS
Scale of Miles
FRANKLIN COUNTY
ORLEANS COUNTY
ESSEX COUNTY
CHITTENDEN COUNTY
CALEDONIA COUNTY
ADDISON COUNTY
ORANGE COUNTY
RUTLAND COUNTY
WINDSOR COUNTY
BENNINGTON COUNTY
WINDHAM COUNTY
HAVERHILL
CLARMONT
CHARLESTOWN
WALPOLE
WESTMORELAND
CHESTERFIELD
HINSDALE
CAMBRIDGE
SALEM
GRANVILLE
HEBRON
HAMPTON
SARATOGA
STILL WATER

HEADS OF FAMILIES

AT THE SECOND CENSUS OF THE UNITED STATES TAKEN IN THE YEAR

1800

VERMONT

CLEARFIELD

Originally Published by the
Vermont Historical Society
Montpelier, 1938

Reprinted with Permission
Genealogical Publishing Company
Baltimore, 1972

Reprinted for
Clearfield Company, Inc. by
Genealogical Publishing Co., Inc.
Baltimore, Maryland
1992, 1995, 2000, 2004

Library of Congress Cataloging in Publication Data

U. S. Census Office. 2d census, 1800.

Heads of families at the second census of the United States taken in the year 1800: Vermont.

Reprint of the 1938 ed.

1. Vermont—Census, 1800. 2. Vermont—Genealogy. I. Title.
F48.A43 1972 929.3 71-39493
ISBN 0-8063-0503-7

Made in the United States of America

THE UNITED STATES CENSUS

The United States Census was first taken in 1790 and it has been taken each decade since, ending in 1930. The enumerated population in 1790 was 3,929,214 and in 1930 it was 122,775,046.

As this foreward has to do mainly with the census of 1790 and 1800 it will treat only on the results of the investigation in those two years. In 1790 the census was taken in the following States: Connecticut, Delaware, Georgia, Kentucky, Maine, Maryland, Massachusetts, New Hampshire, New Jersey, New York, North Carolina, Tennessee, Pennsylvania, Rhode Island, South Carolina, Vermont, and Virginia.

The census of 1800 included the States just mentioned and the following: Indiana, Mississippi, Ohio, and the District of Columbia.

The act providing for the 1790 census was approved March 1, 1790, to commence the coming August, but subsequent legislation extended the enumeration of Vermont and Rhode Island to commence in April, 1791 and it was finished in that year.

An Act of Congress of February 28, 1800 approved the second census. It began in August and was not completed until into the year 1801.

With no further comment concerning the census of 1790, the American Philosophical Society in a memorial signed by its President, Thomas Jefferson, and the Connecticut Academy of Arts and Sciences in a memorial signed by its President, Timothy Dwight, asked of the Senate early in 1800 that much further information be gathered than appeared in the first census. These memorials were referred by the Senate to a committee to whom a preparation of the census law had already been intrusted. The committee apparently made no report on the matter, and nothing came of it.

The information gathered was the names of the heads of families, and the number of free white males and free white females in five sections, under 10 years of age, of 10 and under 16, of 16 and under 26, of 26 and under 45, and of 45 years and upward; the number of all other free persons, except Indians not taxed, and the number of slaves. In 1800 there were no slaves in Vermont.

The Vermont Census of 1790 was published in 1907 under the Department of Commerce and Labor. The 1800 Census has never been printed. The returned sheets in the handwriting of the enumerators are in the Government's possession at Washington, and some years ago, following the generous offer of Mortimer R. Proctor of Proctor, Vermont, the Government allowed photostats made of all the sheets. It was done and the photostats are in the possession of the Vermont Historical Society at Montpelier, Vermont.

In 1929 the contents of all those sheets was typed and carefully compared and from 1930 to 1937 the typed manuscript awaited further action. Then the Vermont Historical Society voted an index be made, the 1800 Census of Vermont be published, and the consent of the Government has been given.

The original work was done long ago, by several different men. Some wrote well, some wrote hastily and poorly, some were careless in the spelling of names, others were quite the reverse and in some cases the names, either sur, or given, are illegible. Such cases have been referred to people at the Vermont State House versed in reading old and new handwriting and they have deciphered many. Those remaining have been looked for in town histories, gazetteers, genealogies and other printed books and the final result leaves comparatively few which cannot be read.

Those are printed at the end of the family names in each town in which they occur.

The work has all been under the direction of Dorman B. E. Kent and his son Richard H. Kent has performed the major portion of the labor.

AN ACT PROVIDING FOR THE SECOND CENSUS, OR ENUMERATION, OF THE INHABITANTS OF THE UNITED STATES, APPROVED FEBRUARY 28, 1800

SECTION 1. Be it enacted by the senate and house of representatives of the United States of America in congress assembled, That the marshals of the several districts of the United States, and the secretaries of the territory of the United States northwest of the river Ohio, and of the Mississippi territory, respectively, shall be and they are hereby, authorized and required, under the direction of the secretary of state, and according to such instructions as he shall give pursuant to this act, to cause the number of the inhabitants within their respective districts and territories to be taken; omitting in such enumeration, Indians not taxed, and distinguishing free persons, including those bound to service for a term of years, from all others; distinguishing also the sexes and colors of free persons, and the free males, under ten years of age; those of ten years and under sixteen, those of sixteen and under twenty-six, those of twenty-six and under forty-five, those of forty-five and upwards. And distinguishing free females under ten years of age, those of ten years and under sixteen, those of sixteen and under twenty-six, those of twenty-six and under forty-five, those of forty-five and upwards; for effecting which purpose, the marshals and secretaries aforesaid shall have power to appoint as many assistants, within their respective districts and territories, as aforesaid, as to them shall appear necessary; assigning to each assistant a certain division of his district or territory, which division shall consist of one or more counties, cities, towns, townships, hundreds or parishes, or of a territory plainly and distinctly bounded by water courses, mountains or public roads: The marshals, or secretaries, as the case may be, and their assistants, shall, respectively, take an oath or affirmation, before some judge or justice of the peace, resident within their respective districts or territories, previous to their entering on the discharge of the duties by this act required. The oath or affirmation of the marshal or secretary shall be: "I, A B, marshal of the district of ______________ (or secretary of the territory of ______________ as the case may be) do solemnly swear, or affirm, that I will, well and truly, cause to be made, a just and perfect enumeration and description of all persons resident within my district or territory, and return the same to the secretary of state, agreeably to the direction of an act of congress, entitled 'An act providing for the enumeration of the inhabitants of the United States,' according to the best of my ability." The oath of affirmation of an assistant shall be: "I, A B, do solemnly swear (or affirm) that I will make a just and perfect enumeration and description of all persons resident within the division assigned to me by the marshal of the district of ______________ (or the secretary of the territory of ______________ as the case may be) and make due return thereof to the said marshal, or secretary, agreeably to the directions of an act of congress entitled 'An act providing for the enumeration of the inhabitants of the United States,' according to the best of my abilities." The enumeration shall commence on the first Monday of August next, and shall close within nine calendar months thereafter. The several assistants shall, within the said nine months, transmit to the marshal or secretaries, by whom they shall be respectively appointed, accurate returns of all persons, except Indians not taxed, within their respective divisions; which returns shall be made in a schedule, distinguishing, in each county, parish, township, town, or city, the several families, by the names of their master, mistress, steward, overseer, or other principal person therein, in the manner following, that is to say: The number of persons within my division, consisting of ______________ appears in a schedule hereto annexed, subscribed by me, this ______________ day of ______________.

A B, assistant to the marshal of ______________
or to the secretary of ______________

Schedule of the whole number of persons within the division allotted to A B.

Name of county, parish, township, town, or city, where the family resides.
Name of head of family.
Free white males, under ten years of age.
Free white males, of ten and under sixteen.
Free white males, of sixteen and under twenty-six, including heads of families.
Free white males, of twenty-six and under forty-five, including heads of families.
Free white males, of forty-five and upwards, including heads of families.
Free white females, under ten years of age.
Free white females, of ten years and under sixteen.
Free white females, of sixteen and under twenty-six, including heads of families.
Free white females, of twenty-six and under forty-five, including heads of families.
Free white females, of forty-five and upwards, including heads of families.
All other free persons, except Indians not taxed.
Slaves.

SECTION 2. And be it further enacted, That every assistant, failing to make a proper return, or making a false return, of the enumeration, to the marshal, or the secretary, (as the case may be) within the time by this act limited, shall forfeit the sum of two hundred dollars.

SECTION 3. And be it further enacted, That the marshal and secretaries shall file the several returns aforesaid, with the clerks of their respective district or superior courts, (as the case may be) who are hereby directed to receive and carefully preserve the same: And the marshals, or secretaries, respectively, shall, on or before the first day of September, one thousand eight hundred and one, transmit to the secretary of state the aggregate amount of each description of persons within their respective districts or territories. And every marshal or secretary failing to file the returns of his assistants, or any of them, with the clerks of their respective courts, as aforesaid, or failing to return the aggregate amount of each description of persons in their respective districts or territories, as the same shall appear from said returns, to the secretary of state, within the time limited by this act, shall, for every such offence, forfeit the sum of eight hundred dollars; all which forfeitures shall be recoverable in the courts of the districts or territories where the offences shall be committed, or in the circuit courts to be held within the same, by action of debt, information, or indictment; the one-half thereof to the use of the United States, and the other half to the informer; but where the prosecution shall be first instituted on behalf of the United States; the whole shall accrue to their use. And for the more effectual discovery of offences, the judges of the several district courts in the several districts, and of the supreme courts in the territories of the United States, as aforesaid, at their next sessions, to be held after the expiration

SECOND CENSUS ACT

of the time allowed for making the returns of the enumeration hereby directed, to the secretary of state, shall give this act in charge to the grand juries, in their respective courts, and shall cause the returns of the several assistants to be laid before them for their inspection.

SECTION 4. And be it further enacted, That every assistant shall receive at the rate of one dollar for every hundred persons by him returned, where such persons reside in the country; and where such persons reside in a city or town, containing more than three thousand persons, such assistant shall receive at the rate of one dollar for every three hundred persons; but where, from the dispersed situation of the inhabitants in some divisions, one dollar for every one hundred persons shall be insufficient, the marshals or secretaries, with the approbation of the judges of their respective districts or territories, may make such further allowance to the assistant in such divisions, as shall be deemed an adequate compensation: Provided, The same does not exceed one dollar for every fifty persons by them returned. The several marshals and secretaries shall receive as follows: The marshal of the district of Maine, two hundred dollars; the marshal of the district of New Hampshire, two hundred dollars; the marshal of the district of Massachusetts, three hundred dollars; the marshal of the district of Rhode Island, one hundred and fifty dollars; the marshal of the district of Connecticut, two hundred dollars; the marshal of the district of Vermont, two hundred dollars; the marshal of the district of New York, three hundred dollars; the marshal of the district of New Jersey, two hundred dollars; the marshal of the district of Pennsylvania, three hundred dollars; the marshal of the district of Delaware, one hundred dollars; the marshal of the district of Maryland, three hundred dollars; the marshal of the district of Virginia, five hundred dollars; the marshal of the district of Kentucky, two hundred and fifty dollars; the marshal of the district of North Carolina, three hundred and fifty dollars; the marshal of the district of South Carolina, three hundred dollars; the marshal of the district of Georgia, two hundred and fifty dollars; the marshal of the district of Tennessee, two hundred dollars; the secretary of the territory of the United States northwest of the Ohio, two hundred dollars; the secretary of the Mississippi territory, one hundred dollars.

SECTION 5. And be it further enacted, That every person whose usual place of abode shall be in any family on the aforesaid first Monday in August next, shall be returned as of such family, and the name of every person, who shall be an inhabitant of any district or territory, but without a settled place of residence, shall be inserted in the column of the aforesaid schedule, which is allotted for the heads of families in that division where he or she shall be on the said first Monday in August next, and every person occasionally absent at the time of the enumeration, as belonging to that place in which he or she usually resides in the United States.

SECTION 6. And be it further enacted, That each and every free person, more than sixteen years of age, whether heads of families or not, belonging to any family within any division, district, or territory, made or established within the United States, shall be, and hereby is, obliged to render, to such assistant of the division, a true account, if required, to the best of his or her knowledge, of all and every person belonging to such family, respectively, according to the several descriptions aforesaid, on pain of forfeiting twenty dollars, to be sued for and recovered by such assistant, the one-half for his own use, and the other half to the use of the United States.

SECTION 7. And be it further enacted, That each assistant shall, previous to making his returns to the marshal or secretary, (as the case may be,) cause a correct copy, signed by himself, of the schedule, containing the number of inhabitants within his division, to be set up at two of the most public places within the same, there to remain for the inspection of all concerned, for each of which copies the said assistant shall be entitled to receive two dollars; Provided, proof of the schedule having been so set up, and suffered to remain, shall be transmitted to the marshal or secretary, (as the case may be,) with the return of the number of the persons; and in case any assistant shall fail to make such proof to the marshal or secretary, as aforesaid, he shall forfeit the compensation by this act allowed him.

SECTION 8. And be it further enacted, That the secretary of state shall be, and hereby is, authorized and required to transmit to the marshals of the several states, and to the secretaries aforesaid, regulations and instructions, pursuant to this act, for carrying the same into effect, and also the forms contained therein of schedule to be returned, and proper interrogatories, to be administered by the several persons who shall be employed therein. (Approved, February 28, 1800.)

SUMMARY OF POPULATION BY COUNTIES AND TOWNS—1800.

Number of Heads of Families

ADDISON COUNTY

Addison	136
Bridport	188
Bristol	118
Cornwall	188
Ferrisburgh	257
Goshen	1
Hancock	28
Kingston	32
Leicester	96
Lincoln	19
Middlebury	212
Monkton	153
Newhaven	199
Panton	63
Ripton	*Not Inhabited*
Salisbury	111
Shoreham	254
Starksboro	71
Vergennes	91
Waltham	39
Warren	11
Weybridge	84
Whiting	73

BENNINGTON COUNTY

Arlington	255
Bennington	380
Bromley	22
Dorset	207
Glastenbury	8
Landgrove	26
Manchester	222
Pownal	284
Readsboro	45
Rupert	256
Sandgate	178
Searsburg	*Not Inhabited*
Shaftsbury	292
Stamford	67
Sunderland	97
Winhall	11
Woodford	27

CALEDONIA COUNTY

Barnet	150
Billymead	26
Burke	22
Cabot	61
Calais	74
Danville	232
Dewey's Gore	26
Groton	37
Hardwick	52
Harris Gore	*Not Inhabited*
Hopkinville	3
Lyndon	94
Marshfield	29
Montpelier	150
Peacham	37
Plainfield	45
Ryegate	69
Sheffield	29
St. Johnsbury	99
Walden	26
Waterford	106
Wheelock	97
Woodbury	5

CHITTENDEN COUNTY

Bolton	34
Burlington	125
Charlotte	197
Colchester	65
Duxbury	32
Essex	135
Fayston	5
Hinesburgh	155
Huntington	66
Jericho	121
Mansfield	1
Middlesex	46
Milton	143
Moretown	32
Richmond	107
Shelburne	118
Stowe	46
Underhill	39
Waitsfield	76
Waterbury	96
Westford	110
Williston	144
Worcester	4

ESSEX COUNTY

Averill	*Not Inhabited*
Brunswick	15
Canaan	8
Concord	52
East Haven	*Not Inhabited*
Ferdinand	*Not Inhabited*
Granby	14
Guildhall	55
Lemington	9
Lewis	*Not Inhabited*
Lunenburgh	66
Maidstone	21
Minehead	5
Newark	1
Norfolk	8
Norton	*Not Inhabited*
Random	*Not Inhabited*
Victory	*Not Inhabited*
Wenlock	*Not Inhabited*
Westmore	*Not Inhabited*

FRANKLIN COUNTY

Alburgh	117
Avery's Gore	8
Bakersfield	36
Belvidere	*Not Inhabited*
Berkshire	29
Cambridge	120
Coit's Gore	11
Enosburgh	20
Fairfax	134
Fairfield	175
Fletcher	36
Georgia	168
Highgate	79
Huntsburgh	48
Isle La Mott	19
Johnson	48
Middle Hero	102
North Hero	54
Montgomery	4
Richford	16
Sheldon	61
South Hero	119
St. Albans	121
Sterling	2
Swanton	140

ORANGE COUNTY

Barre	144
Berlin	112
Braintree	92
Bradford	167
Brookfield	158
Newbury	169
Chelsea	146
Corinth	225
Fairlee	65
Northfield	32
Orange	65
Randolph	292
Roxbury	19
Strafford	273
Thetford	243
Topsham	60
Tunbridge	216
Vershire	169
Washington	97
West Fairlee	65
Williamstown	146

ORLEANS COUNTY

Barton	28
Brownington	23
Caldersburg	*Not Inhabited*
Coventry	1
Craftsbury	42
Derby	40
Duncansboro	10
Eden	5
Elmore	12
Glover	9
Greensboro	52
Holland	*Not Inhabited*
Hyde Park	25
Irasburgh	4
Jay	*Not Inhabited*
Kellyvale	*Not Inhabited*
Lutterloch	3
Morristown	31
Navy	*Not Inhabited*
Salem	3
Westfield	5
Wolcott	7

RUTLAND COUNTY

Benson	101
Benton's Gore	5
Brandon	195
Castleton	192
Chittenden	58
Clarendon	320
Danby	257
Fairhaven	80
Harwich	28
Hubberdton	119
Ira	78
Killington	14
Medway	7
Middletown	194
Mt. Holly	122
Orwell	251
Parker's Gore	*Not Inhabited*
Pawlet	339
Philadelphia	20
Pittsfield	35
Pittsford	275
Poultney	288
Rutland	411
Shrewsbury	129
Sudbury	84
Tinmouth	167
Wallingford	177
Wells	167
Westhaven	85

WINDHAM COUNTY

Athens	76
Brattleboro	271
Brookline	87
Dummerston	252
Grafton	188
Guilford	324
Halifax	237
Hinsdale	54
Jamaica	107
Johnson's Gore	26
Londonderry	60
Marlboro	163
Newfane	162
Putney	233
Rockingham	264
Somerset	24
Stratton	51
Townshend	236
Wardsboro North District	150
Wardsboro South District	113
Westminster	328
Whitingham	154
Wilmington	160
Windham	79

WINDSOR COUNTY

Andover	170
Baltimore	27
Barnard	188
Bethel	149
Bridgewater	135
Cavendish	156
Chester	294
Hartford	224
Hartland	304
Ludlow	73
Norwich	237
Plymouth	87
Pomfret	181
Reading	198
Rochester	87
Royalton	238
Sharon	198
Springfield	327
Stockbridge	84
Wethersfield	288
Windsor	337
Woodstock	337

SUMMARY OF POPULATION, BY COUNTIES AND TOWNS—1800

NAMES OF HEADS OF FAMILIES	TOTAL	FREE WHITE MALES: Under 10 years of age	FREE WHITE MALES: Of 10 and under 16	FREE WHITE MALES: Of 16 and under 26 including heads of families	FREE WHITE MALES: Of 26 and under 45 including heads of families	FREE WHITE MALES: Of 45 and upwards including heads of families.	FREE WHITE FEMALES: Under 10 years of age	FREE WHITE FEMALES: Of 10 and under 16	FREE WHITE FEMALES: Of 16 and under 26 including heads of families	FREE WHITE FEMALES: Of 26 and under 45 including heads of families	FREE WHITE FEMALES: Of 45 and upwards including heads of families	All other free persons except Indians not taxed
ADDISON COUNTY												
TOWN	TOTAL											
Addison	734	142	70	65	86	35	134	40	66	61	35	..
Bridport	1,124	216	80	87	129	50	228	82	85	126	40	1
Bristol	665	141	40	48	72	26	148	53	43	71	23	..
Cornwall	1,163	233	96	114	111	58	193	104	103	105	46	..
Ferrisburgh	956	204	74	79	115	39	168	61	84	90	32	10
Goshen	4	2	..	1	..	..	..	..	1	..	..	..
Hancock	150	33	9	6	17	11	31	11	12	14	6	..
Kingston	185	38	18	18	19	10	33	8	17	16	8	..
Leicester	522	95	49	39	59	30	96	37	40	57	20	..
Lincoln	97	19	2	7	13	3	23	8	8	11	3	..
Middlebury	1,263	242	91	115	159	54	214	83	110	142	45	8
Monkton	880	150	73	66	99	45	181	73	53	99	35	6
Newhaven	1,135	223	91	86	136	52	215	84	91	112	44	1
Panton	363	79	31	29	41	21	57	24	29	33	19	..
Salisbury	644	111	53	64	73	40	113	42	60	58	30	..
Shoreham	1,447	286	101	96	182	60	277	108	106	168	52	11
Starksboro	359	62	21	33	44	18	79	27	24	39	11	1
Vergennes	516	64	24	73	73	19	92	35	45	52	12	27
Waltham	247	41	16	18	32	11	53	23	20	20	13	..
Warren	58	13	2	8	11	1	11	1	7	4	..	..
Weybridge	502	113	41	32	60	25	84	40	36	48	23	..
Whiting	404	77	28	38	42	22	58	36	40	39	23	1
Total	13,418											
BENNINGTON COUNTY												
Arlington	1,597	321	141	129	167	85	297	105	130	155	63	4
Bennington	2,243	328	175	276	211	158	378	202	163	189	138	25
Bromley	130	17	11	13	12	11	26	9	12	11	8	..
Dorset	1,286	222	100	125	126	72	232	114	119	113	63	..
Glastenbury	48	11	4	1	6	2	9	6	2	5	2	..
Landgrove	147	38	7	9	19	4	32	8	9	16	5	..
Manchester	1,397	252	110	142	116	90	233	111	139	116	76	12
Pownal	1,692	296	145	168	138	119	270	117	167	154	101	17
Readsboro	234	45	5	14	26	14	56	13	19	26	16	..
Rupert	1,628	328	137	150	155	88	273	137	136	145	79	..
Sandgate	1,020	179	73	86	110	66	178	84	93	98	48	5
Shaftsbury	1,895	321	166	215	144	130	311	128	194	161	119	6
Stamford	383	70	24	33	39	29	64	33	38	28	25	..
Sunderland	557	111	36	44	59	38	90	35	45	60	30	9
Winhall	202	43	10	11	28	6	46	14	13	24	7	..
Woodford	138	24	15	8	13	13	24	8	11	13	9	..
Total	14,597											
CALEDONIA COUNTY												
Barnet	858	175	68	75	81	71	139	66	48	91	43	1
Billymead	144	32	9	12	21	5	29	7	7	17	5	..
Burke	108	22	3	10	13	7	21	4	9	13	6	..
Cabot	349	70	23	25	46	16	72	21	33	32	10	1
Calais	443	84	28	31	63	11	99	35	36	50	6	..
Danville	1,514	293	94	133	175	79	285	103	133	148	69	2
Dewey's Gore	152	23	14	17	15	8	26	12	19	12	6	..
Groton	248	55	18	10	25	9	60	16	15	27	6	7
Hardwick	260	52	18	30	35	10	39	13	28	26	9	..
Hopkinsville	20	5	3	2	1	1	3	1	2	1	1	..
Lyndon	542	108	25	44	66	26	121	29	47	58	18	..
Marshfield	172	37	14	14	19	6	34	14	12	18	4	..
Montpelier	890	168	60	91	108	38	154	58	84	90	37	2
Peacham	873	158	60	86	118	30	153	55	78	99	35	1
Plainfield	256	55	13	21	33	9	56	8	25	28	7	1
Ryegate	415	82	30	41	45	24	75	27	30	42	19	..
St. Johnsbury	651	129	37	64	82	24	130	40	55	71	18	1
Sheffield	179	40	10	16	18	8	29	6	20	16	6	..
Walden	153	23	12	20	11	7	35	10	17	13	5	..
Waterford	565	133	29	34	74	19	121	34	37	69	15	..
Wheelock	568	118	32	59	58	34	105	33	47	56	26	..
Woodbury	23	3	1	1	3	2	5	1	2	3	2	..
Total	9,383											
CHITTENDEN COUNTY												
Bolton	220	37	21	21	20	15	37	14	23	20	11	1
Burlington	816	144	54	100	122	27	138	49	83	76	14	9
Charlotte	1,231	213	87	117	151	47	229	102	104	120	45	16
Colchester	347	67	25	25	42	18	67	23	27	37	12	4
Duxbury	153	23	9	16	17	8	31	14	18	10	7	..
Essex	729	134	58	62	93	45	123	46	54	79	34	1
Fayston	18	1	..	5	1	2	1	2	4	..	2	..
Hinesburgh	933	195	75	77	102	46	168	57	80	84	40	9
Huntington	405	70	45	42	37	18	89	20	35	34	15	..
Jericho	728	151	42	60	80	35	143	59	52	81	25	..
Mansfield	12	3	1	2	1	..	2	2	..	1	..	..
CHITTENDEN COUNTY, *Continued*												
TOWN	TOTAL											
Middlesex	262	40	15	29	27	11	62	21	22	24	1	
Milton	786	139	58	67	93	34	175	47	69	70	34	..
Moretown	191	33	15	18	22	6	46	18	12	20	6	..
Richmond	718	152	73	55	80	24	119	62	58	74	20	1
Shelburne	723	136	49	80	70	33	130	69	61	64	31	..
Stowe	316	68	23	30	25	16	66	28	27	25	8	..
Underhill	212	35	19	14	27	9	47	16	10	26	9	..
Waitsfield	473	99	42	35	53	17	97	38	33	45	14	..
Waterbury	644	143	62	48	78	20	115	48	43	66	20	1
Westford	648	135	51	50	75	29	124	54	40	65	24	1
Williston	836	161	66	77	98	31	154	54	63	90	42	..
Worcester	25	4	2	1	2	1	9	2	1	2	1	..
Total	11,426											
ESSEX COUNTY												
Brunswick	86	14	7	5	9	5	23	5	5	8	5	..
Canaan	45	5	2	6	8	3	7	2	4	5	2	1
Concord	322	65	26	29	37	16	55	26	21	34	13	..
Granby	69	16	5	4	9	4	14	3	1	9	4	.
Guildhall	296	62	25	19	35	18	46	18	32	24	16	1
Lemington	52	5	6	7	8	3	7	5	3	4	4	..
Lunenburgh	393	70	30	33	50	24	64	31	37	36	17	1
Maidstone	152	30	12	14	14	10	24	13	13	14	8	..
Minehead	27	6	5	2	2	1	4	1	3	3	..	..
Newark	8	2	1	1	1	..	1	1	..	1	..	..
Norfolk	29	8	1	..	7	2	3	..	2	5	1	..
Total	1,479											
FRANKLIN COUNTY												
Alburgh	750	140	64	62	72	48	156	68	38	65	35	2
Avery's Gore	31	3	2	3	4	2	8	1	4	5	..	..
Bakersfield	222	45	17	24	39	4	31	18	15	25	4	..
Berkshire	172	39	13	11	27	5	34	6	11	21	4	1
Cambridge	733	134	49	72	87	28	127	62	63	74	36	1
Coit's Gore	51	10	4	3	7	1	10	5	4	6	1	..
Enosburgh	143	32	14	13	18	5	27	7	12	11	4	..
Fairfax	786	148	52	64	107	29	153	49	65	92	27	..
Fairfield	901	195	66	66	134	29	170	58	62	98	23	..
Fletcher	200	30	25	28	12	7	41	14	22	13	8	..
Georgia	1,068	214	79	76	115	36	223	96	93	104	32	..
Highgate	437	76	29	36	52	36	83	39	31	40	15	..
Huntsburgh	280	62	22	14	38	12	54	13	33	27	5	..
Isle La Mott	135	33	18	10	12	6	23	12	3	13	5	..
Johnson	255	55	14	22	36	6	49	20	23	24	6	..
Middle Hero	611	123	49	46	73	31	119	43	50	54	22	1
Montgomery	36	6	2	5	4	2	5	1	6	3	1	1
North Hero	324	60	28	28	35	18	68	23	27	27	10	..
Richford	113	24	9	17	16	3	12	8	15	7	2	..
St. Albans	901	170	68	130	99	41	146	66	78	80	21	2
Sheldon	408	90	26	36	58	9	69	26	29	44	8	13
South Hero	678	124	43	79	69	40	125	51	52	62	32	1
Sterling	9	..	2	1	1	..	3	..	2	..	..	..
Swanton	858	174	72	83	104	38	146	66	75	75	25	..
Total	10,103											
ORANGE COUNTY												
Barre	919	175	61	107	104	34	176	51	80	104	27	..
Berlin	684	149	51	49	83	24	137	47	58	64	22	..
Bradford	1,062	174	78	85	111	53	235	72	75	110	57	12
Braintree	531	106	40	40	60	26	93	37	32	51	26	20
Brookfield	988	191	83	95	94	58	166	71	71	100	51	8
Chelsea	896	170	51	61	124	34	192	60	67	105	32	..
Corinth	1,413	302	90	96	156	74	272	96	94	156	70	7
Fairlee	386	72	27	30	38	23	79	31	24	37	24	1
Newbury	1,304	236	109	120	132	65	225	96	119	129	59	14
Northfield	204	46	20	16	21	11	31	15	19	19	6	..
Orange	348	82	21	19	55	10	70	21	28	35	7	..
Randolph	1,841	358	155	142	197	88	328	136	163	189	81	4
Roxbury	113	27	5	13	14	4	20	5	10	11	4	..
Strafford	1,642	337	134	130	181	76	313	118	110	169	73	1
Thetford	1,478	285	114	92	154	80	285	118	90	179	70	11
Topsham	344	80	23	22	45	13	78	18	10	44	11	..
Tunbridge	1,324	279	90	103	145	62	273	89	89	140	54	..
Vershire	1,030	214	81	76	116	46	205	64	69	113	46	..
Washington	507	106	29	57	70	23	81	25	41	55	20	..
West Fairlee	391	83	29	23	41	22	69	28	25	42	22	7
Williamstown	839	189	58	67	104	32	165	38	76	80	29	1
Total	18,244											

SUMMARY OF POPULATION, BY COUNTIES AND TOWNS—1800

NAMES OF HEADS OF FAMILIES — TOWN	TOTAL	FREE WHITE MALES: Under 10 years of age	FREE WHITE MALES: Of 10 and under 16	FREE WHITE MALES: Of 16 and under 26 including heads of families	FREE WHITE MALES: Of 26 and under 45 including heads of families	FREE WHITE MALES: Of 45 and upwards including heads of families	FREE WHITE FEMALES: Under 10 years of age	FREE WHITE FEMALES: Of 10 and under 16	FREE WHITE FEMALES: Of 16 and under 26 including heads of families	FREE WHITE FEMALES: Of 26 and under 45 including heads of families	FREE WHITE FEMALES: Of 45 and upwards including heads of families	All other free persons except Indians not taxed
ORLEANS COUNTY												
Barton	128	31	7	17	18	1	23	8	5	15	3	..
Brownington	65	12	4	13	11	1	7	..	14	2	1	..
Coventry	7	3	..	..	1	..	1	1	..	1	..	..
Craftsbury	229	53	21	17	26	13	37	15	14	22	10	1
Derby	178	38	4	32	28	4	31	4	12	19	2	4
Duncansboro	50	12	3	6	4	3	8	..	6	5	3	..
Eden	29	9	1	..	5	..	8	1	1	4	..	..
Elmore	45	7	4	..	10	1	12	2	..	9	..	..
Glover	36	8	1	5	7	..	5	2	5	2	1	..
Greensboro	280	36	24	32	34	7	76	14	22	30	5	..
Hyde Park	110	18	5	5	15	4	17	8	12	9	5	12
Irasburgh	15	1	..	8	1	..	3	..	2	..	..	..
Lutterloch	12	6	..	1	2	1	..	..	..	2	..	..
Morristown	144	20	11	19	17	4	30	12	13	13	5	..
Salem	16	4	1	1	3	..	1	3	1	2	..	..
Westfield	16	2	1	3	3	..	3	1	..	3	..	..
Wolcott	47	8	4	4	5	2	9	4	6	3	2	..
Total	1,407											
RUTLAND COUNTY												
Benson	1,164	240	91	101	127	54	210	88	73	120	49	11
Brandon	1,076	214	82	93	110	50	199	85	98	108	37	..
Castleton	1,039	173	88	84	117	57	193	76	110	96	45	..
Chittenden	327	78	26	22	37	16	65	17	19	35	12	..
Clarendon	1,789	366	141	147	157	109	284	170	168	151	91	5
Danby	1,487	288	117	129	131	87	277	126	123	138	69	2
Fairhaven	411	76	34	48	36	26	63	27	40	35	25	1
Harwich	153	29	7	16	10	11	33	11	16	13	7	..
Hubberdton	641	123	54	55	68	31	115	51	48	61	35	..
Ira	473	117	33	38	50	17	77	32	42	48	19	..
Killington	90	22	9	5	12	4	11	6	7	10	2	2
Medway	39	6	4	2	3	4	6	2	4	6	2	..
Middletown	1,066	195	85	83	108	58	192	90	103	106	45	1
Mt. Holly	668	137	44	53	69	33	143	46	58	61	20	4
Orwell	1,376	256	114	123	165	69	237	94	117	129	59	13
Pawlet	1,938	351	162	170	183	104	371	167	159	171	99	1
Philadelphia	123	17	9	10	11	6	23	11	13	9	5	9
Pittsfield	164	33	7	19	18	9	27	12	16	15	8	..
Pittsford	1,413	268	92	104	160	77	290	101	120	137	63	1
Poultney	1,694	337	138	141	165	85	297	152	134	165	76	4
Rutland	2,125	365	170	189	237	116	385	151	193	203	91	25
Shrewsbury	748	139	69	64	83	37	127	55	66	80	28	..
Sudbury	521	107	40	42	53	19	91	49	45	54	21	..
Tinmouth	973	184	78	87	86	53	200	82	62	91	47	3
Wallingford	912	178	55	77	104	54	165	57	68	100	48	6
Wells	978	190	80	77	89	54	197	71	82	86	52	..
Westhaven	430	84	36	40	49	24	70	29	33	44	19	2
Total	23,818											
WINDHAM COUNTY												
Athens	459	91	36	35	45	27	88	29	36	47	25	..
Brattleboro	1,867	315	168	191	158	130	316	150	165	164	104	6
Brookline	472	87	48	38	35	37	75	42	40	42	28	..
Dummerston	1,692	313	129	138	170	108	306	134	125	171	98	..
Grafton	1,149	237	104	79	130	45	218	81	87	123	45	..
Guilford	2,256	395	192	214	177	163	352	184	235	192	151	1
Halifax	1,600	325	130	118	135	104	289	122	129	152	93	3
Hindsdale	480	88	37	34	43	43	80	35	37	41	41	1
Jamaica	582	112	43	53	64	25	102	49	40	66	28	..
Johnson's Gore	131	26	8	13	12	7	24	8	16	10	7	..
Londonderry	330	68	26	22	38	18	64	24	19	33	18	..
Marlboro	1,087	201	101	93	103	65	183	88	90	104	59	..
Newfane	1,000	176	85	84	94	65	160	78	110	94	53	1
Putney	1,574	226	131	144	134	111	295	127	152	141	100	13
Rockingham	1,684	316	155	165	142	111	248	130	157	160	98	2
Somerset	130	25	6	16	13	9	21	7	11	12	10	..
Stratton	271	50	20	21	32	13	58	19	13	32	13	..
Townshend	1,083	181	96	81	132	58	201	72	72	122	68	..
Wardsboro N. District	868	155	86	63	97	45	171	53	56	94	48	..
Wardsboro S. District	616	122	45	45	74	29	120	34	48	77	21	1
Westminster	1,942	305	174	189	182	128	313	143	191	185	120	12
Whitingham	868	168	73	74	95	49	164	51	54	95	42	..
Wilmington	1,011	203	68	59	104	73	190	66	87	92	69	..
Windham	429	80	29	37	50	22	80	37	30	44	20	..
Total	23,581											
WINDSOR COUNTY												
Andover	1,016	220	78	64	119	33	210	63	89	112	28	..
Baltimore	174	42	10	11	19	8	32	15	11	18	8	..
Barnard	1,236	256	98	90	133	62	231	96	93	126	49	2
Benton's Gore	17	2	..	..	6	..	4	..	..	5	..	..
Bethel	913	168	83	67	89	54	170	70	70	92	50	..
Bridgewater	781	170	47	37	96	36	160	57	54	90	34	..
Cavendish	922	177	83	59	107	47	166	66	57	103	51	6
Chester	1,878	361	144	124	215	82	367	150	127	214	80	14
Hartford	1,494	282	135	165	143	84	218	113	136	135	81	2
Hartland	1,960	357	180	161	188	112	358	158	160	180	104	2
Ludlow	410	78	30	24	56	13	83	24	33	55	13	1
Norwich	1,482	247	128	141	143	100	243	123	126	149	82	..
Plymouth	497	78	46	53	57	21	85	42	40	55	20	..
Pomfret	1,106	187	96	116	96	83	176	81	100	102	69	..
Reading	1,120	210	112	74	133	56	209	64	65	136	56	5
Rochester	524	123	31	38	59	23	104	28	39	59	20	..
Royalton	1,501	331	108	99	158	76	289	109	120	140	70	1
Sharon	1,158	248	85	92	124	57	205	87	83	117	52	8
Springfield	2,032	352	161	166	207	111	416	155	139	208	112	5
Stockbridge	432	80	36	40	57	17	66	30	42	49	15	..
Wethersfield	1,944	371	174	147	208	79	361	146	148	207	85	18
Windsor	2,211	388	167	202	215	128	386	167	200	224	107	27
Woodstock	2,132	403	168	181	205	131	368	176	186	188	126	..
Total	26,940											

GRAND TOTAL OF INHABITANTS IN VERMONT IN 1800 CENSUS, 154,396.

POPULATION, FAMILIES AND AVERAGE POPULATION PER FAMILY

County	Population	Families	Averages per Family
Addison County	13,418	2,424	5.53
Bennington County	14,597	2,377	6.14
Caledonia County	9,383	1,469	6.39
Chittenden County	11,426	1,687	6.66
Essex County	1,479	254	5.59
Franklin County	10,103	1,920	5.19
Orange County	18,244	2,890	6.31
Orleans County	1,407	292	4.80
Rutland County	23,818	4,198	5.67
Windham County	23,581	3,773	6.28
Windsor County	26,940	4,319	6.24
Totals	154,396	25,603	6.03
Population in 1930	359,611	89,188	4.03
Since 1800	Plus 205,215	Plus 63,585	Minus 2.00

In the 130 years the increase in population was 133%, in number of families 248%, and the decrease in the average size of families was 33%.

Were the average population per family in 1930 the same as it was in 1800 the population of Vermont in 1930 would have been 537,803.

Since 1800 the Vermont Counties listed above still bear the same names but sometimes towns in some of those Counties have been set off to form other Counties, and the new Counties added are Grand Isle, Lamoille and Washington.

ADDISON COUNTY

NAMES OF HEADS OF FAMILIES	FREE WHITE MALES					FREE WHITE FEMALES					
	Under 10 years of age	Of 10 and under 16	Of 16 and under 26 including heads of families	Of 26 and under 45 including heads of families	Of 45 and upwards including heads of families.	Under 10 years of age	Of 10 and under 16	Of 16 and under 26 including heads of families	Of 26 and under 45 including heads of families	Of 45 and upwards including heads of families	All other free persons except Indians not taxed
ADDISON											
Abbot, Seth	2	1	..	2	..	1	..	..	1	..	..
Adams, Friend	1	..	..	1	..	..	..	..	1	..	..
Allis, William	1	..	..	1	..	2	..	..	1	..	..
Averist, Joseph	3	3	1	1	..	1	..	..	1	..	..
Averist, William	2	..	..	1	..	3	..	..	1	..	..
Averist, Zadock	1	2	3	..	1	2	1	1	..	1	..
Barber, John	3	..	..	1	..	1	..	..	1	..	..
Bartlet, Ichabod	1	1	1	..	1	..	3	..	1	..	..
Bill, Azariah	..	..	2	..	1	..	1	..	..	1	..
Black, James	..	..	..	1	..	..	..	..	..	..	..
Boyington, Jesse	1	..	..	1	..	..	..	..	1	..	..
Brown, Samuel	1	1	..	1	..	1	..	1	..	..	..
Buck, Isaac	2	1	..	1	..	1	..	..	1	..	..
Burrel, Abraham	..	..	..	1	..	..	..	..	..	1	..
Burrel, Timothy	1	1	..	1	..	2	1	..	1	..	..
Bushnel, James	..	..	2	..	..	..	..	1	..	..	..
Butler, Solomon	..	1	2	..	1	1	1	1	..	1	..
Canada, Henry	1	1	1	..	1	1	..	..	..	1	..
Case, Loudon	2	..	..	1	..	1	..	..	1	..	..
Childs, Samuel	2	2	..	1	..	1	1	..	1	..	..
Clark, Azel	1	1	..	1	..	1	..	..	1	..	..
Clark, Eliphalet	1	..	..	1	..	1	1	..	..	..	..
Clark, Isaiah	2	3	..	..	1	..	..	..	..	1	..
Clifton, Nathaniel	1	..	..	..	1	..	1	..	1	..	..
Crampton, Nathan	2	1	..	1	..	..	1	1	..	..	..
Crandill, Timothy	..	..	1	..	..	1	..	1	..	..	..
Curtis, Zacherias	1	..	..	1	..	1	..	..	1	..	..
Dana, Eleazer	1	..	..	1	..	2	..	..	1	..	..
Day, Jeremiah	1	1	..	1	..	2	2	..	1	..	..
Days, Stephen	1	1	1	..	1	2	..	..	1	1	..
Doran, James	2	2	1	..	1	1	..	..	..	1	..
Doran, John	1	..	..	1	..	..	..	..	1	..	..
Dougy, John	..	..	1	..	..	..	..	1	..	..	..
Dowe, Solomon	2	..	..	1	..	1	..	1	..	..	..
Dozenbery, William	1	1	..	1	..	1	1	..	..	..	..
Dozenbery, William G.	..	..	1	..	..	..	..	..	..	..	..
Eastman, Ezra	1	..	..	1	..	1	..	..	1	..	..
Edgbar, John	2	..	..	1	..	2	2	2	..	1	..
Everts, Benjamin	2	3	..	1	..	3	..	..	1	..	..
Ferguson, Alexander	..	..	1	..	..	..	..	1	..	..	..
Fisher, John	..	1	1	..	1	..	1	..	1	..	..
Fountain, Francis	..	..	..	1	..	3	..	..	1	..	..
Godard, Moses	..	..	2	..	1	..	1	..	..	..	..
Hadley, Jacob	2	..	..	1	..	2	1	..	1	..	..
Haines, James	1	..	2	..	1	..	..	..	..	1	..
Hanks, Stephen	1	1	..	1	..	4	1	..	1	..	..
Harris, John	..	..	..	1	..	..	..	..	..	..	..
Harrymon, John	1	..	1	..	..	..	..	1	..	..	..
Haven, William	1	1	1	..	1	2	3	1	..	1	..
Hitchcock, Buel	1	..	..	1	..	1	..	..	1	..	..
Holcomb, Isaac	..	..	2	1	..	..	..	..	1	..	..
Holsey, John	1	1	..	1	..	2	1	..	1	..	..
Howard, Daniel	2	..	1	1	..	1	..	1	..	..	..
Jackson, Ephraim	1	2	1	..	1	..	..	..	..	1	..
Jones, Amos	1	1	..	1	..	2	1	..	1	..	..
Kimball, William	1	1	..	..	1	1	..	..	1	..	..
Lewis, Edward	1	..	1	..	..	2	..	1	..	..	..
Louis, John	..	..	1	..	..	..	..	1	..	..	..
Louis, Peter	..	..	1	..	..	..	..	1	..	..	..
Lowe, Samuel	3	1	..	1	..	1	..	..	1	..	..
Mauley, Kilbourn	..	..	..	1	..	4	1	..	1	..	..
McLane, John	1	2	..	..	1	3	..	..	1	..	..
McLean, Jacob	3	1	..	1	..	2	1	..	1	..	..
McWheaton, John	2	1	..	1	..	1	..	..	1	..	..
Mead, Ira	1	..	..	1	..	3	..	..	1	..	..
Merihu, William	1	..	..	1	..	..	1	1	..	..	..
Merrils, Conel	1	..	..	1	..	..	..	..	..	..	..
Merrils, Ebenezer	..	..	2	..	1	..	..	2	..	1	..
Mills, William	..	..	..	1	..	..	..	1	..	..	..
Minor, Row	..	..	1	..	..	1	..	1	..	..	..
More, Abraham	..	1	..	1	..	3	2	..	1	1	..
More, Francis	3	..	..	1	..	2	1	..	1	..	..
More, William	..	..	..	1	..	3	..	1	..	..	..
Morm, Aborn	2	..	..	2	..	..	1	..	1	..	..
Murry, Joseph	..	1	..	2	1	1	1	1	..	1	..
ADDISON—con.											
Newton, John	1	1	1	1	1	2	1	1	1	1	..
Norton, Abel	..	..	1	..	..	..	..	..	..	..	..
Norton, Bela	1	..	..	1	..	2	..	..	1	..	..
Norton, Benjamin	..	..	..	1	..	2	..	1	..	..	..
Norton, Jason	4	..	..	1	..	..	..	..	1	..	..
Olin, Gideon	3	3	1	..	1	1	..	1	..	1	..
Pangborn, Stephen	..	..	1	..	1	..	..	2	..	1	..
Payon, Benjamin	..	..	1	..	1	..	1	..	..	1	..
Peacock, Thomas	2	..	..	1	..	1	..	..	1	..	..
Peckett, Ahasel	1	..	..	1	..	..	..	1	..	..	..
Perry, William	1	..	..	1	..	1	..	..	1	..	..
Pond, Samuel	..	1	1	2	1	..	..	1	..	1	..
Post, Caleb	2	..	..	1	..	3	..	..	1	..	..
Post, Jacob	..	1	..	..	1	..	..	..	..	1	..
Post, Jacob	3	1	..	1	..	3	..	..	1	..	..
Post, John	..	..	..	1	..	1	..	1	..	..	..
Pratt, Caleb	..	..	1	..	..	..	..	1	..	..	..
Pratt, Hezekiah	1	..	..	1	..	2	..	..	1	..	..
Pricket, Ebenezer	..	1	1	..	1	2	..	1	..	1	..
Pricket, William	..	..	1	..	..	1	..	1	..	..	..
Randol, Widow Ruth	3	1	1	..	..	..	1	..	1	..	..
Reynold, Nicholas	..	..	1	..	..	..	..	..	..	..	..
Reynolds, Benjamin	3	1	..	1	..	1	1	1	1	..	..
Sacket, Reuben	..	..	..	..	1	..	..	..	..	1	..
Segar, Gideon	..	1	..	..	1	..	..	1	..	1	..
Smith, Amos	1	..	1	..	..	..	..	1	..	..	..
Smith, Daniel	..	3	1	..	..	..	..	1	..	1	..
Smith, Henry	2	..	..	1	..	2	..	1	..	..	..
Smith, Joseph	2	..	..	1	..	4	..	1	..	..	..
Smith, Oliver	1	..	..	1	..	2	..	..	1	..	..
Smith, Simeon	..	1	1	..	1	1	..	1	..	..	..
Smith, Uriah	..	..	..	1	..	2	..	..	1	..	..
Snell, Samuel	3	1	2	..	1	..	1	..	..	1	..
Southerd, Benjamin	1	..	..	1	..	1	..	1	..	..	..
Spencer, Joseph	..	1	..	1	..	2	..	1	..	1	..
Squire, Ashbel	..	..	..	1	..	3	..	1	..	..	..
Squire, Daniel	..	1	..	1	1	..	..	2	..	1	..
Squire, Eli	3	..	..	1	..	..	..	1	..	..	..
Steakle, James	1	..	..	1	..	3	..	..	1	..	..
Steakle, Peter	..	1	..	1	..	..	..	..	1	..	..
Stephens, ———	..	..	..	1	..	..	..	..	1	..	..
Strong, John	1	1	1	..	1	..	..	1	..	1	..
Strong, John Jr.	4	..	1	1	..	..	1	1	1	..	..
Thrickebaker, Bartholomew	3	..	..	1	..	..	1	..	..	..	..
Vallance, James	1	2	1	..	1	..	1	3	..	1	..
Vallance, John	..	..	..	..	1	..	..	..	..	..	..
Ward, John	2	2	1	1	..	2	..	1	1	..	..
Ward, Lyman	1	..	..	1	..	1	..	..	1	..	..
Warner, Aron	1	1	1	..	1	1	1	1	..	1	..
Warner, Nathaniel	..	..	..	1	..	1	..	1	..	..	..
White, Alvin	2	..	..	1	..	..	1	..	..	..	..
Whitney, David	..	1	..	..	1	..	..	..	..	1	..
Williamson, Lewis	1	1	..	1	..	1	..	1	1	..	..
Willmot, Asa	1	1	1	..	1	1	..	..	..	1	..
Willmot, Asa Jr.	2	..	1	..	..	..	..	1	..	..	..
Wilmot, Widow Mary	1	1	2	..	..	..	..	..	1	..	..
Wilmott, Abel	1	..	..	1	..	..	..	2	..	..	..
Woodford, Timothy	2	..	1	1	..	1	..	1	1	..	..
Wright, Daniel	1	..	1	..	..	..	..	1	..	1	..
Wright, Ebenezer	1	..	3	..	1	2	2	1	..	1	..
Wright, Ebenezer 2nd	1	..	1	..	..	..	..	1	..	..	..
BRIDPORT											
Baldwin, John	1	..	..	1	..	1	1	..	1	..	..
Baldwin, Josiah	1	2	..	1	..	3	2	1	1	..	..
Baldwin, Levi	..	..	1	..	1	..	1	2	..	1	..
Baldwin, Martin	3	..	..	1	..	2	..	..	1	..	..
Baldwin, Obadiah	1	..	..	1	..	..	..	..	1	..	..
Baldwin, Stephen	..	..	1	..	1	..	..	1	..	1	..
Baldwin, Thomas	..	..	..	1	1	1	..	..	..	1	1
Baldwin, William	2	..	..	1	..	..	..	..	1	..	..
Ball, Samuel	3	..	..	1	..	1	..	..	1	..	..
Barber, James	2	3	..	1	..	3	..	..	1	..	..
Barber, Joel	3	1	2	1	..	2	1	1	1	..	..
Barber, William	..	..	..	1	..	..	..	..	1	..	..
Barrows, Isaac	2	1	1	..	1	..	2	2	..	1	..
Barrows, Lemuel	1	1	..	1	..	2	2	..	1	..	..
Barrows, Printer	1	1	..	1	1	1	..	1	1	1	..
Barrows, Samuel	4	1	..	1	..	2	..	1	1	..	..

ADDISON COUNTY—Continued

NAMES OF HEADS OF FAMILIES	FREE WHITE MALES: Under 10 years of age	FREE WHITE MALES: Of 10 and under 16	FREE WHITE MALES: Of 16 and under 26 including heads of families	FREE WHITE MALES: Of 26 and under 45 including heads of families	FREE WHITE MALES: Of 45 and upwards including heads of families.	FREE WHITE FEMALES: Under 10 years of age	FREE WHITE FEMALES: Of 10 and under 16	FREE WHITE FEMALES: Of 16 and under 26 including heads of families	FREE WHITE FEMALES: Of 26 and under 45 including heads of families	FREE WHITE FEMALES: Of 45 and upwards including heads of families	All other free persons except Indians not taxed
BRIDPORT—con.											
Bateman, John	..	..	1	..	..	..	..	..	..	..	..
Bean, Abraham	..	..	..	1	..	..	..	..	1	..	..
Benedict, Benijah	1	1	..	1	..	1	..	..	1	..	..
Benjamin, Samuel	2	1	2	1	..	..	2	..	1	..	..
Bennett, John S.	1	1	1	..	1	2	2	..	1	..	..
Boggby, Samuel	..	1	..	1	..	2	1	..	1	..	..
Bosworth, Ira	..	..	1	..	..	1	..	1	..	..	..
Bosworth, James	..	2	..	..	1	..	1	1	..	1	..
Bosworth, James Jr.	1	..	..	1	..	1	..	1	..	..	..
Bott, William	..	..	1	1	1	..	2	..	..	1	..
Bowlsby, Enos	2	..	..	1	..	1	..	..	1	..	..
Breasted, William	2	1	..	1	..	3	..	..	1	..	..
Buck, Samuel	..	1	1	1	..	3	1	..	1	..	..
Buker, Mary	1	..	..	..	..	..	1	..	1	..	..
Burrall, David	4	..	..	1	..	2	1	..	1	..	..
Canven, Handen	1	..	..	1	..	1	..	..	1	..	..
Case, Gamaliel	2	..	..	1	..	3	..	..	..	..	..
Chilles, Timothy	1	..	..	1	..	3	..	..	..	1	..
Chilless, John	1	..	..	1	..	1	..	..	1	..	..
Chilless, Steward	..	..	2	..	..	..	..	..	1	..	..
Clough, David	2	..	..	1	..	1	..	1	..	..	..
Converse, Alfred	1	..	..	1	..	..	..	..	1	..	..
Converse, Barnard	1	2	..	1	..	3	1	..	1	..	..
Converse, Elias	5	1	1	1	..	..	2	1	1	1	..
Converse, Jeremiah	3	1	..	1	..	..	1	..	1	..	..
Converse, Payon	1	..	1	..	..	..	..	1	..	..	..
Cook, Solomon	..	..	1	..	1	3	..	1	1	..	..
Corey, David	3	1	..	1	..	1	..	..	1	..	..
Corey, David Jr.	1	1	2	1	..	3	1	..	1	..	..
Crane, Jesse	4	1	..	1	..	..	1	1	..	..	..
Craw, Isaac	1	2	1	..	1	..	1	..	..	1	..
Cross, David	1	2	1	1	..	..	..	2	1	..	..
Crowfoot, Elijah	1	..	2	1	..	3	1	1	1	..	..
Cummins, Benjamin	1	..	..	1	..	1	..	..	1	..	..
Curtis, David	2	..	..	1	..	2	..	..	1	..	..
Curtis, Zachariah	..	..	1	..	1	..	..	..	..	1	..
Davy, Jacob	1	..	..	2	..	1	2	1	..	..	..
Decamp, Moses	..	..	..	1	..	1	..	1	..	..	..
Decamp, Silas	1	1	..	1	..	3	..	..	1	..	..
Doly, David	1	2	..	1	..	..	..	..	1	..	..
Doty, David, 2nd.	1	3	..	1	..	..	1	..	1	..	..
Dunn, Stephen	..	..	..	1	..	2	..	1	..	..	..
Eldridge, Jonathan	2	2	1	..	1	2	2	2	..	1	..
Ellethrop, John G.	..	..	2	..	..	..	..	..	..	1	..
Ellethrop, Nathaniel	1	..	..	1	..	..	..	..	1	..	..
Ferris, William	3	..	..	1	..	1	..	..	1	..	..
Fitch, Nathaniel	..	..	2	1	..	2	..	..	1	..	..
Fitch, Zoroaster	..	1	..	..	1	..	1	..	..	1	..
Forbes, Charles	1	..	1	..	..	..	..	1	..	..	..
Forbes, John	..	..	..	1	1	..	..	..	..	1	..
Freeman, Hezekiah	..	..	1	..	..	..	..	1	..	..	..
French, Noah	2	2	..	..	1	1	1	..	1	..	..
Frost, Abner	1	1	..	1	..	2	..	..	1	..	..
Frost, Joel	..	1	1	..	1	..	..	..	..	1	..
Frost, Phinehas	..	..	1	1	..	..	1	..	..	1	..
Gale, John	..	2	..	1	..	..	..	1	..	..	..
Gale, Somers	..	..	1	..	..	2	..	1	..	..	..
Graves, Increase	2	..	..	..	1	1	3	3	1	..	..
Gray, Eliot	1	..	1	1	1	..	..	..	2	1	..
Gray, Ewel	1	..	..	1	..	2	..	..	1	..	..
Gray, James	..	1	1	..	1	2	..	..	1	..	..
Gray, James Jr.	1	..	2	..	..	..	..	1	..	..	..
Gray, Lyman	..	2	..	..	1	..	..	1	..	1	..
Gray, Martin	..	..	..	1	..	1	1	1	1	..	..
Gray, Robert B.	3	..	..	1	..	2	..	1	1	..	..
Grovesner, Elijah	2	..	2	..	1	..	2	..	..	1	..
Hall, Henry	..	..	1	1	..	2	..	..	1	..	..
Hall, John	1	..	1	..	..	1	..	1	..	..	..
Hamblin, Daniel	1	..	1	1	..	2	2	1	1	..	..
Hamblin, Isaac	4	..	..	1	..	1	1	..	1	..	..
Hamilton, Arthur	3	..	..	..	1	3	..	..	1	..	..
Hamilton, James	2	..	..	1	..	1	..	..	1	..	..
Hamilton, Michael	1	..	1	1	..	3	..	..	1	..	..
Hamilton, Robert	..	..	..	1	..	..	..	1	..	..	..
Haskins, Daniel	..	..	1	..	1	1	1	..	..	1	..
Haskins, Horatio	1	..	1	..	..	1	..	1	..	..	..
Hayes, Samuel	..	..	..	..	1	1	..	..	1	..	..
Haynes, John	3	..	..	1	..	..	..	..	1	..	..
Heminway, Asa	3	1	2	..	1	3	1	1	1	..	..
Heminway, Jacob	2	..	1	1	..	3	2	1	1	..	..
Heremond, David	2	..	..	1	..	2	..	..	1	..	..
Higgins, James	1	..	..	1	..	2	..	1	..	..	..
Houghton, Nathan	..	..	1	..	1	4	..	1	..	..	..
Howard, Daniel	..	1	2	..	1	2	..	1	..	1	..
Howard, Newton	..	..	1	1	..	2	..	..	1	1	..
BRIDPORT—con.											
Howe, Solomon	2	2	..	1	..	1	2	..	..	1	..
Hubbard, Abijah	2	2	..	1	..	1	..	2	1	..	..
Hurlbut, Bartholomew	3	1	..	1	..	1	1	..	1	..	..
Hurlbutt, John	1	..	..	1	..	1	..	..	1	..	..
Johnson, Jackemiah	..	..	..	1	..	2	..	2	..	..	..
Johnson, Lyman	..	..	1	..	1	..	..	1	..	1	..
Jones, Obadiah	1	1	..	1	..	4	1	..	1	..	..
King, Horace	..	..	..	1	..	3	1	..	1	..	..
Kitchel, Mathew	..	..	..	..	1	1	..	1	1	..	..
Kitchel, Phineas	1	1	1	1	..	1	1	..	1	..	..
Lacey, Widow Betsey	..	..	..	..	..	..	1	..	1	..	..
Lawrence, Abraham	..	1	..	..	1	..	..	1	..	1	..
Lee, Jeremiah	1	..	1	1	..	1	..	..	1	..	..
Lewis, Samuel	2	..	..	..	1	2	..	..	1	..	..
Loomis, Ezra	3	..	..	1	..	..	2	..	1	..	..
Lovelorn, William	..	..	..	..	1	1	..	..	1	..	..
McNeal, Daniel	2	..	..	1	..	3	..	..	1	..	..
Merrick, Barnabas	1	..	..	1	..	2	..	..	1	..	..
Merrick, William	2	..	..	1	..	2	1	..	1	..	..
Merrick, Zenus	1	..	1	1	..	1	1	1	..	..	..
Miller, Benjamin	..	1	..	..	1	..	..	1	..	1	..
Miller, Heman	1	..	1	1	..	..	..	2	1	..	..
Miller, James	2	..	2	..	1	2	1	..	1	..	..
Miner, Benjamin	..	1	3	..	1	..	..	..	..	1	..
Minor, Benjamin	1	..	..	1	..	2	..	..	1	..	..
Minor, William	..	..	..	1	..	1	..	2	1	..	..
More, Abraham	3	..	..	1	..	1	1	..	1	..	..
Morgan, Adame	..	..	..	..	1	..	..	..	1	..	..
Morse, Asa	..	..	..	1	..	1	..	1	..	..	..
Morse, Jonathan	..	..	1	..	..	1	..	1	..	..	..
Morse, Levi	..	..	1	..	1	..	..	1	..	..	..
Morse, Sherman	1	..	..	1	..	1	..	..	1	..	..
Morse, Widow Hannah	2	2	1	..	..	1	..	2	..	1	..
Munn, Daniel	2	1	1	..	1	..	..	2	..	1	..
Nichols, Amos	1	..	1	1	..	2	1	1	1	..	..
Oliver, Andrew	1	..	..	1	..	2	..	..	1	..	..
Oliver, Daniel	1	..	..	1	..	2	..	1	..	..	..
Pagley, Henry	1	..	2	1	..	1	..	2	..	..	..
Perry, David	..	..	..	1	..	..	..	..	..	..	..
Pitt, Ingraham	..	..	..	1	..	2	..	1	..	..	..
Potter, Abel	1	1	..	2	1	2	1	..	1	..	..
Pratt, Asa	..	..	..	1	1	3	..	..	1	..	..
Pratt, David	3	1	1	1	..	3	..	..	1	..	..
Redfield, Richard	4	1	..	..	..	..	..	..	1	..	..
Rice, Widow Ana	2	..	1	..	..	..	1	3	1	..	..
Robins, Joseph	..	..	..	..	1	..	1	..	..	1	..
Roger, John	..	..	2	..	1	1	..	..	1	1	..
Rosbrook, Daniel	3	..	..	1	..	..	2	..	1	..	..
Rouse, Nicholas	2	..	1	1	..	..	..	..	1	..	..
Russel, William	2	..	..	1	..	2	..	..	1	..	..
Sawyer, Ephraim	5	2	..	..	1	..	..	1	1	..	..
Searl, Aron	3	..	..	1	..	2	..	1	1	..	..
Searl, Enoch	1	..	..	1	..	3	1	..	1	..	..
Searl, Luther	..	..	..	1	..	1	..	..	1	..	..
Searl, Philip	..	..	..	1	..	2	..	..	1	..	..
Searl, Samuel	1	..	..	1	..	..	..	..	1	..	..
Searle, Joseph	2	..	..	1	..	2	..	..	1	..	..
Smith, Aaron	2	..	..	1	..	2	..	..	1	..	..
Smith, Asher	1	..	2	..	1	2	1	1	..	1	..
Smith, Caleb	1	..	..	1	..	2	..	..	1	..	..
Smith, Daniel	..	..	..	1	..	4	..	1	..	..	..
Smith, Ephraim	2	..	..	..	1	1	1	..	1	..	..
Smith, Isaac	2	..	1	..	..	..	..	1	..	..	..
Smith, Jacob	1	1	..	1	..	2	..	..	1	..	..
Smith, Marshal	..	1	..	1	1	1	1	1	1	..	..
Smith, Nathan	1	1	..	1	..	1	..	1	1	..	..
Southard, Benjamin	2	1	2	..	1	2	..	..	1	..	..
Stiles, Jacob	3	..	1	..	..	..	..	1	..	..	..
Stone, Ephraim	1	1	..	..	1	2	..	..	..	1	..
Stone, Leonard	..	..	1	..	..	..	..	1	..	..	..
Stone, Phillip	..	1	..	1	..	2	1	..	1	..	..
Swinton, David	1	..	1	1	..	3	1	..	1	..	..
Tichenor, Daniel	3	1	..	1	..	1	1	..	1	..	..
Tichenor, Isaac	..	..	..	1	..	..	..	..	1	..	..
Tichenor, Martin	2	..	2	..	1	2	1	..	1	..	..
Tichenor, Zopher	2	2	..	1	..	2	..	1	1	..	..
Turner, Jeremiah	..	..	..	1	..	1	1	..	1	..	..

ADDISON COUNTY—Continued

NAMES OF HEADS OF FAMILIES	FREE WHITE MALES: Under 10 years of age	FREE WHITE MALES: Of 10 and under 16	FREE WHITE MALES: Of 16 and under 26 including heads of families	FREE WHITE MALES: Of 26 and under 45 including heads of families	FREE WHITE MALES: Of 45 and upwards including heads of families	FREE WHITE FEMALES: Under 10 years of age	FREE WHITE FEMALES: Of 10 and under 16	FREE WHITE FEMALES: Of 16 and under 26 including heads of families	FREE WHITE FEMALES: Of 26 and under 45 including heads of families	FREE WHITE FEMALES: Of 45 and upwards including heads of families	All other free persons except Indians not taxed
BRIDPORT—con.											
Vaughan, William	..	..	..	..	1	1	..	..	..	1	..
Vickerey, Gilbert	..	..	..	1	..	1	..	..	1	..	..
Walker, Russel	1	..	..	1	..	1	..	1	..	..	..
Ward, John	2	2	..	1	..	2	1	..	1	..	..
Wells, Nathaniel	3	2	..	1	..	2	..	2	1	..	..
Wilcox, David	..	..	1	..	..	..	..	1	..	..	..
Wilkinson, Henry	..	..	..	..	1	..	..	..	..	1	..
Williams, Joseph	2	..	1	1	..	3	..	..	1	..	..
Wilson, Samuel	1	..	3	..	..	1	1	2	1	..	2
Wood, Joseph	..	..	1	1	..	3	1	..	1	..	..
Wright, Gilbert	1	..	..	1	..	..	..	..	1	..	..
BRISTOL											
Alen, Johnson	1	..	..	2	..	2	..	..	1	..	..
Allen, Timothy	..	..	..	..	1	..	1	..	..	1	..
Allen, Timothy Jr.	2	..	1	1	..	1	1	1	1	..	..
Alvord, Jonathan	..	..	..	1	1	1	..	..	1	..	..
Andrews, Richard	1	1	..	1	..	1	..	..	1	..	..
Arnold, John	..	4	..	..	1	1	..	..	..	1	..
Bass, William	1	..	..	1	..	..	..	1	..	..	..
Beal, Obadiah	2	..	..	1	..	2	1	..	1	..	..
Bennett, Ezra	..	1	..	1	..	..	..	..	..	..	..
Blanchard, George	2	..	..	..	1	1	..	..	..	1	..
Bond, John	1	..	..	1	..	4	2	1	1	..	..
Brooks, Samuel	..	1	2	..	1	2	..	1	..	1	..
Brown, Nathan	..	..	..	1	..	2	1	..	1	..	..
Burral, Ezra	..	1	1	..	1	..	2	2	..	1	..
Cadwell, Isaac	2	..	..	1	..	2	..	..	1	..	..
Cadwell, Jacob	1	..	..	1	..	..	..	..	..	..	..
Cady, David	..	1	1	..	1	1	1	..	..	1	..
Canfield, Benijah	..	..	..	..	1	..	..	1	..	1	..
Canfield, Benijah Jr.	..	..	1	..	..	2	..	1	..	..	..
Chapel, Andrew	..	..	..	1	..	2	..	..	1	..	..
Chase, Timothy	3	2	1	1	..	1	1	..	1	..	..
Clapp, Benjamin	..	1	1	..	1	..	1	..	..	1	..
Clark, William	1	1	..	1	..	5	..	..	1	..	..
Cook, John	1	..	..	1	..	2	..	..	1	..	..
Copland, David	..	1	..	1	..	3	1	..	1	..	..
Day, James	1	..	..	1	..	..	..	1	..	..	..
Dayfoot, Michael	1	..	..	1	..	2	..	1	..	..	..
Dean, James	2	..	1	1	..	1	..	..	1	..	..
Denton, Ezekiel	..	1	2	1	..	1	2	..	1	..	..
Dicke, John	..	..	..	1	..	..	..	..	1	..	..
Drake, Isaac	..	..	..	1	..	..	1	..	..	1	..
Drake, Oliver	4	..	..	1	..	1	..	1	..	..	..
Dunshee, Robert	3	..	..	1	..	..	1	1	..	..	..
Dunshee, Thomas	4	2	..	1	..	1	1	..	1	..	..
Eastman, Amos	..	..	..	1	..	4	..	..	1	1	..
Eastman, Calvin	1	..	..	1	..	2	1	..	1	..	..
Eastman, Jonathan	3	..	..	..	1	1	..	..	1	..	..
Eastman, Justin	..	..	1	..	..	1	..	1	..	..	..
Eastman, Luther	..	..	1	..	..	..	..	1	..	..	..
Eastman, Oliver	2	2	..	1	..	2	..	..	1	..	..
Elsworth, Chancey	1	..	..	1	..	..	..	..	1	..	..
Elsworth, Oliver	..	1	1	..	1	..	1	1	..	1	..
Ferma, Josa	2	..	..	1	..	..	1	..	1	..	..
Field, Anthony Jr.	..	..	..	1	..	5	..	1	..	..	..
Field, Joseph	1	..	..	1	..	2	..	..	1	..	..
Franklin, Joshua	1	1	1	1	1	1	..	2	..	1	..
Gager, Abraham	1	..	1	..	..	2	..	1	..	..	..
Hall, Gersham	2	..	..	1	..	4	..	..	1	..	..
Hanford, Jesse	1	1	1	..	..	..	..	1	..	..	..
Haskill, David	2	1	1	..	1	3	2	..	..	1	..
Hawley, Manchester	1	..	..	..	1	2	..	..	1	..	..
Hawley, Robert	4	..	1	1	..	..	1	..	1	..	..
Hill, Lewis	..	..	1	..	..	1	..	..	1	..	..
Hitchman, John	..	1	1	..	1	..	2	..	1	..	..
Holcomb, Noah	1	..	..	1	..	1	..	..	1	..	..
Hubbard, Nehemiah	1	..	..	1	..	1	..	1	..	..	..
Huntley, John	1	..	..	1	..	2	1	..	1	..	..
Hurlbut, David	..	..	1	..	..	..	..	1	..	..	..
Hurlbut, Jeremiah	2	..	..	1	..	1	..	..	1	..	..
Isham, David J.	2	..	..	1	..	3	..	..	1	..	..
Isham, Isaac	2	..	..	1	..	1	..	..	1	..	..
Jones, Henry	..	..	2	1	..	..	1	1	..	1	..

NAMES OF HEADS OF FAMILIES	FREE WHITE MALES: Under 10 years of age	FREE WHITE MALES: Of 10 and under 16	FREE WHITE MALES: Of 16 and under 26 including heads of families	FREE WHITE MALES: Of 26 and under 45 including heads of families	FREE WHITE MALES: Of 45 and upwards including heads of families	FREE WHITE FEMALES: Under 10 years of age	FREE WHITE FEMALES: Of 10 and under 16	FREE WHITE FEMALES: Of 16 and under 26 including heads of families	FREE WHITE FEMALES: Of 26 and under 45 including heads of families	FREE WHITE FEMALES: Of 45 and upwards including heads of families	All other free persons except Indians not taxed
BRISTOL—con.											
Keath, Roswel	..	..	1	..	..	2	..	1	..	..	..
Keeler, Jedediah	2	..	..	1	..	..	1	1	..	..	..
Killbourn, John	2	..	..	1	..	1	..	1	..	1	..
Lampson, Amos	1	..	..	1	..	3	..	..	1	..	..
Maccallister, James	..	..	1	..	..	..	..	1	..	..	..
McLathlen, Henry	1	..	4	2	..	..	..	..	1	..	..
Miller, Russel	2	..	..	..	1	..	..	..	..	1	..
Miller, Veris	2	..	..	1	..	1	1	1	1	..	..
Miller, Warren	..	..	..	1	1	..	..	..	..	1	..
Monsil, Jorden	1	1	1	1	..	3	1	..	1	..	..
Mordock, Joshua	..	1	..	1	..	4	1	..	1	..	..
Mordock, Samuel	3	2	..	1	..	1	3	..	1	..	..
More, Seth	1	..	..	1	..	3	..	..	1	..	..
Munson, Ephraim	..	..	..	..	1	..	1	..	..	1	..
Munson, Ephraim Jr.	3	..	..	1	..	..	..	2	..	..	..
Munson, Noble	1	..	..	1	..	1	..	1	..	..	..
Newton, Jonah	3	1	1	..	1	..	1	1	1	..	..
Noise, David	2	1	..	1	..	2	..	..	1	..	..
Norton, Elisha	2	..	..	1	..	..	..	..	1	..	..
Obrien, James	..	..	..	1	..	..	..	..	1	..	..
Obrien, William	..	..	..	1	..	..	..	1	1	..	..
Parmelly, Artemas	4	2	..	1	..	1	1	..	1	..	..
Parmelly, Freeman	2	..	1	..	..	1	..	1	..	..	..
Parmelly, Joseph	1	..	4	..	1	1	1	..	1	..	..
Peterson, John	2	..	..	1	..	1	..	..	1	..	..
Post, Reuben	2	..	..	2	..	2	1	1	1	..	..
Raymond, Paul	3	..	..	1	..	..	..	..	1	..	..
Rich, James	2	..	..	1	..	3	1	..	1	..	..
Richardson, Eleazer	..	..	1	..	..	..	..	1	..	..	..
Rider, John	1	..	..	1	..	..	..	1	..	..	..
Rider, Nathan	..	..	..	1	..	2	..	..	1	..	..
Rugg, Phineas	2	..	..	1	..	2	2	..	1	..	..
Rutherford, Andrew	..	..	..	..	1	..	..	..	..	1	..
Rutherford, Tristram	2	..	..	1	..	2	..	..	1	..	..
Scott, Amos	3	1	2	..	1	4	2	1	1	..	..
Smith, Asa	2	..	..	1	..	4	1	..	1	..	..
Smith, Levi	2	1	..	1	..	2	1	..	1	..	..
Soper, Enos	..	..	1	..	..	..	..	..	1	..	..
Soper, Henry	..	..	1	..	..	..	..	1	..	..	..
Speary, Asahel	..	1	1	..	1	1	..	..	..	2	..
Steadman, John	..	..	..	..	1	..	..	1	..	1	..
Steadman, John Jr.	2	1	2	..	1	2	1	..	..	1	..
Stewart, Samuel	2	..	1	..	1	3	2	..	1	..	..
Stone, Matcher	..	..	..	..	1	..	..	..	1	..	..
Sturdevant, Noah	3	..	..	1	..	2	1	..	1	..	..
Sumner, George	..	..	..	1	..	1	..	..	1	..	..
Sumner, Henry	1	..	..	1	..	..	..	1	..	..	..
Sumner, William	1	..	..	1	..	2	..	..	1	..	..
Sutton, Benjamin	2	..	..	1	..	2	..	..	1	..	..
Thomas, Elijah	2	1	..	1	..	1	..	..	1	..	..
Tibbetts, George	2	..	..	1	..	2	2	..	1	..	..
Tubb, Andrew	1	..	..	1	..	1	..	..	1	..	..
Vrotenbury, Thomas	2	1	..	1	..	1	1	..	1	..	..
White, Moses	1	1	..	1	..	3	1	1	1	..	..
Wilie, Abraham	..	1	1	..	..	..	..	1	..	..	..
UNCERTAIN NAME											
Ebern (?), Reuben	3	..	..	1	..	..	..	..	1	..	..
CORNWALL											
Abbott, Seth	..	..	2	..	1	..	..	..	..	1	..
Abernathy, Cyrus	2	..	..	1	..	..	..	1	..	..	..
Abernathy, Jared	..	..	2	..	1	..	1	..	..	1	..
Alvord, John	1	..	..	1	..	3	..	1	..	..	..
Andrews, Cone	..	1	2	..	..	..	1	1	..	..	..
Andrews, Eldadd	..	1	2	..	1	1	1	2	..	1	..
Andrews, Ephraim	..	..	..	1	..	3	2	..	1	..	..
Andrews, Ethan	1	..	1	1	..	1	..	2	1	..	..
Avery, Roser	2	1	..	1	..	..	..	1	..	..	..
Baker, Timothy	1	1	..	..	1	5	2	..	1	..	..
Bartholomew, Samuel	..	..	..	1	..	..	..	1	..	..	..
Baxter, William	1	1	..	1	..	2	..	..	1	..	..
Benedict, Zachariah	2	..	..	1	..	..	1	..	1	..	..
Benton, Andrew	1	1	..	1	..	1	1	..	1	..	..
Benton, Feelix	2	1	1	1	..	4	1	..	1	..	..
Bingham, James	1	..	1	1	..	1	1	1	..	..	..
Bingham, Jeremiah	..	1	1	..	1	..	1	1	..	1	..

ADDISON COUNTY—Continued

NAMES OF HEADS OF FAMILIES	FREE WHITE MALES					FREE WHITE FEMALES					All other free persons except Indians not taxed
	Under 10 years of age	Of 10 and under 16	Of 16 and under 26 including heads of families	Of 26 and under 45 including heads of families	Of 45 and upwards including heads of families.	Under 10 years of age	Of 10 and under 16	Of 16 and under 26 including heads of families	Of 26 and under 45 including heads of families	Of 45 and upwards including heads of families	
CORNWALL—con.											
Bingham, Jeremiah 2nd	3	..	..	1	..	1	1	..	1	..	..
Bingham, Reuben	2	..	2	..	..	..	..	1	..	..	..
Blanchard, Nathaniel	2	1	1	..	1	2	1	..	1	..	..
Blodget, Samuel	3	1	3		1	2	1	1	1	..	..
Bodfish, Nathan	1	..	1	..	..	..	..	1	..	..	..
Boyington, John	4	1	..	1	..	1	..	..	1	..	..
Cady, Calvin	2	..	..	1	..	..	..	1	..	..	..
Cassel, William	..	..	..	1	1	..	..	..	1	1	..
Chapman, Lemuel	3	..	..	1	..	..	1	..	1	1	..
Chipman, Jesse	3	1	1	..	1	2	2	..	..	1	..
Claflin, Ezra	1	..	..	1	..	2	..	1	..	..	..
Coggswell, Joseph	..	..	1	..	1	..	1	..	..	1	..
Coggswell, Nathaniel	..	..	..	..	1	..	..	..	..	1	..
Cole, Nathaniel	1	1	..	..	1	2	1	..	1	..	..
Cook, Ebenezer H.	1	..	..	1	..	1	..	..	1	1	..
Cook, Joseph	2	1	1	..	1	2	1	1	1	..	..
Daggett, David	..	..	..	1	..	..	..	1	..	..	..
Daggett, Henry	..	..	1	..	..	..	..	1	..	..	..
Daggett, Joseph	1	2	..	1	..	3	..	2	1	..	..
Davis, Abijah	2	1	2	1	..	1	..	1	..	..	..
Delano, Abisha	1	3	4		1	2	1	1	..	1	..
Delong, Aaron	1	..	1	1	..	1	..	1	..	..	..
Delong, Francis	2	..	1	..	..	1	..	1	..	..	..
Douglass, John	..	..	1	..	..	..	..	1	..	..	..
Douglass, Silas	1	..	1	..	..	1	..	1	..	..	..
Durphy, Elijah	4	1	..	1	..	..	..	..	1	..	..
Ealls, Nathan	2	..	..	1	..	..	..	1	..	..	..
Ellsworth, Eliphalet	2	1	..	1	..	1	2	..	1	..	..
Field, Ahasel	..	1	..	1	..	2	..	..	1	1	..
Fields, Elisha	2	..	..	1	..	1	..	..	1	..	..
Finn, Titus	3	2	1	1	..	..	1	2	1	..	..
Finn, Titus Jr.	1	..	1	..	..	..	..	1	..	..	..
Fisher, Isaac	1	..	..	1	..	2	1	1	1	..	..
Foot, Daniel	2	1	1	1	..	1	1	..	1	..	..
Foot, Jared Jr.	3	1	..	1	1	1	..	..	2	..	..
Foot, Nathan	..	..	..	..	1	..	..	1	..	1	..
Foot, Nathan Jr.	1	1	..	1	..	2	..	..	2	..	..
Foot, Solomon	..	..	..	1	..	1	..	..	1	..	..
Ford, David	..	2	1	..	1	2	..	3	1	..	..
Ford, Frederick	..	1	2	1	..	..	..	..	1	..	..
Gibbs, Henry	..	1	..	..	1	..	1	1	..	1	..
Gibbs, Zadock	..	1	..	1	..	1	..	..	1	..	..
Gillet, Reuben	3	..	..	1	..	1	..	..	1	..	..
Goodrich, Moses	1	1	1	..	1	1	..	4	..	1	..
Hall, Reuben	..	..	1	1	..	..	..	1	1	..	..
Hall, Thomas	3	1	1	1	..	1	2	1	..	1	..
Hamblin, John	3	..	2	..	1	2	2	..	..	1	..
Hamblin, Joseph	4	..	..	1	..	1	1	..	1	..	..
Hathway, Erastus	3	1	..	1	..	2	1	..	1	..	..
Hawley, John	2	1	2	..	1	1	2	..	1	..	..
Hawley, Stephen	..	1	1	1	..	1	1	1	1	..	..
Hepburn, Reuben	3	..	..	1	..	..	..	1	..	..	..
Hill, Ambron	..	1	..	..	1	..	1	..	..	1	..
Hill, Moses	2	..	..	1	..	..	..	1	..	..	..
Hill, Titus	2	2	2	..	2	1	..	1	1	1	..
Huntington, Daniel	1	..	1	1	..	1	..	1	..	..	..
Hurlbut, Bartholomew	3	1	..	1	..	1	1	..	1	..	..
Hurlbut, David	..	..	1	..	..	..	..	1	..	..	..
Hurlbut, Elisha	..	..	..	..	1	..	..	..	..	..	..
Hurlbut, Elisha Jr.	3	1	..	1	..	2	2	..	1	..	..
Ingraham, Daniel	..	..	1	..	..	..	..	1	..	..	..
Ingraham, David	3	1	..	..	1	..	1	..	..	1	..
Ingraham, Jabez	..	..	1	..	..	..	..	1	..	..	..
Ingraham, Jacob	..	..	..	..	1	..	1	..	..	1	..
Ingraham, Nathan	..	..	..	..	1	..	1	..	..	1	..
Ingraham, Nathan 2nd	..	..	1	..	..	..	..	1	..	..	..
Ingraham, Samuel	3	1	..	1	1	1	1	1	1	..	..
Ives, Enos	..	..	..	..	1	..	..	..	..	1	..
Ives, Enos Jr.	3	1	..	1	..	1	1	..	1	..	..
Ives, Jared	3	..	..	1	..	1	..	..	1	..	..
Jackson, Nathan	2	..	..	1	..	..	2	1	..	..	..
Jennings, Oliver	..	..	1	..	..	..	..	1	..	..	..
Jennis, Cerdial	1	1	..	1	..	3	..	..	1	..	..
Johnson, Zachariah	..	..	..	..	1	..	1	1	..	1	..
Jones, Amasa	..	..	..	1	..	1	..	1	..	..	..
Jones, Israel C.	1	1	2	1	..	2	..	2	1	..	..
Jones, William	2	1	..	1	..	..	2	..	1	..	..
Jones, Zebulon	..	..	..	1	..	..	..	..	1	..	..
Jones, Zebulon	1	2	..	..	1	1	..	1	..	1	..
Judd, Gideon	3	1	..	1	..	1	..	..	1	..	..
CORNWALL—con.											
Kellogg, Adonijah	..	..	..	1	..	3	..	..	1	..	..
Kellogg, William	..	..	1	1	..	..	..	..	1	..	..
Kingman, Michael	1	1	2	..	1	1	1	1	..	1	..
Lade, James	2	1	1	..	1	..	1	..	1	..	..
Lampson, Daniel	..	1	..	1	..	3	..	..	1	1	..
Landon, Ethan	1	..	..	1	..	..	..	1	..	..	..
Landon, Isaac	1	..	1	..	..	..	..	1	..	..	..
Landon, Thomas	..	1	1	..	1	1	..	..	..	1	..
Lewis, Abraham	1	..	1	..	..	..	..	1	..	..	..
Lewis, John	1	1	..	..	1	1	1	..	..	1	..
Lewis, Mathew	1	..	1	..	1	2	1	..	1	..	..
Lewis, Nathan	2	..	..	..	1	2	2	..	1	..	..
Linsley, David	..	..	..	1	..	1	..	1	..	..	..
Linsley, Joel	5	2	1	1	..	..	1	1	1	..	..
Linsley, Widow Lydia	..	..	..	..	..	..	..	..	..	1	..
Linsley, Simeon	1	..	..	1	..	2	2	..	1	..	..
Linsley, Solomon	..	..	..	..	1	..	..	..	..	1	..
Linsley, Solomon Jr.	1	..	..	1	..	2	2	..	1	..	..
Loomis, Alexander	..	..	1	..	..	..	..	..	..	..	..
Mead, Rufus	1	..	..	1	..	2	..	..	1	..	..
Mead, Solomon	2	..	..	1	..	2	..	..	1	..	..
Minor, Richard	3	..	..	1	..	3	2	1	1	..	..
Nichols, Benjamin	1	1	1	..	1	1	1	..	..	1	..
North, Solomon	1	..	..	1	..	1	1	..	1	..	..
Nowel, Reverius	2	..	2	..	1	1	2	2	1	..	..
Parker, Isaac	3	..	1	..	1	2	3	..	1	..	..
Parker, James	1	..	..	1	..	2	..	..	1	1	..
Parkhill, David	2	..	1	..	1	1	3	..	1	..	..
Payne, Jonathan	1	..	..	1	..	1	..	1	..	..	..
Peck, Jacob	2	2	1	..	1	3	..	1	1	1	..
Peck, Reuben	2	..	1	1	..	..	..	..	1	..	..
Penoyer, Amos	1	..	..	1	..	..	1	..	1	..	..
Post, Roswel	2	1	1	..	1	1	2	1	1	..	..
Pratt, David	2	2	..	1	..	2	..	..	1	..	..
Pratt, Ephraim	..	2	..	1	..	2	1	..	1	..	..
Pratt, Moses	3	1	2	..	1	..	1	1	..	1	..
Prichard, Thomas	6	..	..	1	..	..	1	..	1	..	..
Reaves, Benjamin	1	..	1	..	1	..	1	2	..	1	..
Richards, Samuel	1	2	..	1	..	2	1	1	1	..	..
Richardson, Barzillai	..	..	..	1	..	2	2	..	1	1	..
Richardson, Nathaniel	..	..	1	..	..	1	..	1	..	..	..
Robbins, John	4	..	..	1	..	..	..	..	1	..	..
Rockwell, James	1	..	..	1	..	..	1	..	1	..	..
Rockwell, Jeremiah	2	2	2	1	..	2	..	1	1	..	..
Rockwell, John	1	2	..	..	2	2	..	3	..	1	..
Sampson, Eliphalet	1	..	1	1	..	3	1	1	1	..	..
Sampson, Jonathan	..	..	1	..	..	..	..	1	..	..	..
Sampson, Thomas	..	..	..	1	..	1	..	..	1	..	..
Sampson, William	3	2	..	1	..	1	..	..	1	..	..
Sanfred, Benjamin	3	2	..	1	..	1	1	..	1	..	..
Sanfred, Simon	1	1	1	..	..	..	..	1	..	..	..
Sawyer, Ephraim	..	..	3	2	..	1	..	1	1	..	..
Scott, Aaron	..	3	1	..	1	..	1	..	..	1	..
Scott, Aaron Jr.	1	..	..	1	..	3	..	..	1	..	..
Scott, Ahasel	..	..	1	..	..	1	..	1	..	..	..
Scott, Josiah	1	..	1	1	..	3	..	..	..	..	..
Scovel, Daniel	3	..	..	1	..	1	1	..	1	..	..
Scovel, Ezra	1	..	..	1	..	..	..	1	..	..	..
Sipon, John	1	1	..	1	..	2	..	..	1	..	..
Slade, William	1	1	1	..	1	2	1	1	..	1	..
Smally, Zimri	1	1	..	1	..	1	..	..	1	..	..
Smith, Eliba	..	..	1	..	..	1	..	1	..	..	..
Smith, Ephraim	1	1	..	..	1	1	..	..	1	1	..
Smith, Samuel S.	..	..	..	1	..	1	..	..	1	..	..
Speary, Daniel	1	..	1	1	..	3	..	1	1	..	..
Speary, David	..	2	4	..	1	..	1	..	..	1	..
Speary, Levi	1	..	..	1	..	4	1	..	1	..	..
Squire, Ebenezer	1	1	..	1	..	1	..	..	1	..	..
Squire, Timothy	3	..	..	1	..	1	2	..	1	..	..
Stebbins, Ebenezer	1	..	1	..	1	..	1	2	..	1	..
Stebens, Benjamin	..	1	1	1	..	1	..	1	1	..	..
Stockwell, Joshua	2	1	4	1	..	..	..	1	1	..	..
Stone, Eli	1	1	..	1	..	3	..	..	1	..	..
Stowel, Nathan	..	..	1	1	..	..	..	1	..	..	..
Tamblin, Stephen	..	..	..	..	1	..	2	..	..	1	..
Tamblin, Stephen A.	4	..	..	1	..	2	..	1	..	..	..
Tilden, Calvin	1	2	2	..	1	..	1	1	1	..	..
Tomblin, Lemuel	1	..	..	1	..	1	..	..	1	..	..
Turner, Timothy	..	..	1	..	..	1	..	1	..	..	..
Tyfield, Edward	2	..	..	1	..	3	..	..	1	..	..

ADDISON COUNTY—Continued

NAMES OF HEADS OF FAMILIES	FREE WHITE MALES: Under 10 years of age	FREE WHITE MALES: Of 10 and under 16	FREE WHITE MALES: Of 16 and under 26 including heads of families	FREE WHITE MALES: Of 26 and under 45 including heads of families	FREE WHITE MALES: Of 45 and upwards including heads of families.	FREE WHITE FEMALES: Under 10 years of age	FREE WHITE FEMALES: Of 10 and under 16	FREE WHITE FEMALES: Of 16 and under 26 including heads of families	FREE WHITE FEMALES: Of 26 and under 45 including heads of families	FREE WHITE FEMALES: Of 45 and upwards including heads of families	All other free persons except Indians not taxed
CORNWALL—con.											
Ward, William	1	..	..	1	..	1	1	..	1	..	..
Warner, Thomas	1	..	..	1	..	3	..	..	1	..	..
Waters, Jabez	1	..	..	1	..	..	1	..	1	..	..
Williamson, Abraham Jr.	1	..	1	..	..	1	..	1	..	..	..
Williamson, Alexander	..	1	1	..	1	..	..	..	..	1	..
Williamson, Winart	2	..	1	1	..	2	2	1	1	..	..
Woodward, Asa	1	..	1	1	..	4	1	..	1	..	..
Worcester, Abraham	1	..	..	1	..	3	..	..	1	..	..
Worcester, Benjamin	1	..	1	1	..	1	1	..	1	..	..
Wright, Simeon	1	1	..	1	..	1	..	1	..	..	..
UNCERTAIN NAME											
Mazasen (?), John	..	1	2	1	..	..	1	1	..	..	..
FERRISBURG											
Aikin, James	2	2	2	1	..	1	..	..	1	..	..
Alen, Obediah	2	..	1	1	..	..	1	1	..	..	..
Alfred, Oliver	3	..	..	1	..	2	2	..	1	..	..
Allen, Robert	2	3	1	1	..	2	1	..	1	..	..
Austin, Nathaniel	2	2	..	1	..	1	..	..	1	..	..
Bard, William	..	..	..	1	..	3	..	..	1	..	..
Barns, Joshua	3	1	..	..	1	1	1	..	1	..	..
Barns, Richard	..	..	..	..	1	..	..	..	..	1	..
Barns, Widow Ruth	2	2	4	..	..	1	1	2	..	1	..
Barnum, Barnabas	1	..	1	..	..	..	..	1	..	..	..
Barnum, John	1	1	1	1	..	2	1	..	1	..	..
Barnum, Joseph	1	..	2	..	1	..	..	1	..	1	..
Barnum, Richard	1	1	2	3	..	..	1	1	2	1	..
Bills, John	1	..	..	1	..	1	..	1	..	..	..
Bridia, David	2	2	..	..	1	3	..	1	..	1	..
Brown, John	..	..	1	..	..	..	..	1	..	..	..
Bull, Isaac	..	..	..	1	..	1	1	..	1	..	..
Burden, Nathaniel	..	..	1	..	1	..	2	..	..	1	..
Burdick, Paul	..	..	..	..	1	1	..	..	1	1	..
Cable, Samuel	..	..	..	..	1	..	..	..	..	1	..
Cable, Stephen	1	..	1	..	..	1	..	1	..	..	..
Carpenter, Asa	..	..	..	1	..	..	..	1	..	..	..
Carpenter, Benjamin	2	1	..	1	..	2	..	..	1	..	..
Cavender, Charles	1	..	..	1	..	2	..	1	..	..	..
Champlain, Thomas	5	1	1	1	..	..	1	4	1	..	1
Champlain, Thomas Jr.	2	..	1	..	..	..	..	1	..	..	..
Chatterdon, Abraham	1	..	..	1	..	2	..	1	..	..	..
Chelson, Joseph	1	..	1	..	1	..	..	..	1	..	..
Chittenden, Zebulon	..	..	1	..	1	..	..	1	..	1	..
Clark, Michael	3	1	1	..	1	1	1	..	..	1	..
Clinton, Henry	1	1	..	1	..	2	1	..	1	..	..
Clinton, Sheldon	3	..	..	1	..	1	..	1	..	..	..
Conkite, Peter	..	..	..	1	..	2	..	..	1	..	..
Corbin, David	2	1	..	1	..	1	1	..	1	..	..
Cousins, Jacob	1	..	2	1	..	2	2	..	1	..	..
Cousins, Joshua	..	..	..	..	1	..	..	..	..	1	..
Crampton, Andrew	..	1	..	1	..	1	..	1	..	..	..
Crankite, Lawrence	..	..	..	1	..	1	..	1	..	..	..
Cuiler, Jacob	2	..	..	1	..	2	..	..	1	..	..
Dakin, Timothy	3	1	..	1	..	..	1	..	1	..	..
Davis, Daniel	..	..	..	..	1	..	1	..	..	1	..
Davis, Zophan	1	..	1	1	..	2	..	..	1	..	..
Dewey, Noble	4	..	..	1	..	1	..	1	..	..	..
Ferris Benjamin	1	..	..	1	..	2	1	..	1	..	..
Ferris, Darius	4	..	..	1	..	1	..	..	1	..	..
Field, Anthony	..	..	1	1	1	..	..	2	..	1	..
Field, George	2	..	..	1	..	..	..	..	1	..	..
Field, John	2	2	..	1	..	3	..	..	1	..	..
Field, Stephen	1	..	1	..	..	2	..	1	..	..	..
Fish, Christopher	1	..	..	1	..	1	..	..	1	1	..
Fish, Daniel	2	..	1	2	..	2	..	1	..	..	..
Fish, Stephen	1	1	..	1	..	1	..	..	1	..	..
Fraser, John	2	1	..	2	..	..	..	4	..	..	..
French, Nathan	1	..	..	1	..	2	..	..	1	..	..
Fuller, Ashbel	4	2	..	1	..	1	..	..	1	..	..
Fuller, Isbon	3	2	..	1	..	1	1	..	1	..	..
Gaige, Benjamin	1	..	..	1	..	..	1	1	..	1	..
Gaige, George	1	..	2	2	..	3	2	..	1	..	..
Gaige, Isaac	3	1	1	..	1	1	2	..	1	..	..
Gaige, Peter	1	..	1	..	..	1	..	1	..	..	..
Gaige, Richard	3	..	..	1	..	..	..	1	..	..	..
Gaige, Walter	..	2	2	1	..	..	..	..	..	..	..
Gaige, William	1	..	2	..	1	..	..	1	..	1	..
Ganson, Benjamin	1	1	1	..	1	2	1	1	1	..	..
Gould, Edward	1	2	1	..	1	3	1	..	..	1	..
Gregory, Selah	2	..	..	1	..	2	..	..	1	..	..
Griffin, Jesse	..	..	1	1	..	..	..	..	1	..	..
FERRISBURG—con.											
Halstead, John	3	..	2	1	..	1	1	..	1	..	1
Hamblin, Amos	2	..	..	1	..	2	..	..	1	..	..
Hartshorn, Zephaniah	1	2	..	1	..	1	1	1	..	..	..
Harvey, John	..	1	..	..	1	..	1	..	1	..	..
Hasbrook, Jacob	1	1	..	..	1	..	..	2	..	1	..
Hatch, Ebenezer	1	..	..	1	..	1	..	..	1	..	..
Hatch, Jeremiah	1	..	..	1	..	1	..	..	1	..	..
Hatch, Timothy	1	..	..	1	..	2	..	..	1	..	..
Hawly, Gideon	2	3	..	1	..	2	1	..	1	..	..
Hayes, Michael	1	1	2	..	1	..	1	..	..	1	..
Hazard, John	2	..	..	1	..	1	..	1	..	..	..
Hazard, Robert	2	3	1	..	1	3	..	1	1	..	..
Higbee, William	2	..	..	1	..	1	..	1	..	..	..
Hodges, James	1	1	..	1	..	..	2	..	1	..	..
Hough, John	2	2	2	..	1	1	..	..	1	..	..
Hubble, Jedediah	1	..	3	..	..	1	..	1	..	..	..
Jackson, Bartholomew	1	..	..	1	..	..	..	..	1	..	..
Jaquois, Lewis	2	2	..	..	1	1	..	1	1	..	..
Jaquois, Nathan	..	..	..	..	1	1	2	..	..	1	..
Jaquois, Stafford	2	..	..	1	..	1	..	..	1	..	..
Jaquois, Sylvester	1	..	..	1	..	3	..	..	1	..	..
Johnson Alexander	2	..	1	1	..	..	..	..	1	..	..
Johnson, Isaiah	..	..	..	1	..	3	..	..	1	..	1
Keeler, Jonathan	2	..	..	1	..	2	1	..	1	..	..
Kelley, Bastion R.	..	..	1	..	..	1	..	1	..	..	..
Kellogg, Josiah	2	..	..	1	..	3	..	..	1	..	..
Kellogg, Solomon	3	..	..	1	..	1	..	..	1	..	..
Kellogg, William	..	..	1	..	1	1	1	..	..	2	..
Kerbey, William	..	..	..	1	..	..	..	3	..	..	..
Langworthy, Sheffield	..	..	1	1	..	3	..	2	..	..	..
Locke, Jonathan	3	..	..	1	..	2	..	..	1	..	..
Logg, Thomas	1	..	..	1	..	2	..	..	1	..	..
Meade, Albert	1	..	..	1	..	2	..	1	..	..	..
Meriam, Jonathan	1	2	..	1	..	1	..	..	1	..	..
Miller, Simeon	3	..	..	1	1	..	..	1	..	..	..
Mittlebrook, Theophilas	1	..	1	1	..	2	..	1	1	..	..
Noble, Solomon	..	1	..	1	..	2	1	..	1	..	..
Norris, Isaac	1	..	..	..	1	2	..	..	1	..	..
Odle, Abijah	1	1	..	1	..	1	..	..	1	..	..
Porter, Nathan	2	..	..	1	..	1	..	..	1	..	..
Porter, Noah	..	..	..	..	1	1	1	..	..	1	..
Porter, Noah W.	..	..	1	..	..	1	..	1	..	..	..
Porter, Varsel	1	..	..	1	..	1	..	..	1	..	..
Powers, Joseph	3	..	1	1	..	2	1	..	1	1	..
Powers, Joseph 2nd.	3	..	..	1	..	..	..	1	..	..	..
Powers, Nathan	..	..	1	..	..	1	..	1	..	..	..
Powers, Simeon	..	1	..	..	1	1	..	..	..	1	..
Powers, Whitcomb	2	1	..	1	..	2	1	1	1	..	..
Powers, William	1	..	..	1	..	..	..	1	..	..	..
Prindle, Gideon	1	..	..	1	..	..	..	1	..	..	..
Prindle, Landon	2	..	..	1	..	1	..	..	1	..	..
Prindle, Samuel	3	..	1	..	1	2	1	1	1	..	..
Prindle, Samuel Jr.	1	..	..	1	..	..	..	1	..	..	..
Puck, William	2	2	..	1	..	2	1	..	1	..	..
Reynolds, Shubal	2	..	..	1	..	..	..	..	1	..	..
Robinson, Peter	1	..	..	1	..	2	1	..	1	..	..
Robinson, Thomas R.	1	1	1	2	..	..	1	1	2	..	..
Rogers, Abraham	4	..	..	1	..	1	..	1	1	..	..
Rogers, Ananias	..	..	3	7	..	1	..	3	2	1	2
Rogers, Asa	1	..	1	..	..	..	..	1	..	..	..
Rogers, Timothy	3	1	1	1	1	1	2	1	1	..	..
Rogers, Wing	..	..	..	..	1	1	1	2	..	1	..
Rogers, Wing Jr.	..	..	..	1	..	..	..	..	1	..	..
Saterly, Robert	2	..	..	1	..	3	..	..	1	..	..
Sexton, Jonathan	3	..	2	1	..	1	2	..	1	..	..
Shelden, John	..	..	1	..	..	1	..	1	..	..	..
Shelhouse, Martin	2	1	1	1	..	3	..	..	1	..	..
Slutt, John	2	..	..	..	1	3	1	..	1	..	..
Sprague, Nathan	1	1	..	..	1	..	1	..	..	1	..
Steadman, Job	2	2	..	1	..	2	1	..	1	..	..
Stormes, Primus	..	..	..	..	..	..	..	..	..	..	5
Targett, John	1	..	..	1	..	..	..	1	..	..	..
Thompson, Abel	1	..	2	..	1	..	1	1	..	1	..
Tupper, Absalom	1	1	1	1	..	4	1	1	1	1	..
Vanvliet, Peter	1	..	1	..	..	..	..	..	1	..	..
Varnal, John	1	..	..	1	..	..	..	1	..	..	..

ADDISON COUNTY—Continued

NAMES OF HEADS OF FAMILIES	FREE WHITE MALES: Under 10 years of age	FREE WHITE MALES: Of 10 and under 16	FREE WHITE MALES: Of 16 and under 26 including heads of families	FREE WHITE MALES: Of 26 and under 45 including heads of families	FREE WHITE MALES: Of 45 and upwards including heads of families	FREE WHITE FEMALES: Under 10 years of age	FREE WHITE FEMALES: Of 10 and under 16	FREE WHITE FEMALES: Of 16 and under 26 including heads of families	FREE WHITE FEMALES: Of 26 and under 45 including heads of families	FREE WHITE FEMALES: Of 45 and upwards including heads of families	All other free persons except Indians not taxed
FERRISBURG—con.											
Walker, Daniel	1	1	..	1	..	2	..	..	1	..	..
Walker, Nathan	..	1	3	..	2	..	..	1	..	1	..
Walker, Obadiah	..	1	..	1	..	1	..	1	..	..	..
Walker, William	..	..	1	..	..	1	..	1	..	..	..
Webster, Widow Rachel	..	1	..	..	..	..	..	1	..	1	..
Webster, William	2	3	..	1	..	1	..	1	1	..	..
Weston, Charles	..	1	1	..	1	..	1	..	1	..	..
White, David	1	..	1	..	..	..	..	1	..	..	..
Wing, Gideon	1	..	..	1	..	1	..	..	1	..	..
Wing, Samuel	2	..	..	1	..	1	..	..	1	..	..
Wood, Joseph	..	..	..	1	..	1	..	1	1	..	..
Yale, Moses	2	1	1	..	1	1	1	1	1	..	..
Young, James	..	..	..	1	..	..	..	..	1	..	..
Young, William	1	..	..	1	..	..	..	1	..	..	..
GOSHEN											
Tillotson, Silas	2	..	1	..	..	..	..	1	..	..	..
HANCOCK											
Austin, Daniel	1	..	..	1	..	1	..	1	..	..	..
Barnard, Nathaniel	..	..	..	1	..	..	..	..	..	..	..
Boardman, Isaac	1	1	..	..	1	3	2	..	1	..	..
Butts, Joseph	..	..	..	..	1	..	..	..	..	1	..
Butts, Joseph Jr.	..	..	..	1	..	2	..	1	..	..	..
Butts, Ozias	1	..	..	1	..	..	..	..	1	..	..
Cady, Noah	2	..	1	1	..	..	..	..	1	..	..
Carpenter, Nathan	2	1	..	..	1	1	..	..	1	1	..
Churchman, Nathaniel	..	1	..	1	..	1	1	1	1	..	..
Cummins, William	1	1	..	1	..	2	1	1	..	..	..
Darling, Levi	4	1	..	1	..	1	1	..	1	..	..
Dolbear, Nathan	..	..	1	1	..	1	..	1	..	..	..
Dolbear, Samuel	4	..	1	1	..	..	..	..	1	..	..
Freeman, Constant	2	..	..	1	..	1	..	..	1	..	..
Goodnough, Calvin	2	2	..	1	..	1	..	..	1	..	..
Gould, John	1	1	..	..	1	3	..	1	1	..	..
Lamb, William	1	..	..	1	..	3	..	..	1	..	..
Lane, Henery	..	..	..	1	..	..	..	..	1	..	..
Lards, Abraham	..	..	..	..	1	..	1	1	..	1	..
Larky, Abraham	1	..	1	1	2	5	1	1	..	1	..
McLaughlan, Daniel Jr.	1	..	1	..	..	1	..	1	..	..	..
McLaughlan, James	..	..	..	..	1	..	..	..	..	1	..
McLen, Daniel	3	1	..	..	1	1	..	..	..	1	..
Perkins, Asa	1	..	..	..	1	..	3	..	1	..	..
Piergo, James	..	..	..	1	..	2	..	..	1	..	..
Robins, Zenas	1	..	..	1	..	1	1	1	..	..	..
Simons, Jeremiah	1	..	..	..	1	1	..	1	..	..	..
Washburn, Ezra	1	..	1	..	..	..	..	1	..	..	..
KINGSTON											
Ball, Israel	..	..	1	1	1	..	..	1	..	1	..
Ball, Tyler	..	..	1	1	..	..	..	1	..	..	..
Bemis, Abel	2	..	..	..	..	1	..	1	..	..	..
Carter, John	1	..	1	..	..	..	..	..	1	..	..
Cone, Lemuel	2	1	1	1	..	2	1	1	1	..	..
Farnam, Eliphalet	4	..	..	..	1	..	1	..	1	..	..
Ford, Jonathan	2	..	..	..	..	..	..	..	..	..	..
King, Moses	..	1	1	1	1	1	1	..	1	..	..
King, Thomas	2	..	..	..	..	1	..	1	..	..	..
King, Zenos	2	1	1	1	..	1	..	1	..	..	..
Lamb, Jonathan	..	..	..	1	1	2	1	..	1	..	..
Lamb, Jonathan Jr.	2	2	..	1	..	2	..	..	..	1	..
Lamb, Reuben	2	2	1	..	..	..	..	..	..	1	..
Lamb, Warren	1	..	..	1	..	..	..	1	..	..	..
Lee, Phinehas	..	..	1	..	..	..	..	..	2	..	..
Lee, Sherman	..	..	1	..	..	..	..	1	..	..	..
Lewis, Eli	2	..	..	1	..	3	2	..	1	..	..
Lyman, Richard	1	2	..	2	..	2	1	..	1	..	..
McLaghlin, James	2	..	..	1	..	1	..	1	..	..	..
KINGSTON—con.											
Parker, Abel	2	..	..	..	..	2	1	1	1	1	..
Parker, Joseph	..	1	1	..	1	..	..	1	..	1	..
Patrick, Joseph	1	..	1	1	..	2	..	1	..	..	..
Pierce, Joel	2	..	..	1	1	..	..	..	1	..	..
Safford, Peletiah	1	..	2	..	1	..	..	..	..	..	..
Scarlott, Newman	1	..	..	1	..	1	..	1	..	..	..
Sprague, Night	..	..	1	1	..	3	..	..	1	..	..
Sterlin, Nathan	..	..	1	..	1	..	..	..	..	1	..
Still, Durand	1	..	1	..	1	..	..	1	1	1	..
Swan, John	1	2	2	1	1	3	1	1	..	..	..
Wade, Timothy	3	3	..	1	..	2	..	1	1	..	..
Wood, Asa	2	3	..	1	..	2	..	..	1	..	..
Wood, Oliver	1	..	..	..	..	..	..	1	..	1	..
LEICESTER											
Adams, Samuel	2	2	1	1	..	1	1	..	1	..	..
Adams, Samuel Jr.	2	..	..	1	..	1	..	..	1	..	..
Alden, Enoch	1	..	1	1	..	..	1	..	1	..	..
Alden, Thomas Jr.	..	..	..	..	1	1	..	1	..	..	..
Alden. Thomas Jr.	..	..	..	1	..	..	..	1	..	..	..
Alden, Timothy	1	..	1	..	..	..	..	1	..	..	..
Ames, Calvin	..	2	1	..	1	4	1	..	1	..	..
Barker, John	..	..	3	..	1	1	..	..	..	1	..
Barker, John Jr.	2	..	..	1	..	..	..	1	..	..	..
Bean, Joseph	3	..	..	1	..	..	..	..	1	..	..
Bishop, Thomas	..	..	..	..	1	..	..	..	..	..	..
Brown, Aaron	1	1	..	1	..	..	..	1	..	..	..
Brown, John	2	..	..	1	..	2	..	..	1	..	..
Brown, William	1	..	..	1	..	2	..	..	1	..	..
Capin, Joseph	3	2	1	..	1	1	2	1	1	..	..
Chan, Reuben	1	..	..	1	..	2	..	..	1	..	..
Cole, Allen	1	..	..	1	..	..	1	..	1	..	..
Conger, Codington	1	..	..	1	..	2	..	..	1	..	..
Cook, Widow Elizabeth	..	1	..	..	..	4	..	..	1	..	..
Cook, Elkanah	..	..	..	..	1	1	..	..	1	1	..
Daggett, Widow Judah	1	1	1	..	..	..	..	1	..	1	..
Dow, James	2	..	..	1	..	1	..	..	1	..	..
Dow, Joseph	1	..	1	..	..	..	..	1	..	..	..
Dow, Moses	2	2	1	..	1	3	1	..	1	..	..
Dowe, James	1	..	1	..	1	..	..	..	..	1	..
Easty, Aaron	1	..	..	..	1	..	..	..	..	1	..
Easty, John	2	..	..	1	..	..	..	1	..	..	..
Enos, Abner	2	..	..	1	..	..	..	1	1	..	..
Enos, James	..	..	2	..	1	..	1	1	..	1	..
Fisk, David	3	..	2	..	1	2	2	1	1	..	..
Fisk, Eber	..	..	..	1	..	2	..	1	..	..	..
Fitch, Israel	1	1	..	1	..	1	2	..	1	..	..
Goffield, Benjamin	..	..	..	1	1	..	..	..	..	1	..
Goffield, Elijah	5	..	..	1	..	..	..	1	1	..	..
Goffield, Joshua	1	..	..	1	..	1	..	2	..	..	..
Goffield, Salmon	..	..	1	..	..	2	..	1	..	..	..
Grandy, Asa	1	2	..	1	..	2	1	..	1	..	..
Hitchcock, Ebenezer M.	..	..	1	1	..	..	1	..	1	..	..
Hodgden, John	..	3	..	..	1	1	1	..	..	1	..
Huntley, Bethuel	1	1	..	1	..	1	1	..	1	..	..
Huntley, Samuel	1	..	..	..	1	..	..	..	..	1	..
Jennis, Ebenezer	2	..	..	1	..	..	..	..	1	..	..
Johnson, Moses	1	1	..	..	1	1	..	..	..	1	..
Jones, Richard	1	..	3	1	..	..	..	..	1	..	..
Keep, Samuel	..	..	..	..	1	..	..	..	..	1	..
Kilburn, William	1	1	..	1	..	..	..	..	1	..	..
Kingsley, James	2	1	1	1	..	2	..	..	1	..	..
Ladde, Justin	2	1	..	1	..	2	..	..	1	..	..
Lawson, John	..	1	..	..	1	..	..	1	..	..	..
Mack, James	..	..	..	1	..	..	1	..	1	..	..
Mack, Robert	..	..	..	..	1	..	..	1	..	1	..
McDonald, John B.	2	..	..	1	..	1	..	..	1	..	..
Merrifield, Amos	1	..	..	2	..	1	..	..	1	..	..
Merrifield, Joseph	..	1	1	..	1	..	..	..	..	1	..
Merrifield, Joseph Jr.	2	1	..	1	..	2	1	..	1	..	..
Morse, George	..	1	..	1	..	1	..	..	1	..	..
Morse, Jonathan	1	..	..	..	1	..	2	1	1	..	..
Mulleneaux, Isaac	1	..	..	1	..	..	..	..	1	..	..

ADDISON COUNTY—Continued

NAMES OF HEADS OF FAMILIES	FREE WHITE MALES: Under 10 years of age	FREE WHITE MALES: Of 10 and under 16	FREE WHITE MALES: Of 16 and under 26 including heads of families	FREE WHITE MALES: Of 26 and under 45 including heads of families	FREE WHITE MALES: Of 45 and upwards including heads of families.	FREE WHITE FEMALES: Under 10 years of age	FREE WHITE FEMALES: Of 10 and under 16	FREE WHITE FEMALES: Of 16 and under 26 including heads of families	FREE WHITE FEMALES: Of 26 and under 45 including heads of families	FREE WHITE FEMALES: Of 45 and upwards including heads of families	All other free persons except Indians not taxed
LEICESTER—con.											
Nelson, James	..	..	1	..	..	..	..	1	..	..	..
Noyes, Gilbert	1	..	1	..	..	1	..	1	..	..	..
Olin, Christopher	3	..	1	1	..	2	..	..	1	..	..
Olin, Henry	1	..	..	1	..	3	2	1	1	..	..
Olin, Justus	..	1	1	..	1	..	1	1	..	1	..
Osier, Consider	..	..	1	..	1	1	1	..	..	1	..
Osier, Consider Jr.	1	..	..	1	..	2	..	..	1	..	..
Parker, Jeremiah	..	1	..	..	1	1	1	1	..	1	..
Parks, Ephraim	..	1	..	1	..	4	1	2	1	..	..
Perry, Abijah	3	..	..	1	..	..	..	..	1	..	..
Perry, Nathan	2	..	1	1	..	1	..	2	..	..	..
Pryor, Edward	1	2	..	..	1	2	1	..	1	..	..
Rhodes, Paris	..	..	..	1	..	2	..	..	1	1	..
Roberts, Moses	..	1	..	..	1	2	1	..	1	..	..
Ross, Eleazer	1	2	..	1	..	2	..	1	..	..	..
Round, Nathan	1	1	..	1	..	1	..	..	1	..	..
Sawyer, Stephen	3	1	..	1	..	3	..	..	1	..	..
Smith, Abiel Jr.	..	..	1	..	..	..	..	1	..	..	..
Smith, Abijah	..	3	3	1	1	..	..	..	1	..	..
Smith, Freeman	..	..	1	..	..	1	..	1	..	..	..
Smith, John	1	1	2	..	1	..	1	1	1	..	..
Sparks, Stephen	2	2	..	1	..	5	1	..	1	..	..
Spears, Asa	..	..	1	..	..	..	..	..	..	..	..
Stanley, Jonathan P.	1	..	..	1	..	1	..	..	1	..	..
Stickney, Samuel	3	..	..	1	..	1	1	..	1	..	..
Sweet, Theophilus	1	..	1	..	..	..	..	1	..	..	..
Sweinton, James	..	1	..	1	..	3	2	..	1	..	..
Sweinton, Joseph	1	1	..	1	..	2	..	1	1	..	..
Toby, Sylvanus	2	1	..	1	..	3	1	..	1	..	..
True, Joseph	..	..	..	1	..	..	..	..	1	..	..
Wait, Daniel	1	1	..	..	1	..	..	1	..	1	..
Wait, Joseph	..	..	..	1	..	3	..	..	1	..	..
White, Elisha	..	..	..	1	1	..	..	1	..	1	..
White, Peter	1	..	..	1	..	2	1	..	1	..	..
Whiteman, Benjamin	1	2	1	1	..	1	2	1	1	..	..
Williams, John	1	..	..	1	..	..	..	..	1	..	..
Woodward, Joseph	..	1	..	..	1	..	1	1	..	1	..
Woodward, Othniel	1	..	..	1	..	..	..	..	1	..	..
LINCOLN											
Brooks, Samuel	3	..	..	1	..	2	..	..	1	..	..
Burnam, Wolcot	2	..	..	1	..	2	2	1	1	..	..
Delling, Laurance	..	1	2	..	1	3	..	3	..	..	..
Dellong, Howland	2	..	..	1	..	1	..	..	1	..	..
Durfry, Jedediah	1	1	1	1	..	3	2	..	1	1	..
Durfy, Ebenezer	2	..	..	1	..	1	2	..	1	..	..
Eastman, Samuel	3	..	..	1	..	..	1	..	..	1	..
Goodrich, Thomas	..	..	1	..	..	..	..	..	..	..	..
Heading, James	..	..	..	..	1	..	..	..	..	1	..
Heading, Morris	1	..	1	..	1	1	2	..	..	1	..
Johnson, Robert	..	..	..	1	..	1	..	..	1	..	.
Lee, Thomas	1	..	..	1	..	3	..	..	1	..	.
Leonard, Aron	1	..	..	1	..	..	..	..	1	..	.
Meader, Levi	..	..	..	1	..	1	..	1	..	..	..
Medin, Nathan	..	..	..	1	..	1	..	1	..	..	..
Orvis, Loren	2	..	..	1	..	2	..	..	1	..	..
Peasly, Abraham	..	..	1	..	..	..	..	1	..	..	..
Prisson, Jonathan	..	..	1	..	..	..	..	1	..	..	..
Varney, James	1	..	..	1	..	1	..	..	1	..	..
MIDDLEBURY											
Abbey, Gideon	4	..	..	1	..	2	..	..	1	..	..
Ackley, Philip	1	..	..	..	1	1	..	1	..	..	..
Allen, David	..	..	1	1	..	..	..	2	1	..	..
Allen, Mathew	..	..	..	1	..	..	..	..	1	..	..
Allen, Stephen	1	..	1	..	1	..	1	..	..	1	..
Andrews, James	1	1	1	..	1	1	2	..	1	..	..
Archebald, Thomas	1	1	..	1	..	1	..	..	1	..	..
MIDDLEBURY—con.											
Barber, Reuben	..	..	1	..	..	..	..	1	..	..	..
Barrows, Eleazer	5	..	..	1	..	1	..	..	1	..	..
Bass, Obediah	..	..	1	..	..	1	1	1	..	..	..
Beach, Linus	..	2	1	..	1	3	1	1	1	..	..
Beebe, Asahel	2	..	..	1	..	1	..	..	1	..	..
Bethrong, Abraham	2	..	2	..	1	..	1	..	1	..	..
Bill, Harvey	1	..	..	1	..	2	2	..	1	..	..
Birge, Elijah	1	1	..	1	..	2	1	..	1	..	..
Bishop, Nathaniel	..	2	4	..	1	..	..	1	..	1	..
Blackman, David	..	..	1	1	..	..	..	1	1	..	..
Boardman, Joel	1	..	3	3	..	..	1	..	1	1	..
Boardman, Moses	2	..	..	1	..	2	..	..	1	..	..
Boyington, Jesse	1	..	..	1	..	..	1	1	1	..	..
Brewster, Cyrus	1	1	..	1	..	..	..	..	1	..	..
Brewster, Oliver	..	1	..	1	..	..	..	..	1	..	..
Brooks, Alpheus	..	1	..	3	1	..	..	1	2	2	..
Brooks, Cephas	..	1	1	..	1	1	1	..	1	..	..
Burges, John	2	..	1	1	..	4	..	..	1	..	..
Buttolph, Elijah	2	2	..	..	1	..	..	1	..	1	..
Campbel, Daniel	2	1	1	1	..	2	..	2	1	..	..
Carey, Walter	..	..	..	1	..	3	..	..	1	..	..
Carrigan, Richard	2	..	1	..	..	..	..	..	1	..	..
Case, Abel	1	..	1	..	..	..	..	1	..	..	..
Case, Nathan	1	1	..	1	..	2	1	..	1	..	..
Champlain, Paul	1	..	2	..	..	1	1	1	..	..	..
Chapman, Ezekiel	..	1	..	..	1	..	..	..	..	1	..
Chipman, Daniel	3	1	4	1	..	1	1	1	..	1	..
Chipman, John	..	1	..	..	2	..	1	1	..	1	..
Chipman, Thomas	1	1	1	..	1	..	..	..	1	..	..
Clark, Augustine	..	1	1	..	..	..	1	..	1	..	..
Collard, Ebenezer	2	..	..	1	..	3	..	1	1	..	..
Coller, Asa	1	..	..	1	..	3	..	..	1	..	..
Cook, William	1	..	2	1	..	1	..	1	1	..	..
Cornish, Gabriel	..	..	..	1	..	2	1	1	1	..	..
Crafts, Samuel	3	2	..	1	..	1	..	1	1	1	..
Crane, Asa	1	..	1	..	..	2	..	2	..	..	..
Crane, Ezra	..	..	2	..	1	..	..	..	..	1	..
Crane, James	1	1	1	1	..	1	3	..	1	..	..
Crane, Jeremiah	3	2	..	1	..	2	..	..	1	..	..
Currier, William	3	1	..	1	..	2	1	..	1	..	..
Curtis, John	..	1	..	1	..	..	..	1	..	..	..
Dewey, Chester	3	..	..	1	..	..	..	..	1	..	..
Dewey, Stillman	3	..	..	1	..	2	..	1	..	..	..
Dickenson, David	2	..	..	1	..	1	..	1	..	1	..
Douglass, James	2	1	..	1	1	2	1	..	1	..	..
Dunning, Salmon	2	..	..	1	..	2	..	..	1	..	..
Everts, Eber	2	..	1	..	1	..	..	..	1	1	..
Everts, Martin	..	1	..	1	..	..	..	..	1	..	..
Farr, Samuel	1	2	..	..	1	..	..	1	..	1	..
Foot, Appleton	1	..	..	1	..	2	1	..	1	..	..
Foot, Daniel	..	..	..	..	1	..	2	..	..	1	..
Foot, Freeman	1	..	1	1	..	2	..	1	1	..	..
Foot, Martin	1	..	..	1	..	4	2	..	1	..	1
Foot, Philip	1	..	1	..	1	1	..	2	1	..	..
Foot, Samuel	..	1	1	1	..	..	2	1	1	..	2
Foot, Stillman	1	1	..	1	..	1	..	1	..	1	..
Fuller, Josiah	2	..	2	2	..	4	2	1	..	..	..
Garlick, Daniel	3	..	..	1	..	1	..	..	1	..	..
Garrit, Francis	..	1	..	1	..	..	..	..	1	..	..
Gaylord, Roswell	2	..	1	1	..	3	..	..	1	..	..
Geer, Charles	1	..	..	1	..	1	..	..	1	..	..
Gibbs, Warren	4	..	..	1	..	2	..	..	1	..	..
Goodrich, Bethuel	3	1	..	1	..	1	1	..	1	..	..
Goodrich, Jehiel	..	..	1	1	..	..	..	1	..	..	..
Goodrich, Jonathan	..	1	..	1	..	..	1	..	1	..	..
Goodrich, Lemuel	..	..	..	1	..	1	..	..	1	1	..
Goodrich, Stephen	2	..	..	1	..	2	1	..	1	..	..
Goodrich, William	..	..	..	1	1	..	1	2	1	..	..
Grant, Azariah	..	..	..	..	1	2	1	..	..	1	..
Haines, Philip	1	..	..	1	..	1	..	..	1	..	..
Hale, Jehiel	..	..	..	1	..	2	..	..	1	..	..
Hale, Moses	1	..	..	1	..	..	..	1	..	..	..
Harman, Elnathan	4	1	..	1	..	..	..	..	1	..	..
Harris, Timothy	1	..	..	1	..	1	..	1	..	..	..
Hastings, Aron	..	..	..	1	..	..	2	..	1	..	..
Hawley, Erastus	1	..	2	1	..	..	..	1	..	..	..
Heath, Benjamin	1	..	..	1	..	4	1	..	1	..	..
Henshaw, Joshua	3	2	..	1	..	2	1	..	1	..	3
Hepbourn, Joseph	2	4	..	..	1	1	2	1	1	..	..
Heyer, Hendrick	2	2	1	..	1	4	..	1	1	..	..
Hickock, Nathaniel	1	..	3	..	1	..	..	2	..	..	..
Hide, Joshua	1	..	1	..	1	..	1	..	1	..	..

ADDISON COUNTY—Continued

NAMES OF HEADS OF FAMILIES	FREE WHITE MALES: Under 10 years of age	FREE WHITE MALES: Of 10 and under 16	FREE WHITE MALES: Of 16 and under 26 including heads of families	FREE WHITE MALES: Of 26 and under 45 including heads of families	FREE WHITE MALES: Of 45 and upwards including heads of families.	FREE WHITE FEMALES: Under 10 years of age	FREE WHITE FEMALES: Of 10 and under 16	FREE WHITE FEMALES: Of 16 and under 26 including heads of families	FREE WHITE FEMALES: Of 26 and under 45 including heads of families	FREE WHITE FEMALES: Of 45 and upwards including heads of families	All other free persons except Indians not taxed
MIDDLEBURY—con.											
Hide, Joshua Jr.	1	..	..	1	..	..	..	1	..	..	..
Hill, Elias	3	..	1	1	1	..	..	..	1	..	..
Hill, Festus	1	..	1	1	..	1	..	..	1	..	..
Holton, Moses	3	1	..	..	1	2	1	1	1	..	..
Hooker, Branard	..	1	..	..	1	2	..	1	..	1	..
Hooker, Charles	..	..	1	..	..	..	..	1	..	..	..
Hopkins, Elias	1	..	..	1	..	1	1	..	1	..	..
Howard, Elisha	1	3	..	1	..	3	1	..	1	..	..
Hubbard, Patrick	1	..	1	..	..	..	..	1	..	..	..
Hustin, James L.	1	..	1	1	..	..	..	2	..	..	..
Hustin, Robert	..	1	..	1	1	..	1	..	..	1	..
Hustin, Robert 2nd.	..	..	1	..	..	..	..	1	..	..	..
Janes, Amos	5	..	..	2	..	..	..	..	1	..	..
Johnson, Libeas	..	..	..	1	..	..	..	..	..	..	..
Kirby, John	2	..	..	..	1	..	1	1	..	1	..
Kirby, Joseph	1	..	..	1	..	3	..	..	1	1	..
Knot, Giles	..	..	1	..	..	1	..	1	..	..	..
Ladd, Sampson	2	..	..	1	..	..	..	1	..	..	..
Lawrence, Benjamin	1	1	..	2	..	..	..	1	..	..	..
Lawrence, Nehemiah	3	1	..	1	..	3	1	1	1	..	..
Lawrence, Samuel	1	..	..	1	..	3	..	..	1	..	..
Ledington, Lemuel	2	..	..	1	..	..	..	..	1	..	..
Lee, Daniel	1	..	..	1	..	2	..	..	1	..	..
Lincoln, Nathan	3	..	..	1	..	1	..	..	1	..	..
Loomis, Freedom	2	1	..	1	1	1	..	..	1	1	..
Mallery, James	2	..	..	1	..	3	..	..	1	..	..
Markham, Ebenezer	2	..	..	..	1	1	..	1	1	1	..
Martin, Luther	1	4	4	..	2	..	1	2	..	1	..
Martin, William	2	..	1	..	..	..	..	1	..	..	..
Mathews, Darius	3	..	..	1	..	..	1	1	1	..	..
Mattocks, Samuel	..	..	..	..	1	..	..	1	..	1	..
Mattocks, Samuel Jr.	1	..	1	2	..	2	1	1	1	..	1
McDenad, Joseph	..	..	1	1	..	..	..	1	1	..	..
McDonald, Lewis	..	..	..	2	..	2	1	1	..	..	..
Miller, Epaphrus	..	1	1	1	..	3	..	2	..	..	..
Miller, Samuel	..	1	5	2	..	..	3	1	1	..	..
Monger, Bill Jr.	2	1	..	1	..	1	..	..	..	1	..
Monger, Dudley	1	..	..	1	..	..	..	..	1	..	..
Monger, Nathaniel	1	..	..	..	1	..	..	..	..	1	..
Monger, Reuben	1	..	..	..	1	..	1	1	..	1	..
Monger, Samuel	2	..	..	1	..	1	..	1	..	..	..
Monger, William	..	..	..	..	1	..	..	..	..	1	..
Moultan, Elisha	1	..	1	..	1	2	2	1	1	..	..
Naples, John	1	..	..	1	..	..	..	..	1	..	..
Newton, Abner	2	..	..	1	..	1	2	..	1	..	..
Nichols, Jonathan	1	..	..	..	1	..	..	..	1	1	..
Nichols, Josiah	1	..	..	1	..	1	..	..	1	..	..
Oaks, Isaac	..	..	1	..	1	..	..	..	1	1	..
Obrine, John	1	..	1	..	..	..	..	1	..	..	..
Olmstead, Elijah	..	..	2	..	1	..	..	1	..	1	..
Olmstead, Erastus	1	..	..	1	..	..	..	1	..	..	..
Ormsby, Bela	..	..	..	1	1	1	..	..	2	..	..
Osburn, Alexander	..	1	..	..	1	..	..	..	..	1	..
Painter, Gamaliel	1	..	2	1	1	3	..	2	1	..	..
Pierce, Lyman	1	..	..	1	..	..	..	1	..	..	..
Plumb, Joseph	2	..	..	1	..	3	..	..	1	..	..
Prat, Samuel	..	..	1	..	1	..	1	..	..	1	..
Preston, Asa	2	1	..	1	..	1	..	..	1	..	..
Preston, Jonathan	..	..	..	..	1	..	..	1	..	1	..
Rhodes, Anthony	2	..	..	1	..	2	..	..	1	1	..
Rice, Hosea	..	..	..	1	..	2	..	..	1	..	..
Ripley, Nathaniel	2	1	..	1	..	..	..	1	..	..	..
Rogers, Jabez Jr.	..	..	..	1	..	2	1	1	..	..	..
Rossetter, Josiah	3	1	..	1	..	1	..	..	1	..	..
Rutherford, William	1	1	1	..	..	3	..	..	1	..	..
Sage, David	1	..	1	..	..	..	..	1	..	..	..
Sage, Eleazer	5	..	..	1	..	..	..	..	1	..	..
Sage, Gideon	..	..	..	..	1	..	..	..	1	..	..
Sawyer, Bela	1	..	..	1	..	2	..	..	1	..	..
Sawyer, James	..	1	1	..	1	..	..	..	..	1	..
Scot, Athel	2	1	..	1	..	1	1	..	1	..	..
Seargents, Samuel	..	..	..	1	..	3	..	..	1	..	..
Selick, Seymour	2	..	..	..	1	2	..	..	1	..	..
Sericke, Daniel	2	..	..	1	..	1	..	..	1	..	..
Severance, Ebenezer	..	..	1	..	1	1	..	1	..	1	..
Severance, Enos	..	..	..	1	..	..	..	..	1	..	..
Severance, Moses	..	..	1	..	..	..	..	1	..	..	..
Seymour, Benjamin	..	..	2	..	..	..	..	..	..	..	..
Seymour, Horatio	..	..	2	..	..	..	1	1	..	..	..
Sherman, Jesse	..	..	..	1	..	..	..	..	1	..	..
Sherman, Thomas	..	1	1	..	1	..	..	3	..	1	..
Smally, Zimri	1	1	..	1	..	1	..	..	1	..	..
Smedley, Samuel	1	..	..	2	..	2	..	..	1	..	..
Soolye, Sarah	2	..	..	..	..	1	..	1	1	..	..
Southerland, Tobias	..	..	..	1	..	2	..	..	1	..	..
Spalding, Ephraim	1	..	..	1	..	..	..	..	1	..	..
Spencer, Epaphrus	1	..	1	1	..	1	2	..	1	1	..
Spencer, Jesse	..	..	4	3	..	1	1	..	1	..	..
Spencer, Thomas	1	1	..	1	..	3	..	..	1	..	..
Stanley, Sylvester	..	..	..	1	..	..	..	1	..	..	..
Stephens, Ephraim	..	2	..	..	1	..	1	..	..	1	..
Stevens, Peter	1	1	..	..	1	..	1	1	..	1	..
Stores, Jehiel	1	1	1	1	..	..	1	..	1	1	..
Stores, Seth	2	1	7	1	..	2	1	1	1	..	..
Stowel, Amasa	2	1	..	1	..	2	1	..	1	..	..
Stowel, John	2	1	..	1	..	2	..	..	1	..	..
Sumner, Ebenezer	1	2	1	1	..	3	..	1	1	..	..
Sumner, William B.	1	1	3	2	..	3	1	..	1	1	1
Tailor, Rachel Widow	..	1	..	..	..	2	..	..	1	..	..
Tillotson, John	2	2	..	1	..	2	2	..	1	..	..
Torrence, Roberts	1	..	2	1	..	..	2	2	..	..	..
Troop, Orange	2	..	..	1	..	..	..	1	1	1	..
Troop, Samuel	1	..	1	1	..	..	..	1	..	1	..
Tup, Zephaniah	1	..	..	1	..	1	..	1	..	..	..
Tupper, Darius	2	..	1	1	..	1	1	1	1	..	..
Turner, Isaac	1	..	..	1	..	1	..	..	1	..	..
Turner, Stiles	..	..	..	1	..	..	..	1	..	..	..
Vanduzen, Henry	..	..	..	1	..	3	..	..	1	..	..
Vanduzen, Samuel	1	..	1	1	..	1	..	2	1	1	..
Vanduzin, John	3	1	..	1	..	2	..	..	1	..	..
Wadsworth, Israel	2	4	..	1	..	1	..	1	1	..	..
Warren, John	..	..	3	..	..	1	1	1	..	..	..
Whitney, Joshua	..	..	1	..	..	2	..	1	..	..	..
Wilder, Elias	..	..	..	1	..	1	..	..	1	..	..
Willard, John	2	1	..	1	..	..	1	..	1	..	..
Wood, Charles	2	1	..	1	..	..	2	..	1	..	..
Woodman, Elijah	1	..	..	1	..	..	..	1	..	..	..
Woodworth, Hezekiah	2	3	1	1	..	3	..	1	1	..	..
Wright, Luther	1	..	..	1	..	..	..	1	..	..	..
Wright, Samuel	..	..	..	..	1	..	..	1	..	1	..
Young, William	1	..	1	1	..	1	1	1		..	..
UNCERTAIN NAMES											
Balley (?), Jonathan	1	..	..	1	..	2	1	..	1	..	..
Carieh (?), Richard	1	..	1	..	..	1	..	..	1	..	..
MONKTON											
Alen, Ira	..	..	..	1	..	..	..	1	..	..	..
Allen, Titus	..	..	..	..	1	..	..	..	..	1	..
Ames, David	3	2	..	..	1	..	..	2	1	..	..
Atwood, Paul	4	1	..	1	..	..	..	..	1	..	..
Austin, John	2	..	..	1	..	1	..	1	..	..	..
Austin, Pasque	1	..	1	..	1	..	1	..	..	1	..
Baldwin, Nathan	1	..	..	1	..	1	..	1	..	..	..
Barns, Asa	1	4	..	..	1	..	..	1	..	2	..
Barns, Jaspha	..	..	..	1	..	4	..	..	1	..	..
Barnum, Abijah	..	..	..	1	..	..	..	..	1	..	..
Barnum, Ebenezer	2	2	2	..	1	1	..	1	..	1	..
Barnum, Elihu	..	..	..	1	..	5	..	..	1	..	..
Barnum, Moses	..	..	..	1	..	1	..	..	1	..	..
Barnum, Samuel	..	..	..	..	1	1	..	..	..	1	..
Barnum, Seth	1	..	..	1	..	2	..	..	1	..	..
Barton, Solomon	2	2	..	1	1	..	1	..	1	..	..
Bastwick, Cirus	..	..	..	1	..	1	..	..	1	..	..
Bates, Ichabod	..	2	..	1	..	2	..	..	1	..	..
Been, Eliakim	1	..	1	..	..	..	..	1	..	..	..
Berry, Ebenezer	3	..	..	1	..	..	..	..	1	..	..
Berry, Jehial	2	..	..	1	..	3	..	..	1	..	..
Berry, Joseph	1	..	..	1	..	1	..	..	1	..	..
Bishop, John	..	..	..	..	1	..	..	..	1	1	..
Bishop, John	..	2	..	1	..	4	1	..	1	..	..
Bishop, Samuel	1	..	..	1	..	1	..	1	..	..	..
Branch, Elijah	1	..	1	1	..	5	1	1	1	..	..
Brownson, Lumen	2	..	..	1	..	1	..	1	..	..	..
Bull, William	..	1	1	..	1	..	1	..	..	1	..
Carley, John	1	..	..	..	1	..	2	1	1	1	..
Carter, Frederick	1	2	..	1	..	2	1	..	1	..	..
Carter, Solomon	2	2	..	1	..	1	1	..	1	..	..

ADDISON COUNTY—Continued

NAMES OF HEADS OF FAMILIES	FREE WHITE MALES					FREE WHITE FEMALES					
	Under 10 years of age	Of 10 and under 16	Of 16 and under 26 including heads of families	Of 26 and under 45 including heads of families	Of 45 and upwards including heads of families.	Under 10 years of age	Of 10 and under 16	Of 16 and under 26 including heads of families	Of 26 and under 45 including heads of families	Of 45 and upwards including heads of families	All other free persons except Indians not taxed
MONKTON—con.											
Chamberlain, Jerah	..	1	..	1	..	2	1	..	1	..	..
Chamberlain, Leander	1	..	..	1	..	4	..	..	1	..	..
Chamberlain, Swift	1	..	..	1	..	3	..	1	..	..	..
Coleman, Anthony	1	..	..	1	..	2	2	..	1	..	..
Collins, Archibald	3	..	..	1	..	2	1	..	1	..	..
Collins, Daniel	..	..	1	1	1	..	..	..	..	1	..
Collins, Daniel Jr.	..	1	..	1	..	1	..	..	1	..	..
Collins, David	1	..	1	..	..	..	..	1	..	..	..
Collins, Elisha	2	2	..	1	..	2	1	..	1	..	..
Cook, John	1	..	..	1	..	2	..	..	1	..	..
Curtis, Martin	2	2	..	..	1	2	2	1	1	..	..
Curtis, Silas	2	..	..	1	..	2	2	2	1	..	..
Dart, George	3	3	1	1	..	1	..	..	1	..	..
Day, Joseph	..	1	1	1	..	1	..	..	1	..	..
Dean, Ashbel	2	1	..	2	..	3	..	..	2	..	..
Dean, Nathaniel	..	1	..	..	1	1	1	1	1	..	..
Douglass, Nathan	1	..	..	1	..	1	..	1	..	..	..
Dunham, Isaac	..	..	1	..	1	..	2	..	1	..	..
Ferris, David	2	..	..	1	..	1	..	..	1	..	..
Finny, Eleazer	..	..	2	..	1	..	1	..	..	1	..
Finny, Johnson	1	1	1	..	..	..	..	1	..	..	..
Finny, Moses	..	..	..	1	..	..	..	..	1	..	..
Flagg, Joseph	..	..	..	1	..	1	..	1	..	..	..
Follitt, Joseph	2	1	1	..	1	2	1	..	1	..	..
Follitt, Joseph Jr.	..	..	1	..	..	..	..	..	1	..	..
Frank, Andrew	..	..	..	1	..	2	..	..	1	..	..
Freelove, Stephen	..	..	..	3	1	1	1	2	..	..	1
Fuller, Josiah	2	1	..	1	..	2	1	2	1	..	..
Fuller, Stephen	4	1	..	1	..	1	3	..	1	..	..
Garrett, William	1	1	2	1	..	2	1	..	1	..	..
Gilbert, Thomas D.	3	..	..	1	..	1	2	..	1	..	..
Haight, Benjamin	2	..	2	1	..	2	2	..	1	..	..
Haight, Stephen	..	..	1	..	1	..	..	..	..	1	..
Hard, Henman	..	..	..	1	..	..	..	..	1	..	..
Harde, Samuel	..	1	..	..	1	..	..	..	..	1	..
Hardy, Silas	1	..	..	1	..	3	1	..	1	..	..
Hawley, Ebenezer	3	..	..	1	..	..	..	..	1	..	..
Heath, Josiah	..	..	..	..	1	..	..	..	..	1	..
Hill, Calvin	3	1	1	1	..	1	..	1	1	..	..
Hinnenton, Lymon	..	..	1	..	..	3	1	..	1	..	..
Hitchcock, Ira	2	1	..	1	..	3	1	..	1	..	..
Hodgkiss, Ahaseh	..	..	..	..	1	1	..	..	..	1	..
Holmes, Gershom	1	..	1	..	1	..	1	1	..	1	..
Holmes, Nichols	..	..	2	..	1	..	1	..	..	1	..
Hotchkiss, William	..	..	1	..	..	..	..	1	..	..	..
Hubal, Ephraim	3	1	..	1	..	1	..	..	1	..	..
Hubbel, Jedediah	..	..	..	..	1	..	..	..	..	1	..
Hubbel, Samuel	1	..	..	1	..	1	1	..	..	..	..
Jones, Josiah	1	..	1	..	..	..	1	..	..	..	..
Jones, Nathaniel	..	..	..	1	..	1	..	..	1	..	..
Kendrick, Lemuel	..	..	..	1	..	2	..	..	1	..	..
Knapp, Daniel	..	..	1	..	..	..	..	1	..	..	..
Laurance, Diah	..	..	..	1	..	..	..	1	..	..	..
Laurance, Josiah	2	1	..	1	..	3	..	..	1	..	..
Laurance, Nathan	1	..	..	1	..	1	..	..	1	..	..
Lord, John	..	1	2	..	1	..	..	..	..	1	..
Main, Roswell	1	..	..	1	..	1	1	..	1	..	..
Michael, Joseph	3	..	..	1	..	..	..	1	1	..	..
Mumford, Elijah	..	..	1	..	..	..	..	1	..	..	..
Mumford, Robinson	1	3	..	1	..	3	1	..	1	..	..
Olverd, John	..	..	..	..	1	..	1	..	..	1	..
Page, Ephraim	1	1	..	..	1	2	2	..	1	..	..
Paine, Nathan	..	..	1	..	..	..	..	1	..	..	..
Palmer, John	1	..	1	..	..	..	..	1	..	1	..
Palmer, Taylor	..	1	1	..	1	..	1	..	..	1	..
Payon, Hubbe	..	1	..	1	..	3	..	..	1	..	..
Peck, Ebenezer	2	..	..	..	1	2	1	1	1	..	..
Peck, Jothleel	1	1	..	1	..	3	..	..	1	..	..
Pike, John	1	..	..	1	..	1	..	..	1	..	..
Pingree, Moses	..	1	..	1	..	2	..	..	1	..	..
Potter, Elihu	2	..	..	1	..	1	1	..	1	..	..
Prince, Timothy	..	..	..	..	..	..	..	..	1	..	6
Rusco, David	1	3	1	1	..	2	..	2	1	..	..
Rutherford, Andrew	1	1	..	1	..	2	..	..	1	..	..
Rutherford, Thomas	1	1	..	..	1	1	2	1	1	..	..
Sanford, Josiah	2	..	1	1	..	..	..	1	1	..	..
Sawyer, Isaac	4	..	..	1	..	..	..	..	1	..	..
Scott, Josiah	..	..	1	1	..	..	1	..	1	..	..
Scott, Moses	..	1	..	1	..	2	..	1	..	..	..
Sexton, Ebenezer	2	..	3	..	1	1	1	..	1	..	..
Sherman, Ichabod	1	..	..	1	..	1	..	..	1	..	..
Siple, John	1	..	..	1	..	..	2	..	1	..	..
Skiff, Daniel W.	..	..	1	..	..	..	..	1	..	..	..
Skiff, Elisha	..	..	..	1	..	2	..	1	..	..	..
Smith, Benjamin	1	..	..	1	..	..	..	1	..	1	..
Smith, Champon	2	1	..	1	..	2	..	..	1	..	..
Smith, Daniel	2	..	1	1	..	3	2	..	1	..	..
Smith, Elisha	..	..	2	1	..	..	..	..	1	..	..
Smith, Frederic	2	..	2	1	..	2	..	..	1	..	..
Smith, Hezekiah	..	1	..	1	..	3	1	..	1	1	..
Smith, Joseph	3	1	..	1	..	..	..	..	1	..	..
Smith, Sylvanus	2	..	..	1	..	2	..	1	..	..	..
Smith, Thomas	5	1	..	1	..	..	..	..	1	..	..
Spooner, William	..	2	1	..	1	..	..	1	..	1	..
Stearns, Ebenezer	..	1	2	..	1	..	..	..	..	1	..
Stearns, Ebenezer Jr.	..	..	1	..	..	..	..	1	..	..	..
Stearns, Isaac	..	1	1	..	1	..	..	..	..	1	..
Stearns, John	1	3	..	..	1	..	1	2	1	..	..
Stearns, Joseph	..	..	..	1	..	1	..	..	1	..	..
Stillman, Been	..	..	..	1	..	..	..	1	..	..	..
Stone, Dan	1	..	3	1	..	3	3	..	1	..	..
Swift, Pope A.	1	..	..	1	..	3	..	..	1	..	..
Tafte, Benjamin	..	..	2	..	1	2	2	1	..	1	..
Terrel, Joel	1	..	..	1	..	..	2	..	1	..	..
Terrel, Stephen	..	1	1	..	1	..	1	1	..	1	..
Thompson, Henry	1	..	2	1	1	..	1	2	..	1	..
Tibbets, Jonathan	2	..	1	..	..	..	..	1	..	..	..
Tibbetts, George	..	..	..	..	1	..	..	..	..	1	..
Tibbetts, Widow Sally	2	..	..	..	..	..	..	..	1	..	..
Tibets, John	2	1	..	1	..	2	..	..	1	..	..
Tracy, Daniel	..	..	..	..	1	..	..	..	..	1	..
Tracy, Lemuel	..	1	..	1	..	1	..	..	1	..	..
Tracy, Thomas	1	1	..	1	..	2	..	1	..	..	..
Tupper, John	2	..	..	..	1	4	..	..	1	..	..
Turner, Abraham	..	1	..	..	2	5	..	..	1	..	..
Turner, Artemas	..	..	..	1	..	1	..	..	1	..	..
Tuttle, Gideon	2	..	1	1	1	1	..	..	1	1	..
Tuttle, Samuel	1	..	1	1	..	3	2	..	1	..	..
Webb, Samuel	2	..	..	1	..	3	..	..	1	..	..
Williams, Nathan	..	..	1	..	..	..	..	1	..	..	..
Willorby, Joseph	..	..	..	..	1	..	1	..	..	1	..
Willoughby, Josiah Jr.	1	..	..	1	..	3	..	..	1	..	..
NEW HAVEN											
Abernathy, James P.	2	..	1	1	..	4	1	..	1	..	..
Allis, Stephen	..	..	1	..	1	1	1	..	1	1	..
Alvord, Wilcot	2	..	..	1	..	2	..	..	1	..	..
Ashley, Enoch	2	..	..	1	..	..	1	..	1	1	..
Austin, Rodman	2	1	..	1	..	1	..	..	1	..	..
Badcock, Billings	..	..	..	1	..	2	..	1	..	..	..
Banny, Samuel	1	..	..	1	..	..	1	..	1	..	..
Baron, Hosea	3	1	..	1	..	1	2	..	1	..	..
Barton, Anthony	1	1	2	1	..	1	..	..	1	..	..
Barton, Nathan	1	..	..	1	..	..	..	..	1	..	..
Battolph, Ezekiel	2	1	..	1	..	1	..	1	1	..	..
Beach, Abel	2	2	..	1	..	2	..	1	1	..	..
Berry, Barnabas	2	1	2	1	1	2	..	..	1	..	..
Bird, Joseph	2	2	..	1	..	3	1	..	1	..	..
Bisby, Joseph	2	..	..	1	..	1	..	..	1	..	..
Blanchard, Asahel	..	..	..	..	1	..	..	..	..	1	..
Bostwick, John W.	1	1	..	1	..	3	1	..	1	..	..
Bradly, Miles	..	1	2	..	1	..	1	1	..	1	..
Brateman, Holms	..	..	..	1	..	..	..	1	..	..	..
Brintnal, Thomas	..	1	1	..	1	1	1	..	..	1	..
Broadway, Fraser	1	..	1	..	..	..	..	1	..	..	..
Brown, John	1	..	2	1	..	1	1	1	..	1	..
Brown, Solomon	1	4	1	..	1	5	..	1	1	1	..
Buman, Daniel	1	2	..	1	..	1	1	..	1	..	..
Burbson, John	1	..	1	1	..	4	2	..	1	..	..
Byrd, Amos	1	..	..	1	..	..	..	1	..	..	..
Cadwell, Buckley	2	..	1	2	..	..	1	1	..	..	..
Carr, Roger	..	..	1	..	..	1	..	1	..	..	..
Chalker, Samuel	1	..	..	..	1	2	2	..	..	1	..
Chapman, Phineas	..	..	..	1	..	1	..	1	..	..	..
Chilson, Ahasel	2	..	..	1	..	..	..	1	..	..	..
Chilson, Joseph	2	..	..	1	..	1	..	..	1	..	..
Chittenden, David	3	..	..	1	..	..	..	..	1	..	..
Clark, Josiah	1	1	..	..	1	..	1	..	1	..	..

ADDISON COUNTY—Continued

NAMES OF HEADS OF FAMILIES	FREE WHITE MALES					FREE WHITE FEMALES					All other free persons except Indians not taxed
	Under 10 years of age	Of 10 and under 16	Of 16 and under 26 including heads of families	Of 26 and under 45 including heads of families	Of 45 and upwards including heads of families	Under 10 years of age	Of 10 and under 16	Of 16 and under 26 including heads of families	Of 26 and under 45 including heads of families	Of 45 and upwards including heads of families	
NEW HAVEN—con.											
Cobb, Eliphalet	4	..	..	1	1	1	1	..	1	1	..
Colt, John	..	1	..	..	1	1	1	..	1	..	..
Cook, Jeremiah	1	..	..	1	..	3	1	..	1	..	..
Cook, Samuel	2	1	..	1	2	2	..	1	..	..	..
Cook, Stephen	1	..	2	..	1	2	3	..	1	..	..
Crane, Christopher	..	..	..	1	..	1	..	1	1	..	..
Crane, Martin	2	..	..	1	..	2	1	..	1	..	..
Curtis, Cyrus	2	..	..	1	..	..	1	..	1	..	..
Darley, Eli	..	..	..	1	..	1	..	1	..	..	..
David, David	2	..	..	1	..	2	2	..	1	..	..
David, Isaac	3	..	..	1	..	1	..	..	1	..	..
David, Joel	2	..	..	1	..	..	..	..	1	1	..
David, Silas	2	..	..	1	..	2	..	..	1	..	..
Dennison, Christopher	1	..	..	1	..	..	1	..	1	..	..
Dickenson, Asa	2	1	..	1	..	..	..	..	1	..	..
Dornsin, Philo	3	..	..	1	..	1	1	..	1	..	..
Drake, Elijah	1	..	..	1	..	1	..	2	..	1	..
Dudley, Jonathan	..	..	..	..	1	..	..	..	..	1	..
Dudley, Simeon	1	1	2	..	1	..	..	..	..	1	..
Eadds, Jonathan	..	..	..	1	..	1	..	1	..	..	..
Eaton, Luther A.	3	1	..	1	..	1	2	..	1	..	..
Eldridge, Lemuel	3	2	1	..	1	1	1	..	..	1	..
Eldridge, Lemuel Jr.	..	..	1	..	..	..	..	1	..	..	..
Eno, William	2	1	..	1	..	1	1	..	1	..	..
Everst, Calvin	..	..	..	1	..	1	..	1	..	..	..
Everst, Luther	..	1	1	..	1	..	1	1	..	1	..
Field, Ebenezer	..	1	..	..	1	..	..	1	..	1	..
Field, Ebenezer Jr.	..	..	..	1	..	..	..	1	..	..	..
Field, Simeon	2	1	..	1	..	2	..	1	..	..	..
Finny, John	4	2	..	1	..	2	..	..	1	..	..
Finny, Rufus	..	1	2	1	..	2	..	..	1	..	..
Foot, John	1	..	..	1	..	2	1	..	1	..	..
Foot, Thomas	1	1	..	1	..	1	..	..	1	..	..
Freeman, Elisha	1	..	1	..	..	..	..	1	..	..	..
Fuller, Andrew	1	..	..	1	..	1	..	..	1	..	..
Fuller, Asa	1	2	1	..	1	1	..	1	1	..	..
Fuller, Elisha	..	..	1	1	..	1	1	..	1	..	..
Fuller, Jacob	..	..	..	1	..	1	..	..	1	..	..
Gaslin, Jose	3	1	..	2	..	1	..	..	1	..	..
Gennings, Simeon	1	..	..	1	..	1	..	..	1	..	..
Gray, Isaiah	1	..	..	1	..	3	..	2	..	..	..
Griffin, Ahasel	3	..	..	1	..	1	..	..	1	..	..
Grindle. Reuben	1	3	..	..	1	1	..	1	1	..	..
Griswould, David	..	2	..	1	..	1	..	..	1	..	..
Hall, Richard	3	1	1	1	..	..	..	1	1	..	..
Hamblin, Pierce	..	..	..	..	1	..	..	..	..	1	..
Hamblin, Stephen	..	..	1	..	..	..	..	1	..	..	..
Hantchet, John	2	..	..	1	..	1	2	..	..	..	..
Haskins, Aaron	1	..	1	..	1	3	1	3	..	1	..
Hawley, David	..	..	..	1	..	1	..	..	1	1	..
Henman, John	1	..	1	..	..	..	..	1	..	..	..
Hicock, Austin	..	..	..	1	..	1	..	1	..	..	..
Hill, Billious	..	..	..	..	1	..	..	..	..	1	..
Hill, Reuben	1	..	2	1	..	1	..	1	..	..	..
Hines, Daniel	..	..	1	..	..	..	..	1	..	..	..
Hoit, Ezra	..	..	..	..	1	..	..	1	..	1	..
Hoit, Ezra Jr.	2	..	..	1	..	2	..	1	..	..	..
Hoit, Seymour	1	..	1	..	..	1	..	1	..	..	..
Hoit, Thadeus	..	..	1	..	..	..	..	1	..	..	..
Hoit, Uriah	3	2	..	1	..	2	..	..	1	..	1
Hoyt, Seth	2	1	1	1	..	3	..	1	1	..	..
Hunt, David B.	1	..	1	1	..	..	..	1	..	..	..
Ingal, David	2	..	1	..	..	..	..	1	..	..	..
Jaquays, Joseph	..	..	..	..	1	..	1	..	..	1	..
Jenks, Anthony	..	1	..	..	1	..	..	..	..	1	..
Jones, Joseph	..	..	1	..	1	..	..	..	..	1	..
Jones, Rufus	2	..	..	1	..	1	..	..	1	..	..
Korley, Samuel	4	..	1	1	..	..	1	..	1	..	..
Lampson, William	1	1	..	1	..	3	1	..	1	..	..
Landon, Seth	3	1	..	1	..	1	1	1	1	..	..
Laurance, John	..	..	..	1	..	5	..	..	1	..	..
Laurance, Samuel	2	..	..	..	1	1	..	1	..	..	..
Loomis, Ezra	1	..	..	1	..	1	..	..	1	..	..
Loomis, Samuel	..	..	..	1	..	2	..	..	1	..	..
Loveland, Aaron	1	1	..	1	..	1	..	..	1	..	..
Mason, Elijah	1	1	1	..	1	..	1	2	..	1	..
Mason, Eliphalet	2	..	..	1	..	1	..	..	1	..	..
NEW HAVEN—con.											
Mathews, Isaac	1	1	..	..	1	..	1	..	..	1	..
Mathews, Joseph	1	..	..	..	1	1	..	..	1	..	..
Mead, Hezekiah	2	..	2	1	..	1	..	1	..	..	..
Meggs, Phelix	..	..	..	..	1	..	..	..	..	1	..
Miller, Dan	..	2	..	1	..	2	1	..	1	..	..
Mills, Alvin	..	..	..	1	..	2	..	..	1	..	..
Mills. Andrew	..	..	..	..	1	..	..	..	..	1	..
Mills, Andrew R.	..	..	1	1	..	2	..	1	..	..	..
Mills, Ira	1	..	1	..	..	..	..	..	1	..	..
Mills, Zenos	1	..	..	1	..	1	..	1	..	..	..
Mitone, Roswell I.	..	..	1	1	..	1	..	..	1	1	..
Monross, Jesse	2	1	1	1	..	2	1	..	1	..	..
Nash, Josiah	1	..	..	..	..	1	2	2	1	..	1
Nash, Philips D.	..	..	3	..	..	..	..	2	..	..	..
Nash, William	1	1	..	..	1	..	2	2	..	1	..
Newman, Benjamin	1	..	..	1	..	1	1	..	1	..	..
Nichols, Joshua	..	..	..	1	..	2	..	1	..	..	..
Noble, Roger	1	..	2	..	1	..	2	..	..	1	..
Norris, Rufus	2	..	..	1	..	1	..	1	..	..	..
Norton, Isaachar	3	..	1	1	..	2	..	..	1	..	..
Olmstead, Elijah	1	..	..	1	..	1	..	1	..	..	..
Parker, Joseph	1	..	4	1	..	..	..	..	1	..	..
Parker, Solomon	1	..	..	1	..	3	..	..	1	..	..
Peck, Abel	3	..	1	1	..	1	1	..	1	..	..
Petterson, Jonathan	3	..	1	..	1	2	..	1	..	..	..
Pettibone, Isaac	1	2	1	..	1	1	..	..	..	1	..
Phelps, Lemuel	..	1	..	1	..	..	..	..	1	..	..
Phelps, Mathew	..	3	..	1	1	..	1	..	1	..	..
Phipany, Ahasel	..	..	1	1	..	..	..	1	1	..	..
Pier, Justus	4	..	..	1	..	1	..	..	1	..	..
Pier, Oliver	..	..	2	..	1	..	..	1	..	1	..
Porter, Simeon	1	2	..	..	1	2	..	2	1	..	..
Rennot, Daniel	..	1	1	1	..	..	2	..	1	..	..
Reynolds, James	1	..	1	..	..	1	..	1	..	..	..
Rice, Oney	2	..	..	1	..	1	..	1	..	..	..
Rogers, Chandler	..	1	1	1	..	2	..	..	1	..	..
Rogers, Jabez	..	..	..	..	1	..	..	..	..	1	..
Rogers, Russel	2	..	..	1	..	..	..	..	1	..	..
Rose, Elisha	3	1	1	1	..	1	2	1	1	..	..
Ruble, Andrew	3	..	..	1	..	1	..	1	..	..	..
Russel, Benjamin	1	3	1	..	1	3	..	1	..	1	..
Sabine, Nehemiah	..	..	1	..	1	..	..	1	..	1	..
Seward, Joseph	..	..	..	..	1	..	1	..	..	1	..
Seymour, William	1	2	..	1	..	3	1	1	1	..	..
Shelden, Micah	..	..	..	1	..	1	..	1	..	..	..
Sherman, Amos P.	2	..	..	1	..	2	2	..	1	..	..
Sherman, Wait	2	1	..	1	..	1	2	..	1	..	..
Smith, Alen	2	..	..	1	..	4	2	..	1	..	..
Smith, David	1	1	1	1	..	2	..	1	..	..	..
Smith, Epaphrus	..	..	..	1	..	..	..	1	..	..	..
Smith, George	..	1	..	1	..	..	1	..	1	..	..
Smith, Simon	2	1	..	1	..	1	3	..	1	..	..
Snow, Barras	1	1	1	1	..	1	1	..	1	..	..
Spencer, Asa	..	1	1	..	1	1	..	1	..	..	..
Spint, Robert	1	..	1	..	..	1	..	-1	..	..	..
Sprague, Eseeck	2	..	3	1	..	..	1	..	1	..	..
Sprague, Gideon	1	2	1	..	1	3	2	..	1	..	..
Squire, Andrew	1	1	..	1	..	1	1	1	1	..	..
Squire, Wait	3	..	..	1	..	2	..	..	1	..	..
Stearns, Roswell	..	2	1	1	..	2	1	1	1	..	..
Stowe, Moses	1	..	..	1	..	1	1	..	1	..	..
Strong, John	..	..	1	..	..	..	..	1	1	..	..
Strong, Lemuel	1	..	..	1	..	..	..	..	1	..	..
Strong, Oliver	..	1	..	..	1	..	..	1	..	1	..
Sumner, John A.	1	..	..	1	1	1	..	1	..	..	..
Thayer, Billy	1	..	..	..	1	1	..	..	..	1	..
Thompson, James	2	..	..	1	..	4	..	..	1	..	..
Tobias, Joseph	2	2	2	1	..	2	..	1	1	..	..
Tripp, Augustus	1	..	..	1	..	1	..	..	1	..	..
Turner, Josiah	1	..	1	..	..	1	..	1	..	..	..
Turner, Samuel	1	..	..	1	..	2	..	1	..	..	..
Walker, Samuel	2	..	..	1	..	..	..	1	2	..	..
Ward, Thomas	1	..	..	1	..	2	..	..	1	..	..
Warren, David	..	..	..	1	..	4	..	..	1	..	..
Welch, Michael	..	..	..	..	1	..	..	..	..	1	..
West, Esrael	..	1	..	..	1	..	1	..	..	1	..
West, Joseph	..	..	1	..	..	..	..	1	..	..	..
Wheeler, Ara	..	2	..	1	..	2	..	..	1	..	..
Wheeler, Freeman	2	1	..	1	..	1	1	..	1	..	..
Wheeler, Phillip	1	..	1	1	..	2	..	1	..	..	..
Wheeler, Preserved	..	..	1	..	1	1	..	1	..	..	..

ADDISON COUNTY—Continued

NAMES OF HEADS OF FAMILIES	FREE WHITE MALES: Under 10 years of age	FREE WHITE MALES: Of 10 and under 16	FREE WHITE MALES: Of 16 and under 26 including heads of families	FREE WHITE MALES: Of 26 and under 45 including heads of families	FREE WHITE MALES: Of 45 and upwards including heads of families	FREE WHITE FEMALES: Under 10 years of age	FREE WHITE FEMALES: Of 10 and under 16	FREE WHITE FEMALES: Of 16 and under 26 including heads of families	FREE WHITE FEMALES: Of 26 and under 45 including heads of families	FREE WHITE FEMALES: Of 45 and upwards including heads of families	All other free persons except Indians not taxed
NEW HAVEN—con.											
Wheeler, William	..	1	..	1	..	1	1	..	1	..	..
White, David	2	..	..	1	..	3	..	..	1	..	..
Willa, Widow Susana	..	..	..	..	..	..	..	..	1	1	..
Willcox, Gideon	1	..	..	1	..	2	..	..	1	..	..
Willcox, Roswell	3	..	..	1	..	..	..	1	..	..	..
Williams, Jebediah	..	..	..	1	1	..	..	..	..	1	..
Willy, Calvin	3	..	..	1	..	1	..	1	..	..	..
PANTON											
Bachelor, Reuben	1	2	1	..	1	..	..	2	.	1	..
Bains, Elijah	2	..	..	1	..	2	..	1	1	..	..
Bishop, Jesse	1	1	1	..	1	3	1	2	..	1	..
Bristol, Aaron	..	2	1	..	1	..	..	..	..	1	..
Bristol, Levi	..	..	1	..	..	..	..	1	..	..	..
Bristol, Wait	1	..	..	1	..	1	..	..	1	..	..
Brown, Warren	2	2	..	1	..	..	..	..	1	..	..
Burrel, John	2	1	1	1	..	2	..	1	1	..	..
Chamberlain, Robert	1	..	..	1	..	..	..	..	1	..	..
Chamberlin, Henry	1	2	1	1	1	..	1	3	..	1	..
Champion, Daniel	3	1	1	1	..	2	2	..	1	..	..
Curtis, Ephraim	..	2	2	..	1	..	2	..	..	1	..
Farr, Joel	..	..	1	..	..	1	..	1	..	..	..
Feris, Peter	..	..	..	..	1	..	..	..	..	1	..
Ferris, Darius	3	..	..	1	..	2	..	..	1	..	..
Ferris, James	4	..	..	1	..	1	..	..	1	..	..
Grandy, Edmund	..	1	1	..	1	..	1	1	..	1	..
Grandy, Elijah	1	..	2	..	1	..	1	1	1	..	..
Grandy, Jesse	..	..	1	..	..	..	..	1	..	..	..
Grandy, Lyman	..	..	1	..	..	1	..	1	..	..	..
Hanks, Eleazer	3	..	..	1	..	1	..	..	1	..	..
Hindsdale, William	..	..	1	1	..	..	..	..	..	..	..
Holcomb, Abner	..	2	3	..	1	2	..	..	..	1	..
Holcomb, Darius	1	..	..	1	..	3	..	..	1	..	..
Holcomb, Elisha	1	..	..	1	..	1	1	..	1	..	..
Holcomb, Joseph	2	1	..	1	..	2	..	..	1	..	..
Jackson, Hezekiah	1	..	..	1	..	1	..	1	..	..	..
Jones, Jonathan	..	..	..	1	..	4	..	..	1	..	..
Judd, Thomas	1	..	..	..	1	..	..	..	..	1	..
Newel, Seth	2	2	..	1	..	1	1	..	1	..	..
Nichols, Asa	4	..	..	1	..	1	2	..	1	..	..
Norton, Apolos	2	..	..	1	..	..	..	..	1	..	..
Pangborn, Reuben	2	1	..	1	..	1	1	..	1	..	..
Payon, Samuel	2	..	1	1	1	..	..	1	1	..	..
Pond, Benjamin	2	..	..	1	..	2	1	..	1	..	..
Pond, Jared	..	1	..	1	..	2	..	1	1	..	..
Pond, Silas	2	..	1	1	..	2	1	..	1	..	..
Pond, William	3	..	..	1	..	..	1	..	1	..	..
Porter, Silas	..	1	..	1	..	3	1	..	1	..	..
Post, Asa	3	..	..	1	..	2	..	1	1	..	..
Reynold, John	..	..	..	..	1	..	..	..	..	1	..
Reynold, John Jr.	1	..	1	..	..	1	..	1	..	..	..
Sacket, Abraham	..	..	..	1	..	2	..	1	..	..	..
Sacket, Filer	2	..	..	1	..	1	..	..	1	..	..
Sacket, Joseph	..	..	..	1	..	2	..	1	..	..	..
Sacket, Joseph Jr.	3	..	..	1	..	3	1	..	1	..	..
Sharkie, John A.	2	2	1	..	1	..	..	..	..	1	..
Sharkie, John M.	1	..	1	1	..	..	..	..	1	..	..
Shaw, Stephen	..	..	..	1	..	..	..	..	1	..	..
Shepherd, Abel	..	..	..	1	..	..	1	..	..	..	..
Shepherd, Samuel	2	1	..	1	..	..	1	1	1	..	..
Shepherd, William	..	..	..	..	1	..	..	1	..	1	..
Shoot, Phineas	..	..	..	..	1	..	..	..	..	1	..
Snow, Eli	2	..	..	..	1	1	..	..	1	..	..
Spaulding, Henry	..	1	1	..	1	..	1	1	1	..	..
Spaulding, Philip	1	2	2	1	1	2	1	1	1	..	..
Spaulding, Phineas	1	1	1	..	1	..	1	1	..	1	..
Spencer, Jonathan	3	..	..	1	..	1	..	1	..	..	..
Stephen, Zebulon	2	..	1	..	1	..	1	..	..	1	..
Stephens, Jonathan	3	2	..	1	..	..	1	..	1	1	..
Walker, Johnson	..	..	..	1	..	1	..	1	..	..	..
White, John	2	..	..	1	..	1	1	1	..	..	..
Wilkenson, Christopher	..	..	..	1	..	..	..	..	..	1	..
SALISBURY											
Alden, Nathaniel	..	..	..	1	..	3	..	..	1	..	..
Baker, James	2	..	..	1	..	1	..	..	1	..	..
Barney, Solomon	..	..	1	..	..	1	..	1	..	..	..
Bartemy, Jacob	..	..	1	..	..	..	..	1	..	..	..
Beach, Aaron L.	1	1	..	1	..	1	..	..	1	..	..
Bigelow, Joel	..	1	..	..	1	1	..	1	..	1	..
Blodgett, Asa	..	..	..	..	1	..	..	..	..	1	..
Brown, Thomas	..	..	1	..	..	..	..	1	..	..	..
Brown, William	..	..	1	..	..	..	..	1	..	..	..
Bump, Sadthiel	4	..	..	1	..	2	2	..	1	..	..
Chafey, Nathaniel	2	..	..	..	1	2	1	..	..	1	..
Chase, Henry Jr.	2	2	..	1	..	1	..	..	1	..	..
Chase, Nathaniel	1	2	..	..	1	2	1	..	1	..	..
Cheeney, Joseph	3	2	..	1	..	2	1	..	1	..	..
Claghorn, Elezer	1	..	3	..	1	..	1	..	..	1	..
Clark, Nathan	..	..	..	1	..	4	..	..	1	1	..
Copeland, William	3	2	1	..	1	1	..	..	1	..	..
Crook, Ephraim	1	2	1	1	..	..	..	..	1	..	..
Cudman, Peter	..	2	1	..	1	1	..	..	1	..	..
Dalyrimple, Kelmon	2	..	..	1	..	1	..	..	1	..	..
Daniels, Dan	1	..	..	1	..	..	..	1	..	..	..
Dawson, Thomas	..	1	..	..	1	..	..	..	..	1	..
Deming, Joel	..	..	..	1	..	..	..	1	..	..	..
Deming, John	..	2	..	1	..	2	1	..	1	..	..
Everts, Gilbert	1	1	3	..	1	..	2	1	..	1	..
Everts, Gilbert Jr.	..	..	..	1	..	1	..	..	1	..	..
Everts, Solomon	..	..	..	1	..	1	..	..	1	..	..
Farnum, Bela	1	..	..	1	..	1	..	..	1	..	..
Farnum, Jared	1	1	..	1	1	..	1	..	..	..	..
Farnum, Josiah	..	1	..	..	1	..	..	1	..	..	..
Fife, John	3	1	..	..	1	1	2	..	1	..	..
Flagg, Plinny	..	..	1	..	..	1	..	1	..	..	..
Flagg, Solomon	..	..	..	2	..	..	1	..	1	..	..
Francis, Strong	2	..	..	1	..	1	..	..	1	..	..
Gibbs, Friend	5	1	1	1	..	1	1	..	1	..	..
Gibson, Abraham	4	..	1	..	1	..	1	2	1	..	..
Gibson, Jonathan	..	..	1	..	..	..	..	1	..	..	..
Goodnough, Adenoug	1	2	1	..	1	2	1	..	..	1	..
Goodrich, Amos	2	..	..	1	..	2	..	..	1	..	..
Goodrich, Stephen	..	..	..	..	1	..	..	..	..	1	..
Graves, Barnabus	2	..	..	1	..	1	1	..	1	..	..
Graves, David	..	1	..	..	1	..	2	..	1	1	..
Graves, David 2nd.	..	..	..	1	..	1	..	1	..	..	..
Graves, Jesse	1	1	..	1	1	2	..	..	1	1	..
Graves, Joseph	..	1	..	..	1	..	..	..	..	1	..
Graves, Julius	2	..	..	1	..	3	..	..	1	..	..
Griswold, George	..	..	..	1	..	..	1	..	1	..	..
Hard, Stephen	4	1	..	..	1	3	2	..	1	..	..
Hide, Jonathan	1	..	..	1	..	1	..	1	..	..	..
Hilldrake, Abel	1	1	2	1	1	3	1	1	1	1	..
Holeman, David	2	..	..	1	..	1	..	1	..	..	..
Holeman, Samuel	3	1	..	1	1	..	..	1	..	..	..
Holt, John	..	..	2	..	..	..	..	1	..	..	..
Horseley, Joseph	..	..	1	..	1	..	1	..	..	1	..
Huntley, Asa	2	..	1	..	1	1	1	1	1	..	..
Huntley, Silas	2	..	1	..	..	..	..	1	..	..	..
Huntley, Sterling	2	..	1	..	..	1	..	1	..	..	..
Johnson, Christopher	1	2	2	..	1	2	..	2	1	..	..
Kelsey, Elias	..	1	..	1	1	..	..	..	..	1	..
Kelsey, Elias Jr.	1	..	1	..	..	..	..	1	..	..	..
Kelsey, Gamaliel	..	..	..	1	..	1	..	1	..	..	..
Kelsey, Jeremiah	1	..	..	1	..	..	..	1	..	..	..
Knott, Giles	1	..	1	..	..	1	..	1	..	..	..
Lankin, Loran	3	2	..	..	1	1	..	1	1	..	..
Laurance, Asa	..	1	..	..	1	..	1	1	..	1	..
Laurance, Jedediah	1	..	..	1	..	2	..	1	..	..	..
Livery, Thomas	..	1	..	1	..	..	..	1	1	..	..
Mandego, Jude	2	1	..	1	..	..	..	1	..	..	..
More, Abner	1	1	..	1	..	..	2	..	1	..	..
More, Abner Jr.	1	..	..	1	..	..	..	..	1	..	..
Moreman, Joshua	..	..	..	..	1	..	..	1	2	..	..
Moulton, Jeremiah	..	..	1	..	..	..	..	1	..	..	..
Moulton, Josiah	2	..	..	1	..	3	..	..	3	1	..
Newton, Joel	..	..	2	1	..	1	..	1	..	..	..
Noyes, Daniel	1	..	..	4	1	..	..	1	..	1	..

ADDISON COUNTY—Continued

NAMES OF HEADS OF FAMILIES	FREE WHITE MALES					FREE WHITE FEMALES					
	Under 10 years of age	Of 10 and under 16	Of 16 and under 26 including heads of families	Of 26 and under 45 including heads of families	Of 45 and upwards including heads of families.	Under 10 years of age	Of 10 and under 16	Of 16 and under 26 including heads of families	Of 26 and under 45 including heads of families	Of 45 and upwards including heads of families	All other free persons except Indians not taxed
SALISBURY—con.											
Osier, Joseph	1	..	..	1	..	..	..	1	..	..	..
Owen, Aaron	..	..	..	..	1	..	..	..	..	1	..
Owen, Abner	..	..	..	..	1	..	1	..	..	1	..
Owen, Abner Jr.	..	..	..	1	..	..	..	1	..	..	..
Palmitter, John	..	..	..	1	..	3	..	..	1	..	..
Pierce, Samuel	3	..	..	1	..	1	1	2	1	..	..
Porter, Henry	..	..	..	1	..	1	..	1	..	..	..
Pratt, Levi	1	1	..	1	..	4	1	..	1	..	..
Pratt, Silas	..	..	1	..	..	2	..	1	..	..	..
Pratt, William	2	..	..	1	..	3	..	1	1	..	..
Putnam, Reuben	..	..	..	1	..	1	..	1	..	..	..
Race, John	1	1	..	1	..	3	1	..	1	..	..
Read, Martin	2	..	..	1	..	2	..	..	1	..	..
Reeler, Henry	..	..	..	1	..	1	1	1	..	..	..
Reynold, Jacob	..	..	1	..	..	1	..	1	..	..	..
Sexton, Reuben	..	..	..	1	..	2	..	1	..	..	..
Smalley, Benjamin	..	..	..	..	1	..	..	..	..	1	..
Smalley, William	1	1	..	..	1	2	1	..	..	1	..
Smead, Eli	2	..	..	1	..	3	..	..	1	..	..
Spaulding, Stephen	1	..	..	1	..	1	..	1	..	..	..
Stone, Christopher	2	..	..	1	..	..	..	1	..	..	..
Strong, Simeon	..	..	..	..	1	..	..	..	..	1	..
Strong, Solomon	..	..	..	2	1	1	..	2	..	1	..
Tailor, Samuel	3	1	..	1	..	3	..	..	1	..	..
Thomas, Solomon	..	1	1	..	..	1	..	1	..	..	..
Titus, Luna	3	..	..	1	..	1	..	..	1	..	..
Waters, Widow Phebe	2	..	..	1	..	..	2	..	1	..	..
Weeks, Eliakim	..	..	..	1	..	1	..	1	..	..	..
Weeks, Nolen	..	1	1	..	1	..	1	3	..	2	..
Wells, John	2	1	..	1	1	..	1	3	1	..	..
Wells, Joshua	2	1	1	..	3	1	..	1	..	..	..
Wells, Oliver	1	2	..	1	..	1	..	..	1	..	..
Whitney, Daniel	1	2	..	..	1	..	..	..	1	1	..
Whitney, Silas	2	..	..	1	..	1	1	..	1	..	..
Woodward, Abijah	1	..	..	1	1	5	1	..	1	1	..
Woodward, Stephen	1	1	2	..	1	..	1	1	..	1	..
SHOREHAM											
Adams, John	..	1	3	..	1	1	1	..	..	1	..
Adams, John Jr.	1	..	1	..	..	..	..	1	..	..	..
Ager, James	2	..	..	1	..	3	..	..	1	..	..
Agur, James	1	..	..	1	..	2	..	..	1	..	..
Ames, Barnabus	1	1	..	1	..	3	1	..	1	..	..
Ames, Elijah	1	1	1	1	..	2	..	1	1	..	..
Ames, Henry	1	..	..	1	..	3	..	..	1	..	..
Ames, Samuel	..	..	..	1	..	1	..	..	1	..	..
Ames, William	2	1	..	1	..	2	..	..	1	..	..
Archer, Earl P.	2	..	..	1	..	1	..	..	1	..	..
Armstrong, Eliot	4	..	1	..	..	..	..	1	..	..	..
Atwood, Ebenezer	..	..	1	..	..	..	..	..	1	..	..
Atwood, Jacob	..	..	..	1	..	..	..	1	..	..	..
Atwood, Jacob	1	1	1	..	1	..	1	1	..	1	..
Atwood, Nathaniel	..	..	..	1	..	2	1	1	1	..	..
Baden, Jonathan	..	..	1	..	..	1	..	1	..	..	..
Bailey, Benjamin	3	..	..	1	..	1	..	..	1	1	..
Bailey, Joseph	..	..	2	..	1	2	1	2	..	1	..
Bailey, Joshua	3	..	..	1	1	..	..	..	..	1	..
Bailey, William B.	3	..	..	1	..	2	..	..	1	..	..
Barnum, Jabez	1	..	..	1	..	3	1	..	1	..	..
Barnum, Solomon	2	..	..	1	..	2	1	..	1	..	..
Barnum, Stephen	3	4	1	1	..	3	..	2	..	1	..
Barnum, Thomas	2	1	1	..	1	1	..	2	1	..	..
Barnum, Zacheus	3	..	..	1	..	1	2	1	1	..	..
Bass, Obadiah	..	1	1	..	..	1	..	1	..	..	..
Bateman, Freeman	4	..	..	1	..	1	..	..	1	..	..
Bateman, Thomas	..	..	..	..	1	..	..	..	..	1	..
Beers, Abraham	..	..	..	1	..	1	..	..	1	..	..
Benedict, Peter	1	1	..	1	..	2	..	..	1	..	..
Bennett, Brister	..	..	..	..	..	..	..	..	..	4	..
Bennett, Ephraim	3	1	1	..	1	..	..	1	1	1	..
Benton, Beuman	1	..	..	1	..	3	1	..	1	..	..
Benton, Phinehas	..	..	..	1	..	2	..	..	1	1	..
Benton, Samuel S.	..	..	..	1	..	..	..	..	1	..	..
Bissel, Benjamin	..	1	..	1	..	1	..	..	1	..	..
Bissel, Thomas	..	..	..	1	..	..	..	2	..	..	..
Brookins, Silas	3	1	..	1	..	..	1	1	2	..	..
Brown, Jeremiah	1	..	1	1	..	2	..	..	1	..	..
Burchard, Andrew	2	..	1	2	..	..	..	..	1	..	..
Callender, Amos	..	1	1	..	1	..	..	1	..	1	1
SHOREHAM—con.											
Callender, Gideon	..	..	..	1	..	1	..	..	1	..	..
Callender, Noah	..	..	..	1	..	..	..	1	..	..	..
Cary, Asa	..	..	1	..	..	..	..	1	..	..	..
Cary, Barzilla	..	..	..	1	..	..	..	..	..	..	..
Catlin, Ashbel	..	1	..	..	1	2	1	..	..	1	..
Catlin, John B.	1	..	1	1	..	..	..	1	1	1	..
Chilcot, John	1	3	..	..	1	1	..	..	1	..	..
Chipman, Barnabas	3	..	1	1	..	1	..	1	..	..	..
Chipman, Russel	..	..	..	1	..	..	1	1	..	1	..
Chipman, Timothy F.	1	1	..	1	..	3	1	..	2	..	..
Clark, Daniel	2	2	..	1	..	..	..	..	1	..	..
Cobham, Josiah	3	2	..	1	..	..	..	..	1	..	..
Cooper, Calib	2	..	..	1	..	..	..	..	1	..	..
Cooper, David	2	..	..	1	..	..	..	..	1	..	..
Cooper, Israel	..	1	2	1	..	2	1	2	..	..	..
Cooper, Jonathan	2	..	..	1	..	1	..	..	1	..	..
Cooper, Samuel	..	..	1	..	..	1	..	1	..	..	..
Cooper, Stephen	..	..	..	..	1	..	..	..	..	1	..
Cooper, Stephen Jr.	..	1	2	..	1	..	..	..	..	1	..
Corey, Luther	1	..	..	1	..	3	..	..	1	..	..
Cudworth, Thomas	..	..	..	1	..	1	..	1	..	..	..
Culver, Eliakim	3	2	..	..	1	..	1	2	..	1	..
Cuttin, David	1	..	..	1	..	1	..	..	1	..	..
Cuttin, Samuel	..	..	..	1	..	..	..	1	..	..	..
Dart, Aaron	2	1	..	1	..	2	..	..	1	..	..
Davenport, Thomas	1	..	..	..	1	3	1	1	..	1	..
Davis, John	..	..	2	..	1	..	1	..	1	..	..
Denton, Joseph	2	1	1	..	1	2	1	1	1	..	..
Denton, William	1	1	..	1	..	2	..	..	1	..	..
Doolittle, Ephraim	..	1	1	..	1	..	..	..	..	1	..
Doolittle, Ephraim 2nd.	1	2	1	1	..	2	..	..	1	..	..
Douglass, Domine	..	1	1	..	1	..	1	..	..	1	..
Douglass, Joseph	2	1	..	1	..	2	1	..	1	..	..
Dutton, Jedediah	2	..	..	1	..	3	2	..	1	..	..
Fenton, Bethuel	..	1	..	1	..	3	3	..	1	..	..
Fisk, James	..	..	..	1	..	..	..	1	1	..	..
Forbes, Edward	..	..	..	..	1	..	..	..	..	..	..
Forbes, James	..	..	..	1	..	..	..	..	1	..	..
Forbes, John	1	1	1	1	..	4	2	1	1	..	..
Forbes, Sylvester	..	..	..	2	..	..	..	..	1	..	..
Fuller, Jason	2	..	..	1	..	1	..	..	1	..	..
Fuller, Joseph	1	1	1	1	..	3	2	1	1	..	..
Fuller, Rufus	..	..	1	1	..	1	..	2	1	..	..
Fuller, Widow Mary	..	..	..	..	..	..	..	..	..	1	..
Gennings, Jonathan	1	..	1	1	..	..	2	1	..	1	..
George, Prince	..	..	..	..	..	..	..	..	..	..	2
Goodale, Timothy	..	1	..	..	1	..	..	1	..	1	..
Goodnow, Ebenezer	2	..	..	1	..	1	..	..	1	..	..
Goodwin, Zebod.	2	..	..	1	..	1	2	..	..	..	..
Gould, John	1	1	..	1	..	3	..	..	1	..	..
Griffin, James	2	..	..	1	..	2	..	..	1	..	..
Griffin, Thomas	..	..	..	..	1	..	1	..	..	1	..
Hagle, Francis	2	1	..	..	1	3	..	..	1	..	..
Hagle, John	1	1	..	..	1	3	1	..	1	..	..
Hand, Mathew	..	1	..	1	1	..	1	1	..	1	..
Harrington, Russel	1	1	..	1	..	..	..	..	1	..	..
Haws, Ebenezer	1	..	..	1	..	1	..	1	..	..	..
Healy, Benjamin	2	1	..	..	1	..	1	1	1	..	..
Healy, Caleb	4	2	..	1	..	1	1	..	1	..	..
Healy, Jabez	3	2	..	1	..	..	1	..	1	..	..
Hemenway, Samuel	1	1	2	..	1	3	1	1	1	..	..
Higby, Jesse	1	1	..	1	..	2	..	..	1	..	..
Holcomb, Abraham	1	..	..	1	..	2	..	..	1	..	..
Howe, Job L.	2	..	3	1	..	..	..	..	..	1	..
Howe, Oliver	2	..	..	1	..	..	1	..	1	..	..
Hulbrook, Eleazer	1	..	..	1	..	1	..	..	1	..	..
Hunsden, Allen	1	2	..	1	..	2	1	..	1	..	..
Hunsden, John	1	..	..	1	..	..	..	1	..	..	..
Hunt, Samuel	3	..	..	1	..	2	..	..	1	..	..
Hunter, Jonathan	..	..	..	..	1	..	..	..	1	1	..
Huntley, Davis	1	..	..	1	..	2	..	1	..	..	..
Hutchinson, Benjamin	1	..	1	1	..	3	1	..	1	..	..
Hutchinson, Joseph	3	1	..	1	..	1	..	..	..	..	..
Jenison, Widow Ruth	1	..	..	..	..	2	..	..	1	..	..
Johnson, Gideon	1	1	..	1	..	1	..	..	1	..	..
Johnson, William	..	..	1	1	1	..	1	1	..	..	..
Jones, Asa	1	1	..	1	..	1	2	..	1	..	..
Jones, Noah	2	2	1	1	..	..	1	1	1	..	..
Jones, William	..	..	..	2	..	3	2	1	1	..	..
Jones, William 2nd.	2	2	..	1	..	2	..	1	1	..	..
Kellogg, Elijah	..	..	..	..	1	..	2	..	..	1	..

ADDISON COUNTY—Continued

NAMES OF HEADS OF FAMILIES	FREE WHITE MALES: Under 10 years of age	Of 10 and under 16	Of 16 and under 26 including heads of families	Of 26 and under 45 including heads of families	Of 45 and upwards including heads of families.	FREE WHITE FEMALES: Under 10 years of age	Of 10 and under 16	Of 16 and under 26 including heads of families	Of 26 and under 45 including heads of families	Of 45 and upwards including heads of families	All other free persons except Indians not taxed
SHOREHAM—con.											
Landon, Aqualla	..	2	..	..	1	..	1	..	1	..	..
Landon, Nathan	..	..	..	1	1	..	..	..	1	1	..
Laraby, John S.	1	..	..	2	..	4	..	..	1	..	..
Larrabee, Timothy	3	1	..	1	..	1	1	..	1	..	..
Larraby, John	..	..	..	..	1	..	1	..	..	1	..
Leonard, George	3	1	1	..	1	1	2	..	..	1	..
Leonard, Moses	2	..	..	1	..	1	..	..	1	..	..
Leonard, Moses 2nd	1	..	..	1	..	2	..	..	1	..	..
Leonard, Peter R.	1	..	2	..	..	..	..	1	..	..	..
Linch, David	2	..	..	1	..	..	..	..	1	..	..
Luther, Elisha	3	..	..	1	..	1	1	..	1	..	..
Marsh, Jonas	1	..	..	1	..	3	2	1	1	..	..
Marsh, Leonard	..	..	..	1	..	..	..	1	..	1	..
Mazazen, Mark W.	2	..	..	1	..	1	..	..	1	..	..
McGennis, John	1	..	..	1	..	..	..	1	..	..	..
McGennis, Stephen	..	..	..	..	1	..	..	..	..	1	..
McPherson, Josiah	2	..	..	1	..	1	..	..	1	1	..
Miller, Philip	2	..	..	1	..	1	..	..	1	..	..
More, Daniel	..	..	1	..	..	..	..	1	..	..	..
More, James	1	..	1	..	1	1	..	2	..	1	..
More, Paul	3	1	..	..	1	..	1	..	1	..	..
More, Robert	..	..	1	..	..	..	..	1	..	..	..
Morse, Artemas	3	2	..	1	..	..	..	..	1	..	..
Murdock, Jesse	..	1	2	..	1	..	2	..	..	1	..
Newton, Daniel	..	1	..	1	..	..	1	..	1	..	..
Newton, Lemuel	2	..	..	1	..	3	2	..	1	..	..
Newton, Liberty	2	1	..	2	..	3	1	..	1	1	..
Nicholson, John	1	..	..	1	..	1	..	..	1	..	..
Noble, Asahel	2	..	..	1	..	2	1	..	1	..	..
North, Nathaniel	1	1	2	..	..	..	1	1	1	..	..
Northrop. Jeremiah	2	..	..	2	..	2	1	..	1	..	..
Nothrop, Samuel	..	1	..	1	..	1	..	1	1	..	..
Ormsbee, John	2	..	..	1	..	2	..	1	..	..	..
Page, Timothy	3	1	1	2	..	2	1	1	1	..	..
Paige, Jonathan	3	..	1	..	..	1	..	1	..	..	..
Palmer, William	..	1	..	..	1	1	..	2	1	..	..
Payneham, Widow Elizabeth.	..	..	1	..	..	1	..	..	1	..	..
Payon, Cul	..	..	..	..	..	..	..	..	..	..	3
Peek, Moses	2	..	..	1	..	2	..	..	1	..	..
Perkins, Thomas	1	..	..	1	..	2	..	..	1	..	..
Phillips, Joseph	3	..	1	..	1	2	..	1	1	..	..
Pond, Ira	1	..	..	1	..	1	..	1	..	..	..
Pond, Josiah	1	..	..	..	1	2	1	..	1	..	..
Pond, Munson	..	..	..	1	..	..	..	..	..	..	..
Pond, Nathaniel	2	..	..	1	..	..	2	1	1	..	..
Pourchard, Levi	1	2	..	1	..	2	..	1	1	..	..
Ramsdale, David	1	..	2	1	..	..	..	..	1	..	..
Ramsdale, John	..	1	..	1	..	1	1	..	1	1	..
Ramsdale, Michael	1	..	1	..	1	..	..	1	..	1	..
Reynold, Silas	2	1	..	1	..	1	..	1	..	..	..
Reynolds, Jared	1	1	..	1	..	2	..	..	1	..	..
Rhodes, Obadiah	1	2	1	..	1	1	1	1	1	..	..
Rice, Josiah	2	..	..	..	1	..	..	1	..	1	..
Rich, Charles	3	..	2	1	..	1	..	2	..	..	..
Rich, Thomas	1	..	1	..	1	1	2	2	..	1	..
Riggs, Benjamin	..	..	..	1	..	..	..	..	1	..	..
Robbins, John	1	..	..	1	..	1	..	..	1	..	..
Robinson, John	1	..	..	1	..	2	..	..	1	..	..
Robinson, Rolpheus	1	..	..	1	..	2	1	..	1	..	..
Rood, Briggs	1	..	..	1	..	3	..	..	1	..	..
Rowley, Elisha	1	..	..	1	..	2	..	..	1	..	..
Rowley, Hopkins	1	..	1	1	..	3	1	..	1	..	..
Rowley, Reuben	2	..	1	..	1	1	1	..	1	..	..
Rowley, Thomas	1	1	1	..	1	..	1	1	1	..	..
Russel, David	1	..	1	..	1	..	2	..	..	1	..
Sampson, Anthony	..	..	..	..	..	..	..	..	1	..	1
Scott, James	..	..	..	1	..	..	..	..	1	..	..
Silsby, Enos	1	1	1	1	..	..	..	1	..	..	..
Simons, Andrew	1	..	..	1	..	..	..	1	1	..	..
Sisson, Gideon	..	..	..	1	1	..	..	..	1	..	..
Smith, Benson	..	..	2	..	..	..	..	1	..	..	..
Smith, Calib	2	..	..	1	..	3	..	..	1	..	..
Smith, Eli	..	1	2	..	1	..	2	..	..	1	..
Smith, John	..	1	3	..	1	1	..	2	..	1	..
Smith, John Jr.	3	..	..	1	..	..	1	..	1	..	..
Smith, Joseph	1	1	1	1	..	..	..	1	1	..	..
Smith, Philip	..	..	..	1	..	4	..	..	1	..	..
Smith, Samuel	1	..	..	1	..	1	..	..	1	..	..
Smith, Silas	1	..	..	1	..	1	..	1	..	..	..
Smith, Stephen	..	..	..	..	1	..	1	..	..	1	..
Smith, Stephen Jr.	3	..	..	1	..	2	..	..	1	..	..
Stanley, Amos	..	2	..	1	..	1	..	..	1	..	..
Steward, Mathew	2	1	1	1	..	1	2	..	..	1	..
Stiles, Asa	3	1	..	1	..	..	1	..	1	..	..
Stiles, Ebenezer	..	..	1	..	..	..	..	1	..	..	..
Stiles, Reuben	1	..	..	1	..	..	..	..	1	..	..
Stiles, Stephen	..	..	1	..	1	..	..	1	1	1	..
Stone, Amos	..	..	..	1	1	..	2	..	1	..	..
Tower, Gideon	2	..	1	1	..	2	..	1	..	..	..
Tower, Samuel	..	..	..	1	1	1	1	1	..	1	..
Towner, Benjamin	..	1	..	1	..	2	..	..	1	..	..
Tracy, John	1	1	1	..	1	..	..	..	1	1	..
Tracy, Shelden	1	..	..	1	..	1	..	1	..	..	..
Treadway, Jonathan	1	..	3	1	..	3	1	..	1	..	..
Turrel, Beebee	3	1	..	1	..	2	1	..	1	..	..
Turrel, Daniel	1	..	1	1	..	3	1	..	1	..	..
Turrel, Ebenezer	..	..	1	..	1	1	1	1	..	1	..
Turrel, Ebenezer Jr.	..	..	..	1	..	2	..	1	..	..	..
Veal, Daniel	2	..	1	1	..	1	..	..	1	..	..
Wait, Barton	3	..	..	1	..	..	2	..	1	..	..
Wait, James	1	..	..	1	..	..	..	1	..	..	..
Wait, John	1	..	..	1	..	..	..	1	..	..	..
Wait, Samuel	..	..	..	..	1	..	..	..	..	1	..
Waite, Samuel Jr.	..	1	..	1	..	2	..	..	1	..	..
Wallace, James R.	2	..	1	1	..	2	1	..	1	..	..
Wallace, John	1	..	..	1	..	..	..	1	..	..	..
Wallace, Josiah	1	1	1	1	..	2	..	..	1	..	..
Ward, John	1	..	..	1	..	1	..	..	1	..	..
Watson, William	..	..	..	..	1	..	..	..	1	1	..
Welden, Roswell	2	1	..	1	..	2	..	..	1	..	..
West, Widow Susannah	1	..	..	..	..	2	..	..	1	..	..
White, Widow Sally	1	..	..	..	..	2	..	..	1	..	..
Wilcox, James	2	..	..	1	..	2	..	1	1	..	..
Williams, Elijah	2	..	..	1	..	2	..	..	1	..	..
Willson, Jonathan	5	..	..	1	..	..	..	..	1	..	..
Willson, William	1	..	..	1	..	3	..	..	1	..	..
Witherell, Job	1	..	..	1	..	3	..	..	1	..	..
Witherell, Joseph	..	..	1	..	..	1	..	1	..	..	..
Witherell, Samuel	1	..	1	..	1	..	..	..	1	..	..
Witherell, Samuel Jr.	3	..	..	1	..	..	..	1	..	..	..
Witherell, Sylvanus	1	..	..	1	..	..	..	1	..	..	..
Wolf, Stephen	..	..	1	..	..	4	..	1	..	..	..
Wood, Abel	1	..	..	1	..	2	..	..	1	..	..
Woolcot, Alvin	1	1	..	1	..	3	..	..	1	..	..
Woolcot, Jesse	2	1	..	1	..	1	1	1	1	..	..
Woolcot, Philimon	..	1	..	1	..	2	1	1	..	1	..
Woolcot, Samuel	1	1	2	..	1	..	1	1	..	1	..
Wright, Andrew	1	1	..	1	..	2	2	1	1	..	..
Wright, Ebenezer	1	..	..	1	..	2	1	..	1	..	..
Wright, Elijah	4	..	..	1	..	1	1	..	1	..	..
Wright, Joseph	3	..	..	1	..	..	..	..	1	..	..
UNCERTAIN NAME											
Blayedel (?), Ezra	1	..	1	..	..	..	..	1	..	..	..
STARKSBORO											
Austin, Ezekiel	1	..	..	1	..	3	..	1	..	..	..
Beers, Daniel	3	1	..	1	..	2	1	..	1	..	..
Bidwell, George	..	1	1	..	1	3	1	..	1	..	..
Blaze, Paul	..	..	..	1	..	..	..	..	1	..	..
Blodgett, Aaron	..	..	2	..	1	..	..	..	1	..	..
Bostwick, Joseph	..	..	1	..	1	..	1	..	..	1	..
Bugby, Israel	1	..	1	1	..	4	1	..	1	..	..
Bunker, Dodefind	..	..	1	..	..	..	..	..	..	..	..
Bushnel, Abraham	2	1	..	..	1	1	1	1	..	1	..
Bushnel, John	..	..	1	..	..	1	..	1	..	..	..
Bushnel, Samuel	1	..	..	1	..	1	..	1	..	..	..
Carpenter, Stephen	3	1	..	1	..	1	1	..	1	..	..
Chase, Henry	..	1	1	..	1	..	2	2	..	1	..
Dewey, David	1	..	..	1	..	1	..	..	1	..	..
Eastman, David	..	..	1	..	2	..	..	1	..	..	..
Furguson, Elijah	1	..	1	..	..	1	..	1	..	..	..
Furguson, John	1	..	2	..	1	2	2	..	1	..	..

ADDISON COUNTY—Continued

NAMES OF HEADS OF FAMILIES	FREE WHITE MALES: Under 10 years of age	FREE WHITE MALES: Of 10 and under 16	FREE WHITE MALES: Of 16 and under 26 including heads of families	FREE WHITE MALES: Of 26 and under 45 including heads of families	FREE WHITE MALES: Of 45 and upwards including heads of families	FREE WHITE FEMALES: Under 10 years of age	FREE WHITE FEMALES: Of 10 and under 16	FREE WHITE FEMALES: Of 16 and under 26 including heads of families	FREE WHITE FEMALES: Of 26 and under 45 including heads of families	FREE WHITE FEMALES: Of 45 and upwards including heads of families	All other free persons except Indians not taxed
STARKSBORO—con.											
Furguson, Reuben	..	..	1	..	1	..	..	1	..	..	..
Gay, John	1	1	2	..	1	1	1	..	1	..	..
Griswould, Josiah	2	..	..	..	1	3	3	..	1	..	..
Hall, Abraham	..	..	..	..	1	..	..	..	..	2	..
Hall, Abraham Jr.	2	1	..	1	..	2	..	1	1	..	..
Hall, Samuel	..	2	..	1	..	3	..	..	1	..	..
Hall, Stephen	..	..	1	..	..	..	..	..	..	..	..
Heading, James	1	1	2	1	..	3	3	1	1	..	..
Heath, Samuel	2	2	..	1	..	1	..	1	1	..	..
Hill, John	..	..	..	1	..	..	..	1	..	..	..
Hill, Samuel	4	..	..	1	..	2	..	..	1	..	..
Hill, Thomas	..	..	1	..	..	..	..	..	..	..	..
Hill, William	..	..	..	1	..	..	..	..	..	..	..
Hoagg, David	..	..	..	1	..	4	1	..	1	..	..
Hoagg, Elihu	3	..	2	1	..	..	..	..	1	..	..
Hoagg, Elijah	..	..	..	..	1	..	..	..	..	1	..
Hoagg, Jonathan	2	2	..	1	..	2	..	..	1	..	..
Holcomb, Solomon	1	..	1	1	..	2	1	..	1	..	..
Houghton, Livi	1	..	..	1	..	1	..	..	1	..	..
Kellogg, David	2	..	..	1	..	1	..	1	..	..	..
Kellogg, Elijah I.	..	..	..	..	1	..	..	..	..	1	..
Kellogg, Elijah Jr.	..	1	..	1	..	..	..	1	..	..	..
Knapp, Daniel	..	..	..	1	..	..	..	..	..	..	..
Knapp, Livi	..	1	..	1	..	..	..	..	1	..	..
Knapp, Silas	..	1	..	1	..	4	1	..	1	..	..
Manson, Curtis	..	..	1	..	..	..	..	1	..	..	..
Meader, David	..	..	3	1	..	1	..	..	1	..	..
Meader, Joel	..	..	1	..	..	..	..	1	..	..	..
Miller, Cyrus	2	..	..	1	..	..	..	1	..	..	..
Miller, Thomas	..	..	..	1	..	..	..	1	..	..	..
More, Seth	1	..	..	1	..	2	1	..	1	..	..
Mory, Daniel	..	..	..	1	..	..	..	..	1	..	1
North, Lemuel	..	..	1	..	1	..	..	1	..	1	..
North, Richard	1	..	..	1	..	1	..	..	1	..	..
North, William	2	..	..	1	..	4	1	..	1	..	..
Orvis, Philen	..	..	..	1	..	..	..	..	1	..	..
Peat, Abraham	3	..	..	1	..	1	..	..	1	..	..
Peck, Daniel	1	..	..	1	..	2	..	..	1	..	..
Peck, Forbes	1	..	1	..	..	..	..	1	..	..	..
Peck, John	..	2	..	..	1	..	1	1	..	1	..
Peck, William	..	..	1	..	1	..	..	..	..	1	..
Persons, Enos	3	..	..	1	..	2	..	..	1	..	..
Pierce, Warner	2	..	..	1	..	..	1	..	1	..	..
Smith, Amos	1	..	..	1	..	3	2	..	1	..	..
Swift, Jabez	1	..	1	..	..	1	..	1	..	..	..
Swift, Jirah	..	..	..	1	..	1	..	1	..	1	..
Tucker, Jacob	..	..	1	..	..	..	..	..	..	..	..
Verny, Hezekiah	..	..	..	..	1	..	..	..	..	..	..
Verny, Hezekiah Jr.	..	..	..	1	..	2	..	..	1	..	..
Verny, Isaac	3	1	..	1	..	1	..	..	1	..	..
Verny, Joshua	1	..	1	1	..	2	..	..	1	..	..
Ward, William	4	..	..	1	..	..	1	..	1	..	..
White, Oliver	..	1	..	1	..	3	..	..	1	..	..
Young, Robert	1	..	..	1	..	4	..	..	1	..	..
VERGENNES											
Allen, David	..	..	1	..	..	..	..	1	..	..	..
Avord, Phinehas	1	..	..	1	..	2	..	..	1	..	..
Baldwin, Abraham	..	..	7	4	..	1	2	..	1	..	1
Barber, Stephen	..	..	1	1	..	2	..	1	..	..	..
Bellamy, Justus	2	2	3	1	..	3	..	2	1	..	..
Booth, David	..	..	..	1	1	..	2	1	1	..	4
Booth, Reuben H.	..	..	..	1	..	..	..	..	..	..	..
Brush, Ruth	..	..	..	..	..	1	1	..	1	..	..
Burret, William	..	..	2	..	..	..	..	..	1	..	..
Byrd, Thomas	..	..	2	..	1	2	1	..	1	..	..
Cameron, Triphorn	..	..	..	..	..	1	..	1	1	..	..
Case, Bissel	2	..	1	1	..	3	1	..	1	..	1
Chipman, Samuel Jr.	2	1	3	2	..	4	1	2	1	..	1
Clark, Solomon	..	..	..	1	..	1	..	1	..	..	..
VERGENNES—con.											
Clumb, Jacob	3	..	2	2	..	1	..	..	1	..	..
Cool, Wyman J.	2	..	..	1	..	2	..	..	1	..	..
Cronk, Henry	3	..	..	1	..	..	..	1	..	..	..
Davis, Samuel	..	1	2	1	..	3	1	..	1	..	..
Dibble, Abraham	..	..	..	1	..	1	..	1	..	..	1
Ferris, Alanson	1	..	..	1	..	1	1	..	1	..	..
Ferris, William	..	..	..	..	..	..	..	..	..	..	4
Fitch, Jabez	..	1	..	1	1	1	..	2	..	1	..
Fitch, Jabez G.	..	1	1	1	..	3	1	1	1	..	2
Frank, Jeremiah	1	..	..	..	1	1	..	..	1	..	..
Geer, William	..	1	2	..	..	..	..	..	..	..	..
Goodrich, William	..	..	..	..	1	..	1	..	1	..	..
Hackstaff, John	3	..	..	1	..	1	..	..	1	..	..
Hall, Luther E.	..	..	..	1	..	1	..	..	2	..	..
Harmon, Argalus	..	..	1	1	..	..	..	..	..	..	..
Harmon, Daniel	..	1	2	..	1	..	1	..	..	1	..
Hitchcock, Samuel	3	..	..	2	1	1	1	2	1	..	..
Hoight, John	3	..	..	1	..	..	..	..	1	..	..
Hoisington, Job	1	1	1	2	..	2	..	1	..	..	..
Hopkins, Roswel	1	1	3	2	..	1	1	1	1	..	..
Hopkins, Roswell S.	1	..	..	..	1	1	1	1	..	2	..
Hunter, Peter	..	..	..	..	..	..	..	..	..	..	2
Huntington, Ebenezer	..	1	1	1	..	1	1	..	1	..	1
Jaquois, Darius	..	..	..	..	1	1	..	1	..	1	..
Logan, John	..	..	..	1	..	1	..	..	..	..	..
Lyman, Jesse	1	1	1	1	..	2	2	..	1	..	..
Marsh, Amos	..	..	4	2	..	2	1	2	2	..	2
Mason, John	2	1	..	..	1	2	1	..	1	..	..
McDonald, ———	1	..	..	2	..	1	..	..	1	..	..
McIntosh, Donald	..	..	3	..	1	..	1	..	..	1	..
Miller, John	1	..	..	1	..	..	..	1	..	..	..
Minor, Abet	2	..	..	1	..	2	..	..	1	..	..
Minor, Joseph	..	..	..	1	..	..	1	..	..	1	..
Moulthrop, John	1	..	1	2	..	1	..	1	1	..	..
Newcomb, Azariah	1	1	..	1	..	1	2	1	1	..	..
Newport, Trovo	..	..	..	..	..	..	..	..	..	..	2
Nichols, Brewster	..	..	..	..	..	..	..	..	..	..	2
Nichols, Jonathan Jr.	1	1	1	1	..	3	1	..	1	..	..
Oaks, John	1	1	..	1	..	2	1	..	1	..	..
Osborn, Rebecah	..	1	..	..	..	..	..	..	1	..	..
Painter, Azariah	2	..	2	1	..	1	1	..	1	..	..
Palmer, Eden	3	..	..	1	..	1	..	..	1	..	..
Pemberton, William	..	..	1	..	..	..	..	1	..	..	..
Pousau, Joseph	..	..	1	..	..	1	..	1	..	..	..
Pratt, John	1	..	2	..	..	1	..	1	..	..	..
Pratt, Sevea	1	..	2	..	..	..	..	1	..	..	..
Prime, Benjamin	..	..	..	1	..	..	..	1	..	..	..
Roberts, Eli	..	..	..	..	1	..	..	..	..	1	..
Roberts, Eli 2nd	..	..	2	1	..	2	..	1	..	..	..
Roberts, Seth	1	..	..	1	..	1	..	..	1	..	..
Rogers, Benjamin G.	1	..	..	1	..	1	..	1	..	..	..
Rossetter, Betsey	..	1	..	..	..	2	..	..	1	..	..
Rubblee, John	1	..	..	1	..	..	..	1	..	1	..
Sawyer, Artemas	..	..	1	1	..	..	..	..	..	..	..
Seymor, Belden	1	1	1	1	..	..	..	1	..	..	..
Smith, Josiah	1	1	1	1	..	..	..	2	..	..	2
Smith, William	2	1	1	3	..	2	..	..	2	..	..
Snae, John	2	..	..	..	1	..	..	..	..	1	..
Spencer, Calvin	..	..	..	1	..	2	1	..	..	..	..
Spencer, Elijah	..	..	1	..	1	1	..	..	1	..	..
Spencer, Gideon	..	..	..	1	1	..	..	1	..	1	..
Spencer, Gideon Jr.	1	..	..	1	..	2	..	1	..	..	..
Spencer, Stephen	..	..	1	..	..	1	..	1	..	..	..
Spoor, Charles	2	..	1	1	..	..	..	..	1	..	..
Stockman, Charles	1	..	..	1	..	1	..	..	1	..	..
Strong, Asa	..	..	..	..	1	1	..	..	..	..	..
Strong, Luke	..	..	..	2	..	2	1	1	1	..	..
Strong, Samuel	1	..	6	1	..	2	2	2	2	..	..
Sweet, Sylvester	..	1	..	..	1	1	1	..	1	..	..
Tousaint, Louis	..	..	..	1	..	1	..	..	1	..	..
Train, Robert	1	1	1	..	1	1	..	..	..	1	..
Traverse, Henry	1	..	1	1	..	1	..	1	..	..	..
Tyler, Josiah	..	..	1	1	..	1	..	1	..	..	..
Vaughan, Philander	..	1	..	1	..	..	..	..	1	..	..

ADDISON COUNTY—Continued

NAMES OF HEADS OF FAMILIES	FREE WHITE MALES					FREE WHITE FEMALES					
	Under 10 years of age	Of 10 and under 16	Of 16 and under 26 including heads of families	Of 26 and under 45 including heads of families	Of 45 and upwards including heads of families.	Under 10 years of age	Of 10 and under 16	Of 16 and under 26 including heads of families	Of 26 and under 45 including heads of families	Of 45 and upwards including heads of families	All other free persons except Indians not taxed
VERGENNES—con.											
Wilcot, Abner	1	..	..	1	..	2	1	..	1	..	..
Willcot, John	..	..	1	..	..	..	..	..	..	..	..
Woodbridge, Enoch	..	..	1	..	1	2	2	1	..	..	2
WALTHAM											
Barton, Andrew	..	1	1	..	1	..	..	1	..	1	..
Barton, Andrew Jr.	2	..	1	1	..	3	..	..	1	..	..
Barton, Dyer	..	1	..	1	..	..	1	..	1	..	..
Brown, Phinehas	..	..	2	..	1	2	2	1	..	1	..
Brush, Elkanah	2	1	2	1	..	1	2	..	1	1	..
Chilson, Ezra	2	..	..	1	..	1	..	..	1	..	..
Chipman, Daniel	3	..	..	1	..	2	..	1	..	..	..
Cook, Ichabod	2	3	1	..	1	1	1	3	..	1	..
Daggett, John	..	1	..	..	1	..	..	..	..	1	..
Everts, Luther Jr.	2	..	..	1	..	..	..	1	..	..	..
Griswold, Adonijah	3	..	..	1	..	3	..	..	1	..	..
Griswold, Doctor	..	..	1	2	..	1	..	2	..	..	..
Griswold, Nathan	1	2	..	1	..	..	1	1	1	..	..
Hawkins, Ebenezer	..	..	..	1	..	2	1	..	1	..	..
Hawkins, Roger	2	..	..	1	..	2	..	..	1	..	..
Hawkins, Zebulon	..	..	..	1	..	..	..	..	..	..	..
Hobbs, Elijah	4	..	..	1	..	..	..	..	1	..	..
Hobbs, Isaac	..	..	2	..	1	..	1	1	..	1	..
Hutchinson, John	1	..	..	1	..	4	..	..	1	..	..
Langworthy, Joseph	..	..	1	1	1	..	1	..	..	1	..
Langworthy, Robert	1	..	..	1	..	3	..	..	1	..	..
Lord, Benjamin	1	..	1	1	..	1	2	..	1	..	..
Paddock, Anthony	4	..	..	1	..	2	2	..	1	..	..
Peat, Abraham	..	..	..	..	1	1	2	3	..	1	..
Pier, Moses	..	1	..	1	..	5	..	..	1	..	..
Pier, Oliver Jr.	..	1	..	1	..	3	1	..	1	..	..
Pier, William	..	..	..	2	..	4	1	..	1	..	..
Shelden, Eli	..	2	..	1	..	3	1	1	1	..	..
Spafford, Phinehas	1	..	1	..	..	..	..	1	..	..	..
Spalding, William	..	..	1	..	1	3	1	1	..	1	..
Strong, Solomon	..	2	1	1	1	..	1	1	..	1	..
Tousley, Elephalet	1	..	..	1	..	2	..	1	..	..	..
Tousley, Reuben	..	..	..	1	..	..	..	..	..	..	..
Traver, Nicholas	..	..	..	1	..	..	..	..	..	1	..
Turner, John	..	..	..	..	1	..	..	..	..	1	..
Tyler, David	3	..	..	2	..	2	1	..	1	..	..
Ward, Jesse	4	1	1	1	..	1	..	..	1	..	..
Warner, William Jr.	1	..	..	1	..	2	..	..	1	..	..
Woodridge, William	1	..	2	..	1	..	1	1	..	1	..
WARREN											
Gerish, Thomas	1	..	..	1	..	1	..	1	..	..	..
Kent, William	..	..	1	..	..	3	..	1	..	..	..
Levet, Seth	2	..	1	..	..	..	..	1	..	..	..
Reymond, Joseph	..	..	..	2	..	2	..	..	1	..	..
Rice, Jarius	2	..	..	1	..	..	..	1	..	..	..
Richardson, James	..	..	2	2	..	..	..	1	..	..	..
Rising, Asahel	..	..	3	1	1	1	..	1	..	..	..
Sherman, John	2	..	..	1	..	1	..	1	..	..	..
Sherman, Ruel	1	..	..	1	..	1	..	..	1	..	..
Willock, Simeon	2	1	1	1	..	1	1	..	1	..	..
Wood, John	3	1	..	1	..	1	..	..	1	..	..
WEYBRIDGE											
Bartum, Joel	1	..	..	1	..	1	..	1	..	..	..
Belden, David	1	..	..	1	1	..	..	1	..	..	1
Bell, Amos	..	..	..	1	..	..	..	1	..	..	..
Bell, Jason	2	2	..	1	..	2	..	..	1	..	..
Boyington, David	..	1	1	..	1	2	..	..	..	1	..
Brewster, William	1	1	..	1	..	..	2	2	1	..	..
Brittain, Benjamin	..	1	..	..	1	1	..	1	..	1	..
Brittain, John	3	..	..	1	..	1	..	..	1	..	..
Brown, Brewster	1	..	1	1	..	1	..	1	..	..	..
Childs, Simon	2	..	..	1	..	1	..	..	1	..	..
WEYBRIDGE—con.											
Clark, Benjamin	..	..	1	..	..	..	..	1	..	..	..
Clark, Jonathan	2	..	..	1	..	..	..	..	1	..	..
Clark, Samuel	3	2	1	..	1	1	1	..	..	1	..
Crawfoot, Eleazer	3	..	..	1	..	1	2	..	1	..	..
Dickenson, Widow Sally	1	1	..	..	..	..	1	1	1	..	..
Dickenson, Stoughton	2	2	1	1	..	..	2	..	1	..	..
Drake, Asa	3	..	2	1	..	..	..	..	1	1	..
Dunning, Abraham	4	1	..	1	..	1	1	..	1	..	..
Eastman, Joel	2	..	..	1	..	2	..	..	1	..	..
Easton, James	3	1	1	..	1	1	1	..	1	..	..
Farmer, James	..	..	..	..	1	1	..	..	..	1	1
Field, Daniel	1	1	..	1	..	4	1	..	1	..	..
Fitch, Roswel	..	..	..	1	..	3	1	..	1	..	..
Frost, Frederick	2	1	2	..	1	2	1	1	1	..	..
Gold, William	2	1	..	..	1	2	..	..	..	1	..
Goodale, David	..	2	..	1	..	1	1	..	1	..	..
Gould, William	..	..	..	..	1	..	..	..	..	1	..
Grout, Theodore	3	..	..	1	..	1	..	..	1	..	..
Hager, Benjamin	2	1	2	1	..	1	..	1	..	..	1
Higgins, Solomon	..	..	..	1	..	..	..	..	1	..	..
James, Daniel	2	3	..	..	1	1	..	1	..	1	..
Jewett, Nilam	1	1	..	1	..	1	..	1	..	..	..
Jewett, Samuel	2	1	..	1	..	..	1	1	1	..	..
Judd, Gideon	..	1	..	..	1	..	1	..	..	1	..
Laurance, Asa	1	..	..	1	..	1	1	2	1	..	..
Laurance, Elisha	3	..	..	1	..	1	..	1	..	..	..
Laurance, Jonathan	2	1	..	1	..	2	..	..	1	..	..
Laurance, Zimri	..	..	..	1	..	..	..	..	..	..	..
Lewis, David	1	..	..	1	..	1	..	..	1	..	..
Lewis, John	..	..	..	..	1	..	..	..	1	1	..
Lewis, John Jr.	..	1	..	1	..	..	1	..	..	..	..
Lewis, Thomas	1	..	..	..	1	..	2	1	1	..	..
Lingham, Robert	3	..	..	1	..	2	3	..	1	..	..
Marsh, Amos	1	1	..	1	..	..	1	1	1	..	..
Mecker, Samuel	2	1	1	..	1	1	1	..	..	1	..
Moody, Jeremy	..	..	..	1	..	..	..	1	..	..	..
Palmer, Amos	1	..	1	..	1	1	1	..	1	..	..
Palmer, Jeremiah	2	..	..	1	..	2	..	..	1	..	..
Parmely, Aron	2	..	..	1	1	..	..	..	..	1	..
Parmely, Aron Jr.	..	1	..	1	..	..	1	..	..	..	..
Parmely, Solomon	1	..	..	1	..	2	..	1	..	..	..
Payon, James	..	2	3	..	1	..	..	1	..	1	..
Payon, James Jr.	1	..	..	1	..	..	..	..	1	..	..
Perry, Abner	2	..	..	1	..	1	..	..	1	..	..
Powers, Simeon	2	..	..	1	..	1	..	..	1	..	..
Prichard, William	2	..	..	1	..	1	..	..	1	..	..
Reynold, Silas	1	..	..	1	..	1	..	1	..	..	..
Rowe, Nathan	1	..	..	1	..	2	..	..	2	..	..
Sacket, Joseph	3	..	..	1	..	1	..	..	1	..	..
Sanford, Henry	1	..	..	1	..	3	..	..	1	..	..
Sanford, Thomas	..	..	1	..	1	..	..	1	..	1	..
Scott, Ebenezer	..	1	..	2	..	1	..	..	1	..	..
Smith, Jesse	..	..	..	1	..	4	..	..	1	..	..
Smith, Samuel	1	2	1	1	..	..	..	..	1	..	..
Smith, Samuel	..	..	2	..	1	..	3	..	..	1	..
Southand, Constant	4	..	..	1	..	..	..	2	..	..	..
Sprague, Anthony	4	..	..	1	..	1	..	..	1	..	..
Sprague, David	1	..	..	1	..	2	..	1	..	..	..
Stickney, Lemuel	3	..	1	1	..	2	..	..	1	..	..
Stickney, Zilar	3	1	1	..	1	3	..	..	1	..	..
Stoddard, Samuel	1	1	..	1	..	..	2	2	1	..	..
Stow, Clerk	3	1	..	1	..	3	2	..	1	..	..
Sturdevant, Abner	..	..	..	1	..	1	..	1	..	..	..
Sturdevant, Justus	..	..	1	..	2	..	..	..	..	2	..
Sturdevant, Samuel	..	..	..	1	..	1	..	1	..	..	..
Teilden, Jonah	..	..	1	..	1	1	2	1	..	2	..
Twitchel, Widow Eunice	3	2	..	..	..	1	..	1	1	..	..
Wallis, Roger	1	..	2	1	..	..	..	..	1	..	..
Wardrough, Solomon	2	..	..	1	..	2	1	1	..	..	..
White, Elisha	1	..	..	1	..	4	..	..	1	..	..
Willson, Calvin	2	..	1	1	..	..	..	1	..	..	..
Woodward, Ahasel	..	..	1	..	..	..	..	1	..	..	..
Wright, John	2	1	1	1	..	1	..	..	1	..	..
Wright, Silas	2	..	1	1	..	1	2	..	1	..	..

ADDISON COUNTY—Continued

NAMES OF HEADS OF FAMILIES	FREE WHITE MALES					FREE WHITE FEMALES					
	Under 10 years of age	Of 10 and under 16	Of 16 and under 26 including heads of families	Of 26 and under 45 including heads of families	Of 45 and upwards including heads of families.	Under 10 years of age	Of 10 and under 16	Of 16 and under 26 including heads of families	Of 26 and under 45 including heads of families	Of 45 and upwards including heads of families	All other free persons except Indians not taxed
WHITING											
Adams, Philander	..	..	..	1	..	1	..	1	..	..	..
Allen, Ezra	..	2	1	1	..	2	1	..	1	..	..
Alliss, David	..	..	1	..	..	..	..	1	..	..	..
Andrews, Benjamin	..	..	..	..	1	..	..	..	1	..	..
Baker, Elihu	3	1	1	1	..	3	..	..	1	..	..
Baldwin, Miles	2	2	1	..	1	2	..	1	1	..	..
Beach, Aaron	4	..	..	1	..	..	2	..	1	..	..
Beach, Samuel	1	..	..	..	1	..	1	1	1	..	..
Blackmore, Abel	..	..	1	..	..	2	..	1	..	..	..
Blowers, Charles	1	..	..	1	..	..	..	..	1	..	..
Branch, John	..	..	..	1	1	..	..	1	..	1	..
Branch, Shubel	3	..	..	1	..	1	..	..	1	..	..
Bridges, Ozias	1	..	..	1	..	..	..	..	1	..	..
Carr, Benjamin	4	2	1	1	..	2	..	..	1	..	..
Clark, Benjamin	1	..	..	1	..	..	1	1	..	..	..
Clark, Widow Lydia	..	1	..	..	..	1	..	..	1	..	..
Coben, Benjamin	1	..	..	..	..	2	..	..	1	..	1
Conick, Jonathan	..	1	..	1	..	..	1	1	1	..	..
Curtis, Josiah	1	..	1	..	1	..	2	..	1	1	..
Cushman, Ezra	..	..	..	1	..	3	..	1	..	..	..
Drury, Luther	2	1	1	1	..	2	1	..	2	..	..
Foster, Benjamin C.	1	..	..	1	..	..	..	1	..	..	..
Foster, Ichabod	..	1	2	..	1	1	..	2	..	1	..
Foster, Joel	..	..	1	1	..	1	..	..	1	..	..
Foster, John	..	..	1	..	..	2	..	1	..	..	..
Foster, William	1	..	..	1	..	..	..	1	..	..	..
Griswold, David	3	..	..	1	..	1	..	..	1	..	..
Grovesner, David	1	1	1	..	1	2	..	1	..	1	..
Hall, Clark	..	..	1	..	..	..	..	1	..	..	..
Hows, Asa	..	..	..	..	1	..	..	..	..	..	..
Hubard, Jonas	1	1	..	1	..	..	1	..	1	..	..
Hutchinson, Job	..	1	1	1	..	1	1	..	1	..	..
Jordan, John	..	1	..	..	1	..	1	..	..	1	..
Justin, Benajah	1	..	..	1	..	2	..	1	1	..	..
Justin, Gershom	..	1	1	..	2	..	..	2	..	1	..
Justin, Woolcot	3	..	..	1	..	1	..	..	1	..	..
WHITING—con.											
Kerham, Elijah	1	..	..	1	1	..	..	..	1	1	..
Kitchum Elihu	..	..	1	..	1	..	..	1	..	1	..
Lewis, Christopher	..	2	..	1	..	2	1	..	1	..	..
Mack, Aaron	..	..	1	1	..	..	1	..	1	..	..
McNiel, Thomas	2	2	..	1	..	1	..	..	1	1	..
Medcalf, Philemon	3	1	1	..	1	1	2	1	1	..	..
Monger, Jehiel	..	..	..	..	1	..	1	1	..	1	..
Monger, Moses	1	..	..	1	..	..	..	1	..	..	..
Needham, Joseph	3	1	3	..	1	1	1	1	1	1	..
Parker, Jeremiah	1	1	..	1	..	2	1	..	1	..	..
Patterson, Samuel	..	..	1	..	..	..	2	1	..	1	..
Pierce, Libeus	1	..	..	1	..	..	..	1	..	..	..
Price, Timothy	2	2	..	1	..	2	1	..	1	..	..
Rathbone, Daniel	2	..	..	..	1	3	..	..	1	..	..
Rathburn, David	3	..	1	1	..	1	..	1	1	..	..
Remelee, Stephen W.	..	..	3	..	..	..	..	..	..	2	..
Richards, Nathaniel	4	..	..	1	..	..	2	..	1	..	..
Rowley, Henry	2	..	..	1	..	1	..	..	1	1	..
Shaw, John	..	..	..	..	1	..	..	..	..	1	..
Smith, Benjamin	..	..	..	1	..	1	..	1	..	..	..
Smith, Ellamon	1	1	1	..	1	3	1	2	..	1	..
Stone, Cyrus	1	1	..	1	..	1	1	1	1	..	..
Stone, Joseph	1	..	1	..	..	..	..	1	..	..	..
Stone, Stukely	..	..	1	1	..	..	2	..	..	1	..
Stowel, Samuel	..	..	2	..	1	..	..	..	..	1	..
Thompson, Aaron	4	..	..	1	..	1	2	..	1	..	..
Walker, Ames	2	..	3	..	..	..	..	1	..	1	..
Walker, James C.	1	..	1	..	..	..	..	1	..	..	..
Walker, Jesse	3	..	..	1	..	1	..	1	1	..	..
Walker, Levi	2	..	..	1	..	1	..	1	1	..	..
Washburn, Widow, Jerusha	..	1	..	..	..	..	1	1	..	1	..
Wheelock, Ebenezer	..	..	1	1	..	..	1	..	1	..	..
Wilcox, Nathan	..	..	..	1	..	2	..	1	..	..	..
Willcox, Plinn	2	..	..	1	..	1	1	1	..	..	..
Wilson, Daniel	..	..	..	1	..	..	..	1	..	..	..
Wilson, John	..	..	..	..	1	..	..	..	..	1	..
Wizzle, Henry	..	..	1	..	1	1	3	1	..	1	..

BENNINGTON COUNTY

NAMES OF HEADS OF FAMILIES	FREE WHITE MALES					FREE WHITE FEMALES					
	Under 10 years of age	Of 10 and under 16	Of 16 and under 26 including heads of families	Of 26 and under 45 including heads of families	Of 45 and upwards including heads of families.	Under 10 years of age	Of 10 and under 16	Of 16 and under 26 including heads of families	Of 26 and under 45 including heads of families	Of 45 and upwards including heads of families	All other free persons except Indians not taxed
ARLINGTON											
Ager, John	2	..	..	1	..	..	..	..	1	..	..
Ager, William	1	1	..	1	..	4	..	..	1	..	..
Allen, Amos	2	..	..	1	..	1	..	..	1	..	..
Andrew, Charles	..	..	..	..	1	..	..	..	..	1	..
Andrew, Jonathan	2	1	..	1	..	2	..	1	1	..	..
Andrew, Sylvester	1	2	1	..	1	2	1	1	1	..	..
Andrews, Asa	1	..	..	1	..	2	..	..	1	..	..
Andrews, Ralph	2	..	1	1	..	2	..	..	1	..	..
Arnold, John	..	..	1	1	..	1	..	1	..	..	..
Ash, John	..	..	..	..	1	..	..	..	..	1	..
Austin, Amos	2	..	..	1	..	..	1	..	1	..	..
Austin, Daniel	..	..	1	..	..	1	..	1	..	..	..
Austin, Elijah	2	1	..	1	..	3	..	1	..	1	..
Austin, Jeremiah	2	1	..	1	..	3	..	..	1	..	..
Austin, Thomas	1	..	..	1	..	2	..	..	1	..	..
Babcock, Shubal	2	..	..	1	..	..	..	1	..	..	..
Baker, Amos	2	..	1	..	..	..	1	1	..	..	..
Baker, Daniel M.	1	1	1	1	..	3	1	1	..	2	..
Baker, Eldad	1	2	1	..	1	1	1	..	1	..	..
Baker, Heman	..	..	1	1	..	1	..	1	..	..	..
Baker, Jonathan	..	2	1	..	1	1	..	3	1	..	..
Baker, Ozi	..	2	..	1	..	3	1	..	1	..	..
Baker, Samuel S.	..	2	4	..	..	1	..	1	..	..	..
Barber, William	2	..	..	1	..	3	..	..	1	..	..
Barney, Constant	..	..	..	..	1	..	..	..	..	1	..
Barney, Daniel	3	..	..	1	..	2	..	..	1	..	..
Barney, Reuben	2	..	..	1	..	2	..	..	1	..	..
Barse, Levi	..	..	..	1	..	..	..	1	..	..	..
Bartlett, Eliphalet	..	..	1	..	..	..	..	1	..	..	..
Beatie, William	1	..	..	1	..	2	..	1	..	..	..
Beebee, Jeptha	..	1	1	..	..	..	..	..	1	..	..
Beebee, Reuben	2	..	..	1	1	..	1	..	1	1	..
Benedict, Ichabod	2	..	1	1	1	2	1	3	1	..	..
Bennett, Francis	1	1	..	1	..	2	..	..	1	..	..
ARLINGTON—con.											
Birch, Ezra	..	1	1	1	1	1	..	1	..	1	..
Blowers, Charles	..	2	1	1	..	4	1	1	..	..	..
Blowers, David	2	2	..	..	1	4	..	..	1	..	..
Blowers, Ephraim	3	..	..	1	..	1	2	..	1	..	..
Blowers, Mary	..	..	..	..	..	..	..	..	..	1	..
Blowers, Solomon	..	..	1	..	..	..	..	..	..	1	..
Blowers, William	2	..	..	1	..	1	1	1	..	..	..
Briggs, Bangs	1	..	..	..	1	..	..	..	1	..	..
Buck, Content	..	..	..	..	..	..	1	..	..	1	..
Buck, David	..	..	..	..	1	1	2	..	..	2	..
Buck, Robert	2	1	..	2	..	3	..	2	1	1	..
Buck, Samuel	2	1	1	1	..	1	..	1	1	1	..
Burrall, James	..	..	3	2	..	2	..	1	..	..	..
Caldwell, James	2	..	1	..	1	3	..	1	1	..	..
Canfield, Enos	1	2	1	1	..	1	..	..	2	..	..
Canfield, Israel	..	2	2	..	1	..	..	1	..	1	..
Canfield, Israel Jr.	1	..	..	1	..	..	..	..	1	..	..
Canfield, Nathan	2	3	4	..	1	..	1	1	1	..	..
Carnes, John	..	1	1	..	1	2	1	1	1	..	..
Chase, Abram	2	..	..	1	..	1	1	..	1	..	..
Church, Daniel	..	..	..	1	..	..	..	1	..	..	..
Clark, Daniel	..	..	..	1	..	1	..	..	1	..	..
Clark, Samuel	1	..	..	1	..	4	..	1	1	..	..
Clarke, Nathan	1	1	..	1	..	3	1	..	1	..	..
Compton, David	..	..	1	..	..	2	..	1	..	..	..
Cooper, William	2	1	..	1	..	3	..	..	1	..	..
Corey, David	1	2	..	1	..	2	1	1	1	..	..
Coy, Elisha	2	..	..	1	..	1	3	..	1	..	..
Crowfoot, David	1	..	..	..	1	2	1	..	1	..	..
Cutting, Samuel	1	1	..	1	1	2	..	1	1	..	..
Dana, Samuel	..	..	..	1	..	3	..	..	1	..	..

BENNINGTON COUNTY—Continued

NAMES OF HEADS OF FAMILIES	FREE WHITE MALES: Under 10 years of age	FREE WHITE MALES: Of 10 and under 16	FREE WHITE MALES: Of 16 and under 26 including heads of families	FREE WHITE MALES: Of 26 and under 45 including heads of families	FREE WHITE MALES: Of 45 and upwards including heads of families.	FREE WHITE FEMALES: Under 10 years of age	FREE WHITE FEMALES: Of 10 and under 16	FREE WHITE FEMALES: Of 16 and under 26 including heads of families	FREE WHITE FEMALES: Of 26 and under 45 including heads of families	FREE WHITE FEMALES: Of 45 and upwards including heads of families	All other free persons except Indians not taxed
ARLINGTON—con.											
Daniels, Hosea	..	..	1	..	..	1	..	1	..	..	..
Daniels, John	..	1	..	..	1	..	1	..	..	2	..
Dayton, Caleb	..	1	1	1	1	..	1	1	1	..	..
Dayton, Josiah	2	1	..	1	..	3	..	..	3	..	..
Demming, Gamaliel	..	..	..	..	1	..	..	..	..	1	..
Demming, Martin	1	2	1	1	..	1	..	..	1	..	..
Demming, Sylvester	..	1	1	2	1	..	..	1	1	..	..
Dogharty, William	4	..	1	1	..	..	1	..	1	..	..
Donnely, Owin	2	..	..	1	..	..	..	..	1	..	..
Douly, Darius	..	..	..	1	..	..	..	1	..	..	..
Dunlap, William	3	2	..	..	1	1	1	..	1	..	..
Dwight, Samuel	..	..	..	..	1	..	..	..	..	..	..
Edson, Dean	..	..	1	..	..	..	..	..	..	..	..
Egleston, Benedict	2	1	..	1	..	2	1	..	1	..	..
Elsworth, Abel	1	1	2	..	1	2	1	2	..	1	..
Elsworth, Samuel	..	1	1	..	1	..	..	..	1	..	..
Empee, David	3	1	..	1	..	2	1	..	1	..	..
Empee, George	..	..	2	..	1	..	..	1	..	..	..
Empee, John	1	1	..	1	..	2	..	..	1	..	..
Everitt, Linus	2	..	..	1	..	1	..	..	1	..	..
Fish, Daniel	1	..	..	1	..	..	..	..	1	..	..
Fish, Joseph	..	1	..	..	1	..	..	2	..	1	..
Foot, John	3	2	2	..	1	2	..	1	1	..	..
Freeman, Ebenezer	1	1	2	..	1	2	1	..	..	1	..
Fuller, Shubal	2	..	..	1	..	1	..	..	1	..	..
Fulsom, Samuel	1	..	..	..	1	1	..	2	..	1	..
Gifford, William	3	3	2	1	..	1	..	..	1	..	..
Graham, John	..	..	..	1	..	..	..	1	..	..	..
Gray, Domincus	3	1	..	1	..	1	..	..	1	..	..
Gray, John	..	..	..	..	1	..	..	..	..	1	..
Haight, Sylvanus	4	..	1	1	..	..	..	1	..	..	..
Hall, Ebenezer	1	..	1	..	1	..	..	..	..	1	..
Hall, Ebenezer Jr.	..	2	..	1	..	..	1	..	1	..	..
Hall, Robert	1	1	..	1	..	3	..	..	1	..	..
Hamlin, Levi	2	1	1	1	..	2	1	..	1	..	..
Hard, Belus	1	1	..	1	..	2	..	..	1	..	..
Hard, Noble	3	1	..	1	..	1	..	2	..	..	..
Hard, Zadoc	1	1	3	..	1	..	1	..	1	1	..
Harrington, Job	2	..	..	1	..	2	..	1	..	..	..
Harrington, John	1	..	..	1	..	4	..	..	1	..	..
Harskins, Benjamin	3	2	..	..	1	1	1	..	1	..	..
Hawkes, William	..	..	..	1	..	2	..	..	1	..	..
Hawkins, Benoni	4	1	..	1	..	1	1	..	1	..	..
Hawley, Andrew	1	..	1	..	1	..	1	..	..	1	..
Hawley, Andrew Jr.	..	..	..	2	..	3	..	1	..	..	..
Hawley, Curtis	4	1	1	..	1	..	1	1	..	1	..
Hawley, David	..	1	..	1	..	..	..	1	..	..	..
Hawley, Eli	3	1	..	..	1	1	1	2	..	1	..
Hawley, Philo	1	..	1	1	..	2	2	..	1	..	..
Hawley, Rhoda	..	..	..	..	..	1	2	1	1	..	..
Hawley, Sylvester	2	..	..	1	..	1	..	1	1	1	..
Hewlett, Aaron	4	2	..	1	1	..	2	2	1	..	..
Hewlett, Nathaniel	..	..	..	..	1	1	1	..	1	1	..
Hilldreth, Ben	1	..	2	..	..	..	..	1	..	..	..
Hines, Aden	4	..	2	1	..	2	..	..	1	..	..
Hodges, Abram	2	2	..	1	..	4	1	..	1	..	..
Hulburt, Wait	..	2	..	1	..	2	1	..	1	..	..
Hull, Jeremiah	2	..	..	..	1	2	1	..	1	..	..
Huntington, James	1	..	1	1	..	..	..	1	..	..	..
Hurd, Andrew	1	..	2	1	..	2	..	2	..	..	..
Hurd, Tyrus	3	3	..	1	..	2	..	1	1	1	..
Hyat, Cornelius	..	1	..	1	..	1	..	..	1	..	..
Imes, William	..	..	1	..	1	..	1	..	..	1	..
Imes, William Jr.	1	..	..	1	..	1	1	1	..	..	..
Irish, John	3	2	2	..	1	3	..	..	1	..	..
Jackson, Stephen	4	..	1	1	..	..	..	..	1	..	..
Judson, Joshua	2	..	1	1	..	..	..	2	..	..	..
Kinsman, Thomas	1	2	..	..	1	3	..	1	1	..	..
Lake, James	3	2	1	1	..	..	1	..	1	..	..
Lane, Hezekiah	..	1	..	..	1	..	1	..	..	1	..
Leffingwell, Hezekiah	..	..	1	..	1	..	..	2	..	1	..
Leonard, Benajah	..	..	1	1	1	..	..	..	1	..	..
Littlefield, Simeon	..	..	..	1	..	..	..	1	..	..	..
Lockwood, James	..	..	1	1	..	2	..	1	..	..	..
Loomis, Caleb	1	..	..	1	..	3	1	..	1	..	..
Love, James	2	..	..	1	..	..	..	..	1	..	..
Lylie, John	1	1	..	1	..	2	1	..	1	..	..
Manchester, ———	1	2	1	..	1	1	..	1	..	1	..
Martin, Jeremiah	1	..	..	1	..	1	..	..	1	..	..
Martin, Job	1	..	..	2	1	2	..	1	1	..	..
Matteson, Asa	2	..	..	1	..	2	..	..	1	..	..
Matteson, David	3	1	..	..	1	1	..	..	1	..	..
Matteson, David	3	1	2	..	1	..	1	2	..	1	..
Matteson, Dennis	..	..	1	..	..	..	..	1	..	..	..
Matteson, Stephen	1	1	..	1	..	1	..	..	1	..	..
McKey, James	1	..	..	1	..	1	..	1	..	..	..
McKey, John	..	..	3	..	1	..	..	2	..	1	..
McLaughlin, Thomas	1	..	4	1	..	..	..	1	..	..	..
Merrills, Asahel	3	..	..	1	..	1	..	..	1	..	..
Merrills, Justus	3	..	..	1	..	..	..	..	1	..	..
Merrills, William	3	1	..	1	..	2	..	1	1	..	..
Merwin, Elnathan	..	..	2	..	2	2	2	..	..	2	..
Mix James	2	1	..	1	..	2	..	..	1	..	..
Moffitt, Zebulon	..	..	2	..	1	2	2	1	..	1	..
Montgomery, John	..	1	..	1	..	2	1	1	1	1	..
Moore, Thomas	2	..	1	..	..	1	..	1	..	..	..
Morey, Christopher	..	..	..	..	1	..	..	..	1	..	..
Morey, Christopher Jr.	..	..	..	1	..	1	..	..	1	..	..
Mosmore, Timothy	..	..	..	1	1	..	..	2	1	..	..
Murray, James	2	1	1	1	..	2	..	1	1	..	..
Newton, Henry	1	1	3	..	1	..	..	..	1	..	..
Norton, Henry	2	1	..	1	..	1	..	..	1	..	..
Nouland, John	1	..	..	1	..	..	..	1	..	..	..
Oatman, Daniel	..	1	2	..	1	1	..	1	..	1	..
Oatman, Isaac	3	1	..	1	..	4	..	..	1	..	..
Oatman, Peleg	2	..	2	..	..	..	..	1	..	..	..
Oatman, Samuel	1	1	2	..	1	..	2	..	..	1	..
Odle, William	1	..	..	..	1	3	1	..	1	..	..
Osthonder, John	1	..	1	..	..	..	..	1	..	..	..
Osthonder, Walter	4	..	1	1	..	1	..	..	1	..	..
Park, John	1	1	..	1	..	..	2	..	1	..	..
Park, Reuben	1	1	..	..	1	..	..	1	1	..	..
Patrick, William	2	..	1	1	..	4	1	.	1	..	3
Payne, Simon	..	..	..	..	1	..	..	..	..	1	..
Peck, Simon	..	1	..	1	..	2	1	..	1	..	..
Perry, Davis	1	..	..	1	..	2	..	..	1	..	..
Pitney, Jonathan	..	..	1	..	1	..	1	..	..	1	..
Prentice, James	5	1	1	1	..	1	1	1	1	..	..
Randall, Amos	..	..	1	..	..	2	..	1	..	..	..
Rathban, Gideon	2	..	..	1	..	1	..	1	..	..	..
Rathban, Paris	3	1	..	1	..	1	..	1	1	..	..
Reynolds, Isaac	2	2	..	1	..	1	1	..	1	..	..
Reynolds, John	2	..	..	..	1	..	..	1	..	1	..
Richards, Daniel	2	1	..	1	..	2	..	..	1	..	..
Ross, John	2	..	..	1	..	..	..	1	..	..	..
Rublee, Reuben	2	..	..	1	..	2	..	..	1	..	..
Scott, Eli	2	..	..	1	..	2	..	..	1	..	..
Seaton, James	1	..	..	1	..	1	..	1	..	..	..
Seelye, Austin	1	..	1	..	1	..	2	..	..	1	..
Seelye, David	2	..	1	..	..	..	..	1	..	..	..
Seelye, Salmon	1	..	..	1	..	2	..	1	..	..	..
Sever, William	2	2	..	1	..	1	..	1	1	..	..
Shadock, Rufus	3	..	1	1	..	..	..	..	1	..	..
Sherman, Ezra	2	3	1	1	..	3	..	..	1	..	..
Sherman, Ware	2	..	..	1	1	2	..	..	1	..	..
Silliman, Samuel	2	2	..	1	..	..	..	1	1	..	..
Snyder, John	2	1	..	1	..	2	..	..	1	..	..
Spencer, Rufus	2	1	..	1	..	1	2	..	1	..	..
Spink, Ishmael	2	..	1	..	1	..	1	..	1	..	..
Squire, Abner	2	1	..	1	..	1	..	1	1	..	..
Squire, Deliverance	..	1	..	..	1	..	1	..	..	1	..
Squire, Eli	1	..	..	1	..	..	..	..	1	..	..
Squire, Joseph	2	..	..	1	..	2	1	..	1	..	..
Stearns, Daniel	2	..	..	1	..	2	3	1	1	..	..
Stillson, Henry	..	1	..	1	..	4	1	..	1	..	..
Stoddard, James	1	3	..	1	..	..	2	..	1	..	..
Stone, Abram	2	..	..	1	1	1	..	1	..	..	..
Stone, Betsey	..	..	..	..	..	..	..	1	..	..	..
Stone, Daniel	1	..	..	1	..	..	..	..	1	..	..
Stone, Luther	4	2	..	..	1	..	1	2	1	..	..
Stone, Mary	3	..	..	..	..	1	..	..	1	..	..
Stone, Peleg	..	..	..	..	1	..	..	..	..	1	..
Stone, Samuel	..	..	1	1	..	2	..	..	1	..	..
Stone, Zadoc	1	..	..	1	..	..	..	1	..	..	..
Stoughton, Augustus	1	..	1	1	..	3	2	..	1	..	..
Strong, Selah	2	..	..	1	..	4	..	..	1	..	..
Taft, Aaro	4	..	..	1	..	..	..	..	1	..	..
Thomas, Enoch	..	1	1	1	..	..	1	..	1	..	..
Thompkins, John	..	..	1	..	..	..	..	1	..	1	..
Thorp, Cornelius	1	..	1	..	..	..	..	..	..	..	..
Tidd, Amos	..	..	..	..	1	..	..	1	..	1	..

BENNINGTON COUNTY—Continued

NAMES OF HEADS OF FAMILIES	FREE WHITE MALES: Under 10 years of age	FREE WHITE MALES: Of 10 and under 16	FREE WHITE MALES: Of 16 and under 26 including heads of families	FREE WHITE MALES: Of 26 and under 45 including heads of families	FREE WHITE MALES: Of 45 and upwards including heads of families	FREE WHITE FEMALES: Under 10 years of age	FREE WHITE FEMALES: Of 10 and under 16	FREE WHITE FEMALES: Of 16 and under 26 including heads of families	FREE WHITE FEMALES: Of 26 and under 45 including heads of families	FREE WHITE FEMALES: Of 45 and upwards including heads of families	All other free persons except Indians not taxed
ARLINGTON—con.											
Tidd, Thaddeus	3	..	..	1	..	1	..	..	1	..	..
Torrance, Joseph	1	..	..	1	..	2	..	1	1	..	..
Turk, Hendric	..	2	..	..	1	..	1	..	..	1	..
Turner, Daniel	1	..	1	1	..	..	1	..	1	..	..
Turner, Miller	..	..	..	..	1	2	1	..	1	..	..
Van Buren, Harman	3	1	1	..	1	1	1	2	1	..	..
Wall, William	2	..	..	1	..	2	1	..	1	..	..
Wallace, Isaac H.	..	..	1	..	2	..	..	..	..	2	..
Wallace, Isaac H. Jr.	3	..	..	1	..	2	3	..	1	..	..
Wallace, Joseph	..	..	..	1	..	1	..	1	..	1	..
Wallace, Nathaniel	1	1	1	..	1	..	1	1	..	1	..
Washborn, Phillip	..	2	1	..	1	..	1	..	..	1	..
Wells, William	1	..	..	..	1	2	..	1	1	..	..
Whitehead, Isaac	2	..	..	1	..	2	..	..	1	..	..
Whitehead, James	1	..	..	1	..	2	..	..	1	..	..
Wilcox, Samuel	3	1	1	..	..	..	..	1	..	..	..
Wilmott, Samuel	..	..	1	..	..	..	..	1	..	..	..
Wilson, John	3	1	1	..	1	..	1	..	..	1	..
Wood, Stephen	..	..	..	1	..	1	..	1	..	..	..
Wordon, William	3	..	..	1	..	2	2	1	1	..	..
Work, Robert	..	..	..	..	1	..	..	..	..	..	..
Worrell, John	1	2	..	1	..	4	..	..	1	..	..
Wright, Abram	1	..	1	3	..	4	..	1	1	..	..
Wright, Boardman	..	..	1	..	..	2	..	1	..	..	..
Wright, Nathan	..	1	1	..	1	..	1	1	..	1	..
Young, Andrew	..	..	..	1	1	..	..	3	..	1	..
Young, Ebenezer	2	2	..	1	..	2	1	..	1	..	..
Young, Uriah	..	..	1	..	..	..	..	1	..	..	..
Younglove, Aron	1	..	..	2	..	5	..	..	1	..	..
BENNINGTON											
Abel, Thomas	1	1	1	1	1	3	..	2	..	1	..
Alexander, John	..	..	2	..	1	..	..	1	..	1	..
Armstrong, Hezekiah	..	1	1	..	1	..	1	1	..	1	1
Armstrong, Hopestill	..	..	5	..	1	..	1	1	..	1	..
Armstrong, Zephaniah	1	1	..	1	..	1	..	1	..	..	..
Ashley, Zenas	..	1	2	1	..	1	..	..	1	..	..
Atwood, Moses	..	..	1	1	..	..	..	1	..	..	..
Austin, Abel	1	..	..	1	..	2	..	..	1	..	..
Austin, Caleb	..	..	..	..	1	..	..	1	..	1	..
Austin, John	..	..	..	2	..	1	..	..	1	..	..
Austin, Robert	..	..	1	1	..	..	..	..	..	..	..
Babbitt, James	1	..	..	1	..	3	1	..	1	..	..
Barber, Elihu	1	..	..	1	..	2	..	..	1	..	..
Barney, Elkanah	3	..	1	1	..	1	..	..	1	1	..
Barney, Rufus	..	1	1	..	2	1	1	..	..	1	..
Battles, Jeremiah	..	..	..	..	1	2	..	1	1	1	..
Battles, Reuben	..	1	1	..	..	1	..	1	..	..	..
Beaman, Joseph	1	1	..	1	..	2	..	1	1	..	..
Beebee, Peter	..	..	..	1	..	1	1	..	1	..	..
Beels, Nathan	..	..	..	..	1	2	1	..	..	1	..
Belfield, Mary	..	..	1	..	..	..	..	1	..	1	..
Biddlecomb, Daniel	..	1	..	..	1	..	1	..	..	1	..
Biglow, Cornelius	2	..	..	1	..	..	..	1	..	..	..
Biglow, Elisha	..	..	1	..	..	1	..	1	..	..	..
Biglow, Noah	1	1	..	1	..	3	..	..	1	..	..
Biglow, Roger	2	..	..	1	1	1	..	..	1	..	..
Billing, Beulah	..	..	..	..	..	..	1	..	..	1	..
Bingham, Calvin	2	2	3	..	1	2	1	1	1	..	..
Black, Archibald	3	1	1	1	..	2	2	2	1	1	..
Blackmer, Samuel Jr.	2	..	..	1	..	2	..	..	1	..	..
Blackmore, Jason	..	..	..	1	..	1	..	2	..	..	..
Blackmore, Samuel	..	..	1	..	1	..	..	1	..	1	..
Blackmore, Wilbur	..	..	1	..	..	2	..	1	..	..	..
Bliss, Luther	..	2	..	1	..	3	1	..	1	..	..
Boldery, John	2	..	..	..	1	..	2	..	1	..	..
Booth, Roger	..	..	..	1	..	1	..	2	..	..	..
Brackenridge, Daniel	4	..	..	1	..	..	1	1	1	..	..
Brackenridge, Mary	1	..	1	..	..	2	2	..	2	..	..
Branch, Wheeler	1	..	1	1	..	2	..	..	1	..	..
Brown, James	1	..	..	..	1	..	1	..	1	..	..
Brown, John	..	..	1	..	..	2	..	1	..	..	..
Brown, Zachariah	2	..	..	1	..	2	..	..	1	..	..
Brush, Nathaniel	..	1	..	2	1	2	1	1	1	..	..
Buck, Jonathan	..	1	1	1	..	1	..	1	..	2	..
Buck, Samuel	1	1	..	..	1	1	1	..	..	1	..
Bumford, Thomas	..	..	2	..	1	..	3	..	..	1	3
Burleson, Joseph	2	2	..	1	..	1	1	..	1	..	..
Burrall, Abram	2	..	2	..	..	..	1	1	..	..	..
Burt, William	..	1	2	..	1	..	..	1	2	1	..
Bushnell, James	2	1	..	1	..	2	..	..	1	..	..
BENNINGTON—con.											
Cady, Cornelius	..	1	1	..	1	..	..	1	..	1	..
Camp, Stephen	..	..	..	1	..	..	..	..	..	..	..
Carpenter, Elijah	2	..	..	1	..	1	..	1	..	..	..
Carpenter, Margerette	..	..	2	1	..	1	2	1	1	..	..
Carr, James	..	1	..	1	..	..	..	2	1	..	..
Carson, Alexander	..	..	..	..	1	..	..	..	..	2	..
Chandler, John	..	..	..	..	1	..	..	..	..	1	..
Chandler, Simeon	1	..	..	1	..	2	2	..	1	..	..
Chase, Ebenezer	..	..	1	..	1	1	1	2	..	1	..
Chase, Nathan	1	..	..	1	..	..	1	1	1	..	..
Cheney, William	1	..	..	..	1	1	..	..	1	1	..
Church, Waite	1	..	..	2	..	1	..	2	..	..	..
Clark, Horatio	2	1	1	1	..	..	..	..	1	..	..
Clark, James	1	..	2	1	..	4	..	2	..	..	..
Clark, Washington	1	..	1	..	..	..	1	..	1	..	..
Cleaveland, Solomon	..	1	1	1	..	3	2	1	1	..	..
Clinch, Michael	..	..	1	..	..	..	..	1	..	..	..
Coburn, John	..	..	..	1	..	1	..	1	..	..	..
Colvin, Reuben	1	1	2	..	1	1	..	3	..	2	..
Colvin, Thomas	..	1	..	1	..	..	..	1	..	..	..
Connelly, Stephen	1	..	..	..	1	1	..	..	1	..	..
Cooke, John	..	..	..	..	1	1	..	..	..	1	..
Cooper, Enos	..	..	..	1	..	2	..	..	1	1	..
Crowfoot, James	1	1	..	1	..	3	..	..	1	..	..
Crowfoot, John	3	2	..	1	..	2	1	..	1	..	..
Crowfoot, Joseph	..	..	..	..	1	..	..	..	..	1	..
Crowfoot, Thomas	1	..	..	1	1	..	..	..	..	1	..
Crowfoot, Thomas	1	..	..	1	..	1	..	1	..	..	..
Cummings, William	..	1	..	1	..	3	..	2	..	..	..
Cushman, Charles	..	..	1	..	1	..	1	1	..	1	..
Cushman, John	1	..	..	1	..	2	..	..	1	..	..
Danforth, Nathaniel	1	..	..	1	..	1	..	1	..	..	..
Darling, Joseph	2	..	2	..	1	..	..	..	1	..	..
Davis, Benjamin	2	..	..	1	..	2	..	..	1	..	..
Day, Joseph	..	1	1	1	..	1	..	..	1	..	..
Demic, Austin	..	..	1	..	..	1	..	1	..	..	..
Demming, Aaron	..	..	1	..	1	2	1	1	1	..	..
Demming, George	1	..	..	1	..	2	..	..	1	..	..
Demming, James	2	1	..	1	..	3	1	..	1	..	..
Dewey, Eldad	1	..	4	..	1	1	2	3	..	1	..
Dewey, Elijah	1	1	3	..	2	1	1	2	..	2	..
Dibbel, Benjamin	..	..	..	..	1	1	..	..	..	1	..
Dodge, Benjamin	..	1	..	..	1	..	1	..	..	1	..
Dodge, John	..	..	..	..	1	..	1	..	..	1	..
Dodge, Seth	3	..	..	1	..	2	..	..	1	..	..
Donaldson, Ezrie	2	1	..	..	1	..	1	1	..	1	..
Doty, Amariah	1	1	..	..	1	3	1	..	1	..	..
Doty, Ezra	3	1	..	1	..	2	1	1	1	..	..
Downs, Elisha	..	1	2	..	1	..	..	1	..	1	..
Downs, Jesse	3	..	..	1	..	..	..	..	1	..	2
Edgerton, Eleazer	..	..	2	..	1	1	1	1	..	1	..
Edgerton, Uriah	3	1	1	2	..	1	1	1	1	..	..
Elwell, Amasa	..	..	1	..	..	..	..	1	..	..	..
Elwell, Asa	..	..	1	..	..	1	..	1	..	..	..
Elwell, Stephen	..	..	1	..	..	..	..	1	..	..	..
Fairchild, Sherman	2	..	..	2	1	2	..	..	1	..	..
Farnsworth, Joseph	..	1	1	..	2	..	1	..	..	1	1
Fassett, Benjamin	2	1	1	1	..	2	1	3	1	..	..
Fay, David	..	..	1	1	..	..	1	..	1	2	1
Fay, Elijah	..	1	..	..	1	..	1	2	..	1	..
Fay, Elijah Jr.	..	..	..	1	..	..	..	1	..	..	..
Fay, Jonas	..	1	1	..	1	..	..	1	..	1	..
Fay, Josiah	..	..	..	1	..	..	..	..	..	..	..
Fay, Lydia	..	..	..	..	..	..	..	1	..	..	..
Field, Jesse	..	1	..	..	1	2	2	1	1	..	..
Fillmore, Elijah	1	..	1	..	..	..	..	1	..	..	..
Fillmore, Nathaniel	..	..	2	..	1	..	..	1	..	1	..
Follett, Artemesia	..	1	..	..	..	1	..	..	..	2	..
Follett, Charles	..	1	..	1	..	..	..	..	1	..	..
Follett, Timothy	1	..	2	..	1	..	2	1	1	..	..
French, Samuel	..	1	..	1	..	2	2	..	1	..	..
Frye, John	1	..	..	1	..	1	1	..	1	..	..
Fuller, Josiah	..	1	..	..	1	..	1	..	..	1	..
Garden, Martha	1	..	..	..	..	..	..	1	..	..	..
Geralds, Nials	..	..	1	..	..	..	2	1	..	1	..
Gibbs, Zebulon	1	..	..	1	..	..	..	1	..	..	..
Gladden, Samuel	2	..	..	..	1	1	1	..	1	..	..
Godfrey, George	2	..	1	1	..	1	1	..	1	..	..
Godfrey, Isaac	..	..	1	..	..	..	..	..	..	..	..
Goodenough, David	..	..	1	..	..	..	..	..	..	..	..
Gould, Ely	3	..	..	1	..	2	..	..	2	..	..
Graham, Abraham	..	..	..	..	1	1	1	..	..	1	..
Granger, Jeremiah	3	1	..	1	..	2	1	..	1	..	..
Green, Thomas	1	1	2	4	..	2	3	1	1	1	..

BENNINGTON COUNTY—Continued

NAMES OF HEADS OF FAMILIES	FREE WHITE MALES: Under 10 years of age	FREE WHITE MALES: Of 10 and under 16	FREE WHITE MALES: Of 16 and under 26 including heads of families	FREE WHITE MALES: Of 26 and under 45 including heads of families	FREE WHITE MALES: Of 45 and upwards including heads of families.	FREE WHITE FEMALES: Under 10 years of age	FREE WHITE FEMALES: Of 10 and under 16	FREE WHITE FEMALES: Of 16 and under 26 including heads of families	FREE WHITE FEMALES: Of 26 and under 45 including heads of families	FREE WHITE FEMALES: Of 45 and upwards including heads of families	All other free persons except Indians not taxed
BENNINGTON—con.											
Green, Thomas Jr.	..	..	1	..	..	..	..	1	..	..	..
Green, Willard	1	..	..	1	..	1	..	..	1	..	..
Greenslitt, James	2	1	1	..	1	2	1	..	..	1	..
Griswold, Joshua	4	1	1	1	1	2	1	..	1	1	..
Griswold, William	..	..	..	..	1	1	1	..	1	..	..
Hall, Moses	2	..	..	1	..	2	1	..	1	..	..
Hall, Nathaniel	1	1	..	1	..	2	1	..	1	..	..
Hall, Thomas	..	..	..	..	1	..	..	..	..	1	..
Hammond, Joel	1	..	..	1	..	3	..	1	..	..	..
Harmon, Austin	..	..	2	..	1	..	..	3	..	..	..
Harmon, Ezekiel	1	1	1	..	1	2	1	1	1	1	..
Harmon, Silas	..	..	..	..	1	1	..	1	..	..	..
Harris, George	2	1	..	..	1	..	..	..	1	..	..
Harvey, Phillip	3	1	2	..	1	..	..	1	1	..	..
Harvey, Timothy	1	..	1	..	1	1	..	1	..	..	..
Harwood, Benjamin	..	1	1	1	..	2	..	1	..	..	..
Harwood, Jonas	..	..	..	1	..	2	..	1	..	..	..
Harwood, Joseph	..	..	1	..	..	2	..	1	..	..	..
Harwood, Judah	1	..	1	..	..	1	..	1	..	..	..
Harwood, Oliver	..	..	1	..	..	2	..	1	..	..	..
Harwood, Peter	..	..	1	..	1	..	1	1	..	1	..
Harwood, Stephen	..	..	1	..	1	2	1	..	1	..	..
Harwood, Zachariah	2	1	3	..	1	1	..	1	..	2	..
Haswell, Anthony	1	2	3	1	..	2	..	..	1	1	..
Hathaway, Seth	..	1	..	1	..	2	1	..	1	..	..
Hathaway, Shadrack	..	..	1	2	1	2	1	1	..	1	..
Hathaway, Simeon	..	1	1	..	2	..	..	1	..	2	..
Hawks, Eleazer	3	1	1	..	1	1	..	1	1	..	..
Hawks, William	1	1	1	1	..	3	..	2	1	..	..
Haynes, David	2	..	3	..	2	2	2	2	1	..	..
Henderson, Thomas	..	1	3	2	1	..	4	..	1	..	..
Henderson, Thomas Jr.	1	1	1	1	..	2	1	1	1	..	..
Hendrix, Isaiah	2	..	3	1	..	1	1	..	1	..	..
Henry, David	..	..	2	..	..	..	..	1	..	..	..
Henry, John	1	2	..	1	..	2	..	2	..	..	..
Henry, William	..	1	2	..	1	..	..	1	..	1	..
Henry, William Jr.	2	..	2	1	..	3	1	1	1	..	..
Hicks, James	3	1	..	1	..	3	..	..	1	..	..
Hickson, John	1	..	..	..	1	..	..	..	..	1	..
Hill, Cyrus	2	..	..	1	..	..	..	1	..	..	..
Hill, Parley	..	..	1	..	..	..	..	1	..	..	..
Hills, Elliott	1	..	..	1	..	..	..	1	..	..	..
Hinsdale, Daniel	..	..	1	..	..	..	..	1	..	..	..
Hinsdale, Joseph	..	2	4	1	1	1	..	..	..	1	..
Hopkins, Ebenezer	2	1	1	1	..	2	1	..	1	..	..
Hopkins, Heman	..	..	1	..	..	2	..	1	..	..	..
Houghton, Elias	1	..	1	..	..	..	..	1	..	..	..
House, Joseph	2	1	1	1	1	..	1	1	1	..	4
House, Stephen	2	1	..	2	..	1	1	2	1	..	..
Hubbell, Aaron	..	3	1	1	..	2	2	2	1	..	..
Hubbell, Elnathan	..	1	2	..	1	..	2	..	1	1	..
Hull, Elias	1	1	..	..	1	..	..	..	1	..	..
Hull, John	..	..	1	..	..	1	..	1	1	..	..
Hunt, Ezekiel	1	..	..	1	..	1	..	1	..	..	..
Hunt, Jonathan	1	2	..	1	..	..	1	1	1	..	..
Hunt, Joseph	2	..	..	1	..	1	1	1	1	..	..
Huntley, Solomon	1	..	..	..	1	1	..	..	1	..	..
Hurd, Isaac	3	..	..	1	..	1	1	3	1	..	..
Hurd, Moses	..	1	1	..	1	1	2	1	..	2	..
Jewett, Frederic	..	2	..	1	..	3	1	1	1	..	1
Jewett, Thomas	..	..	..	..	1	..	..	1	..	1	..
Kellogg, Jacob	1	..	..	..	1	1	2	..	1	..	..
Keyes, Wyllys	1	1	..	1	..	2	2	1	2	..	..
King, William	2	..	..	1	..	2	..	..	1	..	..
Kinsley, Abisha	2	1	1	1	1	..	..	3	..	1	..
Laurance, John	..	2	..	1	1	1	..	2	..	1	..
Laurance, Joseph	2	..	2	..	1	3	1	..	1	..	..
Laurance, Josiah	..	..	..	..	1	..	..	..	..	1	..
Laurance, Solomon	..	..	1	..	..	..	..	1	..	..	..
Leach, Micah	1	1	..	1	..	..	..	1	..	..	..
Longworth, William	..	..	..	..	1	1	..	1	1	..	..
Lummis, Jesse	2	..	2	..	1	2	2	1	1	..	..
Lyman, Micah I.	2	1	1	1	..	1	..	1	1	..	..
Lynes, Elijah	3	..	..	1	..	..	..	..	1	..	..
Lyon, Alanson	3	1	..	1	..	2	..	..	1	..	..
Lyon, Simeon	..	1	..	..	1	1	1	..	..	1	..
Mallory, Ephraim	..	..	..	..	1	..	..	..	..	1	..
Mallory, Ephraim Jr.	1	..	..	1	..	4	..	..	1	..	..
Marble, John	..	2	1	..	1	2	1	..	..	1	..
Matteson, Daniel	3	1	..	..	1	2	2	..	1	..	..
Matteson, Samuel	..	..	..	1	..	2	..	..	1	..	..
Matteson, Silas	1	..	1	..	..	..	..	1	..	..	..
BENNINGTON—con.											
McHutchin, John	..	..	..	1	..	..	..	..	..	..	..
McMahan, Patrick	1	..	..	1	..	..	..	..	..	1	..
Merrils, Allen	..	1	..	1	..	..	..	1	..	..	..
Millar, Thomas	2	1	..	..	1	..	2	3	1	..	..
Millar, William	1	..	1	..	..	..	..	1	..	..	..
Millings, Richard	..	1	..	1	..	..	..	..	..	..	..
Millington, Lilie	1	..	..	..	..	1	..	..	1	..	..
Minor, Eunice	..	1	..	..	..	1	..	..	..	2	..
Molton, William	..	..	..	1	..	..	..	2	..	..	..
Moon, Peleg	..	..	2	..	1	..	..	..	..	1	..
Moseley, Rosswell	..	1	1	..	1	..	..	1	1	1	..
Moss, Solomon	..	..	2	..	1	..	..	..	1	1	..
Murray, John	..	..	1	..	..	..	..	..	..	..	..
Nairn, Charles	1	2	..	1	..	1	..	2	1	..	..
Nelson, Joseph	1	..	..	1	..	2	1	..	1	..	..
Newlin, William	..	1	2	1	1	2	..	1	1	..	..
Nichols, Dewey	..	..	1	..	..	1	..	1	..	..	..
Nichols, James	2	1	1	1	..	3	1	1	1	1	..
Nichols, Robert	..	..	..	..	1	..	..	1	..	1	..
North, Asa	..	..	..	1	..	..	1	..	1	..	..
Norton, John	1	2	1	1	..	3	1	..	1	..	..
Norton, Joseph	1	2	1	1	..	..	1	..	1	..	..
Norton, Martin	1	1	1	1	..	2	2	..	2	..	..
Olds, Jonathan	1	..	..	..	1	2	..	..	1	..	..
Orton, Joseph	..	..	1	..	..	..	..	..	..	..	..
Paddock, Ichabod	..	2	1	..	1	1	1	1	..	1	..
Paddock, Zacheus	..	..	1	..	..	1	..	1	..	..	..
Palmer, Joseph	..	..	..	..	1	1	..	1	..	1	..
Palmer, Seth	2	..	..	1	..	..	1	..	1	..	..
Palmer, Thomas	..	1	1	..	..	1	..	1	..	..	..
Palmer, Timothy	..	1	..	..	1	1	2	..	..	..	..
Parker, Henry	..	1	1	1	1	..	..	1	..	1	..
Parling, Lemuel	1	..	3	..	..	..	1	1	..	1	..
Parson, Edward	1	..	..	1	..	1	1	..	1	..	..
Patten, Hugh	..	..	3	1	..	..	..	1	..	1	..
Patten, William	..	..	..	1	..	3	..	..	1	..	..
Pengra, Marshal	2	..	..	1	..	1	..	..	1	..	..
Pierce, Silas	2	..	..	1	..	2	1	..	1	..	..
Pierce, Zadoc	1	..	..	1	..	1	..	..	..	1	..
Plates, Peter	..	..	..	1	..	..	..	..	1	..	..
Pollard, Seth	..	..	..	..	1	3	..	2	1	..	1
Pool, Oliver	1	1	1	..	1	..	4	1	..	1	..
Potter, Honeymon	1	..	5	..	..	..	..	3	..	..	..
Potter, Shadrack	2	2	..	1	..	1	1	1	..	..	..
Pratt, Stephen	2	2	..	..	1	3	..	1	1	1	..
Randall, Gideon	3	..	..	1	..	..	1	..	1	..	..
Rice, Elijah	..	..	..	1	..	1	..	1	..	..	..
Rice, Isaac	..	1	..	1	1	..	..	..	..	..	..
Rice, Sally	..	..	..	..	..	1	..	..	1	..	..
Rice, Silas	1	1	..	..	1	..	1	..	..	2	..
Rice, Stephen	..	2	..	..	1	..	1	1	..	1	..
Richards, William	..	1	3	3	1	1	..	1	..	..	..
Riley, Josiah	2	..	..	1	..	..	..	1	..	..	..
Ritchie, George	..	..	..	1	..	3	..	..	1	..	..
Roach, Israel	1	1	..	2	..	1	..	3	1	..	..
Robinson, Aaron	3	1	1	1	..	1	1	1	1	..	..
Robinson, David	..	1	4	1	1	..	1	3	1	..	..
Robinson, Jonathan	1	1	3	1	..	1	..	2	1	..	..
Robinson, Jonathan E.	..	..	2	1	..	1	1	1	..	..	..
Robinson, Joseph	..	2	3	..	1	..	..	2	..	1	..
Robinson, Moses	..	..	6	1	1	..	2	1	..	1	1
Robinson, Moses Jr.	1	..	..	3	..	1	1	2	..	..	..
Robinson, Samuel	..	1	1	..	1	1	1	1	..	1	..
Robinson, Samuel Jr.	2	..	..	1	..	..	..	1	..	..	..
Robinson, Samuel 2nd.	..	..	..	1	..	..	..	2	1	..	..
Robinson, Silas	..	..	..	..	1	..	..	..	..	1	..
Robinson, Thomas	1	..	..	1	..	..	..	1	..	..	..
Rosier, Joseph	1	..	..	..	1	1	1	1	..	1	..
Rudd, Joseph	..	1	2	..	1	..	..	3	..	1	..
Rugg, Constant	..	..	..	1	..	..	..	1	..	1	..
Rugg, Elijah	1	..	1	..	..	1	..	1	..	..	..
Rugg, Samuel	2	..	..	1	..	2	2	..	1	..	..
Ruttembur, Sylvanus	1	..	..	1	..	..	..	1	1	..	..
Safford, Jacob	..	1	2	..	1	..	2	..	1	..	..
Safford, Joseph	..	..	1	..	1	..	1	1	..	1	1
Safford, Samuel	..	1	1	..	1	..	1	2	..	1	..
Safford, Samuel Jr.	..	..	1	..	..	2	..	1	1	..	..
Safford, Solomon	..	..	1	..	1	1	..	..	..	1	..
Sage, Isaac	1	..	1	..	..	2	..	1	..	..	..
Sage, Jacob	..	..	1	1	..	1	..	1	..	..	..
Sage, Moses	1	2	9	1	2	2	1	2	..	1	1
Sanders, Zelotus	1	..	1	..	1	2	1	2	..	1	..

BENNINGTON COUNTY—Continued

NAMES OF HEADS OF FAMILIES	FREE WHITE MALES: Under 10 years of age	FREE WHITE MALES: Of 10 and under 16	FREE WHITE MALES: Of 16 and under 26 including heads of families	FREE WHITE MALES: Of 26 and under 45 including heads of families	FREE WHITE MALES: Of 45 and upwards including heads of families	FREE WHITE FEMALES: Under 10 years of age	FREE WHITE FEMALES: Of 10 and under 16	FREE WHITE FEMALES: Of 16 and under 26 including heads of families	FREE WHITE FEMALES: Of 26 and under 45 including heads of families	FREE WHITE FEMALES: Of 45 and upwards including heads of families	All other free persons except Indians not taxed
BENNINGTON—con.											
Scott, Phinehas	2	2	2	..	1	1	1	1	..	1	..
Scott, Polly	..	..	1	1	..	2	..	..	1	..	..
Seekins, Paul	..	1	..	1	..	2	3	..	1	..	..
Selden, Andrew	1	1	..	1	1	2	..	..	1	1	..
Shaw, Josiah	2	2	..	1	1	2	..	..	1	..	..
Sherwood, Aaron	1	1	1	1	..	..	..	2	..	..	..
Sickles, William	..	..	1	..	..	1	..	..	1	..	..
Smith, Ephraim	3	1	2	1	..	..	2	2	1	..	..
Smith, Gaius	..	..	..	..	1	..	1	1	1	1	..
Smith, Levi	..	..	..	1	..	3	..	..	1	..	..
Smith, Noah Esq.	2	..	2	..	1	2	..	2	1	..	..
Smith, Olive	..	..	..	..	..	1	..	..	1	..	..
Smith, Rebeckah	..	..	..	1	..	..	2	..	..	1	..
Smith, Samuel Jr.	2	..	..	..	..	..	..	1	..	..	..
Sparrow, Sylvanus	1	..	..	..	..	1	..	..	1	..	..
Squire, Saxton	2	1	3	2	..	1	1	1	1	..	..
Stanley, Anna	..	..	..	..	..	..	..	..	..	1	..
Steele, Joseph	3	1	..	1	..	3	..	..	1	..	..
Stiles, Austin	2	..	1	1	..	3	2	..	1	..	..
Stockwell, Ichabod	2	..	..	..	1	..	1	1	..	1	..
Stockwell, William	2	..	1	..	..	..	..	1	..	..	..
Story, Benajah	2	..	..	..	1	..	2	2	1	..	..
Story, Daniel	..	..	..	1	1	..	..	..	..	1	..
Story, Daniel H.	..	..	..	1	..	..	..	..	1	..	..
Story, Johnson	..	..	1	..	..	..	..	..	..	..	..
Stratton, Joel	2	2	1	1	..	2	..	..	1	..	..
Street, James	1	..	2	1	..	3	..	1	1	1	..
Swift, Job	2	1	3	..	1	1	2	1	1	1	..
Sybley, Elisha	4	1	..	1	..	..	1	..	1	..	..
Tenny, Jesse	1	..	1	..	1	2	2	1	1	1	..
Thayer, Amasa	..	2	..	..	1	..	1	..	..	1	..
Thayer, Amherst	..	..	..	..	1	..	..	..	..	1	..
Thayer, Rufus	2	..	..	1	..	..	..	..	1	..	..
Thayer, Samuel	1	1	1	1	..	4	3	1	1	..	..
Thayer, Simeon	3	..	..	1	..	2	1	..	1	..	..
Thomas, Joel	..	..	1	2	..	1	..	1	..	..	..
Thomas, Joseph	1	..	..	..	1	1	1	..	..	1	..
Thompson, James	..	..	..	..	1	..	..	..	..	1	..
Thurston, Joseph	1	..	1	..	1	..	1	..	..	1	..
Tichenor, Isaac Esq.	..	..	1	1	..	..	1	1	1	..	..
Varnum, Ebenezer	1	..	..	..	1	1	..	..	1	..	..
Vaughan, Job	..	..	1	..	1	..	1	3	..	1	..
Wadsworth, Joseph	1	1	2	1	..	3	..	1	..	1	..
Waite, Thomas G.	2	1	..	1	..	3	..	2	2	..	..
Walbridge, Adolphus	1	..	..	1	..	2	1	..	1	..	..
Walbridge, David	2	..	..	1	..	1	..	..	1	..	..
Walbridge, Ebenezer	1	1	1	..	1	..	2	..	..	1	..
Walbridge, Henry	..	..	..	..	1	..	..	..	1	1	..
Walbridge, Silas	2	1	1	1	..	1	2	..	1	..	..
Walbridge, Stebbins	..	..	2	1	..	2	1	..	1	..	..
Waters, Oliver	1	1	..	..	1	3	1	..	..	1	..
Waters, Samuel	..	..	1	..	..	..	..	..	..	..	..
Watson, Bradock	4	1	..	1	..	1	1	..	1	..	..
Webb, Benjamin	..	1	1	..	1	2	1	1	..	1	..
Webster, Isaac	..	1	..	..	1	3	3	2	1	..	..
Webster, Isaac 2nd	..	..	1	..	..	..	..	..	..	..	..
Webster, Samuel	5	..	1	1	..	..	1	1	1	..	..
Weekes, David	3	1	1	..	2	1	2	1	1	2	..
Wheat, Jonathan	..	..	2	1	1	..	1	..	..	1	..
Whipple, Charles	2	..	..	1	..	..	..	1	..	..	..
Whitcomb, Joseph	..	..	..	1	..	..	..	1	..	1	..
Whitcomb, Samuel	..	1	2	..	1	..	1	..	..	1	..
Whitcomb, Samuel Jr.	..	..	1	..	..	..	..	1	..	..	..
Wickes, John	2	2	1	..	1	2	..	1	1	..	..
Wickwire, Joseph	..	1	..	..	1	..	..	..	..	2	..
Wickwire, Reuben	2	..	1	1	..	..	..	1	..	..	..
Wing, John	3	1	1	..	1	2	1	1	..	1	..
Wood, Andrew	..	1	1	1	..	2	1	..	1	..	5
Wood, Ebenezer	2	..	1	..	1	1	1	..	1	..	..
Wood, Elisha	3	..	..	1	..	1	..	..	1	..	..
Wood, Ephraim	2	1	1	..	1	..	1	..	..	1	..
Wood, Ephraim Jr.	..	..	1	..	..	1	..	1	..	..	..
Wood, Isaac	3	..	..	1	..	1	..	..	1	..	..
Wood, Isaac	..	..	..	1	..	3	..	1	..	..	..
Wood, Job	1	1	1	..	1	1	2	..	..	1	..
Wood, Job	3	..	1	1	..	1	1	..	1	..	..
Wood, John	2	1	2	3	..	1	..	1	1	..	..
Wood, Philippa	..	..	..	..	..	..	..	..	..	1	..
Wright, Eleazer	..	1	..	1	..	3	1	..	1	..	..
Wright, Phinehas	..	2	..	1	1	2	1	..	..	1	..
BROMLEY											
Allen, Amos	1	1	..	1	1	..	1	..	..	..	..
Barnard, Benjamin	1	1	2	..	1	1	1	..	..	1	..
Beebee, Elihu	2	2	1	..	1	..	1	..	..	1	..
Biglow, Reuben	..	..	1	..	..	2	..	1	..	..	..
Brook, John	1	1	..	..	1	2	3	..	1	..	..
Butterfield, Jonathan	..	1	3	..	1	2	1	3	..	1	..
Colson, John	1	..	..	1	..	1	..	..	1	..	..
Dewey, James	2	..	..	1	..	2	..	..	1	..	..
Holt, Silas	1	..	1	..	..	1	..	1	..	..	..
Hurlburt, Ebenezer	..	2	1	..	1	..	..	1	1	..	..
Hurlburt, Simeon	1	..	..	2	..	3	..	..	1	..	..
Ingley, John	1	..	..	1	..	..	..	1	..	..	..
Jackson, Isaac	1	..	..	1	..	2	..	..	1	..	..
Killum, Aaron	..	..	..	1	..	1	..	..	1	..	..
Lincoln, James	1	..	..	1	..	1	..	..	1	..	..
Lincoln, Nehemiah	..	..	..	..	1	..	..	3	..	1	..
More, Jedediah	1	..	..	1	..	3	..	..	1	..	..
Moulton, Joseph	1	..	..	..	1	..	1	..	..	1	..
Richardson, James	2	1	2	1	..	2	1	..	1	..	..
Seaton, George	..	..	..	2	1	..	..	..	..	1	..
White, David	..	2	..	..	2	2	1	..	1	1	..
UNCERTAIN NAME											
Stratton, Enos (?)	..	..	2	..	..	..	..	1	..	1	..
DORSET											
Allen, Lemuel	1	..	2	..	..	..	..	1	..	..	..
Allen, Seth	..	..	..	1	..	2	..	1	..	..	..
Ames, William	1	..	..	1	..	..	..	1	..	..	..
Armstrong, Jonathan	1	..	4	1	1	..	1	2	..	1	..
Austin, John	..	2	1	..	1	2	..	2	..	1	..
Baldwin, Asa	..	1	1	..	1	..	1	1	..	1	..
Baldwin, Asa	2	1	1	1	..	3	1	1	1	..	..
Baldwin, Ben	2	..	3	..	1	..	3	1	1	1	..
Baldwin, Eleazer	3	2	1	1	..	1	3	1	1	..	..
Baldwin, Guy	..	..	2	1	..	2	..	1	..	..	..
Baldwin, Silas	1	..	1	1	..	2	3	1	1	..	..
Barnum, Ashbel	3	1	..	1	..	2	..	..	1	..	..
Barnum, Francis	..	..	..	..	1	..	..	..	..	1	..
Barrows, Aaron	..	..	2	..	..	..	..	..	1	..	..
Bartoe, Francis	..	..	..	1	..	3	1	..	2	..	..
Bartoe, Samuel	1	..	..	..	1	..	..	..	1	..	..
Barton, Gilbert	1	..	1	..	..	..	..	1	..	..	..
Beardsley, Lazarus	1	..	2	1	..	2	..	1	..	..	..
Beardsley, Price	3	2	..	1	..	1	1	1	1	..	..
Beers, Ben	4	1	..	1	..	..	1	..	..	1	..
Blackmer, Abner	..	1	..	..	1	1	..	..	1	..	..
Blackmer, Eseck	1	..	..	1	..	2	..	..	1	..	..
Blackmer, Jonathan	2	..	..	1	..	2	1	1	..	..	..
Blaksby, Samuel	..	1	..	1	..	..	..	..	..	..	..
Blanchard, Benjamin	..	..	..	1	..	4	2	..	1	..	..
Bloomer, Reuben	..	..	1	..	1	..	1	1	..	1	..
Bloomer, Reuben Jr.	..	..	..	1	..	..	..	1	..	..	..
Booth, Zachariah	..	..	1	..	..	..	..	1	..	..	..
Bowen, Daniel	1	2	2	..	1	..	2	..	..	1	..
Bowen, Daniel Jr.	..	..	..	1	..	..	..	1	..	..	..
Bowlin, James	..	..	1	1	..	1	..	1	..	..	..
Burr, Isaac	4	1	..	2	..	1	1	..	1	..	..
Burr, Jonathan	..	..	1	..	1	..	..	..	..	1	..
Cable, Lucy	..	..	..	..	..	3	..	..	1	..	..
Cheney, Howard	2	..	..	1	..	3	1	..	1	..	..
Church, John	..	1	..	1	..	2	1	..	..	1	..
Church, Samuel	1	..	1	1	..	..	1	1	1	..	..
Clark, John	..	1	1	..	1	2	..	1	..	1	..
Clark, John 2nd.	..	..	1	..	..	1	..	1	..	..	..
Clarke, Joseph	1	..	1	..	..	..	..	1	..	..	..
Coffin, Michael	1	1	..	1	..	2	..	..	1	..	..
Collins, Samuel	1	..	1	1	..	3	..	..	1	..	..
Collins, Solomon	..	..	1	..	2	1	2	1	1	..	..
Colson, Andrew	..	..	1	..	..	1	..	1	..	..	..
Cooke, John	..	..	..	..	1	..	..	..	..	1	..
Cooke, Joseph	5	2	..	1	..	..	..	..	1	..	..
Cooke, Shubal	3	1	..	1	..	1	2	..	1	..	..

BENNINGTON COUNTY—Continued

NAMES OF HEADS OF FAMILIES	FREE WHITE MALES: Under 10 years of age	FREE WHITE MALES: Of 10 and under 16	FREE WHITE MALES: Of 16 and under 26 including heads of families	FREE WHITE MALES: Of 26 and under 45 including heads of families	FREE WHITE MALES: Of 45 and upwards including heads of families	FREE WHITE FEMALES: Under 10 years of age	FREE WHITE FEMALES: Of 10 and under 16	FREE WHITE FEMALES: Of 16 and under 26 including heads of families	FREE WHITE FEMALES: Of 26 and under 45 including heads of families	FREE WHITE FEMALES: Of 45 and upwards including heads of families	All other free persons except Indians not taxed
DORSET—con.											
Crane, David E.	3	1	..	1	..	1	1	..	1	..	..
Curtis, Elias	..	2	1	..	1	..	2	..	..	1	..
Curtis, Henry	..	1	1	1	1	..	..	3	1	1	..
Curtis, Joseph	2	1	..	1	..	1	2	..	1	..	..
Curtis, Josiah	2	..	..	1	..	..	..	1	..	..	..
Curtis, Nicholas	1	..	..	1	..	1	2	..	1	..	..
Curtis, Seth	2	..	..	1	..	2	..	..	1	..	..
Curtis, Zachariah	..	..	1	..	1	1	..	1	..	1	..
Day, Ezra	1	..	..	1	..	2	..	..	1	..	..
Demic, Jemina	1	2	1	..	..	1	..	1	1	..	..
Demming, Eli	1	2	2	..	1	..	1	1	..	1	..
Dodge, Thomas	1	2	..	1	..	..	1	..	1	..	..
Draper, David	1	..	..	1	..	2	..	..	1	..	..
Drover, Joseph	..	2	..	..	1	..	..	2	..	1	..
Dunning, Lewis	1	..	..	1	..	1	..	..	1	..	..
Dunning, Richard	..	..	1	..	1	1	..	..	..	1	..
Dunton, Thomas	1	1	1	1	..	4	2	..	1	..	..
Dunton, William	2	2	2	..	1	3	1	2	1	1	..
Durkee, Phinehas	..	..	..	1	..	3	..	1	..	..	..
Fairwell, John	1	..	1	1	1	..	2	1	..	1	..
Fairwell, John Jr.	1	1	..	1	..	2	..	..	1	..	..
Farnsworth, Reuben	1	..	2	1	1	1	2	2	1	..	..
Farwell, Asa	1	..	2	1	..	..	1	..	1	..	..
Farwell, Isaac	1	1	..	..	1	..	1	..	..	1	..
Farwell, Jedutham	..	1	..	1	..	1	1	1	..	..	..
Field, Amos	..	2	1	..	1	3	1	2	..	1	..
French, Andrew	1	1	..	..	1	..	..	..	1	..	..
French, John	1	..	1	..	1	..	2	1	..	1	..
French, Nichols	1	1	1	1	..	1	..	1	..	..	..
Fuller, Noah	2	1	1	1	..	2	1	..	1	..	..
Giddings, Sereno	1	1	1	..	..	..	..	..	1	..	..
Gifford, Humphrey	1	2	2	..	1	2	1	1	..	1	..
Glynn, John	1	..	2	..	1	2	..	..	..	1	..
Gray, Chancey	2	..	1	1	..	1	..	1	..	..	..
Gray, Daniel	..	..	..	1	..	..	..	1	..	..	..
Gray, Isaac	1	2	..	1	..	1	..	..	1	..	..
Gray, John	2	1	1	..	1	..	1	..	..	1	..
Gray, Samuel	4	..	..	1	..	..	1	..	1	..	..
Gray, Zalmon	4	1	..	1	..	1	..	..	1	..	..
Grinnel, Jonathan	1	1	1	..	1	..	1	1	..	1	..
Guyle, Amos	1	2	1	..	1	2	2	1	1	..	..
Hagar, Simeon	..	..	..	..	1	..	..	..	..	1	..
Hagar, Simeon Jr.	2	2	..	1	..	2	..	..	1	..	..
Hanks, Consider	1	..	2	1	..	2	..	..	1	..	..
Harmon, Asahel	..	..	..	..	1	..	..	..	..	1	..
Harrington, Silas	2	2	..	1	..	1	1	2	1	..	..
Harris, Thadeus	2	..	1	..	1	3	2	..	1	..	..
Hawley, Joseph	1	1	..	1	..	1	..	..	1	..	..
Hill, Oliver	..	..	..	1	..	5	..	..	1	..	..
Hills, Joseph	..	1	2	..	1	..	1	2	..	1	..
Hills, Samuel	1	..	1	..	2	..	..	1	..	..	..
Hines, Solomon	1	..	..	..	1	..	..	..	..	1	..
Hoar, James	1	1	..	1	..	1	1	..	1	..	..
Holly, Justus	2	..	..	1	..	3	..	..	1	..	..
Howard, John	1	1	1	..	1	1	1	..	1	..	..
Howe, Ben	1	1	2	..	1	2	1	2	..	1	..
Howe, James	1	..	..	1	..	1	..	..	1	..	..
Hudson, Barzilla	2	..	..	1	..	2	..	..	1	..	..
Huggins, Zadoc	2	1	1	..	1	1	2	2	..	2	..
Hunt, Joseph	1	..	..	1	..	..	..	..	1	..	..
Hyde, Joseph	1	..	..	..	1	2	1	..	1	..	..
Jackson, William	..	..	3	1	..	2	..	..	2	..	..
Kent, Alexander	2	1	..	1	..	2	..	1	1	..	..
Kent, Cephas	..	..	..	..	1	..	..	..	..	1	..
Kent, Cephas Jr.	3	1	1	..	1	1	2	1	1	..	..
Kent, John	..	1	..	..	1	..	..	1	..	1	..
Kent, John	2	..	..	1	..	2	..	..	1	..	..
Kent, Martin	3	..	..	1	..	1	1	1	1	..	..
Kent, Moses	..	2	2	1	..	2	1	2	1	..	..
Kingsbury, Thomas	..	2	..	1	..	4	1	..	1	..	..
Landfair, John	..	1	..	1	..	..	1	2	..	1	..
Langdon, Mathias	..	..	1	..	..	..	..	..	..	..	..
Langdon, Peter	..	..	1	..	..	1	..	1	..	..	..
Leach, Orra	..	..	..	..	..	..	..	1	..	..	..
Livingston, James	..	..	..	..	1	1	..	1	..	1	..
Logan, Hugh	1	1	1	2	..	1	..	1	1	..	..
Lowell, Timothy	2	1	..	1	..	3	..	..	1	1	..
Main, Zadoc	..	..	..	1	..	..	..	1	..	..	..
Mallett, Edmund	..	2	..	..	1	..	..	..	..	1	..
DORSET—con.											
Manley, George	1	..	1	..	1	1	1	3	..	1	..
Manley, John 2nd.	..	1	2	..	1	..	1	1	..	1	..
Manley, John 3rd.	4	..	1	1	..	2	1	..	1	..	..
Manley, William	1	..	..	1	1	1	2	..	1	..	..
Marsh, William	..	1	2	..	1	..	..	..	..	1	..
Martindale, Gershom	..	1	..	1	..	3	2	..	1	..	..
Martindale, Stephen	1	1	1	1	..	1	1	..	1	1	..
Matteson, Benjamin	2	..	4	1	..	2	1	1	1	..	..
Merric, Joseph	..	..	2	..	1	..	1	..	..	1	..
Morse, Alpheus	1	..	..	2	..	1	..	2	1	..	..
Morse, Ebenezer	..	..	..	..	1	..	..	1	1	1	..
Moss, John	2	..	1	1	..	3	..	1	1	..	..
Moss, Joseph	2	..	1	2	..	..	1	1	..	..	..
Moss, Noah	..	..	2	1	1	..	2	..	1	..	..
Nash, Pelatiah B.	2	..	..	1	..	2	..	..	1	..	..
Olds, Stephen	2	1	..	1	..	3	..	..	1	..	..
Paddock, Fauster	1	..	..	1	..	2	..	..	1	..	..
Paddock, Joseph	..	..	..	1	..	3	..	1	..	..	..
Paddock, Prince	..	1	..	1	..	..	1	..	1	..	..
Paddock, Samson	..	..	..	..	..	..	..	..	..	1	..
Page, Achilles	2	..	..	1	..	1	..	..	1	..	..
Palmer, Russell	1	..	1	..	..	2	..	1	..	..	..
Parker, John	2	..	1	..	..	..	1	1	..	..	..
Pettee, John	..	..	1	..	..	..	..	1	..	..	..
Porter, James	1	..	..	..	1	1	..	..	1	..	..
Raymond, Joshua	1	1	..	1	..	2	..	1	..	1	..
Richardson, Humphrey	..	2	1	1	..	1	1	..	1	..	..
Rider, Stephen	1	..	..	1	..	2	..	..	1	..	..
Robinson, Eliab	..	2	2	..	1	2	..	1	..	..	..
Robinson, John	2	2	..	1	..	3	..	1	..	..	..
Rose, Ben	4	2	..	1	..	1	..	..	1	..	..
Sanford, John	..	..	1	..	1	..	..	1	..	1	..
Scofield, Seth	..	..	..	..	1	..	..	1	1	..	..
Sears, Ira	2	..	..	1	..	1	..	1	..	..	..
Sheldon, Joseph	1	..	2	..	1	1	2	1	..	1	..
Shumway, John	..	..	1	..	2	..	..	2	..	1	..
Shumway, Peter	1	..	1	1	..	2	..	..	1	..	..
Sikes, David	..	1	1	..	..	2	..	1	..	..	..
Sikes, Israel	1	..	..	1	..	2	1	..	1	..	..
Sikes, Sylvanus	2	..	1	..	1	..	1	1	..	1	..
Sikes, Sylvanus Jr.	..	..	1	..	..	1	..	1	..	..	..
Sikes, Titus	1	..	..	..	1	1	..	..	1	1	..
Sikes, Titus	1	..	1	..	1	2	3	1	1	..	..
Sikes, Titus 3rd.	1	..	1	..	..	..	..	1	..	..	..
Sikes, Victory	4	..	..	1	..	..	..	..	1	..	..
Slocum, John	3	..	..	1	..	3	..	1	..	..	..
Smith, Calvin	2	..	..	1	..	2	..	..	1	..	..
Smith, Israel	..	..	..	..	1	..	..	..	..	1	..
Smith, Noah	1	..	..	1	..	..	..	..	1	..	..
Soper, John	2	..	..	1	..	1	..	..	1	..	..
Soper, Samuel	..	..	..	..	1	..	..	..	..	1	..
Soper, Samuel Jr.	2	..	..	1	..	..	..	1	..	..	..
Soper, William	..	..	1	..	..	1	..	1	..	..	..
Southerland, Daniel	1	..	..	1	..	..	1	1	..	..	..
Southworth, Chester	2	..	1	1	..	2	2	..	1	..	..
Southworth, Josiah	2	..	..	..	1	..	2	..	1	1	..
Squires, Isaac	2	..	1	..	1	1	2	1	1	..	..
Stewert, James	..	..	..	1	..	..	..	1	1	..	..
Stone, Alexander	1	..	1	..	1	..	2	1	1	..	..
Storrs, Chipman	2	1	..	1	..	2	1	..	1	..	..
Storrs, Prentice	2	1	..	1	..	1	1	..	1	..	..
Thompson, Amos	4	1	..	1	..	1	..	..	1	..	..
Thompson, Nathaniel	2	..	..	..	1	2	1	1	1	..	..
Tousley, Mathew	1	..	..	1	..	1	1	..	1	..	..
Tousley, Nathaniel	..	..	3	..	..	..	..	1	..	..	..
Underhill, Abram	..	..	..	1	..	1	..	1	..	1	..
Underhill, Isaac	2	..	2	1	..	..	1	..	1	..	..
Underhill, James	2	..	..	1	..	..	..	..	1	..	..
Underhill, Nathan	..	..	1	1	..	..	..	1	..	..	..
Vail, John	3	..	..	2	..	1	..	1	1	..	..
Walton, George	..	1	..	..	1	3	..	..	..	1	..
Walton, Thomas	..	..	..	..	1	1	..	1	1	..	..
Weaver, Frederic	3	..	..	1	..	1	..	..	1	..	..
Wells, Abram	1	1	..	1	..	4	1	..	1	..	..
Weston, James	..	..	..	1	..	2	..	1	..	..	..
Wheeler, Nathan	..	..	..	..	1	..	..	..	..	1	..
Wilson, Rust	..	1	..	1	..	1	2	..	1	..	..
Wing, Ephraim	2	..	..	1	..	3	..	..	1	..	..
Woodward, Peter	..	..	1	..	..	..	..	..	..	..	..

BENNINGTON COUNTY—Continued

NAMES OF HEADS OF FAMILIES	FREE WHITE MALES					FREE WHITE FEMALES					
	Under 10 years of age	Of 10 and under 16	Of 16 and under 26 including heads of families	Of 26 and under 45 including heads of families	Of 45 and upwards including heads of families.	Under 10 years of age	Of 10 and under 16	Of 16 and under 26 including heads of families	Of 26 and under 45 including heads of families	Of 45 and upwards including heads of families	All other free persons except Indians not taxed
DORSET—con.											
Worden, Jesse	1	1	..	1	..	6	1	..	1	..	..
UNCERTAIN NAME	..	..	..	..	..	..	..	..	..	..	..
Bartor (?), Thomas	3	..	..	1	..	..	..	..	1	..	..
GLASTENBURY											
Allen, William C.	1	1	..	..	1	2	2	..	..	1	..
Blanchard, Joseph	4	..	..	1	..	1	..	..	1	..	..
Carpenter, Oliver	..	1	..	1	..	2	..	..	1	..	..
Corey, Thomas	2	..	..	1	..	..	..	1	..	..	..
Cutler, Daniel Jr.	..	1	..	1	..	3	2	..	1	..	..
Elwell, Joshua	..	1	1	..	1	..	..	..	..	1	..
Glazier, Ben	1	..	..	1	..	..	1	1	1	..	..
Poolex, George	3	..	..	1	..	1	1	..	1	..	..
LANDGROVE											
Abbott, Barachias	..	1	..	1	..	1	..	..	1	..	..
Archer, Zebina	3	1	1	1	..	1	..	..	1	..	..
Barker, John	..	..	..	1	..	2	..	1	..	1	..
Barker, Jonathan	3	2	..	1	..	1	1	..	1	..	..
Blanchard, Abial	2	..	..	1	..	2	..	..	1	..	..
Blanchard, William	3	..	..	1	..	1	..	1	..	..	..
Carpenter, David	3	..	1	1	..	1	1	1	1	1	..
Chubbuck, Ensign	..	..	..	..	1	..	..	..	..	1	..
Chubbuck, Hosea	..	..	..	..	1	..	..	..	..	1	..
Dale, Joshua	4	..	..	1	..	..	..	..	1	..	..
Davis, Gideon	2	..	2	..	1	2	1	..	1	..	..
Farnum, Joseph	3	..	1	..	..	..	..	1	..	..	..
Fish, Nathan	..	..	..	1	..	..	..	..	..	..	..
Hadley, Jonathan	..	..	..	1	..	3	..	..	1	..	..
Hilldric, Ephraim	1	..	..	..	1	..	1	..	..	..	..
Holt, Joseph	2	..	..	1	..	2	..	..	1	..	..
Morgan, Benjamin	..	..	..	1	..	..	..	..	..	..	..
Pettingil, Peter	1	..	..	1	..	4	..	..	1	..	..
Sheldon, William	2	..	..	1	..	..	..	..	1	..	..
Stiles, Joseph	1	..	..	1	..	3	..	..	1	..	..
Tuthill, Daniel	2	1	1	1	..	..	1	..	1	..	..
Utley, Asa	1	1	1	..	1	2	2	2	..	1	..
Utley, Oliver	..	..	..	1	..	5	..	..	1	..	..
Utley, Peabody	3	..	..	1	..	..	..	1	..	1	..
Whitman, John	2	1	..	1	..	2	1	..	1	..	..
Wylie, David	..	..	1	..	..	..	..	1	..	..	..
MANCHESTER											
Abbott, Erastus	4	..	..	1	..	..	..	1	..	..	..
Allis, Abel	1	..	..	1	..	2	..	1	1	..	1
Anderson, Andrew	2	..	..	1	1	3	..	..	1	..	..
Anderson, James	2	..	..	..	1	..	2	1	..	1	..
Anderson, Robert	2	..	2	..	1	1	1	1	1	..	..
Backus, Nathaniel	..	..	1	1	..	..	..	..	..	..	..
Bailey, Betsey	..	..	..	..	..	..	..	..	1	..	..
Baker, Samuel	1	..	..	1	..	1	..	1	..	..	..
Barlow, Samuel	..	..	..	..	1	..	1	2	..	1	..
Barrett, Zadoc	..	..	..	..	1	2	1	2	..	1	..
Bassett, Samuel	..	..	1	..	..	1	..	1	..	..	..
Beckwith, Daniel	1	..	..	..	1	..	..	..	..	1	..
Beckwith, Robert	..	1	..	..	..	1	..	1	..	..	..
Bedel, William	2	2	1	..	1	1	..	2	..	1	..
Benedict, Jonathan	..	..	..	..	1	..	..	..	..	1	..
Benedict, Jonathan Jr.	2	..	..	1	..	3	..	..	1	..	..
Benedict, Samuel	2	2	..	1	..	2	..	..	1	1	..
Biglow, Ezra	1	1	..	1	..	4	1	1	1	..	..
Birch, Beverly	4	1	..	..	1	..	1	..	1	..	..
Blakesley, Ezra	1	1	..	1	..	1	..	1	1	..	..
Boon, Stephen	1	..	1	..	..	2	..	1	..	..	..
Boorn, Amos	2	..	..	1	..	3	..	..	1	..	..
Boorn, Barnard	2	1	..	..	1	..	..	2	..	1	..

NAMES OF HEADS OF FAMILIES	FREE WHITE MALES					FREE WHITE FEMALES					
	Under 10 years of age	Of 10 and under 16	Of 16 and under 26 including heads of families	Of 26 and under 45 including heads of families	Of 45 and upwards including heads of families.	Under 10 years of age	Of 10 and under 16	Of 16 and under 26 including heads of families	Of 26 and under 45 including heads of families	Of 45 and upwards including heads of families	All other free persons except Indians not taxed
MANCHESTER—con.											
Boorn, Jerad	..	1	..	..	1	..	..	1	1	..	..
Boorn, Nathaniel	1	2	..	1	..	..	..	..	1	..	..
Botteh, Timothy	2	1	..	1	..	2	..	..	1	..	..
Bracket, Christopher	2	2	..	..	1	1	1	1	1	..	..
Bracket, Ezra	2	1	..	3	..	..	..	..	1	..	..
Bronson, Eli	..	1	..	..	1	..	2	1	..	1	3
Brooks, David	2	..	..	1	..	1	..	..	1	..	..
Brown, Timothy	..	..	1	1	1	2	1	2	..	1	..
Bulkley, Joseph	1	..	1	2	1	..	..	1	..	..	..
Bull, Thomas	4	..	..	1	..	1	..	..	1	..	..
Bull, Thomas	1	..	..	2	1	1	..	1	..	1	..
Bulless, Charles	..	..	..	..	1	..	..	..	..	1	..
Bulless, Henry	2	2	2	..	1	1	1	1	..	1	..
Burton, Elijah	3	..	1	1	..	1	..	1	..	..	..
Burton, Isaac	2	..	..	1	..	..	1	1	..	..	..
Butler, John	..	..	1	..	..	..	..	..	..	..	..
Butterfield, Jonas	..	..	1	..	..	..	..	1	..	..	..
Camberlin, Calvin	..	2	..	1	..	..	..	1	1	..	..
Carruth, Jonas	..	..	1	1	..	..	..	..	..	..	..
Cheeseborough, Sylvester	2	1	1	1	..	3	..	..	1	..	..
Clark, Benjamin	..	1	..	..	1	1	1	1	..	1	..
Clark, Ezra	..	..	1	..	..	1	..	1	..	..	..
Cochran, Robert	..	..	..	1	..	1	..	..	1	..	..
Collins, John	1	..	..	1	..	3	..	..	1	..	..
Collins, Nathaniel	1	1	2	..	1	2	3	2	..	1	..
Colvin, Rosana	..	..	1	..	..	..	..	1	..	1	..
Conklin, Benjamin	..	2	..	..	1	..	..	..	1	..	1
Cooke, James	..	..	2	..	..	..	..	..	1	..	..
Corey, Jonathan	1	2	1	1	..	2	..	..	1	..	..
Darby, David	1	..	1	..	1	1	1	..	..	1	..
Darby, Ezra	1	..	1	..	..	..	..	1	..	..	..
Darling, Lyman	..	..	..	1	..	1	..	1	..	..	..
Dedric, Frederic	2	..	..	1	..	2	..	..	2	..	..
Demming, Eliakim	1	2	..	..	1	1	..	1	..	1	..
Doughty, Daniel	3	..	..	..	1	..	..	..	..	1	..
Dudley, Stephen	4	1	..	1	..	1	1	1	1	..	..
Eaton, Ebenezer	1	1	..	1	..	2	..	..	1	..	..
Eaton, Nathan	1	..	1	1	..	2	3	..	1	..	..
Edee, Samuel	1	..	..	1	..	..	..	1	..	..	..
Fairster, Leonard	..	..	1	..	..	1	..	1	..	..	..
Ferguson, Peter	1	2	..	..	1	1	..	..	1	..	..
Field, George	3	..	1	..	1	2	1	..	1	..	..
French, Elijah	1	1	..	..	1	2	1	2	..	1	..
French, Joseph	3	2	..	..	1	2	1	2	1	..	..
French, Joshua	1	..	..	1	..	2	..	..	1	..	..
French, Samuel	..	..	..	..	1	..	..	..	..	1	..
Fuller, Roswell	..	..	..	..	1	..	..	..	..	1	..
Giddings, Job	..	..	..	..	1	..	3	..	..	1	..
Giddings, Moses	..	..	1	..	..	2	..	1	..	..	..
Gilbert, Jonathan	3	..	2	..	1	..	2	2	..	1	..
Glazier, David	..	..	..	..	1	..	..	1	..	1	1
Glazier, David Jr.	2	..	..	1	..	..	..	1	..	..	..
Gould, William Jr.	..	..	1	..	..	..	..	..	..	..	..
Gray, Edward	..	..	..	..	1	..	..	1	..	1	..
Gray, Edward Jr.	3	..	..	1	..	2	..	..	1	..	..
Hacey, John	2	..	..	..	1	1	1	1	..	1	..
Hall, William S.	2	..	..	1	..	..	..	..	1	..	..
Hammond, Daniel	..	..	..	1	..	1	..	..	1	..	..
Harris, Diedame	..	..	1	..	..	..	..	1	..	1	..
Harris, Timothy	..	..	..	1	..	1	..	1	..	..	..
Harrison, Edward	1	1	..	1	..	..	..	..	1	..	..
Hartshorn, Edward	3	..	..	1	..	1	..	..	1	..	..
Hawley, Jabez	2	1	2	..	1	1	1	2	..	1	..
Hawley, Nathan	1	..	1	1	..	1	..	1	..	..	..
Hicks, Benjamin	3	..	1	1	..	3	2	..	1	..	..
Hicks, Daniel	..	..	1	..	1	..	1	..	..	1	..
Hitchcock, Ebenezer	1	..	..	1	..	1	1	..	1	1	..
Hogaboom, John	2	1	1	..	1	2	1	1	..	1	..
Hollistor, Elijah S.	..	1	..	1	..	2	..	..	1	..	..
Holmes, Edward	2	..	1	1	..	1	2	..	1	..	..
Hopkins, John	2	1	..	1	..	2	..	1	1	..	..
Howard, Beriah	..	..	..	1	..	2	..	..	1	..	..
Howe, Joseph	..	..	1	..	..	1	..	1	..	..	..
Hubbell, Silas	..	..	1	..	..	1	..	1	..	..	..
Hurd, Abijah	..	..	..	..	1	..	..	..	..	..	..
Hyde, Nehemiah	..	1	1	1	1	1	..	..	1	1	..
Jacob, Daniel	5	1	..	1	..	2	..	..	1	..	..
Jameson, James	..	..	1	..	1	..	..	1	..	1	..
Jameson, William	1	1	..	1	..	1	..	1	..	..	..
Jewell, Oliver	3	2	1	1	..	3	1	..	1	1	..
Johnson, Aaron	..	..	1	..	..	..	..	..	..	..	..

BENNINGTON COUNTY—Continued

NAMES OF HEADS OF FAMILIES	FREE WHITE MALES: Under 10 years of age	FREE WHITE MALES: Of 10 and under 16	FREE WHITE MALES: Of 16 and under 26 including heads of families	FREE WHITE MALES: Of 26 and under 45 including heads of families	FREE WHITE MALES: Of 45 and upwards including heads of families.	FREE WHITE FEMALES: Under 10 years of age	FREE WHITE FEMALES: Of 10 and under 16	FREE WHITE FEMALES: Of 16 and under 26 including heads of families	FREE WHITE FEMALES: Of 26 and under 45 including heads of families	FREE WHITE FEMALES: Of 45 and upwards including heads of families	All other free persons except Indians not taxed
MANCHESTER—con.											
Johnson, Thomas	..	1	..	..	2	..	1	1	..	2	..
Jones, Daniel	..	..	2	..	1	1	1	..	..	2	..
Jones, Richard	..	..	..	1	..	..	..	1	..	..	..
Joulin, Alexander	1	..	..	1	..	1	..	..	1	..	..
Kimpton, Simeon	2	..	2	1	..	2	..	..	1	..	..
King, Zebulon	2	..	..	1	..	2	..	..	1	..	..
Kyle, William	2	1	1	1	..	1	1	..	1	..	..
Lampheer, Samuel	..	1	1	..	1	1	2	1	..	1	..
Loggan, Robert	1	..	2	..	1	..	..	1	..	1	..
Loveland, Asa	2	..	1	1	..	..	..	..	1	..	..
Mallett, Ely	1	..	..	1	..	1	..	1	..	..	..
Martin, Jonathan	3	..	..	1	..	2	..	..	1	..	..
Mason, Aaron	2	2	..	..	1	3	1	2	1	..	..
Matteson, Samuel	2	2	..	1	..	2	1	1	1	..	..
McColom, David	..	..	2	..	..	..	..	..	..	..	..
McIntyre, Philip	1	1	..	1	..	3	..	..	1	..	..
Meade, Israel	1	..	1	..	..	..	..	1	..	..	..
Meade, Jacob	2	2	..	1	..	4	1	..	1	..	..
Meade, Philip	1	1	2	..	1	2	2	1	1	..	..
Meade, Timothy	1	..	..	..	1	..	..	1	..	1	..
Meade, Timothy	..	1	3	..	1	2	2	1	..	1	..
Meade, Truman	1	1	2	1	..	1	2	..	1	..	..
Miller, Eliza	..	1	..	..	..	..	3	..	1	..	..
Montgomery, Hugh	4	2	2	..	2	..	..	1	1	1	..
Moore, Ambrose	2	1	..	1	..	1	..	..	1	..	..
Munson, Bethia	3	..	..	1	1	..	1	..	..	1	..
Munson, Jared	1	1	..	..	1	..	2	1	..	1	..
Munson, Thaddeus	1	1	1	..	1	1	1	1	..	1	..
Nickeson, Constant	4	2	..	..	1	..	..	..	..	1	..
O'Brien, Timothy	2	..	1	1	..	..	..	..	1	..	..
Odel, Jacob	..	1	1	..	1	1	..	1	..	1	..
Odel, Jacob, Jr.	1	..	..	1	..	..	..	..	1	..	..
Odel, Jeremiah	2	..	..	1	..	2	..	..	1	..	..
Ormsby, Daniel	2	..	..	1	..	3	..	1	1	..	..
Ormsby, Gideon	1	1	2	..	1	..	1	2	..	1	..
Ormsby, Gideon Jr.	1	..	..	1	..	1	..	..	1	..	..
Ormsby, Jacob	1	..	1	1	..	3	..	1	1	..	..
Parish, Oliver	2	..	..	1	..	2	1	..	1	..	..
Pettibone, Abel	1	1	..	1	..	3	3	..	1	..	..
Pettibone, Eli	..	..	1	..	1	1	..	..	1	..	..
Pettibone, Samuel	..	1	2	..	1	..	..	3	..	1	..
Pettibone, Seth	3	3	1	1	1	1	..	1	1	..	..
Pierpoint, Robert	2	..	1	1	..	2	2	1	2	..	..
Place, Ebenezer	2	..	1	..	..	..	..	1	..	..	..
Pratt, Joel 2nd.	1	..	2	..	1	1	..	1	..	..	..
Preston, Samuel	..	1	..	1	..	6	..	1	..	..	..
Prindle, Alexander	..	1	1	..	1	..	1	..	..	1	..
Pritchard, Archibald	1	..	..	1	..	2	..	..	1	..	..
Purdee, Ben	..	..	..	..	1	..	..	..	..	1	..
Purdee, Ben 3rd.	2	..	1	..	..	..	..	1	..	..	..
Purdee, Benjamin Jr.	..	1	2	..	1	2	1	..	..	1	..
Purdee, Charles	1	..	1	..	..	..	..	1	..	..	..
Purdee, Daniel	3	..	2	..	1	..	3	..	2	..	..
Purdee, David	2	1	..	1	..	1	2	..	1	..	..
Purdee, Reuben	1	..	2	..	1	2	2	1	..	1	..
Purdee, Reuben	1	..	1	1	..	..	1	1	..	..	..
Purdee, Samuel	..	..	..	1	..	3	..	..	1	..	..
Purdee, Silas	1	..	1	..	..	1	..	1	..	..	..
Reynold, Philip	3	..	..	..	1	2	1	..	1	..	..
Rhodes, Samuel	2	..	..	1	..	..	..	..	1	..	..
Richardson, Amos	2	1	1	..	1	..	1	1	1	..	..
Richardson, Andrew	1	..	3	..	1	1	1	2	..	..	..
Richardson, John	..	1	1	1	..	..	2	..	1	2	..
Richardson, Nathan	..	..	..	..	1	..	..	..	..	1	..
Roberts, Christopher	1	..	2	1	..	4	1	1	1	1	..
Roberts, James	1	..	1	..	..	1	..	1	..	..	..
Roberts, Martin	1	..	1	..	..	..	..	1	..	..	..
Robinson, Timothy	2	2	..	..	1	1	..	1	1	..	..
Rose, Isaac	1	..	1	..	..	2	1	1	..	..	..
Rose, Joel	..	3	..	..	1	..	1	..	..	2	..
Rose, William	..	..	1	..	..	..	..	1	..	..	..
Seaton, Aron	4	2	..	1	..	1	1	..	1	..	..
Sexton, George	1	1	3	1	..	2	2	1	1	..	..
Shelden, Isaac	..	1	1	..	1	1	..	..	..	1	..
Skinner, Pepperell	2	..	..	1	..	2	..	..	1	..	..
Smith, Enoch	1	..	..	1	..	..	..	1	..	..	..
Smith, Frederic	1	..	..	1	..	1	..	1	1	..	..
Smith, John	2	..	..	1	..	1	..	..	1	..	..
Smith, John	1	2	2	..	1	..	1	1	..	1	..
MANCHESTER—con.											
Smith, Joseph	1	..	..	..	1	..	..	..	..	1	..
Smith, Margarett	..	..	..	..	..	..	1	1	..	1	..
Smith, Noah	1	..	..	1	..	2	1	..	1	..	..
Smith, Seth	..	..	..	..	1	..	2	..	..	1	..
Smith, Seth	4	..	..	1	..	..	..	..	1	..	..
Smith, William	2	..	..	2	..	1	1	1	1	..	..
Soper, Eliza	..	..	..	..	..	1	..	..	..	1	..
Soper, Pelatiah	1	..	1	..	1	..	1	..	..	1	..
Soper, Sarah	..	..	1	..	..	1	..	..	1	2	..
Soper, Solomon	1	..	..	1	..	1	1	1	..	..	..
Soper, Timothy	1	..	..	1	..	..	..	1	..	..	..
Southerland, Ben	..	1	..	1	..	..	..	1	..	..	..
Southerland, Reuben	2	..	1	..	..	1	..	1	..	..	..
Southerland, Roger	1	..	..	1	..	1	..	1	..	..	..
Southerland, Samuel	..	1	3	..	1	1	2	1	..	1	..
Southwick, Chade	..	..	3	..	..	1	..	..	1	..	..
Southwick, Jesse	..	..	2	..	..	2	..	1	..	..	..
Spencer, Seth	..	..	1	..	..	..	..	1	..	..	..
Sperry, Daniel	2	..	1	1	..	2	..	..	1	..	..
Sperry, John	..	..	1	..	..	..	..	1	..	..	..
Sperry, Moses	..	..	..	..	1	..	..	1	..	2	..
Sperry, Moses L.	..	..	..	1	..	..	..	1	..	..	..
Sperry, Philo	..	1	1	..	1	..	..	..	1	..	..
Squire, Samuel	..	..	2	..	..	..	..	1	..	..	..
Squire, Truman	..	..	..	1	..	2	..	..	2	..	..
Stacey, John	2	..	1	1	..	..	..	1	..	..	..
Stewart, Noble	..	..	1	..	..	..	..	..	1	..	..
Stoddard, Stephen	..	..	..	1	..	1	..	..	1	..	..
Strait, Samuel	1	1	2	..	1	3	2	..	1	..	..
Swan, John	1	..	1	..	1	..	2	1	1	..	..
Swift, Serenus	..	1	1	1	..	..	..	..	1	..	..
Tankard, George	..	..	..	..	..	..	..	..	..	..	6
Taylor, Jonathan	..	2	..	..	1	1	1	1	..	1	..
Taylor, Moses	..	..	..	..	1	..	..	..	..	1	..
Taylor, Moses	1	..	..	1	..	3	1	..	1	..	..
Taylor, Samuel	..	1	..	..	1	..	..	2	..	..	..
Thomas, Charles	1	..	..	1	..	2	..	1	1	..	..
Torrance, Thomas	1	1	..	..	1	2	2	2	1	..	..
Vanderlip, John	3	3	..	1	..	1	..	1	1	..	..
Vaughan, James	1	1	3	1	1	..	1	1	..	1	..
Waite, Jeremiah	..	1	1	..	1	3	1	1	1	..	..
West, Clarina	1	..	..	1	..	1	..	..	1	..	..
Wheaton, John	..	1	2	..	1	1	..	1	..	1	..
Whelpley, Joseph	1	..	2	..	1	..	..	1	..	..	..
Whelpley, Margarett	..	3	..	1	..	..	..	1	1	..	..
Willcox, Nathan	..	..	1	..	..	2	..	1	..	..	..
Willcox, Samuel	..	..	1	1	..	4	..	..	1	..	..
Wood, Nichols	2	..	..	1	..	3	2	..	1	..	..
Wyman, William H.	..	..	..	1	..	..	..	1	..	..	..
POWNAL											
Akin, David	..	..	..	..	1	..	..	1	..	..	..
Albis, Martin	3	3	..	..	1	2	..	..	1	1	..
Anderson, Solomon	1	..	..	1	..	..	..	1	..	..	..
Andrews, Noel	..	..	1	1	..	1	1	2	..	1	..
Angel, Abiather	2	1	2	..	1	1	2	1	2	..	..
Angel, Esseek	1	1	1	..	1	2	2	..	1	..	..
Backer, Peter	..	..	..	..	1	1	2	..	1	..	..
Baker, Samuel	2	..	..	1	..	..	..	..	1	..	..
Bannister, Thomas	..	1	..	1	..	1	..	..	1	..	..
Barber, Benjamin	..	..	1	..	..	..	..	..	1	..	..
Barber, Joseph	1	..	..	1	..	3	..	1	..	1	..
Barber, Joseph	3	1	3	..	1	2	1	2	1	..	2
Bates, Daniel	1	..	..	1	..	1	1	..	1	..	..
Bates, Francis	..	..	1	..	1	..	1	..	..	1	..
Bates, Francis Jr.	4	..	1	1	..	1	..	..	1	..	..
Bates, Joab	3	..	..	1	..	1	2	..	1	..	..
Bates, Josiah	1	1	1	..	1	..	1	1	..	1	..
Bates, Stephen	2	1	..	1	..	1	..	..	1	..	..
Becket, Polly	1	..	..	..	..	1	..	..	1	..	..
Bennett, Francis	2	3	..	..	1	2	..	2	..	1	..
Bennett, Stephen	..	..	1	..	..	1	..	..	1	..	..
Bennett, William	..	..	..	1	..	1	..	..	1	..	..
Benson, David	1	..	1	..	2	1	..	..	1	2	..
Blackinton, Jesse	2	..	1	1	..	..	..	1	..	..	..
Blanden, Samuel	..	1	1	1	..	1	..	..	1	..	..
Blinn, Elihu	..	1	..	..	1	..	1	..	..	1	..
Blinn, Nathan	1	..	..	1	..	..	..	1	..	..	..
Blinn, Thomas	..	..	2	..	..	1	1	1	..	..	..
Blood, Jared	1	..	1	1	..	3	2	..	1	..	..
Blue, Stephen	..	..	1	1	1	..	..	..	..	1	..
Bowles, William	1	1	..	1	..	..	1	1	..	1	..

BENNINGTON COUNTY—Continued

NAMES OF HEADS OF FAMILIES	FREE WHITE MALES					FREE WHITE FEMALES					All other free persons except Indians not taxed
	Under 10 years of age	Of 10 and under 16	Of 16 and under 26 including heads of families	Of 26 and under 45 including heads of families	Of 45 and upwards including heads of families.	Under 10 years of age	Of 10 and under 16	Of 16 and under 26 including heads of families	Of 26 and under 45 including heads of families	Of 45 and upwards including heads of families	
POWNAL—con.											
Briggs, Enos	2	1	..	..	1	1	1	1	1	..	..
Broadway, William	2	..	1	..	..	..	..	1	..	..	..
Brown, Isaiah	1	..	1	..	..	..	..	1	..	..	..
Brown, Joseph	..	1	1	..	..	2	..	1	1	..	..
Brown, Richard	3	2	2	..	1	1	1	..	2	..	..
Brownal, Blackman	..	1	1	..	1	2	1	2	1	..	..
Brownal, Thomas	2	1	3	1	..	2	1	1	1	..	1
Brownall, Thomas	2	1	3	1	..	2	1	1	..	1	..
Brumley, Paul	..	..	..	..	1	2	..	..	1	..	..
Buck, Abiathar	..	1	..	..	..	..	2	..	1	..	..
Bucklen, Isaac	..	1	1	..	1	1	2	1	..	1	..
Bulkley, Peter	1	..	..	1	..	2	..	..	1	..	..
Burges, Thomas	2	1	..	1	..	3	1	1	1	..	..
Burleson, Daniel	1	..	..	1	..	4	2	..	1	..	..
Burleson, Job	4	2	..	1	..	..	..	..	2	..	..
Burleson, William	..	..	1	..	..	..	1	..	..	1	..
Burns, Francis	..	..	1	..	1	..	..	..	..	1	..
Burns, Samuel	3	2	..	1	..	..	1	..	1	..	..
Bushnell, Ephraim	1	2	..	1	..	2	1	1	1	..	..
Cald, Jonathan	..	1	..	1	..	3	..	..	1	..	..
Card, Jonathan	1	1	1	1	2	..	..	1	..	1	..
Case, Levi	..	..	1	..	..	..	..	1	1	..	..
Champlain, William	1	..	..	1	..	2	..	..	1	..	..
Choate, Isaac	..	..	..	..	1	..	..	..	..	1	..
Choate, Isaac Jr.	..	1	..	1	..	2	1	..	1	..	..
Choate, Joshua	3	1	..	1	..	1	1	..	1	..	..
Clark, William	1	1	1	..	1	1	1	..	1	..	..
Clark, Zephaniah	1	3	..	..	1	2	..	1	1	..	..
Clarke, Hope	1	..	..	..	..	1	..	1	1	..	..
Clarke, Isaac	..	1	1	1	..	..	1	..	1	..	..
Clarke, Ithamar	2	1	..	..	1	..	..	1	..	..	..
Clarke, Nathaniel	..	..	..	1	..	2	1	1	1	1	..
Cleland, James	..	..	..	..	1	..	..	..	..	1	..
Congdon, Joseph	..	..	1	..	1	1	1	..	1	..	..
Corey, Archibald	4	..	..	1	..	..	..	1	..	..	..
Corey, Benedict	..	..	1	..	1	..	..	1	..	1	..
Cummings, Remington	2	1	..	1	..	2	..	..	1	..	..
Cummings, William	..	..	..	..	1	..	1	1	..	1	..
Curtis, James	..	2	2	..	1	..	1	1	..	1	..
Deal, Bostgoun	..	1	..	..	1	..	1	..	..	1	4
Deal, Peter	..	1	1	1	..	2	..	1	1	..	..
Demic, Abel	..	2	2	..	1	..	2	2	..	1	..
Demic, Keyes	2	..	..	1	..	1	..	1	..	..	..
Demic, Moores	2	1	..	1	..	3	..	..	1	..	..
Downer, John	1	..	1	1	1	..	2	..	1	..	..
Drake, Alexander	1	..	..	1	..	3	..	1	..	..	..
Drake, Josiah	3	2	..	1	..	2	..	..	1	..	..
Dunham, Obadiah	2	..	1	1	..	2	1	..	1	..	..
Dunning, Josiah	3	2	1	..	1	2	1	1	1	1	..
Dunning, Josiah Jr.	..	..	1	..	..	1	..	1	..	..	..
Dunning, Michal	..	..	1	1	1	1	..	1	..	1	..
Eaton, William	..	..	..	..	1	..	..	..	..	..	..
Eldridge, Daniel	1	1	2	..	1	1	2	1	..	1	..
Eldridge, Nathan	..	..	3	..	1	..	1	..	..	1	..
Ellsworth, Judiah	2	..	2	1	..	1	1	..	2	..	..
Ellsworth, Wanton	3	..	..	1	..	1	..	..	1	..	..
Elsworth, Frederic	1	..	1	1	..	..	..	1	..	..	..
Elsworth, James	2	..	..	1	..	3	1	..	1	..	..
Elsworth, Rosanna	..	..	2	..	..	..	..	..	..	2	..
Evans, Barnabas	..	..	..	..	1	..	..	..	..	..	..
Evans, Daniel	2	1	..	1	..	1	2	..	1	..	..
Follett, Joseph	..	..	1	..	..	..	..	..	..	..	..
Fowler, John	2	..	2	1	..	3	2	..	1	..	..
Franklin, Ebenezer	..	..	1	..	..	1	..	1	..	..	..
Frost, Elijah	1	..	2	..	1	2	1	..	1	..	..
Fuller, Ichabod	2	1	..	..	1	3	1	..	..	1	..
Gardener, Abraham	..	1	1	..	1	3	2	1	1	..	..
Gardener, Benjamin	..	1	1	1	..	..	2	1	2	1	..
Gardener, Charles	1	..	1	..	..	1	..	1	..	..	..
Gardener, Daniel	1	..	1	..	..	3	..	1	..	..	..
Gardener, David	1	1	3	..	1	1	1	2	..	1	..
Gardener, George	..	..	..	..	1	..	..	..	..	1	..
Gardener, George Jr.	4	..	..	..	1	..	1	..	2	..	..
Gardner, Benjamin G.	3	..	1	..	1	1	1	2	1	..	..
Gardner, George	..	1	..	1	..	..	1	1	1	..	..
Gardner, Joseph	..	3	2	..	1	2	..	2	..	1	..
Gardner, Phillip	..	..	1	..	..	..	..	1	..	..	..
Gibbs, Caleb	2	1	..	1	..	1	1	1	..	..	..
Gibson, David	3	2	..	1	..	3	..	..	1	..	..
Goodenow, Josiah	2	..	..	1	..	2	..	..	1	..	..
Green, Josias	..	..	..	..	1	..	..	..	..	2	..
Grover, Benjamin	2	..	..	1	..	3	..	..	1	..	..
POWNAL—con.											
Grover, Isaac	2	1	4	1	..	..	..	..	1	1	..
Gulley, Patience	..	..	..	..	..	..	..	2	..	1	..
Hall, James	1	..	..	1	..	1	..	..	1	..	..
Hall, Peleg	1	..	..	1	..	..	..	..	1	..	..
Hall, William	..	1	1	..	1	..	1	1	1	..	..
Hamilton, William	..	..	1	..	1	..	..	..	..	1	..
Harmond, Elisha	1	..	..	1	..	..	..	1	..	..	..
Harvey, Thomas	2	..	1	..	..	..	..	2	..	..	..
Harwood, Daniel	..	..	..	1	..	1	..	1	..	..	..
Hatch, Caleb	3	..	..	1	..	..	1	..	1	..	..
Hendric, Talme	1	..	1	..	..	2	..	1	..	..	..
Higbee, Dexter	1	..	..	1	..	1	..	1	..	..	..
Houghton, Joseph	..	..	..	1	..	..	..	1	..	..	..
Houghton, Martha	..	1	..	..	..	..	..	1	..	1	..
Houghton, Silas	..	2	1	..	1	..	..	2	..	1	..
Hovey, Zaccheus	..	..	1	1	..	..	..	..	..	1	1
Hudson, Benoni	2	1	..	1	..	2	1	1	1	..	..
Hull, Charles	1	..	..	1	..	1	..	..	1	..	..
Hungerford, Amassa	1	..	1	..	..	..	..	1	..	..	..
Hunt, Emery	3	2	1	1	..	1	..	1	1	1	..
Hurd, Ebenezer	..	1	1	..	1	1	..	1	1	..	..
Jenks, Shubal	5	..	1	1	..	..	..	1	1	..	..
Jewett, Erastus	..	1	1	..	..	2	1	2	..	..	..
Johnson, William	3	..	2	..	..	..	..	1	..	..	..
Kenny, Jethro	..	1	..	1	..	2	1	..	1	..	..
Keyes, Seth	1	..	1	1	..	1	..	1	..	..	..
Ladd, James	..	1	2	..	1	..	..	2	1	..	..
Lampson, David	..	1	1	..	1	..	..	..	1	..	..
Larabee, Asaph	1	..	..	1	..	2	..	1	..	..	..
Larabee, Eleazer	1	..	..	..	1	..	..	..	..	1	..
Larabee, Joseph	..	1	1	2	..	4	..	..	1	..	..
Larabee, Ozias	2	..	..	1	..	3	..	1	..	..	..
Larabee, Willet	2	..	..	1	..	..	..	1	..	..	..
Lewis, Abisha	2	1	..	1	1	2	..	1	1	..	..
Lewis, Zenas	..	..	1	..	..	..	..	1	..	1	..
Lovitt, Elijah	3	..	..	1	..	2	..	1	1	..	..
Lovitt, John	..	..	..	..	1	..	..	1	..	1	..
Lylie, Ebenezer	..	1	1	..	1	1	..	1	..	1	..
Magown, John	2	2	..	1	..	2	..	..	1	..	..
Magown, John	..	..	..	1	..	..	..	..	..	..	..
Maiquissee, Lewis	1	..	1	..	..	..	..	3	1	..	..
Manchester, James	3	1	..	1	..	2	..	..	1	..	..
Mann, Ephraim	2	..	2	..	1	1	..	2	1	..	..
Mansfield, Ward	1	..	1	..	..	1	..	2	..	..	..
Marsh, Eleazer	..	..	..	..	1	..	..	..	1	1	..
Marsh, Eleazer Jr.	1	1	1	1	..	1	..	1	1	..	..
Marsh, Nathan	1	1	..	1	..	3	1	..	1	..	..
Marsh, William	2	..	..	1	..	..	..	1	2	..	..
Mason, Aaron	1	..	..	1	..	3	..	1	1	..	..
Matteson, Elizabeth	1	..	1	..	..	1	..	1	..	1	..
Matteson, Francis	2	..	1	..	..	..	1	..	1	..	..
Matteson, Joshua	1	1	1	1	..	..	..	1	..	..	..
Merrills, James	2	1	..	1	..	2	..	..	1	..	..
Montgomery, Charles	1	1	..	1	..	3	..	..	1	1	..
Montgomery, James	1	..	..	1	..	..	..	1	..	..	..
Moon, Asa	..	..	..	1	1	..	..	2	..	1	..
Moon, Jacob	2	..	..	1	..	..	..	..	1	..	..
Morehouse, Philo	1	..	..	1	..	2	..	1	..	..	..
Morgan, Benjamin	..	1	..	..	1	2	1	..	1	1	..
Morgan, Ezra	1	..	..	1	..	1	1	1	..	..	..
Munson, Timothy	..	..	1	..	1	..	1	..	..	1	..
Munson, Timothy Jr.	2	..	..	1	..	1	..	..	1	..	..
Murray, James	..	1	..	..	1	1	..	1	..	1	..
Myers, Elizabeth	1	1	1	..	..	1	1	..	..	1	..
Myers, Gideon	1	2	1	1	..	2	1	..	1	..	..
Myers, Joseph	4	..	..	1	..	1	..	1	..	..	..
Nials, Russel	..	1	1	..	..	..	..	1	1	..	..
Nichols, Caleb	..	1	1	..	1	..	..	1	..	1	1
Noble, Abner	2	1	..	1	..	1	..	..	1	..	..
Noble, Ely	..	..	3	..	1	1	..	..	..	2	..
Noble, Erastus	1	..	1	..	..	..	..	1	..	..	..
Noble, John	..	1	..	..	1	..	..	..	..	1	..
Noble, Josiah	..	..	1	..	1	..	..	2	1	1	..
Noble, Roger	..	1	4	1	..	2	2	..	..	1	..
Norton, George	..	..	1	..	..	1	..	1	..	..	..
Oliver, John	..	1	..	..	1	..	..	..	..	1	..
Osborn, Israel	1	..	..	..	1	..	..	..	..	1	..
Ovaitt, William	1	1	2	..	1	1	1	2	1	..	..

BENNINGTON COUNTY—Continued

NAMES OF HEADS OF FAMILIES	FREE WHITE MALES					FREE WHITE FEMALES					All other free persons except Indians not taxed
	Under 10 years of age	Of 10 and under 16	Of 16 and under 26 including heads of families	Of 26 and under 45 including heads of families	Of 45 and upwards including heads of families.	Under 10 years of age	Of 10 and under 16	Of 16 and under 26 including heads of families	Of 26 and under 45 including heads of families	Of 45 and upwards including heads of families	
POWNAL—con.											
Page, Josiah	..	..	1	..	..	2	..	..	1	..	..
Page, Thomas	2	..	1	1	..	1	..	..	1	1	..
Palmer, Elisha	3	..	..	1	..	1	..	1	..	..	..
Parker, Abel	..	1	2	..	1	2	2	..	..	1	..
Parsons, Aaron	..	..	1	..	1	..	..	..	..	1	..
Peirce, Uriah	2	..	..	..	1	1	..	..	1	..	..
Perkins, Joseph	1	1	..	3	..	3	..	1	2	..	..
Perkins, Moses	1	1	1	..	1	..	..	1	..	1	4
Phillips, Daniel	2	1	..	..	1	1	1	1	1	1	..
Plank, Justice	1	1	..	1	..	3	..	..	1	..	..
Pope, Lydia	..	..	..	..	..	1	..	1	..	..	..
Potter, Abel	..	1	..	..	1	..	..	..	..	1	..
Potter, John	2	..	..	..	1	1	..	2	1	..	..
Potter, Zarah	3	..	..	2	..	1	1	2	1	..	..
Powers, Laurance	4	..	1	1	..	..	2	..	1	..	..
Pratt, Elijah	4	..	..	1	..	1	..	..	1	..	..
Pratt, Silas	1	1	..	1	1	1	..	..	1	..	..
Pratt, Stephen	2	2	..	1	..	3	1	..	1	..	..
Pratt, William	3	1	..	1	..	2	1	..	1	1	..
Pratt, Zadoc	1	..	1	..	..	..	..	1	..	..	..
Primmer, William	..	..	..	..	1	..	..	..	..	1	..
Prosser, John	3	1	2	..	1	1	..	1	1	1	..
Reed, Anna	1	..	..	..	..	..	..	..	1	..	..
Remington, Elisha	..	..	..	..	1	..	..	..	1	..	..
Ripley, Nathaniel	..	..	..	..	..	2	..	1	..	..	..
Roberts, Samuel	..	..	1	..	1	..	..	..	..	1	..
Rogers, Elizabeth	1	1	1	..	..	1	..	..	1	1	..
Rood, Joshua	1	..	..	..	1	..	..	..	1	..	..
Roy, William	..	..	..	..	1	..	..	1	..	1	..
Russel, Jonathan	2	..	..	1	..	..	1	..	1	..	..
Russell, Asa	1	1	..	..	1	1	2	..	..	1	..
Sampson, Isaac	..	..	1	..	1	..	..	..	..	1	..
Sanford, Ezra	1	..	..	2	..	2	1	..	1	..	..
Searls, Isaac	..	..	..	..	1	..	..	..	..	1	..
Seelye, Ebenezer	..	..	..	..	2	..	..	..	..	2	..
Sherman, Benjamin	..	..	1	..	..	1	..	1	..	..	..
Sherman, Jacob	..	..	..	..	1	..	..	..	..	1	..
Sherman, John	2	2	2	..	1	..	1	2	1	1	..
Smith, Alve	..	..	1	..	..	..	..	1	..	..	..
Smith, David	4	..	..	..	1	1	..	..	..	1	..
Smith, Dexter	..	..	..	1	..	..	..	1	..	..	..
Smith, Gilbert	..	1	1	..	..	1	..	1	..	..	..
Smith, Isaac	..	..	1	1	..	..	..	1	..	..	..
Smith, Reuben	1	2	1	..	1	2	..	2	1	..	..
Spencer, Benjamin	..	..	..	1	..	2	..	1	..	..	..
Stanton, John	1	2	1	..	1	1	1	..	..	1	1
Stanton, John Jr.	..	..	..	1	..	2	..	1	..	..	..
Starks, David	..	..	1	..	..	..	..	1	..	..	..
Stevens, John V.	1	..	..	2	..	1	..	2	..	..	..
Stevens, Thomas	..	..	..	..	1	..	..	..	..	2	..
Strait, Asa	1	..	..	1	..	2	..	1	..	..	..
Summers, John	2	..	..	1	..	3	..	..	1	..	..
Tanner, William	..	1	..	1	..	2	..	..	1	..	..
Thompson, Benoni	1	1	3	..	1	1	1	1	1	..	..
Thompson, Levi	1	1	2	..	2	1	2	2	..	1	..
Thorp, Thaddeus	1	2	..	1	..	..	..	..	1	..	..
Tibbetts, George	..	..	1	..	..	2	..	1	..	..	..
Timothy, Daniel	1	1	..	..	1	..	..	2	..	1	1
Tousley, Gideon	2	1	3	..	1	2	1	..	1	..	..
Turner, Amos	1	..	1	1	..	2	..	..	1	..	..
Turner, Solomon	2	..	..	1	..	1	..	..	1	..	..
Vairn, Joseph	..	2	..	..	1	..	..	..	1	..	..
Vosbourgh, Abraham	3	2	..	..	1	..	..	1	..	..	..
Vosbourgh, Peter	..	..	1	..	2	..	..	..	1	1	..
Wallace, Nathaniel	..	1	..	..	1	1	..	1	..	1	..
Wallace, Nathaniel Jr.	..	..	..	1	..	..	..	1	..	..	..
Warren, Moses	2	..	1	1	..	1	1	..	1	..	..
Watson, Freeborn	2	1	1	..	1	..	..	..	1	..	..
Watson, Silas	1	..	1	..	2	..	..	..	1	..	..
Welch, Daniel	1	2	1	..	1	..	..	..	..	1	..
Welch, Ebenezer	2	..	1	1	..	3	..	1	1	1	..
Welch, John	..	..	..	1	..	..	1	..	1	..	..
Wettum, Malachi	1	1	..	..	1	1	..	..	1	..	..
White, Perez	2	1	..	1	..	..	..	..	1	1	..
Williams, Isaiah	3	2	1	1	..	1	2	..	1	..	..
Williams, Joseph	..	..	..	1	1	..	..	..	..	1	..
Williams, Joseph Jr.	..	1	2	..	1	..	1	1	..	1	..
Williams, William	4	..	..	1	..	1	..	..	1	..	..
Wilson, John	1	..	1	..	1	1	..	1	..	1	..
Wistenhouse, John H.	..	..	1	..	1	1	1	1	1	..	..
Woolsey, Thomas	..	1	1	..	1	2	2	..	..	1	..
Wright, Josiah	3	1	2	..	1	1	1	..	1	..	..
Wright, Moses	1	..	..	1	..	1	1	..	1	..	..
Wright, Samuel	1	..	2	..	..	1	2	1	..	..	..
Wright, Solomon	1	2	3	1	..	4	..	..	1	1	2
Young, John	..	..	..	..	1	..	..	..	..	1	..
Young, Stephen	1	..	..	1	..	1	..	..	1	..	..
Youngs, Abraham	1	..	..	1	..	1	2	1	..	..	..
Youngs, Anna	1	..	..	..	2	..	1	..	..	..	..
Youngs, Isaac	2	..	..	1	..	1	..	1	..	..	..
Youngs, John	..	..	1	..	1	2	1	..	1	..	..
Youngs, John Jr.	..	..	1	..	..	..	..	1	..	..	..
UNCERTAIN NAME											
Comar (?), William	1	..	..	1	..	2	..	..	1	..	..
READSBORO											
Adams, Cybele	..	..	..	..	..	..	..	1	..	..	..
Amidon, Ezra	3	..	..	1	..	1	..	..	1	..	..
Amidon, Jedediah	3	..	..	1	..	1	1	..	1	..	..
Amidon, Ralph	..	..	..	1	..	1	..	1	..	..	..
Amidon, Roger	..	..	..	..	1	..	1	1	..	1	..
Amidon, Samuel	..	..	1	1	1	..	1	2	..	2	..
Amidon, Solomon	..	..	1	..	..	1	..	1	..	..	..
Bailey, Elijah	1	..	..	1	..	3	..	..	1	..	..
Bailey, James	..	..	1	..	1	..	..	..	..	1	..
Bailey, James Jr.	..	..	1	..	..	..	..	1	..	..	..
Bailey, Phillip	2	..	..	1	..	2	1	..	1	..	..
Battles, John	3	1	1	..	1	2	..	2	1	..	..
Blanchard, Ebenezer	1	..	1	..	..	1	..	1	..	..	..
Blanchard, Lemuel	1	1	..	..	1	1	1	2	..	1	..
Briggs, Jedediah	..	..	..	1	..	3	..	..	1	..	..
Brown, Abraham	1	..	..	..	1	2	2	..	1	..	..
Cady, Richard	..	..	..	..	1	..	..	..	..	1	..
Chapman, Wilson	..	..	1	..	..	3	..	1	..	..	..
Crumb, Billington	..	..	1	..	1	..	1	2	..	1	..
Cummings, Amos	1	..	..	1	..	6	..	..	1	..	..
Davidson, Henry	1	..	..	1	..	1	..	..	1	1	..
Dupee, Joshua	..	1	..	1	..	..	..	..	1	..	..
Easty, Isaac	..	..	..	..	1	..	1	..	..	1	..
Easty, Isaac Jr.	1	..	..	1	..	2	..	..	1	..	..
Fairbanks, Artemas	..	..	1	..	..	..	..	1	..	..	..
Fairbanks, John	4	..	..	1	..	..	..	..	1	..	..
Goodell, David	1	..	..	1	..	3	..	..	1	..	..
Hartwell, Joseph	1	1	..	1	..	..	1	1	..	1	..
Hewet, Appollus	2	..	..	1	..	1	..	..	1	..	..
Judd, Reuben	2	..	..	1	..	3	..	..	1	..	..
Keyes, Ezra	2	..	..	1	..	2	..	..	2	..	..
Littlefield, Asa	1	1	..	1	..	2	1	1	..	1	..
Myers, Simon	1	..	..	1	..	3	1	..	1	..	..
Ross, Joseph	..	..	1	1	1	..	..	..	..	1	..
Stearns, Ebenezer	..	..	..	1	1	..	..	..	1	1	..
Stearns, George	1	..	..	1	..	1	..	..	1	..	..
Sybley, Jason	1	..	..	1	..	3	..	..	..	1	..
Sybley, Peter	1	..	1	..	..	..	1	..	1	..	..
Thompson, Ebenezer	3	..	..	1	..	1	..	..	1	..	..
Valentine, Robert	..	..	..	..	1	..	..	..	..	1	..
Walker, John	2	..	..	1	..	1	..	..	1	..	..
Walker, Thaddeus	1	..	1	..	..	1	..	..	1	..	..
White, Grant	1	..	..	1	..	2	..	..	1	..	..
Whiting, Caleb	2	..	1	..	1	1	..	..	..	1	..
Whitney, John	1	..	1	..	1	2	..	1	1	..	..

BENNINGTON COUNTY—Continued

NAMES OF HEADS OF FAMILIES	FREE WHITE MALES					FREE WHITE FEMALES					All other free persons except Indians not taxed
	Under 10 years of age	Of 10 and under 16	Of 16 and under 26 including heads of families	Of 26 and under 45 including heads of families	Of 45 and upwards including heads of families.	Under 10 years of age	Of 10 and under 16	Of 16 and under 26 including heads of families	Of 26 and under 45 including heads of families	Of 45 and upwards including heads of families	
RUPERT											
Baily, William	1	2	1	1	..	4	..	1	1	..	..
Baldwin, Eliza	..	..	..	..	..	..	..	1	..	..	..
Barnard, Jacob	..	1	..	..	1	..	..	..	1	..	..
Beebee, Ephraim	2	2	1	1	..	1	..	..	1	..	..
Billings, Christopher	1	3	1	..	1	1	..	2	..	1	..
Billings, Jonas	1	..	..	1	..	2	..	..	1	..	..
Blakesley, Polly	1	..	1	..	..	2	..	1	1	..	..
Bois, James	..	..	1	..	..	..	..	..	..	..	..
Bostwick, Caleb H.	..	..	..	1	..	..	..	1	..	..	..
Bostwick, Israel	1	..	..	..	1	..	1	..	1	1	..
Bragg, Henry	..	..	..	..	1	..	..	..	..	1	..
Brandy, Frederic	2	..	2	..	..	2	..	..	..	1	..
Brown, David	1	..	..	1	..	1	..	..	1	..	..
Bunce, John	1	..	..	1	..	2	..	..	1	..	..
Bunce, William	2	1	1	..	1	..	1	2	..	1	..
Carey, Oliver	2	..	..	1	..	2	1	..	1	..	..
Carl, Thomas	..	..	..	..	1	..	..	..	..	1	..
Carter, David	2	..	..	1	..	2	..	..	1	..	..
Chaffee, Azotus	..	..	1	..	..	1	..	1	..	..	..
Chaffee, Zebediah	..	..	..	..	1	..	..	2	..	1	..
Chapin, David	2	2	..	..	1	1	2	..	..	1	..
Chapin, Jacob	..	1	1	1	..	2	1	1	1	..	..
Church, Jonathan	2	2	..	1	..	3	..	1	1	..	..
Clarke, Andrew	..	..	..	1	..	4	1	..	1	..	..
Clarke, John	1	..	1	..	..	..	..	1	..	..	..
Clarke, Jonas	1	..	..	1	..	..	..	1	..	..	..
Clarke, Nathan	1	..	..	1	..	3	..	..	1	..	..
Clarke, Timothy	3	..	1	1	..	..	1	..	1	..	..
Coley, William	1	2	..	1	..	2	1	..	1	..	..
Colton, David	2	1	1	1	..	2	1	..	1	..	..
Converse, David	3	1	..	1	..	..	2	1	1	..	..
Converse, Samuel	2	..	..	1	..	2	..	1	..	..	..
Cornell, James	1	..	1	..	..	1	..	..	1	..	..
Coulton, Ephraim	1	1	..	1	..	3	..	..	1	..	..
Crane, Rachel	1	1	1	..	..	..	..	..	1	..	..
Cummings, John	..	..	1	1	..	2	..	..	1	..	..
Curtis, Amos	5	1	..	1	..	..	1	2	1	..	..
Curtis, Josiah	3	1	1	1	..	2	1	1	1	..	..
Daley, Jonathan	2	..	1	..	..	..	..	1	..	..	..
Danforth, Samuel	3	..	1	1	..	..	1	..	1	1	..
Darby, Eliab	..	2	2	..	1	..	1	..	..	1	..
Dewey, Cephas	1	..	..	1	..	1	..	1	..	..	..
Dewey, Cyrenus	1	1	1	..	1	3	1	1	1	..	..
Dewey, Hannah	..	..	..	..	..	..	..	..	..	1	..
Dewey, Pell	3	..	..	..	1	..	2	1	1	..	..
Dinsmore, Samuel	..	..	1	..	1	..	..	1	..	..	..
Dixon, Moses	1	1	..	1	..	..	1	1	..	..	..
Doanes, Levi	..	1	1	2	..	1	..	..	..	..	..
Doanes, Levi Jr.	..	..	2	..	..	1	..	1	..	..	..
Draper, John	3	..	..	1	..	1	..	1	..	..	..
Draper, Nathaniel	2	..	..	1	..	2	..	..	1	..	..
Dunham, Eber	..	..	..	1	..	1	..	..	1	..	..
Eastman, Enoch	3	2	3	..	2	2	2	1	1	..	..
Eastman, Stephen	3	2	..	1	..	3	..	1	1	..	..
Edee, Joseph	1	..	2	..	1	1	..	..	..	1	..
Edwards, Cyrus	2	..	..	..	1	2	1	..	1	..	..
Elwell, Harris	3	..	..	1	..	2	..	..	1	..	..
Elwell, Jesse	2	2	..	1	1	2	1	..	1	1	..
Farrar, Jonathan	..	..	1	1	1	..	1	..	..	1	..
Farrar, Jonathan Jr.	..	..	..	1	..	1	..	1	..	..	..
Ferguson, Samuel	3	..	..	1	..	3	..	..	1	..	..
Flowers, Roswell	1	..	2	1	..	2	..	1	..	..	..
Flowers, Timothy	..	..	..	1	..	..	1	..	..	..	..
Fox, Elijah	4	1	1	1	..	..	..	1	1	1	..
Fraker, Philip	2	2	1	..	1	4	1	2	..	1	..
Frara, Orange	4	1	3	1	..	..	1	1	..	1	..
Fuller, Minor	1	1	1	1	..	1	1	..	1	..	..
Galusha, Jonas	..	..	..	1	1	..	..	..	1	1	..
Geurnsey, Seth	..	1	..	1	..	..	1	..	1	..	..
Gillett, David	1	..	..	1	..	1	..	..	1	..	..
Googins, John M.	2	..	..	1	1	1	..	..	1	1	..
Googins, William	3	..	..	1	..	1	2	..	1	..	..
Goph, Caleb	4	1	..	1	..	..	1	3	1	..	..
Goph, Thomas	1	1	..	1	..	2	..	..	1	..	..
Graves, Allen	..	..	2	..	1	..	..	..	..	1	..
Graves, Cyrus	2	1	..	1	..	..	1	..	1	..	..
Graves, John	..	1	1	..	..	..	..	1	..	..	..
Graves, Joseph	2	..	..	1	..	..	..	..	1	..	..
Graves, Josiah	..	..	1	1	..	..	2	2	1	..	..
Graves, Samuel	3	2	2	..	2	3	1	..	1	1	..
Gray, Isaac	..	..	1	..	1	..	1	1	..	1	..
Gray, Lemuel	1	..	1	..	1	1	1	..	1	..	..
Green, David	2	1	..	1	..	2	1	2	1	..	..
RUPERT—con.											
Hamilton, Odadiah	3	..	..	1	..	1	1	..	1	..	..
Hannah, James	1	..	..	1	..	..	..	1	..	..	..
Harmon, Alpheus	2	..	..	..	1	1	1	2	..	..	..
Harmon, Amos	..	..	1	..	1	..	..	..	..	1	..
Harmon, Amos Jr.	3	..	..	1	..	..	1	..	1	..	..
Harmon, Ben	1	..	..	1	..	4	..	..	1	..	..
Harmon, Enos	1	1	1	..	1	..	1	1	..	2	..
Harmon, Nehemiah	1	..	2	..	1	2	2	..	..	1	..
Harmon, Seth	1	1	1	..	1	1	1	..	..	1	..
Harmon, Seth Jr.	..	..	1	..	..	..	..	1	..	..	..
Harwood, Perez	2	1	..	1	..	2	..	..	1	..	..
Harwood, Silas	2	..	..	1	..	..	1	..	1	..	..
Hastings, Jonathan	2	..	..	1	..	2	..	..	1	..	..
Hay, Joseph G.	2	1	2	1	..	..	..	2	1	..	..
Hays, Israel	2	1	2	..	1	..	1	1	..	1	..
Herriman, Jonathan	2	..	..	..	1	1	..	..	1	..	..
Hodge, Abel	..	1	..	..	1	..	..	..	1	1	..
Holcomb, Loami	3	..	1	..	..	..	..	1	..	..	..
Holcomb, Noah	..	..	1	..	1	..	..	..	..	1	..
Holton, Simeon	2	..	..	1	..	1	..	..	1	..	..
Hopkins, Mary	1	3	1	..	..	..	..	1	..	1	..
Hopkins, Samuel	1	..	..	..	..	1	..	..	..	1	..
Hopkins, Samuel	2	1	1	..	1	..	1	..	..	1	..
Hosford, Josiah	..	..	1	..	1	..	1	..	1	1	..
Hough, Justus	2	1	1	1	..	2	2	..	1	..	..
Huggins, Asher	..	1	1	1	..	..	..	1	..	..	..
Hunt, Seth	..	1	..	2	..	3	2	..	1	..	..
Hunt, Simeon	..	..	1	1	1	..	1	2	..	..	1
Ingersoll, Ebenezer	1	3	..	..	1	3	..	1	1	..	..
Jennings, Jonathan	2	..	..	1	..	2	..	1	..	..	..
Jennings, Simeon	..	..	1	..	1	..	..	..	..	1	..
Johnson, Levi	1	2	..	1	..	..	1	2	1	..	..
Johnson, Seth	2	1	..	1	..	2	..	..	1	..	..
Jones, Ephraim	..	1	..	..	1	..	1	..	..	1	..
Kellogg, Titus	2	..	1	1	..	2	..	1	1	..	..
Kenney, Asel	2	..	3	..	1	2	..	..	1	..	..
Kent, Abel	3	1	1	1	..	1	1	1	1	..	..
Kent, Samuel	2	1	1	2	..	1	2	1	1	..	..
Lackey, Simeon	2	..	..	1	..	3	..	1	..	..	..
Lamphere, Ezra	..	1	..	1	..	2	..	..	1	..	..
Leason, Nathaniel	1	..	..	1	..	2	..	1	..	..	..
Leavitt, Asaph	..	..	..	1	..	2	..	1	..	..	..
Leavitt, Eunice	..	..	..	..	..	..	..	1	..	..	..
Leavitt, Joseph	1	1	1	..	1	1	..	1	..	1	..
Leavitt, Samuel	..	..	1	1	..	1	1	..	1	..	..
Lesley, James	2	..	..	1	..	2	..	..	1	..	..
Leslie, Ben	..	..	1	..	..	1	..	1	..	..	..
Linnen, John	..	..	..	1	..	3	1	..	1	..	..
Loggan, John	..	..	..	..	1	..	..	..	..	1	..
Lynn, James	1	..	2	1	1	2	1	..	1	1	..
Martin, Martin	2	..	..	1	..	1	1	..	1	..	..
McChesney, John	4	..	..	1	..	..	2	..	1	..	..
McClary, William	2	..	3	..	1	1	3	1	1	..	..
McClenathan, Josiah	2	1	..	1	..	2	..	..	1	..	..
McClenathan, William	3	..	..	1	..	..	..	..	1	1	..
McCraken, Daniel	..	..	1	..	..	1	..	1	..	..	..
Moore, Grove	4	..	..	1	..	3	..	..	1	..	..
Moore, Jabez	1	1	..	1	..	..	..	..	1	..	..
Moore, James	1	..	1	1	..	1	3	1	1	..	..
Moore, Mary	1	1	..	..	..	1	..	..	1	..	..
Moore, Seth	..	..	1	..	..	..	..	1	..	..	..
Nelson, Calvin	1	..	..	1	..	1	..	..	1	..	..
Nelson, Daniel	1	..	..	..	1	1	1	1	..	..	..
Nelson, Daniel Jr.	1	..	1	..	..	1	..	1	..	..	..
Nelson, Isaac	1	..	..	1	..	1	..	..	1	..	..
Nelson, Moses	..	1	..	..	2	1	1	..	1	1	..
Nelson, Paul	1	2	2	..	1	2	..	..	..	1	..
Noble, David	..	1	..	..	1	1	..	..	..	1	..
Noble, Molly	..	..	..	..	..	..	1	..	..	1	..
Norton, Hosea	..	2	..	1	..	2	..	1	1	..	..
Norton, Joseph	4	1	..	1	1	1	..	2	..	1	1
Norton, William	2	..	..	1	..	2	1	..	1	..	..
Norton, Zadoc	1	1	1	1	..	1	..	..	1	..	..
Olds, Stephen	..	..	..	..	1	..	..	2	..	1	..
Parker, John	2	1	..	1	..	3	1	1	1	..	..
Phillips, Eliza	3	1	1	..	..	1	1	1	1	..	..
Phillips, Samuel	2	3	1	1	..	4	..	..	1	..	..
Pitcher, Nathan	3	..	..	1	..	1	..	..	1	..	..
Preston, John B.	1	..	1	..	..	..	..	1	..	..	..

BENNINGTON COUNTY—Continued

NAMES OF HEADS OF FAMILIES	FREE WHITE MALES: Under 10 years of age	FREE WHITE MALES: Of 10 and under 16	FREE WHITE MALES: Of 16 and under 26 including heads of families	FREE WHITE MALES: Of 26 and under 45 including heads of families	FREE WHITE MALES: Of 45 and upwards including heads of families.	FREE WHITE FEMALES: Under 10 years of age	FREE WHITE FEMALES: Of 10 and under 16	FREE WHITE FEMALES: Of 16 and under 26 including heads of families	FREE WHITE FEMALES: Of 26 and under 45 including heads of families	FREE WHITE FEMALES: Of 45 and upwards including heads of families	All other free persons except Indians not taxed
RUPERT—con.											
Randal, Josiah	..	..	1	..	..	..	..	1	..	..	..
Ransom, Daniel	3	..	1	1	..	2	..	..	1	..	..
Ransom, Moses	2	2	1	..	1	3	..	..	1	..	..
Ransom, Robert	1	..	..	1	1	..	..	1	..	..	..
Raze, Asahel	3	1	1	1	..	3	..	..	1	..	..
Reed, Daniel	..	..	2	..	1	..	..	1	..	1	..
Reed, Jonathan	1	..	..	1	..	2	..	..	1	..	..
Reed, Solomon	3	..	..	1	..	2	..	..	1	..	..
Remmington, Silas	1	..	3	..	..	2	..	1	..	1	..
Remmington, Thomas	3	1	..	1	..	1	..	..	1	..	..
Rising, Aaron	..	..	..	..	1	..	1	..	..	1	..
Rising, Jonah	1	1	..	..	1	1	1	..	..	1	..
Rising, Josiah	1	..	1	1	..	1	..	1	1	..	..
Rising, Simeon	1	..	..	1	..	2	..	..	1	..	..
Robinson, Moses	..	1	1	..	1	1	..	1	1	..	..
Rockwell, Josiah	1	..	..	1	..	1	..	..	1	..	..
Rogers, Isaac	1	1	..	1	..	..	1	..	1	..	..
Rogers, Zephaniah	..	1	..	1	..	3	1	..	1	1	..
Russell, Amasa	3	1	1	1	..	3	1	..	1	..	..
Russell, James	3	..	..	1	..	1	1	..	1	..	..
Sears, Elisha	..	..	1	..	..	..	..	1	..	..	..
Sears, Rachel	..	..	..	..	..	1	..	..	..	..	..
Shelden, Carlos P.	..	..	1	1	..	1	..	1	..	..	..
Shelden, Increase	1	1	..	1	..	2	..	1	1	..	..
Shelden, Isaac	1	1	1	..	1	2	..	1	1	..	..
Shelden, John	..	2	1	1	1	1	..	1	..	1	..
Shelden, John Jr.	1	..	..	1	..	1	..	..	1	..	..
Shelden, Moses	3	3	..	..	1	2	..	2	1	..	..
Shelden, Phinehas	1	..	..	1	1	1	..	2	..	1	..
Shelden, Reuben	..	..	2	..	1	2	2	..	..	2	..
Shelden, Seth	1	1	1	1	..	2	..	..	2	..	..
Sheldon, Asaph	..	2	..	1	..	..	2	..	3	..	..
Sheldon, David	2	3	4	1	..	1	1	1	..	1	..
Sheldon, Ezra	2	1	..	2	..	..	2	..	1	..	..
Sheldon, Joel	1	3	1	..	1	2	..	1	..	1	..
Sikes, Ashbel	2	1	1	1	..	1	1	1	1	..	..
Slater, John	..	..	..	..	1	..	..	2	..	1	..
Smith, Bohan	1	..	1	..	..	1	..	1	..	..	..
Smith, Calvin	2	..	..	1	..	1	1	..	1	..	..
Smith, Ebenezer	1	..	1	..	1	3	1	1	1	..	..
Smith, Enock	..	2	2	1	1	..	..	..	1	..	..
Smith, Stephen	1	..	2	1	..	1	..	1	1	..	..
Smith, Timothy	2	1	..	..	1	2	..	..	..	1	..
Smith, Truman	2	..	1	1	1	1	..	1	1	..	..
Soper, Jonathan	5	1	..	1	..	2	1	..	1	..	..
Southwell, Asahel	..	1	..	1	..	2	1	..	1	..	..
Spears, Nathaniel	..	2	..	1	..	..	1	..	1	..	..
Spencer, Jason	..	..	..	1	..	1	..	..	1	..	..
Spencer, Phinehas	2	..	1	1	..	2	3	..	1	..	..
Sprague, Abram	3	..	..	1	..	1	1	..	1	..	..
Stannard, Libbeus	3	1	1	1	..	2	..	2	1	1	..
Stanyard, Chauncey	..	..	1	..	..	..	..	1	..	..	..
Stanyard, Lemuel	..	..	..	..	1	..	1	2	..	1	..
Stebbins, Samuel	2	..	..	1	..	1	1	..	1	..	..
Stebbins, Selah	2	..	2	1	..	1	2	1	1	..	..
Stone, Moses	..	..	..	..	1	1	..	..	..	1	..
Stone, Putnam	..	..	1	..	..	1	..	1	..	..	..
Stone, Simon	..	..	1	..	..	..	..	1	..	..	..
Stutson, Caleb	..	..	1	2	..	2	..	1	..	..	..
Taylor, Joel	3	..	..	1	..	..	2	..	1	..	..
Teal, Samuel	..	..	..	..	1	..	..	..	..	1	..
Tenant, Rufus	3	..	..	1	..	2	..	..	1	..	..
Thomas, David	..	..	2	1	..	2	1	1	..	..	..
Thompson, John	1	1	..	1	..	3	..	..	1	..	..
Thompson, Joseph	..	1	1	..	1	1	..	..	..	1	..
Tousley, David	3	1	..	..	1	2	..	..	2	1	..
Tousley, David 2nd	2	..	..	1	..	2	..	..	1	..	..
Tousley, Hezekiah	1	1	1	1	..	..	2	1	1	1	..
Tousley, Nathaniel	1	..	1	..	1	1	..	..	..	1	..
Tousley, Thomas	2	..	..	1	..	2	2	1	1	..	..
Tousley, William	..	..	..	..	1	..	1	..	..	1	..
Tousley, William Jr.	1	1	..	1	..	5	..	..	1	..	..
Trumble, Alexander	..	..	1	..	1	..	3	..	..	1	..
Trumble, Horace	1	..	1	..	..	..	..	1	..	..	..
Trumble, Simeon	4	1	..	1	..	1	..	..	1	..	..
Tyrrell, Arad	1	..	1	..	1	1	2	1	..	1	..
Tyrrell, Thaddeus	..	..	1	..	..	..	..	1	..	..	..
Tyrrell, Timothy	1	..	..	1	..	1	..	..	1	..	..
Wade, Edward	2	1	..	..	1	1	2	..	..	..	..
Wade, Solomon	..	..	1	..	1	..	1	1	..	1	..
Walker, Gordon	4	..	..	1	..	..	..	..	1	..	..
Ward, Abner	4	2	..	1	..	1	2	..	1	..	..
Ward, William	2	..	..	1	..	2	..	..	1	..	..
Weaver, Jacob	..	..	..	..	1	1	..	..	..	1	..
Weaver, Jacob Jr.	2	..	..	1	..	2	..	..	1	..	..
Weed, Jehial	..	..	..	..	1	..	..	..	..	1	..
Weed, Jehial Jr.	2	1	..	1	..	1	1	1	1	..	..
Wheeler, Phinehas	2	1	..	1	..	2	1	1	1	..	..
Whitney, Asaph	1	..	..	1	..	1	..	1	..	..	..
Whitney, Caroline	..	..	..	..	..	1	1	..	1	..	..
Wilson, Eber	1	..	1	..	..	1	..	1	..	..	..
Wilson, Josiah	1	..	1	1	1	1	..	1	..	1	..
Wood, John	1	1	1	..	1	..	..	..	..	1	..
Wood, William	..	..	..	1	..	..	..	1	..	..	..
SANDGATE											
Bailey, John	2	..	..	1	..	1	..	..	1	..	..
Baker, Reuben	..	..	1	..	..	1	..	1	..	1	..
Beatie, Walter	..	..	1	..	..	..	..	..	..	..	..
Beers, Jabez	..	..	1	1	..	1	..	2	1	..	..
Bennett, Charles	..	1	..	..	1	..	..	..	..	1	..
Bennett, Silas	1	..	1	1	..	2	1	..	1	..	..
Birch, Nehemiah	2	1	3	..	1	1	..	1	1	..	..
Booth, Andrew	..	..	..	..	1	..	3	..	..	1	..
Bradley, James	..	1	..	..	1	1	1	..	..	1	..
Bradley, James Jr.	2	..	..	2	..	1	2	..	..	..	..
Bristol, Elnathan	1	..	..	..	1	1	..	1	..	1	..
Bristol, James	2	2	..	1	..	..	1	..	1	..	..
Bristol, Nathaniel	..	..	1	1	..	..	3	2	1	..	..
Brown, Asaph	2	..	..	1	..	1	1	..	1	..	..
Brown, Daniel	2	1	..	..	1	1	1	1	..	1	..
Brown, Ebenezer	1	2	1	..	1	3	1	..	1	..	..
Brown, Salmon	..	..	..	1	..	3	..	..	1	..	..
Bucke, Abel	2	1	..	..	..	1	2	..	1	..	..
Bunce, Joseph	3	..	..	1	..	..	..	1	..	..	..
Burke, Josiah	2	1	..	1	..	2	2	..	1	..	..
Burke, Richard	1	..	..	1	1	3	1	..	1	..	..
Burke, William	3	..	..	1	..	..	..	..	1	..	..
Burkingham, Andrew	..	..	..	..	1	..	2	1	..	1	..
Burns, William	2	..	..	1	..	2	..	..	1	..	..
Burt, Joshua	2	1	..	..	1	2	..	..	1	..	..
Cogswell, Daniel	..	..	..	1	..	2	..	..	1	..	..
Cogswell, Ferris	3	1	..	1	..	2	2	1	1	1	..
Cogswell, Joseph	1	..	..	1	..	2	..	..	1	..	..
Cogswell, Sally	2	..	..	..	1	1	..	..	1	..	..
Curtis, Hull	1	..	2	1	..	..	1	..	1	..	..
Davis, William	..	..	..	1	..	3	1	..	1	1	..
Dayton, Daniel	4	..	..	1	..	1	..	..	1	..	..
Dayton, Thomas	1	1	..	1	..	1	..	1	..	..	..
Dunning, Amos	2	..	..	1	..	3	1	..	1	..	..
Dunning, David	..	..	..	..	1	..	..	..	..	1	..
Dunning, Truman	2	1	..	1	..	3	..	..	1	..	..
Fairman, Joseph	1	..	1	..	1	..	2	..	..	1	..
Ferris, Aaron G.	1	..	1	1	..	1	..	1	..	..	..
Field, Francis	2	2	..	..	..	1	1	..	1	..	..
Fields, James	1	1	..	1	..	2	..	..	1	1	..
French, Alpheus	1	..	..	1	..	..	..	1	..	..	..
French, Micah	..	..	..	..	1	..	..	..	..	1	..
French, Micah Jr.	2	1	..	1	..	2	..	1	1	..	..
Frost, John	2	3	1	1	..	1	1	..	1	..	..
Halburt, James	1	..	1	..	..	2	..	..	1	..	..
Hall, Eleazer	..	..	..	1	..	2	1	..	1	..	..
Hall, Samuel	..	..	..	1	..	3	..	..	1	..	..
Hamilton, Alexander	..	..	2	..	1	..	..	1	..	1	..
Hamilton, James	..	1	1	3	1	..	..	2	..	..	..
Hamilton, James	2	..	..	1	..	1	1	1	..	1	..
Hamilton, James Jr.	..	..	..	1	..	..	..	..	1	..	..
Hamilton, Robert	..	..	1	..	..	..	..	1	..	..	..
Hamilton, Thomas	..	..	1	1	1	1	1	1	..	1	..
Hamilton, Thomas Jr.	2	..	..	..	..	..	..	..	1	..	..
Hard, Samantha	..	..	..	..	..	..	..	1	..	..	..
Harrington, Richard	4	1	..	1	..	2	3	1	1	..	..
Hazeltine, Simeon	1	..	1	..	1	..	..	..	..	1	..
Hopkins, Robert	3	1	1	..	1	1	1	1	1	..	..
Hoyt, David	..	2	..	..	1	2	3	1	1	..	..
Hurd, Abner	1	2	2	..	2	..	..	..	..	1	..
Hurd, Abram	1	..	..	1	..	1	..	1	..	..	..
Hurd, Adam	2	..	1	..	1	..	..	2	..	1	..
Hurd, Daniel	..	..	..	..	1	..	..	1	..	1	..
Hurd, Daniel	..	1	..	..	1	..	1	..	..	2	..
Hurd, Edward	2	1	1	..	1	1	1	..	1	..	..
Hurd, Eleazer	2	..	1	1	..	1	2	..	1	..	..
Hurd, Elijah	2	1	1	..	1	..	1	2	1	..	..
Hurd, Frederic	..	2	1	1	..	..	..	..	1	..	..
Hurd, Isaac	..	..	..	..	1	1	..	1	..	1	..
Hurd, James	1	1	..	1	..	2	..	..	1	..	..

BENNINGTON COUNTY—Continued

NAMES OF HEADS OF FAMILIES	FREE WHITE MALES					FREE WHITE FEMALES					
	Under 10 years of age	Of 10 and under 16	Of 16 and under 26 including heads of families	Of 26 and under 45 including heads of families	Of 45 and upwards including heads of families	Under 10 years of age	Of 10 and under 16	Of 16 and under 26 including heads of families	Of 26 and under 45 including heads of families	Of 45 and upwards including heads of families	All other free persons except Indians not taxed
SANDGATE—con.											
Hurd, John	1	1	..	..	1	1	2	2	1	..	4
Hurd, Jonathan	2	..	..	1	..	1	..	1	..	..	..
Hurd, Lewis	3	1	2	1	..	2	..	2	1	..	1
Hurd, Lovell	2	2	..	1	..	1	..	..	1	..	..
Hurd, Lyman	4	..	..	1	..	2	..	..	1	..	..
Hurd, Reuben	..	1	1	..	1	..	3	1	1	1	..
Hurd, Richard	..	1	3	..	1	..	2	..	..	1	..
Hurd, Theophilus	2	..	1	1	1	..	..	2	..	..	..
Hurd, Thomas	1	..	1	1	..	2	..	..	1	..	..
Hurd, Timothy	1	..	1	..	..	..	..	1	..	..	..
Hurd, Winds	3	..	1	1	..	..	..	..	1	..	..
Hurd, Zachariah	..	..	1	1	1	2	..	1	1	..	..
Husted, James	..	..	..	..	1	..	2	1	..	1	..
Johnson, James	2	..	..	1	..	..	..	1	..	..	..
Johnson, Joel	..	..	..	1	..	1	..	1	..	..	..
Johnson, Lyman	1	..	1	..	..	..	..	1	..	..	..
Johnson, Mathew	..	..	1	..	1	..	..	1	..	1	..
Jones, Lorin	..	..	..	..	..	..	1	..	..	1	..
Kelly, John	..	..	..	1	..	..	..	..	..	..	..
Kimberly, Abel B.	..	..	..	1	..	3	..	..	1	..	..
Knapp, James	..	1	..	1	..	..	..	..	1	..	..
Lacey, Ebenezer	..	..	..	..	1	1	2	..	1	..	..
Lakin, Robert	3	..	..	1	..	..	..	1	..	..	..
Lamb, Benjamin	2	2	..	..	1	1	1	1	1	..	..
Larkham, Thomas	1	..	..	1	..	3	..	..	1	..	..
Lucas, Samuel	..	..	1	..	1	..	1	..	1	..	..
Mallery, Isaac	..	1	2	..	1	..	..	1	..	1	..
McNaughton, Daniel	1	..	..	1	..	1	..	1	..	..	..
Meeker, Phinehas	1	..	..	1	1	2	..	..	1	1	..
Merrills, Chillion	..	..	2	..	..	..	..	1	1	..	..
Minor, Josiah	..	..	..	1	..	..	..	1	..	..	..
Morehouse, Ephraim	..	1	1	1	..	2	1	1	1	..	..
Morehouse, Wheelor	1	..	1	1	..	1	..	1	..	..	..
Munn, Hosea	1	..	1	..	..	..	..	1	..	..	..
Murdock, James	2	..	1	..	1	2	2	1	..	1	..
Nelson, Andrew	..	1	..	1	1	4	..	..	1	..	..
Nelson, David	1	..	..	1	..	..	..	1	..	..	..
Nichols, Charles	3	..	1	..	1	..	..	1	..	2	..
Norton, Martin	..	..	1	..	..	..	..	1	..	..	..
Oatman, John	1	..	..	1	..	1	..	1	..	..	..
Olds, David	1	..	..	1	..	1	..	1	..	..	..
Olds, Jacob	..	..	..	1	..	2	..	1	..	..	..
Patterson, Abel	..	..	1	..	..	..	..	1	..	..	..
Peck, George	..	1	3	..	1	..	1	1	..	1	..
Peck, Joel	..	..	..	1	1	..	..	1	..	1	..
Perkins, William	3	3	1	1	1	1	1	1	1	1	..
Perry, Ezekiel	1	..	..	1	..	2	1	..	1	..	..
Porter, William	..	..	..	1	..	2	..	..	1	..	..
Prindle, Nathan	..	..	3	..	1	..	..	..	..	1	..
Prindle, Zalmon	1	2	..	1	..	2	..	..	1	..	..
Ransom, Theophilus	2	1	1	..	1	..	1	..	1	..	..
Raze, Silas	1	..	1	..	..	..	..	1	..	..	..
Reed, Mathias	2	1	..	1	..	2	1	..	1	..	..
Rice, Mathew	1	..	1	..	1	1	..	1	..	1	..
Rice, Simeon	1	..	..	1	..	1	1	..	1	..	..
Richards, Thomas	..	..	2	1	1	..	..	2	..	..	..
Roode, Simeon	1	..	..	1	..	2	3	..	1	..	..
Sabel, Benjamin	2	1	1	..	1	1	1	..	1	..	..
Sanford, Clarke	..	..	..	1	..	1	..	..	1	..	..
Sanford, Ephraim	..	..	..	..	1	..	1	..	..	1	..
Sanford, Nathaniel	..	..	1	..	1	..	..	..	..	1	..
Sherman, Enoch	2	1	1	1	..	1	1	..	1	..	..
Skidmore, Daniel	1	1	..	1	..	3	1	..	1	..	..
Skidmore, James	3	1	..	1	1	..	..	1	1	..	..
Slaten, David	..	1	..	..	1	1	..	..	1	..	..
Smith, Daniel	2	..	..	1	..	2	1	..	1	..	..
Smith, Mathew	1	1	..	1	..	2	..	1	1	..	..
Squire, David	..	2	..	2	1	..	..	1	1	..	..
Squire, Heman	1	..	..	1	..	2	..	..	1	..	..
Squire, Joseph	..	..	..	1	..	2	..	..	1	..	..
Squire, William	..	..	..	1	..	1	..	1	..	..	..
Stillson, Abel	1	..	..	1	..	3	..	..	1	..	..
Stillson, Comfort	..	..	1	..	1	..	..	1	..	1	..
Stillson, Luther	2	..	..	1	..	1	..	..	1	..	..
Stoddard, David	..	..	..	1	..	..	..	..	1	..	..
Stoddard, Gideon	1	..	..	1	..	1	..	..	1	..	..
Stoddard, Jedediah	..	..	..	1	..	1	..	1	..	..	..
Thomas, Jacob	3	..	..	1	..	1	1	1	1	..	..
Thomas, Reuben	..	1	1	1	1	..	..	2	..	1	..
Torrance, Ezra	2	..	..	1	..	2	..	1	..	..	..
Torrance, John	1	..	..	2	..	..	1	..	1	..	..
Torrance, Lewis	..	..	1	..	..	..	1	..	..	..	..
Torrance, William	..	1	1	..	1	1	1	..	1	1	..
Tucker, Daniel	..	..	..	1	1	..	..	1	..	1	..
Tucker, Daniel Jr.	1	1	..	1	..	4	..	..	1	..	..
Tucker, John	3	2	..	1	..	1	..	..	1	..	..
Turrell, David	..	..	..	..	1	..	..	..	..	..	..
Tuttle, Amos	..	..	..	..	1	1	..	..	..	1	..
Tuttle, David	1	..	..	1	..	2	..	..	1	..	..
Tuttle, Joseph	1	..	1	..	..	..	1	..	..	..	..
Wakelin, Platt	2	1	..	1	..	2	1	..	1	..	..
Waklee, Henry	..	..	..	..	1	1	..	..	1	..	..
Warner, Eliphaz	..	1	..	..	1	..	..	2	..	1	..
Warner, William	..	..	..	2	..	1	..	1	..	..	..
Watkins, John	1	..	1	1	..	2	..	1	1	..	..
Watson, James	2	1	1	1	..	2	1	..	1	..	..
White, Timothy	3	1	1	..	1	..	1	..	..	1	..
White, Timothy Jr.	2	..	1	..	..	..	..	1	..	..	..
Wickes, Judah	2	1	1	..	1	1	2	2	1	..	..
Willar, Mathew	1	..	2	..	..	..	..	1	..	..	..
Willson, Delatus	..	..	1	..	..	..	..	..	..	..	..
Willson, Gilbert	1	..	..	1	..	3	..	..	1	..	..
Wolfe, Christian	2	1	..	1	..	2	2	..	1	..	..
Woodward, Alpheus	..	..	2	..	1	..	..	..	1	1	..
Woodward, Noah	..	..	2	1	..	..	..	1	..	1	..
Woodward, Noah	..	..	1	..	..	1	..	1	..	..	..
Woodward, Noble	2	..	..	1	..	3	..	..	1	..	..
Zweres, Daniel	..	..	1	..	..	2	..	..	1	..	..
SHAFTSBURY											
Ames, Jacob	..	..	..	1	..	4	..	..	1	..	..
Ames, Joseph	..	1	..	..	1	1	..	1	..	1	..
Ames, Nathaniel	3	..	..	1	..	1	..	..	1	..	..
Andre, Caleb	2	..	..	1	..	..	..	1	..	..	..
Andrew, John	1	1	..	1	..	2	..	..	1	..	..
Andrews, Isaac	1	..	4	..	1	..	..	1	1	2	..
Andrews, John	3	..	..	1	..	2	..	1	..	..	..
Antizle, Simon	2	..	..	1	1	1	1	2	..	1	..
Baggley, Elijah	1	..	..	1	..	..	..	..	1	..	..
Ball, Nehemiah	1	..	..	1	..	2	..	..	1	..	..
Bartlett, Joseph	4	1	..	1	..	..	..	..	1	..	..
Barton, Gardener	2	1	1	1	..	1	1	..	1	..	..
Barton, Richard	3	1	1	1	..	1	..	1	..	..	..
Bates, Arvin	2	..	1	1	..	2	..	1	1	..	..
Bates, Ebenezer	..	1	..	..	1	..	..	..	1	1	..
Bates, Ebenezer Jr.	2	1	..	1	1	..	..	2	..	..	..
Bates, Joshua	..	1	1	..	1	..	..	1	..	1	..
Bates, Nathan	..	..	..	1	..	1	..	..	1	..	..
Bates, Thomas	1	..	1	..	..	..	..	1	..	..	..
Beardsley, Levi	2	..	1	..	1	3	..	..	..	1	..
Bellknap, John	1	..	..	1	..	..	..	..	1	..	..
Bennett, Eleazer	..	..	1	..	..	1	..	1	..	..	..
Bennett, James	3	1	..	1	..	1	..	..	1	..	..
Bennett, Jediah	..	1	..	..	1	1	1	1	..	1	..
Bennett, John	..	..	1	1	..	1	..	1	..	..	..
Bennett, Joseph	1	1	..	1	..	3	..	..	1	..	..
Bennett, Libbeas	..	..	1	..	..	1	..	1	..	..	..
Blackmer, Jesse	2	..	..	1	..	..	..	1	..	..	..
Blakley, Abram	..	..	3	1	..	2	..	..	1	1	..
Blood, Caleb	..	1	1	..	1	..	..	2	..	..	..
Bloomer, Robert	..	2	..	..	1	..	..	..	..	1	..
Bottom, Ebenezer	3	..	..	1	..	2	..	..	1	..	..
Bottom, Elijah	..	..	..	..	1	..	..	..	..	1	..
Bottom, Pelatiah	..	..	..	..	1	..	..	1	..	1	..
Bottom, Simon	3	1	1	1	..	1	..	1	1	..	..
Bowen, Benjamin	2	1	..	1	..	2	..	..	2	..	4
Bowen, James	4	1	..	1	..	..	1	..	1	..	..
Bowen, Jennings	1	..	..	1	..	4	..	..	1	..	..
Briggs, John	2	2	1	..	1	1	..	1	1	..	..
Brown, Francis	2	..	..	1	1	1	..	2	..	..	..
Brown, James	..	1	..	1	..	1	1	..	1	..	..
Buck, John	2	1	2	..	2	1	..	2	1	1	..
Buel, Josiah	1	2	..	1	1	2	1	1	1	..	..
Burlinggame, William	1	1	..	1	..	2	1	..	1	..	..
Burnham, Asa	..	1	2	..	1	2	2	1	1	..	..
Burnham, Samuel	3	..	..	1	..	1	..	2	..	..	..
Burnham, William	2	..	..	..	2	1	..	..	..	1	..
Carpenter, Daniel	..	..	..	1	1	..	..	..	2	1	..
Carpenter, Hezekiah	2	..	..	1	..	1	..	..	1	..	..

BENNINGTON COUNTY—Continued

NAMES OF HEADS OF FAMILIES	FREE WHITE MALES: Under 10 years of age	FREE WHITE MALES: Of 10 and under 16	FREE WHITE MALES: Of 16 and under 26 including heads of families	FREE WHITE MALES: Of 26 and under 45 including heads of families	FREE WHITE MALES: Of 45 and upwards including heads of families	FREE WHITE FEMALES: Under 10 years of age	FREE WHITE FEMALES: Of 10 and under 16	FREE WHITE FEMALES: Of 16 and under 26 including heads of families	FREE WHITE FEMALES: Of 26 and under 45 including heads of families	FREE WHITE FEMALES: Of 45 and upwards including heads of families	All other free persons except Indians not taxed
SHAFTSBURY—con.											
Carpenter, Isiah	1	..	2	..	1	2	..	1	1	1	..
Carpenter, Oliver	..	1	..	1	..	2	..	..	1	..	..
Caulkins, John	1	2	..	1	..	3	1	..	1	..	..
Chase, Jeremiah	..	..	1	..	1	..	..	..	..	1	..
Church, Timothy	..	1	1	1	..	1	2	..	1	..	..
Clark, Ebenezer	3	1	1	1	..	2	..	2	..	..	..
Clarke, Jeremiah	1	..	2	..	1	..	..	3	..	1	..
Cobb, Matthias	..	1	2	..	..	..	..	1	1	1	..
Cole, Aaron	1	1	1	1	..	..	..	..	1	..	..
Cole, Benjamin	2	1	2	..	1	2	2	1	..	1	..
Cole, David	1	1	1	1	..	2	1	1	1	..	..
Cole, Parker	1	..	1	..	1	..	1	1	..	1	..
Cole, Peleg	3	1	3	1	..	2	..	2	1	..	..
Cole, Seth	1	..	1	1	..	3	..	1	1	..	..
Collins, James	..	1	..	1	..	1	1	1	..	1	..
Colman, Erastus	1	..	1	..	..	1	1	1	..	..	..
Colvin, David	1	1	..	1	..	3	..	1	1	..	..
Corey, Benjamin	..	..	..	..	1	..	..	..	..	1	..
Corey, Benjamin Jr.	3	..	2	..	1	1	1	..	1	..	..
Corey, David	1	..	..	..	1	3	1	..	2	..	..
Cornell, Benjamin	3	..	..	1	..	2	1	..	1	..	..
Cornell, Daniel	4	1	..	1	..	..	1	..	1	..	..
Coy, Joseph	3	..	..	1	..	1	..	..	1	..	..
Cross, Asa	1	..	1	..	..	..	..	1	..	..	..
Cross, Elihu	..	2	2	1	..	..	..	1	1	..	..
Cross, Ichabod	..	..	..	..	1	..	..	1	..	1	..
Cross, Samuel	1	..	4	1	..	3	..	2	1	..	..
Cutler, David	..	..	1	..	1	..	..	..	..	1	..
Daggett, Fanny	..	..	..	..	..	..	..	1	..	..	..
Dailey, Daniel	..	..	..	..	1	..	..	1	..	1	..
Daniels, Ezekiel	..	..	..	1	..	1	..	..	1	..	..
Davis, William	2	1	1	1	..	1	2	..	1	..	..
Day, Ralph	2	..	..	1	..	..	..	..	1	..	..
Denio, Aaron	2	2	..	1	..	2	..	..	1	..	..
Downer, John	..	2	3	..	1	..	1	2	..	1	..
Downer, Zipporan	1	2	1	..	1	..	..	2	..	1	..
Draper, Gideon	3	2	..	1	..	1	..	..	1	..	..
Draper, James	1	..	3	..	3	..	1	2	..	2	..
Draper, Nathan	1	1	1	1	..	2	2	..	1	1	..
Dwinell, Henry	1	..	1	..	..	1	..	1	..	..	..
Dwinell, Stephen	..	2	2	..	1	..	1	..	..	1	..
Dyer, Benjamin	..	1	1	..	..	..	..	1	..	..	..
Dyer, Charles	3	1	2	..	1	1	2	1	2	..	..
Dyer, Eliab	3	..	..	1	..	1	1	..	1	..	..
Dyer, Henry	1	1	..	1	..	2	1	..	1	..	..
Eaton, Richard	..	1	..	1	..	1	..	..	1	..	..
Edwards, Solomon	2	..	..	2	..	1	..	..	1	..	..
Elsworth, Russel	2	..	..	1	..	..	..	1	..	1	..
Elwell, Dearin	1	..	..	1	..	1	..	..	1	..	..
Elwell, Jabez	2	..	..	..	1	1	1	..	..	1	..
Elwell, Jude	3	..	..	..	..	..	1	..	1	..	..
Fanning, Thomas	1	2	1	1	..	1	..	..	..	1	..
Farnum, Reuben	2	1	..	..	1	1	..	1	1	..	..
Fay, Moses	..	..	..	1	..	1	..	1	..	..	..
Fish, David	..	..	1	..	..	..	..	1	..	..	..
Fisher, William	1	..	1	..	..	1	..	1	..	..	..
Fisk, Jeremiah	..	..	..	..	1	..	..	..	..	1	..
Fisk, Jeremiah Jr.	3	..	..	1	..	2	..	..	1	..	..
Fuller, Hosea	..	1	..	..	1	2	1	2	..	1	..
Fuller, Jacob	2	2	1	..	1	..	..	1	..	1	..
Fuller, John	3	1	1	1	..	2	1	..	1	1	..
Fuller, Solomon	2	..	1	..	1	..	2	..	1	..	..
Galloway, George	1	..	1	..	..	..	..	..	1	..	..
Galusha, Amos	1	..	2	..	1	1	1	..	1	1	..
Galusha, David	1	..	3	..	1	2	3	1	2	..	..
Galusha, David 2nd	3	2	..	1	..	1	1	..	1	..	..
Galusha, Jacob	..	1	2	..	1	..	1	2	..	2	..
Galusha, Jonas	1	3	2	..	..	1	1	3	..	1	..
Glass, Alexander	1	1	1	..	2	1	..	1	..	2	..
Gordeneer, John	2	..	..	1	..	2	..	..	1	..	..
Grant, Neverson	3	..	1	..	..	2	1	..	1	..	..
Green, Abner	1	1	..	1	..	1	1	..	1	..	..
Green, Asa	1	..	..	1	..	4	..	..	1	..	..
Green, Nathan	1	..	..	1	..	..	..	1	..	..	..
Gunn, Moses	..	1	..	1	1	3	..	1	1	..	..
Harding, James	2	2	..	..	..	1	1	1	..	1	..
Harpending, Andrew	..	1	..	1	..	..	1	1	1	..	..
Harrington, Abraham	2	2	..	1	..	2	..	..	1	..	..
Harrington, James	..	1	..	..	1	1	..	..	..	..	..
Harrington, Paul	1	..	2	..	1	1	1	1	..	1	..
Harrington, Paul Jr.	1	..	2	1	..	1	..	1	..	..	..
Harrington, Phinehas	..	..	..	1	..	..	..	1	..	..	..
SHAFTSBURY—con.											
Harrington, Squire	1	..	1	1	1	..	..	..	..	2	..
Harrington, William	2	1	..	1	..	3	..	1	1	..	..
Harris, Ebenezer	..	1	..	..	1	..	1	2	..	1	..
Harris, Nathan	2	..	..	1	..	1	..	..	1	..	..
Hawley, William	2	2	1	1	..	1	..	2	1	..	..
Heeling, Alexander	..	1	2	..	1	1	..	..	1	1	..
Hendee, Shubal	..	1	..	1	..	2	..	..	1	..	..
Hewet, Barnabas	..	1	..	1	..	2	2	..	1	..	..
Hibbard, Ahimaar	..	2	..	1	..	4	1	..	1	..	..
Holly, John	..	2	3	..	1	1	2	1	..	1	..
House, Abel	1	..	..	1	..	2	1	..	1	..	..
House, Samuel	..	2	1	..	1	..	1	2	..	2	..
Howard, Otis	..	1	..	1	..	1	..	1	..	..	..
Howlett, Samuel	..	1	..	..	1	2	..	..	..	1	..
Huling, John	1	..	1	1	..	..	..	1	1	..	..
Hunt, Ransom	2	..	..	1	..	2	..	..	1	..	..
Huntington, Amos	..	..	..	..	1	..	..	..	..	1	..
Huntington, Amos Jr.	3	1	1	2	..	1	..	1	1	..	..
Huntington, Daniel	..	..	2	..	..	2	..	2	..	..	..
Huntington, Elias	1	1	3	..	..	..	1	2	..	..	..
Huntington, Henry	..	..	1	1	..	2	..	1	1	..	..
Huntington, Jeremiah	1	2	1	..	1	..	1	1	..	1	..
Huntington, John	..	..	1	1	..	4	2	1	1	..	..
Huntington, Mathew	2	1	2	1	..	1	1	..	2	..	..
James, Samuel	..	..	..	1	..	1	1	..	1	..	..
Janes, Elisha	..	..	2	..	..	..	..	2	..	..	..
Johnson, Freeborn	3	1	..	1	..	1	..	..	2	..	..
Johnson, Jerusha	1	..	..	..	..	2	1	..	1	..	..
Jones, Josiah	..	2	..	..	1	3	1	1	1	..	..
Laurence, Biglow	1	1	2	..	1	..	2	2	..	1	..
Leister, Guy	2	1	..	1	..	1	..	..	1	..	..
Lewis, Peleg	3	1	..	..	1	4	1	..	1	..	..
Loomis, Russell	2	..	2	1	..	2	..	1	1	..	..
Luther, Amos	2	1	..	1	..	1	1	..	1	..	..
Luther, Elizabeth	..	..	1	..	..	..	..	1	..	1	..
Luther, Samuel	..	..	..	1	..	..	..	1	..	..	..
Mack, Joseph	..	..	..	1	1	..	..	1	1	..	..
Marble, Phillip	1	..	..	..	1	2	..	..	1	..	..
Martin, Aaron	1	..	..	1	..	1	1	..	1	..	..
Martin, Ebenezer	1	..	..	1	1	4	..	1	..	..	..
Martin, Mashier	..	..	..	..	1	..	..	..	..	1	..
Martin, Mashier Jr.	..	..	1	..	..	1	..	1	..	..	..
Mathews, David	..	1	2	..	1	2	3	1	..	2	1
Matteson, Abraham Jr.	..	1	1	..	1	2	1	..	1	..	..
Matteson, Abram	..	..	..	..	1	..	..	1	..	1	..
Matteson, Beriah	2	..	..	1	..	1	..	1	1	..	..
Matteson, Caleb	..	1	..	1	..	..	..	..	1	..	..
Matteson, Francis	2	..	..	1	..	1	..	..	1	1	..
Matteson, Francis	1	1	2	..	1	..	2	1	..	1	..
Matteson, Freeborn	1	..	1	..	..	..	..	1	..	..	..
Matteson, George	1	..	1	1	..	1	..	3	..	..	..
Matteson, Henry	2	1	2	1	..	1	2	1	1	..	..
Matteson, Hezekiah	2	..	..	..	1	1	1	..	1	..	..
Matteson, Jeremiah	..	1	1	..	1	..	..	..	..	1	..
Matteson, Johnson	1	1	1	..	..	1	..	1	..	..	..
Matteson, Peleg	..	2	2	..	1	1	..	1	..	1	..
Matteson, Peter	1	1	1	..	1	2	1	2	1	..	..
Matteson, Reuben	4	1	..	1	..	1	..	..	1	..	..
Matteson, Samuel	..	..	1	..	1	1	1	..	..	1	..
Matteson, Solomon	3	1	1	1	..	1	..	..	1	..	..
Matteson, Thomas	..	1	2	..	1	..	1	2	..	1	..
Matteson, Thomas	2	..	2	1	..	3	1	..	1	1	..
Matteson, Zerubbabel	..	1	4	..	..	1	..	2	..	1	..
McClean, Francis	..	..	1	..	..	1	..	1	..	..	..
McDonald, Jereniah	1	1	..	1	..	3	..	..	1	..	..
McGonegal, Dan	1	1	..	1	..	2	..	..	1	..	..
Meads, Israel	1	1	..	..	1	2	..	..	..	1	..
Millington, David	..	..	..	1	..	1	..	..	1	..	..
Millington, Samuel	1	1	2	..	1	1	2	1	1	..	..
Millington, Solomon	1	1	1	..	2	1	1	2	..	2	..
Mills, Solomon	3	..	..	1	..	1	..	..	1	..	..
Moore, Edward	3	..	..	1	..	1	..	..	1	..	..
Munroe, Archibald	2	..	1	1	..	2	..	1	1	..	..
Munroe, Joshua	1	1	2	1	..	5	..	1	1	..	..
Naper, Robert	4	1	..	..	1	1	2	1	1	..	..
Newton, Nathaniel	..	2	..	..	1	4	1	..	..	1	..
Nials, Ebenezer	..	..	..	1	..	1	1	1	..	..	..
Nials, George	..	1	2	..	1	..	1	..	1	1	..
Niles, Joseph	3	2	2	..	1	2	1	..	1	..	..
Olin, Ezra	4	1	1	..	..	1	..	..	1	..	..
Olin, Gideon	..	..	3	..	1	..	2	3	..	1	..
Olin, Giles	..	2	2	..	1	..	..	1	..	2	..

BENNINGTON COUNTY—Continued

Names of heads of families	Free white males: Under 10 years of age	Free white males: Of 10 and under 16	Free white males: Of 16 and under 26 including heads of families	Free white males: Of 26 and under 45 including heads of families	Free white males: Of 45 and upwards including heads of families	Free white females: Under 10 years of age	Free white females: Of 10 and under 16	Free white females: Of 16 and under 26 including heads of families	Free white females: Of 26 and under 45 including heads of families	Free white females: Of 45 and upwards including heads of families	All other free persons except Indians not taxed
SHAFTSBURY—con.											
Olin, Henry	1	1	1	..	..	1	..	1	..	..	..
Olin, John	..	..	2	..	1	..	..	1	..	1	..
Olin, John H.	..	..	..	1	..	2	..	1	..	..	..
Olin, Jonathan	..	1	1	..	1	1	1	..	..	2	..
Olin, Jonathan Jr.	1	2	1	1	..	4	1	..	1	..	..
Olin, Seth	..	..	..	..	1	..	..	1	1	1	..
Pierce, Clothier	..	..	..	..	1	..	..	..	..	1	..
Pike, Jabez	2	..	..	1	..	2	..	..	1	..	..
Potter, Casey	1	..	1	..	..	..	..	1	..	..	..
Powers, Aletta	1	..	..	..	..	1	..	..	1	..	..
Ransom, Newton	3	..	..	1	..	..	1	..	1	..	..
Rathburn, Amos	2	..	..	1	..	2	..	..	1	..	..
Rathburn, Benjamin	1	..	..	1	..	1	..	..	1	..	..
Reynolds, Lucius	..	..	1	..	..	2	..	..	1	..	..
Reynolds, Robert	..	..	..	..	1	..	..	..	..	1	..
Robinson, Nathan	2	1	..	1	..	1	..	..	2	..	..
Robinson, Samuel	2	..	1	..	..	1	..	..	1	..	..
Rogers, Ishmael	..	1	..	..	1	..	..	..	..	1	..
Rose, Rufus	2	1	..	..	1	2	1	1	1	..	..
Russel, Humphry	..	..	1	..	..	..	..	2	..	..	..
Sage, James	..	1	..	1	..	2	..	..	1	..	..
Sage, Jonathan	..	..	..	..	1	..	..	1	..	1	..
Sage, Jonathan Jr.	..	..	..	1	..	1	..	..	1	..	..
Salisbury, Daniel	3	1	1	..	1	1	1	1	1	..	..
Salisbury, Reuben	1	..	1	..	..	..	..	1	..	..	..
Sly, James	1	2	..	1	1	5	2	1	1	2	..
Smith, Benjamin	4	..	..	1	..	1	..	..	1	..	..
Smith, Daniel	..	1	1	1	1	..	..	..	..	1	..
Smith, Ebenezer	..	1	1	..	1	1	..	..	..	1	..
Smith, Gideon	..	..	3	..	1	..	..	..	..	1	..
Smith, Israel	1	..	1	..	1	2	1	1	..	1	..
Southard, Uriah	1	..	..	..	1	1	..	1	..	1	..
Spencer, Charles	2	1	3	..	1	..	1	2	2	1	..
Spencer, Isaac	..	..	..	..	1	..	1	..	..	1	..
Spicer, Dyer	..	..	..	1	..	1	..	1	1	1	..
Stanley, John	2	3	2	..	2	2	1	2	1	..	..
Steward, Leah	..	..	..	..	..	..	1	..	..	1	..
Stone, Nathan	2	..	1	..	1	2	1	1	..	1	..
Stover, Martin	1	..	1	..	..	..	..	1	..	..	..
Stratton, Jonathan	1	..	..	..	2	3	3	2	1	..	..
Sturdevant, John	..	..	1	..	1	..	..	..	..	1	..
Sturdevant, Samuel	..	..	1	..	..	..	..	1	..	..	..
Sturdevant, Steven	2	..	..	1	..	2	..	..	1	..	..
Sweett, James	1	1	..	1	..	2	1	1	1	..	..
Taylor, Jesse	..	..	1	1	..	2	..	2	..	..	..
Thompson, Aaron	..	..	2	..	..	..	..	1	..	..	..
Tinkham, Daniel	1	..	2	..	1	1	2	..	..	2	..
Trumbill, John	..	..	..	..	1	..	..	..	..	1	..
Vaughan, Colonel	2	..	..	1	..	2	..	..	1	1	..
Waite, Benjamin	1	..	1	..	..	1	..	1	..	..	..
Waite, John	2	..	..	..	1	2	1	1	..	1	..
Waite, Richard	..	1	..	..	1	..	1	..	..	1	..
Waite, Thomas	2	..	..	1	..	1	..	1	..	..	..
Waite, William	1	..	1	..	..	..	..	1	..	..	..
Waldo, Abiathar	..	..	2	..	1	..	..	1	..	1	..
Ward, Stephen	..	..	..	1	1	..	1	1	..	1	..
Warren, Thomas	..	1	..	..	1	..	..	2	..	1	..
Watson, Job	1	..	1	..	..	1	..	1	..	..	..
Watson, John	..	1	..	..	1	..	..	..	..	1	..
Weaver, Nichols	1	1	..	1	..	2	1	2	1	..	..
Webster, Rosswell	..	..	..	1	..	1	..	1	..	..	..
Welch, Ebenezer	..	..	..	..	1	1	..	1	..	1	..
Welch, Vine	1	..	2	..	..	..	..	1	..	..	..
Wheeler, Nathan	..	1	1	..	1	..	..	1	..	1	..
Wheelor, Prosper	1	1	..	1	..	..	1	..	1	..	..
Whipple, Oliver	2	..	2	1	..	..	1	..	1	..	..
White, Peregrine	1	1	1	..	1	1	1	..	1	1	..
Whitford, Peleg	..	..	1	..	1	..	1	1	..	1	..
Whitman, Jacob	1	..	..	1	..	1	..	1	..	..	..
Whitman, Valentine	2	..	..	..	1	..	..	2	..	1	..
Willcox, Asher	..	..	2	..	..	2	..	1	..	..	..
Williams, Mark	..	..	..	..	1	..	..	..	..	1	..
Willmarth, Ephraim	..	1	1	..	1	1	1	1	..	1	..
Willoughby, Bliss	1	..	1	..	1	..	1	..	..	1	..
Wood, Joseph	..	..	..	1	..	2	..	..	1	..	..
Wordan, Juda	..	2	..	1	..	1	1	..	1	..	..
Wordan, Rufus	4	1	..	1	..	2	1	..	1	..	..
Wright, Peter	1	..	4	..	1	..	1	1	..	1	..
UNCERTAIN NAME											
Brok (?), Francis	3	1	..	1	..	1	1	..	1	..	..
STAMFORD											
Annis, James	..	1	1	1	1	..	..	1	..	1	..
Baker, Mathew	4	..	..	1	..	1	..	..	1	..	..
Bell, William	1	..	..	1	..	2	..	..	1	..	..
Blake, David	1	..	..	1	..	1	..	1	..	..	..
Blake, James	2	1	..	..	1	1	1	..	1	..	..
Burlingam, Nathan	3	1	..	1	..	2	..	1	1	..	..
Carpenter, Ezekiel	..	..	..	1	..	1	..	1	..	..	..
Carpenter, Otis	3	..	..	1	..	2	1	..	1	1	..
Chafee, James	1	1	..	..	1	1	1	..	..	1	..
Clarke, William	..	..	1	..	..	..	1	..	..	..	..
Coles, Uriah	..	..	..	1	..	..	..	1	..	..	..
Cooke, Silas	..	..	..	1	..	3	..	1	..	..	..
Cooke, Timothy	..	2	..	1	..	3	..	1	1	..	..
Dean, Cybele	..	..	..	..	..	1	1	..	..	1	..
Eaton, Comfort	..	1	..	..	1	..	..	2	..	1	..
Farnum, Joshua	2	..	..	1	..	2	..	..	1	..	..
Farnum, Luther	1	..	..	1	..	1	..	..	1	..	..
Finney, Bethuel	2	1	2	2	..	2	2	1	1	..	..
Gardner, John	..	..	1	..	1	..	..	..	..	1	..
Gilmore, Abram	1	..	..	1	..	1	..	1	..	..	..
Gilmore, Robert	..	..	1	..	1	..	..	..	..	1	..
Gilmore, Robert Jr.	..	..	1	..	..	..	..	1	..	..	..
Goodell, Sylvester	1	..	..	1	..	..	..	..	1	..	..
Harris, Eleazer	1	1	2	1	..	1	1	1	1	..	..
Harris, James	3	..	..	1	..	3	1	1	1	..	..
Lashure, David	2	..	..	1	..	1	..	1	..	..	..
Mallery, Niram	2	..	..	1	..	4	2	..	..	1	..
Marvin, Jesse	3	1	..	..	1	..	..	..	1	..	..
Millerd, James	1	1	1	..	..	..	..	1	..	..	..
Millerd, Squire	1	..	2	..	1	1	1	1	..	1	..
Millerd, Stephen	2	..	..	1	..	2	1	2	..	..	..
Moore, John	..	..	1	..	1	..	..	1	..	1	..
Murray, Sanford	..	..	..	1	..	1	..	1	..	..	..
Nials, Jehiel	..	1	..	..	1	1	1	..	..	1	..
Norton, Abijah	..	..	..	..	1	..	1	1	..	1	..
Phetteplace, Resolved	1	..	..	..	1	..	..	..	..	1	..
Phetteplace, Zilah	..	..	..	1	..	1	..	..	1	..	..
Phillips, Zebedee	1	..	..	1	..	1	..	..	1	..	..
Rare, Benjamin	1	1	..	..	1	4	2	..	1	..	..
Raymond, Elisha	3	..	3	1	1	3	1	..	2	..	..
Rice, Daniel	..	1	..	..	1	..	..	..	..	1	..
Richmond, Edward	1	..	1	1	..	1	..	1	..	..	..
Robinson, Isaac	1	..	..	2	1	1	..	2	..	2	..
Sampson, Jacob	2	1	..	1	..	2	2	..	1	..	..
Smith, Aron	2	..	..	1	..	1	..	..	1	..	..
Smith, Elisha	1	1	..	..	1	..	..	..	1	..	..
Sprague, John	3	..	1	..	1	1	2	..	..	1	..
Stanford, Richard	..	..	2	..	1	..	..	1	1	1	..
Stark, Dyer	..	..	..	..	1	..	..	1	..	1	..
Stearns, David	4	1	1	2	..	3	2	..	1	..	..
Stephens, Shaw	..	..	..	..	1	..	..	..	..	1	..
Stephens, Simeon	1	..	..	1	..	..	..	1	1	..	..
Stoddard, Benjamin	..	..	1	..	1	..	..	1	..	..	..
Stowell, Calvin	3	..	1	1	..	1	..	..	1	..	..
Tucker, Nathan	..	..	1	1	1	..	..	1	..	1	..
Tupper, Benjamin	2	2	1	..	1	1	..	1	..	1	..
Tupper, Josiah	..	..	..	1	..	1	..	1	..	..	..
Turner, Else	1	..	..	..	..	..	..	1	..	..	..
Wallace, Samuel	..	..	..	1	1	..	1	..	..	1	..
Wescoat, Jeffery	..	..	1	..	..	2	..	1	..	..	..
Wescoat, Josiah	..	..	..	1	..	2	..	..	1	..	..
Wheeler, Valentine	3	1	..	..	1	..	..	..	1	..	..
Whipple, John	3	1	1	..	1	..	2	1	1	..	..
Whitney, Daniel	2	2	1	1	1	..	2	..	1	..	..
Whitney, Isaac	1	..	2	..	..	..	1	1	..	..	..
Whitney, Isaac	..	..	2	..	1	..	1	1	..	1	..
Willbur, William	..	2	..	..	1	..	2	..	..	1	..

BENNINGTON COUNTY—Continued

NAMES OF HEADS OF FAMILIES	FREE WHITE MALES					FREE WHITE FEMALES					
	Under 10 years of age	Of 10 and under 16	Of 16 and under 26 including heads of families	Of 26 and under 45 including heads of families	Of 45 and upwards including heads of families.	Under 10 years of age	Of 10 and under 16	Of 16 and under 26 including heads of families	Of 26 and under 45 including heads of families	Of 45 and upwards including heads of families.	All other free persons except Indians not taxed
SUNDERLAND											
Allen, Amos	..	..	..	..	1	..	..	..	1	..	..
Allen, Joseph	1	1	2	..	1	1	1	1	..	1	..
Annis, Jacob	..	1	..	1	..	..	..	..	1	..	..
Avery, Robert	3	..	1	1	..	..	2	1	..	1	..
Bacon, Amos	..	1	1	..	1	..	..	..	..	1	..
Bacon, Benjamin	3	1	..	1	..	..	1	..	1	..	..
Bacon, Daniel	2	1	1	..	1	..	1	..	..	1	..
Bacon, Priscilla	..	..	..	..	..	1	..	..	1	1	..
Barnum, Israel	2	1	..	1	..	2	2	..	1	..	..
Bartlett, Samuel	..	2	1	..	1	..	..	2	1	..	..
Bishop, Lemuel	4	1	..	..	1	..	1	3	1	..	..
Bois, Joseph	1	..	1	1	1	..	..	..	1	..	..
Bradley, Eathan	1	..	1	..	..	1	..	1	1	..	..
Bradley, Francis	..	1	1	..	..	1	..	1	..	..	..
Bradley, Gilbert	1	1	1	2	..	..	1	2	2	..	..
Bradley, John	..	..	..	..	1	..	..	..	..	1	..
Bradley, John F. M.	2	1	..	1	..	2	..	..	1	..	..
Bradley, John Jr.	1	..	..	1	..	1	..	1	..	..	..
Bradley, Joseph	..	..	..	1	1	..	..	..	..	1	..
Bradley, Lemuel	3	..	3	..	1	..	3	..	1	..	..
Bradley, Stephen	..	..	..	..	1	..	..	..	..	1	..
Brunson, Cornelia	..	..	..	..	..	..	..	1	1	1	..
Brunson, Elizabeth	..	..	2	..	..	..	..	1	..	1	..
Brunson, Isaac	2	..	..	1	..	1	2	..	1	..	..
Brunson, Nathan	1	2	1	1	..	..	..	..	1	1	..
Buck, Mathew	..	..	1	..	..	2	..	1	..	..	..
Caldwell, Charles	3	..	..	1	..	3	..	..	1	..	..
Cay, Daniel	..	2	..	..	1	..	..	1	..	1	..
Chipman, Amos	4	2	1	..	1	..	1	2	..	1	4
Chipman, Stephen	2	..	1	..	..	..	..	1	..	..	..
Durfey, Joshua	1	..	..	1	..	2	..	1	..	..	..
Everts, Charles	..	..	2	..	1	..	..	1	..	1	..
Everts, Edward	1	1	..	..	1	..	..	..	1	..	..
Ford, Rosswell	4	..	1	1	..	..	..	..	1	..	..
Godin, John	..	..	..	1	..	1	..	1	..	..	..
Graves, Edmund	2	..	..	2	..	1	..	..	2	..	..
Griffen, Benjamin	..	..	..	..	1	..	..	..	..	1	..
Griffen, Joseph	2	..	..	1	..	2	..	..	1	..	..
Hamilton, George	1	..	..	1	..	1	..	1	..	..	..
Harris, William	..	..	..	..	1	..	..	..	1	..	..
Hawkins, Abial	1	1	..	1	..	1	1	1	1	..	..
Hawkins, Ebenezer	1	..	..	1	..	2	..	..	1	..	..
Hawkins, Robert	..	..	..	..	1	..	..	..	..	1	..
Hicks, Simeon	1	1	2	..	1	2	1	..	1	..	..
Hickson, Samuel	..	..	1	..	1	1	..	2	..	1	..
Hill, Abner	..	1	1	..	1	..	..	..	..	2	..
Hill, Abner Jr.	..	..	1	..	..	..	..	1	..	..	..
Hill, Ezra	1	1	..	..	1	..	1	..	1	..	..
Holden, John	..	..	1	1	..	1	..	1	..	..	..
Howell, John	1	..	2	1	..	..	1	..	1	..	..
Hoyt, Samuel	..	..	..	1	..	2	..	1	..	..	..
Hoyt, Timothy	1	1	..	1	..	1	..	1	..	..	..
Jagger, Josiah	..	..	1	..	..	2	..	..	..	1	..
Judson, Andrew	1	..	..	1	..	2	..	..	1	..	..
Kenny, Benjamin	1	..	..	..	1	..	..	1	1	..	..
King, Caleb	2	..	..	1	..	1	1	..	1	..	..
King, Elisha	1	1	1	..	1	1	1	..	1	..	..
Landon, Elisha	1	1	..	1	..	2	..	..	1	..	..
Laurence, Friend Wickes	..	..	..	1	..	1	1	1	1	..	..
Lewis, Isaac	2	..	1	1	..	3	..	..	1	1	..
Lewis, John	..	..	..	..	1	2	..	..	1	..	..
Lewis, Jonathan	2	..	..	1	..	1	..	..	1	..	..
Lewis, Timothy	..	..	..	..	1	..	..	..	2	1	..
Lewis, Timothy Jr.	2	2	..	1	..	3	..	..	1	..	..
Lockwood, Josiah	1	1	1	2	..	..	2	2	1	..	..
Lothrop, Benjamin	1	..	2	1	..	1	1	1	..	..	..
Miles, Noah	..	1	3	1	..	3	1	..	1	..	..
Millin, Nathan	2	..	..	1	..	1	..	1	1	..	..
Millin, William	..	..	..	..	1	..	..	..	..	1	..
Mole, Joseph	3	..	..	..	1	..	..	..	1	..	..
Munn, Joseph	1	1	1	1	..	1	2	..	1	..	..
Parsons, Aaron	3	..	..	1	..	2	2	..	1	..	..
Parsons, Ephraim	3	..	..	1	..	1	..	..	1	..	..
Peck, Isaac	..	..	..	1	..	3	..	..	1	..	..
SUNDERLAND—con.											
Pike, Joseph	5	..	..	1	..	1	..	..	1	..	..
Porter, John	1	..	..	..	1	..	..	..	1	..	..
Sherwin, Jacob	..	..	1	..	1	..	..	..	..	1	..
Sherwin, Jacob Jr.	2	..	..	1	..	1	..	..	1	..	..
Sherwin, Moses Bartlett	2	..	..	1	..	1	..	1	..	..	..
Smith, Benjamin Y.	..	..	..	..	1	..	1	..	..	1	..
Smith, Isaac S.	1	..	..	1	..	1	..	..	1	..	..
Temple, Palmer C.	1	..	..	1	..	3	..	1	..	..	..
Thayer, Stephen	4	..	..	1	..	2	..	..	1	..	..
Varnum, Joseph	..	..	..	1	..	..	..	..	..	..	4
Waters, James	1	..	1	..	1	1	..	1	..	1	..
Webb, Reuben Jr.	3	..	..	1	1	..	1	..	1	..	..
Weeks, Andrew	..	..	..	1	..	..	1	..	1	..	..
Welch, Luke	1	1	..	..	1	1	..	1	..	1	..
Wellmon, Gideon	3	..	..	1	1	1	..	..	1	1	..
Whipple, Ezra	1	..	2	1	1	..	1	..	1	1	..
White, William	1	..	1	1	..	..	..	3	..	..	1
Williams, Caleb	3	1	..	1	..	1	..	..	1	..	..
Williams, Isaac	..	..	..	1	..	4	1	..	1	..	..
Williams, Joseph J.	..	..	..	1	..	2	..	1	..	..	..
Williams, Thomas	1	..	..	1	..	3	..	1	..	..	..
Withy, Jeduthan	3	2	..	1	..	2	..	..	1	..	..
Woolcott, Giles	..	1	..	..	1	..	..	..	..	1	..
WINHALL											
Barnard, John	1	..	..	1	..	2	..	..	1	..	..
Beebee, Asa	..	..	4	..	1	..	..	..	..	1	..
Beebee, Asa 2nd	1	..	..	1	..	..	..	1	1	..	..
Bogue, Thomas	..	..	..	1	..	2	..	..	1	..	..
Brainard, David	1	..	..	1	..	1	..	..	1	..	..
Brooks, John	1	1	..	1	..	..	1	2	1	..	..
Chubbuck, Job	1	..	..	1	..	2	..	..	..	1	..
Clark, John	..	1	1	1	..	1	..	1	..	..	..
Day, Ephraim	..	1	1	..	1	..	..	..	..	1	..
Day, Ephraim Jr.	2	..	..	1	..	..	..	1	..	..	..
Day, Oliver	3	1	..	1	..	3	1	..	1	..	..
Day, Russell	3	1	..	1	..	1	2	2	1	..	..
Dorance, William	..	..	..	1	..	4	1	..	1	..	..
Hale, Jacob	1	..	..	1	..	2	..	1	..	..	..
Hogaboom, Bartholomew	..	..	..	1	..	2	..	1	..	..	..
Hollis, Thomas	2	..	..	1	..	3	..	..	1	..	..
Kidder, Francis	..	..	..	1	..	3	..	..	1	..	..
Ledyard, Charles	3	1	..	1	..	..	1	1	1	..	..
Millin, James	..	..	1	..	..	..	..	1	..	..	..
Millin, Nathaniel	1	..	..	1	2	1	..	..	..	1	..
Rose, Joseph	2	1	..	1	..	..	..	..	1	..	..
Rose, Nathaniel	2	..	..	1	..	1	1	..	1	1	..
Snow, William	2	..	..	..	1	1	..	..	1	..	..
Sprague, Isaac	1	..	..	1	..	3	..	..	1	..	..
Sprague, John	..	..	1	..	1	..	..	..	1	1	..
Sprague, Jonathan	3	..	..	1	..	1	..	..	1	..	..
Sprague, Wyman	2	..	..	1	..	3	1	..	1	..	..
Taylor, Gershom	..	..	..	1	..	1	..	..	1	..	..
Taylor, Seth	..	..	1	..	1	..	..	..	..	1	..
Vail, Edward	4	..	..	1	..	..	..	1	..	..	..
Vail, Jonathan	..	..	1	1	..	..	..	1	..	..	..
Weatherby, Jonah	2	..	..	1	..	2	..	..	1	..	..
Wheeler, Aaron	2	1	1	1	..	..	2	..	1	..	..
Wheelor, Beriah	1	1	..	1	..	2	2	..	1	..	..
Williams, Isaac	2	1	..	1	..	4	1	..	1	..	..

BENNINGTON COUNTY—Continued

NAMES OF HEADS OF FAMILIES	Free white males: Under 10 years of age	Free white males: Of 10 and under 16	Free white males: Of 16 and under 26 including heads of families	Free white males: Of 26 and under 45 including heads of families	Free white males: Of 45 and upwards including heads of families	Free white females: Under 10 years of age	Free white females: Of 10 and under 16	Free white females: Of 16 and under 26 including heads of families	Free white females: Of 26 and under 45 including heads of families	Free white females: Of 45 and upwards including heads of families	All other free persons except Indians not taxed
WOODFORD											
Crosier, John	..	..	..	1	..	..	..	1	..	..	..
Danforth, Elkanah	1	1	..	..	1	..	1	..	1	1	..
Danforth, Jonathan	..	..	1	..	..	1	..	1	..	..	..
Diver, John	1	1	2	..	1	2	2	1	..	2	..
Edee, Obadiah	1	2	..	..	1	1	..	..	..	1	..
Ferguson, Hezekiah	..	..	..	..	1	2	1	1	1	..	..
Ferguson, John	1	..	1	..	..	..	..	1	..	..	..
Ferguson, Thomas	..	..	1	..	..	1	..	1	..	..	..
Frapwell, James	..	..	..	..	1	..	..	..	1	..	..
Harbower, John	..	1	..	..	1	..	..	..	1	..	..
Hill, John	..	..	..	..	1	..	..	..	..	1	..
Hill, Robert	1	1	..	1	..	1	1	..	1	..	..
Kibbee, Isaac	2	2	..	1	..	3	..	..	1	..	..
Knapp, Jabez	3	2	..	..	1	..	..	..	..	1	..
WOODFORD—con.											
Lyon, Spencer	2	..	..	1	..	1	2	..	1	..	..
Martin, Lemuel	2	..	..	1	..	1	..	..	1	..	..
Oliver, John	2	..	..	1	..	1	..	..	1	..	..
Orcutt, Samuel	..	1	..	1	..	..	..	..	..	1	..
Park, William	..	1	1	..	1	1	1	1	1	..	..
Perry, Elnathan	1	..	..	1	..	1	..	..	1	..	..
Perry, Oliver	..	..	..	3	1	2	..	..	1	1	..
Phelps, Paul	..	1	1	..	1	..	..	..	..	1	..
Pierce, Ely	1	..	..	1	..	1	..	1	..	..	..
Reed, Benjamin	2	2	..	..	1	2	..	1	1	..	..
Shoals, Ebenezer	..	..	..	1	..	2	..	1	..	..	..
Stacey, Samuel	..	..	..	..	1	..	..	..	..	..	..
Sybley, Zadoc	4	..	1	..	..	1	..	1	..	..	..

CALEDONIA COUNTY

NAMES OF HEADS OF FAMILIES	Free white males: Under 10 years of age	Free white males: Of 10 and under 16	Free white males: Of 16 and under 26 including heads of families	Free white males: Of 26 and under 45 including heads of families	Free white males: Of 45 and upwards including heads of families	Free white females: Under 10 years of age	Free white females: Of 10 and under 16	Free white females: Of 16 and under 26 including heads of families	Free white females: Of 26 and under 45 including heads of families	Free white females: Of 45 and upwards including heads of families	All other free persons except Indians not taxed
BARNET											
Abbercromie, Robert	4	2	..	..	1	..	2	1	1	..	..
Adams, William	1	..	..	..	1	..	..	..	1	..	..
Aiken, Samuel	4	..	..	1	..	..	3	..	1	..	..
Backup, John	..	..	3	..	1	..	..	..	..	1	..
Bailey, Jesse	..	..	1	..	..	..	..	2	1	..	..
Bailey, Moses	..	..	..	..	1	1	..	..	..	1	..
Baird, John	..	..	3	..	1	1	2	..	..	1	..
Ballock, William	1	1	1	..	1	..	..	1	..	1	..
Blair, Robert	2	3	..	..	1	2	1	..	..	1	..
Blake, Samuel	..	..	..	1	..	4	..	1	..	..	..
Bonnet, Joseph	..	1	..	1	..	4	..	1	1	..	..
Boynton, Isaac	1	2	..	1	..	1	2	..	1	..	..
Brock, Cloud	..	..	1	..	..	..	..	..	..	..	..
Brock, John	1	..	..	1	..	1	..	1	..	..	..
Brock, Robert	2	1	3	1	1	..	1	..	..	1	..
Brock, Walter	1	..	3	..	1	1	2	..	..	..	..
Buchanan, Alex	..	..	..	1	..	..	..	..	..	..	..
Buchanan, James	..	..	..	1	..	4	..	..	1	..	..
Buchanan, John	..	1	1	..	1	..	..	2	1	1	..
Calder, James	..	2	1	..	1	1	..	1	1	..	..
Carter, Olando	2	..	..	1	1	3	1	1	1	..	..
Cheeck, Nathaniel	2	..	..	1	..	1	..	..	1	..	..
Clerk, Thomas	..	..	1	..	1	..	..	..	..	..	..
Clifford, Jonathan	3	..	..	1	..	2	..	..	1	..	..
Cross, James	..	1	..	..	1	..	2	..	..	1	..
Cushman, Clerk	4	..	..	1	..	1	..	..	1	..	..
Cushman, Paul	..	..	..	..	1	..	1	..	..	1	..
Durrel, Lemuel	2	1	..	1	..	3	1	..	1	..	..
Elmsle, Alexander	..	..	..	..	1	..	..	..	..	..	..
Ferguson, James	..	..	1	1	..	..	..	1	..	..	..
Fowler, Jonathan	..	..	2	..	1	1	..	..	1	1	..
Fowler, Jonathan Jr.	1	..	..	1	..	1	..	..	1	..	..
Garland, George	..	..	..	..	1	..	1	2	..	1	..
Gibson, Widow	1	..	..	..	..	..	..	1	..	..	..
Gilchrist, James	5	1	..	1	1	..	..	..	1	1	..
Gill, Joshua	1	..	..	1	..	2	..	..	1	..	..
Gillfillin, John	..	..	1	..	1	2	..	1	2	..	..
Gillfillin, Robert	4	..	..	1	..	1	..	..	1	..	..
Gillfillin, Thomas	2	1	1	1	..	1	..	1	..	..	..
Gillfillin, William	..	1	..	1	..	1	..	..	1	..	..
Gillfillin, William Jr.	2	..	..	1	..	3	..	..	1	..	..
Gillkorson, John	..	..	3	..	1	..	..	2	..	1	..
Gilson, Abner	1	..	..	1	..	..	..	..	1	..	..
Gilson, Joseph	1	..	..	1	..	1	..	..	1	..	..
Gilson, Samuel	3	..	..	1	..	..	..	..	1	..	..
Goodwillie, David	1	..	..	..	1	2	..	..	1	..	..
Goodwillie, Joseph	2	..	..	..	1	2	2	..	1	..	..
Greenlief, Richard	1	..	..	1	..	1	..	1	..	..	..
Hall, Jacob	..	..	..	..	1	..	..	..	..	1	..
Hall, Moses	1	3	..	1	..	2	1	1	1	..	..
Harriman, John	3	1	..	1	..	2	..	..	1	..	..
BARNET—con.											
Harvey, Alexander	3	1	1	..	1	1	1	2	1	..	..
Harvey, Archbald	1	2	..	1	1	2	..	..	1	..	..
Harvey, Ira	1	..	1	1	2	..	..	2	..	..	..
Hazelton, Joseph	2	..	..	1	..	1	..	2	..	..	..
Hazelton, Thomas	1	1	1	1	..	4	..	..	1	..	..
Hazelton, Timothy	..	1	1	1	..	1	1	..	1	..	..
Henry, Joseph	..	1	..	..	1	1	1	..	..	1	..
Henry, Samuel	3	1	..	1	..	1	..	..	1	..	..
Hosmore, Rufus	1	..	..	1	..	..	..	1	..	..	..
Houghton, Samuel	1	1	..	..	1	..	1	..	..	1	..
Hurd, Tristram	..	1	..	..	1	..	..	..	..	1	..
Hyght, John	2	..	..	1	..	2	..	..	1	..	..
Hynman, John	..	..	2	..	1	..	1	1	..	1	..
Innes, William	..	..	..	1	..	..	..	..	..	..	..
Johnson, Obediah	..	..	..	..	1	..	..	..	1	..	..
Johnson, William	3	..	..	..	1	..	1	..	1	..	..
Kendall, William	..	..	1	..	1	..	..	..	..	1	..
Kendall, William Jr.	..	1	..	1	..	..	..	1	..	..	..
Kensley, William	3	..	..	1	..	2	..	..	1	..	..
Killy, John	1	..	..	1	..	2	..	..	1	..	..
King, Elijah	..	..	..	..	1	..	..	2	..	..	..
Lackey, Andrew	2	1	..	..	1	..	1	..	..	1	..
Laird, Robert	2	1	..	..	1	..	2	1	..	1	..
Lang, Alexander	2	..	..	..	1	3	..	..	1	..	..
Lang, Andrew	..	..	..	1	..	..	..	..	..	..	..
Lindsey, David	2	1	..	1	..	..	2	..	1	..	..
Manchester, Thomas	2	..	..	1	..	..	..	1	..	..	..
Maxwell, William	1	..	..	1	..	3	..	..	1	..	..
McCollum, John	1	..	..	1	..	3	..	..	1	..	..
McEndoe, John	..	..	2	..	1	..	..	..	..	1	..
McFavlin, John	..	1	2	..	1	..	2	..	1	..	..
McLallen, James	2	1	..	2	..	..	..	1	1	..	..
McLallen, John	1	2	..	..	1	2	1	..	1	..	..
McLallen, William	..	..	..	1	1	..	..	..	..	..	..
McLallen, William Jr.	1	1	..	1	..	..	1	..	1	..	..
McNabb, John	2	2	..	1	..	3	..	..	1	..	..
Meadow, Samuel	1	..	..	1	..	2	..	1	..	..	..
Moon, William	..	..	1	..	..	..	..	..	..	..	..
Moore, David	..	..	..	1	..	1	..	..	1	..	..
Moore, James	..	..	..	1	..	..	..	1	..	..	..
Moore, Samuel	..	..	3	1	1	..	2	1	..	1	..
Morrill, Nathaniel	1	..	1	..	..	1	..	..	1	..	..
Morse, John	2	1	..	1	..	3	..	..	1	..	..
Nevens, John	..	2	..	1	..	3	2	1	1	..	..
Nutter, Christopher	..	..	..	..	1	..	..	1	..	1	..
Nutter, Obediah	1	..	..	1	..	..	..	1	1	..	..
Orr, James	..	..	..	..	1	..	..	..	..	..	..
Pierce, Ephraim	..	..	1	..	..	1	..	..	..	1	..
Pierce, Simon	1	1	..	..	1	3	2	..	1	..	..

CALEDONIA COUNTY—Continued

NAMES OF HEADS OF FAMILIES	FREE WHITE MALES					FREE WHITE FEMALES					
	Under 10 years of age	Of 10 and under 16	Of 16 and under 26 including heads of families	Of 26 and under 45 including heads of families	Of 45 and upwards including heads of families.	Under 10 years of age	Of 10 and under 16	Of 16 and under 26 including heads of families	Of 26 and under 45 including heads of families	Of 45 and upwards including heads of families	All other free persons except Indians not taxed
BARNET—con.											
Reynolds, Enoch	3	1	1	..	1	..	1	1	1	..	..
Rider, Stevens	..	2	3	..	1	1	1	..	..	1	..
Rollins, Anthony	1	1	..	1	..	2	1	..	1	..	..
Ross, Hugh	..	..	3	..	1	..	..	..	..	1	..
Ross, John	..	..	1	..	1	..	..	..	..	1	..
Roy, Alexander	1	..	..	1	..	..	..	..	1	..	..
Russel, Reuben	1	..	..	..	1	..	1	..	..	1	..
Sanderland, James	2	..	..	1	..	1	..	..	1	..	..
Shaw, John	..	1	1	..	2	..	1	..	..	1	..
Shaw, William	4	..	1	1	..	..	1	..	1	..	..
Shearrer, William	..	1	1	..	1	1	1	..	..	1	..
Sheldon, Solomon	2	..	..	1	..	2	..	..	1	..	..
Sommers, Bartholomew	1	1	2	..	1	2	..	2	..	1	..
Sommers, Bartholomew 2nd	..	..	1	..	..	..	..	..	..	..	..
Sommers, Bartholomew 3rd.	..	..	1	..	..	..	..	..	..	..	..
Sommers, Cloud	..	1	1	1	2	..	..	1	..	1	..
Sommers, Cloud Jr.	4	..	..	1	..	2	..	..	1	..	..
Stevens, Enos	3	1	2	..	1	1	..	..	2	..	..
Stevens, John	1	..	..	1	..	1	..	..	1	..	..
Stevens, Widow	1	2	..	..	..	2	..	1	1	..	..
Stevenson, William	..	..	1	..	1	..	..	..	..	..	..
Stewart, Alexander	4	..	1	1	..	..	1	..	1	..	..
Stewart, Cloud	..	..	..	..	1	..	1	..	..	1	..
Stewart, James	3	..	1	1	1	2	1	..	1	..	..
Stiles, Caleb	..	..	..	..	1	..	..	..	..	1	..
Stiles, Caleb Jr.	4	1	..	1	..	2	1	..	1	..	..
Stiles, George	5	..	..	1	..	1	1	..	1	..	..
Stocker, John	..	..	1	1	..	1	..	..	1	..	..
Straw, Moses	3	1	..	1	..	1	2	..	1	..	..
Sutton, John P.	3	..	..	..	1	..	1	..	..	1	..
Taylor, Ezra	2	..	..	1	..	..	..	..	1	..	..
Thirstin, Josiah	..	..	2	1	..	1	..	..	1	..	..
Twadel, Robert	..	1	..	..	1	..	..	1	..	1	..
Waddel, John	1	..	..	..	1	..	..	..	3	..	..
Waddel, John Jr.	1	..	..	1	..	2	..	..	1	..	..
Wallace, John	1	..	..	1	..	2	..	..	1	..	..
Warden, William	1	1	1	1	1	1	..	1	1	1	..
Warden, William Jr.	..	..	1	..	..	..	..	..	..	..	..
Watson, Peletiah	..	..	..	..	1	..	..	..	..	1	..
Way, John	..	..	1	..	1	1	..	..	1	..	..
Wells, Paul	2	2	..	..	1	2	1	..	1	..	..
Welly, Bray	1	..	1	..	..	2	..	..	1	..	..
Wesson, Aaron	4	..	..	1	..	1	2	..	1	..	..
Wilson, Silas	3	2	1	1	..	3	1	1	1	..	..
Wood, John	3	2	1	1	..	3	1	1	1	..	..
Wood, Joseph	1	..	1	1	1	1	..	1	..	..	..
Wood, Stephen	2	1	..	..	1	..	1	..	1	..	..
Woolcot, Emerson	..	1	1	..	1	..	..	1	..	1	..
Wright, Abiather	2	..	..	1	..	..	..	..	2	..	..
UNCERTAIN NAME											
Chooelo (?), David	1	..	..	1	..	..	..	..	1	..	..
BILLYMEAD											
Adams, Abner	..	1	..	1	..	2	2	..	1	..	..
Anthony, John	1	..	..	1	..	2	..	..	1	..	..
Atwood, Jesse	2	..	..	1	..	..	..	..	1	..	..
Atwood, John	3	..	..	1	..	1	..	1	1	..	..
Atwood, Peter	2	..	2	..	..	3	..	..	1	..	..
Bacon, James	1	1	1	1	..	3	2	..	1	..	..
Bean, David	2	..	..	1	..	1	..	..	1	..	..
Blake, Enoch	..	2	3	..	1	1	..	..	..	1	..
Blake, Samuel D.	2	..	..	1	..	..	..	..	1	..	..
Bowley, Benjamin	1	..	..	1	..	..	..	..	1	..	..
Brewer, Moses H.	2	..	..	1	..	2	..	..	1	..	..
Cahoon, James	1	1	..	..	1	1	..	..	1	..	..
Cahoon, Samuel	3	1	..	1	..	..	..	1	..	..	..
Calley, Jonathan	..	..	..	1	..	1	..	..	1	..	..
George, Daniel	..	..	..	1	..	1	..	1	..	..	..
Horr, Joshua	..	..	1	2	..	..	..	..	1	..	..
Ladd, John	1	..	..	1	..	..	..	1	..	..	..
Leonard, Charles	..	..	..	1	..	1	..	..	1	..	..
Masefield, Eliphalet	..	..	1	..	1	..	..	..	..	1	..
Norris, David	1	..	..	1	..	3	..	..	1	1	..

NAMES OF HEADS OF FAMILIES	FREE WHITE MALES					FREE WHITE FEMALES					
	Under 10 years of age	Of 10 and under 16	Of 16 and under 26 including heads of families	Of 26 and under 45 including heads of families	Of 45 and upwards including heads of families.	Under 10 years of age	Of 10 and under 16	Of 16 and under 26 including heads of families	Of 26 and under 45 including heads of families	Of 45 and upwards including heads of families	All other free persons except Indians not taxed
BILLYMEAD—con.											
Orcutt, Ephraim	1	..	1	..	..	1	..	1	..	..	..
Orcutt, Samuel	..	1	2	..	1	1	1	1	..	1	..
Richardson, Bradbury	2	1	..	1	..	1	1	..	1	..	..
Richardson, Joseph	2	..	..	2	..	1	..	..	1	..	..
Sanborn, Jethro	3	1	1	..	1	1	1	..	..	1	..
Wasborn, Jeremiah	2	..	..	1	..	2	..	1	..	..	..
UNCERTAIN NAME											
Manfield (?), Eliphalet	..	..	1	..	1	..	..	..	..	1	..
BURKE											
Barber, William	1	..	..	..	1	..	..	1	..	1	..
Boynton, Ammi	..	..	..	1	..	..	..	1	..	..	..
Brokway, John	2	..	..	1	..	2	..	..	1	..	..
Coe, Abner	1	1	..	1	..	1	2	..	1	..	..
Hall, Daniel	1	1	..	..	1	2	..	..	1	..	..
Hicks, Peleg	..	..	1	..	1	..	..	1	..	1	..
Humphrey, Abel	..	..	..	1	..	2	..	..	1	..	..
Leach, John	1	..	..	1	..	2	..	..	1	..	..
McMullin, Ephraim	..	..	..	1	..	..	..	..	1	..	..
Mosses, Reuben	2	1	..	1	..	2	2	..	1	..	..
Nichols, Joshua	1	..	..	1	..	1	..	..	1	..	..
Spencer, Ranney	2	..	..	1	..	..	..	1	..	..	..
Thurber, Barnabas	3	..	..	1	..	1	..	..	1	..	..
Walter, Daniel	2	..	2	..	1	1	..	..	1	..	..
Walter, John	2	..	3	..	1	1	..	1	..	1	..
Walter, Jonathan	1	..	1	1	..	..	..	..	1	..	..
Walter, Lemuel	..	..	..	..	1	..	..	..	..	2	..
Walter, Norris	..	..	1	..	..	1	..	1	..	..	..
Warren Joshua	1	..	1	..	..	..	..	1	..	..	..
Wilder, Zebina	2	..	..	1	..	2	..	..	1	..	..
Woodruff, John	..	..	..	1	..	..	..	1	..	..	..
Woodruff, William	..	..	1	..	1	3	..	1	1	1	..
CABOT											
Adkins, Reuben	4	1	..	1	..	..	1	..	1	..	..
Beardsley, Gershom	1	..	1	..	1	1	2	..	2	..	..
Beardsley, Horrace	..	1	1	1	..	1	..	..	1	..	1
Blanchard, Joseph	3	1	..	1	..	2	..	..	1	..	..
Bruce, John	1	..	..	1	..	1	..	1	..	..	..
Burnum, Nathan	..	..	1	..	..	1	..	1	..	..	..
Butler, James	3	1	2	..	1	..	..	1	1	..	..
Carr, Peter	1	..	1	..	..	..	..	1	..	..	..
Clark, Reuben	1	..	..	1	..	1	..	1	..	..	..
Clark, Stephen	3	1	..	1	..	1	..	..	1	..	..
Coburn, Alepheus	1	2	2	1	..	2	..	..	1	..	..
Coburn, Clement	..	..	1	..	1	..	1	1	..	1	..
Coburn, Elihu	..	..	..	1	..	..	..	1	..	..	..
Covill, Phillip	1	2	1	..	1	2	1	..	1	..	..
Cross, Joseph	2	2	..	2	..	3	1	1	1	..	..
Durgin, Abraham	1	1	..	1	..	2	1	1	1	..	..
Eastman, James	..	..	..	2	..	2	..	..	1	..	..
Edgerton, John	1	2	1	1	..	3	1	1	..	1	..
Fisher, Joseph	2	..	..	2	..	1	..	..	1	..	..
Gunn, Nathan	..	..	2	..	1	..	1	..	..	1	..
Heath, Dearborn	1	..	..	1	..	..	1	..	1	..	..
Heath, Levi	2	..	..	1	..	1	..	..	1	..	..
Hichcock, Elias	1	..	..	1	..	1	..	1	..	..	..
Hichcock, Lyman	2	1	..	..	1	1	..	..	1	..	..
Hill, Isaac	..	..	1	1	..	1	..	1	..	..	..
Hills, Amos	1	..	..	1	..	2	..	1	..	..	..
Hodsdon, Samuel	1	..	..	1	..	4	..	..	1	..	..
Hoit, Enoch	2	..	..	1	..	2	..	1	..	..	..
Huntoon, Joseph	..	..	1	..	1	..	..	2	..	1	..
Huntoon, Joseph Jr.	..	..	..	1	..	2	..	1	..	..	..
Kinerstone, Samuel	..	..	..	1	..	..	..	..	..	..	..

CALEDONIA COUNTY—Continued

NAMES OF HEADS OF FAMILIES	FREE WHITE MALES: Under 10 years of age	FREE WHITE MALES: Of 10 and under 16	FREE WHITE MALES: Of 16 and under 26 including heads of families	FREE WHITE MALES: Of 26 and under 45 including heads of families	FREE WHITE MALES: Of 45 and upwards including heads of families	FREE WHITE FEMALES: Under 10 years of age	FREE WHITE FEMALES: Of 10 and under 16	FREE WHITE FEMALES: Of 16 and under 26 including heads of families	FREE WHITE FEMALES: Of 26 and under 45 including heads of families	FREE WHITE FEMALES: Of 45 and upwards including heads of families	All other free persons except Indians not taxed
CABOT—con.											
Laird, John	2	1	..	1	..	4	1	2	1	..	..
Lyford, David	3	..	..	1	..	1	..	1	..	..	..
Lyford, Fifield	1	..	..	1	1	3	1	..	1	..	..
Lyford, John	2	..	..	1	..	..	..	1	..	..	..
Lyford, Thomas	..	..	..	..	1	1	..	1	..	1	..
Lyford, Thomas Jr.	3	..	..	1	..	..	..	..	1	..	..
Marsh, Ephraim	..	..	2	..	1	..	..	1	..	1	..
Morse, James	1	..	..	1	1	..	..	..	..	1	..
Orcutt, Widow	..	..	1	..	..	..	1	1	..	1	..
Osgood, Amasa	..	..	..	1	..	1	..	..	1	..	..
Osgood, Joshua	..	1	..	1	..	..	..	1	..	..	..
Osgood, Levi	3	..	..	1	..	1	..	..	1	..	..
Osgood, Solomon W.	..	..	1	..	..	1	..	1	..	..	..
Osgood, Thomas	..	2	..	1	..	5	2	..	1	..	..
Osgood, William	..	..	2	..	1	..	1	..	..	1	..
Page, Nathan	4	1	..	1	..	..	1	1	1	..	..
Perry, Anthony	..	..	1	1	..	..	..	1	..	..	..
Reed, John	..	..	..	1	..	..	..	1	..	..	..
Rogers, Anson	..	..	1	..	..	1	..	1	..	..	..
Scott, Pearley	2	..	..	1	..	2	..	..	1	..	..
Seeley, Bradley	1	..	..	..	1	2	1	..	1	..	..
Spillen, John	2	..	..	1	..	1	1	..	1	..	..
Stone, Mathias	1	..	..	1	..	2	..	..	1	..	..
Stone, Moses	1	..	..	1	..	2	1	..	1	..	..
Underhill, Joseph	..	..	..	1	..	1	1	1	..	..	..
Walbridge, Oliver	3	..	..	2	..	2	..	..	1	..	..
Warner, Samuel	2	1	..	..	1	3	..	..	1	..	..
Webster, Benjamin	..	..	1	..	1	..	..	1	..	..	..
Webster, Nathaniel	3	1	1	..	1	1	1	1	..	1	..
Whitier, John	1	1	..	1	..	1	..	..	1	..	..
CALAIS											
Abbot, William	..	1	1	..	..	1	..	..	1	..	..
Ainsworth, Moses	..	..	1	..	1	..	1	1	..	1	..
Albert, Stephen	2	..	..	1	..	3	..	..	1	..	..
Beatis, John	..	..	..	1	..	2	..	..	1	..	..
Beckwith, Joshua	4	1	..	1	..	1	1	1	1	..	..
Bliss, Aaron	..	..	..	1	..	1	..	1	..	..	..
Bliss, Abdial	..	1	1	..	1	..	..	1	..	1	..
Bliss, Alpheus	..	1	1	1	..	3	..	..	1	..	..
Bliss, David	1	..	..	1	..	4	..	..	1	..	..
Bliss, Frederick	3	2	..	1	..	3	..	..	1	..	..
Bliss, Joshua	3	2	..	1	..	1	1	1	1	..	..
Bliss, Joshua 2nd	1	1	..	1	..	2	..	..	1	..	..
Bliss, Noah	..	..	..	1	..	4	..	..	1	..	..
Carpenter, Daniel	2	..	..	1	..	1	..	1	..	..	..
Clark, Noah C.	1	..	..	1	..	..	..	1	..	..	..
Cumins, Jonas	1	..	..	1	..	..	..	1	..	..	..
Curtis, Caleb	1	..	..	1	..	1	..	..	1	..	..
Dagget, David	..	..	1	..	..	1	..	1	..	..	..
Danforth, Samuel	..	..	..	1	..	..	..	1	..	..	..
Davis, Phinehas	3	..	..	1	..	2	1	..	1	..	..
Davis, Salmon	4	1	..	1	..	1	..	..	1	..	..
Davis, Simon	2	..	3	1	..	1	2	..	1	..	..
Done, Elisha	3	..	..	1	..	2	..	..	1	..	..
Eddy, Jonathan	..	..	..	1	..	3	..	1	..	..	..
Emerson, John	1	..	..	1	..	3	..	..	1	..	..
Fay, Jedediah	..	..	..	1	..	1	..	1	..	..	..
Fay, Samuel	..	..	..	1	..	..	..	..	..	..	..
Fuller, David	1	1	..	..	1	1	2	..	1	..	..
Goodall, David	2	..	1	..	..	..	2	..	1	..	..
Goodenough, Ebenezer	1	1	2	1	..	2	..	1	1	..	..
Green, Rufus	3	2	..	1	..	2	..	..	1	..	..
Haskel, Moses	3	..	..	1	..	1	1	..	1	..	..
Hathaway, Elnathan	..	..	..	1	..	2	..	1	..	..	..
Hathaway, Silas	..	..	1	..	1	..	1	1	..	..	..
Hathaway, Thomas	..	..	..	1	..	1	..	..	1	..	..
Howland, Widow	2	..	..	..	..	1	1	..	1	..	..
Janes, Solomon	1	1	1	..	1	1	1	2	1	..	..
Jenins, Amos	..	..	..	1	..	..	..	..	2	..	..
Jenins, James	..	..	1	..	..	1	..	1	..	..	..
CALAIS—con.											
Kendal, Isaac	..	..	..	2	..	2	2	..	1	..	..
Kent, Remember	1	..	..	1	..	1	..	1	..	..	..
Lamb, Aaron	..	..	1	..	1	..	..	1	..	..	..
Lebarron, Frances	1	1	..	1	..	3	..	..	1	..	..
Lilly, Joshua	2	..	1	1	..	2	..	1	1	..	..
Marsh, Jason	2	..	1	2	..	1	..	..	1	..	..
Merrit, Job	1	2	2	..	1	..	1	1	1	..	..
Parmer, Gershom	..	..	..	1	..	2	..	..	1	..	..
Parmer, Oliver	1	..	1	1	..	2	1	..	1	..	..
Pierce, Ashel	1	..	..	1	..	..	..	..	1	..	..
Pierce, Noah	1	..	1	2	..	..	..	1	..	..	..
Pope, Winslow	1	..	..	1	..	2	..	1	..	..	..
Robertson, Joel	1	..	..	1	..	1	..	1	..	..	..
Short, Shubal	2	1	2	1	..	3	2	..	1	..	..
Slayton, Jesse	2	1	1	1	..	3	1	1	1	..	..
Slayton, Simeon	1	..	..	1	..	1	..	..	1	..	..
Sprague, James	2	..	..	1	..	..	2	1	1	..	..
Stewart, Ethel	4	1	..	1	..	1	..	..	1	..	..
Thayer, David	..	..	2	..	1	..	2	1	..	1	..
Thomas, John	..	..	..	1	..	..	..	..	..	..	..
Tobey, Loath	2	..	..	1	..	3	..	..	1	..	..
Tucker, Edward	3	1	..	1	..	2	..	..	1	..	..
Tucker, Jonathan	..	..	..	2	..	..	..	2	..	..	..
Whelock, Abijah	2	1	..	1	..	2	2	..	1	..	..
Whelock, Asa	..	1	1	..	1	..	..	..	..	1	..
Whelock, Gideon	..	..	1	1	..	2	..	1	1	..	..
Whelock, Goddard	1	..	..	1	..	1	..	1	..	..	..
Whelock, Jenison	1	..	..	2	..	2	..	..	1	..	..
Whelock, Peter	2	1	..	..	1	2	4	..	1	..	..
White, Elijah	..	..	..	1	..	1	..	1	..	..	..
White, Samuel	3	1	..	1	..	2	1	2	1	..	..
Wilbar, Holden	..	1	2	1	..	1	..	..	1	..	..
Willis, Edmund	..	..	..	..	1	..	2	1	1	1	..
Wright, Levi	1	..	1	1	..	..	..	1	..	..	..
Young, Duncan	1	1	1	..	1	3	1	..	1	..	..
DANVILLE											
Amsden, Adam	1	..	1	1	..	1	2	..	1	..	..
Babbet, Uri	1	1	..	1	..	2	..	..	1	..	..
Bacheldor, David	4	1	..	1	..	..	1	3	..	..	..
Bacheldor, Jerathmel	1	..	2	..	1	..	1	1	..	1	..
Bacheldor, Joseph	2	..	..	1	..	2	..	..	1	..	..
Bacheldor, Josiah	2	2	..	..	1	2	1	..	1	..	..
Bacheldor, Josiah Jr.	..	..	1	..	..	..	..	1	..	..	..
Bacheldor, Samuel	..	1	..	1	..	3	2	..	1	..	..
Bacheldor, Timothy	2	2	..	1	..	2	..	..	1	..	..
Baldwin, John	1	..	1	3	..	2	..	2	1	..	..
Barker, John	..	..	..	..	1	..	..	..	..	..	..
Barnes, Benjamin	..	..	..	1	..	2	..	..	1	..	..
Barnes, David	..	..	1	..	..	..	..	1	..	..	..
Barnes, George	..	..	2	..	1	1	1	1	1	1	..
Beedey, Joshua	..	..	..	1	..	4	..	..	1	..	..
Bickford, Aaron	1	..	..	1	..	1	..	..	1	..	..
Bickford, Eli	1	1	1	..	1	3	1	1	1	..	..
Blanchard, Peter	..	..	..	1	..	1	2	..	1	..	..
Blanchard, Thomas	3	1	..	1	..	1	2	..	1	..	..
Blunt, Ephraim	..	1	3	..	1	4	2	1	..	1	..
Blunt, Jeremiah A.	..	1	2	1	..	..	1	..	1	1	..
Bowers, Jerathmel	2	..	..	1	..	2	..	..	1	..	..
Bowers, Oliver	2	1	..	1	..	..	..	..	1	..	..
Bradley, Philemon	..	..	3	..	1	..	..	..	..	1	..
Brainard, Asa	1	..	..	1	..	1	..	1	..	..	..
Branard, Israel	..	1	1	..	1	..	1	2	..	1	..
Brown, Samuel	1	..	..	1	..	2	..	..	1	..	..
Canfield, Benjamin P.	1	..	..	1	..	2	..	1	1	..	..
Carr, Timothy	1	1	2	1	1	..	..	..	..	1	..
Chamberlain, Daniel	3	1	..	1	1	..	1	..	1	1	..
Chamberlin, Caleb	1	..	..	1	..	1	..	..	1	..	..
Chamberlin, James	2	1	..	1	1	1	..	..	1	1	..
Chamberlin, John	3	..	..	1	..	1	..	..	1	..	..
Chamberlin, Samuel	2	..	2	..	1	..	..	4	..	1	..
Chesley, Nathaniel	1	2	1	1	..	2	2	..	1	..	..
Clarck, Eli	1	..	..	1	..	1	..	..	1	..	..
Clements, William	2	..	1	1	1	2	2	1	1	..	..
Clifford, John	3	2	..	1	..	..	1	..	2	..	..

CALEDONIA COUNTY—Continued

NAMES OF HEADS OF FAMILIES	FREE WHITE MALES					FREE WHITE FEMALES					
	Under 10 years of age	Of 10 and under 16	Of 16 and under 26 including heads of families	Of 26 and under 45 including heads of families	Of 45 and upwards including heads of families.	Under 10 years of age	Of 10 and under 16	Of 16 and under 26 including heads of families	Of 26 and under 45 including heads of families	Of 45 and upwards including heads of families	All other free persons except Indians not taxed
DANVILLE—con.											
Colby, Thomas	2	1	..	..	1	1	2	..	1	..	..
Cook, Charles	1	..	..	1	..	3	..	1	1	..	..
Crossman, Samuel	4	..	..	1	..	1	..	..	1	..	..
Crown, Jesse	1	..	1	..	1	..	..	1	..	..	..
Dane, Frances	2	1	1	..	1	..	2	..	1	..	..
Danforth, Jonathan	2	..	3	..	1	1	1	1	..	1	..
Danforth, Jonathan Jr.	1	..	..	1	..	1	..	1	..	..	..
Daniels, John	1	..	..	1	..	1	2	..	1	..	..
Daniels, Samuel	1	..	2	..	1	..	..	1	..	1	..
Daniels, Samuel Jr.	4	..	1	1	..	..	1	2	1	..	..
Daniels, Solomon	4	1	..	1	..	1	2	..	1	1	..
Daniels, Stephen	..	..	1	..	..	2	..	1	..	..	..
Davenport, Squire	1	1	..	1	..	2	1	..	1	..	..
Davis, Dudley	..	3	..	..	1	..	1	1	..	1	..
Davis, Mitchel	..	1	1	..	1	1	2	..	..	1	..
Deming, Benjamin	1	1	1	1	1	1	1	1	1	..	..
Dore, Samuel	1	..	..	1	..	3	..	..	1	..	..
Dow, Isaac	..	..	..	1	..	1	..	1	..	..	..
Dow, Richard	1	..	..	1	..	2	..	..	1	..	..
Dow, Thomas	1	..	1	..	1	1	1	2	..	1	..
Dow, Thomas Jr.	5	..	..	1	..	1	..	..	1	..	..
Drew, Francis	..	..	..	1	..	..	..	..	..	..	..
Dunbar, David	1	1	2	3	..	3	..	..	2	..	..
Durgin, Elijah	2	..	..	1	..	2	..	2	..	..	..
Edgely, James	3	1	1	1	..	3	2	1	1	..	..
Edgely, Jonathan	3	..	..	1	..	2	..	1	1	..	..
Ela, Samuel	..	..	..	..	1	..	2	2	1	..	..
Eliott, John	1	..	..	1	..	1	1	..	..	1	..
Eliott, Nathaniel	2	..	..	1	..	..	..	..	1	..	..
Eliott, Samuel	1	..	..	1	1	1	..	1	..	1	..
Emerson, Amos	2	..	..	1	..	2	..	1	..	..	..
Emerson, Cyrus K.	..	..	..	1	..	..	..	..	1	..	..
Emerson, Jonathan	2	..	..	1	..	1	1	..	1	..	..
Farley, Ebenezer	..	..	..	1	..	1	..	1	..	..	..
Farley, Joseph	1	..	1	..	..	..	..	1	..	..	..
Farley, Samuel	2	1	..	..	1	1	1	1	..	1	..
Farley, Samuel Jr.	..	..	..	1	..	2	..	..	1	..	..
Fitch, John	..	..	1	1	..	1	1	2	..	..	..
Flint, Abraham	..	..	1	..	..	..	..	1	..	..	..
Flint, Simeon	..	..	..	1	..	3	..	..	2	..	..
French, William	1	..	..	1	..	..	..	1	..	..	..
Fry, Ezekiel	1	..	..	1	..	2	..	1	1	..	..
Fry, Peter	1	..	1	1	..	..	..	..	1	..	..
Fry, Reuben	2	..	..	1	..	1	..	..	1	..	..
Fuller, Nathan	..	1	..	1	..	..	..	..	1	..	..
Fuller, Samuel	..	..	..	..	1	..	..	..	..	1	..
Gardner, Thomas	2	..	1	1	1	1	2	..	1	..	..
Gibb, John T.	2	2	1	..	1	..	..	2	..	1	..
Glines, James	1	..	..	1	..	4	..	..	1	..	..
Glines, Nathaniel	..	..	2	..	1	..	1	..	..	1	..
Glines, Richard	1	..	1	..	1	1	1	..	1	..	..
Goodwin, William	1	..	..	2	..	..	..	..	..	1	..
Gooken, Daniel	2	1	..	1	..	..	..	1	..	..	..
Gordan, Joseph	..	..	1	..	1	1	..	..	..	1	..
Green, Edmund	..	..	1	2	1	1	..	1	..	1	..
Green, William Jr.	..	..	..	1	..	1	..	1	..	..	..
Griswold, William A.	1	..	..	2	..	1	1	1	..	..	..
Hall, John	1	1	..	1	..	3	..	1	..	..	..
Hardy, David	2	1	..	..	1	..	1	1	..	1	..
Hardy, David Jr.	..	..	1	..	..	..	..	1	..	..	..
Harrington, Leonard	..	..	1	..	..	..	..	1	..	..	..
Harris, Timothy	..	..	2	1	1	..	..	2	..	1	..
Harris, Timothy Jr.	2	..	..	1	..	1	..	..	1	..	..
Hartshorn, Widow	2	..	2	..	..	2	2	1	1	..	..
Harts, Nathaniel	..	..	..	1	..	1	..	1	..	..	..
Harvey, David	2	1	..	1	..	2	..	..	1	..	..
Harvey, Ezra	1	2	..	..	1	..	..	..	..	1	..
Haveland, Benjamin	1	1	3	..	1	..	1	..	..	1	..
Hawley, Samuel	2	..	..	..	1	1	..	..	1	..	..
Heath, Amos	2	..	..	1	..	2	..	..	2	..	..
Heath, Simon	1	..	..	1	..	2	..	1	1	..	..
Herren, James	3	..	..	1	1	1	..	1	1	..	..
Herren, Thomas	..	1	2	..	1	1	2	..	..	1	..
Hill, John	1	..	1	1	..	..	..	..	2	1	..
Hill, Thomas	3	..	1	1	..	2	1	..	1	..	..
Howard, Ephraim	2	..	..	..	1	2	3	..	1	..	..
Hoyt, Thomas	1	..	..	1	..	3	..	..	1	1	..
Hull, Joseph	3	..	..	1	..	1	..	..	1	..	..
Humphrey, Ephraim	3	1	1	1	..	3	..	..	1	..	..
Ingalls, Timothy	1	1	..	1	..	1	1	..	1	..	..
Johnson, David	..	..	..	1	1	..	1	1	..	1	..
Johnson, Robert	..	..	..	1	..	1	..	.	1	1	..
Kelly, James	..	..	..	1	1	..	..	..	..	1	..
Kelsey, James	4	1	1	2	..	1	..	1	1	..	1
Kemp, John	1	1	..	1	..	2	1	..	1	..	..
Kimball, Isaac	3	..	..	1	..	..	..	1	..	..	..
Kitridge, Ezra	2	..	..	1	..	2	..	..	1	..	..
Kitridge, James	2	..	..	1	..	3	..	..	1	..	..
Kitridge, Samuel	1	..	..	1	..	..	..	..	1	..	..
Kitridge, Samuel Jr.	1	..	..	1	..	..	..	..	1	..	..
Lane, Daniel	3	..	..	1	..	1	..	..	1	..	..
Langmaid, Samuel	..	..	..	1	..	1	..	..	..	1	..
Langmaid, Solomon	..	..	..	1	..	2	..	1	..	..	..
Langmaid, Stephen	5	..	..	1	..	..	..	..	..	2	..
Larken, George	1	..	..	1	..	5	..	..	1	..	..
Lawrance, George	..	..	3	..	1	..	2	1	..	1	..
Leavenworth, Jesse	..	..	1	..	1	..	..	2	..	1	..
Leavenworth, Jesse Jr.	1	..	..	1	..	3	..	..	1	..	..
Little, William	3	1	..	1	..	..	1	2	1	..	..
Magoon, Ephraim	..	1	1	1	..	..	1	..	1	..	..
Mansur, Daniel	..	..	..	1	..	1	..	2	..	..	..
Mansur, Joseph	1	..	..	1	..	..	..	..	1	..	..
Marsh, Samuel	3	1	..	1	..	1	..	..	1	..	..
Mathews, Joseph	3	..	..	1	..	..	..	..	1	..	..
McLane, Donald	2	..	..	..	1	3	2	1	1	..	..
Mears, Oliver	3	1	..	1	..	2	..	..	1	..	..
Miles, William	3	1	1	..	1	2	..	..	1	..	..
Moffatt, Joseph	2	1	..	3	..	1	..	2	..	..	..
Morrill, Abel	1	..	2	1	1	1	..	1	..	1	..
Morrill, Ephraim	3	..	..	1	..	..	..	1	1	..	..
Morrill, Isaac	2	2	..	1	..	2	1	..	1	..	..
Morrill, Jacob	1	..	1	1	..	..	..	..	1	..	..
Morrill, Jeremiah	2	..	3	..	1	..	..	1	1	..	..
Morrill, Jonathan	1	..	..	2	..	2	..	..	1	..	..
Morrill, Joseph	2	1	1	..	1	2	1	1	1	..	..
Morrill, Paul	2	..	3	..	1	1	1	1	..	1	..
Morrison, Daniel	2	..	..	1	..	..	..	..	1	..	..
Morrison, John	2	2	..	..	1	2	1	2	..	1	..
Morse, Oliver	1	..	..	1	..	1	..	..	1	..	..
Nicholas, Robert	..	2	1	..	1	1	1	..	..	1	..
Nichols, Charles	1	..	..	1	..	2	..	1	1	..	..
Page, Ebenezer	1	..	..	..	1	3	..	1	..	..	..
Page, Edward	..	..	..	1	..	..	..	1	1	..	..
Page, Peter	2	..	..	1	..	3	..	..	1	..	..
Peck, Peter	1	..	..	1	..	..	..	1	..	..	..
Pell, James	1	1	..	1	..	1	1	..	1	..	..
Petingill, Edmund	1	..	..	1	..	3	..	..	1	..	..
Pope, Eleazer	1	1	2	1	..	..	2	..	1	..	..
Pope, Joseph	1	..	..	1	..	1	..	..	2	..	..
Porter, Elijah	1	..	3	..	1	1	1	2	..	1	..
Preston, Benjamin	..	..	1	..	1	4	..	1	..	..	..
Quimby, Daniel	3	..	1	..	1	1	1	..	1	..	..
Quimby, Eliphalet	1	1	..	1	..	3	1	..	1	..	..
Randal, Israel	..	2	1	..	1	..	1	1	..	1	..
Randal, Israel Jr.	2	..	..	1	..	3	..	..	1	..	..
Randal, Thomas	1	..	2	..	..	..	..	2	..	..	..
Rankin, John	1	..	1	1	..	3	..	2	..	..	..
Richardson, David	4	..	..	1	..	4	..	..	1	..	..
Rogers, Isaac	..	..	1	..	..	..	..	1	..	..	..
Rogers, Joseph	..	1	1	..	1	..	1	1	..	1	..
Root, Curtis	..	..	1	..	..	..	..	1	..	..	..
Root, John	1	..	..	1	..	1	1	1	..	..	..
Russell, Ebenezer	3	1	..	1	..	2	..	..	1	..	..
Russell, Jedediah	1	..	..	1	..	..	..	1	..	..	..
Russell, Jethro	2	1	..	1	..	3	..	1	..	..	..
Russell, Stephen	..	..	2	..	1	1	1	1	..	1	..
Rust, John	2	..	..	1	..	2	..	..	1	..	..
Sabin, Lewis	3	1	..	1	..	2	..	1	1	..	..
Samborn, Jonathan	1	..	..	1	..	..	..	..	1	..	..
Sargeant, Christopher	2	2	2	2	1	1	1	..	1	..	..
Sawyer, Ebenezer	..	..	..	..	1	..	..	..	..	1	..
Sawyer, Ebenezer 2nd	..	..	2	1	..	..	..	1	..	1	..
Senter, David	1	..	..	..	1	..	1	..	..	1	..
Senter, David Jr.	1	..	1	..	..	1	..	2	..	..	..
Sheldon, Jonathan	..	1	..	..	1	..	1	1	..	1	..
Short, John	..	..	1	..	2	..	..	1	..	1	..
Short, John Jr.	2	..	..	1	..	1	1	..	1	..	..
Sias, Benjamin	1	..	..	1	..	2	..	1	..	..	..
Sias, Charles	..	..	5	..	2	1	..	2	..	1	..

CALEDONIA COUNTY—Continued

NAMES OF HEADS OF FAMILIES	FREE WHITE MALES: Under 10 years of age	FREE WHITE MALES: Of 10 and under 16	FREE WHITE MALES: Of 16 and under 26 including heads of families	FREE WHITE MALES: Of 26 and under 45 including heads of families	FREE WHITE MALES: Of 45 and upwards including heads of families.	FREE WHITE FEMALES: Under 10 years of age	FREE WHITE FEMALES: Of 10 and under 16	FREE WHITE FEMALES: Of 16 and under 26 including heads of families	FREE WHITE FEMALES: Of 26 and under 45 including heads of families	FREE WHITE FEMALES: Of 45 and upwards including heads of families	All other free persons except Indians not taxed
DANVILLE—con.											
Sias, Jeremiah	..	..	..	1	..	..	..	1	..	..	..
Sias, Nathaniel	..	..	..	1	..	2	..	..	1	..	..
Sias, Widow	..	1	3	..	..	..	1	..	..	1	..
Silver, Abraham	..	..	..	1	..	..	..	..	..	1	..
Sincler, David	1	..	..	1	..	2	..	..	1	..	..
Sincler, Joseph	2	1	..	1	..	3	..	..	1	..	..
Sleeper, Hezekiah	..	..	..	1	..	2	..	1	..	..	..
Smith, Daniel	..	..	..	1	..	..	..	..	1	..	..
Smith, Jabez	..	1	..	1	..	..	..	1	..	1	..
Smith, Joseph	1	1	..	1	..	3	..	..	1	..	..
Stevens, James	2	..	1	..	..	1	..	..	1	..	..
Stevens, John	3	..	..	1	..	..	..	..	1	..	..
Stevens, Joshua	4	..	..	2	..	..	..	..	1	..	..
Sweesey, Dudley	..	1	1	1	..	3	..	..	1	..	..
Sweesey, Joseph	..	1	1	..	..	1	..	1	..	..	..
Swett, Luke	..	..	..	..	1	..	2	..	1	..	..
Swett, Samuel	1	..	..	1	..	2	..	1	..	..	..
Thorn, Thomas	..	..	..	1	..	3	..	..	1	..	..
Tilton, David	..	1	1	1	..	4	..	..	1	..	1
Tilton, Joseph	1	..	1	..	1	1	1	..	..	1	..
Tole, Jacob	..	..	..	1	..	..	..	1	..	..	..
Truswell, Jacob	2	1	3	..	1	2	1	1	1	..	..
Underwood, Phinehas	1	2	..	1	..	..	..	..	1	..	..
Varnum, Benjamin	3	2	..	1	..	2	..	1	1	..	..
Ward, Aaron	..	..	..	1	..	2	..	1	..	..	..
Watson, Benjamin	1	1	..	1	1	..	..	3	..	1	..
Watson, James Jr.	2	..	..	1	..	3	..	1	..	..	..
Webber, John	1	..	1	1	..	3	..	1	..	..	..
Webster, Moses	..	..	..	1	..	1	1	..	1	1	..
Webster, Moses 2nd	..	..	..	1	..	2	..	1	..	..	..
Webster, Nathan	1	1	..	1	..	2	1	..	1	..	..
Weeks, Samuel	3	..	..	1	..	2	..	..	1	..	..
West, Noah	2	2	..	1	..	1	..	..	1	..	..
Wheeler, Daniel	2	2	2	..	1	2	1	1	1	..	..
Whitier, Abner	..	..	1	..	1	1	..	1	..	1	..
Whitier, Henry	..	..	..	1	..	1	..	1	..	1	..
Whitier, Joseph	2	..	..	1	1	2	..	..	1	1	..
Whitier, Samuel	..	..	1	..	1	1	..	1	..	..	..
Whitier, Sargent	..	2	2	..	1	2	2	2	..	1	..
Whitier, Simeon	2	..	..	1	..	1	..	..	1	..	..
Willa, Abel	1	..	..	1	..	..	3	1	..	1	..
Williams, Isaac	2	..	2	..	..	..	..	1	..	..	..
Willson, David	..	2	2	..	1	..	..	2	..	2	..
Wyman, Aaron	..	..	..	1	..	1	..	..	1	..	..
DEWEY'S GORE											
Barker, Jedediah	3	2	..	..	1	..	1	2	1	..	..
Barker, Levi	1	..	..	1	..	1	..	..	1	..	..
Barker, Silas	3	..	..	1	..	1	..	..	1	..	..
Bayley, Edward	1	..	..	1	..	..	..	1	..	..	..
Carter, Jonas	..	2	..	..	1	..	..	2	..	1	..
Crossman, Stephen	..	..	2	..	1	..	2	..	..	1	..
Dockam, Charles	1	..	..	1	..	..	..	..	1	..	..
Hunt, Abner	..	2	3	..	1	..	1	1	..	1	..
Hunt, Henry	..	1	1	..	1	1	..	1	..	1	..
Laughton, John	..	..	..	1	..	2	..	2	..	..	..
Norris, Benjamin	3	1	1	1	..	2	..	..	1	..	..
Peasley, David	1	1	1	..	1	1	1	2	1	..	..
Peasley, Jedediah	1	..	3	1	..	2	2	1	1	..	..
Plaisted, Ford	..	1	1	..	..	2	..	1	..	..	..
Porter, Elijah	..	..	..	1	..	1	..	..	1	..	..
Porter, John	..	..	..	1	..	3	..	..	1	..	..
Samborn, Simon	1	2	1	..	1	..	1	..	..	1	..
Tice, William	2	..	1	1	..	3	2	1	1	..	..
Whitier, David	..	2	..	..	1	..	1	1	..	..	..
Whitier, David Jr.	2	..	..	1	..	1	..	1	..	..	..
Woodward, Amaziah	1	..	..	1	..	2	..	1	..	..	..
Woodward, Benjamin	..	..	..	1	..	1	..	..	1	..	..
Woodward, Clergy	1	..	1	..	..	1	..	1	..	..	..
Woodward, Darius	..	..	1	..	..	..	..	1	..	..	..
Woodward, Jepther	..	..	1	1	..	..	1	..	..	1	..
Woodward, Nathaniel	2	..	..	1	..	2	..	..	1	..	..

NAMES OF HEADS OF FAMILIES	FREE WHITE MALES: Under 10 years of age	FREE WHITE MALES: Of 10 and under 16	FREE WHITE MALES: Of 16 and under 26 including heads of families	FREE WHITE MALES: Of 26 and under 45 including heads of families	FREE WHITE MALES: Of 45 and upwards including heads of families.	FREE WHITE FEMALES: Under 10 years of age	FREE WHITE FEMALES: Of 10 and under 16	FREE WHITE FEMALES: Of 16 and under 26 including heads of families	FREE WHITE FEMALES: Of 26 and under 45 including heads of families	FREE WHITE FEMALES: Of 45 and upwards including heads of families	All other free persons except Indians not taxed
GROTON											
Abott, James	2	2	1	..	1	..	..	..	..	1	..
Alexander, Abram	..	..	1	..	..	2	1	..	1	..	..
Bacheldor, Jeremiah	..	..	..	1	..	2	..	1	..	..	..
Bailey, Benjamin	3	1	..	1	..	2	2	..	1	..	..
Bailey, Israel	1	..	..	1	..	2	1	..	1	..	..
Darling, John	..	2	..	1	..	..	1	1	..	1	..
Darling, Robert	2	1	..	1	..	3	2	..	1	..	..
Darling, Samuel	2	..	..	1	..	1	..	1	..	..	..
Emery, Charles	..	..	..	..	1	..	..	..	..	1	..
Emery, John	4	1	..	1	..	4	..	1	1	..	..
Emery, Timothy	1	..	..	1	..	2	..	1	1	1	..
Frost, William	1	..	..	1	..	4	..	..	1	..	..
Gary, Ephraim	1	..	..	1	..	..	..	..	1	..	..
Gray, Domincan	1	..	1	1	1	3	1	..	..	1	..
Hatch, Jacob	5	..	..	1	..	..	1	..	1	..	..
Heath, Jesse	3	3	1	..	1	2	..	1	1	..	..
Hill, John	..	..	..	1	..	2	..	..	1	..	..
Hooper, James	..	..	..	1	..	3	..	..	1	..	..
Hosmore, Aaron	1	..	..	1	1	2	1	3	..	..	..
James, Jonathan	1	..	1	..	1	3	..	1	1	..	..
Knight, Nathan	2	..	..	1	..	2	..	..	1	..	..
Lund, Cilas	2	1	..	1	..	..	..	..	1	..	..
Manchester, Enoch	1	1	1	..	..	..	..	1	..	..	..
Martin, Truman	..	1	..	1	..	3	..	..	1	..	..
McOmber, Jonathan	2	1	..	..	1	3	1	1	..	..	..
Monro, Daniel	3	..	..	1	..	2	..	..	1	..	..
Morrison, Bradbury	2	..	..	1	..	2	1	..	1	..	..
Morse, Edmund	1	..	..	1	..	4	1	..	1	..	..
Noyes, Susanna	3	..	..	..	..	1	1	1	1	..	..
Phelps, John	..	..	..	..	..	..	..	..	1	..	1
Pollard, Edward	3	..	..	1	..	1	..	..	1	..	..
Remick, John	2	1	..	1	..	..	..	..	1	..	..
Tassy, Robert	2	1	..	1	..	2	..	..	1	..	..
Tassy, William	..	..	1	..	1	..	..	..	..	1	..
Thurston, Ruke	..	..	2	..	..	..	..	1	..	..	..
Welch, Edmund	3	1	1	..	1	1	1	1	1	..	..
Welch, Jonathan	1	1	..	1	..	2	1	..	1	..	..
HARDWICK											
Addams, Stephen	..	..	..	1	..	1	..	1	..	..	..
Bailey, Charles	2	..	1	..	1	..	..	1	..	1	..
Bailey, Charles Jr.	..	1	..	1	..	1	..	..	1	..	..
Bailey, Enoch	..	..	..	1	..	..	..	..	..	..	..
Bailey, Whitefield	..	..	1	..	..	..	..	1	..	..	..
Bridgeman, Jesse	..	..	..	1	..	..	..	..	..	..	..
Bridgeman, John	2	..	..	1	..	1	..	..	1	..	..
Bundy, Aaron	1	..	..	1	..	1	..	..	1	..	..
Bundy, James	1	..	..	1	..	1	..	..	1	..	..
Cheever, Nathaniel	..	..	1	..	1	..	1	..	..	1	..
Cheever, William	..	..	1	..	1	..	1	..	..	1	..
Colton, Gideon	1	..	1	..	..	..	..	1	..	..	..
Cone, William M.	..	..	1	..	..	..	..	1	..	..	..
Davis, Elisha	..	..	..	1	..	..	..	..	1	..	..
Ferrington, Isaac	1	..	..	..	1	..	..	..	1	..	..
Filbrook, Benjamin	2	..	..	1	..	1	..	..	1	..	..
Filbrook, David	1	1	..	1	..	..	..	..	1	..	..
French, Samuel	2	1	2	1	1	..	..	2	1	..	..
Fuller, Thomas	2	2	2	1	..	1	1	1	1	1	..
Goodrich, Asahel	2	..	1	..	..	..	..	1	..	..	..
Goodrich, Levi	1	..	1	1	1	1	1	1	..	1	..
Goram, Silas	1	1	..	1	..	1	1	1	1	..	..
Holmes, John	1	..	..	1	..	..	..	1	..	..	..
Nay, Jonathan	..	..	..	1	..	1	..	1	..	..	..
Norris, David	1	1	2	..	1	..	1	1	..	1	..

CALEDONIA COUNTY—Continued

NAMES OF HEADS OF FAMILIES	FREE WHITE MALES: Under 10 years of age	FREE WHITE MALES: Of 10 and under 16	FREE WHITE MALES: Of 16 and under 26 including heads of families	FREE WHITE MALES: Of 26 and under 45 including heads of families	FREE WHITE MALES: Of 45 and upwards including heads of families.	FREE WHITE FEMALES: Under 10 years of age	FREE WHITE FEMALES: Of 10 and under 16	FREE WHITE FEMALES: Of 16 and under 26 including heads of families	FREE WHITE FEMALES: Of 26 and under 45 including heads of families	FREE WHITE FEMALES: Of 45 and upwards including heads of families	All other free persons except Indians not taxed
HARDWICK—con.											
Norris, David Jr.	2	..	..	1	..	1	..	1	..	..	..
Norris, Mark	1	..	..	1	..	1	..	..	1	..	..
Norris, Nathaniel	3	..	..	1	..	2	..	..	1	..	..
Norris, Nathaniel 2nd	1	..	1	..	..	1	..	1	..	..	..
Page, Foster	..	3	..	1	..	2	..	..	1	..	..
Page, Peter	3	2	..	1	1	1	1	..	1	..	..
Perkins, Timothy	2	1	1	..	1	1	1	2	..	1	..
Randall, Robert O.	..	..	1	..	..	2	..	1	..	..	..
Ruggles, Benjamin	1	..	..	1	..	2	..	..	1	..	..
Sabin, Elihu	1	..	..	1	..	2	..	..	1	..	..
Sabin, Elijah	..	..	..	1	..	..	..	..	1	..	..
Sabin, Elisha	3	..	..	1	..	1	..	..	1	..	..
Sabin, Gideon	1	2	2	1	1	1	1	..	1	..	..
Sambon, Israel	1	..	1	1	..	2	..	..	1	..	..
Sheppard, Elisha	1	..	1	..	..	..	2	..	1	..	..
Sincler, Benjamin	1	1	..	..	1	..	1	1	..	1	..
Sincler, Nathaniel	1	..	1	..	..	2	..	..	1	..	..
Stephens, Jacob	1	..	1	..	..	2	..	..	1	..	..
Thomas, William	..	..	1	..	..	..	..	1	..	..	..
True, Benjamin	1	..	..	1	..	1	..	1	..	..	..
True, Elijah	1	1	1	..	1	..	2	2	..	1	..
True, Samuel	2	..	1	..	..	..	..	1	..	..	..
Tuttle, Amos	..	1	1	1	..	..	2	..	1	..	..
Warner, Alpheus	1	..	2	2	..	1	..	..	1	..	..
Webber, Levi	1	..	1	..	..	..	..	1	..	..	..
West, Gilman	..	..	..	1	..	..	..	..	1	..	..
UNCERTAIN NAME											
Tarssoth (?), Josiah	2	..	..	1	..	1	..	..	1	..	..
HOPKINSVILLE											
Bailey, Richard	3	1	..	1	..	1	1	..	1	..	..
Grant, Theophilus	2	..	1	..	..	2	..	1	..	..	..
Page, Peter	..	2	1	..	1	..	..	1	..	1	..
LYNDON											
Bemas, Elias	3	..	..	1	..	..	..	2	..	..	..
Bemas, Joel	..	..	..	1	..	2	..	..	1	..	..
Bemas, Wait	2	..	..	1	..	1	..	..	1	..	..
Blake, William	1	..	..	1	..	1	..	1	1	..	..
Bligh, John	..	..	1	..	1	1	..	..	..	1	..
Brown, John	1	1	..	1	..	..	1	1	1	..	..
Brown, Josiah	..	..	..	1	..	1	..	1	..	..	..
Buckland, Benjamin	..	..	..	1	..	3	..	..	1	..	..
Cahoon, Daniel	1	1	2	1	1	..	..	1	1	1	..
Carpenter, Abel	1	1	..	..	1	3	1	1	1	..	..
Clark, Joseph	..	1	..	1	..	4	1	..	1	..	..
Coburn, Joseph	3	1	2	..	1	2	1	1	1	..	..
Coburn, Stephen	..	..	3	..	..	..	..	1	..	..	..
Cole, Jesse	..	..	1	1	..	1	1	2	1	..	..
Cumins, Adams	..	..	..	1	..	1	..	..	1	..	..
Deckermon, Eli	3	..	..	1	1	1	..	..	1	..	..
Doolittle, Jesse	1	..	1	1	..	2	1	..	1	..	..
Easterbrook, Benjamin	1	..	1	..	1	..	..	3	..	1	..
Easterbrook, Benjamin Jr.	3	..	..	1	..	1	..	..	1	..	..
Evans, Joseph	2	..	..	1	..	3	..	..	1	..	..
Evans, Moses	..	1	1	..	1	..	1	..	..	1	..
Evans, Zera	1	1	..	1	..	4	..	..	1	..	..
Fay, Samuel	2	..	..	1	..	3	..	..	1	..	..
Field, Francis	..	..	..	1	..	..	..	1	..	..	..
Fisher, Jeremiah	..	1	..	1	1	..	..	1	..	1	..
Fisher, William	1	..	..	1	..	1	..	..	1	..	..
Fisk, Isaiah	2	..	1	1	..	..	1	..	1	..	..
Fletcher, Joel	1	..	1	2	..	4	..	1	1	..	..
Gates, John	2	..	..	1	..	..	..	1	..	..	..
Gates, Josiah	3	..	1	..	1	..	3	..	..	1	..
Hackett, Ebenezer	2	..	..	1	..	2	..	..	1	..	..
Hackett, George	..	..	..	1	..	1	..	..	..	..	..
Hackett, Stilson	3	2	1	1	..	2	1	..	1	..	..
Harris, Joseph	..	..	..	1	..	..	..	..	1	..	..
Harvey, Daniel	2	..	..	1	..	..	..	1	..	..	..
Harvey, William	1	1	1	..	1	2	1	..	1	..	..
LYNDON—con.											
Healey, Comfort	..	..	..	1	..	1	..	..	1	1	..
Hooffman, Henry	1	1	2	..	1	1	1	1	..	1	..
Houghton, Daniel	3	2	..	..	1	2	..	..	1	..	..
Houghton, Jacob	1	..	..	1	..	3	..	..	1	..	..
Houghton, Luther	2	..	..	1	..	3	..	..	1	..	..
Howland, Eber	1	..	..	1	..	2	..	..	1	..	..
Hubbard, Ephraim	2	..	..	1	..	2	..	..	1	..	..
Huchins, Amasa	3	..	..	1	..	1	..	1	1	..	..
Ide, Timothy	2	..	..	1	..	..	..	1	..	..	..
Jenks, Nathaniel	2	1	1	..	1	1	..	..	1	..	..
Jenks, Nehemiah	2	..	..	1	..	2	..	1	1	..	..
Jenks, Welcome	1	..	1	1	..	1	1	..	1	..	..
Johnson, John	1	1	..	1	..	1	..	1	..	..	..
Johnson, Roswell	1	1	..	1	..	2	..	..	1	..	..
Jones, Abner	..	..	..	1	..	1	..	..	1	..	..
Jones, Jeremiah	..	..	..	..	1	..	..	2	..	1	..
Kent, Jacob	..	..	1	..	..	1	..	1	..	..	..
Kimball, Jude	3	1	..	1	..	..	..	1	..	..	..
Lockling, Levi	1	..	1	..	1	1	1	..	1	..	..
Madison, Thomas	..	..	1	..	..	1	..	1	..	..	..
McGaffey, Andrew	3	..	1	1	..	2	..	..	1	..	..
McGaffey, James	1	..	1	..	..	1	..	1	..	..	..
McGaffey, John	..	1	1	..	1	..	..	1	..	..	..
McGaffey, William W.	4	..	1	1	..	1	..	..	1	..	..
Norris, Zebulon	..	..	1	..	..	1	..	..	1	..	..
Olney, Job	1	..	..	..	1	..	..	1	..	..	..
Parker, Caleb	..	1	..	1	..	..	..	2	..	..	..
Parker, Nathan	2	..	1	..	..	..	1	1	..	..	..
Parker, Noah	..	..	1	..	1	..	1	..	..	1	..
Parks, Jonathan	..	..	1	..	..	1	..	1	..	..	..
Peck, Ebenezer	..	..	..	1	..	2	..	1	..	..	..
Peck, Eleazer	..	..	..	1	..	..	..	..	1	..	..
Peck, Gaius	2	..	1	1	..	2	1	..	1	..	..
Reniff, Daniel	2	1	..	1	..	2	..	..	1	..	..
Ripley, Daniel	2	..	..	1	..	3	..	..	1	..	..
Root, Moses	2	1	1	..	1	2	1	..	..	1	..
Ross, Elijah	2	..	..	1	..	1	1	..	1	..	..
Ross, Joel	..	1	..	1	..	3	..	..	1	..	..
Ruggels, William	1	..	..	1	..	1	..	..	1	..	..
Scott, Jeremiah	2	..	1	1	..	3	2	..	1	..	..
Shelden, Pardon	1	..	1	..	1	2	2	..	..	1	..
Sheldon, Job	3	..	1	1	..	2	..	1	1	..	..
Smith, David	..	..	1	..	1	..	..	..	..	1	..
Smith, Israel	..	..	1	..	..	3	..	1	..	..	..
Smith, Simeon	..	..	..	1	..	5	..	..	1	..	..
Sprague, Jones	..	..	1	..	1	..	..	1	..	1	..
Thurston, Thomas	..	1	1	..	1	..	..	..	1	..	..
Tibbits, Peter	1	..	..	1	..	..	..	..	1	..	..
Tucker, Nehemiah	3	..	..	2	..	1	..	..	1	..	..
Tute, Ziba	2	..	..	1	..	2	..	..	1	..	..
Walter, Enos	..	..	..	2	..	1	..	..	1	1	..
Watson, Henry	..	..	..	1	..	2	..	1	..	..	..
Watson, Leonard	..	..	..	1	..	..	1	..	1	..	..
Wilmot, Abel	3	..	..	1	..	1	1	..	1	..	..
Wilmot, Joseph	..	1	1	..	1	1	1	3	..	1	..
Winslow, Samuel	2	..	..	..	1	3	1	2	1	..	..
Winsor, William	..	..	1	..	1	..	..	..	..	1	..
Wood, Benjamin	1	..	..	1	..	1	..	..	1	..	..
MARSHFIELD											
Benjamin, David	2	..	..	1	..	..	..	1	..	..	..
Benjamin, Elisha	..	..	1	..	1	..	2	..	..	1	..
Benjamin, Elisha Jr.	1	..	..	1	..	3	..	..	1	..	..
Cole, Russell	..	..	..	1	..	3	..	..	1	..	..
Cutler, John	..	..	..	1	..	2	..	..	1	..	..
Dodge, Ebenezer	..	..	..	..	1	..	1	..	1	1	..
Dodge, Ebenezer Jr.	1	..	1	1	..	..	..	2	..	..	..
Dodge, Nathaniel	..	..	1	..	..	1	..	1	..	..	..
Elmore, Aaron	2	1	..	1	..	3	1	..	1	..	..

CALEDONIA COUNTY—Continued

NAMES OF HEADS OF FAMILIES	FREE WHITE MALES					FREE WHITE FEMALES					
	Under 10 years of age	Of 10 and under 16	Of 16 and under 26 including heads of families	Of 26 and under 45 including heads of families	Of 45 and upwards including heads of families.	Under 10 years of age	Of 10 and under 16	Of 16 and under 26 including heads of families	Of 26 and under 45 including heads of families	Of 45 and upwards including heads of families	All other free persons except Indians not taxed
MARSHFIELD—con.											
Gilman, Solomon	1	2	1	..	1	2	1	..	..	1	..
Goodall, John	..	..	1	..	..	..	..	..	1	..	..
Olmsted, Stephen	2	..	1	..	..	..	..	1	..	..	..
Page, Joseph P.	2	..	..	1	..	1	..	..	1	..	..
Patterson, Samuel	1	2	1	1	..	3	..	..	1	..	..
Pitkin, Caleb	1	..	..	1	..	..	..	2	..	..	..
Pitkin, Joshua	3	1	..	1	..	..	1	..	1	..	..
Pitkin, Nathaniel	2	1	1	1	..	1	2	..	1	..	..
Pitkin, Stephen	3	1	..	1	..	..	1	..	1	..	..
Rich, Stephen	..	1	..	1	..	2	1	..	1	..	..
Roberts, Hart	2	..	..	1	..	..	..	1	..	..	..
Simons, Uriah	..	..	..	1	..	2	..	..	1	..	..
Skiner, Giles	4	..	..	1	..	..	1	..	1	..	..
Spencer, Gideon	2	..	..	1	..	2	..	1	..	..	..
Taylor, Joab	..	1	..	1	..	1	..	..	1	..	..
Waugh, John	1	1	..	..	1	3	1	1	1	..	..
Waugh, Robert	3	..	..	1	..	1	1	..	1	..	..
Wells, Joseph	1	..	1	..	..	1	..	1	..	..	..
Wells, Sealer H.	..	1	2	..	1	1	1	..	..	1	..
Wilson, Samuel	3	2	3	..	1	2	..	1	1	..	..
MONTPELIER											
Allen, Thomas	1	1	..	..	1	..	1	2	1	..	..
Ames, Edmond	..	1	..	1	..	..	1	..	1	..	..
Andrews, Widow	1	2	2	..	..	..	..	2	..	1	..
Bancraft, John	2	..	1	..	1	..	..	1	1	..	..
Bennett, Caleb	4	1	..	1	..	1	..	1	..	..	..
Blush, Joseph	4	2	..	1	..	2	1	..	1	..	..
Boyden, Darius	..	..	..	1	..	3	2	..	1	..	..
Brooks, Lemuel	..	..	2	1	..	2	..	1	..	..	..
Brooks, Thomas	2	..	..	1	..	2	1	..	1	..	..
Burges, Anthony	3	..	..	1	..	1	..	1	..	1	..
Burgh, Benjamin	1	..	..	1	..	..	..	..	1	..	..
Bush, Benjamin	3	1	..	..	1	..	..	1	1	..	..
Cadwell, Willis Jr.	1	..	1	2	..	..	..	1	..	..	..
Cameron, Daniel	1	..	1	..	..	..	..	1	..	..	..
Cate, Enoch	3	2	..	..	1	..	1	2	1	..	..
Church, Ichabod	..	1	..	1	..	3	..	..	1	..	..
Clark, Nathaniel	2	..	..	1	..	2	..	..	1	..	..
Clerk, Theouphilus	1	..	..	1	..	1	..	..	1	..	..
Cobourn, Asa	1	..	1	1	..	..	..	1	1	..	..
Cummins, Elisha	1	..	..	1	..	1	..	..	1	..	..
Cummins, John	1	..	..	1	..	..	..	1	..	..	..
Cutler, John	..	..	..	1	..	4	..	1	..	..	..
Cutler, Jonathan	4	1	2	1	1	..	..	1	..	1	..
Cutler, Jonathan Jr.	2	..	1	1	..	..	..	..	1	..	..
Cutler, Stephen	..	..	..	1	1	..	..	1	1	..	..
Dagget, Arthur	..	..	2	..	1	1	..	1	..	2	..
Dagget, Arthur Jr.	..	..	1	1	..	..	..	1	..	..	..
Darling, William	1	..	2	1	..	..	..	1	..	..	..
Davis, Hezekiah	1	..	..	1	1	1	..	2	..	1	..
Davis, Jacob	..	..	1	..	1	..	1	1	..	1	..
Davis, Jacob Jr.	3	..	..	1	..	1	1	..	1	..	..
Davis, Nathaniel	..	..	..	2	..	3	..	1	1	..	..
Davis, Parley	1	1	..	1	..	3	..	1	1	1	..
Davis, Thomas	..	..	..	1	..	1	..	..	1	..	..
Dodge, Solomon	2	2	..	1	..	3	1	..	1	..	..
Doty, Barnabas	..	1	1	..	1	..	1	3	..	1	..
Doty, Barnabas Jr.	..	..	..	1	..	2	..	..	1	..	..
Doty, Edmond	..	..	..	1	..	3	..	..	1	..	..
Doty, Thomas	2	1	..	1	..	2	1	..	1	..	..
Edwards, David	1	2	1	..	1	1	..	1	..	1	..
Ellis, Reuben	1	1	1	..	1	1	1	..	1	..	..
Freeman, Elijah	..	..	..	1	..	2	..	1	1	..	..
Freeman, Josiah	..	..	..	1	..	1	..	..	1	..	..
Gallison, John	..	..	1	..	..	1	..	1	..	..	..
Gifford, Robertson	..	..	..	1	..	1	1	..	1	..	..
Gilbert, Moses	3	..	..	1	..	..	..	..	1	..	..
Gould, Daniel	2	..	3	..	1	..	1	..	..	1	..
Gould, John	..	..	2	..	1	..	..	..	1	2	..
Gould, John Jr.	..	..	1	..	..	..	..	..	1	..	..
Gray, Benjamin	..	..	1	..	..	..	..	1	..	..	..
Gray, Hugh	1	..	..	1	..	2	..	..	1	..	..
Gray, John	..	1	2	..	1	2	1	2	..	1	..
MONTPELIER—con.											
Gray, Kalso	..	..	..	1	..	..	..	..	..	..	..
Gray, Mathew	1	..	..	1	..	1	..	..	1	..	..
Gray, Reuben	1	..	..	1	..	..	..	1	..	..	..
Hamblin, Asa	..	1	2	..	..	1	1	1	..	1	..
Hamblin, Isaac	1	3	2	..	1	..	..	1	..	1	..
Hamblin, Silvanus	2	..	..	1	..	2	..	..	..	..	..
Hammet, Barnabas	..	..	1	..	1	..	1	2	..	1	..
Hammond, Salathial	4	1	..	1	..	2	1	..	1	..	..
Hatch, Timothy	..	1	3	..	1	..	2	..	1	..	..
Hathaway, Lott	1	1	..	..	1	..	2	5	..	1	..
Hawkins, James	1	1	1	1	..	2	2	..	1	..	..
Hill, Joseph	..	..	1	..	..	1	..	1	..	..	..
Homes, John	..	..	1	1	..	2	1	..	1	..	..
Homes, William	2	..	1	1	..	..	..	1	1	..	..
Howland, Eseek	1	2	..	..	1	2	1	..	..	1	..
Humphrey, Levi	3	..	..	1	..	2	..	..	1	1	..
Hutchins, William	1	..	..	2	..	1	..	1	..	..	..
Jacob, Stephen	3	..	..	1	..	..	..	1	..	..	..
Knap, Paul	1	..	..	1	..	1	..	1	..	..	..
Lamb, Learned	2	..	2	1	..	1	..	..	1	..	..
Lebarron, Isaac	2	..	..	1	..	3	2	..	1	..	..
Lewis, Solomon	2	1	1	..	1	2	..	1	..	1	..
Lumberd, Justus	4	1	2	1	..	..	1	..	1	..	..
Mash, William	..	..	1	..	..	..	..	1	..	..	..
McCloud, Thomas	2	2	1	..	1	1	..	2	1	..	..
McKnight, Kimball	1	..	1	..	..	1	..	1	..	..	..
McKnight, Lemuel	..	..	2	..	..	2	..	2	..	..	..
Moseley, Luther	3	1	1	..	1	..	3	..	1	..	..
Moss, Ebenezer	..	..	..	1	..	1	..	..	1	..	..
Moss, Silvanus	2	1	..	1	..	1	..	..	1	..	..
Nash, Benjamin	1	1	..	1	..	2	..	..	1	..	..
Neley, Andrew	2	1	2	..	1	..	1	1	..	1	..
Nelson, John	1	2	..	1	..	2	..	..	1	..	..
Nelson, Mark	2	..	..	1	..	2	..	..	1	..	..
Nye, Irum	2	1	2	..	1	..	1	..	..	1	..
Ormesby, Caleb	2	..	..	1	..	2	..	..	1	..	..
Parker, Alexander	..	1	..	..	1	1	1	2	..	1	..
Parsons, David	3	..	..	1	..	..	..	..	1	..	..
Peck, Joshua	..	..	..	1	..	2	1	..	1	..	..
Peck, Nathaniel	1	..	..	1	..	2	..	..	1	..	..
Persons, Eliacum	..	1	..	1	..	3	1	..	1	..	..
Phinny, Benjamin	1	..	1	..	..	2	..	1	..	..	..
Pope, Elnathan	1	1	..	1	..	3	1	..	1	..	..
Preston, Samuel	1	..	..	1	..	..	..	..	1	..	..
Proctor, Henry	2	..	..	1	..	2	..	1	..	..	..
Proctor, Nathaniel	..	..	1	..	..	..	..	..	..	1	..
Putnam, Benjamin	..	..	1	..	..	2	..	1	..	..	..
Putnam, Isaac	1	1	..	1	..	1	..	..	1	..	..
Putnam, Levi	1	2	..	1	..	2	..	..	1	..	..
Richardson, Samuel	2	..	2	2	..	..	..	..	1	..	..
Richardson, William	3	1	..	2	..	..	1	..	1	..	..
Robbins, David	..	..	1	1	..	2	1	1	1	..	..
Robinson, Samuel	..	..	..	2	..	1	..	1	..	..	..
Sanders, Gideon	..	..	..	..	1	..	..	..	1	1	..
Sears, Paul	2	..	..	1	..	3	1	..	1	..	..
Shepard, Jonathan	1	..	1	..	..	..	..	1	1	..	..
Sherman, Daniel	..	..	1	..	..	..	..	1	..	..	..
Snow, Freeman	..	..	..	2	1	1	1	1	..	1	1
Snow, Jonathan	3	..	..	1	..	3	..	..	1	..	..
Snow, Jonathan	3	..	..	1	..	3	..	..	1	..	..
Staples, William	..	..	..	..	1	..	..	..	..	1	..
Stevens, Charles	..	..	..	1	..	..	..	1	..	..	..
Stevens, Clark	2	..	..	1	..	2	..	..	1	..	..
Stevens, Hinkley	1	..	..	1	..	..	..	1	..	..	..
Stevens, John	3	..	..	1	..	3	..	..	1	..	..
Stevens, Prince	..	..	1	..	1	..	..	2	..	1	..
Stevens, Smith	..	..	..	1	..	1	..	..	1	..	..
Stoddard, Phinehas	3	..	..	1	..	2	..	..	1	..	..
Stone, Moses	1	..	..	1	..	1	..	..	1	..	..
Stone, Uriah	..	1	2	..	1	..	1	..	..	2	..
Taber, Ebenezer	..	1	1	1	..	2	..	..	1	..	..
Taber, Elihu	3	..	1	2	..	1	..	..	1	..	..
Taber, Thomas	2	1	1	..	1	1	2	..	..	1	..
Taylor, Jonah	1	..	..	1	..	1	..	..	1	..	..
Templeton, John	5	1	1	1	1	1	..	..	1	1	..
Templeton, William	1	2	..	1	1	..	1	..	2	1	..

CALEDONIA COUNTY—Continued

NAMES OF HEADS OF FAMILIES	FREE WHITE MALES					FREE WHITE FEMALES					
	Under 10 years of age	Of 10 and under 16	Of 16 and under 26 including heads of families	Of 26 and under 45 including heads of families	Of 45 and upwards including heads of families.	Under 10 years of age	Of 10 and under 16	Of 16 and under 26 including heads of families	Of 26 and under 45 including heads of families	Of 45 and upwards including heads of families.	All other free persons except Indians not taxed
MONTPELIER—con.											
Thomas, Warren	1	..	1	..	..	1	..	1	..	..	..
Tolman, David	..	..	1	1	..	2	1	1	1	..	..
Tresfethen, George	1	..	..	1	..	..	..	..	1	..	..
Vinson, Phillip	..	2	..	1	..	1	2	..	1	..	..
Wakefield, Rufus	1	..	2	1	..	3	2	..	1	..	..
Watrous, Erastus	1	..	2	2	..	1	..	2	..	..	1
West, Thomas	..	..	1	..	1	..	..	..	..	1	..
West, Thomas	1	..	3	..	..	..	..	2	..	..	..
West, Widow	2	..	..	..	..	2	..	..	1	..	..
Wheeler, Benjamin	2	..	..	1	..	2	..	..	1	..	..
Wheeler, Jerathmel	2	..	..	1	..	3	..	..	1	..	..
Wheeler, Philip	..	..	1	1	..	..	2	..	1	..	..
Whelock, Salem	1	..	..	1	..	1	..	1	..	..	..
Wiggin, Joshua	..	1	2	1	1	..	..	1	..	1	..
Williams, Daniel	1	..	3	1	..	..	..	1	1	..	..
Wing, David	..	..	1	..	1	..	..	..	1	..	..
Wing, David Jr.	3	..	..	1	..	..	1	1	1	..	..
Wing, Joseph	..	..	..	1	..	1	1	..	1	..	..
Winn, Nathan	1	1	1	..	..	..	..	1	..	..	..
Wood, Daniel	1	..	..	1	..	..	..	..	1	..	..
Woodworth, Benjamin	..	..	..	..	1	..	..	..	..	1	..
Woodworth, Joseph	1	2	..	1	..	1	2	..	1	..	..
Woodworth, Ziba	2	..	1	1	..	1	..	..	1	..	..
PEACHAM											
Abbot, Jeremiah	2	1	..	1	..	3	..	..	1	..	..
Ames, John	1	..	..	1	..	1	..	1	..	..	..
Bacon, Samuel	..	..	..	1	..	2	2	..	1	..	..
Bailey, Cyrus	..	..	2	1	1	..	1	..	..	1	..
Bailey, Ebenezer	2	2	..	1	..	..	1	..	1	..	..
Bailey, James	..	..	2	1	1	..	1	..	..	1	..
Bailey, Luther	3	2	1	1	1	1	1	2	1	1	..
Bayley, Abijah	4	1	2	1	..	1	1	..	1	..	..
Blanchard, Abial	2	2	1	1	..	2	1	..	1	..	..
Blanchard, Abiel	3	3	..	1	..	2	..	1	1	..	..
Blanchard, Joel	4	1	..	1	..	3	1	..	1	..	..
Blanchard, Reuben	..	1	..	1	..	2	..	1	1	..	..
Blanchard, Simon	2	..	1	1	..	1	..	..	1	..	..
Blasdel, David	1	..	..	1	..	1	..	..	1	..	..
Brown, James	1	1	..	1	..	3	..	..	1	..	..
Brown, Joseph	..	2	2	..	1	..	1	2	..	1	..
Buckminster, William	..	..	2	2	..	..	..	1	..	1	..
Buel, Abraham	1	..	..	1	..	1	..	..	1	..	..
Burbank, Benjamin	1	1	1	1	..	1	1	..	1	..	..
Buswel, Nicolas	2	..	..	1	..	3	..	..	1	..	..
Capron, John	1	..	..	1	..	..	..	1	..	..	..
Carter, Levi	..	..	..	..	1	..	..	1	1	..	..
Chamberlin, Abiel	..	1	1	..	1	..	1	2	..	1	..
Chamberlin, Ebenezer	2	..	..	1	..	2	..	..	1	..	..
Chamberlin, Ephraim	..	..	..	1	..	..	..	1	..	..	..
Chamberlin, Samuel	..	..	..	..	1	..	..	..	1	1	..
Chamberlin, William	3	1	..	1	..	2	1	1	1	..	..
Chandler, John W.	2	..	1	1	..	1	..	1	1	1	..
Clark, John	..	..	1	1	..	..	..	1	..	2	..
Cotes, Perez	2	..	..	1	..	..	..	..	1	..	..
Cross, James	..	..	..	1	..	1	1	1	1	..	..
Currier, David	2	2	..	1	..	1	1	..	..	1	..
Dana, Lemuel	..	..	..	1	..	..	..	1	..	..	..
Davidson, Daniel	..	..	..	..	1	..	..	..	..	1	..
Doty, Daniel	1	1	..	1	..	1	..	..	1	..	..
Elkins, David	1	..	..	1	..	3	..	..	1	..	..
Elkins, Jonathan Jr.	2	1	2	1	1	2	..	1	1	1	..
Fairchild, Seth	1	1	1	1	..	2	2	2	1	..	..
Field, James	3	..	..	1	..	1	..	..	1	..	..
Field, Nathan	..	1	..	1	..	1	..	..	1	..	..
Fife, John	..	..	1	..	1	..	..	1	..	1	..
Foster, Enoch	2	..	..	1	..	..	..	1	..	..	..
Foster, Ephraim	..	..	1	..	1	..	..	..	1	1	..
Foster, Ephraim Jr.	..	..	..	1	..	4	..	..	1	..	..
Foster, Josiah	..	..	..	..	1	..	..	..	..	1	..
Gerould, Asahel	2	..	1	..	..	..	..	1	..	..	..
Gibson, William	3	..	2	1	..	3	2	..	1	..	..
Gilbert, Atemas	..	..	2	1	..	..	..	..	..	..	..
Gilbert, John	2	1	..	1	..	1	1	..	1	..	..
Goodnough, Levi	3	..	..	1	..	1	..	1	..	..	..
Goodnough, Stephen	1	..	..	1	..	..	..	1	..	..	..
Gould, Amos	3	..	..	1	..	..	..	1	1	..	..
PEACHAM—con.											
Guy, Jacob	..	..	2	..	1	..	1	1	1	1	..
Guy, James	1	..	2	..	1	..	1	1	..	1	..
Hall, Timothy	3	1	..	1	..	..	1	2	1	..	..
Hand, Reuben	..	1	2	..	..	..	..	1	..	1	..
Heaton, Solomon	..	..	3	2	..	1	1	..	1	..	..
Hill, Samuel	1	..	1	..	1	1	1	2	..	1	..
Hoit, Benjamin	3	1	1	1	..	1	2	..	1	..	..
Hurd, Nathan	1	..	..	1	..	3	..	..	1	..	..
Hutchins, Hannah	1	1	..	..	..	..	1	2	..	1	..
Jenison, William	..	..	..	3	..	..	..	1	..	..	..
Jenyns, Jacob	2	..	..	1	..	1	..	..	1	..	..
Johnson, Daniel	2	..	..	1	..	2	..	..	1	..	..
Johnson, Dole	..	2	1	..	1	1	..	1	..	1	..
Johnson, Jedediah	2	..	..	1	..	1	..	..	1	..	..
Johnson, Solomon	..	..	1	..	..	1	..	1	..	..	..
Johnson, Ziba	2	..	..	1	..	1	..	..	1	..	..
Kellogg, Erastus	..	..	4	..	..	..	..	1	..	..	..
Keyes, John	1	2	..	..	1	3	..	1	1	..	..
Kimball, Joab	1	..	..	1	..	..	1	..	1	..	..
Kimball, Smith	2	1	1	1	..	1	..	1	1	..	..
Knox, William	4	1	..	1	..	1	1	1	1	..	..
Lakeman, Amos	1	..	..	1	..	2	..	..	1	..	..
Lyndsay, Alexander	..	..	..	1	1	..	..	..	..	1	..
Lyndsay, Ephraim	1	1	..	1	..	3	3	..	1	..	..
Lyndsay, James	..	..	1	1	..	1	..	..	2	..	..
Mackey, Benjamin	4	..	..	1	..	1	..	..	1	..	..
Mackey, Widow	..	..	..	..	..	..	..	..	1	1	..
Martin, Andrew	1	2	2	1	..	2	1	2	1	..	..
Martin, Ashbel	4	..	..	1	..	1	..	..	1	1	..
Martin, David	1	..	..	1	..	1	..	..	2	..	..
Martin, Elijah	..	..	2	1	1	1	..	1	1	1	..
Martin, Nathan	1	..	2	..	1	2	..	1	1	..	..
Martin, Samuel	1	..	..	1	..	1	..	..	1	..	..
Mathews, Hugh	..	..	..	1	..	2	1	..	..	..	..
Mathews, Joseph	..	..	..	1	..	..	..	..	1	1	..
McDonold, Alexander	2	..	..	1	..	1	..	1	..	..	..
McLachlin, John	1	1	2	2	..	1	..	1	..	1	..
Meade, Nathan	1	1	..	..	1	3	2	..	1	..	..
Mears, Richard	2	..	..	1	..	..	1	..	1	..	..
Melvin, Nathaniel	..	..	..	..	1	..	..	1	1	..	..
Merrill, David	..	..	..	2	..	..	..	1	..	..	..
Merrill, Jesse	4	1	..	1	..	1	..	..	1	..	..
Merrill, Moses	1	..	..	1	2	..	4	..	1	1	..
Miner, Abner	2	..	..	1	..	2	1	..	1	..	..
Miner, James	..	1	1	1	..	1	1	1	1	..	..
Miner, Reuben	..	..	1	..	1	..	..	2	..	1	..
Miner, Reuben Jr.	2	..	..	1	..	..	1	..	1	..	..
Miner, Samuel	..	..	..	1	..	..	..	2	1	..	..
Moore, William	1	1	1	1	..	1	..	..	..	..	1
Morse, Moody	1	..	1	..	1	1	3	2	1	..	..
Nortrop, Lemuel	2	..	..	..	1	1	..	..	..	1	..
Page, Israel	2	..	1	..	..	..	..	1	..	..	..
Parker, William	1	1	4	1	..	1	1	3	..	1	..
Patterson, Ebenezer	2	..	1	..	..	2	..	1	1	..	..
Patterson, Joseph	2	..	..	1	..	..	..	..	1	..	..
Phelps, Elisha	1	..	1	1	..	..	..	2	..	..	..
Poor, Noah	1	..	..	1	..	1	..	..	1	..	..
Pratt, Isaiah	..	..	3	..	..	1	..	1	..	..	..
Pratt, Lot	1	..	..	1	..	2	2	..	1	..	..
Putney, Jewett	2	..	..	..	..	2	1	..	1	..	..
Sargeant, Asa	1	..	4	1	..	..	1	..	1	..	..
Scales, Aaron	1	..	..	1	..	..	..	1	..	..	..
Scott, Dr. William	1	..	1	1	..	3	..	1	1	..	..
Skeels, John	1	1	2	..	1	3	1	2	1	..	..
Spencer, Ebenezer	..	1	..	1	..	6	..	..	1	..	..
Spencer, John	3	1	1	2	..	2	..	..	1	..	..
Stewert, John	..	..	1	2	..	2	..	..	1	..	..
Stillwell, Elisha	..	..	..	1	..	..	..	..	1	..	..
Sumner, Edward C.	..	1	..	1	..	3	..	1	1	..	..
Thayer, Benoni	2	3	2	1	..	1	..	..	1	1	..
Tuttle, Reuben	..	..	..	1	..	2	..	..	1	..	..
Varnum, Abraham	1	1	..	1	..	2	..	1	1	..	..
Varnum, William	..	..	2	..	1	..	1	..	..	1	..
Walker, Caleb	1	..	..	1	..	3	..	..	1	..	..
Walker, Simeon	1	2	1	1	..	2	1	..	1	..	..
Ware, Jonathan	2	..	..	1	..	..	..	..	1	..	..
Watts, Moses	..	2	..	1	..	2	..	1	1	..	..

CALEDONIA COUNTY—Continued

NAMES OF HEADS OF FAMILIES	FREE WHITE MALES					FREE WHITE FEMALES					
	Under 10 years of age	Of 10 and under 16	Of 16 and under 26 including heads of families	Of 26 and under 45 including heads of families	Of 45 and upwards including heads of families.	Under 10 years of age	Of 10 and under 16	Of 16 and under 26 including heads of families	Of 26 and under 45 including heads of families	Of 45 and upwards including heads of families	All other free persons except Indians not taxed
PEACHAM—con.											
Weeks, William D.	..	1	..	1	..	1	..	1	..	..	..
Wells, Abraham	..	..	1	3	..	..	..	..	..	..	..
Wesson, Ephraim	..	..	1	1	1	..	..	1	..	1	..
White, Corporal Robert	1	..	1	1	..	1	..	..	2	..	..
Willey, Abel	..	2	1	1	1	3	..	2	..	..	..
Willey, Jared	1	1	..	1	..	2	3	..	1	..	..
Willey, Seth	4	..	..	..	1	1	1	..	2	2	..
Wilson, Nathaniel	..	..	..	1	..	1	..	..	1	..	..
Worcester, Leonard	2	..	..	2	..	1	..	1	1	..	..
PLAINFIELD											
Bacheldor, Joseph	1	1	2	..	1	2	1	2	..	1	..
Bacheldor, Joseph Jr.	1	..	..	1	..	1	..	1	..	..	..
Bacheldor, Molton	3	1	1	1	..	1	..	1	1	..	..
Bacheldor, Nathaniel	2	..	..	1	..	1	..	1	1	..	..
Bancraft, Asa	1	..	..	1	..	..	..	1	..	..	..
Bancraft, David	..	..	1	..	1	..	..	1	..	1	..
Bancraft, Moses	1	2	1	..	1	..	..	..	..	1	..
Benedict, David	1	..	1	..	..	..	..	1	..	..	..
Boutwell, James	3	..	..	1	..	2	..	..	1	..	..
Chace, John	1	..	..	1	..	..	..	1	..	..	..
Chapman, John	1	..	..	1	..	3	..	..	1	..	..
Freeman, Alden	2	..	..	1	..	3	..	..	1	..	..
Freeman, Ebenezer	1	..	3	1	1	..	1	..	1	1	..
Freeman, Ebenezer Jr.	1	..	..	1	..	1	..	..	1	..	..
Hopkins, David	2	..	..	1	..	4	..	..	1	..	..
Kenney, Bradford	1	..	..	1	..	3	1	..	1	..	..
Kenney, Jonathan	3	1	..	..	1	1	1	..	1	..	..
Kenney, Sanford	2	..	..	1	..	1	..	..	1	..	..
Lamson, Joseph	2	1	..	1	..	2	1	..	1	..	..
Lawrence, Joshua	2	1	1	..	1	2	1	2	..	1	..
Mack, Nehemiah	1	3	1	..	1	1	..	1	1	..	..
McClowd, Charles	..	..	..	1	..	1	..	..	1	..	..
McClowd, Charles 2nd	1	1	..	1	..	1	..	1	..	..	..
McClowd, John	..	..	..	2	1	..	..	1	1	..	..
McClowd, John Jr.	..	..	..	1	..	1	..	1	..	..	..
Millin, John	..	..	..	1	..	4	..	..	1	..	..
Millin, Robert	2	..	..	1	..	2	1	..	1	..	..
Moore, John	2	..	..	1	..	2	..	..	1	..	..
Niles, Benjamin	..	..	..	1	..	1	..	..	1	..	..
Nye, Elijah	1	..	..	1	..	1	..	..	1	1	..
Nye, Joseph	..	..	1	..	..	1	..	1	..	..	..
Perkins, Jacob	..	..	2	..	..	1	..	1	..	..	..
Perry, Elijah	3	1	..	1	..	2	1	..	1	..	..
Perry, James	4	1	1	1	..	..	..	2	1	..	..
Shepherd, Willard	..	..	1	1	..	1	..	2	..	..	..
Stone, Jeremiah	..	..	1	..	..	1	..	1	..	..	..
Sturtevant, Zopher	1	..	..	1	..	..	..	..	1	..	..
Vinson, John	1	..	..	1	..	2	..	..	1	..	..
Vinson, Thomas	1	..	1	..	..	..	..	..	1	..	1
Washburn, Asa	..	..	2	..	..	1	..	1	..	..	..
Washburn, Isaac	2	..	..	1	1	2	..	..	1	1	..
Washburn, Niles	2	..	..	1	..	1	..	..	1	..	..
White, Jonathan	..	..	1	..	..	..	..	1	..	..	..
Whitrige, Thomas	2	..	..	1	..	2	..	..	1	..	..
Wolson, Charles R.	1	..	..	1	..	1	..	1	..	..	..
RYEGATE											
Bigelow, Jabez	..	1	1	1	..	3	1	..	1	..	..
Brock, Andrew	2	1	..	1	1	1	2	1	1	1	..
Buchannan, Moses	..	..	1	..	..	..	..	..	..	..	..
Cammeron, John	1	1	4	2	..	..	1	..	2	..	..
Crage, William	..	..	2	..	1	..	2	1	..	1	..
Crage, William Jr.	2	..	..	2	..	..	..	1	..	..	..
Currier, Ezra	..	..	2	..	1	..	..	2	1	..	1
Darling, Jonathan	..	..	..	2	..	1	..	..	1	..	..
Darling, Josiah	..	..	..	2	..	..	..	1	..	..	..
Darling, Moses	4	2	..	1	..	1	..	3	1	..	..
Dow, Job	1	..	..	1	..	2	..	..	1	..	..
Dunn, John	2	..	1	..	..	..	..	..	1	..	..
Easelen, James	1	..	..	1	..	1	..	..	1	..	..
RYEGATE—con.											
Gardner, Hugh	..	..	..	..	1	5	..	..	1	..	..
Gates, Ezra	..	..	..	1	..	2	..	..	1	..	..
Gates, Jonathan	3	..	..	1	..	2	..	..	1	..	..
Gibson, William	1	..	1	1	..	1	..	1	1	..	..
Gray, John	..	2	1	..	1	..	..	1	..	1	..
Hall, Robert	1	..	..	1	..	1	..	1	..	..	..
Harvey, John	2	1	..	1	..	..	..	..	1	1	..
Harvey, William	..	..	..	..	1	..	..	..	..	..	..
Heath, Daniel	3	..	..	1	..	..	..	1	..	..	..
Heath, Ebenezer	1	1	..	1	..	3	1	..	1	..	..
Heath, Nathan	1	..	..	1	..	2	..	..	1	..	..
Heath, Simon	2	2	..	1	..	2	..	..	1	..	..
Henderson, James	1	1	2	..	1	1	..	1	1	..	..
Holmes, Alexander	..	..	..	1	..	3	..	..	1	..	..
Holmes, John	..	..	..	1	..	1	..	..	1	..	..
Hunt, Joshua	4	..	..	1	1	..	1	..	1	..	..
Huntin, John	..	..	1	..	..	..	..	..	..	..	..
Ingills, Samuel	2	..	..	1	..	3	..	..	1	..	..
Johnson, Elihu	2	..	..	1	1	1	..	..	1	1	..
Johnson, John	..	1	..	..	1	..	1	..	..	1	..
Johnson, Samuel	2	2	..	1	..	2	..	..	1	..	..
Johnson, William	2	..	3	..	1	1	2	2	..	1	..
Laughlin, Hugh	2	..	..	1	..	2	..	..	1	..	..
Lockir, Andrew	1	..	1	..	1	..	..	1	..	1	..
Manchester, Ezekiel	1	..	..	1	..	2	..	..	1	..	..
McDonald, Alexander	1	..	..	1	..	1	..	1	..	..	..
McKinley, James	4	..	..	1	..	..	..	..	1	..	..
Miller, Alexander	2	..	1	..	1	4	1	1	1	..	..
Nelson, James	1	2	..	..	1	3	1	1	1	..	..
Nelson, William	..	1	2	..	1	..	1	..	..	1	..
Nelson, William Jr.	..	..	..	1	..	..	..	..	..	..	..
Orr, John	1	..	1	..	1	1	..	..	1	..	..
Page, Barker	4	1	..	1	..	1	1	..	1	..	..
Page, Jacob	..	1	..	..	1	2	..	3	..	1	..
Page, Jonathan	2	..	..	1	..	2	1	..	1	..	..
Page, Jonathan P.	2	..	..	1	..	..	..	..	1	..	..
Page, Josiah	..	1	2	..	1	..	1	..	..	1	..
Park, John	..	1	2	..	1	..	..	..	..	1	..
Reed, David	..	..	..	..	1	..	..	..	..	..	..
Reed, Widow	..	..	..	..	..	..	..	..	..	..	1
Richie, Widow	..	..	..	..	..	..	..	..	..	..	1
Ronalds, George	1	..	..	1	..	4	..	..	1	..	..
Shield, Alexander	..	1	1	..	1	..	2	2	..	1	..
Smith, John	1	..	..	1	..	1	..	..	1	..	..
Stewart, Allen	2	1	1	1	..	1	1	..	1	..	..
Syme, Cambell	5	..	1	1	..	1	1	..	1	..	..
Taylor, Widow	..	..	1	..	..	..	..	..	..	1	..
Thomas, James	2	..	..	1	..	3	..	..	1	..	..
Thomas, John	2	..	..	1	..	2	..	..	1	..	..
Warden, Andrew	..	..	1	..	..	..	..	1	..	..	..
Whitelaw, James	..	..	2	..	1	..	1	1	..	1	..
Whither, Foxwell	1	3	2	1	..	2	..	..	1	..	..
Whither, James	..	..	2	..	1	..	..	..	1	..	..
Whithill, Abraham	3	2	..	1	..	..	2	..	1	..	..
Whithill, James	1	1	2	..	1	2	..	2	1	..	..
Wright, Benjamin	3	..	..	1	..	2	..	1	1	..	..
SHEFFIELD											
Allard, Joseph	1	..	..	..	1	1	..	..	1	..	..
Daniels, Samuel	2	..	1	..	..	1	1	..	1	..	..
Drown, David	..	..	1	..	..	..	..	1	..	..	..
Drown, Enoch	1	..	1	..	..	..	..	..	1	..	..
Drown, Joseph	..	..	1	1	1	2	..	1	1	..	..
Drown, Stephen	2	..	..	1	1	1	..	..	1	1	..
Durbin, Benjamin	..	..	1	..	..	2	..	..	1	..	..
Foss, Moses	4	1	..	1	..	..	1	2	1	..	..
Foy, James	4	..	..	1	..	1	..	1	..	..	..
Gray, Henry	1	..	..	1	..	3	..	..	1	..	..
Gray James	1	1	1	..	1	..	1	..	..	1	..
Gray, Jonathan	2	..	..	1	..	1	..	..	1	..	..
Gray, Joseph	2	..	3	..	1	2	1	1	1	..	..

CALEDONIA COUNTY—Continued

NAMES OF HEADS OF FAMILIES	FREE WHITE MALES					FREE WHITE FEMALES					
	Under 10 years of age	Of 10 and under 16	Of 16 and under 26 including heads of families	Of 26 and under 45 including heads of families	Of 45 and upwards including heads of families.	Under 10 years of age	Of 10 and under 16	Of 16 and under 26 including heads of families	Of 26 and under 45 including heads of families	Of 45 and upwards including heads of families	All other free persons except Indians not taxed
SHEFFIELD—con.											
Hall, Moses	1	..	..	1	..	1	..	1	..	..	..
Hawkins, William	2	2	..	1	..	4	..	1	1	..	..
Heard, Daniel	..	..	..	2	..	..	1	..	..	1	..
Heath, Caleb	3	..	..	1	..	..	..	..	1	..	..
Hodgeden, James N.	1	..	1	..	..	1	..	..	1	..	..
Jenings, David	2	..	..	1	..	1	..	1	..	..	..
Jenings, Richard	1	..	..	1	..	3	..	..	1	..	..
Jennings, John	..	1	3	..	1	..	..	3	..	1	..
Keniston, Isaac	2	..	..	1	..	1	..	1	..	..	..
Miles, Archelus	..	1	1	..	1	..	..	2	..	1	..
Miles, Archelus Jr.	2	..	..	1	..	..	..	1	..	..	..
Miles, Reuben	2	..	..	2	..	2	..	..	1	..	..
Pearl, Isaac	1	..	1	..	..	..	..	1	..	..	..
Pearl, William	2	2	1	..	1	..	..	1	..	1	..
Twombley, Samuel	..	..	..	1	..	1	..	1	..	..	..
Willey, John	1	2	..	1	..	2	1	1	1	..	..
ST. JOHNSBURY											
Abbot, George	..	..	..	1	..	..	..	1	..	..	..
Aldridge, Ariel	..	..	..	1	..	1	..	..	1	..	..
Aldridge, Samuel	1	..	..	1	..	1	..	..	1	..	..
Aldridge, Squir	1	1	..	1	..	1	2	..	1	..	..
Alexander, Reuben	..	..	..	1	..	4	..	2	..	..	..
Allen, Mathew	..	..	2	..	..	..	..	1	..	..	..
Arnold, William	..	..	2	2	..	1	..	2	..	..	1
Ayre, Hezekiah	3	..	..	1	..	2	..	..	1	..	..
Ayre, James	1	..	..	1	..	1	..	1	..	..	..
Ayre, John	2	1	..	1	..	2	2	..	1	..	..
Ayre, John 2nd	3	1	..	1	..	1	..	..	1	..	..
Ayre, Samuel	..	..	2	..	1	..	..	1	..	1	..
Ayre, Samuel Jr.	3	2	..	1	..	2	..	1	1	..	..
Balch, Josiah	1	..	..	1	..	1	..	1	..	..	..
Barker, Barnabus	1	1	..	1	..	3	1	1	1	..	..
Barker, John	..	..	..	1	..	..	..	..	1	..	..
Barker, John Jr.	2	..	..	1	..	2	..	..	1	..	..
Barker, Samuel	..	1	..	1	..	..	..	1	..	..	..
Bishop, Nathaniel H.	4	..	..	1	..	1	..	..	1	..	..
Bradley, Reuben	..	..	1	2	1	..	..	2	..	1	..
Britt, Ephraim	1	..	1	..	..	..	..	1	..	..	..
Brown, Nathaniel	2	..	..	1	..	1	1	..	1	..	..
Chandler, Barnabus	2	..	..	1	..	1	..	..	1	..	..
Cobb, Simeon	..	1	..	1	..	..	1	..	1	..	..
Colbey, Ezekiel	1	..	..	1	..	4	..	1	..	..	..
Cushing, Benjamin	1	..	..	1	..	2	..	..	1	..	..
Edson, Nathaniel	..	..	1	4	..	4	3	..	1	1	..
Flint, Jonas	4	1	..	1	..	..	..	..	1	..	..
Freeman, Caleb	1	..	1	1	..	1	..	..	1	..	..
Fuller, Daniel	..	..	..	1	..	2	3	..	1	..	..
Gardner, Paris	2	..	..	1	1	2	..	..	1	..	..
Gilbert, Gideon	1	1	2	..	1	1	1	1	1	1	..
Gilchrist, Alexander	3	..	..	1	..	1	..	..	1	..	..
Gilson, Daniel	2	1	..	1	..	1	..	..	1	..	..
Gilson, Jonathan	3	..	..	1	..	1	..	..	1	..	..
Goss, Alpheus	1	..	..	1	..	1	..	1	..	..	..
Goss, David	3	1	1	1	..	1	..	..	1	..	..
Hastens, Joel	1	..	..	1	..	2	..	..	2	..	..
Hawes, Daniel	1	..	..	1	..	2	..	..	1	..	..
Hawkins, Jonah	..	1	1	..	1	1	1	1	1	..	..
Healey, John	3	..	1	1	..	1	1	1	..	1	..
Hicks, Peleg	2	..	..	1	..	3	..	..	1	..	..
Hidden, Otis	1	..	..	1	..	..	..	1	..	..	..
Higgins, John	..	1	3	..	1	..	1	1	..	1	..
Higgins, Joseph	..	1	..	..	1	..	..	..	..	1	..
Higgins, Peletiah	2	2	..	1	..	3	..	..	1	..	..
Hoit, William	5	..	..	1	..	2	1	..	2	1	..
Houghton, Alpheus	2	..	1	1	..	3	..	..	1	..	..
Houghton, Elijah	2	..	1	1	1	..	..	..	2	1	..
Ide, John	1	..	1	..	1	..	1	3	..	1	..
Johns, Marshal	1	..	..	1	..	1	..	..	1	..	..
Jones, Godfrey	3	..	..	1	..	2	..	..	1	..	..
Juit, Luther	2	..	1	..	..	..	..	..	1	..	..
ST. JOHNSBURY—con.											
Kelly, Daniel	..	1	1	..	1	..	..	..	..	1	..
Kuch, Philip	2	2	1	1	..	..	..	..	1	..	..
Ladd, John	1	2	3	..	1	1	..	..	..	1	..
Lathan, Asa	1	..	..	1	..	2	..	..	1	..	..
Lawrence, Hubart	..	..	..	2	..	..	..	1	..	..	..
Lee, Asa	1	..	1	1	..	2	..	1	1	..	..
Lord, Joseph	2	1	1	1	2	1	..	1	1	..	..
Mann, James	2	1	1	..	1	1	..	1	..	1	..
Martin, Isaac	4	..	..	1	..	2	1	1	1	..	..
McGaffey, John	1	1	..	1	..	1	1	..	1	..	..
McMenas, Patrick	1	..	1	..	1	4	3	..	1	..	..
Melvin, Moses	..	..	..	1	..	1	..	2	..	..	..
Minot, Benjamin	..	..	1	..	..	1	..	1	..	..	..
Minot, Straton	..	..	..	1	..	1	..	2	..	..	..
Peck, Thomas	1	1	6	1	..	..	..	2	..	..	..
Pierce, Aratus	2	..	..	1	..	1	..	..	1	..	..
Pierce, Daniel	..	1	2	..	1	..	1	..	1	1	..
Pierce, Daniel Jr.	..	1	..	1	..	..	2	..	1	..	..
Pierce, Israel	1	..	..	1	..	..	..	1	..	..	..
Pierce, John	2	..	..	..	1	..	2	..	..	1	..
Pierce, Thomas	..	..	2	1	..	2	1	..	1	..	..
Roberts, Joel	1	1	..	1	..	3	..	1	1	..	..
Root, Issac	..	1	1	1	..	4	1	2	1	..	..
Rowlin, Hopkins	2	..	..	1	..	2	..	..	1	..	..
Sanderson, Ebenezer	2	..	3	..	1	..	2	1	..	1	..
Sanger, Eleazer	1	1	1	1	..	3	..	..	1	..	..
Shins, Oliver	4	1	..	1	..	2	..	..	1	..	..
Smith, John	1	1	..	1	2	..	..	1	..	..	..
Spaldan, Reuben	1	..	..	1	..	3	..	1	1	..	..
Spaldan, Samuel	2	..	..	1	..	..	3	..	1	..	..
Stoel, Isaac	1	..	1	..	1	1	1	1	..	..	..
Thayer, John	1	..	..	1	..	1	..	..	1	..	..
Trolcutt, Jonathan	..	..	..	1	..	2	..	..	1	..	..
Tute, Moses	..	..	..	..	1	..	..	1	..	1	..
Vinson, Joseph	2	1	1	..	1	..	1	3	..	1	..
West, Presbry	3	..	1	1	..	2	..	1	1	..	..
Weston, Caleb	1	..	..	1	..	1	..	..	1	..	..
Wheeler, Gardner	..	..	1	1	..	3	..	1	1	..	..
Wheeler, Martin	2	..	1	1	..	2	..	..	1	..	..
Wheeler, Samuel	..	..	1	..	..	..	..	1	..	..	..
Wheston, James	2	..	..	1	..	1	..	..	1	..	..
Whipple, Jeremiah	1	2	1	..	1	1	..	3	1	..	..
Wilder, Peter	1	..	..	2	..	2	..	..	1	..	..
Wilson, Samuel	1	1	2	1	..	3	2	..	1	..	..
Wing, Isaac	1	..	..	1	..	3	..	..	1	..	..
Wright, Benjamin	3	1	2	..	1	3	..	1	1	..	..
WALDEN											
Adye, Caleb	..	..	2	..	1	..	1	3	..	1	..
Barker, Nathan	..	2	..	1	..	5	..	..	1	..	..
Blanchard, James	3	1	1	..	1	1	..	1	1	..	..
Burbank, Nathaniel	1	2	1	..	1	2	..	1	..	1	..
Carr, Robert	2	..	1	..	1	2	1	..	1	..	..
Carr, Samuel	..	..	1	..	..	..	..	1	1	..	..
Cate, Benjamin	2	..	..	1	..	3	1	..	1	..	..
Cate, Elisha	1	..	..	..	1	..	2	2	..	1	..
Dow, Nathaniel	3	2	..	..	1	..	1	..	1	..	..
Edwards, David	1	..	..	1	..	2	..	..	1	..	..
Edwards, Timothy	1	..	1	..	..	2	..	1	..	..	..
Farrington, Nathaniel	2	1	3	1	..	..	..	..	1	..	..
Fulsom, Enoch	..	..	1	..	..	..	..	1	..	..	..
Gilman, David	1	..	..	1	..	3	1	1	..	..	..
Gilman, Edward	..	1	1	1	..	1	..	1	..	..	..
Gilman, Joseph	1	..	1	1	..	2	..	..	1	..	..
Gilman, Peter	..	1	..	..	1	..	..	..	..	1	..
Gilman, Widow	..	..	..	..	..	..	..	1	..	1	..
Haynes, Timothy	..	..	1	..	..	1	..	1	..	..	..
Johnson, Daniel	..	..	2	..	..	2	..	1	..	..	..
Perkins, Nathaniel	1	1	..	1	..	4	1	..	1	..	..

CALEDONIA COUNTY—Continued

NAMES OF HEADS OF FAMILIES	FREE WHITE MALES: Under 10 years of age	FREE WHITE MALES: Of 10 and under 16	FREE WHITE MALES: Of 16 and under 26 including heads of families	FREE WHITE MALES: Of 26 and under 45 including heads of families	FREE WHITE MALES: Of 45 and upwards including heads of families	FREE WHITE FEMALES: Under 10 years of age	FREE WHITE FEMALES: Of 10 and under 16	FREE WHITE FEMALES: Of 16 and under 26 including heads of families	FREE WHITE FEMALES: Of 26 and under 45 including heads of families	FREE WHITE FEMALES: Of 45 and upwards including heads of families	All other free persons except Indians not taxed
WALDEN—con.											
Ransom, Thomas	..	..	1	..	..	..	..	..	1	..	..
Smith, Benjamin	..	..	..	1	..	1	..	1	..	..	..
Spaldon, Amos	1	..	3	..	..	1	1	1	..	..	..
Weeks, John	1	2	..	1	..	2	1	..	1	..	..
White, William	2	..	..	1	..	1	..	..	1	..	..
WATERFORD											
Addams, Charles	..	..	..	1	..	2	..	1	..	..	
Allen, Zadock	..	..	1	..	..	1	..	1	..	..	..
Armington, John	1	..	1	..	..	1	..	..	1	..	..
Armington, Joseph	2	1	1	1	..	2	1	..	1	..	..
Badger, James	..	..	1	..	..	1	..	1	..	..	..
Brigham, Aaron	1	..	..	1	..	2	..	..	1	..	..
Brigham, Ephraim	1	..	..	..	1	1	1	1	..	1	..
Brigham, Ephraim	..	1	..	..	1	1	1	..	..	1	..
Brown, Daniel	..	..	..	1	..	2	..	1	..	..	..
Brown, Joshua	..	..	1	..	..	1	..	1	..	..	..
Brown, Peleg	3	2	1	1	..	2	2	..	1	..	..
Buck, Reuben	3	..	..	1	..	1	..	..	1	..	..
Buck, Walter	2	..	..	1	1	2	..	..	1	1	..
Bugbee, Alpheus	1	..	..	1	..	2	..	1	..	..	..
Carpenter, Asa	..	..	..	1	..	2	..	1	..	..	..
Carpenter, Jonah	..	..	1	..	..	..	..	1	..	..	..
Case, John	..	..	1	..	..	..	..	1	..	..	..
Caswell, Andrew	3	1	..	1	..	1	..	..	1	..	..
Caswell, John	..	..	..	1	..	1	..	1	..	..	..
Chafee, Oliver	..	..	..	1	..	..	..	1	..	..	..
Chancy, Abial	..	..	..	1	..	..	..	..	1	..	..
Chaplin, John	2	1	..	1	..	1	1	..	1	..	..
Church, Bela	..	..	1	..	..	..	..	..	..	..	..
Church, David	..	..	..	1	..	2	..	..	1	..	..
Church, Pearly	1	..	..	1	..	3	1	..	1	..	..
Cleavland, Elijah P.	1	..	..	1	..	1	..	..	1	..	..
Cole, Nathan	2	..	..	1	..	1	..	..	1	..	..
Cole, Stephen	1	1	..	..	1	2	1	..	..	1	..
Cole, Stephen Jr	1	..	1	..	..	..	..	1	..	..	..
Collins, Daniel	..	..	1	..	..	1	..	..	1	..	..
Cushman, Comfort	..	..	..	1	..	..	..	1	..	..	..
Cushman, Delano	1	..	1	..	..	..	..	1	..	..	..
Davison, Asahel	3	..	..	1	..	1	..	1	1	..	..
Davison, Silas	2	1	..	1	..	2	..	..	1	..	..
Dutton, Zaconiah	..	..	..	1	..	2	..	..	1	..	..
Eaton, Eliphalet	2	..	..	1	..	2	..	..	1	..	..
Eddy, Abraham	2	..	..	1	..	1	..	..	1	..	..
Farnum, Ebenezer	4	1	1	..	1	1	1	..	..	1	..
Farrington, Joseph	2	..	..	1	..	1	..	..	1	..	..
Fisher, Nathan	2	..	..	1	..	2	..	..	1	..	..
Fitteh, Joseph	1	1	..	1	..	2	..	..	1	..	..
Fletcher, Samuel	3	..	2	1	1	4	2	1	1	..	..
Freeman, Elijah	1	2	1	1	..	1	..	..	1	..	..
Fuller, Benjamin	1	..	..	1	..	1	..	..	1	..	..
Goodall, Alva	..	..	..	1	..	1	..	..	1	..	..
Goodall, Shubell	3	..	..	1	..	1	..	..	1	..	..
Goodall, Summer	1	..	..	1	..	1	..	1	..	..	..
Goodall, Zedediah	..	..	..	1	..	..	..	..	1	..	..
Goss, Abel	3	1	..	1	..	1	1	..	1	..	..
Goss, Levi	3	..	..	1	..	..	..	..	1	..	..
Green, Samuel	2	..	1	..	1	..	1	1	..	1	..
Grow, Asa	1	..	1	1	1	1	..	..	3	1	..
Grow, John	1	2	2	..	1	..	1	..	..	1	..
Hadley, Nehemiah	..	..	..	1	..	..	..	..	1	..	..
Hadley, Stephen	1	1	1	..	..	1	..	1	..	..	..
Harvey, Ezra	3	..	..	1	..	2	..	..	1	..	..
Hastens, Amasa	..	..	..	1	..	..	..	1	..	..	..
Hemingway, Silvanus	3	..	..	1	..	2	..	..	1	..	..
Hendrick, Widow	..	..	..	..	..	1	..	1	..	..	..
Higgins, Nathaniel F.	..	..	..	1	..	2	..	..	1	..	..
Hill, David	1	1	2	..	1	..	1	1	..	1	..
Hill, Thomas	2	..	1	..	..	..	..	1	..	..	..
Holbrook, Henry	..	..	..	1	..	4	2	..	1	..	..
Holbrook, William	..	1	..	1	..	2	..	..	1	..	..
Hull, Elijah	..	1	..	..	1	..	1	1	..	1	..
Hull, Elijah Jr.	2	..	..	1	..	2	..	..	1	..	..
Hull, Ephraim	2	..	1	1	..	..	..	..	1	..	..
Hull, Levi	2	..	..	1	..	1	..	..	1	..	..
Hurlbutt, Elisha	..	..	2	..	1	..	2	..	..	1	..
WATERFORD—con.											
Hurlbutt, Hezekiah	4	..	..	1	..	..	..	1	..	..	..
Hurlbutt, Nathaniel	5	1	..	1	..	..	..	..	1	..	..
Hutchinson, Benjamin	..	..	..	1	..	..	..	1	..	..	..
Jacobs, Amisiah	..	..	..	1	..	2	..	..	1	..	..
Joslin, James	2	1	..	1	..	1	..	..	1	..	..
Kenney, Amos	..	..	..	1	..	1	..	1	..	..	..
Kenny, Nathan	1	..	..	1	..	1	..	..	1	..	..
Kidder, Luther	1	..	..	1	..	4	..	..	1	..	..
Knight, Joseph	..	1	2	1	..	1	1	..	1	..	..
May, Dexter	4	..	..	1	..	2	..	..	1	..	..
Morgan, Cornelius	2	1	1	..	1	..	1	1	1	1	..
Morgan, David	..	..	..	1	..	..	..	..	1	..	..
Newton, Silas	..	..	..	1	..	1	..	..	1	..	..
Niles, John	..	..	..	1	..	3	..	..	1	..	..
Pain, Thomas	3	..	..	1	..	1	2	..	1	..	..
Pike, Luther	1	..	..	1	..	1	..	..	1	..	..
Pike, Nathan	4	..	..	1	..	..	..	..	1	..	..
Pomroy, Eleazer	1	..	1	..	..	1	..	..	1	..	..
Pomroy, Solomon	1	..	1	1	1	2	3	..	1	..	..
Potter, Barnabas	1	1	..	..	1	1	1	..	..	1	..
Potter, Thaddeus	1	..	..	1	..	2	..	..	1	..	..
Richards, Jonathan	2	..	..	1	..	..	..	..	1	..	..
Richardson, Abial	2	..	..	1	..	..	..	..	1	..	..
Rin, Squire	..	..	1	..	..	1	..	1	..	..	..
Ross, Jonathan	2	..	..	1	..	..	..	1	..	..	..
Silvester, Peter	3	..	..	..	1	3	1	..	1	..	..
Smith, Thomas	..	..	1	..	1	..	1	2	..	1	..
Soapper, Joseph	2	..	1	..	..	..	..	1	..	..	..
Soapper, Samuel	..	..	..	..	1	..	..	..	1	1	..
Soapper, Samuel Jr.	..	..	..	1	..	2	..	1	..	..	..
Trescott, William	1	..	..	1	..	2	1	..	1	..	..
Underwood, Samuel	1	1	..	..	1	2	..	..	1	..	..
Waren, Jonas	2	1	..	1	..	2	..	..	1	..	..
Woods, Ebenezer	3	1	..	1	..	1	..	..	1	..	..
Woods, Joseph	2	1	..	1	..	2	3	2	1	..	..
Woods, Oliver	2	..	..	1	..	3	..	..	1	..	..
UNCERTAIN NAME											
Clark, Leavent (?)	1	..	..	1	..	1	..	..	1		..
WHEELOCK											
Adams, David	..	..	..	1	..	..	..	..	1	..	..
Allard, Joseph	1	..	1	..	..	..	..	1	..	1	..
Allen, John	1	..	..	..	1	1	..	..	1	..	..
Bangs, Joshua	2	1	..	1	..	1	1	..	1	..	..
Bean, John	1	2	2	..	1	1	..	2	..	1	..
Bean, Joseph	3	..	1	1	..	1	..	..	1	..	..
Bean, Samuel	..	..	1	..	..	1	..	1	..	..	..
Bickford, Ebenezer	..	1	3	..	1	2	..	..	..	1	..
Bickford, Hezekiah	1	..	1	..	..	..	..	1	..	..	..
Boyington, John	4	1	..	1	..	3	..	..	1	..	..
Bracket, Ichabod	..	..	1	..	1	..	..	..	..	1	..
Bracket, Levi	4	..	..	1	..	..	..	..	1	..	..
Bracket, Simeon	2	1	1	1	..	2	..	..	1	..	..
Brown, Nathaniel	2	..	1	1	..	1	..	..	1	..	..
Brown, Robert	2	..	..	1	..	1	..	..	1	..	..
Cate, James	1	..	1	..	..	..	..	1	..	..	..
Cate, Widow	1	..	..	..	..	3	1	1	..	1	..
Chandler, Ebenezer	2	2	..	1	2	1	1	1	..	..	..
Chandler, Joseph	1	2	1	..	1	1	..	..	1	..	..
Clemont, Merrill	2	..	1	1	..	2	..	..	1	..	..
Cochrin, Peter W.	..	1	..	1	..	1	..	..	1	..	..
Cochrine, John	1	..	..	1	..	2	..	..	1	..	..
Conner, Joseph	1	..	2	1	..	1	3	1	1	1	..
Cross, Nathaniel	1	..	1	1	..	1	..	1	..	..	..
Curtis, John	..	..	..	1	..	3	..	..	1	..	..
Derbon, Sherbon	..	1	1	..	1	..	..	..	..	1	..
Dow, Jonathan	1	..	3	..	1	..	..	1	1	..	..
Dow, Perkins	1	..	..	1	..	2	..	..	1	..	..
Elkins, John	..	..	..	1	..	..	..	1	..	..	..
Elkins, Nathaniel	..	..	2	..	1	..	..	1	..	1	..

CALEDONIA COUNTY—Continued

NAMES OF HEADS OF FAMILIES	FREE WHITE MALES: Under 10 years of age	FREE WHITE MALES: Of 10 and under 16	FREE WHITE MALES: Of 16 and under 26 including heads of families	FREE WHITE MALES: Of 26 and under 45 including heads of families	FREE WHITE MALES: Of 45 and upwards including heads of families	FREE WHITE FEMALES: Under 10 years of age	FREE WHITE FEMALES: Of 10 and under 16	FREE WHITE FEMALES: Of 16 and under 26 including heads of families	FREE WHITE FEMALES: Of 26 and under 45 including heads of families	FREE WHITE FEMALES: Of 45 and upwards including heads of families	All other free persons except Indians not taxed
WHEELOCK—con.											
Fifield, Samuel	1	..	2	..	1	..	..	..	..	1	..
Foster, Daniel	2	..	..	1	..	2	1	..	1	..	..
French, Elisha	..	..	..	..	1	..	..	..	..	1	..
Fuller, Samuel	..	..	1	1	1	..	1	..	1	..	..
Fuller, Simeon	..	..	..	..	1	..	1	..	..	1	..
Fuller, William	..	..	..	1	..	2	..	1	..	..	..
Fulsom, Daniel	2	..	..	1	..	..	..	1	..	..	..
Fulsom, Jonathan	..	1	3	..	1	1	1	..	..	1	..
Fulsom, Theophilus	1	1	1	..	1	..	..	..	1	..	..
Gilman, Daniel	2	..	1	..	..	..	..	..	1	..	..
Glidden, Simeon	1	..	1	..	..	2	..	1	..	..	..
Gray, Jeremiah	..	..	3	..	1	..	1	..	..	1	..
Gray, John	1	..	..	1	..	3	..	1	..	..	..
Gray, Joshua	..	..	..	1	..	1	..	1	..	..	..
Guy, Jacob	2	..	..	1	..	1	..	..	1	..	..
Harris, Joseph	1	..	..	1	..	..	..	1	..	..	..
Heath, John	2	..	..	1	..	3	..	..	1	..	..
Hines, Nathan	2	..	..	1	..	1	..	..	1	..	..
Hoit, Abner	1	1	2	..	1	2	2	..	1	..	..
Hoit, Barret	2	..	..	2	..	..	..	1	..	..	..
Hoit, Daniel	..	..	..	..	1	1	..	..	1	..	..
Holladay, Noah	4	1	1	..	1	1	..	1	1	..	..
Howard, Nathaniel	..	..	..	1	..	1	1	..	1	..	..
Howard, William	1	..	..	1	..	2	..	..	1	..	..
Hutchins, Samuel	2	..	1	1	..	2	2	..	1	..	..
Ingalls, Joseph	..	..	1	..	1	..	..	1	..	1	..
Leach, Samuel	2	..	..	1	..	1	..	..	1	..	..
Leavitt, Gideon	1	..	3	..	1	1	2	2	1	..	..
Little, David	3	3	..	1	..	1	1	..	1	..	..
Lock, Moses	1	..	..	1	..	..	..	1	..	..	..
Lock, Thomas	..	1	1	..	1	..	1	..	..	1	..
Louge, Nehemiah	..	..	..	1	..	1	..	..	1	..	..
Love, John	1	..	..	1	..	1	..	1	..	..	..
Lyman, Elijah	1	..	..	1	..	1	..	..	1	..	..
Mash, Henry	1	..	..	1	..	4	..	..	1	..	..
McClaran, Andrew	2	1	..	1	..	2	..	..	1	..	..
Miles, Josiah	1	1	3	..	1	1	..	1	..	1	..
Morrill, Abner	1	..	..	1	..	..	..	1	..	..	..
Morrill, Abraham	1	..	1	..	1	4	2	2	1	..	..
Morrill, Benjamin	2	..	..	1	..	1	..	..	1	..	..
Mosher, Michael	..	1	1	..	1	..	1	2	..	1	..
Mosher, Richard	1	..	..	1	..	2	..	1	..	..	..
Niles, Ephraim	2	2	1	..	1	1	1	2	..	1	..
Noyse, Thomas	4	..	..	1	..	1	..	..	1	..	..
Omans, Thomas	1	1	1	1	..	2	1	1	1	..	..
Otis, Joshua	4	..	..	1	..	..	2	..	1	..	..
Otis, Thomas	2	1	..	1	..	..	1	..	1	..	..
Philips, Nehemiah	2	..	..	1	..	1	..	..	1	..	..
Potter, William	1	..	..	1	..	..	..	1	..	..	..
Sanbon, Elisha	3	..	..	1	..	..	1	1	1	..	..
Sanbon, Jonathan H.	2	..	1	..	1	3	2	1	1	..	..
Shattock, Obel	2	..	..	1	..	3	..	..	1	..	..
Shattock, Shubel	1	..	1	..	..	..	..	1	..	..	..
Shattock, Simeon	1	..	..	1	..	..	..	..	1	..	..
Sherbon, James	1	1	2	..	1	1	1	..	1	..	..
Sly, David	1	..	..	1	..	1	..	1	..	1	..
Smith, Nathan	2	..	..	1	..	..	..	1	1	..	..
Thomson, Ebenezer	1	..	1	..	..	1	..	1	..	..	..
Townson, Thomas	1	1	1	..	1	1	1	1	..	1	..
Trunt, James	1	..	..	1	..	2	..	..	1	..	..
Verry, Joseph	2	..	..	1	..	1	..	..	1	..	..
Ward, Samuel	..	1	..	..	1	3	..	..	1	..	..
Weeks, Joshua	..	2	1	1	1	1	..	3	1	1	..
Willey, John	..	..	..	..	1	..	..	..	1	1	..
Willey, Paul	1	..	..	1	..	3	..	..	1	..	..
Woodmorn, John	3	..	..	1	1	2	1	..	1	1	..
Wright, Thomas	..	..	..	..	1	..	..	..	..	1	..
WOODBURY											
Ainsworth, Ephraim	..	..	..	..	1	..	..	1	1	1	..
Ainsworth, Smith	..	..	..	1	..	..	..	..	1	..	..
Carr, Joseph	1	1	1	..	1	..	1	..	..	1	..
Sabin, Gideon	1	..	..	1	..	2	..	1	..	..	..
Smith, Daniel	1	..	..	1	..	3	..	..	1	..	..

CHITTENDEN COUNTY

NAMES OF HEADS OF FAMILIES	FREE WHITE MALES: Under 10 years of age	FREE WHITE MALES: Of 10 and under 16	FREE WHITE MALES: Of 16 and under 26 including heads of families	FREE WHITE MALES: Of 26 and under 45 including heads of families	FREE WHITE MALES: Of 45 and upwards including heads of families	FREE WHITE FEMALES: Under 10 years of age	FREE WHITE FEMALES: Of 10 and under 16	FREE WHITE FEMALES: Of 16 and under 26 including heads of families	FREE WHITE FEMALES: Of 26 and under 45 including heads of families	FREE WHITE FEMALES: Of 45 and upwards including heads of families	All other free persons except Indians not taxed
BOLTON											
Algier, Aaron	..	1	..	..	1	2	..	..	1	1	..
Barnet, Job	2	..	..	1	..	3	1	..	1	..	..
Barnet, Samuel	..	1	..	..	1	..	..	..	..	1	..
Beach, Joseph	..	..	..	1	..	..	1	1	1	..	..
Bigford, Abner	..	..	1	..	..	2	..	1	..	..	..
Camwell, Isaac	1	..	1	..	..	1	..	1	..	..	..
Canada, Robert	..	..	..	1	..	2	..	..	1	..	1
Colbath, Winthrop	..	..	..	..	1	5	..	..	1	..	..
Craig, James	2	1	1	..	..	..	..	..	1	..	..
Hinxton, Samuel	1	2	..	..	1	2	..	..	..	1	..
Hunt, Jonas	..	..	2	1	1	1	2	1	1	..	..
Joiner, Francis	..	3	..	1	1	3	1	..	1	..	..
Joiner, Nathan	2	..	..	1	..	1	..	..	1	..	..
Jones, Jabez	1	..	..	1	..	..	..	1	..	..	..
Kennada, John	1	1	1	..	1	..	..	2	..	1	..
Lavake, Augustin	3	1	2	1	..	1	..	1	1	..	..
Lewis, Asa	1	..	..	1	..	2	..	1	..	..	..
Miller, Robert	3	1	1	1	..	2	..	3	1	..	..
Montgomery, Thomas	2	..	..	1	..	2	..	..	1	..	..
Moor, Ezra	..	1	1	1	..	1	..	..	1	..	..
Moore, John	4	1	..	1	..	1	2	..	1	..	..
Morris, Thomas	4	..	..	1	..	..	..	3	1	1	..
Mows, John	..	1	2	..	1	..	1	..	..	1	..
O'Bryan, Daniel	1	1	1	1	..	2	..	..	1	..	..
Pineo, Andrew	..	..	..	1	..	..	..	..	..	..	..
Pineo, Daniel	..	1	2	1	1	..	2	..	..	1	..
Preston, John	1	1	1	..	1	..	..	2	..	1	..
Preston, John Jr.	..	..	1	..	..	..	..	1	..	..	..
BOLTON—con.											
Stillson, Robert	2	..	2	..	1	1	1	1	1	..	..
Stockwell, Asa	2	..	..	1	..	..	..	..	1	..	..
Stockwell, Eleazer	1	1	..	..	1	1	2	..	..	1	..
Webster, Samuel	1	1	..	..	1	..	1	2	..	1	..
Willson, John	1	..	..	1	..	..	..	..	1	..	..
Wood, Joseph	1	..	..	1	1	..	..	..	2	..	..
BURLINGTON											
Adams, Benjamin	2	..	..	1	..	3	..	..	1	..	..
Adams, John	..	1	1	2	..	2	1	..	1	..	..
Allen, Daniel	1	..	1	1	..	..	..	1	..	..	..
Allen, Levi	..	..	..	..	1	..	..	..	1	..	..
Allen, Samuel	..	2	1	..	1	2	1	..	1	..	..
Ames, Thomas	..	..	2	1	..	2	..	..	1	..	..
Ames, Walter	2	..	1	2	..	..	1	1	1	..	..
Atwater, Thomas	1	..	2	..	..	..	..	1	..	..	..
Avery, Walter	1	1	1	1	..	2	..	1	1	..	..
Backus, Simon	2	1	1	1	..	..	1	..	1	..	..
Baker, Nahum	..	..	..	1	..	2	..	..	1	..	..
Bean, Eliphalet	4	..	..	1	..	1	..	..	1	..	..
Bennett, Seeley	2	..	..	1	..	3	..	1	1	..	..
Bernard, Eli	..	1	1	2	..	..	1	..	1	..	..
Berry, John	..	..	..	1	..	..	..	..	..	..	..
Bostwick, Reuben	..	..	1	1	1	2	..	..	1	..	..
Boynton, Job	1	1	3	2	1	1	1	1	..	1	..
Brimsmaid, James	..	..	..	2	..	..	1	..	1	..	..
Brown, Ebenezer	4	..	1	1	..	..	2	1	1	..	..
Brownson, Amos Jr.	1	..	2	2	..	3	1	1	1	..	1
Burnham, Amos	3	2	1	1	..	..	..	1	..	..	..
Butler, Alpheus	4	..	..	1	..	1	..	..	1	..	..
Callender, John	..	..	3	..	1	1	..	..	..	1	..
Castle, Daniel	..	..	2	..	1	1	2	..	..	1	..
Catlin, Moses	..	1	4	4	..	1	..	1	1	..	..
Chamberlin, Ebenezer	2	2	2	1	..	3	1	2	1	..	

CHITTENDEN COUNTY—Continued

NAMES OF HEADS OF FAMILIES	FREE WHITE MALES					FREE WHITE FEMALES					
	Under 10 years of age	Of 10 and under 16	Of 16 and under 26 including heads of families	Of 26 and under 45 including heads of families	Of 45 and upwards including heads of families	Under 10 years of age	Of 10 and under 16	Of 16 and under 26 including heads of families	Of 26 and under 45 including heads of families	Of 45 and upwards including heads of families	All other free persons except Indians not taxed
BURLINGTON—con.											
Christie, Lawrence	..	..	1	2	..	3	..	..	1	..	..
Coit, William	2	..	..	1	..	2	..	1	1	..	..
Colamore, Samuel	1	1	1	1	..	4	..	..	1	..	..
Cole, Matthew	..	..	..	1	..	..	..	..	..	..	..
Collard, John	..	..	..	1	..	..	..	..	..	..	..
Comstock, Jason	3	1	1	1	..	2	..	..	1	..	..
Comstock, Peter	3	..	..	1	..	1	..	1	..	..	..
Converse, Asa	3	1	..	..	1	2	..	2	..	1	..
Curry, John	..	..	2	1	..	..	..	1	1	..	..
Davison, Alexander	..	..	..	1	..	..	..	..	..	..	..
Dodge, Paul	..	..	1	..	..	..	..	..	..	..	..
Doxy, John	1	1	..	1	2	2	1	1	1	..	..
Eaton, Jesse	..	..	1	1	..	1	..	1	..	..	..
Eaton, William	1	..	..	1	..	3	..	..	1	..	..
Eldridge, John	..	1	3	..	1	..	..	1	1	1	..
Farnum, Barikias	2	..	..	1	..	2	1	..	1	..	..
Farwell, Edward	..	..	1	..	..	..	..	1	..	..	..
Fay, John Esq.	1	1	2	1	..	2	..	2	1	..	..
Fay, Moses	..	..	1	..	..	..	..	1	..	..	..
Featoks, Richard	..	..	..	1	1	3	..	..	2	..	..
Ferris, Peter	..	..	1	..	..	2	..	1	..	..	..
Finch, Zimri	..	..	1	..	..	1	..	1	..	..	..
Fletcher, Thomas	..	..	4	1	1	..	..	..	1	..	..
Fobes, Eliab	2	..	..	1	..	2	1	..	1	..	..
Galusha, Ezra	..	..	1	1	..	..	..	..	1	..	..
Harrington, Joseph	1	..	..	1	..	1	..	1	1	..	..
Harrington, William C.	2	1	5	..	1	1	..	3	..	..	..
Harris, Seth	..	2	..	1	..	..	..	..	..	..	..
Hecock, Samuel	..	1	2	1	..	..	..	1	1	..	..
Hilton, Winthrop	2	1	..	1	..	1	..	..	1	..	..
Hollister, Jesse	2	..	1	1	..	..	1	1	1	..	2
Hoose, Barnabas	5	1	..	1	..	..	..	..	1	..	..
Hoyt, David	..	..	..	1	..	2	..	..	1	..	..
Humphry, Emery	1	2	..	1	..	..	..	..	1	..	..
Hurlbut, Daniel	3	1	1	1	..	1	1	3	1	..	..
Hurlbut, Enos	2	..	..	1	..	1	1	1	1	..	..
Hurlbut, Ephraim	1	1	..	2	..	1	..	2	..	..	..
Hurlbut, Samuel	..	..	..	..	1	..	..	..	..	..	..
Johnson, Asa	3	..	..	1	..	2	..	..	1	..	..
Judson, Lyman	2	..	..	1	..	1	..	2	..	..	..
Kennan, Isaac	4	2	1	1	..	2	1	..	1	..	..
Keyes, Elnathan	2	1	1	2	..	1	..	2	1	..	1
King, Gideon	..	..	4	3	1	2	1	..	..	1	..
King, Gideon Jr.	..	..	..	1	..	..	..	..	..	..	..
King, Lyman	1	1	..	2	2	1	1	..	1	..	..
Lawrence, Stephen	1	1	1	1	..	3	..	..	1	..	..
Leak, Ephraim	1	..	2	..	1	..	..	1	..	..	..
Loomis, Horace	..	..	2	2	..	2	..	1	..	..	..
Loomis, Phineas	..	..	3	..	1	..	3	1	2	1	..
Mansfield, Alpheus	4	..	..	1	..	1	..	1	..	..	..
Moors, Stephen	2	1	2	1	..	3	1	1	..	..	..
Nichols, Levi	5	1	..	1	..	2	1	..	1	..	..
Ormsby, Jonathan	2	..	1	1	..	2	2	..	1	..	..
Osgood, Moses	..	..	2	1	..	2	..	..	1	..	..
Owens, Abel	1	..	1	..	..	..	..	1	..	..	..
Paine, Samuel	..	..	1	..	..	..	..	..	..	..	..
Pardo, Thomas	2	..	..	1	..	2	..	1	..	..	..
Pearl, Stephen	..	1	1	..	1	..	1	1	1	1	..
Peaslee, Zacheus	2	2	..	3	..	..	1	2	..	..	..
Peters, David	..	..	..	1	1	..	..	..	1	..	..
Pitcher, Isaac	3	..	1	1	..	1	1	2	1	..	..
Pomeroy, John	3	1	2	2	..	1	..	1	1	..	..
Reed, Job	1	1	2	1	..	1	1	2	..	..	..
Rice, Isaac	..	..	..	1	..	3	..	..	1	..	..
Rice, Mark	..	1	..	1	..	..	..	2	..	..	..
Richards, Jeremiah	..	..	1	..	..	3	..	1	..	..	..
Root, James B.	2	..	..	1	..	..	..	2	..	..	1
Russell, David	2	..	1	1	..	1	..	2	1	..	..
Russell, Stephen	..	..	1	1	1	..	..	1	..	1	..
Sanders, Rev. D. C.	..	..	..	1	..	3	..	2	1	..	1
Sawyer, James	4	..	..	1	1	..	1	..	1	..	..
Shea, Daniel	2	2	..	1	..	1	..	..	1	..	..
BURLINGTON—con.											
Sheffield, Charles	2	1	..	1	..	..	..	..	1	..	..
Simonds, James	1	..	..	1	..	3	1	..	1	..	..
Smith, Ezra	1	..	..	1	..	..	..	1	..	..	..
Smith, Lydia	..	..	..	..	..	..	..	1	..	1	..
Smith, Nathan	2	..	..	1	..	3	..	..	1	..	..
Smith, Peter B.	2	..	..	1	..	..	..	2	..	..	..
Snell, Calvin	1	1	..	1	..	1	2	..	1	..	..
Staniford, Daniel	..	..	2	2	..	..	..	..	..	..	..
Swift, Wyat	2	..	1	..	..	..	1	1	..	..	..
Thatcher, David	1	..	1	..	..	..	..	1	..	..	..
Thompson, Samuel	..	..	..	1	..	2	..	1	..	..	..
Tuttle, Thaddeus	..	1	..	1	..	3	..	1	1	..	..
Vansicklin, John	2	2	..	1	..	3	1	..	1	..	..
Wallace, Daniel	2	..	..	1	..	2	..	1	1	..	..
Ward, Aaron	..	1	..	2	..	2	..	1	..	..	..
Wares, Richard	1	..	..	1	..	..	2	..	1	..	..
Warner, Justus	1	..	1	1	..	..	..	..	1	..	..
Webb, Isaac	1	1	..	1	..	1	2	..	1	..	..
Webster, Nathan	..	..	..	1	..	..	2	..	1	..	..
Wells, John Jr.	2	..	..	1	..	2	3	..	1	..	..
Wilder, Daniel	2	..	1	3	..	2	..	..	1	..	..
Willard, Dubartis	1	2	2	1	2	..	..	..	..	1	..
Winslow, Luther	1	1	..	1	..	1	..	..	1	..	..
Woodward, Thomas	2	1	..	..	1	..	1	1	1	1	..
Woodworth, Joel	..	..	2	..	1	1	2	..	..	1	..
Wright, Cornelius	2	1	..	1	..	2	1	..	1	..	..
Young, Jenks	1	..	1	..	..	..	..	1	..	..	..
CHARLOTTE											
Adams, Allen	1	1	..	1	..	2	..	..	1	..	..
Adams, John	..	..	..	..	1	..	..	..	..	1	..
Allen, Joseph	..	..	1	..	1	..	..	..	..	1	..
Allen, Joseph Jr.	2	..	..	1	..	..	1	1	1	..	..
Allen, Moses	..	..	3	..	..	..	..	1	..	..	..
Allin, James	..	..	..	1	..	1	..	..	1	..	..
Andres, Denison	2	..	..	1	..	..	..	2	..	..	..
Andres, Samuel	1	..	..	1	..	..	..	1	..	..	..
Atwood, Jonathan	1	1	..	1	..	..	..	1	..	..	..
Awood, David	..	..	..	1	..	..	..	..	..	..	5
Baker, Eliab	3	..	..	1	..	1	1	..	1	..	..
Barker, Samuel	3	2	..	1	..	1	..	..	1	..	..
Barnam, Nathaniel	..	..	..	..	1	..	..	..	..	1	..
Barns, Asa	..	..	..	..	1	..	..	..	..	1	..
Barns, Asa Jr.	2	..	1	1	..	1	..	1	..	..	..
Barns, Daniel	..	..	1	1	..	..	1	1	1	1	..
Barns, Hezekiah	2	1	2	1	..	1	2	..	1	..	1
Barns, Joseph	1	..	1	..	..	2	..	2	..	..	..
Barton, Andrew	..	..	1	..	..	2	..	2	..	..	..
Barton, Caleb	..	1	..	..	1	..	..	1	..	1	..
Barton, Jeremiah	2	..	1	1	..	..	..	..	1	..	..
Beach, Ebenezer	1	..	1	1	..	1	1	..	1	..	..
Bears, James	1	..	..	1	..	1	..	..	1	..	..
Beers, Matthew	1	..	..	1	..	2	1	..	1	..	..
Bell, John	..	1	..	..	1	..	3	..	..	1	..
Bills, Joshua	2	1	..	1	..	1	2	..	1	..	..
Blanchard, Abial	1	1	..	..	1	..	2	1	..	1	..
Boughton, Stephen	..	..	..	1	..	1	..	1	..	..	..
Breakenridge, Francis	..	..	..	1	..	1	..	..	1	..	..
Breakenridge, Jonathan	3	1	2	1	..	1	1	..	1	..	..
Brown, Samuel	..	..	..	1	..	1	..	..	1	..	1
Buffum, Stephen	3	1	..	1	..	1	2	..	1	..	..
Burch, Thomas	2	..	..	1	..	1	2	..	1	..	..
Burgess, James	1	..	..	1	..	..	..	2	..	..	..
Burt, Thomas	3	..	..	1	..	1	..	..	1	..	..
Butterfield, James	..	..	1	..	1	2	1	1	..	..	..
Butterfield, James Jr.	3	1	..	1	..	1	..	..	1	..	..
Canfield, Thomas	..	..	2	..	..	..	..	..	..	..	..
Castle, Elijah	..	..	..	1	..	1	..	..	1	..	..
Chandler, Hill	..	..	1	1	..	1	..	1	1	1	..
Chandler, Philo	2	..	..	1	..	2	..	..	1	..	..
Chatfield, Joseph	..	..	..	1	..	1	..	1	..	..	..
Clark, Amos	1	..	..	1	..	..	..	..	1	..	..
Clark, John	1	1	..	1	..	..	..	..	1	..	..
Clark, Lamberton	1	..	..	1	..	..	3	2	1	1	..
Clarke, Jonah	1	..	..	1	..	2	1	1	..	..	..
Clarke, Reuben	1	..	1	1	..	1	2	1	1	..	..
Clarke, Zenas	4	1	..	1	..	2	2	1	1	..	..
Cobb, John	..	1	..	1	..	..	..	..	1	..	..

CHITTENDEN COUNTY—Continued

NAMES OF HEADS OF FAMILIES	FREE WHITE MALES					FREE WHITE FEMALES					All other free persons except Indians not taxed
	Under 10 years of age	Of 10 and under 16	Of 16 and under 26 including heads of families	Of 26 and under 45 including heads of families	Of 45 and upwards including heads of families.	Under 10 years of age	Of 10 and under 16	Of 16 and under 26 including heads of families	Of 26 and under 45 including heads of families	Of 45 and upwards including heads of families	
CHARLOTTE—con.											
Cogswell, Isaac	..	..	1	..	1	..	1	1	..	1	..
Cogswell, Levi	2	1	..	..	1	2	..	..	..	1	..
Cogswell, Seth	..	1	..	1	..	2	..	1	..	..	..
Conger, Moses	3	..	..	1	..	1	..	..	1	..	..
Coon, Jacob	2	1	..	1	..	2	1	..	1	..	..
Davis, Abel	..	1	..	1	..	3	1	..	1	..	..
Davis, William	..	..	..	1	..	1	1	2	..	..	..
Davison, William	..	..	..	1	..	..	..	..	..	1	..
Dudley, Moses	..	..	1	..	..	..	..	1	..	..	..
Eady, Thomas	..	2	..	1	..	2	..	..	1	..	..
Eaton, John	..	..	1	..	..	..	..	1	..	..	..
Fanches, John G.	..	..	1	..	..	1	..	1	..	..	..
Ferris, Walter	1	..	..	1	..	2	..	..	1	..	..
Fisher, John	..	..	..	1	..	..	..	..	1	..	..
Floyd, William	1	..	..	1	..	3	1	1	1	..	..
Foot, Isaac	2	..	1	1	..	1	..	..	1	..	..
Foot, Simeon	..	..	2	..	..	..	..	1	..	..	..
Foot, Uri	..	1	..	1	..	1	..	1	..	..	..
Fuller, Ammi	..	1	1	1	..	1	1	..	2	..	..
Fuller, Luther	1	..	2	..	..	..	..	1	..	1	..
Gentle, Andrew	1	..	..	..	1	2	2	..	2	..	..
Gibbs, Abel	1	2	..	1	..	4	1	..	1	..	..
Gillet, Ellal	..	..	..	1	..	..	..	..	1	..	..
Gillet, Jonathan	2	..	..	1	1	..	1	..	1	..	..
Gillet, Wheeler	..	1	1	..	1	..	1	2	1	1	..
Ginnins, Darius	..	..	1	1	..	3	1	1	..	..	..
Grant, Dinah	1	..	1	..	..	1	..	1	..	1	..
Hadlock, Samuel	..	..	..	..	1	..	..	..	..	1	..
Hall, Joseph	2	..	1	1	..	3	1	..	2	..	..
Hatch, Rufus	1	..	1	..	..	..	..	1	..	..	..
Heath, John	..	..	..	1	..	..	..	1	..	..	..
Heath, Josiah	2	..	1	..	1	..	..	2	..	..	..
Henman, Calvin	..	..	..	1	..	..	..	1	..	..	..
Herbert, Samuel	..	..	..	1	..	3	..	..	1	..	..
Hewitt, Ezekiel	..	..	1	..	..	2	..	1	..	..	..
Hide, Samuel D.	2	1	1	..	1	..	1	..	1	..	..
Hill, Elisha	2	..	..	1	..	1	..	1	..	..	..
Hill, James	1	1	2	..	1	1	..	1	1	..	..
Hill, John	1	..	..	..	2	..	1	..	1	1	..
Hill, Zimri 1st	2	1	..	1	..	1	..	1	..	..	..
Hill, Zimri 2nd	1	1	1	1	..	3	1	1	1	..	..
Hinman, Daniel	..	..	..	..	1	1	..	1	..	2	..
Hoag, Joseph	1	1	1	1	..	2	2	1	1	..	..
Hollace, Elijah	4	1	..	..	1	1	1	..	1	..	..
Horsford, Daniel	..	..	2	..	1	..	..	..	..	1	..
Horsford, Daniel Jr.	2	1	..	..	1	2	..	1	1	..	..
Horsford, Roger	4	2	1	2	..	..	1	..	1	..	..
Hoskins, Eli	..	1	..	1	..	1	..	1	..	..	..
Hough, Caleb	4	2	1	1	..	2	..	..	1	..	..
Hough, Daniel	..	2	..	1	..	2	1	1	1	..	..
Howard, Stephen	1	2	..	1	..	2	..	..	1	..	..
Hubbell, Benjamin	..	..	..	1	..	5	..	..	1	..	..
Hubbell, David	2	1	1	..	1	1	1	..	1	..	..
Hurlbut, Elisha	1	1	1	1	1	..	1	1	1	..	..
Hurlbut, Isaiah	3	..	..	1	..	2	2	..	1	..	..
Hurlbut, Salmon	..	..	..	..	1	..	2	1	..	1	..
Hurlbut, Samuel	..	1	..	..	1	1	1	..	..	1	..
Hurlbut, Samuel Jr.	1	..	3	1	..	..	1	..	..	..	..
Irish, David	3	..	1	1	..	1	..	1	1	..	..
Judson, Phineas	..	..	..	1	..	2	2	..	1	..	..
Keeler, Ebenezer	..	1	..	..	1	..	..	..	..	1	..
Keeler, Elijah	3	2	..	..	1	1	..	..	1	..	..
Keeler, Thomas	1	2	..	1	..	3	..	1	1	..	..
Keep, William	..	..	2	1	..	..	1	..	1	..	..
Latham, William	2	..	..	1	..	..	..	..	1	..	..
Leavensworth, Abel	2	..	..	2	..	1	..	..	1	..	..
Lemon, Ezekiel	1	..	1	..	..	1	..	1	..	..	..
Lockwood, Israel	3	2	..	1	..	2	1	..	1	..	..
Loomer, Samuel	1	..	1	..	..	..	..	1	..	..	..
Loomis, Joseph	3	1	2	..	1	1	..	..	..	1	..
Lorey, Nehamiah	1	1	..	1	1	2	..	..	1	1	..
Lyman, Gad	1	..	..	1	..	2	..	..	1	..	..
Lyman, Medad	1	..	..	1	..	1	..	1	..	..	..
Lyman, Medad 2nd	..	..	1	3	..	2	..	..	1	..	..
Mallery, Gideon	..	..	..	1	..	3	2	..	1	..	..
Marble, Nathan	2	..	..	1	..	2	1	..	1	..	..
Martin, Jonas	..	..	1	..	..	1	..	1	..	..	1
Martin, Nathaniel	..	..	2	..	..	1	..	1	..	..	..

NAMES OF HEADS OF FAMILIES	FREE WHITE MALES					FREE WHITE FEMALES					All other free persons except Indians not taxed
	Under 10 years of age	Of 10 and under 16	Of 16 and under 26 including heads of families	Of 26 and under 45 including heads of families	Of 45 and upwards including heads of families.	Under 10 years of age	Of 10 and under 16	Of 16 and under 26 including heads of families	Of 26 and under 45 including heads of families	Of 45 and upwards including heads of families	
CHARLOTTE—con.											
Martin, Reuben	2	1	2	..	1	2	1	..	1	..	..
Martin, Wait	1	1	1	..	1	1	1	1	1	..	..
Martin, Zadock	1	..	1	..	..	..	..	1	..	..	..
McNeil, Charles	2	1	4	..	1	1	..	3	..	1	..
McNeil, John 1st	..	2	2	..	1	..	..	2	..	1	1
McNeil, John 2nd	..	..	..	1	..	3	..	..	1	..	..
Merchant, Ezra	..	..	..	..	1	..	..	..	..	1	..
Moger, Jesse	..	..	1	..	1	1	2	..	..	1	..
Moger, Truman	1	..	1	..	..	1	..	1	..	..	..
Morgan, David	1	..	1	1	..	2	..	1	..	..	..
Morse, Perce	1	..	1	1	..	..	..	..	1	..	..
Naramore, Asa	1	..	..	1	..	4	..	..	1	..	..
Newell, Abel	..	..	1	1	1	..	1	..	..	1	..
Newell, Abel Jr.	2	1	..	1	..	2	..	1	..	..	..
Newell, John	2	..	2	1	..	..	1	1	..	..	..
Newell, Lot	..	..	..	1	..	..	1	1	..	..	..
Newell, Nathaniel	1	1	2	1	..	2	2	1	..	..	..
Nicholds, Robert	3	..	..	1	..	2	1	..	1	..	..
Niles, William	1	1	2	..	1	..	2	1	..	1	..
Noles, David	3	..	..	1	..	1	..	1	..	..	..
Noss, Jacob	1	..	..	1	..	1	..	..	1	..	..
Noys, Oliver	..	..	..	1	..	1	..	..	1	..	..
Packard, Abijah	2	2	..	1	2	2	..	1	..	..	..
Pain, Dan	..	..	2	1	..	1	..	1	1	1	..
Palmer, John	1	2	1	..	1	2	..	..	1	..	..
Parmer, Joel	2	..	..	1	..	1	2	..	1	..	..
Pease, William	2	..	3	1	..	2	..	1	..	1	..
Penfield, Samuel	1	..	..	1	..	3	..	..	1	..	..
Pitts, Richard	2	..	..	1	..	3	..	..	1	..	..
Place, Thomas	2	..	..	1	..	2	1	1	..	..	..
Powell, Calvin	1	..	1	..	..	..	..	1	..	..	..
Powell, Elijah	1	1	3	1	..	3	1	..	1	..	..
Powell, William	1	1	1	1	..	1	1	1	1	..	..
Pray, Nehemiah	1	..	1	1	..	1	..	..	1	..	..
Prindle, Gideon	..	1	2	1	..	1	..	1	1	..	..
Prindle, Lucy	1	1	1	1	..	1	1	..	1	..	..
Raxford, Benjamin	..	1	1	..	1	..	..	..	..	1	..
Read, Michael	2	..	..	1	..	3	..	..	1	..	..
Read, Thomas	..	..	..	1	..	1	..	..	1	..	..
Read, Timothy	..	1	1	1	..	..	1	..	..	..	..
Reynolds, David	..	..	1	..	..	2	..	1	..	..	..
Reynolds, Jeremiah	..	..	1	..	..	1	..	1	..	..	..
Rich, Ruth	1	..	..	..	..	..	3	..	1	..	..
Rich, Samuel	3	..	..	1	..	1	..	..	1	..	..
Root, Gad	1	1	1	..	..	..	..	1	..	..	..
Rowell, William	..	..	1	..	..	..	..	1	..	..	..
Sanlord, Zacharius	1	1	..	1	..	6	2	..	1	..	..
Sawyer, Manassa	..	2	1	1	..	3	1	..	1	..	..
Shelton, Peter	..	..	..	..	..	..	..	..	..	..	3
Sherman, George	3	..	2	1	..	..	..	..	1	..	..
Simonds, Joseph	1	..	2	2	..	2	1	..	1	..	..
Smith, Thomas	..	..	..	1	..	..	..	..	1	..	..
Soper, Cyrus	1	..	..	1	..	2	2	..	1	..	..
Squire, Heber	2	1	..	1	..	1	..	1	1	..	..
Squire, James	..	..	..	1	..	1	..	..	..	..	..
Steward, Joseph	..	..	..	1	..	2	..	1	..	..	..
Stone, Jacob	2	..	2	..	1	1	..	2	..	1	..
Straight, Henry	1	1	..	1	..	2	1	..	1	..	..
Sweat, Nicholas	4	..	..	1	..	..	..	..	1	..	..
Taft, Moses	2	..	2	1	..	3	3	1	1	..	..
Talor, John	2	..	..	1	..	2	..	..	1	..	..
Tharp, Betsey	1	1	1	1	..	1	1	2	1	..	..
Towner, Erastmas	2	..	..	1	..	2	1	1	..	..	..
Towner, Zacheus	..	..	1	..	1	..	..	2	..	1	..
Tucker, Daniel	3	..	..	1	1	..	..	..	1	..	..
Tucker, John	1	..	..	1	..	2	..	..	1	..	..
Ufford, Benjamin	..	..	..	3	..	..	..	..	..	2	..
Warren, Bethuel	2	..	..	1	..	2	1	..	1	..	..
Webb, Abraham	4	..	..	1	1	..	..	..	1	1	..
Webb, Isaac	..	..	1	1	..	1	..	1	1	..	..
Wheeler, Peter	2	..	..	1	..	1	..	..	1	..	..
Wheeler, Sheldon	..	1	1	..	..	2	..	1	..	..	..
White, Edward	3	1	..	2	..	1	1	1	1	..	..
Willcox, Joseph	..	1	2	1	..	3	..	..	1	..	..
Williams, Johannah	..	..	..	..	..	1	..	..	..	2	..
Williams, William	..	2	..	3	..	..	3	..	1	..	4
Woolcott, Elijah	1	..	..	..	1	..	..	1	..	1	..
Wooster, Ephraim	..	1	..	1	1	..	1	1	1	..	..
Yale, Aaron	..	..	..	1	..	4	..	..	1	..	..
Yale, Lyman	..	1	..	1	1	..	1	2	..	..	..

CHITTENDEN COUNTY—Continued

NAMES OF HEADS OF FAMILIES	Free white males: Under 10 years of age	Free white males: Of 10 and under 16	Free white males: Of 16 and under 26 including heads of families	Free white males: Of 26 and under 45 including heads of families	Free white males: Of 45 and upwards including heads of families	Free white females: Under 10 years of age	Free white females: Of 10 and under 16	Free white females: Of 16 and under 26 including heads of families	Free white females: Of 26 and under 45 including heads of families	Free white females: Of 45 and upwards including heads of families	All other free persons except Indians not taxed
COLCHESTER											
Allen, Elisha	..	..	1	..	1	4	1	..	1	..	..
Allen, Jerusha	1	1	1	..	..	2	1	1	1	..	..
Allen, Samuel	..	..	..	..	1	..	..	..	..	..	..
Ames, Charles	3	..	1	1	..	1	..	..	1	..	..
Austin, Paul	2	1	..	1	..	1	..	..	1	..	..
Austin, Samuel	..	..	1	..	1	..	..	..	..	1	..
Austin, Solomon	1	..	..	1	..	1	..	..	1	..	..
Baker, Eli	1	1	2	..	1	1	2	1	1	..	..
Barker, Solomon	2	..	..	..	1	2	..	..	1	..	..
Barney, Paul	1	..	..	1	..	..	..	1	..	..	..
Bartlet, Phillip	2	1	..	..	1	1	..	..	..	..	1
Bates, Moses	1	..	1	..	..	..	..	1	..	..	..
Bean, Enoch	..	..	..	1	..	..	1	..	1	..	..
Bee, Jube	..	..	..	..	..	..	..	..	..	..	4
Belding, Moses	4	1	..	1	..	..	..	..	1	..	..
Bellows, David	..	..	..	1	..	1	..	1	..	..	..
Blanchard, Moses	..	..	1	..	1	..	1	..	..	1	..
Boardman, Benjamin	3	1	4	1	..	3	1	..	1	..	..
Brownell, Aaron	1	2	..	1	..	1	..	1	1	..	..
Brownell, Ichabod	..	1	..	..	1	1	1	1	1	..	..
Camp, Luke	1	1	..	1	..	3	1	..	1	..	..
Cary, Seth	2	..	..	1	..	1	..	1	..	..	..
Chance, Evans	..	..	1	..	1	1	..	2	..	1	..
Chase, Samuel	..	1	1	..	1	..	..	1	..	1	..
Conway, John	..	..	..	1	..	2	1	..	1	..	..
Downing, Dennis	2	..	..	1	..	..	..	1	..	..	..
Downing, John	1	..	..	1	..	..	..	..	1	..	..
Ellis, Zebidiah	1	1	..	..	1	..	..	2	..	1	..
Enos, Roger Jr.	..	..	..	1	..	..	..	..	..	1	..
Farnam, Benjamin	..	1	..	..	1	..	2	1	..	1	..
Farren, David	1	..	..	1	1	1	..	..	1	..	..
Farren, Friend	..	..	..	1	..	..	..	..	1	..	..
Farren, Timothy	1	..	..	1	..	3	..	..	1	..	..
Fountain, Richard	1	..	..	1	..	..	..	1	..	..	..
Fulsom, Josiah	4	..	..	1	..	..	..	..	1	..	..
Gill, Thomas	2	..	..	1	..	..	..	..	1	..	..
Greno, Thomas	1	..	..	1	..	2	..	1	..	..	..
Griffin, Nathan	1	1	..	1	..	2	1	1	1	..	..
Harris, Laban	2	..	..	1	..	2	..	..	1	..	..
Harris, Stephen	2	1	..	1	..	1	1	..	1	..	..
Hibbard, Reuben	..	..	..	1	..	1	..	1	..	..	..
Hicks, Comfort	..	..	..	1	..	..	..	..	1	..	..
Hicks, Levi	1	2	..	1	..	1	..	..	1	..	..
Hide, William	1	1	..	1	..	3	1	..	1	..	..
Hill, David	..	..	2	..	..	1	..	1	..	..	..
Hill, Ruth	..	..	2	..	..	..	1	..	1	1	..
Hine, Simeon	1	1	2	..	1	2	2	1	1	..	..
Hyde, James	..	1	1	..	1	..	2	1	..	1	..
Johnson, Dorman	1	..	..	1	..	3	..	..	1	..	..
Law, John	..	..	..	1	..	..	..	..	..	..	..
Leak, Collins	1	1	..	1	..	1	..	..	1	..	..
Loomis, Roger	1	..	..	1	..	1	..	..	..	1	..
Lyon, Eleazer	1	..	..	1	..	..	..	1	..	..	..
Mansfield, Amos	4	..	..	1	..	2	..	..	1	..	..
Matthew, John	..	1	..	..	1	..	1	..	1	..	..
McFarling, Jesse	..	..	..	..	1	1	..	1	..	1	..
Morehouse, Elish	1	..	2	..	1	2	1	..	..	1	..
Munson, William	..	..	..	1	1	3	..	1	..	..	..
Newel, Daniel	..	..	..	1	..	1	..	1	..	..	..
Place, John	3	1	1	1	..	3	1	..	1	..	..
Preston, Levi	4	..	..	1	..	1	..	..	1	..	..
Stanton, Joshua Jr.	..	1	..	1	..	..	..	..	..	..	..
Thomas, John	..	..	1	..	..	1	..	1	..	..	..
Wily, Joseph	2	1	..	1	..	2	1	..	1	..	..
Woolcot, Ebenezer	2	..	..	1	..	1	..	1	..	..	..
DUXBURY											
Ames, Jesse	1	..	..	1	..	..	..	1	..	..	..
Bryant, Benjamin	2	..	..	1	..	2	1	..	1	..	..
Clark, Joseph	..	..	..	1	..	..	..	1	..	..	..
Coss, Ebenezer	1	..	..	1	..	3	..	..	1	..	..
Coss, Isaac	1	..	..	1	..	..	1	..	1	..	..
Crofoot, David	..	..	1	..	..	..	..	1	..	..	..
Cross, Dan	..	..	1	..	1	..	..	..	1	..	..
Davis, Amos	2	..	1	..	..	..	..	1	..	..	..
Davis, Benjamin Jr.	..	1	..	1	..	1	1	1	1	..	..
Eaton, Moses	..	1	3	..	1	..	..	..	1	..	..
Fola, Josiah	..	..	..	1	..	1	..	1	..	..	..
Graves, Elihue	2	..	..	1	..	1	..	..	1	..	..
Heaton, Reuben	..	..	..	1	..	3	..	1	..	..	..
Heaton, Samuel	..	..	1	..	1	..	2	1	..	1	..
Hobbs, Caleb	2	..	..	1	..	..	3	3	..	1	..
Kennady, David	..	..	2	..	1	..	..	..	..	1	..
Kennady, John	..	..	..	1	..	1	..	1	..	..	..
Mows, Daniel	..	..	..	1	..	1	..	1	..	..	..
Nash, Danjel	..	..	1	..	..	..	..	1	..	..	..
Nash, Joseph	2	2	1	1	..	2	..	..	1	..	..
Perry, Francis	..	1	1	..	1	..	..	1	..	1	..
Roberts, Luke	1	1	..	..	1	..	4	..	..	1	..
Roby, Josiah	..	..	..	..	1	..	..	..	..	..	..
Sandin, Samuel	1	..	1	..	..	..	..	1	..	..	..
Smattey, James	..	..	1	..	..	..	..	1	..	..	..
Spalding, John	1	1	..	1	..	2	..	..	1	..	..
Stimson, Abijah	..	..	..	..	1	..	..	..	..	1	..
Taplin, John	1	..	..	1	..	1	..	1	..	..	..
Wallace, Corbin	3	1	..	1	..	3	1	..	1	..	..
Wells, Eleazer	..	1	..	1	..	5	1	..	1	..	..
Wells, Elias	..	..	..	1	..	1	1	1	..	1	..
Wells, Simeon	..	..	1	..	..	..	..	1	..	..	..
ESSEX											
Andrus, Isaac	..	..	..	..	1	..	..	..	..	1	..
Atherton, Samuel	3	..	..	1	..	2	..	..	1	..	..
Babcock, Silas	..	..	1	1	..	2	1	1	..	..	..
Baker, Ezra	..	..	2	..	1	..	..	1	1	..	..
Bates, Elijah	..	..	..	1	..	..	..	..	..	..	..
Bates, Joshua	2	..	..	1	1	2	..	..	1	1	..
Bates, Reuben	1	..	1	..	..	1	..	1	..	..	..
Bellow, Zadock	1	..	1	1	..	..	..	..	1	..	..
Bigsby, Jonathan	1	2	3	..	1	..	..	1	..	1	..
Bigsby, Samuel	2	..	..	1	..	1	..	..	1	..	..
Blin, Charles	..	..	..	1	..	..	..	..	..	..	..
Blin, Charles	..	..	1	..	1	..	..	..	..	1	..
Bliss, Amos	1	..	..	1	..	2	..	..	1	..	..
Bliss, Elias	..	1	..	1	..	1	..	1	..	..	..
Bliss, Samuel	1	..	..	1	..	1	..	..	1	..	..
Bliss, Timothy	..	..	1	..	1	1	..	1	..	1	..
Bliss, William	1	..	1	..	1	1	..	1	..	..	..
Blood, Nathan	5	3	..	1	..	..	..	1	1	1	..
Blood, William	..	1	..	1	..	3	..	..	1	..	..
Bradley, Harden	..	..	..	1	..	2	..	..	1	..	..
Bradley, Jay	..	..	..	1	..	1	..	..	1	..	..
Bradley, Samuel	1	1	1	1	..	2	2	1	1	..	..
Brady, Hardy	..	..	1	..	..	..	2	..	1	..	..
Bryant, Nathan	..	1	..	..	1	..	1	2	..	1	..
Buck, Benton	..	..	..	1	..	..	..	..	1	..	..
Buel, Samuel	3	..	..	1	..	..	2	..	1	..	..
Bull, Samuel	1	..	..	1	..	1	1	1	..	..	..
Bullard, Gardner	..	1	..	1	1	2	..	..	1	1	..
Butler, Stephen	1	..	..	1	..	..	2	1	1	..	..
Camp, David	..	..	1	..	..	..	..	..	..	..	..
Castle, David	4	3	..	1	..	..	1	..	1	..	..
Castle, David	3	2	2	1	1	2	..	..	1	..	..
Castle, Nathan	2	..	2	1	..	1	1	..	1	..	..
Chipman, Thomas	2	..	..	1	1	..	..	1	..	1	..
Collins, Asa	..	..	..	1	..	..	1	..	1	..	..

CHITTENDEN COUNTY—Continued

Names of heads of families	Free white males					Free white females					
	Under 10 years of age	Of 10 and under 16	Of 16 and under 26 including heads of families	Of 26 and under 45 including heads of families	Of 45 and upwards including heads of families.	Under 10 years of age	Of 10 and under 16	Of 16 and under 26 including heads of families	Of 26 and under 45 including heads of families	Of 45 and upwards including heads of families	All other free persons except Indians not taxed
ESSEX—con.											
Collins, Henry	..	..	..	1	..	1	..	1	1	..	..
Collins, John	..	1	..	..	1	..	1	..	..	1	..
Curtis, Gideon	1	..	..	1	..	3	1	1	..	..	..
Davenport, John	2	..	..	1	..	2	1	..	1	..	..
Davenport, Thomas	..	..	..	..	1	..	..	..	..	1	..
Day, Asa	4	..	1	1	2	..	..	..	1	..	..
Day, David	2	1	..	1	..	2	1	..	1	..	..
Day, Hezekiah	2	..	..	1	..	1	..	..	1	..	..
Day, Justin	2	2	..	1	..	3	..	1	1	..	..
Day, Roderick	1	..	..	1	..	1	..	..	1	..	..
Ellet, William	1	..	..	1	..	3	..	..	1	..	..
Evans, Edmund	..	1	..	1	..	4	1	..	1	..	..
Evans, Oliver	..	..	..	..	1	..	..	..	..	1	..
Evans, Oliver Jr.	2	..	1	..	3	..	1	..	..	..	..
Farow, Prentice	..	..	..	1	..	..	..	..	..	..	..
Fisher, Comfort	..	..	..	1	..	3	..	..	1	..	..
Fisher, Edmund	1	1	..	1	..	..	1	2	..	1	..
Garlick, Reuben	1	1	2	..	1	1	..	..	..	1	..
Girbin, Samuel	..	..	..	1	..	..	..	1	..	..	..
Griffen, John	..	..	1	..	..	..	..	1	..	..	..
Griffen, Samuel	..	..	..	..	1	..	..	..	..	1	..
Griffen, Samuel	..	..	1	..	..	..	..	1	..		..
Hamilton, Charles	2	1	1	1	1	2	1	..	1	1	..
Hares, Ezra	1	..	1	1	..	1	..	..	1	..	..
Hatch, William	1	..	..	1	..	..	..	..	1	..	..
Holgate, Curtis	..	1	..	2	..	..	..	1	..	..	..
Hubbard, Peter	..	..	..	1	..	..	..	..	1	..	..
Hurd, Nehemiah	..	..	1	..	..	..	..	..	..	..	..
Hyde, Ephraim	4	..	..	1	..	1	..	..	1	..	..
Ingraham, William	1	..	..	..	1	..	..	2	1	..	..
Johnson, John	1	2	..	1	..	..	..	..	1	..	..
Keeler, James	..	2	1	..	1	1	..	..	..	1	..
Kellog, David	..	..	2	..	1	1	1	1	1	1	..
Kellog, Russel	1	..	..	1	..	2	..	..	1	..	..
Knickerbacker, John	..	..	1	..	1	..	..	1	..	..	..
Lambson, Joel	..	..	..	1	..	2	..	1	..	..	..
Lamson, Daniel	..	..	..	1	..	1	..	1	..	..	..
Lane, Jedidiah	..	2	1	..	1	..	..	..	..	1	..
Lane, Jedidiah Jr.	1	..	..	1	..	..	..	..	1	..	..
Lane, Roger	1	..	1	1	..	5	..	..	1	..	..
Lawrence, Noah	1	..	..	1	..	..	..	..	..	1	..
Leavens, Elijah	..	..	1	1	..	..	..	1	1	1	..
Littlefield, Daniel	..	..	1	..	..	..	..	..	..	..	..
Lloyd, John	1	1	..	..	1	..	1	..	1	..	..
Man, Asa	..	..	1	..	..	..	..	..	..	1	..
McEvony, Cornelius	1	..	..	1	..	4	..	..	1	..	..
Meigs, Julius	..	1	..	1	..	..	..	1	..	..	..
Messenger, John	1	..	1	..	..	1	..	..	1	..	..
Messenger, Lemuel	1	1	..	1	..	4	1	..	1	..	..
Morgan, Daniel	..	..	2	1	1	..	..	1	..	1	..
Morgan, Daniel Jr.	..	1	..	1	..	2	1	1	..	..	..
Night, Datheniel	1	1	..	..	1	4	2	..	1	..	..
Nobles, Ariel	1	..	..	1	..	1	..	..	1	..	..
Nobles, Matthew	4	..	..	1	..	..	1	..	1	..	..
Nobles, Morgan	..	1	2	..	1	..	..	1	..	1	..
Nobles, Stephen	..	1	..	1	..	..	..	1	1	..	..
Obery, John F.	..	..	1	..	..	..	..	1	..	..	..
Olds, Caleb	..	..	1	..	..	1	..	1	..	..	..
Palmeter, William	2	..	..	1	..	2	..	..	1	..	..
Parmele, Hezekiah	1	..	..	..	1	1	..	1	..	1	..
Peirson, Moses	1	..	..	1	..	2	..	..	1	..	..
Pelton, James	1	..	1	1	..	..	..	..	1	..	..
Pelton, James	..	..	1	1	1	..	1	1	2	1	..
Pelton, Samuel	..	1	..	1	..	..	..	1	..	..	..
Reed, John	..	..	1	1	..	1	..	..	1	..	..
Reed, Stephen	3	..	..	1	..	1	2	..	1	..	..
Rice, Lemuel	..	..	1	1	..	..	..	1	..	..	..
Richards, William	..	..	..	1		..	..	..	..	..	..
Sinkler, John	3	1	..	1	1	1	1	1	1	1	..
Sinkler, Joseph	..	..	1	..	..	1	..	1	..	..	..
Sinkler, Samuel	2	..	..	1	1	1	1	..	1	1	..
Slater, Ezra	3	..	..	1	..	1	..	..	1	1	..

Names of heads of families	Free white males					Free white females					
	Under 10 years of age	Of 10 and under 16	Of 16 and under 26 including heads of families	Of 26 and under 45 including heads of families	Of 45 and upwards including heads of families.	Under 10 years of age	Of 10 and under 16	Of 16 and under 26 including heads of families	Of 26 and under 45 including heads of families	Of 45 and upwards including heads of families	All other free persons except Indians not taxed
ESSEX—con.											
Slater, Henry	3	1	..	1	..	1	..	..	1	..	..
Smith, Samuel	1	1	1	1	..	..	..	..	..	1	..
Spafford, Nathan	3	2	..	1	..	..	2	2	1	..	..
Spellman, Robert	1	..	..	1	1	..	1	..	1	..	..
Stanton, David	..	2	1	1	..	..	1	..	1	..	..
Stanton, Solomon	1	..	..	1	..	3	1	..	1	..	..
Stevens, Abram	3	1	..	1	..	..	1	1	1	..	..
Taft, Benjamin	1	..	1	..	..	1	..	1	..	..	..
Thatcher, George	..	..	1	..	..	..	..	1	..	..	..
Thompson, James	3	1	..	1	1	2	..	..	1	..	..
Tubbs, Dan	4	..	..	..	1	..	1	..	1	..	..
Tubbs, Simon	3	2	..	1	1	1	1	1	1	..	..
Tyler, David	1	..	..	1	..	1	..	..	1	..	..
Tyler, George	..	1	1	1	..	1	..	..	1	..	..
Tylor, Royal	2	..	..	1	..	2	..	..	1	..	..
Warner, Parle	..	..	1	1	1	1	..	1	..	..	..
White, Jacob	..	..	3	..	1	1	1	..	1	1	..
Whitney, Samuel	1	1	..	1	..	2	1	..	1	..	..
Wicks, John	2	1	..	1	..	..	..	..	1	..	..
Woodbury, Nathan	2	1	..	1	..	2	..	..	1	..	..
Woodworth, Amasa	..	..	..	1	..	..	..	..	..	..	..
Woodworth, Eliza	2	2	1	..	1	2	..	..	..	1	..
Woodworth, Ezra	3	1	..	1	..	5	..	..	1	..	..
Woodworth, Josiah	2	1	2	1	..	2	1	..	1	..	..
Woodworth, Nathan	1	..	..	1	1	1	..	1	..	..	..
Woodworth, Rachel	..	..	..	..	..	..	..	1	..	..	..
Wright, William	2	1	..	..	1	..	..	..	..	1	..
Yemmans, Elisha	..	..	2	..	1	..	2	..	1	1	..
FAYSTON											
Bennet, Rufus	..	..	1	..	..	..	..	1	..	..	..
Clouds, John	..	..	1	..	..	..	..	1	..	..	..
Minor, Nathaniel	1	..	2	..	1	1	2	1	..	1	..
Pike, Samuel	..	..	..	..	1	..	..	..	..	1	..
Wait, Sandy	..	..	1	1	..	..	..	1	..	..	..
HINESBURGH											
Adams, Arculus	2	..	..	1	..	1	..	..	1	..	..
Allen, Edward	..	..	..	1	..	1	..	..	1	..	..
Ames, Thamer	1	..	1	..	..	..	..	1	..	..	..
Andrus, Amos	..	..	1	..	1	..	..	..	..	1	..
Andrus, Nerus	1	..	..	1	..	..	..	1	..	..	..
Baldwin, Orange F. E.	3	..	2	..	..	2	..	2	..	..	..
Barnum, Daniel	..	1	..	1	..	1	..	..	1	..	..
Barto, Benjamin	..	..	1	..	1	1	..	1	..	1	..
Bassett, Daniel	1	..	..	1	..	2	..	1	..	..	..
Bassett, Seth	..	1	..	..	1	..	1	2	..	1	..
Baxter, Jedediah	1	2	..	1	1	1	..	..	1	..	..
Beach, Robert	2	1	1	1	..	2	..	1	1	..	..
Benedict, Leve	..	..	3	..	..	1	1	2	2	..	1
Bennett, Daniel	..	..	1	..	..	..	..	1	..	..	..
Bideto, James	2	..	..	1	..	1	..	..	1	..	..
Bishop, Daniel	2	..	..	1	..	2	2	..	1	..	..
Bishop, Napthali	3	..	1	1	..	1	..	1	1	..	..
Booth, Elisha	1	1	..	1	..	2	1	1	1	..	..
Bostwick, Doctor	2	2	..	1	..	..	..	..	1	..	..
Bostwick, Edmund	1	..	..	..	1	..	1	..	..	1	3
Bostwick, Erastus	1	..	..	1	..	1	..	1	..	..	..
Bostwick, Gershom	2	1	..	1	..	4	..	..	1	..	..
Bostwick, Heman	1	..	1	..	..	..	..	1	..	..	..
Bostwick, Isbon	..	..	1	2	..	2	..	1	..	..	..
Bostwick, Lemuel	2	..	1	1	1	1	1	..	1	1	..
Bostwick, Lyman	2	..	..	1	..	2	..	..	1	..	..
Boyington, Justus	3	1	..	1	..	2	1	..	1	..	..
Brand, Robert	..	2	..	1	..	4	..	..	1	..	..
Burritt, Andrew	..	1	3	1	1	1	..	1	..	1	..
Butler, Thomas	..	..	1	..	1	..	2	1	..	1	..
Calkins, Charles	..	..	..	1	..	2	..	..	1	1	..
Calkins, Durgee	..	1	1	1	..	1	..	..	1	..	..
Canfield, Levi	2	..	1	1	..	..	..	1	1	..	..
Cattin, Russell	1	..	..	1	..	2	..	..	2	..	..
Church, Isaac	1	..	1	..	..	..	..	1	..	..	..
Church, Othello	..	..	1	..	..	..	..	1	..	..	..
Clapp, Thomas	3	..	..	1	..	2	..	..	1	..	..
Clark, Daniel	1	1	2	..	1	..	..	1	..	1	..
Clark, Milton	3	..	1	..	..	..	..	..	..	1	..
Clark, Shubel	..	..	..	..	..	..	..	..	..	..	5

CHITTENDEN COUNTY—Continued

NAMES OF HEADS OF FAMILIES	FREE WHITE MALES					FREE WHITE FEMALES					
	Under 10 years of age	Of 10 and under 16	Of 16 and under 26 including heads of families	Of 26 and under 45 including heads of families	Of 45 and upwards including heads of families.	Under 10 years of age	Of 10 and under 16	Of 16 and under 26 including heads of families	Of 26 and under 45 including heads of families	Of 45 and upwards including heads of families	All other free persons except Indians not taxed
HINESBURGH—con.											
Conger, Asher	3	2	..	1	..	1	1	..	1	..	..
Conger, John	2	..	..	1	..	4	..	..	1	..	..
Crossman, Rufus	..	..	..	1	..	2	..	..	1	..	..
Cummings, James	3	1	1	1	..	2	..	1	..	..	..
Darr, Samuel	..	1	1	..	1	..	..	..	..	1	..
Day, William	..	1	..	1	..	3	..	..	1	..	..
Durham, Zeriah	..	1	..	..	..	..	1	..	1	..	..
Eddy, Josiah	3	1	..	..	1	..	..	1	..	..	..
Edwards, Calvin	2	..	..	1	..	..	..	1	..	..	..
Farling, Thomas	1	1	1	..	1	..	1	..	1	2	..
Farren, Joseph	..	..	1	..	1	..	..	..	..	1	..
Farren, Joseph Jr.	1	1	..	1	..	2	..	1	1	..	..
Farren, Samuel	..	1	1	..	1	..	..	1	..	1	..
Febrick, Andrew	1	..	..	1	..	2	..	..	1	..	..
Ferris, Anglice	2	1	..	1	..	1	1	..	1	..	..
Ferris, Joseph	3	..	..	1	..	..	1	..	1	..	..
Ferry, Ebenezer	..	1	..	..	1	..	..	..	..	1	..
Field, Michael	1	..	..	1	..	2	..	..	1	..	..
Fipeny, Joel	1	1	1	..	..	..	..	1	..	..	..
Gates, Ira	1	2	1	..	1	..	..	1	..	1	..
Gates, James	2	..	..	..	1	..	2	1	1	..	..
Gillet, Reuben	1	..	1	1	..	3	1	..	1	..	..
Gould, Nathaniel	2	..	..	1	..	1	..	1	..	..	..
Green, Jonathan	3	..	..	1	..	1	4	..	1	1	..
Griffice, Daniel	..	1	..	..	1	..	..	..	..	1	..
Hagar, James	..	..	1	1	..	2	..	1	..	..	..
Hinsdale, Aaron	2	..	..	1	1	3	..	..	1	..	..
Hollister, Stephen	..	..	1	1	..	..	..	1	..	..	..
Howard, Dan	3	..	..	1	..	2	2	..	1	..	..
Hull, Calep	1	..	..	1	..	4	..	..	1	..	..
Hull, Paphrus	3	1	..	1	..	2	1	..	1	..	..
Hunt, Theophilus	..	..	..	1	1	..	..	..	..	..	..
Huntington, Jonathan	..	..	1	..	..	..	1	1	..	..	..
Hurlbut, Cornelius	2	..	..	1	1	2	..	1	1	..	..
Hurlbut, Timothy	1	..	1	..	..	..	..	1	..	..	..
Irish, Benjamin	5	..	..	1	..	..	..	..	1	..	..
Leonard, Amos	..	..	..	1	..	1	..	1	..	..	..
Levensworth, Nathan Jr.	1	1	2	1	1	1	..	1	..	1	..
Lockwood, Nathaniel	1	1	1	..	1	2	1	1	..	1	..
Love, George W.	..	..	1	..	..	..	..	1	..	..	..
Loveley, Perry	3	..	..	1	..	3	..	..	1	..	..
Lovely, Valentine	3	..	..	1	..	2	..	..	1	..	..
Marsh, Daniel	1	..	..	1	..	2	1	..	1	..	..
Marsh, Thomas	..	..	..	1	..	2	..	..	1	..	..
Marsh, William B.	3	1	1	1	..	2	1	..	1	..	..
Marshal, Silas	2	..	..	1	..	2	..	1	..	..	..
Marshall, Jonathan	2	2	1	1	..	3	2	1	1	..	..
McUne, George	3	3	..	..	1	2	1	..	1	..	..
McUne, Robert	2	2	..	1	..	1	1	..	1	..	..
Meach, Elisha	1	1	2	2	1	1	1	..	1	1	..
Mead, Alpheus	3	1	..	1	..	2	1	..	1	..	..
Mead, Lockwood	..	1	..	1	..	4	1	..	1	..	..
Monger, Reuben	3	1	..	1	..	2	1	..	1	..	..
Moon, Asa	1	..	..	1	..	1	..	..	1	..	..
Morey, Samuel	..	..	1	..	1	..	1	..	1	..	..
Morgan, Asa	1	..	..	1	..	..	..	1	..	..	..
Moses, John	2	1	..	1	..	1	1	1	1	..	..
Norton, Daniel	2	..	..	1	..	1	..	1	..	..	..
Norton, Eli	..	..	1	..	..	1	..	1	..	..	..
Norton, John	..	..	..	..	1	..	..	..	1	1	..
Olmsted, Lewis	3	..	1	1	..	..	..	1	1	..	..
Palmer, Azariah	..	1	..	..	1	..	1	..	..	1	..
Palmer, George	3	1	..	1	..	..	2	1	1	..	..
Palmer, Pardon	..	..	..	1	..	..	..	1	..	..	..
Parker, William	2	2	..	..	1	2	..	..	1	..	..
Patch, Thompson	2	1	3	..	1	..	..	..	1	..	..
Patrick, Daniel	1	1	..	1	..	..	1	..	1	..	..
Peck, Elijah	..	..	2	1	..	..	2	1	1	..	..
Peck, Ezra	2	..	..	1	1	..	..	..	1	..	..
Peck, Joel	1	..	..	1	..	1	..	1	..	..	..
Perry, Valentine	1	..	..	1	..	1	1	1	..	..	..
Pierce, Luther	2	..	1	1	..	1	..	..	1	..	..
Place, Griffin	2	1	1	1	1	3	1	..	1	..	..
Place, Job	1	2	..	1	..	3	..	..	1	..	..
Ransley, William	1	..	..	1	..	1	..	..	1	..	..
Roundy, Hiram	..	..	1	..	..	..	..	1	..	..	..
Russell, Charles	2	1	1	1	..	..	..	1	1	..	..
Scovel, Hezekiah	2	..	1	..	..	..	..	1	..	..	..
Sherman, Olly	2	1	..	..	..	2	..	..	1	..	..
Skinner, Zenos	3	..	..	1	..	1	..	1	..	..	..
Smeadley, Elisha	2	1	..	1	..	..	..	2	..	..	..
Smith, Nathan	1	1	1	..	..	1	..	1	..	..	..
Smith, Norris	3	..	1	1	..	..	..	1	1	..	..
Spalding, Silas	..	..	1	..	..	1	..	1	..	..	..
Spalding, Stephen	..	1	1	..	1	..	..	2	..	2	..
Spencer, Moses	2	..	..	1	..	1	..	1	..	..	..
Spencer, Noah	2	3	..	1	..	2	1	..	1	..	..
Stacy, Samuel	..	1	..	1	1	..	1	..	..	2	..
Steel, Eliphus	2	1	..	1	1	1	1	..	1	1	..
Sterns, Jonathan	..	..	..	..	1	1	1	..	..	1	..
Sterns, Jonathan Jr.	1	..	1	..	..	1	1	1	..	..	..
Sterns, Peter	1	1	1	..	1	2	..	1	..	1	..
Steward, Thaddeus	..	1	..	1	1	1	..	..	1	1	..
Stone, Ebenezer	..	1	1	1	1	1	..	..	..	1	..
Stone, Ebenezer Jr.	2	1	..	1	..	..	..	..	1	..	..
Stone, Nathan	1	..	..	1	..	1	..	..	1	..	..
Sweat, Abram	1	1	..	1	..	3	..	..	1	..	..
Taylor, Amos	2	..	..	1	..	2	..	..	1	..	..
Tibile, Adam	1	..	..	..	1	1	..	1	..	..	..
Tracy, Bela	1	..	..	1	..	..	1	..	1	..	..
Turrel, Caleb	2	..	..	..	1	..	..	2	..	..	..
Tuttle, Hezekiah	1	..	..	1	..	..	..	..	1	..	..
Videto, Justus	2	..	1	..	..	..	..	..	1	..	..
Wait, Nathaniel	1	..	..	1	..	2	..	1	..	..	..
Walker, Asa	..	..	..	1	..	4	..	1	..	..	..
Weed, John	3	..	1	1	..	4	1	..	1	..	..
Welles, David	2	..	1	..	..	..	..	1	..	..	..
Welles, John	..	1	..	..	1	..	..	..	1	..	..
Welles, Seth	..	..	1	..	..	1	..	1	..	..	..
Wells, Thomas	2	1	3	1	..	2	..	1	..	..	..
Wells, William	2	2	2	..	1	1	1	..	..	1	..
Wheeler, Nathan	..	..	1	..	1	3	2	1	..	1	..
Willson, John	..	..	1	..	1	..	1	..	..	1	..
Willson, John Jr.	3	1	..	1	..	..	..	1	1	..	..
UNCERTAIN NAME											
Dauks (?), Benjamin	2	..	..	1	1	..	..	1	..	..	..
HUNTINGTON											
Ambler, Ebenezer	..	1	..	1	..	1	..	..	1	..	..
Ambler, Frederick	1	..	..	1	..	..	..	1	..	..	..
Ambler, James	1	1	1	..	1	..	1	1	1	..	..
Barrett, Benjamin	2	..	..	1	..	2	..	..	1	..	..
Barrett, Squire O.	1	2	1	1	..	2	..	..	1	..	..
Benham, Enos	3	1	..	1	..	1	..	..	1	..	..
Blackman, Stephen	..	..	..	..	1	4	..	..	1	..	..
Brewsters, Charles	2	1	1	1	..	2	..	2	1	..	..
Brownell, Benjamin	2	2	2	1	..	2	..	..	1	..	..
Buel, Elias	..	1	..	1	1	..	..	..	..	1	..
Buel, Elias Jr.	..	..	..	1	..	2	..	..	1	..	..
Buel, Solomon	2	..	..	1	..	1	..	..	1	..	..
Bull, Elijah	..	1	2	..	..	..	..	1	..	..	..
Bull, Elijah	1	1	1	..	..	1	..	1	..	..	..
Bumpus, Joel	1	..	..	1	..	1	..	1	..	..	..
Burtt, Alpheus	2	..	1	..	..	..	..	1	..	..	..
Carpenter, Beriah	1	..	1	..	..	2	..	1	..	..	..
Carpenter, Joseph	..	2	2	..	1	4	1	1	..	1	..
Castle, Daniel	1	..	1	..	..	2	..	1	..	..	..
Castle, David	..	1	1	1	..	4	1	1	1	..	..
Clark, Joseph	..	2	1	..	1	1	1	..	..	1	..
Cunningham, Elijah	2	..	..	1	..	1	..	1	..	1	..
Dyke, Jonathan	1	1	2	..	1	1	..	1	1	..	..
Far, Elias	..	3	..	1	..	2	1	1	..	1	..
Fargo, Aron	..	..	..	..	1	..	..	..	..	1	..
Fargo, Darius	2	..	..	1	..	1	..	1	..	..	..
Fargo, Jabez	..	2	..	1	..	1	1	1	1	..	..
Fargo, Samuel	4	..	..	1	..	1	1	..	1	..	..
Ferrin, Abel 2nd	3	..	1	1	..	..	..	1	..	..	..
Fitch, John	2	..	..	1	..	1	..	..	1	..	..
Freeman, Jacob	1	1	2	..	1	..	..	1	..	1	..
Gillet, Asa	2	..	..	1	..	1	..	..	1	..	..

CHITTENDEN COUNTY—Continued

NAMES OF HEADS OF FAMILIES	FREE WHITE MALES: Under 10 years of age	FREE WHITE MALES: Of 10 and under 16	FREE WHITE MALES: Of 16 and under 26 including heads of families	FREE WHITE MALES: Of 26 and under 45 including heads of families	FREE WHITE MALES: Of 45 and upwards including heads of families.	FREE WHITE FEMALES: Under 10 years of age	FREE WHITE FEMALES: Of 10 and under 16	FREE WHITE FEMALES: Of 16 and under 26 including heads of families	FREE WHITE FEMALES: Of 26 and under 45 including heads of families	FREE WHITE FEMALES: Of 45 and upwards including heads of families	All other free persons except Indians not taxed
HUNTINGTON—con.											
Hill, William	1	..	..	..	1	1	..	..	1	..	..
Jones, Jehiel	3	2	..	1	..	..	1	1	..	..	..
Joslin, Zebediah	1	1	1	1	..	5	2	..	1	..	..
Lamb, Ebenezer	1	2	..	..	1	1	..	..	..	1	..
Marshal, Joseph	..	..	1	..	..	1	..	..	1	..	..
Martin, John	3	..	..	1	..	2	..	..	1	..	..
Nixton, Spencer	1	..	1	..	..	..	..	1	..	..	..
Pierce, Ebenezer	..	..	..	1	..	..	..	1	..	..	..
Pierce, Jacob	..	..	..	..	..	1	..	..	..	..	..
Pierce, Nathaniel	1	..	..	1	..	..	..	1	..	..	..
Powers, Isaac	2	1	1	1	..	2	..	..	1	..	..
Ravelin, Lawrence	..	1	2	..	1	..	..	..	..	1	..
Russell, Sylvester	..	..	1	1	..	..	1	..	1	..	..
Shattuck, James	..	2	..	1	..	3	1	..	1	..	..
Sherman, David	1	..	3	..	1	..	..	..	..	1	..
Sherman, David Jr.	1	..	..	1	..	2	..	1	..	..	..
Slate, John	..	..	1	..	..	..	..	..	..	..	..
Smith, Isaac	..	1	..	1	..	2	1	1	1	..	..
Snider, Jacob	2	1	..	1	..	4	1	2	1	..	..
Squires, Stephen	1	2	1	1	..	2	..	..	1	..	..
Steward, Nathaniel	2	1	1	1	..	2	1	1	1	1	..
Sweat, William	3	1	..	1	..	3	..	..	1	..	..
Taft, Gideon	..	..	1	..	..	1	..	1	..	..	..
Terry, Jonathan	..	1	..	..	1	..	..	1	..	1	..
Thomas, John	..	..	..	1	..	2	1	..	1	..	..
Tift, John	..	..	1	..	1	1	..	..	..	1	..
Turner, Abel	1	1	..	1	..	2	2	1	1	..	..
Turner, John	..	..	1	..	1	2	..	2	..	1	..
Turrel, Enoch	..	..	1	..	1	1	..	..	..	1	..
Walker, John	..	..	1	..	..	..	..	1	..	..	..
Wells, James	3	2	..	..	1	2	..	..	1	..	..
Williams, John	2	..	..	1	..	2	1	..	1	..	..
Williams, Lyman	..	..	1	..	..	1	..	..	1	..	..
Williams, Rufus	4	3	2	..	1	2	1	..	1	..	..
JERICHO											
Allen, Heber	..	..	..	1	..	1	1	1	1	1	..
Arwin, John	1	..	1	..	..	1	..	2	..	..	..
Babcock, Paul	1	..	..	1	..	1	..	1	..	..	..
Bartlet, Benjamin	..	..	1	..	1	..	2	1	..	1	..
Bartlet, William	2	..	..	2	..	1	..	..	1	..	..
Benedict, Moses	3	1	..	..	1	..	..	..	1	..	..
Benham, Isaac	2	2	1	1	..	..	..	1	1	..	..
Bentley, Elisha	2	..	..	1	..	2	1	1	1	..	..
Bentley, Samuel Jr.	1	1	..	1	..	1	..	..	1	..	..
Billings, Moses	..	..	1	1	..	..	1	..	1	..	..
Billings, Silas	1	1	1	1	..	2	..	1	1	..	..
Birchard, Elisha	2	1	..	1	..	2	1	..	1	..	..
Bird, Jesse	2	1	..	1	..	..	1	..	1	..	..
Blaid, John	1	..	..	1	..	..	..	1	1	..	..
Blair, James	2	..	..	1	..	3	2	..	1	..	..
Bliss, Daniel	2	..	..	1	..	1	1	..	..	1	..
Bliss, Timothy	3	..	..	1	..	2	..	1	1	..	..
Boswick, Nathaniel	..	1	2	1	1	1	2	1	1	1	..
Brown, Charles	1	1	..	1	1	2	1	..	1	1	..
Brown, Joseph	3	..	1	1	..	1	..	..	1	..	..
Brown, Samuel	1	..	..	1	..	1	..	1	..	..	..
Brown, Timothy	3	..	1	..	1	1	1	1	1	..	..
Butler, Ebenezer	..	..	..	1	1	1	..	1	1	1	..
Castle, David	..	..	..	..	1	..	..	..	..	1	..
Castle, Jonathan	..	..	1	..	1	..	1	1	1	..	..
Casy, Edward	2	1	3	1	..	2	1	..	1	..	..
Chapin, Ichabod	1	1	..	1	..	1	1	..	1	..	..
Chapins, Lewis	..	2	..	1	..	3	2	..	1	..	..
Chipman, Joseph	1	..	..	1	..	2	1	..	1	..	..
Chittenden, Martin	1	1	1	1	..	1	..	2	1	..	..
Chittenden, Noah	1	1	2	..	1	1	..	2	1	..	..
Curtis, Leven	..	1	1	..	..	1	1	..	1	..	..
Cutler, Willard	..	..	..	..	1	2	..	..	1	..	..
Daile, Jedidiah	4	..	..	1	..	..	1	..	1	..	..
Day, Edward	1	..	..	..	1	..	1	..	..	1	..
Day, Edward	2	..	..	1	..	..	..	..	1	..	..
Day, Samuel	2	..	..	1	..	1	..	..	1	..	..
Day, Thomas	1	..	..	1	..	1	..	1	..	..	..
JERICHO—con.											
Fay, Samuel	2	1	..	1	..	3	3	..	1	..	..
Ferris, Hannah	..	..	1	..	..	..	..	..	..	2	..
Fields, David	..	1	..	1	..	3	..	..	1	..	..
Fish, David	..	..	..	1	..	2	1	..	..	..	..
French, Samuel	1	..	1	1	..	2	..	..	1	..	..
Gaffil, Thomas	1	1	..	1	..	3	..	..	1	..	..
Gould, Peter	1	..	1	..	1	1	..	1	..	..	..
Haskins, Nathan	1	1	..	1	..	1	..	..	1	..	..
Hatch, David	..	..	2	1	1	..	..	..	..	1	..
Hatch, Joseph	..	..	1	..	..	1	..	1	..	..	..
Hill, Winthrop	..	..	1	1	..	2	..	..	1	..	..
How, Charles	..	..	..	..	1	..	..	..	..	1	..
How, Uri	2	1	3	..	1	..	..	3	1	..	..
Hubbell, Eleazer	..	..	2	..	1	1	1	1	..	1	..
Hurlbut, Jube	1	..	..	1	..	2	1	..	..	1	..
Hutchinson, Ebenezer	3	..	..	1	..	1	..	..	1	..	..
Hutchinson, Nathaniel	1	..	..	1	..	3	..	1	1	1	..
Kingsbury, Rev. E.	1	..	..	1	..	2	..	..	1	..	..
Lane, John	2	..	..	1	..	..	..	1	1	..	..
Lee, Ezariah	..	..	1	..	1	..	..	..	..	1	..
Lee, John	..	..	..	1	..	2	..	..	1	..	..
Lee, Linus	..	..	..	1	..	1	..	1	..	..	..
Lee, Lucy	..	..	2	..	..	..	..	..	1	..	..
Lee, Reuben	..	1	..	1	..	4	1	..	1	..	..
Lee, Solomon	1	..	..	1	..	1	..	..	1	..	..
Lowrey, Thomas	1	..	1	..	1	..	..	1	..	2	..
Lyman, John	4	..	..	1	..	1	2	..	1	..	..
Lymon, Noah	4	1	1	1	..	..	1	..	1	..	..
Marsh, Thomas	3	..	..	1	..	1	..	..	1	..	..
Martin, James	..	..	..	1	..	..	..	..	1	..	..
Martin, William	2	1	..	..	1	2	1	3	1	..	..
Matthew, Anne	..	..	..	..	..	..	..	2	..	1	..
Matthew, Seth	..	..	1	..	..	..	..	1	..	..	..
Matthews, Walter	2	..	1	..	..	1	..	1	..	..	..
McArthur, Nicholas	2	..	1	1	..	1	..	..	1	..	..
Merril, Peter	..	2	..	1	..	..	1	..	1	..	..
Messenger, Roderick	2	1	3	..	1	1	2	1	..	1	..
Morse, Benoni	2	..	..	1	..	4	1	..	..	1	..
Morton, Smart	..	..	1	..	..	1	..	1	..	..	..
Nash, Caleb	..	1	1	..	1	1	..	..	..	1	..
Nash, Caleb Jr.	1	..	..	1	..	..	..	..	1	..	..
Nash, Elias	1	..	..	1	1	..	..	..	1	..	..
Orr, James	1	..	..	1	..	..	..	1	..	..	..
Packard, Carpus	..	1	1	..	..	3	..	..	1	..	..
Packard, George Jr.	1	1	..	1	1	2	2	..	1	1	..
Pease, Ganes	2	..	..	1	1	..	..	..	1	..	..
Pelton, Ithamer	1	..	..	1	3	..	..	1	..	..	..
Porter, John	3	1	1	..	..	3	..	..	1	..	..
Portley, Samuel	2	..	..	..	1	4	..	..	1	..	..
Potter, James A.	3	..	..	1	..	2	..	..	1	..	..
Prouty, Nehemiah	..	1	..	..	1	..	..	..	..	1	..
Prouty, Nehemiah Jr.	..	..	..	1	..	3	3	1	..	..	..
Reed, Ebenezer	1	1	1	1	..	2	2	..	1	..	..
Rice, Seth	2	..	..	1	..	3	..	..	1	..	..
Ripley, John	..	..	1	..	..	2	1	..	1	..	..
Rockwell, Reuben	2	..	1	..	..	1	1	1	..	..	..
Rood, Thomas T.	4	1	1	1	1	..	2	1	..	..	..
Rood, William	3	..	..	1	..	1	1	..	1	..	..
Root, Simeon	2	2	..	..	1	3	1	1	1	..	..
Shaw, Benjamin	..	..	..	1	..	4	..	..	1	..	..
Shaw, Jonathan	..	1	1	..	..	3	..	..	1	..	..
Shaw, Peter	3	..	..	1	..	..	..	..	..	1	..
Shaw, Stephen	..	..	1	..	1	..	..	2	..	1	..
Skinner, Asbel	3	1	..	..	1	1	1	2	1	..	..
Smalley, Alford	1	..	1	1	..	2	1	..	1	..	..
Smith, William	3	..	..	1	..	2	1	..	1	..	..
Staples, Joseph	3	1	..	1	..	..	2	..	1	..	..
Stevens, Roger	1	..	1	..	1	..	..	1	..	..	..
Stone, David	2	..	..	1	..	1	..	..	1	..	..
Strong, Ariel	4	1	..	1	..	..	..	..	1	..	..
Thatcher, Arsy	2	..	..	1	..	3	..	..	1	..	..
Thompson, John	..	1	1	..	1	..	3	..	..	1	..
Thompson, John Jr.	1	..	..	1	..	2	..	..	1	..	..
Tony, Timothy	3	..	..	1	..	1	1	..	1	..	..

CHITTENDEN COUNTY—Continued

NAMES OF HEADS OF FAMILIES	FREE WHITE MALES					FREE WHITE FEMALES					All other free persons except Indians not taxed
	Under 10 years of age	Of 10 and under 16	Of 16 and under 26 including heads of families	Of 26 and under 45 including heads of families	Of 45 and upwards including heads of families.	Under 10 years of age	Of 10 and under 16	Of 16 and under 26 including heads of families	Of 26 and under 45 including heads of families	Of 45 and upwards including heads of families	
JERICHO—con.											
Wait, Thomas	2	..	1	..	..	1	..	1	..	..	..
Warner, Samuel	..	..	1	..	..	..	..	..	..	..	..
Wells, Shipley	1	..	1	..	..	..	..	..	1	..	..
Whitmash, David	..	..	..	1	1	..	1	..	..	1	..
Whitmash, Oliver	..	1	..	1	..	2	..	1	..	..	..
Wilder, Oliver	2	..	1	1	..	1	..	..	1	..	..
Willson, Nathaniel	1	..	1	1	..	1	..	1	..	..	..
Wood, Peter	..	..	1	..	..	..	..	1	..	..	..
Young, William	1	..	..	1	..	1	..	..	1	..	..
MANSFIELD											
Luce, Zimri	3	1	2	1	..	2	2	..	1	..	..
MIDDLESEX											
Allen, David	..	..	..	1	..	..	..	1	1	..	..
Atherton, Oliver	..	..	..	1	1	3	1	..	1	..	..
Ball, Amos	1	..	1	..	..	..	..	1	..	..	..
Bates, Simeon	..	..	..	..	1	..	..	..	..	1	..
Bates, Stephen	2	..	..	1	..	2	2	..	1	..	..
Benton, Nathan	1	..	..	1	..	3	..	..	1	..	..
Bullock, Preserved	..	..	1	..	..	..	..	1	..	..	..
Chamberlin, Rufus	2	..	..	1	..	2	..	..	1	..	..
Chipan, Joseph	1	..	..	1	..	..	1	1	..	..	..
Comstock, Noah	1	2	1	1	..	2	1	2	1	..	..
Convers, Josiah	2	..	..	1	..	1	..	..	1	..	..
Cutler, Artemus	..	..	1	..	..	2	..	1	..	..	..
Davis, John	..	..	1	..	1	..	..	..	..	..	..
Dear, Jediah	2	1	3	1	..	2	2	1	1	1	..
Grigs, Isaac	1	..	1	..	..	..	..	1	..	..	..
Harrington, David	..	..	1	1	..	..	..	..	..	..	..
Harrington, Dennis	2	1	2	1	..	..	1	2	..	2	..
Harris, Samuel	1	1	1	..	1	2	..	..	1	..	..
Hatch, Michael	..	1	1	1	..	2	1	..	1	..	..
Hawk, Ira	1	..	1	1	..	3	2	..	1	..	..
Holden, John	1	..	..	1	..	4	..	..	1	..	..
Holden, William	3	..	..	1	..	1	..	..	1	..	..
Holding, Edmund	..	..	..	1	..	4	1	..	1	..	..
Hoyt, John	1	..	..	2	..	..	..	1	..	..	..
Hubbard, James	..	..	1	..	1	..	..	..	..	1	..
Hubbard, Joseph	1	..	..	1	..	2	..	..	1	..	..
Hutchins, Joseph	..	1	1	..	1	..	..	1	..	1	..
Johnson, Joseph	3	3	..	1	..	2	..	1	1	..	..
Kelkit, Jonathan	..	..	1	..	..	..	..	1	..	..	..
Landers, Obed	..	..	..	..	1	..	2	..	..	..	..
Lewis, Levi	..	..	1	..	..	1	..	1	..	..	..
Lincoln, Henry	2	..	1	1	..	3	..	..	1	..	..
McClena, Thomas	..	..	1	..	..	2	..	1	..	..	..
Meads, Thomas	1	3	2	..	1	1	1	..	..	1	1
Meads, Thomas Jr.	..	..	1	..	..	1	..	1	..	..	..
Meltire, Lewis	2	..	1	..	1	..	1	..	..	1	..
Phelps, David	2	..	..	1	..	1	1	..	1	..	..
Preston, Anson	..	..	..	1	..	1	..	..	1	..	..
Putnam, Ebenezer	1	..	..	1	1	2	1	..	..	1	..
Putnam, Ebenezer Jr.	2	..	1	..	..	..	..	1	..	..	..
Putnam, Seth	2	1	1	..	1	1	1	2	1	..	..
Stanton, Joseph	2	..	..	1	..	2	..	..	1	..	..
Wentworth, Levi 3rd	..	..	..	1	..	2	..	..	1	..	..
Willey, Ephraim	..	1	1	1	..	3	2	..	1	..	..
Woodbury, Thomas	..	..	..	1	1	3	..	..	1	1	..
Woolcott, Joseph	1	..	1	..	..	2	..	1	..	..	..
MILTON											
Ashley, Elisha	4	3	2	1	..	1	..	2	1	..	..
Austin, David	1	2	..	1	2	..	..	..	1	..	..
Austin, Job	1	1	..	1	..	2	..	..	1	..	..
Austin, Joseph	2	..	..	..	1	1	..	..	1	1	..
Austin, Peleg	..	..	1	..	..	..	..	1	..	..	..
Baarney, Jacob	..	..	..	1	..	3	..	..	1	..	..
Babcock, Jonathan	2	1	..	1	..	2	..	..	1	..	..
Barney, Jonathan	2	..	..	1	..	2	..	..	1	..	..
Bascomb, John	2	1	..	1	..	..	1	1	..	..	..
Basdel, Nathan	2	1	..	1	..	4	1	..	1	..	..
Baskum, Joel	2	..	..	1	..	3	..	1	..	..	..
MILTON—con.											
Bean, John	1	1	1	1	..	..	1	..	1	..	..
Beman, Friend	..	..	..	..	1	..	..	..	..	1	..
Beman, Friend Jr.	..	..	1	..	..	1	..	1	..	..	..
Beman, Reuben	3	..	..	1	..	1	1	..	1	..	..
Beman, Sheldon	..	..	..	1	..	1	..	1	..	..	..
Bibbins, Thomas	3	..	..	1	..	1	..	..	1	..	..
Blakeley, James	..	..	..	1	..	1	..	1	..	..	..
Bond, Calvin	1	..	..	..	1	3	..	..	1	..	..
Boyd, William	2	1	..	1	..	2	2	1	..	..	..
Brigham, Edward	2	2	2	..	1	2	1	1	1	..	..
Brigham, Leonard	2	2	3	..	1	2	1	..	1	1	..
Camel, Rufus	..	..	1	..	..	1	..	1	..	..	..
Campbell, Asa	..	..	1	..	..	..	..	1	..	..	..
Campbell, Nathan	..	1	3	..	1	2	3	..	..	1	..
Carpenter, Aaron	1	..	..	1	..	3	1	..	1	..	..
Castle, Isaac	1	..	1	..	..	..	1	1	..	..	..
Castle, Solomon	1	1	..	1	..	3	1	..	1	1	..
Chapins, Jesse	..	..	..	1	1	4	..	..	1	..	..
Church, Samuel	1	..	..	1	3	..	1	..	1	..	..
Cooe, John	2	..	..	1	..	1	..	1	..	..	..
Cooley, Solomon	2	..	1	..	1	2	1	2	..	1	..
Coon, Peleg	..	1	..	..	1	1	..	..	..	1	..
Coon, Thomas	1	..	..	1	..	1	..	..	1	..	..
Coy, Daniel	1	..	..	1	..	1	..	..	1	..	..
Davis, Moses	1	..	1	1	..	1	..	1	..	..	..
Day, Enos	2	..	..	1	..	..	..	..	1	..	..
Dean, Josiah	..	..	..	1	..	3	..	..	1	..	..
Dean, William	..	..	1	1	..	..	1	1	..	..	..
Dewey, Thomas	..	2	..	1	..	1	1	..	1	..	..
Dewey, Zebediah	1	..	..	1	..	3	..	1	1	..	..
Drake, Festus	..	..	2	..	1	..	1	..	..	1	..
Drean, William	1	..	1	..	1	1	..	1	..	..	..
Drury, Abel	1	..	..	1	..	3	..	..	1	..	..
Drury, Isaac	..	1	..	1	..	2	..	1	..	..	..
Frost, Bela F.	..	..	..	1	..	2	1	..	1	..	..
Giffin, Luther	..	..	..	1	..	..	..	1	..	..	..
Gifford, Gideon	..	1	..	1	..	..	1	..	1	..	..
Gifford, Reuben	..	..	..	1	..	1	..	..	1	..	..
Giler, Felix	1	2	1	1	..	1	..	2	..	1	..
Grannis, Levi	2	1	2	1	..	1	..	..	1	..	..
Hall, Edward	3	..	..	1	..	2	..	..	1	..	..
Hall, Joseph	2	..	2	..	1	1	2	2	..	1	..
Harrington, Ammi	3	..	..	1	..	1	..	..	1	..	..
Harris, Uri	..	1	..	1	1	2	..	..	1	1	..
Hawkins, John	4	..	1	..	..	..	..	..	..	..	..
Henry, Ebenezer	..	..	3	..	1	2	..	1	..	1	..
Hentley, Daniel	2	1	..	1	..	3	1	..	1	..	..
Hickok, Elisha	..	1	..	1	..	3	..	..	1	..	..
Hill, Benjamin	2	..	..	1	..	3	1	..	1	..	..
Holgate, Asa	..	..	..	..	1	..	..	..	..	1	..
Holgate, Samuel	3	..	..	1	..	..	..	1	..	..	..
How, Wyat	1	..	..	1	..	1	..	1	..	..	..
Howard, William	1	1	..	1	..	1	..	..	1	1	..
Hoxie, Gideon	1	..	..	1	..	2	1	..	1	..	..
Hull, Samuel	2	..	1	..	1	1	2	2	1	..	..
Hunt, William	2	..	..	1	..	3	..	..	1	..	..
Hurlbutt, William	1	1	3	..	1	1	..	..	1	..	..
Hyde, Henry	..	..	1	..	2	..	1	..	..	..	..
Inman, Stephen	..	..	..	1	..	1	..	1	..	..	..
Irish, Jesse	3	..	..	1	..	..	..	1	1	..	..
Irish, Stephen	1	2	..	1	..	2	..	..	1	..	..
Irish, William	..	..	3	..	1	..	..	1	..	1	..
Jackson, John	2	2	..	1	..	3	..	..	1	..	..
Jackson, Sarah	..	..	..	..	..	1	..	1	..	1	..
Jared, John	..	1	..	1	..	1	1	..	1	..	..
Knapp, Eleazer	..	1	..	..	1	2	..	..	..	1	..
Leet, Miles	2	1	..	1	..	2		..	2	1	..
Leonard, Joseph	2	1	1	1	..	3	1	..	1	..	..
Levitt, Samuel	..	..	..	1	..	1	..	1	..	..	..
Lewin, Robert	..	2	..	1	..	3	2	..	1	..	..
Lloyd, Peter	2	..	..	1	..	1	..	..	1	..	..
Logan, Samuel	..	..	..	..	1	1	..	..	..	1	..
Logan, Samuel Jr.	2	..	..	1	..	1	1	..	1	..	..
Loveland, Mehitabel	4	2	..	..	..	..	..	1	..	..	..
Manley, Nathan	..	..	1	..	1	..	1	1	..	1	..
Mansfield, Amasa	2	..	..	1	..	3	..	..	1	..	..
Mansfield, Amos	1	..	..	1	..	3	..	..	1	..	..
Mansfield, David	..	..	1	..	..	..	1	..	1	..	..

CHITTENDEN COUNTY—Continued

NAMES OF HEADS OF FAMILIES	FREE WHITE MALES: Under 10 years of age	FREE WHITE MALES: Of 10 and under 16	FREE WHITE MALES: Of 16 and under 26 including heads of families	FREE WHITE MALES: Of 26 and under 45 including heads of families	FREE WHITE MALES: Of 45 and upwards including heads of families.	FREE WHITE FEMALES: Under 10 years of age	FREE WHITE FEMALES: Of 10 and under 16	FREE WHITE FEMALES: Of 16 and under 26 including heads of families	FREE WHITE FEMALES: Of 26 and under 45 including heads of families	FREE WHITE FEMALES: Of 45 and upwards including heads of families	All other free persons except Indians not taxed
MILTON—con.											
Mansfield, Elias	..	..	1	..	..	..	..	1	..	..	1
Mansfield, Jacob	3	1	1	1	..	2	..	1	1	..	..
Mansfield, James	3	..	..	1	..	1	1	..	1	..	..
Mansfield, Lewis	..	..	..	..	..	..	1	..	..	1	..
Mansfield, Nathan	1	..	..	1	..	2	..	1	..	..	..
Mansfield, Samuel	..	..	1	1	..	..	..	1	..	..	..
Mansfield, Samuel	..	..	1	..	..	..	..	1	..	..	..
Mansfield, Stephen	1	..	1	..	..	1	1	1	..	..	..
Mansfield, Theophilus	..	..	1	..	1	..	..	..	..	1	..
Marble, John	2	..	1	..	..	..	..	1	..	..	..
Meaker, Daniel	..	..	1	1	..	4	..	..	1	..	..
Mears, John	2	..	..	1	..	2	..	..	1	..	..
Mears, Stephen	3	..	..	1	..	1	..	..	1	..	..
Naye, James	1	..	..	1	..	..	..	1	..	..	..
Naye, William A.	..	..	..	1	..	1	..	1	..	..	..
Newel, Asa	1	1	..	1	..	2	..	1	1	..	..
Newel, Medad	..	1	..	..	1	1	..	..	..	1	..
Newton, Jonas	1	1	..	1	..	2	1	..	1	..	..
Owen, Abigail	2	1	..	..	..	1	..	..	1	..	..
Owens, Elish	..	..	1	1	..	..	..	..	..	1	..
Owens, Ethan	..	..	1	..	..	..	..	1	..	..	..
Owens, Isaac	..	..	2	1	..	..	2	1	..	1	..
Owens, James	..	..	1	..	1	1	..	1	..	..	..
Parrish, William	..	3	..	1	..	2	1	..	1	..	..
Partridge, Richard	..	..	1	..	..	..	..	1	1	..	..
Pierce, David	2	..	..	..	2	2	..	..	1	1	..
Pierce, Peter	1	..	1	..	..	..	..	1	..	..	..
Ploof, Fanaway	1	..	..	1	..	1	..	..	1	..	..
Rich, William	2	..	..	1	..	2	..	..	1	..	..
Rood, Silas	1	1	..	1	..	3	..	..	1	..	..
Salmon, Samuel	1	1	..	1	..	3	1	..	1	..	..
Smith, Eleazer	1	..	..	1	..	..	..	1	..	..	..
Smith, Nehemiah	..	..	..	1	..	..	..	..	..	..	..
Soper, Mordecai	2	2	..	1	2	2	..	1	..	1	..
Swan, John	1	..	..	1	..	..	..	1	..	..	..
Taylor, Elisha	1	..	1	..	..	..	..	..	..	..	..
Taylor, Luther	..	..	1	..	..	..	..	1	..	..	..
Taylor, Samuel	..	1	2	1	..	1	..	1	..	..	..
Tomblin, Levi	..	..	..	1	..	..	..	1	..	..	..
Waters, Abel	..	1	..	..	1	..	1	1	..	1	..
Waters, Daniel	1	..	1	..	..	..	..	1	..	..	..
Waters, Truman	1	..	..	1	..	1	..	..	1	..	..
Wheeler, Zebediah	5	1	..	1	..	..	..	..	1	..	..
Willcox, William	2	..	2	..	1	..	2	..	..	1	..
Williams, Joseph	..	1	..	1	..	1	..	1	1	..	..
Williams, Joseph	1	..	..	1	..	..	..	..	1	..	..
Wood, Sanders	1	..	1	..	..	1	..	1	..	..	..
Woodruff, Jesse	1	..	..	1	..	1	..	1	..	..	..
Woodruff, Wier	1	..	..	1	1	3	1	..	1	..	..
Woods, Isaac	..	..	1	..	..	..	..	1	..	..	..
Woods, William V.	..	..	2	4	..	1	..	1	1	..	..
Wright, Phineas	2	2	..	..	1	1	..	..	..	1	..
Wyman, Solomon	..	1	..	1	..	1	..	1	..	..	..
Yale, Aaron	..	..	..	..	1	..	..	..	..	1	..
MORETOWN											
Atherton, Adonijah	..	..	1	..	..	2	..	1	..	..	..
Benton, Nathan	..	1	1	..	1	..	2	..	..	1	..
Bracker, Israel	3	..	..	1	..	1	..	1	1	..	..
Bruce, Hezekiah	2	1	..	1	..	..	..	..	1	..	..
Cady, Jonathan	2	..	..	1	..	..	..	..	1	..	..
Drake, Andrew	..	..	..	1	..	5	..	..	1	..	..
Drown, Pent	..	..	1	..	..	..	..	..	..	..	..
Foster, Isaac	1	..	1	..	..	1	..	1	..	..	..
Foster, John	2	..	..	1	..	3	1	..	1	..	..
Hambleton, Eli	1	..	..	1	..	2	..	..	1	..	..
Hawks, Eliakim	..	..	1	..	..	1	..	1	..	..	..
Hawks, Reuben	..	..	1	..	1	..	1	1	..	1	..
Hazeltine, Ebenezer	..	..	..	1	..	2	..	..	1	..	..
Hazeltine, Joseph	1	..	..	1	..	1	..	..	1	..	..
Heaton, Elijah	..	..	..	1	..	1	..	..	1	..	..
Heaton, John	..	..	3	1	1	..	..	2	..	1	..
Howard, Jonathan	3	2	..	1	..	2	..	..	1	..	..
MORETOWN—con.											
Knapp, Matthew	..	2	1	..	..	..	..	1	..	1	..
Lyon, Nathan	..	..	..	1	..	1	..	1	..	..	..
Mayo, Ebenezer	..	..	..	1	..	3	..	..	1	..	..
Munson, Seth	1	1	1	1	..	2	..	..	1	..	..
Perkins, Ariel	1	2	..	1	..	1	1	..	1	..	..
Pressy, James	..	..	..	1	..	2	..	..	1	..	..
Robinson, Zelotus	3	1	..	1	..	1	1	..	1	..	..
Server, Jonathan	..	..	1	..	..	1	..	1	..	..	..
Smith, Roswell	..	..	3	..	1	1	2	..	..	1	..
Spalding, Nersal	1	..	1	..	..	..	..	1	..	..	..
Spalding, Royal	2	..	1	1	..	2	..	..	1	..	..
Spalding, Wright	1	2	..	1	1	2	..	..	1	1	..
Sterns, Asa	2	2	..	1	..	3	2	1	..	..	..
Sterns, Asa	3	1	..	..	1	3	3	..	1	..	..
Thrasher, James	1	..	1	..	..	..	..	..	..	..	..
RICHMOND											
Alger, Nathaniel	6	3	..	1	..	..	..	..	1	..	..
Algier, Abraham	3	2	..	1	..	..	..	..	1	..	..
Algier, Asa	3	2	..	1	..	1	..	..	1	..	..
Andrus, Isaac	2	1	..	1	..	2	..	..	1	..	..
Arnold, Dan	..	..	..	1	..	2	..	..	1	..	..
Arnold, Elisha	3	..	..	1	..	1	..	..	1	..	..
Arnold, James	..	..	..	..	1	..	1	..	..	1	..
Arnold, James Jr.	2	..	..	1	..	..	..	1	..	..	..
Barber, Martin	2	1	1	1	..	2	1	..	1	..	..
Bates, Solomon	1	1	1	1	..	..	..	..	1	1	..
Betty, James	2	..	..	1	..	3	1	..	1	..	..
Betty, Joseph	1	..	..	1	..	..	2	..	1	..	..
Bishop, Benjamin	..	1	..	1	..	2	..	1	..	..	..
Bishop, Daniel	1	..	1	..	1	..	1	..	1	1	..
Boselby, Joshua	..	1	1	..	1	2	1	1	..	1	..
Brewster, Ozer	3	..	2	..	1	3	2	2	1	..	..
Brownson, Amos	1	..	..	..	1	..	..	..	..	1	..
Brownson, Asa	..	2	1	..	1	..	1	1	1	..	..
Brownson, Ebenezer	2	..	1	1	..	2	..	1	1	..	..
Brownson, Joel	2	2	1	2	..	1	1	..	1	..	..
Butler, James	..	..	1	1	..	2	..	..	1	..	..
Butler, Joseph	..	..	..	..	1	..	..	2	..	1	..
Chamberlin, Isaac	2	..	..	1	1	2	..	1	..	1	..
Chamberlin, Joshua	1	2	1	1	..	3	..	1	1	..	..
Chamberlin, Samuel	..	1	1	1	..	2	1	1	..	1	..
Church, Sylvanus	..	..	..	1	..	2	1	..	1	..	..
Closson, Jonathan	..	1	1	..	1	..	2	1	..	1	..
Closson, Josiah	..	1	..	1	..	1	..	1	..	..	..
Cole, Seth	1	..	..	1	..	1	..	..	1	..	..
Cooper, Abel	1	1	3	..	1	..	..	1	..	1	
Cooper, John	1	..	..	1	..	..	..	..	1	..	..
Cox, Matthew	2	1	..	1	..	2	1	..	1	..	..
Crague, Richard	2	..	..	1	..	2	..	..	1	..	..
Crane, James	1	..	1	1	..	1	..	..	1	..	..
Crane, Peter	1	1	..	1	..	2	2	1	1	..	..
Dart, James	3	..	..	1	..	1	..	..	1	..	..
Davenrix, John	3	1	..	..	1	1	1	1	1	..	..
Densmore, Eliph	..	1	1	1	..	..	..	1	..	..	..
Dills, Peter	2	1	..	1	..	1	..	..	1	..	..
Douglass, William	1	2	3	1	..	2	..	1	..	1	..
Dutton, Timothy	..	..	1	..	..	..	..	1	..	..	..
Egly, Aaron	..	..	1	1	..	2	..	1	..	..	..
Everitts, Jesse	4	..	..	1	..	1	1	..	1	..	..
Evets, William	2	..	..	1	..	1	..	1	..	..	..
Farnsworth, Benjamin	4	2	..	1	..	2	3	..	1	..	..
Fay, Henry	1	1	1	1	..	3	..	1	..	..	..
Fay, Nathan	3	2	1	1	..	1	..	1	1	..	..
Flag, Ebenezer	2	1	..	1	..	4	..	..	1	..	..
Flemming, Asa	1	2	1	1	..	2	1	..	1	..	..
Gay, Abner	..	..	..	1	..	3	..	1	..	..	..
Gay, Zebulon	..	..	..	1	..	1	..	1	..	..	..
Graves, William	..	1	..	1	..	..	1	..	1	..	1
Green, Jesse	1	2	..	1	..	2	..	..	1	..	..
Guthardy, Ezra	3	..	..	1	..	1	..	..	1	..	..

CHITTENDEN COUNTY—Continued

NAMES OF HEADS OF FAMILIES	FREE WHITE MALES					FREE WHITE FEMALES					All other free persons except Indians not taxed
	Under 10 years of age	Of 10 and under 16	Of 16 and under 26 including heads of families	Of 26 and under 45 including heads of families	Of 45 and upwards including heads of families.	Under 10 years of age	Of 10 and under 16	Of 16 and under 26 including heads of families	Of 26 and under 45 including heads of families	Of 45 and upwards including heads of families	
RICHMOND—con.											
Hall, Abijah	..	..	1	..	..	1	..	1	..	..	..
Hall, James	4	..	1	1	..	..	2	1	1	..	..
Hall, Jeremiah	..	..	..	1	..	1	..	..	1	..	..
Hall, Joseph Jr.	..	1	2	..	1	..	..	1	..	1	..
Hallock, Content C.	2	..	..	1	..	2	..	..	1	..	..
Hallock, John	3	..	..	1	..	1	..	..	1	..	..
Hallock, Joseph	..	..	..	1	..	3	..	..	1	..	..
Hallock, Stephen	..	1	1	..	1	..	..	2	..	1	..
Hallock, Stephen	2	2	..	1	..	1	..	..	1	..	..
Hitchcock, Nathaniel	..	..	..	..	1	2	..	..	1	..	..
Hodges, Leonard	1	3	..	1	..	1	..	..	1	..	..
Holenbeck, John	..	1	..	..	1	..	..	1	..	1	..
Hollenbeck, Abram	3	..	1	1	..	1	..	..	1	..	..
Hoyt, Flemen	..	1	1	..	1	1	3	..	..	1	..
Hoyt, Martin	1	..	1	..	..	..	..	1	..	..	..
Hoyt, Samuel	1	..	1	..	..	1	..	1	..	..	..
Hunt, Silas	1	..	..	1	..	..	..	1	..	..	..
Hurlbut, Elijah	1	1	..	..	1	..	1	1	..	1	..
Jackson, Asa	3	..	..	1	..	1	2	..	1	..	..
Jackson, Rial	1	..	..	1	..	1	..	..	1	..	..
Janes, Edward	1	..	..	1	1	..	..	1	1	..	..
Linscot, Samuel	3	1	..	1	..	2	..	..	1	..	..
Mallard, John	1	..	..	1	..	2	..	..	1	..	..
Martin, Samuel	2	..	..	1	..	..	..	2	1	..	..
McFarson, Amasa	..	1	..	..	..	1	2	1	1	..	..
Nichols, Andrew	3	1	2	1	..	..	..	..	1	..	..
Nichols, James	3	2	..	1	..	1	..	..	1	..	..
Palmer, Thomas	1	1	1	..	1	2	1	..	1	..	..
Reynols, Daniel	3	..	2	..	..	..	..	1	..	..	..
Ridley, Samuel	1	1	..	1	..	1	..	..	1	..	..
Robins, Daniel	..	1	..	1	..	..	2	..	1	..	..
Russell, John	1	1	3	1	..	3	1	..	1	..	..
Sherman, George	1	..	1	..	..	2	..	1	..	..	..
Smith, Abram	2	3	..	1	..	1	3	..	1	..	..
Smith, Ezra	1	2	1	..	1	2	2	2	..	1	..
Smith, James	3	1	..	1	..	..	2	..	1	..	..
Spafford, Jacob	3	..	1	1	..	1	1	..	1	..	..
Spafford, Job	1	1	..	1	..	2	..	..	1	..	..
Spooner, Bigford	2	1	2	1	..	1	2	3	1	..	..
Star, Parley	..	..	..	..	1	..	..	..	..	..	..
Stephens, Arnold	1	..	..	1	..	1	..	..	1	..	..
Stevens, James	..	1	2	..	1	..	3	2	..	1	..
Stevens, James Jr.	..	1	..	1	..	1	2	..	1	..	..
Stockwell, Abner	2	..	..	1	..	1	..	..	1	..	..
Tomlinson, Eliphalet	2	..	..	1	..	2	..	..	1	..	..
Torrington, Thomas	2	1	2	..	1	2	1	1	1	..	..
Tyler, Abraham	3	2	..	1	..	1	1	..	2	1	..
Warren, Aaron	2	..	1	1	..	1	..	..	1	..	..
Wells, Reuben	1	..	1	1	..	1	4	5	1	..	..
Whitcomb, James	2	..	..	1	..	..	1	1	1	..	..
Whitcomb, Robert	..	..	1	..	1	..	..	..	..	1	..
Willson, Joseph	2	..	..	1	..	1	..	1	1	..	..
Wright, Thaddeus	3	1	..	1	..	..	1	..	1	..	..
Wright, Zebulon	2	..	..	1	..	1	..	..	1	..	..
SHELBURNE											
Allen, Abijah	..	..	..	1	..	..	1	1	..	..	..
Allen, Richard	..	..	..	1	..	..	..	..	1	..	..
Atwater, Ambrose	..	1	1	..	1	..	1	1	..	1	..
Bacon, John	..	..	2	1	..	3	..	1	..	..	..
Barber, Daniel	..	..	1	1	1	..	1	..	1	..	..
Barber, Daniel Jr.	1	..	..	1	..	2	..	1	..	..	..
Benson, Benoni	..	..	1	..	..	..	..	1	..	..	..
Bidgood, Remington	1	..	..	1	..	3	2	..	1	..	..
Blair, Francis	..	1	2	1	..	..	..	1	..	..	..
Blair, William	2	..	1	..	1	1	..	1	..	..	..
Blinn, Samuel	1	..	..	1	..	2	..	1	..	..	..
Blinn, Simon	2	1	..	1	..	1	1	..	1	..	..
Blinn, William	..	1	..	1	1	..	..	..	..	1	..
Boynton, Jedediah	..	1	2	..	..	2	..	1	..	..	..
Burrite, Israel	..	1	1	..	1	1	..	..	1	..	..
Chittenden, Bethuel	..	..	1	..	1	..	..	..	..	1	..
Chittenden, Luther	..	..	..	1	..	2	..	..	1	1	..
Chittenden, William	2	..	..	1	..	2	..	1	..	..	..
Choat, Storey	3	..	2	1	..	..	2	1	..	1	..

NAMES OF HEADS OF FAMILIES	FREE WHITE MALES					FREE WHITE FEMALES					All other free persons except Indians not taxed
	Under 10 years of age	Of 10 and under 16	Of 16 and under 26 including heads of families	Of 26 and under 45 including heads of families	Of 45 and upwards including heads of families.	Under 10 years of age	Of 10 and under 16	Of 16 and under 26 including heads of families	Of 26 and under 45 including heads of families	Of 45 and upwards including heads of families	
SHELBURNE—con.											
Clark, Zadock	2	..	..	..	1	1	..	1	..	..	..
Clark, Zadock Jr.	..	..	1	..	..	2	..	1	..	..	..
Clarke, Samuel	..	..	..	..	1	1	1	1	..	1	..
Cobb, Ebenezer	2	1	..	..	1	..	1	2	..	1	..
Comstock, Daniel	1	1	1	2	1	1	1	1	..	1	..
Comstock, Levi	1	..	1	1	..	1	..	..	1	..	..
Cook, David	1	..	..	1	..	3	..	..	1	..	..
Cook, Israel	1	..	1	..	..	..	..	1	..	..	..
Drew, Isaac	1	..	1	..	..	..	..	1	..	..	..
Drew, John	1	1	1	..	1	1	..	1	..	1	..
Drew, Mary	1	..	1	..	..	1	2	..	1	..	..
Drew, Salmon	..	..	1	..	..	..	..	1	..	..	..
Fairchild, Dan	..	..	2	..	1	..	..	..	..	1	..
Fish, Nathan	2	..	..	1	..	..	..	1	..	..	..
Frisby, Asa	1	..	1	..	..	..	..	1	..	..	..
Gage, Nathaniel	1	..	..	1	..	1	..	..	1	..	..
Gage, Richard	1	..	..	1	..	4	..	..	1	..	..
Green, Martin	..	..	1	..	..	..	..	1	..	..	..
Gregory, Salmon	2	1	..	1	..	3	..	..	1	1	..
Hall, Thomas	..	2	2	..	1	..	2	1	..	1	..
Hambleton, Joseph	1	..	..	1	..	3	..	..	1	..	..
Harrington, Benjamin	2	..	3	2	..	1	2	2	1	..	..
Hawley, James	2	..	1	..	1	1	2	1	..	1	..
Helms, Samuel	..	..	..	1	..	3	..	..	1	..	..
Higby, Elnathan	1	2	1	1	..	2	1	..	1	..	..
Higby, Wheeler	1	2	..	1	..	2	1	..	1	..	..
Hill, Phinehas	..	1	..	1	..	2	2	..	1	..	..
Hixton, John	1	..	1	..	..	1	..	1	..	..	..
Hopkins, Joseph	3	..	2	1	..	..	..	1	..	1	..
Horslord, William	1	..	1	..	1	1	..	1	..	1	..
Hurlbut, Timothy	..	1	1	..	1	1	3	..	..	1	..
Isham, Jeremiah	1	..	..	1	..	3	3	..	1	..	..
Isham, Joshua	1	..	3	1	..	2	2	..	1	..	..
Lathrop, Thomas	1	..	2	..	1	1	2	1	..	1	..
Lemaly, Luma	1	..	..	..	2	2	..	..	1	..	..
Lyon, Asa	1	..	1	..	..	..	..	1	..	..	..
Lyon, Gene	..	..	..	..	..	..	1	1	..	1	..
Lyon, Gershom	2	2	1	..	1	..	1	2	..	2	..
Lyon, Jonathan	2	..	1	..	..	1	..	1	..	..	..
Lyon, Robert	2	..	..	1	..	1	1	..	1	..	..
Lyon, Timothy	1	..	..	1	..	2	..	1	..	..	..
Lyon, William	2	1	..	1	..	2	..	..	1	..	..
Mick, Frederick	2	..	1	1	..	2	..	..	1	..	..
Mills, Alexander	..	..	2	..	1	..	..	1	..	1	..
Mills, Ebenezer	..	..	1	..	..	..	1	..	1	..	..
Mills, Samuel	3	1	..	1	..	1	..	..	1	..	..
Morehouse, Sterges	2	1	2	1	..	1	1	1	1	..	..
Morgan, Joshua	2	2	1	..	2	1	1	2	1	..	..
Morgan, Skiff	3	..	..	1	..	..	3	..	1	..	..
Nash, Asel	3	2	..	1	..	3	..	..	1	..	..
Packer, Eldridge	..	..	1	1	..	..	..	..	..	..	..
Paine, Nehemiah	..	..	1	..	..	1	..	1	..	..	..
Palmer, Simeon	2	..	..	1	..	1	..	..	1	..	..
Pangman, Amos	2	..	..	1	..	..	1	1	..	..	..
Patrol, John	..	..	..	..	1	..	..	..	..	1	..
Payne, Dan	1	..	..	1	..	2	1	..	1	..	..
Peck, Sarah	1	..	..	..	..	1	1	..	..	1	..
Perkins, Philo	2	..	..	1	..	2	1	..	1	..	..
Pierson, Moses	..	..	..	..	1	..	..	..	..	1	..
Pierson, Samuel	2	..	2	1	..	2	1	..	1	..	..
Pierson, Ural	3	1	1	1	..	3	..	..	1	..	..
Pierson, William	2	2	1	1	..	..	..	2	..	..	..
Pierson, Ziba	1	..	3	1	..	3	1	..	2	..	..
Post, Zeley	..	1	..	..	..	..	2	2	..	1	..
Prowty, Caleb	1	..	..	..	1	..	..	..	1	..	..
Reed, Joshua	2	1	..	1	..	2	..	..	1	1	..
Roback, F. B.	..	..	1	..	..	..	..	..	..	..	..
Roberts, David	1	..	..	1	..	3	2	..	1	..	..
Robinson, Claghorn	3	..	2	..	1	..	2	..	1	..	..
Robinson, Samuel	..	..	1	..	..	1	..	..	1	..	..
Roswell, Minor	3	1	2	..	1	1	2	..	1	..	..
Rowley, Aaron	3	2	3	3	..	2	1	..	1	..	..
Sexton, Horace	..	..	2	..	..	..	1	1	..	1	..
Sexton, Nehemiah	2	..	1	1	..	2	..	..	1	..	..
Sheldon, Israel	2	1	1	1	..	2	1	..	1	..	..
Slawson, Asa	1	..	..	1	..	4	..	..	1	..	..

CHITTENDEN COUNTY—Continued

NAMES OF HEADS OF FAMILIES	Free white males: Under 10 years of age	Free white males: Of 10 and under 16	Free white males: Of 16 and under 26 including heads of families	Free white males: Of 26 and under 45 including heads of families	Free white males: Of 45 and upwards including heads of families	Free white females: Under 10 years of age	Free white females: Of 10 and under 16	Free white females: Of 16 and under 26 including heads of families	Free white females: Of 26 and under 45 including heads of families	Free white females: Of 45 and upwards including heads of families	All other free persons except Indians not taxed
SHELBURNE—con.											
Smith, Noah	2	..	..	1	..	..	..	1	..	..	..
Smith, Sylvanus	..	..	1	..	..	..	..	2	..	..	..
Smith, William	..	..	..	..	1	..	1	..	..	1	..
Smith, Zadock	2	..	..	1	..	2	1	..	1	..	..
Spears, Barnabus	2	..	..	1	..	2	..	..	1	..	..
Spears, Betsey	..	..	1	..	..	..	..	1	1	1	..
Spears, Polly	3	1	..	..	..	1	..	1	1	..	..
Steward, Asher	..	..	..	..	1	..	..	..	1	1	..
Sulivan, Adam	1	..	..	..	1	2	..	..	1	..	..
Sutton, Benjamin	6	4	..	1	..	..	..	1	1	..	..
Sutton, James	3	..	..	1	..	..	..	..	1	1	..
Tabor, John	3	..	1	1	..	1	..	..	1	..	..
Thayer, Dan	..	..	..	1	..	2	2	..	1	..	..
Thayer, Eli	1	..	..	1	..	1	..	1	..	..	..
Tiny, Richard	..	..	..	1	..	..	1	..	1	..	..
Tracy, Hezekiah	..	3	1	..	1	..	1	2	..	1	..
Tracy, Isaac	1	..	..	1	..	1	..	1	..	..	..
Trobridge, Keeler	1	1	..	1	1	2	1	1	..	1	..
Tuttle, Levi	1	..	3	1	..	2	2	..	1	..	..
VanOrnum, John	..	..	1	..	..	1	..	1	..	..	..
Vester, Ebenezer	2	2	..	1	..	3	1	1	1	..	..
White, Nathaniel	2	1	..	1	..	..	..	1	1	..	..
Whitley, John	1	..	..	..	1	1	..	..	1	..	..
STOWE											
Bement, Asa	..	..	..	1	..	1	..	1	..	..	..
Bennett, Stephen	4	..	..	1	..	..	..	..	1	..	..
Bigford, Abner	3	2	1	..	1	3	2	..	1	..	..
Bigford, John	1	1	1	..	1	2	1	..	1	..	..
Chapel, Noah	1	..	1	..	..	1	1	..	..	..	..
Chatman, Israel	2	..	..	1	..	1	..	..	1	..	..
Cutchins, Hugh	..	..	1	..	1	2	2	2	..	1	..
Done, Joshua	1	1	1	1	..	1	2	1	1	..	..
Downing, Thomas B.	1	..	..	1	..	1	..	1	..	..	..
George, Caleb	..	..	1	..	..	2	..	1	..	..	..
George, Jared	2	..	..	1	..	..	1	..	..	..	..
Harris, Joel	2	1	..	1	..	1	..	1	..	..	..
Haydon, Chandler	1	..	..	1	..	2	..	..	1	..	..
Haydon, Elijah	..	..	1	..	1	..	..	1	..	1	..
Henderson, Nicholas	1	..	..	1	..	2	..	1	..	..	..
Henderson, Samuel	2	1	2	..	1	..	..	..	1	1	..
Henderson, Samuel Jr.	..	..	1	..	..	..	..	1	..	..	..
Hurlbut, Isaiah	2	2	..	1	..	3	2	..	1	..	..
Kimbal, Isaac	..	..	1	..	..	..	..	1	..	..	..
Lamb, Josiah	..	1	2	..	1	1	..	..	1	..	..
Lathrop, Daniel	..	..	1	..	..	2	..	1	..	..	..
Luce, Andrew	3	2	2	..	1	1	..	1	..	1	..
Luce, Oliver	1	..	..	1	1	3	1	..	1	1	..
Luce, Wiram	..	..	1	..	..	1	..	1	..	..	..
Marshal, Clement	2	1	3	..	1	1	2	2	1	1	..
Moody, Clement	1	..	1	1	1	..	1	1	..	1	
Moody, Clement Jr.	2	..	..	1	..	1	..	..	1	..	..
Moody, Phillip	4	1	..	1	..	1	..	2	1	..	..
Parker, Dexter	..	..	1	..	1	1	..	1	..	..	..
Pierce, Samuel	5	..	..	1	..	..	..	..	1	..	..
Pike, John	..	..	1	..	..	2	..	1	..	..	..
Robinson, Nathan	1	1	..	..	1	3	1	1	1	..	..
Sambon, Levi	1	..	1	..	1	3	2	..	..	..	..
Sambon, Paul	1	..	1	1	..	4	2	..	1	..	..
Smith, Jethro	1	2	..	1	..	1	..	..	1	..	..
Smith, Thomas	4	1	..	1	..	1	1	..	1	..	..
Stiles, Abiel	..	..	..	1	..	2	1	1	..	..	..
Storey, Francis	3	1	..	1	..	3	..	..	1	..	..
Tabor, John	3	..	..	1	..	2	..	..	1	..	..
Town, Edmund	3	1	..	1	..	2	..	..	1	..	..
Town, James	2	1	2	..	1	1	3	2	..	1	..
Utley, William	2	..	..	1	1	1	2	..	1	..	..
Wakefield, Ebenezer	1	..	1	1	1	2	..	..	1	..	..
Walder, Elias	2	..	..	1	..	..	..	..	1	..	..
Waters, Stephen	1	..	1	..	..	1	..	1	..	..	..
Wilbur, Israel	2	3	1	1	..	3	1	..	1	..	..

NAMES OF HEADS OF FAMILIES	Free white males: Under 10 years of age	Free white males: Of 10 and under 16	Free white males: Of 16 and under 26 including heads of families	Free white males: Of 26 and under 45 including heads of families	Free white males: Of 45 and upwards including heads of families	Free white females: Under 10 years of age	Free white females: Of 10 and under 16	Free white females: Of 16 and under 26 including heads of families	Free white females: Of 26 and under 45 including heads of families	Free white females: Of 45 and upwards including heads of families	All other free persons except Indians not taxed
UNDERHILL											
Barney, William	..	1	..	1	..	1	..	..	1	..	..
Benedict, Elijah	..	..	..	..	1	1	..	..	1	1	..
Bigsby, Salmon	1	..	..	1	..	1	..	1	..	..	..
Blood, James	..	..	1	..	..	..	..	1	..	..	..
Brookins, Phillip	..	..	..	1	..	1	..	..	1	..	..
Brown, Deliverance	..	1	1	..	1	..	..	..	..	1	..
Bung, David	2	2	2	1	1	1	1	1	..	1	..
Clark, Daniel	..	..	..	1	..	..	1	..	1	..	..
Coleman, John	1	..	..	1	..	1	..	..	1	..	..
Dixon, Elenor	..	..	..	..	..	..	..	..	..	1	..
Dixon, Jared	2	2	..	1	..	2	1	..	1	..	..
Dixon, Luther	..	..	1	1	..	1	..	1	1	..	..
Eaton, Abner	2	..	..	1	2	2	..	..	1	..	..
Frink, William E.	..	..	..	1	..	..	1	..	..	1	..
Graves, Bennett	..	..	..	1	..	1	..	..	1	..	..
Graves, Chauncey	2	1	1	1	..	2	3	..	1	..	..
Graves, Simeon	..	..	..	..	1	..	..	..	1	..	..
Hawley, Stephen	1	1	..	1	..	2	1	..	1	..	..
Hay, Udney	..	1	1	..	1	1	..	2	..	..	..
Hurlbut, Adam	..	1	1	1	1	..	..	..	..	1	..
Jones, Moses	..	..	..	1	..	2	..	..	1	..	..
Loomer, Dexter	..	..	1	..	4	1	..	..	1	1	..
Martin, Peter	1	1	..	1	..	1	..	1	..	..	..
Mead, Ezra	3	..	..	1	..	2	..	..	1	..	..
Mead, Josiah	1	..	..	1	..	1	..	..	1	..	..
Mead, Levi	3	..	..	1	..	3	..	..	1	..	..
Naramore, Justin	..	..	..	1	..	2	..	..	1	1	..
Oak, Benjamin	..	..	..	1	..	2	1	..	1	..	..
Oles, George	1	2	3	..	1	2	1	1	1	..	..
Palmer, Solomon	1	..	..	1	..	2	1	..	..	..	..
Prior, Heman	5	1	..	1	..	2	..	..	1	..	..
Safford, William	..	1	..	1	..	4	1	..	1	..	..
Sheldon, Caleb	3	..	1	1	..	..	1	..	1	..	..
Spalding, Sylvester	1	..	..	1	..	1	..	..	1	..	..
Stephens, Zenas	3	2	..	1	..	1	..	..	1	..	..
Ward, Dexter	1	..	..	1	..	2	..	1	1	..	..
Wood, Bernard	..	2	..	1	..	..	1	..	1	..	..
Worden, Nathaniel	1	..	1	..	..	1	..	1	..	..	..
Wordon, Gabriel	..	..	1	..	..	..	..	1	1	..	..
WAITSFIELD											
Abbot, Eli	3	..	..	1	..	2	..	1	1	..	..
Allen, William	2	2	1	1	..	..	1	1	1	..	..
Baislee, Samuel	3	1	..	1	..	1	1	..	1	..	..
Barnard, Samuel	1	..	1	..	1	2	2	..	..	1	..
Bartlet, Nathaniel	2	2	1	1	..	1	..	..	1	..	..
Bemon, John	..	1	..	..	1	1	1	..	..	1	
Bliss, Thatcher	1	..	1	1	..	3	..	1	..	..	..
Burdick, Ashbel	1	..	..	1	..	5	..	..	1	..	..
Burdick, John	2	1	..	1	..	2	1	1	1	..	..
Bushnel, David	2	1	..	1	..	1	..	..	1	..	..
Butterfield, Stephen	1	..	..	1	..	3	..	..	1	..	..
Chace, Moses	3	1	1	1	..	1	1	..	1	..	..
Childs, Robert	2	1	..	1	..	3	..	..	1	..	..
Dana, Foster	..	..	1	1	..	..	..	1	..	..	..
Dana, Frenus	..	..	1	..	1	..	..	2	..	..	..
Dana, Henry	4	..	..	1	..	..	1	1	1	..	..
Durfe, Rufus	..	..	1	..	..	..	..	..	..	..	..
Eaton, James	2	2	2	..	1	1	1	1	..	1	..
Freeman, Alpheus	..	..	..	1	..	..	..	..	1	..	..
Gandy, Elijah	2	..	1	..	..	..	..	1	..	..	..
Hambleton, Joseph	2	2	1	..	..	2	..	1	..	1	..
Hawley, Hezekiah	1	1	1	..	1	3	1	..	1	..	..
Hitchcock, Granis	2	1	..	1	..	3	1	..	1	..	..

CHITTENDEN COUNTY—Continued

NAMES OF HEADS OF FAMILIES	FREE WHITE MALES					FREE WHITE FEMALES					All other free persons except Indians not taxed
	Under 10 years of age	Of 10 and under 16	Of 16 and under 26 including heads of families	Of 26 and under 45 including heads of families	Of 45 and upwards including heads of families.	Under 10 years of age	Of 10 and under 16	Of 16 and under 26 including heads of families	Of 26 and under 45 including heads of families	Of 45 and upwards including heads of families	
WAITSFIELD—con.											
Joiner, William	..	1	..	..	1	1	2	..	1	..	..
Jones, Ezra	..	..	..	1	..	..	..	..	..	..	..
Jones, Ginson	..	..	1	..	..	..	..	..	..	..	..
Jones, Matthias	..	..	1	..	..	..	..	..	..	..	..
Joslin, James	1	..	1	..	..	1	..	1	..	..	..
Joslin, Joseph	..	..	1	..	..	..	..	1	..	..	..
Lamb, John	..	..	..	1	..	..	..	1	..	..	..
Lee, Josiah	..	..	1	..	..	..	..	..	..	..	..
Lee, Roswell	..	..	..	1	..	1	..	1	..	..	..
Lyon, Joseph	..	..	1	..	..	..	..	..	..	..	..
Minor, Aaron	1	1	1	1	..	..	..	1	1	..	..
Mix, Jesse	..	..	..	1	..	1	..	1	..	..	..
Moniston, William	..	..	1	..	..	..	..	..	..	..	..
Moor, Peleg	1	..	..	1	..	2	..	1	..	..	..
Palmer, William	..	..	..	1	1	..	..	..	1	..	..
Pellmer, Jonathan	..	1	..	1	..	3	2	..	1	..	..
Phelps, Aaron	1	..	1	..	..	..	..	..	1	..	..
Phelps, Bissel	..	..	1	..	1	..	1	..	..	1	..
Phinny, Elijah	1	2	1	..	1	2	1	1	..	1	..
Pierce, Joseph	2	..	..	1	..	1	..	1	1	..	..
Pike, Joshua	..	..	..	1	..	3	..	..	1	..	..
Rider, Phineas	3	..	..	1	..	2	1	..	1	..	..
Rider, Salma	2	..	..	1	..	2	1	..	1	..	..
Savage, Samuel	1	1	..	1	..	1	1	..	1	1	..
Sherman, Beriah	..	1	2	..	1	..	..	1	..	1	..
Simons, David	..	..	..	1	..	..	..	1	..	..	..
Skinner, Amasa	2	1	..	1	..	2	1	..	1	..	..
Skinner, Eli	1	1	1	1	..	4	1	..	1	..	..
Skinner, Jared	..	1	1	..	1	..	1	1	..	1	..
Smith, Elijah	..	..	..	1	..	2	..	..	1	..	..
Smith, Lesley	3	2	..	1	..	1	1	..	1	..	..
Smith, Moses	4	..	..	1	..	..	1	..	1	..	..
Smith, Moses	1	..	..	1	..	1	..	..	1	..	..
Spalding, Abel	3	..	..	1	..	3	..	..	1	..	..
Spalding, James	3	1	..	1	..	1	1	..	1	..	..
Sterling, Nathan	2	1	..	1	..	3	..	..	1	..	..
Stewart, Moses	1	..	..	1	..	..	..	1	..	..	..
Stoddard, Simeon	4	1	..	1	..	..	1	..	1	1	..
Stowel, Nathan	1	..	..	1	..	3	..	..	1	..	..
Taylor, Daniel	1	1	..	..	1	4	2	..	1	..	..
Taylor, Elias	2	1	2	1	..	2	1	1	1	..	..
Taylor, Jabez	3	1	..	1	..	1	1	..	1	..	..
Trask, Isaac	..	1	..	..	1	1	2	1	..	..	..
Trask, Silas	..	..	..	1	..	..	..	..	..	..	..
Tuksbury, Isaac	1	..	..	1	..	1	..	..	1	..	..
Wait, Benjamin	..	1	1	1	1	1	..	..	1	..	..
Wait, Benjamin Jr.	2	..	..	1	..	1	..	1	..	..	..
Wait, Ezra	3	1	..	1	..	2	2	..	1	..	..
Wait, Jedrathan	3	1	..	..	1	1	..	..	1	..	..
Wait, Robert	..	..	1	..	..	2	..	1	..	..	..
Wells, John	..	..	..	..	1	1	..	..	..	1	..
Wheeler, William	3	..	..	1	..	2	..	..	1	..	..
Wilder, Samuel	1	1	1	1	1	..	1	2	..	1	..
WATERBURY											
Adkins, Daniel	2	1	..	1	..	..	1	1	1	1	..
Adkins, David	2	1	1	..	1	1	2	..	..	1	..
Allen, Joseph	2	2	1	..	1	1	..	1	1	..	..
Austin, David O.	3	1	1	1	1	2	2	..	1	1	..
Barber, Isaac	1	..	2	1	..	3	..	..	1	..	..
Bates, Edward	2	..	..	1	1	1	2	2	..	1	..
Bates, Moses	2	1	1	1	..	1	1	1	..	..	..
Battles, Ezra	1	1	1	1	..	4	1	1	1	..	..
Beming, Amos	1	3	..	..	1	4	2	..	..	1	..
Bigford, James	3	..	..	1	..	2	..	..	1	..	..
Bigford, Thomas	..	..	1	..	1	..	..	1	..	1	..
Blair, Hugh	..	..	1	..	1	1	2	1	..	2	..
Bliss, Daniel	4	..	..	2	..	1	1	..	1	..	..
Brown, William	2	..	..	1	..	..	..	..	1	..	..
Bryant, James	2	..	..	1	..	1	..	..	1	..	..
Bryant, Samuel	2	..	..	1	..	..	..	1	..	..	..
Burke, David	1	..	..	1	..	1	..	1	..	..	..
Burns, Joseph	4	1	..	1	..	1	..	..	1	..	..
Cady, Jason	1	1	2	..	1	1	1	2	..	1	..
Calkins, John B.	3	2	2	..	1	..	1	1	1	..	..
Chafy, Amos	1	..	..	1	..	2	..	..	1	..	..
Chapman, John	2	..	..	1	..	1	..	..	1	..	..
WATERBURY—con.											
Clark, Carpus	2	..	1	..	2	3	..	..	1	..	..
Claushlin, Timothy	..	..	..	..	1	..	..	..	..	1	..
Claushlin, Timothy Jr.	1	2	1	2	..	1	..	..	1	..	..
Coffin, Moses	3	..	..	1	..	1	..	..	..	..	..
Cotton, William	2	2	2	..	1	1	1	..	1	..	..
Craig, John	..	1	..	1	..	1	1	..	..	2	..
Craig, Uriah	1	..	1	..	..	..	..	1	..	..	..
Danfier, Moses	2	1	2	..	1	1	1	..	..	1	..
Daniels, Joshua	1	..	1	2	..	1	..	..	1	1	..
Darling, Joseph	..	..	..	1	..	3	..	1	..	..	..
Edmonds, William	1	..	1	..	..	..	..	1	..	..	..
Fay, David	2	..	..	1	..	1	..	..	1	..	..
Fiske, Job	..	1	..	1	..	3	..	..	1	..	..
Freeman, Elijah	..	..	..	2	..	2	..	..	1	..	..
Freeman, John	2	1	1	1	..	..	2	..	1	..	..
Freeman, Zebediah	4	..	..	1	..	1	..	..	1	..	..
Frink, Stoughton	1	..	1	..	1	1	..	..	1	1	..
Gilbert, Josiah	..	2	1	1	..	..	1	..	1	..	..
Gubtail, Humphrey	..	..	1	1	..	3	..	..	1	..	..
Gubtail, Thomas	..	1	..	1	..	1	2	..	1	..	..
Hastings, Samuel	..	..	..	1	..	..	..	..	..	..	..
Henderson, John	..	2	..	1	..	4	..	..	1	..	..
Hill, Joshua	3	..	..	1	..	2	..	..	1	1	..
Holding, Richard	2	2	1	1	..	1	1	..	1	..	..
Hudson, John	2	1	..	1	..	1	2	1	1	..	..
Hunt, William	1	..	1	..	..	..	..	1	..	..	..
Jenkins, Elijah	3	1	1	1	..	2	1	..	1	..	..
Jones, Stephen	1	2	1	1	..	..	1	..	1	..	..
Kannan, Thomas	2	..	..	1	..	1	..	..	1	..	..
Kemman, Daniel	2	1	2	1	..	1	1	..	..	1	..
Kennan, George Jr.	..	..	1	..	..	..	..	1	..	..	..
Loomis, Silas	1	..	..	1	..	3	..	..	1	..	..
Lyon, Lemuel	2	..	..	1	..	1	1	..	1	..	..
Marsh, Elias	3	..	..	1	..	..	..	..	1	..	..
Marshal, Amasa	2	2	..	..	1	2	1	1	1	..	..
Marshal, Joseph	1	..	..	1	..	1	..	1	1	..	..
Merrils, Joseph	1	..	2	2	..	..	1	..	3	..	..
Mows, Daniel	2	1	..	1	..	2	2	1	1	..	..
Nelson, Daniel	..	..	1	1	..	..	..	..	..	..	..
Nelson, Moses	3	1	1	1	..	2	1	1	1	..	..
Nights, Isaac	..	..	..	1	..	2	..	..	1	..	..
Nights, Joseph	..	..	1	..	..	1	..	1	..	..	..
Parcher, Daniel	4	3	..	1	..	..	..	..	1	..	..
Parcher, Robert	2	..	..	1	..	1	..	..	1	..	..
Peck, John	2	1	..	2	..	..	..	1	1	..	..
Perry, James	..	..	2	..	..	..	..	1	..	..	..
Pickering, Timothy	1	1	..	..	1	..	1	..	..	1	..
Pierce, Francis	..	..	..	..	1	..	..	1	..	1	..
Polin, Asa	..	1	..	1	..	2	1	1	1	..	..
Proctor, Josiah	2	..	..	1	..	..	1	1	1	..	..
Rich, Jonathan	2	1	..	1	..	1	1	..	1	..	..
Robins, Jonathan	..	..	..	1	..	1	..	..	1	..	..
Schedule, George	2	..	..	1	..	2	..	1	1		..
Sherman, Samuel	2	1	1	1	..	2	1	..	1	..	..
Simpson, William	..	..	..	1	..	1	2	..	1	..	..
Sinclair, Joseph	..	1	..	1	..	..	..	1	1	..	..
Slaight, Amos	2	..	..	1	..	1	..	..	1	..	..
Slaight, Samuel	1	..	1	..	..	1	..	1	..	..	..
Stevens, Isaac	..	..	..	1	..	1	..	1	..	..	..
Stone, Uri	2	..	..	1	..	2	..	1	..	..	..
Straw, David	2	1	..	1	..	..	..	..	1	..	..
Straw, Valentine	..	1	1	..	1	1	..	1	..	1	..
Straw, William	2	2	..	1	..	1	..	2	1	..	..
Town, Asa	2	2	2	..	1	1	1	1	..	1	..
Town, Asa Jr.	..	1	..	1	..	2	..	1	..	..	..
Town, David	4	2	..	1	..	1	1	1	..	1	..
Tyler, Joseph	3	..	..	1	..	1	..	..	1	..	..
Waters, Amos	..	..	..	1	..	..	..	..	..	..	..
Welch, John	1	..	1	1	..	2	..	..	1	..	..
Wilson, Isaac	3	1	..	1	1	1	1	1	1	..	..
Woods, Hezekiah	1	..	..	1	..	2	1	..	..	..	..
Woolson, Simeon	..	..	..	1	..	..	..	..	1	..	..
Wright, Jonathan	1	2	..	1	..	2	..	..	1	..	..
Wyat, Swift	2	..	1	..	..	..	..	1	..	..	..

CHITTENDEN COUNTY—Continued

NAMES OF HEADS OF FAMILIES	FREE WHITE MALES: Under 10 years of age	FREE WHITE MALES: Of 10 and under 16	FREE WHITE MALES: Of 16 and under 26 including heads of families	FREE WHITE MALES: Of 26 and under 45 including heads of families	FREE WHITE MALES: Of 45 and upwards including heads of families.	FREE WHITE FEMALES: Under 10 years of age	FREE WHITE FEMALES: Of 10 and under 16	FREE WHITE FEMALES: Of 16 and under 26 including heads of families	FREE WHITE FEMALES: Of 26 and under 45 including heads of families	FREE WHITE FEMALES: Of 45 and upwards including heads of families	All other free persons except Indians not taxed
WESTFORD											
Austin, James	3	1	3	1	..	2	1	1	1	..	..
Austin, Jeremiah	2	1	1	1	..	2	..	..	1	..	..
Ball, Erastus	2	1	..	1	..	1	1	..	1	..	..
Barnaby, Harlow	3	..	..	1	..	3	1	1	1	..	..
Bates, Job	2	..	..	1	..	3	1	..	1	..	..
Baxter, Daniel	2	..	..	1	..	..	..	1	..	..	..
Beach, Barnabas	..	..	1	..	..	1	..	..	1	..	..
Beach, Elizabeth	..	1	1	..	..	1	1	..	1	..	..
Beach, Truman	..	..	..	1	..	..	..	1	..	..	..
Booth, John	1	1	1	..	1	2	1	1	1	..	..
Brown, Roswel	..	..	1	..	..	1	..	1	..	..	..
Brown, Thomas	1	..	..	1	..	2	1	1	1	..	..
Burdick, Ebenezer	3	1	..	1	..	1	..	..	1	1	..
Burdit, Elijah	3	1	..	1	..	2	..	1	..	..	..
Burdit, Nicholas	..	..	..	1	..	2	..	..	1	..	..
Burdit, Reuben	..	..	2	..	1	1	1	..	..	1	..
Burdit, Samuel	..	..	1	..	..	..	1	..	1	..	..
Case, Benajah	..	1	1	..	1	1	..	1	..	1	..
Chase, Isaac	3	1	..	1	..	..	1	..	1	..	..
Chase, Jonathan	1	1	..	2	..	1	..	..	..	..	..
Clark, Solomon	2	..	..	1	..	2	..	..	1	..	..
Cook, Frederick	2	2	..	1	..	2	..	..	1	..	..
Cook, Neilson	..	..	..	1	..	..	..	..	..	1	..
Cook, Pelham	2	..	..	1	..	1	..	..	1	..	..
Coon, Benjamin	1	1	1	..	1	1	1	..	..	1	..
Coon, Benjamin Jr.	..	..	1	..	..	..	..	1	..	..	..
Coon, Benjamin 3rd	1	..	..	1	..	..	..	1	..	..	..
Coon, Eber	1	..	2	..	..	..	..	..	..	..	..
Coon, Joseph	1	..	1	..	..	..	1	1	..	..	..
Crandall, David	..	..	1	..	1	..	1	1	..	..	..
Crandall, David Jr.	1	..	..	1	..	2	..	..	1	..	..
Crandall, Elias	2	..	..	1	1	2	..	..	1	..	..
Crandell, John	1	..	1	..	..	..	..	1	..	..	..
Crandell, Timothy	2	1	..	1	..	2	..	..	1	..	..
Crandell, Zelah	..	..	1	..	..	..	..	1	..	..	..
Cunningham, William	1	1	1	1	1	..	1	1	..	1	..
Cunningham, William Jr.	..	..	..	1	..	1	..	..	1	..	..
Davison, John	1	..	..	..	1	1	..	..	1	..	..
Dryer, Samuel	3	..	..	1	..	3	..	..	1	..	..
Eager, Paul	..	..	..	1	..	..	..	..	1	..	..
Farnsworth, Joel	2	1	..	1	..	1	..	1	..	..	..
Farnsworth, Levi	1	1	..	1	..	4	1	1	1	..	..
Fisk, Amos	2	..	1	..	..	1	..	1	..	..	..
Frisby, David	2	1	..	..	1	1	2	..	..	1	..
Frisby, Eliakim	3	1	..	1	..	2	..	..	1	..	..
Gale, David	..	..	1	..	..	..	..	1	..	..	..
Hacket, John	1	2	1	1	..	2	..	..	1	..	..
Hall, Simeon	1	..	..	1	..	2	..	..	1	..	..
Hart, Benjamin	..	..	1	..	..	..	..	1	..	..	..
Henderson, William	4	..	..	1	..	..	..	..	1	..	..
Hill, Isaac	1	..	..	1	..	2	..	..	1	..	..
Hooker, Simeon	..	..	1	..	1	..	1	1	..	1	..
Howe, Aaron	1	..	..	1	..	3	..	..	1	..	..
Hoyt, Joseph	2	..	..	1	1	..	..	1	1	..	..
Hyde, Luther	..	..	..	1	..	2	..	..	1	..	..
Johnson, Stephen	1	2	..	1	..	3	2	..	1	..	..
Joslin, Amasa	2	..	..	1	..	..	..	1	..	..	..
King, Robert	..	..	..	1	..	..	..	..	1	..	..
Knapp, Obadiah	3	1	..	1	..	2	2	..	1	..	..
Lanfier, John	..	..	..	1	..	3	..	..	1	..	..
Lawrence, John	2	..	1	1	1	3	..	..	1	..	..
Lincoln, William	2	2	1	..	2	2	1	..	1	..	..
McClallen, David	1	1	1	1	..	..	1	..	..	..	..
Morgan, Timothy	2	3	2	..	1	..	..	1	..	1	..
Neils, Peter	3	1	..	1	..	1	..	1	..	..	..
Nichols, William	1	..	1	2	..	1	..	..	1	..	..
Northaway, Francis	2	..	1	..	1	2	2	..	1	..	..
Northaway, George	1	1	..	1	..	1	1	..	1	..	..
Nye, Rufus	..	..	1	..	..	..	..	1	..	..	..
Osgood, Manassah	..	..	..	1	..	1	..	1	..	..	..
Partridge, Amos	..	..	4	..	1	..	2	1	1	1	..
Perrigo, Elijah	1	..	..	1	..	1	..	..	1	..	..
Perrigo, John	..	..	..	..	1	..	..	..	..	1	..
WESTFORD—con.											
Pierce, Samuel	..	..	..	1	..	..	..	..	..	..	..
Powel, Martin	..	1	..	1	..	1	..	..	1	..	..
Powel, Martin	1	1	1	..	1	..	1	2	..	1	..
Richards, Nathan	..	1	1	1	..	2	2	..	1	..	..
Richards, William	3	1	..	1	..	1	1	..	1	..	..
Robinson, Levi	..	..	..	1	..	..	..	..	..	..	..
Rogers, Thomas	2	..	..	1	..	1	..	..	1	..	..
Seeley, John	..	..	..	..	1	..	..	..	..	1	..
Seeley, John Jr.	..	2	1	1	..	1	1	1	1	..	..
Seeley, Jonas	3	..	..	1	..	2	1	..	1	..	..
Smith, Reuben	..	1	1	..	1	3	2	1	..	1	..
Stackhouse, Joseph	..	2	..	..	1	1	1	..	..	1	..
Stanford, Joshua	..	..	..	..	1	..	..	..	..	1	..
Stevens, Samuel	3	..	..	1	..	2	..	..	1	..	..
Steward, James	..	1	..	..	1	..	..	2	..	1	..
Stewart, Urial	1	..	..	1	..	4	..	..	1	..	..
Stone, Honeymoon	3	..	..	1	..	1	1	..	1	..	..
Stone, Jeremiah	1	1	..	1	..	3	2	..	1	..	..
Washburn, Ezra	..	..	..	1	..	1	..	..	1	..	..
Wickery, Jonathan	3	..	..	1	..	1	..	..	1	1	..
Willcox, Collins	..	2	2	..	1	..	2	1	..	1	..
Willcox, David	2	3	1	..	1	2	..	1	..	1	..
Willcox, William	..	..	1	..	1	..	2	1	..	..	..
Williams, Hiel	4	..	..	1	..	1	..	..	1	..	..
Willis, Jonathan	..	..	..	1	..	2	..	..	1	..	..
Willis, Stoughton	..	..	1	..	1	..	..	..	..	..	..
Willmoth, Benjamin	2	..	..	1	..	1	1	..	..	1	..
Willmoth, James	2	..	..	1	..	2	1	..	1	..	..
Willson, David	..	..	..	1	..	..	..	..	1	..	..
Witherell, Aaron	1	..	..	1	..	..	..	..	1	..	..
Witherell, Aaron	1	1	..	1	..	..	..	..	1	..	..
Woodruff, Chauncey	..	..	..	1	..	..	..	..	..	..	..
Woodruff, Joseph	2	2	2	1	1	1	1	2	..	1	..
Woodruff, Josiah	..	..	..	..	1	..	1	..	..	1	..
Woodward, Shubal	2	..	..	1	..	2	2	..	1	..	..
Woodworth, Lemuel	3	..	..	1	..	1	1	..	1	..	..
Woodworth, Uri Jr.	2	..	..	1	..	3	1	..	1	..	..
WILLISTON											
Adams, Samuel	1	..	..	1	..	1	..	..	1	..	..
Allen, Elihu	..	..	..	..	1	..	..	..	..	1	..
Allen, Elihu Jr.	2	..	..	1	..	2	..	..	1	..	..
Allen, Nathan	3	1	1	1	..	2	..	..	1	..	..
Atwater, Jonathan	..	..	..	1	..	..	..	..	1	..	..
Atwater, Linus	2	..	..	1	..	..	..	2	2	..	..
Auger, Phillip	1	1	..	1	..	1	1	..	1	..	..
Barber, John	1	2	1	..	1	2	..	1	1	..	..
Barber, Oliver	2	..	1	1	..	1	..	..	1	..	..
Barney, Heman	2	..	..	1	..	1	1	1	..	..	..
Barney, Ira	2	..	..	1	..	..	..	..	1	..	..
Barney, Simeon	2	..	1	..	..	..	..	1	..	..	..
Barney, Thomas	..	1	1	..	1	..	3	..	..	1	..
Barns, Joseph	1	2	1	1	..	1	..	1	1	1	..
Bartholomew, Levi	..	..	..	1	..	..	..	..	1	..	..
Bates, David	2	..	..	1	..	2	..	..	1	..	..
Bates, David Jr.	..	..	1	..	1	..	..	1	..	1	..
Beach, John	..	1	2	1	..	..	..	..	1	..	..
Bean, Sanbon	2	..	..	1	..	..	1	..	1	..	..
Beeley, Joseph	2	2	1	1	..	2	1	..	1	..	..
Bennett, William	..	..	1	..	..	..	..	2	..	1	..
Bottum, Lemuel	..	..	..	1	..	1	1	..	1	1	..
Bradley, Elisha	2	1	1	1	..	2	1	1	1	..	..
Bradley, Ezra	1	2	..	1	..	1	1	..	1	..	..
Bradley, James	..	..	..	..	1	..	..	..	..	1	..
Bradley, Joseph	2	2	1	1	..	3	..	..	1	..	..
Bradley, Stillman	4	1	..	1	..	1	1	..	1	..	..
Brown, George	..	..	2	..	..	..	..	1	..	..	..
Brown, Jesse	..	1	1	..	..	1	..	1	..	..	..
Bushnel, John	3	..	..	1	..	1	..	..	1	..	..
Carpenter, Allen	1	1	1	..	1	1	2	1	..	..	..
Castle, Asher	1	3	..	1	..	2	2	..	1	..	..
Castle, John	..	1	..	1	..	..	..	..	..	1	..
Catlin, Roswel	1	..	..	1	..	2	1	..	1	..	..
Chittenden, Bethuel	1	..	..	1	..	1	..	..	1	..	..
Chittenden, Elizabeth	..	..	..	..	..	..	1	..	..	1	..
Chittenden, Giles	2	1	1	1	..	4	1	..	1	..	..
Chittenden, Truman	3	1	1	1	..	1	..	1	1	..	..
Cleveland, Samuel	1	..	..	1	..	2	..	1	..	..	..
Cobb, Asahel	1	..	..	1	..	2	..	..	1	..	..

CHITTENDEN COUNTY—Continued

NAMES OF HEADS OF FAMILIES	FREE WHITE MALES					FREE WHITE FEMALES					All other free persons except Indians not taxed
	Under 10 years of age	Of 10 and under 16	Of 16 and under 26 including heads of families	Of 26 and under 45 including heads of families	Of 45 and upwards including heads of families.	Under 10 years of age	Of 10 and under 16	Of 16 and under 26 including heads of families	Of 26 and under 45 including heads of families	Of 45 and upwards including heads of families	
WILLISTON—con.											
Colby, Ellet	1	..	1	..	..	1	..	..	1	..	..
Collins, A. C. Rev.	2	1	..	1	..	2	1	..	1	..	..
Colman, Zadok	1	..	1	..	1	..	1	1	..	1	..
Coming, Noah	..	..	1	..	..	..	..	1	..	..	..
Coming, Richard	1	..	3	1	..	1	..	..	1	..	..
Cook, Silas	..	1	..	..	1	..	..	..	..	1	..
Dart, Obadiah	..	1	..	..	1	1	..	2	1	2	..
Dart, Simeon	..	1	..	1	..	1	..	1	1	..	..
Davis, William	1	..	1	..	..	1	..	1	..	..	..
Doolittle, Theophillus	3	..	..	1	..	1	..	..	1	..	..
Downer, Anne	..	..	2	..	..	..	..	..	..	1	..
Downer, Caleb	1	1	1	..	..	1	..	1	..	..	..
Downer, John	..	..	..	1	..	2	..	..	1	..	..
Downer, Samuel	1	..	..	1	..	3	..	..	1	..	..
Dudley, William	3	1	..	1	..	1	1	..	1	..	..
French, Isaac	1	1	..	1	..	..	..	..	1	..	..
French, Jeremiah	1	..	1	1	..	1	..	1	..	..	..
Galusha, Daniel	1	1	..	1	..	2	..	1	1	..	..
Glinds, Eli	..	1	..	1	..	..	1	..	1	..	..
Graves, Thaddeus	..	2	..	1	..	3	1	2	1	..	..
Hall, John	1	1	1	..	1	1	..	1	..	1	..
Howard, Ebenezer	3	..	..	1	..	2	..	..	1	..	..
Hoyt, Josiah	1	..	..	1	..	3	2	..	1	..	..
Isham, Isaac C.	2	1	3	..	1	1	..	..	..	1	..
Johnson, Dan	1	..	1	1	..	..	1	..	1	1	..
Jones, John	..	..	..	1	..	2	..	..	1	..	..
Joslin, Amasa	2	..	..	1	..	..	..	1	..	..	..
Judson, Enoch	2	..	..	1	..	2	..	..	1	..	..
Kimball, Amos	2	1	..	1	..	1	..	..	1	1	..
Lafardy, James	1	..	..	1	1	2	2	..	1	..	..
Latch, Lasdol	..	..	..	1	..	1	..	..	1	..	..
Lawrence, Abijah	..	..	..	1	..	1	..	..	1	..	..
Leach, Ephraim	3	2	..	1	..	1	1	..	1	..	..
Lee, Simeon	..	..	..	1	1	1	..	1	..	1	..
Lee, Timothy	2	..	..	1	..	2	3	..	1	..	..
Lincoln, John	1	1	1	..	1	3	3	..	..	1	..
Martin, Deodat	..	2	1	1	..	3	1	..	1	..	..
Marvin, Matthias	..	1	1	..	1	1	..	..	..	1	..
McNeil, Isaac	..	1	..	1	..	1	..	1	..	..	..
Miller, Elisha	2	2	..	1	..	3	..	1	1	..	..
Miller, Solomon	2	..	..	1	..	1	1	1	1	1	..
Minor, John	2	..	..	1	..	2	..	..	1	..	..
Moulton, Rufus	2	..	..	1	..	2	..	..	1	..	..
Munson, Caleb	..	..	1	..	..	..	..	1	..	..	..
Munson, John	1	..	1	..	..	..	..	1	..	..	..
Murry, Asel	..	..	..	1	..	1	..	1	..	..	..
Murry, Beriah	..	2	1	..	1	..	1	2	..	1	..
Murry, Calvin	1	..	..	1	..	2	..	..	1	..	..
Murry, Curtis	2	..	1	1	..	2	..	..	1	..	..
Murry, Mack	..	..	..	1	..	2	..	1	..	..	..
Newland, Abner	4	..	1	1	..	1	..	..	1	..	..

NAMES OF HEADS OF FAMILIES	FREE WHITE MALES					FREE WHITE FEMALES					All other free persons except Indians not taxed
	Under 10 years of age	Of 10 and under 16	Of 16 and under 26 including heads of families	Of 26 and under 45 including heads of families	Of 45 and upwards including heads of families.	Under 10 years of age	Of 10 and under 16	Of 16 and under 26 including heads of families	Of 26 and under 45 including heads of families	Of 45 and upwards including heads of families	
WILLISTON—con.											
Parker, Carde	1	..	..	1	..	1	..	..	1	..	..
Perkins, Andrew	2	..	2	1	..	1	2	..	..	..	..
Place, Robert	1	..	..	1	..	..	1	..	..	..	..
Pulford, Elisha	..	..	..	..	1	1	..	..	1	..	..
Redfield, Reuben	1	..	1	1	..	3	..	..	1	..	..
Seeley, Stephen	3	..	..	1	..	2	1	..	1	..	..
Segar, Jonathan	..	..	1	..	..	..	..	..	..	..	..
Segar, Joseph	..	1	..	..	1	..	1	1	..	1	..
Shaw, Daniel	..	..	3	..	1	..	..	1	..	1	..
Shaw, Rufus	1	..	1	..	..	1	..	1	..	..	..
Smith, Alby	2	..	..	1	..	2	..	1	..	..	..
Smith, Caleb	..	..	1	..	1	..	..	1	..	1	..
Smith, Elijah	1	1	..	1	..	..	1	..	1	..	..
Smith, John	1	1	..	1	..	1	1	..	1	..	..
Smith, Sarah	1	..	1	..	..	1	..	1	..	..	..
Spafford, Jonathan	..	1	..	..	1	..	..	1	..	1	..
Spafford, Jonathan Jr.	2	..	1	..	..	..	..	..	1	..	..
Squires, Richard	..	..	..	1	..	1	1	..	1	..	..
Stearns, Eleazer	..	..	..	..	1	..	..	1	..	1	..
Stearns, Pierce	3	2	..	1	..	..	..	..	1	..	..
Stearns, Ralph	..	..	1	..	..	..	1	1	..	1	..
Stevens, Andrew	2	..	..	1	..	2	..	..	1	..	..
Stevens, John	1	..	1	1	..	..	..	..	1	..	..
Stevens, Safford	..	1	..	1	1	..	..	..	..	1	..
Stewart, Calvin	1	..	..	..	1	..	5	1	..	1	..
Talcott, David	1	..	..	..	1	..	..	..	..	1	..
Talcott, David Jr.	2	1	2	1	..	3	..	1	1	..	..
Talcott, Jonathan	1	..	1	1	..	..	..	1	..	..	..
Talcott, Josiah	2	1	..	1	..	..	..	..	1	..	..
Talcott, Parker	2	2	..	1	..	2	..	..	1	..	..
Talcott, Timothy	1	1	2	..	1	1	..	..	..	1	..
Talcott, Zela	2	..	..	1	..	1	..	..	1	..	..
Taylor, Edward	2	..	3	1	..	..	3	3	..	1	..
Taylor, Ester	..	..	1	..	..	..	..	..	..	1	..
Taylor, Ezra	..	..	..	1	..	..	..	..	1	..	..
Taylor, John	2	..	..	1	..	1	3	..	1	..	..
Taylor, Joseph	..	1	..	..	1	1	..	2	1	..	..
Taylor, Willis	2	2	1	1	..	..	..	1	1	..	..
Thatcher, Abothy	1	..	1	..	..	1	..	1	..	..	..
Thatcher, Elisha	..	..	1	..	..	..	..	..	..	..	..
Thatcher, John	2	..	..	1	..	2	..	..	1	1	..
Thatcher, Levi	1	2	2	..	1	..	..	..	..	1	..
Townes, Edmond	1	..	..	1	..	..	..	..	1	..	..
Tyler, Nathan	1	..	..	1	..	2	..	..	1	..	..
Walker, Phillip	2	..	..	1	..	1	1	1	..	..	..
Walstom, Obadiah	2	..	1	..	..	1	..	1	..	..	..
Ward, Timothy	..	..	..	1	1	2	..	..	..	1	..
Warren, Stephen L.	1	..	..	1	..	3	1	..	3	..	..
Washburn, Isaac	..	..	2	..	1	..	..	..	1	1	..
Winslow, John	1	2	..	1	..	3	1	..	1	..	..
Winslow, Lemuel	..	..	3	..	1	..	..	1	1	1	..
Winslow, Nathaniel	2	..	..	1	..	2	1	..	1	..	..
Wright, Elisha	2	..	..	1	..	1	..	..	1	..	..
WORCESTER											
Johnson, Benjamin	1	..	1	..	..	3	1	..	1	..	..
Martin, George	2	1	..	..	1	2	1	..	..	1	..
Rice, Ebenezer	..	..	..	1	..	2	..	1	..	..	..
Ridley, John	1	1	..	1	..	2	..	..	1	..	..

ESSEX COUNTY

NAMES OF HEADS OF FAMILIES	FREE WHITE MALES					FREE WHITE FEMALES					All other free persons except Indians not taxed
	Under 10 years of age	Of 10 and under 16	Of 16 and under 26 including heads of families	Of 26 and under 45 including heads of families	Of 45 and upwards including heads of families.	Under 10 years of age	Of 10 and under 16	Of 16 and under 26 including heads of families	Of 26 and under 45 including heads of families	Of 45 and upwards including heads of families	
BRUNSWICK											
Bishop, Enos	1	..	..	1	..	1	..	..	1	..	..
Blake, James	1	..	..	1	..	1	..	..	1	..	..
Cargill, Itheil	..	..	3	..	..	..	..	1	..	..	..
Cofman, Frederick	1	..	..	1	..	2	..	..	1	..	..
Grapes, Elizabeth	1	..	..	..	..	..	..	..	..	2	..
Grapes, Jacob	..	..	..	1	..	1	..	1	..	..	..
Hide, David	2	1	..	1	..	2	..	2	..	..	..
BRUNSWICK—con.											
Lamkin, Joshua	2	..	..	1	..	2	1	..	1	..	..
Merrill, John	..	1	..	..	1	..	1	1	..	1	..
Moulton, Nathaniel	..	..	..	1	..	3	..	..	1	..	..
Schoff, Jacob	1	..	..	1	1	..	..	..	..	1	..
Smith, Gideon	1	4	1	1	1	2	..	..	1	..	..
Wait, Benjamin	..	..	..	..	1	..	..	..	..	1	..
Wait, Joseph	1	1	..	..	1	6	2	..	1	..	..
Wait, Nathaniel	3	1	..	1	..	3	1	..	1	..	..

ESSEX COUNTY—Continued

NAMES OF HEADS OF FAMILIES	FREE WHITE MALES					FREE WHITE FEMALES					All other free persons except Indians not taxed
	Under 10 years of age	Of 10 and under 16	Of 16 and under 26 including heads of families	Of 26 and under 45 including heads of families	Of 45 and upwards including heads of families.	Under 10 years of age	Of 10 and under 16	Of 16 and under 26 including heads of families	Of 26 and under 45 including heads of families	Of 45 and upwards including heads of families	
CANAAN											
Beech, Nathaniel	..	..	3	2	1	..	..	1	..	1	..
Beech, Samuel	..	..	1	1	..	3	1	..	1	..	..
Chamber, James	1	1	1	2	..	1	1	..	1	..	..
Frizzle, Benjamin	..	1	..	..	1	..	..	..	..	1	..
Frizzle, Nathan	1	..	..	1	..	..	..	1	..	..	..
Frizzle, Samuel	1	..	..	1	..	1	..	..	1	..	..
Gates, Elias	..	..	1	..	1	1	..	2	1	..	..
Hugh, Joab	2	..	..	1	..	1	..	..	1	..	..
CONCORD											
Ames, Jonathan	1	..	..	1	..	..	..	1	..	..	..
Ames, Thomas	..	1	1	..	1	..	..	1	..	1	..
Babcock, Solomon	1	1	1	..	1	..	2	..	..	2	..
Ball, Joseph	2	1	..	1	..	2	1	..	1	..	..
Ball, Levi	3	..	..	1	..	..	1	..	1	..	..
Billings, John	1	..	2	..	1	..	..	..	..	1	..
Bingham, Elisha	1	3	..	1	..	..	..	..	1	..	..
Booty, Joseph	1	..	..	..	1	..	..	..	1	..	..
Chase, Francis	..	..	1	..	..	2	..	1	..	..	..
Chase, Moses	1	..	..	1	..	3	2	..	1	..	..
Cutting, Oliver	..	..	1	..	..	..	..	1	..	..	..
Foster, William	..	..	..	1	..	..	..	..	1	..	..
Fry, John	..	1	2	..	1	3	1	1	1	..	..
Fry, John Jr.	2	..	1	..	..	..	..	1	..	..	..
Grigory, Daniel	2	1	..	1	..	3	..	..	1	..	..
Hamlet, David	..	1	..	..	1	..	2	..	..	1	..
Hardy, Benjamin	1	1	..	2	..	..	1	..	1	..	..
Hibbard, David	1	1	2	..	1	5	2	..	..	1	..
Hill, Isaac	2	..	1	1	..	2	..	1	..	..	..
Holton, Bela	2	..	..	1	..	..	..	..	1	..	..
Holton, Buck	1	1	3	1	..	..	..	..	1	..	..
Hopkins, John	2	..	..	1	..	2	..	..	1	..	..
Hunter, Jonathan	5	..	..	1	..	..	..	1	..	..	..
Hutchinson, David	1	..	..	1	..	1	..	1	..	..	..
Hutchinson, Jonathan	1	..	2	..	1	..	..	1	1	2	..
Hutchinson, Samuel	..	..	..	1	..	2	..	1	..	..	..
Lewis, Jonathan	3	1	..	..	1	1	..	..	1	..	..
May, Benjamin	..	1	4	1	1	..	..	1	..	1	..
May, James	..	..	..	1	..	1	1	..	1	..	..
Morse, Amasa	1	1	..	1	..	..	..	..	1	..	..
Morse, James	..	3	..	1	..	..	..	..	1	1	..
Noiee, Lucy	..	..	..	..	..	2	..	..	1	..	..
Olcott, Simeon	2	..	..	1	..	..	..	..	1	..	..
Page, Eunice	3	..	..	..	..	1	1	..	1	..	..
Perry, Oliver	..	..	..	1	..	..	..	1	..	..	..
Powers, Jonathan	2	2	..	1	..	2	1	..	1	..	..
Scot, Andrew	1	..	1	..	1	1	1	1	1	..	..
Streeter, Ben	3	2	..	..	1	2	..	..	1	..	..
Streeter, Benjamin	1	1	..	1	..	1	..	..	1	..	..
Streeter, David	..	..	1	1	..	..	..	..	..	..	..
Streeter, Joseph	4	..	..	1	..	1	..	..	1	..	..
Taggard, Robert	..	..	..	1	..	..	..	..	1	..	..
Temple, Richard	1	..	..	1	..	1	..	..	1	..	..
Underwood, Amos	..	1	..	1	..	1	..	1	..	1	..
Vilas, Noah	..	..	..	1	..	1	..	..	1	..	..
Walker, John	..	..	..	1	..	2	..	..	1	..	..
Wetherbee, Samuel	1	1	3	..	1	2	3	3	..	1	..
Wilder, Nathan	2	..	..	1	..	1	..	..	1	..	..
Wilkins, Archelus	..	..	1	..	1	..	..	1	..	..	..
Willard, James	1	..	..	1	..	2	..	..	1	..	..
Williams, Azarias	..	..	..	1	1	..	1	..	1	..	..
Woodbury, Jesse	2	1	1	1	1	2	2	1	1	..	..
GRANBY											
Barrows, Ansel	2	..	..	1	..	1	..	..	1	..	..
Bugbee, Elijah	..	..	1	..	1	..	1	..	..	1	..
Bugbee, Elijah Jr.	..	..	..	1	..	..	..	..	1	..	..
Cheaney, Benjamin	2	2	..	1	..	3	1	..	1	..	..
Curtis, Clark	2	1	..	1	..	2	1	..	1	..	..
Elcott, James	..	2	1	..	1	1	..	..	..	1	..
Hart, Samuel	1	..	1	..	2	..	..	1	..	..	..
Herrick, Joseph	3	..	..	1	..	3	..	..	1	..	..
Herrick, Nathaniel	..	..	..	..	1	..	..	..	..	1	..
Herrick, Nathaniel Jr.	2	..	..	1	..	1	..	..	1	..	..
Herrick, Zadock	2	..	..	1	..	1	..	..	..	1	..
Learned, David	1	..	1	..	1	1	1	..	..	1	..
Muerhead, James	..	..	2	..	1	..	..	1	..	1	..
Pike, Robert	2	..	..	1	..	..	..	..	1	..	..
GUILDHALL											
Amy, Caleb	..	..	1	..	..	1	..	1	..	..	..
Amy, John	2	..	..	1	..	3	..	..	1	..	..
Amy, Micah	..	..	..	..	1	..	..	..	..	1	..
Amy, Micah Jr.	..	..	1	..	..	..	..	1	..	..	..
Amy, William	3	..	..	1	..	1	2	..	1	..	..
Babb, Nathaniel	..	..	..	1	..	2	..	..	1	..	..
Barry, John	1	..	..	1	..	..	..	2	..	..	..
Barry, Joseph	2	2	..	..	1	1	..	1	1	..	..
Bartlet, Benjamin	2	..	..	1	..	2	..	..	1	..	..
Basset, Heman	1	..	2	..	1	2	1	..	..	1	..
Benjamin, Jonathan	..	1	1	..	1	..	..	..	..	2	..
Bothell, James	1	..	1	..	..	..	..	1	..	..	..
Bundy, David	1	..	..	1	..	..	..	..	1	..	..
Bundy, Isaac	..	2	1	..	1	..	1	..	..	1	..
Bundy, Isaac Jr.	..	..	1	..	..	1	..	1	..	..	..
Burns, Edward	3	1	..	1	..	2	..	..	1	..	..
Button, Augustus	1	..	..	1	..	1	..	..	1	..	..
Call, Caleb	3	..	..	1	..	1	1	..	1	..	..
Cass, Nathan	4	2	..	2	..	1	..	..	1	1	..
Caswell, Nathan	..	1	..	..	1	1	..	1	..	1	..
Caswell, Nathan Jr.	2	1	..	1	..	1	..	1	..	..	..
Chaplin, Moses	2	..	..	1	..	..	..	1	..	..	..
Cheaney, John	2	..	..	1	..	1	..	..	1	..	..
Cook, Benjamin	1	1	..	1	..	1	..	1	..	..	..
Cook, Lemuel	..	..	..	1	..	..	..	1	..	..	..
Crawford, John	..	..	1	..	1	..	1	2	..	1	..
Cutler, Benoni	..	1	2	1	1	..	..	2	..	1	..
Cutler, Charles	2	..	..	1	..	2	..	..	1	..	..
Cutler, Theophelus	2	..	..	1	..	3	..	..	1	..	..
Cutler, William	..	..	..	1	..	..	..	..	..	..	..
Dana, Daniel	1	1	..	1	..	3	2	..	1	..	..
Flanders, Israel	..	..	..	1	..	1	..	1	..	..	..
Grout, Elijah	1	..	..	1	..	1	..	..	1	..	..
Hall, Samuel R.	2	1	..	..	1	1	1	..	..	1	..
Hews, William	2	..	..	1	..	1	..	1	..	..	..
Holms, Timothy	2	1	..	1	..	1	..	1	..	..	..
Hopkinson, David	1	2	1	..	1	1	..	1	..	1	..
Hopkinson, David Jr.	1	..	1	..	..	..	..	1	..	..	..
Hopkinson, Joshua	1	..	..	1	..	..	..	1	..	..	..
How, Reuben	2	1	..	..	1	1	1	..	1	..	1
How, Samuel	2	..	1	2	..	1	1	..	1	..	..
How, Simon	4	1	..	..	1	1	1	3	1	..	..
Johnson, Eben	..	..	..	1	..	..	..	..	1	..	..
Johnson, Joseph	1	1	..	..	1	1	..	..	..	1	..
Linsey, John	..	..	..	..	1	..	..	1	..	..	..
Linsey, Simeon	3	1	..	1	..	..	..	1	..	..	..
Nash, Samuel	1	1	..	..	1	1	1	3	1	1	..
Perkins, Calvin	2	..	..	1	..	2	..	..	1	..	..
Perkins, Ephraim	..	..	..	1	..	1	..	..	1	..	..
Perkins, Zepheniah	..	1	3	2	..	2	1	..	1	..	..

ESSEX COUNTY—Continued

NAMES OF HEADS OF FAMILIES	FREE WHITE MALES					FREE WHITE FEMALES					All other free persons except Indians not taxed
	Under 10 years of age	Of 10 and under 16	Of 16 and under 26 including heads of families	Of 26 and under 45 including heads of families	Of 45 and upwards including heads of families.	Under 10 years of age	Of 10 and under 16	Of 16 and under 26 including heads of families	Of 26 and under 45 including heads of families	Of 45 and upwards including heads of families	
GUILDHALL—con.											
Rosbrook, James	..	..	..	..	2	..	..	..	..	1	..
Samson, Lanor	..	1	..	..	..	..	..	..	..	1	..
Sanborn, John	..	..	1	..	..	..	..	1	..	..	..
Whipple, John	1	1	1	..	1	..	2	..	..	1	..
Wooster, Moses	1	..	..	1	..	..	2	..	1	..	..
LEMINGTON											
Bailey, Ward	..	1	3	2	1	..	1	1	..	1	..
Blodget, Howard	..	1	..	1	..	1	..	1	..	..	..
Buckman, Asa	2	1	..	1	..	..	1	..	1	..	..
Forrest, Mills D.	..	1	1	1	..	..	1	..	..	1	..
McAllister, Andrew	..	1	..	1	..	..	..	..	1	..	..
Mills, Peter	..	..	2	..	1	..	1	..	..	1	..
Morgan, Isaac	2	1	1	..	2	1	1	..	1	..	..
Smeridge, Lewis	..	..	..	1	..	3	..	..	1	..	..
Whiting, Hale	1	..	..	1	..	1	..	..	1	..	..
LUNENBURGH											
Allis, Abel	..	..	1	..	..	..	..	1	..	..	..
Ames, Aaron	3	..	..	1	1	..	..	..	1	..	..
Ayers, William	..	..	..	1	..	1	1	1	..	..	..
Balch, Benjamin	2	2	..	2	1	1	1	..	1	..	..
Belknap, Ebenezer	1	1	..	..	1	1	..	..	..	1	..
Boston, Gershom	..	1	..	..	1	2	..	..	..	..	..
Bowker, Gideon	3	1	1	2	..	..	1	..	1	..	..
Braden, Robert	..	..	1	..	1	..	..	2	..	..	..
Cheaney, Daniel	1	1	3	..	1	..	..	..	1	..	..
Cheaney, Eliphlet	..	1	1	1	..	..	1	..	1	..	..
Clark, Dan	..	..	..	1	..	3	..	..	1	..	..
Clark, Ebenezer	3	1	2	1	1	1	1	3	..	1	..
Cook, Warren	2	..	..	2	1	1	..	..	2	..	..
Currier, Joseph	1	..	..	1	..	4	..	..	1	..	..
Eager, Zerubabel	1	..	..	..	1	3	..	..	1	..	..
Edson, Jonah	..	..	..	1	..	1	..	1	..	..	..
Egrey, Daniel	1	1	..	2	..	1	..	..	1	..	..
Emerson, Jacob	2	..	..	1	1	1	1	1	..	1	..
Everitt, John	..	..	..	1	..	..	..	1	..	..	..
Everitt, Nathaniel	1	..	..	1	..	..	..	..	1	..	..
Fay, Levi	..	..	1	..	1	..	1	2	..	1	..
Gates, Samuel	..	1	2	1	..	..	1	1	1	..	..
Goodnough, Banister	1	..	..	1	..	2	..	1	..	..	..
Graves, Samuel	..	..	1	..	..	..	..	1	..	1	..
Gustin, Thomas	..	1	..	..	1	..	2	..	1	..	..
Hannum, Luther	1	..	..	1	..	1	..	..	1	..	..
Hartshorn, Ebenezer	2	..	3	..	1	1	3	2	..	1	..
Hinman, Amos	..	..	1	..	..	1	..	1	..	..	..
Hope, Joseph	..	1	..	1	..	..	..	..	1	..	..
How, Aaron	..	..	..	1	..	..	..	..	1	..	..
How, Jedediah	1	..	..	1	..	..	..	..	1	..	..
How, Stephen	3	..	1	2	..	3	..	2	..	..	..
Jacob, Solomon	1	1	..	1	..	1	1	..	1	..	..
Kimball, Joshua	..	1	..	..	1	..	1	1	..	1	..
Kimball, Josiah	1	..	..	1	..	..	..	..	1	..	..
Lamson, Reuben	1	1	1	1	..	..	1	..	1	..	..
Lane, Ebenezer	2	1	2	..	1	..	1	1	..	1	..
Littlefield, Timothy	2	..	1	..	1	1	1	1	1	..	..
Lovewell, Nathan	2	..	..	2	..	..	..	..	2	..	..
Lyon, Eliphelet	..	..	..	1	1	..	..	1	..	1	..
McKoy, Robert	2	..	1	1	..	2	..	..	1	1	..
Messer, John	1	..	..	1	..	..	..	1	..	..	..
Mills, James	2	..	..	1	..	1	..	..	1	..	..
Morse, Joseph	1	2	..	..	1	1	1	..	1	..	..
Parker, Josiah	2	1	1	..	1	..	1	1	..	1	..
Phelps, Samuel	3	2	..	1	..	1	..	..	1	..	..
Phelps, William	..	1	..	1	..	1	1	1	1	..	..
Powers, Joseph	4	..	..	1	..	..	1	..	1	..	..
LUNENBURGH—con.											
Quimby, Moses	..	..	1	..	1	3	3	2	..	1	..
Quimby, Richard	..	..	..	1	..	..	..	1	..	..	..
Rice, Caleb	2	..	..	1	..	..	..	1	..	..	..
Sanders, John	..	..	2	..	1	..	1	..	..	1	..
Savage, Ozias	2	..	..	1	..	3	..	..	1	..	..
Shepard, Nathaniel	..	..	..	1	1	..	..	..	..	..	..
Shepard, Otis	1	..	..	1	..	2	..	..	1	..	..
Snow, Barzilai	3	..	..	1	..	2	..	..	1	..	..
Spafford, Elijah	1	1	..	1	..	4	..	..	1	..	..
Sunbury, Henry	2	2	2	..	1	1	1	1	..	1	..
Thompson, Abner	..	..	1	..	..	..	..	1	..	..	..
Waldron, Thomas	..	..	..	1	..	1	..	1	..	..	..
Webb, Ashbel	1	1	..	1	..	3	..	..	1	..	..
Webb, Azariah	1	1	2	..	1	1	1	1	..	1	..
Wheeler, George	..	2	1	..	1	..	..	2	..	1	..
Williams, Abraham	1	1	..	1	..	1	1	..	1	..	..
Williams, Smith	2	..	..	1	..	3	1	..	1	..	..
Winklar, John	1	..	..	1	..	4	1	..	1	..	..
MAIDSTONE											
Brown, Silas	1	..	..	1	..	1	..	..	1	..	..
Byran, Benjamin	1	..	2	..	1	..	..	..	1	1	..
Clifford, Zachariah	2	1	..	1	..	1	2	..	1	..	..
Frazer, James P.	4	..	..	1	..	1	2	..	1	..	..
French, Hains	2	..	1	1	..	1	1	..	..	1	..
Gaskill, Asa	..	..	1	..	..	..	..	1	..	..	..
Gaskill, David	1	2	..	..	1	1	..	1	..	1	..
Hall, Moses	2	1	..	..	1	2	..	..	1	..	..
Hawkins, Reuben	2	..	..	1	..	2	1	..	..	1	..
Hugh, John	1	..	..	1	1	..	1	1	..	1	..
Linsey, John	..	..	1	..	..	..	..	1	..	..	..
Lucas, James	3	1	1	1	1	1	..	1	1	..	..
Merril, Joseph	..	..	1	..	..	..	..	1	..	..	..
Rich, Jacob	1	1	..	1	..	2	..	..	1	..	..
Rich, John	1	..	1	..	1	..	..	1	..	..	..
Rich, John Jr.	1	..	1	1	1	2	1	2	2	..	..
Rich, Moody	..	..	1	..	..	..	..	1	..	..	..
Smith, Isaac	1	2	..	2	..	3	1	..	1	..	..
Smith, Jonathan	1	1	..	..	1	3	2	1	1	..	..
Stevens, Isaac	1	2	3	..	1	2	..	2	1	1	..
Wooster, Joseph	1	..	..	3	..	..	1	..	1	..	..
MINEHEAD											
French, John	4	1	..	1	1	..	..	..	1	..	..
Fuller, Ayers	..	..	..	1	..	2	..	1	..	..	..
Fuller, Raymond	1	..	1	..	..	..	..	1	..	..	..
Johnson, Harvey	..	1	1	..	..	..	1	..	1	..	..
Lamkin, Thomas	1	3	..	1	..	2	..	1	1	..	..
NEWARK											
Ball, James	2	1	1	1	..	1	1	..	1	..	..
NORFOLK											
Beech, Gilbert	1	..	..	1	..	1	..	..	1	..	..
Bennet, Abel	3	..	..	1	..	..	..	..	1	..	..
Dunning, Harmon	..	1	..	1	..	1	..	..	1	..	..
Godard, Joseph	..	..	..	1	..	..	..	..	1	..	..
Kimball, Joshua	3	..	..	1	..	..	..	..	1	..	..
Nichols, Mansfield	..	..	..	..	1	..	..	..	..	1	..
Nichols, Nathaniel	1	..	..	1	..	1	..	1	..	..	..
Osbom, Samuel	..	..	..	1	1	..	..	1	..	..	..

FRANKLIN COUNTY

NAMES OF HEADS OF FAMILIES	FREE WHITE MALES: Under 10 years of age	FREE WHITE MALES: Of 10 and under 16	FREE WHITE MALES: Of 16 and under 26 including heads of families	FREE WHITE MALES: Of 26 and under 45 including heads of families	FREE WHITE MALES: Of 45 and upwards including heads of families.	FREE WHITE FEMALES: Under 10 years of age	FREE WHITE FEMALES: Of 10 and under 16	FREE WHITE FEMALES: Of 16 and under 26 including heads of families	FREE WHITE FEMALES: Of 26 and under 45 including heads of families	FREE WHITE FEMALES: Of 45 and upwards including heads of families	All other free persons except Indians not taxed
ALBURGH											
Alexander, Gideon	..	..	..	1	..	1	..	..	1	..	..
Andrews, James	1	..	1	1	..	1	..	..	1	..	..
Andrews, Thomas	..	..	..	1	..	..	..	..	1	..	..
Aubury, Edward	2	..	2	..	1	2	..	..	..	1	..
Austin, Wait	1	1	..	1	..	1	..	..	1	..	..
Babcock, George	1	..	..	1	..	2	..	..	..	1	..
Babcock, Ichabod	1	1	1	1	1	1	..	1	..	..	..
Babcock, John	1	..	..	1	..	2	..	..	1	..	..
Bell, William	2	..	..	1	..	1	..	1	..	..	..
Brame, George	..	..	..	1	..	3	..	..	1	..	..
Brandige, William	..	..	1	1	..	..	..	..	1	..	..
Brayton, Mathew	4	3	..	1	..	2	..	..	1	..	..
Brown, Robert	..	2	..	1	..	2	1	..	1	..	..
Burgit, Cornood	..	..	..	..	1	..	1	..	..	1	..
Calkins, Salmon	1	..	1	..	..	1	..	1	..	..	..
Calkins, Samuel	2	..	1	..	1	4	1	..	1	..	..
Calkins, Seth	..	..	..	1	..	..	..	..	1	..	..
Carogan, Patrick	..	..	..	1	1	..	..	..	..	1	..
Caroo, Charles	1	..	..	1	1	1	1	..	1	..	..
Carr, Charles	..	..	1	..	..	..	..	1	..	..	..
Chetton, John R.	2	..	1	1	..	2	2	..	1	..	..
Clarck, Daniel	2	..	1	..	..	2	..	..	1	..	..
Clark, Elizabeth	..	..	..	1	..	..	1	..	..	1	..
Clark, John	1	1	..	1	..	1	1	..	1	..	..
Conklin, Abraham	3	1	1	..	1	3	2	..	..	1	..
Cook, Phillip	2	1	..	1	..	3	1	..	1	..	..
Cory, Silas	1	..	..	1	1	1	..	..	..	..	..
Covey, Samuel	4	3	2	..	1	3	2	..	1	..	..
Cowing, James	2	..	..	1	..	2	..	..	1	..	..
Cowing, Moses	..	..	..	1	2	..	..	..	1	1	..
Danar, James	2	1	..	1	2	3	1	..	1	2	..
DeLimback, Henry	4	..	4	..	1	..	2	..	..	1	..
Deniah, Eli	2	2	..	1	..	1	1	..	1	..	..
Dewitt, Michael	2	..	3	..	1	..	2	..	..	1	..
Dewitt, William	2	1	..	1	..	1	..	1	..	..	..
Doody, John	3	..	1	..	..	1	..	1	1	..	..
Duby, John	1	..	..	1	..	2	..	..	1	..	..
Dugan, Peter	..	..	..	..	1	..	..	..	..	1	..
Fisher, James	2	..	..	1	..	2	1	1	1	..	..
Freeman, Peter	2	2	..	..	1	3	1	..	..	1	..
Grant, John M.	1	..	..	1	..	1	..	..	1	..	..
Hammond, Benjamin	1	1	1	..	1	..	1	..	..	1	..
Hammond, Consider	1	..	1	..	..	..	..	1	..	..	..
Hammond, Lyon	2	..	1	..	..	1	..	1	..	..	..
Harvey, David	..	1	1	..	1	1	..	..	..	2	..
Hogan, Edward	4	..	..	..	1	..	..	..	1	..	..
Holbrook, Abraham	3	1	..	1	..	2	2	..	1	..	..
Holmes, Sands	3	2	..	1	..	1	1	..	1	..	..
Honsinger, Frederick	1	1	3	..	1	1	3	..	..	1	..
Honsinger, Manuel	5	1	..	1	..	..	1	..	1	..	..
Honsinger, Michall.	..	..	..	1	..	..	..	..	1	..	..
Hoxie, Frederick	2	1	1	1	..	4	..	1	1	..	..
Huxby, Silas	..	..	..	1	..	6	..	..	1	..	..
Kilburn, Charles	2	1	..	1	..	..	2	..	1	..	..
Lane, Elizabeth M.	..	..	1	..	..	..	..	..	..	1	..
Leader, John	3	1	..	1	..	2	..	..	1	..	..
Libbey, John	3	1	..	1	..	..	1	..	1	..	..
Logan, Device	..	..	..	..	1	1	1	..	1	..	..
Manning, Gabriel	1	..	1	1	1	4	1	2	1	..	..
Manning, Jacob	..	1	1	..	..	..	..	1	..	..	..
Manning, Joshua	4	2	1	..	1	1	2	1	1	..	..
Martin, James	1	1	1	..	1	..	1	1	..	1	..
Marvin, Benjamin	2	1	1	1	1	1	..	2	..	1	..
McGregor, Duncan	3	2	1	1	1	2	1	..	..	1	..
McGregor, John	..	..	..	..	1	..	1	..	..	1	..
Miller, Henry	1	..	..	..	1	..	1	..	..	1	..
Miller, John	1	..	1	..	..	..	..	1	..	..	..
Miller, Samuel	1	..	1	..	1	1	..	1	..	1	..
Miller, William	1	..	1	..	..	..	..	1	..	..	..
Mott, Ephraim	..	..	..	1	..	1	..	1	..	..	..
Mott, Jacob	3	1	..	1	..	..	3	..	1	..	..
Mott, John	1	..	..	1	..	1	..	..	..	..	..
Mott, Joseph	4	1	1	1	..	..	1	..	1	..	..
Mott, Joseph S.	2	..	..	1	..	2	..	1	..	..	..
Mott, Samuel	1	2	2	..	1	..	..	1	..	1	..
Mott, Samuel	1	1	1	1	..	..	..	1	..	..	..
Munroe, Elijah	..	..	..	..	1	..	2	..	..	..	..
ALBURGH—con.											
Niles, Ichabod	1	..	..	1	..	2	..	..	1	..	..
Niles, Nathan	1	1	1	1	..	3	2	..	1	..	..
Niles, Stephen	1	..	2	..	1	1	..	1	..	..	..
Palmer, James	..	..	..	..	2	..	..	..	..	1	..
Par, Abel	..	..	..	1	..	1	..	..	1	..	..
Par, Moses	..	..	..	..	1	3	2	..	..	1	..
Par, Moses Jr.	..	2	..	1	..	2	..	..	1	..	..
Par, Thomas	1	..	1	..	..	..	..	1	..	..	..
Pike, Ezra	3	..	..	1	..	2	2	..	1	..	..
Proboat, Henry	..	1	..	..	1	..	1	..	..	1	..
Reynolds, Elisha	..	2	2	1	..	1	1	2	1	..	..
Scott, Abraham	1	..	..	..	1	3	..	..	1	..	..
Searls, Daniel D.	2	1	..	1	..	2	1	..	1	..	..
Sherman, Abner	2	..	..	1	..	1	..	..	..	1	..
Smith, Daniel	..	..	1	..	1	..	1	1	..	1	..
Souls, John	1	..	..	1	..	2	..	1	..	..	..
Souls, Stephen	1	..	..	2	..	5	2	..	1	..	..
Souls, Stephen	1	2	..	1	..	4	1	..	1	..	..
Souls, Sylvester	..	1	..	..	1	..	1	2	..	1	..
Souls, Timothy	1	1	..	1	..	3	..	..	1	..	2
Souls, William	2	..	..	1	1	1	..	1	..	1	..
Spencer, Daniel	..	..	2	1	..	3	..	..	1	..	..
Sweet, James	1	1	..	1	..	..	..	..	1	..	..
Sweet, Joseph	1	..	1	..	1	..	..	1	..	..	..
Sweet, Sylvester	1	1	..	1	..	3	..	..	1	..	..
Taylor, John	..	..	1	1	1	..	..	..	..	1	..
Utley, Jeremiah	..	1	..	..	1	2	..	..	1	1	..
Vaughn, William	1	..	..	1	..	2	..	..	1	..	..
Waggoner, Francis	2	..	1	1	..	..	1	..	1	..	..
Way, Abraham	1	..	..	1	..	2	..	..	1	..	..
Weeks, Joseph	..	1	..	1	..	4	1	..	1	..	..
West, Peter	..	1	..	1	..	4	..	..	1	..	..
Wing, Giles	..	1	1	..	1	2	..	..	..	1	..
Wing, John	..	..	1	..	..	..	..	1	..	..	..
Wing, Samuel	1	..	1	..	..	1	..	1	..	..	..
Wright, Samuel	1	1	..	1	..	1	1	..	1	..	..
UNCERTAIN NAMES											
Hull (?), John Farr(?)	1	1	..	1	..	4	1	..	1	..	..
Hymkbanack (?), Benjamin	1	1	1	1	1	3	1	..	1	..	..
Lunna (?), William	1	1	1	..	1	2	1	..	1	..	..
Wheaton, Eliam (?)	..	..	1	1	..	2	1	..	1	..	..
AVERY'S GORE											
Bartlet, Gideon	..	..	..	..	1	..	..	2	1	..	..
Blasdell, Thomas	..	..	1	..	..	..	..	..	..	..	..
Cross, Daniel	2	1	..	1	..	3	1	1	1	..	..
Fletcher, Jonathan	1	..	..	1	..	2	..	..	1	..	..
Holden, ———	..	..	1	..	..	..	..	..	..	..	..
Morrell, Sargeant	..	1	..	1	..	3	..	..	1	..	..
Rinds, Josiah	..	..	..	1	1	..	..	1	1	..	..
Underhill, ———	..	..	1	..	..	..	..	..	..	..	..
BAKERSFIELD											
Adams, Ephraim	..	..	4	2	..	..	..	2	..	..	..
Allen, Thomas	1	..	..	1	..	..	..	..	1	..	..
Baker, Joseph	..	..	..	..	1	..	..	..	..	1	..
Barnes, Joshua	3	1	3	1	..	2	1	..	1	..	..
Bays, Elisha	1	1	1	..	1	1	..	..	1	..	..
Brigham, Jonas	1	2	1	1	1	..	1	1	..	1	..
Brigham, Uriah	3	..	..	1	..	2	..	..	1	..	..
Brown, Levi	2	1	..	1	..	1	2	..	1	..	..
Cobb, Isaac	2	..	..	1	..	1	..	..	1	..	..
Cushman, Samuel	3	..	3	1	..	1	3	..	1	..	..
Cutler, Amos	..	..	..	1	..	1	1	..	1	..	..
Davis, Joel	..	..	2	..	..	..	..	1	..	..	..
Davis, Solomon	3	..	..	1	..	..	..	..	1	..	..
Deniah, Seth	..	1	2	..	1	..	..	1	..	1	..

FRANKLIN COUNTY—Continued

NAMES OF HEADS OF FAMILIES	FREE WHITE MALES					FREE WHITE FEMALES					All other free persons except Indians not taxed
	Under 10 years of age	Of 10 and under 16	Of 16 and under 26 including heads of families	Of 26 and under 45 including heads of families	Of 45 and upwards including heads of families.	Under 10 years of age	Of 10 and under 16	Of 16 and under 26 including heads of families	Of 26 and under 45 including heads of families	Of 45 and upwards including heads of families	
BAKERSFIELD—con.											
Done, Benjamin	..	..	..	1	..	3	..	..	1	..	..
Dunn, James	2	1	..	1	..	1	..	..	1	..	..
Dunn, John	2	..	1	1	..	1	..	..	1	..	..
Farnsworth, Jonathan	1	2	..	2	..	2	..	..	1	..	..
Farr, William	..	..	1	..	..	1	..	1	..	..	..
Freeman, Isaac	..	1	..	2	..	1	..	..	2	1	..
Goodale, Jonathan	..	1	..	1	..	..	1	..	1	..	..
Hart, Moses	..	..	..	1	..	2	..	..	1	..	..
Hazletine, Silas	..	1	..	4	..	2	1	1	1	..	..
Huntley, Jacob	3	..	..	2	..	..	..	1	..	..	..
Manor, John	..	..	2	1	..	1	..	1	..	..	..
Manor, Stephen	2	2	1	1	..	1	1	..	1	..	..
Potter, Thomas	3	2	1	1	..	1	1	1	1	..	..
Pratt, Jeremiah	..	..	..	2	..	1	1	1	1	..	..
Saunderson, Aaron	1	..	1	..	..	1	..	1	..	..	..
Saunderson, Abraham	1	1	..	1	..	2	2	..	1	..	..
Smith, Aaron	2	..	..	1	..	..	..	..	1	..	..
Stebbins, David	3	..	..	1	..	..	2	..	1	..	..
Underwood, Amos	..	..	..	1	..	1	..	1	..	..	..
Webster, Joel	..	..	..	1	..	..	..	1	..	..	..
Willson, Ichabod	3	..	..	2	..	..	..	1	..	..	..
Wright, David	3	..	1	1	..	1	1	..	1	..	..
BERKSHIRE											
Adams, Amos	..	1	1	..	1	..	..	1	1	..	..
Adams, James	2	1	..	1	..	1	..	..	1	..	..
Austin, Oliver	2	1	..	1	..	1	1	..	1	..	..
Babcock, Jesse	3	..	..	1	..	1	1	1	1	1	..
Baker, Job	1	..	..	1	..	3	..	..	1	..	..
Bell, Salmon	1	..	..	1	..	..	..	1	..	..	..
Dingman, Dolfus	2	1	..	2	..	2	..	..	1	..	..
Durham, Allen	2	..	..	1	..	1	1	..	1	..	..
Freeman, Joseph	..	1	..	1	..	3	..	..	1	..	..
Gibbs, Nathan	2	..	..	1	..	..	..	..	1	..	..
Heard, Abraham	1	..	..	1	..	3	..	..	1	..	..
Hill, Mills	2	..	..	1	..	..	..	..	1	..	..
Jewit, Elvin	..	1	1	..	1	1	..	..	..	1	..
Johnson, Abel	3	1	3	..	1	1	1	1	1	..	..
Kindal, Silas	..	..	..	1	..	..	..	1	..	..	..
McCay, Daniel	1	1	..	1	..	3	..	..	1	..	..
More, Chancey	1	1	..	1	..	..	..	1	..	..	..
Owing, Daniel	1	..	..	1	..	2	..	..	1	..	..
Phelps, Barnabas	1	1	..	1	..	..	..	1	..	..	..
Phelps, Elijah	..	..	1	..	..	..	..	1	..	..	..
Pollard, Silas	2	..	..	1	..	..	..	..	1	..	..
Porter, Stephen	..	..	..	..	1	..	..	..	..	1	..
Prince, Moses	3	..	1	1	..	1	..	1	..	..	..
Richards, John	..	..	..	1	1	..	..	..	..	1	..
Richards, Russell	1	..	..	1	..	4	..	..	1	..	..
Royce, Stephen	2	1	2	2	..	2	1	..	2	..	..
Rublee, Hiram	2	..	1	1	..	2	..	1	..	..	..
Searls, Benjamin B.	2	1	..	1	..	1	1	..	1	..	..
Smith, Ira	..	..	1	..	..	1	..	1	..	..	..
Stone, Samuel	2	..	..	1	..	1	..	..	1	..	..
Willoby, Armhurst	..	1	..	1	..	..	..	..	1	..	..
CAMBRIDGE											
Baker, Joseph	..	1	1	..	1	..	1	..	..	1	..
Baker, Joseph Jr.	..	..	..	1	..	2	..	..	1	..	..
Baker, Zebulon	2	2	1	..	1	3	2	..	..	1	..
Barber, John	..	..	..	1	..	..	..	1	..	..	..
Bennet, Charles	1	..	..	1	..	..	..	1	..	..	..
Billings, Daniel	..	..	1	..	1	..	..	2	..	..	..
Blasdel, Daniel	1	1	1	..	..	1	..	1	..	..	..
Blasdel, Jonathan	..	..	1	..	..	..	..	1	..	..	..
Blasdel, Miriam	..	..	1	..	..	..	..	1	1	1	..
CAMBRIDGE—con.											
Brewster, Jonah	1	2	2	..	1	..	1	1	..	1	..
Brush, Abner	3	..	..	2	..	..	..	1	1	..	..
Brush, Reuben	1	1	..	1	..	..	..	1	..	1	..
Burnham, Samuel	4	1	..	1	..	2	..	..	1	..	..
Cady, Amasa	2	2	..	1	..	..	..	..	1	..	..
Cady, Joseph	3	..	..	1	..	..	..	..	1	..	..
Cady, Walter	..	..	..	1	..	2	3	..	1	..	..
Calton, Enoch	3	..	..	1	..	1	..	1	1	..	..
Campbell, William	1	1	..	1	..	3	2	..	1	..	..
Carpenter, Barned	..	1	1	1	..	..	1	..	1	..	..
Chadwick, David	1	..	..	1	..	2	..	..	1	..	..
Cohren, Robert	..	1	2	..	1	..	1	..	..	1	..
Curtis, Beriah	..	..	1	..	..	1	..	1	..	1	..
Cutler, Oliver	..	..	..	1	..	..	..	1	..	..	..
Dewey, Anahabald	3	..	..	1	..	3	..	..	1	1	..
Dickinson, Nathaniel	..	1	1	..	2	1	1	..	1	1	..
Dukinson, John	2	..	..	1	..	1	1	..	1	..	..
Eaton, Sylvanus	2	1	..	1	..	4	..	..	1	..	..
Elsworth, Jonathan	..	..	2	2	..	..	1	..	1	..	..
Fassett, Elias	2	..	1	2	..	1	..	..	2	..	..
Fassett, John	1	..	..	1	..	1	..	1	..	..	..
Fassett, John Esq.	..	..	1	..	1	..	2	..	..	1	..
Fassett, Jonathan	1	..	2	1	1	..	..	3	..	1	..
Fassett, Moses	1	..	1	..	..	1	..	1	..	..	..
Fassett, Nathan	1	..	3	..	1	1	2	1	..	1	..
Fisk, Anna	1	..	1	..	..	..	..	1	..	1	..
Flood, Joseph	1	1	1	..	1	3	2	2	1	..	..
Flood, Moses	..	..	..	..	1	1	..	1	..	1	..
Fullington, Ephraim	1	..	..	1	..	2	..	..	1	..	..
Fullington, Ezekiel	..	2	..	1	..	1	1	..	1	..	..
Gallup, Joseph	..	1	..	1	..	2	..	1	..	..	..
Gillmore, James	..	..	..	..	1	..	..	1	..	..	..
Gillmore, James B.	2	..	..	1	..	..	..	..	1	..	..
Goodwin, Daniel	1	..	..	1	..	3	..	..	1	..	..
Goodwin, James	..	..	1	..	..	..	..	1	..	..	..
Goodwin, John	1	..	..	..	1	..	..	..	..	1	..
Gove, Frederick	2	1	..	1	..	1	..	..	1	1	..
Green, Elias	1	1	..	1	..	1	..	1	1	..	..
Green, Jonathan	1	1	..	1	..	2	..	..	1	..	..
Griswold, Benjamin	3	1	1	1	..	..	1	1	..	1	..
Hawley, Elisha	3	1	3	..	..	1	1	1	..	1	..
Hawley, Thomas R.	..	..	..	2	..	2	..	..	1	..	..
Hodgekiss, Nathaniel	4	..	..	2	..	2	..	..	1	..	..
Hopkins, Frederick	2	..	1	1	..	1	2	..	1	..	..
Horner, James	1	..	..	1	..	1	..	..	1	..	..
Horner, John	3	..	..	1	..	1	..	..	1	..	..
Horner, Thomas	4	2	..	1	..	..	1	..	1	..	..
Howe, Micah	1	1	2	..	1	2	1	..	..	1	..
Ingram, Phillip	2	1	1	1	..	2	..	..	1	..	..
Jefferson, Christopher	2	..	..	1	..	2	3	1	1	..	..
Johnson, Augustus	..	..	1	1	..	1	..	..	1	..	..
Joslin, Jonas	2	..	1	1	..	..	..	..	1	..	..
Keyes, Solomon	..	..	..	1	..	1	..	2	..	..	..
Kibbee, Bildad	1	1	..	1	..	2	1	1	1	..	..
Kingmen, Alexander	1	..	..	1	..	1	2	..	1	..	..
Kinsley, Daniel Jr.	2	..	..	1	1	3	1	..	1	..	..
Massey, John	1	1	..	1	..	1	2	1	1	..	..
McLaughlin, James	..	..	..	..	1	..	..	..	..	1	..
Melvin, Moses	..	..	1	..	..	..	..	1	..	..	..
Melvin, Nathan	..	..	..	..	1	..	..	1	..	1	..
Melvin, Theodore	..	..	..	1	..	2	..	1	..	..	..
Montague, Nathaniel	1	..	..	1	..	3	1	..	1	..	..
Montague, Rufus	3	..	..	1	..	2	1	..	1	..	..
Montague, Samuel	..	1	1	1	1	2	..	2	..	1	..
Mudget, Ezra	..	2	..	1	..	1	..	..	1	..	..
Murray, Joseph	2	..	..	..	1	..	1	1	1	..	..
Page, Amos	..	1	3	..	1	..	..	..	..	1	..
Page, John	..	..	..	1	..	1	..	..	2	1	..
Page, Parker	3	..	..	1	..	2	..	..	1	..	..
Pamile, Giles	2	..	..	1	..	..	2	..	1	1	..
Parker, Frederick	1	..	..	1	..	4	..	..	1	..	..
Parker, Samuel Holmes D.	3	1	1	1	..	..	2	1	1	..	..
Parker, Solomon Walbridge	1	2	3	..	1	2	..	1	..	1	..
Peabody, Stephen	1	..	..	1	..	..	..	..	1	..	..
Pearle, John	2	..	..	1	..	1	..	..	1	..	..
Perkins, Daniel	3	1	..	1	..	1	2	..	1	..	..

FRANKLIN COUNTY—Continued

NAMES OF HEADS OF FAMILIES	FREE WHITE MALES					FREE WHITE FEMALES					All other free persons except Indians not taxed
	Under 10 years of age	Of 10 and under 16	Of 16 and under 26 including heads of families	Of 26 and under 45 including heads of families	Of 45 and upwards including heads of families	Under 10 years of age	Of 10 and under 16	Of 16 and under 26 including heads of families	Of 26 and under 45 including heads of families	Of 45 and upwards including heads of families	
CAMBRIDGE—con.											
Phillips, Micah	1	..	1	..	..	..	..	1	..	..	..
Piny, Josiah	1	..	..	1	..	2	..	1	..	..	..
Piny, Richard	1	..	1	..	..	..	..	1	..	1	..
Pitt, Thomas C.	..	..	..	1	..	..	..	..	1	..	..
Poor, Enoch	1	..	..	1	..	2	..	..	1	..	..
Prior, William	2	..	1	1	1	..	2	1	1	1	..
Read, Daniel	..	..	..	1	..	..	..	1	..	..	..
Read, Nathaniel	4	2	..	1	..	1	1	..	1	..	..
Reynols, Benjamin	..	..	1	..	..	3	..	1	..	..	..
Reynols, William	3	1	..	1	..	2	..	..	1	..	..
Rice, Abner	..	..	1	..	1	1	..	2	..	1	..
Robinson, Isaac	2	..	..	1	..	2	2	..	1	..	..
Robinson, John	..	..	1	..	1	..	..	1	..	1	..
Robinson, Robert	2	1	..	1	..	2	1	..	1	..	..
Safford, David	1	1	4	..	1	1	1	..	1	1	..
Safford, John	2	..	..	2	..	2	..	..	2	..	..
Spafford, John	1	1	1	..	1	1	3	1	..	1	..
Stearns, Peleg	3	..	1	1	..	..	..	..	1	..	..
Stoddard, John	..	..	..	1	..	..	..	1	..	1	..
Taylor, Joseph	1	..	2	1	..	1	2	..	1	..	..
Thomas, Richard	..	..	2	..	..	1	..	..	1	..	..
Walbridge, Asa	2	..	1	1	..	3	1	..	1	..	..
Wells, Thomas	..	1	1	..	..	..	..	2	1	..	..
Wilcox, William	1	..	..	1	..	..	..	..	1	..	..
Willowby, Zirah	..	..	..	1	..	1	..	2	1	1	1
Wires, John	1	..	..	1	..	1	..	1	..	1	..
Woods, John	..	1	1	..	1	..	1	..	..	1	..
Woods, John Jr.	..	1	..	1	..	1	..	..	1	..	..
Woodworth, Charles	1	..	3	1	..	..	..	1	..	..	..
Woolsey, Jonathan	2	..	..	1	..	..	2	..	1	..	..
Worthen, Nathan	..	..	1	1	..	..	..	2	..	..	..
UNCERTAIN NAMES											
Farrel (?), Josiah	..	1	..	1	..	4	..	1	1	..	..
Holmes (?) D. (?)	3	1	1	1	..	..	2	1	1	..	..
Inman (?), Powell	..	1	3	1	..	4	1	..	1	..	..
COIT'S GORE											
Brown, Timothy	2	1	..	1	..	1	1	..	1	..	..
Farnum, Timothy	..	2	..	..	1	..	1	..	..	1	..
Hale, Hewitt	1	..	..	1	..	1	..	..	1	..	..
Masson, Jonathan	1	..	..	1	..	..	..	1	..	..	..
Oaks, John	1	..	1	..	..	1	..	1	..	..	..
Olmstead, James	..	1	..	1	..	3	1	..	1	..	..
Page, Thomas	1	..	..	1	..	2	2	..	1	..	..
Pinny, Peter	1	..	..	1	..	..	..	..	1	..	..
Twiss, Samuel	2	1	..	1	..	1	..	..	1	..	..
Willey, Amos	..	..	1	..	..	..	..	1	..	..	..
Willey, Barnabas	1	..	1	..	..	1	..	1	..	..	..
ENOSBURGH											
Baker, Edward	1	..	3	1	..	2	..	1	..	..	..
Balch, Amos	2	..	1	1	..	1	..	..	1	..	..
Balch, Cyrus	2	..	..	1	..	2	..	..	1	..	..
Barber, William	..	..	..	3	..	1	..	1	..	..	..
Clark, Amaziah	3	..	..	1	..	2	..	..	1	..	..
Clark, Moody	1	..	..	1	..	..	..	1	..	..	..
Davis, David	2	1	..	1	..	1	..	..	1	..	..
Deming, Martin	2	3	..	1	..	4	2	1	1	..	..
Fassett, Amos	3	2	1	..	1	1	1	2	..	1	..
Fassett, David	..	..	2	..	1	2	2	..	..	1	..
Follett, Martin	3	..	2	1	..	2	..	..	1	..	..
Gilbert, Solomon	3	3	1	..	1	1	..	..	1	..	..
Griswold, Nathaniel	1	..	1	1	..	..	..	1	..	..	..
Hopkins, Henry	3	1	..	1	..	2	..	..	1	..	..
Little, Samuel	..	..	1	1	..	1	..	..	2	..	..
ENOSBURGH—con.											
Peete, Wheelock	1	..	1	..	..	..	..	1	..	..	..
Richards, Thomas	5	2	..	..	1	..	..	3	1	..	..
Rosier, Charles	..	1	..	1	..	3	1	..	1	..	..
Safford, Charles	..	..	..	2	..	2	..	1	..	..	..
Sweatland, Lucos	..	1	..	1	1	..	1	..	..	1	..
FAIRFAX											
Andrews,———	..	..	..	..	1	..	..	..	1	..	..
Balch, Caleb	..	..	..	..	1	..	..	..	1	..	..
Barlow, Warren	1	..	..	1	..	1	..	1	..	1	..
Barnet, Robert	..	..	1	..	1	..	..	1	..	1	..
Beeman, Asa	..	1	..	..	..	..	..	1	..	..	..
Beeman, Jedediah	1	..	..	1	..	..	..	..	1	..	..
Beeman, Joseph	..	1	..	..	1	..	..	1	..	1	..
Beeman, Joseph Jr.	1	..	2	1	..	2	..	1	1	..	..
Bellows, James	3	1	2	1	..	..	1	1	1	..	..
Bidwell, Phineas	..	..	1	1	..	3	1	..	1	..	..
Blake, Bradbury	..	1	1	1	..	3	1	..	1	..	..
Blake, John	..	..	1	1	1	..	..	..	1	..	..
Blake, Theophilus	1	..	2	1	..	..	..	1	1	..	..
Blasdil, Phillip	1	1	1	..	1	1	..	..	1	..	..
Bowen, Shubal	..	..	..	1	..	1	..	..	1	..	..
Buck, George	1	..	1	1	..	4	..	..	1	..	..
Buck, Gould	3	1	..	1	..	2	..	..	1	..	..
Buck, Nathan	..	1	..	1	..	1	..	1	..	..	..
Buck, Zadock	..	1	1	1	..	..	..	1	..	..	..
Chadwick, Moses	..	..	..	1	..	2	..	1	..	1	..
Chadwick, Samuel	2	..	..	1	..	3	..	..	1	..	..
Chadwick, William	2	1	1	1	..	2	1	..	1	..	..
Chiney, Greanleaf	1	..	..	3	..	1	..	..	1	..	..
Churchill, Amos	2	..	1	1	..	1	..	..	2	..	..
Churchill, William	1	..	1	1	..	2	..	2	1	1	..
Colegrove, Nathan	2	..	..	1	..	3	1	..	1	..	..
Cooper, Enos	..	..	..	1	..	2	..	1	..	..	..
Crissey, James	1	1	..	1	..	1	1	..	1	..	..
Crissey, John	..	..	..	..	1	..	..	..	..	1	..
Crissey, John Jr.	1	1	1	..	1	1	1	2	..	1	..
Crissey, Samuel	..	..	..	1	..	..	..	..	1	..	..
Crissey, Sylvanus	..	..	..	1	..	1	..	..	1	..	..
Danforth, Jonathan	2	2	1	1	..	2	1	1	1	..	..
Dow, Jonathan	2	..	..	1	..	..	..	..	1	..	..
Dowen, Samuel	1	..	..	1	..	1	..	1	..	..	..
Duckin, James	4	1	..	1	..	1	..	..	1	..	..
Eastman, Peter	1	..	3	1	..	3	1	..	1	..	..
Ellis, Andrew	4	..	..	1	..	1	..	..	1	..	..
England, Stephen	3	1	..	1	..	1	1	..	1	..	..
Farewell, Eldridge	..	..	..	2	..	2	..	1	..	..	..
Farewell, Oliver	1	1	..	1	..	1	1	..	1	..	..
Farnsworth, James	2	1	..	1	..	..	..	1	..	1	..
Farnsworth, Josiah	..	..	..	1	..	3	..	1	..	..	..
Farnsworth, Oliver	..	..	..	..	1	..	..	..	..	1	..
Farnsworth, Oliver Jr.	3	..	..	1	..	2	1	..	1	..	..
Farnsworth, Thomas	2	1	..	1	..	1	1	1	..	..	..
Farrar, Isaac B.	2	..	1	2	..	1	..	1	1	..	..
Fisk, Aaron	..	..	2	..	1	..	..	3	..	..	..
Ford, Seth	3	1	..	1	..	1	1	2	1	..	..
Fullington, Francis	1	..	2	..	1	1	1	2	..	1	..
Fullington, Jonathan	1	..	1	..	..	1	..	1	..	..	..
Fullington, Joseph	..	..	..	1	..	2	2	..	..	1	..
Gale, Benjamin	..	..	..	1	..	..	1	..	..	..	..
George, Michael	2	2	..	1	..	1	1	..	1	..	..
Gillet, Ebenezer	..	..	..	1	..	2	..	..	1	..	..
Gove, Nathaniel	1	..	..	1	..	3	..	..	1	..	..
Grosvenor, Bethsheba	1	1	..	..	..	1	1	..	1	..	..
Grosvenor, Leicester	1	..	..	1	..	..	..	1	1	..	..
Grosvenor, Resolved	..	2	..	1	..	2	1	1	..	1	..
Grosvenor, Richard	1	..	..	1	1	2	..	..	1	1	..
Grout, Josiah	1	..	1	1	..	1	..	..	1	..	..
Hampton, Lovegrove	..	2	..	1	..	..	1	..	1	..	..
Hapgood, Asa	3	2	..	1	..	3	1	..	1	..	..
Harmon, Luther	..	..	1	1	1	2	..	1	..	1	..
Hart, John	..	1	..	..	1	..	..	..	1	..	..
Hastings, Joseph	2	..	..	1	..	1	..	..	1	..	..
Hawley, Abijah	..	1	..	2	..	2	1	..	1	..	..
Hodgeman, Jonathan	..	..	..	1	..	3	..	..	1	..	..
Holmes, James	..	..	..	1	..	..	..	..	1	..	..
Holmes, Stephen	2	..	1	1	..	2	2	1	1	..	..

FRANKLIN COUNTY—Continued

NAMES OF HEADS OF FAMILIES	FREE WHITE MALES: Under 10 years of age	FREE WHITE MALES: Of 10 and under 16	FREE WHITE MALES: Of 16 and under 26 including heads of families	FREE WHITE MALES: Of 26 and under 45 including heads of families	FREE WHITE MALES: Of 45 and upwards including heads of families	FREE WHITE FEMALES: Under 10 years of age	FREE WHITE FEMALES: Of 10 and under 16	FREE WHITE FEMALES: Of 16 and under 26 including heads of families	FREE WHITE FEMALES: Of 26 and under 45 including heads of families	FREE WHITE FEMALES: Of 45 and upwards including heads of families	All other free persons except Indians not taxed
FAIRFAX—con.											
Hopkins, Gamaliel	1	..	..	1	..	..	..	..	1	..	..
Hopkins, Read	1	1	2	..	..	..	..	1	..	1	..
Howard, Charles	..	3	2	..	..	..	2	..	..	..	..
Kingsbury, Joseph	1	..	1	1	..	3	..	..	1	..	..
Kingsbury, Zriah	..	..	..	1	..	..	..	..	1	..	..
Larabee, Joshua	..	..	..	1	..	..	..	..	1	..	..
Larnard, Silas	..	..	..	1	..	..	..	1	..	..	..
Magoes, George	1	1	1	..	1	3	1	..	..	1	..
Mankant, James	..	..	1	..	..	..	..	1	..	..	..
Marble, Simeon	..	..	..	1	..	1	..	1	..	..	..
Maxfield, William	2	1	1	1	..	2	..	..	1	..	..
McMaster, Moses	2	..	..	1	..	2	..	..	1	..	..
Millinton, Samuel	1	..	1	..	..	1	..	1	1	..	..
Mirril, Jedediah	1	..	2	..	1	..	..	1	..	..	..
Mudget, Benoni	2	..	..	1	..	2	1	..	2	..	..
Orton, Gideon	2	..	..	1	..	2	1	..	1	..	..
Orton, Oliver	1	..	..	1	..	1	..	..	1	..	..
Owen, James	1	..	..	1	..	..	..	1	..	..	..
Page, Phineas	..	1	2	..	1	1	1	1	1	..	..
Palmer, Zeras	3	..	..	1	..	1	2	..	1	..	..
Pamile, Ebenezer	2	1	..	1	..	1	..	..	1	..	..
Pamile, Jonathan	..	..	..	1	..	..	..	..	1	..	..
Pamile, Moses	1	..	..	1	..	2	..	1	..	..	..
Pamile, Oliver	..	..	..	1	..	1	..	..	..	..	1
Pamile, Samuel	..	..	..	1	..	..	1	1	1	..	..
Parsins, Medad	..	..	1	..	..	..	..	1	..	..	..
Parsons, Medad	3	..	2	1	1	2	1	1	1	1	..
Perry, Daniel	2	..	..	1	..	1	..	..	1	..	..
Pierce, Nathan	1	..	..	1	..	..	..	1	..	..	..
Plumb, Joseph	1	2	..	..	1	1	..	..	1	..	..
Powers, Simon	..	1	1	..	..	..	..	1	..	..	..
Safford, Erastus	5	..	..	2	..	..	1	..	1	..	..
Safford, Jabez	3	..	..	1	..	1	..	1	..	1	..
Safford, Josiah	..	1	2	..	1	1	1	..	1	..	..
Saundeson, Amos	1	..	..	1	..	3	..	2	..	..	..
Smith, Ebenezer	3	2	..	1	..	1	1	1	1	..	..
Smith, Isaac	..	..	..	1	..	2	1	..	1	..	..
Smith, John	2	..	..	..	1	3	..	1	..	1	..
Soul, Isaac N.	1	..	1	..	..	2	..	1	..	..	..
Spafford, Broadhurst	..	..	..	..	1	..	1	..	..	1	..
Spafford, Broadhurst Jr.	2	..	..	1	..	1	..	1	1	..	..
Spafford, Ephraim	3	..	..	1	..	1	..	..	1	..	..
Squire, Silas	1	..	..	1	..	2	1	..	1	..	..
Stickney, Thomas	3	1	..	1	..	1	2	..	1	..	..
Stone, Isaac	..	..	..	1	1	..	..	1	..	1	..
Stone, Mijah	1	..	1	2	..	3	..	..	2	..	..
Storey, Jacob	3	2	..	1	..	1	1	..	1	..	..
Storey. James	1	..	..	1	..	1	..	1	..	..	..
Story, Elisha	..	..	1	..	..	2	..	1	..	..	..
Story, Thomas	..	1	..	..	1	..	1	1	..	1	..
Thomas, Joel	3	..	2	..	1	2	1	..	1	..	..
Thompson, James	5	..	..	1	..	1	..	..	1	..	..
Thornton, Irad	1	..	2	..	..	1	..	..	1	1	..
Thurston, Joseph	2	1	..	1	..	1	..	..	1	..	..
Tracy, Samuel	1	1	..	1	..	1	..	1	..	..	..
Tracy, Stephen	..	1	..	1	1	..	1	1	..	1	..
Ufford, Shoers	..	..	..	1	1	..	..	2	..	1	..
Walker, Jacob	2	..	..	1	..	4	..	..	1	..	..
Warner, Anna	1	1	1	..	..	..	1	1	1	..	..
Wilkins, Asa	2	..	3	1	..	2	2	..	1	..	..
Wills, Elijah	2	..	1	..	..	..	..	1	..	..	..
Willson, Joel	1	..	..	1	..	1	..	..	1	..	..
Wood, William	1	..	..	1	..	..	..	..	1	..	..
Wright, Hezekiah	..	3	..	..	1	1	..	..	1	..	..
FAIRFIELD											
Abel, John	2	..	..	1	..	1	..	..	1	..	..
Ayres, Benjamin	1	..	..	1	..	1	..	..	1	..	..
Baker, David	4	..	..	1	..	1	1	..	1	..	..
Baker, Solomon	3	2	1	..	1	2	1	..	..	1	..
Barber, Elisha	..	1	1	..	1	..	..	2	..	1	..
Barber, Francis	1	..	1	..	..	..	..	1	..	..	..
Barber, Hiram	..	1	..	1	..	..	..	..	1	..	..
Barber, Isaac	3	1	..	1	..	2	2	..	1	..	..
Barber, Jesse	1	1	1	1	..	3	1	..	1	..	..
FAIRIELD—con.											
Barber, Joel	1	..	..	1	..	..	..	..	1	..	..
Barber, Philo	1	..	..	1	..	..	..	1	..	..	..
Barkum, John	2	..	..	1	..	..	..	..	1	..	..
Barlow, Bradley	2	..	..	4	..	1	1	..	1	..	..
Barlow, David	..	..	..	1	..	..	..	1	..	..	..
Barlow, Dimond	3	..	..	1	..	2	..	..	1	..	..
Barlow, Eleanor	..	..	..	1	..	1	1	..	1	..	..
Barlow, Hubbard	1	1	2	1	..	..	1	..	1	..	..
Bartham, David	1	..	..	1	..	1	..	..	1	..	..
Beaden, William	5	1	..	..	1	..	1	..	1	..	..
Beardsley, Demming	2	..	..	1	..	2	2	..	1	..	..
Beardsley, Nathaniel	2	2	..	1	..	1	..	..	1	..	..
Beardsley, Whitmore	2	1	..	1	..	2	..	..	1	..	..
Bingham, Solomon	2	..	..	1	..	2	..	1	..	..	..
Bliss, Rufus	2	..	..	1	..	1	..	1	..	..	..
Blood, Abner	1	..	..	1	..	..	..	1	..	..	..
Boardman, Amos	2	..	..	1	..	2	..	..	1	..	..
Bostwick, Andrew	1	..	..	1	..	1	1	..	1	..	..
Bostwick, Noble	1	..	..	1	..	2	..	1	..	..	..
Bostwick, Oliver	2	..	..	1	..	..	1	..	1	..	..
Bowdish, Joseph	..	1	..	1	..	3	..	..	1	..	..
Bradley, Andrew	..	1	2	..	1	..	2	..	1	..	..
Bradley, Ephraim	..	..	2	1	1	..	..	..	..	1	..
Bradley, Ezekiel	1	1	2	..	1	..	2	..	..	1	..
Bradley, Ezekiel Jr.	3	1	..	1	..	2	..	1	1	..	..
Bradley, Loyd	3	..	..	1	..	2	..	..	1	..	..
Briggs, Joseph	2	..	..	1	..	2	..	..	1	..	..
Briggs, Joseph	..	2	..	1	1	3	2	..	1	..	..
Briggs, Michael	..	..	..	1	..	..	..	1	..	..	..
Briggs, Thomas	..	..	..	..	1	..	..	..	..	1	..
Brown, Barzilla	1	..	..	..	1	1	1	..	1	..	..
Buck, William	2	1	1	1	..	2	..	..	1	..	..
Burr, Jabez	..	..	1	1	..	..	..	..	1	..	..
Bush, Lydiat	..	..	1	..	..	1	..	1	..	..	..
Butler, Samuel	2	..	..	1	..	2	..	..	1	..	..
Case, Abijah	3	1	..	1	..	..	..	1	1	..	..
Chamberlin, Thomas	2	1	..	1	..	1	1	..	1	..	..
Chandler, Benjamin	2	..	2	1	..	2	..	..	1	..	..
Childs, Stephen	..	..	..	1	..	2	..	1	..	..	..
Churchill, David	1	..	..	1	..	2	..	..	1	..	..
Clark, Amaziah	3	..	..	1	..	2	..	1	..	..	..
Clauson, Nathan	..	..	..	1	..	..	..	..	..	..	..
Cooley, Luther	..	..	..	1	..	..	..	..	..	..	..
Cooley, Moses	..	..	1	..	..	..	..	1	..	..	..
Cotton, William	2	1	..	2	..	2	1	..	1	..	..
Cowles, Eli	..	..	1	..	1	..	..	..	1	..	..
Craw, Reuben	4	1	1	..	1	..	1	1	1	..	..
Cutler, Benjamin	1	..	..	1	..	2	1	..	1	..	..
Day, Reuben	..	1	1	..	..	..	1	..	1	..	..
Dimon, Moses	..	..	1	..	..	..	..	1	..	..	..
Dolph, Joseph	..	1	..	1	..	..	..	..	1	..	..
Dowgle, David	..	..	..	1	..	..	..	1	..	..	..
Draper, David	1	..	..	1	..	2	..	..	1	..	..
Ebo, Francis	1	..	..	1	..	2	..	..	1	..	..
Farnsworth, Joseph D.	..	..	..	1	..	2	..	1	..	..	..
Farrand, Thomas	1	..	..	1	..	2	..	..	1	..	..
Fitch, Hezekiah	..	..	1	..	..	..	..	1	..	..	..
Foot, Elijah	2	2	..	..	1	..	1	..	1	..	..
Foot, Russell	..	..	..	1	..	1	..	..	1	..	..
Giddings, William	..	..	1	..	..	1	..	1	..	..	..
Gilbert, John	..	..	..	..	1	..	..	..	..	1	..
Gilbert, Louis	2	2	..	1	..	3	1	..	1	..	..
Gilbert, Nathan	..	..	..	1	1	..	..	1	..	1	..
Gilbert, Samuel	..	..	..	1	..	1	..	..	1	..	..
Gilbert, Thomas	1	..	..	1	..	1	..	1	..	..	..
Gorham, John	1	..	1	1	..	1	..	..	1	..	..
Grant, Joseph	..	..	..	1	..	..	..	..	..	..	..
Gregory, Amos	..	..	..	1	..	2	..	1	..	..	..
Gregory, Keeler	4	1	..	1	..	1	..	..	1	..	..
Gregory, Levi	1	..	..	1	..	..	..	..	..	..	..
Gregory, Lois	..	1	2	..	..	3	1	1	1	..	..
Gregory, Stephen	..	..	1	..	..	..	..	..	..	1	..
Hall, Edmund	..	..	..	1	..	1	..	1	..	..	..
Hall, Lewis	..	..	1	..	1	..	1	..	..	1	..
Hall, Thomas	1	..	..	1	..	2	..	1	..	..	..
Hatch, Henry	..	1	..	1	..	2	1	..	1	..	..
Hawley, Isaac	..	..	..	1	..	..	..	..	1	..	..
Hawley, James	2	..	..	..	1	2	..	..	1	..	..
Hawley, James	..	..	..	1	..	3	..	..	1	..	..
Hawley, Thomas	3	..	..	1	..	..	..	1	..	..	..
Hendrick, Andrew	..	..	..	1	..	..	..	1	..	..	..

FRANKLIN COUNTY—Continued

NAMES OF HEADS OF FAMILIES	FREE WHITE MALES					FREE WHITE FEMALES					All other free persons except Indians not taxed
	Under 10 years of age	Of 10 and under 16	Of 16 and under 26 including heads of families	Of 26 and under 45 including heads of families	Of 45 and upwards including heads of families.	Under 10 years of age	Of 10 and under 16	Of 16 and under 26 including heads of families	Of 26 and under 45 including heads of families	Of 45 and upwards including heads of families	
FAIRFIELD—con.											
Hendrick, Benjamin	..	1	..	1	..	..	1	..	1	..	..
Hide, Robert	..	..	..	1	..	1	..	1	..	..	..
Hind, Joseph	1	..	..	1	..	2	..	..	1	..	..
Hoit, Nathan	2	..	1	1	..	1	..	..	1	..	..
Hoit, Nehemiah	..	..	..	2	..	..	..	..	1	..	..
Holbbut, Job	..	1	..	1	..	2	1	1	1	..	..
Holister, Lemuel	2	..	..	1	..	2	..	..	1	..	..
Howard, Benjamin	1	..	..	1	..	3	..	..	1	..	..
Howard, John	..	..	1	..	1	..	..	..	..	1	..
Howard, Jonas	1	..	..	1	..	2	..	..	1	..	..
Hoyt, David	1	..	..	1	..	3	1	..	1	..	..
Hubble, Timothy	1	..	..	1	..	1	..	..	..	..	..
Hull, Jehiel	2	1	..	1	..	2	1	..	1	..	..
Hull, Levi	..	..	..	1	..	..	..	..	..	..	..
Hull, Samuel P.	1	..	..	1	..	2	..	..	1	..	..
Hurlburt, Job	..	1	..	1	..	2	1	1	1	..	..
Johnson, Nathaniel	1	..	..	1	..	2	..	1	..	..	..
Johnson, Thomas	2	..	1	..	..	..	..	1	..	..	..
Judson, Eli	2	2	..	1	..	..	..	..	1	..	..
Judson, Jonathan	1	..	..	1	..	..	1	..	1	1	..
Kinsley, Nathan	2	1	..	1	..	1	3	..	1	..	..
Labaree, Alexander	..	..	..	1	..	..	..	..	1	..	..
Leach, Asa	1	..	1	..	..	..	..	1	..	..	..
Leach, James	..	..	..	..	1	..	..	..	..	1	..
Leach, John	2	1	3	..	1	1	..	..	1	..	..
Leach, John Jr.	3	6	..	..	1	1	1	..	1	..	..
Lee, John	3	..	..	1	..	1	2	..	1	..	..
Lobdell, Ebenezer	..	..	1	1	1	..	..	..	..	1	..
Lobdell, Nathan	1	..	..	1	..	2	..	..	1	..	..
Madison, David	1	..	..	1	..	..	..	1	..	..	..
Meachum, Isaac	1	..	..	1	..	..	..	1	..	..	..
Meachum, Jeremiah	..	..	1	..	..	1	..	1	..	..	..
Meachum, Samuel	2	1	..	1	..	2	..	1	..	..	..
Mitchel, John B.	4	1	..	1	..	3	2	..	1	..	..
Morey, William	1	..	..	1	..	1	..	..	1	..	..
Morse, Daniel	..	1	1	..	1	1	..	1	..	1	..
Mott, Samuel	..	..	..	1	..	1	..	..	1	..	..
Nelson, Solomon	1	..	..	1	..	1	..	1	..	..	..
Northrop, Abraham	1	..	1	..	..	..	..	1	..	..	..
Northrop, Amos	3	..	..	1	..	2	..	1	..	..	..
Northrop, Thomas	1	..	..	1	..	2	2	..	1	..	..
Osgood, Josiah	..	..	..	1	..	..	4	..	1	..	..
Page, Solomon	1	..	1	..	..	..	..	1	..	..	..
Phelps, Ebenezer	2	..	..	1	..	..	..	..	1	..	..
Phelps, Elkanah	..	..	1	..	..	..	..	..	..	..	..
Phelps, Martin	..	..	..	1	..	..	..	..	..	..	..
Phelps, Philo	2	..	..	1	..	2	..	..	1	..	..
Phelps, Phineas	2	..	..	1	..	2	..	1	..	..	..
Pierce, Daniel	2	..	..	1	..	1	..	1	..	..	..
Pittiss, William	1	1	1	1	..	1	1	..	1	1	..
Prindle, Martins	..	..	1	..	..	1	..	1	..	..	..
Ramsdale, Girsham	..	..	1	..	..	1	..	1	..	..	..
Randal, John	2	..	..	1	..	1	..	..	1	..	..
Richardson, John	..	..	1	1	1	..	..	..	..	1	..
Sherwood, Gabriel	3	..	..	1	..	1	..	..	1	..	..
Sherwood, Jedediah	2	1	..	1	..	..	1	..	1	..	..
Sherwood, Nathan	1	1	1	..	1	..	1	..	..	1	..
Sherwood, Willlam	1	..	..	1	..	2	..	1	..	..	..
Sloan, James	2	..	..	1	..	3	..	..	1	..	..
Smith, David	..	..	..	1	..	..	..	..	..	..	..
Smith, John	..	..	1	..	..	..	..	1	..	..	..
Smith, William	..	5	5	..	1	..	1	2	..	1	..
Soul, Joseph	..	2	2	..	1	..	..	1	..	1	..
Soul, Solomon	1	1	..	1	..	2	..	..	1	..	..
Soul, Timothy	3	..	..	1	..	2	1	..	1	..	..
Squire, Asa	1	..	..	1	..	3	..	..	1	..	..
Stone, Othniel	..	..	..	1	..	2	..	..	1	..	..
Storey, Francis	2	2	2	1	..	2	..	..	1	..	..
Sturdevant, John	..	..	3	..	1	..	1	1	..	1	..
Thompson, John	2	1	..	1	..	1	..	..	1	..	..
Wakemen, Nathan	3	..	..	1	..	2	..	1	..	..	..
Wanzer, Moses	3	..	..	1	..	..	..	..	1	..	..
Waring, Samuel	1	1	2	..	1	..	..	..	1	..	..
Warner, Daniel	..	..	..	1	..	2	..	..	1	..	..
Warren, Daniel	..	..	1	..	..	..	..	1	..	..	..
Wheaton, Joseph	2	1	..	1	..	1	..	..	1	..	..
FAIRFIELD—con.											
Wheeler, (Widow) Hannah	2	2	..	..	..	1	1	..	1	..	..
Wheeler, Joseph	..	..	1	..	1	..	..	2	1	1	..
Whitehead, Aaron	2	..	..	1	..	1	..	1	..	..	..
Whitehead, Isaac	1	..	..	1	..	..	..	..	1	..	..
Whitney, Sherwood	1	..	..	1	..	1	1	..	1	..	..
Willard, Windsor	..	..	..	1	..	..	..	1	..	..	..
Wright, Abram	2	1	1	..	1	..	1	1	..	1	..
Wright, Asahel	..	..	1	..	..	1	..	1	..	..	..
Wright, Doratius	3	..	..	1	..	1	..	..	1	..	..
FLETCHER											
Alen, Christopher	2	1	..	..	1	..	1	..	..	1	..
Armstrong, Reuben	1	..	2	..	..	2	..	2	..	..	..
Bailey, Daniel	..	1	3	..	1	1	1	..	..	1	..
Blair, Elias	..	1	1	1	..	1	..	1	..	..	..
Call, Joseph	..	2	..	..	1	..	..	..	..	1	..
Campbell, Daniel	1	..	..	1	..	1	..	..	1	..	..
Church, Samuel	..	..	2	1	..	..	..	..	1	..	..
Daley, Elijah	3	2	..	..	1	2	..	..	..	1	..
Daley, Elijah Jr.	..	..	1	..	..	1	..	1	..	..	..
Danforth, Peter	..	2	1	..	..	..	..	1	..	..	..
Davis, Elisha	..	..	1	..	..	1	..	1	..	..	..
Ellis, Joseph	..	2	..	..	1	1	1	..	..	..	..
Ellsworth, Ezra	1	..	1	..	..	3	1	1	..	..	..
Hall, John	2	..	..	1	..	..	..	..	1	..	..
Haynes, Jonathan	1	..	2	..	..	1	..	1	..	..	..
Hinman, Seth	2	..	1	1	..	2	..	..	1	..	..
Holmes, Widdow	..	..	2	..	..	..	2	..	1	..	..
Kendal, John	1	..	1	..	..	1	..	1	..	..	..
Kinsley, John	1	..	1	..	..	2	1	1	..	..	..
Kinsley, John B.	..	..	..	1	..	2	..	2	..	..	..
Law, John	..	2	1	..	1	1	..	..	1	..	..
Layton, John	..	..	1	1	..	..	1	..	1	..	..
Leach, Asaph	1	..	1	..	..	..	..	1	..	..	..
Leach, James	..	..	..	1	..	..	..	1	1	..	..
Leats, Zebulon	1	..	1	..	..	1	..	1	..	..	..
Meacham, Thomas	3	..	1	..	..	2	..	1	..	..	..
Mulsel, Moses	..	1	1	..	..	2	1	1	..	..	..
Pevar, Nathaniel	..	..	1	..	..	..	1	..	..	..	..
Reynols, Widdow	2	2	..	..	..	..	2	1	1	..	..
Scott, Lemuel	2	4	..	1	..	3	..	..	1	..	..
Thomas, William	1	1	..	1	..	3	..	..	1	1	..
Thurston, Peter	1	2	..	1	..	3	..	..	1	2	..
Tubbs, Samuel	1	2	..	1	..	4	..	1	..	..	..
Warren, Theophilus	..	..	1	..	..	..	..	1	..	..	..
Wheeler, John	3	..	..	..	1	..	1	1	1	..	..
Woodworth, Widdow	..	..	..	..	..	1	1	..	..	1	..
GEORGIA											
Baily, Ebenezer	..	..	1	..	..	..	1	..	..	..	..
Baker, Elijah	..	1	2	..	1	1	1	1	..	1	..
Ballard, Henry	1	..	..	1	..	1	..	..	1	..	..
Ballard, James	1	..	1	..	..	1	..	1	..	..	..
Ballard, Joseph	2	..	..	1	..	1	..	1	1	..	..
Ballard, William	1	..	1	1	..	..	1	1	..	..	..
Barber, Moses	1	1	..	1	..	1	..	..	1	..	..
Barron, Joseph	..	..	..	1	..	2	..	..	1	..	..
Bartlet, Elisha	1	..	1	..	1	3	..	..	1	..	..
Basford, Benjamin	1	2	1	..	1	..	2	..	1	..	..
Bentley, James	3	2	..	1	..	..	2	2	1	..	..
Bishop, Ebenezer	..	1	..	..	1	..	2	..	..	1	..
Blair, Abel	1	..	..	1	..	2	..	..	1	..	..
Blair, Mathew	1	..	..	1	..	1	..	1	..	..	..
Blair, Young	3	..	..	1	..	3	..	..	1	..	..
Blake, Samuel	..	1	..	..	..	3	3	1	1	..	..
Blakesley, Darius	1	1	..	1	..	1	..	..	1	..	..
Blanchard, Phillip	..	..	1	..	..	1	..	1	..	..	..
Bliss, Abner	1	..	..	1	..	3	..	..	1	..	..
Bliss, Eli	..	..	1	..	..	..	..	1	..	..	..
Bliss, Frederick	..	..	1	1	..	..	..	..	1	..	..
Bliss, Solomon	1	..	1	..	..	3	..	1	..	..	..
Blodget, Sardius	1	..	..	1	1	..	3	3	..	1	..

FRANKLIN COUNTY—Continued

NAMES OF HEADS OF FAMILIES	FREE WHITE MALES: Under 10 years of age	FREE WHITE MALES: Of 10 and under 16	FREE WHITE MALES: Of 16 and under 26 including heads of families	FREE WHITE MALES: Of 26 and under 45 including heads of families	FREE WHITE MALES: Of 45 and upwards including heads of families	FREE WHITE FEMALES: Under 10 years of age	FREE WHITE FEMALES: Of 10 and under 16	FREE WHITE FEMALES: Of 16 and under 26 including heads of families	FREE WHITE FEMALES: Of 26 and under 45 including heads of families	FREE WHITE FEMALES: Of 45 and upwards including heads of families	All other free persons except Indians not taxed
GEORGIA—con.											
Bouge, Samuel C.	2	1	1	..	1	..	..	..	1	..	..
Bowkir, Nathaniel	2	..	..	1	..	4	1	..	1	..	..
Brooks, Roger	2	..	..	1	..	1	..	..	1	..	..
Brush, Thomas	1	1	2	..	1	..	1	1	..	1	..
Buck, David	..	..	..	1	..	1	..	1	..	..	..
Buck, Moses	..	3	..	..	1	2	..	..	1	..	..
Burnall, Titus	2	..	1	1	..	1	..	1	..	..	..
Castle, Thadius	1	1	..	1	..	3	2	..	1	..	..
Chadsey, James	2	..	..	1	..	..	2	..	1	..	..
Chester, Moses	1	1	1	1	..	..	..	1	1	..	..
Churchill, Jonathan	..	..	2	..	1	1	2	1	..	1	..
Clark, David	1	1	..	1	..	2	..	..	1	..	..
Clark, Noble	1	..	1	..	..	..	..	1	..	..	..
Cloice, Cornelius	2	1	..	1	..	2	2	..	1	..	..
Cook, Nathaniel	3	..	..	1	..	2	2	..	1	..	..
Cookman, Frederick	1	..	1	1	..	3	..	..	2	1	..
Cotton, Walter	2	..	..	1	..	3	..	..	1	..	..
Davis, Francis	2	1	..	..	1	2	2	1	1	1	..
Davis, Stephen	..	1	..	1	1	..	..	1	..	1	..
Dee, Elijah	..	..	1	..	..	..	..	1	..	..	..
Dee, Elijah	..	1	2	..	1	1	2	1	..	1	..
Dee, John	2	..	..	1	..	1	..	1	..	..	..
Densmore, Joseph	..	1	..	..	1	..	2	..	..	1	..
Densmore, Joseph Jr.	1	..	1	..	..	..	..	1	..	..	..
Doty, Reuben	..	..	1	..	..	2	..	1	..	..	..
Drew, Daniel	1	..	1	..	..	..	..	1	..	..	..
Dunton, Stephen	3	..	..	1	..	1	..	1	..	..	..
Ellis, Phillip	1	..	..	1	..	2	1	..	1	..	..
Ellis, Widdow	1	..	1	..	..	1	1	1	..	..	..
Evarts, James	..	1	3	..	1	1	2	..	..	1	..
Evarts, Reuben	..	1	..	1	..	3	..	..	1	..	..
Fairchild, Daniel	1	..	..	1	..	2	..	..	1	..	..
Fairchild, Joel	2	1	..	1	..	1	..	..	1	..	..
Fairchild, Stephen	..	..	..	1	..	4	2	..	1	..	..
Fairchild, Truman	2	..	..	1	1	3	..	..	1	1	..
Finton, Samuel	1	1	..	1	..	..	..	..	1	..	..
Gilbert, Eber	1	..	1	..	1	..	1	2	..	1	..
Goodman, Stephen	..	2	1	2	..	2	..	3	..	..	..
Goodrich, Ebenezer	2	..	..	1	..	1	..	..	1	..	..
Goodrich, Edmund	2	..	1	..	..	..	..	1	..	..	..
Goodrich, Solomon	2	..	..	1	..	2	..	..	1	..	..
Goodwin, Nathan	1	..	..	1	..	1	..	..	1	..	..
Graves, Luman	2	2	..	1	..	2	1	..	1	..	..
Guilder, Andrew	1	..	..	1	..	1	..	..	1	..	..
Guilder, Daniel	1	..	..	..	..	..	1	1	..	..	..
Guilder, David	1	2	..	1	..	2	2	..	1	..	..
Guilder, Jacob	3	..	..	1	..	1	3	..	1	..	..
Guilder, Joseph	2	1	..	1	..	1	2	..	1	..	..
Hale, Jeriah	2	1	..	1	..	3	..	..	1	..	..
Hill, Howard	1	..	1	1	..	2	..	..	1	..	..
Hill, Jonathan	3	..	..	..	1	3	..	..	..	1	..
Hill, Reuben	1	..	1	..	..	..	..	1	..	..	..
Hills, Obadiah	1	1	1	..	..	2	..	..	..	..	..
Himes, Darius	..	..	1	..	..	3	..	1	..	..	..
Himes, Elisha	..	..	1	..	..	1	..	1	..	..	..
Hinckley, Ira	1	1	1	1	..	..	..	1	1	..	..
Hodgekiss, James	2	..	..	1	..	2	..	..	1	..	..
Holmes, Benjamin	1	1	..	..	1	2	2	1	1	..	..
Holoburt, Ebenezer	1	..	..	1	..	2	..	..	1	..	..
Hopkins, Joseph	3	1	1	1	..	1	2	..	1	..	..
Hubble, Abijah	1	..	..	1	..	2	1	..	1	..	..
Hubble, Samuel	1	..	..	1	..	..	..	1	..	..	..
Hull, Isaac	2	1	1	1	..	2	1	1	1	..	..
Hull, Jeremiah	..	..	1	..	..	1	..	1	..	..	..
Hurlburt, William	2	..	..	1	..	..	1	..	1	..	..
Ingerson, Ambrose	2	..	..	1	..	3	..	..	1	..	..
Joslin, Israel	1	..	1	..	..	2	1	..	..	..	..
Keeler, Hezekiah	2	2	..	1	..	1	..	..	1	..	..
Laflin, Abraham	1	1	..	1	..	1	..	..	1	..	..
Laflin, Samuel	2	1	1	1	..	2	1	..	1	..	..
Lamb, Edmond	5	1	..	1	1	2	..	..	1	..	..
Lamb, George	1	..	..	1	..	..	..	..	1	..	..
Lay, Daniel	2	1	..	..	1	1	..	3	..	1	..
Lay, Nathaniel	1	..	..	1	..	2	..	1	..	..	..
Lewis, Zriah	1	..	..	1	..	1	..	..	1	..	..
Lockwood, John	4	1	..	1	..	..	..	..	1	..	..
Loomis, Noah	2	2	1	..	1	1	..	..	..	1	..
Loomis, Roger	..	..	1	..	..	..	..	..	..	1	..
Loomis, Roswell	1	..	1	..	..	..	..	1	..	..	..
GEORGIA—con.											
Maitane, John	1	..	..	1	..	..	..	1	..	..	..
Maxfield, Anna	..	1	..	..	1	5	..	..	..	1	..
Maxfield, David	..	1	4	2	1	..	..	..	1	1	..
Maxfield, Isaac	1	..	..	1	..	3	..	1	..	..	..
McLaughlin, Henry	1	..	1	..	..	..	..	1	..	..	..
Merrit, Ansel	1	..	..	1	..	1	..	..	1	..	..
Merrit, Martin	1	..	..	1	..	4	..	1	..	..	..
Merrit, Nathaniel	1	..	..	1	..	..	..	..	1	..	..
Minor, Peter	..	..	1	..	..	3	..	1	..	..	..
Mitchel, John	..	2	1	..	..	..	2	1	1	..	..
Mitchel, Samuel	2	1	..	..	..	..	3	1	1	..	..
Murray, James	..	..	..	..	1	..	1	..	..	1	..
Murray, Silas	..	..	1	1	..	1	..	1	..	..	..
Newton, Hemon	1	..	1	..	..	..	..	..	1	..	..
Nichols, Reuben	..	..	1	1	..	1	..	1	..	..	..
Parmont, Joseph	1	1	..	..	..	..	..	1	1	..	..
Patrick, Moses	1	..	1	..	..	1	..	1	..	..	..
Pattee, Loammi	2	..	..	1	..	1	3	..	1	..	..
Patterson, John	2	..	..	1	1	..	..	..	1	1	..
Pease, Ebenezer	2	..	1	..	1	1	..	1	..	1	..
Pease, Ebenezer Jr.	2	..	..	1	..	2	..	1	..	..	..
Peck, Joseph	3	..	1	1	..	..	..	1	1	..	..
Perigo, David	2	1	..	1	..	3	1	..	1	..	..
Perry, Abigal	..	..	..	..	..	2	..	..	1	..	..
Phelps, Samuel N.	1	..	..	..	1	2	2	1	1	1	..
Pierce, Abel	3	1	..	1	..	2	..	..	1	..	..
Post, Jesse	2	..	..	1	..	1	..	1	..	..	..
Post, Noah	2	..	..	1	..	2	..	1	..	..	..
Post, William	..	..	2	3	1	..	1	..	..	1	..
Pratt, Nathan	2	..	..	1	..	..	..	1	..	..	..
Pratt, Paul	1	..	..	1	..	3	..	..	1	..	..
Roberts, Daniel	..	..	..	..	..	1	1	1	..	..	..
Rodgers, Ziriah	1	..	..	1	..	1	..	..	1	..	..
Ruggles, Charles	1	1	..	..	..	1	1	..	..	..	..
Saunderson, William	..	..	..	..	1	..	2	1	..	1	..
Shaw, John	..	..	..	..	1	..	..	1	..	1	..
Shepard, Bohem	3	..	..	1	..	..	..	2	..	..	..
Shepard, Levi	2	1	..	1	..	1	1	..	1	..	..
Shipman, Ezekiel	2	1	..	1	..	4	2	..	1	..	..
Sluys, Justus	1	..	1	1	..	2	..	..	1	..	..
Sluys, Lewis	3	1	..	1	..	..	1	..	1	..	..
Smeadley, Joshua	..	1	..	..	1	2	1	2	..	1	..
Smith, ———	1	1	..	1	..	1	1	1	1	..	..
Smith, Silas	2	..	..	..	..	1	1	1	..	..	..
Soul, Amos	1	..	1	..	..	1	..	1	..	..	..
Southwick, Caleb	1	..	..	1	..	1	..	1	..	..	..
Stannard, Abner	1	..	..	1	1	..	..	1	1	1	..
Stannard, Joseph	1	..	..	2	..	2	1	2	1	..	..
Stephen, Orange	1	..	..	1	..	3	..	1	..	..	..
Stevens, David	1	1	..	1	..	2	1	..	1	..	..
St. John, John	2	2	..	1	..	2	..	..	1	..	..
Taylor, Hannah	..	..	..	..	..	1	1	..	1	..	..
Thair, Oliver	1	..	1	..	..	1	..	1	..	..	..
Todd, John	2	..	..	..	1	1	..	1	..	..	..
Torrance, Thomas	..	1	..	..	1	..	1	..	1	1	..
Torry, Nathaniel B.	3	..	1	1	..	2	..	2	1	..	..
Town, Polly	2	2	..	..	..	2	..	1	1	..	..
Tupper, Asahel	..	..	..	1	..	2	..	..	1	..	..
Washburn, Jedediah	..	2	..	1	..	..	..	..	1	..	..
Watkins, Jared	2	2	..	1	..	..	2	1	1	..	..
Weeks, Frederick	3	..	..	1	..	1	..	..	1	..	..
White, David	..	..	..	..	1	..	1	..	..	1	..
White, John	..	1	..	..	1	..	1	1	..	1	..
White, John Jr.	..	..	1	..	..	1	..	1	..	..	..
White, Sylvester	1	..	..	1	..	2	..	1	..	..	..
Williams, Amarriah	2	..	1	..	..	1	1	1	..	..	..
Willis, John	..	..	..	1	..	..	1	..	1	..	..
Wills, Joseph	1	1	2	..	..	..	..	1	1	..	..
Willson, Deliverence	1	..	..	1	..	2	1	..	1	..	..
Winchel, Hezekiah	1	2	1	..	..	..	1	..	..	..	..
Winchell, Elijah	1	..	..	1	..	1	..	..	1	..	..
Winters, Hawley	2	..	..	1	..	1	..	..	1	..	..
Winters, John	1	..	..	1	..	1	..	..	1	..	..
Wood, Sanders	1	..	..	1	..	..	..	1	..	..	..
Wright, Isaac	1	..	1	1	..	4	1	1	1	..	..
Wright, Obadiah	3	..	..	1	..	1	..	..	1	..	..

FRANKLIN COUNTY—Continued

NAMES OF HEADS OF FAMILIES	FREE WHITE MALES					FREE WHITE FEMALES					
	Under 10 years of age	Of 10 and under 16	Of 16 and under 26 including heads of families	Of 26 and under 45 including heads of families	Of 45 and upwards including heads of families.	Under 10 years of age	Of 10 and under 16	Of 16 and under 26 including heads of families	Of 26 and under 45 including heads of families	Of 45 and upwards including heads of families	All other free persons except Indians not taxed
HIGHGATE											
Assletine, Abraham	..	..	2	..	1	1	1	..	..	1	..
Bessey, Elias	..	2	..	..	1	2	1	..	1	..	..
Bessey, Moses	..	1	..	1	..	2	..	1	1	..	..
Best, Thomas	..	..	..	1	..	2	..	..	1	..	..
Beur, Conrad T.	1	..	1	..	1	5	1	..	1	..	..
Brewer, Jeremiah	1	..	2	..	1	1	2	1	..	1	..
Brown, Joseph	..	..	..	1	..	2	..	..	1	..	..
Bunday, James	..	..	..	1	..	1	..	1	..	..	..
Butterfield, Jonathan	..	1	..	1	..	..	1	..	1	..	..
Canard, Nathan	..	..	1	..	1	..	..	..	1	..	..
Cannan, Abraham	1	1	..	..	1	3	2	..	1	..	..
Chappel, John	3	2	..	1	..	3	..	..	1	..	..
Christie, John	..	1	..	1	..	3	..	..	1	..	..
Claw, John	1	..	1	..	..	2	2	..	..	1	..
Cobb, Sylvester	1	2	..	1	..	3	1	..	1	..	..
Cray, Jacob	..	..	..	1	..	1	..	1	..	..	..
Cray, Lawrence	..	..	..	..	1	..	..	..	..	1	..
Croix, John	3	1	..	1	..	1	..	..	1	..	..
Dewey, Samuel	..	..	..	1	1	..	..	1	..	1	..
Donalson, Henry	1	..	..	1	..	1	..	..	1	..	..
Donalson, John	..	..	1	5	1	..	..	..	..	1	..
Fisher, Henry	3	..	..	..	2	..	2	..	1	..	..
Frazer, Daniel	..	..	1	..	1	..	..	..	..	1	..
Griffith, David	..	..	1	..	..	..	..	..	..	..	..
Gunman, Samuel	..	..	..	1	..	2	..	1	..	..	..
Helm, Peleg	1	..	..	..	1	2	..	..	1	..	..
Higgins, Elisha	2	..	..	1	..	1	..	1	..	..	..
Hill, Isaac	2	..	1	1	..	1	..	..	1	..	..
Hilliker, John	2	2	..	..	1	..	1	..	1	..	..
Hockstadt, Jacob	2	..	1	..	1	1	..	1	..	..	..
Hodge, John	2	..	..	1	..	1	..	..	1	..	..
Hoffman, Henry	..	..	..	..	1	1	1	..	1	..	..
Hogeboom, James	2	1	1	2	1	..	1	..	1	..	..
Hoyle, John	2	..	2	..	1	2	1	..	1	..	..
Hungerford, Levi	2	..	..	1	..	..	1	..	..	..	..
Johnson, John	2	1	1	..	1	1	1	1	..	1	..
Kelly, William	4	1	..	1	..	1	1	..	1	..	..
Lampkin, Nothrip	..	..	..	1	..	1	..	1	1	..	..
Lampman, Henry	1	..	..	1	..	2	..	..	1	..	..
Lampman, Stephen	2	..	..	1	..	2	..	..	1	..	..
Landon, Jonathan	..	1	1	..	1	..	1	2	..	1	..
Lent, Hercules	3	..	..	1	..	2	..	..	1	..	..
Mantle, Wyant	..	..	..	3	1	1	1	1	..	1	..
Moor, David	..	..	..	1	..	..	..	..	..	..	..
Moor, Richard	2	2	..	..	1	..	1	..	1	..	..
Mower, Henry	..	1	1	..	1	..	..	..	1	..	..
Mudget, David	1	2	1	..	1	..	1	1	..	1	..
Nokes, John	1	..	..	1	..	1	..	1	..	..	..
Odle, Nathan	2	..	..	1	..	1	..	1	..	..	..
Perrey, David	..	..	1	..	1	3	3	1	..	1	..
Perrey, Salmon	..	..	..	1	..	2	..	..	1	..	..
Pickle, Christopher	1	..	..	1	..	1	..	1	..	..	..
Potter, Andrew	3	2	1	2	..	1	..	1	1	..	..
Proper, Henry	..	..	..	..	1	..	1	..	..	1	..
Proper, Isaac	..	..	1	..	..	..	..	..	..	..	..
Proper, James	2	..	1	..	..	..	..	1	..	..	..
Proper, James	..	..	1	..	1	..	..	1	..	..	..
Proper, Peter	1	..	..	1	..	..	..	1	..	..	..
Proper, Tunis	..	..	..	1	..	1	..	1	..	..	..
Race, Thomas	..	..	..	1	..	..	..	..	..	..	..
Rampson, Richard	..	..	..	1	..	1	..	1	..	..	..
Richards, David	1	..	1	..	1	..	1	1	..	1	..
Rood, Elisha	..	..	..	1	..	..	..	1	..	..	..
Sax, John	..	..	5	..	1	..	1	..	..	..	..
Scheyer, Simeon	2	..	1	..	..	2	1	1	..	1	..
Shepard, James	..	..	..	..	1	..	1	..	..	1	..
Shidler, John	3	..	..	1	..	1	..	..	1	..	..
Stearns, Solomon	2	2	..	1	..	2	1	..	1	..	..
Steenhawker, George	2	1	3	1	..	4	1	1	1	..	..
Stienmetz, John	..	..	..	..	2	3	..	..	1	..	..
HIGHGATE—con.											
Teachout, Jacob Jr.	3	..	..	1	..	..	..	1	..	..	..
Teachout, Minard	2	..	..	1	..	1	..	1	..	..	..
Williams, Christopher	..	..	..	..	1	..	..	..	..	..	..
Willson, George	..	..	1	..	1	..	..	..	..	..	..
Willson, George Jr.	2	..	..	1	..	1	1	..	1	..	..
Willson, John	2	..	..	1	..	1	..	1	..	..	..
Winters, Timothy	..	2	..	1	..	3	2	..	1	..	..
Youngman, Thomas	..	..	..	..	1	2	1	..	1	..	..
UNCERTAIN NAME											
Minels (?), John	1	..	1	..	1	2	2	..	1	..	..
HUNTSBURGH											
Barnum, Heman	3	..	..	1	..	1	..	..	1	..	..
Bridgeman, John	2	..	..	1	..	..	..	1	..	..	..
Brown, Jude	1	2	2	..	1	1	..	1	..	1	..
Burnside, William	1	..	1	1	..	..	1	..	1	..	..
Coburn, Amasa	..	..	1	..	1	2	1	..	1	..	..
Curtis, Samuel	..	..	..	1	..	1	..	..	1	..	..
Dorson, Ziba	..	..	..	1	..	1	..	1	..	..	..
Fay, Asa	..	..	..	1	..	2	..	1	..	..	..
Flagg, Samuel	1	..	..	1	..	1	..	2	..	..	..
Gates, Paul	5	1	..	1	..	..	..	..	1	..	..
Hart, Lysander	1	..	..	1	..	3	..	..	1	..	..
Hockins, Enoch	..	1	..	1	1	..	1	..	1	..	..
Holbrook, John	..	..	1	1	1	1	..	1	..	1	..
Hubbart, Samuel	4	..	1	1	..	3	..	1	1	..	..
Jared, Silas	..	..	..	..	1	..	..	1	..	1	..
Jewit, Abel	3	1	..	1	..	1	..	2	1	..	..
Joy, Benjamin	2	1	..	1	..	2	..	1	..	..	..
Joy, Ephraim	..	1	2	..	..	..	1	2	..	..	..
Lake, Reuben	2	..	..	1	..	2	..	..	1	..	..
Loster, David	..	..	..	1	..	3	..	..	1	..	..
Marvin, Ebenezer	1	..	3	1	1	..	1	2	..	1	..
Millings, John	2	2	..	..	1	1	..	..	1	1	..
Moor, Nathan	2	..	..	1	..	1	..	1	..	..	..
Noble, Eli	1	..	..	1	..	1	..	2	..	..	..
Noross, John	..	..	..	1	..	..	..	1	..	..	..
Palmer, Joseph	..	..	..	1	..	2	..	1	..	..	..
Peckham, Josiah	2	1	..	1	..	1	2	1	1	..	..
Peckham, Samuel	1	2	2	..	1	..	..	1	2	..	..
Pomeroy, Enoch	2	..	..	1	..	..	..	1	..	..	..
Pratt, Elijah	2	1	..	1	..	1	1	..	1	..	..
Prowtee, Simeon	2	..	..	..	1	..	..	1	..	..	..
Randal, Joseph	2	3	..	1	..	2	..	..	1	..	..
Roberts, Lemuel	..	1	1	..	1	5	2	1	1	..	..
Saunderson, Sally	2	1	..	..	..	1	1	..	..	1	..
Sleeper, Josiah	1	..	..	1	..	2	..	1	..	..	..
Spaldin, Joseph	1	..	..	1	..	..	1	..	..	..	..
Stevens, James	4	..	..	..	1	..	..	..	1	..	..
Tarbor, Peter	2	..	..	1	..	1	..	1	..	..	..
Vincent, Noah	2	..	..	1	..	..	..	1	..	..	..
Warner, Salmon	2	..	..	1	1	2	1	..	1	..	..
Webbs, Joseph	..	..	..	1	..	1	..	1	..	..	..
Webster, John	1	2	..	1	..	3	1	..	1	..	..
Weed, Amasa	..	..	..	1	..	2	..	..	1	..	..
Weed, Hezekiah	3	1	..	1	..	..	..	1	1	..	..
Whitor, Daniel	..	1	..	1	..	..	..	..	1	..	..
Wright, William	..	..	..	1	..	..	..	1	1	..	..
UNCERTAIN NAMES											
Hall, Nehemiah (?)	..	..	..	1	..	2	..	..	1	..	..
Hindrince (?), John	2	..	..	1	..	2	..	..	1	..	..

FRANKLIN COUNTY—Continued

NAMES OF HEADS OF FAMILIES	FREE WHITE MALES: Under 10 years of age	Of 10 and under 16	Of 16 and under 26 including heads of families	Of 26 and under 45 including heads of families	Of 45 and upwards including heads of families	FREE WHITE FEMALES: Under 10 years of age	Of 10 and under 16	Of 16 and under 26 including heads of families	Of 26 and under 45 including heads of families	Of 45 and upwards including heads of families	All other free persons except Indians not taxed
ISLE LA MOTT											
Anderson, Benjamin	1	..	..	..	1	3	..	..	1	..	..
Baker, Daniel	2	2	..	1	..	1	2	..	1	1	..
Barber, Isaac	1	..	..	1	..	..	..	..	1	..	..
Blancher, William	2	1	2	..	1	..	3	1	..	1	..
Bravort, Isaac	3	1	..	1	..	1	..	..	1	..	..
Clark, Truman	..	..	..	1	..	1	..	1	1	..	..
Cooper, Enoch	2	1	..	1	..	1	..	..	1	..	..
Dean, Richard	1	1	1	1	..	1	..	..	1	..	..
Fisk, Ichabod E.	..	1	3	..	1	2	1	..	..	1	..
Hoit, Elisha	4	1	..	1	..	..	1	..	1	..	..
Holcum, Carmi	2	1	..	1	..	..	1	..	1	..	..
Horcumb, Amos	1	1	..	1	..	2	..	..	1	..	..
Horcumb, Jesse	1	..	..	1	..	1	..	..	1	..	..
Jourdan, Samuel	1	..	1	..	..	3	1	1	..	..	..
Knapp, Abraham	3	1	1	..	1	..	..	..	1	1	..
Knapp, Abraham Jr.	..	2	..	1	..	3	1	..	1	..	..
Langley, David	3	2	1	..	1	3	1	..	..	..	..
Noakes, Morris	3	..	..	1	..	..	1	..	1	..	..
Wait, Gardiner	3	3	1	..	1	1	..	..	1	1	..
JOHNSON											
Atwell, Jonathan	2	..	..	1	..	1	..	..	1	..	..
Atwell, Nathan	2	..	..	1	..	2	..	..	1	..	..
Balch, Moses	..	..	..	1	..	1	..	1	..	..	..
Balch, Robert	..	1	..	1	..	..	..	..	1	..	..
Balch, Solomon	..	..	..	1	..	..	..	..	..	..	..
Boaz, Samuel	2	..	..	1	..	..	..	..	..	1	..
Brooks, Ebenezer	2	..	..	1	..	..	..	..	1	..	..
Clark, Levi	1	..	1	..	..	1	..	1	..	..	..
Cram, Ezekiel	2	..	..	1	..	..	..	1	..	..	..
Davis, Moses	1	1	..	1	..	2	1	1	..	..	..
Dodge, Amos	1	..	1	..	..	2	..	1	..	..	..
Dodge, Elisha	..	..	..	1	..	..	..	1	..	..	..
Eaton, Henry	..	..	..	1	..	2	..	..	..	..	..
Eaton, Samuel	4	1	1	1	..	1	1	..	1	..	..
Eaton, Samuel	..	..	1	..	1	..	..	1	..	1	..
Ellingwood, Ralph	2	2	..	1	..	3	2	..	1	..	..
Erwin, David	1	..	2	..	1	4	1	..	1	1	..
Ferry, Daniel	1	..	1	1	..	1	..	1	..	..	..
Ferry, Ebenezer	..	..	1	..	..	2	..	1	..	..	..
Ferry, Joel	1	..	..	1	..	..	..	1	..	..	..
Foster, David	3	..	3	..	1	..	1	2	..	1	..
Foster, Obadiah	1	..	..	1	..	1	..	..	1	..	..
Garvin, Ephraim	4	1	..	..	1	1	2	..	..	1	..
Gragg, George	2	1	..	1	..	1	1	..	1	..	..
Gragg, Isaac	2	..	..	1	..	2	1	..	1	..	..
Gragg, Thomas	..	..	..	1	..	..	1	..	..	1	..
Griswold, John	..	2	1	1	..	2	2	..	1	..	..
Hall, George	..	..	1	1	..	..	1	..	1	..	..
Heath, Lupkir	1	..	1	..	..	1	..	1	..	..	..
Heath, William	2	1	4	..	1	..	1	..	1	1	..
Hunkins, John	..	1	..	1	..	2	1	1	1	..	..
Larabee, William H.	1	..	..	1	..	..	..	1	..	..	..
McComall, Jeremiah M.	3	..	..	..	1	..	..	..	1	..	..
McConnel, David	1	..	..	1	..	..	..	1	..	..	..
McConnel, John	..	..	1	1	..	2	1	..	1	..	..
McConnel, Moses	..	..	..	1	..	1	..	1	..	..	..
McCoy, John	1	..	..	1	..	2	..	..	1	..	..
Merril, Jonathan	..	..	..	1	..	..	..	..	1	..	..
Miller, Samuel	2	..	..	1	..	2	3	..	1	..	..
Page, James	2	..	..	1	..	1	..	..	1	..	..
Prince, John	1	..	..	1	..	..	..	..	1	..	..
Redington, Daniel	1	1	..	1	..	4	..	..	1	..	..
JOHNSON—con.											
Semins, John	3	..	..	1	..	1	..	..	1	..	..
Smith, Aaron	2	1	1	1	..	1	..	2	..	..	..
Wheelock, Joel	..	..	1	..	..	..	..	1	..	..	..
Whipple, Jonas	1	..	..	1	..	1	..	1	..	..	..
Willson, Robert	..	..	1	..	..	2	..	1	..	..	..
Wire, John	..	1	..	1	..	..	..	..	..	..	..
JOHNSON'S GORE											
Booth, Henry	1	..	1	..	..	1	..	1	..	..	..
Butler, David	1	..	2	..	..	1	..	..	1	..	..
Covey, Joseph	3	1	2	..	1	1	1	1	..	1	..
Evans, Abel	3	..	..	1	..	2	..	1	..	..	..
Farnsworth, Ebenezer	..	1	..	1	..	1	..	1	1	..	..
Farr, Joshua	1	..	1	..	..	2	..	1	..	..	..
Farr, Samuel	..	..	..	..	1	..	..	..	..	1	..
Farr, Samuel Jr.	1	..	1	..	..	..	..	1	..	..	..
Farr, Thomas	2	1	..	1	..	1	..	..	1	..	..
Farr, Thomas 2nd	..	..	..	1	..	1	..	1	..	..	..
Fisher, Isaac	2	..	..	1	..	1	..	..	1	..	..
Fisher, Noah	..	..	1	..	1	..	..	..	..	1	..
Fisher, Noah Jr.	..	..	..	1	..	..	..	1	..	..	..
Fisher, Timothy	..	1	..	1	..	..	2	..	1	..	..
Gennison, William	..	1	..	..	1	3	1	..	..	1	..
Hale, Amos	1	..	..	1	..	..	..	2	..	1	..
Heiks, John	..	1	..	..	1	..	..	..	..	1	..
Holden, Philemon	4	1	1	1	..	..	..	1	1	..	..
Johnson, Elisha	..	..	1	..	..	2	..	1	..	..	..
Kathan, Rufus	..	1	..	1	..	2	..	..	1	..	..
Kingsbury, Philip	3	..	1	1	..	1	3	1	1	..	..
Knapp, Aaron	..	..	..	..	1	..	..	..	..	1	..
Prentice, Joseph	2	..	..	..	1	1	1	1	1	..	..
Scott, Wait	1	..	1	..	..	2	..	1	..	..	..
Scott, Wooderd	..	..	..	1	..	..	..	..	1	..	..
Streeter, Otis	1	..	1	..	..	2	..	1	..	..	..
MIDDLE HERO											
Adams, Joseph	2	1	..	2	..	..	1	..	1	..	..
Adkins, Isaac	2	1	..	1	..	2	..	..	1	..	..
Allen, Ebenezer H.	1	1	..	1	..	3	..	..	1	..	..
Allen, Enoch	..	1	..	1	..	..	..	1	..	1	..
Allen, Lamberton	1	1	..	..	1	..	1	1	..	1	..
Allen, Lamberton Jr.	..	..	1	..	..	..	..	1	..	..	..
Allen, Samuel	1	..	1	1	..	2	..	1	1	..	..
Ames, Adon	2	1	1	1	..	2	2	..	1	..	..
Armstrong, Jeremiah	2	2	..	1	..	3	1	..	1	..	..
Baker, Matthew	3	..	..	1	..	..	..	1	..	..	..
Barnes, Robert	..	..	..	..	1	3	..	1	..	..	..
Barney, William	..	..	..	1	..	..	1	..	1	..	..
Beedle, Nathaniel	..	..	..	..	1	1	..	..	..	1	..
Belden, Noah	1	1	..	1	..	1	..	..	1	..	..
Belden, Samuel	..	..	2	..	..	..	..	..	..	..	..
Bell, Benjamin	1	1	..	..	1	1	..	..	..	1	..
Benedict, Joshua	2	..	..	1	..	1	1	..	1	..	..
Brigham, John	2	..	..	1	..	1	..	..	1	..	..
Bristol, Abel	..	1	2	..	1	2	3	..	..	1	..
Brown, James	1	..	..	1	..	1	1	..	1	..	..
Buckman, Elijah	3	..	..	1	..	2	..	2	1	..	..
Burnes, Samuel	1	1	..	..	1	2	..	..	..	1	..
Campbell, James	2	..	..	1	..	1	1	2	1	..	..
Chamberton, Wyman	..	..	..	1	..	2	1	1	..	..	..
Clapp, Reuben	1	..	1	1	..	5	2	1	1	..	..
Clark, Charles	3	1	1	..	1	1	..	..	1	..	..
Clark, Cheney	1	..	1	1	..	1	..	..	1	..	..
Clark, Simeon	1	..	..	1	..	..	..	1	..	..	..
Clark, Uzziel	..	..	..	..	1	..	..	..	..	1	..
Collins, Warren	2	..	..	1	..	3	..	..	1	..	..
Conkee, Jonas	3	..	1	..	1	2	..	..	1	..	..
Coonley, David	..	1	..	1	..	3	2	..	1	..	..
Cooper, Thomas	1	..	1	..	1	..	..	1	..	..	..
Cooper, Thomas	..	1	1	..	1	..	..	1	..	1	..
Davis, Daniel	2	..	1	..	..	..	..	1	..	..	..
Delong, Francis	2	..	..	1	..	1	..	..	1	..	..
Doody, Obadiah	1	1	1	..	1	..	..	1	1	..	..

FRANKLIN COUNTY—Continued

NAMES OF HEADS OF FAMILIES	FREE WHITE MALES: Under 10 years of age	FREE WHITE MALES: Of 10 and under 16	FREE WHITE MALES: Of 16 and under 26 including heads of families	FREE WHITE MALES: Of 26 and under 45 including heads of families	FREE WHITE MALES: Of 45 and upwards including heads of families.	FREE WHITE FEMALES: Under 10 years of age	FREE WHITE FEMALES: Of 10 and under 16	FREE WHITE FEMALES: Of 16 and under 26 including heads of families	FREE WHITE FEMALES: Of 26 and under 45 including heads of families	FREE WHITE FEMALES: Of 45 and upwards including heads of families	All other free persons except Indians not taxed
MIDDLE HERO—con.											
Farnsworth, William	..	..	3	..	1	..	..	..	..	..	..
Ferris, Zebulon	2	1	..	1	..	2	..	..	1	..	..
Fox, Ira	..	..	..	1	..	..	..	..	..	..	..
Fulsom, John	..	..	..	..	1	..	..	..	..	1	..
Gibson, John	2	1	..	..	1	2	1	1	..	..	..
Gilbert, Benjamin	..	..	..	1	1	..	..	1	..	1	..
Gilbert, James	..	..	..	1	..	..	..	1	..	..	..
Gordan, Alexander	..	1	..	..	2	1	..	1	1	..	..
Gordan, Willard	2	1	..	1	..	1	..	1	..	..	..
Hazen, Andrew	2	..	..	1	..	1	1	..	1	..	..
Hill, Nathan	..	..	1	..	..	..	..	1	..	..	..
Hoag, Daniel	3	..	..	1	..	2	3	1	1	..	..
Hyde, Elijah	3	1	1	..	1	2	1	1	..	..	..
Hyde, Jedidiah	1	3	..	1	..	3	..	..	1	..	..
Hyde, Jonathan	2	1	..	1	..	2	..	1	..	..	..
Jenkins, Valentine	2	2	1	2	..	1	1	1	..	1	..
Ladd, Andrew	3	..	..	1	..	1	..	..	1	..	..
Lambson, Daniel	1	..	1	1	..	3	..	..	1	..	..
Lanes, John	3	1	..	1	..	2	..	..	1	..	..
Lent, Abram	2	..	2	..	1	1	..	..	..	1	..
Lent, Peter	..	..	1	..	..	..	..	1	..	..	..
Linsey, James	1	1	..	1	..	3	..	..	1	..	..
Loveland, Zibe	..	..	1	1	..	..	..	..	..	..	..
Lyn, Abram	..	..	..	1	..	1	..	..	..	..	..
Lyon, Asa Rev.	..	..	..	1	..	1	..	..	1	..	..
Makman, Weson	2	3	2	1	..	3	1	..	1	..	..
Meker, Christopher	1	..	..	1	..	1	..	..	1	..	..
Merrihue, Joseph	..	..	..	1	..	..	..	1	..	..	..
Minckler, Barnabas	1	..	2	1	..	2	2	..	1	..	..
Minkler, Jacob	2	..	..	1	..	1	..	1	..	1	..
Minkler, Jeremiah	4	..	..	1	..	..	..	..	1	..	..
Minkler, Peter	3	..	..	1	..	1	1	..	1	..	..
Moors, Mark	1	..	1	..	..	1	..	1	..	..	..
Mow, Jacob	1	2	1	1	..	3	1	..	1	..	..
Peck, Nicholas	4	1	1	1	1	2	..	..	1	..	..
Peters, Abel	..	1	..	..	1	..	..	..	..	1	..
Pickering, Joseph	1	..	..	1	..	..	1	..	..	..	..
Rennels, Charles	..	1	..	1	..	1	1	1	1	..	..
Reynolds, Grenold	3	..	1	2	1	2	1	1	1	..	..
Roback, Jacob	..	..	..	..	1	..	..	1	..	..	..
Rosey, John	..	..	..	1	..	..	..	1	..	..	..
Rosman, Bostem	..	1	1	..	1	1	1	..	..	1	..
Rosman, Conrad	..	..	..	..	1	..	..	1	..	1	..
Sawyer, Ephraim	1	2	1	..	1	1	2	1	1	..	..
Scott, Henry	3	2	1	1	..	3	3	..	1	..	..
Shaw, Cypius	1	..	..	1	..	1	..	1	..	..	..
Simpson, William	1	..	1	..	1	1	..	1	..	..	..
Slason, Eleazer	1	..	1	..	1	..	..	1	..	1	..
Stark, Benajah	1	..	..	..	1	1	2	2	..	1	..
Stoson, David	1	..	..	1	..	3	..	..	1	..	..
Stoson, William	1	..	..	1	..	1	..	1	..	..	..
Thomas, Beriah	..	..	1	..	1	..	..	..	..	1	..
Thomas, John	2	2	..	1	..	1	1	..	1	..	..
Thomas, Leonard	..	..	1	..	..	1	..	1	..	..	..
Thomas, Matthew	2	..	..	1	..	1	..	..	1	..	..
Tiffany, Recompence	..	..	..	1	..	..	..	2	..	..	..
Tobias, James	3	1	..	1	..	2	..	..	1	..	..
Vaughan, Elisha	..	2	..	1	..	3	..	..	1	..	..
Vaughan, John	..	..	1	..	..	..	..	1	..	..	..
Vaughan, Levi	..	..	1	1	..	1	..	1	..	..	..
Weaver, Peter	..	..	..	1	..	1	..	..	1	..	..
Wilber, Stephen	1	..	1	..	..	..	..	1	..	..	..
Willcox, Daniel	1	..	1	1	..	..	..	..	1	1	..
Woodley, Samuel	1	..	..	1	1	..	..	1	..	..	..
UNCERTAIN NAME											
Atwell (?), Joseph	2	..	..	1	..	1	..	..	1	..	..
NORTH HERO											
Ayers, Ebenezer	..	..	..	..	1	1	..	1	..	..	..
Babcock, Ebenezer	..	1	1	..	1	2	3	..	..	1	..
Babcock, Elias	1	..	1	..	..	..	..	1	..	..	..
Baylo, Francis	..	..	..	..	1	..	..	..	..	1	..
Burnsen, Simeon	..	1	..	1	..	2	..	1	..	..	..
Butler, Benjamin	2	3	..	1	..	2	..	..	1	..	..
Butler, James	2	1	..	1	..	2	1	..	1	..	..
Cochran, Thomas	..	..	..	1	..	4	1	..	1	..	..
Demery, Roswell	..	..	1	..	1	..	..	1	..	1	..
Dowd, Ebenezer	..	1	1	..	1	..	..	..	..	..	..
Dowd, Roger	..	..	..	..	1	..	..	..	1	..	..
Hart, Thomas	1	..	2	..	..	..	..	1	..	..	..
Haynes, Jonathan	..	..	1	1	..	2	..	2	..	..	..
Haynes, Nathan	2	2	..	1	..	1	1	1	1	..	..
Haynes, William	..	..	..	1	..	1	..	..	1	..	..
Hayzen, Andrew	1	1	..	1	..	1	..	..	1	..	..
Hayzen, Andrew 2nd	2	..	..	1	..	1	1	..	1	..	..
Hayzen, Asahel	3	..	..	1	..	1	..	..	1	..	..
Hayzen, Joseph Jr.	3	..	1	..	..	1	1	1	..	..	..
Hayzen, Solomon	3	1	..	1	1	..	..	1	..	1	..
Hayzin, Don	..	2	..	..	5	..	2	..	..	..	..
Howard, Alexander D.	1	..	..	2	..	2	..	1	..	..	..
Hubbard, Elisha	2	..	1	..	1	2	..	3	..	1	..
Hutchins, Asel	2	1	1	1	1	2	..	..	1	..	..
Hutchins, Nathan	..	1	1	..	1	..	..	1	..	..	..
Junchon, Francis	1	2	..	1	..	2	..	1	1	..	..
Kinsley, Stephen	3	2	1	..	1	2	3	..	1	..	..
Knight, John	1	1	1	..	1	1	2	..	..	1	..
Knoulton, Elijah	..	1	1	1	..	2	..	..	..	..	..
Ladd, Jedediah P.	2	1	..	1	..	1	2	..	1	..	..
Martin, John	..	1	2	1	..	4	1	..	1	..	..
Martin, Peter	..	..	2	..	..	2	..	1	..	..	..
More, John	1	..	..	1	..	..	..	..	1	..	..
Pain, Roger	..	..	..	1	..	2	..	..	1	1	..
Pain, Stephen	2	1	..	1	..	2	..	1	1	..	..
Parker, Abel	1	..	..	1	..	4	..	1	1	..	..
Patch, Stephen	1	..	..	1	1	1	..	..	1	..	..
Pearl, Asalph	..	..	..	1	..	..	..	..	..	..	..
Perkins, Samuel	3	..	1	1	..	..	1	..	1	..	..
Pixley, Asa	2	1	1	..	1	2	..	1	1	..	..
Pixley, Peter	2	1	2	..	1	1	1	1	1	..	..
Pudoo, Joseph	2	..	..	1	..	2	..	..	1	..	..
Rice, Abner	2	1	..	1	..	..	..	1	..	..	..
Russell, Oliver	3	..	..	1	..	1	..	..	1	..	..
Squires, Algin	..	2	1	..	..	..	1	1	..	..	..
Stewart, James	1	..	..	1	..	2	..	..	1	..	..
Stoddard, David	..	..	1	1	1	..	..	..	..	1	..
Strong, William	..	..	1	..	1	..	2	..	..	1	..
Town, Silas	4	..	..	1	..	..	..	..	1	..	..
Trumble, Levi	..	..	..	1	..	1	..	1	..	..	..
Waiscoat, Joseph	1	..	..	1	..	..	..	1	..	..	..
Williams, Ansel	2	..	..	1	..	3	..	..	1	..	..
Wood, John	..	1	1	..	1	..	1	..	..	1	..
Wood, Lois	1	..	..	1	..	1	1	..	..	..	..
MONTGOMERY											
Barnard, Samuel	..	1	1	..	2	..	..	3	..	1	1
Clapp, Joshua	1	..	2	1	..	2	1	3	1	..	..
Clapp, Reuben	2	..	1	1	..	2	..	..	1	..	..
Upham, James	3	1	1	2	..	1	..	..	1	..	..
RICHFORD											
Barron, Nathan	2	..	1	1	..	..	..	1	..	..	..
Blasdell, Stephen	2	1	..	3	1	2	1	..	1	..	..
Brown, Francis	..	..	2	..	..	..	..	..	..	..	..
Canada, Robert	..	..	..	1	..	..	..	1	..	..	..
Carpenter, Stephen	1	1	2	1	..	1	..	1	..	..	..
Davis, Daniel	4	1	..	1	..	1	1	..	1	..	..

FRANKLIN COUNTY—Continued

NAMES OF HEADS OF FAMILIES	Free white males: Under 10 years of age	Free white males: Of 10 and under 16	Free white males: Of 16 and under 26 including heads of families	Free white males: Of 26 and under 45 including heads of families	Free white males: Of 45 and upwards including heads of families	Free white females: Under 10 years of age	Free white females: Of 10 and under 16	Free white females: Of 16 and under 26 including heads of families	Free white females: Of 26 and under 45 including heads of families	Free white females: Of 45 and upwards including heads of families	All other free persons except Indians not taxed
RICHFORD—con.											
Hastings, Theophilus	3	..	..	1	..	2	..	1	1	..	..
Jane, Jonathan	2	2	3	3	..	1	2	2	1	..	..
Janes, Daniel	1	2	1	1	..	1	..	1	1	..	..
Miller, Hugh	..	..	2	..	1	1	..	3	..	1	..
Page, Moses	..	..	..	1	..	..	1	1	..	..	..
Powell, Bradford	..	..	3	..	..	..	..	1	..	..	..
Powell, Rowland	2	1	2	..	1	1	2	2	..	1	..
Shepard, Thomas	..	..	..	1	..	..	..	..	..	..	..
Stanhope, Joseph	4	1	1	1	..	..	..	1	1	..	..
Wright, Phineas Z.	3	..	..	1	..	2	1	..	1	..	..
SHELDON											
Alexander, Eliakin	1	..	..	1	..	..	..	1	..	..	..
Avery, Josiah	2	1	1	..	1	2	1	..	1	..	..
Barnet, John	1	1	..	..	1	1	2	..	..	1	..
Barton, Jesse	2	..	..	1	..	1	..	..	1	..	..
Bowles, John	..	..	1	1	..	1	2	2	1	..	..
Bran, Jesse	1	..	2	2	1	1	1	..	..	1	..
Buckley, Asa	1	..	..	2	..	2	..	1	..	..	..
Burt, Joseph	2	..	1	1	..	..	..	..	1	..	..
Chapman, Timothy	2	..	..	2	..	1	3	..	1	..	..
Cooper, Samuel	1	..	..	1	..	..	..	1	..	..	..
Coutton, Lucius	1	..	..	1	..	1	..	..	1	..	..
Demmon, Frederick	2	..	..	1	..	1	..	1	..	..	..
Demmon, Tully	2	..	..	1	..	2	..	..	1	..	..
Dewing, Luke	3	1	..	1	..	2	..	1	1	..	..
Dixon, Alexander	3	1	1	1	..	1	..	..	1	..	..
Draper, Gideon	1	..	2	..	..	..	..	1	..	..	..
Elderthorp, Jacob	3	..	..	1	..	..	..	..	1	..	..
Elderthorp, Salmon	2	..	..	1	..	..	1	..	1	..	..
Fellows, Daniel	1	..	1	1	..	1	..	1	1	..	..
Foster, David	2	1	..	1	..	1	..	1	1	..	..
Grant, Asa	1	..	..	1	..	..	..	1	..	..	..
Hawley, James	2	1	1	1	..	1	..	..	1	..	..
Herrick, James	..	..	..	1	..	1	..	1	..	..	..
Holobut, Samuel	2	..	..	1	..	1	..	..	1	..	..
Hoskins, John	..	..	..	1	..	1	..	1	..	..	..
Hoskins, Seth	2	..	..	1	..	2	..	..	1	..	..
Iram, William	4	..	..	1	..	2	..	..	1	..	..
Keith, Alfred	2	..	7	1	..	2	..	1	1	..	..
Keith, Anson	1	1	..	1	..	..	..	2	..	..	..
Keys, Elnathan	3	1	3	1	..	2	1	..	1	..	8
Kimball, James	..	1	1	..	1	1	..	1	..	1	..
Kimball, John	..	1	..	1	..	2	..	..	1	..	..
Kimball, Solomon F.	1	..	1	1	..	2	..	1	1	..	..
Lewis, John	1	..	..	1	..	1	..	1	..	..	..
Mann, Corlis	2	..	1	1	..	..	..	1	1	..	..
Marsh, John	2	..	..	1	..	1	..	..	1	..	..
Parker, Peter	2	..	..	1	..	2	..	..	1	..	..
Pentland, Thomas	1	..	..	1	..	..	..	..	1	..	..
Pottir, John	3	1	..	1	..	..	2	..	1	..	..
Powel, Stephen	..	1	2	1	..	3	1	..	1	1	..
Prince, Joseph	2	1	1	1	1	2	1	..	1	1	..
Read, Isaac	..	1	..	..	1	..	..	..	..	1	..
Read, Leonard	2	2	1	1	..	2	..	..	1	..	..
Remington, Benjamin	..	..	..	1	..	..	1	1	1	..	..
Ross, Parent	1	1	1	..	..	1	..	1	..	..	..
Sarles, James	2	..	..	1	..	1	..	..	1	..	..
Shattock, Consider	1	..	..	1	..	1	..	..	1	..	..
Shattock, Samuel	1	..	..	1	..	1	..	..	1	..	..
Shattock, Seth	..	..	..	1	..	2	..	..	1	..	..
Sheldon, Elisha	..	..	..	..	1	..	..	..	..	1	..
Sheldon, Elisha Jr.	2	2	..	1	..	..	1	..	1	..	..
Sheldon. George	2	..	..	1	..	3	1	..	1	..	..
Sheldon, Samuel B.	3	..	3	1	..	..	1	3	1	..	2
SHELDON—con.											
Tuttle, Josiah	..	1	4	1	..	2	1	1	..	..	..
Wait, Nathaniel	2	2	..	1	..	2	2	..	1	..	..
Wallace, Moses	2	..	..	1	..	2	..	..	1	..	..
Webster, Charles	2	1	..	1	..	1	..	..	1	..	..
Willard, Alexander	1	..	1	1	..	1	..	1	..	..	..
Wood, Robert	2	1	..	..	1	..	1	..	1	..	..
Wright, Jehu	1	1	..	1	..	3	1	..	1	..	..
Young, Elijah	1	1	..	2	1	1	1	2	1	1	..
SOUTH HERO											
Adams, Isaac	2	2	..	1	..	3	1	..	1	..	..
Aldridge, John	2	2	1	..	1	2	1	..	1	..	..
Allen, Ebenezer	..	..	..	..	1	..	1	..	..	1	..
Allen, Levi	2	..	..	1	..	1	..	1	..	..	..
Allen, Samuel	..	..	1	..	1	..	1	1	..	..	..
Allen, Timothy	1	..	..	1	..	3	1	..	1	..	..
Allis, Ebenezer	..	..	..	1	..	..	..	1	..	..	..
Ames, Barzilla	..	..	..	1	..	4	1	..	1	..	..
Bacon, Abel	1	..	1	..	1	1	1	..	..	1	..
Baldwin, Jabz	1	3	..	..	1	2	1	..	1	..	..
Barnes, Mary	..	..	..	..	..	1	..	..	1	..	..
Barns, Edward	1	..	1	..	..	..	..	1	..	..	..
Barns, Melvin	2	..	1	1	..	1	..	1	..	..	..
Barns, William	2	..	..	1	..	..	..	1	..	..	..
Bedient, William	3	..	..	..	1	1	..	..	1	..	..
Bingham, Aaron	1	..	..	1	..	..	..	2	1	..	..
Boardman, Elisha	..	..	4	..	..	..	..	1	..	..	..
Boardman, Joseph	..	1	1	..	..	1	..	..	1	..	..
Boardman, Samuel	2	..	..	1	..	2	..	..	1	..	..
Brown, Benjamin	2	1	..	1	..	3	1	..	1	..	..
Brown, Chester	1	..	1	..	..	..	..	1	..	..	..
Brown, Enos	1	..	1	..	1	1	..	2	..	..	..
Brown, Jesse	..	..	1	..	..	..	..	1	..	..	..
Brown, Joshua	1	..	3	..	1	..	2	1	..	1	..
Brown, Simeon	..	..	2	..	..	1	..	1	..	..	..
Brown, Thomas	3	..	..	1	..	..	..	..	1	..	..
Bunnel, Solomon	1	..	1	1	1	..	1	1	..	1	..
Butler, Joseph	..	..	..	..	1	..	..	..	..	1	..
Cady, William	2	..	..	..	1	2	2	1	1	..	..
Campbell, Samuel	3	..	..	1	..	1	..	..	1	..	..
Campbell, William	3	1	..	1	..	2	..	..	1	..	..
Clark, Benjamin	..	..	..	1	..	..	..	..	1	..	..
Coiney, Stephen	1	..	..	1	..	1	1	2	..	..	..
Cook, Benjamin	1	2	..	..	1	4	..	1	1	..	..
Davison, John	..	..	1	1	1	..	..	..	..	1	..
Davison, Samuel	1	1	..	1	..	2	..	..	1	..	..
Davison, Stephen	1	..	1	1	..	..	1	..	1	1	..
Dennis, George	..	..	1	..	..	..	..	1	..	..	..
Dennis, Jesse	..	1	1	..	1	1	..	..	..	1	..
Dixon, Joseph	..	..	1	..	..	..	..	1	..	..	..
Dixon, Thomas	..	..	..	1	1	2	1	..	1	..	..
Dunham, William	2	1	..	1	..	3	1	..	1	..	..
Eldridge, Amos	1	..	1	..	1	1	1	..	1	..	..
Fairchile, Isaac	..	..	1	..	..	..	..	1	..	..	..
Fairchile, Jesse	..	..	..	1	1	..	..	..	..	1	..
Fletcher, Calvin	..	..	2	..	..	..	..	1	..	..	..
Fletcher, Elias	2	..	..	1	..	2	..	1	1	..	..
Griffin, Jonathan	..	2	1	..	2	2	1	1	..	2	..
Hacket, Allen	1	1	1	1	..	2	2	..	1	..	..
Hale, Elijah	..	..	1	..	..	..	..	..	..	..	..
Hall, Alpheus	2	1	2	..	..	2	2	2	1	..	..
Harrington, Hezekiah	..	..	1	..	1	..	1	..	..	1	..
Harris, Nathaniel	..	..	..	1	1	..	..	..	1	1	..
Hastings, Samuel	2	1	..	1	..	..	..	..	1	1	..
Herrick, Elijah	1	..	4	1	..	3	1	..	1	..	..
Hines, Abel	..	1	..	..	1	..	..	1	..	1	..
Hinne, Asa	..	..	1	..	1	..	..	..	..	1	..
Hodges, William	2	1	1	1	..	1	1	..	1	..	..
Janes, Elijah	..	..	2	..	1	..	1	..	..	1	..
Kinne, Asa	..	..	1	..	..	..	..	..	..	..	..
Kinne, Ezra	..	..	1	1	..	2	..	1	..	..	..
Kinne, Jonas	4	..	..	1	..	..	1	..	1	..	1
Kinne, Kimbal	..	..	2	1	..	..	..	1	..	..	..

FRANKLIN COUNTY—Continued

NAMES OF HEADS OF FAMILIES	FREE WHITE MALES: Under 10 years of age	FREE WHITE MALES: Of 10 and under 16	FREE WHITE MALES: Of 16 and under 26 including heads of families	FREE WHITE MALES: Of 26 and under 45 including heads of families	FREE WHITE MALES: Of 45 and upwards including heads of families.	FREE WHITE FEMALES: Under 10 years of age	FREE WHITE FEMALES: Of 10 and under 16	FREE WHITE FEMALES: Of 16 and under 26 including heads of families	FREE WHITE FEMALES: Of 26 and under 45 including heads of families	FREE WHITE FEMALES: Of 45 and upwards including heads of families	All other free persons except Indians not taxed
SOUTH HERO—con.											
Laflin, Matthew	2	..	..	1	..	1	..	..	1	..	..
Landon, Asel	2	..	1	1	..	..	..	1	..	..	..
Landon, Benjamin	..	..	2	..	1	..	1	1	..	1	..
Landon, Thaddeus	2	2	..	1	..	1	1	..	1	..	..
Lanes, Humphrey	4	1	..	1	..	2	..	..	1	..	..
Lanes, John	1	..	..	1	..	4	..	..	1	..	..
Looner, Joseph	1	1	..	1	..	4	1	..	1	..	..
Martin, Caleb	1	..	..	1	..	1	..	..	1	..	..
Martin, Ebenezer	2	..	1	..	1	2	1	1	1	..	..
Martin, Ebenezer Jr.	..	..	1	..	..	..	..	1	..	..	..
Martin, Isaac	1	..	1	1	..	..	..	1	..	..	..
Martin, Jonas	2	..	..	2	..	2	1	..	1	..	..
Merrium, Daniel	2	..	1	..	..	1	..	1	..	..	..
Minkler, Isaac	2	..	..	1	..	3	..	..	1	..	..
Minkler, John	..	..	..	1	1	1	..	..	..	2	..
Minkler, John Jr.	1	1	1	1	..	3	..	1	1	..	..
Mix, Samuel	1	..	1	1	..	2	1	..	1	..	..
Moors, Ephraim	3	2	..	1	..	4	1	..	1	..	..
Mott, Richard	3	..	..	2	..	1	1	1	1	..	..
Pearl, Timothy	..	1	1	..	1	2	1	..	..	1	..
Peters, Ashbel	..	..	2	..	1	..	..	..	..	1	..
Peters, Ebenezer	..	..	2	..	..	1	1	..	..	1	..
Peters, James	2	..	..	1	..	..	..	..	1	..	..
Peters, Levi	..	..	1	1	..	..	..	1	..	..	..
Peters, Timothy	1	..	3	..	1	..	1	..	..	1	..
Petton, James	3	1	..	1	..	1	..	1	1	..	..
Phelps, Abel	..	..	..	..	1	..	1	..	..	1	..
Phelps, Abel Jr.	2	..	..	1	..	..	1	..	1	..	..
Phelps, Alexander	2	..	..	1	..	2	..	..	1	..	..
Phelps, Benajah	..	..	..	1	..	3	..	..	1	1	1
Phelps, Elijah	..	..	1	..	1	..	1	..	..	1	..
Phelps, Joseph	1	2	2	..	1	1	1	..	..	1	..
Phelps, Joseph Jr.	..	..	1	..	..	..	..	..	..	..	..
Phelps, Salmon	..	..	2	1	..	2	..	..	1	..	..
Plumb, Samuel	..	..	2	..	1	1	..	..	..	1	..
Remington, Joseph	..	..	..	1	..	..	..	..	1	..	..
Rennels, Content	1	..	..	1	..	3	..	..	1	..	..
Rennels, Joseph	1	3	..	..	1	1	..	..	1	..	..
Robinson, Ebenezer	1	..	..	1	..	..	..	1	..	..	..
Robinson, Simeon	..	1	3	..	1	..	1	..	..	1	..
Rockwell, Jabez	2	1	1	1	..	..	1	..	1	..	..
Sawyer, Daniel J.	3	..	..	1	..	1	..	1	..	..	..
Sawyer, Ephraim	..	..	..	..	1	..	..	..	..	1	..
Sawyer, Peter	1	1	..	1	..	3	..	..	1	..	..
Snickall, Joseph	1	..	..	1	..	..	..	1	1	..	..
Starks, Ebenezer	4	..	1	..	1	..	..	1	..	..	..
Starks, John	..	..	..	..	1	..	2	3	..	1	..
Steward, William	2	3	..	..	1	2	1	..	1	..	..
Stiles, Jonathan	1	..	1	..	..	2	..	1	..	..	..
Stiles, Jonathan	1	..	..	1	..	2	..	..	1	..	..
Stone, John	..	..	..	1	..	2	..	1	..	..	..
Wadsworth, Daniel	1	..	..	1	..	2	..	..	1	..	..
Welch, James	1	..	1	1	..	..	..	1	1	..	..
Welch, Mala	2	..	..	1	..	..	..	..	1	..	..
Welch, Timothy	1	..	..	2	..	..	..	..	1	..	..
Wells, Daniel	1	..	1	..	..	1	..	1	..	..	..
ST. ALBANS											
Armstrong, John	2	..	..	1	..	1	..	1	..	..	..
Aylesworth, Lemuel	1	..	..	1	..	..	..	1	..	..	..
Baker, Ira	3	..	..	2	..	1	1	1	1	..	..
Boardman, Elijah	2	1	..	..	1	..	1	..	1	..	..
Bonney, Jethro	2	..	..	1	..	2	..	1	..	..	..
Bradley, Benjamin	3	1	..	1	..	1	1	..	1	..	..
Brooks, Adonijah	1	..	2	1	1	..	1	..	..	1	..
Brooks, Eleazer	1	..	1	1	..	2	..	1	..	..	..
Brooks, Ezariah	..	2	..	1	..	1	..	..	1	..	..
Brown, Elijah	3	1	1	..	1	2	..	1	1	..	..
Burton, Nathaniel	1	..	2	1	..	1	..	..	1	..	..
Burton, Samuel	2	..	1	1	..	..	..	1	1	..	..
Butler, Eldad	2	1	1	1	..	3	1	..	1	..	..
Calkins, Solomon	2	1	1	..	..	2	2	1	..	..	..
Campbell, David	2	2	..	..	1	3	1	1	1	..	..
Carter, Joseph	1	..	1	1	..	..	..	2	..	..	..
Chance, Josiah	..	..	1	1	..	...	2	1	1	..	..
Chapin, Thomas	1	..	..	2	..	1	..	..	1	..	..
Chapman, Eben	3	..	..	..	1	1	2	1	1	..	..
Church, Azel	2	..	4	1	1	..	1	1	1	1	..
Church, Ira	..	..	3	..	1	2	..	1	1	..	..

NAMES OF HEADS OF FAMILIES	FREE WHITE MALES: Under 10 years of age	FREE WHITE MALES: Of 10 and under 16	FREE WHITE MALES: Of 16 and under 26 including heads of families	FREE WHITE MALES: Of 26 and under 45 including heads of families	FREE WHITE MALES: Of 45 and upwards including heads of families.	FREE WHITE FEMALES: Under 10 years of age	FREE WHITE FEMALES: Of 10 and under 16	FREE WHITE FEMALES: Of 16 and under 26 including heads of families	FREE WHITE FEMALES: Of 26 and under 45 including heads of families	FREE WHITE FEMALES: Of 45 and upwards including heads of families	All other free persons except Indians not taxed
ST. ALBANS—con.											
Clark, Daniel	3	..	..	1	..	2	..	..	1	..	..
Clark, David	2	..	..	1	..	2	..	1	..	..	..
Colfix, John	1	1	2	1	..	3	..	..	1	..	..
Colony, Josiah	2	..	1	1	..	1	..	1	..	..	..
Conger, Job	2	1	3	..	1	5	1	1	..	1	..
Cook, Parsons	..	2	2	1	..	1	1	1	1	..	..
Cort, Daniel	1	1	..	1	..	3	..	..	1	..	..
Crippin, Alpheus	1	3	..	..	1	1	1	..	1	..	..
Curtis, Orringe	..	..	1	1	..	2	..	1	..	..	..
Davis, Elijah	3	..	..	..	1	1	3	..	1	..	..
Day, Oliver	2	..	..	1	..	2	1	..	1	..	..
Dean, Josiah D.	1	..	1	..	1	1	..	..	1	..	..
Delano, Jabez	1	1	2	1	..	..	1	1	..	..	..
Dotee, David	..	1	..	1	..	..	..	1	..	..	..
Dotee, Timothy	2	1	..	1	..	..	1	..	1	..	..
Dutcher, Christopher	1	1	6	1	1	..	2	..	1	..	..
Dutcher, Ruluff	1	1	..	1	..	3	2	1	1	..	..
Emery, Richard	1	2	2	..	1	4	1	..	2	..	..
Frary, Elisha	2	..	..	1	..	2	1	..	..	..	..
Fuller, Asa	1	..	1	1	1	2	..	..	1	..	..
Fuller, Reuben	3	1	2	..	1	..	..	2	..	1	..
Gates, John	2	..	..	1	..	3	..	..	1	..	..
Gibbs, Thomas	2	3	..	..	1	..	..	..	1	..	..
Gillman, John	1	..	2	1	..	2	1	..	1	..	..
Goodwin, Benjamin	1	1	1	..	1	..	..	2	..	2	..
Goodwin, Gillman	1	..	1	1	1	2	1	..	..	..	..
Green, Job	3	..	4	1	..	2	1	..	1	..	..
Green, Nathan	2	1	..	1	..	2	..	1	1	..	..
Griffith, William	3	..	..	..	1	1	2	..	1	..	..
Hall, Prince B.	..	1	..	1	..	..	..	1	..	..	..
Hatch, Barnabas	..	..	4	..	1	1	2	..	..	1	..
Hathaway, Alfred	2	1	1	..	1	3	1	1	1	..	..
Hathaway, Silas	3	..	2	1	..	1	2	1	2	..	..
Healy, Ebenezer	1	..	..	2	1	4	..	..	1	..	..
Hendrix, Eli	..	..	1	..	..	1	..	1	..	..	..
Hickcoth, Eliza	2	2	1	1	..	1	3	..	1	..	..
Hide, Asahel	3	..	5	1	1	1	1	1	2	1	..
Hilbard, Uriah	1	2	..	..	1	1	..	1	1	..	..
Hoadly, James	..	..	3	..	1	..	1	2	1	..	..
Hoit, Jonathan	2	2	3	..	1	1	..	2	1	..	..
House, Levi	1	1	3	1	..	..	..	1	..	..	..
Isham, William	1	3	..	1	..	1	1	..	1	..	..
Jewit, Eleazer	1	..	..	1	..	1	..	2	..	1	..
Johnson, William	..	..	..	..	..	..	..	..	..	..	2
Jones, Joseph	2	..	6	2	1	2	2	2	1	..	..
Kittle, Charles	2	..	..	1	..	..	..	1	..	..	..
Kittle, William	..	1	..	1	..	3	..	..	1	1	..
Lane, Samuel	1	1	..	..	1	2	1	1	1	2	..
Langdon, Barnabus	2	1	..	2	..	1	..	..	1	..	..
Lowell, Robert	2	1	..	..	1	2	..	..	1	..	..
Marsh, Lemuel	2	..	..	1	..	3	..	1	..	..	..
Meirs, Joseph	..	..	..	1	..	2	..	..	1	..	..
Moody, Noah	1	..	..	1	..	..	..	..	1	..	..
Morgan, Solomon	1	..	..	1	..	..	1	1	..	..	..
Morril, Amos	..	3	4	..	1	1	..	2	..	2	..
Nason, William	..	..	5	..	1	..	4	..	..	1	..
Oliver, Robert	3	..	..	1	..	3	..	..	1	..	..
Parsons, Samuel	1	..	1	1	..	..	..	2	..	..	..
Pitcher, Benjamin	1	..	1	1	..	..	..	1	1	..	..
Pitcher, Thomas	..	..	..	1	..	..	..	1	..	..	..
Pomeroy, Seth	..	..	3	1	..	..	..	2	..	..	..
Potter, Freeborn	3	1	..	2	..	2	..	1	1	..	..
Powers, David	1	..	2	4	1	..	2	2	..	1	..
Powers, David Jr.	2	..	..	1	..	1	1	..	..	..	..
Prentice, Jonathan	2	1	2	..	1	1	2	1	..	..	..
Ray, John	1	1	..	..	1	1	..	..	1	..	..
Reynols, Isaac	2	1	1	1	1	3	..	1	..	1	..
Rice, Thaddeus	..	..	2	2	..	1	1	2	..	1	..
Ryan, Daniel	..	2	..	1	..	..	..	2	..	..	..
Spencer, John	..	..	..	1	..	..	..	1	..	1	..
Spoor, Abraham	1	1	2	..	1	1	1	..	1	..	..
Spoor, Abraham 2nd	2	1	..		1	1	1	..	1	..	..

FRANKLIN COUNTY—Continued

NAMES OF HEADS OF FAMILIES	FREE WHITE MALES: Under 10 years of age	FREE WHITE MALES: Of 10 and under 16	FREE WHITE MALES: Of 16 and under 26 including heads of families	FREE WHITE MALES: Of 26 and under 45 including heads of families	FREE WHITE MALES: Of 45 and upwards including heads of families	FREE WHITE FEMALES: Under 10 years of age	FREE WHITE FEMALES: Of 10 and under 16	FREE WHITE FEMALES: Of 16 and under 26 including heads of families	FREE WHITE FEMALES: Of 26 and under 45 including heads of families	FREE WHITE FEMALES: Of 45 and upwards including heads of families	All other free persons except Indians not taxed
ST. ALBANS—con.											
Spoor, Isaac	1	..	2	1	..	..	..	1	..	..	..
Stevens, David	..	..	5	2	1	..	..	..	1	..	..
Stratton, David	2	1	2	..	..	2	3	1	..	..	..
Taylor, Hollaway	1	1	10	1	..	..	1	1	..	..	..
Taylor, John	..	..	1	..	1	..	..	1	..	1	..
Thurstin, Benjamin	1	..	..	1	..	2	..	..	1	..	..
Tibbitts, Henry	1	..	..	1	..	1	..	1	..	..	..
Tuller, Reuben Jr.	2	..	..	1	..	1	..	1	..	..	..
Turner, Bates	1	..	..	2	..	..	..	..	1	..	..
Walker, Lewis	2	..	..	1	..	2	..	1	1	..	..
Wares, William	1	..	1	1	..	..	..	1	1	..	..
Warner, John	2	1	4	..	1	1	1	1	1	..	..
Wells, Ezekiel	2	..	..	1	..	1	1	..	1	..	..
Wells, Russell	5	..	..	1	..	2	..	..	1	..	..
Wells, Samuel	3	..	..	1	..	2	..	..	1	..	..
Wentworth, John	3	..	..	1	..	1	..	..	1	..	..
Wetmore, Seth	..	..	..	1	..	..	..	1	..	..	..
Whittimore, John	2	1	..	2	..	1	1	..	1	..	..
Whittimore, Richard	1	..	..	1	..	2	..	..	1	..	..
Wickwire, Roswell	2	..	..	1	..	1	..	..	1	..	..
Willson, Bradley	1	..	..	1	..	1	..	..	1	..	..
Winchel, Jonathan	..	1	..	..	1	1	..	1	..	1	..
Winslow, Jared	3	..	..	1	..	..	..	..	1	..	..
Winslow, Jonathan	1	1	1	1	..	1	..	..	1	..	..
Withy, Francis	1	..	..	1	..	1	..	..	1	..	..
Wood, Enos	2	3	..	1	..	1	..	2	1	..	..
Wood, Nathan	1	..	2	1	..	3	1	1	1	..	..
UNCERTAIN NAME											
Swan (?), Augustus	1	..	1	1	..	2	..	1	1	..	..
STERLING											
McColister, Peter	..	..	1	..	..	1	..	1	..	..	..
McColister, William	..	2	..	1	..	2	..	1	..	..	..
SWANTON											
Abels, Asa	1	1	1	..	..	..	..	1	..	..	..
Abels, Jesse	1	..	..	1	..	1	..	..	1	..	..
Addams, John	..	1	2	1	1	..	1	1	..	1	..
Alford, Ashley	4	1	..	1	1	..	1	1	..	..	..
Andrews, Joseph	1	..	..	1	..	3	..	..	1	..	..
Arnold, Randol	4	1	1	1	..	..	..	1	..	..	..
Assletine, Hendrick	..	..	1	1	..	1	..	..	1	..	..
Assletine, Issac	1	..	..	1	..	..	2	..	1	..	..
Assletine, Peter	..	1	..	..	1	..	1	..	..	1	..
Assletine, Peter Jr.	..	1	1	..	1	..	1	..	1	..	..
Austin, John	2	1	..	1	..	1	4	..	1	..	..
Baker, Absalom	..	1	..	..	1	1	..	..	1	..	..
Baker, Constant	..	1	2	..	1	1	2	..	..	1	..
Baker, John	2	1	1	1	..	3	2	..	1	..	..
Baptist, John	3	1	1	1	..	1	1	3	..	..	..
Barney, Elisha	1	..	..	1	..	2	..	1	..	..	..
Barney, Rufus	..	..	6	1	2	..	..	..	..	..	..
Benton, Noah F.	1	..	1	2	..	1	..	1	..	..	..
Billings, Enoch	1	1	..	..	1	3	1	1	1	..	..
Bowers, Benjamin	2	..	..	1	..	1	..	..	1	..	..
Brooks, Jonathan	1	1	..	..	1	1	..	1	1	1	..
Brown, Benjamin	2	..	2	..	..	..	..	1	..	..	..
Brown, James	..	..	2	1	..	..	1	..	..	..	..
Brown, Purchis	3	1	1	1	..	1	1	..	1	..	..
Brown, Reuben	..	..	..	1	..	1	..	1	..	..	..
Burnard, Manassah	1	1	..	1	..	3	2	..	1	..	..
Butterfield, Thomas	..	1	2	..	1	3	..	..	1	..	..
Cady, ———	2	1	..	..	1	..	..	..	..	..	..
Calkins, Daniel	..	..	1	..	..	1	..	1	..	..	..
Calkins, John	..	..	..	1	1	1	..	1	..	1	..
Calkins, Joshua	1	..	..	..	1	..	1	2	1	1	..
Calkins, Mathias	1	1	..	1	..	2	..	1	..	..	..
Campbell, John	..	..	..	1	..	..	..	1	..	..	..
Clark, Card	2	1	..	1	..	1	..	..	1	..	..
Clark, Joseph	2	1	..	1	..	2	1	..	1	..	..
Clark, Thomas	2	1	..	1	..	2	1	..	1	..	..
Crawford, Andrew	..	1	1	3	..	..	..	1	..	..	..
Crawford, John	2	1	..	1	..	2	..	..	1	..	..
Daleo, Joseph	..	..	1	..	..	..	..	1	..	..	..
Duker, Brewer	..	..	2	..	1	..	..	..	1	..	..
SWANTON—con.											
Duker, John	1	..	..	1	..	..	..	1	..	..	..
Dunbar, John	..	..	..	1	..	3	..	..	2	..	..
Eastman, Amos	1	..	1	..	..	..	..	1	..	..	..
Eastman, Peter	2	1	..	1	..	1	1	..	1	..	..
Eastman, William	..	..	1	..	1	1	1	..	..	1	..
Eastman, William Jr.	2	..	..	1	..	1	..	1	..	..	..
Eastman, Zitton	..	..	..	1	..	1	..	..	1	..	..
Easton, William	2	..	..	1	..	3	2	..	1	..	..
Fay, Benjamin	..	..	2	..	..	..	..	1	..	..	..
Ferguson, Alexander	..	..	1	..	..	1	..	1	..	..	..
Foster, George W.	1	1	..	1	..	1	1	..	1	..	..
Foster, William	1	2	..	1	..	1	..	1	..	..	..
Francis, Lewis	..	..	..	1	..	..	..	..	1	..	..
Frelick, Merry	..	..	..	..	..	..	..	..	1	..	..
Goaff, John	..	..	2	..	1	..	..	1	..	..	..
Graham, James	..	..	..	1	..	2	..	..	1	..	..
Green, Asa	2	..	1	1	..	1	..	2	..	..	..
Green, William	2	..	..	1	..	3	..	..	1	..	..
Griffin, Joel	3	..	..	1	..	2	..	1	..	..	..
Griswold, Joseph	1	1	..	1	..	..	..	1	1	..	..
Hall, George	5	2	1	1	..	..	..	1	1	..	..
Harrington, Daniel	..	..	..	1	1	..	..	..	..	1	..
Harrington, Daniel Jr.	..	..	..	..	1	..	..	..	..	1	..
Hathaway, Levi	2	1	1	..	1	1	1	..	..	1	..
Herrick, Leonard	1	..	1	1	..	1	..	1	1	..	..
Holgall, James	..	1	..	..	..	..	1	1	..	..	..
Howe, Amasa	3	1	..	1	..	2	..	..	1	..	..
Howe, Charles	..	..	1	1	..	1	..	1	..	..	..
Hubbard, Clark	1	1	1	1	..	..	1	1	..	..	..
Hubbart, Moses	..	..	1	..	..	..	..	1	..	..	..
Hungerford, Levi	2	..	..	1	..	1	..	1	..	..	..
Hungerford, Simeon	4	..	1	1	..	1	1	..	1	..	..
Ingols, Daveris	..	2	1	..	1	2	..	1	1	..	..
Ingols, Parker	..	..	1	..	..	..	..	1	..	..	..
Jackson, Jacob	2	..	..	3	..	1	..	1	1	..	..
Johnson, Samuel	..	2	1	1	..	..	..	..	1	1	..
Lackey, Isaac	3	2	1	1	..	2	1	..	1	..	..
Lackey, Isaac Jr.	1	..	1	..	..	..	..	1	..	..	..
Lampkin, Philo	..	1	..	1	..	..	..	..	2	..	..
Lasell, Joshua	2	..	..	1	..	2	..	..	1	..	..
Lasell, Lemuel	2	..	1	1	..	2	1	..	1	..	..
Lewis, Asa	2	3	1	1	..	4	1	..	1	..	..
Lewis, John	..	1	..	..	..	..	..	1	..	..	..
Lewis, William	2	1	1	..	1	2	1	1	..	1	..
Lummis, Joseph	..	..	1	..	1	..	1	..	..	..	..
Manger, Martin	2	1	..	1	..	3	1	..	1	..	..
Mason, Robert	1	..	..	1	1	1	..	1	..	1	..
McClure, John	..	..	1	..	1	..	..	..	..	1	..
McClure, Moses	1	..	1	..	..	1	..	1	..	..	..
McNamara, John	1	..	..	..	1	1	2	..	1	..	..
Mead, Caleb	2	..	..	1	..	..	..	1	1	..	..
Meigs, Benjamin	3	1	..	1	..	..	..	..	1	..	..
Meigs, Daniel B.	2	2	2	1	..	..	1	..	1	..	..
Meigs, Elisha	3	1	3	1	1	..	1	1	..	1	..
Moor, Thomas	3	1	2	..	1	1	..	1	1	..	..
More, John	..	..	..	1	..	..	..	1	..	..	..
Nothrip, David	..	..	1	..	1	2	1	..	1	..	..
Oaks, John	1	2	1	..	1	1	..	1	..	1	..
Orcutt, Ebenezer	..	1	1	..	1	3	1	..	1	1	..
Orcutt, William	2	..	1	..	..	..	..	1	..	..	..
Owen, Ephraim	..	..	1	1	1	1	..	..	..	1	..
Pirrey, Earl	2	..	..	1	..	1	..	1	1	..	..
Potter, Noel	2	..	1	1	..	2	1	..	1	..	..
Pratt, John	2	1	1	..	1	3	..	2	1	..	..
Roberts, James	2	..	..	2	1	2	..	..	1	..	..
Robinson, Israel	2	..	..	1	..	2	..	1	..	..	..
Robinson, Joseph	2	..	2	..	..	2	..	1	..	..	..
Robinson, Leonard	..	1	2	..	1	1	1	1	..	1	..
Robinson, Paul	2	..	2	1	..	2	..	..	1	..	..
Rowley, Daniel	3	2	..	1	..	..	1	..	1	1	..
Rowley, Elijah	2	..	..	..	1	1	..	..	1	..	..
Scott, Levi	1	..	1	..	..	..	..	1	..	..	..
Scovil, Daniel	1	..	..	1	..	..	..	1	..	..	..
Scovil, Nathaniel	..	1	1	3	..	3	..	1	1	..	..

FRANKLIN COUNTY—Continued

NAMES OF HEADS OF FAMILIES	FREE WHITE MALES					FREE WHITE FEMALES					
	Under 10 years of age	Of 10 and under 16	Of 16 and under 26 including heads of families	Of 26 and under 45 including heads of families	Of 45 and upwards including heads of families.	Under 10 years of age	Of 10 and under 16	Of 16 and under 26 including heads of families	Of 26 and under 45 including heads of families	Of 45 and upwards including heads of families	All other free persons except Indians not taxed
SWANTON—con.											
Sheldon, Jonathan	2	..	..	1	..	1	2	..	1	..	..
Smith, John	..	..	..	1	..	1	1	..	1	..	..
Smith, Lemuel	..	1	1	1	..	1	..	1	1	..	..
Smith, Nathan	1	..	..	1	..	3	..	1	..	..	..
Smith, Orringe	2	1	1	1	..	..	2	1	..	..	..
Smith, Perez	3	1	..	1	..	1	1	..	1	..	..
Spoor, John	..	1	..	..	1	1	..	1	..	1	..
Stearns, Benjamin	3	..	..	1	..	1	1	..	1	..	..
Stewart, David	1	1	..	2	..	1	2	..	1	1	..
Taylor, James	3	1	..	1	..	..	1	..	1	..	..
Thomas, Henry	1	1	..	1	..	2	1	..	1	..	..
Tracy, James	3	..	..	1	..	1	..	..	1	..	..
Wadkins, George	..	..	..	1	..	1	..	1	..	..	..
Wait, Oliver	2	2	..	1	..	2	..	1	1	..	..
Warner, Isaac	1	..	..	1	..	..	..	1	..	..	..
Warner, John Jr.	..	..	..	1	..	1	..	1	..	..	..
Weed, Benjamin	2	1	..	..	1	2	..	..	1	..	..
White, Nathan	2	..	1	..	1	..	1	1	..	1	..
Willer, Jonathan	3	..	..	1	..	2	..	..	1	..	..
Willson, Asa	1	1	..	1	..	1	2	..	1	..	..
Witherell, Asa	1	..	..	1	..	2	1	..	1	..	..
Wood, Daniel	3	1	..	1	..	..	1	..	1	..	..
Wood, John	3	1	..	2	..	..	1	1	1	..	..
Wood, John	1	..	3	1	..	3	1	..	1	..	..
Wood, Silas	..	..	1	..	1	3	2	..	1	..	..
UNCERTAIN NAME											
Ruil (?), Hezekiah	..	..	..	1	..	..	..	1	..	..	..

ORANGE COUNTY

NAMES OF HEADS OF FAMILIES	FREE WHITE MALES					FREE WHITE FEMALES					
	Under 10 years of age	Of 10 and under 16	Of 16 and under 26 including heads of families	Of 26 and under 45 including heads of families	Of 45 and upwards including heads of families.	Under 10 years of age	Of 10 and under 16	Of 16 and under 26 including heads of families	Of 26 and under 45 including heads of families	Of 45 and upwards including heads of families	All other free persons except Indians not taxed
BARRE											
Abbot, Abijah	1	..	..	1	..	2	..	1	..	..	..
Adams, ———	..	1	..	..	..	2	..	..	1	..	..
Albee, Amaniah	..	..	..	1	..	2	..	..	1	..	..
Aldrich, Phinehas	2	..	1	..	..	..	1	1	..	..	..
Baker, John	2	..	..	1	..	1	..	1	..	..	..
Barton, James	..	..	..	1	..	2	..	..	1	..	..
Batchelder, Nathaniel	2	..	3	1	..	2	2	1	1	..	..
Bates, Carver	2	..	..	1	..	1	..	..	1	..	..
Bell, William	..	..	..	..	1	2	..	2	..	1	..
Bigelow, Addi	1	..	1	1	..	1	1	1	1	..	..
Bishop, Joel	..	..	1	..	1	2	..	2	..	1	..
Bixby, Roger	..	..	1	..	..	2	..	..	1	..	..
Bizzy, John	1	..	..	1	..	2	1	..	1	..	..
Blanchard, Asa	..	1	..	1	..	1	..	..	1	1	..
Blodget, Phillip	..	..	1	..	..	..	..	1	..	..	..
Boutwell, Asa	2	2	..	1	..	1	..	1	1	..	..
Brady, Patrick	..	..	..	..	1	..	..	1	..	1	..
Browning, Joseph	2	1	..	1	..	2	1	..	1	..	..
Burke, Elijah	1	..	3	1	..	..	..	1	1	1	..
Cameron, Daniel	1	..	1	..	..	..	..	1	..	..	..
Cameron, Duncan	..	..	1	..	1	..	..	..	..	1	..
Carleton, Jeremiah	1	..	1	1	..	..	..	1	..	..	..
Carpenter, Jetham	2	..	..	1	..	1	1	..	1	..	..
Carpenter, Nathaniel	3	1	..	1	..	1	..	..	1	..	..
Carpenter, Rembrance	2	..	..	1	..	3	..	..	1	..	..
Carpenter, Reuben	2	..	..	1	..	1	2	1	1	..	..
Carpenter, William B.	2	1	2	1	..	1	..	..	1	..	..
Chase, Levi	2	..	..	1	..	1	..	..	1	..	..
Clark, Francis	..	1	..	1	..	2	..	1	..	..	..
Conant, Amos	1	1	1	..	1	..	1	1	..	1	..
Conant, Charles	4	..	..	1	..	1	..	..	1	..	..
Cook, Samuel	2	..	2	1	..	..	..	1	..	..	..
Cook, Samuel D.	..	1	2	..	1	1	..	1	1	1	..
Culver, Jonathan	1	1	..	1	..	1	..	..	1	..	..
Dodge, Asa	3	..	..	1	..	..	..	..	1	..	..
Dodge, John	2	..	1	1	..	3	..	..	2	..	..
Dodge, Nathaniel B.	..	..	1	..	1	..	..	..	1	1	..
Dodge, Thomas	2	1	1	1	..	..	1	1	1	..	..
Dwight, Joseph	..	..	2	..	1	..	..	1	1	..	..
Everett, Stephen	..	..	1	..	..	1	..	1	..	..	..
Ewin, Josiah	1	..	1	1	..	1	..	..	1	..	..
Farewell, Lemuel	1	1	1	..	..	..	..	1	..	..	..
Farewell, William	..	..	2	..	1	..	1	..	1	..	..
Fiske, James	1	1	..	1	..	3	..	..	1	..	..
Freeman, Southwick	..	..	..	1	..	..	..	..	1	..	..
French, Bartholomew	..	2	2	..	1	6	1	1	1	..	..
Frost, Daniel	2	2	1	1	..	1	..	1	1	..	..
Fuller, Ignatius	1	..	..	1	..	3	1	..	1	..	..
Fuller, Nathaniel	2	..	..	1	..	2	..	1	..	..	..
Fuller, William	1	..	..	1	..	1	..	..	..	..	..
Gaffill, Aaron	3	..	..	1	..	1	..	..	1	..	..
Gale, Ebenezer B.	1	..	..	1	..	1	..	..	1	..	..
Gale, Elisha	1	..	4	1	1	1	1	2	..	1	..
Gale, Henry	2	3	3	..	1	1	1	..	1	..	..
Gale, Paul	2	1	..	1	..	3	2	1	1	..	..
BARRE—con.											
Gale, Peter	2	..	2	..	2	1	3	..	..	1	..
Glidden, Asa	..	..	3	..	..	1	..	1	..	..	..
Glitton, Joseph	2	..	1	..	1	2	3	2	1	..	..
Goodale, Edward	..	..	..	1	..	..	..	..	1	..	..
Gould, John	..	..	..	1	..	2	..	1	..	..	..
Gould, John Jr.	1	..	1	..	1	1	..	2	..	1	..
Gould, William	2	..	..	1	..	..	..	1	..	..	..
Gould, William	1	..	..	1	..	1	..	1	..	..	..
Gouldsbury, John	..	1	..	1	1	..	..	..	..	1	..
Gouldsbury, Sylvanus	2	..	..	1	..	1	..	..	1	..	..
Gouldsbury, William	3	..	..	1	..	..	..	1	1	..	..
Hale, Apollos	2	1	1	1	..	1	..	1	1	..	..
Harrington, Nathaniel	1	2	..	1	..	3	..	1	1	..	..
Herrick, John	1	..	..	1	..	3	1	..	1	..	..
Howard, Nathaniel	1	1	..	1	..	3	..	..	1	..	..
Howard, Sheffield	4	..	..	1	..	1	..	..	1	..	..
Ingalls, Joseph	1	1	..	1	..	..	1	..	1	..	..
Johannet, Peter	1	..	1	1	..	1	..	..	1	..	..
Kellogg, Joseph	2	..	..	1	..	1	..	..	1	..	..
Kellum, Nathaniel	2	1	3	..	1	2	1	..	1	..	..
Kellum, Samuel	1	..	1	..	..	..	..	1	..	..	..
Kingsley, Ebenezer	1	2	1	..	1	2	1	..	1	..	..
Leason, Nathaniel	2	..	..	1	..	1	..	..	1	..	..
May, Asa	2	..	..	1	..	1	..	..	1	..	..
May, John	..	..	..	..	1	..	..	..	..	1	..
Minard, Sherman	1	..	..	1	..	1	..	..	1	1	..
Moor, Thomas	1	..	..	1	..	2	..	..	1	..	..
Neilson, John D.	3	1	1	1	..	1	1	..	1	..	..
Nichols Thomas	2	1	1	1	..	..	..	..	1	..	..
Paddock, James	2	..	..	1	..	1	..	..	1	..	..
Paddock, James	2	..	..	1	..	1	..	1	..	..	..
Paddock, Robert	..	..	2	1	..	1	1	..	2	..	..
Patterson, Ansel	..	1	..	1	..	3	..	..	1	..	..
Patterson, Levi	..	..	..	1	..	..	..	1	..	..	..
Patterson, Timothy	..	..	..	..	1	..	..	..	..	1	..
Patterson, Timothy Jr.	..	..	..	1	..	..	..	1	..	..	..
Pearsons, Cornelius	2	..	1	1	..	2	..	..	1	..	..
Peck, Amaziah	..	2	1	..	1	1	..	1	1	..	..
Pettingill, Joshua	1	1	..	1	..	1	..	..	..	2	..
Phelps, Nathaniel	..	..	3	..	1	..	1	2	..	..	..
Pickering, Theophilus	..	..	2	..	..	1	..	1	..	..	..
Powers, Abraham	1	..	..	1	..	3	1	..	1	..	..
Rice, Israel	3	1	1	1	..	1	2	..	1	..	..
Richardson, Asa	3	..	..	1	..	1	..	..	1	..	..
Richardson, Benjamin	1	..	..	1	..	4	1	1	1	..	..
Richardson, David	2	..	1	1	..	3	..	2	1	..	..
Richardson, Phinehas	2	..	..	1	..	..	..	1	..	..	..
Robinson, William	3	1	2	..	1	..	1	..	..	1	..
Robinson, William Jr.	2	..	1	..	..	..	..	1	..	..	..
Rood, Joseph	1	..	..	1	..	4	..	..	2	..	..
Rood, Moses	..	2	2	..	1	..	..	2	..	1	..
Ross, Paul	..	..	1	..	..	..	..	1	..	..	..

ORANGE COUNTY—Continued

NAMES OF HEADS OF FAMILIES	FREE WHITE MALES: Under 10 years of age	FREE WHITE MALES: Of 10 and under 16	FREE WHITE MALES: Of 16 and under 26 including heads of families	FREE WHITE MALES: Of 26 and under 45 including heads of families	FREE WHITE MALES: Of 45 and upwards including heads of families	FREE WHITE FEMALES: Under 10 years of age	FREE WHITE FEMALES: Of 10 and under 16	FREE WHITE FEMALES: Of 16 and under 26 including heads of families	FREE WHITE FEMALES: Of 26 and under 45 including heads of families	FREE WHITE FEMALES: Of 45 and upwards including heads of families	All other free persons except Indians not taxed
BARRE—con.											
Scott, Jacob	1	..	..	1	..	..	..	..	1	..	..
Scott, Phillip	2	..	..	1	..	1	..	..	1	1	..
Sherman, Asaph	1	..	..	..	1	1	..	..	..	1	..
Sherman, Asaph Jr.	..	..	1	..	..	..	..	1	..	..	..
Sherman, Jonathan	2	1	..	1	..	2	1	..	1	..	..
Sherman, Nathan	..	..	1	..	1	..	1	1	..	1	..
Sherman, Samuel	2	..	..	1	..	1	..	..	1	..	..
Sinclair, Barnabas	1	1	2	..	1	2	..	..	1	..	..
Sisson, Elisha	..	1	..	1	..	1	1	..	1	..	..
Smith, Calvin	3	..	..	1	..	1	..	1	1	..	..
Smith, Jonathan	..	1	1	..	..	1	..	1	..	..	..
Southwick, Samuel	..	1	3	..	1	..	1	1	..	1	..
Stacy, Malam	..	..	..	1	..	2	..	1	1	..	..
Stacy, Warham	1	..	..	1	..	1	..	..	1	..	..
Sterling, Joseph	3	..	..	1	..	1	1	..	1	..	..
Taft, Caleb	..	..	1	..	..	..	..	1	..	..	..
Taft, Henry	..	..	2	1	1	..	..	2	..	1	..
Taft, Peter	1	..	..	1	..	1	..	..	1	..	..
Thompson, Joseph	2	..	..	1	..	1	..	..	2	..	..
Thompson, Phinehas	..	1	1	1	..	1	..	..	1	..	..
Thurston, Benjamin	..	..	2	..	1	..	..	..	1	..	..
Tinkum, Abel	2	1	2	..	1	3	2	..	1	..	..
Town, Enos	2	2	..	1	..	2	1	..	1	..	..
Trow, George	1	..	4	1	..	2	..	1	1	..	..
Twing, James	1	2	..	1	..	1	1	2	1	..	..
Walker, Benjamin	1	2	1	1	..	..	..	..	1	..	..
Walker, Benjamin Jr.	..	..	2	..	..	..	..	1	..	..	..
Waters, Timothy	..	1	1	1	..	2	3	1	1	..	..
Watson, Joseph	3	1	2	2	..	2	..	..	2	..	..
Webster, David	1	..	..	1	..	2	..	..	1	..	..
Wheaton, John	..	1	3	..	1	..	..	1	..	1	..
Wheeler, Ezekiel D.	..	..	1	1	..	4	1	..	1	..	..
Wheeler, Gardner	3	..	..	1	..	1	1	..	1	..	..
Willey, Judah	..	1	1	..	1	..	..	2	..	1	..
Wilson, James	2	..	..	1	..	1	..	1	..	..	..
Woods, Ezekiel	1	..	1	..	..	..	..	2	..	..	..
Woods, Israel	..	..	..	1	..	..	..	1	1	..	..
BERLIN											
Andrews, Abel	3	..	..	1	..	1	1	..	1	..	..
Andrews, Allen	1	..	..	1	..	2	..	..	1	..	..
Andrews, Elijah	1	3	1	1	..	2	..	..	1	..	..
Andrews, Josiah	..	..	..	1	..	..	..	..	1	..	..
Ayer, Jonathan	1	..	1	1	..	..	..	1	..	..	..
Bachelder, Increase	1	..	..	1	..	2	..	..	1	..	..
Baxter, Timothy	2	..	..	1	..	2	..	..	1	..	..
Bayley, Ebenezer	2	1	1	1	..	2	2	..	1	1	..
Bayley, Joshua	3	1	1	1	..	2	2	1	1	..	..
Benjamin, Josiah	1	..	..	1	..	3	..	..	1	..	..
Black, Jacob	2	..	1	..	1	2	2	1	..	1	..
Black, John	..	1	..	..	1	..	..	3	..	1	..
Black, John Jr.	1	..	..	1	..	1	..	1	..	..	..
Black, Paul	1	..	..	1	..	1	..	1	..	..	..
Brayman, James	2	1	..	1	..	2	..	..	1	..	..
Brown, Eliada	4	2	..	1	..	2	..	..	1	..	..
Brown, Gustus	..	..	..	1	..	4	..	..	2	..	..
Buck, William	3	1	2	1	..	1	1	..	1	..	..
Bulkeley, Charles	..	1	1	1	..	..	1	..	1	..	..
Clark, Moseley	1	..	1	..	..	1	..	..	1	..	..
Clark, Silas	4	1	..	1	..	1	1	..	1	..	..
Cole, Jesse	3	..	..	1	..	..	..	..	1	..	..
Collins, Calvin	2	1	1	..	1	2	..	1	..	..	..
Cotes, John	1	1	2	..	1	..	1	1	..	1	..
Coxe, Asa	..	..	..	1	..	2	..	..	1	..	..
Coxe, Jonathan	..	2	..	1	..	2	1	1	1	..	..
Culver, Jeremiah	1	..	..	1	..	1	1	..	1	..	..
Cummins, Jacob	1	1	..	1	..	1	..	..	1	..	..
Currier, Samuel	..	..	..	1	..	1	1	..	..	1	..
Dice, Simeon	2	..	1	1	..	1	..	..	1	..	..
Dice, William	..	..	1	1	..	..	..	1	..	..	..
Ellis, Jabez	2	..	..	1	..	3	..	1	1	..	..
Emerson, Jonathan	2	..	1	1	..	2	2	..	1	..	..
Emerson, Samuel	1	..	1	..	..	..	..	1	..	..	..
Field, Bennett	1	1	1	..	1	..	1	2	..	1	..
Flagg, William	1	2	..	1	..	..	1	1	..	1	..
Foster, Josiah	1	..	..	1	..	..	..	1	..	..	..
Fowler, Jacob	..	..	2	..	1	3	2	1	..	1	..
BERLIN—con.											
Goff, Aaron	..	..	..	1	1	..	..	1	..	1	..
Goodale, Thomas	2	..	..	1	..	2	1	..	1	..	..
Goodenough, Jonathan	..	1	2	..	1	..	..	2	..	1	..
Goodenough, Josiah	2	..	..	1	..	1	..	1	..	..	..
Gray, Richard M.	..	..	1	..	..	..	..	1	..	..	..
Greeley, Zebulon	1	..	..	1	..	1	..	..	1	..	..
Hidden, Gersham	..	..	..	1	..	..	..	..	..	..	..
Hill, Levi	2	3	1	1	..	1	..	1	..	..	..
Hollister, Jonathan	..	..	..	1	..	1	..	1	..	..	..
Hollister, Nathaniel	3	..	..	1	..	1	..	..	1	..	..
Holt, Ephraim	1	..	..	1	..	..	..	..	1	..	..
Holt, Maiston	..	..	..	..	1	..	1	..	1	..	..
Holt, Moses	2	..	..	1	..	1	..	1	..	..	..
House, Israel	2	2	1	1	..	3	..	..	1	..	..
Hubbard, Eliezer	1	..	1	..	1	..	1	..	..	1	..
Hubbard, Eliezer Jr.	1	1	..	..	1	2	1	2	..	1	..
Hubbard, Peter	1	..	1	1	..	..	..	..	1	..	..
Hubbard, Tilley	1	2	..	1	..	2	1	..	1	..	..
Johnson, John	..	..	..	1	3	..	1	1	..	..	..
Johnson, Seth	..	..	1	..	1	..	2	1	..	1	..
Johnson, Silas	2	..	..	1	..	1	..	..	1	..	..
Jones, Samuel	3	..	..	..	1	1	1	1	1	..	..
Knap, Abel	1	..	1	1	..	1	..	1	1	..	..
Leonard, Henry	..	..	..	1	..	1	..	1	..	..	..
Martin, Daniel	2	..	..	1	..	2	..	..	1	..	..
McCollister, James	2	..	..	1	..	3	..	..	1	..	..
McCollister, William	..	..	2	..	1	..	1	2	..	1	..
McCollister, William Jr.	1	..	..	1	..	1	..	1	..	..	..
Miller, Jonathan	..	..	..	1	..	..	..	..	..	..	..
Nye, David	1	1	1	1	..	..	1	1	1	..	..
Nye, Elijah	2	1	..	1	..	2	..	..	1	..	..
Nye, Solomon	2	..	..	..	1	2	1	1	1	..	..
Parker, Jonah	2	..	..	1	..	2	..	..	1	..	..
Paul, Abner	..	..	1	..	..	..	..	1	..	..	..
Pearsons, Stephen	2	1	1	1	..	1	..	1	..	..	..
Perley, James	3	..	..	1	..	1	1	..	1	..	..
Perley, John	4	1	..	1	..	..	2	1	1	..	..
Perrin, Zacchariah	2	2	1	..	1	1	2	1	1	..	..
Phelps, Joel	1	..	..	1	..	..	..	1	..	..	..
Phelps, John	..	..	..	1	..	2	..	1	..	..	..
Pierce, Asaph	1	..	..	1	..	2	..	1	..	..	..
Pierce, Gurdon	2	..	..	1	..	1	..	..	1	..	..
Poor, Jesse	1	..	..	1	..	1	..	1	..	..	..
Poor, Job	3	..	..	1	..	1	..	1	..	..	..
Rice, Peleg	..	..	..	..	1	..	1	..	..	1	..
Richardson, Jonathan	1	..	..	1	..	2	..	..	1	..	..
Sawyer, Abel	1	1	..	1	..	4	..	..	1	..	..
Sawyer, James	..	..	..	..	1	..	..	..	..	1	..
Sawyer, James Jr.	..	..	..	2	..	..	..	..	..	..	..
Scott, Elotas	..	..	1	..	..	..	..	..	..	..	..
Scott, Samuel	1	..	..	1	..	..	..	..	1	..	..
Scott, Samuel Jr.	4	..	..	1	..	..	..	..	1	..	..
Shirtleaf, Carver	1	..	..	1	..	3	..	1	..	..	..
Shirtleaf, Joel	2	..	..	1	..	3	..	..	1	..	..
Shirtleaf, Troas	..	..	..	1	..	3	..	..	1	..	..
Silliway, Aaron	5	1	..	1	..	1	..	..	1	..	..
Silliway, Hezekiah	..	2	3	..	1	..	..	..	1	1	..
Smith, Enoch	3	1	..	1	..	2	2	..	1	1	..
Smith, Ephraim	1	..	..	1	..	3	..	..	1	..	..
Smith, Samuel	3	1	..	1	..	1	2	..	1	..	..
Stewert, Simpson	..	1	1	..	1	3	1	..	..	1	..
Stickney, Lemuel	..	1	1	..	1	1	1	1	..	1	..
Strong, Aaron	1	..	..	1	..	2	1	..	1	..	..
Strong, Amos	1	..	3	..	..	2	..	1	..	..	..
Strong, Reuben	1	..	..	1	..	..	..	1	..	..	..
Taplin, John	4	1	1	..	1	1	..	1	1	..	..
Taylor, Daniel	3	2	..	1	..	2	..	..	1	..	..
Thompson, Stephen	1	..	1	1	..	2	..	1	..	..	..
Ticktum, Elizabeth	..	..	..	..	..	1	..	1	..	1	..
Urbuckle, Joseph	4	1	2	..	1	2	1	..	1	..	..
Wallace, Matthew	..	1	2	..	1	..	..	3	..	1	..
Warren, Joel	1	..	..	1	..	..	..	..	..	..	..
Wright, Elijah	3	1	..	1	..	3	..	..	1	..	..
UNCERTAIN NAME											
Cose (?), Robert	1	2	..	1	..	3	2	..	1	..	..

ORANGE COUNTY—Continued

NAMES OF HEADS OF FAMILIES	FREE WHITE MALES					FREE WHITE FEMALES					
	Under 10 years of age	Of 10 and under 16	Of 16 and under 26 including heads of families	Of 26 and under 45 including heads of families	Of 45 and upwards including heads of families.	Under 10 years of age	Of 10 and under 16	Of 16 and under 26 including heads of families	Of 26 and under 45 including heads of families	Of 45 and upwards including heads of families	All other free persons except Indians not taxed
BRAINTREE											
Banister, Levi	2	..	1	..	1	2	3	..	..	1	..
Bass, Isaac	..	..	..	1	..	..	..	1	1	..	..
Bass, Samuel	..	2	3	..	1	..	2	1	..	1	..
Bass, William	..	..	1	..	..	..	..	..	..	..	..
Belcher, Elisha	1	..	..	1	..	1	..	..	1	..	..
Bracket, Henry	3	..	..	1	..	2	1	..	1	..	..
Bradley, Hope	3	1	..	1	..	2	1	..	1	..	..
Brownson, Sylvester	2	..	..	1	..	1	..	..	1	..	..
Burke, John	..	..	1	..	1	..	..	..	..	..	1
Burrage, John	1	..	2	..	1	2	..	..	..	1	..
Copeland, Zion	3	..	..	1	..	1	..	..	1	..	..
Curtis, Simeon	3	..	..	1	..	..	1	..	1	..	..
Doleby, Exeter	..	..	..	..	..	..	..	..	..	..	4
Doleby, Peter	..	..	..	..	..	..	..	..	..	..	6
Dubois, Joseph	1	..	1	..	..	..	..	1	..	..	..
Dunbar, Zebulon	..	..	..	..	..	..	..	..	..	..	8
Dyer, Ichabod	..	1	..	..	1	..	1	..	..	1	..
Dyer, Ichabod Jr.	2	..	..	1	..	2	..	..	1	..	..
Dyer, Samuel	2	..	1	..	..	..	..	1	..	..	..
Fish, Nathan	1	1	..	1	..	2	1	..	1	..	..
Fitz, Clark	2	..	..	1	..	1	..	1	..	..	..
Fitz, Samuel	1	3	..	..	1	2	1	..	..	1	..
Flint, Asahel	..	..	..	1	..	..	..	..	..	..	..
Flint, Daniel	1	1	..	1	..	3	1	..	1	..	..
Flint, Phinehas	..	2	1	..	1	4	1	..	..	1	..
Flint, Rufus	1	..	..	1	..	..	..	..	1	..	..
Ford, Phinehas	..	..	..	1	..	..	..	..	1	..	..
Ford, Stephen	..	..	..	1	..	..	..	..	1	..	..
Ford, William	..	1	3	..	1	..	..	1	..	1	..
Ford, William Jr.	2	..	..	1	..	1	..	1	1	..	..
Frazier, Charles	1	..	..	1	..	1	..	..	1	..	..
Freeman, Edward	2	1	..	1	..	..	..	..	1	..	..
French, Jedidiah	2	..	..	1	..	2	..	..	1	..	..
French, John	1	2	1	..	1	3	1	1	..	1	..
French, Sarah	3	..	1	1	..	1	1	..	..	1	..
Fuller, Stephen	3	2	..	1	..	1	1	..	1	..	..
Garner, Robert	2	1	..	1	..	1	2	..	1	..	..
Gouge, John	..	..	..	1	1	2	..	..	1	1	..
Green, Alpha	1	..	..	1	..	1	..	..	1	..	..
Green, William	..	1	..	..	1	..	1	..	..	1	..
Harwood, Samuel	..	1	4	..	1	..	..	1	1	..	..
House, Stephen	2	..	..	1	..	..	..	..	1	1	..
Howard, Abiel	1	..	..	1	..	2	..	..	1	..	..
Hunt, Seth	2	1	..	1	..	2	..	..	1	..	..
Huntington, Asa	3	..	..	..	2	3	2	1	..	1	..
Hutchinson, John	2	..	..	1	..	2	..	..	1	..	..
Hutchinson, Lot	..	..	2	..	1	..	..	..	..	1	..
Kidder, Francis	..	..	..	1	..	..	..	1	..	..	..
Kidder, John	1	3	..	..	1	..	..	3	..	1	..
Kidder, Lyman	..	..	1	1	..	1	..	1	..	..	..
Kinney, James	1	..	..	1	..	..	..	..	1	..	..
Kinney, Nathan	1	1	1	..	..	..	..	1	..	..	..
Kinney, Rufus	3	..	..	1	..	1	..	..	1	..	..
Kinney, Thomas	..	1	..	..	1	..	..	..	..	1	..
Lamb, Amos	1	..	..	1	..	1	..	..	1	..	..
Leason, Bezahel	1	..	..	..	1	2	..	..	1	..	..
Lovewell, Joseph	..	..	..	1	..	..	..	..	1	..	..
Mann, Job	..	1	..	1	..	3	..	..	1	..	..
Mann, Seth	5	2	1	..	1	3	1	2	..	1	..
May, David	..	..	1	..	..	1	..	1	..	..	..
Nichols, Caleb	..	..	1	..	..	..	..	1	..	..	..
Nichols, Isaac	..	1	..	1	..	1	..	..	..	..	1
Nichols, Isaac Jr.	1	..	..	1	..	2	..	..	1	..	..
Nichols, Sampson	3	1	..	1	..	..	1	..	1	..	..
Pamilee, Eliezer	2	2	..	1	..	2	..	..	1	..	..
Parker, James	1	..	..	1	1	..	..	..	1	..	..
Parker, (Widow)	..	..	2	..	..	..	..	..	..	1	..
Parmelee, Jehiel	..	..	1	1	1	..	..	1	..	1	..
Pratt, Martha	3	1	..	1	..	4	2	..	1	..	..
Presson, Charles	1	1	..	1	..	2	..	..	1	..	..
Reed, John	2	..	..	1	..	2	1	..	1	..	..
Rice, John	1	..	..	1	..	1	1	..	1	..	..
Ryeford, Joseph	4	1	..	1	..	1	1	1	..	1	..
Smith, David	2	..	..	1	..	..	..	..	2	..	..
Smith, Seth	..	..	1	1	..	..	..	..	..	1	..
Spear, Jacob	4	..	2	..	1	..	1	..	1	..	1
BRAINTREE—con.											
Spear, Jacob Jr.	1	..	1	1	..	..	1	1	1	..	..
Spear, Joseph	..	1	..	1	..	1	..	1	..	..	..
Spear, Samuel	..	..	..	..	1	1	2	1	..	1	..
Spears, Nathaniel	2	2	2	..	1	..	1	..	..	1	..
Stacy, Joseph	..	1	1	1	..	..	..	..	1	..	..
Stedman, Henry	..	..	..	1	..	1	..	1	..	..	..
Trask, Peter	1	..	..	1	..	1	..	..	1	..	..
Tucker, Elisha	..	..	..	1	..	..	..	..	..	..	..
Wait, Daniel	1	..	..	1	..	1	..	1	1	..	..
Wakefield, Asahel	1	..	..	1	..	3	..	..	1	..	..
Wells, Samuel	1	..	..	1	..	2	..	..	1	..	..
White, Ebenezer	1	..	1	1	..	2	..	1	..	..	..
Whiting, Azias	..	..	..	1	..	2	3	..	..	1	..
Willington, Benjamin	2	..	..	1	..	1	..	..	1	..	..
UNCERTAIN NAMES											
Fais (?), Benjamin	2	..	..	1	..	2	..	2	1	..	..
Masey (?), Robert	..	1	1	..	1	3	1	2	..	1	..
BRADFORD											
Aldrich, Silas	1	2	1	..	1	1	1	1	..	1	..
Andrews, John	3	1	..	1	..	..	1	..	1	..	..
Andrews, Levi	1	1	1	..	2	2	1	..	1	..	..
Aspinall, John	..	..	2	..	..	..	..	1	..	..	..
Ayer, Timothy	1	1	1	..	1	..	1	2	..	1	..
Bachelder, Isaiah	2	..	1	..	1	3	..	2	..	2	..
Baldwin, Benjamin	..	1	2	1	1	2	..	1	..	2	..
Baldwin, Theophilus	1	1	..	1	..	..	..	..	1	..	..
Banfill, Sarah	..	..	..	1	..	..	..	..	..	1	..
Barker, Theodore	1	1	..	1	..	3	2	..	1	..	..
Barron, John	1	..	1	..	1	1	1	3	..	1	..
Barron, Joshua	1	..	2	..	1	2	..	..	1	..	..
Barron, Micah	..	2	1	1	..	2	1	1	2	..	..
Bartlet, Edmund	3	..	..	1	..	2	1	..	1	..	..
Bliss, David	1	..	..	1	..	1	..	..	1	..	..
Bliss, Ellis	2	1	1	1	..	..	1	1	1	..	..
Bliss, John	..	1	1	1	..	..	1	..	1	..	..
Brown, Edmund	..	..	2	..	2	..	2	..	..	2	..
Bullock, Squire	1	1	..	1	..	2	..	..	1	..	..
Burt, Francis	1	..	..	1	..	..	..	1	..	..	..
Burt, Joseph	..	..	..	1	..	..	..	..	1	..	..
Cady, Cyrall	1	1	..	1	..	2	..	1	1	..	..
Cady, Zadock	..	..	..	1	..	1	..	..	1	..	..
Carter, Noah	..	..	..	1	..	1	2	..	1	..	..
Casco, Silas	..	..	..	..	..	..	..	..	..	..	3
Cass, Chandler	2	1	..	1	..	2	..	..	1	..	..
Cass, Samuel	2	..	..	1	..	..	..	..	1	..	..
Chadwick, John	..	1	..	1	..	..	1	..	1	..	..
Chamberlin, Moses	1	1	1	..	1	3	..	1	2	..	..
Chase, Moses	1	1	..	1	..	1	..	..	1	..	..
Chase, Simeon	1	..	..	1	..	3	2	..	1	..	..
Cheeney, Elias	..	1	..	1	..	1	..	..	2	..	..
Chenniday, Patrick	1	3	..	..	1	3	..	..	..	1	..
Clark, John	1	..	..	..	1	3	..	..	1	..	..
Clark, John	1	1	2	1	..	..	..	1	..	1	..
Clark, Joseph	2	1	2	..	1	1	2	..	..	2	..
Colby, Joseph	1	1	1	..	1	1	..	1	..	1	..
Collins, Ephraim	..	..	1	..	..	..	1	1	..	..	..
Collins, Ichabod	..	3	..	..	1	1	1	2	..	1	..
Collins, Levi	3	..	..	1	..	2	1	..	1	..	..
Collins, Moses	..	..	1	..	..	..	..	1	..	..	..
Collins, Richard	..	..	1	..	..	2	..	1	..	..	..
Colman, Jacob	1	1	..	1	..	2	1	..	1	..	..
Corlis, Pelatiah	2	1	..	1	..	3	1	..	1	..	..
Corliss, David	..	..	..	1	..	..	..	1	1	1	..
Corliss, Emerson	1	..	..	1	..	2	1	..	1	..	..
Crane, Daniel O.	1	..	..	1	..	2	..	..	1	1	..
Darling, Peter	1	..	1	..	1	1	..	1	..	1	..
Davis, Obediah	..	1	..	..	1	..	..	..	..	1	..
Davis, Samuel	3	1	..	1	..	3	2	..	1	..	..
Davis, William	..	1	1	..	..	2	..	1	..	1	..
Dean, Leonard	1	1	1	1	..	1	..	1	..	1	..
Dick, Stephen	1	..	..	1	..	2	..	..	1	..	..
Dickey, Samuel	..	..	..	1	..	..	1	..	1	..	..
Eastman, Josiah	..	1	..	1	..	2	2	..	1	..	..

ORANGE COUNTY—Continued

NAMES OF HEADS OF FAMILIES	FREE WHITE MALES					FREE WHITE FEMALES					
	Under 10 years of age	Of 10 and under 16	Of 16 and under 26 including heads of families	Of 26 and under 45 including heads of families	Of 45 and upwards including heads of families.	Under 10 years of age	Of 10 and under 16	Of 16 and under 26 including heads of families	Of 26 and under 45 including heads of families	Of 45 and upwards including heads of families	All other free persons except Indians not taxed
BRADFORD—con.											
Fifield, David	2	1	..	1	..	3	..	..	1	..	..
Flanders, James	..	..	..	1	..	..	..	1	..	..	..
Flanders, John	1	..	..	1	1	1	..	..	1	..	..
Fuller, Lemuel	2	..	..	1	..	2	1	..	1	..	..
Garfill, John	1	..	..	1	..	3	..	..	1	..	..
George, Gideon	2	1	..	..	1	1	1	1	1	..	..
George, Stephen	1	..	1	..	..	..	..	1	..	..	..
Gerry, Joshua	1	..	..	1	..	3	3	..	1	..	..
Gerry, William	1	..	..	1	..	2	..	..	1	..	..
Hall, Roland C.	1	..	..	1	..	2	..	..	1	..	..
Heath, Amos	..	..	1	..	1	..	..	..	..	1	..
Heath, Daniel	1	..	1	1	..	2	..	..	1	..	..
Heath, Isaac	1	1	2	..	1	3	..	1	..	1	..
Heath, Isaac Jr.	..	..	1	..	..	..	..	1	..	..	..
Heath, Thomas	1	..	..	1	..	..	..	1	..	..	..
Hidden, Ebenezer	2	..	1	1	..	1	..	1	..	..	..
Hinks, John	..	2	2	..	1	2	1	..	..	1	..
How, Eliakim	2	..	..	1	..	2	1	..	1	..	..
Howe, Jonathan	..	..	..	1	..	1	..	..	1	..	..
Hunkins, Robert	..	1	2	1	1	1	1	2	..	1	..
Jenkins, Joseph	2	..	..	1	..	2	..	..	1	..	..
Jenkins, Stephen	..	1	1	1	..	3	1	..	1	..	..
Johnson, David	1	..	..	1	..	1	..	..	1	..	..
Johnson, Joseph	3	..	1	1	..	..	..	..	1	..	..
Kellogg, Gardner	..	..	1	1	..	1	1	1	..	..	..
Kelly, Benjamin	1	..	..	1	..	..	..	..	1	..	..
Kelly, Daniel	..	1	..	..	1	1	1	..	..	1	..
Kimball, Daniel	1	..	..	1	..	2	..	..	1	..	..
Kinney, Henry	..	..	1	..	1	..	..	1	..	1	..
Lamb, John	1	..	..	1	..	..	..	..	1	..	..
Leach, James	..	..	1	..	1	..	..	2	..	1	..
Lee, Stephen	2	1	1	1	..	3	2	..	1	..	..
Little, Benjamin	..	1	..	..	1	..	..	..	..	1	..
Martin, Ephraim	..	..	..	..	1	..	..	1	..	1	..
Martin, Ephraim Jr.	2	..	1	..	1	3	..	1	..	1	..
Martin, Jonathan	3	..	..	1	..	2	..	..	1	..	..
Martin, Moses	1	..	..	1	..	1	..	..	1	..	..
Martin, Nathaniel	2	1	..	1	..	2	..	1	1	..	..
Martin, Reuben	..	1	1	1	..	6	2	..	1	..	..
Martin, Samuel	3	..	1	..	..	3	..	..	1	..	..
May, Thomas	3	..	2	1	..	3	..	1	1	..	..
McConnell, Stevens	1	1	2	..	1	1	..	1	..	1	..
McDuffe, Daniel	..	..	2	..	1	1	1	2	..	1	..
McDuffe, John	1	..	..	1	..	..	..	1	1	..	..
McDuffe, Samuel	1	..	..	1	..	1	..	..	1	..	..
McIntire, Hugh	2	..	..	..	1	3	1	..	1	..	..
McKellup, Samuel	1	2	1	..	1	2	1	..	..	1	..
Merrill, David	..	..	..	1	..	4	..	..	1	..	..
Merrill, Jesse	1	..	..	1	..	..	..	1	1	..	..
Merrill, Nathaniel	..	..	..	1	..	2	..	..	1	..	..
Moor, John	1	1	..	1	..	2	1	..	1	..	..
Moor, Robert	1	..	..	1	..	1	..	1	1	1	..
Munn, Ralph	..	..	..	1	..	..	1	..	1	..	..
Nasmith, Benjamin	2	2	3	..	1	..	1	..	..	1	..
Newell, Joshua	2	..	1	1	..	2	1	..	1	..	..
Nouross, David	2	..	..	1	..	1	..	..	1	..	..
Obrey, Frederick	2	..	..	..	1	2	1	1	1	1	..
Olmstead, Ebenezer	3	1	..	1	..	2	1	..	1	..	..
Olmstead, Joseph	..	2	2	..	1	..	..	2	..	1	..
Olmsted, John	..	..	..	1	1	4	..	..	1	..	..
Osborne, Lemuel	..	..	..	1	..	1	..	1	1	1	..
Palmer, Daniel	1	..	..	1	..	2	..	..	1	..	..
Peters, Andrew B.	3	..	..	1	..	1	..	..	1	..	..
Picket, William	..	..	..	1	..	..	..	1	..	1	..
Pratt, Edward	1	1	..	1	..	2	1	..	1	..	..
Putnam, John	2	1	..	1	..	2	..	..	1	..	..
Ring, Issacher	..	..	..	..	1	1	..	..	..	1	..
Ring, Stephen	..	..	1	..	..	2	..	1	..	..	..
Rogers, Elizabeth	..	..	..	..	..	..	..	..	..	1	..
Rogers, Perly	2	1	..	1	..	1	1	..	1	..	..
Rollins, Stephen	..	..	1	..	1	..	1	1	..	1	..
Rowe, Elijah	2	..	..	1	..	2	..	..	1	..	..
Rowell, Elijah	2	..	..	1	..	2	..	..	1	..	..
Rowell, Thomas	4	..	1	2	1	2	1	..	2	2	..
Sawyer, Ezekiel	1	..	2	..	1	1	..	2	..	1	..
Seavey, William	..	..	..	1	..	1	..	..	1	..	..
Severance, Peter	1	1	2	..	1	..	1	1	1	1	..
Sharp, Jeptha	..	..	..	..	..	..	..	..	..	..	6
Simpson, Alexander	3	..	1	2	..	3	..	..	2	..	..
Simpson, Willliam	..	1	..	3	1	..	1	..	..	2	3
Smith, Aaron	..	2	2	..	1	1	1	2	..	1	..
Stearns, Elias	1	2	2	..	1	3	..	1	..	1	..
Stearns, Zenas	..	1	..	1	..	1	..	..	1	..	..
Stebbins, Arad	..	1	3	1	..	5	..	2	1	..	..
Stebbins, Eli	3	..	..	1	..	1	..	..	1	..	..
Stevens, Daniel	..	..	1	..	..	..	..	1	..	..	..
Stevens, Eliphalet	1	..	..	1	..	4	2	..	1	..	..
Stevens, Nicholas	1	..	..	..	1	3	1	..	1	..	..
Stevens, Otho	1	1	..	1	..	3	..	..	1	..	..
Stone, Isaiah	2	1	..	1	..	2	1	..	1	..	..
Sweat, Paul	3	..	1	..	..	..	..	1	..	..	..
Sweat, Silas	..	1	2	..	2	..	..	1	..	1	..
Tabor, Stephen	2	2	1	..	1	3	1	3	1	..	..
Taylor, John	1	1	..	..	1	3	1	1	1	1	..
True, Joshua	1	..	..	1	..	1	..	..	1	..	..
Underwood, John	4	2	2	..	1	..	1	1	..	1	..
Wallace, Joseph	..	..	..	1	..	2	..	..	1	..	..
Warren, Benjamin	3	..	..	1	..	3	..	..	1	..	..
Warthen, Thomas	2	1	..	1	..	..	3	2	..	1	..
Welton, Peter	..	1	1	..	1	..	1	1	..	1	..
Welton, Peter Jr.	2	..	..	1	..	1	..	..	1	..	..
Wheaton, Jeremiah	1	..	..	1	..	1	..	..	1	..	..
Whitcomb, Benjamin	..	..	..	1	..	3	..	..	1	..	..
White, Nicholas	1	..	1	..	1	3	..	..	1	..	..
Wild, Asa	2	..	..	..	1	1	..	..	..	1	..
Willson, James	1	1	..	2	..	2	..	..	1	..	..
Wilson, David	4	..	..	1	..	..	..	..	1	..	..
Woodward, Joseph	3	..	..	1	..	3	..	1	..	..	..
Worthley, Jesse	..	..	..	1	..	1	..	..	1	..	..
Wright, Locke	..	..	..	1	..	1	..	..	1	..	..
Wright, Simeon	1	..	..	1	..	..	..	1	..	..	..
BROOKFIELD											
Abbott, Henry	..	1	2	..	1	1	..	2	..	2	..
Adams, Reuben	1	2	..	1	..	1	..	3	1	..	..
Adams, Thomas	..	2	2	..	1	..	..	..	..	1	..
Ainsworth, Ebenezer	4	..	..	1	..	..	2	..	1	..	..
Allen, Nathan	2	1	..	1	..	1	..	..	1	..	..
Alvord, Enos	1	..	..	1	..	1	..	..	1	..	..
Alvord, Nathan	..	..	..	..	1	..	..	..	..	1	..
Alvord, Nathan Jr.	2	..	1	..	..	..	..	1	..	..	..
Arnold, Phinehas	1	..	..	1	..	1	..	..	1	..	..
Bagley, Samuel Jr.	3	..	..	1	..	..	..	1	..	..	..
Barlow, Timothy	1	..	..	1	..	2	..	..	1	..	..
Bayley, Josiah	..	..	1	..	..	1	..	..	1	..	..
Bayley, Samuel	..	3	2	..	1	..	..	1	1	1	..
Bean, Fulsome	4	..	..	2	..	1	..	..	1	..	..
Belden, Paul	1	2	1	1	..	2	..	..	1	..	..
Bigelow, Amasa	..	..	2	..	1	1	..	..	..	1	..
Bigelow, Barna	1	..	5	1	..	1	..	1	1	..	..
Bigelow, David	2	..	..	2	..	2	1	..	1	..	..
Bigelow, Josiah	1	1	..	1	..	2	2	..	1	..	..
Bigelow, Timothy	3	2	..	1	..	..	1	..	1	..	..
Bigelow, Zelotus	1	..	..	1	..	2	..	..	1	..	..
Bodwell, Daniel	1	..	1	..	..	..	..	1	..	..	..
Bodwell, John	3	..	..	1	..	..	..	..	1	..	..
Bottom, Joseph	..	1	..	1	..	2	..	..	1	..	..
Bradford, Robert	2	..	1	1	..	1	..	..	1	..	..
Burnham, Elijah	4	1	1	1	..	1	2	..	1	..	..
Burnham, Walter	1	..	1	1	..	1	..	..	1	..	..
Burrows, Timothy	1	1	1	..	1	1	1	2	..	1	..
Carby, Ichabod	..	..	..	..	1	..	..	..	..	1	..
Carleton, Ruchard	1	3	..	..	1	..	..	..	..	1	..
Carpenter, Comfort	1	..	..	1	..	1	..	1	..	..	..
Clark, Luke	3	..	..	2	..	2	..	..	1	..	..
Colburn, Micajah Jr.	..	..	..	1	..	1	..	..	1	..	..
Colburn, Silas	..	2	..	..	1	..	..	2	1	1	..
Colburn, William	3	..	..	1	..	1	..	..	1	..	..
Cole, Abner	1	..	1	..	..	1	..	..	1	..	..
Cole, Timothy	2	2	3	..	1	1	..	..	..	1	..
Colt, Benjamin	1	..	..	1	..	3	1	..	1	..	..
Converse, Nathaniel	1	..	1	..	1	..	2	..	..	1	..
Craniker, John	..	..	..	..	1	..	..	3	..	1	..
Davidson, Paul	1	..	1	..	1	2	2	..	..	1	..
Dawing, Francis	..	..	..	1	..	3	1	..	1	..	..
Durkee, Oliver	..	..	..	..	1	..	..	..	..	1	..

ORANGE COUNTY—Continued

NAMES OF HEADS OF FAMILIES	FREE WHITE MALES: Under 10 years of age	FREE WHITE MALES: Of 10 and under 16	FREE WHITE MALES: Of 16 and under 26 including heads of families	FREE WHITE MALES: Of 26 and under 45 including heads of families	FREE WHITE MALES: Of 45 and upwards including heads of families.	FREE WHITE FEMALES: Under 10 years of age	FREE WHITE FEMALES: Of 10 and under 16	FREE WHITE FEMALES: Of 16 and under 26 including heads of families	FREE WHITE FEMALES: Of 26 and under 45 including heads of families	FREE WHITE FEMALES: Of 45 and upwards including heads of families	All other free persons except Indians not taxed
BROOKFIELD—con.											
Easterbrooks, Nehemiah	2	1	..	..	1	1	1	3	..	1	..
Edgerton, David	2	..	..	1	..	..	2	1	1	..	..
Edgerton, Uriah	4	2	..	..	1	..	..	2	1	..	..
Edson, Amasa	2	1	..	1	..	2	..	..	1	..	..
Edson, Daniel	1	..	2	..	1	..	..	1	..	1	..
Edson, Daniel	1	..	2	..	1	..	1	..	..	1	..
Edson, Jonathan	1	2	..	1	..	2	..	1	1	..	..
Edson, Timothy	1	..	..	1	..	1	..	1	..	..	..
Ellis, Elisha	2	..	2	..	1	..	1	2	..	1	..
Ferry, Lyman	1	..	..	1	..	2	2	..	1	..	..
Fiske, Experience	3	..	2	..	1	1	2	..	1	..	..
Freeman, Samuel	1	2	..	..	1	1	..	..	1	..	..
Gallup, Joseph	3	2	..	1	..	2	..	1	1	..	..
Gaylor, Hezekiah	1	1	1	1	1	3	1	1	..	1	..
Gaylor, Hezekiah Jr.	4	..	..	1	..	..	..	..	1	..	..
Gould, Daniel	1	..	..	1	..	..	..	..	1	..	..
Green, Arby	2	..	..	1	1	2	..	..	1	1	..
Green, Lampson	1	..	..	1	..	..	..	..	1	..	..
Griswold, Frederick	..	..	1	1	..	..	..	..	1	..	..
Grover, Amaziah	..	..	..	..	1	1	1	..	..	1	..
Guster, Josiah	2	1	1	..	1	2	1	..	..	1	..
Hamilton, Oliver	..	1	1	..	1	1	1	1	..	1	..
Harding, Samuel	2	..	..	1	..	3	..	..	1	..	..
Harrington, John	2	2	..	1	..	..	1	..	1	..	..
Hatch, Ashur	2	1	..	1	..	2	..	..	1	..	..
Herrick, David	..	..	..	1	..	2	..	..	1	..	..
Hibbard, John	3	..	..	1	..	1	..	..	1	..	..
Hibbard, Roger	2	1	2	..	1	1	1	..	1	..	..
Hopkins, Stephen	1	..	..	1	..	2	1	..	1	..	..
Hovey, Rufus	2	..	..	1	..	2	..	1	..	..	..
Hovey, Samuel	..	1	2	..	1	..	1	2	..	1	..
Hovey, Samuel Jr.	..	..	1	..	..	..	1	..	1	..	..
Hubbard, Moses	1	..	1	..	1	2	2	1	..	1	..
Humphrey, Amos	1	1	1	1	..	..	1	..	1	..	..
Humphrey, James	3	..	2	..	1	1	2	2	1	..	..
Humphrey, Lewis	2	..	..	1	..	2	..	..	1	..	..
Humphrey, Nathaniel	..	..	..	..	1	..	..	..	..	1	..
Humphrey, Nathaniel Jr.	2	..	..	1	..	2	1	..	1	..	..
Hyde, Asahel	1	..	1	..	..	..	..	1	..	..	..
Hyde, Benjamin	..	1	..	..	1	..	1	3	..	1	..
Hyde, Ichabod	..	1	..	..	1	1	1	3	..	1	..
Hyde, Jacob	..	..	1	..	..	..	..	1	..	..	..
Hyde, Samuel	1	..	..	1	..	1	..	..	1	..	..
Ingraham, Micajah	..	2	..	1	..	1	..	2	1	..	..
Kellog, Enoch	3	2	..	1	..	1	1	..	1	..	..
Kellogg, Phinehas	2	1	1	1	..	4	..	..	1	..	..
Kingsbury, Daniel	1	1	2	..	1	1	..	1	1	1	..
Knight, Stephen	..	..	1	..	..	2	..	..	1	..	..
Lord, Ichabod	2	1	..	1	..	2	2	..	1	..	..
Lyman, Abel	1	2	3	..	1	2	..	..	2	2	..
Lyman, Elijah	1	1	1	1	..	1	..	1	..	..	..
Lyman, John	..	..	..	..	1	..	1	..	..	1	..
Lyndes, John	..	..	..	..	..	..	..	..	..	..	8
Malry, Caleb	..	1	..	..	1	..	1	..	..	1	..
Manly, Eli	3	..	..	1	..	2	1	..	1	..	..
Martin, Walker	1	..	1	1	..	2	..	..	1	..	..
Matton, Lemuel	1	..	..	1	..	1	..	..	1	..	..
Morgan, Isaac	1	..	..	1	..	..	..	1	..	..	..
Newton, Simon	..	1	..	..	1	..	..	..	..	1	..
Nichols, Abner	1	1	..	1	..	2	..	..	1	..	..
Paine, John	3	1	2	1	..	1	1	1	1	..	..
Paine, Lemuel	1	1	1	..	1	1	2	..	..	1	..
Paine, Noah	1	1	1	1	..	2	..	..	1	..	..
Parish, Nathan	1	..	..	1	..	2	1	..	1	..	..
Partridge, Aaron	2	..	1	1	..	1	..	1	1	..	..
Pease, Edward	2	2	..	1	..	1	1	..	1	..	..
Peck, Thomas	2	..	1	1	..	2	..	..	1	..	..
Phinney, John	1	..	..	1	..	1	..	..	1	..	..
Pike, Seth	2	..	..	1	..	1	..	..	..	1	..
Pride, Abner	1	1	2	..	1	..	..	..	2	1	..
Pritchard, John	1	..	..	..	1	2	..	..	1	..	..
Reed, Jonathan	1	1	1	..	1	1	..	..	1	..	..
Robinson, Ashur	1	..	1	..	1	..	1	1	1	..	..
Rood, Simeon	1	..	2	..	1	1	2	1	..	1	..
Rood, Simeon Jr.	1	..	..	1	..	..	..	..	1	..	..
BROOKFIELD—con.											
Sanderson, James	..	..	1	1	..	3	..	..	1	..	..
Seber, Benjamin	1	..	1	..	1	2	1	1	..	1	..
Sexton, Charles	..	1	2	..	1	..	..	1	..	1	..
Shepard, Roswell	..	..	1	..	..	1	..	1	..	..	..
Skiff, Sanders	3	..	..	1	..	..	1	..	1	..	..
Slap, Simon	..	1	..	..	1	2	2	1	..	1	..
Sled, John	1	..	..	..	1	1	..	..	1	..	..
Smalley, Benjamin	2	..	..	1	..	..	..	1	..	..	..
Smalley, Joseph	..	1	2	..	1	..	1	..	..	1	..
Smith, Abraham	..	..	1	1	..	2	..	..	1	..	..
Smith, Elkin	1	..	2	1	..	..	2	1	..	1	..
Smith, Isaac	..	1	1	..	..	..	..	2	..	1	..
Smith, Josiah	3	1	1	1	..	2	1	..	1	..	..
Smith, Josiah 2nd	1	1	..	1	..	3	..	..	1	..	..
Smith, Paul	..	..	..	1	..	..	..	..	..	..	..
Smith, Shubel	..	1	..	1	..	3	..	..	1	..	..
Smith, Solomon	3	..	..	1	..	2	..	..	1	..	..
Smith, Sylvanus	2	1	..	1	..	3	..	..	1	..	..
Smith, Thomas	..	1	1	..	1	..	..	..	..	1	..
Smith, Timothy	..	..	2	..	1	..	..	1	..	1	..
Smith, Zephaniah	1	..	..	1	..	..	..	..	..	1	..
Steele, Zadock	3	2	..	1	..	1	1	..	1	..	..
Stickney, Lemuel	2	..	..	1	..	2	..	..	1	..	..
Stickney, Solomon	..	..	1	..	1	..	..	..	..	1	..
Stickney, Solomon	..	..	..	1	..	1	..	1	..	..	..
Stratton, Ebenezer	1	1	3	1	..	..	1	1	1	..	..
Thatcher, Samuel	2	..	..	1	..	1	..	..	1	..	..
Tyler, Asahel	3	..	..	1	..	1	..	..	1	..	..
Tyler, Phinehas	..	..	1	..	1	..	..	1	..	1	..
Wakefield, Elijah	2	2	..	1	..	1	2	..	1	..	..
Wakefield, William	..	..	1	1	1	..	..	..	..	1	..
Walder, Roswell	..	..	1	..	..	1	..	1	..	..	..
Walder, Samuel	..	..	..	1	..	2	..	1	..	..	..
Waterman, John O.	1	1	1	..	1	2	1	..	1	..	..
Wells, Simeon	1	2	..	..	1	2	..	..	1	..	..
Wheatley, Nathaniel	1	2	1	..	1	1	2	1	1	..	..
White, William	2	..	..	1	..	2	..	..	1	..	..
Wood, Elisha	..	..	..	..	1	1	1	1	..	..	..
UNCERTAIN NAME											
Durkee, Zina (?)	2	..	..	1	..	1	..	..	1	..	..
CHELSEA											
Allen. Shuman	..	..	1	1	..	4	2	..	1	..	..
Anderson, John	..	..	1	..	..	1	..	2	..	..	..
Annis, Daniel	..	..	2	..	1	..	..	1	..	1	..
Annis, Daniel Jr.	..	..	..	1	..	2	..	1	..	..	..
Annis, Solomon	3	..	..	1	..	1	..	..	1	..	..
Ashley, Calvin	1	1	..	1	..	1	1	1	..	..	..
Badger, Samuel	..	1	..	..	1	..	..	1	..	1	..
Barker, Lemuel	..	..	..	2	1	3	1	..	1	..	..
Barnes, Daniel	1	..	1	..	1	..	..	..	..	1	..
Barnes, John	2	2	..	1	..	2	2	..	1	..	..
Barret, Benjamin	2	..	..	1	..	..	..	..	1	..	..
Barret, Nathan	3	..	..	1	..	1	1	..	1	..	..
Bennet, Elisha	1	..	..	1	..	1	..	1	..	..	..
Berry, David	1	..	1	..	1	2	..	1	..	1	..
Berry, Peleg	2	..	..	1	..	2	..	..	1	..	..
Bicknell, Kent	..	..	..	1	..	..	..	1	..	..	..
Bixby, Ichabod	3	1	..	..	1	2	1	..	..	1	..
Bliss, Israel	3	..	..	1	..	3	..	..	1	..	..
Blodget, Benjamin	1	..	..	1	..	2	..	..	1	..	..
Blodget, Daniel	2	1	1	1	..	1	1	1	..	..	..
Boardman, Stephen	1	..	1	1	..	..	..	..	1	..	..
Bosworth, Nathaniel	1	1	1	..	1	3	1	1	1	..	..
Brigham, Abraham	..	2	1	..	1	2	..	..	..	1	..
Burges, Benjamin	1	1	1	..	..	1	..	..	..	..	1
Chamberlin, Henry	1	..	1	1	..	..	..	1	..	..	..
Church, Asa	3	..	..	1	..	2	..	..	1	..	..
Corkins, Frederick	..	..	1	..	1	3	..	1	..	1	..
Crocker, David	3	1	1	1	..	..	1	..	..	1	..
Dearborne, Asa	3	1	1	..	1	2	..	1	1	..	..
Densmore, Abel	2	1	..	1	..	1	..	..	1	..	..
Densmore, Amos	2	..	..	1	..	1	..	..	1	..	..
Dewey, David	2	..	1	..	..	..	..	1	..	..	..
Dodge, Phinehas	1	..	..	1	..	2	..	..	2	..	..
Dodge, Shubal	1	..	..	1	..	..	..	1	..	1	..
Douglass, Caleb	4	2	..	1	..	..	2	..	1	..	..
Douglass, Ivory	3	2	..	1	..	3	2	1	1	..	..
Downing, Benjamin	1	..	..	..	1	2	1	1	..	1	..
Downing, Henry	1	..	..	1	..	3	..	..	1	1	..
Downing. Rufus	..	..	1	..	..	..	..	1	..	..	..
Drew, Noah	1	..	..	1	..	2	..	..	1	..	..

ORANGE COUNTY—Continued

NAMES OF HEADS OF FAMILIES	FREE WHITE MALES					FREE WHITE FEMALES					All other free persons except Indians not taxed
	Under 10 years of age	Of 10 and under 16	Of 16 and under 26 including heads of families	Of 26 and under 45 including heads of families	Of 45 and upwards including heads of families	Under 10 years of age	Of 10 and under 16	Of 16 and under 26 including heads of families	Of 26 and under 45 including heads of families	Of 45 and upwards including heads of families	
CHELSEA—con.											
Eaton, Levi	1	1	..	..	1	3	2	..	1	..	..
Eldrikin, Joshua B.	..	1	..	..	1	..	1	..	..	1	..
Elliott, John	3	..	..	1	..	1	..	..	1	..	..
Emerson, Jonathan	..	..	..	1	..	1	..	..	1	..	..
Emerson, Nathaniel	2	..	..	1	..	2	..	..	1	..	..
Emerson, Theophilus	..	..	1	..	..	1	..	1	..	..	..
Evadone, John	1	..	..	1	..	..	..	..	1	..	..
Farrar, Joseph	..	..	..	1	..	..	2	..	..	..	..
Field, John	..	..	1	..	..	..	..	1	..	..	..
Fish, Thomas	1	..	..	1	..	..	..	..	1	..	..
Flint, Nathan	1	..	..	1	..	1	2	..	1	..	..
Fox, Nehemiah	..	..	..	1	..	2	2	..	1	..	..
Franklin, Ichabod	..	1	..	..	1	..	..	..	..	1	..
Franklin, Ichabod Jr.	4	..	..	1	..	1	..	..	1	..	..
Fuller, Daniel	..	..	..	2	..	..	..	1	..	..	..
Fyfield, Moses	4	..	..	1	..	..	1	..	1	..	..
Gilman, Zebe	1	..	..	1	..	..	1	..	1	..	..
Griswold, Benjamin	2	..	..	1	..	2	..	1	1	..	..
Gunnerson, Henry	2	..	..	1	..	2	1	..	1	..	..
Gustin, Sebra	..	..	..	3	..	2	..	..	1	..	..
Haschel, Rufus	..	..	..	1	..	..	..	..	1	..	..
Hatch, Elijah	1	..	1	1	..	1	..	..	1	1	..
Hatch, John	2	..	..	1	..	..	..	..	1	..	..
Hatch, Joseph	1	..	..	1	..	1	..	1	..	..	..
Hatch, Joseph	1	..	..	1	..	1	..	..	1	..	..
Hatch, Michawl	..	2	2	..	1	1	..	3	1	1	..
Hatch, Reuben	..	2	4	1	..	5	1	1	1	..	..
Hatch, Rufus	3	..	..	1	..	2	..	..	1	..	..
Hibbard, Vina	..	..	..	1	..	..	..	..	..	..	..
Hollibut, Ashur	4	1	..	1	..	1	2	..	1	..	..
Hood, Amos	1	..	..	1	..	3	..	..	1	..	..
Hood, Enos	1	1	..	1	1	2	..	..	1	1	..
Hood, Nathan	2	..	..	1	..	2	..	..	1	..	..
Hood, Nathaniel	1	..	..	1	..	..	..	..	1	..	..
Hood, Thomas	..	..	..	1	..	2	..	..	2	..	..
Howard, Samuel	2	1	..	1	..	2	1	..	1	..	..
Hoyt, Joseph	1	..	..	1	..	1	1	..	1	..	..
Huntington, Hiram	2	..	..	1	..	1	..	1	1	..	..
Huntington, Theophilus	1	..	1	1	..	1	..	2	1	..	..
Hyde, Elisha	..	..	..	1	..	..	..	1	..	..	..
Ingraham, Reuben	1	..	2	1	..	2	1	..	1	..	..
Jaquish, Amos	2	..	..	1	..	3	..	..	1	1	..
Jones, James	1	..	..	1	..	1	..	..	1	..	..
King, Joseph	3	2	..	..	1	1	..	1	1	..	..
King, Oliver	1	2	..	..	1	4	..	5	1	..	..
Ladd, Daniel	1	..	..	1	..	1	1	..	1	..	..
Ladd, James	3	..	1	1	..	2	..	..	1	..	..
Lathrop, Elias	1	..	..	1	..	1	..	1	..	..	..
Lathrop, Elisha	3	..	..	1	..	2	1	..	1	..	..
Lathrop, Joshua	2	1	1	..	1	2	1	..	1	..	..
Lathrop, Rufus	1	..	1	2	..	2	..	..	1	..	..
Lathrop, Urban	2	..	..	1	..	..	..	..	1	..	..
Lincoln, Samuel	1	..	1	2	1	..	..	..	1	..	..
Lincoln, Samuel Jr.	..	2	..	..	1	1	1	1	1	..	..
Lincoln, Shubel	1	..	..	1	..	2	..	1	..	..	..
Little, Hazen	1	..	..	1	..	2	..	1	..	..	..
Little, Noah	2	..	..	1	..	3	1	..	1	..	..
Lyndsey, Daniel	..	..	..	1	..	1	..	..	1	..	..
Marston, Thomas	..	..	..	1	..	1	..	..	1	1	..
McCole, William	2	..	..	1	..	1	1	..	1	..	..
Merrill, John	..	..	1	..	..	1	..	1	..	..	..
Moor, Samuel	..	1	1	1	..	1	1	1	1	..	..
Moor, Thomas	3	2	1	1	1	..	1	1	1	..	..
Norris, Jacob	1	..	1	1	..	2	1	..	1	..	..
Norris, John	3	1	..	1	..	..	..	1	..	1	..
Norris, Moses	..	..	1	..	1	1	1	..	..	1	..
Nutt, John	3	..	..	1	..	3	..	..	1	..	..
Oak, Nathaniel	1	1	4	4	2	1	2	2	..	1	..
Parker, Thomas	..	..	2	1	..	3	2	2	1	..	..
Perigo, William	1	1	..	..	1	1	2	..	..	1	..
Perkins, Benjamin	1	..	..	1	..	..	..	1	..	..	..
Perkins, Daniel	..	1	..	1	..	1	2	..	1	..	..
Perkins, David	..	..	1	..	..	..	..	1	..	1	..
Perkins, Elisha	2	..	..	1	..	1	..	..	1	..	..
Powers, Abner H.	..	..	1	..	..	..	..	1	..	..	..
Prentiss, Robert	1	..	..	1	..	2	..	..	1	..	..
CHELSEA—con.											
Reddington, Isaac	..	..	..	2	..	1	..	..	2	..	..
Richardson, Ananiah	1	..	..	1	..	2	..	..	2	..	..
Seaver, Richard	..	1	1	1	..	2	..	1	1	..	..
Sleeper, Ephraim	1	1	..	1	1	1	..	1	..	1	..
Smith, Ebenezer	1	..	..	1	..	3	1	..	1	..	..
Smith, Enos	2	1	..	1	..	2	..	..	1	..	..
Smith, Nathaniel	..	..	1	..	1	..	..	2	..	1	..
Smith, Oliver	..	..	..	2	..	4	..	..	2	1	..
Spalding, Elisha	..	1	..	1	..	4	..	..	1	..	..
Spiler, Joseph	..	..	..	1	..	3	..	..	1	..	..
Stone, Eli	1	..	1	1	..	..	..	1	..	..	..
Thayer, Joseph	..	..	2	1	1	2	3	1	1	..	..
Thompson, Lathrop	..	..	..	1	..	1	..	..	1	..	..
Throop, Benjamin	1	..	..	1	..	1	..	..	1	..	..
Tracy, Elias	1	..	..	1	..	4	1	..	1	..	..
Tracy, Oliver	2	..	2	1	..	2	..	..	1	..	..
Wiggin, David	..	1	..	2	..	1	..	..	1	..	..
Wiggin, John	1	1	..	1	..	1	1	..	1	..	..
Williams, Elisha	3	1	..	1	..	1	1	..	1	..	..
Wills, Jesse	1	..	..	1	..	1	..	..	1	..	..
Wills, John	..	1	..	1	..	3	..	..	1	..	..
Wills, Jonathan	3	1	1	..	1	2	..	3	..	1	..
Wood, Gideon	1	..	1	1	..	1	1	..	..	1	..
Woodward, Henry	..	..	2	..	1	..	1	2	..	1	..
Woodworth, Isaac	1	..	..	1	..	2	..	..	1	..	..
Woodworth, Jabez	1	..	..	1	..	..	..	..	1	..	..
Wright, Benjamin	1	1	3	..	1	..	1	1	..	1	..
Wright, John	..	..	..	1	..	1	..	..	1	..	..
Young, Isaac	2	..	..	1	..	1	..	..	1	..	..
Young, Thomas	2	..	1	1	..	..	..	..	1	..	..
CORINTH											
Adams, Joel	2	2	1	..	1	1	..	..	..	1	..
Adams, Joel Jr.	2	..	1	..	..	1	1	1	..	..	..
Adams, Moses	2	1	1	..	1	1	..	1	..	1	..
Allen, Elijah	1	1	..	1	..	1	..	1	..	..	..
Amy, Heman	1	2	..	1	..	1	1	..	1	..	..
Amy, John	2	..	..	1	..	3	..	..	1	..	..
Armon, John	1	1	..	..	1	2	1	..	..	1	..
Avery, Amos	2	..	..	1	..	1	..	..	1	..	..
Avery, Andrew	2	..	..	1	..	3	1	..	1	..	..
Avery, Christopher	2	..	..	1	..	1	..	..	2	..	..
Ayer, John	2	2	..	1	..	2	..	..	1	..	..
Ayer, Richard	3	..	..	1	..	2	..	..	1	..	..
Bachelder, Daniel	1	..	..	1	..	4	..	..	1	..	..
Bagley, Jesse	..	2	2	..	1	2	2	..	..	1	..
Banfill, George	1	..	..	..	1	2	2	..	..	1	..
Banfill, John	2	..	..	1	..	2	..	..	1	..	..
Banks, Thomas	2	..	..	1	..	1	..	..	1	..	..
Berry, David	1	..	..	1	..	1	1	..	1	..	..
Berry, Simon	..	..	1	1	1	..	..	1	..	1	..
Berry, Thomas	1	..	1	..	1	5	1	..	1	..	..
Bigelow, Joshua	..	..	..	1	.	3	..	..	1	..	..
Bond, Joseph	3	1	..	1	..	1	1	..	1	..	..
Bowen, Jeremiah	2	..	..	1	..	..	..	..	2	..	..
Bowen, John	1	..	..	1	..	4	..	..	1	..	..
Bowen, Peter	..	..	2	..	2	..	..	..	..	1	..
Bowen, Peter Jr.	..	1	..	1	..	2	..	..	1	..	..
Bowen, Taplin	..	..	1	..	..	1	..	1	..	..	..
Boyden, Jonathan	3	1	..	1	..	1	..	..	1	..	..
Boyden, (Widow)	..	..	..	..	..	..	..	3	..	1	..
Brown, Benjamin	1	1	..	1	..	..	..	..	1	..	..
Brown, Daniel	3	..	..	1	..	2	..	..	1	..	..
Brown, Elias	..	..	..	1	1	..	1	..	..	1	..
Brown, John 1st	3	..	..	1	..	3	1	..	1	..	..
Brown, John 2nd.	..	..	..	1	..	3	..	..	1	..	..
Caldwell, James	2	2	..	1	..	2	..	..	1	..	..
Carr, Abner	2	..	..	1	..	1	1	..	1	..	..
Carr, Benjamin	..	..	..	1	..	3	..	..	1	..	..
Chubb, John	2	1	..	1	..	1	..	..	1	1	..
Clement, Job	1	..	..	1	..	1	..	..	1	..	..
Clifford, Israel	2	..	3	..	1	1	2	..	..	1	..
Clough, Zacchariah	2	1	..	..	1	3	1	..	..	1	..
Colby, Ezekiel	3	2	..	1	..	1	..	2	1	..	..
Colby, John	2	..	..	1	..	3	..	..	1	..	..
Colby, John Jr.	3	..	..	1	..	1	..	..	1	..	..
Colby, Jonathan	..	..	..	1	..	..	..	..	1	..	..
Colby, Joseph	..	..	..	1	..	2	..	..	1	..	..
Colby, Nicholas	2	1	..	..	1	2	1	1	..	1	..
Colby, Sarah	..	1	2	..	..	..	..	1	..	1	..

ORANGE COUNTY—Continued

NAMES OF HEADS OF FAMILIES	FREE WHITE MALES					FREE WHITE FEMALES					All other free persons except Indians not taxed
	Under 10 years of age	Of 10 and under 16	Of 16 and under 26 including heads of families	Of 26 and under 45 including heads of families	Of 45 and upwards including heads of families.	Under 10 years of age	Of 10 and under 16	Of 16 and under 26 including heads of families	Of 26 and under 45 including heads of families	Of 45 and upwards including heads of families	
CORINTH—con.											
Collyer, Chapman	1	..	..	1	..	..	..	1	..	..	..
Collyer, Thomas	..	..	2	..	1	1	..	..	1	2	..
Collyer, Thomas Jr.	2	..	..	1	..	1	..	..	1	..	..
Conner, David	2	1	..	1	..	1	..	..	1	..	..
Conner, John	..	..	1	..	..	1	..	1	..	..	..
Conner, Nathan	..	..	..	1	..	1	..	1	1	..	..
Cook, Daniel	2	1	1	3	..	1	..	1	1	..	1
Cooper, Joseph	2	..	..	..	1	3	..	..	1	..	..
Copse, Paul	..	..	..	1	..	2	..	..	1	..	..
Corliss, Daniel	..	..	1	..	..	..	..	1	..	..	..
Corliss, Samuel	1	1	1	..	2	..	1	1	..	1	..
Corliss, Willoughby	2	..	..	1	..	..	..	..	1	..	..
Crook, Charles	3	1	2	..	1	2	1	1	1	..	..
Crook, Reuben	2	..	1	1	..	1	..	..	1	..	..
Crook, Thomas	2	..	1	..	1	..	1	1	..	1	..
Currier, Aaron	5	..	..	1	..	1	..	..	1	..	..
Currier, Joseph	1	2	1	..	1	1	1	1	..	1	..
Currier, Samuel	2	1	..	1	..	4	..	..	1	..	..
Davis, John	..	1	..	..	1	4	2	..	1	1	..
Davis, Joshua	3	2	1	1	..	2	1	..	1	..	..
Davis, Simeon	3	..	..	1	..	2	..	..	1	..	..
Davis, Thomas	3	..	..	1	..	2	..	..	1	..	..
Dearborne, John	2	..	..	1	..	..	..	..	1	1	..
Dearborne, Samuel	..	..	..	1	1	..	..	..	..	1	..
Dickey, Adam	..	..	1	..	1	..	..	1	..	1	..
Dow, Illsley	1	..	..	1	..	..	1	..	1	..	..
Drew, Daniel	2	1	1	..	1	2	1	3	..	1	..
Drew, Daniel 2nd	1	1	..	1	..	1	2	..	1	..	..
Drew, Samuel	2	..	..	1	..	2	..	..	1	..	..
Dustin, Paul	..	..	..	..	1	..	1	..	..	1	..
Dustin, Timothy	2	..	1	1	..	2	1	..	2	..	..
Eastman, Edmund	2	1	3	1	1	..	2	3	..	1	..
Eastman, Ezekiel	1	..	..	1	..	..	..	..	1	..	..
Eastman, James	2	..	1	..	..	1	..	1	..	..	..
Eastman, Jesse	..	1	1	1	..	2	..	1	..	..	..
Farr, Jacob	1	..	..	..	1	1	..	..	1	..	..
Fellows, Joseph	3	..	..	1	..	1	..	..	1	..	..
Fellows, William	..	1	1	..	1	..	1	2	..	1	..
Ford, Robert	1	..	1	..	1	1	1	1	..	1	..
Forsythe, Robert	1	2	..	1	..	1	..	..	1	..	..
French, Samuel	1	1	..	1	..	2	..	..	1	..	..
Fuller, Timothy	1	..	1	..	..	..	..	1	..	..	..
Fulsome, Joshua	1	1	..	1	..	..	..	..	1	..	..
Gitchel, Zebulun	2	1	..	1	..	2	1	1	1	..	..
Gould, Nathaniel	1	..	..	1	..	..	1	..	1	..	..
Graves, James	..	..	..	1	..	3	..	..	1	..	..
Hadley, Jonathan	2	1	..	..	1	2	1	2	..	1	..
Hadlock, Hezekiah	..	..	1	..	..	..	..	1	..	..	..
Hale, Henry	2	1	..	1	..	1	..	..	1	..	..
Hale, Joshua	..	..	..	2	..	..	..	..	1	..	..
Harriman, Rufus	2	1	..	1	..	..	1	..	1	..	..
Hazeltine, Samuel	..	..	1	..	1	..	1	1	2	1	..
Heath, Abel	2	..	..	1	..	3	..	..	1	..	..
Heath, David	1	..	..	1	..	2	..	..	1	..	..
Heath, Joseph	2	..	..	1	..	2	..	..	1	..	..
Heath, Moses	1	1	..	1	..	2	1	..	1	..	..
Higgins, Joseph	3	1	..	1	..	1	..	..	1	..	..
Horn, Amos	..	..	..	2	..	1	..	..	1	..	..
Horn, Joseph	1	..	..	..	1	1	1	..	..	1	..
Horn, Joseph	2	..	..	1	..	2	..	..	1	..	..
Howard, William	2	..	..	1	..	1	..	..	1	..	..
Humphrey, Ebenezer	3	..	..	1	..	..	..	..	1	..	..
Hunkins, Moses	2	..	..	1	..	3	..	..	1	..	..
Hurd, Elisha	..	..	1	1	..	..	..	..	1	..	..
Ingalls, Nathaniel	2	..	..	1	..	1	..	..	1	..	..
Jackman, Abel	2	..	..	1	..	3	..	..	1	..	..
Jackman, Sarah	4	1	..	..	..	..	..	..	1	..	..
Jennison, Lydia	..	..	..	..	..	3	..	..	1	..	..
Johnson, Simon	1	..	3	..	1	..	..	1	..	1	..
Knight, Joseph	3	..	..	1	..	..	..	..	1	..	..
Ladd, Caleb	2	..	..	1	..	1	1	..	1	..	..
Ladd, Jonathan	3	1	..	..	1	..	1	..	1	..	..
Lamb, Nathan	1	..	..	..	1	1	..	3	..	1	..
Locke, Reuben	2	..	..	1	..	3	..	..	1	..	..
Loverain, Simeon	..	1	1	..	1	..	1	2	..	1	..
Lovwell, John	2	..	..	..	2	3	1	..	1	..	..
Lovwell, Jonathan	..	..	1	2	1	..	..	..	..	1	..
Lucas, Benjamin	..	..	1	..	..	..	..	1	..	..	..
CORINTH—con.											
Lucas, James	..	..	..	..	1	..	1	1	..	1	..
Lund, Noah	2	1	..	1	..	1	2	..	1	..	..
Luther, Benjamin	2	..	..	1	..	..	..	..	1	..	..
Mann, Nathan	3	..	..	1	..	..	..	..	1	..	..
Marshall, Moses	2	..	..	1	..	2	2	1	1	..	..
Martin, Benjamin	1	2	..	..	1	2	1	2	..	1	..
McCreliss, Daniel	..	..	1	..	..	1	1	1	..	..	..
McCreliss, Robert	..	1	..	..	1	..	1	2	..	1	..
McFarlane, John	1	..	1	1	..	2	..	..	1	..	..
McFarlane, Moses	..	..	..	..	1	1	..	..	2	..	1
McKeen, Daniel	1	..	..	2	..	..	..	2	..	..	..
McKeen, David	2	..	2	..	1	2	2	..	..	1	..
McKeen, Robert	..	1	..	..	1	..	1	..	..	1	..
Merrick, Joseph	1	..	1	..	..	1	..	1	..	..	..
Merrill, Joshua	2	..	1	1	..	2	..	1	1	..	..
Merrill, Stephen	..	1	..	1	..	2	..	..	1	..	..
Meserve, James	..	..	..	2	..	1	..	..	1	..	..
Metcalf, Samuel	1	..	..	1	..	1	..	..	1	..	..
Metcalf, Thomas	2	1	..	1	..	2	1	..	1	..	..
Miles, Joseph	2	1	..	1	..	2	..	..	1	..	..
Miller, Samuel	1	..	..	2	..	2	..	..	2	..	..
Moor, Henry	..	..	..	1	1	..	..	..	..	..	..
Morrill, Peter	1	..	3	..	1	..	2	1	..	1	..
Moulton, David	..	..	2	..	1	..	..	1	..	1	..
Moulton, Micajah	5	..	..	1	..	..	1	..	1	..	1
Muzzy, Benjamin	..	..	2	..	1	..	..	3	..	1	..
Norris, Benjamin	1	2	2	..	1	4	1	..	1	..	..
Norris, Benjamin Jr.	..	..	2	1	..	3	2	..	1	..	..
Norris, John	2	..	..	2	..	..	..	..	1	..	..
Norris, Jonathan	3	..	..	1	..	1	..	..	1	..	..
Norris, Levi	2	..	..	1	..	2	..	..	1	..	..
Norris, Moses	3	..	..	1	..	1	1	..	1	..	..
Norris, Samuel	..	..	..	..	1	..	..	..	..	1	..
Noyes, James	1	..	1	..	..	..	..	1	..	..	..
Nutting, John	1	..	2	..	1	..	1	3	..	1	..
Ober, John	4	1	2	1	..	..	1	..	1	..	..
Ordway, Richard	..	..	..	1	..	2	..	..	1	..	..
Orr, Robert	..	2	1	..	1	4	1	..	..	1	..
Page, Reuben	2	1	..	..	1	2	..	..	1	..	..
Paine, Richard	3	1	..	1	..	2	1	..	1	..	..
Parker, Silas	2	1	..	1	1	1	1	..	1	..	..
Peck, Simeon	1	..	..	1	..	4	..	..	1	1	..
Pike, ———	..	..	..	2	..	..	..	..	..	..	..
Poor, John	1	..	..	2	..	..	..	1	1	..	..
Rawling, Jonathan	1	..	..	1	..	3	..	..	1	..	..
Rawling, Richard	..	..	2	..	1	..	1	1	1	..	..
Rawling, Richard Jr.	2	..	1	1	..	1	..	..	1	..	..
Rent, Joseph	3	..	..	1	..	1	..	..	1	..	..
Richardson, Caleb	1	2	..	1	..	2	2	..	1	..	..
Richardson, James	3	2	..	1	..	1	1	..	1	..	..
Richardson, Samuel	3	..	2	1	..	2	1	..	1	1	..
Ring, David	1	..	..	1	..	2	..	..	1	..	..
Ring, Elijah	..	..	1	..	1	..	1	1	..	1	..
Robinson, Jonathan	..	1	1	..	1	1	1	1	..	1	..
Roby, Edward	2	..	..	1	..	2	1	..	1	..	..
Roby, Jonathan	4	..	..	1	..	..	..	..	1	..	..
Rollins, Josiah	1	..	..	1	..	1	..	..	1	..	..
Rowe, Robert	..	1	1	..	1	..	..	1	..	1	..
Rowel, Aaron	..	..	1	..	1	..	..	..	..	1	..
Rowel, Elijah	1	..	..	1	..	..	..	..	1	1	..
Rutter, Job	1	1	..	..	1	1	..	..	..	1	..
Sanborn, Reuben	1	2	..	1	..	3	..	..	1	1	..
Sandborn, Moses	2	..	..	1	..	2	..	..	1	..	..
Sawyer, Richard	1	..	3	..	1	..	1	2	..	2	..
Scribner, Benjamin	2	1	..	1	..	1	..	..	1	..	..
Sleeper, Ezekiel	..	..	..	1	..	1	..	..	1	..	..
Sleeper, Ezra	..	..	..	1	..	..	1	..	1	..	..
Sleeper, Jacob	1	1	..	1	..	3	2	..	1	..	..
Sleeper, Jethro	3	..	..	1	..	..	..	..	1	..	..
Sleeper, John	..	..	1	..	..	1	..	1	1	1	..
Sleeper, Robert	3	1	..	1	..	1	..	..	1	..	..
Smith, Alexander	1	..	1	..	1	3	2	..	..	1	..
Stephens, John	1	1	..	1	..	1	..	..	1	..	..
Stevens, Caleb	4	..	..	1	..	2	..	..	1	..	..
Stevens, Daniel	1	1	..	1	..	2	2	..	1	..	..
Stevens, Moses	2	..	..	1	..	..	..	..	1	..	..
Swift, Stephen	3	..	..	1	..	1	2	..	1	..	..
Taplin, Gouldsbury	1	1	..	1	1	2	..	..	1	..	..
Taplin, John	..	..	..	1	1	..	..	..	..	1	..
Taplin, Mansfield	2	..	2	..	1	2	1	1	..	1	..

ORANGE COUNTY—Continued

NAMES OF HEADS OF FAMILIES	FREE WHITE MALES: Under 10 years of age	FREE WHITE MALES: Of 10 and under 16	FREE WHITE MALES: Of 16 and under 26 including heads of families	FREE WHITE MALES: Of 26 and under 45 including heads of families	FREE WHITE MALES: Of 45 and upwards including heads of families.	FREE WHITE FEMALES: Under 10 years of age	FREE WHITE FEMALES: Of 10 and under 16	FREE WHITE FEMALES: Of 16 and under 26 including heads of families	FREE WHITE FEMALES: Of 26 and under 45 including heads of families	FREE WHITE FEMALES: Of 45 and upwards including heads of families	All other free persons except Indians not taxed
CORINTH—con.											
Taplin, Nathan	1	..	1	..	1	1	..	3	..	1	..
Taplin, William	2	2	1	..	1	2	1	2	..	1	..
Tenny, Jonathan	..	..	..	1	1	..	..	1	..	1	..
Tenny, Jonathan Jr.	1	..	..	1	..	1	..	..	1	..	..
Tenny, Joshua	2	..	1	1	..	..	1	..	1	..	..
Thurston, John	..	..	1	..	..	2	..	1	..	..	..
Tilletson, Widow	..	1	..	..	..	..	..	..	..	1	..
Towle, Bracket	2	2	..	..	1	2	1	3	..	1	..
Twilight, Ichabod	..	..	..	..	..	..	..	..	..	..	6
Wasson, Caldwell	2	..	..	1	..	1	..	..	1	..	..
Wasson, Thomas	3	..	..	1	..	..	..	..	1	..	..
Wells, Jacob	..	..	1	..	1	1	..	1	..	1	..
Wells, Jacob	..	..	1	..	..	..	..	1	..	..	..
Whitcher, Reuben	..	..	..	..	1	..	1	1	..	1	..
White, George	3	..	..	1	..	..	..	..	1	..	..
Wilson, John	2	1	..	1	..	2	1	..	1	..	..
Wilton, Josiah	1	..	1	..	..	..	..	2	..	..	..
Woods, Daniel	1	1	1	..	1	1	1	1	..	1	..
Wright, Darius	1	..	..	1	..	3	2	..	1	..	..
FAIRLEE											
Ames, David	1	..	2	..	1	1	1	1	..	..	..
Ames, Thaddeus	1	..	..	..	1	..	1	..	..	1	..
Baldwin, Ebenezer	..	..	3	..	1	..	..	..	..	1	..
Baldwin, Ebenezer Jr.	1	..	..	1	..	1	..	..	1	..	..
Banon, Moses	1	1	..	..	1	2	2	..	1	..	..
Bissell, Noadiah	..	..	..	1	..	..	..	1	1	..	..
Bissel, Simon B.	2	..	2	2	..	1	1	..	2	..	..
Bliss, Samuel	..	..	..	..	1	..	..	..	..	1	..
Bliss, Samuel Jr.	1	..	..	1	..	5	..	..	1	..	..
Bliss, Solomon	1	..	1	1	..	2	..	..	1	..	..
Brown, Benjamin	2	1	1	1	..	1	3	..	1	..	..
Brown, William	1	..	..	1	..	4	..	..	1	..	..
Cady, Rannibus	2	..	1	1	1	..	..	..	1	1	..
Carpenter, Ephram	3	..	..	1	..	1	1	..	..	1	..
Child, Phinehas	2	..	..	1	..	2	2	..	..	1	..
Clark, Roswell	1	1	..	1	..	2	1	2	1	..	..
Coburn, Samuel	1	1	..	..	1	2	1	..	..	1	..
Coburn, Samuel Jr.	3	..	..	1	..	1	..	..	1	..	..
Cook, Ebenezer	..	1	1	..	1	..	..	2	..	1	..
Cook, Ebenezer Jr.	..	1	..	1	..	1	..	..	1	..	..
Dodge, Samuel	2	2	..	..	1	2	..	..	1	..	..
Follet, Giles	..	..	..	..	1	2	..	..	..	1	..
Gay, Rufus	..	..	1	..	..	1	..	1	..	..	..
Goodale, Lemuel	1	..	..	1	..	..	..	..	1	..	..
Hammond, Calvin	..	..	2	..	..	..	..	1	..	..	..
Hilldrake, Ephram	2	1	..	1	..	2	1	..	1	..	..
Horner, Jesse	..	..	..	1	..	..	..	1	..	..	..
Houghton, Samuel	..	1	..	1	..	2	..	..	1	..	..
Ivers, John	..	..	..	..	1	..	..	1	..	1	..
Lamb, Asa	3	..	..	1	..	2	1	..	1	..	..
Langley, Joseph	2	..	..	1	..	1	..	..	1	..	..
Marston, John	..	1	1	..	1	2	..	1	..	1	..
Marston, Peter	3	2	..	1	..	..	1	..	1	1	..
Martin, Phillip	1	..	..	1	..	2	..	..	1	1	..
Morey, Darius L.	2	1	1	..	..	..	..	1	..	..	..
Morey, Israel	2	..	..	1	..	..	..	..	1	..	..
Morey, Moultan	2	1	..	1	1	..	..	1	1	1	..
Morey, Solomon	..	1	2	..	1	1	1	..	..	1	..
Morey, Solomon Jr.	1	..	..	1	..	3	..	..	1	..	..
Morey, William P.	2	1	1	..	..	..	..	1	..	..	..
Nichols, Widow	..	..	..	..	..	..	..	..	1	..	1
Northey, Abraham	3	..	..	1	..	1	2	..	1	..	..
Ormsbee, Ichabod	..	..	..	..	1	..	..	1	..	1	..
Ormsbee, Joseph	..	..	1	..	1	1	1	..	..	1	..
Ormsbee, Rufus	1	..	1	..	..	..	1	1	..	..	..
Ormsbee, Thomas	..	..	..	..	1	..	..	..	..	1	..
Pierce, George	1	..	1	..	..	1	..	1	..	..	..
Pierce, James Jr.	1	..	..	1	..	2	1	..	1	..	..
Pierce, Jedidiah	2	..	1	..	..	..	..	1	..	..	..
Pollet, Benjamin	1	..	..	..	2	3	1	..	..	1	..
FAIRLEE—con.											
Rogers, John	1	..	..	1	..	3	..	..	1	..	..
Ross, Ephram	3	3	2	..	1	1	1	..	..	1	..
Russ, Horatio	..	..	..	..	1	..	..	..	..	1	..
Smith, Samuel	1	..	3	..	1	..	..	2	..	1	..
Stratton, Benjamin	2	1	..	1	..	2	..	3	1	..	..
Stratton, Samuel	..	..	..	1	..	..	..	1	..	..	..
Swift, Joshua	2	1	1	..	1	..	2	..	..	1	..
Terbut, Phillip	3	1	..	1	..	..	2	..	1	..	..
Trusdale, Aaron	1	1	..	1	..	2	..	..	1	1	..
Trusdale, Thomas D.	1	1	..	1	..	4	..	..	1	..	..
Tyler, Samuel	..	..	..	1	..	..	..	..	..	..	..
Wiggins, William	..	1	..	1	..	5	..	..	1	..	..
Williams, James	..	..	1	..	..	3	1	..	1	..	..
Woodward, Asa	2	2	..	1	..	3	2	..	1	..	..
Woodward, Benjamin	1	..	..	1	..	1	..	..	1	..	..
NEWBURY											
Abbot, Bancroft	3	2	..	1	..	1	..	..	1	..	..
Abbot, Ezra	1	1	..	1	..	1	1	..	1	..	..
Abbot, James	..	..	..	..	1	..	..	..	..	1	..
Avery, Nathan	2	3	..	1	..	1	1	1	1	..	..
Banfill, Mark	..	1	1	..	..	..	..	1	..	..	..
Barnet, David	..	..	2	1	..	..	..	1	..	..	..
Barnet, Nehemiah	1	1	..	1	..	3	2	..	1	..	..
Barnet, Samuel	..	..	..	2	1	..	..	..	1	1	..
Bartlet, Solomon	2	..	..	1	..	1	..	..	1	..	..
Bayley, Abner	2	..	1	1	..	1	..	..	1	..	..
Bayley, Enoch	1	..	1	1	..	..	..	1	..	..	..
Bayley, Frye	2	2	1	..	1	2	..	2	..	1	..
Bayley, Isaac	3	..	1	1	..	2	2	..	2	..	..
Bayley, Jacob	..	..	..	1	1	..	..	..	..	1	..
Bayley, Jacob Jr.	2	3	1	1	..	3	..	1	1	..	..
Bayley, James	1	..	..	1	..	2	..	..	1	..	..
Bayley, John	2	..	..	1	..	4	1	1	2	..	..
Bayley, John G.	1	1	1	..	1	2	1	1	..	1	..
Bayley, Joshua	3	1	4	..	1	1	1	2	..	1	..
Bayley, Moses L.	2	..	..	1	..	2	..	..	1	..	..
Bayley, Webster	1	1	2	..	1	2	2	2	1	..	..
Bliss, Davenport	..	..	1	..	..	..	..	1	..	..	..
Bliss, Ruth	1	..	..	..	..	..	..	1	1	..	..
Bowers, Benjamin	1	..	1	1	..	..	1	..	1	..	..
Boyes, James	2	..	..	1	..	..	..	..	1	..	..
Boyes, William	..	1	1	1	1	..	..	1	..	1	1
Bricket, Abraham	1	1	..	1	..	..	..	..	1	..	..
Brock, Thomas	1	2	2	..	1	1	1	2	..	1	..
Brown, John	1	..	2	1	..	..	1	2	1	1	..
Buel, Ashbel	3	1	..	1	..	1	..	..	1	..	..
Bullock, Richard	1	..	..	1	..	..	..	..	1	..	..
Burnham, Mary	2	..	..	..	..	3	..	..	1	..	..
Burroughs, Thomas	..	..	1	1	..	3	..	1	1	..	..
Burroughs, Williams	..	..	2	..	..	1	..	1	..	..	..
Butterfield, Aaron	1	..	..	1	..	..	..	..	1	..	..
Butterfield, Samuel	3	..	..	1	..	1	..	..	1	..	..
Carby, Joel	4	..	..	1	..	..	..	..	1	..	..
Carleton, Dudley	2	1	1	..	1	1	2	1	..	1	..
Carter, Andre	4	1	..	1	..	2	..	..	1	..	..
Carter, John	4	..	..	1	..	1	..	..	1	..	..
Carter, Moses	1	..	..	1	..	1	..	..	1	..	..
Carter, Samuel	3	3	..	..	1	1	..	1	1	..	..
Carter, William	1	1	..	2	..	4	..	1	1	..	..
Challis, William	..	..	..	..	1	..	..	..	..	1	..
Chamberlin, Benjamin	1	2	..	..	2	..	2	2	..	1	..
Chamberlin, Blanchard	2	..	..	1	..	5	..	..	1	..	..
Chamberlin, Charles	2	..	1	..	..	..	..	1	..	..	..
Chamberlin, Eri	1	..	..	1	..	..	..	..	1	..	..
Chamberlin, Err	2	..	2	..	1	3	2	..	..	1	..
Chamberlin, Joseph	..	1	3	..	1	..	2	2	..	1	..
Chamberlin, Nathaniel	..	1	8	..	1	2	2	1	..	1	..
Chamberlin, Raymond	1	..	..	1	..	2	1	1	1	..	..
Chamberlin, Remembrance	..	2	2	..	2	1	1	2	..	3	..
Chamberlin, Rodolphus	..	..	..	1	..	..	..	..	..	..	..
Chamberlin, Silas	2	2	2	..	1	1	1	1	..	1	..
Chamberlin, Thomas	1	..	1	..	1	..	1	1	..	1	..
Chamberlin, Uriah	1	..	1	..	2	1	..	1	..	1	..
Chapman, Jonah	2	2	..	..	1	2	2	2	..	1	..
Chase, Stephen	2	1	1	1	..	1	1	1	1	..	..
Clark, Choate	1	..	..	1	..	1	..	..	1	..	..
Clark, John	..	..	..	..	1	..	..	..	1	1	..
Clark, Timothy	..	1	..	1	..	5	..	1	1	..	..
Clough, Samuel	1	2	..	1	..	1	..	..	1	..	..
Coburn, Lawrence	2	..	..	1	..	2	..	..	1	..	..

ORANGE COUNTY—Continued

NAMES OF HEADS OF FAMILIES	FREE WHITE MALES: Under 10 years of age	FREE WHITE MALES: Of 10 and under 16	FREE WHITE MALES: Of 16 and under 26 including heads of families	FREE WHITE MALES: Of 26 and under 45 including heads of families	FREE WHITE MALES: Of 45 and upwards including heads of families	FREE WHITE FEMALES: Under 10 years of age	FREE WHITE FEMALES: Of 10 and under 16	FREE WHITE FEMALES: Of 16 and under 26 including heads of families	FREE WHITE FEMALES: Of 26 and under 45 including heads of families	FREE WHITE FEMALES: Of 45 and upwards including heads of families	All other free persons except Indians not taxed
NEWBURY—con.											
Corliss, Timothy	1	..	..	..	1	1	3	..	..	1	..
Crown, John	..	..	3	..	1	..	..	1	..	1	..
Crown, William	1	..	1	..	..	1	..	1	..	..	..
Cunningham, Nathaniel	..	..	1	..	1	..	..	..	..	1	..
Currier, Ebenezer	..	..	1	..	1	..	..	..	..	1	..
Danah, Arthur	1	2	1	1	..	3	..	..	1	..	..
Davis, Enoch	1	1	..	1	..	3	..	..	1	..	..
Dodge, James	1	..	1	..	1	2	..	..	1	1	..
Dow, William	4	1	2	1	..	1	..	..	1	..	..
Downer, Andrew	..	2	..	..	1	..	..	1	1	1	..
Downer, Solomon	1	2	..	1	..	1	1	..	1	..	..
Duffs, Isaac	..	..	1	1	..	1	..	..	1	..	..
Dustin, Nathaniel	2	3	..	1	..	1	1	..	1	..	..
Dustin, Zaccheus	..	1	..	2	..	2	1	1	1	..	..
Eastman, David	2	..	..	1	..	2	..	1	1	..	..
Eastman, Thomas	1	..	1	..	1	1	1	1	..	1	..
Ewen, John	1	..	1	..	1	1	..	1	1	..	..
Fellows, Samuel	2	1	..	1	..	2	..	..	1	..	..
Flanders, Josiah	3	..	..	1	..	2	..	..	1	..	..
Foggerson, John	..	..	..	1	1	..	..	1	..	1	..
Ford, Paul	..	1	..	..	1	1	..	1	1	..	..
Foster, Asa	2	1	1	..	1	2	2	..	1	..	..
Fowler, Jacob	2	1	1	1	..	3	1	1	1	..	..
Gibson, David	2	..	..	1	..	..	..	..	1	..	..
Gibson, Matthew	1	2	1	..	1	1	..	2	..	1	..
Goodwin, Jonathan	1	..	1	..	1	2	..	4	..	1	..
Green, Hannah	1	..	..	..	..	..	1	..	..	1	..
Greenleaf, Samuel	3	1	..	1	..	3	1	..	1	..	..
Grow, Samuel	2	2	..	..	1	2	..	..	..	1	..
Hadley, Parrit	1	1	..	1	..	2	1	..	1	..	..
Hamblet, William	3	..	..	1	..	2	1	..	1	..	..
Hazeltine, David	2	2	..	1	..	2	1	..	1	..	..
Heath, Azubah	..	..	1	..	..	..	1	1	..	1	..
Heath, James	2	..	..	1	..	2	..	..	1	..	..
Heath, Joseph	2	..	1	..	..	..	..	1	..	..	..
Hibbard, Jacob	1	1	..	..	1	3	1	1	1	..	..
Hibbard, Joseph	..	..	..	..	1	..	..	1	..	1	..
Holt, Daniel	2	..	1	1	..	2	..	..	1	..	..
Ingalls, Jeremiah	3	..	1	1	..	2	..	1	1	1	..
Johnson, James	1	1	1	1	..	2	..	..	1	..	..
Johnson, Jonathan	1	..	..	2	..	..	..	..	1	..	..
Johnson, Moses	1	1	1	2	..	..	1	1	1	..	..
Johnson, Rasmus	..	..	1	..	1	..	..	..	1	..	..
Johnson, Robert	1	1	3	..	1	3	1	2	1	1	..
Johnson, Thomas	..	1	4	..	1	1	2	2	..	1	1
Kelly, Nehemiah	2	..	..	1	..	..	..	1	..	..	..
Kent, Jacob	..	..	..	1	1	..	1	..	..	1	..
Kent, Jacob Jr.	3	..	..	1	..	..	1	1	2	..	..
Kent, Joseph	..	..	..	1	..	..	..	1	..	..	..
Kincaid, Charles	1	..	..	1	..	3	..	..	1	..	..
Kincaid, Robert	1	..	..	1	..	1	..	..	1	..	..
Kinsman, Aaron	..	..	..	2	..	..	..	..	..	..	1
Lambert, Nathaniel	2	..	..	1	..	..	1	1	1	..	..
Lancaster, Samuel	1	1	..	1	..	..	3	..	1	..	..
Lovewell, Nehemiah	..	1	2	1	..	..	1	..	2	..	..
Lyndsey, Samuel	3	1	..	..	1	1	1	1	1	..	..
Martin, James	1	..	..	1	..	1	..	..	1	..	..
McKeith, Thomas	2	1	..	..	1	..	1	2	1	..	..
McLaughlin, Alley	1	..	..	1	..	1	..	..	1	..	..
Mellen, Thomas	4	3	..	1	..	..	2	1	..	..	..
Messervy, Samuel	2	..	..	1	..	2	..	..	1	..	..
Metcalf, Ephram	2	..	..	1	..	2	..	..	1	..	..
Mills, John	..	..	3	..	1	..	..	1	..	1	..
Mills, John Jr.	1	1	1	1	..	3	2	3	..	1	..
Ober, Henry	..	1	..	1	..	1	..	..	2	..	..
Peach, William	..	1	2	..	1	1	1	..	..	1	..
Peach, William Jr.	1	..	1	..	..	..	..	1	..	..	..
Powers, Samuel	1	1	..	1	..	1	..	..	1	..	..
Powers, Stephen	2	1	..	1	..	3	1	..	1	..	..
Pratt, Daniel	..	..	..	1	..	2	..	..	1	..	..
Pratt, Josiah	2	2	..	1	..	3	1	..	1	..	..
Putnam, Daniel	2	..	1	1	..	2	..	..	1	..	..
Putnam, Farrant	1	..	1	..	1	..	1	2	..	1	..
Putnam, Israel	1	..	..	1	..	1	1	..	1	1	..
NEWBURY—con.											
Quimby, John	2	..	1	1	..	..	..	..	1	..	..
Randall, Lemuel	..	..	1	1	1	..	..	1	..	1	..
Randall, Mason	1	..	1	..	..	2	..	1	..	..	..
Randall, Samuel	1	..	..	1	..	2	1	1	1	..	..
Raymond, Joseph	2	..	..	..	1	..	..	..	1	..	..
Rhoades, Eliezer	..	..	..	1	..	..	..	..	..	..	..
Ricker, Joseph	1	1	..	1	..	4	..	1	1	..	..
Rogers, Daniel	1	..	1	..	..	4	1	..	1	..	..
Rogers, John D.	..	2	1	..	1	..	..	3	..	1	..
Rogers, Josiah	..	1	1	1	1	..	1	2	..	1	..
Rogers, Samuel	1	..	..	1	..	..	..	1	..	..	..
Rogers, Stephen	..	1	..	1	..	..	..	..	1	..	..
Salter, Ebenezer	..	..	..	..	1	..	..	1	..	1	..
Sanders, John	1	1	..	1	..	2	1	2	1	..	..
Sawyer, Elliott	1	..	1	1	..	3	1	..	1	..	..
Sawyer, Sylvanus	..	1	..	1	..	5	1	..	1	..	..
Scott, John	2	1	1	..	1	2	2	..	1	..	..
Seagel, Elijah	1	..	..	1	..	1	..	..	1	..	..
Seagel, Jacob	..	..	..	..	1	..	..	..	..	1	..
Sleeper, Joseph	1	1	..	..	1	3	1	1	..	1	..
Sly, John	1	..	1	..	1	..	..	1	..	1	..
Smith, James	1	..	..	..	1	..	..	2	..	1	..
Smith, Joseph	1	..	..	1	..	..	..	2	..	..	..
Spear, James	..	2	..	1	..	1	..	1	1	..	..
Spencer, Hobart	2	..	1	1	..	..	..	1	..	..	..
Stebbins, Horace	1	..	..	1	..	2	..	1	..	..	..
Stevens, Otho	3	..	..	1	..	1	2	..	1	..	..
Stevens, Simeon	3	3	1	1	..	1	..	1	2	..	..
Swazey, Moses	1	..	1	1	..	2	..	..	1	..	..
Swazey, Obadiah	1	..	1	1	..	..	..	1	..	..	..
Sylvester, Levi	..	..	1	..	1	..	..	1	1	1	..
Sylvester, Levi Jr.	3	..	1	..	1	1	..	1	..	..	..
Taplan, Brigham	2	..	..	1	..	2	1	..	1	..	..
Taylor, Jonathan	2	..	..	1	..	2	..	..	1	..	..
Temple, Ebenezer	..	..	..	1	..	1	..	1	..	..	..
Tenny, Asa	1	1	1	1	..	..	1	..	1	..	..
Thompson, Samuel	1	1	..	1	..	3	1	..	1	..	..
Tucker, Samuel	1	..	2	..	1	..	1	1	..	1	..
Tucker, Samuel Jr.	..	1	1	1	..	2	..	..	1	..	..
Tuxbury, Gideon	2	..	..	2	..	..	..	..	1	..	..
Tuxbury, Jacob	2	1	..	1	..	3	1	..	1	..	..
Tuxbury, Phillip	1	1	..	1	..	2	..	..	1	..	..
Vance, James	..	1	..	..	1	1	..	..	..	1	..
Vance, John	3	1	..	1	..	1	2	1	1	..	..
Virginia, Jeremiah	..	..	..	..	..	..	..	..	..	..	10
Wallace, William	..	2	9	..	1	1	1	2	1	1	..
Webster, Peter	..	..	1	..	..	..	..	1	..	..	1
Weed, Joseph	1	..	1	..	..	..	..	1	..	..	..
Weston, Abel	..	..	1	..	..	..	..	1	..	..	..
White, Ebenezer	1	1	1	..	1	..	1	..	..	1	..
White, Ebenezer Jr.	..	..	1	1	..	..	..	1	1	..	..
White, Nicholas	1	..	1	1	..	..	..	1	1	..	..
White, Nicholas Jr.	..	..	..	1	..	1	..	..	1	..	..
White, Samuel	3	..	1	1	..	1	1	..	1	..	..
White, Samuel Jr.	1	..	1	..	..	1	..	..	1	..	..
White, Timothy	1	..	..	1	..	2	1	..	1	..	..
Williams, Joseph	..	1	..	1	..	2	..	..	1	..	..
Willlson, Caleb	..	..	..	1	..	..	..	1	..	..	..
NORTHFIELD											
Allen, Ithemer	2	1	2	1	1	1	1	3	..	1	..
Ashcroft, William	1	2	2	..	1	1	1	3	..	1	..
Baron, Israel	3	1	..	1	..	..	1	..	1	..	..
Black, John	1	..	1	..	..	1	..	1	..	..	..
Brown, Elisha	..	1	..	1	..	..	..	1	..	..	..
Burnham, Justus	1	..	1	1	..	2	1	..	1	..	..
Carpenter, Roswell	1	..	..	1	..	2	..	1	..	..	..
Cathan, John	2	..	..	1	..	..	..	1	..	..	..
Cobley, Oliver	1	..	..	1	..	1	..	..	1	..	..
Emerson, John	3	..	..	1	..	1	..	1	1	..	..
Fox, Ebenezer	..	..	1	..	1	..	1	..	..	1	..
French, Thomas	..	1	1	..	1	..	..	..	1	..	..
Hedges, Daniel	4	..	..	2	..	1	..	1	1	..	..
Hedges, David	..	2	1	..	1	..	..	..	..	1	..

ORANGE COUNTY—Continued

NAMES OF HEADS OF FAMILIES	FREE WHITE MALES					FREE WHITE FEMALES					
	Under 10 years of age	Of 10 and under 16	Of 16 and under 26 including heads of families	Of 26 and under 45 including heads of families	Of 45 and upwards including heads of families.	Under 10 years of age	Of 10 and under 16	Of 16 and under 26 including heads of families	Of 26 and under 45 including heads of families	Of 45 and upwards including heads of families	All other free persons except Indians not taxed
NORTHFIELD—con.											
Jones, Aquilla	1	..	2	..	1	..	1	2	..	1	..
Keyes, Abel	1	1	..	1	..	1	..	..	1	..	..
Lyndes, Isaac	2	2	..	..	1	..	1	..	1	..	..
Paul, James	1	..	..	1	..	2	1	..	1	..	..
Pierce, Ezekiel	3	1	..	1	..	2	..	..	1	..	..
Rice, Merrick	..	..	..	..	1	..	..	..	..	..	..
Richardson, Lemuel	1	..	..	1	..	1	..	1	..	..	..
Richardson, Samuel	2	1	..	..	1	1	1	..	1	..	..
Richardson, Stanton	2	2	1	..	1	2	..	..	1	..	..
Robinson, Amos	3	1	1	1	..	2	2	..	1	..	..
Robinson, Ezekiel	3	1	1	1	..	1	1	..	1	..	..
Robinson, Nathaniel	1	1	..	1	..	3	2	..	1	..	..
Shipman, Abraham	2	..	..	1	..	1	..	..	1	..	..
Shipman, Eliphalet	1	1	.	1	..	2	..	2	1	..	..
Stockwell, Amos	..	1	..	1	..	1	1	..	1	..	..
Tubes, Lemuel	..	..	1	..	1	..	..	1	..	1	..
Tubes, William	3	..	..	1	..	1	..	..	1	..	..
Waters, Stephen	1	..	1	..	..	1	..	1	..	..	..
ORANGE											
Bachelder, Jonah	..	..	..	1	..	1	..	1	..	..	..
Barker, William	2	1	..	1	1	1	..	..	1	..	..
Bliss, Enos	1	..	..	1	..	1	..	..	..	..	..
Buell, Brown	..	..	2	..	..	..	..	..	..	..	..
Bush, Fairbank	1	..	..	1	..	1	..	1	..	..	..
Bush, Timothy	4	..	..	1	..	2	..	..	1	..	..
Camp, Abel	..	..	..	..	1	..	..	..	..	1	..
Camp, Gould	..	1	..	2	..	3	..	..	2	..	..
Camp, William	3	1	..	1	..	1	1	..	1	..	..
Chamberlin, Amos	2	..	1	1	..	2	..	..	1	..	..
Chamberlin, Ira	..	..	..	1	..	1	..	1	..	..	..
Cheeney, John	4	..	..	1	..	1	1	..	1	..	..
Clapp, Paul	1	..	1	1	..	1	..	1	..	..	..
Conant, Jonathan	..	..	..	..	1	..	..	..	..	1	..
Conant, Josiah	3	..	..	1	..	1	2	..	1	..	..
Currier, Ezekiel	..	..	1	..	..	1	..	1	..	..	..
Currier, Joseph	3	..	..	1	..	3	..	..	1	..	..
Divine, Joseph	1	..	1	..	..	..	..	1	..	..	..
Dyer, Waterman	1	..	..	1	..	1	..	1	..	..	..
Everett, Francis	1	..	..	1	..	1	..	..	1	..	..
Fish, Levi	..	..	..	2	..	..	..	1	..	..	..
Freeman, Alfred	..	..	1	..	..	1	..	..	1	..	..
Fullington, George	..	..	..	1	..	1	..	1	..	..	..
Fullington, Jonathan	..	..	..	1	..	..	..	..	..	..	..
Fyfield, Samuel	2	..	..	1	..	..	..	2	..	..	..
Garfill, Asa	1	..	..	1	..	..	..	1	..	..	..
Goodale, Ezra	..	1	..	1	..	..	..	..	1	..	..
Goodrich, David	2	..	3	..	1	1	..	1	..	1	..
Goodrich, David Jr.	1	..	1	..	..	1	..	1	..	..	..
Griswold, Aaron	2	..	2	..	1	1	1	..	2	..	..
Hastings, Medad	3	2	..	1	..	2	..	2	1	..	..
Hill, Ebenezer	1	..	..	1	..	2	..	1	..	..	..
Hoff, Alexander	6	1	..	..	1	1	2	..	2	..	..
Hoff, John	5	2	..	..	1	1	2	..	1	..	..
Holbrooks, Nathaniel	..	..	..	1	..	1	..	..	1	..	..
Howard, Solomon	1	1	..	1	..	..	..	..	1	..	..
Hunt, Ephram	1	..	..	1	..	3	1	..	1	..	..
Hunt, Humphrey	2	..	..	1	..	2	1	..	1	..	..
Jones, Amos	3	..	..	1	..	1	2	..	1	..	..
Judkins, Samuel	4	..	..	1	..	2	..	..	1	..	..
King, George	..	..	..	1	..	1	..	1	..	..	..
Lord, Porter	..	..	1	1	..	1	1	..	1	..	..
Neilson, Charles	2	1	..	2	1	3	..	1	..	1	..
Neilson, David	..	..	..	1	..	2	..	1	..	..	..
Noyes, Aaron	..	..	..	1	..	1	..	1	..	..	..
Noyes, Friend	3	2	..	1	..	..	..	..	1	..	..
Paine, Ezra	2	1	..	1	..	2	1	1	..	..	..
Paine, Thomas S.	..	1	..	1	..	3	1	..	1	..	..
ORANGE—con.											
Pike, Lemuel	..	..	..	1	..	3	..	..	1	..	..
Pineo, James	..	1	..	1	..	3	..	..	1	..	..
Pope, Thomas	..	..	..	1	..	1	..	1	..	..	..
Richardson, James	3	..	..	1	..	1	..	..	1	..	..
Richardson, Nathaniel	2	..	..	1	..	1	..	..	1	..	..
Rising, David	1	..	..	2	..	1	..	1	..	..	..
Salter, Peter	3	1	..	1	..	..	1	..	1	..	..
Sandborn, Amariah	..	..	..	1	..	..	..	1	..	..	..
Sloane, John	..	..	..	1	..	..	..	..	..	1	..
Sloane, Matthew	1	2	1	1	..	2	2	..	1	..	..
Spafford, Abraham	..	..	1	1	..	1	..	1	..	..	..
Stacy, John	4	..	..	1	..	1	1	..	1	..	..
Strong, Absolom	..	..	..	1	..	..	..	..	1	..	..
Waterman, Daniel	..	1	..	1	..	1	..	1	..	..	..
Waterman, John	..	1	2	..	1	..	..	1	..	1	..
West, John	..	..	1	..	..	..	..	..	..	..	..
Williams, Joseph	..	..	..	..	1	..	..	..	..	1	..
RANDOLPH											
Abbott, Benjamin	4	..	..	1	..	..	2	..	1	..	..
Adams, Phineas	1	..	..	1	..	..	..	..	1	..	..
Adams, Silas	..	..	..	1	..	..	..	..	1	..	..
Ainsworth, Edward	2	2	..	1	..	2	1	..	1	..	..
Allen, Woolcot	..	1	..	1	..	4	..	1	1	..	..
Ammidown, Jonathan	2	2	..	1	..	2	..	1	1	..	..
Ammidown, William	3	..	..	1	..	3	..	..	1	..	..
Annis, Hannah (Widow)	..	..	..	..	..	..	1	..	..	1	..
Arnold, Gamaliel	..	..	3	..	1	..	..	..	..	1	..
Arnold, Henry	1	..	5	1	..	4	..	..	1	..	..
Averill, Samuel	..	..	1	..	..	..	..	2	..	..	..
Bacon, John	1	1	1	..	1	1	1	1	..	1	..
Banister, Eli	2	..	2	..	1	3	1	1	..	1	..
Barnes, Comfort	1	..	..	1	..	2	..	..	1	..	..
Bates, David	1	..	1	..	1	..	2	1	..	1	..
Bates, Eliphalet	4	..	..	1	..	..	..	..	1	..	..
Bates, Joseph	..	2	1	1	..	2	..	..	1	..	..
Bates, Robert	1	..	..	1	..	1	..	..	1	..	..
Bates, Thomas	1	..	..	1	..	..	..	..	1	..	..
Bayliss, Timothy	1	..	..	1	..	2	2	..	1	..	..
Belknap, David	3	1	1	1	..	1	1	..	1	..	..
Belknap, Moses	3	..	2	..	1	2	1	4	..	1	..
Belknap, Simeon	3	1	1	1	..	1	1	..	1	..	..
Benedit, Samuel	..	1	2	..	1	1	1	..	..	1	..
Biam, Mary	..	..	1	..	..	..	..	2	..	1	..
Birch, Ephram	2	..	..	1	..	2	1	1	1	..	..
Bissel, Daniel	..	..	..	1	1	..	..	..	..	2	..
Bissel, Daniel Jr.	2	..	..	1	..	2	..	..	1	..	..
Bissel, Elias	2	1	..	1	..	4	2	..	1	..	..
Bissel, Ezekiel	2	..	..	1	..	..	..	..	1	..	..
Blakely, Moses	2	1	..	1	..	2	2	1	1	..	..
Bliss, Corliss	..	1	2	..	1	..	1	1	1	..	..
Bliss, Shubael	1	..	2	..	..	..	..	2	..	..	..
Blodget, Benjamin	3	2	3	..	1	2	..	..	1	1	..
Blodget, Caleb	4	1	1	..	1	..	2	..	1	..	..
Blodget, Ezra	2	..	..	1	..	..	..	..	1	..	..
Blodget, Henry	2	1	..	1	..	2	1	..	1	..	..
Blodget, James	..	..	..	..	1	..	..	..	..	1	..
Blodget, James Jr.	1	1	1	..	1	2	1	..	1	..	..
Blodget, John	2	1	..	1	..	2	1	..	..	..	..
Blodget, Joshua	2	1	1	1	..	3	1	..	1	..	..
Blodget, Sylvanus	..	1	..	1	..	1	..	..	1	..	..
Blodgett, Seth	..	..	..	1	..	..	..	1	..	..	..
Bradford, John	1	..	..	1	..	1	..	1	..	..	..
Brag, Moses	..	..	..	1	..	3	1	..	1	..	..
Braynard, Asahel	1	..	..	1	..	..	..	..	1	..	..
Braynard, Elijah	2	..	1	..	1	2	1	..	..	1	..
Braynard, Isaac	5	3	..	1	..	..	..	..	2	1	..
Brooks, John	1	..	..	1	..	..	..	..	1	..	..
Brooks, Joshua	1	..	..	1	..	..	..	..	1	..	..
Brooks, Timothy	1	..	..	1	..	1	..	..	1	..	..
Brown, John H.	2	..	..	1	..	..	..	..	1	..	..
Brown, Nathaniel	..	..	..	..	1	..	1	1	..	1	..
Call, Rufus	4	..	..	1	..	..	1	..	1	..	..
Carpenter, Comfort	1	..	1	..	..	..	..	1	..	..	..
Carpenter, David	1	2	1	1	..	1	1	..	1	..	..
Carpenter, John	..	1	..	..	1	..	..	1	..	..	..
Carpenter, Jonathan	3	1	..	..	1	..	1	1	1	..	..
Carpenter, Joseph	1	1	1	1	..	1	..	1	..	..	..
Chadwick, Amos	2	..	1	..	..	..	..	1	..	..	..
Chadwick, Isaac	1	..	..	1	..	1	..	..	1	..	..
Chadwick, Joseph	..	1	1	..	1	1	1	2	..	1	..

ORANGE COUNTY—Continued

NAMES OF HEADS OF FAMILIES	FREE WHITE MALES: Under 10 years of age	FREE WHITE MALES: Of 10 and under 16	FREE WHITE MALES: Of 16 and under 26 including heads of families	FREE WHITE MALES: Of 26 and under 45 including heads of families	FREE WHITE MALES: Of 45 and upwards including heads of families.	FREE WHITE FEMALES: Under 10 years of age	FREE WHITE FEMALES: Of 10 and under 16	FREE WHITE FEMALES: Of 16 and under 26 including heads of families	FREE WHITE FEMALES: Of 26 and under 45 including heads of families	FREE WHITE FEMALES: Of 45 and upwards including heads of families	All other free persons except Indians not taxed
RANDOLPH—con.											
Chadwick, Lot	3			1					1		
Chase, Dudley	1		1	1				2			
Chase, Seth	1		1		1	1			2		
Clark, Jeremiah	2	1	1	1	2			2	1		
Cleveland, Enoch				1		3			1		
Cloe, Phineas	1			1		1			1		
Cobb, Jacob	3		1	1		2	2		1		
Coburn, Solomon				1					1		
Cogswell, Bersheba	3								1		
Cogswell, Jesse	2	1		1		2			1		
Cole, John	1		1	1		3			1		
Cole, Joseph	1			1		3			1		
Cole, Samuel					1	1	1	2	1		
Conkey, Joel	1			1		1			1		
Converse, Frederick	3			1		2		1	1		
Converse, Israel	3	1	3		1	1	2	3		1	
Converse, Israel Jr.				1		1		1			
Converse, Shubael			1	1		2		1	1		
Corbin, Daniel	1			1		2	1		1	1	
Crocker, Abraham	2	1		1			1		1		
Cross, Ebenezer	2	1	1	1			2		1		
Cross, Nathan	1			1				1	1	1	
Curtis, Nehemiah	1	1	1	1		2	1		1		
Cushman, Elieza	1	1		1		2	2		1		
Cushman, William				1		3		1	1		
Cushman, William P.	2			1					1		
Darby, John	1	1			1	1	1			1	
Day, Horace	1			1				1			
Day, Stephen	2			1					1		
Device, Barzillai		1	1		1	2	2			1	
Device, Ephram		1		1		1		1			
Device, Experience	1				1					1	
Dibble, Charles	1		1	1		2		1			
Dotey, Isaac	2			1		2			1		
Dryer, Jesse		1		1		2	1	2			
Dudley, Nicholas			1		1			1		1	
Eaton, Daniel				1		3			1		
Edgerton, Benjamin		1	3						1		
Edgerton, Ezra	1	1			1	1				1	
Edgerton, Libbeus		1		1				1	1		
Edgerton, Oliver	1	2		1		1	1		1		
Edgerton, William	3			2	2	2			1		
Edson, Abiel				1		1			1		
Edson, Eliab	2	1		1		2	1	1	1		1
Edson, Josiah	2	2	3	2		2	1	3	1		
Edson, Peter		1	1		1			2		1	
Edson, Samuel					1					1	
Edson, Simon	2	1		1					1		
Edson, Timothy	2	2	3		1			2		1	
Edy, James	2				1	1	1			1	
Edy, Polly								1		1	
Ellis, Elijah	1	1		1		4			1		
Ellis, Gedeon			3		1					1	
Ellis, Nathaniel	3			1					1		
English, John	1	1		1		1			1		
English, Zephaniah	2	1		1		2			1		
Evans, Edward	1	1	1		1	1	1	1		1	
Evans, John	1	1	2		1	1				1	
Evans, Nathaniel		1	1			1		2			
Evans, Robert	1	1		1					1		
Evans, William					1		1	2		1	
Fenton, Peleg			1		1				1		
Fish, Elias	1	1	2		1	1	2	1		1	
Fish, Elvin	1	1		1		2			1		
Fish, Stephen	1	2			1	1	1	3		1	
Fiske, David	1		1	1		1		1	1		
Fiske, Stephen	3			2		2	1	1	1		
Flint, Dyer	2		1	1				2			
Flint, James			2		1	2	2			1	
Flint, Samuel		1	1		1		1	2		1	
Gasson, Michael	1			1		1			1		
Gauze, John	2	2		1			1	2		1	
Gauze, John Jr.	1			1		2		1			
Geer, John				1		1		1			
Gifford, John	1			1		2			1		
Gilbert, Othniel	3			1		2			1		
Glazier, John			1					1			
Granger, Washington	1		2					1			
Green, David	1	1	1		1	3	1	1	1		
Green, James	3	1		1		1			1		
Grimes, James		1	1		1					1	
Griswold, Benjamin				1		1			1		
Griswold, John	3	1		1			1	1	1		
RANDOLPH—con.											
Griswold, Joseph					1					1	
Gullet, Joseph				1		1			1		
Hanks, Benjamin	1	1				1		1	1		
Hanks, Theophilus	1			1		2		1			
Heath, Abraham				1		5			1		
Heath, Isaac	1			1		1			1		
Heath, Jacob			1					1			
Herrick, Israel	2	1			1	1	1	1		1	
Herrick, Stephen	2			1		2	3		1		
Hibbard, Millen	2	1		1		2	1		1		
Hidden, Cheeney	1			1					1		
Honeyday, Joshua	1	1			1		1	2		1	
Hovey, Jonathan			2		1	3	2	2	1		
Hubbard, Zebulon	1	1	4		1		1	1	1	1	
Huntington, Christopher	1	1	1	1		3	2		1		
Hutchinson, Aaron	2			1				1			
Hyde, Joshua	2			1		1			1		
Hyde, William			1		1	1		2			
Jones, Simon	3	1		1		1	2		1		
Kibbee, Ambrose	1			1		4		1	1		
Kibbee, Israel	1	1		1		2	1	1	1		
Kibbee, James	1			1		1		1		1	
Kibbee, Josiah	2			1		1		1		1	
Kidder, John	1			1					1		
Kidder, John Jr.	1			1				1			
Kimball, Richard	2			1		1			1		
Knight, Joseph			1					1			
Lamb, Joseph	3			1		3		1			
Lamb, Nathan	2	2		1		1			1		
Lamson, Jonathan	3	2			1	3	2		1		
Lamson, Samuel	1	2		1		3	2		1		
Lamson, Thomas	2	1		1		3	1		1		
Lilley, Elisha	2			2		4		2	1		
Lovett, Joseph	1		1					1			
Lyon, Phillip		1		1		1		1	1		
Martin, Gideon	1	2	1		1			1		1	
Maxley, John		1	3	1	1				1		
McMurphy, Alexander	4		1			1		1			
Miles, Stephen	1	1		1		2			1		
Miles, Timothy	3	1	1		1	1	1	2		1	
Miller, Daniel			1						1	1	
Miller, Moses				1		1			1		
Morgan, Noah			1	1	1	1	1	3	2		1
Morris, James	1	1	1		1	1		1	1		
Morton, Joseph				1		1		1			
Moses, Abner	2			1		2			1		
Moultan, Daniel	1			1		1		1			
Moultan, Jude	2		1			1		1			
Moultan, Nathaniel	2	1		1		1	1		1		
Moultan, Phineas	2	1	2		1		1		1		
Neff, Thomas					1				1	1	
Newton, Isaac		2	2		1		1			1	
Nichols, Reuben			2	1				2			
Nye, Nathan	1	1	1	1		2			1		
Olds, John	4	2		1		1			1		
Olds, Joseph	2			1		1			1		
Orcutt, Jacob	1	1	1	1		1	1		1		
Orcutt, Lemuel				1		1			1		
Orcutt, Solomon					1				1	1	
Osgood, Abijah	2			1		1			1		
Paine, Daniel	1		1	1		2		1	1		
Palmer, Isaac S.			1		1		2			2	
Parker, Robert	3	1	1	1		1	1		1		
Parker, Stephen	1	2	1	1		1	1		1		
Parmilee, Benjamin	2	1	1		1	1				1	
Parrish, Daniel			1					1			
Parrish, Jacob	1				1					2	
Parrish, William P.	1		1	1				2			1
Partridge, Harper		2		1		1	1		1		
Pearson, Elias	1	2	1		1			2		1	
Pearson, Moses		1			1		1			1	
Pearson, Moses Jr.	1		1			2		1			
Peck, Jonathan	2			1		3			1		
Peckham, Jonathan	4	3	1	1	1		1	2	2		
Pember, Samuel	2				1		1	2		1	
Pember, Stephen			1	1		3	2		1		
Perrin, Noah			1					1			
Perrin, Samuel				1				1			
Phinney, Joshua	1			1				1			

ORANGE COUNTY—Continued

NAMES OF HEADS OF FAMILIES	FREE WHITE MALES					FREE WHITE FEMALES					
	Under 10 years of age	Of 10 and under 16	Of 16 and under 26 including heads of families	Of 26 and under 45 including heads of families	Of 45 and upwards including heads of families.	Under 10 years of age	Of 10 and under 16	Of 16 and under 26 including heads of families	Of 26 and under 45 including heads of families	Of 45 and upwards including heads of families	All other free persons except Indians not taxed
RANDOLPH—con.											
Pickens, Thomas	..	..	..	1	..	2	..	..	1	..	..
Pike, Jonathan	..	2	..	..	1	..	..	..	..	1	..
Ramsay, William	1	1	..	1	..	1	2	..	1	..	..
Riddle, John	..	1	..	1	..	4	1	..	1	..	..
Russell, Cornelius	2	2	..	1	..	1	..	..	1	..	..
Scott, William	3	2	..	1	..	..	1	..	1	..	..
Sisco, James D.	1	..	..	1	..	1	..	..	1	..	..
Smalley, Justus	..	2	..	1	..	1	..	..	1	..	..
Smith, Aaron	..	..	1	..	1	..	..	1	..	1	..
Smith, Abijah	2	..	..	1	..	2	1	1	1	..	..
Smith, Jedidiah	3	1	..	1	..	1	1	..	1	..	..
Smith, Joel	2	..	..	1	..	2	..	..	1	..	..
Smith, John	3	1	..	1	..	1	1	2	1	..	..
Smith, Jonathan	2	..	..	1	..	4	..	2	..	1	..
Smith, Oliver	3	..	..	1	..	2	..	1	1	1	..
Smith, William	..	1	..	1	..	3	1	..	1	..	..
Snow, Zephaniah	2	1	..	1	..	2	1	..	1	..	..
Sprague, John	2	..	..	1	..	..	..	1	..	..	..
Sprague, Jonathan	..	1	1	..	1	..	..	1	..	1	..
Sprague, William	2	1	..	1	..	1	1	..	1	..	..
Steele, Andrew	2	1	..	1	..	2	..	..	1	..	..
Steele, James	..	2	..	..	1	1	..	..	..	2	..
Steele, Samuel	1	1	..	1	..	1	..	1	1	..	..
Stoddard, Clement	1	..	..	1	..	3	1	..	1	..	..
Storey, Asa	..	2	1	..	1	..	1	1	..	1	..
Storrs, Aaron	1	1	1	1	1	..	2	2	..	1	..
Storrs, Huckins	1	1	..	1	..	1	2	1	1	..	..
Sturtevant, Elisha	..	..	..	1	..	1	..	..	1	..	..
Tarbox, James	3	2	..	..	1	2	..	..	1	..	..
Thayer, Isaac	2	..	..	1	..	..	..	..	2	..	..
Thomas, Aaron	4	1	..	1	..	1	..	..	1	1	..
Thompson, John	1	..	..	1	..	2	..	..	1	..	..
Tiffany, Benjamin	1	1	..	..	1	1	..	2	1	..	..
Tiffany, James	2	1	..	1	..	3	1	..	1	..	..
Tinkum, Nathaniel	1	2	..	1	..	1	..	..	1	..	..
Tracy, Perez	2	..	..	1	..	..	..	..	1	..	..
Tracy, Timothy	2	1	..	1	..	1	..	..	1	..	..
Trusdale, Thomas	1	..	..	..	1	1	..	1	..	1	..
Turner, David	..	1	3	..	1	2	2	1	..	1	..
Tyler, John	2	..	2	1	..	2	..	..	1	..	..
Tyler, Oliver	1	..	3	..	1	1	2	1	..	1	..
Vaughan, Jabez	1	..	..	1	..	1	1	1	1	..	..
Vilas, Moses	1	..	..	1	..	1	..	1	..	..	..
Walbridge, Eliezer	1	..	1	..	1	..	1	2	..	1	..
Walbridge, Henry	1	2	1	1	1	..	..	2	..	1	..
Waldo, Abner	3	..	..	1	..	..	..	1	..	..	..
Warner, Ellen	1	..	1	..	..	1	..	1	..	..	..
Warner, Joshua	..	..	1	..	1	3	3	1	1	..	..
Washburn, Abner	..	1	..	1	..	4	..	1	1	..	..
Washburn, Jonah	..	1	..	..	1	..	..	..	..	1	..
Washburn, Jonah Jr.	1	..	1	1	..	1	2	..	1	..	..
Washburn, Josiah	4	..	..	1	..	2	..	..	1	..	..
Wesson, Abner	2	1	..	1	..	2	1	..	1	..	..
Wesson, John	..	..	..	1	..	2	..	..	1	..	..
Wheeler, Moses	..	..	1	1	..	1	..	..	..	..	..
Williams, Henry D.	2	..	1	..	..	1	..	1	..	..	..
Wood, Amasa	..	1	..	..	1	2	..	1	..	1	..
Wood, Jacob	2	..	..	1	..	..	..	..	1	..	..
Wood, Lemuel	..	..	1	..	..	2	..	1	..	..	..
Wood, Thomas	1	..	..	1	..	1	..	..	1	..	..
Wood, Thomas	..	..	1	..	1	..	..	..	..	1	..
Wood, Thomas Jr.	..	..	..	1	..	2	..	..	1	..	..
Woodward, Asahel	2	..	..	1	..	2	..	..	1	..	..
Woodward, Benjamin	2	1	1	1	..	1	1	1	1	..	..
Woodward, Eliezer	3	1	..	..	1	1	..	1	1	..	..
Woodward, Jahael	1	..	1	..	2	3	3	..	1	1	..
Woodward, ———	..	..	..	1	1	3	..	..	1	1	..
York, Joseph	1	1	..	1	..	2	1	1	..	1	..
ROXBURY											
Adams, Joseph	3	1	..	1	..	1	..	..	1	..	..
Adams, Roswell	2	1	..	1	..	1	..	..	1	1	..
Bachelder, Christopher	..	..	1	..	..	1	..	1	..	..	..
Corbin, Daniel	1	..	..	1	..	1	..	1	..	..	..
Cram, David	3	..	..	1	..	1	..	..	1	..	..
Emerson, Timothy	..	..	1	..	..	..	..	..	..	..	..
ROXBURY—con.											
Ford, Benjamin	1	1	1	..	1	1	..	1	1	..	..
Freeman, Daniel	..	..	1	..	..	..	..	1	..	..	..
Huntington, Christopher	1	..	..	1	1	..	..	2	..	1	..
Huntington, Thomas	2	..	..	2	..	1	..	..	1	..	..
Lewis, Isaac	2	..	1	1	..	3	..	..	1	..	..
Moffitt, Eber	2	..	..	1	..	2	..	..	1	..	..
Newton, Joseph	1	..	..	1	..	..	..	1	..	..	..
Rice, Obadiah	..	..	1	..	1	..	1	..	..	1	..
Richardson, Samuel	1	..	2	..	1	1	2	2	..	1	..
Spalding, Darius	2	1	4	1	..	2	..	..	1	..	..
Stafford, John	1	..	..	1	..	..	..	..	1	..	..
Webster, Benoni	2	..	..	1	..	3	..	..	1	..	..
Willcox, Elisha	3	1	..	1	..	2	2	..	1	..	..
STRAFFORD											
Adams, Moses	..	..	..	1	..	1	..	..	1	..	..
Algur, Benjamin	2	..	..	1	..	1	..	..	1	..	..
Algur, Jared	1	1	..	1	..	..	1	..	1	..	..
Algur, John	..	..	1	..	1	..	1	..	..	1	..
Algur, John Jr.	2	1	..	1	..	2	..	..	1	..	..
Algur, Nathaniel	..	..	..	1	..	1	..	1	..	..	..
Algur, Silas	1	..	1	..	1	1	1	..	..	1	..
Algur, Silas Jr.	..	..	..	1	..	3	1	..	1	..	..
Allen, John	2	1	..	1	..	1	..	1	..	..	..
Ames, Amos	1	1	..	1	1	1	..	1	..	1	..
Avery, Israel	2	..	..	1	..	..	2	2	1	..	..
Bachelder, Jethro	..	1	..	1	..	2	2	..	1	..	..
Backer, Daniel	2	1	..	1	..	1	..	..	1	..	..
Bacon, Benjamin	1	..	..	..	1	1	..	..	..	1	..
Bacon, Daniel	3	..	..	1	..	..	..	..	1	..	..
Bacon, Daniel	2	..	1	1	1	1	..	..	1	1	..
Bacon, Levi	3	1	1	1	..	2	1	..	1	..	..
Badcock, Richard	2	..	..	1	..	1	..	..	1	..	..
Barrett, David S.	1	1	..	1	..	1	..	..	1	..	..
Barrett, Joseph	..	..	1	1	..	1	..	..	1	..	..
Batchelder, Isaac	2	..	1	1	..	..	..	..	1	..	..
Bean, Nathaniel	2	1	..	1	..	1	..	..	1	..	..
Bean, Sampson	3	..	..	1	..	..	..	..	1	..	..
Bedee, Azariah	..	1	..	1	..	..	1	..	1	..	..
Bedee, Barzillai	1	1	..	1	..	1	1	1	1	..	..
Beeman, Elijah	..	..	2	..	1	..	..	2	..	1	..
Blake, Elijah	1	..	1	1	..	..	2	..	1	..	..
Blake, Timothy	..	..	3	..	1	..	1	1	..	1	..
Blasdel, Hovey	..	2	1	..	1	..	..	2	1	..	..
Blasdel, John	3	..	..	1	..	..	..	..	1	..	..
Blasdel, Ezra	1	..	1	1	..	1	1	..	1	..	..
Bliss, Samuel	1	1	2	..	1	2	2	1	1	..	..
Booth, Isaiah	1	2	..	1	..	1	1	..	..	1	..
Brown, Absalom	3	1	..	1	..	2	1	1	1	..	..
Brown, Amos	3	..	1	1	..	1	..	..	1	..	..
Brown, Heman	4	..	1	1	..	3	2	1	1	..	..
Brown, Joshua	3	..	..	1	..	4	..	..	1	..	..
Brown, Josiah	3	1	1	..	1	2	1	1	..	1	..
Brown, Moses	3	3	4	..	1	1	..	1	..	1	..
Brown, Nathaniel	2	2	..	1	..	1	1	..	1	..	..
Brown, Nathaniel	..	..	..	..	1	..	..	..	..	1	..
Brown, William	3	..	..	1	..	1	..	..	1	..	..
Buel, Abel Jr.	1	..	1	..	..	1	..	1	..	..	..
Buel, Joseph	4	..	..	..	1	1	1	..	1	..	..
Bullock, John	3	..	1	..	1	1	1	1	1	..	..
Burbank, Aaron	..	2	1	..	1	1	..	..	..	1	..
Burroughs, Thomas	1	1	..	..	1	2	1	..	..	1	..
Buzzel, Israel	2	..	..	1	..	..	..	..	1	..	..
Camber, John H.	1	..	..	1	..	3	1	..	1	..	..
Carpenter, Asa	..	1	..	1	..	2	2	..	1	..	..
Carpenter, Elias	1	..	..	1	..	..	..	1	..	..	..
Carpenter, Ephram	..	..	1	..	1	..	..	1	..	1	..
Carpenter, Willard	3	..	..	1	..	1	..	..	1	..	..
Carr, Bradbury	..	..	..	1	..	3	..	..	1	..	..
Carrier, Isaac	..	1	..	1	..	..	..	1	..	..	..
Chamberlin, Amasa	3	2	1	..	1	2	1	..	..	1	..
Chamberlin, Amasa, Jr.	2	..	..	1	..	1	..	..	1	..	..
Chamberlin, Asahel	..	2	3	..	1	..	1	2	1	..	..
Chamberlin, Elias	1	1	1	..	1	3	..	..	..	1	..
Chamberlin, Isaac	..	1	..	1	..	1	..	..	1	1	..
Chamberlin, Joseph	..	..	1	..	..	..	..	1	..	..	..
Chamberlin, Warren	1	..	1	..	..	..	..	..	1	..	..
Chandler, Andrew	2	2	..	1	..	2	..	..	1	..	..

ORANGE COUNTY—Continued

NAMES OF HEADS OF FAMILIES	FREE WHITE MALES					FREE WHITE FEMALES					
	Under 10 years of age	Of 10 and under 16	Of 16 and under 26 including heads of families	Of 26 and under 45 including heads of families	Of 45 and upwards including heads of families.	Under 10 years of age	Of 10 and under 16	Of 16 and under 26 including heads of families	Of 26 and under 45 including heads of families	Of 45 and upwards including heads of families	All other free persons except Indians not taxed
STRAFFORD—con.											
Childs, Asa	..	..	..	..	1	..	1	..	..	1	..
Clark, Benjamin	1	..	1	..	..	..	..	1	..	..	..
Clark, Eli	2	1	..	1	..	1	1	..	1	..	..
Clark, Ezra	1	..	..	1	..	..	..	1	..	..	..
Clark, Joseph	1	..	..	1	..	2	..	..	1	..	..
Clark, Richard	..	..	1	..	..	..	..	1	..	..	..
Clogstone, Silas	1	..	..	1	..	2	..	1	..	..	..
Clogstone, Thomas	3	..	..	1	..	..	..	1	1	..	..
Clough, John	..	..	1	..	..	..	..	1	..	..	..
Clough, Josiah	3	1	..	1	..	..	..	..	1	..	..
Clough, Wadley	..	..	..	1	..	3	..	..	1	..	..
Comstock, John	2	..	..	1	..	..	1	..	1	..	..
Day, Alpheus	2	..	1	..	..	2	..	1	..	..	..
Day, Elkanah	..	..	..	..	1	..	..	..	..	1	..
Day, Sylvester	1	..	1	..	..	..	..	1	..	..	..
Dennison, Susannah	1	1	2	..	..	..	..	1	..	1	..
Dowe, Jeremiah	1	4	..	1	..	2	..	2	..	1	..
Downing, Richard	1	..	..	1	..	1	..	1	..	..	..
Drew, Ezekiel	..	..	1	1	..	6	1	1	1	..	..
Drew, Silas	2	..	..	1	1	1	..	..	1	1	..
Evans, Abner	1	..	2	..	1	1	2	..	..	1	..
Evans, Laban	..	..	1	..	..	..	..	1	..	..	..
Evans, Paul	2	1	..	1	..	1	..	..	1	..	..
Farmer, Oliver	1	..	..	1	..	2	1	..	1	..	..
Flanders, Daniel	1	..	..	1	..	3	..	..	1	..	..
Flanders, Jesse	2	..	..	1	..	8	..	..	1	..	..
Flanders, Joseph	..	..	1	1	..	1	..	2	..	1	..
Foggerson, John	1	2	..	1	..	3	1	..	1	..	..
Garnsey, Cyrall	2	..	..	2	..	2	1	1	1	..	..
George, Benjamin	1	1	1	..	1	2	1	1	..	1	..
George, Benjamin	..	..	..	..	1	..	..	..	..	1	..
George, Isaac	1	1	1	1	..	2	..	1	1	..	..
George, James	..	..	..	..	1	..	..	1	..	1	..
George, Joseph	2	..	..	1	..	1	..	..	1	..	..
George, Moses	..	..	1	..	..	..	..	1	..	..	..
Gilbert, Ezra	3	1	..	1	..	..	1	..	1	..	..
Gilbert, Heber	3	2	..	1	..	1	..	..	1	..	..
Gilbert, Joseph	2	1	..	1	..	1	..	..	1	..	..
Gilman, Daniel	..	1	..	..	1	..	1	..	..	1	..
Gilman, Edward	..	1	1	..	..	..	..	1	..	1	..
Gilman, John	..	..	..	1	..	1	..	1	..	..	..
Gilman, Nicholas	..	..	1	..	1	..	..	1	..	..	..
Goodale, Bartholomew	1	..	..	1	1	..	..	..	..	1	..
Green, Elijah	..	..	2	..	1	1	..	1	..	1	..
Green, John	2	1	..	1	..	1	..	..	1	..	..
Griffin, David	2	..	..	1	..	1	..	..	1	..	..
Griffin, Isaac	..	1	..	2	..	..	..	..	1	1	..
Grow, Nathaniel	2	2	3	1	..	1	..	1	1	..	..
Hacket, Moses	3	3	1	..	1	2	1	..	1	..	..
Hall, William	2	1	..	1	..	2	1	..	1	..	..
Hardy, Burley	2	..	1	..	1	2	1	..	..	1	..
Harris, James	2	..	..	1	..	1	..	1	..	..	..
Harris, John	1	1	..	1	1	..	..	..	1	1	..
Harris, William	..	..	..	1	..	..	..	1	..	..	..
Haskell, Job	..	..	2	..	1	..	..	..	..	1	..
Haskell, Thomas	1	..	..	1	..	1	..	..	1	..	..
Hatch, Joel	..	..	..	1	..	1	1	..	2	..	..
Hayes, Comfort	2	..	..	1	..	2	..	1	..	..	..
Hayes, Eleazer	2	..	..	1	..	3	1	..	1	..	..
Hayes, Robert	2	1	..	1	..	1	1	..	1	..	..
Hazeltine, Thomas	2	..	..	1	..	3	1	..	1	1	..
Heath, Daniel	4	..	..	1	..	1	2	..	1	..	..
Hogan, John	..	1	..	..	1	..	..	..	..	1	..
Holmes, Perly	2	1	..	1	..	3	..	1	1	..	..
Hopkins, Asa	2	2	..	1	..	2	1	..	1	..	..
Hopkins, Daniel	..	..	..	..	1	..	..	..	..	1	..
Hopkins, John	2	..	..	1	..	1	..	..	1	..	..
Hopkins, William	2	..	1	1	..	2	1	..	1	..	..
Howes, Benjamin	3	..	..	2	..	2	2	..	1	..	..
Hunt, Moses	1	..	..	1	..	3	..	..	1	..	..
Huntington, Roger	1	..	..	1	..	2	..	..	1	..	..
Huntington, Zebulon	..	..	1	1	..	..	..	..	1	..	..
Hutchins, John	3	..	..	1	..	..	..	..	1	..	..
Hyde, Asa	..	2	2	..	1	..	1	1	..	1	..
Hyde, James	3	1	..	1	..	..	..	..	1	..	..
Jenkins, Enos	2	1	..	1	..	3	1	..	1	..	..
Jewett, Nathaniel	1	..	1	..	..	..	..	1	..	..	..
Jewett, William	..	1	1	..	1	1	1	2	..	1	..
Johnson, Willis	..	1	1	..	1	2	1	..	1	..	..
Jude, Ira	..	..	..	1	..	3	..	..	1	..	..
Jude, Liberty	2	..	1	..	..	1	..	1	..	..	..
STRAFFORD—con.											
Jude, Phillip	4	2	..	1	..	1	..	..	1	1	..
Jude, William	3	..	..	1	..	2	1	..	1	..	..
Kelly, Addi	2	..	..	1	..	..	..	1	..	..	..
Kent, Charles	1	..	1	..	..	1	..	1	..	..	..
Keyes, Peter	2	1	..	1	..	2	..	1	1	..	..
Kimball, Caleb	..	1	1	..	1	..	1	1	..	1	..
Ladd, Oliver	..	1	..	1	..	2	2	..	1	..	..
Libbee, Bennet	1	..	3	..	1	2	2	..	..	1	..
Libbee, Isaac	..	1	2	1	1	..	1	..	..	1	..
Libbee, Job	1	2	..	1	..	2	..	..	1	..	..
Lilly, Benjamin	1	1	..	1	..	1	..	..	1	..	..
Lougee, William	..	..	..	1	..	1	..	1	..	..	..
Lucas, Thomas	2	..	1	..	..	2	1	..	1	..	..
May, Hezekiah	..	..	1	..	1	..	..	..	..	1	..
McIntire, Benjamin	..	1	..	..	1	1	..	3	..	1	..
McNeal, John	1	..	..	..	1	..	..	..	1	..	..
Miller, William	1	2	..	..	1	2	1	..	..	1	..
Moor, Joshua	3	..	..	1	..	2	..	..	1	..	..
Morey, Zenas	..	..	1	..	1	1	..	..	..	1	..
Morey, Zenas Jr.	2	..	..	1	..	2	..	..	1	..	..
Morrell, Smith	1	2	2	..	1	1	1	..	1	..	..
Munsel, Benjamin	2	..	1	1	..	..	..	1	..	1	..
Munsel, Ichabod	..	..	1	..	..	..	..	..	1	..	..
Newell, Esa	..	1	..	1	..	3	..	1	1	..	..
Newman, John	2	..	..	1	..	1	..	..	1	..	..
Newman, William	..	1	2	..	1	1	..	1	..	1	..
Newton, Asahel	2	1	..	1	..	1	1	2	..	1	..
Norton, Azariah	3	1	..	1	..	2	1	..	1	..	..
Norton, Joseph	..	1	..	1	..	3	1	1	1	..	..
Norton, Nathan	2	1	1	1	..	1	1	..	1	..	..
Norton, Noah	..	..	1	..	..	1	..	1	..	..	..
Norton, Seth	..	..	1	1	1	1	..	..	1	1	..
Ordeway, Aaron	4	..	..	1	..	1	..	..	1	..	..
Ordeway, Isaac	1	..	1	..	..	..	..	1	..	..	..
Patterson, Daniel	..	..	1	1	..	2	..	..	1	..	..
Percival, Azel	3	..	..	1	..	2	1	..	1	..	..
Pingree, John	1	..	..	1	..	3	1	..	1	..	..
Pinnick, Aaron	..	..	..	..	1	3	..	1	..	1	..
Pinnick, Adonijah	..	..	1	..	..	..	..	1	..	..	..
Pinnick, Alexander	..	1	3	1	..	1	1	1	1	..	..
Pinnick, Haman	2	..	..	1	1	4	1	..	1	..	..
Pinnick Ira	2	2	..	1	..	..	1	..	1	..	..
Pinnick, Isaac	2	..	..	1	..	2	..	..	1	..	..
Pinnick, Oliver	..	1	..	1	..	3	3	..	1	..	..
Pinnick, Peter	1	2	..	..	1	..	..	1	..	1	..
Pinnick, Peter Jr.	1	..	1	..	..	..	..	1	..	..	..
Pinnick, William	2	..	..	1	..	2	..	1	..	..	..
Polly, Benoni	1	..	..	1	..	1	..	..	1	..	..
Post, Israel	..	1	..	1	..	1	1	..	1	..	..
Powel, Calvin	1	1	..	1	..	2	1	..	1	..	..
Powel, Elisha	1	1	..	1	..	1	2	2	1	..	..
Powell, John	3	..	..	..	1	1	..	..	1	..	..
Prescott, James	1	..	1	..	1	..	..	2	..	1	..
Prescott, James Jr.	2	..	1	..	..	3	..	1	..	..	..
Presson, Alexander	..	..	..	1	..	4	2	..	1	..	..
Presson, Benjamin	2	1	..	1	..	2	2	..	1	..	..
Presson, Edward	1	..	..	1	..	1	..	..	1	..	..
Presson, Joseph	1	..	..	1	..	1	..	1	..	..	..
Presson, Robert	3	2	..	1	..	..	..	..	1	..	..
Presson, William	..	..	1	..	1	..	..	..	..	1	..
Preston, John	3	..	1	..	..	..	..	1	..	..	..
Randall, Reuben	1	..	..	1	..	..	..	..	1	..	..
Reddington, William	1	..	..	2	..	..	..	..	1	..	..
Rich, Abel	..	..	..	1	..	1	..	1	..	..	..
Rich, David	2	2	2	1	..	2	..	..	1	..	..
Rich, James	..	..	..	1	..	..	..	..	1	..	..
Rich, Jonathan	..	1	1	..	1	2	1	..	2	..	..
Richardson, Jeremiah	1	..	..	1	..	2	..	..	1	..	..
Ripley, Nehemiah	2	..	..	1	..	2	..	..	1	..	..
Robinson, Abraham	..	1	..	..	1	..	1	1	..	1	..
Robinson, Apollos	..	..	1	..	..	1	..	1	..	..	..
Robinson, Daniel	..	..	1	..	1	..	..	..	..	1	..
Robinson, Daniel Jr.	1	..	..	1	..	4	..	..	1	..	..
Robinson, Zadock	3	..	..	1	..	1	1	..	1	..	..
Rogers, Robert	2	..	..	1	..	2	..	..	1	..	..
Root, Daniel	3	1	..	1	..	1	..	..	2	1	..
Root, Levi	1	..	3	..	1	..	..	1	..	1	..
Root, Levi Jr.	..	..	1	1	..	..	..	1	..	..	..
Root, Oliver	3	1	..	1	..	1	..	..	1	..	..
Root, Solomon	3	..	..	1	..	2	2	..	1	..	..

ORANGE COUNTY—Continued

NAMES OF HEADS OF FAMILIES	FREE WHITE MALES: Under 10 years of age	FREE WHITE MALES: Of 10 and under 16	FREE WHITE MALES: Of 16 and under 26 including heads of families	FREE WHITE MALES: Of 26 and under 45 including heads of families	FREE WHITE MALES: Of 45 and upwards including heads of families.	FREE WHITE FEMALES: Under 10 years of age	FREE WHITE FEMALES: Of 10 and under 16	FREE WHITE FEMALES: Of 16 and under 26 including heads of families	FREE WHITE FEMALES: Of 26 and under 45 including heads of families	FREE WHITE FEMALES: Of 45 and upwards including heads of families	All other free persons except Indians not taxed
STRAFFORD—con.											
Root, William	2	2	..	1	..	1	1	..	1	..	..
Root, William B.	..	..	..	1	..	..	..	..	..	..	..
Rowel, Jonathan	1	1	1	..	1	1	..	1	1	..	..
Sabins, John	1	..	..	1	..	..	..	..	1	..	..
Sandborn, Enoch	1	..	1	..	..	1	..	1	..	..	..
Sandborn, Moses	2	1	1	1	..	2	1	..	1	..	..
Sandborn, Theophilus	2	..	..	1	..	1	1	..	1	..	..
Seavey, Joseph	..	..	..	1	..	1	..	1	..	..	..
Seckins, Martin	3	..	..	1	..	3	1	1	1	..	..
Sessions, Samuel	..	..	1	..	1	..	2	..	..	1	..
Shepard, Elisha	2	1	..	1	..	..	1	..	..	1	..
Simons, Nathaniel	..	1	..	1	..	1	..	..	1	..	..
Sinclair, John	1	..	1	..	..	..	..	..	1	..	..
Smith, Frederick	2	..	2	..	1	2	1	1	..	1	..
Smith, Isaac	1	..	..	1	..	2	..	..	1	..	..
Smith, Joseph	2	1	..	..	1	2	1	1	1	..	..
Stevens, Abel	2	..	..	1	..	1	..	..	1	..	..
Stevens, Abiel	..	1	2	..	1	..	2	..	..	2	..
Stevens, Jacob	3	..	..	1	..	2	..	..	1	..	..
Stoddard, Nathan	2	..	..	..	1	1	..	..	1	..	..
Straw, Joseph	..	..	..	1	..	..	..	1	..	..	..
Straw, Moses	2	..	..	1	..	1	..	..	1	..	..
Taft, Reserve	..	..	..	1	..	1	1	..	1	..	..
Thomas, Eliphalet	2	..	..	1	..	..	..	1	1	..	..
Tucker, Benjamin	..	..	..	1	..	1	..	..	1	..	..
Tucker, John	2	..	..	1	..	1	..	..	1	..	1
Tyler, Roswell	1	1	1	..	1	1	..	1	1	1	..
Walker, Freeman	..	1	1	1	..	3	1	1	1	..	..
Walker, Leonard	1	1	..	1	..	3	..	..	1	..	..
Warner, Eliezer	..	1	..	..	1	..	..	..	..	1	..
Wedge, Ezra	1	..	1	..	..	..	..	1	..	..	..
Wedge, John	1	1	..	..	1	..	..	..	..	1	..
Wedge, John Jr.	1	..	..	1	..	1	..	..	1	..	..
Wells, David	..	2	1	1	..	4	1	..	1	..	..
Wells, Nicholas	1	..	..	1	..	1	..	..	1	..	..
West, Daniel	3	1	4	..	1	2	1	..	1	1	..
West, Gilman	1	1	1	..	1	..	2	..	..	1	..
West, Jonathan	..	3	..	..	1	1	..	..	..	1	..
West, Samuel	1	..	..	1	..	..	..	..	1	..	..
White, Ebenezer	1	1	1	1	..	3	..	..	1	..	..
White, Joel	1	..	1	..	1	1	2	..	1	..	..
White, William	1	..	..	1	..	3	..	2	..	..	..
Whittaker, Ezra	1	..	..	1	..	2	..	1	..	..	..
Williams, Asa	1	..	1	..	1	..	..	..	..	1	..
Williams, John	2	..	..	1	..	2	..	..	1	..	..
Wood, Jesse	1	..	1	..	..	..	..	1	..	..	..
Wood, Joseph	..	..	..	1	..	1	1	..	1	..	..
Young, Guy	..	1	..	..	1	1	2	..	..	1	..
Young, Joab	2	..	1	2	..	1	1	1	1	..	..
THETFORD											
Abbot, Catharine	1	..	..	..	..	1	..	1	1	..	..
Abbot, Walter	..	2	3	..	1	..	..	1	..	1	..
Amesdale, Joseph	1	..	1	1	..	..	..	..	1	..	..
Amesdale, Noah	3	1	..	1	..	2	2	..	1	..	..
Annis, Frederick	..	..	..	..	1	..	..	..	..	1	..
Annis, Jacob	..	..	..	..	1	..	..	..	..	1	..
Annis, Jesse	2	..	..	1	..	..	..	1	..	..	..
Annis, John	1	2	..	1	..	2	1	1	1	..	..
Annis, Phinehas	3	1	..	..	1	1	..	1	1	..	..
Atkinson, Samuel	2	..	..	1	..	2	1	1	1	..	..
Avery, Charles	3	1	..	1	..	1	2	..	1	1	..
Avery, Josiah	2	..	..	1	..	2	..	..	1	..	..
Barlet, Samuel	..	1	..	1	..	..	..	..	1	..	1
Barret, Oliver	..	1	2	..	1	..	..	1	..	..	..
Bartholomew, Timothy	..	..	2	..	1	1	1	1	..	1	..
Bartlet, Gideon	..	..	..	2	1	..	..	1	..	..	..
Bennet, James	3	4	2	..	1	2	..	..	1	..	..
Bird, Ira	1	..	1	..	..	..	..	1	..	..	..
Bliss, Asahel	1	..	..	1	..	1	..	..	1	..	..
Bliss, Beriah	1	..	..	1	..	2	..	..	1	..	..
Bliss, James	3	..	..	1	..	1	1	..	1	..	..
Bliss, John	..	1	..	1	1	..	..	..	..	1	..
Brown, Amos	1	2	..	1	..	2	..	..	1	..	..
Brown, Thomas	..	..	1	..	..	..	..	1	..	..	..
Brown, William	3	1	..	1	..	1	1	..	1	..	..
Bryant, Daniel	3	1	..	1	..	..	1	..	1	..	..
Buckingham, Jedidiah P.	..	..	..	..	1	..	1	..	..	1	..
Burgoyne, Augustus	..	..	..	..	1	1	2	1	..	1	..
Burnham, Caleb	1	..	..	1	..	1	1	..	1	..	..
Burnham, William	..	..	..	1	..	1	..	..	1	..	..
THETFORD—con.											
Burroughs, John	3	..	..	1	..	..	1	..	1	..	..
Burton, Asa	..	1	1	..	1	..	1	1	..	..	..
Cadwell, Aaron	1	..	..	1	..	3	..	..	1	..	..
Cadwell, Moses	..	..	..	..	1	1	..	..	1	1	..
Cadwell, Moses, Jr.	1	..	..	1	..	4	1	..	1	..	..
Chamberlin, Abner	..	..	1	..	2	..	1	1	..	1	..
Chamberlin, Ashur	..	1	3	..	1	1	1	..	..	1	..
Chamberlin, Benjamin	..	1	..	..	1	..	..	..	..	1	..
Chamberlin, Benjamin Jr.	1	..	..	1	..	1	..	..	1	..	..
Chamberlin, Charles	2	..	..	1	..	3	2	3	1	..	..
Chamberlin, Ebenezer	2	..	..	1	..	1	..	..	1	..	..
Chamberlin, Ezekiel	2	..	..	1	..	1	..	..	1	..	..
Chamberlin, Joel	3	..	1	..	1	..	2	..	1	..	..
Chamberlin, John	4	2	..	1	..	..	..	..	1	..	..
Chamberlin, Samuel	2	..	..	1	..	1	..	..	1	..	..
Chamberlin, Timothy	1	..	1	..	..	..	..	1	..	..	..
Chapel, Joseph	..	1	..	1	..	2	..	..	1	..	..
Childs, Aaron	2	..	..	1	..	1	..	..	1	..	..
Childs, Jonathan	..	..	..	..	1	..	..	..	..	1	..
Childs, William	1	2	1	1	..	2	1	1	1	..	..
Clark, David	1	..	..	1	..	3	..	..	1	..	..
Clark, Elijah	1	1	1	..	1	2	..	1	1	1	..
Clark, Jonah	1	..	..	1	..	1	..	..	1	..	..
Clossen, Simon	3	..	..	1	..	2	1	..	1	1	..
Cook, Samuel	1	..	..	1	..	..	..	1	..	..	..
Coster, Thomas	1	..	1	..	..	..	..	1	..	..	..
Courser, Jonathan	1	..	1	..	..	1	..	1	..	..	..
Courser, Simeon	2	2	..	1	..	3	..	..	1	..	..
Crandell, Richmond	1	..	..	..	1	..	..	..	1	..	..
Critchet, Josiah	1	..	..	1	..	3	..	..	1	..	..
Critchet, Thomas	..	..	..	..	1	..	..	..	..	1	..
Crosset, Israel	..	..	..	1	..	4	1	..	1	..	..
Cummins, Eliezer	1	..	..	1	..	1	..	..	1	..	..
Cummins, Ezra	2	..	..	1	..	2	..	..	1	..	..
Cummins, Israel	1	..	..	1	..	1	..	..	1	..	..
Cummins, Nathaniel	2	..	..	1	..	2	..	..	1	..	..
Curtis, Ephram	..	..	1	..	1	..	1	2	..	1	..
Cushman, William	..	..	1	..	1	..	..	..	..	1	..
Davenport, Thomas	..	..	..	1	..	3	1	..	1	..	..
Device, Eliezer	..	..	1	..	..	1	..	1	..	..	..
Device, Isaac	..	1	..	..	1	1	..	..	..	1	..
Downer, Cushman	3	1	..	1	..	..	1	..	1	..	..
Downer, James	..	1	..	1	..	3	..	..	1	..	..
Downer, Joseph	..	..	1	..	1	..	..	..	1	..	..
Duffee, Martha	..	..	..	..	..	3	..	..	1	..	..
Elkins, Moses	1	..	..	1	..	1	..	..	1	..	..
Ellsworth, William	1	..	..	1	..	2	..	..	1	..	..
Fish, Ephram	..	..	..	1	..	2	..	..	1	..	..
Flanders, Stephen	2	2	1	..	1	2	1	..	1	..	..
Fletcher, Jonathan	..	1	..	1	..	3	..	..	1	..	..
Fletcher, Leonard	2	1	..	1	..	..	1	2	1	..	..
Foss, Josiah	1	..	..	1	..	3	..	..	1	..	..
Fowler, Philip	2	1	..	1	..	2	1	..	1	..	..
Freeman, William	..	1	..	..	1	2	..	2	..	1	..
Frizzle, John	..	1	..	1	..	3	2	..	1	..	..
Galush, Samuel	2	1	1	..	1	1	1	..	..	1	..
Garwin, Ebenezer	2	..	..	1	..	1	..	..	1	1	..
Gerry, Loved	2	..	..	1	..	1	..	1	1	..	..
Gillet, Simon	3	1	..	..	1	1	2	..	1	..	..
Gould, Israel	..	1	..	1	..	2	..	..	1	..	..
Gould, Stephen	2	..	..	1	..	..	..	..	1	..	..
Green, Chauncy	..	..	..	1	..	..	..	..	1	..	..
Green, Joseph	1	..	..	..	1	..	..	..	..	1	..
Green, Samuel	..	..	1	..	..	..	..	1	..	..	..
Hammond, Elijah	1	..	..	1	..	2	..	..	1	..	..
Hanks, Asa	4	1	..	1	1	..	1	..	1	..	..
Hardy, Daniel	2	1	..	..	1	2	1	..	1	..	..
Haskel, Andrew	..	..	..	..	1	1	2	..	..	1	..
Hawley, Emanuel	..	..	..	1	..	3	..	..	1	..	..
Hawley, Experience	3	1	..	1	..	1	3	..	1	..	..
Heaton, Benjamin	2	..	..	1	..	2	1	..	1	..	..
Heaton, James	..	..	1	..	..	..	..	1	..	..	..
Heaton, Orange	1	1	..	1	..	2	..	..	1	..	..
Heaton, William	..	1	..	..	1	..	1	1	1	1	..
Heaton, William Jr.	..	..	1	1	..	1	1	1	..	..	..
Hinckley, Gershom	1	1	1	..	1	..	2	1	..	1	..
Hinckley, Joseph	1	..	..	1	..	1	..	..	1	..	..
Hinckley, Oramel	3	..	1	1	..	2	2	..	1	..	1
Horn, Ephram	1	..	..	1	..	1	..	..	1	..	..
Hosford, Aaron	..	..	1	..	1	..	..	..	..	1	..
Hosford, Aaron	1	1	..	1	..	3	..	..	1	..	..

ORANGE COUNTY—Continued

NAMES OF HEADS OF FAMILIES	FREE WHITE MALES					FREE WHITE FEMALES					
	Under 10 years of age	Of 10 and under 16	Of 16 and under 26 including heads of families	Of 26 and under 45 including heads of families	Of 45 and upwards including heads of families.	Under 10 years of age	Of 10 and under 16	Of 16 and under 26 including heads of families	Of 26 and under 45 including heads of families	Of 45 and upwards including heads of families	All other free persons except Indians not taxed
THETFORD—con.											
Hosford, Elihu	3	..	1	..	1	2	2	1	..	1	..
Hosford, Joseph	1	1	2	..	1	..	2	1	..	1	..
Hosford, Joseph 2nd	3	..	..	1	..	1	..	..	1	..	..
Hosford, Obadiah	2	..	1	..	1	1	1	..	1	..	..
House, John	..	1	3	..	1	..	1	..	..	1	..
Hovey, Amos	1	..	..	..	1	1	1	2	..	1	..
Hovey, William	2	..	2	..	1	3	2	1	..	1	..
Howard, Abijah	..	1	2	..	1	1	2	3	..	1	..
Howard, Abner	..	..	1	..	1	..	..	..	1	1	..
Howard, Elijah	..	..	..	..	1	..	..	1	..	1	..
Howard, Elijah Jr.	1	2	..	1	..	1	1	..	1	..	..
Howard, Jonathan	..	2	..	1	..	..	..	..	..	1	..
Hubbard, Jacob	3	..	..	1	..	1	..	..	1	..	..
Hubbard, Josiah	..	2	..	1	..	..	1	..	1	..	..
Illsley, Israel	..	..	..	2	..	3	..	..	1	..	...
Jackman, Samuel	3	..	2	..	1	1	..	2	..	1	..
Jaquish, Moses	..	1	..	1	..	3	1	..	1	..	..
Johnson, Charles	2	..	1	..	1	4	..	1	..	1	..
Kendall, Benjamin	1	..	..	1	..	1	..	..	1	..	..
Kendall, Peter	2	..	..	1	..	3	1	1	1	..	..
Kendall, Samuel	..	1	..	1	..	1	1	..	1	..	..
Kidder, John	..	..	..	..	1	..	1	..	..	1	..
Kilburn, Nathaniel	1	..	..	1	..	3	1	..	1	..	..
Kingsbury, Benjamin	..	..	..	..	1	..	..	..	2	..	..
Kinney, David	2	1	..	1	..	1	..	..	1	..	..
Knight, Levi	3	..	..	1	..	2	..	..	1	..	..
Knight, Seth	1	..	..	1	..	3	..	..	1	..	..
Knox, George	..	..	..	..	..	..	..	..	1	..	6
Ladd, Thaddeus	1	..	..	1	..	4	3	..	1	..	..
Loomis, Beriah	1	2	5	..	1	1	2	2	..	1	..
Lord, Russell	1	..	1	..	..	..	..	1	..	..	..
Lucas, Edmond	2	..	..	1	..	2	..	..	1	..	..
Mann, Frederick	3	1	1	1	1	..	..	..	1	1	..
Manuel, David	2	..	2	..	..	..	..	1	..	..	..
Marstin, Josiah	1	..	..	1	..	1	..	..	1	..	..
McLary, John	2	1	1	..	1	..	2	2	..	1	..
McLellan, Lucy	1	..	..	..	..	..	1	..	1	..	1
Messenger, Nathaniel	1	..	..	2	1	1	..	1	..	1	..
Moor, Hannah	..	..	1	..	..	..	..	2	1	1	..
Moor, James 1st.	2	..	..	1	..	2	1	..	1	..	..
Moor, James	..	2	..	1	..	4	..	..	1	..	..
Moor, James	2	..	..	1	..	..	..	..	1	..	..
Moor, William	..	..	1	..	1	..	1	2	..	1	..
Murdock, Asahel	..	1	1	..	1	1	1	1	..	1	..
Newcomb, Bethuel	2	1	1	..	1	2	1	1	..	1	..
Newcomb, Justus	5	1	..	1	..	..	..	..	1	..	..
Newcomb, Simon	2	..	..	1	1	2	..	..	1	1	..
Newton, Samuel	..	..	..	1	..	1	..	..	1	..	..
Nichols, Francis	1	2	..	1	..	2	..	1	1	1	..
Nichols, John	1	..	..	1	..	1	1	..	1	..	..
Nichols, Jonathan	3	..	..	..	1	2	..	..	1	..	..
Nichols, Thomas	1	..	..	1	..	1	..	..	1	..	..
Osborne, John	1	1	..	1	..	1	1	..	1	..	..
Osmore, Aaron	..	1	..	2	..	..	..	..	1	..	..
Page, Charlotte	3	..	..	..	..	1	1	..	1	..	..
Page, Samuel	3	..	..	1	..	1	..	..	1	..	..
Parker, Levi	1	2	..	1	..	2	1	..	1	..	..
Patterson, Josiah	1	2	..	..	1	2	2	..	1	..	..
Penny, Martin	..	..	..	1	..	1	..	..	1	..	..
Pettigrew, Stephen	3	..	..	1	..	1	1	1	1	..	..
Phillip, Alpheus	..	..	..	1	1	..	..	1	..	1	..
Post, Aaron	2	1	..	1	..	3	..	..	1	..	..
Post, Daniel	1	..	..	1	..	4	..	..	1	..	..
Post, Eldad	..	..	..	..	1	..	..	..	1	..	..
Post, John	2	1	2	1	..	1	2	1	1	..	..
Post, Russell	1	..	..	1	..	1	..	..	1	..	..
Powers, Nahum	3	..	..	1	..	3	..	..	1	..	..
Pratt, Daniel	3	3	..	1	..	..	..	..	1	..	..
Ransted, Roger	1	..	1	1	..	1	..	1	1	..	..
Rice, John	..	..	1	..	..	..	..	1	..	..	..
Rice, John Jr.	..	1	1	..	1	..	1	..	..	1	..
Right, Daniel	2	2	..	1	..	2	..	..	1	..	..
Riley, John	1	..	..	1	..	3	..	..	1	1	..
Riley, Simeon	..	..	..	1	..	1	..	1	1	..	..
Robins, Benjamin	1	..	..	1	..	1	..	..	1	..	..
Robinson, James	1	..	..	..	1	3	1	..	..	1	..
Robinson, Samuel	1	..	..	1	..	..	..	..	1	..	..
Rogers, John	..	1	..	..	1	..	..	..	..	1	..
THETFORD—con.											
Rogers, Samuel	2	1	2	..	1	..	1	2	..	1	..
Rogers, Zenos	4	..	..	1	..	..	..	..	1	..	..
Russell, Peter	..	..	..	1	..	1	..	..	1	..	..
Sacket, William	1	2	1	..	1	2	1	1	1	..	..
Sanborn, Thomas	1	..	1	..	..	1	..	1	..	..	..
Sawyer, James	1	1	..	..	1	..	1	..	..	1	..
Sealy, Deborah	2	..	..	..	..	..	..	..	1	..	..
Seers, Sylvanus	..	..	..	1	..	4	..	..	1	1	..
Severance, Nicholas	3	1	..	1	..	1	..	..	1	..	..
Sexton, Benjamin	1	..	..	1	..	2	..	..	1	..	..
Shattuck, Benjamin	1	..	..	1	..	2	..	..	1	..	..
Shepard, Phillip	4	1	..	1	..	..	..	..	1	..	..
Smith, Israel	..	..	1	1	1	..	..	..	1	..	..
Smith, Israel B.	2	..	..	1	..	..	..	..	1	..	..
Stowel, Ira	2	..	..	1	..	1	1	..	1	..	..
Strong, Deliverance	..	1	..	..	..	..	..	1	..	1	..
Strong, Elisha	3	..	..	1	..	2	2	1	1	..	..
Strong, Joel	2	..	1	..	1	1	2	2	..	1	..
Strong, Oliver	..	2	..	1	..	..	..	1	1	..	..
Strong, Solomon	..	..	..	..	1	..	2	1	..	1	..
Strong, Walter	1	..	..	1	..	2	1	..	1	..	..
Strong, Walter Jr.	1	..	..	1	..	1	..	..	1	..	..
Sweatland, Molly	..	1	2	..	..	..	..	2	..	1	..
Swift, Ebenezer	..	..	..	..	1	..	..	..	..	1	..
Swift, Ebenezer Jr.	2	..	..	1	..	2	1	..	1	..	..
Taylor, Jeremiah	3	2	..	1	..	2	1	..	1	..	..
Tyeler, Oliver	1	..	..	1	..	1	..	..	1	..	..
Tyler, Gould	1	..	1	..	..	..	..	1	..	..	..
Tyler, James	..	..	..	1	..	..	..	1	..	..	..
Tyler, James	2	1	1	1	..	2	1	1	1	..	..
Tyler, John	..	..	..	1	..	1	..	..	1	..	..
Tyler, Joshua	..	..	1	..	1	..	..	1	1	1	..
Tyler, Moses	3	2	..	1	..	1	..	1	1	..	..
Tyler, William	..	..	1	..	1	..	1	..	..	1	..
Walker, Eli	1	..	..	1	..	4	2	..	1	..	..
Wallace, Richard	1	2	..	..	1	3	2	1	..	1	..
Waterman, Levi	1	2	..	1	..	2	1	..	1	..	..
Welch, John	..	..	..	..	1	..	..	..	..	1	..
Welch, Percith	1	..	..	..	..	1	..	..	1	..	..
Wetherbee, Danforth	2	1	..	1	..	..	..	..	1	..	..
Wetherbee, Silas	2	..	..	1	..	1	..	..	1	..	..
Wheeler, Amos	3	1	..	1	..	1	1	..	1	..	..
White, Isaac	..	..	..	1	..	1	..	..	1	..	..
White, James	1	2	2	..	1	1	..	..	1	..	..
White, Samuel	1	..	..	1	..	1	..	..	1	..	..
Wire, Joseph	1	1	2	..	1	3	..	1	1	..	..
Wood, Abiel	1	..	..	1	..	1	..	..	1	..	..
Wood, Israel	1	..	..	..	1	1	..	..	..	1	..
Wood, Jacob	..	1	2	1	..	1	..	1	..	..	..
Wood, Jonathan	2	..	3	..	1	3	3	..	..	1	..
Woodward, Samuel	1	1	..	1	..	3	1	..	1	..	..
Woodworth, ———	1	..	..	..	..	4	..	..	1	1	..
Woodworth, Elijah	1	..	..	1	..	..	..	1	..	..	2
Young, Samuel	2	1	..	1	..	2	1	..	1	..	..
TOPSHAM											
Bagley, Aaron	2	1	..	1	..	2	..	..	1	..	..
Bagley, David	..	..	..	1	..	1	..	..	1	..	..
Bagley, Nathaniel	2	..	..	1	..	2	1	..	1	..	..
Baldwin, Jonathan	1	..	..	1	..	2	..	..	1	..	..
Barnet, James	..	..	..	1	..	..	..	1	..	..	..
Boyes, William	1	..	..	1	..	..	..	1	..	..	..
Brown, John	1	..	1	1	..	1	..	..	1	..	..
Brown, Timothy	..	1	1	..	1	..	1	..	..	1	..
Bullard, Ebenezer	3	1	..	..	1	1	1	..	1	..	..
Chapman, Abraham	..	..	1	..	..	..	..	1	..	..	..
Crown, Samuel	1	..	..	1	..	3	1	..	1	..	..
Cunningham, James	2	..	..	1	..	2	..	..	1	..	..
Devils, Asa	1	..	..	1	..	..	..	..	1	..	..
Dickey, Adam	2	..	3	..	1	2	2	..	1	..	..
Dowe, John	..	..	..	1	..	..	..	..	1	..	..
Farren, Joseph	..	..	..	1	..	2	..	..	1	..	..
Fellows, John	2	1	..	1	..	3	..	..	1	..	..
Gentleman, William	..	..	..	1	..	1	..	..	1	..	..
George, James	1	..	..	1	..	1	..	..	1	..	..
Harding, Richard	1	..	1	..	1	3	1	..	..	1	..
Holman, Ezekiel	2	..	..	1	..	2	1	..	1	..	..

ORANGE COUNTY—Continued

NAMES OF HEADS OF FAMILIES	FREE WHITE MALES					FREE WHITE FEMALES					All other free persons except Indians not taxed
	Under 10 years of age	Of 10 and under 16	Of 16 and under 26 including heads of families	Of 26 and under 45 including heads of families	Of 45 and upwards including heads of families.	Under 10 years of age	Of 10 and under 16	Of 16 and under 26 including heads of families	Of 26 and under 45 including heads of families	Of 45 and upwards including heads of families	
TOPSHAM—con.											
Huckins, Jonathan	..	..	..	..	1	..	..	..	..	1	..
Huckins, Moses	..	..	..	1	..	..	..	..	1	..	..
Huntley, Richard	2	..	1	1	..	1	..	..	1	..	..
Jones, Charles	2	2	1	..	1	2	..	1	..	1	..
Jones, Daniel	1	..	..	1	..	3	..	..	1	..	..
Jones, David	..	..	1	..	..	1	..	1	..	..	..
Kenniston, Francis	2	..	..	1	..	1	..	..	1	..	..
Kent, Jacob	2	1	..	..	1	2	..	..	1	..	..
Mann, Robert	..	1	..	..	1	..	..	..	..	1	..
Mann, Robert Jr.	..	..	..	1	..	3	..	..	1	..	..
May, John	..	1	..	1	..	..	..	1	..	..	..
McCrelis, Robert	2	..	..	1	..	1	..	..	1	..	..
McCrelis, Stephen	1	..	..	1	..	1	..	1	..	..	..
Mills, Nathaniel	2	2	..	1	..	1	..	..	1	..	..
Moor, Elisha	1	..	..	1	..	1	..	..	1	..	..
Nasmith, John	3	1	..	1	..	2	..	..	1	..	..
Nasmith, Robert	..	..	..	..	1	..	..	..	2	1	..
Nasmith, Stephen	2	..	..	1	..	1	..	..	1	..	..
Nutt, John	4	..	..	1	..	2	..	..	1	..	..
Nutt, William	2	2	..	1	..	2	..	1	..	1	..
Putnam, Porter	1	2	..	1	..	1	..	..	1	..	..
Richardson, Zacchariah	2	..	2	..	1	1	1	..	..	1	..
Rider, Seth	1	1	..	1	..	2	..	..	1	..	..
Rockwell, Joseph	1	..	..	1	..	3	..	..	1	..	..
Sandborn, Ebenezer	3	..	..	1	..	1	..	..	1	..	..
Sandborn, William	..	..	..	1	..	3	1	..	1	..	..
Sawyer, John	3	..	..	1	..	3	1	..	1	..	..
Severance, Daniel	5	1	2	..	1	..	..	..	..	1	..
Silly, William	2	..	..	1	..	2	..	..	1	..	..
Smith, James	1	..	..	1	..	2	1	..	1	..	..
Stevens, John	3	1	..	1	..	..	..	..	1	..	..
Stevens, Samuel	2	..	..	1	..	2	1	..	1	..	..
Tabor, Lemuel	4	2	1	..	1	1	..	..	1	..	..
Thompson, Samuel	..	..	1	1	..	..	1	..	..	1	..
Vance, John	1	1	..	..	1	1	..	..	..	1	..
Walden, John	..	..	3	1	..	2	..	1	1	..	..
White, Jesse	..	..	1	1	..	..	..	..	..	..	..
Wild, Jacob	2	1	..	1	..	1	1	..	1	..	..
Wood, William	1	..	2	..	1	1	2	2	..	1	..
TUNBRIDGE											
Adams, Benjamin	..	1	1	..	1	..	1	..	1	..	..
Adams, Jonathan	2	..	..	1	..	1	1	..	1	..	..
Adams, Robert	..	..	4	..	1	2	..	1	..	1	..
Adams, Samuel	..	..	..	..	1	2	..	..	..	1	..
Ainsworth, Ammi	1	..	2	1	..	3	1	..	1	..	..
Alexander, William	2	1	..	1	..	3	..	..	1	..	..
Allen, Amos	2	..	1	..	1	1	2	..	..	1	..
Allen, Oliver	2	..	..	1	..	1	..	..	1	..	..
Andrews, James	3	..	2	..	1	1	1	..	..	1	..
Austin, Abiel	..	..	1	1	..	..	..	1	..	..	..
Austin, Samuel	2	..	..	1	..	1	1	1	..	..	..
Austin, Seth	3	1	1	..	1	2	1	..	..	1	..
Austin, Thomas	..	..	1	..	..	2	..	..	1	..	..
Banks, Josiah	1	..	1	..	..	1	..	1	..	..	..
Barret, Thomas	2	1	..	1	..	3	1	..	1	..	..
Bates, Jacob	1	2	..	1	..	2	..	..	1	..	..
Bean, Enoch	..	..	..	..	1	..	..	1	..	1	..
Bean, John	1	..	1	..	..	2	..	1	..	..	..
Beeman, Samuel	1	..	1	1	..	1	..	1	1	..	..
Beeman, Silas	1	..	..	1	..	..	..	1	..	..	..
Belden, David	4	..	..	1	..	..	..	..	1	..	..
Bell, Ezekiel	1	1	..	1	..	1	..	..	1	..	..
Benson, Henry	1	..	..	1	..	..	..	1	..	..	..
Bliss, Jonathan	2	2	..	..	1	2	1	2	1	..	..
Blodget, Nathaniel	1	..	1	..	..	..	..	1	..	..	..
Blodget, William	..	..	1	..	..	1	..	1	..	..	..
Blue, William	1	2	..	1	..	2	..	..	1	..	..
Branch, Peter	..	..	1	..	1	1	3	..	..	1	..
Branch, Phineas	2	..	..	..	..	..	..	1	..	..	..
Brewer, David	3	..	..	1	..	1	..	1	1	..	..
Brigham, Sylvanus	1	..	1	1	..	..	..	2	..	..	..
Brigham, William	1	..	..	1	1	..	..	1	1	1	..
Broughton, John	3	..	..	1	..	2	..	..	1	..	..
Broughton, John	2	1	..	1	..	1	..	..	1	..	..
TUNBRIDGE—con.											
Brown, Deliverance	3	1	..	1	..	2	..	2	2	..	..
Burroughs, Abel	1	..	..	1	..	1	..	..	1	..	..
Burroughs, Asa	1	..	..	1	..	1	..	1	..	..	..
Burroughs, Daniel	1	..	..	1	..	1	..	1	..	..	..
Button, Louis	..	..	2	..	..	..	..	..	..	2	..
Camp, Abel	1	2	1	1	..	3	..	1	1	..	..
Camp, Joel	2	2	..	..	1	1	1	1	1	..	..
Camp, Major	3	..	..	1	..	2	..	1	1	..	..
Chamberlin, Joseph	..	1	..	1	..	1	2	..	1	..	..
Chambers, Robert	2	..	..	1	..	1	..	..	1	..	..
Chambers, William	2	1	1	..	1	1	..	2	..	1	..
Chapman, Becket	..	..	2	..	1	..	2	1	..	1	..
Cheeney, Thomas	1	1	..	1	..	3	2	..	1	..	..
Clemens, Stephen	..	1	..	1	..	3	..	..	1	..	..
Clemens, William	1	2	..	..	1	2	..	1	..	1	..
Colburn, Asa	1	..	..	..	1	2	1	..	..	1	..
Colburn, Gustin	..	..	1	..	..	1	..	1	..	..	..
Colby, John	2	1	..	1	1	3	1	..	1	1	..
Conkey, Ezekiel	1	1	..	1	..	2	1	1	..	..	..
Conkey, Joel	1	..	..	1	..	1	..	1	..	..	..
Cowder, Edward	2	1	1	1	..	2	..	..	1	..	..
Cowder, Jabish	..	..	1	..	1	..	1	..	..	1	..
Cowder, Zacchariah	1	..	1	..	..	..	..	..	1	..	..
Coy, Reuben	..	..	..	1	..	1	..	1	..	..	..
Currin, Hubbard	2	1	..	1	..	1	1	..	1	..	..
Curtis, Asahel	1	..	..	1	..	1	..	1	..	..	..
Curtis, Elias	..	..	3	..	1	1	1	..	1	..	..
Curtis, Elias Jr.	1	..	1	1	..	..	..	1	..	..	..
Curtis, Samuel	4	..	..	1	..	2	1	..	1	..	..
Curtis, Simeon	..	1	2	..	1	..	..	1	..	1	..
Cushman, (Widow)	..	..	2	..	..	..	1	..	..	1	..
Cushman, Willard	1	..	..	1	..	..	..	1	..	..	..
Device, Samuel	1	3	..	1	..	..	..	..	1	..	..
Dewey, Timothy	1	1	1	..	1	..	1	..	1	..	..
Dodge, Ammi	1	..	..	1	..	1	..	..	1	..	..
Dresser, Alanson	2	..	..	1	..	1	..	..	1	..	..
Durkee, Solomon	2	..	..	1	..	2	2	..	1	..	..
Dwinald, Amos	2	..	1	1	..	1	1	1	1	..	..
Eaton, Daniel	1	..	..	1	..	..	..	..	1	..	..
Eaton, James	2	..	..	1	..	2	..	..	1	..	..
Eaton, Samuel	4	..	..	1	..	1	1	..	1	..	..
Emery, Joel	1	1	..	..	1	1	1	1	1	..	..
English, David	..	..	2	1	1	..	..	..	1	1	..
English, David Jr.	1	..	..	1	..	3	..	..	1	..	..
Field, Patrick	..	..	1	..	1	2	1	..	..	1	..
Forrest, Robert	2	..	..	..	1	3	2	..	1	..	..
Foster, Joshua	2	..	..	1	..	3	2	..	1	..	..
Freeman, Phillip	2	1	..	1	..	1	..	..	1	..	..
Fulsome, Daniel	..	..	..	1	1	2	..	..	1	1	..
Fulsome, David	2	1	..	1	..	1	..	..	1	..	..
Fulsome, Jacob	2	..	1	..	..	2	..	..	1	..	..
Fulsome, John	..	..	1	..	..	2	..	1	..	..	..
Fulsome, Stephen	1	..	1	..	..	3	..	..	1	..	..
Gay, Gideon	1	..	1	1	..	..	..	1	1	1	..
Gay, Nathan	..	..	..	1	..	..	..	..	1	..	..
Goodwin, Nathan	4	1	2	..	1	1	1	..	1	..	..
Goodwin, Richard	2	..	..	1	..	1	2	1	1	..	..
Griswold, Jedidiah	2	..	..	1	..	3	..	..	1	..	..
Grow, David	..	1	..	1	..	2	..	..	1	..	..
Grow, Deborah	2	..	..	..	..	2	1	..	1	..	..
Grow, Edward	..	..	2	..	1	..	..	..	..	1	..
Hacket, Daniel	..	2	2	..	1	..	..	1	1	..	..
Hadley, Daniel	3	..	..	1	..	2	1	..	1	..	..
Hall, John	..	1	..	1	..	4	..	..	1	..	..
Hall, Nathaniel	1	..	..	1	..	1	..	..	1	..	..
Hall, Obadiah	1	..	1	..	1	..	..	..	..	1	..
Harriman, Buck B.	3	..	..	1	..	2	..	..	1	..	..
Harriman, Stephen	1	1	2	1	..	2	1	1	1	..	..
Haskel, Thomas	..	..	..	1	..	..	..	..	1	..	..
Holmes, Miah	1	..	..	1	..	1	..	..	1	..	..
Howard, Abijah	..	..	..	..	1	..	..	..	..	1	..
Howard, Brooks	1	..	..	1	..	1	..	..	1	..	..
Hudson, Brooks	2	..	..	1	..	2	..	..	1	..	..
Hunt, Daniel	2	1	..	..	2	2	1	1	..	2	..
Hunt, Daniel	2	1	..	2	..	2	..	..	1	..	..
Hunt, Simeon	2	..	..	1	..	2	..	..	1	..	..
Hutchins, John	..	2	..	1	..	3	..	..	1	..	..
Hutchinson, Abijah	..	1	..	..	1	..	..	..	1	..	..
Hutchinson, Elisha	1	..	..	1	..	3	..	..	1	..	..
Hutchinson, Hezekiel	1	1	1	..	1	1	2	..	..	1	..

ORANGE COUNTY—Continued

NAMES OF HEADS OF FAMILIES	FREE WHITE MALES					FREE WHITE FEMALES					All other free persons except Indians not taxed
	Under 10 years of age	Of 10 and under 16	Of 16 and under 26 including heads of families	Of 26 and under 45 including heads of families	Of 45 and upwards including heads of families.	Under 10 years of age	Of 10 and under 16	Of 16 and under 26 including heads of families	Of 26 and under 45 including heads of families	Of 45 and upwards including heads of families.	
TUNBRIDGE—con.											
Johnson, Willis	2	..	..	1	..	1	..	..	1	1	..
Kendall, Merrill	1	..	..	1	..	1	..	1	..	..	..
Kilburn, William	2	2	..	1	..	2	..	..	1	..	..
Kimball, Andrew	3	..	3	..	2	1	2	..	..	2	..
King, Joshua	2	..	..	1	..	2	..	..	1	..	..
King, Nathaniel	..	..	..	1	..	3	..	..	1	..	..
Kingsbury, Nathaniel	2	..	2	1	..	3	1	..	1	..	..
Kneal, William	2	..	..	1	..	1	..	..	1	..	..
Knox, David	2	..	1	..	1	2	2	1	..	1	..
Ladd, John	1	..	..	1	..	2	..	1	..	..	..
Ladd, Jonathan	..	..	..	..	1	..	1	2	1	..	..
Ladd, Robert	..	..	1	..	..	..	..	1	..	..	..
Lasdel, John	..	1	..	1	1	..	..	1	..	1	..
Lilly, John	..	..	3	1	1	..	1	..	1	1	..
Lougee, William	2	1	..	1	..	2	..	..	1	..	..
Lunt, Ezekiel	..	..	..	..	1	2	2	..	..	1	..
Lunt, Moses	..	..	1	..	..	..	..	2	..	..	..
Lyon, James	3	1	2	..	1	2	..	1	1	..	..
Lyon, William	1	..	1	..	..	..	..	1	..	..	..
Mack, Solomon	..	..	..	1	1	..	..	..	1	1	..
Mack, Stephen	1	1	5	1	..	6	1	..	1	..	..
Manning, Aaron	1	..	1	..	..	..	..	1	..	..	..
Marshall, Daniel	1	..	..	1	..	2	..	1	..	..	..
Merrill, John	2	2	..	..	1	..	..	1	..	..	..
Minor, Luke	3	..	..	1	..	1	..	..	1	..	..
Moody, Elisha	3	..	..	1	..	1	..	..	1	..	..
Moody, John	4	..	..	1	..	1	2	..	1	..	..
Mudget, John	1	..	1	1	..	..	..	..	1	..	..
Muxley, Nathan	1	..	..	1	..	2	..	..	1	..	..
Muxley, Seth	..	1	..	1	..	2	1	..	1	..	..
Muxley, Thomas	..	..	..	1	1	1	..	1	..	1	..
Nichols, Jonathan	2	2	..	1	..	2	2	..	1	..	..
Noyes, Aaron	3	..	..	..	1	..	1	1	..	1	..
Noyes, Nathan	2	3	2	..	1	1	..	..	1	..	..
Noyes, True	1	..	..	1	..	1	..	1	..	..	..
Ordeway, Benjamin	1	1	..	1	..	3	..	..	1	..	..
Ordeway, Michael	..	1	..	1	..	3	1	..	1	..	..
Ordeway, Moses	..	1	1	..	1	..	1	1	..	1	..
Ordeway, Moses Jr.	1	..	1	..	..	..	1	1	..	..	..
Otis, Edward	2	1	..	1	..	2	1	..	1	..	..
Paine, Seth	..	..	2	..	1	2	1	1	1	1	..
Peabody, John	1	1	..	1	..	2	..	1	1	..	..
Perkins, Seth	1	..	..	1	..	2	..	..	1	..	..
Pratt, Daniel	..	..	..	..	1	..	..	..	..	1	..
Pudney, James	2	1	..	1	1	1	..	..	1	..	..
Putnam, Abijah	1	..	..	1	..	..	..	..	1	..	..
Putney, James	2	1	..	1	1	..	1	..	1	..	..
Rayno, Samuel	..	..	..	1	..	..	..	..	1	..	..
Riddle, John	3	1	..	1	..	2	1	..	1	..	..
Riley, James	2	..	..	1	..	1	2	1	1	..	..
Roberts, Jonathan	1	1	..	..	1	3	..	2	..	1	..
Rollins, Levi	1	..	..	1	..	3	..	..	1	..	..
Ruff, James	2	..	..	1	..	..	..	..	1	..	..
Sargeant, Robert	1	1	..	1	..	4	..	1	1	..	..
Seavey, Joseph	..	2	1	..	1	..	..	1	..	1	..
Seavey, William	2	2	..	1	..	2	2	..	1	..	..
Seeley, Ebenezer	2	..	..	1	..	2	..	..	1	..	..
Seely, Jacob	..	..	1	..	..	..	..	1	..	..	..
Silly, Daniel	..	1	..	1	..	1	..	..	1	..	..
Smith, Asahel	..	1	2	1	1	..	1	1	..	1	..
Smith, Jesse	3	..	..	1	..	1	..	..	1	..	..
Smith, Joseph	1	..	1	..	..	2	..	..	1	..	..
Smith, Obadiah	1	1	2	..	1	..	1	..	..	1	..
Smith, Stephen	1	..	..	1	..	2	..	..	1	..	..
Spalding, Duty	1	..	..	1	..	1	..	..	1	..	..
Stanley, Jacob	2	..	1	1	..	2	..	1	1	..	..
Stanley, Joseph	..	..	..	1	..	4	..	..	1	..	..
Stanley, Matthew	6	1	..	1	..	1	1	..	1	..	..
Stanley, Nathaniel	3	..	..	1	..	..	..	..	1	..	..
Stanley, Phineus	..	..	1	..	..	1	..	1	..	..	..
Stedman, Alexander	2	1	2	..	1	1	1	1	..	1	..
Stedman, Dorothy	..	..	..	..	..	3	..	1	..	..	..
Stedman, Eli	1	..	1	..	..	..	..	1	..	..	..
Storey, Ezekiel	1	..	1	..	..	1	..	1	..	..	..
Swan, Caleb	..	..	..	1	..	1	..	1	..	..	..
Thompson, Nathan	..	..	3	..	1	..	..	..	..	1	..
Thompson, Richard	1	..	1	..	..	..	..	1	..	..	..
Tracy, Cynes	2	1	..	..	1	2	..	..	1	..	..
Tracy, Elijah	..	2	..	1	..	1	1	1	..	1	..
Tracy, Hannah	..	..	..	..	1	..	..	1	..	1	..
Train, Lemuel	1	1	..	1	..	1	..	..	1	1	..
True, Jonathan	..	..	..	1	..	2	..	1	..	..	..
Tubes, Ananias	2	..	..	1	..	2	..	2	..	1	..
Tucker, Sargeant	1	..	..	1	..	1	..	..	1	..	..
Tuttle, Timothy	1	..	..	1	..	2	..	..	1	..	..
Tuxbury, Sargeant	1	..	..	1	..	..	..	..	1	..	..
Tyler, James	2	1	..	1	..	..	..	..	1	..	..
Wait, William	3	..	..	1	..	1	1	..	1	..	..
Waldo, Edward	..	1	..	1	..	1	..	..	1	..	..
White, Henry	..	..	1	..	1	..	..	1	..	1	..
White, Simon	1	1	..	1	..	2	..	..	1	..	..
White, William	1	..	..	1	..	4	..	..	1	..	..
Whitney, Abel	2	..	..	1	..	1	..	..	1	..	..
Whitney, Benjamin	1	..	..	1	..	4	1	..	1	..	..
Whitney, David	3	..	..	1	..	1	1	..	1	..	..
Whitney, Jonathan	2	..	..	1	..	..	..	1	..	..	..
Whitney, Peter	..	..	..	..	1	..	2	..	..	1	..
Whitney, Thomas	..	..	..	1	..	..	..	1	..	..	..
Willard, Solomon	3	1	..	1	..	..	..	..	1	..	..
Williston, Howe D.	1	..	..	1	..	..	..	..	1	..	..
Wright, William	4	..	..	1	..	..	..	..	1	..	..
York, Gushom	1	1	1	1	..	3	2	..	1	..	..
VERSHIRE											
Aldrich, Aaron	1	..	1	..	..	..	..	..	1	..	..
Aldrich, Wales	1	..	..	1	..	1	..	..	1	..	..
Alexander, Hugh	2	..	1	..	1	1	1	1	..	1	..
Allen, Asaph	..	..	..	1	..	1	..	..	1	..	..
Annis, Jesse	1	2	..	..	2	..	2	1	..	1	..
Annis, Joseph	1	1	..	1	..	1	..	..	1	..	..
Ashley, Luke	2	..	..	1	..	..	..	..	1	..	..
Ayer, Joseph	1	1	..	1	..	3	1	..	1	..	..
Ayer, Nathaniel	..	..	..	..	1	..	..	..	..	1	..
Bachelder, Josiah	2	..	..	1	..	1	..	..	1	..	..
Baldwin, Asa	2	..	..	1	..	3	1	..	1	..	..
Baldwin, Eliam	..	..	..	1	..	1	..	1	..	..	..
Baldwin, Jabez	2	1	..	1	..	1	..	..	1	1	..
Baldwin, Stephen	2	..	1	1	..	1	..	..	1	..	..
Baldwin, Zadock	2	..	..	1	..	..	..	..	1	1	..
Barret, Benjamin	..	..	2	..	1	..	..	1	..	1	..
Barret, Lemuel	2	..	..	1	..	2	..	..	1	..	..
Barret, Luke	4	1	..	1	..	3	..	..	1	..	..
Barret, Thaddeus	1	..	..	1	..	1	..	1	1	..	..
Bartholomew, Moses	..	1	2	..	..	1	..	1	..	1	..
Batchelder, Jonathan	3	..	..	1	..	..	..	..	1	..	..
Bichford, Paul	3	2	..	1	1	1	..	..	1	..	..
Bixby, John	2	..	..	1	..	..	..	..	1	..	..
Black, Nehemiah	1	..	..	1	..	2	..	..	1	..	..
Black, Nicholas	..	..	..	..	1	..	..	1	..	1	..
Bond, Amasa	1	..	2	..	1	2	..	..	1	..	..
Bowman, Oliver	..	..	..	1	..	1	1	..	1	..	..
Brown, Ebenezer	1	..	..	1	..	1	..	..	1	..	..
Burnham, James	2	1	..	1	..	2	1	..	1	..	..
Butterfield Amos	2	..	..	1	..	2	..	..	1	..	..
Cadwell, Jonathan	1	1	..	1	..	..	..	..	1	..	..
Carpenter, Ezra	1	2	1	1	..	2	1	1	1	..	..
Carr, John	..	..	2	..	1	..	..	2	..	1	..
Carr, John Jr.	1	1	..	1	..	2	..	..	1	..	..
Childs, Joseph	1	..	..	1	..	..	..	..	1	..	..
Childs, Samuel	2	..	..	1	..	1	..	..	1	..	..
Childs, Samuel	1	..	..	1	..	3	..	..	1	..	..
Church, Asa	..	1	2	..	1	..	..	1	..	1	..
Church, Isaac	..	1	3	..	1	..	..	..	..	1	..
Church, Jacob	3	1	..	..	1	1	1	1	..	1	..
Colby, Jonah	..	3	1	..	1	..	1	2	..	1	..
Colton, Daniel	1	..	..	1	..	1	..	1	1	..	..
Colton, Enoch	1	1	..	1	..	1	1	..	1	..	..
Colton, Julius	..	1	..	1	..	3	..	..	1	..	..
Comstock, Daniel	..	..	1	..	..	1	..	1	..	..	..
Comstock, Israel	3	..	..	1	..	1	..	..	1	..	..
Comstock, Michael	2	..	..	1	..	2	..	..	1	..	..
Comstock, Samuel	..	..	..	1	..	2	..	..	1	1	..
Corse, Asaph	..	1	..	2	..	1	..	..	1	..	..
Currier, John	1	1	..	1	..	1	1	..	1	..	..
Dake, Joseph	2	1	1	..	1	..	..	..	..	1	..
Darby, William	..	1	1	..	1	..	..	..	..	1	..
Davis, Paul	3	..	..	1	..	..	..	..	1	..	..
Demming, John	2	..	1	1	..	..	..	..	1	..	..
Downing, Robert	2	..	..	1	..	1	..	..	1	..	..

ORANGE COUNTY—Continued

NAMES OF HEADS OF FAMILIES	FREE WHITE MALES: Under 10 years of age	Of 10 and under 16	Of 16 and under 26 including heads of families	Of 26 and under 45 including heads of families	Of 45 and upwards including heads of families	FREE WHITE FEMALES: Under 10 years of age	Of 10 and under 16	Of 16 and under 26 including heads of families	Of 26 and under 45 including heads of families	Of 45 and upwards including heads of families	All other free persons except Indians not taxed
VERSHIRE—con.											
Drake, Ebenezer	..	1	1	1	..	2	..	1	1	..	..
Drake, James	..	..	..	1	..	1	..	..	1	..	..
Durant, Alexander	3	1	..	2	..	1	..	..	1	..	..
Durgin, Samuel	2	..	..	1	..	2	..	..	1	..	..
Evans, Isaac	1	1	..	1	..	4	1	..	..	1	..
Foster, Thomas	1	1	2	..	1	1	1	1	..	1	..
Fuller, Abraham	..	..	..	1	..	..	..	..	1	..	..
Fuller, Ezekiel	2	..	1	1	..	1	..	..	1	..	..
Fuller, James	2	1	..	1	..	3	..	..	1	..	..
Fuller, Nathan	..	..	2	..	1	..	1	2	..	1	..
Fuller, Nathan Jr.	1	1	..	1	..	1	1	..	1	..	..
Fuller, Stephen	3	1	..	..	1	3	..	..	2	..	..
Garvin, John	..	..	2	..	..	..	..	1	..	1	..
Gilman, John	2	..	..	1	..	2	..	..	1	..	..
Gilman, Jonathan	3	2	..	1	..	4	..	..	1	..	..
Godfrey, Henry	1	..	..	1	..	2	..	..	1	..	..
Godfrey, James	1	..	..	1	..	3	1	..	1	..	..
Godfrey, Jonathan	3	..	..	1	..	..	..	..	1	..	..
Godfrey, Moses	..	..	..	..	1	..	..	..	..	1	..
Godfrey, Simeon	3	..	..	1	..	1	1	..	1	..	..
Gray, Matthew	..	..	..	1	..	2	1	..	1	..	..
Hoit, Joseph	2	1	..	1	..	..	1	1	..	..	..
Hull, Moses	2	..	..	1	..	1	..	..	1	..	..
Humphrey, Arthur	..	..	..	1	..	1	..	..	1	..	..
Humphrey, Josiah	1	..	..	1	..	1	..	..	1	..	..
Jones, Nathaniel	3	..	1	1	..	..	1	1	1	..	..
Jones, Samuel	1	1	..	1	..	1	..	..	1	..	..
Langdon, James	3	2	1	1	..	..	..	..	1	..	..
Langdon, John	3	2	..	1	..	3	2	..	1	..	..
Layton, Phinehas	2	..	..	1	..	2	..	..	1	..	..
Maltbie, Jonathan	..	1	2	..	1	..	1	3	..	1	..
Maltbie, Jonathan Jr.	1	..	..	1	..	1	1	..	1	..	..
Maltbie, Noah	..	1	1	..	..	..	..	1	..	..	..
Maltbie, Stephen	..	..	1	1	..	1	..	..	1	..	..
Maltbie, William	1	1	2	..	1	2	1	..	1	..	..
Marston, John	1	2	..	1	..	2	1	1	1	..	..
Matson, Amos	..	..	1	..	1	..	..	1	1	1	..
Matson, Howel	1	..	..	1	..	2	..	..	1	..	..
Matson, Israel	..	..	2	1	..	3	..	..	1	..	..
Mattoon, John	1	..	..	1	..	2	..	..	1	..	..
Mattoon, Nathaniel	3	1	..	1	..	1	..	..	1	..	..
Mattoon, Phillip	1	..	..	1	..	2	..	..	1	..	..
Moody, Elisha	2	..	..	1	..	3	..	..	1	..	..
Moody, Elisha	..	..	2	..	1	3	2	1	..	1	..
Moody, Elisha Jr.	..	..	1	..	..	..	..	1	..	..	..
Morey, Charles	2	1	2	1	..	2	2	1	1	..	..
Morey, Simeon	..	2	..	..	1	1	1	..	..	1	..
Morse, Noah	..	2	..	..	1	2	..	1	..	1	..
Norris, James	1	1	..	1	..	2	..	..	1	..	..
Paine, Jesse	3	1	1	1	..	3	2	..	1	..	..
Palmer, Elijah	..	1	..	..	1	4	..	..	..	1	..
Palmer, Joseph	1	..	..	1	..	1	..	..	1	..	..
Patterson, William	1	1	..	1	..	1	..	..	1	..	..
Perkins, Peter	1	1	..	1	..	3	..	..	1	..	..
Peters, Andrew	3	1	1	1	..	3	1	1	1	..	..
Phillips, Elisha	1	2	1	..	1	1	1	1	..	1	..
Pierce, Elisha	1	2	2	..	1	1	..	2	..	1	..
Pierce, William	..	..	1	..	..	..	..	1	..	..	..
Pomeroy, Elisha	1	..	..	1	..	3	1	..	1	..	..
Porter, Caleb	2	..	..	1	..	..	..	..	1	..	..
Porter, Nathan	1	1	..	..	1	1	1	..	..	1	..
Porter, Thomas	..	..	..	1	..	1	..	1	1	..	..
Powell, John	1	..	..	1	..	1	..	..	1	..	..
Powell, William	2	..	..	1	..	2	..	..	1	..	..
Prescott, Elisha	..	1	1	..	1	..	1	1	..	1	..
Prescott, Elisha 2nd.	..	..	1	..	..	1	..	1	..	..	..
Prescott, Jeremiah	2	..	1	1	..	2	1	1	1	..	..
Prescott, Samuel Jr.	2	..	1	1	..	..	..	..	1	..	..
Prescott, William	..	1	2	..	2	..	..	..	..	2	..
Richardson, John	2	..	..	1	..	..	..	..	1	..	..
Rockley, Pelatiah	2	..	1	..	..	2	..	1	..	..	..
Russ, John	2	..	..	..	1	2	1	..	..	1	..
Scales, Matthew	1	..	..	1	..	1	..	..	1	..	..
Senter, Ebenezer	2	..	1	1	..	..	1	1	1	...	..
Skinner, Daniel	2	1	..	1	..	2	..	..	1	..	..
Smith, Asa	1	..	1	..	1	..	1	2	..	1	..

NAMES OF HEADS OF FAMILIES	FREE WHITE MALES: Under 10 years of age	Of 10 and under 16	Of 16 and under 26 including heads of families	Of 26 and under 45 including heads of families	Of 45 and upwards including heads of families	FREE WHITE FEMALES: Under 10 years of age	Of 10 and under 16	Of 16 and under 26 including heads of families	Of 26 and under 45 including heads of families	Of 45 and upwards including heads of families	All other free persons except Indians not taxed
VERSHIRE—con.											
Smith, Asa Jr.	1	..	..	1	..	..	..	1	..	..	..
Smith, Stephen	3	..	..	1	..	..	..	1	1	..	..
Spencer, Daniel	1	..	..	1	..	1	..	1	..	..	..
Spencer, Ebenezer	..	..	..	..	1	..	..	..	..	1	..
Spencer, Ebenezer, Jr.	..	..	1	1	..	1	..	1	..	..	..
Stebbins, Aaron	..	1	2	..	2	1	..	2	..	1	..
Stebbins, Abraham	2	1	1	..	1	2	..	1	..	7	..
Stevens, Willliam	1	..	1	..	..	..	..	1	..	..	..
Stratton, Eliezer	1	..	..	1	..	2	..	..	1	..	..
Taft, Eliezer	3	2	..	1	..	2	1	..	1	..	..
Thompson, Seth	2	3	..	1	..	2	1	..	1	..	..
Titus, Beverly	1	..	1	..	..	..	..	1	..	..	..
Titus, Ephram	..	..	..	1	..	5	..	..	1	..	..
Titus, Joseph	1	..	..	1	..	2	..	..	1	..	..
Titus, Lenox	..	1	..	..	1	..	1	1	..	1	..
Titus, Michael	..	1	..	..	1	..	1	2	..	..	..
Titus, Silas	1	..	..	1	..	2	1	..	1	..	..
Tolman, Abner	1	..	..	1	..	2	1	..	1	..	..
Tracy, James	..	..	1	..	..	..	..	1	..	..	..
True, Daniel	1	..	1	..	..	..	..	1	..	..	..
Walker, Aaron	2	..	1	1	..	..	..	1	..	..	..
Walker, Eliakim	4	..	1	..	1	..	2	2	..	1	..
Walker, Elijah	3	..	..	1	..	3	..	..	1	..	..
Walker, Joel	..	1	1	..	1	..	1	1	..	1	..
Wallace, William	2	..	..	1	..	..	..	..	1	..	..
Ward, Shadrach	2	..	2	1	..	2	..	..	1	..	..
Warriner, Reuben	2	1	..	1	..	3	1	..	1	..	..
West, Gilman	2	..	1	..	..	..	..	1	..	..	..
West, John	1	..	..	1	..	4	2	..	1	..	..
West, Jonathan	3	..	1	..	1	1	1	2	..	1	..
West, William	3	..	..	1	..	..	..	..	1	..	..
White, Hugh	..	..	..	..	1	..	..	..	..	1	..
White, Samuel	..	..	1	1	..	3	2	..	1	..	..
Whittaker, Abraham	3	1	..	1	..	1	1	..	1	..	..
Winchester, Benjamin	1	1	2	..	1	2	1	1	..	1	..
Woodward, Elijah	2	1	..	1	..	1	1	..	1	..	..
Woodward, Thaddeus	1	..	..	1	..	1	1	..	1	..	..
Yates, Barzillai	3	1	..	..	1	3	1	1	..	1	..
WASHINGTON											
Abbot, Nathan	2	1	..	1	..	1	..	..	1	..	..
Allen, Pelatiah	1	..	..	1	..	1	..	1	..	..	..
Allen, William	4	1	3	1	1	3	1	..	1	..	..
Austin, Thomas	..	..	1	1	..	1	..	1	..	..	..
Bacon, Asa	..	..	2	..	1	..	..	..	..	1	..
Bacon, Nathan	1	..	..	1	..	1	..	1	1	..	..
Barron, Eliezer	..	..	1	..	..	..	..	..	1	..	..
Bartholomew, Peter	..	1	1	2	1	2	..	1	1	1	..
Beales, William	..	..	..	..	1	..	..	..	..	1	..
Bedee, Rezai	1	2	..	1	..	..	..	..	1	..	..
Billings, Benjamin	..	1	4	..	..	..	..	1	..	..	..
Black, Tristram S.	3	..	..	1	..	..	..	..	1	..	..
Blakely, Eber	1	..	..	..	1	..	..	..	1	..	..
Bliss, Jacob	..	1	..	1	..	..	..	1	..	..	..
Bliss, Samuel	..	..	..	..	1	..	..	..	..	1	..
Bohonnan, Ananias	1	2	2	..	1	..	..	..	1	1	..
Bowles, Joseph	..	1	2	..	1	..	..	1	1	1	..
Buckminster, Richard	2	..	..	1	..	1	1	..	1	..	..
Burton, Amos	1	..	..	1	..	..	1	..	1	..	..
Burton, Jacob	2	1	1	1	..	1	..	..	2	..	..
Calf, Joseph	2	..	2	..	..	..	..	1	..	..	..
Campbell, Jesse	1	..	1	..	..	..	..	1	..	..	..
Campbell, Robert	1	..	1	..	1	2	1	1	..	1	..
Campbell, Robert	2	..	1	..	..	..	..	1	..	..	..
Campbell, William	..	..	1	..	..	..	..	1	..	..	..
Carr, Benjamin	1	..	..	1	..	1	..	1	..	..	..
Cheeney, Enoch	2	1	..	1	..	3	..	1	1	..	..
Cheeney, Giles	4	..	..	1	..	1	..	..	1	..	..
Chesimore, Abner	..	..	..	1	..	2	..	1	..	..	..
Chesimore, William	1	..	..	1	..	2	..	..	1	..	..
Clough, Moses	..	..	..	1	..	3	..	1	..	..	..
Coggswell, Nathan	1	..	..	1	..	..	..	1	1	..	..
Cook, Joshua	..	2	..	..	1	..	1	1	..	1	..
Cook, Lemuel	..	..	..	1	..	3	..	..	1	..	..
Cook, Silas	..	..	..	1	..	1	..	1	..	..	..
Craft, Samuel	..	..	..	1	..	..	..	1	..	..	..
Cummins, Ebenezer	..	..	..	3	..	2	..	1	..	..	..
Currier, David	..	1	..	..	1	1	1	..	1	..	..
Currier, James	1	..	1	..	..	2	..	1	..	..	..

ORANGE COUNTY—Continued

NAMES OF HEADS OF FAMILIES	FREE WHITE MALES: Under 10 years of age	FREE WHITE MALES: Of 10 and under 16	FREE WHITE MALES: Of 16 and under 26 including heads of families	FREE WHITE MALES: Of 26 and under 45 including heads of families	FREE WHITE MALES: Of 45 and upwards including heads of families.	FREE WHITE FEMALES: Under 10 years of age	FREE WHITE FEMALES: Of 10 and under 16	FREE WHITE FEMALES: Of 16 and under 26 including heads of families	FREE WHITE FEMALES: Of 26 and under 45 including heads of families	FREE WHITE FEMALES: Of 45 and upwards including heads of families	All other free persons except Indians not taxed
WASHINGTON—con.											
Darling, Moses	..	..	1	..	..	1	..	1	..	..	..
Dickinson, Gideon	..	1	1	1	1	1	2	..	1	..	..
Evans, Andrew	..	..	..	1	..	1	..	..	1	..	..
Fellows, Rodolphus	1	..	1	2	..	2	..	..	1	..	..
Fuller, Simeon	1	2	1	1	..	2	2	..	1	..	..
George, Asa	4	1	..	1	..	..	1	..	1	..	..
Glidden, Joseph	2	1	2	..	1	1	1	..	..	1	..
Glitton, Samuel	..	..	2	..	..	..	..	..	1	1	..
Hart, Jonathan	1	..	1	..	..	1	..	1	..	..	..
Hubbard, Gershom	..	..	1	..	1	..	..	..	..	1	..
Hubbard, Gershom Jr.	2	..	1	..	..	..	..	1	..	..	..
Huntington, William	3	..	1	..	..	..	..	1	..	..	..
Ingraham, Gershom	3	..	..	1	..	1	..	..	1	..	..
Ingraham, John	..	..	..	..	1	..	..	..	..	1	..
Ingraham, Robert	2	..	..	1	..	4	..	..	1	..	..
Jones, Ephram	1	..	2	1	..	..	..	..	1	1	..
Jones, John	1	1	..	..	1	..	1	1	..	1	..
Jones, Stephen	5	..	..	1	..	..	..	..	1	..	..
Leavit, Joseph	1	..	..	1	..	3	..	..	1	..	..
Matthew, Levi	..	..	..	1	..	..	..	1	..	..	..
McIntrie, Samuel	2	..	..	1	..	1	..	..	1	..	..
McKellup, Stephen	1	..	1	..	..	..	..	1	..	..	..
Merrill, Dudley	..	..	1	..	1	1	1	2	..	1	..
Merrill, Eliphalet	..	..	..	1	..	..	..	1	..	..	..
Morey, Sylvester	3	..	..	1	..	..	..	1	..	..	..
Nichols, Humphrey	1	1	..	1	..	2	1	1	1	..	..
Page, John	1	..	..	1	..	..	..	..	1	..	..
Palmer, Nathan	1	..	..	1	..	1	..	..	1	..	..
Partridge, Payson P.	..	..	..	1	..	1	..	..	1	..	..
Peasley, Daniel	..	1	1	1	..	1	2	..	1	..	..
Powers, Stephen	2	..	..	1	..	..	..	..	1	..	..
Ramsdale, Robert	2	..	..	1	..	1	2	..	1	..	..
Randall, Daniel	2	..	..	1	..	1	..	1	1	..	..
Ring, Moses	1	..	..	1	..	2	..	..	1	..	..
Robinson, Jonathan	..	..	1	..	..	1	..	1	..	..	..
Scoggins, Thomas	..	..	..	..	1	..	..	..	..	..	..
Scribner, Samuel	1	..	..	1	..	1	..	1	..	..	..
Simons, Samuel	3	..	..	1	..	2	1	..	1	..	..
Sleeper, Samuel	1	..	1	1	..	..	..	1	..	..	..
Smith, Elisha	..	..	..	..	1	..	..	..	..	1	..
Smith, Gideon	1	..	1	..	1	..	..	..	..	1	..
Smith, Henry	2	..	1	1	..	1	1	1	1	..	..
Smith, Shubal	3	2	..	1	..	..	..	..	1	..	..
Squires, Benjamin	1	..	..	1	..	2	..	..	1	..	..
Stoddard, Solomon	1	..	..	1	..	1	..	1	..	..	..
Strong, Stephen	..	..	..	1	..	1	1	..	1	..	..
Styles, Aaron	..	..	..	1	..	..	..	..	..	1	..
Tracy, Robert	..	..	..	1	..	1	..	..	1	..	..
Tracy, Safford	1	1	..	1	..	2	..	..	1	..	..
Tracy, Samuel	..	..	..	..	1	..	..	..	..	1	..
Truphant, Joseph	..	..	..	1	..	..	..	..	1	..	..
Walker, John	3	..	..	1	..	2	..	..	1	..	..
Wheatley, John	5	..	..	..	1	1	1	..	1	..	..
Whitcomb, Ephram	..	..	..	1	..	..	..	1	..	..	..
Whitcomb, Reuben	2	2	2	2	1	1	1	..	..	1	..
Whitcomb, Stephen	1	..	..	1	..	1	..	..	1	..	..
White, Thaddeus	1	1	1	1	..	2	1	..	1	..	..
Worthley, William	1	..	3	1	..	..	..	..	1	..	..
Wright, Abel	1	..	..	1	..	..	..	..	1	..	..
WEST FAIRLEE											
Allord, Peter	..	..	1	1	..	..	..	1	..	..	..
Basset, Elnathan	1	..	4	..	1	..	2	2	..	1	..
Bixby, George	4	1	..	1	..	2	1	..	1	1	..
WEST FAIRLEE—con.											
Bliss, Simeon	3	..	..	1	..	3	..	..	1	1	..
Blood, Comfort	2	2	..	1	..	2	..	..	1	..	..
Blood, Elijah	2	..	..	..	1•	..	2	..	1	..	..
Brown, Nicholas	..	..	2	..	1	..	..	..	..	1	..
Brown, Samuel	1	..	..	1	..	..	..	..	1	..	..
Burr, Sylvanus	2	..	..	1	..	4	..	..	1	..	..
Carpenter, Rufus	1	..	..	1	..	2	..	..	2	..	..
Caseo, Nero	..	..	..	..	..	..	..	..	..	..	3
Churchill, Francis	6	2	..	1	..	..	..	1	1	..	..
Churchill, Jonathan	..	2	..	..	1	..	1	..	..	1	..
Colton, John	..	..	..	..	1	..	..	..	..	1	..
Colton, John Jr.	2	1	..	1	..	1	1	..	1	..	..
Colton, Oliver	1	..	..	1	..	..	..	..	1	..	..
Dickinson, Reuben	..	..	..	..	1	..	..	..	..	1	..
Dickinson, Solomon	2	..	..	..	1	..	..	..	..	1	..
Durget, Joseph	1	..	..	1	..	4	..	..	1	..	..
Ford, Timothy	1	..	..	1	..	..	..	1	..	..	..
Giles, John	2	1	..	1	..	..	..	..	1	..	..
Hadley, Humphrey	2	..	..	1	..	3	..	..	1	..	..
Holbrook, Parker	..	..	..	2	..	1	..	2	..	..	..
House, Francis	1	1	..	..	1	1	1	1	..	1	..
House, William	2	..	..	1	..	..	..	..	1	..	..
House, William Jr.	1	..	1	..	..	..	..	1	..	..	..
Jaquish, John	..	1	2	..	1	..	1	3	1	..	..
Kidder, Aaron	1	..	..	1	..	3	..	..	1	..	..
Kidder, David	1	..	..	1	..	1	1	..	1	..	..
Landfair, Jabez	2	1	..	..	1	..	2	1	..	1	..
Lawrence, Levi	3	1	..	1	..	1	1	1	1	..	..
Martin, Elisha	1	..	..	1	..	3	..	..	1	..	..
Martin, Thomas	3	1	1	1	..	1	2	..	1	..	..
Maxfield, Thompson	1	..	..	1	..	..	..	..	1	..	..
May, Asa	1	1	..	1	..	1	1	..	2	..	..
May, Stephen	2	2	..	1	..	..	1	..	1	..	..
Moor, Daniel	3	1	..	1	..	1	1	..	1	..	..
Morrison, Samuel	..	2	..	..	1	1	1	1	..	1	..
Morse, Amos	1	..	..	1	..	1	..	..	1	..	..
Morse, Calvin	1	1	..	1	..	2	1	1	..	1	..
Niles, Nathaniel	3	..	2	..	1	1	1	2	..	1	1
Niles, Samuel	..	2	1	..	1	..	..	1	..	1	..
Ormsbee, Ichabod	..	..	..	..	1	..	..	1	..	1	..
Palmer, Joseph	..	..	1	..	1	..	1	1	..	1	..
Peabody, Dudley	..	..	..	1	..	3	..	..	1	..	..
Pelham, Martin	..	..	..	..	..	..	..	..	..	..	3
Pierce, Charles	..	..	2	1	..	2	..	..	1	..	..
Pierce, James	..	..	..	..	1	..	..	..	..	1	..
Pierce, John	1	..	..	1	..	1	..	..	1	..	..
Reid, Henry	3	..	..	1	..	4	..	..	1	..	..
Robinson, David	2	..	..	1	..	1	..	..	2	..	..
Robinson, Jesse	..	..	..	1	..	1	..	..	1	..	..
Robinson, Samuel	1	..	..	1	..	..	1	..	1	..	..
Rowell, Asa	..	..	3	..	1	..	..	2	..	1	..
Rowell, Benjamin	1	..	1	..	..	1	..	1	..	..	..
Russ, Nathan	1	..	..	1	1	1	..	..	1	1	..
Sessions, David	1	..	..	..	1	..	2	..	..	1	..
Southward, Asa	2	2	1	..	1	2	..	..	..	1	..
Southward, Lemuel	3	2	..	1	..	2	1	..	1	..	..
Southward, Ralph	2	..	..	1	..	3	..	..	1	..	..
Streeter, Jonathan	..	..	..	..	1	1	..	..	1	..	..
Wheeler, Abijah	2	1	1	..	1	..	..	1	..	1	..
Wheeler, Tuttle	..	..	..	1	..	3	..	..	1	..	..
Wild, Andrew	2	..	..	1	..	2	2	..	1	..	..
Wild, Elisha	2	1	..	1	..	3	..	..	1	..	..

ORANGE COUNTY—Continued

NAMES OF HEADS OF FAMILIES	FREE WHITE MALES: Under 10 years of age	FREE WHITE MALES: Of 10 and under 16	FREE WHITE MALES: Of 16 and under 26 including heads of families	FREE WHITE MALES: Of 26 and under 45 including heads of families	FREE WHITE MALES: Of 45 and upwards including heads of families	FREE WHITE FEMALES: Under 10 years of age	FREE WHITE FEMALES: Of 10 and under 16	FREE WHITE FEMALES: Of 16 and under 26 including heads of families	FREE WHITE FEMALES: Of 26 and under 45 including heads of families	FREE WHITE FEMALES: Of 45 and upwards including heads of families	All other free persons except Indians not taxed
WILLIAMSTOWN											
Abel, Simon	2	..	1	1	..	1	..	..	1	..	..
Bacon, Edmund	2	..	..	1	..	3	1	1	1	..	..
Bass, Joel	3	..	1	1	..	..	..	2	..	..	..
Bates, Jonathan	..	2	1	..	1	..	1	..	..	1	..
Becket, Reuben	3	..	..	1	..	1	..	..	1	..	..
Bigelow, Timothy	2	..	..	1	..	2	1	..	1	..	..
Briggs, Calvin	1	..	..	1	..	2	..	..	1	..	..
Briggs, Enos	1	..	..	1	..	1	..	1	..	..	..
Briggs, Henry	3	1	1	1	1	..	..	..	1	..	..
Briggs, Israel	..	..	..	1	..	1	..	1	..	..	..
Briggs, Luther	..	..	..	1	..	2	..	1	..	..	..
Brown, Ephram	..	1	1	..	1	..	..	..	..	1	..
Brown, Jonathan	1	1	2	..	1	2	1	..	..	1	..
Brown, Josiah	1	..	1	..	..	..	..	1	..	..	..
Brown, William	..	1	..	1	..	..	..	..	1	..	..
Buck, Asa	..	..	1	1	..	..	..	..	1	..	..
Buck, Isaac	3	1	..	1	..	1	1	..	1	..	..
Buck, William	3	..	..	1	..	1	1	..	1	..	..
Burnham, Adonijah	..	..	..	1	..	..	..	1	..	..	..
Burnham, Enoch	2	1	1	..	..	1	..	1	..	..	..
Burnham, Rufus	1	..	..	1	..	1	..	1	..	..	..
Burroughs, Daniel	1	2	2	1	..	2	1	..	1	..	..
Burroughs, David	2	..	1	..	..	1	..	1	..	..	..
Burroughs, Joel	1	..	1	..	..	1	..	1	..	..	..
Campbell, John	..	2	3	..	1	..	..	1	..	..	..
Case, Thaddeus	1	..	1	..	..	..	..	1	..	..	..
Chase, Moses	..	..	..	1	1	..	..	..	..	1	..
Clark, Abijah	2	2	..	1	..	2	..	1	1	..	..
Clark, John	1	1	..	1	..	1	..	1	..	..	..
Coburn, Hezekiah	..	1	..	..	1	..	1	1	..	1	..
Coburn, Joel	2	..	..	1	..	2	..	1	..	..	..
Coburn, Jonathan	1	..	1	1	..	..	..	1	..	..	..
Coburn, Roswell	..	..	1	..	..	..	..	1	..	..	..
Coleman, Eliphalet	..	2	2	..	1	..	1	1	..	1	..
Comstock, Abner	1	1	..	1	..	1	..	..	1	..	..
Conner, Edmund	5	..	..	1	..	..	..	2	1	..	..
Crane, John	..	..	1	1	..	2	..	1	..	..	..
Crane, Joseph	5	1	1	..	1	1	2	1	..	..	..
Crane, Zebulon	..	1	..	1	..	1	1	1	1	..	..
Davenport, Amos	3	1	..	1	..	2	1	..	1	..	..
Davenport, Daniel	3	2	..	1	..	2	..	..	1	..	..
Davenport, John	1	..	1	..	..	1	..	1	..	..	..
Davenport, Lemuel	..	..	..	..	1	..	..	..	..	1	..
Davenport, Thomas	..	..	..	1	..	3	..	..	1	..	..
Delanoe, Barnet	2	..	..	1	..	1	..	1	1	..	..
Diamond, Penuel	..	..	1	..	1	..	..	1	..	1	..
Durkee, Samuel	1	..	..	1	..	1	..	1	..	..	..
Durkee, William	1	..	..	1	..	1	..	..	1	..	..
Elliot, Stephen	..	..	1	..	..	..	..	1	..	..	..
Farnesworth, Thomas	1	..	..	1	..	3	..	1	..	..	..
Fiske, Jonathan	2	1	2	..	1	1	2	..	..	1	..
Fiske, Nathaniel	1	..	1	..	..	1	..	..	1	..	..
Franklin, Samuel	2	..	..	1	..	2	2	..	1	..	..
Gifford, Moses	1	1	..	1	..	2	..	..	1	..	..
Gilbert, James	..	..	..	1	..	2	..	..	1	..	..
Gillet, Abner	..	1	..	1	..	4	1	..	1	..	..
Gillman, Josiah	1	2	1	..	1	1	1	1	..	1	..
Gillson, Isaac	2	..	..	1	..	1	..	1	..	..	..
Gould, Waterman	1	..	..	1	1	3	..	..	1	..	..
Green, Jared	4	1	..	1	..	..	1	..	1	..	..
Harding, Perry	1	..	..	1	..	2	..	..	1	..	..
Harrington, Daniel	1	..	..	1	..	1	..	1	..	..	..
Hassington, Vespatian	4	2	..	1	..	..	..	..	1	1	..
Hatch, Asa	5	1	1	1	..	2	..	1	1	..	..
Hopkins, James	2	1	..	..	1	..	1	1	..	1	..
Hopkins, Robert	1	..	..	1	..	1	..	..	1	..	..
Horsley, Ira	..	..	1	..	..	..	..	1	..	..	..
Howard, Amasa	2	..	..	1	..	..	..	3	..	1	..
Howe, Perly	3	2	..	..	1	2	..	1	..	1	..
Jafford, Darius	2	..	..	1	..	..	..	..	1	..	..
Jafford, Jacob	..	..	..	1	..	4	..	..	1	..	..
Johnson, Henry	4	..	..	1	..	1	..	..	1	..	..
WILLIAMSTOWN—con.											
Kendall, Timothy	..	1	1	..	1	3	1	1	..	2	..
Kilburn, James	..	..	..	1	..	..	..	..	1	..	..
Kilburn, Joseph	1	1	..	1	..	2	..	..	1	..	..
Kimball, Jared	1	..	1	1	..	3	..	..	1	..	..
Kingsley, Elias	..	..	..	1	..	..	..	..	1	..	..
Leason, William	..	..	2	1	..	..	..	1	1	..	..
Lyman, Josiah	..	2	..	1	..	..	2	1	1	..	..
Lyndes, Cornelius	2	..	1	..	1	1	1	..	1	..	..
Martin, Aaron	2	..	..	1	..	2	..	2	..	..	..
Martin, Daniel	1	1	..	1	1	3	..	..	1	..	..
Martin, James	2	1	..	1	..	1	..	..	1	..	..
Martin, Jonathan	1	..	..	1	..	2	..	..	1	..	..
Martin, Smith	1	..	..	1	1	1	..	1	..	..	..
Martin, ———	..	..	..	1	..	..	..	1	..	..	..
Montgomery, William	..	1	..	1	..	1	..	1	..	..	..
Moor, Jeptha	1	1	..	1	..	2	..	1	..	..	..
Morse, Moses	2	..	..	1	..	2	..	..	1	..	..
Newman, Thomas	2	..	1	..	1	..	..	..	..	1	..
Olds, Phinehas	4	1	..	1	..	..	..	1	..	..	..
Paine, Elijah	3	1	3	1	..	1	1	..	2	..	1
Phillips, Zedekiah	..	1	3	..	..	3	..	1	..	..	..
Pool, Warren	2	..	..	1	..	1	..	..	1	..	..
Pool, William	3	1	3	1	..	2	..	..	1	..	..
Pratt, Josiah	1	..	..	1	..	2	..	1	..	..	..
Rice, John	..	..	..	..	1	..	..	..	..	1	..
Rice, John Jr.	3	..	..	1	..	2	..	..	1	..	..
Rice, Nathan	1	..	..	1	..	1	..	..	1	..	..
Risley, Asahel	1	..	1	..	..	..	..	1	..	..	..
Robinson, Isaac	4	..	..	1	..	1	..	..	1	..	..
Robinson, Solomon	..	..	1	..	1	..	1	..	..	1	..
Root, Thomas	..	1	..	1	..	..	1	..	..	1	..
Russ, Elijah	1	..	..	1	..	..	..	..	1	..	..
Russ, Joseph	..	..	..	..	1	..	..	2	..	1	..
Sabins, William	..	..	..	1	..	3	..	..	1	..	..
Seaver, Robert	6	..	..	1	..	..	..	..	1	..	..
Sexton, Levi	1	..	..	1	..	..	..	..	1	..	..
Sherman, Stiles	3	2	..	1	..	2	..	1	1	..	..
Sible, Ebenezer	4	..	..	1	..	1	..	..	1	..	..
Silly, William	..	..	1	..	..	2	..	1	..	..	..
Simons, Shubal	1	..	1	..	1	..	1	3	..	1	..
Smith, Abiel	1	1	..	1	..	1	..	..	1	..	..
Smith, Asa	1	..	..	1	..	..	..	..	1	..	..
Smith, James	1	1	..	1	..	2	1	..	1	..	..
Smith, Jediah	2	..	..	1	..	1	..	1	..	..	..
Smith, John	2	1	..	..	2	3	..	..	1	..	..
Smith, Levi	4	..	1	1	..	1	..	..	1	..	..
Smith, Sylvester	3	1	..	1	..	..	1	..	1	..	..
Snow, Timothy	1	..	..	1	..	1	..	..	1	..	..
Stebbins, Braynard	..	1	1	1	..	1	..	2	..	..	..
Stockwell, Daniel	..	..	..	1	..	2	..	1	..	..	..
Stockwell, Moses	..	2	..	1	..	2	..	..	1	..	..
Symmonds, Shubal	2	..	..	1	..	1	..	1	..	..	..
Tilden, Ithamer	..	..	2	..	1	..	..	1	1	..	..
Tilden, Lenard	1	..	..	1	..	..	..	1	..	..	..
Townsend, John	1	..	2	1	..	3	1	1	1	..	..
Trexbury, Moses	..	..	1	..	..	..	..	..	..	..	..
Tricklin, Jonas	..	1	..	1	..	3	1	1	1	..	..
Tyler, Nehemiah	1	..	..	1	..	1	..	1	1	2	..
Walcott, Eliezer	1	..	1	..	..	1	..	1	..	..	..
Walcott, Elijah	..	..	..	1	1	..	..	..	..	2	..
Walcott, Eliphalet	1	..	..	1	..	2	..	..	1	..	..
Walder, Anson	2	..	1	1	..	1	..	..	1	..	..
Walker, Asahel	3	1	..	1	..	1	2	..	1	..	..
Watson, David	..	..	4	..	..	1	..	1	..	..	..
Whitney, Elijah	1	1	..	..	1	2	1	2	..	1	..
Whitney, Elijah Jr.	1	..	1	..	..	2	..	..	1	..	..
Willington, Nathan	2	..	..	1	..	1	..	..	1	..	..
Wilson, David	2	..	..	1	..	1	..	..	1	..	..
Wilson, John	..	..	..	1	..	3	..	..	1	..	..
Wilson, Jonathan	2	..	..	1	..	3	..	..	1	..	..
Wilson, Reuben	3	..	..	1	..	1	..	..	1	..	..
Wise, Abner	1	..	1	1	..	2	1	..	1	..	..
Wise, Benjamin	2	..	..	1	..	1	..	1	..	..	..
Withrington, Daniel	1	..	1	1	1	..	1	2	..	1	..

ORLEANS COUNTY

NAMES OF HEADS OF FAMILIES	FREE WHITE MALES: Under 10 years of age	FREE WHITE MALES: Of 10 and under 16	FREE WHITE MALES: Of 16 and under 26 including heads of families	FREE WHITE MALES: Of 26 and under 45 including heads of families	FREE WHITE MALES: Of 45 and upwards including heads of families.	FREE WHITE FEMALES: Under 10 years of age	FREE WHITE FEMALES: Of 10 and under 16	FREE WHITE FEMALES: Of 16 and under 26 including heads of families	FREE WHITE FEMALES: Of 26 and under 45 including heads of families	FREE WHITE FEMALES: Of 45 and upwards including heads of families	All other free persons except Indians not taxed
BARTON											
Abbot, David	1	..	..	1	..	..	1	..	1	..	..
Allyn, Abner Jr.	..	..	..	1	..	..	..	..	..	..	..
Allyn, Jonathan	1	..	1	1	..	1	..	..	1	..	..
Ames, John	2	..	..	1	..	..	1	..	1	..	..
Beard, James	..	..	1	..	..	..	..	..	..	..	..
Beard, John	..	..	1	..	..	..	..	..	..	..	..
Benton, Joel	2	2	..	1	..	1	1	..	1	..	..
Blodget, David	3	..	..	1	..	..	..	..	1	..	..
Blodget, Oliver	1	..	..	1	..	..	..	..	1	..	..
Brown, Jeremiah	..	..	1	..	..	..	..	..	..	..	..
Brown, John	..	1	3	..	1	2	2	..	..	1	..
Brown, Welcome	..	..	1	..	..	..	..	..	..	..	..
Dexter, Stephen	2	..	..	1	..	1	..	..	1	..	..
Fuller, Charles	..	..	1	..	..	..	..	..	..	..	..
Green, Joseph	1	..	1	..	..	3	..	1	..	..	..
Grimes, James	..	..	1	..	..	..	..	..	..	..	..
Kimball, Asa	..	..	..	2	..	2	..	2	1	..	..
Kimball, Stephen	..	..	1	..	..	..	..	..	..	..	..
Lord, Samuel	2	..	1	..	..	1	..	..	1	..	..
May, James	2	..	1	..	..	2	..	1	..	..	..
Nichols, Samuel	3	..	..	1	..	1	..	..	1	..	..
Pillsbury, David	2	1	..	1	..	2	1	..	1	..	..
Redman, James	3	..	..	1	..	1	..	..	1	1	..
Robinson, Jonathan	4	1	..	1	..	1	1	..	1	..	..
Salisbury, James	..	..	..	1	..	..	..	..	..	..	..
Sturdivant, Lemuel	2	..	3	1	..	4	1	1	1	..	..
Wadhams, Solomon	..	..	..	1	..	..	..	..	1	..	..
Young, Daniel	..	2	..	1	..	1	..	..	..	1	..
BROWNINGTON											
Clark, Peter	..	..	..	1	..	..	..	1	..	..	..
Cole, Carlos	..	..	1	..	..	1	..	1	..	..	..
Dart, Obed	..	..	1	..	..	..	..	..	..	..	..
Drew, George	..	..	1	..	..	..	..	..	..	..	..
Gilbert, Like	1	..	..	1	.	..	..	2	..	..	..
Gridley, Eben	..	..	1	..	..	..	..	..	..	..	..
Kingsbury, Eleazer	1	..	1	..	..	..	..	1	..	..	..
Knox, David	..	..	1	..	..	..	..	..	..	..	..
Markham, John	3	2	..	1	..	2	..	..	1	..	..
McGraff, Michael	..	..	1	..	..	..	..	..	..	..	..
Newell, Benjamin	..	..	..	1	..	..	..	2	..	..	..
Porter, Amos	..	..	..	1	..	..	..	..	..	..	..
Porter, James	..	..	1	..	..	..	..	..	..	..	..
Seavy, Thomas	1	..	..	1	..	..	..	1	..	..	..
Smith, Jonathan	1	..	..	1	..	..	..	1	..	..	..
Smith, Justus	..	..	1	..	..	..	..	..	..	..	..
Smith, Samuel	..	2	1	..	1	1	..	2	..	1	..
Smith, Samuel Jr.	..	..	..	1	..	..	..	..	..	..	..
Spencer, Elijah	3	..	..	1	..	1	..	1	..	..	..
Spencer, Erastus	1	..	1	..	..	1	..	1	..	..	..
Strong, Elijah	1	..	..	1	..	1	..	1	1	..	..
Sweat, Luther	..	..	..	1	..	..	..	..	..	..	..
Willcocks, Obadiah	..	..	2	..	..	..	..	..	..	..	..
COVENTRY											
Morse, John	3	..	1	..	1	1	..	1	..	..	..
CRAFTSBURY											
Allen, Elijah	4	1	1	1	..	2	2	..	1	..	..
Babcock, John	..	..	..	1	..	..	..	..	..	..	..
Babcock, Nathaniel	..	..	..	..	1	..	..	..	..	2	..
CRAFTSBURY—con.											
Chapin, Calvin	3	..	..	1	..	2	..	..	1	..	..
Collins, Samuel Rev.	2	..	1	..	1	2	2	..	..	1	..
Corbin, Royal	1	1	..	1	..	..	1	..	1	..	..
Corey, John	..	1	3	..	1	..	1	..	..	1	..
Crafts, Ebenezer	..	..	..	..	1	..	..	..	..	1	..
Crafts, Samuel C.	1	..	1	1	..	..	..	1	..	1	1
Cutler, Nathan	..	2	1	..	1	1	..	..	..	1	..
Davison, Daniel	1	1	..	1	1	2	..	..	1	..	..
Drew, Clark	..	2	..	..	1	2	1	..	..	1	..
Flood, Daniel	1	1	1	1	..	1	1	1	..	1	..
French, Samuel	2	..	..	1	..	1	..	..	1	..	..
Gerald, Willliam	2	..	1	..	..	..	..	1	..	..	..
Hayden, William	1	..	1	..	..	..	..	1	..	..	..
Holmes, Leonard	..	1	..	1	..	1	1	..	1	..	..
Hoyt, Benjamin	4	2	..	1	..	..	..	..	1	..	..
Jennings, Benjamin	2	..	..	..	1	1	2	..	1	..	..
Johnson, Isaac	1	..	..	1	..	2	..	..	1	..	..
Leach, Sylvanus	..	..	..	1	..	2	..	..	1	..	..
Lyon, Nehemiah	2	1	1	..	1	1	1	1	1	..	..
Mason, Daniel	1	..	..	1	..	3	..	..	1	..	..
Mason, Hiram	1	..	1	1	..	..	..	2	..	..	..
Mason, Wareham	2	..	..	1	..	2	..	..	1	..	..
Merrifield, Mills	3	1	..	1	..	1	..	..	1	..	..
Morse, Ephraim	2	1	..	1	..	1	..	..	..	1	..
Nelson, Arba	3	..	..	..	1	1	..	..	1	..	..
Norris, Jonathan	..	..	..	1	..	1	..	..	1	..	..
Paddock, James	2	..	1	1	..	..	..	2	..	..	..
Scott, Joseph	..	..	..	1	..	3	..	..	1	..	..
Sever, Daniel	4	3	1	..	1	..	..	1	1	..	..
Shumway, William F.	..	..	1	..	..	1	..	1	..	..	..
Stratton, Samuel	1	..	..	1	..	..	..	1	..	..	..
Trumbull, Robert	2	1	..	..	1	2	1	..	1	..	..
Trumbull, Thomas	..	1	1	..	1	..	1	..	..	..	..
White, Hervey	1	..	..	1	..	..	..	1	..	..	..
White, Hezekiah	2	..	..	1	..	..	1	..	..	1	..
White, Jacob	..	..	..	..	1	..	..	..	1	..	1
White, James	2	1	..	..	1	2	..	..	1	..	..
White, Lemuel	..	..	1	..	..	..	..	..	..	..	..
Works, Samuel	..	..	..	..	1	..	..	..	..	..	..
DERBY											
Abel, Dustin	..	..	1	..	..	..	..	..	..	..	..
Bangs, Eliphalet	1	..	2	1	1	2	..	..	1	..	..
Barret, Benjamin	2	..	..	1	..	1	..	..	1	..	..
Benham, Japhet	..	..	..	1	..	2	..	..	1	..	..
Boardman, Jehiel	3	..	1	1	..	2	1	..	1	..	..
Bunnel, Job	1	..	1	..	..	..	..	2	..	..	..
Buzzel, Henry	3	1	1	1	..	2	1	..	1	..	..
Colby, Samuel	1	1	..	1	..	1	..	..	2	..	..
Cowell, Joseph	..	..	..	1	..	..	..	..	..	..	..
David, Dustin	..	..	1	..	..	..	..	..	..	..	..
Drakeley, William	..	..	1	..	..	..	..	..	..	..	..
Elliot, ———	2	..	2	1	..	1	..	1	..	..	..
Goodenough, James	2	..	..	1	..	1	..	..	1	..	..
Goodenough, Levi	..	..	..	1	..	1	..	..	1	..	..
Greenleaf, James	1	..	2	..	..	3	..	1	..	..	..
Hickok, Amos	..	..	1	..	..	..	..	..	..	..	..
Hinman, Benjamin	..	1	..	1	..	..	..	..	..	..	..
Hinman, Isaac	..	..	2	2	1	..	..	1	..	..	..
Hinman, Timothy	3	1	3	2	1	2	1	..	1	..	..
Hinman, William	..	..	1	..	..	..	..	..	..	..	..
Holmes, Prentiss	..	..	..	1	..	1	..	..	1	..	..
Kingsbury, Charles	..	..	..	1	..	..	..	1	..	..	..
Ludden, Luther	3	..	..	1	..	1	..	..	1	..	..
Lunt, Charles C.	4	..	..	1	..	3	..	..	1	..	..
Lyman, Elisha	2	..	..	1	..	1	1	..	1	..	..

ORLEANS COUNTY—Continued

NAMES OF HEADS OF FAMILIES	FREE WHITE MALES					FREE WHITE FEMALES					
	Under 10 years of age	Of 10 and under 16	Of 16 and under 26 including heads of families	Of 26 and under 45 including heads of families	Of 45 and upwards including heads of families.	Under 10 years of age	Of 10 and under 16	Of 16 and under 26 including heads of families	Of 26 and under 45 including heads of families	Of 45 and upwards including heads of families	All other free persons except Indians not taxed
DERBY—con.											
Merrit, John	..	..	2	..	1	..	..	..	..	1	..
Merrit, John Jr.	1	..	1	..	..	1	..	1	..	..	..
Nash, Elisha	1	..	..	1	..	1	..	..	1	..	..
Newcomb, Luther	..	..	..	1	..	..	..	1	..	..	..
Pomeroy, Samuel	2	..	1	..	..	1	..	1	..	..	..
Richard, Isaac W.	..	..	2	1	..	..	..	..	1	..	..
Richardson, Jedediah	2	..	..	1	..	..	..	..	1	..	..
Severance, ———	..	..	1	..	..	..	..	..	..	..	..
Spencer, Amasa	3	..	..	1	..	1	..	..	2	..	..
Stewart, Rufus	..	..	2	..	..	2	..	1	..	..	..
Sweatland, John	..	..	3	..	..	..	..	1	..	..	..
Villers, Aaron	..	..	..	1	..	..	..	..	..	..	..
Wood, John	..	..	1	..	..	..	..	..	..	..	..
Wood, Oliver	1	..	..	2	..	..	1	1	..	..	..
Youngman, Peter	..	..	..	..	..	..	..	..	..	1	4
DUNCANSBORO											
Adams, James C.	..	..	..	1	..	2	..	1	1	..	..
Bartlet, Enos	3	..	..	1	..	1	..	..	1	..	..
Carpenter, Simeon	..	..	1	..	..	..	..	..	..	..	..
Chapin, Luther	3	1	1	..	1	..	..	1	..	1	..
Dagget, Nathaniel	3	..	..	1	..	..	..	..	1	..	..
Horton, Widow	1	..	2	..	..	..	..	..	..	1	..
Page, Joshua	1	..	..	1	..	..	..	..	1	..	..
Parkhurst, Abel	..	..	1	..	..	1	..	1	..	..	..
Prouty, John	1	1	..	..	1	2	..	2	1	..	..
Sawyer, Amos	..	1	1	..	1	2	..	1	..	1	..
EDEN											
Brown, Josiah	3	1	..	1	..	2	..	..	1	..	..
Hinman, Benjamin	4	..	..	1	..	1	..	..	1	..	..
Hudson, William	..	..	..	1	..	5	1	..	1	..	..
Parker, Thomas H.	1	..	..	1	..	..	..	..	1	..	..
Pond, Ezra	1	..	..	1	..	..	..	1	..	..	..
ELMORE											
Carter, John	1	2	..	1	..	1	..	..	1	..	..
Carter, Samuel	1	..	..	1	..	3	1	..	1	..	..
Elmore, Jesse	..	1	..	1	..	1	1	..	1	..	..
Elmore, Martin	..	..	..	1	..	..	..	..	..	..	..
Elmore, Molly	..	..	..	..	..	..	..	..	1	..	..
Elmore, Samuel Col.	..	..	..	..	1	..	..	..	..	..	..
Gibbs, Job	..	..	..	1	..	..	..	..	..	..	..
Leach, Isaac	1	1	..	1	..	2	..	..	1	..	..
Leach, Joseph	..	..	..	1	..	1	..	..	1	..	..
Olmstead, Seth	2	..	..	1	..	3	..	..	1	..	..
Tucker, Reuben	1	..	..	1	..	..	..	..	1	..	..
Whitney, Zadock	1	..	..	1	..	1	..	..	1	..	..
GLOVER											
Bean, Samuel	1	..	1	..	..	..	..	1	..	..	..
Conant, John	..	1	1	1	..	1	2	1	..	1	..
Haney, Elijah	1	..	1	1	..	1	..	1	..	..	..
Moore, Andrew	2	..	..	1	..	1	..	..	1	..	..
Parker, Ralph	1	..	1	1	..	..	..	1	..	..	..
Sturdivant, John	1	..	..	1	..	2	..	1	..	..	..
Vance, James	2	..	..	1	..	..	..	..	1	..	..
GLOVER—con.											
White, John	..	..	1	..	..	..	..	..	..	..	..
Woodward, Noah	..	..	..	1	..	..	..	..	..	..	..
GREENSBORO											
Andrew, James	1	..	..	1	..	4	..	..	2	..	..
Babbet, Jacob	1	1	1	..	1	1	1	1	..	1	..
Bills, Israel	..	..	1	..	..	2	..	1	..	..	..
Blanchard, Amos	1	1	..	1	..	1	..	1	1	..	..
Blanchard, Edmund	..	..	1	..	..	..	..	..	..	..	..
Blanchard, James	1	..	..	1	..	1	..	1	..	..	..
Burbank, Hazen	..	..	..	1	..	..	..	..	1	1	..
Carpenter, John	..	..	..	1	..	4	..	..	1	..	..
Cutler, Nathan Jr.	..	..	1	..	..	..	..	..	..	..	..
Cutler, Obed	1	..	1	..	..	3	..	..	1	..	..
Dagget, Ichabod	..	..	1	1	..	2	..	..	1	..	..
Eddy, Seth	1	1	2	1	..	1	2	1	1	..	..
Elkins, Salmon	1	..	..	1	..	1	..	1	..	..	..
Ellsworth, John	2	..	1	1	..	3	..	1	1	..	..
Farnham, Aaron	..	..	2	..	..	1	..	1	..	..	..
Farren, Aaron	2	..	..	1	..	..	..	1	..	..	..
Glidden, Joseph	..	..	..	1	..	..	..	..	..	..	..
Haines, Moses	..	..	1	..	1	1	..	1	..	..	..
Hatch, Nathan	1	..	..	1	..	3	..	..	1	..	..
Hill, Anne	..	..	..	..	..	..	..	..	..	1	..
Hill, James	2	..	..	1	..	2	1	..	1	..	..
Hill, Peleg	3	2	..	1	..	1	1	..	1	..	..
Huntington, Samuel	..	1	2	1	..	2	2	..	1	..	..
Lincoln, Willard	..	1	1	..	..	..	..	..	..	..	..
McComber, Isaiah	..	..	..	1	..	1	..	1	..	..	..
Moore, William	1	2	..	1	..	..	1	..	1	..	..
Peck, Barney	2	..	..	1	..	3	..	..	1	..	..
Pettengill, Jonathan	1	..	..	..	1	..	..	..	1	..	..
Phipps, John	1	1	..	1	..	2	..	..	1	..	..
Randall, Peter	..	..	1	..	..	2	..	1	..	..	..
Randall, Thomas	..	..	..	1	..	2	..	..	1	..	..
Randall, William	..	2	..	..	1	..	..	..	..	1	..
Ring, Jonathan	..	..	1	..	1	..	1	..	..	1	..
Ring, Jonathan Jr.	..	..	1	..	..	1	..	2	..	..	..
Risley, George	1	2	..	1	..	3	1	..	1	..	..
Sanborn, William	2	..	1	1	..	1	..	1	..	..	..
Shepard, Aaron	1	2	..	1	..	3	..	..	1	..	..
Shepard, Ashbel	2	1	..	1	..	1	..	1	1	..	..
Shepard, Horace	2	..	..	1	..	3	1	..	1	..	..
Shepard, James	..	..	1	..	..	..	..	..	..	..	..
Smith, Amos	..	1	..	1	..	1	..	..	1	..	..
Smith, Ezra	..	..	1	..	..	1	..	1	..	..	..
Stanley, Joseph	1	..	3	1	..	2	..	1	..	..	..
Stanley, Timothy	3	..	3	2	..	1	1	..	1	..	..
Stevens, Levi	..	1	1	..	..	4	..	..	1	..	..
Stone, David	..	1	..	1	..	2	..	1	1	..	..
Tolman, Thomas	..	2	..	1	..	4	2	..	1	..	..
Ufford, Michael	..	..	1	..	..	1	..	1	..	..	..
Underhill, James	..	..	..	1	..	..	..	1	..	..	..
Vance, David	3	1	..	1	1	3	..	..	1	..	..
Vance, John	..	1	1	1	..	2	..	..	1	..	..
Walton, Simeon	..	..	2	..	1	..	..	1	..	1	..
HYDE PARK											
Billings, Thomas	..	..	..	..	..	..	..	..	1	..	3
Dick, Anthony	..	..	..	..	..	..	..	..	..	..	2
Ferren, Reuben	2	..	..	1	..	1	..	..	1	..	..
Fisher, ———	..	..	..	..	..	..	..	..	..	1	2
Fitch, Darius	..	..	..	1	..	1	..	..	1	..	..
Fitch, Jabez	1	..	..	2	1	..	..	1	..	1	..

ORLEANS COUNTY—Continued

NAMES OF HEADS OF FAMILIES	FREE WHITE MALES: Under 10 years of age	FREE WHITE MALES: Of 10 and under 16	FREE WHITE MALES: Of 16 and under 26 including heads of families	FREE WHITE MALES: Of 26 and under 45 including heads of families	FREE WHITE MALES: Of 45 and upwards including heads of families.	FREE WHITE FEMALES: Under 10 years of age	FREE WHITE FEMALES: Of 10 and under 16	FREE WHITE FEMALES: Of 16 and under 26 including heads of families	FREE WHITE FEMALES: Of 26 and under 45 including heads of families	FREE WHITE FEMALES: Of 45 and upwards including heads of families	All other free persons except Indians not taxed
HYDE PARK—con.											
Hadley, Eliza	1	1	..	..	..	..	2	..	1	..	..
Hastings, John	2	1	..	1	..	1	..	..	1	..	..
Hastings, Timothy	..	..	..	1	..	3	2	..	1	..	..
Hyde, Jedediah	2	1	..	..	1	..	1	2	..	1	..
Hyde, Pitt W.	1	..	1	..	..	1	..	1	..	..	..
Keeler, Aaron	3	1	..	1	..	1	1	1	..	..	..
Kinney, ———	2	..	1	..	..	..	..	1	..	..	..
Lattimer, Henry	..	..	..	1	..	1	..	1	..	..	..
Martin, Peter	..	1	1	..	1	..	..	..	..	1	..
McDaniel, John	..	..	1	..	1	..	..	1	..	1	..
Newland, Jabez	2	..	..	1	..	1	2	..	1	..	..
Parker, David	..	..	1	..	..	1	..	1	..	..	..
Pond, Ezekiel	1	..	..	1	..	1	..	..	1	..	..
Sawyer, Nathaniel P.	..	..	..	1	..	2	..	1	..	..	..
Sawyer, Truman	1	..	..	1	..	..	..	..	1	..	..
Searl, John	..	..	..	1	..	1	..	1	..	..	..
Taylor, Gamaliel	..	..	..	1	..	2	..	1	..	..	..
Williams, Nehemiah	..	..	..	1	..	..	..	..	..	..	..
———, Worcester	..	..	..	..	..	..	..	..	..	..	5
IRASBURGH											
Horam, Daniel	..	..	1	..	..	..	..	..	..	..	..
Horam, Timothy	..	..	1	..	..	..	..	..	..	..	..
Humphrey, Solomon	..	..	1	..	..	1	..	1	..	..	..
Leach, Caleb	1	..	5	1	..	2	..	1	..	..	..
LUTTERLOCH											
Fairfield, Isaac	2	..	..	1	..	..	..	..	1	..	..
Fairfield, Jacob	4	..	..	1	..	..	..	..	1	..	..
Fairfield, Nathan	..	..	1	..	1	..	..	..	..	..	..
MORRISTOWN											
Boardman, Elisha	1	..	..	1	..	..	..	1	..	..	..
Boardman, Lydia	..	..	2	..	..	..	..	..	..	1	..
Boardman, William	..	..	1	..	..	..	..	1	..	..	..
Borris, Joseph	2	..	..	1	..	2	..	..	1	..	..
Brigham, Abner	2	1	2	..	..	..	..	1	1	..	..
Burke, Joseph	2	1	..	1	..	3	1	..	1	..	..
Childs, Stephen	1	..	..	1	..	2	1	..	1	..	..
Cole, Asa	..	..	1	..	..	..	..	..	..	..	..
Cole, Ebenezer	..	..	..	1	..	..	..	..	..	..	..
Dunham, Micajah	2	..	1	1	..	..	..	1	1	..	..
Goodale, Alpheus	..	..	..	1	..	..	..	..	..	..	..
Goodale, Cyril	..	..	..	1	..	..	..	1	..	..	..
MORRISTOWN—con.											
Goodale, Nathaniel	..	..	..	1	..	2	..	1	..	..	..
Gosslin, Samuel	2	..	..	1	..	3	..	..	1	..	..
Hill, Cyrus	1	..	..	1	..	..	..	..	1	..	..
Hurd, Aaron	..	1	..	..	1	..	1	..	1	..	..
Kenfield, George	1	1	2	..	1	4	..	2	1	..	..
Keyzer, John	2	1	..	1	..	1	1	..	1	..	..
Little, James	..	1	1	1	..	2	3	..	1	..	..
Matthews, James	..	..	4	..	1	..	1	..	..	1	..
Olds, Comfort	1	1	..	1	..	1	1	..	1	..	..
Perry, Sylvanus	1	2	..	1	..	3	..	..	1	..	..
Rood, Samuel	..	..	1	..	..	..	..	1	..	..	..
Safford, John	2	..	1	..	1	1	..	2	..	1	..
Scrivner, David	..	..	1	..	..	..	..	1	..	..	..
Scrivner, Samuel	2	1	..	1	..	3	1	..	..	1	..
Shaw, Crispus	..	1	..	1	..	3	1	..	1	..	..
Silewar, Redfield	1	..	..	1	1	1	..	..	1	..	..
Sumner, Asa	..	..	..	1	..	..	..	..	..	..	..
Sumner, Daniel	..	..	1	..	..	2	1	1	..	1	..
Williams, Joseph	..	..	1	..	..	..	..	..	..	..	..
SALEM											
Blake, Ephraim	1	..	..	1	..	..	..	1	..	..	..
Paddock, Bradford	1	..	..	1	..	..	2	..	1	..	..
Woodman, Archelaus	2	1	1	1	..	1	1	..	1	..	..
WESTFIELD											
Bancroft, John	..	..	1	..	..	..	..	..	..	..	..
Burgess, Anthony	..	..	1	..	..	..	..	..	..	..	..
Hobbs, William	1	1	1	1	..	..	1	..	1	..	..
Hume, Ezra	1	..	..	1	..	..	..	..	1	..	..
Olds, Jesse	..	..	..	1	..	3	..	..	1	..	..
WOLCOTT											
Guyer, John	2	..	1	..	..	..	..	1	..	..	..
Guyer, Luke	..	..	..	..	1	..	..	..	..	1	..
Hubbel, Seth	2	..	..	1	..	2	2	3	1	..	..
Sinclair, James	1	2	..	1	..	5	1	..	1	..	..
Taylor, Thomas	2	2	..	1	..	1	..	1	1	..	..
Whitney, Hezekiah	..	..	3	1	1	..	1	..	..	1	..
Whitney, William	1	..	..	1	..	1	..	1	..	..	..

RUTLAND COUNTY

NAMES OF HEADS OF FAMILIES	FREE WHITE MALES: Under 10 years of age	FREE WHITE MALES: Of 10 and under 16	FREE WHITE MALES: Of 16 and under 26 including heads of families	FREE WHITE MALES: Of 26 and under 45 including heads of families	FREE WHITE MALES: Of 45 and upwards including heads of families.	FREE WHITE FEMALES: Under 10 years of age	FREE WHITE FEMALES: Of 10 and under 16	FREE WHITE FEMALES: Of 16 and under 26 including heads of families	FREE WHITE FEMALES: Of 26 and under 45 including heads of families	FREE WHITE FEMALES: Of 45 and upwards including heads of families	All other free persons except Indians not taxed
BENSON											
Abbott, Timothy	..	1	..	..	1	..	..	..	1	..	..
Adams, Abraham	1	..	..	1	..	1	..	1	..	..	..
Adkins, Robert	1	..	..	1	..	3	..	..	1	..	..
Akins, Edward	..	..	..	1	..	..	..	..	1	..	..
Arnold, Epaphas	..	..	..	..	1	..	..	1	..	1	..
Arnold, Epaphas Jr.	..	..	1	..	..	..	..	1	..	..	..
Arnold, Francis	2	1	..	1	1	..	..	..	1	..	..
Austin, Frederick	..	..	1	..	..	..	..	..	..	..	..
Barber, Daniel	2	1	..	1	..	1	1	1	1	..	..
Barber, Levi	3	..	..	1	..	..	1	..	1	..	..
Barber, Margaret	..	..	2	..	..	..	..	1	..	1	..
Barber, Mathew	..	..	..	1	..	..	..	..	..	..	..
Barber, Robert	2	1	..	1	..	1	2	..	1	..	..
Barker, Cyrus	..	..	1	..	..	1	..	1	..	..	..
Barker, Oliver	..	..	..	..	1	..	..	..	..	1	..
Barlow, James	..	..	1	..	..	..	..	1	..	..	..
Barlow, Nathaniel	2	1	..	1	..	1	..	..	1	..	..
Bebee, Simeon	3	1	..	1	..	3	1	..	1	..	..
Belden, Abraham	..	..	..	1	..	..	1	..	1	..	..
Belden, Charles	..	..	3	..	1	..	..	..	..	1	..
Belden, Elisha	2	..	2	1	..	2	2	..	1	..	..
BENSON—con.											
Belden, Levi	2	1	1	..	1	3	1	1	1	..	..
Belden, Phinehas	2	..	..	1	1	3	..	..	1	1	..
Belden, Solomon	..	1	..	1	..	1	..	..	1	..	..
Benson, Ellis Jr.	2	..	..	1	..	2	..	..	1	..	..
Benson, John	2	2	..	1	..	..	1	..	..	..	1
Blossom, Benjamin	..	..	1	..	..	1	..	1	..	1	..
Branch, Israel	1	..	1	..	..	..	..	1	..	..	..
Branch, Jephtha	2	..	..	1	..	1	..	..	1	..	..
Branch, Joseph	..	..	..	1	..	..	..	..	..	..	..
Branch, Massey	1	1	2	..	1	..	..	..	..	1	..
Branch, Vine	2	..	..	1	..	2	..	..	1	1	..
Briggs, Arnold	..	..	1	..	1	1	..	1	..	1	..
Briggs, Simeon	2	..	..	1	1	1	..	1	..	1	..
Brooks, Thomas	2	1	..	1	..	2	2	..	1	..	..
Brown, Daniel	3	2	2	..	1	..	1	..	..	1	..
Buck, Justice	1	..	..	1	..	1	..	1	..	..	..
Buck, Seth	..	..	2	..	..	..	..	..	..	1	..
Campbell, John	2	..	..	1	..	1	..	1	1	..	..
Carter, Jabez	2	1	3	..	1	1	1	..	1	..	..
Carter, John	1	..	..	1	..	1	..	1	..	..	..
Chapin, Perry	1	1	2	..	1	1	1	1		1	..
Chittenden, Solomon	2	1	..	1	..	1	2	..	1	..	..

RUTLAND COUNTY—Continued

NAMES OF HEADS OF FAMILIES	FREE WHITE MALES					FREE WHITE FEMALES					
	Under 10 years of age	Of 10 and under 16	Of 16 and under 26 including heads of families	Of 26 and under 45 including heads of families	Of 45 and upwards including heads of families.	Under 10 years of age	Of 10 and under 16	Of 16 and under 26 including heads of families	Of 26 and under 45 including heads of families	Of 45 and upwards including heads of families	All other free persons except Indians not taxed
BENSON—con.											
Churchel, John	..	..	1	1	..	1	2	1	..	1	..
Clark, Josiah	1	2	1	..	1	2	..	..	1	..	..
Cooley, Alfred	..	1	..	1	..	3	..	1	..	..	..
Couch, Stephen	..	..	1	..	..	1	..	1	..	..	..
Cramer, Peter	..	..	..	1	..	..	..	1	..	..	..
Crammer, Bishop	2	..	1	1	..	..	..	1	1	..	..
Crofoot, Stephen	..	1	1	..	1	..	1	..	..	1	..
Crofoot, Stephen Jr.	..	..	..	1	..	1	1	..	1	..	..
Cudworth, Paul	1	1	1	..	1	..	..	..	..	3	..
Curtis, Levi	2	..	..	1	..	2	..	1	..	..	..
Denison, Andrew	2	..	1	1	..	..	1	..	1	..	..
Denison, Robert	..	..	..	1	..	..	..	..	..	..	..
Dill, Edward	..	..	..	1	..	2	..	..	1	..	..
Dowd, Peleg	..	1	..	1	..	4	..	..	1	..	..
Dunning, John	1	..	..	1	..	1	..	..	1	..	..
Dunning, Stephen	3	2	..	..	1	1	1	..	1	..	..
Durfey, Walter	2	..	1	..	1	2	..	..	1	1	..
Dyar, Solomon	1	1	..	1	..	2	..	..	1	..	..
Dyar, Thomas	2	1	..	1	..	2	..	..	1	..	..
Dyar, Uzziah	3	..	..	1	..	1	..	..	1	..	..
Farnham, Asa	1	2	2	1	..	3	1	1	2	..	..
Fisher, John	1	..	1	..	1	..	1	..	..	1	..
Ford, William	..	..	1	..	1	..	..	1	..	1	..
Fordam, Barnabas	2	..	1	..	1	1	..	..	1	..	..
Fordam, Gideon	..	1	3	..	1	1	2	..	..	1	..
Fordam, Paul	..	..	..	1	..	..	1	1	..	1	..
Fordam, Silas	..	..	1	..	..	..	..	1	..	..	..
Fowler, Thomas	2	1	..	1	..	3	1	..	1	..	..
Fuller, James	3	..	..	1	..	1	..	1	..	..	..
Fuller, Josiah	..	..	1	..	..	2	..	1	..	..	..
Garrett, Theodore	2	..	..	1	..	2	..	..	1	..	..
Gibbs, Aaron	1	..	..	1	..	2	..	1	..	..	..
Gibbs, Darius	5	2	1	1	..	..	1	..	1	..	..
Gibbs, Solomon	3	1	..	1	..	..	1	..	1	..	..
Gleason, Benoni	2	..	..	1	..	2	1	..	1	..	..
Gleason, Enoch	..	..	1	..	..	..	..	1	..	..	..
Gleason, Jacob	..	1	1	..	1	..	..	2	..	1	..
Gleason, Jared	2	1	..	1	..	..	..	..	1	..	..
Gleason, Jonah	3	..	..	1	..	1	..	..	1	..	..
Gleason, Putnam	1	..	..	1	..	..	..	1	..	..	..
Goodrich, Allen	2	1	..	1	..	3	1	..	1	..	..
Goodrich, Anna	..	..	..	..	..	2	..	..	1	..	..
Goodrich, Josiah	1	1	1	1	..	1	1	..	1	..	..
Goodrich, Othniel	2	..	..	1	..	1	..	..	1	..	..
Goodrich, Simeon	4	1	..	1	..	..	1	..	1	..	..
Goodrich, Thomas	1	..	..	1	..	3	..	..	1	..	..
Gregg, Ebenezer	..	..	..	1	..	..	..	1	..	..	..
Gregory, John	2	..	1	1	..	2	2	..	1	..	..
Harrison, Lemuel	..	..	1	..	1	..	1	..	..	1	..
Harvey, Josiah	2	1	..	1	..	1	..	1	1	..	..
Harvey, Loved	..	..	1	..	..	..	..	..	..	..	..
Haywood, Daniel	2	..	..	1	..	..	..	..	1	..	..
Haywood, James	1	2	..	1	..	3	1	..	1	..	..
Haywood, Samuel	3	..	1	1	..	1	2	..	1	1	..
Henderson, Abner	2	..	..	1	..	2	..	..	1	..	..
Higgins, Ichabod	1	..	..	1	..	1	..	..	1	..	..
Higgins, Samuel	1	..	2	..	1	1	2	..	1	..	..
Hinman, Abijah	..	..	..	..	1	..	..	..	..	1	..
Hinman, Simeon	2	..	..	1	..	1	..	1	1	..	..
Hinman, Timothy	2	..	..	1	..	1	..	1	..	..	..
Hodgkins, David	2	1	..	1	..	4	..	..	1	..	..
Holten, Benjamin	2	..	..	1	..	..	1	..	1	..	..
Hooker, John	3	..	1	..	..	..	..	1	..	..	..
How, Asaph	1	..	..	1	..	4	1	..	1	..	..
How, Joshua	1	..	..	1	..	..	1	1	..	..	..
Hurlbut, Abijah	..	1	..	..	1	..	1	..	1	..	..
Hurlbut, Amos	3	..	..	1	..	2	1	..	1	..	..
Hurlbut, Samuel	..	..	..	1	..	..	..	1	..	..	..
Johnson, Brown	..	..	..	1	..	3	..	..	1	..	..
Johnson, David	1	..	..	1	..	2	..	1	..	..	..
Johnson, Ozias	..	1	..	1	..	..	..	1	1	1	..
Jones, Asa	1	1	..	11	..	2	..	1	..	..	..
Kent, Dan	1	1	1	1	..	2	..	1	1	..	..
Killicot, David	1	1	..	1	..	2	..	..	1	..	..
King, Amos	..	..	1	..	1	..	1	1	1	..	..
King, Elias	1	2	..	1	..	1	2	..	1	..	..
King, Peletiah	2	1	1	..	1	1	1	..	..	1	..
King, Stephen	..	1	1	1	..	2	..	..	1	..	..
Kinson, Daniel	1	..	1	..	1	2	2	2	1	..	..
Knapp, Ebenezer	2	..	..	1	..	1	..	..	1	..	..
Ladd, Peregrine	..	..	1	1	..	..	..	..	1	..	..
Lebanen, David	..	1	1	..	1	..	1	..	..	1	..
Manley, Calvin	2	..	..	1	..	2	..	..	1	..	..
Manley, William	..	..	1	..	..	..	..	..	1	..	..
Maynard, Shubal	..	..	..	1	..	..	..	..	1	..	..
McCotter, Alexander	3	..	..	1	..	1	1	..	1	..	..
McCotter, James	..	..	1	..	..	..	..	..	..	1	..
Meacham, David	3	..	..	1	..	..	..	..	1	..	..
Meacham, Isaac	1	..	..	1	..	..	..	1	..	..	..
Meacham, John	..	..	3	..	1	1	2	..	..	1	..
Meacham, Jonathan	..	..	1	..	1	..	..	1	..	1	..
Meacham, Josiah	..	..	..	1	..	4	..	..	1	..	..
Meacham, William	2	2	..	..	1	3	2	..	1	..	..
Merritt, Bartholomew	2	..	..	1	..	..	1	..	1	..	..
Merritt, Michael	..	..	..	1	..	2	..	..	1	..	..
Merritt, Nathaniel	3	1	1	..	1	1	1	1	1	..	..
Miller, Ebenezer	2	..	..	1	..	2	..	..	1	1	..
Morgan, Thomas	1	..	..	1	..	..	..	1	..	1	..
Narrimore, Joel	1	..	..	1	..	2	..	..	1	..	..
Nash, Reuben	2	..	1	1	..	2	2	1	1	..	..
Nelson, Jonas	..	1	1	..	..	..	..	1	..	..	..
Nerin, Loam	2	..	2	..	1	1	2	1	1	..	..
Noble, James	1	1	1	1	..	2	1	..	1	..	..
Omstead, Asher	3	1	..	..	1	1	..	..	1	..	..
Omstead, Asher Jr.	1	..	..	1	..	1	..	1	..	..	..
Omstead, Jesse	3	1	..	1	..	1	..	1	1	..	..
Omstead, Stephen	..	1	..	..	1	..	..	..	..	1	..
Pain, Sparrow J.	1	1	..	1	..	3	..	..	1	..	..
Parker, James	..	..	1	..	..	..	..	..	..	..	..
Parker, Prince	..	1	..	1	..	1	1	..	..	1	..
Parkill, James	1	1	1	..	1	..	1	2	..	1	..
Parsons, Reuben	..	1	..	1	..	2	..	..	1	..	..
Pattason, John	..	2	..	..	1	..	1	1	..	1	..
Pattason, William	1	..	..	1	..	..	..	..	1	..	..
Peters, Comfort	3	1	..	1	..	1	..	..	1	..	..
Pitts, Hanover	1	..	..	..	1	2	..	1	..	..	..
Potter, Aaron	3	1	..	1	..	1	..	..	1	..	..
Rising, Elijah	2	..	..	1	..	2	1	..	1	..	..
Root, Amos	..	..	2	..	1	..	1	..	..	..	..
Root, Amos Jr.	1	2	..	..	1	1	1	..	..	1	..
Root, Oliver	1	..	..	1	..	..	..	..	1	..	..
Root, Silas	..	..	1	..	..	..	..	..	..	..	..
Rynolds, Simeon	1	1	..	1	..	2	..	..	1	..	..
Shared, Stephen	1	..	..	..	1	..	1	3	..	1	..
Shared, Stephen Jr.	..	..	1	..	..	..	..	1	..	..	..
Shaw, Benjamin	1	..	..	1	..	..	..	..	1	..	..
Shaw, John	1	..	1	1	..	1	3	..	..	1	..
Smith, Chauncey	4	1	..	1	..	1	1	..	1	1	..
Smith, Elihu	3	1	..	1	..	1	..	..	1	..	..
Smith, Jiles	2	..	..	1	..	1	..	1	1	..	..
Smith, Loins	2	1	..	1	..	2	..	..	1	..	..
Southwick, Daniel	..	1	1	..	..	..	..	1	..	..	..
Southwick, David	2	2	..	2	..	2	1	..	1	..	..
Stacey, Benjamin	3	..	..	1	..	2	1	..	1	..	..
Stacey, Joseph	2	1	..	1	..	2	1	1	1	..	..
Standish, Lemuel	2	1	..	1	..	2	1	..	2	..	..
Starns, John	..	..	1	..	1	..	..	..	..	1	..
Stevens, Albert	..	..	1	..	..	..	..	..	..	..	..
Stevens, Czarr	..	..	1	..	..	1	..	..	1	..	..
Stiles, Asael	3	2	..	1	..	1	1	..	1	..	..
Stiles, Silas	1	1	..	1	..	4	1	..	1	..	..
Strong, Russel	2	..	..	1	..	3	..	..	1	..	..
Taylor, Amos	..	..	..	1	..	..	..	..	..	..	..
Taylor, Jonathan	3	1	..	1	..	2	3	..	1	..	..
Vaughn, John A.	1	..	..	1	..	2	..	1	..	..	..
Wallis, Harriman	..	1	..	..	1	4	1	1	1	..	..
Watson, Timothy	1	1	1	1	..	..	1	..	1	..	..
Webb, Reuben	..	..	1	..	..	..	..	1	..	..	..
Welch, Nathaniel	2	1	1	..	1	2	..	..	1	..	..
Wheeler, Isaac	1	1	1	1	..	1	..	1	1	..	..
Wilcox, Elijah	..	..	3	..	1	..	..	..	..	1	..
Wilcox, Levi	..	..	1	..	..	..	..	..	..	..	..
Wilcox, Martin	1	..	..	1	..	3	..	1	1	..	..
Wilkinson, Lewis	..	1	2	..	1	..	1	..	..	1	..
Wilkinson, Lewis Jr.	2	..	..	1	..	..	..	1	..	..	..
Wilkinson, Reuben	4	1	1	..	1	1	1	..	1	..	..
Woodard, Benaiah	1	..	1	1	..	1	..	..	1	..	..
Woodard, Josiah	..	..	..	1	1	2	..	..	1	1	..

RUTLAND COUNTY—Continued

NAMES OF HEADS OF FAMILIES	FREE WHITE MALES: Under 10 years of age	FREE WHITE MALES: Of 10 and under 16	FREE WHITE MALES: Of 16 and under 26 including heads of families	FREE WHITE MALES: Of 26 and under 45 including heads of families	FREE WHITE MALES: Of 45 and upwards including heads of families.	FREE WHITE FEMALES: Under 10 years of age	FREE WHITE FEMALES: Of 10 and under 16	FREE WHITE FEMALES: Of 16 and under 26 including heads of families	FREE WHITE FEMALES: Of 26 and under 45 including heads of families	FREE WHITE FEMALES: Of 45 and upwards including heads of families	All other free persons except Indians not taxed
BENTON'S GORE											
Farrington, Daniel	..	..	..	1	..	..	..	..	1	..	..
Greele, Samuel	1	..	..	1	..	..	..	..	1	..	..
Parker, Joel	..	..	..	1	..	1	..	..	1	..	..
Perry, Shubael	1	..	..	1	..	2	..	..	1	..	..
Ridout, David	..	..	..	2	..	1	..	..	1	..	..
BRANDON											
Amblor, William	2	..	..	1	..	..	1	..	1	..	..
Arnold, John	3	1	..	1	..	1	2	..	1	..	..
Avery, Daniel	1	1	..	1	..	1	1	..	1	..	..
Avery, Simeon	3	1	..	1	..	..	1	..	1	..	..
Bacon, James	..	..	1	..	..	..	..	..	..	..	..
Bacon, Nathaniel	2	..	..	1	..	1	..	..	1	..	..
Bacon, Philp.	..	..	..	1	..	5	2	1	1	..	..
Bakon, David	..	..	..	1	..	..	..	..	..	..	..
Barnard, Joel	2	..	..	1	..	1	1	1	1	..	..
Barnett, James	1	2	..	..	1	1	1	..	1	..	..
Barns, Moses	1	..	..	1	..	1	3	..	1	..	..
Bascom, Susanna	..	..	..	..	..	2	..	..	1	..	..
Battles, Nathan	1	..	..	1	..	2	..	..	1	..	..
Bemus, Joshua	2	..	1	1	..	4	1	..	1	..	..
Bigalow, Nathan	..	..	..	1	..	1	..	1	1	..	..
Bigalow, Simeon	3	3	..	..	1	3	1	..	1	..	..
Bigsby, John	1	..	..	1	..	1	..	1	..	..	..
Broughton, Samuel	1	..	1	..	..	..	..	1	..	..	..
Brown, Michael	..	..	1	..	..	..	..	..	..	..	..
Brownson, Philander	..	1	2	..	..	2	2	1	1	..	..
Buckland, Abner	2	..	..	1	..	..	..	..	1	..	..
Buckland, David	3	..	..	1	..	1	..	..	1	..	..
Buckland, David	..	2	1	..	..	1	..	1	..	2	..
Buckland, Timothy	1	1	1	..	..	..	..	1	..	..	..
Burnell, Samuel	3	1	1	1	..	4	3	..	1	..	..
Buttles, John	1	..	..	1	..	..	..	1	..	..	..
Carver, Rufus	1	..	..	..	1	3	1	..	..	1	..
Cary, Seth	..	1	1	..	1	1	2	1	1	..	..
Chena, Edward	1	1	..	..	1	..	1	1	..	1	..
Chena, Edward Jr.	..	..	1	..	..	..	..	1	..	..	..
Chena, Ephraim	2	..	..	1	..	1	..	..	1	..	..
Chena, Samuel	3	..	..	1	..	..	..	1	..	..	..
Childs, Ebenezer	2	..	..	1	..	1	..	..	1	..	..
Childs, Pearly	1	..	..	1	..	1	1	..	1	1	..
Childs, Penuel	1	2	1	1	..	1	..	..	1	..	..
Churchel, Winslow	1	..	..	1	..	1	..	1	..	..	..
Clark, John	..	..	1	..	..	..	..	..	..	..	..
Conant, John	2	..	..	1	..	2	..	..	1	..	..
Coos, Joshua	..	2	1	..	1	..	1	1	..	1	..
Crooks, John	..	..	1	..	1	..	1	1	..	1	..
Cutler, Amos	1	..	1	..	1	1	1	..	1	..	..
Darling, David	1	1	1	..	1	3	..	..	1	..	..
Davis, Simeon	1	1	..	1	..	3	..	..	1	..	..
Dimmick, Shubal	1	..	..	1	..	1	..	1	..	..	..
Dodge, Asa	..	..	2	..	1	1	..	1	..	1	..
Dodge, Jonathan	2	1	..	1	..	2	..	..	1	..	..
Dodge, William	..	..	1	..	1	1	..	..	..	1	..
Douglass, Benair	2	1	1	..	1	1	2	1	1	..	..
Dow, Joel	1	..	..	1	..	1	..	..	1	..	..
Downey, Charles	3	..	..	1	..	..	..	1	..	..	..
Downey, Robert	..	..	1	..	..	..	..	1	..	..	..
Downey, Thomas	1	..	..	1	..	1	..	1	..	..	..
Durkee, Shubal	2	..	..	1	..	1	..	..	1	..	..
Durkee, Stephen	..	1	2	..	1	..	..	1	..	1	..
Eastman, Ira B.	..	..	..	1	..	2	..	..	1	..	..
Eno, James	..	..	..	1	..	3	..	..	1	..	..
Farr, Salmon	2	2	..	1	..	1	..	3	1	..	..
Farrington, Daniel	..	1	1	..	..	1	..	..	1	..	..
Farrington, Jacob	..	..	..	..	1	..	..	..	..	1	..
Field, Joshua	..	1	3	..	1	..	..	1	..	1	..
Finney, David	..	..	..	..	1	..	..	..	..	1	..
Finney, David Jr.	1	2	..	1	..	3	..	1	1	..	..
Fisk, Bateman	..	..	1	..	..	..	..	1	..	..	..
Fisk, Nathaniel Jr.	..	2	1	..	1	..	1	1	..	1	..
Fisk, Nathaniel Jr.	..	..	..	1	..	2	..	1	..	..	..
Fisk, Rufus	..	..	1	..	..	..	..	1	..	..	..
Flint, Ephraim	3	..	..	1	..	2	..	..	1	..	..
Flint, Lemuel	..	..	..	1	..	..	..	..	..	..	..
Flint, Nathan	..	..	..	..	1	..	..	1	..	1	..
BRANDON—con.											
Flint, Nathan Jr.	1	..	..	1	..	..	..	..	1	..	..
Flint, Roswell	1	1	..	1	..	2	..	..	1	..	..
Gilbert, Abraham	..	1	..	..	1	..	..	..	..	1	..
Gilbert, Elan	4	..	..	1	..	..	..	..	1	..	..
Gilbert, Moses	1	..	..	..	1	..	..	..	1	..	..
Gilbert, Moses Jr.	..	1	1	..	1	..	2	..	1	..	..
Gilbert, Richard	2	..	2	..	..	1	..	1	..	..	..
Ginna, Robert	..	..	..	..	1	..	..	..	..	..	..
Ginnings, Joseph	4	1	1	1	..	..	1	2	1	..	..
Goodenow, Abel	..	..	..	1	..	..	..	..	..	..	..
Goodenow, Asa	..	..	..	1	..	..	..	1	..	..	..
Goodenow, Elijah	..	2	1	1	..	..	1	..	1	..	..
Grandy, Asa	2	1	..	1	..	3	..	..	1	..	..
Grandy, Reuben	1	1	..	..	1	1	1	..	..	1	..
Graves, Asa	3	..	..	1	..	1	2	2	1	..	..
Gray, Samuel	2	2	2	..	1	2	..	..	1	..	..
Hach, Joseph	2	..	1	..	..	..	..	1	..	..	..
Hach, Zephaniah	1	..	..	1	..	..	1	..	1	1	..
Hall, David	1	1	..	1	..	1	..	..	2	..	..
Hal!, John	..	1	..	1	..	..	..	..	1	..	..
Hall, Stephen	1	2	..	2	..	1	1	..	1	..	..
Handley, James	..	..	..	..	1	..	..	1	..	1	..
Harris, Nathaniel	..	1	3	..	1	3	1	..	1	..	..
Hawley, David	..	..	..	..	1	..	1	..	..	1	..
Hawley, Joseph	..	2	1	..	1	1	..	..	1	..	..
Henry, Daniel	1	1	1	..	..	..	..	1	..	2	..
Hibbord, Ebenezer Rev.	3	1	..	1	..	1	..	..	1	..	..
Hibbord, Ithamar	..	..	1	..	..	..	..	..	..	..	..
Hill, John	..	..	..	..	1	..	..	..	..	1	..
Hill, William	1	2	1	1	..	4	1	1	1	..	..
Hines, Jesse	1	1	2	1	..	3	3	..	1	..	..
Hines, John	..	..	..	1	..	..	..	..	1	..	..
Hitchcock, Martin	..	..	1	..	..	1	..	1	..	..	..
Hollyday, Nehemiah	..	..	1	..	..	..	..	..	..	..	..
Hollyday, Richard	2	..	1	..	..	..	..	1	..	..	..
Holt, Benjamin Jr.	..	..	..	..	..	..	..	..	..	..	..
Holt, Seth	..	..	1	..	..	..	..	1	..	..	..
Holt, Silas	..	..	..	..	1	..	..	1	..	1	..
Hooker, John	..	..	1	..	..	..	..	..	..	..	..
Horton, Gideon	1	..	..	..	1	..	..	..	..	1	..
Horton, Gideon Jr.	3	..	1	1	..	2	1	1	1	..	..
Horton, Hiram	3	..	..	1	..	2	3	..	1	..	..
Horton, John	..	..	1	..	..	..	..	..	..	..	..
Hudson, Abijah	..	..	..	1	..	1	..	..	1	..	..
Hudson, Stephen	2	..	..	1	..	1	..	..	1	..	..
Hurlbert, Benjamin	..	..	..	1	..	1	..	1	..	..	..
Hurlbert, Benjamin	..	1	3	..	1	1	1	..	1	..	..
Hurlbert, Nathaniel C.	1	..	1	..	..	..	..	1	..	..	..
Jacobs, David	1	..	..	..	1	..	..	1	..	1	..
Jacobs, Levi	2	..	..	1	..	3	..	..	1	..	..
Johnson, Charles	..	1	..	1	..	1	..	1	..	..	..
Jones, Philip	2	1	..	1	..	3	1	..	1	..	..
Judd, Asa	..	..	..	1	..	..	..	1	..	..	..
June, Asael	..	..	1	..	..	2	..	1	..	..	..
June, Daniel	2	..	..	1	..	..	..	1	1	..	..
June, David	..	..	..	..	1	3	1	..	..	1	..
June, Joshua	3	1	1	..	1	2	..	2	1	..	..
June, Stephen	1	..	1	..	..	1	..	1	..	..	..
Keiler, Seth	..	..	2	..	..	..	..	1	..	..	..
Keiler, Silas	3	..	..	1	..	..	..	1	..	..	..
King, Simeon	1	1	..	..	1	..	1	3	..	1	..
King, Simeon Jr.	3	..	..	1	..	3	1	..	1	..	..
Ladd, Dustin	3	1	..	..	1	1	1	..	..	1	..
Langdon, David	2	..	..	1	..	1	..	1	..	..	..
Larkin, Joseph	1	1	..	1	..	1	1	..	1	..	..
Love, John	4	..	..	1	..	1	1	..	1	..	..
Loveland, Jonathan	2	1	..	..	1	..	..	..	1	..	..
Lyon, Jabez	1	1	1	..	1	3	1	3	1	..	..
McCollum, David	1	..	..	1	..	3	..	..	1	..	..
McCollum, Henry	2	..	..	1	..	..	2	..	1	..	..
McCollum, John	..	..	..	..	1	..	..	1	..	1	..
Meriam, Benjamin	1	..	..	1	..	..	..	1	..	..	..
Meriam, David	1	3	..	1	..	1	..	3	..	1	..
Merriam, Jonathan	2	1	1	1	..	2	..	..	1	..	..
Moseley, Abishai	..	..	..	..	1	..	..	1	..	1	..
Moseley, John	1	..	..	1	..	2	1	..	1	..	..
Moseley, Nathaniel	2	..	..	1	..	2	..	..	1	..	..
Mott, Gideon	1	..	..	1	..	..	2	..	1	..	..
Mott, John	1	1	2	..	1	1	2	1	1	..	..
Mott, Samuel	1	1	..	..	1	2	..	..	..	1	..
Muzzy, Amos	2	..	..	1	..	1	..	..	1	..	..

RUTLAND COUNTY—Continued

NAMES OF HEADS OF FAMILIES	FREE WHITE MALES					FREE WHITE FEMALES					
	Under 10 years of age	Of 10 and under 16	Of 16 and under 26 including heads of families	Of 26 and under 45 including heads of families	Of 45 and upwards including heads of families.	Under 10 years of age	Of 10 and under 16	Of 16 and under 26 including heads of families	Of 26 and under 45 including heads of families	Of 45 and upwards including heads of families	All other free persons except Indians not taxed
BRANDON—con.											
Nelson, Andrew	1	2	..	1	..	..	1	..	1	..	..
Nelson, James	..	..	1	..	..	..	1	..	..	..	..
Parmerton, Josiah	..	..	1	..	..	2	..	1	..	..	..
Parmerton, Nathan	..	..	1	..	..	1	..	..	1	..	..
Pease, Samuel	..	..	1	..	..	..	..	..	..	..	..
Pomroy, Daniel	1	1	1	1	..	1	..	1	..	..	..
Pond, Zebulon	1	..	..	1	..	2	..	..	1	..	..
Powers, Simeon	1	..	..	1	..	1	..	1	..	..	..
Prout, Jesse	3	..	1	1	..	2	2	1	1	..	..
Purdy, Israel	3	..	..	..	1	1	1	..	1	..	..
Randal, Ichabod	6	..	1	1	..	1	..	1	1	..	..
Rice, Justice	..	..	..	1	..	..	..	..	..	..	..
Scovil, Frederick	1	..	..	1	..	2	..	1	..	..	..
Scovil, Samuel	3	..	..	1	..	2	1	..	1	1	..
Seaton, James	..	..	12	..	..	..	..	..	..	..	..
Seaton, John	..	..	1	..	1	..	..	..	..	1	..
Seaton, John Jr.	..	..	2	1	..	1	..	1	..	..	..
Simons, Jacob	3	..	..	1	..	2	..	..	1	..	..
Smith, Oliver	2	2	1	..	1	1	1	1	1	..	..
Snow, Jesse	..	..	..	1	..	2	1	..	1	..	..
Soaper, Prince	2	1	1	1	..	1	1	..	1	..	..
Squier, Ebenezer	1	..	..	1	..	2	1	2	1	..	..
Starkweather, Roger	3	..	..	1	..	3	2	..	1	..	..
Stewert, Abraham	..	..	2	1	..	1	1	..	1	..	..
Stewert, Benjamin	..	..	1	..	..	..	..	1	..	..	..
Stiles, John	2	..	..	1	..	4	1	..	1	..	..
Strong, Ephraim	..	1	..	1	..	1	..	..	1	..	..
Thorndich, Paul	..	..	..	1	..	..	..	1	..	..	..
Tinkum, Isaac	2	1	..	..	1	..	1	2	1	..	..
Tracy, Arza	2	..	..	1	..	1	..	..	1	..	..
Tracy, Solomon	..	1	..	1	..	4	1	..	1	..	..
Tucker, Stephen	2	..	..	1	..	3	..	..	1	..	..
Warner, Samuel	2	..	1	..	1	1	2	4	1	..	..
Warren, Jacob	..	..	1	1	..	..	..	..	1	..	..
Weatherby, Jonathan	2	..	..	1	..	..	..	1	..	..	..
Weed, Jacob	..	..	3	..	..	..	..	1	..	..	..
Welch, David	3	..	..	1	..	2	..	..	1	..	..
Whaland, James	..	..	..	1	..	..	..	..	1	..	..
White, James	3	1	1	1	..	2	1	1	1	..	..
Winchester, Henry	..	1	..	..	1	2	1	..	1	1	..
Winslow, Justin	3	..	..	1	..	1	..	..	1	..	..
Wolcott, Oliver	3	..	..	1	..	..	..	..	1	..	..
Worster, Barzillai	..	..	1	..	..	..	..	1	..	..	..
Worster, Ebenezer	..	1	1	..	1	3	..	3	..	1	..
Wright, Gardner	1	1	1	..	..	1	..	1	..	..	..
CASTLETON											
Adams, Pelatiah	1	..	..	..	1	2	..	1	1	..	..
Adams, Zopha	1	..	1	..	..	1	..	1	..	..	..
Barber, Eli	..	1	1	..	..	..	..	1	..	1	..
Barber, Zimr	1	..	..	1	..	1	..	1	..	..	..
Bates, Andrew	..	..	1	..	..	1	..	1	..	..	..
Belnap, Jesse	..	2	..	..	1	..	1	1	..	1	..
Blackmore, Lewis	..	..	..	1	..	..	..	..	..	..	..
Bliss, Ephraim	..	..	1	..	..	..	..	1	..	..	..
Bliss, Philetus	2	1	..	1	..	..	1	1	..	..	..
Boland, Noah	..	..	..	1	..	..	..	1	..	..	..
Boland, William	..	..	1	..	1	..	..	2	..	1	..
Bond, Moses	..	2	..	1	1	..	1	..	1	1	..
Bord, Cornelius	1	..	..	1	..	2	..	1	..	..	..
Bord, David	..	..	..	1	..	..	..	..	..	..	..
Branch, Artemas	..	..	1	..	..	..	..	..	..	..	..
Branch, Rufus	..	1	..	..	1	..	1	1	..	1	..
Branch, Seth	1	..	1	..	..	..	..	1	..	..	..
Branch, Wait	..	..	1	..	..	..	..	..	..	..	..
Brockway, Timothy	1	1	1	1	..	3	..	..	..	1	..
Brown, Jeremiah	2	3	2	..	1	1	1	2	..	1	..
Brownson, Abijah	1	2	2	..	1	..	..	..	1	..	..
Brownson, Benjamin	2	2	..	1	..	1	..	..	..	..	..
Brush, Josiah	2	2	1	..	1	..	..	1	1	..	..
Calkins, Simeon	1	..	..	..	1	..	..	1	..	1	..
Carver, Benjamin	..	1	..	2	1	..	..	1	..	1	..
Carver, Ralph	1	1	..	1	..	2	1	..	1	..	..
Charter, James	..	..	..	1	..	3	..	..	1	..	..
Clark, Bildad	..	2	..	1	..	1	2	1	1	..	..
Clark, Isaac	1	3	2	..	1	1	2	1	..	1	..
Clark, Robert	..	1	..	..	1	1	2	4	..	1	..
Coggswel, Peter	..	..	..	..	1	..	..	..	..	1	..
Coggswell, Eli	1	1	..	1	..	1	2	1	1	..	..

NAMES OF HEADS OF FAMILIES	FREE WHITE MALES					FREE WHITE FEMALES					
	Under 10 years of age	Of 10 and under 16	Of 16 and under 26 including heads of families	Of 26 and under 45 including heads of families	Of 45 and upwards including heads of families.	Under 10 years of age	Of 10 and under 16	Of 16 and under 26 including heads of families	Of 26 and under 45 including heads of families	Of 45 and upwards including heads of families	All other free persons except Indians not taxed
CASTLETON—con.											
Cool, Samuel	..	..	..	1	..	2	1	1	..	..	..
Couch, Samuel	1	..	..	1	..	1	..	..	1	..	..
Culver, Joel	1	..	..	1	..	2	1	..	1	..	..
Cushman, Daniel	1	1	1	1	..	2	1	1	1	..	..
Cushman, William	1	1	1	..	1	..	..	1	..	1	..
Cushman, William Jr.	..	..	..	1	..	..	..	1	..	..	..
Danby, James	..	..	..	..	1	..	..	..	..	1	..
Darby, Oliver	..	..	..	1	..	2	..	..	1	..	..
Dart, Justice	..	1	2	..	1	1	1	1	1	..	..
Davis, Alden	1	..	..	1	..	2	1	1	..	..	..
Deming, Jonathan	3	..	..	1	..	2	2	..	1	1	..
Denison, Daniel	..	1	1	1	..	2	1	..	1	..	..
Denison, Eber	2	..	..	1	1	1	1	..	1	1	..
Denison, Jedediah	2	2	..	1	..	2	..	..	1	..	..
Down, Zina	2	..	1	..	..	1	..	1	..	..	..
Drake, Eli	4	1	..	1	..	2	..	1	1	..	..
Drake, Joel	..	..	..	1	1	..	..	..	1	1	..
Dudley, Ephraim	4	..	..	1	..	1	..	..	1	..	..
Dunehu, Alexander	..	..	..	1	..	..	..	..	..	..	..
Dunehu, Jeffrey	..	..	..	1	1	..	..	..	..	1	..
Dunning, Betsey	..	..	..	..	..	..	1	..	..	1	..
Dunning, Eli	1	..	..	1	..	..	..	1	..	..	..
Dunning, Moses B.	..	..	1	..	..	..	..	..	..	..	..
Dyar, William	2	..	..	..	1	..	2	..	..	1	..
Eastman, Newel	..	..	1	..	..	..	..	..	..	..	..
Eastman, Peasley	..	..	..	1	..	2	..	..	1	..	..
Eaton, Daniel	..	1	..	1	..	3	2	1	..	..	..
Eaton, Elihu	1	..	..	1	..	3	..	..	1	..	..
Eaton, Enoch	2	..	..	1	..	..	..	..	1	..	..
Eaton, Jonathan	1	..	..	1	..	1	..	..	1	..	..
Eaton, Rebecca	..	..	1	..	..	..	..	1	..	2	..
Eaton, Stephen	1	..	..	1	..	2	1	..	1	..	..
Ellis, John	..	..	1	..	..	..	..	..	..	..	..
Erwin, Joseph	..	..	..	1	..	3	..	..	1	..	..
Everts, Jonas	1	..	..	1	..	1	..	2	..	..	..
Everts, Timothy	..	..	..	..	1	1	2	1	1	..	..
Fisher, Peter	1	..	1	1	..	..	2	..	1	..	..
Frisby, Luther	1	..	..	1	..	2	..	..	1	..	..
Gains, James	..	..	1	..	..	..	..	1	..	..	..
Gary, Stephen	1	..	1	..	..	2	..	..	1	..	..
Gates, Cyrus	1	1	..	1	1	1	..	1	1	..	..
Gernsey, Sylvanus	2	1	..	1	..	..	..	1	..	..	..
Gilder, Van James	2	..	..	1	..	1	..	1	..	..	..
Gill, Daniel	1	..	..	1	..	4	..	..	1	..	..
Gill, William	..	1	..	1	..	3	1	..	1	..	..
Goram, James	1	..	..	1	..	2	..	..	1	..	..
Gould, John	..	..	1	..	..	..	..	..	..	..	..
Granger, Dyar	1	..	1	..	..	..	..	1	..	..	..
Gregory, Elijah	1	..	..	1	..	2	..	1	..	..	..
Gregory, Nathan	1	..	..	1	..	..	..	..	1	..	..
Gridley, Selah	..	..	..	1	..	..	1	..	1	..	..
Griswold, Asael	1	..	..	1	..	..	..	2	..	..	..
Griswold, Azariah	3	2	3	..	1	2	..	..	1	..	..
Hall, Elias	1	1	..	..	1	1	1	1	1	1	..
Hall, Silas	..	..	1	..	1	1	1	1	..	1	..
Hammon, Nathan	3	2	1	1	..	1	1	..	1	1	..
Harris, Josiah G.	1	..	..	1	..	..	..	1	..	..	..
Hartwell, Ebenezer	2	1	4	..	1	1	2	1	..	1	..
Hawkins, Joseph	1	..	..	1	..	..	..	1	1	..	..
Hawkins, Moses	4	2	..	1	..	1	2	..	1	..	..
Hawley, Israel Rev.	..	..	..	..	1	..	..	..	..	..	..
Heading, Oliver	..	..	..	..	1	1	..	2	..	1	..
Heading, Oliver Jr.	..	..	..	1	..	..	1	..	..	..	..
Hedges, Lewis	..	1	2	..	1	..	..	..	..	1	..
Hide, Aruna W.	3	1	..	1	..	2	..	2	..	..	..
Higley, Brewster	1	..	..	..	1	..	..	2	..	1	..
Higley, Erastus	1	..	..	1	..	1	1	..	1	1	..
Hoit, Nehemiah	..	1	..	..	1	..	..	3	..	1	..
Hoit, Noah	1	..	..	1	..	..	1	..	1	..	..
Holmes, Zerah	..	..	..	1	..	..	..	..	..	..	..
Huit, Asa	2	..	..	1	..	1	2	1	1	..	..
Hurlbut, Curtiss	1	..	1	..	..	3	..	..	1	..	..
Hurlbut, Israel	..	..	1	..	1	..	..	1	..	1	..
Hurlbut, Israel Jr.	..	..	..	1	..	1	..	..	1	..	..
Jewet, Jared	1	..	..	1	..	1	..	..	1	..	..
Johnson, Adam	2	1	..	..	1	1	1	..	1	..	..
Johnson, Durfee	..	..	1	..	..	..	..	..	..	..	..
Johnson, Orange	1	..	..	1	..	..	..	..	1	..	..
Jones, Peletiah	1	..	..	1	..	1	..	1	..	..	..
Joyce, John	..	..	..	1	..	1	..	..	1	..	..

RUTLAND COUNTY—Continued

NAMES OF HEADS OF FAMILIES	FREE WHITE MALES					FREE WHITE FEMALES					All other free persons except Indians not taxed
	Under 10 years of age	Of 10 and under 16	Of 16 and under 26 including heads of families	Of 26 and under 45 including heads of families	Of 45 and upwards including heads of families.	Under 10 years of age	Of 10 and under 16	Of 16 and under 26 including heads of families	Of 26 and under 45 including heads of families	Of 45 and upwards including heads of families	
CASTLETON—con.											
Kellogg, Edward	1	..	..	1	..	2	..	..	1	..	..
Kellogg, Orsimus	1	..	..	1	..	1	..	..	1	..	..
Kellogg, Preserved	..	1	2	..	1	..	1	1	..	1	..
Kellogg, Saxton	4	..	..	1	..	..	..	..	1	..	..
Kilburn, Roswell	2	1	..	1	..	..	2	..	1	..	..
Kimberly, Samuel	..	..	..	1	..	..	..	..	..	..	..
Lake, Daniel	2	..	..	1	..	..	..	1	..	..	..
Lake, John	1	..	..	1	..	2	..	..	1	..	..
Lake, Sevia	..	..	..	..	..	..	..	3	..	1	..
Langdon, Chauncy	2	..	..	1	..	1	..	..	1	..	..
Lee, Noah	..	2	2	..	1	1	..	2	1	1	..
Lincoln, Charles	1	1	..	1	..	3	1	..	1	..	..
Lincoln, Sylvester	3	2	1	..	1	1	1	1	1	..	..
Lusk, Samuel	..	2	2	..	1	2	..	1	..	1	..
Mann, William	..	..	..	..	..	..	1	..	..	..	..
Marks, Jesse	..	..	..	1	..	..	..	..	..	..	..
Mason, John	1	1	..	1	..	4	..	1	1	1	..
McIntosh, Dunkan	..	2	2	1	..	2	..	..	1	..	..
McKenster, Amos	1	1	..	1	..	4	1	..	1	..	..
McKenster, John	3	..	..	1	..	..	..	1	..	..	..
Mead, Jeremiah	1	1	1	..	1	2	1	1	..	..	..
Mead, Reed	..	..	1	..	..	1	..	1	..	..	..
Merrill, Enos	2	2	..	1	..	2	..	2	..	..	..
Merrill, Jonathan	2	1	..	1	..	2	1	..	1	..	..
Merwin, John	..	..	1	..	..	..	..	..	..	..	..
Mills, Aaron	..	..	..	1	..	1	..	1	..	..	..
Mills, Sarah	..	..	..	..	..	..	1	..	1	..	..
Mills, Silas	4	..	..	1	..	..	..	..	1	..	..
Molton, Abel	..	..	1	..	..	..	..	2	..	..	..
Molton, Gershom	..	..	..	..	1	1	3	..	1	..	..
Molton, Heman	1	..	..	1	..	1	..	..	2	..	..
Molton, Rachel	..	..	1	..	..	..	..	..	..	1	..
Molton, Reuben	..	1	2	..	1	..	..	1	..	1	..
Murdock, Troop	..	..	1	1	..	3	..	..	1	..	..
Northrop, Ira	..	..	1	..	..	1	..	1	..	..	..
Northrop, Nathaniel	1	2	1	..	1	..	1	2	..	1	..
Olvord, Amasa	2	1	..	1	..	..	..	1	1	..	..
Palmer, Jared	..	..	1	1	1	..	1	..	..	1	..
Parker, Ebenezer	3	1	..	1	..	..	1	..	1	..	..
Parsons, Abraham	..	..	..	1	..	1	..	1	..	..	..
Parsons, Ludland	..	1	2	..	1	..	1	1	..	..	..
Pattason, David	4	3	..	1	..	1	..	..	1	..	..
Pattason, Thomas	3	..	..	1	..	2	1	..	1	..	..
Peck, Ithel	1	..	..	1	..	3	..	..	1	..	..
Perkins, Joseph	..	..	..	1	..	2	..	1	..	..	..
Perry, Judson	..	..	1	..	..	..	..	..	..	..	..
Pond, Benjamin	..	..	2	..	1	..	..	2	..	1	..
Pond, Samuel	2	2	..	1	..	2	..	..	1	..	..
Porter, John	1	1	2	..	1	3	..	..	1	..	..
Pratt, Adonijah	1	..	..	1	..	4	..	..	1	..	..
Ransom, Lemuel	..	..	..	1	..	1	1	1	..	..	..
Remington, Zadock	..	1	2	..	1	1	..	1	1	..	..
Roberts, Lebbius	2	1	..	..	1	1	..	..	1	..	..
Rogers, Joseph	..	1	..	..	1	1	1	..	1	..	..
Sanford, David	1	..	..	1	..	3	..	1	1	..	..
Shaw, Samuel	..	1	..	1	1	1	2	..	1	..	..
Shepard, David	1	2	..	1	..	2	..	1	1	..	..
Simmons, James	1	..	..	1	..	2	..	..	1	..	..
Smith, Abijah	..	..	1	..	..	..	..	1	..	..	..
Smith, Gilbert	..	..	1	..	..	..	..	..	..	..	..
Snell, John	..	..	..	1	..	2	..	1	..	..	..
Southmaid, Ebenezer	2	..	1	..	..	..	..	1	..	..	..
Spaulding, William	1	..	..	1	..	..	..	..	1	..	..
Sprague, John	..	..	1	..	..	..	..	..	..	..	..
Stanton, Robert	1	..	..	1	1	2	2	..	1	..	..
Statia, Cornelius	2	..	..	1	..	3	..	..	1	..	..
Stevens, Luke	..	..	..	..	1	..	..	..	..	1	..
Stevens, William	1	..	..	1	..	3	..	..	1	..	..
Stiles, Bliss	..	..	1	..	..	..	..	1	..	..	..
Stiles, Job	1	..	..	..	1	..	..	..	1	..	..
Taylor, Richard	2	..	..	1	..	2	..	..	1	..	..
Trall, Jesse	4	..	..	1	..	1	..	..	1	..	..
Tucker, Isaac	..	..	..	..	1	..	..	1	..	..	..
Tuttle, Joseph	..	..	..	1	..	3	..	1	..	..	..
Ware, Samuel	..	..	..	1	..	..	..	..	..	..	..
Warner, Wright	..	..	1	..	..	..	..	..	..	..	..
Whipple, James	2	..	..	1	..	2	..	1	..	..	..
Whipple, William	1	..	..	1	..	3	..	1	1	..	..
Whitlock, Hezekiah	1	..	..	1	..	1	..	..	1	..	..
Whitlock, John	2	1	2	..	1	..	1	1	1	1	..
Whitlock, John Jr.	1	1	..	1	..	1	1	1	..	..	..
Whitlock, Levi	1	..	..	1	..	1	1	1	..	..	..
Wood, Hezekiah	1	1	2	..	1	3	1	..	1	..	..
Woodard, Aruna	1	1	..	..	1	2	1	1	1	..	..
Wright, Elihu	1	..	..	1	..	1	..	..	1	..	..
CHITTENDEN											
Andrus, Kellogg	3	..	..	1	..	1	..	..	1	..	..
Baird, Earl	3	..	..	1	..	1	..	..	1	..	..
Baird, John	1	1	1	..	1	1	..	1	..	1	..
Bancraft, John	..	1	..	..	1	..	..	1	..	1	..
Bancraft, Nathaniel	..	..	1	..	..	1	..	1	..	..	..
Bardard, Roger	..	1	..	1	..	5	..	1	1	..	..
Barnard, Andrew	4	1	..	1	..	1	..	..	1	..	..
Barnard, Dan	..	..	..	..	1	..	..	..	..	1	..
Beach, Donas	2	..	..	..	..	..	..	..	1	..	..
Bebee, Ezekiel	..	..	..	..	1	3	..	..	..	1	..
Bigalow, Russel	2	..	..	1	..	4	1	..	1	..	..
Booge, Jeffrey A.	2	1	..	1	..	3	..	..	1	..	..
Bowen, Consider	3	1	1	1	..	1	1	..	1	..	..
Brown, Noah	3	..	..	1	..	..	..	..	1	..	..
Bullis, John	..	1	..	1	..	2	..	..	1	..	..
Burpee, Nathan	2	1	..	1	..	2	..	..	1	..	..
Burpee, Stephen	3	1	..	1	..	..	..	..	1	..	..
Carpender, Daniel	1	1	2	..	1	..	..	..	1	..	..
Castle, Amasa	..	1	1	..	1	1	1	1	1	..	..
Chaffee, Simeon	3	..	..	1	..	..	..	1	..	..	..
Chaffee, Stephen	2	..	..	1	..	1	..	1	..	..	..
Coke, John	1	1	..	1	..	2	..	..	1	..	..
Cren, Josiah	1	..	1	..	1	2	1	..	1	..	..
Dike, Jonathan	2	2	1	..	2	..	1	..	1	1	..
Dresser, David	..	..	..	1	..	1	..	1	..	..	..
Eggleston, Freeman	1	1	..	1	..	..	..	..	1	..	..
Eggleston, James	2	..	..	1	..	1	..	..	1	..	..
Farrar, Asa	2	2	..	1	..	..	2	..	1	..	..
Goff, Enoch	1	..	..	1	..	3	..	..	1	..	..
Goram, Wakeman	2	..	..	1	..	2	..	..	1	..	..
Grandy, Beriah	1	..	..	1	..	1	..	1	..	..	..
Green, Zeeb	3	..	1	1	1	2	1	1	1	..	..
Harrison, Joseph	..	..	1	1	..	..	..	..	1	1	..
Harrison, Samuel	..	2	1	1	..	2	1	1	1	..	..
Hobbs, Jonas	3	..	..	1	..	2	..	..	1	..	..
Huet, Nathan	4	1	..	1	..	1	..	..	1	..	..
Ladd, Nathaniel	1	..	3	..	1	1	3	..	..	1	..
Lawrence, Amos	1	1	..	1	..	2	1	..	1	..	..
Leggett, James	..	..	..	..	1	..	..	..	..	1	..
Leonard, Jacob	..	..	1	..	1	..	..	..	..	1	..
Manley, Thomas	..	..	1	..	..	..	..	1	..	..	..
McCurdee, Richard	..	..	1	..	..	..	..	1	..	..	..
Mead, Mathew	..	..	..	1	..	..	..	..	..	..	..
Ormstead, Jabez	2	1	2	1	..	1	1	..	1	..	..
Powers, Moses	..	..	1	..	..	1	..	1	..	..	..
Rann, William	1	..	1	..	..	..	..	1	..	..	..
Russel, David	..	..	..	1	..	1	..	1	..	..	..
Scovel, Benjamin	2	1	..	1	1	2	1	..	1	..	..
Shays, David	3	..	..	1	..	1	..	..	1	..	..
Simmons, Nathaniel	..	..	..	1	..	1	..	1	..	..	..
Taylor, Solomon	..	1	..	..	1	1	1	..	..	1	..
Thomas, Ebenezer	4	..	..	1	..	2	..	..	1	..	..
Thomas, Joseph	4	1	..	1	..	1	1	..	1	..	..
Thomas, Odoardo	..	..	2	..	1	..	..	1	..	1	..
Wheeler, Nathaniel	..	..	..	..	1	..	..	..	..	1	..
Wheeler, Obadiah	..	..	..	1	..	2	..	1	1	..	..
Wheeler, Otis	2	..	..	1	..	1	..	1	..	..	..
Wood, Jonathan	1	1	..	1	..	3	..	..	1	..	..

RUTLAND COUNTY—Continued

NAMES OF HEADS OF FAMILIES	FREE WHITE MALES: Under 10 years of age	FREE WHITE MALES: Of 10 and under 16	FREE WHITE MALES: Of 16 and under 26 including heads of families	FREE WHITE MALES: Of 26 and under 45 including heads of families	FREE WHITE MALES: Of 45 and upwards including heads of families.	FREE WHITE FEMALES: Under 10 years of age	FREE WHITE FEMALES: Of 10 and under 16	FREE WHITE FEMALES: Of 16 and under 26 including heads of families	FREE WHITE FEMALES: Of 26 and under 45 including heads of families	FREE WHITE FEMALES: Of 45 and upwards including heads of families	All other free persons except Indians not taxed
CLARENDON											
Abbey, Amasa	3	..	1	..	..	1	..	1	..	..	..
Allen, Samuel	..	..	2	..	1	..	..	..	..	1	..
Andrus, Reuben	..	..	1	..	..	..	..	1	..	..	..
Angel, Nedabiah	..	..	1	..	1	..	..	..	..	1	..
Arnold, Caleb	2	..	..	1	..	..	1	..	1	..	..
Arnold, Oliver	2	..	3	..	1	..	1	1	..	1	..
Arnold, Stephen	..	..	1	..	1	..	1	1	..	1	..
Arnold, Stephen Jr.	..	..	1	..	..	..	1	..	..	..	..
Austin, Sarah	3	..	..	..	..	2	..	..	1	..	..
Babbott, Charles	3	3	..	1	..	2	..	..	1	..	..
Babbott, Dyar	5	..	..	1	..	..	..	..	1	..	..
Bala, Thomas	..	..	..	1	..	2	..	1	..	..	..
Barney, Joseph	..	1	1	1	..	..	1	1	..	..	..
Bassett, Caleb	..	1	..	1	1	..	..	2	..	..	..
Bassett, James	..	..	..	1	..	..	..	1	..	..	..
Baxter, Stephen	3	..	..	1	..	1	..	..	1	..	..
Beach, George	2	..	1	..	1	2	1	..	1	..	..
Beall, Isaac Rev.	..	..	2	..	1	..	..	1	..	1	..
Bevens, Joseph	1	..	..	1	..	..	..	1	..	..	..
Bigalow, John	1	..	..	1	..	3	2	..	1	..	..
Bishop, George	..	..	..	..	1	..	1	..	..	1	..
Bishop, Joseph	2	..	..	1	..	1	..	1	..	..	..
Black, Peter	1	..	..	..	1	..	..	..	..	1	..
Blancher, Caleb	1	1	1	1	..	2	1	..	1	..	..
Blancher, Reuben	3	1	..	1	..	1	..	..	1	..	..
Bordman, Ebenezer	5	..	..	1	..	..	1	..	1	..	..
Bordman, Elisha	..	1	1	1	..	..	1	..	..	1	..
Bordman, John	..	1	..	..	1	..	..	2	..	1	..
Braddish, Aaron	1	..	..	1	..	2	1	..	1	..	..
Briggs, Daniel	..	..	..	..	1	..	..	1	1	1	..
Briggs, Philip	..	..	1	..	1	..	2	..	..	1	..
Briggs, William	2	..	..	1	..	1	..	1	..	..	..
Brooks, Peter	4	..	..	1	..	1	..	..	1	..	..
Brown, William	..	..	..	..	1	1	..	..	..	1	..
Buck, Alvin	..	..	1	..	..	..	..	..	..	..	..
Buck, Moses	2	..	..	1	..	1	..	..	1	..	..
Buck, Nathan	..	..	1	..	..	..	..	..	..	..	..
Burdett, Joshua	2	..	..	1	..	1	..	..	1	..	..
Burlingham, Solomon	..	1	1	1	..	3	3	2	..	1	..
Burt, Henry	..	2	..	1	..	..	..	1	1	..	..
Button, Frederick	3	2	..	1	..	2	..	..	1	..	..
Button, Jacob	1	..	1	..	..	..	..	1	..	..	..
Cappel, Stephen	2	..	..	..	1	..	3	..	..	1	..
Carpender, Comfort	..	..	1	..	..	..	..	1	..	..	..
Carpender, Stephen	1	1	..	1	..	3	1	1	1	..	..
Carpender, William	..	1	2	..	2	..	..	..	1	1	..
Cary, Samuel	..	..	..	..	1	..	1	..	..	1	..
Cassey, Michael	..	..	..	1	..	..	..	..	1	..	..
Chaffee, Comfort	4	2	1	1	..	..	1	1	1	..	..
Chapman, Joseph	..	..	..	1	..	1	..	1	..	..	..
Chapman, Lemuel	2	..	..	1	..	1	1	..	1	..	..
Chapman, Obadiah	..	1	1	..	1	..	..	..	..	..	..
Chapman, William	1	1	..	1	..	4	1	..	1	..	..
Clark, Jedidiah	..	1	..	..	1	..	..	1	..	1	..
Clark, Jedidiah Jr.	1	..	..	1	..	2	..	1	1	..	..
Colvin, Alfred	1	..	..	1	..	3	..	1	..	..	..
Colvin, Daniel	1	2	..	..	1	1	..	..	..	1	..
Colvin, Jonathan	3	..	1	..	2	1	..	1	..	..	..
Colvin, Levi	1	1	..	..	1	..	..	..	..	1	..
Colvin, Sanford	2	..	..	1	..	2	1	..	1	..	..
Congwell, George	4	..	1	..	..	..	..	..	1	..	..
Congwell, Job	5	2	..	1	..	..	1	..	1	..	..
Congwell, John	3	1	..	1	..	1	1	..	1	..	..
Congwell, Joseph	..	..	..	..	1	..	..	..	..	1	..
Cook, Peter	..	..	..	1	..	1	..	1	1	..	..
Cooper, John	..	..	..	..	1	..	..	..	..	1	..
Cooper, Samuel	2	..	..	1	..	2	..	..	1	..	..
Cotton, Luther	..	1	..	1	..	..	1	..	..	1	..
Crary, Ezra	..	..	..	..	1	..	..	1	..	1	..
Crocker, Mary	..	2	..	..	..	..	2	..	..	1	..
Crosman, William	1	2	..	..	1	2	..	..	1	1	..
Cross, Benjamin	..	..	1	..	..	..	..	..	..	..	..
Cumber, John	1	..	..	1	..	..	..	..	1	..	..
Curtiss, Philo	4	..	1	..	..	1	..	1	..	..	..
Curtiss, Thaddeus	..	1	..	..	1	1	1	1	..	1	..
Cushman, Benjamin	..	..	1	..	..	..	1	..	..	..	..
Davis, Jeffrey	3	1	..	..	1	1	2	2	1	..	..
Davis, John	1	1	..	1	..	1	1	..	1	..	..
Davis, John	1	1	..	..	1	1	..	..	..	1	..
Dean, David	1	..	..	1	..	1	2	..	1	..	..
Dean, Perry	1	..	..	1	..	1	..	1	..	..	..
Dexter, Dilno	1	..	..	1	..	1	..	1	..	..	..
Doke, Nathaniel	..	..	..	1	..	..	1	..	..	..	..
CLARENDON—con.											
Drake, Adin	1	..	..	1	..	..	..	1	..	..	..
Drinkwater, Warren	..	..	..	..	1	2	..	..	1	..	..
Dunkin, John	2	..	..	..	1	1	1	1	1	..	..
Durkee, David	1	..	..	1	..	1	..	..	1	..	..
Dyar, Daniel	2	..	..	1	..	..	1	2	1	..	..
Dyar, Edward	1	..	2	..	..	1	..	1	..	..	..
Eastman, Deliverance	3	2	..	1	..	1	1	..	1	..	..
Eastman, Eli	3	1	..	..	1	..	2	..	1	..	..
Eddy, James	3	..	..	1	..	3	1	..	1	..	..
Eddy, Jonathan	4	1	..	1	..	2	1	..	1	1	..
Eddy, Thomas	1	1	1	1	..	..	1	2	..	1	..
Edmond, James	1	2	1	1	..	3	1	..	1	1	..
Emmons, Solomon	1	2	1	..	1	1	1	2	1	..	..
Failes, Joseph	3	1	1	1	..	..	..	1	..	..	..
Fairfield, John	3	..	1	..	1	1	2	..	1	..	..
Fassett, Samuel	3	..	..	1	..	..	..	..	1	..	..
Fassett, Sarah	..	1	1	..	..	..	..	..	..	1	..
Fisk, Azariah	..	..	1	..	..	..	..	1	..	..	..
Flagg, Eleazer	..	..	1	..	..	..	..	..	..	..	..
Forbbs, John	..	..	..	..	1	..	..	..	1	..	..
Foster, Asaph	1	1	1	..	..	1	..	2	..	..	..
Foster, Benjamin	2	1	1	..	1	3	1	..	1	..	..
Foster, Whitefield	..	..	..	2	..	1	1	..	1	..	..
French, Zeba	3	2	..	2	..	..	1	1	1	..	..
Frisby, Noah	..	..	..	1	..	..	..	..	..	..	..
Fuller, Roger	2	1	2	..	..	1	1	1	1	..	..
Gaut, Calvin	1	..	..	1	..	..	..	1	..	..	..
Gideon, Dan	3	1	..	..	2	..	2	1	2	..	..
Goff, Christopher	1	..	1	..	..	..	..	1	..	..	..
Goff, Daniel	..	..	1	..	1	..	2	..	1	..	..
Gould, Benjamin	..	..	1	..	1	..	1	..	..	1	..
Gould, Benjamin	3	..	..	1	..	..	2	1	..	..	..
Gould, Jacob	..	..	..	..	1	..	..	..	..	..	..
Gould, Jacob Jr.	1	..	..	1	1	3	..	..	1	..	..
Gould, Joseph	1	..	1	..	..	1	..	2	..	..	..
Green, Peleg	1	..	1	..	2	1	1	2	..	1	..
Green, Philip	3	..	1	1	..	1	2	1	1	..	..
Green, William	1	..	..	1	..	1	1	1	..	..	..
Hall, Luke	1	..	..	1	..	1	..	..	1	..	..
Hammon, Asaph	..	..	..	..	1	..	..	..	..	..	..
Hammon, John	..	..	1	..	..	3	..	1	..	..	..
Hammon, Lyman	3	..	..	1	..	..	..	1	..	..	..
Harrington, Caleb	..	1	1	..	1	1	1	..	1	..	..
Harrington, Gardner	3	1	..	1	..	..	..	..	1	..	..
Harrington, Israel	..	..	..	..	1	..	..	..	..	..	..
Harrington, James	3	1	..	1	..	..	2	..	1	..	..
Harrington, Theophilus	4	..	2	1	..	..	1	..	1	..	..
Harrington, William Rev.	2	2	1	1	..	3	1	1	1	..	..
Havens, John	1	2	..	1	..	..	..	..	1	..	..
Hawley, Lemuel	..	..	1	..	..	1	1	1	..	..	..
Haynes, James	..	..	1	..	..	..	..	..	..	..	..
Haywood, Josiah	3	..	..	1	..	1	..	..	1	..	..
Hifflon, William	1	..	..	1	..	1	..	1	..	..	..
Hill, Daniel	2	..	1	1	..	..	..	2	..	..	..
Hill, Erastus	2	1	..	1	..	2	1	1	..	..	..
Hill, John	1	1	1	1	..	2	..	..	1	..	..
Himes, Cleveland	3	..	..	1	..	1	..	1	..	..	..
Hobbs, Abraham	1	..	..	1	..	3	..	..	1	..	..
Hodges, Silas	..	3	3	..	1	1	1	2	1	..	..
Hogg, Hamilton	..	..	1	..	..	..	..	..	..	..	..
Horton, Hezekiah	1	1	..	..	1	..	..	1	1	..	..
Howard, Christopher	1	..	1	..	1	1	1	1	1	1	..
Howard, Samuel	..	..	1	..	..	..	..	1	..	..	..
Howard, Simeon	2	..	1	1	..	1	..	..	1	..	..
Howland, Banister	..	..	1	..	..	..	..	1	..	..	..
Howland, Caleb	3	..	2	1	..	1	..	..	1	1	..
Howland, Samuel	..	1	1	1	..	5	2	..	1	..	..
Huit, Gideon	2	1	1	..	1	2	1	..	1	..	..
Huit, John	..	..	1	..	..	..	..	..	..	..	..
Hutchinson, Thomas	..	2	..	..	1	2	..	1	1	1	..
Ide, Otis	1	..	..	1	..	..	..	1	..	..	..
Ide, Squier	1	1	..	..	1	1	1	1	..	1	..
Ingols, Caleb	..	..	..	..	1	5	2	..	1	..	..
Jenks, Edmond	..	..	..	..	1	2	1	..	..	..	..
Jenks, James	1	1	..	..	1	..	1	2	..	1	..
Jewel, David	1	..	..	..	1	..	1	..	2	2	..
Johnson, John	..	..	..	1	..	..	..	..	..	..	..
Johnson, Zachariah	5	..	..	1	..	..	..	..	1	..	..
Jones, John	..	..	..	1	..	..	..	..	..	..	..

RUTLAND COUNTY—Continued

NAMES OF HEADS OF FAMILIES	FREE WHITE MALES					FREE WHITE FEMALES					
	Under 10 years of age	Of 10 and under 16	Of 16 and under 26 including heads of families	Of 26 and under 45 including heads of families	Of 45 and upwards including heads of families.	Under 10 years of age	Of 10 and under 16	Of 16 and under 26 including heads of families	Of 26 and under 45 including heads of families	Of 45 and upwards including heads of families	All other free persons except Indians not taxed
CLARENDON—con.											
Kendal, John	1	1	..	1	..	..	..	..	1	1	..
Kimbol, John	2	..	1	..	..	..	1	..	..	..	..
King, Jesse	1	..	..	1	..	2	..	1	..	..	..
King, Nathan	..	..	1	..	..	..	..	..	..	..	..
King, Seth	..	..	1	..	..	..	1	..	..	..	..
Knoulton, Joseph	1	2	..	..	1	2	2	..	1	..	..
Lanford, Daniel	2	..	1	..	1	3	1	..	1	..	..
Lawrence, Garret	..	..	..	1	..	1	..	..	1	..	..
Learnard, John	..	..	1	..	..	..	..	..	..	..	..
Lewis, Abner	..	..	1	..	1	..	..	..	..	1	..
Lewis, Asael	4	1	..	1	..	1	2	..	1	..	..
Lingfield, Edward	2	..	1	..	..	1	2	1	..	..	..
Loomis, Epaphas	..	..	1	1	..	..	2	1	1	..	..
Luther, Elisha	..	1	..	1	..	2	1	1	1	..	..
Marsh, Daniel	..	..	2	1	1	1	..	2	..	1	..
Marsh, William	..	..	1	..	..	..	..	1	..	..	..
Mattason, Chapman	..	..	..	1	..	1	..	..	1	..	..
Mattason, Francis	2	..	1	..	1	1	2	..	1	..	..
McCoy, David	..	..	2	..	1	..	..	..	..	1	..
McCoy, William	..	1	2	..	1	..	2	2	..	1	..
Meacham, Seth	..	..	..	1	..	..	..	..	..	..	..
Millington, Solomon	2	..	..	..	1	5	..	..	1	..	..
Miner, Lamson	..	..	1	..	..	..	..	..	..	..	..
Mix, Collins	..	..	1	..	..	..	..	..	..	..	..
Munsill, Joseph	..	1	..	1	..	1	..	1	..	..	..
Munsill, Thomas	2	..	..	1	..	3	..	..	1	..	..
Nichols, Caleb	..	..	1	..	..	..	..	..	..	..	..
Olds, Jasper	2	..	..	..	1	2	1	1	1	..	..
Ormsby, Joseph	2	..	..	1	..	2	..	..	1	..	..
Ormsby, Samuel	3	..	..	1	..	1	..	..	1	..	..
Palmer, James	1	1	..	1	..	4	..	..	1	..	..
Parker, Benjamin	1	4	..	1	..	4	..	..	1	..	..
Parker, Ephraim	3	..	1	..	..	1	..	1	..	..	..
Parker, Jonathan	..	..	..	..	1	..	..	..	..	..	..
Parker, Jonathan	1	1	2	1	1	1	2	1	..	1	..
Parker, Levi	..	..	..	..	1	..	1	..	..	1	..
Parker, Peter	2	1	..	1	..	1	1	..	1	..	..
Parker, Philip	..	..	..	..	1	..	1	..	..	1	..
Parker, Samuel	1	1	..	..	1	2	..	..	2	1	..
Parmer, David	..	..	..	..	1	1	..	1	3	1	..
Pearl, John	..	..	..	..	1	..	..	..	..	1	..
Pearse, George	..	..	..	..	1	..	..	..	..	..	..
Pearse, Giles	1	1	..	1	..	4	2	..	1	..	2
Peck, Lewis	1	2	..	1	..	2	..	..	1	..	..
Peck, Noah	1	..	1	..	..	3	1	1	..	..	..
Pell, Thomas	1	..	..	1	..	3	3	..	1	..	..
Perigo, Ranscom	3	..	..	1	..	1	..	..	1	..	..
Pettingell, Joseph	..	..	..	1	1	..	..	..	..	1	..
Pitcher, Ebenezer	..	..	..	..	1	..	..	..	..	1	..
Pitcher, Ebenezer Jr.	3	1	1	1	..	1	1	..	1	..	..
Platt, Daniel	..	1	1	1	..	..	1	..	1	..	..
Platt, Dolly	2	1	..	..	..	1	..	..	1	..	..
Pope, Stephen	1	..	..	1	1	3	..	..	1	1	..
Potter, David	1	1	..	1	..	4	2	..	1	..	..
Potter, Noel	1	2	..	1	..	1	1	..	1	..	..
Pratt, Abijah	..	1	1	..	1	..	..	2	1	1	..
Pratt, Edmund	2	..	..	1	..	1	4	1	1	..	..
Preast, Joseph	1	..	1	..	..	1	..	1	..	..	..
Preast, Joshua	3	1	1	..	1	3	1	2	..	1	..
Rice, Amos	3	..	..	1	..	2	..	2	..	..	..
Rice, Nathan	2	1	..	..	1	1	1	2	..	..	..
Rice, Nathan Jr.	..	..	1	..	..	..	..	..	..	..	..
Rice, Randal	2	..	..	1	..	..	1	1	..	..	..
Rice, Thomas	..	1	1	..	1	..	1	2	..	1	..
Robbins, Collins	2	2	..	..	1	2	..	..	..	1	..
Robinson, Amos	..	..	1	..	1	..	..	..	1	1	..
Robinson, Amos Jr.	1	..	1	..	..	..	..	1	..	..	..
Robinson, Stephen	2	2	..	1	..	2	1	..	1	..	..
Roger, Jedediah	..	..	1	..	..	..	..	1	..	..	..
Rose, John	..	1	..	..	1	3	1	1	1	1	..
Rounds, George	3	2	1	..	1	1	..	..	..	1	..
Rounds, James	..	1	..	..	1	..	2	2	..	1	..
Rounds, Stephen	..	..	..	1	..	1	1	..	1	..	..
Russel, Isaac	..	..	..	..	1	1	1	..	..	1	..
Salsbury, Abram	2	2	1	..	1	..	1	2	..	1	..
Salsbury, Ezekiel	2	..	1	..	..	1	..	1	..	..	..
Salsbury, Gardner	5	1	..	1	..	..	1	..	..	..	..
Saxton, Elizabeth	..	..	..	..	..	..	..	..	1	..	..
Scovil, John	1	..	1	..	..	..	..	1	..	..	..
CLARENDON—con.											
Scovil, Michael	2	2	..	1	..	1	..	..	1	..	..
Scovil, Molly	..	..	..	..	..	1	..	..	1	..	..
Shaw, Elijah	1	1	..	1	..	..	..	..	1	..	..
Shepard, Jonathan	2	..	..	1	..	2	..	..	1	..	..
Shepard, Stephen	1	..	..	1	..	1	..	1	..	..	..
Shepardson, Noah	1	..	..	1	..	..	..	1	..	..	..
Sherman, Joshua	1	1	4	..	1	2	1	1	..	1	..
Sherman, Nathan	1	1	1	..	..	..	..	1	..	..	..
Simmons, Charles	3	1	..	1	..	3	1	1	1	1	..
Simmons, John	1	..	..	..	1	..	..	1	..	1	..
Simmons, Oliver	2	..	..	1	..	..	..	..	1	..	..
Sliter, Nicholas	3	..	..	1	..	2	..	..	1	..	..
Smith, Anna	..	..	1	..	..	..	..	1	..	..	..
Smith, Arima	2	1	..	1	..	2	1	1	..	..	..
Smith, Asa	..	..	..	..	1	..	..	..	..	2	..
Smith, Charles	..	1	1	..	1	..	..	1	..	1	..
Smith, Daniel	2	1	..	..	1	2	1	..	1	..	..
Smith, Elihu	..	..	3	..	1	..	1	1	..	1	..
Smith, Sally	..	..	..	..	..	1	..	..	1	..	..
Smith, Sarah	..	..	..	..	..	..	..	..	..	2	..
Smith, Silas	..	..	..	1	..	..	..	1	..	..	..
Spalding, Hannah	..	..	..	..	..	..	..	..	..	..	1
Spencer, Caleb	4	..	..	1	..	1	..	..	1	1	..
Spencer, John	..	..	1	..	1	2	1	..	..	1	..
Spencer, Pearce	..	1	1	..	1	..	..	2	..	1	..
Spencer, Simeon	1	..	..	1	..	3	..	..	1	..	..
Spencer, Thomas	1	..	..	1	..	1	1	1	..	..	..
Sprague, Abraham	1	..	..	1	..	3	..	..	1	..	..
Sprague, Durram	2	..	..	1	..	..	..	1	..	..	..
Sprague, Jesse	..	1	..	..	1	..	..	..	..	1	..
Spring, Amos	1	..	..	1	..	1	1	2	..	..	..
Stewart, Daniel	..	..	..	1	..	..	..	..	..	..	..
Stewart, John	..	..	..	..	1	..	..	..	..	..	..
Stewart, Oliver	1	1	2	..	1	1	1	2	..	1	..
Stewart, Thomas	3	1	1	..	..	..	..	1	..	..	..
Stowel, David	3	1	1	1	..	2	1	2	1	..	..
Stratton, Isaac	3	1	..	1	..	3	..	..	1	..	..
Tanner, Josiah	2	..	1	1	..	1	..	..	1	..	..
Taylor, Levi	1	..	..	1	..	1	..	1	..	..	..
Titus, Abel	..	..	1	..	..	..	..	..	..	..	..
Titus, Robert	..	..	1	1	..	..	3	1	1	..	..
Tomms, John	3	..	..	1	..	2	2	..	1	..	..
Tomms, Joseph	..	..	1	..	..	..	..	..	1	1	..
Torrance, John	..	..	..	1	..	1	1	..	1	..	..
Townsend, Samuel	2	..	..	1	..	3	..	1	1	..	..
Tripp, Abial	..	1	..	1	..	..	2	..	..	1	..
Tripp, Palmer	1	1	1	1	..	1	1	1	..	1	..
Tubbs, Isaac	..	..	1	..	..	..	..	..	..	..	..
Tubbs, Zephaniah	1	1	1	..	1	1	..	2	..	1	..
Vary, John	..	..	..	..	1	..	..	..	..	..	..
Walker, Ichabod	2	1	1	..	1	2	1	1	..	1	..
Walker, Lewis	..	..	2	..	1	..	..	1	..	2	..
Walker, Simon	1	..	..	1	..	1	..	1	1	..	..
Weaver, Richard	4	1	1	..	1	1	2	2	1	..	..
Weaver, Thomas	1	1	1	..	1	2	1	1	1	..	..
Wells, Alexander	..	..	1	..	..	..	..	..	..	..	..
Wescott, Ephraim	2	..	..	1	..	..	..	1	..	1	..
Wescott, Johnson	1	..	1	..	..	1	..	1	..	..	..
Wescott, Nicholas	2	..	1	..	..	1	..	1	..	..	..
Wescott, Oliver	2	1	..	..	1	1	1	1	1	1	..
Wescott, Peleg	2	..	..	1	..	2	..	1	..	..	..
Wescott, Phebe	1	1	..	..	..	2	2	..	1	..	..
Wescott, Thomas	3	..	..	1	..	1	1	..	1	1	..
Whitcomb, Reuben	1	1	1	1	..	3	2	1	1	..	..
White, Timothy	..	..	..	1	..	..	..	..	..	..	..
Whitmore, Asael	..	..	1	..	..	..	..	..	..	..	..
Whitney, David	3	3	..	1	..	2	1	..	1	..	..
Whitney, Oliver	1	2	..	1	..	1	1	1	..	..	..
Whitney, Samuel	1	..	..	1	..	2	..	..	1	..	..
Whitney, Solomon	..	..	1	1	..	..	..	2	..	..	..
Wicks, Friend	3	..	..	1	..	2	..	..	1	..	..
Wicks, John	..	1	1	..	1	..	1	..	..	1	..
Wicks, William	..	..	1	..	..	..	..	1	..	..	..
Wilcox, Jehiel	1	..	..	1	..	1	..	1	..	..	..
Wild, James	..	1	1	..	1	..	..	2	..	1	..
Wyman, Israel	1	..	1	..	1	1	2	..	1	1	..
Wyman, Nehemiah	..	..	1	..	..	..	..	..	..	..	..
UNCERTAIN NAMES											
Hermes (?), Barnum	1	1	..	1	..	1	..	..	1	..	..
Wilcox (?), Solomon	..	..	..	1	..	..	..	..	..	..	..

RUTLAND COUNTY—Continued

NAMES OF HEADS OF FAMILIES	FREE WHITE MALES: Under 10 years of age	FREE WHITE MALES: Of 10 and under 16	FREE WHITE MALES: Of 16 and under 26 including heads of families	FREE WHITE MALES: Of 26 and under 45 including heads of families	FREE WHITE MALES: Of 45 and upwards including heads of families.	FREE WHITE FEMALES: Under 10 years of age	FREE WHITE FEMALES: Of 10 and under 16	FREE WHITE FEMALES: Of 16 and under 26 including heads of families	FREE WHITE FEMALES: Of 26 and under 45 including heads of families	FREE WHITE FEMALES: Of 45 and upwards including heads of families	All other free persons except Indians not taxed
DANBY											
Abbey, Benjamin	3	..	..	1	..	1	..	..	1	..	..
Abbott, Daniel	..	..	1	..	..	1	..	1	..	..	..
Abott, Israel	..	..	1	..	..	..	..	..	..	..	..
Allen, John	2	..	..	1	..	..	2	1	1	..	..
Allen, Jude	1	..	..	1	..	..	..	1	..	..	..
Allen, Prince	3	1	..	..	1	1	1	..	1	..	..
Allen, Zoath	1	..	..	1	..	2	1	..	1	..	..
Andrus, John	2	..	..	1	1	3	..	..	1	2	..
Arnold, Hadwin	..	..	2	..	..	..	..	..	..	..	..
Babcock, Champlain	2	..	..	..	1	1	1	..	1	..	..
Barlow, John	..	..	..	..	1	..	..	..	..	1	..
Barlow, William	..	..	1	..	..	1	..	1	1	..	..
Barns, Bradford	..	1	2	..	1	1	..	..	1	..	..
Barns, Eli	3	1	2	1	..	2	1	2	..	2	..
Barnum, Gideon	..	..	1	1	1	1	1	1	..	1	..
Barrett, Alexander	1	1	..	1	..	3	1	..	1	..	..
Bartlett, Abner	3	2	1	..	1	2	..	1	1	..	..
Bartlett, Jacob	2	1	..	..	1	..	1	..	..	1	..
Bates, Hezekiah	..	..	1	..	2	..	1	1	1	1	..
Benson, Elihu	4	2	1	1	..	1	1	..	1	..	..
Blackmore, Abner	2	..	..	1	1	1	..	..	1	..	..
Bollard, Ezekiel	..	..	..	..	1	..	..	1	2	..	..
Bollard, Isaac	1	1	1	1	..	3	1	..	1	..	..
Bollard, Nathaniel	..	..	1	..	..	..	..	1	..	..	..
Braman, Benjamin	1	..	..	1	..	3	..	1	..	..	..
Brayford, Eli	..	..	..	1	..	..	..	1	..	1	..
Bromley, Daniel	2	2	..	..	1	..	1	1	..	1	..
Bromley, Joshua	2	..	..	1	..	1	..	..	1	..	..
Brown, Amos	..	1	1	1	..	2	1	1	..	1	..
Brown, Asa	2	..	..	1	..	1	..	1	..	..	..
Brown, Daniel	..	..	..	..	1	..	..	..	..	1	..
Brown, Elisha	2	..	..	..	1	1	2	1	..	1	..
Brown, Perez	1	..	1	..	..	1	..	1	..	..	..
Brumley, Barton	4	..	..	1	..	1	1	1	1	..	..
Brumley, Betheul	..	2	1	..	1	1	..	..	1	..	..
Brumley, William	..	..	..	..	1	..	..	..	..	..	..
Brumley, William Jr.	..	1	1	1	..	4	1	..	1	..	..
Brumley, William 2nd.	2	..	..	1	..	1	..	..	1	..	..
Buckstone, John	1	1	3	..	1	3	1	1	..	1	..
Buckstone, Timothy	1	..	1	..	..	..	..	1	..	..	..
Bull, Crispan	2	..	1	..	2	..	2	1	..	1	..
Bull, Joseph	2	..	1	..	1	3	2	4	1	..	..
Bull, Timothy	..	..	..	1	..	2	..	1	..	..	..
Bush, Benjamin	4	1	..	1	..	..	2	1	1	..	..
Bushee, Stephen	4	1	..	1	..	1	1	1	1	..	..
Button, Joseph	3	2	..	1	..	..	1	..	1	..	..
Canada, William	3	..	..	1	..	1	..	1	..	..	..
Canfield, Darius	1	2	1	1	..	..	1	..	..	1	..
Chatsey, Richard	..	..	..	..	1	..	..	..	..	1	..
Clark, Henry	..	..	3	..	1	..	1	1	..	1	..
Clark, John	..	..	..	1	..	2	..	..	1	..	..
Clark, Moses	..	..	1	1	..	2	..	1	..	..	..
Clark, Nathan	1	..	..	1	..	2	..	1	..	..	..
Colvin, Amos	1	1	3	..	1	3	1	..	1	..	..
Colvin, Caleb	..	..	..	1	..	1	..	..	1	..	..
Colvin, Joshua	1	..	..	1	..	2	..	..	1	..	..
Colvin, Levi	4	..	..	1	..	1	2	..	1	..	..
Colvin, Luther	1	1	..	..	1	..	..	4	1	1	..
Colvin, Reuben	1	..	1	..	..	..	..	1	..	..	..
Colvin, Stephen	3	3	..	1	..	2	1	..	1	..	..
Colvin, Titus	..	..	2	..	1	..	3	1	1	..	..
Conger, David	..	..	1	..	..	1	..	1	..	..	..
Conger, Enoch	1	1	..	1	..	..	1	..	1	..	..
Conger, Gershom	2	..	1	1	..	..	2	..	1	..	..
Conger, John	..	..	1	..	..	..	..	..	..	..	..
Cook, Daniel	..	..	..	1	..	..	1	..	..	1	..
Cook, John	1	..	..	..	1	2	2	..	1	..	..
Cook, Seth	..	..	2	..	1	..	..	..	..	1	..
Cook, Sylvanus	3	1	..	1	..	1	3	..	1	..	..
Cook, William	2	..	..	1	..	2	..	..	1	..	..
Corkins, Nathaniel	..	..	1	..	..	..	..	1	..	..	..
Corkins, Stephen	..	..	1	..	1	..	..	..	..	1	..
Daley, Laban	..	..	..	1	..	1	..	..	1	..	..
Dart, John	1	..	..	1	..	1	..	1	..	..	..
Dart, Roswell	2	..	..	1	..	3	..	..	1	..	..
Davis, Josiah	..	1	..	1	..	..	1	..	1	..	..
Dodge, Hannah	3	..	3	..	..	..	2	1	..	1	..
Dow, Samuel	1	..	1	1	..	2	..	..	1	..	..
Eddy, David	..	1	1	..	..	..	..	1	..	..	..
Eddy, Jacob	1	..	1	1	1	1	3	1	..	1	..
Eddy, Ruth	2	..	..	..	..	..	1	1	1	..	..
DANBY—con.											
Edmonds, Obadiah	1	2	..	1	..	..	..	1	..	2	..
Edmonds, William	..	2	2	1	..	6	1	1	1	..	..
Edmonds, William Jr.	1	..	1	..	..	1	..	..	1	..	..
Fay, John	..	1	..	1	..	2	..	1	1	..	..
Fish, Elisha	1	1	..	1	..	2	1	..	1	1	..
Fisk, Benjamin	1	..	..	1	..	3	..	..	1	..	..
Fisk, Benoni	3	..	..	1	..	1	..	..	1	..	..
Fisk, Reuben	..	1	..	1	..	4	..	..	1	..	..
Flint, Porter	2	1	..	1	..	1	..	1	..	..	..
Folger, Daniel	..	..	1	..	..	..	..	1	..	..	..
Frost, Henry	1	1	2	1	..	1	1	..	1	..	..
Frost, Jonathan	1	..	1	..	..	..	..	1	..	..	..
Gardner, Thomas	..	..	..	1	1	1	..	..	1	..	..
Gilbert, Zebina	1	..	1	..	..	..	..	..	1	..	..
Gilmore, David	3	..	..	1	..	..	..	..	1	..	..
Griffin, David	2	..	..	1	..	3	..	..	1	..	..
Griffin, Lemuel	..	1	1	..	1	1	..	..	..	1	..
Grippin, Thomas	..	..	..	1	..	2	1	1	..	..	..
Harrington, Elisha	..	..	1	1	..	..	..	..	..	1	..
Harrington, Hezekiah	1	..	..	1	..	1	2	..	1	..	..
Harrington, Israel	..	..	..	..	1	..	..	..	..	1	..
Harrington, John	1	..	2	1	..	2	2	..	1	..	..
Harrington, John	1	1	..	..	1	..	..	..	..	1	..
Harrington, Oliver	4	1	..	..	1	..	1	..	1	..	..
Harrington, Peter	1	3	..	1	..	1	..	..	1	..	..
Harrington, Thomas	1	..	..	..	1	..	1	..	..	1	..
Harrington, William	2	..	..	..	1	1	..	1	..	1	..
Harris, Jason	2	..	..	1	..	3	..	..	1	..	..
Harris, Joseph	1	..	..	1	..	..	..	1	..	..	..
Hatheway, James	1	..	1	..	1	1	2	1	1	..	..
Herick, Henry Jr.	..	1	..	1	..	4	1	..	1	..	..
Herrick, Henry	..	1	..	..	1	..	1	..	..	1	..
Herrick, Joshua	..	..	1	..	..	..	1	..	..	..	..
Hill, Aaron	..	..	1	..	1	..	..	..	..	1	..
Hill, Daniel	1	..	..	..	1	..	..	..	..	1	..
Hill, George	..	..	..	1	..	2	1	..	1	..	..
Hill, Henry D.	..	..	2	..	..	..	..	1	..	..	..
Hilyard, Miner	1	1	..	1	..	2	..	..	1	..	..
Horton, Abel	3	1	..	1	..	2	..	1	1	..	..
Hoskins, Abel	..	1	2	..	1	1	1	..	..	1	..
Hulett, Paul	..	..	1	..	..	..	..	1	..	..	..
Irish, Abel	3	2	..	..	1	1	2	..	1	..	..
Irish, David	..	..	..	..	1	..	..	..	1	1	..
Irish, John	..	..	1	..	..	..	..	..	..	..	..
Irish, Jonathan	2	..	..	1	..	2	..	..	1	..	..
Irish, Joseph	1	1	..	1	..	3	2	..	1	..	..
Irish, Zadock	1	..	1	..	..	..	..	1	..	..	..
Johnson, Adam	..	..	..	..	1	1	..	2	..	1	..
Johnson, John	..	1	..	..	1	..	..	..	..	1	..
Keith, Moses	..	..	..	1	..	..	1	..	..	..	..
Kelly, Benjamin	..	1	1	..	1	1	3	..	1	1	..
Kelly, Daniel	..	1	..	..	1	2	..	..	1	..	..
Kelly, Hattel	2	..	..	1	..	..	..	1	..	..	..
Kelly, Pardon	..	1	..	1	..	2	..	..	1	..	..
King, Job	..	..	..	..	1	..	1	2	1	1	..
King, Joseph	..	..	..	1	..	..	..	2	..	..	..
King, Nathan	1	2	..	..	1	4	..	..	1	..	..
Kingsbury, Charles	4	2	..	1	..	..	..	..	1	..	..
Lake, William	2	2	..	1	..	2	1	..	1	..	..
Lappam, Nathan	3	1	..	1	..	1	..	2	1	..	1
Lee, William	1	..	1	..	..	2	..	2	..	..	..
Lewis, Jacob	..	1	..	1	..	4	..	..	1	..	..
Lewis, John	..	1	..	..	1	..	..	..	1	..	..
Lily, Emmons	..	..	..	1	..	1	..	1	..	..	1
Lincoln, Elisha	3	2	..	..	1	1	1	..	1	..	..
Lincoln, Leonard	..	..	1	..	..	..	..	1	..	..	..
Lobdin, Darius	1	1	1	1	..	1	1	..	1	..	..
Lobdin, Jared	1	..	..	1	..	2	1	..	1	..	..
Lobdin, John	..	..	1	..	..	1	..	1	..	1	..
Mattason, Ishimael	2	..	..	1	..	2	..	1	..	..	..
Mattason, Jabez	..	..	..	1	..	3	..	1	..	..	..
McCurdee, Richard	..	..	1	..	..	..	..	1	..	..	..
Newbury, John	1	1	..	1	..	2	..	..	1	..	..
Nichols, Anthony	2	1	..	..	1	1	..	..	1	..	..
Nichols, Charles	..	2	1	..	1	3	2	..	..	1	..
Nichols, James	3	..	..	1	..	1	..	..	2	..	..
Northrop, John	5	..	..	1	..	1	..	..	1	..	..

RUTLAND COUNTY—Continued

NAMES OF HEADS OF FAMILIES	FREE WHITE MALES					FREE WHITE FEMALES					
	Under 10 years of age	Of 10 and under 16	Of 16 and under 26 including heads of families	Of 26 and under 45 including heads of families	Of 45 and upwards including heads of families.	Under 10 years of age	Of 10 and under 16	Of 16 and under 26 including heads of families	Of 26 and under 45 including heads of families	Of 45 and upwards including heads of families	All other free persons except Indians not taxed
DANBY—con.											
Otis, Harris	3	..	..	1	..	..	..	1	..	..	..
Palmer, Gilbert	..	..	2	..	1	3	..	2	..	1	..
Palmer, Jehiel	3	..	1	..	1	1	1	1	1	..	..
Palmer, Job	3	1	..	1	..	1	..	..	1	..	..
Palmer, John	4	1	..	1	..	..	..	..	1	..	..
Parmerton, John	2	1	..	..	1	1	1	..	1	..	..
Parrish, Daniel	5	..	..	1	..	1	..	..	1	..	..
Parrish, Elkanah	..	1	..	1	1	..	..	2	1	1	..
Perkins, Holmes	..	1	..	1	..	2	1	..	1	..	..
Peters, Nathan	2	..	..	1	..	1	..	..	1	..	..
Phillips, Barzillai	..	..	..	1	..	..	..	..	..	..	..
Phillips, Benjamin	..	..	1	..	..	1	..	1	..	..	..
Phillips, Caleb	..	1	..	..	1	..	..	1	..	2	..
Phillips, Chad	..	..	..	1	..	2	..	..	1	..	..
Phillips, Israel	1	..	..	1	..	..	1	..	1	1	..
Phillips, John	2	1	..	..	1	1	1	1	..	1	..
Phillips, Noah	..	..	1	..	..	..	..	1	..	..	..
Phillips, Stephen	..	1	..	..	1	1	..	1	..	1	..
Potter, Edmund	2	1	2	..	1	2	1	..	..	1	..
Potter, Thomas	1	..	..	..	1	1	2	1	..	1	..
Pratt, James	2	1	1	1	..	1	..	..	1	..	..
Prince, Job	..	..	..	..	1	..	..	..	..	1	..
Randal, Benjamin	..	..	..	1	..	..	..	1	..	1	..
Randal, Caleb	1	..	1	..	..	..	..	1	..	..	..
Rixford, Samuel	3	1	..	1	..	1	..	..	1	..	..
Rogers, Aaron	..	..	1	..	..	1	..	1	..	..	..
Rogers, Deliverance	1	..	..	1	..	2	..	..	1	..	..
Rogers, Isaac	2	..	..	1	..	1	..	..	1	..	..
Rogers, John	..	..	..	1	..	3	..	..	1	..	..
Rogers, Joseph	..	1	..	1	..	2	..	..	1	..	..
Rogers, Stephen	..	1	1	..	1	1	2	..	..	1	..
Ross, Joseph	..	..	2	..	1	..	..	1	..	1	..
Ross, Joseph Jr.	1	..	..	1	..	2	1	1	..	..	..
Salsbury, Brigget	..	..	..	..	..	1	..	..	1	..	..
Salsbury, Nathan	..	2	2	..	1	1	1	..	..	1	..
Sava, Stephen	1	1	..	1	..	4	1	..	1	1	..
Sayles, John	..	2	1	..	1	..	..	1	1	..	..
Seley, Israel	2	1	..	..	1	1	..	1	..	1	..
Seley, John	2	1	..	1	..	2	..	..	1	..	..
Seley, Jonathan	4	..	1	1	..	1	2	..	1	..	..
Session, Richard	1	..	1	..	..	..	..	1	..	..	..
Sherman, Edmond	1	..	1	..	..	1	..	1	..	..	..
Sherman, Elihu	1	1	..	..	1	1	1	2	1	..	..
Sherman, Levi	3	..	1	..	1	3	1	1	1	..	..
Sherman, Solomon	..	..	1	..	..	..	..	..	..	..	..
Shippee, Hezekiah	..	..	1	..	..	..	..	1	..	..	..
Shippee, Jacob	1	..	..	..	1	2	2	1	1	..	..
Signer, John	..	1	..	..	1	..	..	..	..	2	..
Smith, Amasa	..	..	1	..	..	2	..	1	..	..	..
Smith, Ezekiel	2	..	4	..	1	1	2	..	1	1	..
Smith, Howland	1	..	1	..	..	1	..	1	..	..	..
Smith, Nathan	3	1	..	..	1	1	1	..	1	..	..
Soule, James	4	..	..	1	..	..	..	1	1	..	..
Southwick, Daniel	2	..	..	1	..	3	..	..	1	..	..
Southwick, Elisha	..	1	..	1	..	2	1	..	1	..	..
Southwick, Isaac	..	..	..	1	..	..	..	..	..	..	..
Sprague, Martin	2	..	1	..	..	1	..	1	..	..	..
Sprague, Zebulon	..	..	..	1	..	..	..	1	..	..	..
Stanford, David	2	..	..	1	..	1	1	..	1	..	..
Stanley, Daniel	2	..	..	1	..	2	1	..	1	..	..
Stanley, Samuel	1	..	..	2	..	..	1	..	..	1	..
Staples, Abraham	..	..	1	1	..	3	..	1	1	..	..
Staples, Jonathan	2	1	1	..	1	..	1	..	..	1	..
Streeter, Josiah	..	..	1	1	..	2	1	..	2	..	..
Streeter, Solomon	..	..	1	..	..	1	..	1	..	..	..
Sumner, Edward	..	..	1	..	..	..	..	..	..	..	..
Taft, Levi	1	1	..	..	1	1	1	1	..	1	..
Thare, Oliver	1	..	..	1	..	..	..	..	1	..	..
Thomson, Benjamin	2	1	1	1	..	3	2	..	1	..	..
Tift, Mattason	2	..	..	1	..	1	..	1	..	..	..
Torrey, Philip	..	..	1	..	..	..	..	..	..	..	..
Trafton, Abial	..	..	1	..	1	..	..	..	1	..	..
Tryon, Elisha	2	..	..	1	..	2	..	..	1	..	..
Vaughn, William	..	..	1	..	..	..	..	..	..	..	..
Veale, Edward	1	3	2	1	..	1	..	..	1	..	..
Veale, Moses	1	1	1	..	1	1	1	..	..	1	..
Vial, Constant	1	1	..	..	1	2	1	..	1	..	..
Wallin, Thomas	1	..	..	1	..	..	..	1	..	..	..
Warner, Asa	2	..	..	1	..	1	..	..	1	..	..
Waters, David	4	1	..	..	1	1	1	1	1	..	..
Webber, William	2	..	..	1	..	2	..	1	1	..	..
Webster, Jehiel	..	..	1	..	..	..	..	..	..	..	..
Webster, Samuel	..	..	..	1	..	2	..	1	..	..	..
Weed, Micajah	..	..	..	1	..	3	..	1	..	..	..
Wellow, Nathan	3	1	..	1	..	1	2	..	1	..	..
Wells, Charles	3	..	..	1	..	..	..	..	1	..	..
Wheeler, Ebenezer	1	..	..	1	..	3	..	..	1	..	..
White, Reuben	3	..	..	1	..	2	..	1	..	..	..
Wilber, Henry	..	..	1	..	1	..	1	2	..	1	..
Wilber, Isaac	..	1	2	..	1	3	1	..	1	..	..
Williams, Hosea	1	..	1	..	..	1	..	1	..	..	..
Williams, Stephen	..	2	..	..	1	3	1	..	1	..	..
Wing, Matthew	..	..	..	..	1	..	..	..	..	1	..
Wing, Matthew Jr.	3	1	..	1	..	..	..	..	1	..	..
Winn, Jacob	3	1	1	..	1	2	1	1	..	1	..
Winn, Jacob Jr.	..	..	1	..	..	..	..	1	..	..	..
Worton, Abraham	1	..	1	..	..	1	..	1	..	..	..
Worton, Walter	..	..	1	..	1	1	2	..	1	..	..
UNCERTAIN NAME											
Blens (?), David	..	..	1	..	..	..	..	..	..	1	..
FAIRHAVEN											
Ainsworth, Danforth	..	..	1	..	..	..	..	1	..	..	..
Ainsworth, Henry	3	1	1	..	1	1	..	..	1	..	..
Andrus, Ephraim	..	..	..	1	..	..	..	1	..	..	..
Artherton, Abiah	2	..	..	..	..	..	1	1	1	..	..
Ashley, Noah	1	..	1	..	..	..	1	..	..	..	..
Biado, Richard	3	2	..	1	..	1	..	..	1	..	..
Bordem, William	..	..	1	..	..	..	..	1	..	..	..
Braynard, Timothy	1	1	2	..	1	1	1	1	..	1	..
Brown, John	2	..	..	1	..	2	..	..	1	..	..
Brownson, Amos	..	..	2	..	..	..	1	..	..	..	..
Bullock, Shubal	1	..	1	..	..	..	..	1	..	..	..
Cleveland, James	1	..	1	..	..	..	..	1	..	..	..
Cleveland, Josiah	1	1	..	1	..	4	2	..	1	..	..
Cleveland, Oliver	..	..	..	..	1	..	1	..	..	2	..
Cleveland, Olvord	1	..	..	1	..	1	..	1	..	..	..
Corbin, Edward	..	..	..	1	..	..	..	1	..	..	..
Cutler Isaac	..	1	..	1	..	..	1	..	1	..	..
Dibble, Thomas	..	1	..	1	..	2	..	..	1	..	..
Dickinson, Nathaniel	..	..	..	1	..	1	1	..	1	..	1
Dowland, Thomas	..	..	1	..	..	..	..	..	1	..	..
Durand, Jeremiah	1	2	..	..	1	..	..	2	..	1	..
Durand, Martha	..	..	1	..	..	..	1	3	..	1	..
Erwin, David	1	3	1	1	..	2	1	1	1	..	..
Evetts, Eli	1	..	..	..	2	1	1	..	..	1	..
Gifford, Paul	..	..	1	..	1	1	..	..	..	1	..
Gilbert, Tilla	3	..	..	1	..	..	..	1	..	..	..
Goodrich, Timothy	2	..	2	1	..	1	..	..	1	..	..
Hall, John	..	..	1	..	..	..	..	1	..	..	..
Hamilton, Joel	..	..	..	1	..	..	..	..	1	..	..
Hawkins, Charles	..	..	2	..	1	..	1	1	..	1	..
Hawkins, Olney	1	1	..	1	..	2	..	1	..	1	..
Hawkins, William	..	..	..	1	..	4	..	1	..	..	..
Holt, Stephen	..	1	..	..	1	..	..	1	1	..	..
Kelsey, Curtiss	..	..	1	..	1	..	..	..	..	1	..
Kelsey, Orin	..	..	1	..	..	..	..	1	..	..	..
King, Rufus	..	..	..	1	..	..	..	..	..	..	..
Leonard, Gamaliel	4	2	..	1	..	1	1	..	1	..	..
Lewis, Josiah	2	..	1	..	..	..	..	1	..	..	..
Long, Alexander	..	..	1	..	1	..	..	..	..	1	..
Long, Jacob	3	..	1	..	..	..	..	1	..	..	..
McCarter, Charles	3	1	..	..	2	2	..	..	1	2	..
McCarter, Dunkin	1	1	1	..	..	1	..	1	..	..	..
McWeva, Hannah	1	..	..	..	..	..	1	..	1	..	..
McWeva, Isaac	4	..	..	1	..	..	..	..	1	..	..
McWeva, Simeon	..	..	..	..	1	..	..	..	..	1	..
Miller, Elihu	1	3	1	..	1	1	..	1	..	1	..
Monger, Asael	1	..	..	1	..	2	..	..	1	..	..
Monger, Daniel	..	..	..	..	1	..	..	..	..	1	..
Morril, Michael	..	..	1	..	1	..	..	2	..	1	..
Morrison, John	..	..	1	..	..	..	..	..	..	..	..
Norton, Josiah	1	1	2	..	1	1	..	1	..	1	..

RUTLAND COUNTY—Continued

NAMES OF HEADS OF FAMILIES	FREE WHITE MALES: Under 10 years of age	FREE WHITE MALES: Of 10 and under 16	FREE WHITE MALES: Of 16 and under 26 including heads of families	FREE WHITE MALES: Of 26 and under 45 including heads of families	FREE WHITE MALES: Of 45 and upwards including heads of families	FREE WHITE FEMALES: Under 10 years of age	FREE WHITE FEMALES: Of 10 and under 16	FREE WHITE FEMALES: Of 16 and under 26 including heads of families	FREE WHITE FEMALES: Of 26 and under 45 including heads of families	FREE WHITE FEMALES: Of 45 and upwards including heads of families	All other free persons except Indians not taxed
FAIRHAVEN—con.											
Orbs, Jonathan	1	1	..	1	..	3	..	1	1	..	..
Parmerton, Benjamin	3	..	..	1	..	1	..	2	1	..	..
Perkins, Ethel	..	..	..	..	1	..	..	..	..	1	..
Preast, Aaron	1	..	1	..	..	1	1	..	..	..	..
Preast, Philip	..	..	1	..	1	1	..	..	..	1	..
Rice, Isaac	1	3	1	1	..	1	..	2	1	..	..
Rogers, Ambrose	..	..	..	1	..	..	1	1	..	..	..
Rogers, Beriah	2	..	2	1	..	..	1	1	..	..	..
Rogers, Jared	..	1	2	..	..	..	..	1	..	..	..
Rogers Stephen	1	..	1	1	..	1	..	..	1	..	..
Safford, Silas	3	1	..	1	..	2	1	..	1	1	..
Scribner, John	2	1	..	..	1	1	1	..	1	1	..
Sharp, Abraham	3	..	..	1	..	1	..	..	1	..	..
Sharp, James	1	..	..	1	..	3	..	..	1	..	..
Sheldon, Joseph	..	..	1	..	..	..	..	..	..	..	..
Smith, James	..	..	1	..	1	..	..	..	..	1	..
Snow, Joseph	2	..	..	1	..	..	2	..	1	..	..
Solger, Thomas	..	..	2	..	..	..	1	1	..	..	..
Stanford, Joshua	..	..	..	..	1	..	..	..	..	..	..
Stannard, Daniel	1	..	..	1	..	1	..	..	1	..	..
Stannard, Samuel	..	..	1	..	1	..	..	..	..	1	..
Stevens, Benjamin	1	..	..	1	..	1	..	..	1	..	..
Trobrige, Levi	3	2	..	1	..	1	..	..	1	..	..
Walker, Ebenezer	..	..	..	1	..	..	..	..	2	..	..
Warren, Ahijah	..	2	3	..	1	2	1	1	..	1	..
Whipple, Ethan	1	..	1	1	..	3	1	..	1	..	..
Whitehouse, Thomas	1	..	..	..	1	1	..	1	..	..	..
Wilder, Solomon	..	1	..	1	..	3	2	..	1	..	..
Witherell, James	3	..	1	1	1	3	1	..	1	..	..
HARWICH											
Baker, Gideon	2	1	3	..	1	1	2	1	1	..	..
Booth, Rowland	3	..	..	1	..	1	..	..	1	..	..
Carpender, William	..	..	1	..	..	1	..	1	..	..	..
Dewey, Aaron	..	..	..	..	1	..	..	..	..	2	..
Fish, Thomas	..	..	..	..	1	..	..	..	1	..	..
Gorton, Amos	..	..	1	..	..	..	..	1	..	..	..
Gorton, Samuel	1	..	1	..	..	..	..	1	..	..	..
Grippen, George	3	..	..	1	..	1	..	..	1	..	..
Halbee, Eleazer	2	2	..	..	1	1	1	..	1	..	..
Harris, Asael	1	1	..	1	..	1	1	..	1	..	..
Hill, Stephen	..	1	2	..	1	1	1	..	..	1	..
Hill, Stephen Jr.	2	..	..	1	..	2	..	..	1	..	..
May, John	..	..	..	..	1	..	..	..	..	1	..
McIntire, Nathaniel	..	..	1	..	..	1	..	1	..	..	..
Phillips, Seth	2	..	..	1	..	4	..	..	1	..	..
Randal, Snow	1	..	..	..	1	1	1	..	1	..	..
Remington, Stephen	..	..	..	1	..	2	..	1	..	..	..
Sherman, Daniel	3	..	1	1	..	2	1	..	1	..	..
Smith, Peleg	1	..	..	1	..	3	..	1	..	..	..
Sweet, David	..	..	1	..	..	..	..	1	..	..	..
Sweet, John	1	..	1	..	1	3	2	1	1	..	..
Tabor, Gideon	2	1	..	1	..	2	2	..	1	..	..
Tabor, Peleg	..	..	1	..	..	1	..	2	..	..	..
Tabor, Water	..	..	..	..	1	..	..	1	..	1	..
Tabor, Water Jr.	1	..	1	..	..	..	..	1	..	1	..
Tift, Oliver	2	1	2	..	1	..	..	2	..	1	..
Wheeler, Jacob	2	..	..	..	1	2	..	1	..	..	..
Williams, John	..	..	..	1	..	3	..	..	1	..	..
HUBBERDTON											
Ashley, Abner	..	1	1	..	1	3	1	..	..	1	..
Baldwin, Nathan W.	2	..	..	1	..	2	1	..	1	..	..
Balus, Eunice	..	2	..	..	..	1	2	..	1	1	..
Barber, David	3	..	..	1	..	..	..	1	..	..	..
Barse, Joshua B.	..	1	..	1	..	1	..	..	1	..	..
Bisbrow, Simeon	3	..	1	..	1	2	1	1	1	..	..
Bordman, Josiah	..	..	..	..	1	..	1	..	..	1	..
HUBBERDTON—con.											
Churchel, Anna	1	..	1	..	..	..	1	..	1	..	..
Churchel, Ezekiel	1	1	..	1	..	4	1	..	1	2	..
Churchel, Ithamar	1	..	1	..	..	..	..	1	..	..	..
Churchel, Jesse	3	1	..	1	..	1	1	..	1	..	..
Churchel, John	2	2	..	1	..	2	1	..	1	..	..
Churchel, Joseph	3	1	1	..	1	1	2	2	..	1	..
Churchel, Josiah	..	1	..	1	1	..	..	..	..	1	..
Churchel, Lovell	1	..	1	..	..	1	..	1	..	..	..
Churchel, Nathaniel	2	1	1	1	..	1	1	..	1	..	..
Churchel, Silas	..	1	..	1	..	1	1	..	1	..	..
Churchel, William	4	1	..	1	..	2	1	..	1	..	..
Colvin, Benjamin	2	1	..	1	..	..	1	..	1	..	..
Dana, Nathan Rev.	3	1	..	1	..	..	..	1	1	..	..
Davis, Henry	..	..	1	..	..	..	..	..	..	..	..
Dewey, John	..	1	..	1	..	1	..	..	1	..	..
Dewey, Moseley J.	..	..	1	..	..	..	..	..	..	..	..
Dikeman, Frederick	1	2	..	1	..	2	..	2	..	1	..
Dowd, Peleg	..	..	..	..	1	..	..	..	..	1	..
Dowd, Seymour	2	..	..	1	..	2	1	..	1	..	..
Finney, Luther	2	1	1	..	..	1	..	1	..	..	..
Flagg, Theophilus	..	1	..	1	..	1	..	..	1	..	..
Foster, Edward	3	..	..	1	..	2	..	..	1	..	..
Foster, Samuel	..	1	1	..	..	..	..	1	..	..	..
Freeman, Elisha	..	1	1	..	1	..	..	..	..	1	..
Freeman, Elkanah	1	..	1	..	..	..	..	1	..	..	..
Gilliff, Benjamin	..	1	..	1	..	3	1	..	1	..	..
Gilliff, Thomas	2	..	..	1	..	2	..	..	1	..	..
Goodrich, Noah	..	1	..	1	..	2	1	..	1	..	..
Gregory, Ithamar	1	1	3	..	1	2	1	1	..	1	..
Hammon, David	..	..	1	..	..	..	..	..	..	..	..
Hibbord, Ithamar Rev.	4	1	1	..	1	2	1	..	1	..	..
Hichock, Elijah	..	..	..	1	..	..	..	1	..	..	..
Hicock, Benjamin	..	..	1	1	1	..	1	..	..	1	..
Hicock, Mathew	1	..	..	1	..	1	1	..	1	..	..
Hicock, Moses	..	1	..	1	..	..	..	1	..	..	..
Hicock, Uriah	1	..	..	..	1	1	1	..	..	1	..
Hicock, Uriah Jr.	..	..	..	1	..	..	..	..	..	..	..
Higby, Silas	..	..	1	..	..	..	..	..	..	..	..
Hogg, David	4	1	1	..	1	..	..	2	..	..	..
Holmes, Water	2	..	..	1	..	2	..	..	1	..	..
Hunt, Elnathan	2	..	..	1	..	1	1	..	1	..	..
Hunt, John	1	1	..	1	..	..	..	1	1	..	..
Hurlbert, Samuel	1	1	1	..	1	1	1	1	..	1	..
Hurlbert, Stephen	..	..	..	1	..	1	..	1	..	..	..
Hurlburt, John	..	..	..	..	1	..	..	..	..	1	..
Jennings, Joseph	2	..	..	1	..	1	..	..	1	..	..
Johnson, Martha	..	..	1	..	..	1	..	..	..	1	..
Jones, Asael	1	1	..	1	..	3	..	..	1	..	..
Kellogg, Enos	..	1	2	..	1	..	1	2	1	1	..
Lawrence, Bigalow	3	1	..	1	..	3	1	2	1	..	..
Lewis, Ebenezer	..	1	..	..	1	..	..	..	..	1	..
Meeker, Daniel	..	1	..	1	..	1	..	1	..	..	..
Merrills, Roswell	2	..	..	1	..	1	..	1	..	..	..
Nichols, Charles	2	..	..	1	..	1	..	..	1	..	..
Nichols, David	1	..	1	..	..	..	..	1	..	..	..
Nichols, John	..	..	..	..	1	..	..	1	..	1	..
Parsons, Samuel	1	..	..	1	..	1	1	..	1	..	..
Parsons, Samuel	1	..	..	1	..	1	1	..	1	..	..
Patrige, Amos	2	..	..	1	..	1	..	1	..	..	..
Pease, George	..	..	1	..	..	1	..	1	..	..	..
Petty, James	..	..	..	1	..	..	..	..	1	..	..
Petty, Samuel	1	..	..	1	..	3	2	..	1	..	..
Ranger, Cyrus	1	..	1	..	..	..	..	1	..	..	..
Rickey, William	1	..	1	..	..	..	..	1	..	..	..
Robinson, Isaiah	2	1	3	1	..	1	1	1	1	..	..
Rumsey, Daniel	..	..	1	..	1	..	2	1	..	1	..
Rumsey, David	2	2	2	1	..	3	1	..	1	..	..
Rumsey, Ebenezer	1	1	..	1	..	2	..	1	1	2	..
Rumsey, Ephraim	..	1	1	..	1	..	..	..	1	..	..
Rumsey, Hezekiah	1	1	..	..	1	3	1	..	1	..	..
Rumsey, John	1	1	..	1	..	1	..	..	1	..	..
Rumsey, Joseph	1	1	2	..	1	..	1	..	1	1	..
Rumsey, Nathan	2	..	..	1	..	2	2	..	1	..	..
Rumsey, Smith	..	1	..	1	..	1	..	..	1	..	..
Rumsey, William	1	2	1	..	1	4	1	..	1	..	..
Rumsey, William Jr.	1	1	..	1	..	2	..	..	1	..	..
Rusha, Isaac	..	..	1	..	..	1	..	1	..	..	..

RUTLAND COUNTY—Continued

NAMES OF HEADS OF FAMILIES	FREE WHITE MALES					FREE WHITE FEMALES					All other free persons except Indians not taxed
	Under 10 years of age	Of 10 and under 16	Of 16 and under 26 including heads of families	Of 26 and under 45 including heads of families	Of 45 and upwards including heads of families.	Under 10 years of age	Of 10 and under 16	Of 16 and under 26 including heads of families	Of 26 and under 45 including heads of families	Of 45 and upwards including heads of families	
HUBBERDTON—con.											
Scovil, Daniel	2	..	..	1	..	3	..	..	1	..	..
Sellock, Benjamin	4	..	..	1	..	2	1	..	1	..	..
Sellock, John	..	..	..	..	1	..	..	..	..	1	..
Sellock, Jonas	2	..	1	1	..	1	..	..	1	..	..
Sellock, Joseph	1	..	..	1	..	2	..	..	1	..	..
Sellock, Philo	..	..	..	1	..	..	..	..	..	..	..
Sension, Nehemiah	..	..	..	..	1	..	..	..	..	1	..
Sension, Seth	2	..	..	1	..	1	1	1	..	..	..
Sessions, Timothy	1	..	..	1	..	..	1	..	1	..	..
Smith, Eliel	1	..	1	..	..	2	..	1	..	..	..
Smith, Ithamar	..	1	..	1	..	..	1	1	1	..	..
Spalding, Dyar	..	..	1	..	..	..	..	..	..	..	..
Spalding, Hiram	2	1	..	1	..	..	..	..	1	..	..
Spalding, Joseph	..	..	..	1	..	1	..	..	..	1	..
Spalding, Zebulon	1	..	..	1	1	2	..	..	1	..	..
Spooner, John	2	1	..	1	..	2	1	..	1	..	..
Stutton, Ezra	1	1	..	1	..	3	..	..	1	..	..
Wadkins, Joseph	..	..	1	..	..	..	..	..	..	..	..
Walker, Rufus	2	..	..	1	..	..	..	1	..	..	..
Wallace, Ebenezer	..	1	3	..	1	..	..	1	..	1	..
Wallis, Gilbert	1	..	1	..	..	..	..	1	..	..	..
Ware, Samuel	..	..	..	1	..	..	..	..	..	..	..
Warren, Nehemiah	2	1	..	1	..	2	..	1	..	..	..
Webster, Abdiel	..	..	..	..	1	..	..	..	..	1	..
Webster, Benajah S.	..	..	1	..	..	..	..	1	..	..	..
Whelpley, James	..	..	..	..	1	..	..	..	..	1	..
Whillock, David	..	..	1	..	1	..	..	..	..	1	..
Willard, Joseph	..	..	2	1	..	2	..	..	1	1	..
Wolcott, Erastus	3	..	..	1	..	2	2	..	1	..	..
Wood, Abijah	1	..	..	1	..	1	..	1	..	..	..
Wood, Ezra	1	..	1	..	..	..	..	..	1	..	..
Wood, Joseph	1	..	..	1	..	..	1	1	1	..	..
Wood, Lemuel	..	..	1	..	1	..	1	..	..	1	..
Wright, Asael	1	1	2	..	1	..	2	..	1	..	..
Wright, Elisha	1	..	..	1	..	4	..	..	1	..	..
IRA											
Akin, John	..	..	1	..	..	..	..	..	..	..	..
Ames, Zebulon	..	..	..	1	..	2	..	..	1	..	..
Anderson, John	2	2	..	1	..	3	..	2	1	..	..
Anderson, Mathew	1	1	..	1	..	2	..	..	1	..	..
Bala, Edward	2	..	1	..	1	..	2	1	..	1	..
Bates, John	..	..	2	..	1	..	..	..	..	1	..
Bebee, Sino	1	..	1	..	..	..	..	..	1	..	..
Bebee, Theodeus	..	..	1	..	1	..	..	..	..	1	..
Brooks, Joseph	3	1	..	1	..	1	..	..	1	..	..
Brown, Joseph	..	..	1	..	..	..	..	..	..	..	..
Brown, Prentice	1	..	..	1	..	1	..	1	..	..	..
Brown, Ruth	1	..	..	..	..	3	..	..	1	..	..
Burlingame, John	3	1	..	1	..	1	..	..	1	..	..
Carpender, Aaron	3	..	..	1	..	1	..	..	1	..	..
Carpender, Cephas	2	1	1	..	1	2	2	1	1	..	..
Carpender, Wilson	4	..	..	1	..	1	1	..	1	..	..
Cleft, Hezekiah	6	..	..	1	..	1	2	..	1	1	..
Collins, Benoni	1	..	2	..	1	2	2	1	..	1	..
Collins, John	3	1	1	..	1	1	3	1	1	..	..
Collins, Joseph	2	..	..	1	..	..	..	1	..	..	..
Collins, Justice	1	2	..	1	..	2	..	1	1	..	..
Collins, Nathan	3	..	..	1	..	2	1	..	1	..	..
Collins, Thomas	1	..	..	1	..	2	..	1	..	1	..
Colvin, Jonathan	1	..	1	..	..	..	..	1	..	..	..
Colvin, Rufus	4	..	..	1	..	1	2	1	1	..	..
Davis, Samuel	2	..	..	1	..	1	..	1	..	..	..
Dutton, James	..	..	..	1	1	..	1	1	..	..	..
Eddy, John	1	..	..	1	..	1	..	..	1	..	..
Eddy, William	2	1	1	1	..	1	..	..	1	..	..
Fish, Preserved	4	..	..	1	..	1	..	..	1	..	..
Fish, Robert	..	..	1	..	..	..	..	..	..	..	..
Gates, Seth	1	..	1	1	..	2	..	..	1	..	..
Gilmore, James	..	2	..	1	..	2	1	..	1	..	..
Gilmore, William	2	1	..	1	..	..	..	1	2	1	..
Graves, Daniel	2	..	1	1	..	1	..	..	1	..	..
Graves, William	2	3	..	1	..	2	..	..	1	..	..
Huet, Gideon	2	1	..	1	..	1	..	..	1	..	..
Hunter, Daniel	1	2	1	..	1	1	..	1	1	1	..
Hunter, Samuel	2	1	..	1	..	2	1	..	1	..	..
IRA—con.											
Jackman, Moses	..	..	1	..	..	..	..	..	..	..	..
Joiner, Erastus	..	..	1	..	..	..	..	..	..	..	..
Joiner, Martin	..	..	..	1	..	1	..	1	..	..	..
Kile, Daniel	..	..	1	..	..	..	..	..	..	..	..
Kinsley, Solomon	5	1	3	1	..	..	2	1	1	..	..
Linley, Abiathar	2	..	..	1	..	..	..	1	..	..	..
Martin, James	1	1	..	1	..	1	..	..	1	..	..
Mason, Isaiah	2	1	1	1	..	3	..	2	1	..	..
Mason, Nathaniel	1	2	1	1	..	2	1	..	1	..	..
Miles, John	..	..	1	..	..	..	..	..	..	..	..
Miles, Samuel	..	..	1	..	..	..	..	..	..	..	..
Molton, John	3	1	..	..	1	3	2	3	1	..	..
Morey, Edward	3	..	..	..	1	..	1	..	..	1	..
Newton, Jason	2	1	..	1	..	2	2	1	..	..	..
Newton, Samuel	1	..	1	1	..	..	1	..	1	..	..
Noble, Enoch	2	1	..	1	..	2	..	..	1	..	..
Ormsby, Joseph	..	..	..	..	1	..	..	..	..	1	..
Owen, Ebenezer	3	..	..	1	..	1	..	1	..	..	..
Owen, Jonathan	3	1	..	1	..	1	..	..	1	1	..
Parker, David	3	..	..	1	..	..	..	..	1	..	..
Prindle, Elias	..	..	..	1	..	..	..	1	..	..	..
Rice, Daniel	1	..	1	..	..	..	..	1	..	..	..
Roberts, Purchase	..	..	..	1	1	3	..	1	1	1	..
Sherman, George	2	1	1	..	1	2	..	3	..	1	..
Sherman, James	1	..	..	1	..	2	..	..	1	..	..
Sprague, Jesse	..	..	..	1	..	..	..	..	..	..	..
Taylor, Mathew	1	..	..	1	..	..	..	..	1	..	..
Thornton, Stuteley	1	..	1	..	..	..	..	1	1	1	..
Tower, Joseph	..	1	1	..	1	..	..	4	..	1	..
Tower, Joseph Jr.	2	..	..	1	..	1	..	1	..	..	..
Tower, Nathaniel	3	..	..	1	..	2	1	..	1	..	..
Warner, Asa	..	..	..	1	..	3	..	..	1	..	..
Warner, Charles	..	..	1	..	1	..	..	..	2	1	..
Warner, Omri	4	..	..	1	..	..	1	1	1	..	..
Whipple, Christopher	..	1	..	1	1	1	1	2	..	1	..
Whitmore, John	..	..	2	..	1	2	..	..	..	1	..
Whitmore, Samuel	1	..	..	1	..	2	..	..	1	..	..
Williams. Erastus	..	..	1	..	..	..	..	..	..	..	..
Wilmott Nathaniel	..	..	1	1	..	..	1	..	1	1	..
Woodard, Rufus	4	1	1	1	..	..	1	..	1	..	..
KILLINGTON											
Anthony, John	1	..	1	2	1	..	..	1	2	1	..
Barnett, Levi	1	..	..	1	..	2	..	1	..	..	..
Barns, Simeon H.	1	..	1	..	1	1	..	..	..	..	..
Bisby, Isaac	..	..	..	1	..	3	2	1	..	..	..
Bissel, Aaron	1	..	..	1	..	1	..	..	1	..	..
Briggs, Asa	3	..	2	1	..	1	2	1	..	..	..
Easterbrooks, Richard	3	1	..	1	..	1	..	..	1	..	..
Easterbrooks, Robert	..	..	..	..	1	..	..	..	1	1	..
Fuller, Amasa	1	3	..	1	..	1	..	..	1	1	..
Fuller, John	1	2	..	1	..	1	..	..	1	..	..
Johnson, Ichabod	3	2	..	1	..	1	..	..	1	..	..
Tripp, William	5	..	2	..	1	..	..	..	2	..	2
Wood, Josiah	..	1	..	..	1	..	..	1	..	..	..
Wood, Josiah Jr.	2	..	..	1	..	..	1	..	1	..	..
MEDWAY											
Bettis, William	3	2	..	..	1	..	..	1	2	1	..
Eggleston, Jonathan	..	..	1	..	1	..	1	..	1	1	..
Farmer, Benjamin	..	..	..	..	1	..	..	..	1	..	..
Farmer, Benjamin Jr.	1	1	..	..	1	2	1	1	1	..	..
Farmer, Emerson	..	..	..	1	..	2	..	1	..	..	..
Rawson, Simeon	1	..	1	1	..	..	..	1	..	..	..
Richardson, Johnson	1	1	..	1	..	2	..	..	1	..	..

RUTLAND COUNTY—Continued

NAMES OF HEADS OF FAMILIES	FREE WHITE MALES					FREE WHITE FEMALES					
	Under 10 years of age	Of 10 and under 16	Of 16 and under 26 including heads of families	Of 26 and under 45 including heads of families	Of 45 and upwards including heads of families.	Under 10 years of age	Of 10 and under 16	Of 16 and under 26 including heads of families	Of 26 and under 45 including heads of families	Of 45 and upwards including heads of families	All other free persons except Indians not taxed
MIDDLETOWN											
Austin, Horrington	3	..	..	1	..	..	..	..	1	..	..
Barse, Jonathan	2	..	..	1	..	2	..	..	1	..	..
Bateman, Joseph	4	1	..	1	..	1	2	2	1	..	..
Bazley, Cyrus	4	..	..	1	..	1	1	1	1	..	..
Benedick, Eunice	..	..	..	..	..	..	..	..	1	..	..
Benson, Seth	..	..	..	..	1	2	..	1	1	..	..
Bigalow, Edmund	1	..	..	..	1	2	2	2	..	1	..
Blunt, Asher	1	1	2	1	..	2	1	1	1	..	..
Brewster, Eliphas	3	..	1	..	1	1	1	..	1	..	..
Brewster, Jonathan	..	1	1	..	1	..	1	..	..	1	..
Brewster, Ohel	1	..	..	1	..	..	..	1	..	..	..
Brewster, Oriman	..	..	1	..	..	2	..	1	..	..	..
Brewster, Orson	1	..	..	1	..	1	..	1	1	..	..
Brown, Joseph	..	1	1	..	1	2	1	2	..	1	..
Buckingham, William	1	..	..	1	..	3	..	..	1	..	..
Buel, Gideon	1	1	..	1	..	1	..	..	1	..	..
Burham, Jacob	3	..	..	1	..	..	..	..	1	..	..
Burnham, John	..	1	1	..	1	..	..	1	..	1	..
Burnham, Nathan	..	..	..	1	..	1	..	1	..	..	..
Burnham, William	1	..	..	1	..	..	..	..	..	..	..
Butler, Orman	1	..	1	..	..	..	..	1	..	..	..
Butler, Orrimond	1	..	1	..	..	..	2	1	..	1	..
Butler, Russel	1	..	..	1	..	1	..	..	1	..	..
Button, Nathan	1	..	..	1	..	1	..	1	..	..	..
Button, Susanna	..	..	..	..	..	..	..	2	..	1	..
Carr, Ephraim	2	2	1	..	1	..	..	..	1	..	..
Castle, Beal	..	..	..	..	1	..	1	2	..	1	..
Castle, Jesse	1	..	1	..	..	..	..	1	..	..	..
Castle, Josiah	1	1	..	1	..	1	..	1	1	..	..
Castle, Zeba	..	1	..	1	..	..	..	1	..	..	..
Chubb, Joseph	1	1	..	1	..	3	2	1	1	..	..
Clark, Ashbel	1	..	..	1	..	3	1	..	1	..	..
Clark, Enos	3	..	..	1	..	1	..	1	..	..	..
Clark, Ezra	2	1	..	1	..	1	..	..	1	..	..
Clark, Jonas	..	..	..	..	1	..	..	..	..	1	..
Clark, Jonas Jr.	..	..	1	..	..	..	..	1	..	..	..
Clark, Roswell	1	..	..	1	..	2	..	1	1	..	..
Clark, Rufus	1	2	1	1	..	2	..	..	1	..	..
Clark, Theophilus	3	..	1	1	..	2	1	..	1	..	..
Cleveland, Benajah	..	..	..	1	1	..	..	..	..	1	..
Cleveland, Lemuel	3	2	..	1	..	1	..	..	1	..	..
Cleveland, Stephen	..	1	..	..	1	2	..	..	1	..	..
Cluff, Phinehas	1	..	2	..	1	..	..	1	..	1	..
Colegrove, Calvin	1	..	..	1	..	1	..	1	..	..	..
Colegrove, Nathan	..	..	..	..	1	..	..	..	..	1	..
Corbin, Edward	..	..	..	..	1	..	..	1	1	1	..
Corbin, Elihu	1	..	..	1	..	3	..	1	..	..	..
Coy, Benjamin	3	1	1	1	..	1	1	2	..	1	..
Coy, Benjamin Jr.	1	..	1	..	..	..	..	1	..	..	..
Darby, Elias	..	..	1	..	..	..	..	1	..	..	..
Dart, Olie	2	..	..	1	..	2	..	..	1	..	..
Davinson, Abigail	2	..	..	..	..	..	..	..	1	..	..
Davinson, Jonathan	..	..	..	1	..	..	..	..	1	1	..
Doan, Ephraim	4	..	..	1	..	1	..	1	..	1	..
Downey, James	2	..	..	..	1	1	..	1	..	..	..
Downey, William	4	1	..	1	..	1	1	..	1	..	..
Drinkwater, Elizabeth	..	..	..	..	..	..	..	..	1	..	..
Everts, Thomas	1	2	1	..	1	..	2	1	..	1	..
Farr, Salmon	1	2	1	..	1	2	1	..	1	..	..
Filmore, Etha	..	..	1	..	..	1	..	1	..	..	..
Filmore, Luther	..	1	3	..	1	2	1	..	1	1	..
Ford, Daniel	..	..	2	..	1	..	..	1	1	1	..
Ford, Nathan	1	..	..	1	..	1	2	..	1	..	..
Franklin, Nathan	..	..	..	..	1	..	..	..	1	..	..
French, Thomas	1	1	1	1	..	1	..	..	1	..	..
Frisby, Eli	..	..	1	..	..	..	..	1	..	..	..
Frisby, Joel	..	1	2	..	1	..	..	2	1	..	..
Frisby, Jonathan	..	..	2	..	1	..	2	..	1	..	..
Frisby, William	..	1	1	..	1	..	..	2	..	1	..
Fuller, Jonathan	..	..	..	1	..	..	..	..	..	..	..
Gardner, Asa	3	..	..	1	..	2	1	1	1	..	..
Gates, Benjamin	1	1	..	1	..	..	..	1	..	..	..
Gilman, John	3	..	..	1	..	2	..	..	1	..	..
Graves, Gideon	..	..	1	..	..	..	..	1	..	..	..
Griswold, Andrew	1	..	..	1	..	2	2	..	1	..	..
Griswold, David	2	..	..	..	1	2	1	..	1	..	..
Griswold, Jonathan	3	..	1	1	..	2	1	1	1	..	..
Griswold, Willis	..	..	..	1	..	2	..	1	..	..	..
Grovener, Israel	3	..	..	1	..	2	..	..	1	..	..
MIDDLETOWN—con.											
Harmon, Nehemiah	..	..	..	..	1	..	..	..	..	1	..
Harmon, Selah	..	1	..	..	1	..	1	..	..	1	..
Harrington, Brooks	..	..	1	..	..	..	1	1	1	..	..
Haynes, Jonathan	..	1	1	..	1	3	2	2	1	..	..
Haynes, Sylvanus Rev.	1	..	..	1	..	2	..	..	1	..	..
Hazleton, Daniel	..	1	..	1	..	2	2	..	1	..	..
Hazon, Reuben	..	..	1	..	1	1	..	2	..	..	..
Herrick, Daniel	..	..	1	..	..	1	..	1	..	..	..
Herrick, David	..	..	1	..	..	..	1	..	..	..	..
Herrick, Denison	..	..	1	..	..	..	..	..	..	1	..
Hill, Libbeus	..	..	..	1	..	3	..	1	..	..	..
Hoskins, Benjamin	..	3	1	..	1	1	1	1	1	..	..
Hoskins, Richard	4	2	..	1	..	..	2	..	1	..	..
Hubbard, Abel	1	1	..	..	1	3	1	1	1	..	..
Hubbard, Jesse	1	2	1	..	2	..	1	1	..	1	..
Hubbard, Selah Jr.	..	1	..	1	..	1	1	1	1	..	..
Huff, Samuel	..	..	1	..	..	..	..	..	..	..	..
Huntington, Thomas	3	..	1	1	..	1	2	..	1	..	..
Hutchins, Samuel	3	..	..	1	..	1	..	1	1	..	..
Ingolson, Josiah J.	1	..	..	1	..	4	..	..	1	..	..
Jones, Oliver	2	..	..	1	..	1	..	..	1	..	..
Keyes, David	1	2	1	..	1	3	..	..	1	..	..
Leach, Moses	2	..	..	1	..	..	2	1	1	..	..
Leffingwell, Dyer	..	..	..	1	..	..	..	1	..	..	..
Leffingwell, Jeremiah	1	1	1	1	..	1	..	2	..	..	..
Leonard, Jared	..	..	..	1	..	..	..	..	..	..	..
Loomis, Fitch	1	..	..	1	..	2	..	..	1	..	..
Loomis, Reuben	..	..	..	..	1	1	..	..	..	1	..
Lovell, Joseph	2	..	1	..	1	1	..	1	1	..	..
Mahanna, Silas	..	..	1	..	..	..	..	..	..	..	..
Mahuram, Amasa	1	..	..	1	..	3	..	..	1	..	..
Mahuram, David	1	1	1	..	1	..	1	..	1	..	..
Mahuram, Hezekiah	..	..	1	..	..	..	1	..	1	1	..
Mahuram, John	1	..	..	1	..	3	..	..	1	..	..
Mahuram, Jonathan	2	..	..	1	..	..	1	..	1	..	..
Mallory, Silas	3	2	..	..	2	2	..	..	..	1	..
Mattason, Elijah	1	..	..	1	..	1	..	..	1	..	..
Mattason, Obadiah	2	2	1	1	..	1	1	..	1	..	..
McCluer, James	1	..	2	..	1	..	1	2	..	1	..
Mear, Richard	..	..	2	..	..	..	..	..	..	..	..
Miner, Gideon, Jr.	2	..	..	1	..	2	..	1	..	..	..
Miner, Joel	..	..	1	1	1	..	..	1	..	1	..
Miner, Lewis	1	1	..	1	..	1	1	..	1	..	..
Morgan, Nathan	..	..	..	1	..	2	..	..	1	..	..
Morgan, Thomas	1	..	1	..	1	..	1	..	..	1	..
Murrey, Alexander	..	..	..	1	..	1	1	..	1	..	..
Newel, Darius	..	..	..	1	1	1	..	..	1	1	..
Newland, Briar	..	..	1	..	..	..	..	..	..	..	..
Northrop, Samuel	1	..	1	1	..	1	1	..	1	..	..
Oatman, Eli	..	..	1	..	..	..	1	..	..	..	..
Oatman, Eliakim	..	..	1	..	..	..	..	1	..	..	..
Oatman, George	..	1	..	1	..	..	1	..	1	..	..
Paige, John	2	..	..	1	..	..	..	1	..	..	..
Perkins, Frances	2	1	1	1	..	2	1	..	1	..	..
Perry, Azer	..	1	1	1	..	4	2	1	1	..	..
Perry, Ezekiel	2	1	..	..	1	3	2	2	1	..	..
Pickle, John	..	..	1	..	..	..	..	..	..	..	..
Pratt, Samuel	1	2	1	1	..	1	..	..	1	..	..
Rathbun, Wait	2	..	1	..	..	..	..	1	..	..	..
Record, Ambrose	1	..	..	1	..	1	..	..	1	1	..
Record, Nathan	..	1	..	1	..	..	1	..	1	..	..
Record, Uriah	..	..	..	..	1	..	..	..	..	..	..
Richardson, Stephen	..	..	..	1	..	1	..	..	1	..	..
Roberts, Asher	..	..	1	..	..	..	..	..	..	..	..
Rockwell, Solomon	2	..	..	1	1	1	..	..	1	1	..
Rudd, Baruck	2	..	..	1	..	2	1	..	1	..	..
Rudd, Increase	..	..	1	..	1	..	1	..	..	1	..
Rudd, Johnson	1	..	..	1	..	..	..	1	..	..	..
Rudd, Silas	2	1	2	..	1	3	2	1	1	..	..
Satchel, Jeremiah	1	2	1	1	..	..	2	..	1	..	..
Scott, Jonathan	..	..	1	..	..	..	..	1	..	..	..
Scott, Oliver	3	..	..	1	..	..	..	1	..	..	..
Semple, John	2	..	..	1	..	..	..	1	..	..	..
Semple, William	..	..	..	1	..	..	..	..	..	..	..
Shepardson, Ansil	2	2	..	1	..	1	..	..	2	1	..
Skinner, Zeri	3	1	..	1	..	1	..	..	1	..	..
Smith, Amos	..	..	1	..	..	1	..	1	..	..	..

RUTLAND COUNTY—Continued

NAMES OF HEADS OF FAMILIES	FREE WHITE MALES: Under 10 years of age	FREE WHITE MALES: Of 10 and under 16	FREE WHITE MALES: Of 16 and under 26 including heads of families	FREE WHITE MALES: Of 26 and under 45 including heads of families	FREE WHITE MALES: Of 45 and upwards including heads of families.	FREE WHITE FEMALES: Under 10 years of age	FREE WHITE FEMALES: Of 10 and under 16	FREE WHITE FEMALES: Of 16 and under 26 including heads of families	FREE WHITE FEMALES: Of 26 and under 45 including heads of families	FREE WHITE FEMALES: Of 45 and upwards including heads of families	All other free persons except Indians not taxed
MIDDLETOWN—con.											
Smith, James	2	1	1	1	..	3	3	1	1	..	..
Smith, Peter	..	..	..	..	1	1	..	..	..	1	..
Smith, Reuben	..	..	..	1	..	..	..	1	..	1	..
Smith, Timothy	3	..	..	1	..	2	2	1	1	..	..
Spalding, Jeremiah	3	1	..	1	..	..	..	1	..	..	..
Spalding, John	..	..	..	1	..	..	..	1	..	..	..
Spalding, Joseph	..	..	1	..	1	1	..	..	..	2	..
Spalding, Joseph Jr.	4	..	..	..	1	1	..	..	1	..	..
Spicer, Samuel	2	..	1	..	..	1	..	..	1	..	..
Squier, Amasa	..	..	..	1	..	..	..	..	..	..	..
Squier, Gardner	..	1	..	1	..	3	..	..	1	..	..
Squier, Noble	..	..	..	1	..	2	..	..	1	..	..
Steven, Isaac	..	..	..	..	1	..	..	..	..	1	..
Stevens, Sperry	2	..	..	1	..	3	..	..	1	..	..
Stoddard, Philo	3	2	..	1	..	2	..	..	1	..	..
Stoddard, Samuel	..	1	..	1	..	..	2	1	1	..	..
Sumner, Shubal	2	1	..	1	..	2	1	..	1	..	..
Sunderlin, John	2	..	..	..	1	2	1	1	1	..	..
Sunderlin, Samuel	1	2	1	..	1	3	1	..	1	1	..
Thorn, Eliakim	1	..	..	1	..	2	1	..	..	..	..
Tisdall, Samuel	..	..	1	..	..	..	..	..	..	..	..
Townsend, Ambrose	2	..	..	1	..	1	1	..	1	..	..
Waldo, Gamaliel	..	2	..	1	..	1	1	2	..	1	..
Walker, Luther	2	..	..	1	..	2	..	..	1	..	..
Walton, Henry	2	2	..	1	..	2	..	..	1	..	1
Walton, Nathan	..	1	..	..	1	..	1	..	1	..	..
Wascott, Preserved	1	..	1	..	..	..	..	1	..	..	..
Wetherby, Simonnagus	..	..	..	..	1	..	..	1	..	1	..
White, Caleb	..	1	..	1	..	4	1	..	1	..	..
Williams, Obadiah	..	..	..	1	..	..	..	1	..	..	..
Wood, Ebenezer	2	1	..	1	..	1	..	1	1	..	..
Wood, Ephraim	..	2	..	1	..	5	1	1	1	..	..
Wood, Ephraim Jr.	..	..	1	..	..	..	..	1	..	..	..
Wood, Jacob	..	1	..	..	1	1	..	1	..	2	..
Wood, Moseley	..	1	..	1	..	1	..	1	..	1	..
Wood, Nathaniel	..	..	..	..	1	..	..	1	..	1	..
Wood, Nathaniel Jr.	3	..	..	1	..	..	1	..	1	..	..
UNCERTAIN NAME											
Garet (?), Alexander	..	2	..	1	..	3	1	..	1	..	..
MOUNT HOLLY											
Adams, Alden	1	..	..	1	..	4	3	..	1	..	..
Andrus, Titus	2	..	2	..	1	1	1	2	1	..	..
Barber, Hoxxy	1	1	..	1	..	2	..	..	1	..	..
Barns, Nathaniel	3	..	..	1	..	1	..	1	..	..	..
Beall, George	2	..	..	1	..	1	..	..	1	..	..
Benson, Benoni	2	2	..	..	1	1	1	1	1	..	..
Bent, David	3	1	1	2	..	1	3	1	1	..	..
Bent, Peter	1	..	1	..	..	..	..	1	..	..	..
Bigalow, Levi	..	..	..	1	..	1	..	..	1	..	..
Bigalow, Nathan	1	3	1	..	1	1	..	2	..	1	..
Bigsby, David	..	1	..	1	..	..	..	..	..	1	2
Bigsby, Joseph	3	..	..	1	..	..	..	..	1	..	..
Bingham, Silas	..	..	..	1	..	..	..	..	1	..	..
Boice, Lucius	..	..	..	1	..	2	..	..	1	..	..
Brown, Benjamin	1	..	..	1	..	..	..	1	1	..	..
Brown, William	..	..	1	..	..	..	..	..	..	..	..
Bruce, Thomas	..	..	..	1	..	1	..	1	..	..	..
Chase, Solomon	..	..	..	1	..	2	..	1	..	..	..
Chatterton, David	1	..	..	1	..	2	..	..	1	..	..
Clark, Chauncey	2	1	..	1	..	1	2	..	1	..	..
Clark, Googer	1	1	3	..	1	2	1	..	1	..	..
Clark, Levi	..	..	1	..	..	..	..	1	..	..	..
Clark, Levi	1	..	..	1	..	1	..	..	1	..	..
Clark, Stephen	..	1	4	..	1	3	1	..	1	..	..
Cook, George	..	..	..	..	1	..	..	..	..	1	..
Cook, Peter	1	..	1	..	..	..	..	1	..	..	..
Cook, Samuel	4	..	..	1	..	1	..	..	1	..	..
Crandal, Pardon	1	1	..	1	..	1	..	..	1	..	..
Croley, George	..	..	..	1	..	1	..	1	..	..	..
Crowley, Abraham	..	1	..	..	1	..	2	..	..	1	..
Crowley, John	3	..	..	1	..	1	..	..	1	..	..
Crowley, Royal	2	..	..	1	..	2	..	..	1	..	..
Crowley, Walter	2	..	1	..	..	1	..	1	..	..	..
Davenport, Clark	..	..	..	1	..	1	..	1	..	..	..
Davenport, Daniel	..	1	..	..	1	..	..	1	..	1	..
Dawley, Perrigrine	2	1	2	1	..	4	1	..	1	..	..
Dickerman, Amasa	1	1	..	1	1	..	..	1	..	..	..
Dickerman, Isaac	2	..	..	1	..	..	..	1	..	..	..
MOUNT HOLLY—con.											
Dickerman, Lyman	2	..	..	1	..	1	..	1	..	..	..
Dickerman, Simeon	2	..	..	1	..	1	..	1	..	..	..
Dickinson, Dan	3	..	..	1	..	1	..	..	1	..	..
Doolittle, Nathan	1	..	1	..	..	1	..	1	..	..	..
Douglass, William	1	..	..	..	1	1	..	..	..	1	..
Farewell, Abel	..	1	1	..	1	..	1	1	..	1	..
Farewell, Solomon	..	..	..	1	..	1	..	1	..	..	..
Fish, Isaac	3	..	..	1	..	1	..	..	1	..	..
Fletcher, Gershom	1	1	..	..	1	..	1	1	..	1	..
Fletcher, Stephen	1	..	1	..	..	1	..	1	..	..	..
Foster, Daniel	3	1	..	..	..	1	1	1	..	1	..
Freman, Daniel	..	..	..	..	1	1	..	..	..	1	..
Frost, Benjamin	1	..	..	1	..	2	..	..	1	..	..
Frost, Joseph	2	1	2	1	..	3	..	..	1	..	..
Gardner, John	1	..	..	..	1	1	..	..	1	..	..
Gernsey, Oliver	1	..	1	..	..	..	..	1	..	..	..
Gillet, Moses	2	2	..	1	..	2	..	..	1	..	..
Gipson, John	..	1	..	1	..	1	1	1	1	..	..
Gould, Isaac	..	..	..	..	1	..	..	..	..	1	..
Gould, Reuben	..	..	1	..	..	1	..	1	..	..	..
Green, Absolom	..	..	1	..	..	1	..	1	..	..	..
Green, Gardner	1	..	..	..	1	1	..	..	1	..	..
Green, John	1	1	1	..	1	3	3	1	..	..	..
Green, Parker	4	..	..	1	..	1	..	..	1	..	..
Hadley, John	..	..	1	..	2	..	..	1	..	..	..
Hadley, Jonas	2	1	1	1	1	2	2	..	1	1	..
Hammon, Jedediah	2	1	..	1	..	3	..	..	1	..	..
Hill, David	..	..	1	..	..	..	..	..	..	..	..
Hines, Collins	1	..	1	..	..	2	..	1	..	..	..
Holden, Jonas	2	1	1	..	1	2	..	1	..	..	..
Horton, Aaron	1	1	..	1	..	4	1	..	1	..	..
Ives, Ebenezer	..	..	..	1	..	1	..	..	1	..	..
Ives, Jonah	3	2	..	..	1	2	..	..	1	..	..
Jackson, Abraham	..	1	2	..	1	..	1	..	..	1	..
Kinney, Joseph	1	..	..	1	..	..	..	..	1	..	..
Lawrance, Richard	..	..	..	1	..	1	1	..	..	..	..
Lawrence, Simeon	..	1	..	1	..	1	2	..	..	1	..
Loomis, Joseph	..	..	..	..	1	..	..	..	1	..	..
Loomis, Silas	1	..	..	1	..	..	..	..	1	..	..
Loomis, Solomon	1	1	..	1	..	4	1	..	1	1	..
Mattason, James	1	..	..	1	..	2	..	..	1	..	..
Miller, Ebenezer	1	..	..	1	..	2	1	..	1	..	..
Miller, Hannah	..	..	..	..	..	3	..	1	..	..	..
Monger, Joshua	..	..	1	..	..	..	..	..	..	..	..
Moore, Abraham	2	1	..	1	..	2	..	..	1	..	..
Moore, Hezekiah	1	..	1	..	..	1	..	1	..	..	..
Moore, John	..	1	1	..	1	..	2	1	..	1	..
Parker, Elias	..	..	..	1	..	1	..	1	..	..	..
Parker, Leonard	2	1	..	1	..	2	1	..	1	..	..
Patch, John	3	1	..	1	..	2	1	..	1	..	..
Peck, Elijah	2	1	1	1	..	2	1	..	1	..	..
Pengry, Jonathan	1	1	..	1	..	3	..	1	1	..	..
Pengry, Joseph	1	..	..	1	..	3	1	..	1	1	..
Pengry, Nathaniel	5	..	..	1	..	2	..	..	1	..	..
Peters, Israel	2	..	..	..	1	3	2	1	1	..	..
Prescott, Zachariah	1	..	..	1	..	1	..	1	..	..	..
Procktor, Silas	1	2	..	..	1	3	..	..	1	..	..
Randall, Samuel	..	..	2	..	..	..	..	1	..	..	..
Russel, Benjamin	1	..	1	..	..	1	..	..	1	..	..
Russel, Henry	1	..	1	..	..	..	..	1	..	..	..
Russel, John	..	..	1	..	1	..	..	..	..	..	..
Russel, Samuel	..	..	..	..	1	..	..	1	..	1	..
Russel, Samuel B.	1	..	..	1	..	1	1	..	1	..	..
Sadler, Benjamin	1	..	..	1	..	1	..	1	..	..	..
Sanford, Peter	..	..	1	..	..	..	..	..	..	..	..
Sargant, Enoch	..	..	1	..	..	1	..	1	..	..	..
Sargant, Samuel	1	..	..	1	..	..	..	1	..	..	..
Sargant, Timothy	1	2	..	..	1	..	1	..	..	1	..
Sargant, Timothy Jr.	2	..	1	..	..	..	..	..	1	..	..
Shaw, John	3	..	..	1	..	..	..	1	..	..	..
Spencer, Jabez	3	..	..	1	..	1	3	..	1	..	..
Tarble, Edmund	..	..	..	1	..	3	..	1	..	..	..
Tarble, James	..	..	1	..	..	..	..	..	..	..	..
Todd, Jared	..	..	1	..	..	1	..	1	..	..	..
Todd, Job	1	..	1	1	1	1	..	1	..	1	..

RUTLAND COUNTY—Continued

NAMES OF HEADS OF FAMILIES	FREE WHITE MALES: Under 10 years of age	FREE WHITE MALES: Of 10 and under 16	FREE WHITE MALES: Of 16 and under 26 including heads of families	FREE WHITE MALES: Of 26 and under 45 including heads of families	FREE WHITE MALES: Of 45 and upwards including heads of families	FREE WHITE FEMALES: Under 10 years of age	FREE WHITE FEMALES: Of 10 and under 16	FREE WHITE FEMALES: Of 16 and under 26 including heads of families	FREE WHITE FEMALES: Of 26 and under 45 including heads of families	FREE WHITE FEMALES: Of 45 and upwards including heads of families	All other free persons except Indians not taxed
MOUNT HOLLY—con.											
Todd, Ruel	2			1		1			1		
Townsend, Joshua				1		1			1		
Tucker, Stephen	3			1		2			1		
Wells, Perry	1			1		1		1			
White, Daniel	2		1			2		1			
White, Hosea	3			1		1		1			
Wilcox, Jacob	2	1		1		2	1	2	1		
Wilson, Abner			2			2		1			
UNCERTAIN NAME											
Miller, E———(?)			1		1	2	1		1		
ORWELL											
Abbott, Seth	1			1		2			1		
Abel, Daniel B.	2			1					1		
Abel, Henry	2	1	1			1		1	1		
Abel, Isiah			1		1		1		1	1	
Allen, Elisha	2	1		1		2	1		1	1	
Ames, Abner	1	1		1		2	1	1	1		
Appollos, Austin			1	1		1		3			
Ashley, Zebulon	2			1		3			1		
Austin, Josiah	1			1							
Babcock, John	2		1	1		2	1		2		
Bacon, Nathaniel	4			1				1	1		
Baker, Israel			1								
Bakeworth, Ezekiel					1				1		
Ballard, Luke	1	1			1	2			1	1	
Barker, William				1							
Barnett, Barnabas	2		1						1		
Bascom, Dorus				1				1		1	
Bascom, Elias			2		1			1	2		
Bascom, Elias Jr.	2	1		1		2		1		1	
Bascom, Zeri	1			1					1		
Bebee, Avery I.	3			1		1			1		
Becket, Levi			1								
Becket, Walter				1					1		
Belcher, William					1		1			1	
Benson, Elliss			1	1	1	1		1		1	
Benson, Prince	5			1		1			1		
Benson, Seth				1			1	1			
Bisby, Benjamin			1	1	1		1	1		1	
Bisby, Joseph	1		1					1			
Bisby, Robert	1			1		3			1		
Blake, Obadiah		2		1					1		
Blakely, Jonathan			1		1			1			
Blanchard, John					1		1			1	
Blandon, Daniel	1			1		2			1		
Blinn, Jonathan				1	1	1			1		1
Booth, Reuben	3			1				1			
Bottom, Jesse	1	1		1		1	1		1		
Bottom, Roswell	1	1		1				1			
Bowers, John				1		2			1		
Bowers, Samuel	1			1		1	1	2	1		
Bramble, Dan	3			1		1			1		
Branch, Darius	3			1		1	1		1		
Brewer, Archibald	2			1		3			1		
Brewer, Samuel					1					1	
Bridge, Jesse	2			1		4	1		1		
Bridge, Reuben			1								
Brooks, Jonas	1			1				1			
Brown, David	1			1		2	1		1		
Brown, Luther	3			1		2	2	1	1		
Brundige, Joseph	1	1		1		2			1		
Brush, Stephen		3	1		1	1		2		1	
Brush, Stephen Jr.	1			1		1		1	1		
Buel, Daniel	3	1		1	1	1	1	1	1	1	
Castle, Joel	1	1	1		1	1			1		
Catlin, Hosea			1								
Chamberlin, Reuben	1			1		2			1		
Chapin, Syrenus Rev.	1			1		1	1	1	1		
Charter, John	2	1	1		1	1			1		
Choat, Alpheus				1				1			
Choat, William					1					1	
Choat, William Jr.	1	2		1		3	1		1		
Clark, Cyrus		1	3		1	1	2			1	
Clark, Josiah	1	1	1		1	1	1	1	1		
Clark, Lemuel		1	3		1		2	2		1	
Clark, Lemuel Jr.			1					1			
Clark, Smith		1	1		1	2	1			1	
Conkey, Asaph	1	1	1		1	3				1	
Conkey, James	1			1		1		1			
Conkey, Joshua	4	2			1	2	2		1		
ORWELL—con.											
Cook, David	3			1		3			1		
Cook, Ivory	3			1		2	1		1		
Cook, Reuben					1		1			1	
Cook, Samuel			2		1				1		
Cook, Samuel Jr.			1								
Crouch, Richard			1	1			1			1	
Cutteen, David	2		2		1	1		1	1	1	
Cutteen, Elijah	1	1		1		1					
Cutts, Thomas	2			1		1		1			
Darby, Roger	1			1		1		1			
Darby, William				1	1				1	1	
Dickinson, John				1				2			
Dow, Isaiah	1	1		1		1			1		
Dresser, Moses	1			1		1	1		1		
Dunham, Caleb	2			1		2	1		1		
Eggleston, Ebenezer			2					1			
Fisher, Ephraim	1	2	1		1	3	1		1		
Fisher, William		1	1	1					1		
Fisk, David	2	1			1			1		1	
Fuller, Asa			1					1			
Fuller, Benjamin				1		4		1			
Fuller, Jacob					1	1				1	
Fuller, William	2	2	1	1		1			1		
Galpin, William			1			1			1		
Gleason, Ebenezer	1			1	1	1			1		
Griswold, Alvin	1			1		1			1		
Griswold, Ebenezer	2		2		1		1			1	
Griswold, Jedediah	1			1	2	1			1		
Griswold, Rufus	2			1		2		1			
Griswold, Samuel	4	2	1	1					1		
Hale, Gershom			1	1	1				1		1
Hale, Israel	2				1			1		2	
Hale, Samuel	1	1	2		1			1	1		
Hall, Asael	1	2			1		1	1		1	
Hall, Bethuel	1			1		1			1		
Hall, Elihu	2	1		1			2		1		
Hall, Peter	2	2	1	1			1		1		
Hall, Peter P.			1			1		1			
Harris, John		1	1	1		1	1			1	
Hibbord, Jere	1	2	1			2	1	1	1		
Hibbord, Timothy	3			1		1	1		1		
Higgliston, Thomas	2	2			1	1	1			1	
Hill, Moses	1			1		1			1		
Hinman, Adonijah	2		1	1		2	1		1		
Hollenbeck, John	1			1			1			1	
Holt, Joshua	1		1					1			
Humphrey, Rufus	3			1					1		
Humphrey, Thomas	1	1	1		1	1				1	
Hurlbert, Ebenezer	4	1	1		1	1	2	1	1		
Judd, Allen			2			1		1			
Kelly, William				1				1			
Kelsey, Isaac	1	2		1		2	1			1	
Kendal, Smith				1							
Keyes, Pebody		1		1		2			1		
Kidar, Ephraim			2								
Kinsley, Jason	2		1	1		1			1		
Knapp, Jabez	1		1	1	1		1	1			1
Knapp, Joshua	1			1		1		1			
Knapp, Moses	1			1				1			
Knapp, William		2	2	1		4		1	1		
Lapish, John					1						
Lathrop, Solomon		1		1		2		1			
Leonard, David		2	1		1	1		2		1	
Leonard, Moses				1				1			
Linsey, Amherst				1				1			
Linsey, John	2	1		1		2		1			
Long, Stephen	1			1		2		1			
Lyon, Moses	2			1			1	1			
Mallory, Eleazer					1						
Martin, Wheeler	2			1		1		1			
Mayo, Nathaniel	1	1	2			1		2		1	
Miner, Christopher	1	1	1	1		2			1		
Moffit, Eli				1				1			
Molton, Salmon			1								
Monger, Joseph		3	2		1		1		1		
Moon, Jesse	3			1					1		
Morton, Martin					1		1			1	
Morton, Martin Jr.	1			1				1			

RUTLAND COUNTY—Continued

NAMES OF HEADS OF FAMILIES	FREE WHITE MALES					FREE WHITE FEMALES					
	Under 10 years of age	Of 10 and under 16	Of 16 and under 26 including heads of families	Of 26 and under 45 including heads of families	Of 45 and upwards including heads of families.	Under 10 years of age	Of 10 and under 16	Of 16 and under 26 including heads of families	Of 26 and under 45 including heads of families	Of 45 and upwards including heads of families	All other free persons except Indians not taxed
ORWELL—con.											
Morton, Richard	..	1	..	..	1	..	1	..	..	..	..
Mott, John	..	..	2	..	1	3	2	1	..	1	..
Motton, Ephraim R.	..	1	..	1	..	3	1	1	1	..	..
Murrey, Eber	..	2	1	..	1	..	1	1	..	2	..
Needam, John	2	..	..	1	..	1	..	1	..	..	..
Noble, James	..	..	1	..	1	..	..	..	..	1	..
Noble, Russel	..	1	..	1	..	1	..	1	..	..	..
Ormsby, James	..	..	..	1	..	..	..	..	..	..	..
Osburn, Joseph	1	..	..	1	..	..	..	1	..	..	..
Owen, Frederick	3	1	..	..	1	..	1	1	..	1	..
Palmer, Amos	..	..	..	..	1	..	1	..	..	1	..
Palmer, Asa	..	..	1	..	..	..	..	1	..	..	..
Parks, Asa	4	1	2	1	..	..	1	..	1	1	..
Parks, Jesse	1	..	..	1	..	..	1	..	..	..	..
Parks, Nathan	..	1	..	1	..	1	1	..	1	..	..
Pearce, John	1	..	2	..	1	1	1	1	..	1	..
Pebble, Samuel	1	..	..	1	..	3	2	..	1	..	..
Perkins, Westly	..	2	..	1	..	3	..	1	1	..	..
Peters, Bunsley	3	..	..	1	..	2	..	2	1	..	..
Pettebone, Luman	4	..	..	1	..	..	1	..	1	..	..
Phelps, Elnathan	..	..	..	..	1	..	..	1	..	1	..
Phelps, Elnathan Jr.	2	..	..	1	..	1	..	1	..	..	..
Phelps, Jacob	..	..	1	..	..	..	..	1	..	..	..
Pike, Timothy	..	..	..	1	..	..	..	..	..	..	..
Ranney, William	..	1	3	1	..	2	..	1	..	..	..
Reynolds, Peter	4	1	..	1	..	2	1	2	1	..	..
Rice, Eli	2	..	..	1	..	3	1	..	1	..	..
Rice, Jacob	..	..	..	..	1	..	..	..	..	1	..
Rice, Jonas	..	1	1	..	1	..	1	1	1	..	..
Rice, Nehemiah	1	2	..	1	1	1	1	..	1	..	..
Root, Eli	1	..	..	1	..	1	1	..	1	..	..
Rowley, Parsons	1	..	..	1	..	2	..	..	1	..	..
Rust, Daniel	..	..	1	1	1	..	..	..	..	1	..
Rust, Daniel Jr.	..	..	..	1	..	..	..	1	..	..	..
Rust, Quartus	..	..	1	1	..	1	..	1	..	..	..
Sanford, Clark	..	..	..	1	..	1	..	1	..	..	..
Sanford, Joseph	1	..	2	1	1	..	..	2	..	1	..
Scovel, Ephraim	2	..	..	1	..	1	1	..	1	..	..
Scovel, Nathan	1	..	..	1	1	1	..	1	..	..	..
Scovel, Thomas	1	1	2	1	..	2	..	1	..	1	..
Sears, Abram	4	1	..	..	1	..	..	..	..	1	..
Seymour, Roger	..	1	..	1	..	..	..	2	1	..	..
Slicer, John	..	1	2	..	1	..	2	..	..	1	..
Slutson, Thomas	1	..	..	1	..	3	..	..	1	..	..
Smith, Abijah	2	..	..	1	..	1	1	..	1	..	..
Smith, Daniel	..	..	..	1	..	..	..	1	..	..	..
Smith, Feron	..	..	1	..	..	..	..	1	..	..	..
Smith, Jehiel	1	3	1	1	..	2	..	1	1	..	..
Smith, Joab	1	..	1	1	..	2	..	..	1	..	..
Smith, Joel	1	..	..	1	..	1	..	..	1	..	..
Smith, Plinny	2	1	1	1	..	1	1	..	1	..	..
Smith, Reuben	..	1	..	1	..	..	1	..	1	..	..
Southwick, Jonathan	..	..	..	1	..	1	..	1	..	..	..
Spalding, Samson	..	1	2	..	1	4	..	..	1	..	..
Spalding, Simeon	2	1	1	1	..	2	1	..	1	..	..
Spencer, Rachel	2	1	..	..	..	1	..	..	1	..	..
Spooner, Paul	3	..	..	1	..	1	..	..	1	..	..
Stacey, Ebenezer	4	..	..	1	..	1	..	..	1	..	..
Staples, William	1	..	..	1	..	..	..	1	..	..	..
Starns, Starling	..	1	..	1	..	4	..	..	1	..	..
Stevens, Adam	..	..	..	..	1	..	..	..	1	..	..
Stevens, Darius	1	..	1	..	3	..	..	1	..	..	..
Stevens, Michael	..	..	1	..	..	1	..	1	..	..	..
Stewert, Charles	2	1	..	1	..	1	..	..	1	..	..
Story, Asa	4	..	..	1	..	..	..	1	..	..	..
Thare, Daniel	..	..	1	..	..	..	..	..	..	..	..
Thare, Ezra	..	..	..	1	..	..	..	1	..	1	..
Thatcher, James	..	..	..	1	..	..	..	..	..	..	..
Thomas, Joseph	1	1	..	1	..	2	..	..	1	..	..
Thomson, David	1	..	..	1	..	2	..	1	..	..	..
Thomson, Jonathan	1	..	..	1	..	1	..	..	1	..	..
Tinney, Isaac	..	..	1	..	..	..	..	1	..	..	..
Toles, John	..	..	..	1	..	1	..	1	..	..	..
Tracey, Abdiel	1	..	..	1	..	1	..	..	1	..	..
Wait, Henry	2	2	1	1	..	2	..	..	1	..	..
Wallace, John	..	1	2	..	1	1	..	..	..	1	..
Ward, Ruggles	1	1	..	1	..	3	2	1	1	..	..
Warren, David	..	..	1	..	..	..	1	..	..	..	..
Warren, David	1	1	3	..	1	1	1	1	1	..	..
Warren, Jabish	2	1	1	1	..	1	2	..	1	..	..
Warren, Jabish Jr.	..	..	1	..	..	1	..	1	..	..	..
Weaver, William	1	..	..	1	..	..	..	1	..	1	..
Webb, Ebenezer	1	1	1	1	..	2	1	..	1	..	..
Webster, Samuel Rev.	1	1	2	..	1	..	1	1	1	..	..
White, John	..	..	..	1	..	..	..	..	..	..	..
White, Joshua	3	1	..	..	1	1	1	2	1	..	..
White, Ruluff	2	1	..	1	..	2	3	..	1	..	..
Wilcox, Ebenezer	3	..	..	1	..	1	..	1	..	..	..
Williams, Ezra	..	..	2	1	1	3	..	..	1	..	..
Williams, John	2	2	..	1	..	1	1	..	1	..	..
Wilson, Ebenezer	2	1	1	..	1	2	1	..	1	..	..
Wilson, Isaac	..	..	1	..	..	..	..	1	..	..	..
Wilson, Michael	..	..	..	..	1	..	..	..	..	1	..
Wilson, Michael Jr.	2	1	..	1	..	2	1	..	1	..	..
Winchester, James	3	1	..	1	..	..	1	..	1	..	..
Wood, Charles	2	..	..	1	..	2	..	1	..	..	..
Woodard, James	..	2	3	1	1	1	1	1	..	1	..
Wright, Asael	..	..	1	..	..	1	..	1	..	..	..
Wright, Benjamin	..	..	..	1	..	..	..	1	..	..	..
Wright, Eliphalet	..	1	..	1	..	2	..	..	1	..	..
Wright, Isaac	..	..	1	..	..	..	..	..	..	..	..
Wright, Jacob	1	1	..	1	..	3	..	..	1	..	..
Young, John	2	..	..	1	..	1	1	..	1	..	..
Young, Simeon	2	2	..	1	..	..	1	..	1	..	..
PAWLET											
Adams, Cyrus	..	..	..	1	..	..	..	..	..	..	..
Adams, Gideon	..	..	..	..	1	1	1	..	1	1	..
Adams, Israel	2	..	..	1	..	2	..	..	1	..	..
Adams, Jesse	1	1	2	1	..	1	2	..	1	..	..
Adams, John	..	1	..	1	..	1	..	..	1	..	..
Adkins, Isaiah	1	1	..	1	..	1	1	..	1	..	..
Allen, Caleb	1	..	2	..	1	..	..	2	1	..	..
Alten, Epenetus	..	..	2	..	..	2	..	..	1	1	..
Andrus, Asa	..	..	..	..	1	..	1	1	..	1	..
Andrus, Asa Jr.	1	..	1	..	..	..	..	1	..	..	..
Andrus, Desire	..	..	1	..	..	..	1	..	..	1	..
Andrus, William	..	..	1	..	..	..	..	..	..	..	..
Andrus, Zebadiah	1	1	2	..	2	..	1	..	..	1	..
Armstrong, Joseph	..	2	1	..	1	..	2	2	..	1	..
Arnold, Jonathan	2	1	1	1	..	2	..	..	1	..	..
Ashley, Noah	1	..	..	1	..	1	..	1	..	..	..
Aspinwall, Eleazer	1	1	1	..	1	2	..	1	1	..	..
Avery, Elisha	2	..	1	..	1	2	2	1	1	..	..
Avery, Moses	2	1	..	1	1	3	1	..	1	1	..
Baker, Ebenezer	1	1	..	1	..	2	1	..	1	..	..
Baker, Elijah	..	..	..	..	1	..	..	..	..	1	..
Baker, Ichabod	1	..	1	1	..	1	1	..	1	..	..
Baker, Rufus	1	2	1	..	1	1	2	1	..	1	..
Baldrige, Daniel	..	..	..	1	..	3	..	1	..	..	..
Baldrige, Edward	1	1	..	1	..	..	..	1	..	..	..
Baldrige, Polly	..	..	..	..	..	..	2	2	..	1	..
Baldwin, Isaac	..	..	..	1	1	..	..	1	..	1	..
Baldwin, Isaac Jr.	3	1	..	1	..	3	..	..	1	..	..
Baldwin, Jeremiah	2	1	..	1	..	2	1	..	1	..	..
Baldwin, Jonas	..	..	..	1	..	3	..	..	1	..	..
Baldwin, Samuel	1	1	..	1	..	2	1	..	1	..	..
Barlow, John	..	..	..	1	..	1	..	1	..	..	..
Barns, Jared	1	1	..	1	..	1	..	..	1	..	..
Barr, Samuel	2	..	..	1	..	3	1	..	1	..	..
Bennet, Aaron	1	1	..	1	..	2	..	1	1	..	..
Bennet, Banks	..	..	1	..	1	..	..	1	..	1	..
Bennet, Lemuel	..	1	1	1	1	..	1	..	1	1	..
Bennet, Oliver	..	..	1	..	..	..	..	..	..	..	..
Bennett, Roswell	..	..	..	..	1	3	..	1	..	1	..
Betts, Selah	2	..	1	1	..	2	..	..	1	..	..
Blakeley, David	2	1	..	..	1	1	1	3	1	..	..
Blakeley, Jonathan	1	..	..	1	..	..	..	1	..	..	..
Blossom, Seth	2	..	..	1	..	3	..	..	1	..	..
Bradford, Joseph	2	..	..	1	..	..	..	1	1	..	..
Branch, Daniel	1	..	1	1	1	..	..	2	1	1	..
Brewster, Lydia	..	..	..	..	..	1	..	1	1	..	..
Brewster, Nathaniel	..	2	..	..	1	1	1	4	1	..	..
Brewster, Timothy	1	1	1	1	..	1	..	1	1	..	..
Brezie, William	..	2	1	..	1	3	..	..	..	1	..
Broughton, Ebenezer	5	..	..	1	..	1	..	1	1	..	..
Brown, Elijah	1	2	1	1	..	2	..	..	1	..	..
Brown, Selah	1	1	..	1	..	3	..	..	1	..	..
Brownson, Eldad	2	1	..	..	1	1	..	..	1	..	..
Buchet, Nathan	2	1	1	..	1	2	1	2	..	1	..
Buker, Miriam	3	..	..	..	..	2	2	..	..	1	..
Burns, David	2	..	..	1	..	..	..	1	..	..	..
Burton, Samuel	..	..	..	..	1	..	..	..	..	1	..
Bushnell, Abishai	2	..	1	..	1	..	2	..	1	..	..
Bushnell, Benajah	..	..	1	..	1	..	..	..	..	1	..

RUTLAND COUNTY—Continued

NAMES OF HEADS OF FAMILIES	FREE WHITE MALES: Under 10 years of age	FREE WHITE MALES: Of 10 and under 16	FREE WHITE MALES: Of 16 and under 26 including heads of families	FREE WHITE MALES: Of 26 and under 45 including heads of families	FREE WHITE MALES: Of 45 and upwards including heads of families	FREE WHITE FEMALES: Under 10 years of age	FREE WHITE FEMALES: Of 10 and under 16	FREE WHITE FEMALES: Of 16 and under 26 including heads of families	FREE WHITE FEMALES: Of 26 and under 45 including heads of families	FREE WHITE FEMALES: Of 45 and upwards including heads of families	All other free persons except Indians not taxed
PAWLET—con.											
Bushnell, Jay	..	..	1	..	1	..	..	1	..	1	..
Butts, Joshua	..	..	1	..	..	..	..	1	..	..	..
Butts, Nathaniel	1	..	..	1	..	2	1	..	1	..	..
Butts, Samuel	..	1	..	..	1	..	2	..	..	1	..
Butts, Samuel Jr	1	..	..	1	..	3	..	..	1	..	..
Carver, Nathaniel	2	1	..	1	..	1	1	..	1	..	..
Church, Titus	..	..	1	..	1	..	2	..	..	1	..
Clark, Daniel	5	..	..	1	..	..	1	..	1	1	..
Clark, Jehiel	..	..	1	..	..	..	..	1	..	..	..
Clark, Joseph	..	..	1	..	..	2	..	1	..	..	..
Clark, Ozias	1	1	1	1	..	2	1	..	1	..	..
Cleveland, Augustus	1	..	1	..	..	..	..	1	..	..	..
Cleveland, Calvin	..	..	..	2	..	..	..	..	1	1	..
Cleveland, David	1	1	1	..	..	1	..	1	..	..	..
Cleveland, David	..	..	..	1	..	..	1	1	..	..	..
Cleveland, Luther	..	..	..	1	..	..	..	1	..	..	..
Cleveland, Moses	1	1	..	..	1	..	1	..	..	1	..
Cleveland, Tracey	..	1	..	..	1	2	1	..	..	1	..
Cobb, John	2	2	1	..	1	2	3	1	1	1	..
Cobb, Joshua	2	..	2	..	1	2	3	1	1	..	..
Cobb, Mary	..	1	..	..	..	2	..	..	..	1	..
Coburn, Ebenezer	1	..	1	..	1	2	2	1	1	..	..
Colegrove, Jeremiah	..	3	1	..	1	1	..	1	..	1	..
Comstock, David	2	1	..	1	..	1	1	..	1	..	..
Conant, John	4	1	..	1	..	..	..	..	1	..	..
Cenklin, John	..	..	..	1	..	1	1	..	1	..	..
Cook, Titus A.	1	1	3	1	..	4	1	1	..	..	..
Cox, Robert	1	..	..	1	..	1	2	..	1	..	..
Crocker, Josiah	3	1	..	1	..	2	..	..	1	..	..
Curtiss, Aaron	1	..	1	..	..	1	1	1	..	..	..
Curtiss, David	..	..	1	..	..	..	..	..	..	..	..
Curtiss, Eldad	..	..	..	..	1	..	..	..	..	1	..
Davis, Edward	..	..	..	1	..	3	..	..	1	..	..
Denison, Daniel	1	1	1	..	1	..	..	..	..	1	..
Dimick, Thomas	..	..	..	..	1	..	..	..	..	1	..
Dixonson, Lewis	1	..	1	..	..	..	..	1	..	..	..
Dutton, Calvin	2	1	..	1	..	1	1	..	1	..	..
Eaton, Rice	1	..	1	..	..	..	..	1	..	..	..
Edgerton, Jacob	1	1	..	1	..	1	1	..	1	..	..
Edgerton, Jedidiah	2	2	1	1	..	2	1	..	1	..	..
Edgerton, John	..	..	1	..	..	..	..	1	..	..	..
Edgerton, Simeon	..	1	..	1	1	2	1	..	..	1	..
Ethrige, Thomas	..	..	..	..	1	1	..	..	..	1	..
Evans, Abiathar	..	..	..	..	1	1	..	..	..	1	..
Evans, Abiathar Jr.	..	..	1	..	..	..	..	1	..	..	..
Evans, Frederick	2	..	1	..	..	2	..	1	..	..	..
Field, Asa	3	..	..	1	..	1	1	1	1	..	..
Fitch, Benjamin	3	..	1	1	..	1	..	1	1	..	..
Fitch, Daniel	..	2	2	..	1	1	1	1	..	1	..
Fitch, Ephraim	..	2	..	1	..	2	..	2	..	..	..
Fitch, Israel	1	..	..	1	..	1	..	2	..	..	..
Fitch, Joseph	1	..	..	..	1	2	..	..	..	1	..
Fitch, Richard	..	1	..	..	1	..	1	..	..	1	..
Foster, Dan	2	..	..	1	..	2	1	..	1	..	..
Foster, Jeremiah	..	..	..	..	1	..	1	..	..	1	..
Foster, Thomas	..	..	1	..	..	..	..	1	..	..	..
Frasar, Simeon	1	..	..	1	..	3	..	..	1	..	..
Fullor, John	2	1	..	1	..	4	1	1	1	..	..
Gernsey, Amos	1	1	..	1	..	2	..	..	1	..	..
Gibbs, Harmon	1	..	..	1	..	1	..	1	..	..	..
Gibbs, Zebulon	1	..	1	..	..	1	..	..	1	..	..
Gifford. Gideon	3	..	..	1	..	2	..	..	1	..	..
Gilbert, John	1	2	..	1	..	4	..	1	1	..	..
Gillett, Samuel	..	..	..	..	1	..	..	..	..	1	..
Gilmore, David	2	1	1	..	1	3	1	..	1	..	..
Ginnings, Ebenezer	..	..	1	..	..	..	..	..	..	..	..
Goodspeed, Samuel	2	1	..	1	..	4	2	..	1	..	..
Googins, Samuel	2	..	..	1	..	..	3	..	1	..	..
Gordon, Samuel	..	1	..	1	..	2	..	..	1	..	..
Gould, Edmund	3	2	..	1	..	3	1	..	1	..	..
Gould, Joseph	3	..	..	1	..	..	..	1	..	..	..
Gould, Willard	..	2	..	1	..	..	..	..	..	1	..
Grant, John	2	2	..	..	1	2	1	..	1	..	..
Gregory, Sylvanus	1	1	2	1	..	2	1	1	1	..	..
Griswold, Ahira	..	..	1	..	..	..	..	..	..	..	..
Griswold, John Rev.	1	..	..	1	1	3	1	1	1	..	..
Grovnor, Elizabeth	..	..	..	..	..	2	..	..	1	..	..
Hale, Benjamin	..	..	..	1	..	..	..	1	1	1	..
Hale, Gershom	2	..	1	..	1	1	..	..	..	1	..
Hall, James	1	..	..	1	..	..	..	..	..	..	..
Hamilton, John	..	..	2	..	1	3	2	..	..	1	..
PAWLET—con.											
Hancock, Amasa	1	..	1	..	..	1	..	..	..	..	..
Hanks, Aruna	1	..	..	1	..	2	..	..	1	..	..
Hanks, Oliver	..	..	1	..	..	..	..	1	..	..	..
Hanks, William	..	..	..	..	1	..	..	..	..	1	..
Harmon, Ezekiel	3	..	2	..	1	1	2	1	..	1	..
Harmon, Joel	..	1	3	..	1	1	1	3	..	1	..
Harmon, Joel Jr.	1	..	1	1	..	1	1	1	..	..	..
Harmon, Oliver	1	..	..	1	..	2	1	..	1	..	..
Harmon, Thaddeus	..	2	..	1	..	2	1	..	..	1	..
Haskill, Joseph	..	2	2	..	1	2	..	2	..	1	..
Hastins, Heman	2	..	..	1	..	2	..	..	1	..	..
Hatheway, Reuben	..	..	1	..	..	..	..	..	..	..	..
Havens, Nathaniel	2	..	..	1	..	2	1	..	1	..	..
Hawley, Benjamin	3	..	..	1	..	1	..	..	1	..	..
Hawley, Phinehas	..	..	..	1	..	4	..	..	1	..	..
Hawley, Silas	1	1	1	..	..	..	..	..	1	..	..
Henry, Andrew	1	..	..	1	..	2	..	..	1	..	..
Herskins, James	..	..	..	1	..	2	1	..	1	..	..
Hitchcock, Philip	..	..	1	..	..	..	..	..	..	..	..
Hollister, Ashbel	6	..	..	1	..	..	1	..	1	..	..
Hollister, Elijah	..	..	1	1	1	1	1	..	1	1	1
Hollister, Innitt	2	1	..	1	..	1	1	..	1	..	..
Huet, Dan	3	..	..	1	..	..	1	..	1	..	..
Hulet, Daniel	..	..	2	..	1	3	3	..	..	1	..
Hurd, Bethuel	2	2	1	..	1	2	1	1	1	1	..
Hutchins, Buckley	1	2	..	1	..	1	..	..	1	..	..
Ingram, Eliphalet	1	..	..	1	..	1	..	1	..	..	..
Ingram, Ephraim	1	..	..	..	1	..	..	1	..	1	..
Ingram, Joseph	1	..	1	1	..	..	..	1	..	..	..
Johnson, Gordon	2	2	..	1	..	2	..	1	..	1	..
Jones, Ephraim	3	..	..	1	..	1	..	..	1	..	..
Jones, Joseph	..	..	..	1	..	2	..	..	1	..	..
Jones, Roswell	3	1	..	1	..	1	..	..	1	..	..
Jones, Silas	2	2	1	1	..	..	1	..	1	..	..
Keigwell, Joseph	1	..	..	1	..	..	1	..	1	..	..
Kellogg, Joseph	1	1	..	..	1	..	..	..	..	1	..
Kellogg, Joseph Jr.	1	..	1	..	..	1	..	1	..	..	..
King, Chauncy	2	..	..	1	1	..	..	..	1	..	..
Kinsley, Ebenezer	..	..	2	..	1	..	1	..	..	1	..
Kinsley, Elias	1	..	..	1	..	2	..	1	..	..	..
Lake, William	3	1	..	1	..	1	..	..	1	..	..
Leach, James	2	1	1	1	..	..	1	1	1	..	..
Lewis, David	2	1	..	1	..	1	1	..	..	1	..
Lombard, Abner	..	..	..	1	..	2	1	1	..	..	..
Loomis, Abner	1	..	..	1	..	1	..	..	1	..	..
Loomis, Oliver	..	1	..	1	..	..	1	..	1	..	..
Loomis, Roswell	1	..	..	1	..	2	1	..	1	..	..
Lounsbury, Nathan	..	..	..	1	..	2	..	1	..	..	..
Love, Jonathan	..	..	1	..	..	1	..	1	..	..	..
Loveland, Hosea	..	..	1	..	..	..	..	..	..	..	..
Lowell, David	3	1	..	1	..	..	1	..	2	..	..
Lowell, Josiah	3	1	..	1	2	..	..	1	1	..	..
Marks, Cornwal	2	1	..	1	..	2	..	..	1	..	..
McCrackin, Luke	1	..	1	..	..	1	..	1	..	..	..
McDonald, John	..	1	..	..	1	..	..	..	..	1	..
McNorton, Sarah	..	1	..	..	..	4	2	..	1	..	..
Meacham, Abraham	1	1	2	..	1	2	1	..	1	..	..
Meacham, Isaac	2	1	3	..	1	1	1	..	1	..	..
Merriman, Abel	1	..	..	1	..	1	..	1	..	..	..
Moffett, Jude	3	..	1	1	..	..	1	..	1	..	..
Montague, Adonijah	2	1	..	1	..	..	1	1	..	1	..
Mooseman, Timothy	1	..	..	1	..	1	1	..	1	..	..
Mott, Martha	..	..	..	..	..	..	..	..	..	1	..
Mullikin, Joseph	2	..	..	1	..	2	..	..	1	..	..
Munn, Isaiah	..	..	..	1	..	1	..	1	..	..	..
Munroe, Jesse	1	..	..	1	..	1	..	1	..	..	..
Munroe, Josiah	3	..	..	1	..	2	1	..	1	..	..
Nye, Timothy	..	..	..	1	..	1	..	1	..	..	..
Ormsby, Jeremiah	3	..	1	1	..	1	2	..	1	..	..
Osburn, Justice	2	..	..	1	..	1	..	1	..	..	..
Palmer, James	2	4	2	..	1	1	..	1	..	1	..
Palmer, Jonathan	..	..	..	1	..	..	..	..	..	..	..
Palmer, Josiah	1	..	1	..	..	..	..	1	..	..	..
Palmer, Susanna	..	..	..	..	..	..	..	..	1	..	..
Parker, Abijah	1	..	..	1	..	4	..	..	1	..	..
Pattason, Robert	..	1	..	..	1	..	..	..	..	1	..
Pattason, Thankful	..	1	..	..	..	..	..	1	..	1	..
Pepper, Simeon	3	1	..	..	1	1	2	..	1	..	..
Perkins, Erastus	..	..	1	..	..	..	..	1	..	..	..

RUTLAND COUNTY—Continued

NAMES OF HEADS OF FAMILIES	FREE WHITE MALES: Under 10 years of age	FREE WHITE MALES: Of 10 and under 16	FREE WHITE MALES: Of 16 and under 26 including heads of families	FREE WHITE MALES: Of 26 and under 45 including heads of families	FREE WHITE MALES: Of 45 and upwards including heads of families.	FREE WHITE FEMALES: Under 10 years of age	FREE WHITE FEMALES: Of 10 and under 16	FREE WHITE FEMALES: Of 16 and under 26 including heads of families	FREE WHITE FEMALES: Of 26 and under 45 including heads of families	FREE WHITE FEMALES: Of 45 and upwards including heads of families	All other free persons except Indians not taxed
PAWLET—con.											
Perkins, Jacob	..	..	1	..	1	..	1	..	..	1	..
Perkins, William	..	..	1	..	..	..	1	1	..	..	..
Pettingell, Lemuel	..	..	..	1	..	..	..	..	..	..	..
Pettingill, William	2	..	..	1	..	2	..	..	1	..	..
Pitts, Luke	..	..	1	..	..	..	..	..	..	..	..
Pomroy, John	..	..	..	..	1	..	..	1	..	1	..
Porter, Eleazor	..	..	..	..	..	2	..	1	..	..	..
Porter, Joseph	..	..	1	..	..	..	..	1	..	..	..
Porter, Moses	..	1	..	..	1	1	..	..	..	1	..
Porter, Samuel	2	2	..	..	1	1	1	..	1	..	..
Porter, Seth	..	..	..	..	1	..	..	1	..	1	..
Porter, Zoroster	..	..	..	1	..	1	..	1	..	2	..
Potter, John	2	..	..	1	..	..	..	1	..	..	..
Potter, William	1	..	3	..	1	1	2	..	..	1	..
Pratt, Elisha	..	..	..	..	1	..	..	..	1	..	..
Pratt, James	1	1	..	1	..	4	..	1	1	..	..
Pratt, Samuel	..	..	..	..	1	2	..	..	1	1	..
Prindle, Jonathan	..	..	..	..	1	..	..	..	..	..	..
Reed, Daniel	4	1	..	1	..	..	1	..	1	..	..
Reed, Jedediah	..	1	2	..	1	..	..	1	..	..	..
Reed, Simeon	1	2	3	..	1	2	2	..	1	1	..
Rice, Aaron	..	..	..	1	..	1	..	1	..	..	..
Risdem, John	..	1	..	..	1	..	..	..	..	2	..
Robinson, Aaron	2	2	..	..	1	..	1	..	1	..	..
Robinson, Abel	1	1	..	1	..	1	1	..	..	..	..
Robinson, Ephraim	2	..	..	1	..	3	1	..	1	..	..
Robinson, Richard	3	1	..	1	..	..	1	..	1	..	..
Rockwell, Adonijah	..	..	2	..	1	1	2	2	1	..	..
Roe, Abijah	1	..	..	1	..	2	..	..	1	..	..
Rose, John	..	..	..	1	..	..	..	..	..	..	..
Rose, Samuel	..	..	..	..	1	1	..	..	..	1	..
Rush, Appollos	..	..	..	1	1	1	..	1	..	..	..
Rush, Jacob	2	1	..	1	..	2	..	1	1	..	..
Safford, Jonathan	1	1	1	1	..	3	..	1	1	..	..
Sage, Benjamin	1	..	1	..	..	..	..	1	..	..	..
Sanford, Aaron	..	2	1	..	1	1	..	2	..	1	..
Sanford, Aaron, Jr.	..	..	..	1	..	1	..	..	1	..	..
Sanford, Amos	..	..	1	..	..	..	1	..	..	1	..
Sargant, John	4	1	..	1	..	1	2	1	1	..	..
Sawyer, Elias	..	..	..	..	1	..	..	..	1	..	..
Sheldon, Joel Jr.	..	..	1	..	..	1	..	1	..	..	..
Sheldon, Seth	..	..	2	..	1	..	1	1	..	1	..
Sheldon, Seth Jr.	..	..	1	..	..	..	..	1	..	..	..
Sheppard, Silas	2	1	..	1	..	2	1	1	1	..	..
Sikes, Jacob	1	1	..	1	..	5	2	..	1	..	..
Simons, Joel	1	1	1	2	1	2	1	1	..	1	..
Smith, Abigail	1	..	1	..	..	1	1	..	1	..	..
Smith, Eliphalet	1	..	..	1	..	3	1	..	1	..	..
Smith, Josiah	2	1	..	1	..	2	1	..	1	..	..
Smith, Nathaniel	1	2	2	..	1	..	1	1	..	1	..
Smith, Reuben	3	..	..	1	..	1	1	..	1	..	..
Smith, Sarah	1	..	..	..	..	1	..	1	1	..	..
Smith, Whiting	1	..	1	..	..	2	..	1	..	..	..
Spencer, Stephen	3	..	..	1	..	1	1	..	1	..	..
Stacey, Joseph	2	..	..	1	..	..	1	1	..	..	..
Stanford, Wait	1	..	..	1	..	1	..	1	..	..	..
Stannard, Roswell	..	..	1	..	..	..	..	1	..	..	..
Starks, Samuel	1	1	..	1	..	4	..	..	1	..	..
Starkweather, Elisha	2	..	..	1	..	1	1	1	..	..	..
Starns, David	..	..	1	..	..	..	..	..	..	..	..
Stedman, Charles	..	..	1	..	..	2	..	..	1	..	..
Stevens, Peter	4	1	..	..	1	1	..	..	..	1	..
Stevens, William	2	..	2	..	..	1	..	..	1	..	..
Stocking, Howel	..	..	1	..	..	..	..	..	..	..	..
Stoddard, Benjamin	..	..	..	1	..	2	..	..	1	..	..
Stone, James	..	..	1	..	..	..	..	..	..	..	..
Stratton, Jabez	..	1	1	..	1	..	..	..	1	..	..
Stratton, Joseph	..	1	..	1	1	..	..	..	1	..	..
Stratton, Samuel	3	..	..	1	1	1	2	..	1	1	..
Strong, Return	2	1	2	..	1	1	..	1	1	..	..
Taylor, Samuel	3	1	..	1	..	1	..	..	1	..	..
Thomas, Benajah C.	..	..	1	..	..	..	..	..	..	..	..
Thomas, Ebenezer	1	..	..	..	1	1	1	..	1	..	..
Thomson, John	..	1	1	..	1	..	1	1	..	..	..
Toby, Eleazer	..	..	1	..	..	..	..	..	..	..	..
Toby, Josiah	1	1	..	1	..	2	1	..	1	..	..
Toby, Reuben	..	..	..	1	..	2	..	..	1	..	..
Tryon, Jesse	3	1	1	1	..	1	..	..	1	..	..
Tubbs, Clement	3	1	..	1	..	1	1	..	1	..	..
Uran, Abigail	..	1	1	..	..	..	..	1	..	1	..
Uran, Jams	1	..	1	1	..	..	..	..	..	1	..
PAWLET—con.											
Wade, Alpheus	..	..	1	..	..	..	..	..	..	..	..
Walden, Miner	..	..	2	1	..	2	..	..	1	..	..
Warner, Gad	1	1	1	1	..	1	1	..	1	..	..
Warner, Zadock	1	..	..	1	..	2	..	..	1	..	..
Waterhouse, William	3	..	1	1	..	2	..	..	1	..	..
Welch, Daniel	2	..	2	..	1	3	1	2	1	..	..
Welch, Daniel Jr.	..	..	1	..	..	..	..	1	..	..	..
Wells, Cyrus	2	..	2	1	..	1	..	..	1	..	..
Wheaten, Ansil	2	2	..	1	..	1	..	1	1	..	..
Wheaten, Edmund	..	1	..	1	..	2	3	1	1	..	..
Whitman, Edward	3	2	..	..	1	1	1	..	1	..	..
Wickam, Isaac	2	..	1	1	..	..	..	1	..	..	..
Wicks, Samuel	2	..	..	1	..	1	..	..	1	1	..
Wilcox, Jared	1	1	..	1	..	4	1	1	1	..	..
Wilcox, John	2	1	1	..	1	1	2	1	1	..	..
Wilcox, Sarah	..	..	..	..	..	1	..	..	..	1	..
Willard, Edward	1	1	..	1	..	1	..	..	1	..	..
Willard, John	2	1	..	1	1	2	1	..	1	1	..
Willard, Jonathan	..	1	1	1	1	2	..	..	1	..	..
Willard, Jonathan Jr.	2	..	..	1	..	1	..	1	..	..	..
Willard, Joseph	2	1	..	..	1	..	2	..	..	1	..
Willard, Samuel	..	..	2	..	..	..	..	2	..	..	..
Williams, Abel	2	1	..	1	..	2	1	1	..	1	..
Williams, Nathan	4	1	..	1	..	2	1	..	1	..	..
Willow, Benjamin	..	..	1	..	..	1	..	1	..	..	..
Wily, Asa	..	1	2	..	1	1	3	2	..	1	..
Wily, Moses	..	1	1	1	..	2	..	..	..	1	..
Wily, Samuel	..	..	1	..	..	1	..	1	..	..	..
Winchester, Andrew	..	1	..	..	1	1	2	1	..	1	..
Wing, Elisha	..	..	1	..	..	..	..	..	..	..	..
Wiseman, John	1	..	..	1	..	2	..	1	..	..	..
Wood, David	..	2	1	..	1	..	..	1	..	1	..
Wood, John	2	..	1	..	..	..	..	1	..	..	..
Wood, Otis	1	..	..	1	..	1	..	1	..	..	..
Worstiff, Henry	..	..	1	1	..	1	1	1	..	1	..
Worstiff, Henry Jr.	..	..	1	..	..	..	..	..	1	..	..
Wright, Preserved	3	..	..	1	..	1	..	..	1	..	..
Wright, Samuel	2	..	1	..	1	1	1	3	..	1	..
Wyman, Joseph	..	..	..	1	..	..	..	1	..	..	..
PHILADELPHIA											
Axtell, Ezra	3	1	..	..	1	1	..	..	1	..	..
Bancraft, John	..	..	..	1	..	2	1	..	1	..	..
Bancraft, Samuel	..	..	..	1	..	1	..	1	..	..	..
Bisby, Isaac	3	2	..	1	..	..	..	..	1	..	..
Bisby, Issachar	..	1	..	..	1	1	1	1	..	1	..
Church, Seth	..	..	..	1	..	1	..	1	..	..	..
Churchel, Caleb	3	..	..	1	1	2	1	..	1	..	..
Churchel, Isaac	..	..	2	..	1	..	1	2	..	1	..
Churchel, Michael	1	..	..	1	..	4	..	..	1	..	..
Clark, John	..	..	1	..	1	2	2	2	..	1	..
Hawley, Nathan	1	..	..	1	..	2	..	1	1	..	..
Henry, Nathan	..	..	1	..	..	1	..	..	..	..	..
Keiler, Thomas	..	..	1	..	..	1	..	1	..	..	..
Lyman, Ebenezer	..	1	..	..	1	1	1	2	..	1	..
Osburn, Isaac	1	1	1	1	..	2	1	..	1	..	..
Osburn, Jacob	..	..	1	..	..	1	..	..	..	..	..
Plumley, Jonathan	4	1	..	1	..	1	..	..	1	..	..
Seger, Elijah	1	2	2	1	..	..	1	..	..	..	..
Starns, Elias	..	..	..	1	..	..	..	..	1	..	..
UNCERTAIN NAME											
Streeter, Lesley (?)	..	..	1	..	..	..	2	1	..	1	..
PITTSFIELD											
Blossom, Benjamin	..	1	..	1	1	..	2	..	1	..	..
Bon, Daniel	3	..	..	1	..	2	..	..	1	..	..
Bryant, Samuel	2	..	..	1	..	..	1	..	1	..	..
Campbell, Abel	..	..	1	..	..	..	..	1	..	..	..
Crosman, Jacob	..	..	1	..	1	1	1	1	..	1	..
Crosman, Robert	..	..	1	..	..	..	..	1	..	..	..
Daley, David	..	..	..	1	..	4	..	..	1	..	..
Davis, William	3	..	..	1	..	2	1	..	1	..	..
Durkee, Albia	2	..	1	..	..	1	..	..	1	1	..

RUTLAND COUNTY—Continued

NAMES OF HEADS OF FAMILIES	FREE WHITE MALES: Under 10 years of age	FREE WHITE MALES: Of 10 and under 16	FREE WHITE MALES: Of 16 and under 26 including heads of families	FREE WHITE MALES: Of 26 and under 45 including heads of families	FREE WHITE MALES: Of 45 and upwards including heads of families	FREE WHITE FEMALES: Under 10 years of age	FREE WHITE FEMALES: Of 10 and under 16	FREE WHITE FEMALES: Of 16 and under 26 including heads of families	FREE WHITE FEMALES: Of 26 and under 45 including heads of families	FREE WHITE FEMALES: Of 45 and upwards including heads of families	All other free persons except Indians not taxed
PITTSFIELD—con.											
Durkee, David	..	1	1	..	1	..	..	1	..	..	..
Durkee, Ebenezer	..	1	..	1	..	1	1	..	1	..	..
Durkee, Timothy	2	..	1	..	..	1	..	..	1	1	..
Eddy, Nathan	..	..	..	..	1	..	..	..	..	1	..
Eddy, Nathan Jr.	3	1	..	1	..	..	..	1	..	..	..
Gains, Asa	2	..	..	1	..	..	..	..	1	..	..
Gains, John	..	..	..	1	..	..	..	1	..	..	..
Goodrich, James	..	..	1	..	..	..	..	..	..	..	..
Green, Uzziah	3	..	1	..	1	2	2	..	1	..	..
Harlow, Lewis	..	..	..	1	..	1	..	1	..	..	..
Hodgkins, Thomas	1	..	1	1	..	1	1	1	1	..	..
Holt, Stephen	1	1	2	..	1	..	1	..	1	..	..
Jeperson, Jacob	1	..	..	1	..	2	..	1	..	..	..
Jones, Amos	1	1	1	..	1	1	1	1	..	2	..
Lovett, David	..	..	1	..	1	..	1	..	..	1	..
Lyman, James Jr.	1	..	1	..	..	1	..	1	..	..	..
Lyman, James Jr.	1	1	1	1	..	..	..	1	1	..	..
Martin, George	..	..	..	..	1	..	..	..	..	1	..
Martin, Washington	1	..	1	..	..	..	..	1	..	..	..
Rogers, Benjamin	..	..	1	..	..	..	..	..	..	..	..
Sanger, Isaac	2	..	..	1	..	2	..	..	1	..	..
Stone, Jonas	1	..	1	1	..	1	..	..	1	..	..
Warren, Bethuel	1	..	..	1	..	..	..	..	..	..	..
Washbun, Libbius	..	..	1	..	..	..	..	1	..	..	..
Whitcomb, Anthony	1	..	..	1	..	3	..	..	1	..	..
Wolcott, William	1	..	..	1	..	1	..	..	1	..	..
PITTSFORD											
Adams, Elijah	1	1	..	1	4	..	..	1	..	..	..
Adams, Samuel	..	1	..	1	1	1	1	1	..	1	..
Adams, Thomas	2	..	..	1	..	1	..	1	..	..	..
Allen, William	1	1	..	..	1	1	2	2	..	1	..
Andrus, Zelotes	..	1	..	1	..	1	..	1	..	..	..
Anthony, Abraham	1	1	..	..	1	1	..	1	..	1	..
Armstrong, Libbeus	1	..	..	1	..	..	..	1	..	..	..
Avery, Elijah	..	..	..	1	..	2	..	1	..	..	..
Avery, Stephen	1	..	..	1	..	..	1	1	..	..	..
Ayers, Joseph	2	..	..	1	..	1	..	1	1	..	..
Bachelor, Benjamin	1	..	..	1	..	1	..	..	1	..	..
Baker, Jonathan	1	2	..	1	..	4	1	..	1	..	..
Barlow, Giles	..	..	1	1	..	..	..	..	..	..	..
Barlow, William W.	4	..	..	1	..	1	..	1	1	..	..
Barns, Ithel	..	..	..	1	..	3	2	..	1	..	..
Barns, John	..	1	1	..	1	1	..	..	..	1	..
Barns, John	2	1	..	1	..	2	..	..	1	..	..
Barns, Vintin	2	1	..	1	..	2	1	..	1	..	..
Barnum, Ephraim	3	..	..	1	..	..	..	1	..	..	..
Basset, Samuel	..	..	1	..	..	..	..	..	..	..	..
Bates, Eliphalet	..	..	1	..	..	..	..	..	..	..	..
Bates, Michael	2	..	1	1	..	2	..	1	1	..	..
Baxter, Hiram	..	..	..	1	..	..	..	..	1	..	..
Baxter, William	..	1	..	1	..	4	1	1	1	..	..
Beall, John	2	..	..	1	..	1	..	..	1	..	..
Belch, Nathan	2	..	1	..	..	1	..	1	..	..	..
Bentley, John	1	..	..	1	1	1	..	2	..	1	..
Blackmore, Asa	..	..	..	1	..	..	..	..	..	..	..
Blanchard, Clark	..	..	..	1	..	3	1	..	1	..	..
Booge, Oliver	1	..	3	..	1	3	1	..	..	1	..
Booth, Benjamin	1	..	..	1	..	..	..	..	1	..	..
Bradford, Elisha	3	..	..	..	1	3	..	..	1	..	..
Brewster, David	1	..	..	..	1	2	1	2	..	1	..
Brewster, Israel	..	..	..	..	1	..	..	..	..	1	..
Brewster, Israel Jr.	..	..	..	1	..	..	..	..	1	..	..
Brewster, Justice	1	..	..	1	..	3	..	..	1	..	..
Brewster, Peter	1	..	..	1	..	2	..	..	1	..	..
Bristol, Nathan	..	..	1	..	..	..	..	..	..	..	..
Bristol, Richard	..	..	1	..	..	..	..	..	..	..	..
Brizie, Christopher	1	3	2	1	..	4	1	..	1	..	..
Brizie, Nicholas	3	..	..	1	..	1	2	..	1	1	..
Brizie, Peter	2	1	1	1	..	3	1	1	1	..	..
Brizie, Peter Jr.	..	..	1	..	..	..	..	..	..	..	..
Brown, Elijah	..	..	..	..	1	..	..	..	..	1	..
Brown, Elisha	1	..	..	1	..	..	..	1	..	..	..
Brown, Elisha Jr.	3	..	1	1	..	2	1	..	1	..	..
Brown, Ephraim	3	..	..	1	..	1	..	1	..	..	..
Brown, Syrenus	..	..	..	1	..	..	..	1	..	..	..
Buck, Alfred	1	..	..	1	..	1	..	..	1	..	..
PITTSFORD—con.											
Buel, Samuel	..	..	1	1	..	..	..	1	..	..	..
Butter, Anthony	2	..	..	1	..	2	..	1	..	..	..
Caffee, Benjamin	2	..	..	1	..	1	..	..	1	..	..
Call, Anna	1	..	..	..	..	..	..	..	1	..	..
Carr, Hezekiah	1	1	..	1	..	2	1	..	1	1	..
Chase, Isaac	1	..	..	..	1	1	..	1	..	..	..
Churchel, Amos	..	..	1	..	..	1	..	1	..	..	..
Clark, Isaac	1	..	1	..	..	..	..	1	..	..	..
Clifford, Edward	..	..	..	..	1	1	..	1	..	1	..
Clifford, Edward Jr.	4	..	..	1	..	1	..	..	1	..	..
Clifford, Simeon	2	..	..	1	..	2	..	1	1	..	..
Cobb, Allen	2	..	..	1	..	1	..	1	..	..	..
Cooley, Benjamin	..	..	2	..	1	3	2	..	1	..	..
Cooley, Caleb	2	..	..	1	..	3	3	..	1	..	..
Cooley, Samuel	..	..	1	..	..	1	..	1	..	..	..
Copley, Samuel	1	1	1	1	..	2	3	1	1	..	..
Cox, William	..	1	..	..	1	..	..	..	..	1	..
Crispen, Amos	..	..	1	..	..	..	..	..	..	1	..
Demon, Noadiah	1	..	..	..	1	..	1	1	..	..	..
Downey, John	..	..	1	..	..	2	..	1	..	..	..
Drewry, Abraham	1	..	..	..	1	2	1	..	1	..	..
Drewry, Calvin	2	..	..	1	..	1	..	1	..	..	..
Drewry, Ebenezer	..	2	..	..	1	..	..	..	..	1	..
Drewry, Lewis	1	1	..	1	..	1	1	..	..	..	..
Dunlap, Ephraim	..	..	..	..	1	2	..	..	1	..	..
Dutton, John	3	..	..	1	..	1	2	..	1	..	..
Ewings, Alexander	1	1	..	1	..	2	..	..	2	..	..
Ewings, Benjamin	1	..	1	..	..	..	..	1	..	..	..
Ewings, James	..	1	..	..	1	3	..	2	1	..	..
Fanfield, Nathaniel	..	..	..	..	1	..	..	..	..	2	..
Farefield, Samuel	..	2	..	..	1	3	3	1	1	..	..
Finn, John	..	..	2	..	1	..	..	..	..	1	..
French, Abel	2	..	..	1	..	1	..	1	..	..	..
Frisby, William	1	..	..	1	..	..	..	..	1	..	..
Gates, William	1	..	..	1	..	1	..	..	1	..	..
Gibbs, Nathan	3	2	2	1	..	1	1	3	1	..	..
Gibbs, Thomas	2	..	..	2	..	2	..	1	1	..	..
Gilbert, Simeon	..	1	..	1	..	1	1	..	1	..	..
Gillet, John	2	1	..	..	1	2	2	..	1	..	..
Ginna, Asa	2	..	1	..	..	..	..	1	..	..	..
Gitchel, David	1	..	2	..	1	1	1	..	1	..	..
Goff, Joshua	..	..	..	1	..	..	..	..	1	..	..
Hall, Elias	2	1	..	..	1	..	1	..	..	1	..
Hammon, Thomas	4	..	2	1	..	1	2	1	1	..	..
Harwood, Eleazer	..	..	..	..	1	..	1	..	..	1	..
Hawks, John	..	1	..	1	..	2	2	2	1	..	..
Hay, William	..	1	..	..	1	..	..	..	..	1	..
Hendee, Caleb	2	2	..	..	1	..	1	..	..	1	..
Hendee, Caleb Jr.	1	1	..	1	..	1	1	..	2	..	..
Hendee, Daniel	..	..	1	..	..	2	..	1	..	..	..
Hendee, Jonathan	2	..	..	1	..	..	..	1	..	..	..
Henry, Aaron	1	..	1	..	1	..	1	..	..	1	..
Heron, Simon Rev.	3	..	..	1	..	2	1	..	1	..	..
Herrick, Elijah	..	..	..	1	..	..	..	..	..	..	..
Hewet, James	1	..	..	1	..	1	..	1	..	..	..
Hewings, Elijah	..	..	..	1	..	2	..	2	1	..	..
Hicock, Deborah	..	1	..	..	..	1	..	..	..	1	..
Hicock, James	1	..	1	..	..	..	..	1	..	..	..
Hicock, Stephen	..	..	..	1	..	..	..	..	..	..	..
Hitchcock, Chapman	..	..	..	1	..	..	..	..	..	..	..
Hitchcock, John	1	1	..	1	..	1	..	1	1	..	..
Hitchcock, John	..	..	..	1	2	..	..	..	1	2	..
Hitchcock, Moses	1	..	1	..	..	..	..	1	..	..	..
Hitchcock, Remembrance	..	..	..	1	..	1	..	1	..	..	..
Hooper, Joseph	..	..	1	..	..	..	..	..	..	..	..
Hopkins, Ebenezer	2	2	..	1	1	3	1	1	1	1	..
Hopkins, Hiram	2	..	..	1	..	1	..	1	..	..	1
Hopkins, Martin	1	..	..	1	..	2	1	1	1	..	..
Hopkins, Mathew	1	..	..	1	..	..	..	..	..	..	..
Hopkins, Nehemiah	2	1	..	1	..	1	..	..	1	..	..
Hopkins, Noah	..	..	..	1	..	..	..	..	..	..	..
Hopkins, Samuel	1	1	..	1	1	3	..	1	1	1	..
Hopkins, Stephen	1	1	..	1	..	3	..	..	1	..	..
Hoten, Walter	2	..	..	1	..	1	..	..	1	..	..
Hudson, Eli	1	..	1	..	..	..	..	1	..	..	..
Hudson, Lot	3	..	..	1	..	1	..	..	1	..	..
Ives, Reuben	3	..	1	..	1	..	1	1	1	..	..
Jackson, James	2	..	..	1	..	1	..	..	1	..	..
Jackson, Jonathan	1	..	..	..	1	1	2	..	1	..	..
Jackson, Samuel	3	..	..	1	..	1	..	..	1	..	..

RUTLAND COUNTY—Continued

NAMES OF HEADS OF FAMILIES	FREE WHITE MALES					FREE WHITE FEMALES					All other free persons except Indians not taxed
	Under 10 years of age	Of 10 and under 16	Of 16 and under 26 including heads of families	Of 26 and under 45 including heads of families	Of 45 and upwards including heads of families.	Under 10 years of age	Of 10 and under 16	Of 16 and under 26 including heads of families	Of 26 and under 45 including heads of families	Of 45 and upwards including heads of families	
PITTSFORD—con.											
Jenner, Stephen	1	1	1	..	1	3	..	1	..	1	..
Jenner, Timothy	2	..	1	..	..	..	..	1	..	..	..
Johnson, Heman	..	..	1	..	..	..	..	..	..	..	..
Johnson, Joseph	1	1	..	..	1	..	1	..	1	1	..
Jones, Samuel	..	..	..	1	..	4	..	..	1	..	..
Keiler, David	1	..	..	1	..	..	..	1	..	..	..
Keiler, Ebenezer	..	..	..	1	..	1	..	1	..	..	..
Keiler, Lot	1	..	..	1	1	..	..	..	1	1	..
Keith, Israel	..	..	..	..	1	..	..	..	1	..	..
Keith, Ruel	2	1	..	..	1	1	2	..	1	..	..
Keith, Union	1	1	..	1	..	..	..	1	..	..	..
Keith, Unite	2	2	..	1	..	2	2	..	1	..	..
Keith, Zephaniah	..	1	..	..	1	..	..	..	..	1	..
Kellogg, Amos	1	..	1	1	..	1	1	1	1	..	..
Kinsley, Joshua	..	..	1	..	..	..	1	..	..	..	..
Kinsley, Nathaniel	..	..	1	..	1	1	2	2	..	1	..
La Clare, Frances	2	..	..	..	1	1	..	..	..	1	..
Ladd, Hammon	1	..	..	1	..	1	..	..	1	..	..
Lake, Israel	1	..	..	1	..	..	..	1	1	..	..
Lamson, John	..	..	..	1	..	3	2	..	1	..	..
Lathrop, Adgate	2	..	..	1	..	1	..	1	1	..	..
Leach, Andrew	..	1	..	1	..	..	..	..	..	..	..
Lee, Ashbel	3	1	..	1	..	1	..	..	1	..	..
Lewis, Daniel	2	..	..	1	..	3	1	..	1	..	..
Loveland, Robert	1	..	..	1	..	3	..	..	1	..	..
Lucas, Paul	..	..	..	1	..	3	..	..	1	..	..
Lucas, Samuel	..	..	1	..	..	..	..	..	..	..	..
Luther, Samuel	1	..	1	..	..	..	..	1	..	..	..
Lyman, John	..	..	1	..	..	..	..	..	..	..	..
Mather, Thomas	1	..	..	1	..	1	1	..	1	..	..
Mattason, Isaac	..	..	..	1	..	2	..	..	2	..	..
Mattason, James	..	..	1	..	..	..	..	1	..	..	..
McCarter, Alexander	..	..	..	1	..	2	..	..	1	..	..
Mead, John	..	2	3	..	1	..	..	..	..	1	..
Mead, Martin	1	..	..	1	..	1	..	..	1	..	..
Mead, Polly	..	..	..	..	..	2	..	1	..	..	..
Mead, Stephen	..	..	..	..	1	..	..	..	..	1	..
Mead, Stephen Jr.	..	..	2	1	..	2	..	..	1	..	..
Merrifield, Bethiah	1	1	1	..	..	1	..	..	..	1	..
Millard, Abeathar	..	3	..	..	1	..	..	..	..	1	..
Miller, John	..	..	..	1	..	..	..	..	..	..	..
Molton, Solomon	..	..	1	1	..	..	..	1	..	..	..
Mooseman, Oliver	..	..	..	1	..	1	..	..	1	1	..
Morgan, Benjamin	3	..	..	1	..	2	1	..	1	..	..
Morgan, Israel	..	1	..	..	1	2	1	2	..	1	..
Morgan, Samuel	..	..	..	1	..	2	..	1	..	..	..
Morgan, William	..	..	1	..	..	1	..	1	..	..	..
Morse, Jeremiah	1	..	..	1	..	3	..	..	1	..	..
Moses, Rufus	2	..	1	..	..	..	..	..	1	1	..
Needam, Jeremiah	3	..	..	1	..	..	..	1	..	..	..
Needham, Abner	..	..	..	1	..	3	..	1	..	..	..
Nelson, Nathan	1	..	1	1	..	..	..	1	..	..	..
Orcott, Bildad	..	..	..	1	..	3	..	..	1	..	..
Osburn, Isaac	2	1	1	..	1	2	1	1	1	..	..
Osgood, Oliver	1	..	..	1	..	1	..	1	..	..	..
Owen, Abraham	1	2	1	1	..	3	1	..	1	..	..
Parker, Jonas	1	..	..	1	..	2	..	1	..	..	..
Parmele, Simeon	..	2	2	..	1	1	1	..	..	1	..
Pawley, Amasa	1	..	1	..	..	1	2	2	1	..	..
Pearce, David	2	..	..	1	..	2	..	..	1	..	..
Pearce, Eliphalet	..	..	..	1	..	..	..	..	..	..	..
Penfield, John	..	2	1	..	1	..	1	2	..	1	..
Penfield, John Jr.	..	..	1	..	..	..	..	1	..	..	..
Philips, Anthony	1	..	1	..	1	1	..	2	..	..	..
Phillips, Hiram	..	..	1	..	..	..	..	..	..	..	..
Phillips, Jacobs	2	..	..	1	..	..	..	1	..	..	..
Phillips, Joel	..	..	1	..	..	..	..	..	..	..	..
Porter, James	3	..	..	1	..	1	..	..	1	..	..
Potter, Milton	..	2	1	1	..	4	..	..	1	..	..
Powers, Jeremiah	1	..	..	..	1	..	..	..	..	1	..
Powers, Jeremiah	..	..	..	1	..	1	1	1	1	..	..
Powers, Joab	..	..	..	..	1	..	..	..	..	..	..
Powers, Justice	..	..	..	1	..	..	..	1	..	..	..
Powers, Montgomery	2	..	..	1	..	..	..	1	..	..	..
Powers, Peters	2	1	..	1	..	1	1	..	1	..	..
Pratt, John	2	..	..	1	..	1	..	..	1	..	..
Rawson, Leonard	1	..	1	1	..	..	..	1	..	..	..
Rice, Peter	3	1	2	..	1	..	1	1	1	..	..
Rich, Elisha Rev.	..	..	1	..	1	..	..	1	..	1	..
Ripley, Phinehas	..	1	1	..	1	4	1	1	..	1	..
PITTSFORD—con.											
Rowley, Jonathan	..	..	..	..	1	1	..	..	..	1	..
Rowley, Joseph	1	1	..	1	..	2	..	..	1	..	..
Saunders, Michael	..	..	1	..	..	2	..	1	..	..	..
Saunders, William	..	..	..	..	1	1	2	..	..	1	..
Saunders, William	..	..	1	..	..	..	..	..	..	..	..
Simmons, Ezekiel	..	..	1	..	..	..	..	..	..	..	..
Simmons, John	3	2	1	1	..	1	2	..	1	..	..
Smith, David	3	1	..	1	..	1	1	..	1	..	..
Smith, Reuben	1	..	1	..	1	1	1	1	1	..	..
Spencer, William	2	2	..	1	..	2	1	1	1	..	..
Squier, Darius	1	..	..	1	..	1	..	..	1	..	..
Squier, Phinehas	..	..	1	..	..	..	..	..	..	..	..
Stanford, William	1	..	..	1	..	2	..	1	..	..	..
Stanton, Abraham	..	..	..	1	..	..	..	..	..	2	..
Starks, David	1	1	..	1	..	1	..	..	1	..	..
Stevens, Aaron	..	3	..	..	1	1	1	1	1	..	..
Stevens, Asa	..	..	..	..	1	..	1	..	1	..	..
Stevens, Benjamin	..	..	..	..	1	..	1	..	..	1	..
Stevens, Simeon	3	..	..	1	..	..	1	1	1	..	..
Stowers, Abijah	2	..	..	1	..	1	..	..	1	..	..
Strong, Ozem	2	1	..	1	..	2	1	..	1	..	..
Taff, Josiah	1	..	..	1	..	1	..	..	1	..	..
Taff, Timothy	..	1	..	..	1	..	..	..	..	1	..
Tedder, James	2	..	..	1	..	2	..	..	1	..	..
Tisdall, James	3	..	..	1	1	1	..	..	1	1	..
Titus, John	..	..	2	..	1	..	..	..	..	1	..
Tupper, Ebenezer	2	..	1	..	..	..	..	1	..	..	..
Tupper, Simeon	1	..	..	..	1	..	..	..	1	1	..
Tupper, Simeon Jr.	1	..	..	1	..	3	..	..	1	..	..
Tuttle, David	..	..	1	..	..	..	..	..	..	..	..
Walker, Abraham	..	1	..	..	1	..	..	..	1	2	..
Walker, Tilla	..	1	..	1	..	..	..	..	1	..	..
Ward, Daniel	2	..	..	1	..	1	..	..	1	..	..
Ward, Rufus	1	..	..	1	..	2	2	..	1	..	..
Warner, Eleazer	2	1	..	1	..	2	1	..	1	..	..
Warner, Jonathan	1	..	1	..	1	..	1	..	..	1	..
Warren, Daniel	2	..	..	1	..	1	..	..	1	..	..
Waters, John	..	..	1	..	..	3	..	1	..	..	..
Weed, Jacob	..	..	1	..	1	..	..	1	..	1	..
Wetherby, David	1	..	..	1	..	1	..	..	1	..	..
Wetherell, Rufus	..	..	1	..	..	..	..	..	..	..	..
Wheaten, Isaac	..	..	..	1	..	1	..	1	..	..	..
Whipple, Abner	..	..	..	1	..	2	..	..	1	..	..
Whipple, Wright	..	..	1	..	..	1	..	1	..	..	..
White, Edward	..	..	..	1	..	..	..	..	..	..	..
Whitmore, Andrew	1	..	..	1	..	1	..	..	1	..	..
Whitmore, Nathan	4	..	..	1	..	1	2	..	1	..	..
Wicker, James	..	..	1	..	1	1	1	..	1	..	..
Wicker, Luther	1	1	1	..	1	2	1	..	1	..	..
Wilder, Calvin	1	..	..	1	..	3	..	1	..	..	..
Williams, Eli	2	2	..	1	..	1	..	..	1	..	..
Williams, Theophillus	..	..	..	..	1	..	..	..	..	1	..
Willow, Amos	1	2	1	1	..	2	2	..	1	..	..
Winslow, Thomas	..	..	1	..	..	..	..	..	..	..	..
Wood, Calvin	2	..	..	1	..	1	..	..	1	..	..
Wood, Elijah	..	..	1	..	..	..	..	..	..	..	..
Wood, Jeremiah	2	..	1	..	1	3	..	1	1	1	..
Wood, Josiah	1	..	1	1	1	1	..	..	..	1	..
Woodard, John	2	..	..	1	..	2	..	2	..	..	..
Woodruff, Asher	1	..	1	..	..	1	..	..	1	..	..
Woodruff, Elisha	..	2	..	..	1	2	..	..	..	1	..
Woodruff, Elisha Jr.	..	..	1	..	..	..	..	..	..	..	..
Woodruff, Januel	1	..	..	1	..	1	..	1	..	..	..
Wright, Abel	..	..	1	..	1	..	..	..	1	..	..
Wright, Nathan	..	..	1	..	..	..	..	1	..	..	..
Wright, Robert	2	..	..	1	..	2	..	1	..	..	..
POULTNEY											
Adams, Abner	2	2	1	1	..	1	1	..	..	1	..
Adams, Jeremiah	..	1	..	..	1	1	..	..	..	2	..
Adams, Samuel	..	1	3	1	..	1	1	..	..	..	1
Aldrige, Abraham	..	..	1	..	..	..	..	1	..	..	..
Ames, Elijah	3	..	..	1	..	2	2	..	1	..	..
Andrus, Isaac	3	2	..	1	..	..	..	..	1	..	..
Andrus, Roswell	2	..	..	1	..	1	..	..	1	..	..
Andrus, Rufus	2	..	1	..	..	1	..	1	..	..	..
Angeline, Aaron	1	..	..	1	..	3	..	..	1	..	..
Angeline, Anthony	..	..	1	..	1	..	..	1	..	1	..
Angeline, Moses	1	..	1	1	..	..	..	1	..	..	..
Arnold, Shubal	1	1	..	1	1	1	..	1	1	1	..
Ashley, Elkanah	..	..	..	1	..	..	..	1	..	..	..

RUTLAND COUNTY—Continued

NAMES OF HEADS OF FAMILIES	FREE WHITE MALES: Under 10 years of age	FREE WHITE MALES: Of 10 and under 16	FREE WHITE MALES: Of 16 and under 26 including heads of families	FREE WHITE MALES: Of 26 and under 45 including heads of families	FREE WHITE MALES: Of 45 and upwards including heads of families	FREE WHITE FEMALES: Under 10 years of age	FREE WHITE FEMALES: Of 10 and under 16	FREE WHITE FEMALES: Of 16 and under 26 including heads of families	FREE WHITE FEMALES: Of 26 and under 45 including heads of families	FREE WHITE FEMALES: Of 45 and upwards including heads of families	All other free persons except Indians not taxed
POULTNEY—con.											
Ashley, John	1	..	1	..	1	..	2	1	..	1	..
Ashley, Thomas	..	1	..	..	1	..	..	1	1	1	..
Atwater, Abraham	2	..	..	1	..	2	..	..	1	..	..
Babcock, Elias	..	..	..	1	..	2	..	..	1	..	..
Babcock, Ichabod	..	..	1	1	..	2	1	1	..	..	..
Babcock, Moses	..	..	..	1	..	..	..	..	..	..	..
Bachelor, Benjamin	1	..	..	1	..	2	..	..	1	..	..
Baker, Joseph	..	..	..	1	..	2	..	1	..	..	1
Baker, Seth	..	..	1	..	1	..	1	2	2	1	..
Baker, Seth	..	..	..	1	..	..	..	..	..	..	..
Baker, Thaddeus	..	..	..	2	..	4	..	..	1	..	..
Bazley, James	..	..	1	..	..	..	..	..	..	..	..
Beach, Bennet	3	..	..	1	..	1	..	..	1	..	..
Bishop, Benoni	3	1	..	1	..	1	2	..	1	..	..
Blackmore, Elijah	2	..	1	1	..	2	..	..	1	..	..
Bradley, Thomas	..	1	..	..	1	2	1	..	1	..	..
Branch, Rufus	1	..	..	1	..	..	..	..	1	..	..
Brookins, Boze	..	..	..	..	1	..	..	..	..	1	..
Brookins, Cyrus	..	1	..	..	1	..	..	..	..	1	..
Brookins, Ithamar	..	..	3	..	1	..	1	1	..	1	..
Brougton, John	4	..	2	..	1	..	2	..	1	1	..
Brown, John	..	..	1	..	..	..	..	..	..	..	..
Brown, Philip	2	2	..	..	1	2	1	1	1	..	..
Brownson, Peleg	1	..	..	1	..	4	..	1	1	..	..
Buckland, Ebenezer	2	..	..	1	..	..	1	..	1	..	..
Buckland, Samuel	2	..	..	1	..	2	1	..	1	..	..
Buckley, Roswell	2	..	..	1	..	..	..	1	..	..	..
Buckley, William	1	..	..	1	..	2	1	..	1	1	..
Buel, Ezekiel	..	..	4	..	..	1	1	1	..	..	..
Bukus, Timothy	..	..	..	..	1	..	..	..	..	..	..
Bullock, Asa	1	..	..	1	1	..	..	..	1	1	..
Calkins, Eleazer	4	2	2	1	..	..	..	..	1	..	..
Canfield, Ebenezer	1	..	..	..	1	..	1	2	..	1	..
Canfield, Lewis	2	..	..	1	..	2	..	..	1	..	..
Chittenden, Seymour	2	..	1	..	1	1	1	..	..	1	..
Chittenden, Timothy	1	..	1	..	1	2	1	1	1	..	..
Chubb, Simon	2	..	..	1	..	2	1	..	1	..	..
Clark, Jonathan	1	1	1	..	1	1	1	..	1	..	..
Cleveland, Solomon	2	1	1	..	1	2	1	1	1	..	..
Colman, Thomas	..	1	..	1	1	..	..	..	2	1	..
Cone, Abner	..	1	2	..	1	..	..	2	..	1	..
Cone, Enoch	1	..	..	1	..	2	1	..	1	..	..
Cone, Timothy	1	..	1	..	..	..	..	1	..	..	..
Craw, Seth	1	1	..	1	..	1	3	..	1	..	..
Crittenden, Jarus	..	..	1	..	..	..	..	..	1	..	..
Cross, Abishai	..	..	..	1	..	1	..	..	2	..	..
Dank, Daniel	..	..	1	..	..	..	..	..	..	..	..
Darby, Phinehas	1	2	..	..	1	..	..	2	..	1	..
Darby, Phinehas Jr.	..	..	1	..	..	1	..	1	..	..	..
Dewey, Azariah	2	..	..	1	..	..	..	..	1	..	..
Dewey, David	..	..	1	..	..	..	..	..	..	..	..
Dewey, Jonathan	1	..	1	..	..	..	..	1	..	..	..
Dewey, Zebadiah	..	1	1	..	1	..	..	2	..	1	..
Dickinson, Thomas A.	1	1	..	1	..	4	..	..	1	..	..
Dike, Motimus	..	..	..	1	..	1	..	..	1	..	..
Dixon, David	..	1	..	1	..	3	..	..	1	..	..
Doolittle, Abner	2	2	..	1	..	..	..	..	1	..	..
Doolittle, Thomas	2	..	..	1	..	1	..	..	1	..	..
Dowd, Samuel	2	1	..	1	..	1	..	..	1	..	..
Dye, Jonathan	1	..	..	1	..	2	..	..	1	..	..
Farewell, Benjamin	..	2	1	1	..	..	2	1	1	..	..
Farnel, Edward	1	2	1	..	1	4	1	..	1	..	..
Farnham, Bazaliel	..	1	..	1	..	2	2	..	1	..	..
Farnham, Benair	..	..	..	1	..	2	..	1	..	..	..
Farnham, David	2	..	..	1	..	1	..	..	1	..	..
Fellows, Nathan	..	..	1	1	..	..	2	2	..	1	..
Fifield, Josiah	3	..	..	1	..	1	1	..	1	1	..
Fifield, Samuel	..	..	..	1	..	1	..	..	1	..	..
French, Obadiah	3	..	..	1	..	1	..	..	1	..	..
Frisby, Amos	1	1	..	1	..	..	..	3	1	1	..
Frisby, Ebenezer	1	..	1	1	..	3	2	..	1	..	..
George, Sally	1	..	..	..	..	1	..	..	1	..	..
Gideons, Benjamin	1	2	2	..	1	2	1	1	1	..	..
Gilman, Amos	4	..	..	1	..	1	..	..	1	..	..
Gipson, Daniel	..	..	1	..	..	..	..	1	..	..	..
Gipson, Simeon	..	..	2	..	1	..	..	1	1	1	..
Glass, Silas	..	1	..	..	1	..	1	..	..	1	..
Goodspeed, Cornelies	..	..	..	1	..	1	1	1	..	..	..
Goodwin, Elijah	5	1	..	1	..	1	1	..	1	..	..
Goodwin, Silence	..	..	..	..	..	..	..	..	..	1	..
Gorum, James	1	1	..	1	..	..	..	..	1	..	..
Gorum, Seth	3	..	..	1	..	1	1	..	1	..	..
POULTNEY—con.											
Gorum, Seth	3	1	..	1	..	1	1	..	1	..	..
Gorum, Seth 2nd	2	2	..	1	..	..	1	..	1	..	..
Grant, John	..	1	..	2	1	..	1	1	..	..	..
Grant, Orante	..	..	..	1	..	..	..	1	..	..	..
Grant, Thomas	2	..	..	1	..	2	..	..	1	..	..
Green, William	1	..	..	1	..	2	..	..	1	..	..
Herick, Ephraim	..	1	1	1	..	1	..	..	1	..	..
Herick, Rufus	..	..	..	..	1	..	..	..	..	1	..
Herrick, Edward	..	..	..	1	..	4	2	..	1	..	..
Herrick, John	4	..	..	1	..	1	2	..	1	..	..
Hicock, Simeon	2	1	..	1	1	..	1	2	1	1	..
Hicock, Thaddeus	..	..	1	..	1	..	..	1	1	..	..
Hide, Ebenezer	..	..	1	..	..	..	..	1	..	..	..
Hide, Fay	..	..	1	..	..	..	..	1	..	..	..
Hide, Henry	1	2	1	..	1	..	..	2	1	..	..
Hide, Jabez	1	1	..	..	1	..	1	..	..	1	..
Hide, Samuel	..	..	1	..	..	..	..	..	..	..	..
Hide, Samuel	2	..	..	1	..	1	..	1	..	..	..
Hide, Walton	2	..	1	..	..	1	..	1	..	..	..
Hill, Warren	..	..	1	..	..	..	..	..	..	..	..
Hitchcock, Asael	..	..	1	..	..	..	..	..	..	..	..
Hitchcock, Jesse	1	..	1	..	..	1	..	1	..	1	..
Hodgkiss, Miles	..	..	..	1	..	1	..	1	..	..	..
Holembeck, Buelah	..	..	..	..	..	2	..	..	1	..	..
Hooker, James	3	1	..	1	..	1	1	..	1	..	..
Hooker, Thomas	4	1	1	..	1	1	2	..	2	..	..
Hosford, Aaron	1	2	..	..	1	2	1	..	1	..	..
Hosford, Isaac	..	..	..	1	..	..	..	..	..	1	..
Hosford, Reuben	..	1	1	..	1	1	1	..	1	..	..
Hosington, James	..	..	1	1	..	1	2	..	..	1	..
Hough, Ruth	..	..	..	..	..	..	..	..	1	..	..
How, Jacob	..	..	..	1	..	..	1	2	1	..	..
How, John	1	1	1	1	..	..	..	..	1	..	..
How, Peter	2	..	..	1	..	1	3	2	1	..	..
How, Silas	..	..	..	1	1	..	..	..	..	1	..
Hubbard, Daniel	2	..	..	1	..	1	..	1	..	..	..
Hull, William	..	1	..	1	..	..	..	..	1	..	..
Hurlbert, David	2	1	..	1	..	2	1	1	1	1	..
Jenny, Prince	2	1	1	1	..	2	2	..	1	..	..
Jones, Solomon	..	..	..	1	..	3	..	..	1	..	..
Jordan, Joseph	2	..	1	..	..	..	..	1	..	..	..
Jordan, Stephen	1	1	1	..	1	1	1	..	1	..	..
Jordan, Stephen Jr.	4	..	..	1	..	1	..	1	..	..	..
Joslin, James	1	2	..	..	1	3	1	1	..	2	..
Kellogg, Nehemiah	..	..	..	..	1	..	..	..	..	1	..
Kellogg, Samuel	1	1	..	1	1	2	1	1	1	..	..
Kilburn, Abraham	4	1	..	1	..	2	..	..	1	..	..
King, Joseph	4	1	..	1	..	1	..	..	1	..	..
King, Theodore	3	..	..	1	..	1	1	..	1	..	..
Kingsbury, George	1	..	..	1	..	..	..	1	..	..	..
Kingsbury, William	..	..	1	..	..	..	..	..	..	..	..
Kinney, Pebody	2	2	..	1	..	2	1	1	1	..	..
Lamson, Edmund	3	..	1	1	..	2	1	..	1	..	..
Lee, Samuel	1	1	1	..	1	..	3	1	1	..	..
Lewis, Benjamin C.	..	..	..	1	..	..	..	..	..	..	..
Lewis, John	4	1	..	1	..	1	1	1	1	..	..
Lewis, William	3	1	2	..	1	..	1	..	..	1	..
Lewis, Zuriel	..	1	..	1	..	5	1	..	1	..	..
Lincoln, Benjamin	..	1	2	..	1	3	..	1	..	2	..
Lincoln, John	2	..	2	1	..	1	1	..	1	..	..
Linsey, Mathew	2	..	..	1	..	1	..	..	1	..	..
Linsey, William	..	..	1	..	..	..	..	..	..	..	..
Lovel, Thomas	..	..	1	..	..	..	..	1	..	..	..
Mahuran, Seth	3	..	..	1	..	2	..	1	..	..	..
Mallory, Calvin	2	..	..	1	..	3	1	..	1	1	..
Mallory, Daniel	2	1	1	1	..	..	..	1	1	..	..
Manning, Dan	1	2	1	..	1	1	1	1	1	..	..
Marshal, Abijah	..	..	1	..	..	..	1	1	..	..	..
Marshal, Joseph	2	1	1	..	1	1	..	..	1	..	..
Marshal, Lydia	..	2	..	..	..	2	2	..	..	1	..
Marshal, Moses	..	..	1	..	..	2	..	1	..	..	..
Marshal, Timothy	1	..	..	1	..	2	..	..	2	..	..
McGraw, John	1	..	2	1	..	1	..	2	..	..	..
Meacham, John	..	..	1	..	..	..	..	..	..	..	..
Meacham, William	2	..	..	1	..	2	..	1	..	1	..
Mears, John	..	..	1	..	1	..	..	..	..	..	1
Mix, Stephen	..	..	1	..	..	..	..	..	..	..	..
Mix, Theophilus	1	1	1	1	..	1	2	..	1	..	..
Moranville, Lewis	1	..	..	1	..	2	..	1	..	..	..
Moranville, Stephen	1	1	2	1	..	..	1	2	..	1	..
Morgan, Caleb	1	1	..	..	1	..	1	1	1	..	..
Morgan, Jonathan	..	..	2	..	1	..	..	..	..	1	..

RUTLAND COUNTY—Continued

NAMES OF HEADS OF FAMILIES	FREE WHITE MALES: Under 10 years of age	FREE WHITE MALES: Of 10 and under 16	FREE WHITE MALES: Of 16 and under 26 including heads of families	FREE WHITE MALES: Of 26 and under 45 including heads of families	FREE WHITE MALES: Of 45 and upwards including heads of families	FREE WHITE FEMALES: Under 10 years of age	FREE WHITE FEMALES: Of 10 and under 16	FREE WHITE FEMALES: Of 16 and under 26 including heads of families	FREE WHITE FEMALES: Of 26 and under 45 including heads of families	FREE WHITE FEMALES: Of 45 and upwards including heads of families	All other free persons except Indians not taxed
POULTNEY—con.											
Morgan, Jonathan	1	..	..	1	..	3	1	..	1	..	..
Morse, Joseph	3	1	..	1	..	..	1	1	1	..	..
Munsill, Erastus	3	2	..	1	..	1	..	..	1	..	..
Newton, John	..	..	..	1	..	3	..	..	1	..	..
Newton, William	..	..	..	..	1	2	1	1	..	1	..
Noble, Ezekiel	..	..	..	1	..	2	..	1	1	1	..
Norton, Solomon	2	1	2	..	1	1	1	1	1	..	..
Olds, Aaron	2	1	1	..	1	1	2	..	..	1	..
Olds, Horace	..	1	..	1	..	1	..	1	1	..	..
Olds, Robert	2	..	1	..	..	1	..	1	..	..	..
Oney, Davis	..	..	2	..	..	..	..	..	..	1	..
Otis, Barnabas	2	2	..	1	..	2	..	..	1	..	..
Palmer, Joseph	3	2	..	1	..	1	..	..	1	..	..
Pardy, Amos	1	..	..	1	..	1	..	1	..	..	..
Parker, Abel	1	..	..	1	..	..	..	1	..	..	1
Parsons, John	1	..	..	..	1	2	3	1	1	..	..
Parsons, Oliver	3	..	..	1	..	2	..	..	1	..	..
Pearce, Simeon	1	1	2	..	1	..	1	1	..	1	..
Pepkin, Stephen	3	3	..	..	1	1	1	..	1	..	..
Pettingell, Joseph	..	..	1	..	1	..	1	..	..	1	..
Petty, Eliphalet	3	1	..	..	1	2	..	..	1	..	..
Pond, Abel	3	..	2	..	1	1	..	2	..	1	..
Pond, Elijah	2	..	1	..	..	..	..	1	..	..	..
Pond, Samuel	..	1	1	..	1	..	1	1	..	1	..
Pond, Thaddeus	2	..	..	1	..	..	..	1	..	..	..
Popple, Samuel	2	..	..	..	2	2	2	..	1	1	..
Powers, Sarah	..	..	..	..	..	2	..	1	..	..	..
Pratt, Lemuel	..	..	1	..	..	..	..	..	1	..	..
Pratt, Robert	1	..	1	1	..	2	..	..	1	..	..
Preson, John	1	2	1	..	..	2	1	1	..	..	..
Prouty, Lucas	1	..	1	..	..	..	..	..	1	..	..
Rann, Olive	..	1	2	..	..	1	1	1	..	1	1
Ransom, John	1	..	2	..	1	..	1	..	..	1	..
Redmond, Zephaniah	..	..	..	..	1	..	..	..	..	1	..
Reed, Josiah	1	1	..	1	..	4	1	1	1	..	..
Rice, Jason	2	2	..	1	..	2	1	..	1	..	..
Rice, Levi	3	..	..	1	..	1	1	..	1	..	..
Rice, Nathan	..	..	..	1	..	2	..	..	1	..	..
Richards, John	2	2	1	..	1	2	1	3	..	1	..
Richmond, Anah	2	..	..	..	..	..	..	..	1	..	..
Richmond, Barnabas	..	..	2	..	1	2	1	1	1	..	..
Richmond, Trajan	..	..	1	..	..	..	..	1	..	..	..
Riley, John	2	3	..	2	..	1	..	..	1	..	..
Roberts, Moses	2	..	..	1	..	1	..	..	1	..	..
Robinson, Asher	..	..	1	..	..	..	..	..	..	..	..
Rockwell, Daniel	3	..	..	1	..	1	..	..	1	..	..
Safford, Jonas	3	1	..	1	..	2	1	..	1	..	..
Sanford, Oliver	..	..	..	..	1	1	..	1	..	1	..
Sanford, Oliver Jr.	3	..	..	1	..	2	..	1	..	..	..
Satterly, James	..	..	1	..	..	..	..	..	..	..	..
Scilly, Moses	..	..	1	..	..	..	..	..	..	..	..
Scribner, Peter	1	..	..	1	..	2	..	..	1	..	..
Severance, Stephen	1	..	1	..	..	..	..	1	..	..	..
Seward, Timothy	2	1	..	1	..	1	..	..	1	..	..
Sheldon, Thaddeus	2	..	1	..	..	..	..	1	..	..	..
Shumway, John	3	..	..	1	..	2	1	1	1	..	..
Sliter, Jacob	..	2	3	..	1	..	1	..	..	1	..
Sliter, Walter	1	1	..	1	..	3	1	..	1	..	..
Smawley, Adoniram	..	..	..	1	..	..	..	..	..	..	..
Smawley, Elijah	1	..	..	..	1	..	1	..	..	1	..
Smawley, Porter	2	..	1	..	..	..	..	1	..	..	..
Smedley, Aaron	1	..	..	..	1	1	2	..	..	1	..
Smith, Daniel	2	..	..	1	..	2	..	1	..	..	..
Smith, Ebenezer	..	..	..	1	..	1	1	1	..	1	..
Smith, Ezra	2	..	..	1	..	1	..	1	..	..	..
Smith, Joel	4	1	2	..	1	..	1	..	1	..	..
Smith, Joseph	1	..	..	1	..	3	2	..	1	..	..
Sooper, Gilbert	1	2	..	..	1	1	..	1	1	..	..
Spooner, Joshua	1	..	..	1	..	..	..	1	..	..	..
Sprage, Daniel	1	..	1	1	..	2	..	1	..	..	..
Stanley, John	3	1	..	1	..	2	2	..	1	1	..
Stevens, Reuben	..	..	..	..	1	1	..	..	1	1	..
Stevens, Reuben Jr.	1	1	..	1	..	2	..	..	1	..	..
Stewart, Samuel	3	..	2	..	1	..	1	2	..	1	..
Stone, Samuel	..	..	1	..	..	..	..	..	..	..	..
Stone, William	..	..	..	1	..	..	..	..	..	..	..
Streeter, John	3	1	..	1	1	3	1	..	1	..	..
Strong, Darius	3	1	..	1	..	1	2	..	1	..	..
Sweet, Jonathan	1	1	1	..	1	..	1	2	..	1	..
Taylor, Edward	..	..	1	..	1	1	1	..	1	..	..
Thatcher, Amasa	1	..	..	..	1	..	2	..	..	1	..

NAMES OF HEADS OF FAMILIES	FREE WHITE MALES: Under 10 years of age	FREE WHITE MALES: Of 10 and under 16	FREE WHITE MALES: Of 16 and under 26 including heads of families	FREE WHITE MALES: Of 26 and under 45 including heads of families	FREE WHITE MALES: Of 45 and upwards including heads of families	FREE WHITE FEMALES: Under 10 years of age	FREE WHITE FEMALES: Of 10 and under 16	FREE WHITE FEMALES: Of 16 and under 26 including heads of families	FREE WHITE FEMALES: Of 26 and under 45 including heads of families	FREE WHITE FEMALES: Of 45 and upwards including heads of families	All other free persons except Indians not taxed
POULTNEY—con.											
Thatcher, Amasa Jr.	1	..	..	1	..	2	..	1	..	..	..
Thomson, Amos	1	..	..	1	..	..	..	1	..	..	..
Thomson, David	..	..	..	1	1	1	..	2	..	1	..
Thomson, John	1	..	..	..	1	3	1	..	1	..	..
Todd, Thomas	2	..	2	1	..	2	2	..	1	..	..
Torrey, Aaron	..	..	1	..	..	..	..	1	..	..	..
Torrey, Ripley	1	1	1	..	1	1	1	1	..	1	..
Turner, Moses	1	..	..	1	..	2	..	..	1	..	..
Turner, Pain	2	1	1	..	1	3	1	1	..	1	..
Turner, William	4	..	..	1	..	..	..	..	2	..	..
Tuttle, Calvin	2	..	..	1	..	1	1	1	..	..	..
Tyler, Asa	..	1	..	1	..	4	2	..	1	..	..
Wadkins, Bodewell	3	2	..	1	..	1	..	..	1	..	..
Walker, Ezra	1	..	..	1	..	2	..	..	1	..	..
Ward, William	1	2	2	..	1	..	..	1	..	..	1
Wares, Reuben	1	..	..	1	..	3	..	..	1	..	..
Webster, Elijah	..	1	..	1	..	2	2	..	1	..	..
Wells, Enos	..	..	1	1	..	2	1	3	1	1	1
Wheeler, Nicholas	2	..	1	1	..	2	..	..	1	..	..
Wheeter, Reuben	1	1	1	1	..	..	1	..	1	..	..
Whitcomb, Joshua	2	1	..	1	..	2	..	..	1	..	..
Whitmore, Philip	..	..	1	..	..	..	..	..	..	..	..
Whitney, Solomon	4	..	..	1	..	2	1	..	1	..	..
Wood, Daniel	..	2	..	1	..	2	..	1	1	..	..
Wood, John	1	..	..	1	..	2	..	..	1	..	..
Wood, Samuel	3	1	..	1	..	..	2	..	1	..	..
Woodman, Samuel	..	1	1	1	..	1	2	..	1	..	..
Yates, William	..	2	..	..	1	..	1	1	1	..	..
Yemmons, Elisha	1	1	..	1	..	..	1	..	1	..	..
UNCERTAIN NAME											
Stevens, Parada (?)	..	..	..	..	1	1	..	1	..	1	..
RUTLAND											
Adams, Horace	1	..	..	1	..	3	..	..	1	..	..
Adams, Titus	1	..	1	..	1	..	1	..	..	1	..
Adams, Titus Jr.	1	..	1	..	..	..	..	1	..	..	..
Allen, Nathaniel	2	..	..	1	..	2	..	..	1	..	..
Ames, Matthias	..	..	1	..	1	..	..	1	2	1	..
Andrus, Ebenezer	1	..	1	..	1	3	..	1	1	..	..
Andrus, Ezekiel	..	..	..	..	1	..	..	..	..	2	..
Andrus, Moses	1	..	1	..	1	1	..	..	1	..	..
Atkins, David	..	..	1	..	..	..	..	..	..	..	..
Atwell, Richard	..	..	1	..	1	..	..	1	..	1	..
Atwell, Thomas H.	..	..	1	1	..	..	..	..	1	..	..
Atwood, Benjamin	2	1	..	1	..	1	1	..	1	..	..
Avery, Bebee D.	1	..	1	1	..	2	..	..	1	..	..
Baker, Daniel	..	..	1	1	..	..	..	..	1	..	..
Baker, William	..	..	..	..	1	..	..	..	..	..	..
Baker, William Jr.	..	..	..	1	..	..	..	..	..	..	..
Bala, Moses	1	..	..	1	..	..	..	..	2	..	..
Ball, Daniel	..	..	..	1	..	..	..	..	..	..	..
Ball, Heman Rev.	..	..	..	1	..	..	..	..	..	..	..
Barns, James	1	..	1	..	1	..	1	1	..	1	..
Barns, William	2	..	..	1	..	2	3	2	1	..	..
Barr, William	..	..	1	..	1	..	1	1	..	1	..
Barr, William Jr.	..	1	..	1	..	1	..	1	..	..	..
Bassett, David	..	..	..	1	..	1	..	..	1	..	..
Bates, Christopher	2	1	1	1	..	2	1	2	1	..	..
Bates, Daniel	..	..	..	..	1	..	..	..	..	1	..
Bates, Daniel Jr.	1	..	..	1	..	..	..	..	1	..	..
Beach, Gershom	1	1	1	1	..	1	..	1	..	..	..
Bebee, Allen	4	2	..	..	1	..	..	..	1	..	..
Bebee, Ezekiel	..	2	..	1	..	3	1	..	1	..	..
Bebee, Guy	3	..	..	1	..	1	..	1	..	..	..
Bebee, Mary	..	..	..	..	..	1	..	..	..	1	..
Bebee, Solomon	1	1	..	1	..	1	1	1	1	..	..
Beeman, Nathaniel	1	3	2	..	1	2	..	..	..	1	..
Bell, Jonathan	1	1	1	..	1	1	..	1	1	..	..
Bidwell, Elijah	1	1	..	1	..	4	1	..	1	..	..
Billington, Betty	..	..	..	..	..	..	..	..	..	1	..
Billington, Frederick	..	..	..	1	..	..	..	..	..	..	..
Bird, Michael	2	1	..	1	..	2	..	..	2	..	..
Bisby, Ephraim	..	..	1	..	..	..	..	..	..	..	..
Bissel, Benjamin	1	..	..	1	..	1	..	1	..	..	..
Bissel, John	..	1	1	..	1	..	..	..	1	..	..
Bissel, John Jr.	1	..	..	1	..	1	..	1	..	..	..
Blanchard, Benjamin	1	..	..	1	..	2	..	..	1	..	..
Blanchard, Benjamin	..	..	..	..	1	..	..	..	..	1	..
Blanchard, Bryan	1	..	..	1	..	..	..	..	1	..	..
Blanchard, Eber	..	..	1	..	1	..	..	..	..	1	..
Blanchard, Ephram	..	1	1	..	..	2	1	1	..	..	..

RUTLAND COUNTY—Continued

NAMES OF HEADS OF FAMILIES	FREE WHITE MALES: Under 10 years of age	Of 10 and under 16	Of 16 and under 26 including heads of families	Of 26 and under 45 including heads of families	Of 45 and upwards including heads of families	FREE WHITE FEMALES: Under 10 years of age	Of 10 and under 16	Of 16 and under 26 including heads of families	Of 26 and under 45 including heads of families	Of 45 and upwards including heads of families	All other free persons except Indians not taxed
RUTLAND—con.											
Blanchard, Timothy	2	..	..	1	..	1	1	1	..	..	..
Bordman, Timothy	3	1	..	1	..	1	2	..	1	..	..
Bowen, James	..	..	..	1	..	..	..	..	..	..	..
Brewster, Josiah	1	..	..	1	..	3	..	..	1	..	..
Bridge, Benjamin	..	..	1	..	4	..	1	1	..	..	..
Briggs, Varda	..	..	1	..	..	2	2	..	..	1	..
Brown, Simeon	..	..	1	..	..	..	..	..	..	..	..
Brownson, John	..	..	1	..	..	..	..	1	..	..	..
Buck, George	..	..	..	1	..	..	..	..	..	..	..
Bush, William	2	1	..	1	..	..	..	1	..	..	..
Butler, James	..	..	..	1	..	..	..	1	..	..	..
Butler, John	..	..	1	1	..	2	..	1	..	..	..
Butman, William	2	..	1	1	..	2	..	2	..	..	..
Campbell, Daniel	3	..	..	1	1	..	..	1	..	..	..
Campbell, David	2	..	..	1	..	3	..	..	1	..	..
Campbell, Joseph	..	..	..	1	..	3	..	..	1	..	..
Campbell, Samuel	2	1	..	1	..	4	1	..	1	..	..
Capron, Benjamin	3	2	3	..	1	1	..	1	1	..	..
Carpender, Cyrus	..	..	1	..	..	..	..	..	..	..	..
Carpender, Jabish	..	2	..	..	1	..	..	..	1	1	..
Carter, David	1	2	..	1	..	1	..	1	1	1	..
Chapman, John	1	..	1	..	..	..	1	..	1	..	..
Chapman, Lemuel	2	..	..	1	..	1	1	..	1	..	..
Chapman, Nathaniel	2	1	1	..	1	1	1	1	1	..	..
Chatterton, Isaac	..	1	1	1	..	2	2	..	1	..	..
Chatterton, Wait	1	1	1	1	..	2	1	..	1	..	..
Cheney, Benjamin	..	..	..	..	1	..	..	..	..	1	..
Cheney, Benjamin Jr.	1	..	..	1	..	1	..	..	1	..	..
Cheney, Eliakim	1	..	1	..	..	1	..	1	..	..	..
Cheney, Gershom	..	1	..	1	..	..	..	1	..	..	..
Cheney, Samuel	..	..	..	1	..	..	..	..	..	..	..
Cheney, Timothy	..	1	3	..	1	1	..	1	1	1	..
Cheney, Timothy Jr.	1	..	..	1	..	..	..	1	..	..	..
Chipman, Darius	1	1	..	1	1	2	2	1	1	..	..
Claghorn, Eleazer	..	..	..	1	..	..	..	..	1	..	..
Claghorn, James	..	1	..	..	1	..	1	..	..	1	..
Claghorn, John	1	..	..	1	..	3	..	1	..	..	..
Clark, Asa	2	..	..	..	1	2	..	..	1	..	..
Clark, Elisha	1	1	1	..	1	2	1	..	1	..	..
Cleveland, John	..	..	1	..	..	..	..	..	..	..	..
Coburn, Dyar	..	..	..	..	1	..	..	..	..	..	..
Coffin, Ralph	2	..	..	1	..	1	..	..	1	..	..
Cook, Ashbel	6	..	..	..	1	..	..	..	..	1	..
Cook, John	..	..	..	1	..	..	..	..	..	..	..
Cook, John	3	1	..	..	1	1	1	1	1	..	..
Cook, Munson	..	1	..	1	..	..	1	1	..	..	..
Cook, Simeon	..	..	3	..	..	1	..	1	..	..	..
Cornish, Benjamin	1	1	..	..	1	..	1	..	2	1	..
Cornish, Gabriel	4	..	..	1	..	2	..	1	..	..	..
Craft, Royal	1	..	..	1	..	1	1	1	..	..	..
Cray, Daniel	3	..	..	1	..	..	..	..	1	..	..
Crofts, Christopher	3	..	2	1	..	1	2	..	1	..	..
Crosman, Elijah	..	1	1	..	1	3	..	3	1	..	..
Cross, Isaac	..	..	1	1	..	..	..	..	..	..	..
Cushman, Ethel	2	..	..	1	..	3	..	..	2	..	..
Daniels, Gad	1	..	..	1	..	5	..	..	1	..	..
Daniels, John	1	..	1	..	..	1	..	1	..	..	..
Daniels, John	2	1	..	..	1	1	1	2	..	1	..
Darling, Abel	..	1	2	..	1	2	1	..	..	1	..
Davis, Samuel	..	..	..	..	1	..	..	..	..	1	..
Dealing, Rufus	3	2	..	1	..	..	1	..	1	..	..
Deers, William	2	..	..	1	..	1	..	1	..	..	..
Denison, William	..	1	2	..	..	..	..	1	..	..	..
Densmore, David	..	..	1	..	..	..	1	1	..	..	..
Densmore, Samuel	..	..	1	..	..	..	..	..	..	..	..
Dewey, Barzillai	3	2	..	1	..	2	..	..	1	..	..
Dewey, Jeremiah	2	2	..	1	..	..	..	..	1	..	..
Dickinson, Hannah	1	..	..	..	..	1	..	1	..	..	..
Dickinson, Heman	..	..	1	..	..	..	..	..	..	..	..
Dickinson, Versail	1	..	..	1	..	2	..	1	..	..	..
Dicks, John	..	..	1	..	..	..	..	1	..	..	..
Dow, Samuel	2	1	1	..	1	..	..	..	1	..	..
Driver, Thomas	..	..	1	..	..	..	..	..	..	..	..
Dutton, Samuel	1	..	1	1	..	..	..	1	1	..	..
Dyar, George	1	..	..	1	..	1	..	1	..	..	..
Eno, Benjamin	..	..	1	..	..	..	..	1	..	..	..
Fenn, Gideon	2	..	..	1	..	2	1	..	1	..	..
Fenton, John	..	..	1	1	1	..	2	1	..	1	..
Fenton, Mathew	1	1	..	..	1	..	..	1	1	..	..
Fenton, Samuel	1	..	..	..	1	2	..	2	..	1	..
Fessenden, Samuel	..	..	1	..	..	..	..	..	..	..	..
Fessenden, Thomas	..	..	1	..	..	..	..	..	..	..	..
Foot, Levi	..	..	..	1	..	..	..	..	..	..	..
RUTLAND—con.											
Forbes, Samuel	1	..	..	1	..	1	1	..	1	..	..
Ford, Benjamin	..	..	1	..	..	..	..	..	..	..	..
Ford, Daniel	..	..	..	1	..	..	1	..	1	..	..
Frost, David	1	..	..	1	..	2	..	1	..	..	..
Fuller, Ozias	1	..	..	1	..	1	..	1	..	..	..
Fuller, Samuel	2	..	..	1	..	2	..	..	1	..	..
Gage, Isaac	..	..	..	1	..	..	..	..	..	..	..
Gates, Jeremiah	..	..	1	..	..	..	..	..	..	..	..
Gates, Nehemiah	1	2	..	..	1	..	1	1	..	1	..
Goddard, Nichols	..	..	..	1	..	1	..	1	..	1	..
Goodrich, Francis	..	1	..	1	..	..	..	..	1	..	..
Gould, Henry	1	2	..	1	..	1	1	..	1	..	..
Gove, Nathaniel	..	..	1	..	1	..	..	..	..	..	..
Graham, Burr	1	1	..	1	..	1	1	1	..	..	..
Graves, Asa	1	..	..	1	..	..	2	1	1	..	..
Green, Ezekiel	3	2	..	1	..	..	1	..	1	..	..
Greno, Daniel	1	2	2	..	1	2	..	..	1	..	..
Greno, Moses	1	..	..	1	..	..	..	..	1	..	..
Grinols, Noah	1	2	..	1	..	1	..	..	1	..	..
Hagar, William	1	..	..	1	..	1	..	1	..	..	..
Hale, Asa	3	..	..	1	..	3	3	..	1	..	..
Hale, Thomas	2	..	..	..	2	..	1	1	1	..	..
Hale, William	2	..	..	1	..	2	..	1	1	..	..
Hall, Abijah	2	..	..	1	..	1	..	..	1	..	..
Hamblin, Lewis	1	..	..	1	..	..	..	1	..	..	..
Hamblin, Nathaniel	..	..	1	..	..	..	..	..	..	..	..
Harmon, Oliver	..	2	..	1	..	1	..	1	1	1	..
Harris, Israel	..	1	3	..	1	..	1	2	..	1	..
Hart, Hawkins	..	1	..	1	..	2	..	1	..	..	..
Hart, Josiah	..	..	1	..	1	..	..	1	..	1	..
Hart, Lombard	3	..	..	1	..	2	1	..	1	..	..
Hartwell, Joseph	..	..	1	..	1	..	1	..	..	1	..
Haskins, Daniel	2	1	1	1	..	1	1	..	1	..	..
Hawks, Moses	1	1	..	1	..	1	1	1	1	..	..
Hazard, Robinson	..	..	..	1	..	4	..	..	1	1	..
Hazleton, John	..	..	1	..	..	..	..	..	..	..	..
Hazleton, Joseph	..	..	1	..	..	..	..	..	..	..	..
Hendrick, Asa	2	..	..	1	..	1	..	..	1	..	..
Henry, William	..	..	1	..	..	..	..	..	..	..	..
Herrick, Elijah	4	1	..	1	..	..	..	..	1	..	..
Hill, Frederick	2	..	..	..	1	1	..	..	..	1	..
Hill, Lyman	..	..	1	..	..	..	..	..	..	..	..
Hobbs, Jacob	..	..	1	1	1	..	..	2	..	1	..
Holbrook, Abel	..	..	..	1	..	..	..	..	..	..	..
Holbrook, John	1	..	..	1	..	2	..	..	1	..	..
Holmes, Amos	..	1	1	..	1	..	1	2	..	..	..
Hooker, Thomas	..	..	1	1	..	1	..	1	1	..	1
Horn, James	..	..	1	..	..	1	1	1	..	..	..
Hoten, Luther	..	..	1	..	..	..	..	..	..	..	..
How, John	1	1	..	1	..	1	..	..	1	..	..
Huet, Amos	2	..	..	1	..	2	..	..	1	..	..
Humphrey, Joseph	1	1	..	1	..	1	..	1	..	..	..
Jackson, David	2	3	..	1	1	3	1	..	1	..	..
Jenkins, Simeon	1	..	1	1	1	..	..	..	1	1	..
Johnson, Elisha	1	2	..	1	..	1	..	..	1	..	..
Johnson, John	..	..	2	..	1	1	..	..	..	1	..
Johnson, Libbius	3	2	1	1	..	3	..	..	1	..	..
Johnson, Silas	2	..	..	1	..	2	1	..	1	..	..
Keiler, Eli	1	..	..	1	..	1	..	..	1	..	..
Keiler, Martin	1	..	..	1	..	2	..	1	..	..	..
Keiler, Samantha	..	1	1	..	..	2	2	1	1	..	..
Kimbol, John	4	1	..	..	1	1	1	..	1	..	..
Kinsley, Phinehas	1	1	..	..	1	2	3	..	..	1	..
Knott, William	1	..	..	1	..	2	..	1	..	..	..
Larkin, Abel	..	..	..	1	..	..	..	..	2	1	..
Larkin, Joseph	..	..	..	1	..	..	..	..	..	..	..
Lathrop, Abijah	..	..	2	..	..	..	..	..	..	..	..
Lee, William	..	..	1	1	..	..	1	1	1	..	1
Lewis, Henry	..	..	..	1	..	..	..	..	1	..	..
Lily, Richard	3	1	..	1	..	4	1	..	1	..	..
Lister, Moses	..	..	..	1	..	..	..	1	..	..	..
Lister, Simeon	1	..	1	1	..	1	..	..	1	..	..
Long, Levi	5	2	..	1	..	1	..	..	1	..	..
Loomis, John	..	..	..	..	1	..	..	..	..	1	..
Lord, Benjamin	..	..	1	1	..	..	..	1	..	..	..
Loveland, Joseph	..	..	2	..	..	..	..	1	..	..	..
Marsh, Asaph	..	..	..	1	..	2	..	..	1	..	..
Maynard, Trobrige	..	..	4	1	..	1	1	1	..	..	..
McCarter, John	2	..	..	1	..	3	..	1	1	..	..
McConnel, John	2	..	..	1	..	2	1	..	1	..	..
McConnel, Mary	..	..	..	..	..	..	..	1	1	..	..

RUTLAND COUNTY—Continued

NAMES OF HEADS OF FAMILIES	FREE WHITE MALES: Under 10 years of age	FREE WHITE MALES: Of 10 and under 16	FREE WHITE MALES: Of 16 and under 26 including heads of families	FREE WHITE MALES: Of 26 and under 45 including heads of families	FREE WHITE MALES: Of 45 and upwards including heads of families.	FREE WHITE FEMALES: Under 10 years of age	FREE WHITE FEMALES: Of 10 and under 16	FREE WHITE FEMALES: Of 16 and under 26 including heads of families	FREE WHITE FEMALES: Of 26 and under 45 including heads of families	FREE WHITE FEMALES: Of 45 and upwards including heads of families	All other free persons except Indians not taxed
RUTLAND—con.											
McConnel, Samuel	2	..	1	1	..	..	..	1	..	..	..
McConnel, William	3	..	..	1	..	..	1	..	1	..	..
Meacham, Jacob	2	1	..	..	1	1	..	1	1	..	..
Meacham, Lewis	..	..	..	1	..	..	..	..	..	..	..
Mead, Abner	1	2	1	1	..	1	1	..	..	..	..
Mead, Henry	4	..	1	1	1	1	1	..	1	1	..
Mead, James	1	..	..	..	1	..	..	..	..	1	..
Mead, James Jr.	1	..	..	1	..	..	1	1	..	..	..
Mead, Silas	..	1	..	1	..	4	1	..	2	..	..
Mead, Stephen	3	2	..	1	..	..	..	1	1	..	..
Mead, William	..	..	..	1	..	2	..	2	..	..	..
Mead, Zebulon	1	..	..	..	1	1	2	1	1	..	..
Miller, Aaron	1	1	..	..	1	1	..	1	..	1	..
Miller, Sally	..	..	..	..	..	2	..	..	1	..	..
Miller, Thomas	2	..	..	1	..	3	..	1	1	1	1
Miner, John	2	1	..	1	..	2	1	..	1	..	..
Molthrop, Jude	..	2	..	1	..	1	1	..	1	..	..
Montague, Zenas	..	..	1	..	..	..	..	..	..	..	..
Moon, Abner	..	..	1	..	..	..	..	..	..	..	..
Moon, Moses	..	..	1	..	..	..	..	..	..	..	..
Moorey, Philemon	..	..	1	..	1	..	..	1	..	1	..
Morey, Abraham	1	..	1	..	..	2	..	1	..	..	..
Morey, Joseph	2	..	..	1	..	2	..	..	1	..	..
Morgan, David	1	..	1	..	..	..	..	1	..	..	..
Morgan, Elias	..	..	..	1	..	..	..	..	..	..	..
Moses, Charles	..	..	..	1	..	2	..	..	1	1	..
Moses, Ezekiel	1	..	..	1	..	3	..	..	1	..	..
Moses, Levi	1	..	..	1	..	2	..	..	1	..	..
Moses, Nathan	..	1	1	..	1	..	3	..	..	1	..
Muzzy, Ebenezer	2	..	3	1	..	..	1	1	..	..	..
Newcomb, Asaph	..	..	..	1	..	..	..	1	..	..	..
Newcomb, Bradford	..	..	1	..	..	..	..	..	..	..	..
Noble, Obadiah	..	..	1	..	..	..	..	..	..	..	..
Norton, Benjamin	1	2	1	..	1	..	1	2	..	1	..
Olvord, William	..	..	..	1	..	1	..	1	..	..	..
Ormsby, Ezekiel	..	..	..	..	1	..	..	..	..	1	..
Ormsby, Joseph	..	..	..	1	..	5	..	1	..	..	..
Osgood, David	..	..	..	..	1	..	..	1	..	1	..
Osgood, Joshua	..	..	1	..	..	..	..	..	..	..	..
Osgood, Josiah	..	..	1	..	..	..	..	1	..	..	..
Osgood, Nathan	1	..	..	1	..	3	..	1	1	..	..
Paige, Nathaniel	1	1	1	..	..	..	..	1	..	..	..
Paige, Polly	..	2	3	..	..	1	..	1	..	1	..
Paige, Ralph	..	1	3	1	..	5	1	..	1	..	..
Parker, Abel	..	..	..	..	1	..	..	..	..	1	..
Parsons, Daniel	1	..	..	1	..	..	..	1	..	..	..
Parsons, Hovey	3	..	..	1	..	1	..	..	1	..	..
Parsons, Josiah	2	3	..	1	..	1	..	2	1	..	..
Patrige, Jonathan	1	..	..	..	1	3	..	..	1	..	..
Pearson, Bartholomew	..	..	..	..	1	..	..	..	..	1	..
Pearson, Hovey	2	..	1	..	..	2	..	1	..	..	..
Perkins, Luther	..	..	1	..	..	..	..	1	..	..	..
Perry, Daniel	1	..	..	1	1	1	..	2	..	1	..
Perry, Joshua	..	..	2	..	..	2	..	1	..	..	..
Perry, Joshua	..	..	..	..	1	..	..	1	..	1	..
Phillips, James	..	..	1	..	..	..	..	..	..	..	..
Pier, Ethan	..	1	..	..	1	..	..	..	..	1	..
Pike, John	2	..	..	1	..	..	1	..	1	..	..
Pincheon, John	..	..	1	..	..	..	..	..	..	..	..
Poor, Elizabeth	3	..	..	..	..	1	..	1	..	..	..
Porter, Ezekiel	3	..	1	1	..	1	..	1	..	..	..
Porter, Stephen	2	..	..	1	..	..	..	..	1	..	..
Post, Elias	1	1	..	1	..	2	1	..	1	..	..
Post, Roswell	..	..	1	..	1	..	..	..	..	1	..
Post, Simeon	1	..	..	..	1	2	2	..	1	..	..
Pratt, Benjamin	..	..	1	..	..	..	..	1	..	..	..
Pratt, Ebenezer	..	..	1	..	1	1	..	1	1	1	..
Pratt, John	1	..	..	1	..	..	..	1	..	..	..
Pratt, Joshua	1	..	..	1	1	..	2	..	1	..	..
Pratt, Nathan	2	..	1	..	1	4	1	2	1	..	..
Pratt, Silas	..	1	..	1	..	..	1	..	1	..	..
Prentice, Samuel	..	..	..	1	..	..	..	..	..	..	..
Purdy, Smith	1	..	..	1	..	2	..	..	1	..	..
Purdy, Solomon	..	1	2	..	1	..	..	1	..	1	..
Ramsdal, John	2	..	..	1	..	1	..	..	1	..	..
Rattz, Jerusha	..	..	1	..	..	1	..	..	..	1	..
Reed, Daniel	2	..	..	1	..	3	1	..	1	..	..
Reed, Issachar	2	1	..	1	..	4	..	2	1	..	..
Reynold, Silas	1	..	..	1	..	3	1	..	1	..	..
Reynolds, James	..	..	..	1	..	..	1	1	..	..	..
Reynolds, Jonathan	..	2	1	..	1	..	..	1	..	1	..
Reynolds, Joshua	1	2	2	..	1	..	..	2	1	..	..
Rice, Adam	..	1	1	..	1	1	..	..	..	1	..
RUTLAND—con.											
Rice, Ephraim	1	..	..	1	..	..	..	..	1	..	..
Rolfe, Moses	4	1	..	1	..	1	..	..	1	..	1
Roots, Benajah G.	..	..	1	1	1	3	2	1	1	1	..
Ruggles, John	..	1	..	1	..	..	..	3	..	..	..
Russel, Peter B.	..	..	..	1	..	1	..	..	1	..	..
Sabins, David	..	1	..	1	1	1	1	..	1	1	..
Sawin, Luther	..	..	1	..	..	..	..	..	..	..	..
Sawyer, Jacob	1	1	..	1	..	2	..	1	1	..	..
Scott, Elijah	..	..	1	1	..	..	..	1	..	..	..
Scovel, Rufus	..	..	1	..	..	..	..	..	..	..	..
Sessions, Abner	1	..	..	1	..	..	..	1	..	..	..
Seward, Stephen	3	1	..	1	..	2	..	..	1	..	..
Shared, Ethan	2	1	1	..	..	..	..	1	..	..	..
Shaw, John	3	..	..	1	..	1	..	..	1	..	..
Shaw, Luther	..	1	..	1	..	1	..	..	1	..	..
Shaw, William	..	..	..	1	..	..	..	..	..	..	..
Shedd, William	2	..	..	1	..	1	..	1	1	..	..
Sheldon, Medad	..	1	..	1	..	..	1	1	..	..	..
Smith, Alexander	..	..	1	..	..	..	..	..	..	..	..
Smith, Cephas	..	..	..	..	1	1	1	..	1	1	..
Smith, Cephas Jr.	..	..	..	1	..	2	1	2	..	..	1
Smith, David	1	..	1	..	..	..	1	1	..	..	..
Smith, Elias	..	..	1	..	..	..	..	..	..	..	..
Smith, Elijah	1	1	..	1	..	2	1	..	1	..	..
Smith, Israel	..	2	..	1	..	1	2	2	1	..	..
Smith, Joel	2	..	..	1	..	3	1	..	1	..	..
Smith, John	..	..	..	..	1	..	..	..	..	1	..
Smith, John	2	..	2	1	..	3	..	1	1	..	..
Smith, John Jr.	2	1	2	1	..	1	2	..	1	..	..
Smith, Moses	1	..	..	1	..	2	..	..	1	..	..
Smith, Sally	..	1	..	..	..	1	1	..	..	1	..
Smith, Samuel	..	..	..	..	1	1	..	..	1	..	..
Smith, Samuel	..	..	1	..	..	..	..	..	..	..	..
Smith, Solomon	..	2	2	..	1	1	1	2	..	1	..
Smith, Willliam	..	..	1	..	..	..	..	..	..	..	..
Southerlin, James	..	..	..	1	1	3	2	..	1	..	..
Southerlin, Peter	1	1	..	1	..	3	2	..	1	..	..
Southworth, Isaac	1	2	..	1	..	2	1	..	1	..	..
Spalding, Joel D.	2	..	..	1	..	..	..	1	..	..	..
Spencer, Abel	3	..	1	1	..	2	1	1	..	..	..
Squier, Asa	..	..	..	1	..	..	..	1	..	..	..
Squier, Daniel	..	1	1	..	1	..	..	..	..	1	..
Squier, Daniel Jr.	2	..	..	1	..	2	..	..	1	..	..
Staples, Asa	1	1	..	1	..	2	2	1	1	1	..
Starkweather, Elijah	1	1	..	1	..	1	2	..	1	..	..
Stevens, Josiah	..	1	..	..	1	..	..	..	..	1	..
Stewart, Charles	..	..	1	..	..	..	..	..	..	..	..
Stewart, James	..	..	1	..	1	..	..	1	1	..	..
Stoddard, Isaac	..	..	..	1	..	..	..	..	..	..	..
Story, William	2	..	1	1	..	1	..	..	1	..	..
Stowers, Jacob	1	1	..	1	..	1	..	..	1	..	..
Stratton, John	..	1	1	..	1	..	..	1	..	1	..
Strong, David	..	..	2	..	1	..	1	1	..	1	..
Strong, Enos	..	..	..	1	..	..	..	..	..	..	..
Strong, Henry	1	1	1	..	1	2	..	2	..	..	..
Strong, Return	1	1	..	1	..	..	..	1	..	..	..
Strong, Rhoda	..	..	..	..	..	2	..	..	1	..	..
Sweet, Samuel	..	..	..	..	1	..	..	..	..	..	..
Tanter, Benjamin	..	..	1	..	1	..	..	..	..	1	..
Thare, Zenas	..	..	..	1	..	..	..	..	..	..	..
Thomas, John	..	..	1	..	..	..	..	1	..	..	..
Todd, Timothy	3	..	..	1	..	2	2	..	1	..	..
Tooley, Joseph	1	..	1	..	..	1	..	1	..	..	..
Train, John	..	..	..	1	..	..	..	..	..	..	..
Trall, Aaron	3	1	..	1	..	..	1	..	2	..	..
Trall, Chauncey	1	..	..	1	..	2	..	..	1	..	..
Trall, Eliphaz	4	..	..	1	..	1	..	..	1	..	..
Trall, Samuel	..	..	..	..	1	..	..	..	..	1	..
Tuttle, Benjamin	..	..	..	1	..	..	..	1	..	..	..
Tuttle, David	2	2	..	..	1	..	1	1	1	..	..
Tuttle, Ebenezer	2	2	..	1	..	..	1	..	1	1	..
Tuttle, Nathaniel	2	1	..	1	..	3	..	..	1	..	..
Wadkins, Moses	1	1	..	1	1	4	1	..	1	..	..
Walker, Benjamin	..	..	..	..	1	..	..	..	..	1	..
Walker, Jedediah	2	..	..	1	..	4	2	..	1	..	..
Walker, Samuel	..	..	..	1	..	2	..	1	1	1	..
Ward, Jabez	4	3	..	1	..	..	..	..	1	..	..
Warner, Aaron	..	..	..	1	..	..	..	..	..	..	..
Warren, Abram	..	..	..	..	1	..	..	..	..	1	..
Warren, Lyman	4	..	..	1	..	1	1	..	1	..	..
Washbun, Isaiah	..	2	1	..	1	2	1	1	1	..	..
Washbun, Reuben	..	..	1	..	..	..	..	..	..	..	..
Webber, Christopher	2	..	..	1	..	..	..	1	..	..	..
Wells, Jonathan	..	..	..	1	..	..	..	..	..	..	..

RUTLAND COUNTY—Continued

NAMES OF HEADS OF FAMILIES	FREE WHITE MALES: Under 10 years of age	FREE WHITE MALES: Of 10 and under 16	FREE WHITE MALES: Of 16 and under 26 including heads of families	FREE WHITE MALES: Of 26 and under 45 including heads of families	FREE WHITE MALES: Of 45 and upwards including heads of families	FREE WHITE FEMALES: Under 10 years of age	FREE WHITE FEMALES: Of 10 and under 16	FREE WHITE FEMALES: Of 16 and under 26 including heads of families	FREE WHITE FEMALES: Of 26 and under 45 including heads of families	FREE WHITE FEMALES: Of 45 and upwards including heads of families	All other free persons except Indians not taxed
RUTLAND—con.											
Wells, Joseph	..	2	..	1	..	2	1	..	1	..	..
Wheeler, Wilder	2	1	..	1	..	2	1	..	1	..	..
Wheelock, Eleazar	1	1	..	1	..	1	1	1	1	..	..
Whipple, Caleb	..	..	..	1	..	..	..	..	..	..	..
Whipple, Davis	2	1	..	1	..	3	3	1	1	..	..
Whipple, Ephraim	..	1	..	1	..	..	..	1	..	..	..
Whipple, Jonathan	1	..	..	1	..	2	1	..	1	..	..
Whipple, Joseph	..	1	1	..	1	1	..	2	..	1	..
Whipple, Nehemiah	2	1	1	..	1	1	..	2	..	2	..
Whipple, Thomas	..	..	1	..	..	..	..	1	..	..	..
Whitcomb, Rufus	..	..	1	..	..	..	..	..	..	..	..
White, Otis	..	..	..	1	..	3	..	..	1	..	..
White, Silas	..	..	1	..	..	..	..	..	..	..	..
Whitman, Jeremiah	1	2	1	1	..	2	1	..	1	..	..
Whitmore, Zolva	2	1	..	1	..	2	..	..	1	..	..
Whitney, Nathaniel	..	..	..	1	1	4	2	..	1	..	..
Whittaker, Gideon	..	..	..	1	..	..	..	2	..	2	..
Willard, Timothy	1	..	1	..	1	2	2	1	1	..	..
Williams, John	..	..	1	..	..	..	..	..	..	..	..
Williams, Polly	2	..	..	..	..	1	..	..	1	..	..
Williams, Samuel	..	1	2	..	1	..	..	1	..	1	..
Williams, Stephen	..	..	2	..	1	..	1	1	1	..	..
Willis, Adam	2	..	1	..	2	..	1	..	..	2	..
Wilmott, Thomas	1	..	..	1	..	1	..	2	..	..	..
Winchel, Nathaniel	3	2	..	..	1	..	1	..	..	1	..
Wolfe, Putnam	..	..	1	..	..	..	..	1	..	..	..
Woodard, William	1	..	..	1	..	3	1	1	1	..	..
Wright, Simeon	..	1	1	..	1	2	2	1	..	1	..
Wycott, James	2	1	..	..	1	..	..	..	..	1	..
Wycott, William	..	..	1	..	..	..	..	..	..	..	..
Wyman, Seth	1	..	..	..	1	1	..	..	1	..	..
UNCERTAIN NAME											
Biere (?), Luke	1	..	..	1	..	2	..	..	1	..	..
SHREWSBURY											
Adams, Philemon	..	1	1	1	..	1	1	..	1	..	..
Aldrige, Nicholas	1	..	..	1	..	2	..	..	1	..	..
Aldrige, Ziber	..	1	2	..	1	2	1	1	..	1	..
Allen, Joseph	..	..	..	1	..	..	..	..	1	..	..
Alson, Nehemiah	..	1	..	1	..	..	1	..	1	..	..
Andrus, Elijah	..	..	..	1	..	..	..	..	..	..	..
Andrus, Nathaniel	..	1	..	..	1	..	..	..	1	1	..
Ashley, Martin	..	1	..	1	..	3	..	..	1	..	..
Barney, Barney A.	..	1	1	1	..	2	..	1	1	..	..
Bassett, Asa	..	..	..	1	..	..	..	..	1	..	..
Billings, Philip	..	1	..	1	1	..	1	..	1	1	..
Bishop, Bethuel	1	2	1	..	1	..	2	1	1	1	..
Bishop, Robert	2	..	..	..	1	3	..	..	1	..	..
Blews, John	3	..	..	1	..	1	..	..	1	..	..
Briggs, Ebenezer	..	..	1	..	..	2	..	1	..	..	..
Brown, Christopher	1	1	..	1	..	1	..	..	1	..	..
Brown, James	..	..	1	..	..	..	..	..	..	..	..
Brown, Moses	1	..	..	1	..	3	1	..	1	..	..
Brown, Reuben	..	..	3	..	1	..	2	1	..	1	..
Brown, William	1	..	..	1	..	..	1	..	1	..	..
Buckminster, Job	4	..	..	1	..	2	2	..	1	..	..
Bullard, Asa	3	..	..	1	..	1	..	..	1	..	..
Bullard, John	1	..	1	..	..	1	1	..	..	..	..
Cass, Susannna	..	..	2	..	..	1	1	..	1	..	..
Chaplin, Jonathan	..	..	..	1	..	..	..	..	1	..	..
Cheney, Ephraim	1	..	1	..	1	..	2	2	..	1	..
Clark, Rufus	2	..	..	1	..	2	..	..	1	..	..
Colburn, Moses	3	..	..	1	..	..	..	..	1	..	..
Colburn, Willard	2	..	1	1	..	2	..	1	..	..	..
Cook, Uriah	3	1	..	1	..	1	1	..	1	..	..
Curtiss, Amariah	1	1	..	1	..	2	1	2	1	..	..
Dawson, Martin	..	1	1	1	..	1	1	..	1	..	..
Dennis, Samuel	1	1	..	1	..	1	..	..	1	..	..
Deriket, George	1	..	..	1	..	2	..	..	1	..	..
Dickerman, Jesenial	2	1	2	..	1	1	1	1	..	1	..
Elson, Nehemiah	1	3	..	..	1	1	..	..	1	..	..
Finney, Charles	..	..	..	..	1	..	..	..	..	1	..
Finney, Nathan	1	2	..	1	..	1	1	1	1	..	..
Gile, Jacob	..	..	..	1	.	..	..	..	..	..	..
SHREWSBURY—con.											
Hamilton, Adam	2	..	..	1	..	2	..	1	1	..	..
Hathum, Peter	2	..	..	1	..	..	..	1	..	..	..
Holden, David	2	..	1	1	..	1	..	1	1	..	..
Holden, Elijah	2	..	..	1	..	..	1	..	..	..	..
Holton, Asael	..	..	..	1	..	..	..	..	..	..	..
Hull, Ebenezer	1	..	1	..	..	..	..	1	..	..	..
Ives, Amos	2	1	..	..	1	1	1	1	1	..	..
Jenison, Abijah	1	..	1	..	1	1	..	..	1	..	..
Johnson, Ebenezer	..	1	3	..	1	..	..	2	..	1	..
Johnson, Ebenezer	..	..	2	..	..	1	..	1	..	..	..
Johnson, Elisha	3	..	..	1	..	2	..	..	1	..	..
Johnson, Timothy	2	4	2	..	1	..	..	..	..	1	..
Jones, Archelaus	3	..	..	1	..	1	..	..	1	..	..
Jones, Jonathan	..	1	1	..	1	..	1	1	..	1	..
Keyes, Nathaniel	1	..	..	1	..	2	..	..	1	..	..
Kilburn, John	..	..	..	..	1	..	..	..	..	2	..
Kilburn, John Jr.	2	..	..	1	..	2	..	..	1	..	..
Knights, Amos	1	1	2	..	1	1	..	1	..	1	..
Knights, Joseph	2	..	..	1	..	1	..	1	..	..	..
Knights, Luther	..	..	1	..	..	..	..	..	..	..	..
Laland, Benjamin	4	..	..	1	..	..	..	1	..	..	..
Lathrop, Abijah	..	..	1	..	..	..	..	..	..	..	..
Lathrop, John	1	..	..	1	..	2	..	1	..	..	..
Lathrop, Nathan	..	..	1	..	..	..	..	..	..	..	..
Lincoln, Daniel	2	1	..	1	..	3	..	..	1	..	..
Lincoln, William	2	..	..	1	..	2	..	..	1	..	..
Lord, William	..	2	2	..	1	4	..	2	1	..	..
Low, Samuel	1	1	..	..	1	..	2	2	1	..	..
Marsh, William	2	..	1	1	..	..	..	2	1	..	..
Mather, Samuel	..	2	..	1	..	..	..	..	1	..	..
McClarren, Moses	..	2	..	1	..	2	1	..	1	..	..
Merriam, John	1	1	..	1	..	..	..	..	1	..	..
Misser, Daniel	..	..	..	1	..	..	..	..	..	..	..
Morse, Squier	..	..	..	1	..	..	..	..	..	..	..
Needam, Benjamin	1	..	1	..	1	1	2	..	..	1	..
Needam, Benjamin	..	..	1	..	..	1	..	1	..	..	..
Newel, Jacob	3	..	1	1	1	..	3	..	1	1	..
Newell, James	..	..	..	1	..	2	..	..	1	..	..
Niles, David	3	1	..	1	1	1	1	1	1	1	..
Onion, Jonathan	..	1	1	..	1	..	..	1	..	1	..
Paige, Phinehas	..	1	1	1	..	4	2	2	1	..	..
Parker, James	2	1	..	1	..	3	2	..	1	..	..
Parker, Joseph	2	..	..	1	..	..	..	..	1	..	..
Pearce, Caleb	..	..	..	1	..	3	1	..	1	..	..
Pearce, Ephraim	..	..	..	1	..	..	..	..	1	..	..
Perkins, Philip	3	..	..	1	..	2	..	1	..	..	..
Perry, William	1	..	2	1	..	4	..	..	1	..	..
Plummer, Asa	4	..	..	1	..	..	..	..	1	..	..
Plummer, Joseph	..	..	..	..	1	..	1	..	..	1	..
Pollard, William	..	..	..	1	..	..	..	..	1	..	..
Pratt, Benjamin	..	3	1	..	1	..	..	2	..	1	..
Pratt, Benjamin Jr.	3	..	..	1	..	1	..	..	1	..	..
Preast, Samuel	1	2	..	1	3	1	..	1	..	..	..
Randal, Joseph	1	..	1	..	1	2	..	..	1	..	..
Richardson, David	1	1	1	..	..	1	..	1	..	..	..
Richardson, Jesse	2	1	..	1	..	1	..	1	1	..	..
Richardson, Rufus	2	..	..	1	..	1	2	..	1	..	..
Ritter, Reuben	2	..	..	1	..	1	..	..	1	..	..
Robinson, Calvin	..	..	1	..	..	..	..	..	..	..	..
Robinson, Daniel	..	..	4	..	..	..	..	2	..	..	..
Robinson, Ichabod	..	1	..	..	1	1	..	1	..	1	..
Russel, Nathan	1	..	..	1	..	2	..	1	..	..	..
Russel, William	..	..	1	..	1	..	..	1	..	1	..
Sanders, Moses	4	2	..	1	..	..	1	2	1	..	..
Shaw, Jarus	..	..	..	1	..	..	..	..	1	..	..
Shippee, John	3	2	..	..	1	..	1	..	1	..	..
Shirtliff, Jonas	1	..	..	1	..	2	..	..	1	..	..
Simmons, John	..	..	1	..	1	..	..	..	1	..	..
Smith, Abraham	4	1	..	1	..	1	1	..	1	..	..
Smith, Elijah	..	..	..	1	..	1	..	1	..	..	..
Smith, Elisha	1	..	1	..	..	2	..	1	..	..	..
Smith, John	4	1	..	1	..	1	..	..	1	..	..
Smith, Nehemiah	1	2	..	1	1	1	2	1	..	1	..
Smith, Reuben	..	..	1	..	..	..	..	..	..	..	..
Snow, John	2	..	..	1	..	..	1	..	1	1	..

RUTLAND COUNTY—Continued

NAMES OF HEADS OF FAMILIES	FREE WHITE MALES: Under 10 years of age	FREE WHITE MALES: Of 10 and under 16	FREE WHITE MALES: Of 16 and under 26 including heads of families	FREE WHITE MALES: Of 26 and under 45 including heads of families	FREE WHITE MALES: Of 45 and upwards including heads of families.	FREE WHITE FEMALES: Under 10 years of age	FREE WHITE FEMALES: Of 10 and under 16	FREE WHITE FEMALES: Of 16 and under 26 including heads of families	FREE WHITE FEMALES: Of 26 and under 45 including heads of families	FREE WHITE FEMALES: Of 45 and upwards including heads of families	All other free persons except Indians not taxed
SHREWSBURY—con.											
Sparrock, Noah J.	2	1	..	1	..	1	2	2	1	..	..
Swift, Barnabas	..	1	..	1	..	..	1	1	1	..	..
Swift, David	1	2	..	1	1	3	..	..	1	..	..
Underwood, David	2	..	..	1	..	..	..	..	1	..	..
Washbun, Salathiel	2	..	1	1	..	3	2	..	1	..	..
Waterman, David	2	1	1	1	1	1	..	2	1	..	..
Webber, Benedick	..	..	..	..	1	..	..	..	1	1	..
White, John	..	..	1	..	1	..	..	1	..	..	..
White, Lemuel	1	2	1	..	1	..	1	2	..	1	..
Whitmore, James	2	2	..	1	..	2	..	..	1	..	..
Wilber, Charles	..	..	..	1	..	1	1	1	..	..	..
Wilber, Philip Jr.	..	1	..	1	..	1	..	1	1	..	..
Wilber, Robert	..	..	..	1	..	1	..	..	1	..	..
Wilberm, Philip	..	..	..	..	1	..	1	1	..	1	..
Wilboby, John	..	1	1	1	..	..	2	..	..	1	..
Willis, Amasa	..	..	2	..	..	..	..	..	..	..	..
Witherly, Asa	..	..	1	..	..	..	..	1	..	..	..
Witherly, Noah	..	..	..	1	..	1	..	..	1	..	..
SUDBURY											
Adams, Elisha	..	..	1	..	..	..	..	..	..	..	..
Allen, Noah	1	..	..	1	..	1	..	1	..	..	..
Allen, Reuben	2	..	..	1	..	2	..	..	1	..	..
Austin, Seth	2	..	..	1	..	1	..	..	1	..	..
Baker, Moses	2	2	..	..	1	2	1	1	1	..	..
Barr, Alexander	2	1	..	..	1	..	2	..	1	..	..
Bassett, Samuel	..	..	1	..	..	..	..	..	..	..	..
Blakeman, Abel H.	..	..	..	1	..	2	..	..	1	..	..
Blanchard, Amasa	3	..	1	1	..	2	2	2	1	..	..
Bratten, David	..	..	1	..	..	..	..	..	..	..	..
Bratten, Samuel	2	..	..	1	..	1	..	1	..	1	..
Burr, Roger	4	1	..	1	..	..	..	..	1	..	..
Cattle, John	..	..	1	..	..	..	..	1	..	..	..
Chandler, Levi	1	..	1	..	..	..	..	1	..	..	..
Field, Othniel	..	..	..	1	..	..	..	..	..	..	..
Foster, Alpheus	2	..	..	1	..	3	1	..	1	..	..
Fuller, John	..	1	..	..	1	2	2	1	..	1	..
Gage, Ellis	1	..	..	1	..	1	..	..	1	..	..
Gage, Jesse	..	..	..	1	..	..	..	1	..	..	..
Gage, John	1	1	2	..	1	1	1	3	..	1	..
Graves, Elijah	1	..	..	1	..	2	..	..	1	..	..
Green, Moses	1	..	1	..	..	3	..	..	1	..	..
Greno, Daniel	2	..	1	..	..	1	..	1	..	..	..
Griffin, Benoni	2	..	..	1	..	..	..	1	..	..	..
Haff, Isaac	2	1	1	..	1	..	1	1	1	..	..
Hall, Aaron	3	..	..	1	..	1	..	..	1	..	..
Hall, Abner	2	1	..	1	..	4	..	..	1	1	..
Hall, Emerson	..	..	1	..	..	..	..	1	..	1	..
Hall, Moses	1	1	..	1	..	1	1	..	1	..	..
Hamilton, Benjamin	1	2	2	1	..	1	1	..	1	..	..
Hendee, Ephraim	..	..	1	..	..	..	..	..	..	..	..
Hurlbut, John	..	..	..	1	..	1	..	1	1	..	..
Jackson, Aaron	..	1	1	1	..	..	..	1	1	..	..
Jackson, Nathan	2	..	..	1	..	1	..	..	1	..	..
Ketcham, Platt	2	..	..	1	..	2	..	..	1	..	..
Ketcham Thomas	1	..	2	..	1	..	1	3	..	1	..
Kinsley, Benjamin	1	1	1	..	1	1	2	1	..	1	..
Lathrop, George	..	..	..	1	..	1	..	1	..	..	..
Little, Joseph	1	..	..	1	..	3	1	..	1	..	..
Little, Joseph	..	..	2	..	1	..	..	1	..	1	1
Little, Rufus	1	..	..	1	..	1	..	1	..	..	..
Merritt, Noah	1	..	1	1	..	2	2	1	1	..	..
Miller, Timothy	3	..	2	..	1	1	3	1	1	..	..
Mills, Stephen	1	..	..	1	..	2	1	1	1	..	..
Morton, Asa	..	..	1	..	..	..	..	..	..	..	..
Morton, Bala	3	..	..	1	..	..	..	2	..	..	..
Murrey, Daniel	1	..	1	1	..	..	..	..	..	1	..
Murrey, Stephen	1	1	..	1	..	2	2	1	1	..	..
Nichols, Aaron	1	1	..	1	..	2	1	1	1	..	..
Palmer, William	2	1	..	1	..	2	2	..	1	..	..
Parks, Aaron	2	1	..	1	..	2	1	1	1	..	..
Pearce, Richard	2	2	1	1	..	2	1	..	1	..	..
Pond, Paul	2	2	..	1	..	3	..	..	1	..	..
SUDBURY—con.											
Ranger, Samuel	..	..	1	1	1	..	1	1	..	1	..
Ranger, Samuel Jr.	..	1	..	..	..	..	..	..	..	..	..
Ray, William	1	1	1	1	..	1	1	..	1	1	..
Rice, Eli	2	..	..	1	1	2	1	..	1	1	..
Salsbury, Ephraim	2	1	..	..	1	..	1	..	..	1	..
Salsbury, Ephraim Jr.	1	..	..	1	..	2	1	..	1	..	..
Sanders, Asael	1	2	..	1	..	..	1	..	1	..	..
Saunders, Benjamin	..	..	..	..	1	..	..	..	..	1	..
Saunders, Sebrina	2	..	1	1	..	2	1	..	1	..	..
Smith, Asa	1	1	..	1	..	2	..	..	1	..	..
Smith, Benjamin	..	1	..	1	..	1	1	..	..	1	..
Smith, Daniel	4	..	1	1	..	1	..	..	1	..	..
Smith, Enoch	1	1	..	1	..	1	1	..	2	1	..
Smith, Oliver	2	..	1	..	..	..	..	..	1	..	..
Smith, Phinehas	..	..	..	1	..	1	..	..	1	..	..
Telton, Daniel	1	2	1	..	1	..	..	2	2	1	..
Torrey, Abel	2	..	..	1	..	2	..	..	1	..	..
Torrey, Samuel	3	1	..	..	1	1	1	1	1	..	..
Walker, David	..	..	1	..	..	..	..	..	..	..	..
Warner, Joseph	3	1	1	1	..	1	2	..	1	..	..
Warner, William	..	1	..	1	..	..	1	1	1	1	..
Wentworth, Elijah	4	1	1	1	..	..	1	1	1	..	..
Wheeler, Seth	3	1	2	..	1	1	2	..	..	1	..
Whitney, Israel	2	1	..	1	..	2	..	..	1	..	..
Williams, Asael	1	1	..	1	..	3	..	..	1	1	..
Williams, Joseph	..	..	..	1	..	..	..	..	..	..	..
Wilson, Jacob	1	..	..	..	1	5	..	..	1	..	..
Wissel, Benjamin	2	1	2	..	1	..	..	3	..	1	..
Wissel, Moses	..	..	1	..	..	..	..	1	..	..	..
Wood, Abel	2	2	..	..	1	3	2	1	1	..	..
Wood, Joseph	1	..	..	1	..	..	1	2	1	..	..
TINMOUTH											
Adams, Abel	..	..	1	..	..	..	..	..	..	..	..
Allen, Samuel	..	2	..	[illegible]	..	3	1	..	1	..	..
Allen, Waldo	..	..	1	..	..	..	..	..	..	..	..
Allen, Zenas	2	..	1	1	..	2	..	..	1	1	..
Ambler, Moses	..	..	..	1	..	..	..	1	1	1	..
Andrus, Elihu	..	1	2	..	1	1	1	1	..	1	..
Andrus, Joseph	1	1	..	..	1	..	2	1	1	..	..
Bala, John	1	..	..	1	..	3	..	..	1	..	..
Baldwin, Joel	..	1	..	..	1	2	..	..	..	1	..
Bal!, Jonathan	2	..	1	..	1	..	2	1	1	..	..
Ballard, Daniel	2	2	..	..	1	..	1	2	..	1	..
Ballard, Tilla	1	..	1	1	..	3	1	..	1	..	..
Barker, Erastus	..	..	1	1	..	2	..	..	1	..	..
Barker, Pitman	1	..	..	1	..	..	..	1	..	..	..
Barker, Samuel	..	..	1	..	1	..	..	..	..	1	..
Bartholomew, Isaac	3	1	..	1	..	3	2	..	1	..	..
Beach, David	3	..	..	1	..	1	..	2	..	..	1
Bebee, Eli	..	2	1	..	1	..	1	..	1	..	..
Bell, Oliver	1	1	..	..	1	2	1	..	1	..	..
Benham, Asaph	..	..	..	..	1	1	..	1	..	..	..
Benham, Samuel	1	2	3	..	1	1	1	..	..	1	..
Benjamin, James	..	..	..	..	1	..	..	..	..	1	..
Benjamin, Polly	..	1	..	..	..	3	1	..	1	..	..
Bingham, Solomon	2	1	1	..	1	..	..	..	1	1	..
Bishop, Edward	1	..	1	..	..	..	..	1	..	..	..
Bishop, Gideon	2	..	..	..	1	..	..	1	..	1	..
Bloggett, Artimus	4	3	..	..	1	2	..	1	..	1	..
Brewer, Jonathan	1	1	..	..	1	2	..	2	..	..	..
Brown, Dexter B.	..	..	..	1	..	2	..	1	..	..	..
Brown, John	..	..	..	1	..	4	..	..	1	..	..
Brown, Nathan	2	..	..	1	..	1	..	1	..	..	..
Calkins, Elisha	1	..	1	..	..	..	..	..	1	..	..
Calkins, Levi	3	1	..	1	..	2	1	..	1	..	..
Calkins, Thomas	2	1	..	1	..	1	..	..	1	..	..
Campbell, Ebenezer	..	1	1	..	1	..	..	1	..	2	..
Chandler, Asa	2	..	1	..	..	1	..	1	..	..	..
Chandler, Jesse	2	1	..	1	..	2	1	..	1	..	..
Chansey, Elijah	..	..	1	..	..	1	..	1	..	..	..
Clark, Elisha	2	1	1	..	1	2	2	..	1	..	..
Clark, Jasper	..	..	..	1	..	..	..	1	..	..	..
Coleman, Phinehas	3	..	..	1	..	2	..	..	1	..	..
Comstock, Daniel	..	..	1	..	..	..	..	..	..	..	..
Cramton, Augustus	3	..	..	1	..	1	..	..	1	..	..
Cramton, Buzi	..	..	..	1	..	1	..	1	..	..	..
Cramton, Neri	1	1	2	..	1	..	1	1	..	1	..
Croffield, Simeon	..	..	2	..	..	1	..	1	..	..	..
Cummings, John	..	..	..	1	..	1	..	1	..	..	..

RUTLAND COUNTY—Continued

NAMES OF HEADS OF FAMILIES	FREE WHITE MALES					FREE WHITE FEMALES					All other free persons except Indians not taxed
	Under 10 years of age	Of 10 and under 16	Of 16 and under 26 including heads of families	Of 26 and under 45 including heads of families	Of 45 and upwards including heads of families.	Under 10 years of age	Of 10 and under 16	Of 16 and under 26 including heads of families	Of 26 and under 45 including heads of families	Of 45 and upwards including heads of families	
TINMOUTH—con.											
Daley, William J.	4	..	..	1	..	..	1	..	1	..	..
Dean, Moses	..	..	..	1	..	..	..	..	..	..	..
Dodge, Richard	..	..	1	..	..	..	..	..	..	..	..
Downs, Noah	4	..	1	1	..	1	1	..	1	..	..
Ford, Isaiah	2	2	..	1	..	2	2	..	..	1	..
Gaut, John	..	1	..	..	1	..	..	1	..	1	..
Gillett, Abraham	..	..	1	..	1	1	1	..	..	1	..
Gillett, Sarah	..	..	..	..	..	1	..	..	1	..	..
Goff, Squier	..	..	1	..	..	1	..	1	..	..	..
Gould, Isaac	1	..	..	1	..	3	..	..	1	..	..
Gould, Joseph	..	..	..	1	..	2	..	..	1	..	..
Graham, William	1	..	..	..	1	2	1	..	..	1	..
Green, David	2	..	1	1	..	2	2	1	1	..	..
Hamilton, Aaron	..	..	1	1	..	2	..	1	..	..	..
Hamilton, Elisha	..	..	1	..	1	..	1	1	..	1	..
Hamilton, Nathaniel	1	1	..	1	..	..	..	..	1	..	..
Hamilton, Ziber	2	1	..	1	..	2	..	..	1	..	..
Harkins, John	2	..	..	..	1	3	..	..	1	..	..
Hazleton, Paul	..	..	..	1	..	..	..	..	..	..	..
Hazleton, Royal	1	2	..	1	..	3	..	..	1	..	..
Hazleton, Thaddeus	3	1	..	1	..	2	1	..	1	..	..
Henderson, David	..	..	1	..	..	..	..	..	..	..	..
Hill, Erastus	..	..	..	1	..	2	..	..	1	..	..
Hill, Ira	1	2	..	..	1	2	..	..	1	..	..
Hill, Luke	..	..	1	..	1	..	..	..	1	1	..
Hill, Zenus	..	..	..	..	1	..	..	..	1	1	..
Hiscock, William	6	2	..	1	..	..	1	1	..	1	..
Hooker, Martin	3	..	..	1	..	2	2	..	1	1	..
Hooker, Rowland	3	1	1	..	1	..	1	..	1	..	..
Huet, William	1	..	..	1	..	1	..	..	1	..	..
Hurd, Daniel	3	1	1	1	..	1	2	..	1	..	..
Hutchinson, Thomas	1	..	1	..	2	..	1	1	..	1	..
Ives, David	3	..	..	..	1	1	..	..	..	1	..
Ives, James	..	..	1	..	..	..	..	..	..	..	..
Ives, Jared	1	..	1	..	..	..	..	1	..	..	..
Jackson, Zerah	1	..	..	1	..	1	..	..	1	..	..
Johnson, Jesse	2	1	..	1	..	..	..	..	1	..	..
Jones, Reuben	2	..	..	1	..	1	..	..	1	..	..
Kent, Peleg	..	..	..	1	..	..	..	..	..	..	..
Kinney, Seth	..	..	2	..	1	..	1	..	..	1	..
Lansing, Robert	..	..	1	..	..	1	..	1	..	..	..
Lathrop, Elijah	..	..	1	..	..	..	..	..	..	..	..
Leete, Polly	..	1	1	..	..	..	..	1	1	..	..
Lily, Elijah	..	..	1	1	..	..	..	..	1	..	..
Linley, David	..	..	1	..	..	1	..	1	..	..	..
Linley, Jere	2	..	..	1	..	..	..	..	1	..	..
Miles, Charles	1	3	1	..	1	2	..	..	1	..	..
Morey, Abel	..	..	1	..	..	1	..	1	..	..	..
Mosure, Aaron	2	..	1	..	..	..	..	1	..	..	..
Mosure, Daniel	2	1	1	..	1	1	1	..	1	..	..
Mosure, Daniel	..	..	1	..	..	..	..	..	..	..	..
Mulford, Nathan	2	1	1	1	..	2	1	1	1	..	..
Newel, Daniel Jr.	2	1	2	1	..	1	2	1	1	..	..
Newel, Joseph	1	..	1	1	..	3	3	..	1	..	..
Nicholson, Ashbel	2	..	..	1	..	1	..	..	1	..	..
Nicholson, Glover P.	..	..	..	1	..	1	..	..	..	1	..
Nicholson, Henry	..	..	..	..	1	..	..	..	..	1	..
Nicholson, John	2	..	..	1	..	1	..	..	1	..	..
Noble, Obadiah	..	..	1	..	1	..	1	..	..	1	..
Noble, Shubal	2	..	..	1	..	2	..	..	1	..	..
Okeman, Joseph	..	..	..	1	..	1	1	..	1	..	..
Osburn, Benjamin	..	..	..	..	1	..	1	1	1	..	..
Owen, Joseph	2	..	..	1	..	2	2	..	1	..	..
Owin, Samuel	1	1	..	1	..	2	..	1	1	..	..
Palmer, Jeroniah	1	1	..	1	..	3	..	..	1	..	..
Palmer, Jerub	2	1	..	1	..	3	1	..	1	..	..
Paul, Joshua	3	1	..	1	..	2	..	..	1	..	..
Perry, Eliakim	..	1	1	..	1	..	1	..	..	1	..
Perry, Ozias	2	1	..	1	..	4	2	..	1	..	..
Perry, Seth H.	1	..	1	..	..	..	..	1	..	..	..
Pier, Chauncy	3	..	..	1	..	2	..	..	1	..	..
Porter, Thomas	1	..	..	1	..	1	..	..	1	..	1
Porter, Thomas	..	2	1	..	1	..	..	..	..	1	..
Pratt, Abner	1	..	..	1	..	2	..	1	..	..	..
Pratt, John	..	1	..	1	..	..	1	1	..	..	..
TINMOUTH—con.											
Rice, Eber	2	1	..	1	..	3	..	..	1	..	..
Rice, Levi	1	..	..	1	1	2	..	1	1	1	..
Ridley, John	..	..	1	..	..	..	..	..	..	..	..
Ripley, Vinis	1	1	..	1	..	1	..	..	1	..	..
Roe, John	2	1	..	1	..	..	1	..	1	..	..
Rogers, Thomas	2	1	..	1	..	3	1	..	1	..	..
Roys, Caleb	..	..	1	..	..	..	..	1	..	..	..
Roys, Charles	..	..	..	..	1	..	..	..	..	..	..
Roys, Samuel	2	1	..	..	1	2	2	1	1	..	..
Sawyer, David	1	..	..	1	..	2	..	..	1	..	..
Shaiss, Molly	..	..	..	..	..	..	..	..	1	..	1
Shepard, Elisha	1	..	..	1	..	5	1	..	1	..	..
Smith, Caleb	..	1	1	..	1	2	1	..	..	1	..
Smith, Daniel B.	3	..	..	1	..	..	1	1	..	..	..
Smith, Elisha	2	..	..	1	..	1	3	..	1	..	..
Smith, Jedediah	1	1	..	1	..	4	..	..	1	..	..
Smith, John	2	..	..	1	..	1	..	1	..	..	..
Smith, Nathan	..	..	1	..	1	..	..	..	..	1	..
Southworth, Jasher	..	1	..	1	..	3	..	..	1	..	..
Southworth, Obed	1	..	4	..	1	..	1	1	..	1	..
Sprage, Ebenezer	..	2	4	..	1	1	2	..	1	..	..
Sturdefant, Caleb	3	..	1	1	..	2	..	1	1	..	..
Sunderlin, Wallace	1	2	1	1	..	3	2	..	1	1	..
Taylor, Eldad	..	..	..	1	..	5	..	..	1	..	..
Tracey, Solomon	1	1	2	..	1	3	..	1	..	1	..
Train, Orange	..	..	1	..	1	2	2	..	..	2	..
Turner, Samuel	1	1	..	1	1	..	1	..	..	1	..
Utley, Elisha	..	..	2	..	1	..	..	..	..	1	..
Waldo, Beulah	2	..	1	..	1	..	1	2	..	1	..
Warriner, Samuel	..	..	..	1	..	4	1	1	1	..	..
Wheeler, Joseph	..	..	..	1	..	2	..	..	1	..	..
White, Gregory	2	1	1	1	1	1	3	..	1	1	..
Wilford, Joseph	1	1	2	..	1	2	..	1	..	1	..
Willard, Charles	..	1	1	..	..	..	..	1	1	..	..
Willard, Lura	2	..	..	..	..	3	..	1	1	..	..
Wood, Ezra	2	..	..	1	..	2	..	..	1	..	..
Wood, John	..	..	1	..	..	1	..	1	..	..	..
Wood, Samuel	3	2	1	..	..	1	..	..	1	..	..
Wood, Seth	1	..	..	1	..	4	..	..	1	..	..
Woodhouse, Henry	3	1	..	1	..	2	1	..	1	..	..
Woodman, Peter	3	..	..	1	..	..	2	..	1	1	..
Woodruff, Oliver	1	1	1	..	1	..	2	2	..	1	..
Wright, Chester	..	..	1	..	..	..	..	..	..	..	..
Wyman, John	3	..	..	1	..	1	..	..	1	..	..
Young, David	..	1	..	1	..	..	..	..	1	..	1
WALLINGFORD											
Aldrige, Arial	1	..	..	1	..	2	..	1	..	..	..
Aldrige, Oney	..	..	..	1	..	2	..	..	1	..	..
Aldrige, Philip	..	..	..	..	1	..	1	1	..	1	..
Aldrige, Royal	3	1	..	1	..	1	2	..	1	..	..
Aldrige, Solomon	2	..	2	1	..	1	1	..	1	..	..
Amidon, Horatio	..	..	1	..	..	..	..	..	..	..	..
Amidon, Jacob	..	..	..	1	..	1	..	1	..	..	..
Anderson, Ahira	3	..	..	1	..	1	..	..	1	..	..
Anderson, Asa	3	1	..	1	..	2	..	..	1	..	..
Anderson, John	..	..	1	..	..	..	..	..	..	..	..
Andrus, Jesse	3	..	..	1	..	..	..	1	..	..	..
Andrus, Lincoln	2	1	..	1	..	2	..	..	1	..	..
Andrus, Roswell	..	..	1	..	..	..	..	1	..	..	..
Babcock, Joseph	..	1	..	2	1	..	..	1	2	1	..
Baldwin, Jared	..	..	..	..	1	1	1	..	1	..	..
Bigalow, Jonathan	..	..	1	..	..	..	..	1	..	..	..
Bishop, Agabus	5	..	..	1	..	1	..	..	1	..	..
Bollard, Seth	1	..	1	..	..	..	..	1	..	..	..
Bradley, Benjamin	..	..	..	..	1	..	1	..	1	..	..
Bradley, Stephen	1	1	..	1	..	..	..	..	1	..	..
Brown, Abraham	3	1	1	..	1	4	1	1	1	..	..
Brown, Isaac	..	..	1	..	1	..	..	..	..	1	..
Bucklin, Nathaniel	..	..	1	..	1	..	..	..	..	1	..
Bucklin, Nathaniel Jr.	2	..	..	1	..	2	..	..	1	..	..
Bucklin, Rufus	3	..	2	..	1	1	1	..	1	..	..
Bump, Eben	..	1	..	..	1	..	..	1	..	2	..
Bump, Edward Jr.	..	..	1	..	..	2	..	1	..	..	..
Bump, James	2	1	2	..	1	1	1	1	..	1	..
Busby, William	..	..	..	1	..	..	1	..	1	..	..
Button, Asa	1	..	..	1	..	..	..	..	1	..	..
Button, Elisha	2	1	2	..	1	..	..	1	1	..	..
Button, Elisha Jr.	2	..	..	1	..	2	..	..	1	..	..
Button, Joseph	..	..	..	1	..	2	..	..	1	..	..
Button, Kinney	..	..	1	..	..	..	..	..	1	..	..

RUTLAND COUNTY—Continued

NAMES OF HEADS OF FAMILIES	FREE WHITE MALES					FREE WHITE FEMALES					All other free persons except Indians not taxed
	Under 10 years of age	Of 10 and under 16	Of 16 and under 26 including heads of families	Of 26 and under 45 including heads of families	Of 45 and upwards including heads of families.	Under 10 years of age	Of 10 and under 16	Of 16 and under 26 including heads of families	Of 26 and under 45 including heads of families	Of 45 and upwards including heads of families	
WALLINGFORD—con.											
Campbell, Ebenezer Jr.	..	..	..	1	..	1	..	1	..	..	..
Carpender, Beriah	2	1	1	..	1	1	..	1	..	1	..
Carter, Jonas	..	1	..	1	..	3	..	..	1	..	..
Cavenaugh, Martin	..	..	..	1	..	..	..	..	..	..	..
Chaplain, Rowland	1	1	..	1	..	2	..	..	1	..	..
Clark, Clemant	..	..	..	1	..	..	..	1	1	..	..
Clark, Edmond	..	2	1	..	1	2	..	1	1	..	..
Clark, Gardner	1	..	..	1	..	..	..	..	1	..	..
Clark, James	..	..	..	..	1	..	..	..	2	..	..
Clark, William	1	..	..	1	..	1	..	..	1	..	..
Congwell, Hadley	..	..	1	..	..	..	..	..	..	..	..
Congwell, Joseph	..	..	..	1	..	..	1	..	..	..	..
Conkright, Abraham	..	..	..	1	..	1	..	..	1	..	..
Conkright, James	1	..	1	..	1	..	1	1	1	..	..
Constantine, Jacob	1	..	..	1	..	..	..	..	1	..	..
Cook, Nicholas	2	..	..	1	..	1	..	2	..	..	..
Cook, Peter	1	..	1	..	..	..	..	1	..	..	..
Cook, Samuel	..	..	1	..	..	..	1	..	..	..	..
Cook, Zephaniah	..	..	..	1	..	..	1	..	1	..	..
Crandall, Luke	2	1	1	1	..	2	1	..	1	..	..
Crary, Elias	3	1	..	1	..	1	1	1	1	..	..
Crary, William	..	2	1	1	..	..	..	1	1	..	..
Cutiss, John	1	..	..	1	..	1	..	..	1	..	..
Darby, Amasa	..	..	..	1	..	1	..	1	..	..	..
Darby, Benjamin	3	1	1	..	1	1	1	..	1	..	..
Dennison, Nathan	3	..	1	1	..	1	2	..	1	..	..
Doty, Isaac	1	..	..	1	..	2	..	1	..	..	..
Doty, Joseph	1	..	..	1	..	..	..	1	..	..	..
Doty, Orman	1	1	2	..	1	1	1	1	..	1	..
Douglass, Daniel	1	3	2	..	1	1	..	1	..	2	..
Earl, William	2	..	..	1	..	1	..	2	..	..	..
Eddy, Andrew	..	1	..	1	..	..	1	..	1	..	..
Eddy, Enoch	2	..	1	1	..	2	..	..	1	..	..
Eddy, James	3	..	1	1	..	1	1	..	1	..	..
Eddy, John	1	..	..	1	..	1	..	1	..	..	..
Edgerton, Daniel	3	..	..	1	..	1	..	..	1	..	..
Edgerton, Phillip	2	..	1	..	..	..	..	..	1	..	..
Edgerton, Robert	2	..	..	1	..	..	2	..	..	..	..
Finney, Isaac	..	..	..	1	..	..	2	..	1	..	..
Fox, William	2	..	2	1	..	3	2	..	1	..	..
Fuller, William	..	..	..	..	1	2	..	1	..	..	..
Gardner, John	2	..	..	..	1	..	..	1	..	..	..
Ginney, Aaron	2	2	..	1	..	1	..	1	1	..	..
Ginney, George	..	..	..	..	1	..	..	..	..	1	..
Gould, Eli	1	..	..	1	..	..	..	1	..	..	..
Gould, Nathan	2	1	..	1	..	1	..	..	1	..	..
Green, Benjamin	2	..	..	1	..	3	..	..	1	..	..
Green, Henry	4	1	..	1	..	1	1	..	2	..	..
Green, Nathan	..	..	..	1	..	4	..	..	1	..	..
Hall, Abner	2	..	..	1	..	2	1	..	1	..	..
Hall, Isaac	..	..	..	1	..	..	..	..	..	..	..
Hall, Moseley	1	..	1	1	..	1	..	1	..	..	..
Hamalton, Silas	1	..	..	1	1	..	..	1	..	..	..
Hawkins, Abraham	2	2	1	1	..	2	..	1	..	1	..
Harris, Oliver	3	..	..	1	..	..	..	..	1	..	..
Hart, Jesse	..	..	1	..	..	..	..	..	..	..	..
Hawley, Abner	1	1	..	1	..	2	..	..	1	..	..
Hill, John	1	..	2	..	1	2	..	2	1	1	..
Hill, William	1	..	..	1	..	..	..	1	..	..	..
Hopkins, John	1	1	..	..	1	2	1	..	1	..	..
Hoten, Jacob	..	..	1	..	..	..	..	..	..	..	..
Huet, Andrew	1	..	..	1	..	2	..	..	1	..	..
Huet, Joel	3	..	..	1	..	..	..	1	..	..	..
Hull, Josephas	..	1	..	1	..	..	..	1	..	2	2
Hull, Zephaniah	2	1	..	1	..	1	..	..	1	..	..
Ives, Lent	1	..	..	1	..	2	..	..	1	..	..
Ives, Nathaniel	1	1	..	..	1	2	1	1	..	1	..
Jackson, Isaac	..	1	1	1	..	3	1	..	1	..	..
Jackson, Pharez	1	..	1	..	..	1	..	1	..	..	..
Jackson, Stephen	..	1	..	..	1	1	..	..	..	1	..
Johnson, Eliakim	..	..	1	..	..	..	..	..	..	..	..
Johnson, Miles	..	..	2	1	..	..	..	..	1	..	..
Jones, Jeremiah	1	..	1	..	..	..	..	1	..	..	..
Jones, Samuel	..	1	..	..	1	..	..	..	..	1	..
Kelly, Seth	1	..	..	1	..	2	..	..	1	..	..
Kent, Charles	1	1	..	1	..	3	1	1	1	2	..
Kent, William	1	..	1	..	..	..	..	1	..	..	..
Ketcham, Jonathan	..	..	1	..	1	..	..	..	..	1	..
Korah, William	2	..	..	..	1	..	1	..	..	1	..
WALLINGFORD—con.											
Lane, John	2	..	..	1	..	..	..	..	1	..	..
McCluer, Samuel	1	1	1	1	..	1	..	..	1	..	..
Meacham, David	1	..	..	..	1	3	..	1	..	..	..
Miles, Eleazer	1	..	..	1	..	3	3	..	1	..	..
Miles, Ezekiel	..	..	..	..	1	..	..	..	..	1	..
Miles, James	1	..	..	1	..	..	..	1	..	..	..
Miles, Thomas	..	1	..	1	..	2	1	..	..	..	..
Miller, Frederick	..	..	1	..	..	..	..	..	..	1	..
Miller, Solomon	..	..	1	..	1	..	..	..	..	1	..
Mix, Joel	..	..	1	1	..	2	..	1	..	..	..
Moon, Daniel	2	..	..	1	..	2	..	..	..	1	..
Moon, Sanford	..	..	..	..	1	..	..	..	..	1	..
Parker, Joseph	1	..	..	..	1	..	2	..	..	1	..
Phillip, William	..	..	..	..	1	2	..	..	1	..	..
Preson, Colburn	..	..	..	..	1	..	..	1	..	1	..
Preson, Daniel	2	..	1	..	..	1	..	..	1	..	..
Randal, John	1	1	1	1	..	3	1	2	1	..	..
Randal, Joseph	1	..	1	..	1	2	..	..	1	..	..
Randal, Joseph Esq.	1	..	..	1	..	..	1	..	1	..	..
Remmington, Daniel	4	..	..	1	..	1	..	..	1	..	..
Remmington, Jonathan	..	2	..	1	..	3	..	..	1	..	..
Remmington, Joshua	3	..	1	1	..	2	1	..	1	..	..
Rhodes, Judah	..	1	..	..	..	..	..	1	..	1	..
Richmond, Eliakim	..	..	..	..	1	..	..	..	..	1	..
Richmond, George	1	1	..	1	..	1	..	..	1	..	..
Richmond, Howland	..	..	..	1	..	2	..	..	1	..	..
Rogers, Nehemiah	..	1	..	..	1	..	1	1	..	1	..
Ross, Ezekiel	..	..	1	1	..	..	..	..	1	..	..
Ross, James	1	1	..	1	..	3	2	..	1	..	..
Scott, George	1	..	..	..	1	..	..	..	..	1	..
Scott, Justice	3	..	..	1	..	2	1	..	1	..	..
Shaw, Ichabod	3	..	..	1	..	..	..	..	1	..	..
Sherman, George	1	..	3	1	..	..	2	1	1	1	..
Smith, Moses	..	..	..	..	1	..	..	..	..	1	..
Smith, William	2	..	..	1	..	1	..	..	1	..	..
Southerlin, Aral	..	..	..	1	..	3	..	1	..	..	..
Southerlin, John	1	..	1	..	1	3	..	..	1	..	..
Southerlin, John Jr.	3	..	..	1	..	..	1	..	1	..	..
Stafford, Stuteley	2	1	..	1	..	1	1	1	1	..	..
Stewert, Vinol	2	..	1	..	..	..	..	..	1	..	..
Stewert, William	2	..	..	..	1	2	1	2	1	..	..
Streeter, Jonathan	1	..	..	1	..	3	..	1	..	..	..
Sweet, Benjamin	..	..	..	1	..	..	..	..	..	..	..
Sweet, James	1	..	..	..	1	..	1	1	1	..	..
Sweet, John	..	..	..	..	1	..	..	..	..	2	..
Swetland, John	..	..	..	1	..	1	1	..	..	1	..
Swift, Rowland	1	..	2	1	..	1	1	..	2	1	..
Terris, David	..	1	..	..	1	..	..	..	..	1	..
Thomson, Jonathan	..	..	..	..	1	..	..	..	..	1	..
Tift, Samuel	..	1	2	..	1	1	..	..	..	1	..
Towner, Ebenezer	..	..	1	..	..	1	..	1	..	..	..
Vaughn, George	1	..	1	..	1	..	..	..	..	1	..
Vaughn, Thomas	..	..	..	1	..	..	..	..	1	..	..
Vaughn, William	1	..	..	..	1	..	..	..	..	1	..
White, Abraham	1	1	2	1	..	1	..	1	1	..	..
White, Coolige	2	..	..	1	..	2	..	..	1	..	..
White, Elijah	..	1	1	..	1	1	..	..	1	..	..
White, Nehemiah	1	1	..	1	..	2	..	..	1	..	..
White, Nicholas	..	..	..	..	1	..	..	..	..	1	..
White, Philip	..	..	1	..	1	..	..	..	..	1	..
White, Simeon	2	..	..	1	..	1	..	..	1	1	..
Whitehorn, Clark	..	..	2	1	..	2	1	1	..	..	..
Whitehorn, John	..	..	..	1	..	3	2	..	1	..	..
Wily, Joseph	..	1	..	..	1	..	..	1	..	1	..
WELLS											
Andrus, Isaac	..	..	..	..	1	..	..	1	..	1	..
Atwater, Simeon	1	..	..	..	1	3	..	..	1	..	..
Baker, Reuben	..	1	..	1	..	..	1	1	1	..	..
Bebee, Ephraim	1	1	1	..	1	..	..	1	..	1	..
Bell, Andrew	2	..	..	..	1	1	1	..	1	1	..
Bellamy, Samuel J.	..	1	..	1	..	1	1	..	1	..	..
Blossom, David	2	3	..	..	1	1	1	1	1	..	..
Blossom, Peter	1	3	..	1	..	..	1	1	1	1	..
Bodfish, Joseph	3	..	..	1	..	1	..	..	1	..	..
Bow, Amos	1	1	..	1	..	2	..	..	1	..	..
Broughton, John	2	..	..	1	..	1	..	1	..	..	..
Broughton, Michael	1	4	..	1	..	..	..	..	1	..	..
Broughton, Samuel	..	..	..	1	..	2	..	..	1	..	..

RUTLAND COUNTY—Continued

NAMES OF HEADS OF FAMILIES	FREE WHITE MALES					FREE WHITE FEMALES					
	Under 10 years of age	Of 10 and under 16	Of 16 and under 26 including heads of families	Of 26 and under 45 including heads of families	Of 45 and upwards including heads of families	Under 10 years of age	Of 10 and under 16	Of 16 and under 26 including heads of families	Of 26 and under 45 including heads of families	Of 45 and upwards including heads of families	All other free persons except Indians not taxed
WELLS—con.											
Brown, William	2	..	..	..	1	1	1	..	1	..	..
Button, Joseph	1	..	3	..	1	2	1	1	..	1	..
Button, Joseph	1	..	1	..	..	1	..	1	..	..	..
Butts, Ebenezer	2	1	..	1	..	1	..	..	1	..	..
Cass, Isaac	2	2	..	1	..	1	2	..	1	..	..
Clark, Andrew	3	..	2	..	1	1	1	1	..	2	..
Clark, Reuben	3	..	..	1	..	..	..	..	1	..	..
Clark, Roswell	..	1	1	1	..	4	1	..	1	..	..
Clark, Stephen	..	1	..	..	1	1	1	1	..	1	..
Clemmans, Joel	1	1	1	1	..	4	..	..	1	..	..
Clemmans, Michael	..	..	..	1	..	3	2	..	1	..	..
Clemmans, Thomas	..	..	..	..	1	..	..	1	..	1	..
Cole, Anthony	2	..	..	1	..	2	..	..	1	..	..
Cook, Giles	..	..	1	..	1	1	2	..	..	1	..
Cowdre, William	3	1	..	1	..	1	..	..	2	..	..
Crosman, William	1	..	..	..	1	1	..	1	..	..	..
Cross, Daniel	4	1	..	1	..	1	..	..	1	..	..
Cross, Josiah	1	..	..	1	..	1	..	1	..	..	..
Culver, Daniel	..	..	..	1	..	..	..	..	1	1	..
Culver, Joshua	1	1	1	..	1	3	1	1	..	1	..
Culver, Samuel	..	2	1	..	1	1	..	2	1	..	..
Culver, Timothy	..	..	1	..	..	1	..	..	1	..	..
Darby, Jedediah	1	1	..	1	..	3	..	..	1	..	..
Davis, George	3	1	..	1	..	2	1	..	1	..	..
Dow, Jesse	1	2	..	..	1	3	..	..	1	..	..
Dunning, David	1	..	1	..	..	1	..	..	1	..	..
Dunskin, James	1	..	..	1	..	1	..	1	..	..	..
Dunton, Elijah	..	..	..	1	..	1	..	..	1	..	..
Dunton, Thomas	..	..	..	1	..	..	..	1	..	..	..
Dunton, William	1	..	1	..	..	1	..	2	..	..	..
Fenton, Walter	1	..	..	1	..	2	..	1	..	..	..
Fillmore, Henry	..	..	..	..	1	..	1	..	..	1	..
Fish, William	2	..	..	1	..	1	..	1	..	..	..
Foster, Talcott	5	..	..	1	..	..	..	..	1	..	..
Francis, Abigail	..	1	..	..	..	2	2	2	1	..	..
Francis, Daniel	2	..	..	1	..	1	1	..	1	..	..
Francis, Joel	2	..	..	1	..	1	..	..	1	..	..
Francis, John	1	..	..	1	..	3	2	1	1	..	..
Francis, Simon	2	1	..	1	..	2	1	..	1	..	..
Freeman, Benjamin	3	..	..	1	..	2	..	..	1	..	..
Fry, David	..	..	..	1	..	..	..	2	..	1	..
Fry, Sylvanus	1	..	..	1	..	1	..	1	..	..	..
Fuller, Timothy	2	..	..	1	..	2	..	..	1	..	..
Gears, Albergins	4	..	..	1	..	2	1	..	1	..	..
Gears, Israel	..	1	..	..	1	..	..	1	..	1	..
Gears, Israel Jr.	2	..	1	..	..	..	..	1	..	..	..
Gifford, John	..	..	1	..	..	..	..	..	..	..	..
Gillett, Jonathan	..	2	1	1	..	4	..	..	1	..	..
Glass, Rufus	1	1	1	..	1	1	2	1	1	..	..
Glass, Samuel	1	2	..	1	..	3	1	1	1	..	..
Goodrich, Daniel	1	2	..	..	1	3	1	1	1	..	..
Goodsill, Daniel	2	..	..	1	..	1	2	..	1	..	..
Goodspeed, Ansel	2	..	..	1	..	2	2	..	1	1	..
Goodspeed, Josiah	..	..	1	..	1	..	..	..	..	1	..
Goodspeed, Josiah Jr.	1	..	1	..	..	..	..	1	..	..	..
Goodspeed, Stephen	..	..	1	..	..	..	..	..	..	..	..
Graves, Ebenezer	1	1	..	..	1	1	..	..	..	1	..
Gray, David	1	..	..	1	..	2	..	1	..	..	..
Green, David	2	..	1	..	..	..	..	1	..	..	..
Grovenor, Nathaniel	3	..	1	1	..	1	..	1	..	..	..
Harmon, Caleb	..	1	..	..	1	..	..	..	..	1	..
Hicks, John	2	..	..	1	..	3	1	..	1	..	..
Hicks, Solomon	..	..	1	..	..	..	..	..	..	..	..
Hodgkins, Ramon	..	..	1	..	..	..	..	1	..	..	..
Hodgkins, Robert	..	..	..	..	1	..	1	..	..	1	..
Hodgkiss, Secretus	..	1	..	1	..	2	..	1	..	..	..
Hopsom, John C.	1	..	..	1	..	2	..	1	1	..	..
How, Benjamin	1	..	..	1	..	..	..	1	..	..	..
How, David	1	..	1	..	1	2	1	..	..	1	..
How, Joshua	..	..	1	..	1	..	..	1	..	1	..
How, Samuel	3	3	1	1	..	2	..	..	1	1	..
Hunt, William	..	..	..	1	..	..	..	..	1	..	..
Ives, Aaron	..	..	2	..	1	3	1	1	..	..	..
Johnson, Comfort	2	1	1	1	..	4	..	..	1	..	..
Johnson, Israel	2	1	1	1	1	2	1	..	1	1	..
Johnson, Samuel	1	..	1	..	..	1	..	1	..	..	..
Kellogg, Aaron	3	1	..	..	1	1	..	..	1	..	..
WELLS—con.											
Lamb, Gares	1	..	..	1	..	4	..	..	1	..	..
Lamb, Joseph	..	1	1	..	1	..	..	..	..	2	..
Lamb, Shubal	2	..	..	1	..	1	..	1	..	..	..
Lamb, William	3	1	..	1	..	..	..	1	1	..	..
Lane, Allen	1	1	1	..	..	..	..	1	..	1	..
Lathrop, Azariah	..	..	..	1	..	3	..	1	1	..	..
Lathrop, Robert	1	..	1	..	..	..	..	1	..	..	..
Lathrop, Samuel	..	..	..	..	1	1	..	..	..	1	..
Law, John	2	1	1	..	1	3	..	..	1	1	..
Lewis, David	1	1	..	1	..	1	..	1	1	..	..
Lewis, Enos	..	..	..	1	..	1	..	..	1	..	..
Lewis, John	2	..	..	1	..	..	..	..	1	..	..
Lewis, Mary	1	..	1	..	..	1	..	1	..	1	..
Lewis, Nathaniel	..	2	1	..	1	..	..	..	..	1	..
Lewis, William	..	..	2	..	1	..	..	..	1	1	..
Lily, Benjamin	..	..	1	..	..	1	..	1	..	..	..
Lily, Joseph	1	..	..	1	..	2	..	1	..	..	..
Lombard, Benjamin	1	1	2	1	..	..	1	..	1	..	..
Mallory, Gill	3	..	1	1	1	4	2	1	..	..	..
Mallory, Stephen	3	1	..	1	..	2	1	..	1	..	..
Mansford, Amos	..	1	2	1	..	1	1	..	1	..	..
McGraw, Thomas	1	..	1	..	1	1	1	..	1	..	..
McTosh, Daniel	2	..	..	1	..	2	..	1	..	1	..
Merrils, Nathaniel	2	1	..	1	..	..	1	..	1	..	..
Merrils, Oliver	1	1	1	..	1	..	..	1	1	..	..
Merriman, Israel	1	..	1	1	..	1	2	..	..	1	..
Merriman, Samuel	..	1	..	1	1	4	..	..	1	..	..
Miner, Ichabod	1	..	..	1	..	2	1	..	..	1	..
Morey, Walton	3	..	..	1	..	1	..	..	1	..	..
Moseley, Prince	1	1	..	..	1	2	1	2	1	..	..
Moss, Timothy	1	..	..	..	1	..	..	..	..	1	..
Parker, Eliphalet	..	..	1	..	..	1	..	1	..	..	..
Parks, Elijah	2	..	1	1	..	1	2	..	1	..	..
Parks, Simeon	3	..	..	1	..	1	..	1	1	..	..
Parsons, Jesse	1	2	..	..	1	4	1	..	1	..	..
Paul, James	1	..	..	..	1	..	1	..	..	1	..
Paul, Jonathan	2	1	..	1	..	2	..	..	1	..	..
Paul, Stephen	3	..	1	1	..	..	..	1	..	..	..
Pember, John	1	1	3	..	1	..	1	1	..	1	..
Potter, Seth	1	..	1	..	..	1	..	1	..	..	..
Potter, William	2	..	..	1	..	..	..	1	..	..	..
Prey, John	2	..	..	1	..	1	..	..	1	..	..
Reynolds, John	1	..	..	..	1	..	..	2	..	1	..
Reynolds, Joshua	1	..	1	..	1	1	..	1	..	2	..
Rider, Benjamin	..	..	..	1	..	2	..	..	1	..	..
Robinson, William	2	..	..	1	..	2	..	..	1	..	..
Ross, Friend	..	2	1	..	1	1	1	..	..	1	..
Rust, Elona	2	..	..	1	..	1	..	..	1	..	..
Rust, Obed	..	..	1	..	..	..	..	..	..	..	..
Snow, Amos	..	..	1	..	1	..	..	..	..	1	..
Starks, Abel	..	..	..	..	1	..	1	..	..	1	..
Stevens, Abner	2	..	..	1	..	2	..	..	1	..	..
Stevens, Asa	4	1	..	1	..	1	1	1	1	..	..
Stevens, James	1	..	..	1	..	..	..	..	..	..	..
Stevens, Peter	..	1	1	..	1	..	..	1	..	1	..
Stevens, Samuel	..	..	1	..	..	1	1	..	1	..	..
Stone, Nathan	..	..	1	..	..	..	..	1	..	..	..
Stratton, Benjamin	..	..	1	..	..	..	..	1	..	..	..
Strong, Seth	..	1	..	..	1	1	..	1	..	1	..
Sumner, Daniel	1	..	..	1	..	3	1	..	1	..	..
Sumner, Josiah	1	..	1	..	..	..	..	1	..	..	..
Terry, Elijah	2	..	..	1	..	2	..	1	..	..	..
Thomson, Jeremiah	..	..	..	1	..	2	..	..	1	..	..
Toby, Allen	..	..	..	1	..	..	..	1	..	..	..
Todd, Joseph	1	..	..	1	..	2	..	1	..	..	..
Turner, Jonathan	..	1	..	..	1	1	1	1	..	1	..
Tyler, Jason	..	..	1	..	1	1	1	1	..	1	..
Ward, David	3	1	2	1	..	2	1	..	1	..	..
Williams, Abijah	3	2	2	1	..	..	1	..	1	..	..
Winters, Thomas	2	..	..	1	..	1	..	1	..	..	..
Wolcott, Abel	..	..	..	..	1	..	..	1	..	1	..
Wolcott, Abel Jr.	..	..	1	..	..	1	..	1	..	..	..
Wolcott, John	1	..	1	..	..	..	..	1	..	..	..
Woodworth, Roswell	3	2	..	..	1	3	2	..	1	1	..
Wyman, Betty	..	..	1	..	..	..	1	..	..	1	..
Wyman, Daniel	1	1	..	1	..	2	2	..	1	..	..
Wyman, Nahum	..	..	1	..	..	..	..	..	..	..	..

RUTLAND COUNTY—Continued

NAMES OF HEADS OF FAMILIES	FREE WHITE MALES: Under 10 years of age	Of 10 and under 16	Of 16 and under 26 including heads of families	Of 26 and under 45 including heads of families	Of 45 and upwards including heads of families	FREE WHITE FEMALES: Under 10 years of age	Of 10 and under 16	Of 16 and under 26 including heads of families	Of 26 and under 45 including heads of families	Of 45 and upwards including heads of families	All other free persons except Indians not taxed
WESTHAVEN											
Adams, Samuel	1	1	..	1	..	1	1	..	1	..	..
Barber, Joseph	2	..	..	1	..	2	1	..	1	..	..
Barker, Cyrus	..	..	1	..	..	1	..	1	..	..	..
Barns, John	3	..	..	1	..	1	1	..	1	..	..
Bates, David	2	..	..	1	..	1	..	1	..	..	..
Bates, Oliver	2	1	1	..	1	..	1	2	..	1	..
Bates, Oliver Jr.	..	..	1	..	..	..	..	..	..	..	..
Bazley, Levi	1	..	..	1	..	2	..	1	..	..	..
Benjamin, Drake	..	..	1	..	..	..	..	1	..	..	..
Benjamin, Joseph	..	..	1	..	..	1	..	1	..	..	..
Bozworth, Hezekiah	..	..	1	..	..	..	..	..	..	..	..
Brownson, John	1	..	..	1	..	..	..	..	..	..	..
Camp, Heath	..	1	..	..	1	1	..	..	1	..	..
Chelsey, Elihu	3	1	2	..	1	..	..	1	1	..	..
Church, Elizabeth	1	1	1	..	..	..	..	..	..	1	..
Church, Oliver	..	..	..	..	1	..	..	1	..	..	..
Collins, Tyrannus	..	1	1	..	1	..	1	..	..	1	..
Cone, Azel	..	3	..	1	..	2	2	..	1	..	..
Crammer, Henry	..	..	1	1	..	1	2	..	1	..	..
Dickinson, Joel	3	2	1	..	1	1	..	1	..	1	..
Downs, Simeons	..	1	..	1	..	1	..	..	1	..	..
Farr, Arad	..	..	1	..	..	..	..	..	..	..	..
Field, Joseph	..	..	1	..	..	..	..	..	..	..	..
Fippeny, Benjamin	..	..	..	..	1	..	..	..	..	1	..
Fippeny, David B.	..	1	1	..	..	1	..	1	..	..	..
Foscott, Jesse	2	..	..	..	1	1	2	..	1	..	..
Foscott, John	..	..	..	1	..	..	..	..	1	1	..
Frances, Joseph	1	1	..	1	..	1	..	1	..	..	..
Frances, Samuel	1	..	1	1	..	..	..	1	..	..	..
Ginnings, John	1	1	1	..	1	..	1	..	..	1	..
Goodale, Ezekiel	..	..	..	1	..	..	..	..	..	..	..
Goodrich, Asa	1	..	..	1	..	..	..	..	1	..	..
Hard, Gilbert	1	..	1	..	..	1	..	..	1	..	..
Hicks, Comfort	3	1	..	1	..	..	..	..	1	1	..
Hide, Diana	1	1	2	..	..	1	1	..	1	..	..
Horton, Jesse	2	..	..	..	1	2	1	2	..	..	..
How, Isaac	..	..	..	..	1	..	..	..	..	1	..
How, John	2	..	..	1	..	..	..	..	1	..	..
How, Philo	2	..	..	1	..	1	..	..	1	..	..
How, Uriah	..	..	..	1	..	..	..	..	1	..	..
Howel, Edward	1	..	1	..	1	..	..	..	..	1	..
Jones, Enos	1	..	..	..	1	2	1	..	..	1	..
Jones, Joel	2	..	..	1	..	1	..	..	1	..	..
Jones, Samuel E.	1	..	..	1	..	..	..	..	1	..	..
WESTHAVEN—con.											
Kelsey, Parsons	2	..	..	1	..	..	1	..	1	..	..
Kinney, Hezekiah	2	2	..	1	..	1	..	..	1	..	..
Korah, Ebenezer	1	1	..	1	..	1	1	1	1	..	..
Lewes, Barrett	..	2	1	1	1	1	1	..	..	1	..
Martin, John	1	..	1	..	..	1	..	..	1	..	..
Martin, Solomon	..	..	2	..	1	..	..	..	..	1	..
Martin, Timothy	3	..	..	1	..	1	..	..	1	..	..
Maynard, Cyrus	..	..	1	..	1	..	..	1	..	1	..
McAllister, William	..	..	..	1	..	..	1	..	..	..	..
McCaleb, David	..	..	..	1	..	..	..	..	..	..	..
McLain, Jacob	1	..	..	1	..	1	..	1	..	..	..
Mitchel, Ichabod	2	1	..	1	..	2	1	1	1	..	..
Orton, Eloiada	1	1	..	..	1	..	..	1	2	1	..
Parkins, Nathan	1	..	..	..	1	1	1	..	1	..	..
Pearce, Amos	2	..	..	1	..	3	1	..	1	..	..
Peat, Abijah	..	..	..	1	..	3	..	1	1	..	..
Peat, Benjamin	..	..	1	..	1	..	..	..	..	1	..
Petebone, Cephas	..	1	..	1	..	..	..	..	1	..	..
Preast, Noah	4	..	..	1	..	2	..	..	1	..	..
Rice, Charles	1	..	1	1	..	1	..	..	1	..	..
Sanford, David	1	..	..	1	..	3	..	..	1	..	..
Smith, Clement	..	..	..	1	..	1	..	1	..	..	..
Smith, Dan	..	1	1	1	..	..	2	1	1	..	..
Smith, James	2	..	1	..	..	..	..	1	..	..	..
Smith, Joel	1	1	..	1	..	1	..	..	1	..	..
Smith, Joseph	4	..	..	1	..	1	..	..	1	..	..
Smith, Simeon	.	1	3	1	1	1	1	1	1	1	2
Stevens, Daniel	.	2	1	..	1	..	..	1	1	..	..
Stevens, Ebenezer	..	..	..	1	1	..	..	1	..	1	..
Stevens, Joel	..	..	..	1	..	1	..	1	..	..	..
Strong, Yirum	1	..	..	1	..	3	1	1	1	..	..
Tammage, William	3	..	..	1	..	2	1	..	1	..	..
Tryon, Elijah	2	1	..	1	..	2	1	..	1	..	..
Tupper, Reuben	..	2	1	1	..	2	..	..	1	..	..
Wallis, Joseph	..	..	..	1	..	3	..	..	1	..	..
Washman, Hope	2	1	2	..	1	3	..	..	..	1	..
Wheeler, Nehemiah	1	2	..	1	..	1	..	..	1	..	..
Woodarad, Polly	3	..	..	..	1	..	1	..	..	..	..
Wyght, Potter	3	..	..	1	..	1	..	..	1	..	..
Wyman, Artemas	..	..	1	..	..	1	..	1	..	..	..
Wyman, William	..	..	1	1	..	..	..	1	..	..	..

WINDHAM COUNTY

NAMES OF HEADS OF FAMILIES	FREE WHITE MALES: Under 10 years of age	Of 10 and under 16	Of 16 and under 26 including heads of families	Of 26 and under 45 including heads of families	Of 45 and upwards including heads of families	FREE WHITE FEMALES: Under 10 years of age	Of 10 and under 16	Of 16 and under 26 including heads of families	Of 26 and under 45 including heads of families	Of 45 and upwards including heads of families	All other free persons except Indians not taxed
ATHENS											
Alexander, Thaddeus	2	1	..	1	..	1	..	..	1	..	..
Bailey, Edward	3	..	..	..	1	1	..	..	..	1	..
Bailey, Samuel	1	1	2	..	1	2	..	2	..	1	..
Balch, Samuel	..	..	2	..	1	..	..	2	..	1	..
Balch, Samuel Jr.	3	..	..	1	..	2	..	..	1	..	..
Ball, Abraham	1	1	..	1	..	2	2	..	1	..	..
Beal, Abel	2	..	..	1	1	2	..	1	..	1	..
Beal, Reuben	2	..	1	..	..	..	..	1	..	..	..
Beal, William	2	1	1	..	1	1	2	2	..	1	..
Carpenter, Eliphalet	2	..	..	1	..	..	1	..	1	1	..
Carpenter, Lewis	1	..	..	1	..	3	..	..	1	1	..
Carpenter, Timothy	..	2	..	1	..	1	..	..	1	..	..
Chaffee, Amos	..	..	2	..	1	..	..	..	..	1	..
Chaffee, Charles	..	..	..	1	..	2	..	..	1	..	..
Chaffee, David	3	..	..	1	..	1	..	..	1	..	..
Chaffee, Ezra	..	1	1	..	1	..	2	4	..	1	..
Chaffee, Rufus	2	..	..	1	..	..	..	1	..	..	..
Chamberlin, Aaron	3	..	..	1	..	..	..	1	..	..	..
Chamberlin, Moses	..	..	..	1	..	..	..	1	..	..	..
Chickering, Luther	1	..	1	..	..	1	..	1	..	..	..
Cowle, Elias	2	3	1	1	..	4	..	..	1	..	..
Davis, David	3	..	..	1	..	..	1	..	1	..	..
Davis, Oliver	3	..	1	..	1	3	1	1	..	1	..
ATHENS—con.											
Edwards, Abraham	3	..	..	..	1	1	..	1	..	1	..
Evans, Roswell	2	..	..	1	..	1	..	..	1	..	..
Evans, Simeon	..	1	2	..	1	..	1	1	..	2	..
Evans, Willard	2	..	..	1	..	3	..	..	1	..	..
Ferrington, Elijah	1	1	..	1	..	2	1	1	1	..	..
Ferrington, Stephen	1	2	1	..	1	..	..	1	1	..	..
Field, Bennett	..	..	..	..	1	..	..	..	..	..	..
Field, Bennett Jr.	..	..	1	..	..	..	..	..	..	..	..
Field, Pedajah	..	..	..	1	..	2	..	..	1	..	..
Fisher, Widow	2	..	1	..	..	..	..	1	..	1	..
Fletcher, Antipas	1	..	..	1	..	1	..	..	1	..	..
Fuller, Daniel	1	..	..	1	..	4	2	..	1	..	..
Holden, Ephraim	1	..	..	..	1	2	2	1	1	..	..
Hooker, Israel S.	2	1	1	..	1	1	1	2	..	1	..
Hooker, Jabez	..	..	..	1	..	..	1	..	1	..	..
Hooker, John	4	..	..	1	..	1	..	..	1	..	..
Mattoon, Sylvanus	1	..	..	1	..	1	..	..	1	..	..
Newton, Alpheus	..	..	..	..	1	..	..	..	..	1	..
Nichols, James	1	1	2	..	1	..	..	..	..	1	..
Nichols, Joshua	1	..	..	1	..	2	1	..	1	..	..
Oaks, Calvin	..	1	..	1	..	3	1	1	1	..	..
Oaks, Nathaniel	2	..	..	1	..	2	..	..	1	..	..

WINDHAM COUNTY—Continued

NAMES OF HEADS OF FAMILIES	FREE WHITE MALES: Under 10 years of age	FREE WHITE MALES: Of 10 and under 16	FREE WHITE MALES: Of 16 and under 26 including heads of families	FREE WHITE MALES: Of 26 and under 45 including heads of families	FREE WHITE MALES: Of 45 and upwards including heads of families	FREE WHITE FEMALES: Under 10 years of age	FREE WHITE FEMALES: Of 10 and under 16	FREE WHITE FEMALES: Of 16 and under 26 including heads of families	FREE WHITE FEMALES: Of 26 and under 45 including heads of families	FREE WHITE FEMALES: Of 45 and upwards including heads of families	All other free persons except Indians not taxed
ATHENS—con.											
Perham, Joel	3	1	1	1	..	1	..	..	1	..	..
Perkam, Ezekiel	1	1	..	1	..	2	1	..	1	..	..
Perkam, John	2	..	..	1	..	1	1	..	1	..	..
Perkam, Jonathan Jr.	2	..	..	1	..	1	..	..	1	..	..
Pierce, Sherman	2	1	..	1	..	2	1	..	2	..	..
Porter, George	..	1	..	1	..	3	..	..	1	..	..
Porter, Joshua	..	..	..	..	1	..	..	..	1	..	..
Porter, Joshua Jr.	..	1	..	..	1	4	..	..	1	..	..
Powers, Silas	3	1	..	1	..	2	..	..	1	..	..
Preham, Jonathan	..	..	1	..	1	..	..	1	..	1	..
Priest, John	2	1	..	1	..	2	2	..	1	..	..
Richmond, Amaziah	2	1	..	1	..	1	..	..	1	1	..
Richmond, Elias	..	..	1	..	..	..	..	1	..	..	..
Rosier, Jonathan	..	1	..	..	1	..	2	..	..	1	..
Shafter, James	1	2	..	1	..	1	..	1	1	..	..
Shattuck, Moody	2	..	..	1	..	1	..	..	1	..	..
Thayer, Zephaniah	3	2	..	1	..	2	..	1	1	..	..
Thrasher, Benjamin	1	1	1	..	2	..	1	..	..	1	..
Tillotson, Ebenezer	..	..	..	1	..	..	..	..	1	..	..
Tinckham, Jeremiah	..	..	2	..	1	..	..	..	1	..	..
Tinckham, Warren	..	..	1	..	..	..	..	1	..	..	..
Walker, Timothy	..	..	2	..	1	2	..	1	..	1	..
Wells, Asa	2	..	..	1	..	2	..	..	2	..	..
Wells, Daniel	..	1	2	..	1	..	1	1	1	1	..
Wells, Ezra	1	1	..	1	..	1	..	..	1	..	..
Wells, Israel	..	..	..	1	..	2	..	1	..	..	..
Wells, Joel	..	..	..	1	..	1	..	1	..	..	..
Wells, Reuben	2	2	1	1	..	2	..	..	1	..	..
Wells, Thomas	..	1	1	..	1	1	..	1	..	1	..
Wells, Thomas Jr.	1	..	1	1	..	2	1	..	1	..	..
Whitney, Ezra	..	..	1	..	1	..	..	..	..	1	..
BRATTLEBORO											
Akeley, Thomas	4	3	..	1	1	2	2	..	1	1	..
Alexander, John	..	1	..	..	1	2	..	2	..	1	..
Alexander, Jonathan	1	2	1	..	1	2	1	2	..	1	..
Allen, Elnathan	1	..	..	..	1	..	..	1	1	..	..
Arms, John	2	..	2	1	..	1	..	1	1	1	..
Arms, Josiah	1	2	2	..	2	1	1	1	1	2	..
Attridge, George	..	..	1	..	1	..	..	1	..	1	..
Avery, Elisha	1	1	..	1	..	3	..	..	1	..	..
Avery, William	..	..	..	1	..	1	..	..	1	..	..
Bailey, Samuel	1	..	..	..	1	1	1	..	..	1	1
Baker, Benjamin	3	2	1	..	1	2	1	2	1	..	..
Banister, Calvin	..	1	1	1	..	..	..	1	..	..	1
Barber, Nathaniel	1	..	2	1	..	1	..	1	1	..	..
Barns, James	..	..	..	1	..	1	..	..	1	..	..
Barrett, Benjamin	3	..	1	1	..	3	..	..	1	..	..
Barrett, Whitmore	3	..	1	..	..	..	1	1	..	..	..
Bassett, Joseph	2	1	..	1	..	1	1	..	1	..	..
Beebea, Timothy	1	..	..	..	1	2	2	1	..	1	..
Bemis, John	3	2	..	..	1	2	1	..	1	..	..
Bennett, Derastus	..	1	..	1	..	1	..	..	1	..	..
Bennett, Noah	..	2	2	..	1	1	1	4	..	1	..
Bennett, Rodolphus	1	..	1	1	..	2	..	1	..	..	..
Bennett, Stephen	3	..	1	1	1	..	..	..	2	1	..
Bennett, Uriah	..	..	..	1	..	..	..	..	1	..	..
Blake, John W.	2	1	2	2	..	2	..	2	1	..	..
Blakeslee, David	2	..	..	1	..	2	..	..	1	..	..
Blakeslee, James	1	..	..	1	..	1	..	1	1	..	..
Blakeslee, Nathaniel	..	1	2	1	..	2	1	..	1	..	..
Blakeslee, William	1	..	..	1	..	1	..	..	1	..	..
Bliss, Joel W.	..	..	2	1	..	1	..	..	1	..	..
Blodgett, Isaiah	..	2	..	1	..	3	1	..	1	..	..
Bootle, Thomas	2	..	..	1	..	1	1	..	1	..	..
Bordwell, Moses	1	..	..	1	..	3	2	..	1	..	..
Briggs, Elisha	1	..	1	1	..	1	1	..	1	..	..
Briggs, Gideon	1	2	..	..	1	3	1	1	..	1	..
Briggs, Noah	..	..	1	..	..	1	..	1	..	..	..
Briggs, Samuel	1	2	..	..	1	3	2	1	1	..	..
Briggs, Solomon	..	1	..	..	1	3	1	1	1	..	..
Brown, Jesse	1	2	..	1	..	3	4	..	1	..	..
Brown, Luke	1	1	..	1	..	..	..	1	..	..	..
Bump, Isaac	..	..	1	..	1	..	..	..	..	1	..
Burt, Jonathan	2	..	..	1	..	..	1	..	1	..	..
Butterfield, Benjamin	..	2	1	..	1	1	1	2	..	1	..
Butterfield, Jesse	2	2	1	1	..	2	..	1	1	..	..
Carpenter, Abel	2	..	..	1	..	3	..	..	1	..	..
Carpenter, Asa	1	..	..	1	..	..	..	1	1	..	..
Carpenter, James	2	1	1	..	1	..	..	1	..	2	..
Carpenter, John	1	1	..	..	1	1	3	..	..	1	..
BRATTLEBORO—con.											
Carpenter, Josiah	4	..	1	1	..	..	..	1	..	..	..
Carpenter, Peter	..	..	2	..	1	1	..	..	..	1	..
Castle, Joseph	..	2	..	..	1	..	..	..	1	..	..
Chamberlain, Benjamin	3	1	1	1	..	1	2	..	1	..	..
Chamberlain, Selah	..	1	..	2	..	1	..	1	1	..	..
Chandler, Gardner	..	1	3	..	2	..	..	1	..	1	..
Chandler, Henry	4	..	..	1	..	..	2	..	1	..	..
Chandler, Nathaniel	3	2	..	1	..	1	..	..	1	..	..
Childs, Isaac	3	1	1	..	1	2	..	..	..	1	..
Church, Jonathan	1	..	1	..	1	1	..	2	..	1	..
Church, Malashi	2	..	..	1	..	2	..	1	..	..	..
Church, Reuben	1	1	1	1	..	3	1	1	1	..	..
Church, Timothy	1	..	1	1	1	1	..	1	..	1	..
Clark, Joseph	2	2	2	..	1	1	2	..	1	..	..
Cole, Nathaniel	..	1	2	1	..	..	2	1	1	..	..
Collins, Sylvanus	..	..	..	1	..	..	..	1	..	..	..
Cook, Ephraim	2	..	..	1	..	2	..	..	7	..	..
Cook, Joseph	2	1	1	1	..	1	2	..	1	..	..
Cook, Oliver	..	..	..	..	1	..	..	..	..	1	..
Cook, Oliver Jr.	..	..	..	1	..	1	..	1	..	..	..
Cook, Solomon	..	..	1	..	1	..	..	1	..	1	..
Covil, Peter	..	1	..	..	1	..	1	..	..	1	..
Cranny, William	..	1	..	..	1	..	2	..	..	1	..
Crosby, Eleazer	2	..	..	1	..	1	..	..	1	..	..
Crosby, Isaac	1	..	3	..	1	..	..	..	1	1	..
Crosby, Isaac Jr.	2	..	..	1	..	1	..	1	..	..	..
Crosby, W. R.	..	..	1	..	..	..	..	1	..	1	..
Cune, Isaac	2	1	..	..	1	..	1	1	..	1	..
Cune, John	2	1	..	1	1	..	..	2	..	..	..
Cune, William Jr.	3	1	1	1	..	3	1	2	1	..	..
Demander, James	..	..	1	..	1	..	..	..	..	1	..
Denison, George	2	..	..	1	..	..	..	..	1	..	..
Dickerman, John	1	2	2	1	..	3	1	..	1	..	..
Dickerman, Lemuel	2	..	2	..	1	1	2	1	1	..	..
Dickerman, William	..	..	..	1	..	..	..	..	..	..	..
Dickinson, Samuel	1	..	6	1	2	..	..	1	2	..	1
Dudley, Benajah	2	2	..	1	..	1	..	..	1	..	..
Duncklee, Jonathan	3	1	1	1	..	2	2	..	1	..	..
Duncklee, Joseph	1	..	2	..	1	3	1	1	..	1	..
Earl, Samuel	4	..	..	1	..	..	..	..	1	..	..
Easterbrook, James	..	1	1	..	..	1	..	1	..	..	..
Easterbrook, Warren	2	1	1	..	1	..	1	..	..	1	..
Eaton, Simeon	..	..	2	..	1	3	1	1	..	1	..
Ellas, John	..	1	1	..	1	..	..	1	..	1	..
Ellas, Thankful	3	..	1	..	..	..	..	1	1	..	..
Farrand, Andrew	3	3	..	..	1	1	..	..	1	..	..
Field, John	..	..	..	..	..	..	..	..	..	..	..
Field, Reuben	..	2	..	..	1	1	..	..	..	1	..
Field, Samuel	2	1	..	..	1	3	2	1	1	..	..
Fisher, Ebenezer	3	..	1	..	1	..	1	3	..	1	..
Fitch, Russel	..	..	1	..	..	1	..	1	..	..	..
Forbes, Simeon	1	2	..	1	..	1	1	..	1	..	..
Fox, Ebenezer	..	..	1	..	1	1	..	1	..	1	..
Fraser, Daniel	1	..	1	1	1	4	1	1	..	1	..
French, Asa	3	2	..	1	..	1	..	..	1	..	..
French, John	2	..	..	1	1	1	1	..	1	1	..
Frost, Jesse	..	..	2	1	1	2	..	1	1	1	..
Frost, Jesse Jr.	2	1	1	1	..	2	2	1	1	..	..
Gardner, Abner	..	..	..	1	1	..	..	..	..	1	..
Gill, Obadiah	2	..	..	1	..	1	..	..	1	..	..
Gladden, Royal	2	..	..	1	..	1	..	..	1	..	..
Goodale, Joseph	1	..	..	1	..	2	..	..	1	..	..
Goodenough, Jonathan	1	1	1	..	1	2	1	1	1	..	..
Goodenough, Levi	3	3	..	1	..	..	..	..	1	..	..
Gorton, Benjamin	..	..	..	..	1	1	..	..	..	1	..
Gould, Benjamin	1	2	..	..	1	1	..	..	1	1	..
Gould, John	..	1	2	..	1	1	..	1	..	1	..
Gould, Nathan	2	1	1	..	2	2	1	..	..	1	..
Greenleaf, Samuel	2	1	..	1	..	1	..	1	1	..	..
Greenleaf, Stephen	..	..	1	..	1	..	..	1	..	1	..
Greenleaf, Stephen Jr.	1	..	1	1	..	..	1	..	1	..	..
Griffith, Lot	2	..	2	..	..	1	..	2	..	..	..
Grimes, Charles	1	..	..	..	1	..	1	..	..	1	..
Grout, Abel	4	2	..	1	..	..	2	..	1	..	..
Hadley, Ebenezer	..	..	..	..	1	..	..	1	..	1	..
Hadley, Jacob	3	1	1	1	..	2	..	..	1	..	..
Hadley, Jesse	3	1	3	..	1	1	1	..	..	1	..
Hadley, John	1	1	..	1	..	2	1	..	1	..	..
Hadley, Josiah	..	..	..	..	1	..	..	..	..	1	..
Hale, William	..	..	1	..	1	1	1	..	..	1	..
Hall, George H.	2	1	2	1	..	3	..	1	1	..	..
Harris, Calvin	3	..	..	1	1	1	..	..	1	1	..

WINDHAM COUNTY—Continued

NAMES OF HEADS OF FAMILIES	FREE WHITE MALES: Under 10 years of age	FREE WHITE MALES: Of 10 and under 16	FREE WHITE MALES: Of 16 and under 26 including heads of families	FREE WHITE MALES: Of 26 and under 45 including heads of families	FREE WHITE MALES: Of 45 and upwards including heads of families	FREE WHITE FEMALES: Under 10 years of age	FREE WHITE FEMALES: Of 10 and under 16	FREE WHITE FEMALES: Of 16 and under 26 including heads of families	FREE WHITE FEMALES: Of 26 and under 45 including heads of families	FREE WHITE FEMALES: Of 45 and upwards including heads of families	All other free persons except Indians not taxed
BRATTLEBORO—con.											
Harris, Ezra	2	..	..	1	..	1	1	..	1	..	..
Harris, James	..	3	2	1	..	2	..	1	..	..	..
Harris, Salathiel	4	..	..	1	..	..	1	..	1	..	..
Harris, Valentine	..	1	1	1	..	..	1	1	..	..	..
Harris, William	3	..	..	1	..	2	1	..	1	1	..
Hawes, Ebenezer	..	1	2	..	1	..	1	3	..	1	..
Hayes, Jeremiah	1	..	2	..	1	3	2	1	1	..	..
Hayes, Jeremiah Jr.	2	..	1	..	..	..	..	1	..	..	..
Hayes, Luke	2	..	..	1	..	..	..	1	1	..	..
Hayes, Rutherford	..	2	2	2	1	2	1	2	1	..	..
Haynes, Nathaiel	1	..	1	..	..	..	..	1	..	..	..
Higgins, Isaac	4	..	1	..	1	2	3	..	1	..	..
Holbrook, John	1	..	1	1	..	4	1	2	1	..	1
Holton, William	4	..	2	..	1	..	1	..	2	..	..
Hopkins, John	..	..	1	..	1	..	1	2	..	1	..
Horton, David	1	1	1	..	2	..	..	1	..	2	..
Horton, Jonathan	1	..	..	1	..	2	..	..	1	..	..
Horton, Nehemiah	1	3	1	1	..	2	2	1	1	..	..
Hotchkiss, Elihu	..	1	1	1	1	..	1	..	2	1	..
Houghton, Hiram	..	1	1	1	..	4	1	..	1	..	..
Houghton, John	..	..	2	..	1	..	1	1	..	1	..
Houghton, Phinehas	1	..	..	1	..	3	..	..	1	..	..
Howard, Joseph	2	1	..	1	1	2	..	..	1	1	..
Jones, Henry W.	..	1	1	..	..	..	2	..	..	..	..
Jones, Income	2	1	2	..	1	1	1	..	1	..	..
Jones, Oliver	..	1	..	1	..	2	1	..	..	1	..
Joy, Abel	1	1	1	..	1	1	1	2	1	..	..
Joy, Jesse	1	2	..	1	..	2	..	..	1	..	..
Joy, Lewis	1	1	1	1	1	1	..	..	1	1	..
Kelsey, John	1	..	1	1	..	1	..	..	1	..	..
Kimball, Francis	1	..	3	..	..	..	..	1	..	..	..
King, Adonijah	..	1	1	1	..	..	1	1	1	..	..
King, William	2	..	..	1	..	2	..	..	1	..	..
Knapp, Ebenezer	..	..	..	..	1	..	..	..	..	1	..
Knapp, James	1	..	..	..	1	2	..	..	1	..	..
Knight, John	2	..	..	1	..	2	..	1	..	..	..
Knight, John 2nd	1	..	..	1	..	..	..	..	1	..	..
Knight, Samuel	1	..	2	1	1	1	..	1	1	1	..
Larrabee, Asa	..	2	..	1	..	2	..	..	1	..	..
Larrabee, Stephen	1	1	..	..	2	1	1	..	..	1	..
Lewis, Isaac	..	1	..	1	..	2	1	..	..	..	..
Lincoln, Michael	2	1	..	..	1	..	1	..	1	..	..
Lowater, Stephen	..	..	1	..	..	1	..	2	..	..	..
Marsh, Israel	1	1	..	..	1	1	1	1	..	1	..
Metcalf, Reuben	1	..	..	1	..	3	..	..	2	..	..
Mixer, Daniel	1	1	..	1	..	5	..	..	1	..	..
Mixer, Jonas	..	..	..	1	..	..	..	..	1	..	..
Mixer, Joseph	..	..	..	..	1	..	..	..	..	1	..
Mixer, Samuel	2	1	2	1	..	2	1	1	1	..	..
Monroe, Rosbotham	..	..	..	1	1	1	..	1	..	1	..
Morgan, Caleb	..	..	1	..	1	..	..	..	..	1	..
Nash, Aaron	..	..	3	..	1	..	..	1	..	2	..
Nash, Moses	..	1	..	..	1	3	1	1	1	..	..
Nash, Oliver	1	1	1	1	1	2	1	2	1	..	..
Nash, Pliny	..	..	1	..	..	1	..	1	..	..	..
Newton, Samuel	1	1	..	..	1	..	1	2	..	1	..
Nichols, James	2	..	..	1	..	2	..	1	..	..	..
Orvis, Waitstill	4	2	3	1	..	1	..	..	1	1	..
Otis, James	..	..	..	..	1	3	2	..	1	..	..
Partridge, Larnard	1	..	..	1	..	1	..	1	..	..	..
Paterson, Jonathan	..	1	..	..	1	..	..	..	..	1	..
Patterson, Eleazer	..	..	..	..	1	..	..	..	..	1	..
Peabody, Jonathan	..	..	..	..	1	..	..	..	..	1	..
Pettis, John	2	1	..	..	1	1	2	1	1	..	..
Pierce, Cyprian	..	..	..	..	1	..	..	..	..	1	..
Pierce, Widow Anna	3	..	..	..	..	2	1	..	1	1	..
Plummer, John	1	..	3	..	1	1	1	1	..	1	..
Plummer, John Jr.	..	..	1	..	..	1	..	1	..	..	..
Potter, Reuben	1	2	1	..	3	1	1	1	..	1	..
Pratt, Barney	2	..	1	..	..	1	..	1	..	..	..
Pratt, Benjamin	5	1	1	..	1	..	..	1	1	..	..
Pratt, Levi	..	..	..	1	..	..	..	1	..	..	..
Pratt, Nathaniel	1	..	..	1	..	1	..	1	..	..	..
Prouty, Elijah	..	..	1	1	1	2	1	2	..	1	..
Redfield, Levi	..	1	1	..	1	1	..	..	..	1	..
Redfield, Theophilus	1	..	..	1	..	..	..	2	..	..	..
Reeves, Silas	2	..	1	1	..	2	1	..	1	..	..
Richardson, Isaiah	2	..	1	1	..	2	2	1	1	..	..
Roberts, Giles	1	2	..	1	..	4	..	..	1	1	..
Robertson, Archebald	3	..	..	1	..	..	..	..	1	..	..
Robertson, William	..	3	1	..	2	1	1	1	..	1	..
Root, Samuel	..	1	1	..	1	2	2	1	1	..	..
BRATTLEBORO—con.											
Sabin, Noah 3rd	..	..	2	2	..	1	1	1	..	..	1
Salisbury, Gardner	1	..	1	..	..	..	..	1	..	..	..
Salisbury, Hale	1	..	..	1	..	4	1	..	1	..	..
Salisbury, Hezekiah	1	1	2	1	..	4	2	..	1	..	..
Salisbury, James	..	..	1	1	1	..	..	..	2	1	..
Salisbury, Joseph	..	..	1	..	..	..	..	1	..	..	..
Sargeant, Eli	1	1	..	1	..	2	1	..	1	..	..
Sargeant, Elihu	1	2	..	1	..	..	1	1	1	..	..
Sargeant, Levi	1	..	..	1	..	..	..	..	1	..	..
Sargeant, Luther	..	1	..	1	..	..	..	1	1	..	..
Sargeant, Widow Anna	..	..	1	..	..	..	..	..	..	1	..
Sargeant, Widow Polly	..	..	1	..	..	..	..	..	1	1	..
Sartwell, Nathaniel	..	..	..	..	1	..	..	..	..	1	..
Sartwell, Sylvanus	1	..	..	1	..	3	3	..	1	..	..
Scovil, Abner	..	..	..	..	1	..	..	..	..	1	..
Shaw, William	1	..	..	..	1	3	1	..	1	..	..
Smead, Benjamin	1	..	3	..	..	..	1	1	..	..	..
Smith, David	2	..	1	..	2	3	1	1	1	1	..
Smith, Josiah	2	..	..	1	..	1	..	..	1	..	..
Smith, Phinehas	2	..	..	1	..	..	..	1	..	..	..
Stacey, Nymphas	..	1	..	1	..	1	1	..	..	1	..
Stearns, Reuben	3	1	2	1	..	1	2	1	1	..	..
Stebbins, Edward	2	..	1	1	..	2	..	1	1	..	..
Stebbins, Levi	2	1	..	1	..	3	1	..	1	..	..
Stebbins, Zebediah	..	..	..	..	1	..	..	..	..	1	..
Steene, James	2	..	..	1	..	..	..	..	1	..	..
Steward, Daniel	..	..	1	1	..	2	1	2	1	..	..
Stewerd, John	1	2	1	..	1	1	..	2	..	1	..
Stockwell, Asaph	..	..	..	1	..	2	..	..	1	..	..
Stoddard, Asa	2	..	..	1	..	1	..	..	1	..	..
Stoddard, Jacob	3	1	..	1	..	1	..	..	1	..	..
Stoddard, Jonathan Jr.	1	1	..	1	1	3	1	..	1	..	..
Stow, William	1	1	..	1	..	..	..	2	..	..	..
Thayer, Thompson	..	..	..	1	..	1	..	1	..	..	..
Thomas, John	2	..	..	..	1	3	1	1	1	..	..
Thornton, Sheldon	..	..	2	..	..	1	..	2	..	..	..
Thurber, Hardin	1	..	..	1	..	1	1	..	1	..	..
Townsend, Jonathan	..	1	..	1	..	3	..	1	1	..	..
Townsend, Micah	..	2	2	..	1	2	3	1	1	..	..
Underwood, John	1	..	..	1	..	..	..	1	..	..	..
Walkup, Thomas	2	..	..	1	..	3	..	..	1	..	..
Ward, Josiah	2	..	..	1	..	2	..	..	1	..	..
Warriner, Samuel	..	2	..	2	1	..	1	1	2	1	..
Wells, John	4	1	..	1	..	..	1	..	2	..	..
Wells, William	..	1	6	..	1	..	..	5	..	2	..
Wheaton, Benjamin	..	..	..	..	..	..	..	..	..	..	1
Whipple, William	2	..	1	1	..	4	..	..	1	1	..
Whitney, Ephraim	..	..	1	..	1	..	..	..	..	1	..
Whitney, Lemuel	2	1	..	2	..	1	1	..	..	1	..
Whitney, Samuel W.	..	1	1	1	..	2	1	..	1	..	..
Wilder, John	1	..	..	1	..	2	..	..	1	..	..
Wilder, Joshua	..	1	..	..	1	..	3	..	..	1	..
Williams, John	..	..	..	..	1	..	..	..	..	1	..
Williams, William	..	1	1	..	..	1	..	1	..	..	..
Winchester, Benjamin	2	3	..	1	..	2	..	..	1	..	..
Winchester, Joshua	3	..	..	1	1	..	..	..	1	1	..
Wood, Jabez	3	3	2	..	1	1	..	..	1	..	..
Wood, Philip	2	1	1	1	..	3	1	..	1	..	..
Yeaw, Joseph	1	..	1	..	..	..	..	..	1	..	..
BROOKLINE											
Alden, Phinehas	1	..	..	1	..	2	..	..	1	..	..
Austin, Appollos	1	..	..	1	..	2	..	..	1	..	..
Austin, Ebenezer	..	..	2	..	..	..	..	1	..	1	..
Austin, Nathaniel	..	..	..	..	1	..	..	..	..	..	..
Austin, Nathaniel Jr.	1	1	..	..	1	3	..	..	1	..	..
Benson, Daniel	2	..	1	..	1	3	..	..	1	..	..
Benson, Moses	1	..	..	..	1	..	..	1	..	1	..
Benson, Peter	2	..	2	1	..	1	3	..	1	..	..
Blake, William	1	..	..	..	1	1	2	..	1	..	..
Blandin, Jonathan	1	1	..	1	..	2	2	1	1	..	..
Blandin, Lemach	1	1	..	..	1	3	3	2	..	1	..
Blandin, Samuel	2	..	..	1	..	1	..	..	1	..	..
Bond, William	..	..	..	1	..	..	..	..	1	..	..
Briggs, Delius	1	..	..	..	1	1	4	1	..	2	..
Brown, Daniel E.	..	..	1	..	..	1	..	1	..	..	..
Bugbee, Abel	..	..	1	..	..	..	..	1	..	..	..
Bugbee, Ebenezer	1	..	..	..	1	..	1	..	..	1	..
Burdon, Widow	..	1	..	..	..	..	..	..	..	2	..

WINDHAM COUNTY—Continued

NAMES OF HEADS OF FAMILIES	FREE WHITE MALES: Under 10 years of age	FREE WHITE MALES: Of 10 and under 16	FREE WHITE MALES: Of 16 and under 26 including heads of families	FREE WHITE MALES: Of 26 and under 45 including heads of families	FREE WHITE MALES: Of 45 and upwards including heads of families.	FREE WHITE FEMALES: Under 10 years of age	FREE WHITE FEMALES: Of 10 and under 16	FREE WHITE FEMALES: Of 16 and under 26 including heads of families	FREE WHITE FEMALES: Of 26 and under 45 including heads of families	FREE WHITE FEMALES: Of 45 and upwards including heads of families	All other free persons except Indians not taxed
BROOKLINE—con.											
Carey, Seth	..	1	1	..	1	..	1	..	..	..	..
Cheney, Cornelius	3	..	..	1	..	2	..	..	1	..	..
Cheney, Oliver	..	..	..	..	1	..	..	..	..	1	..
Churchell, Samuel	..	..	2	..	..	..	1	..	..	1	..
Collins, David	..	1	..	..	1	..	..	..	1	..	..
Costley, James	2	..	..	1	..	1	..	..	1	..	..
Cummins, Joshua	2	1	..	1	..	2	..	..	1	..	..
Cutting, Robert	..	..	1	..	..	..	..	1	..	..	..
Cutting, Zadock	..	2	..	..	1	..	..	..	..	1	..
Daggett, James	1	..	..	1	..	1	..	1	..	..	..
Derry, Peter	2	2	1	..	1	..	1	2	..	1	..
Drake, Abijah	..	..	..	..	1	..	..	..	..	1	..
Drake, Abijah Jr.	2	2	..	1	..	3	1	..	1	..	..
Drake, Francis	1	1	..	1	..	1	1	..	1	..	..
Drake, Seth	..	1	..	1	..	2	..	..	1	..	..
Elenwood, Jonathan	2	1	..	1	..	2	..	..	1	..	..
Farmer, Benjamin	2	..	2	..	1	1	1	1	..	1	..
Flemming, David	4	1	..	1	..	..	1	..	1	..	..
Flint, Asa	1	..	1	..	..	..	..	1	..	..	..
Freeman, Jonathan	2	2	..	1	..	2	1	..	1	..	..
Fries, John	..	..	1	..	..	..	..	1	..	..	..
Harwood, Ebenezer	1	2	..	..	1	..	..	2	..	1	..
Holden, Josiah	..	..	1	..	..	1	..	1	..	..	..
Leonard, John	1	1	1	..	1	..	1	..	..	1	..
Marritt, Joseph	1	..	..	1	..	3	..	..	1	..	..
Millett, Nathaniel	1	..	2	..	1	..	2	..	..	1	..
Moore, Abijah	1	1	..	1	1	3	1	..	1	..	..
Moore, Hezkiah	2	..	1	1	..	..	1	..	1	..	..
Moore, Jonas	2	..	..	..	1	1	..	..	1	..	..
Moore, William	1	3	..	..	1	2	2	..	1	..	..
Negus, Jonas	..	..	1	..	..	..	..	1	..	..	..
Phillip, Charles	3	3	..	..	1	2	..	1	1	..	..
Pollard, Sally	..	..	..	..	..	..	..	1	..	..	..
Pool, Ebenezer	..	..	..	1	..	..	..	..	..	..	..
Remmington, Dyer	4	..	..	1	..	1	..	..	1	..	..
Rhodes, John	1	1	1	..	1	..	..	..	1	..	..
Richardson, Francis	1	..	1	..	..	1	..	1	..	..	..
Richardson, Jonathan	3	..	..	1	..	..	1	..	1	..	..
Rist, Thomas	..	..	1	1	1	..	2	..	1	..	..
Rollins, William	..	1	..	1	..	5	2	..	1	..	..
Rownds, Isaiah	1	..	..	1	..	1	..	..	1	..	..
Skinner, Eliphalet	1	1	..	1	..	1	..	1	1	..	..
Skinner, William	..	..	1	..	1	..	..	..	..	1	..
Stebbins, Jotham	..	1	1	1	..	1	..	..	1	..	..
Stone, Benjamin	2	2	..	..	1	1	1	1	1	..	..
Taft, Josiah	2	..	..	1	..	1	..	1	1	..	..
Tarble, Zackariah	..	..	1	..	1	..	..	..	..	1	..
Thomas, William	..	1	..	..	1	..	..	1	..	1	..
Tillotson, Ebenezer	..	..	1	..	1	..	..	1	..	1	..
Tillotson, Isaac	2	3	..	1	..	2	..	..	1	..	..
Walker, Jesse	1	..	1	..	..	1	..	1	..	..	..
Walker, Thomas	..	1	..	..	1	3	2	3	..	1	..
Waters, Jonathan	..	1	..	..	1	..	1	..	..	1	..
Wellman, Daniel	..	1	1	..	..	..	..	..	1	..	..
Wellman, Darius	1	..	..	1	..	3	1	1	1	..	..
Wellman, Ebenezer	1	2	..	..	1	1	1	..	..	1	..
Wellman, Isaac	4	2	..	1	..	1	..	..	1	..	..
Wellman, John	..	..	..	1	..	..	..	1	1	..	..
Wellman, Timothy	..	..	..	..	1	..	..	..	..	1	..
Wellman, Timothy Jr.	4	1	1	..	1	1	1	..	1	..	..
Whitcomb, Cyrus	2	..	1	..	1	..	..	2	..	1	..
Whticomb, Cyrus Jr.	..	..	1	..	..	..	..	1	..	..	..
Whitcomb, Silas	..	..	..	..	1	..	..	..	..	..	..
Whitney, Ebenezer	..	..	1	..	..	..	..	1	..	..	..
Whitney, Israel	1	..	..	1	..	1	..	..	1	..	..
Whitney, Richard	..	1	2	..	1	1	2	..	..	1	..
Whitney, Timothy H.	1	..	1	..	..	..	..	..	1	..	..
Woods, Jotham	3	..	..	1	..	..	1	..	..	..	..
Woodward, Abel	..	..	..	1	..	..	..	..	1	..	..
DUMMERSTON											
Adams, Nathan	2	..	..	1	..	2	3	1	1	1	..
Allen, Charles	3	1	..	1	..	1	..	..	1	..	..
Allen, Josiah	..	..	1	..	1	..	1	1	..	1	..
Alvord, Benjamin	2	1	..	1	..	2	2	..	1	1	..

NAMES OF HEADS OF FAMILIES	FREE WHITE MALES: Under 10 years of age	FREE WHITE MALES: Of 10 and under 16	FREE WHITE MALES: Of 16 and under 26 including heads of families	FREE WHITE MALES: Of 26 and under 45 including heads of families	FREE WHITE MALES: Of 45 and upwards including heads of families.	FREE WHITE FEMALES: Under 10 years of age	FREE WHITE FEMALES: Of 10 and under 16	FREE WHITE FEMALES: Of 16 and under 26 including heads of families	FREE WHITE FEMALES: Of 26 and under 45 including heads of families	FREE WHITE FEMALES: Of 45 and upwards including heads of families	All other free persons except Indians not taxed
DUMMERSTON—con.											
Alvord, Moses	2	..	..	..	1	..	..	..	1	..	..
Arnold, Camaliel	2	1	..	1	..	2	..	..	1	..	..
Ash, Ebenezer	1	..	..	1	..	1	..	..	1	..	..
Bailey, Dudley	..	1	3	..	1	..	..	..	..	1	..
Baker, Mrs.	..	..	1	..	..	2	2	..	..	1	..
Baldwin, John	..	..	1	..	1	1	1	1	1	..	..
Barnett, Isaac	..	..	2	..	1	..	..	..	1	1	..
Barrns, John	..	..	..	..	1	..	..	1	1	1	..
Barrns, Moses	..	..	..	1	..	2	..	1	..	..	..
Barrus, Jonathan	..	1	..	..	1	1	..	..	..	1	..
Bartlet, Silas	1	2	..	1	..	3	1	..	1	..	..
Belknap, Calvin	1	1	..	1	..	3	1	..	1	..	..
Belknap, Charles	1	..	..	1	..	1	..	1	..	..	..
Belknap, Daniel	1	1	..	1	..	1	..	..	1	..	..
Bemis, Benjamin	2	..	..	1	..	2	..	..	1	..	..
Bemis, David	..	..	..	1	1	..	..	..	..	1	..
Bemis, Elias	2	..	..	1	..	3	..	..	1	..	..
Bemis, Joseph	..	1	1	1	..	1	1	2	..	1	..
Bemis, Philip	2	..	..	1	1	1	1	..	1	..	..
Bennett, John	3	1	..	..	1	..	1	1	1	..	..
Bennett, Joseph	2	1	..	..	1	2	1	1	..	1	..
Bennett, Samuel	..	1	2	..	1	..	2	..	..	1	..
Bennett, Stephen	1	..	..	1	..	4	..	..	1	..	..
Bigelow, Isaac	..	1	..	1	..	3	1	..	1	..	..
Bixby, Nathaniel	2	2	..	1	..	1	1	..	1	..	..
Black, Steward	2	1	1	..	1	2	1	..	1	..	..
Bond, William	2	1	..	..	1	..	1	..	..	1	..
Boyden, Isaac	..	1	1	..	2	..	..	..	..	2	..
Boyden, Josiah	..	..	1	..	1	..	..	1	..	1	..
Boyden, William	1	..	1	..	1	1	..	1	..	1	..
Briggs, Seth	1	..	..	1	..	4	3	..	1	..	..
Brooks, Dan	3	2	..	1	1	2	1	..	1	1	..
Brown, Elijah	1	1	..	1	..	..	1	1	1	1	..
Buck, Elijah	1	..	..	1	..	2	1	1	1	..	..
Burnham, Gideon	1	..	1	..	1	1	1	1	..	1	..
Burnham, John	1	..	..	1	..	2	..	1	1	..	..
Burnham, Thomas	1	1	..	1	..	4	2	1	..	1	..
Burnham, Washington	..	..	1	..	..	1	..	1	..	..	..
Butler, Calvin	2	1	..	1	1	1	1	..	1	..	..
Butler, Silas	2	..	..	1	2	1	1	..	1	1	..
Butler, Simeon	2	..	1	1	..	2	..	..	1	..	..
Butterfield, Ezra	3	1	3	1	..	2	1	..	1	..	..
Butterfield, Luke	1	..	..	1	..	3	1	..	1	..	..
Cambridge, John	1	1	..	1	..	1	2	2	1	..	..
Carryl, Abijah	1	..	..	1	..	3	..	1	..	..	..
Carryl, Asa	..	..	1	..	1	..	..	1	..	1	..
Carryl, Levi	2	..	..	1	..	2	..	..	1	..	..
Clark, Thomas	1	1	4	..	1	..	2	..	1	1	..
Cobleigh, Jonathan	4	..	1	..	1	3	..	..	1	..	..
Cobleigh, Jonathan Jr.	..	..	1	..	..	..	..	1	..	..	..
Colby, Simeon	1	..	..	1	..	3	..	..	1	..	..
Cook, Enoch	..	1	..	1	..	4	..	..	1	2	..
Cresey, Henry	3	1	..	1	..	3	1	..	1	..	..
Crosby, Aaron	..	1	1	..	1	..	..	2	..	1	..
Crosby, Timothy	..	2	..	1	..	5	1	..	1	..	..
Cummings, William	2	..	..	1	..	1	2	..	1	..	..
Cutler, Widow Polly	..	..	..	..	1	1	..	1	..	..	..
Cutting, Joel	..	..	..	1	..	1	..	..	1	..	..
Davenport, Charles	..	..	..	..	1	..	..	..	..	1	..
Davenport, Charles Jr.	2	1	..	1	..	2	1	1	1	..	..
Davis, Calvin	4	..	..	1	..	..	..	..	1	..	..
Day, Eli	1	..	..	1	..	..	..	..	1	..	..
Dean, Richard	..	..	..	1	..	1	..	..	1	..	..
Dickinson, Paul	..	..	1	1	..	1	..	2	..	..	..
Duncan, Jason	2	1	..	..	1	1	..	1	..	2	..
Duncan, Jonas	1	..	1	..	..	..	..	1	..	..	..
Duncan, Joseph	1	..	1	..	..	1	..	1	..	..	..
Duncan, Samuel	1	..	1	..	1	2	3	2	1	1	..
Dutton, Asa	1	..	..	1	1	3	3	..	1	1	..
Dutton, David	..	1	2	..	1	2	1	..	1	..	..
Dutton, Samuel	..	1	..	..	1	1	1	3	..	1	..
Easterbrook, Benjamin	1	..	2	..	1	..	1	2	..	2	..
Ellis, Benjamin	1	..	1	1	..	1	..	1	..	1	..
Enos, Joseph	1	1	1	..	1	..	1	2	..	1	..
Fairchild, Silas	4	1	..	1	..	2	..	..	1	..	..
Farr, William	..	..	1	..	..	1	..	1	..	..	..
Fitts, Abraham	..	2	1	1	1	..	..	..	..	1	..
Flarraty, Widow S.	..	1	3	..	..	1	..	1	..	1	..
Foster, Skelton	..	1	..	..	1	1	..	..	..	1	..
French, Joel	2	..	..	1	..	..	..	..	1	..	..
French, Nathaniel	..	1	2	..	1	..	1	2	..	1	..
French, Samuel	..	..	1	..	..	..	..	1	..	..	..

WINDHAM COUNTY—Continued

NAMES OF HEADS OF FAMILIES	FREE WHITE MALES: Under 10 years of age	FREE WHITE MALES: Of 10 and under 16	FREE WHITE MALES: Of 16 and under 26 including heads of families	FREE WHITE MALES: Of 26 and under 45 including heads of families	FREE WHITE MALES: Of 45 and upwards including heads of families	FREE WHITE FEMALES: Under 10 years of age	FREE WHITE FEMALES: Of 10 and under 16	FREE WHITE FEMALES: Of 16 and under 26 including heads of families	FREE WHITE FEMALES: Of 26 and under 45 including heads of families	FREE WHITE FEMALES: Of 45 and upwards including heads of families	All other free persons except Indians not taxed
DUMMERSTON—con.											
Gansey, Samuel	2	2	..	1	..	2	..	..	1	..	..
Gates, Daniel	..	2	2	1	1	..	..	2	..	1	..
Gates, John S.	..	1	4	..	1	..	2	1	..	1	..
Gates, Phinehas	4	..	1	1	..	1	2	..	1	..	..
Gibbs, Elijah	..	..	..	1	..	2	..	..	1	..	..
Gibbs, Samuel	3	..	..	1	..	2	..	..	1	..	..
Gleason, Joseph	1	..	1	..	1	2	2	..	1	..	..
Goddard, Levi	3	..	1	1	..	1	..	1	..	..	..
Goss, Daniel	1	..	..	1	..	4	..	1	1	..	..
Goss, Henry	..	..	..	1	..	1	..	1	1	..	..
Goss, Zebulon	..	..	2	..	..	..	..	1	..	..	..
Gowen, Samuel	4	..	..	1	..	..	..	..	1	..	..
Graham, Caleb	1	..	1	1	..	..	1	..	1	..	..
Graham, Lemuel	2	1	1	1	..	3	1	..	1	..	..
Graves, Reuben	2	4	..	1	..	2	..	1	1	..	..
Griffith, Ellis	1	1	..	1	..	2	1	..	1	..	..
Grout, Ebenezer	..	..	..	1	..	1	..	1	..	..	..
Hadley, Benjamin	2	..	..	1	1	1	..	..	1	..	..
Hall, Ephraim	..	..	..	1	..	1	..	..	1	..	..
Hartwell, Oliver	3	3	1	1	..	3	..	1	1	..	..
Haven, Abel	3	2	..	1	..	1	1	..	1	..	..
Haven, David	1	..	..	1	..	1	..	..	1	..	..
Haven, Joseph	1	..	..	1	..	4	..	..	1	..	..
Healey, James	2	..	..	1	..	2	1	..	1	..	..
Herrick, Jonathan	..	..	..	1	..	2	..	..	1	..	..
Higgins, Alpheus	1	..	1	..	..	..	..	1	..	..	..
Higgins, Polly	2	..	..	1	..	1	..	..	2	..	..
Hildreth, Ezekiel	1	..	1	..	..	1	..	1	..	..	..
Hildreth, Jesse	1	1	1	..	1	..	..	..	1	..	..
Hildreth, Joseph	..	..	1	..	1	..	1	..	2	..	..
Hildreth, Wilson	1	..	..	1	..	3	..	..	1	..	..
Hilliard, Joseph	..	..	..	..	1	..	..	..	..	2	..
Hillick, John	..	..	..	1	..	..	..	1	..	..	..
Holton, Arad	2	2	1	..	2	1	1	2	..	..	..
Hopkins, Jeremiah	..	..	1	..	1	..	..	..	1	1	..
Hudson, Enos	3	..	1	..	1	1	2	..	1	1	..
Hudson, Seth	..	1	1	1	..	1	1	3	..	2	..
Jenks, Obadiah	2	1	..	..	1	2	..	..	..	1	..
Jilson, Sylvester	..	..	..	1	..	..	..	..	1	..	..
Johnson, Ashbel	2	2	2	1	1	1	1	3	..	1	..
Johnson, E. F.	2	..	..	1	..	2	..	..	1	..	..
Johnson, James	1	..	..	1	..	2	..	..	1	..	..
Johnson, John	..	..	1	..	..	..	..	1	..	..	..
Johnson, Simeon	1	..	..	1	1	1	1	..	1	..	..
Jones, Cornelius	1	..	..	..	1	1	1	2	..	..	..
Kathan, Alexander	..	1	..	1	1	..	..	1	1	1	..
Kathan, Daniel	1	1	1	..	1	..	1	1	..	1	..
Kathan, Daniel 2nd	2	1	..	1	..	2	1	..	1	..	..
Kathan, Gardner	2	..	..	1	..	1	..	..	1	..	..
Kathan, John	2	..	2	1	1	1	..	1	1	1	..
Kathan, John 2nd	..	..	..	1	..	1	1	..	1	..	..
Kelley, Richard Jr.	1	..	..	1	1	1	..	1	1	..	..
Kellogg, Ebenezer	2	1	..	..	1	2	..	..	1	..	..
Kelly, Alexander	1	1	..	..	1	..	1	2	..	1	..
Kendall, Isaac	2	1	..	..	1	1	..	..	1	..	..
Kendall, Luke	..	..	1	..	..	1	..	1	..	..	..
Kilbary, John	..	..	..	..	1	..	..	..	..	1	..
Kilbary, Richard	2	..	..	1	..	1	..	1	..	..	..
Knapp, Ichabod	1	1	2	1	..	2	2	..	1	..	..
Knapp, John	4	..	..	1	..	..	..	..	1	..	..
Knight, Jesse	2	1	1	1	..	2	2	..	1	..	..
Knight, Joel	2	..	..	1	..	2	1	1	1	..	..
Knight, Jonathan	..	..	..	..	1	..	..	..	..	1	..
Knight, Jonathan Jr.	2	1	..	1	1	..	..	2	..	..	..
Knight, Samuel	2	1	..	1	..	1	..	1	1	..	..
Lamb, Peter	2	1	..	1	..	2	1	..	1	..	..
Larrabee, James	1	..	..	1	..	1	..	..	1	..	..
Larrabee, John	..	..	..	..	1	..	1	..	..	1	..
Laughton, David	2	2	..	1	..	..	1	..	1	..	..
Laughton, John	3	..	..	1	..	2	..	1	1	..	..
Laughton, John 2nd	2	..	..	1	1	1	..	1	1	1	..
Laughton, Samuel	..	..	..	..	1	5	2	..	1	..	..
Leonard, William	..	..	..	..	1	..	..	..	..	2	..
Manley, James	..	1	1	..	1	..	..	2	..	1	..
Manley, Jesse	1	1	1	..	2	1	2	1	1	3	..
Manley, John	..	..	1	..	2	..	1	..	..	1	..
Mann, Nathaniel	2	..	..	1	..	..	..	..	1	..	..
Mann, Stephen	..	..	1	..	..	1	..	1	..	..	..
Mann, Timothy	..	..	..	..	1	..	..	..	..	1	..
Mansfield, Amos	2	..	..	1	..	..	..	..	1	..	..
Merrick, Ebenezer	1	..	1	..	1	..	..	..	1	1	..
Miller, Hosea	1	1	..	1	..	..	..	1	..	..	..
Miller, John	1	..	2	1	..	3	1	..	1	..	..
Miller, Marshal	2	2	4	..	1	2	1	1	..	1	..
Miller, Rebecca	1	..	..	1	..	2	..	..	..	..	..
Miller, Solomon	1	..	..	2	1	1	1	2	..	2	..
Miller, Vespasian	..	..	3	..	1	..	..	2	..	1	..
Miller, Vespasian 2nd	4	..	..	1	..	1	..	..	1	..	..
Miller, William	4	3	..	1	..	1	1	1	1	..	..
Moore, Jonathan	1	1	..	1	..	1	1	1	1	1	..
Morse, John	..	..	..	1	..	..	..	..	1	..	..
Morse, Samuel	1	..	..	1	..	..	..	..	1	..	..
Negus, John	1	1	..	1	..	4	1	..	1	..	..
Negus, William	..	..	1	..	1	..	..	1	..	1	..
Newton, James	1	2	1	1	1	..	..	2	1	..	..
Newton, John	..	..	..	1	..	1	..	..	1	..	..
Norgross, Nathan	..	..	..	1	..	1	..	..	1	..	..
Nurse, Joseph	4	2	1	..	1	..	1	1	..	1	..
Nurse, Solomon	..	..	..	..	1	3	2	1	..	1	..
Parish, Asa	1	..	..	1	..	1	1	..	1	..	..
Parmerter, Aaron Jr.	2	..	..	1	1	2	1	..	2	1	..
Phillips, Daniel	4	1	..	1	..	1	1	..	1	..	..
Phillips, Ezekiel	2	..	..	1	..	1	..	..	1	..	..
Pierce, Benjamin	1	1	4	5	..	1	1	..	1	1	..
Pierce, Henry	..	..	..	1	..	3	..	..	1	..	..
Pierce, Josiah	3	..	..	1	..	..	..	..	1	..	..
Pierce, William	..	..	2	..	1	..	..	1	..	1	..
Porter, Samuel	4	1	..	3	..	1	..	..	2	..	..
Pratt, Asa	2	..	..	1	..	2	1	..	1	..	..
Prentiss, Elkanah	1	1	..	1	..	2	..	..	1	..	..
Prouty, Abel	4	..	..	1	..	..	..	..	1	..	..
Read, Isaac	2	..	..	1	..	2	..	..	1	..	..
Rice, Amos	..	..	1	..	1	..	..	..	..	1	..
Rice, Elijah	4	2	..	1	1	1	2	..	1	1	..
Rice, Elijah	1	..	..	1	..	2	..	..	1	..	..
Rice, Gardner	1	..	..	2	..	5	..	1	1	..	..
Rice, Nathan	2	1	..	1	..	1	..	..	1	..	..
Rider, David	..	..	2	1	..	2	..	..	1	..	..
Rodes, Ebenezer	1	2	..	..	1	2	1	..	..	1	..
Sargeant, Rufus	1	2	2	..	1	..	1	1	..	..	..
Sargeant, Thomas	2	..	..	1	..	2	..	..	1	..	..
Sargeant, William	3	2	1	1	..	1	..	2	1	..	..
Shaw, Bela	2	2	..	1	..	1	..	..	1	..	..
Stevens, Daniel	2	..	1	1	..	4	2	..	1	..	..
Stevens, Henry	2	..	1	1	1	1	1	..	2	1	..
Stickney, Peter	..	1	..	1	..	..	1	1	..	1	..
Stimpson, Amos	..	2	2	..	1	3	..	..	..	1	..
Stockwell, Joel	2	..	..	1	..	1	1	..	1	..	..
Stockwell, Jonas	2	1	..	..	1	2	1	..	1	..	..
Stoddard, Samuel	1	..	..	1	..	..	..	1	..	..	..
Stone, Nathaniel	3	..	..	1	..	1	..	..	1	..	..
Sweetzer, William	..	..	1	1	..	..	..	..	1	..	..
Taft, Asahel	2	..	..	1	..	1	2	3	1	..	..
Taft, Silas	..	1	1	1	1	1	1	1	1	..	..
Taylor, Daniel	2	..	1	1	1	1	..	1	1	1	..
Taylor, Eleazer	..	..	1	..	1	..	..	..	1	1	..
Taylor, Isaac	..	..	..	1	..	..	..	..	1	..	..
Temple, Joseph	..	1	1	..	1	..	..	1	..	1	..
Thayer, Thaddeus	4	2	1	1	..	1	1	..	1	..	..
Thomas, Eliab	1	..	..	1	..	..	..	1	..	..	..
Thompson, Benoni	2	..	..	1	..	1	1	..	1	..	..
Townsend, Nathaniel	1	1	..	1	..	2	..	..	1	..	..
Turner, John	..	..	2	..	1	..	..	2	..	1	..
Twitchell, Joshua	2	..	..	..	1	2	..	1	1	..	..
Vial, Mason	..	..	..	1	..	1	..	..	1	..	..
Wait, Ebenezer	..	..	..	1	1	..	..	..	2	..	..
Wakefield, Samuel	1	..	2	..	1	3	1	..	..	1	..
Walker, Jonas	2	2	3	..	1	..	1	..	..	1	..
Warner, Daniel	2	1	..	1	..	1	1	..	1	..	..
Webster, Asahel	1	..	1	1	..	2	..	..	1	..	..
Welch, Silas	..	..	..	1	..	2	..	..	1	..	..
Whipple, John	3	..	..	1	..	2	1	..	1	..	..
White, Asa	3	..	..	1	..	2	..	..	1	..	..
Whitney, Benjamin	1	..	..	..	1	..	1	1	1	..	..
Wilder, Elias	..	2	..	..	1	3	1	..	1	1	..
Wilder, Holeb	..	1	1	..	1	..	..	1	..	1	..
Wilder, Joshua	5	1	2	1	..	1	1	1	1	..	..
Willard, Henry	..	1	1	1	..	4	1	..	1	..	..
Williams, Asa	2	..	1	..	1	..	2	1	1	..	..
Wood, Seth	2	..	1	..	1	2	1	1	..	1	..
Woodbury, Stephen	1	1	..	1	..	..	..	1	..	..	..
Wooley, Asa	..	..	..	1	..	..	..	..	1	..	..

WINDHAM COUNTY—Continued

NAMES OF HEADS OF FAMILIES	FREE WHITE MALES: Under 10 years of age	FREE WHITE MALES: Of 10 and under 16	FREE WHITE MALES: Of 16 and under 26 including heads of families	FREE WHITE MALES: Of 26 and under 45 including heads of families	FREE WHITE MALES: Of 45 and upwards including heads of families.	FREE WHITE FEMALES: Under 10 years of age	FREE WHITE FEMALES: Of 10 and under 16	FREE WHITE FEMALES: Of 16 and under 26 including heads of families	FREE WHITE FEMALES: Of 26 and under 45 including heads of families	FREE WHITE FEMALES: Of 45 and upwards including heads of families	All other free persons except Indians not taxed
DUMMERSTON—con.											
Wyman, John	..	..	1	..	1	..	..	..	..	1	..
Wyman, John Jr.	1	1	..	1	..	2	1	..	1	..	..
Zwears, Benjamin	..	..	1	..	..	..	..	1	..	..	..
Zwears, Daniel	2	1	..	..	1	1	..	..	1	1	..
GRAFTON											
Adams, James	2	1	..	1	..	..	..	..	1	1	..
Alexander, Zuiel	2	..	..	1	..	1	2	..	1	..	..
Archer, Jacob	..	..	..	1	..	3	..	1	..	..	..
Axtell, Alexander	3	1	..	1	..	1	1	..	1	..	..
Axtell, Joseph	5	..	1	1	..	..	..	1	1	1	..
Baird, Abijah	..	..	..	..	1	..	..	..	..	1	..
Baird, Abijah Jr.	3	..	..	1	..	..	..	..	1	..	..
Baird, John	1	..	..	1	..	2	..	1	..	..	..
Baird, Jonathan	1	..	1	..	..	2	..	1	..	..	..
Baird, Josiah	..	1	..	..	1	..	1	..	..	1	..
Baker, Cornelius	3	..	..	1	..	2	..	..	1	..	..
Baker, Daniel	2	1	..	1	..	1	1	..	1	1	..
Beeman, Peter	3	..	..	1	..	2	2	..	1	..	..
Bixby, Aaron	1	1	..	1	..	1	2	..	1	..	..
Blodget, Ruil	2	..	1	..	..	..	..	1	..	..	..
Blodget, Silas	..	..	..	1	..	1	..	..	1	1	..
Bond, Henry	..	1	1	..	1	..	..	1	..	1	..
Bond, Josiah	1	..	..	1	..	1	..	1	..	..	..
Bond, William	1	..	1	..	..	..	..	1	..	..	..
Burdit, Ebenezer	2	3	..	1	..	1	..	..	1	..	..
Burdit, Thomas	3	2	1	1	..	1	1	..	1	..	..
Burgis, Barzillia	..	..	..	1	..	3	..	1	..	..	..
Burgis, Benjamin	1	..	..	1	..	1	..	..	1	..	..
Burgis, Ebenezer	..	2	2	..	1	1	..	2	..	1	..
Burgis, Ebenezer Jr.	2	..	..	1	..	..	1	..	1	..	..
Chaffee, Alfred	1	..	..	1	..	..	..	..	1	..	..
Challis, Nathaniel	2	..	..	1	..	3	..	1	1	..	..
Chapman, Benjamin	1	1	..	1	..	3	1	..	1	..	..
Chapman, David	3	..	..	1	..	1	..	..	1	..	..
Chapman, Jonathan	..	..	..	1	..	3	1	..	1	..	..
Convers, Robert	..	..	..	1	..	2	..	1	..	..	..
Cooper, Zebede	2	1	1	1	1	3	..	1	1	..	..
Crowell, Mahue	3	..	..	1	..	1	..	..	1	..	..
Crumb, Joseph	1	2	..	1	..	4	1	..	1	..	..
Darling, John	3	2	..	..	1	2	..	..	..	1	..
Darling, Oliver	1	..	..	..	1	3	..	..	1	..	..
Davis, Oliver	2	..	..	1	..	3	1	..	1	..	..
Davis, Thomas	4	..	..	1	..	1	..	..	1	..	..
Dean, James	3	1	..	1	..	1	1	2	1	..	..
Death, Caleb	2	..	..	1	..	1	..	..	1	..	..
Dennison, Amos	1	1	..	..	1	..	2	1	..	1	..
Dole, Thomas	1	..	..	1	..	1	..	..	1	..	..
Downs, Samuel	..	..	1	..	1	..	..	1	..	1	..
Downs, Thomas	1	..	..	1	..	1	..	1	..	..	..
Dutton, Thomas	..	1	1	..	1	..	..	1	..	1	..
Dwinnell, Benjamin	1	1	..	1	..	4	1	..	1	..	..
Edson, Ezra	1	3	1	1	..	2	1	..	1	..	..
Edson, Jonathan	1	2	..	..	1	2	1	..	..	1	..
Edson, Robert	1	..	..	1	..	2	1	3	1	..	..
Ellis, Asa	..	..	1	..	..	..	..	..	..	..	..
Emery, Asa	3	..	..	1	..	1	..	..	1	..	..
Everest, Widow Eliza	1	2	..	..	..	1	1	..	1	..	..
Everitt, Jared	3	..	..	1	..	2	2	..	1	..	..
Farmer, Joseph	2	1	1	..	1	..	1	..	1	..	..
Fisher, Amos	1	1	1	1	..	1	..	..	1	..	..
Fisher, Ezra	..	..	1	1	..	..	..	1	1	1	..
Fisher, Jephet	..	1	..	1	..	1	..	..	1	..	..
Flemmons, John	..	..	1	..	1	..	..	1	..	1	..
Franklin, Joseph	1	..	..	1	..	1	..	1	..	..	..
Franklin, Vial	1	..	..	1	..	2	..	..	1	..	..
French, William	3	..	..	1	..	2	1	..	1	..	..
Fuller, Bartholomew	2	2	..	1	..	2	..	2	1	..	..
Gibson, Abraham	1	2	1	1	..	3	1	..	1	..	..
Gibson, David	5	..	..	1	1	1	..	..	1	1	..
Gibson, Isaac	..	..	1	..	..	..	..	1	..	..	..
Gibson, Jonathan	1	1	2	1	..	..	..	2	1	1	..
Gibson, Nathan	..	..	1	..	..	..	..	..	..	..	..
Gibson, Nathaniel	1	2	2	..	1	2	1	2	1	..	..
Gibson, Silas	..	..	1	..	..	..	..	..	..	..	..
Gilson, David	2	1	1	1	..	1	1	..	1	..	..
Gilson, Simon	..	1	..	1	..	..	..	1	..	..	..
Gilson, Solomon	..	3	..	1	..	1	..	..	1	..	..
Gilson, Zachariah	3	..	..	1	..	2	1	1	1	..	..
GRAFTON—con.											
Goodrich, John	2	..	..	1	..	..	..	..	1	..	..
Goodrich, Moses	4	..	..	1	1	1	..	..	1	1	..
Goodrich, Samuel	1	..	2	1	..	1	..	..	1	..	..
Gowen, Samuel	1	..	..	1	..	..	1	..	1	..	..
Guile, Ephraim	3	2	..	1	..	1	1	1	1	..	..
Haedley, Charles	..	1	2	..	1	4	1	..	..	1	..
Hale, Enoch	..	..	1	..	1	..	1	1	..	1	..
Hall, Caleb	..	..	..	1	..	..	..	..	..	..	..
Hall, William	1	1	1	..	1	2	..	1	1	..	..
Hall, William Jr.	..	..	..	1	..	..	..	..	..	..	..
Harris, William	1	1	..	1	..	1	..	1	1	..	..
Haywood, Stephen	2	2	..	..	1	1	1	1	..	1	..
Haywood, Stephen Jr.	..	..	1	..	..	..	..	..	..	..	..
Haywood, Ziba	3	2	..	1	..	1	..	..	1	..	..
Heaton, William	1	2	1	..	1	1	..	1	..	1	..
Hill, Abraham	..	..	..	1	..	4	2	..	1	..	..
Holden, Isaac	1	..	..	1	..	2	..	1	..	..	..
Holmes, Given	1	..	2	..	..	..	..	1	..	..	..
Houghton, Abel	1	..	..	1	..	2	..	1	..	..	..
Houghton, Eleazer	..	..	..	1	..	..	..	1	..	..	..
Houghton, Manassah	1	..	..	1	..	..	..	1	..	..	..
How, Asa	..	..	1	..	..	..	..	1	..	..	..
How, Ezekiel	3	..	2	..	1	3	3	..	1	..	..
Kelsey, Jonathan	2	..	..	1	1	..	1	1	..	..	..
Kidder, John	1	1	..	1	..	4	1	..	1	..	..
Knight, Silas	2	..	1	..	..	..	..	1	..	..	..
Lane, Joel	3	..	..	1	..	..	..	..	1	..	..
Lane, Jonathan	1	..	1	..	..	..	..	1	..	1	..
Lane, Matthew	..	..	..	..	2	..	..	2	1	..	..
Loveland, Aaron	1	..	..	1	..	..	..	1	..	..	..
Loveland, Israel	..	..	..	1	..	3	..	..	1	..	..
Loveland, Jared	..	..	..	1	..	3	..	..	1	..	..
Lovell. Enos	1	1	3	1	..	2	1	..	1	..	..
Mastic, Nathaniel	..	..	..	1	..	3	..	..	1	..	..
Mastic, William	3	..	1	1	..	1	1	..	1	..	..
Mastick, Benjamin	2	..	1	..	1	..	1	..	1	..	..
Noyce, Philip	2	..	..	1	..	1	..	..	1	..	..
Palmer, David	2	1	2	1	..	2	2	1	1	..	..
Palmer, Thomas K.	5	1	1	1	..	1	1	2	1	..	..
Park, James	..	..	1	..	..	..	..	..	..	..	..
Park, Robert	2	..	..	1	..	2	..	..	1	..	..
Park, Thomas K.	1	2	..	1	..	..	..	1	1	..	..
Parker, Timothy	..	..	1	..	..	..	..	..	..	..	..
Parks, Widow Lucy	1	1	..	..	..	2	1	..	1	..	..
Perkins, Newland	..	..	..	1	..	..	..	..	..	..	..
Pettingill, Peter	1	..	..	1	..	..	..	..	1	..	..
Phelps, Elijah	1	1	1	1	..	3	..	1	1	..	..
Pierce, Benjamin	2	1	..	1	..	1	1	1	1	..	..
Pike, William	2	2	..	1	..	2	1	1	1	..	..
Pollard, Jeremiah	3	..	..	1	..	3	..	..	1	..	..
Priest, Jonathan	..	1	..	..	1	..	..	1	..	1	..
Putnam, Daniel	3	..	1	1	..	2	..	..	2	..	..
Putnam, Edward	..	1	2	1	..	..	..	2	..	2	..
Putnam, Jonathan	2	..	1	1	..	..	..	..	2	1	..
Rand, Artimas	2	..	..	1	..	2	2	..	1	..	..
Rand, Henry	..	..	..	..	..	..	..	..	..	..	..
Reed, Isaac	1	..	..	1	..	1	..	..	1	..	..
Rhodes, James	1	1	..	..	1	1	1	1	1	..	..
Rhodes, Joseph	..	1	2	..	1	1	..	1	..	1	..
Rice, Rufus	2	..	..	1	..	..	..	1	..	..	..
Richmond, Ephraim	..	..	1	..	1	..	..	2	..	1	..
Richmond, Simeon	..	..	..	1	..	3	..	..	1	..	..
Rider, John	1	..	..	1	..	..	..	1	..	..	..
Ripley, Charles	2	..	..	1	..	2	2	..	1	..	..
Ross, Benjamin	1	..	..	1	..	1	..	1	..	..	..
Ross, James Jr.	1	..	..	1	..	..	..	1	..	..	..
Rugg, Levi	1	1	1	..	1	3	..	..	1	..	..
Shed, David	2	1	..	1	..	2	2	..	1	..	..
Sherar, John	..	..	1	..	3	..	..	1	..	..	..
Smith, Ephraim	2	..	..	1	..	..	..	1	..	..	..
Smith, George	1	..	..	1	..	4	2	..	1	..	..
Smith, John	4	3	..	1	..	..	..	1	1	..	..
Smith, Rogers	2	..	..	1	..	2	..	..	1	..	..
Smith, Samuel	2	..	..	1	..	..	..	..	1	..	..
Spaulding, Samuel	..	1	..	1	..	1	..	1	1	1	..
Spring, Luther	3	..	..	1	..	1	..	..	1	..	..
Spring, Samuel	..	..	1	..	1	..	..	..	..	1	..
Spring, Samuel Jr.	1	..	..	1	..	..	..	1	..	..	..
Stearns, Jonathan	..	1	..	1	..	3	..	..	1	..	..

WINDHAM COUNTY—Continued

NAMES OF HEADS OF FAMILIES	FREE WHITE MALES					FREE WHITE FEMALES					
	Under 10 years of age	Of 10 and under 16	Of 16 and under 26 including heads of families	Of 26 and under 45 including heads of families	Of 45 and upwards including heads of families.	Under 10 years of age	Of 10 and under 16	Of 16 and under 26 including heads of families	Of 26 and under 45 including heads of families	Of 45 and upwards including heads of families	All other free persons except Indians not taxed
GRAFTON—con.											
Stickney, David	..	..	..	..	1	..	..	..	..	1	..
Stickney, David Jr.	1	..	..	1	..	2	..	..	1	..	..
Stickney, William	..	1	1	..	1	..	1	1	..	1	..
Stickney, William Jr.	1	..	..	1	..	1	..	..	1	..	..
Tarbel, Peter	2	1	..	1	..	1	2	..	1	..	..
Taylor, David	..	..	..	1	..	..	1	..	..	..	..
Taylor, Thaddeus	2	..	..	1	..	..	..	..	1	..	..
Thacher, Joseph	1	1	..	1	..	1	3	..	1	..	..
Thompson, James	1	1	3	..	1	1	..	2	..	1	..
Thompson, Samuel	1	..	1	..	..	..	..	..	1	..	..
Tinney, David	1	..	1	1	1	2	..	..	1	1	..
Tucker, Caleb	..	..	1	..	1	..	1	1	..	1	..
Walker, Samuel	..	..	2	..	1	..	..	2	..	1	..
Walker, Timothy Jr.	2	1	..	1	..	4	..	..	1	..	..
Walton, Rufus	1	2	..	1	..	4	1	..	1	..	..
Wheeler, Jonathan B.	1	1	..	1	..	1	..	1	..	..	..
Whitcomb, Joseph	..	1	..	..	1	..	..	..	..	1	..
Whitcomb, Joseph Jr.	2	1	..	1	..	..	1	..	1	..	..
Whitcomb, Luke	..	..	..	1	..	..	..	..	..	..	..
Whitcomb, Peter	1	..	..	1	..	2	1	..	1	..	..
Whitney, Lemuel	3	..	..	1	..	1	..	..	1	..	..
Wilder, Daniel	1	2	..	1	..	2	2	..	1	..	..
Willington, John	..	1	..	..	1	..	..	..	..	1	..
Willington, William	..	..	1	..	..	..	..	1	..	..	..
Wills, David	..	..	1	..	..	..	..	..	..	..	..
Willson, Benjamin	2	1	..	1	..	..	..	..	1	..	..
Willson, Robert	2	1	1	1	..	2	1	1	1	..	..
Wise, John	..	1	..	1	..	4	1	..	1	..	..
Wise, Widow	..	2	1	..	..	..	1	2	1	..	..
Wise, William	1	..	..	1	..	2	..	..	1	..	..
Witherby, Hezekiah	1	1	1	1	..	4	1	..	1	1	..
Wooley, Samuel	1	..	..	1	1	1	..	1	2	1	..
Wooley, Thomas	..	3	1	1	..	4	..	..	1	..	..
Wright, Josiah	..	..	..	..	1	2	..	..	..	1	..
Wyman, Stephen	2	2	1	..	1	2	..	1	1	..	..
GUILFORD											
Aldrich, Jonathan	1	2	4	..	1	2	4	5	..	2	..
Aldrich, Jonathan Jr.	1	..	1	..	..	1	..	1	..	..	..
Aldrich, Joseph	..	..	1	..	1	..	1	..	..	1	..
Aldrich, Peter	2	2	2	1	1	4	2	1	..	1	..
Aldrich, Roger	1	..	..	1	..	1	..	1	..	..	..
Allen, Samuel	1	1	..	..	1	1	1	1	..	1	..
Andrews, Benjamin	..	..	..	..	..	..	..	..	..	..	..
Andrews, John	..	..	2	..	1	..	..	2	..	1	..
Andrews, Nehemiah	..	4	1	..	1	1	..	1	1	..	..
Ashcraft, Daniel	..	..	2	1	1	..	1	..	..	1	..
Ashcraft, Uriah	1	..	..	1	..	..	..	..	1	..	..
Aylesworth, Robert	..	..	1	..	1	..	..	..	..	1	..
Ayres, David	..	..	2	1	1	1	..	3	..	1	..
Ayres, Ezra G	..	..	1	..	..	1	..	1	..	..	..
Babcock, Harris	3	..	..	1	..	1	..	..	1	..	..
Baker, Samuel	2	2	..	..	2	..	..	2	..	1	..
Baker, Silas	..	..	1	..	..	2	..	1	..	..	..
Ballou, Benjamin	..	..	..	..	1	..	2	1	..	1	..
Ballou, Martin	..	..	1	..	..	..	..	1	..	..	..
Bangs, Herman	1	1	..	1	..	4	..	..	1	..	..
Barber, Isaac	4	..	..	1	..	..	..	..	1	..	..
Barnard, John	2	..	3	1	..	1	1	1	..	..	..
Barney, Aaron	2	1	..	1	1	..	..	1	..	1	..
Barney, Edward	2	2	2	..	1	..	1	..	1	..	..
Barney, Edward Jr.	1	..	..	1	..	1	..	..	1	..	1
Barney, Sylvanus	2	1	1	1	..	1	1	..	1	..	..
Barney, Widow Ruth	..	1	1	..	..	1	2	..	1	..	..
Barns, Russel	..	..	..	1	..	1	..	..	1	..	..
Barns, Simeon	2	1	..	1	..	1	3	..	1	1	..
Barrows, James	..	1	3	..	1	..	..	..	1	1	..
Bennett, Aaron	4	..	..	1	..	..	..	..	1	..	..
Bennett, Matthew	1	..	..	..	1	..	..	..	1	..	..
Bennett, Moses	2	..	1	1	..	..	..	2	..	1	..
Bigelow, Joel	1	2	4	..	1	1	..	2	..	1	..
Bigelow, William	1	1	1	2	1	2	1	..	2	..	..
Billings, Amos	..	1	4	..	1	1	2	2	..	1	..
Bixby, Daniel	..	1	1	1	..	3	1	..	1	..	..
Bixby, David	..	..	1	..	1	1	..	1	..	1	..
Bixby, Manassa	..	1	1	..	1	..	1	1	..	1	..
Bixby, Manassa	3	1	..	1	..	2	2	..	1	..	..
Blanchard, Joshua	1	1	2	..	1	2	..	1	..	1	..
Bolster, John	1	..	..	1	1	1	..	..	1	1	..
Bowen, Asa	2	..	..	..	1	2	1	..	..	1	..
Bowen, Asa Jr.	..	..	1	..	..	1	..	1	..	..	..
Bowler, Charles R.	1	1	..	..	1	1	1	..	1	..	..
Boyden, Daniel	..	..	1	..	1	..	1	..	..	1	..
GUILFORD—con.											
Boyden, Daniel Jr.	1	1	..	1	..	2	..	..	1	..	..
Boyden, James	5	..	..	1	..	1	1	..	1	..	..
Boyden, Joseph	1	1	..	1	..	3	1	..	1	..	..
Boyden, Levi	3	..	1	1	..	..	..	..	1	1	..
Briggs, Peter	2	2	2	..	1	1	1	1	..	1	..
Briggs, Thomas	3	..	..	1	..	1	..	..	1	..	..
Brooks, Ephraim	2	..	..	1	..	3	2	..	1	..	..
Brooks, Israel	..	..	1	..	..	..	..	1	..	..	..
Brown, Isaac	..	1	2	..	1	1	1	2	..	1	..
Brown, Isaac Jr.	2	2	..	..	1	..	1	..	1	..	..
Brown, James	..	1	..	..	1	..	1	..	..	1	..
Buckland, Benjamin	2	1	1	..	1	1	1	2	..	1	..
Buckland, James	1	..	1	..	..	1	..	1	..	..	..
Bullock, Elkanah	2	..	..	..	1	..	2	2	..	1	..
Bullock, Joseph	1	1	1	..	1	3	1	..	2	..	..
Bullock, Lovel	1	..	3	..	1	2	1	1	..	1	..
Bullock, William	3	..	..	1	..	2	1	..	1	..	..
Burnett, John	..	..	..	1	1	3	..	1	..	..	..
Burrows, Joseph	3	..	..	1	..	1	1	..	1	..	..
Burrows, Joshua	..	..	..	1	..	..	..	..	1	..	..
Burrows, Solomon	..	..	1	..	1	1	..	..	1	..	..
Burt, Ithamar	1	1	1	1	..	1	1	1	1	..	..
Carpenter, Benjamin	3	2	..	1	1	3	..	..	1	1	..
Carpenter, Jacob	3	1	..	..	1	1	1	..	1	..	..
Carpenter, John B.	4	..	..	1	..	2	1	..	1	..	..
Carpenter, Joseph	..	1	..	..	1	1	..	1	..	1	..
Carpenter, Seral	2	..	..	..	1	3	1	1	1	..	..
Chapin, Eddy	..	..	..	1	..	2	..	1	..	..	..
Chapin, Solomon	1	..	..	1	..	..	..	1	..	..	..
Chase, Dean	2	2	2	..	1	..	..	3	1	..	..
Chase, Elisha	..	..	1	..	..	1	..	1	..	..	..
Chase, James	..	2	..	..	1	1	..	2	..	1	..
Chase, Paul	1	2	1	..	1	..	..	2	..	1	..
Chase, Rufus	..	1	..	..	1	2	..	1	..	1	..
Chase, Slade	1	..	..	1	..	1	..	..	1	..	..
Chickering, Timothy	1	2	..	..	1	..	1	2	..	1	..
Clark, John	3	..	..	1	..	1	1	..	1	..	..
Clark, Samuel	1	1	..	1	..	3	..	1	1	..	..
Clark, Seth	2	2	..	1	..	2	..	1	1	..	..
Cleaver, William	1	..	..	1	..	2	1	..	1	..	..
Cobb, James	1	1	..	1	..	3	..	..	1	..	..
Cole, Amos	2	1	2	..	1	1	1	..	1	..	..
Cole, Caleb	1	..	..	1	..	1	1	2	1	..	..
Cole, Daniel	2	..	..	1	..	1	2	1	1	..	..
Cole, Ephraim	..	..	..	1	..	..	..	..	1	..	..
Cole, Henry	4	2	..	1	..	1	..	1	1	..	..
Colegrove, Reuben	..	1	2	..	1	1	..	1	..	1	..
Collins, John	..	..	3	..	1	..	1	..	..	1	..
Crandall, Sylvester	..	1	..	..	1	3	1	..	..	1	..
Crouch, James	..	1	..	..	1	..	..	1	..	1	..
Crowningshield, John	1	..	..	1	..	..	..	1	..	..	..
Cudworth, James	..	..	..	..	1	..	..	..	2	..	..
Cudworth, Samuel	1	..	..	..	1	..	..	..	2	..	..
Culver, Joshua	..	1	..	1	1	3	2	..	1	1	..
Cutler, Thomas	..	1	3	1	1	..	1	3	1	2	..
Cutting, Jonah	4	..	1	1	..	..	1	..	1	..	..
Davis, David	..	..	..	..	1	..	2	3	..	2	..
Davis, Joseph	1	..	..	1	..	2	..	1	1	..	..
Dean, Benjamin	1	1	3	1	1	2	3	1	1	1	..
Denison, Gilbert	2	1	1	1	..	1	1	1	1	..	..
Denison, Jabez	..	1	..	..	2	3	1	..	2	1	..
Denison, William	2	1	1	..	1	1	1	2	..	1	..
Dennis, James	1	..	..	1	..	1	..	..	1	2	..
Dennis, John	4	..	..	1	..	..	..	..	1	..	..
Dewey, David	..	..	1	..	1	1	..	1	..	1	..
Dickinson, John	2	2	..	1	..	3	..	1	1	..	..
Dunham, Ephraim	..	2	1	..	1	..	..	..	..	1	..
Dwyer, John	..	..	3	..	1	..	..	2	..	1	..
Eddy, Benjamin	..	..	..	..	1	..	..	..	..	1	..
Eddy, Joel	2	..	..	1	..	1	..	1	..	..	..
Edwards, Joseph	..	..	..	..	1	..	..	..	..	2	..
Edwards, William	4	..	2	..	1	..	..	..	2	1	..
Ellenwood, Ephraim	..	..	2	..	1	..	1	1	..	1	..
Elliott, Joseph	2	..	..	..	1	..	1	..	1	..	..
Ellithrop, Azeriah	2	2	1	1	..	2	1	..	1	1	..
Farnsworth, Jonas	1	..	2	2	..	..	..	..	..	1	..
Farril, Isaac	..	1	1	..	1	..	..	1	..	1	..
Field, Elihu	..	..	1	..	1	1	1	1	..	1	..
Fisher, Edmund	..	..	..	..	1	..	..	..	2	1	..
Fisher, Ichabod	2	..	1	1	..	1	2	2	1	..	..
Fitch, Ebenezer	..	..	..	..	1	..	..	..	1	1	..
Fitch, John	..	..	..	1	..	4	..	..	1	..	..
Forrest, David	3	1	1	..	1	1	2	1	..	1	..

WINDHAM COUNTY—Continued

NAMES OF HEADS OF FAMILIES	FREE WHITE MALES: Under 10 years of age	FREE WHITE MALES: Of 10 and under 16	FREE WHITE MALES: Of 16 and under 26 including heads of families	FREE WHITE MALES: Of 26 and under 45 including heads of families	FREE WHITE MALES: Of 45 and upwards including heads of families.	FREE WHITE FEMALES: Under 10 years of age	FREE WHITE FEMALES: Of 10 and under 16	FREE WHITE FEMALES: Of 16 and under 26 including heads of families	FREE WHITE FEMALES: Of 26 and under 45 including heads of families	FREE WHITE FEMALES: Of 45 and upwards including heads of families	All other free persons except Indians not taxed
GUILFORD—con.											
Fosdick, James	..	1	1	1	..	..	..	..	1	..	..
Franklin, Aaron	1	..	..	1	1	1	..	1	..	1	..
Franklin, Aaron Jr.	2	1	1	1	..	1	1	..	1	..	..
Franklin, Benjamin	2	..	..	1	..	2	..	..	1	..	..
Franklin, Jabez	1	1	1	..	1	1	1	2	1	..	..
Franklin, Philip	..	2	1	..	1	1	..	..	..	1	..
Frink, Samuel	..	..	..	1	..	..	1	..	1	..	..
Gains, David	2	..	..	..	1	1	2	2	..	1	..
Gains, Joseph	2	2	1	1	..	1	..	2	1	..	..
Gale, Ephraim	2	2	1	1	..	1	..	1	1	..	..
Gallup, Joseph	..	1	..	..	1	..	..	..	1	1	..
Goodenough, Ebenezer	1	1	2	..	1	1	..	2	1	1	..
Goodenough, Levi	1	..	2	..	1	..	1	..	..	1	..
Goodenough, Liberty	2	..	..	1	..	3	..	..	1	..	..
Goodspeed, Gideon	1	1	..	1	..	2	1	..	1	..	..
Goodwin, Joseph	..	1	..	..	1	2	..	2	..	1	..
Gould, Stephen	3	1	1	..	1	..	..	2	..	1	..
Gould, Thomas	1	..	..	1	..	2	..	1	..	..	..
Graves, Jeremiah	3	..	..	..	1	3	1	1	1	..	..
Greenleaf, Daniel	3	..	..	1	..	2	..	..	1	..	..
Gregory, Elisha	1	..	2	1	..	1	..	..	1	..	..
Grover, Jacob	1	..	1	..	1	2	1	..	1	..	..
Grow, Nathaniel	..	1	2	..	2	1	..	2	..	2	..
Haley, Belcher	2	..	..	1	..	2	..	2	..	..	..
Hammond, John	..	1	1	..	1	1	1	..	..	1	..
Hammond, Thomas	..	..	..	1	..	2	..	..	1	..	..
Haynes, Nathaniel	..	..	1	..	..	1	..	1	..	..	..
Haynes, Vine	..	..	1	..	1	..	..	2	..	..	..
Hicks, Ezra	1	1	..	1	..	..	1	..	1	..	..
Hicks, Henry	..	..	..	..	1	..	..	..	..	..	..
Hill, Asahel	..	1	1	..	1	..	..	2	..	1	..
Hill, Fisher	1	..	..	1	..	3	..	..	1	..	..
Horton, Nathan	1	1	..	1	1	1	..	2	1	..	..
Houghton, Edward	1	..	2	2	..	4	..	..	2	..	..
Houghton, James	2	..	..	1	..	1	..	1	1	..	..
Houghton, Richardson	1	..	..	1	..	2	..	1	..	..	..
Houghton, Widow L.	..	..	..	..	..	1	..	..	..	1	..
Hudson, Henry	..	..	..	1	..	..	..	1	..	..	..
Hyde, Dana	2	..	1	1	..	3	1	1	1	..	..
Hynds, William	1	..	1	..	1	1	..	2	..	1	..
Ingraham, Elisha	1	1	..	1	..	2	..	..	1	..	..
Jackson, Widow	..	..	1	..	..	..	..	1	..	1	..
Jacobs, Joseph	2	1	3	..	2	1	1	2	..	1	..
Jacobs, Peter	2	1	1	1	..	2	1	..	1	..	..
Jilson, David	2	..	..	1	..	3	..	1	1	..	..
Johnson, Jedidiah	1	..	..	1	..	4	..	1	..	..	..
Johnson, Jonathan	..	1	1	..	1	..	..	1	..	1	..
Jones, Anthony	..	..	1	..	1	..	2	..	..	2	..
Jones, Eliakim	1	..	..	1	..	1	..	1	1	..	..
Joy, Abithar	2	..	1	1	..	3	1	1	1	..	..
King, James	..	1	..	..	1	1	..	..	..	1	..
King, James Jr.	1	..	..	1	..	..	..	..	2	..	..
King, John	2	..	2	1	..	2	..	1	..	1	..
King, Jonas	1	..	1	..	..	2	..	1	..	..	..
Lamb, Nathan	3	1	..	1	..	..	..	1	1	..	..
Larrabee, Samuel	1	..	..	1	..	6	1	..	2	1	..
Leonard, David	2	..	3	..	1	1	2	2	1	..	..
Littlefield, Thomas	..	..	..	..	1	..	..	..	..	1	..
Lynde, Daniel	..	1	1	..	1	..	1	2	..	1	..
Lynde, Joshua	4	..	1	1	..	1	2	1	1	1	..
Lynde, Lemuel	3	1	..	1	..	1	..	1	1	..	..
Lynde, Thomas	..	..	..	1	..	..	..	..	1	..	..
Marsh, William	2	..	..	1	1	..	..	2	..	1	..
Marsh, William Jr.	2	1	..	1	..	1	2	..	1	..	..
Martin, Cyrus	1	2	..	1	..	2	..	..	1	..	..
Maxwell, Philip	2	1	1	..	2	2	..	1	1	..	..
Melenday, Jonathan	1	..	..	1	..	1	1	2	1	..	..
Melenday, Samuel	..	..	3	..	1	2	3	..	..	1	..
Millet, Nathaniel	..	..	..	1	..	3	..	..	1	..	..
Minor, James	1	1	1	1	..	2	1	..	1	..	..
Morgan, Henry	1	..	..	1	..	..	..	..	1	1	..
Newell, Oliver	1	1	1	..	1	1	1	..	..	1	..
Nichols, Ephraim	1	..	1	1	..	1	3	1	1	..	..
Nichols, Jonas	3	2	..	1	..	2	..	2	1	..	..
Nichols, Paul	3	1	..	..	1	..	1	1	1	..	..
Noyes, Gershom	2	1	..	1	..	2	1	..	1	..	..
Noyes, Isaac	..	1	1	1	..	..	..	2	..	..	..
Noyes, John	..	1	2	..	1	..	1	1	..	1	..
Noyes, John Jr.	1	..	1	1	..	1	..	1	1	..	..
Nye, William	3	1	..	1	..	..	3	1	..	..	..
GUILFORD—con.											
Olden, Joseph	..	..	1	..	1	..	..	1	..	1	..
Palmer, Charles	1	1	..	1	..	2	2	1	1	..	..
Palmer, Humphrey	1	1	..	..	1	2	..	2	..	1	..
Parker, Eleazer	..	1	..	1	..	2	..	1	..	..	..
Parker, James	..	..	..	..	1	1	..	1	..	1	..
Parker, James Jr.	3	2	1	1	..	2	2	1	1	..	..
Parker, Jeremiah	2	2	..	1	..	2	2	..	1	..	..
Parker, William	3	2	..	1	1	..	..	1	2	1	..
Partridge, Jasper	3	..	1	1	1	1	..	..	1	1	..
Paul, Henry	1	1	..	1	..	1	..	..	1	..	..
Peck, Seth	..	..	..	..	1	..	1	3	..	1	..
Penny, Jonathan	2	2	1	..	1	1	..	..	..	1	..
Pierce, Ichabod	4	..	..	1	..	3	..	..	1	..	..
Porter, Elisha	1	1	1	..	1	1	2	..	1	..	..
Pullen, John	..	..	..	..	1	..	..	..	..	1	..
Pullen, Mathew	..	..	1	..	1	..	..	..	..	1	..
Putnam, Asa	..	1	3	1	..	1	..	2	1	1	..
Ramsdale, Elijah	..	1	1	1	..	1	..	1	..	1	..
Ramsdale, William	2	..	..	1	..	1	..	..	1	..	..
Redington, Widow S.	..	..	..	..	..	..	..	1	1	..	..
Rice, Asa	3	..	..	..	1	1	..	..	1	..	..
Rice, Asa Jr.	..	..	1	1	..	..	1	..	1	..	..
Rice, Josiah	..	..	3	..	1	2	..	2	..	1	..
Rice, Micah	..	..	..	..	1	1	..	2	1	1	..
Rice, Phinehas	3	2	..	..	1	..	..	1	..	1	..
Richardson, William	..	..	1	1	..	..	..	1	1	..	..
Roberts, Ebenezer	1	..	..	2	1	..	1	1	1	1	..
Rogers, Abijah	..	..	..	..	1	..	1	2	..	1	..
Root, Elihu	1	2	1	..	1	..	2	1	..	1	..
Root, Timothy	..	1	1	..	1	..	..	..	..	1	..
Rose, Thomas	2	3	1	..	1	3	1	..	1	..	..
Russel, Jonathan	1	..	..	1	..	1	1	..	1	..	..
Russel, Jonathan 2nd	2	1	..	1	..	1	..	..	1	..	..
Salisbury, Edward	..	2	..	1	..	3	1	..	1	..	..
Salisbury, James	2	..	2	..	1	..	2	1	1	..	..
Severance, John	..	1	..	..	1	..	..	..	..	..	..
Shaw, Thomas	..	..	1	1	..	2	..	1	1	..	..
Shepardson, John	..	..	..	..	1	..	..	..	..	1	..
Shepardson, Noah	1	..	1	..	1	1	1	..	..	1	..
Shepardson, Samuel	3	2	1	2	..	1	..	2	2	..	..
Shepardson, Stephen	4	..	..	1	..	1	1	..	1	..	..
Shepardson, William	3	1	2	1	1	3	3	..	1	1	..
Shepardson, Zephaniah	4	1	2	..	1	2	1	..	1	..	..
Shippee, Nathan	1	2	1	..	1	2	..	2	1	..	..
Slater, John	1	1	..	..	1	1	1	3	..	1	..
Slater, Joseph	..	1	1	..	1	..	..	1	..	1	..
Slater, Joseph 2nd.	1	..	..	1	..	2	..	..	1	..	..
Smead, Amasa	2	1	4	1	1	3	1	1	2	..	..
Smith, Amos	2	1	..	1	..	2	..	..	1	..	..
Smith, Daniel	2	1	1	2	..	..	1	1	1	..	..
Smith, Eli	6	..	..	1	..	..	..	..	1	..	..
Smith, Isaac	2	2	..	1	..	2	..	2	1	..	..
Smith, Jonas	1	..	..	1	..	1	..	1	..	..	..
Smith, Solomon	3	1	1	..	1	1	2	1	..	1	..
Snow, Simeon	..	1	1	..	1	4	..	..	1	..	..
Spaulding, Jonathan	..	..	..	1	..	..	..	..	1	..	..
Spears, Widow	..	..	1	..	..	..	..	..	..	1	..
Stafford, Isaac	2	1	..	1	..	2	2	..	1	..	..
Stark, Jedidiah	1	..	..	1	..	1	..	1	..	..	..
Stark, Morgan	..	..	1	..	..	..	..	1	..	..	..
Stark, Nathan	2	1	1	..	1	1	1	1	..	1	..
Starr, Timothy	1	..	..	1	1	1	..	..	2	1	..
Stebbins, Abner	2	1	1	..	1	1	..	1	..	1	..
Stevens, Simeon	2	2	3	1	..	1	..	2	1	..	..
Steward, Antipas	..	..	1	..	1	..	1	..	..	1	..
Stone, Reuben	1	..	1	..	1	..	..	2	..	2	..
Stowell, David	..	..	2	..	1	..	2	2	..	1	..
Streeter, Benjamin	1	..	1	..	..	1	..	..	1	..	..
Streeter, Enoch	1	..	1	..	..	..	..	1	..	..	..
Streeter, Rufus	2	..	..	1	..	3	1	..	1	..	..
Thurber, David	..	..	..	..	1	..	..	1	..	1	..
Thurber, Edward	1	1	..	1	..	4	1	..	3	..	..
Tinker, Almerin	1	..	..	1	..	1	..	..	1	..	..
Tisdale, Otis	1	1	..	1	1	..	..	1	..	1	..
Toby, Eleazer	2	1	1	..	1	1	..	1	..	1	..
Torry, Abel	..	..	1	..	1	..	..	..	..	1	..
Torry, Jones	..	1	..	1	..	1	1	..	1	..	..
Trivott, Benjamin	2	1	1	..	1	1	1	..	..	1	..
Tubbs, Isaac	3	2	4	..	1	3	1	1	..	1	..
Tubbs, Nehemiah	..	..	..	1	..	1	..	..	1	..	..
Tyler, Royal	3	..	..	1	..	1	1	3	..	..	..

WINDHAM COUNTY—Continued

NAMES OF HEADS OF FAMILIES	FREE WHITE MALES					FREE WHITE FEMALES					
	Under 10 years of age	Of 10 and under 16	Of 16 and under 26 including heads of families	Of 26 and under 45 including heads of families	Of 45 and upwards including heads of families.	Under 10 years of age	Of 10 and under 16	Of 16 and under 26 including heads of families	Of 26 and under 45 including heads of families	Of 45 and upwards including heads of families	All other free persons except Indians not taxed
GUILFORD—con.											
Underwood, John	1	..	..	..	1	..	..	..	..	1	..
Upham, Jonathan	2	..	..	1	..	4	1	..	1	..	..
Wadliegh, Theophilas	1	..	1	1	1	3	1	2	1	..	..
Wallen, John	1	..	..	1	..	..	..	1	1	..	..
Walsworth, Elijah	2	..	..	1	..	2	1	..	1	..	..
Ward, Henry	2	..	..	1	..	2	..	..	1	..	..
Waterhouse, Nathan	1	3	1	..	1	2	1	1	1	..	..
Weld, Calvin	1	1	..	1	..	..	1	..	1	1	..
Weld, Luther	2	1	..	1	..	1	..	..	1	..	..
Welman, Jedidiah	1	..	1	..	1	..	..	1	..	1	..
West, Robert	1	..	..	2	..	1	2	..	2	2	..
Wetherhead, Jeremiah	2	..	1	1	..	..	..	1	..	..	..
Wheeler, Daniel	..	1	1	..	1	..	1	1	..	1	..
White, David	2	..	..	1	..	..	1	1	..	..	..
White, Jacob	1	1	..	1	..	3	1	..	..	1	..
Whitney, Abel	1	4	..	..	1	..	1	..	1	..	..
Whitney, Job	2	..	..	..	..	..	1	2	..	1	..
Wilder, Aaron	1	1	..	..	1	1	2	1	..	1	..
Wilkins, Andrew	1	..	..	1	..	2	1	..	1	..	..
Wilkins, Daniel	..	..	..	..	1	..	..	..	..	1	..
Williams, Barzillai	2	..	..	1	..	..	..	1	..	..	..
Williams, Davis	1	1	..	..	1	..	..	..	..	1	..
Williams, Israel	2	1	..	1	..	1	..	..	1	..	..
Williams, Singleton	4	..	..	1	..	..	..	..	1	..	..
Williams, Solomon	3	1	..	1	..	..	..	..	1	..	..
Willis, Beriah	..	..	..	..	1	..	..	2	..	1	..
Willis, Stoughton	1	..	..	1	..	3	..	..	1	..	..
Wilson, John	..	..	1	..	1	1	3	1	1	..	..
Wilson, Samuel	1	..	..	1	..	..	..	1	..	..	..
Wood, Charles	3	1	2	..	1	..	1	1	..	1	..
Yaw, Amos	1	..	..	1	..	1	2	..	1	..	..
Yaw, Moses	3	1	..	1	..	2	1	..	1	1	..
Yaw, William	2	..	..	1	..	1	1	1	..	1	..
Younglove, John	..	1	2	..	1	3	1	2	1	..	..
HALIFAX											
Adams, Levi	3	1	3	1	..	1	..	..	1	..	..
Akeley, Francis	1	3	3	..	1	..	..	..	..	1	..
Alexander, Jonathan	1	..	..	1	..	..	..	..	1	..	..
Allen, David	..	2	..	1	1	2	..	1	2	1	..
Allen, David 2nd	1	2	1	..	1	..	1	2	..	1	..
Allen, David 3rd	3	..	..	1	..	2	1	1	1	..	..
Alvason, David	..	..	2	..	1	..	1	1	..	1	..
Alvason, Jonathan	1	..	1	1	..	1	..	..	1	1	..
Alvason, William	..	1	..	1	..	..	1	..	1	..	..
Baldwin, Daniel	1	..	..	1	..	2	..	..	1	..	..
Ballou, Asahel	1	..	..	1	..	1	..	..	1	..	..
Barber, Benjamin	1	..	2	..	1	2	1	1	..	1	..
Barney, James	3	1	2	1	..	1	1	2	1	..	..
Barney, James Jr.	..	..	..	1	..	2	..	..	1	..	..
Barney, John	1	..	..	1	..	..	..	1	..	..	..
Bell, David	..	..	..	1	..	2	..	..	1	..	..
Bell, James	1	..	..	1	..	..	..	..	1	..	..
Bell, Joseph	..	..	2	..	1	1	1	2	..	1	..
Boardman, George	..	..	..	1	..	3	..	..	1	..	..
Bolster, Joel	2	..	..	..	1	3	..	..	..	1	..
Breed, Oliver	2	1	3	..	1	3	..	..	1	..	..
Brooks, Asa	3	1	..	1	..	2	1	..	1	..	..
Brown, Joseph	1	..	1	..	..	..	..	1	..	..	..
Bullock, Darius	3	..	1	1	..	2	2	1	1	..	..
Calf, Stephen	2	2	..	1	..	2	..	..	1	..	..
Carpenter, Asaph	..	..	1	..	1	..	..	1	..	1	..
Carpenter, Caleb	..	..	..	1	..	3	..	..	1	..	..
Carpenter, Stutely	1	..	1	..	1	..	..	1	..	1	..
Chase, Asaph	..	..	..	1	..	1	..	1	..	..	..
Chase, Cyrus	..	..	..	1	..	2	..	1	1	..	..
Clark, Archibald	1	..	1	..	..	..	..	1	..	..	..
Clark, Asa	..	1	2	..	1	3	1	1	..	1	..
Clark, Ebenezer	2	1	..	..	1	..	1	2	..	1	..
Clark, Elisha	..	..	2	..	1	2	2	..	1	..	..
Clark, James	..	..	..	1	1	..	2	1	3	1	..
Clark, Josiah	..	2	1	..	1	1	..	..	..	1	..
Clark, Samuel	1	..	..	..	1	1	1	..	..	1	..
Clark, Samuel 2nd	4	1	..	1	..	2	..	1	1	..	..
Clark, Thomas	..	1	1	..	1	1	1	2	..	1	..
Conant, Amos	..	..	2	1	1	..	2	..	..	1	..
Cook, Stephen	3	..	..	..	1	..	1	1	..	1	..
Crain, Isaac	..	1	1	..	1	..	..	2	..	1	..
Crozer, Artemas	1	1	1	..	1	2	..	..	1	1	..
Crozer, John	..	..	1	..	1	..	..	1	1	1	..
Crozer, Robert	..	..	1	..	1	1	..	3	..	..	2
Cutler, Joel	..	..	1	..	1	..	..	1	..	1	..

NAMES OF HEADS OF FAMILIES	FREE WHITE MALES					FREE WHITE FEMALES					
	Under 10 years of age	Of 10 and under 16	Of 16 and under 26 including heads of families	Of 26 and under 45 including heads of families	Of 45 and upwards including heads of families.	Under 10 years of age	Of 10 and under 16	Of 16 and under 26 including heads of families	Of 26 and under 45 including heads of families	Of 45 and upwards including heads of families	All other free persons except Indians not taxed
HALIFAX—con.											
Dalrymple, William	2	1	..	..	1	..	1	..	..	1	..
Darling, Peter	1	..	1	..	1	3	1	1	1	..	..
Davis, Benajah	..	..	..	..	1	..	..	..	..	1	..
Dean, Pardee	3	1	..	1	1	..	1	..	1	1	..
Dunagan, Andrew	..	1	..	..	1	1	..	..	..	1	..
Edson, Howard	2	..	1	..	..	..	..	1	..	..	..
Edson, Jesse	..	1	..	1	..	2	..	1	1	..	..
Everett, Jeremiah	1	..	1	..	1	..	1	..	..	1	..
Farnsworth, Thomas	1	2	2	..	1	2	1	1	1	..	..
Fessenden, Solomon	5	3	..	2	..	..	..	..	1	..	..
Fish, Nathan	1	2	..	..	1	2	1	2	..	1	..
Fish, Samuel	1	1	2	..	1	1	2	1	1	..	..
Fisher, Isaac	1	..	..	1	..	..	..	..	1	..	..
Fisher, Timothy	3	..	..	..	1	3	1	..	..	1	..
Fowler, Elias	..	..	1	..	..	..	..	1	..	..	..
Fowler, Luther	1	..	1	..	..	1	..	1	..	..	..
French, Eleazer	2	..	..	1	..	3	..	..	1	..	..
French, Jesse	..	..	..	1	..	3	1	..	1	..	..
Gates, Stephen	2	..	3	..	1	1	1	1	..	1	..
Gault, Archibald	3	..	..	1	1	1	..	..	1	..	..
Gault, William	3	1	..	1	..	2	..	..	1	..	..
Gleason, Ezra	2	..	..	1	..	3	..	..	1	..	..
Gore, Amos	2	..	1	1	..	1	2	1	1	..	..
Gore, Ezekiel	1	..	1	1	1	3	1	..	1	1	..
Green, John	3	2	..	..	1	2	2	..	1	..	..
Grover, Aaron	1	..	..	1	..	3	..	..	1	..	..
Guild, Jesse	4	1	..	1	..	1	..	..	1	..	..
Hall, Azariah	1	1	..	..	1	..	1	2	..	1	..
Hall, Erastus	..	..	1	..	..	..	..	1	..	..	..
Hall, Joel	1	2	2	..	1	..	2	..	..	1	..
Hall, John	..	1	1	..	1	..	1	2	1	1	..
Hall, Widow	1	2	..	..	..	..	1	..	1	..	..
Hamilton, John	3	..	..	1	..	2	..	..	1	..	..
Hammond, Bela	2	1	..	..	1	..	1	2	..	1	..
Hardy, Samuel	..	..	..	..	..	..	..	..	..	..	2
Harris, John	1	..	..	1	..	1	..	..	1	..	..
Harris, Joshua	2	..	..	1	..	3	..	..	1	..	..
Harris, William	4	..	..	..	1	..	1	..	1	..	..
Hasket, Asa	..	..	..	1	..	1	..	..	1	..	..
Hastings, Jacob	..	..	2	2	..	2	1	2	..	..	..
Hatch, James	2	1	1	1	..	2	3	2	1	..	..
Hatch, Nathan	2	1	..	1	..	2	1	..	1	..	..
Haven, Clark	..	1	..	..	1	..	1	..	..	1	..
Haven, Elijah	..	..	..	1	..	3	..	..	1	..	..
Henderson, Henry	5	2	..	..	1	..	..	..	..	1	..
Henry, Benjamin	1	..	1	1	1	1	1	1	1	1	..
Henry, James	..	..	1	1	..	3	..	2	..	..	..
Herrington, Job	2	..	..	1	..	1	..	1	..	1	..
Herrington, Widow S.	2	..	..	..	..	1	..	..	1	..	..
Hewes, William	2	2	..	1	..	1	1	1	1	..	..
Holms, Samuel	2	..	..	1	1	1	..	..	1	1	..
Houghton, Philemon	..	1	..	1	..	2	1	..	1	..	..
Hudson, Elisha	1	2	..	..	1	2	..	..	..	1	..
Hunt, Jonathan	3	..	2	..	1	1	2	..	..	1	..
Jackson, Ebenezer	2	..	..	1	..	2	..	1	..	..	..
Johnson, Seth	..	1	..	..	1	..	1	..	..	1	..
Jones, Israel	..	2	..	1	..	3	1	..	1	..	..
Kellogg, Jonathan	2	1	1	..	1	1	2	..	1	..	..
Kenneday, Alexander	3	..	..	1	..	2	..	1	..	..	..
Kenneday, Hugh	..	..	1	..	1	..	..	3	..	1	..
Kenneday, Thomas	2	..	..	1	..	1	..	..	1	..	..
Kingsbury, John	..	1	2	..	1	..	1	..	..	1	..
Kirkley, John	..	..	..	..	1	..	..	2	..	1	..
Lamb, Aaron	1	..	..	1	..	3	..	..	1	..	..
Lamb, David	1	2	1	..	1	1	..	..	1	..	..
Lamphere, Jlatham	1	1	..	1	..	..	1	..	1	..	..
Larnard, Moses	3	1	..	1	..	2	2	..	1	..	..
Little, Thomas	2	1	1	1	..	1	..	1	..	..	..
Littlefield, Jesse	3	..	..	1	..	2	..	..	1	..	..
Littlefield, Josiah	3	1	..	1	..	2	1	..	1	..	..
Long, David	2	..	2	1	..	..	..	1	..	..	..
Marble, Jonathan	2	..	..	..	1	1	..	1	..	1	..
Marsh, Jacob	5	..	..	1	..	..	..	..	1	..	..
Marsh, Osburn	1	..	..	1	..	3	2	..	1	..	..
Mason, Ashbel	..	..	..	1	..	..	..	..	..	1	..
Mason, George	1	..	..	1	..	1	..	..	1	..	..
Mason, Peter	..	..	..	..	1	2	1	..	1	1	..
Mathews, Benjamin	3	3	..	..	1	1	..	..	..	1	..
McAllister, Benjamin	..	..	1	..	..	1	..	1	..	..	..

WINDHAM COUNTY—Continued

NAMES OF HEADS OF FAMILIES	FREE WHITE MALES: Under 10 years of age	FREE WHITE MALES: Of 10 and under 16	FREE WHITE MALES: Of 16 and under 26 including heads of families	FREE WHITE MALES: Of 26 and under 45 including heads of families	FREE WHITE MALES: Of 45 and upwards including heads of families	FREE WHITE FEMALES: Under 10 years of age	FREE WHITE FEMALES: Of 10 and under 16	FREE WHITE FEMALES: Of 16 and under 26 including heads of families	FREE WHITE FEMALES: Of 26 and under 45 including heads of families	FREE WHITE FEMALES: Of 45 and upwards including heads of families	All other free persons except Indians not taxed
HALIFAX—con.											
McCluer, Joseph	..	2	1	..	1	..	1	3	..	1	..
Mines, Perez	2	..	..	1	..	1	..	..	1	..	..
Minor, Adam	1	..	..	1	..	..	..	..	1	..	..
Minor, Ephraim	2	..	..	1	..	1	1	..	1	..	..
Mullet, James	3	3	..	1	..	2	1	..	1	..	..
Nichols, Samuel	2	..	..	1	..	2	2	1	1	..	..
Nichols, Samuel 2nd	1	..	2	1	..	4	2	2	1	..	..
Niles, Henry	2	..	2	1	..	1	..	1	1	..	..
Niles, Oliver	2	..	1	1	..	1	..	..	1	..	..
Niles, Samuel	2	..	..	1	..	1	..	..	..	1	..
Orr, Isaac	..	..	1	..	1	..	1	3	..	1	..
Orr, Isaac Jr.	..	..	..	1	..	2	..	..	1	..	..
Orvis, Oliver	1	..	1	..	1	2	1	1	..	1	..
Pennel, Widdow, Jane	..	2	..	..	..	1	1	..	1	..	..
Pennell, Andrew	3	..	..	1	..	1	1	..	1	..	..
Pennell, James	..	..	2	..	1	1	..	1	1	..	..
Perry, Benjamin	..	1	..	1	..	..	1	..	1	..	..
Perry, Joseph	..	..	1	..	1	..	..	2	..	1	..
Phelps, Francis	2	3	..	..	1	1	2	..	..	1	..
Phillips, Ezekiel	..	..	..	..	1	..	..	..	..	1	..
Pierce, Allen	2	..	..	1	..	1	..	..	1	..	..
Pierce, Amasa	..	..	4	..	..	..	..	1	..	1	..
Pierce, Benjamin	3	..	..	1	..	3	1	..	1	..	..
Pierce, James	1	..	..	1	..	..	..	..	1	..	..
Pierce, Joseph	1	..	..	..	1	..	..	1	..	1	..
Pierce, Nathaniel	2	..	..	1	..	..	..	..	1	..	..
Pierce, Reuben	1	..	..	1	..	4	1	..	1	..	..
Pike, David	..	..	..	1	..	2	..	1	..	..	..
Plumb, George	4	..	..	1	..	..	..	..	1	..	..
Plumb, James	2	2	1	..	1	1	..	1	1	..	..
Putnam, Jesse	3	1	..	..	1	..	1	2	..	1	..
Randall, Stephen	1	..	..	1	..	4	..	1	1	..	..
Ransom, Luther	1	1	..	..	1	3	1	..	1	..	..
Raymond, Benjamin	2	..	..	1	..	1	..	1	..	1	1
Read, George	2	..	..	..	1	1	..	..	..	1	..
Rich, Jethniel	1	..	..	..	1	..	..	..	1	1	..
Richardson, Jonathan	1	1	1	..	1	1	1	..	..	1	..
Richardson, Samuel	2	..	1	1	..	2	..	1	1	..	..
Rugg, Joseph	..	..	..	..	1	..	..	..	1	1	..
Russel, Samuel	..	1	..	..	1	5	2	..	1	..	..
Sabin, Ebenezer	..	..	1	..	1	..	1	1	..	1	..
Sabin, Ebenezer Jr.	2	..	..	1	..	..	1	..	1	..	..
Saunders, Aaron	2	1	1	1	..	2	2	..	1	..	..
Saunders, Jones	2	1	..	1	..	..	2	..	1	..	..
Sawyer, Darius	..	..	..	..	1	..	..	..	..	1	..
Scott, Abel	2	..	1	..	..	..	1	..	1	..	..
Scott, Asahel	..	1	..	1	..	2	..	..	1	..	..
Scott, Thomas	..	2	1	..	1	..	1	1	..	1	..
Scott, Thomas Jr.	..	..	..	1	..	..	..	..	1	..	..
Seaver, Joshua	..	..	..	1	..	1	..	..	1	..	..
Shepard, Abel	2	..	1	1	..	2	..	1	1	..	..
Shepardson, Jared	..	..	..	1	..	2	..	..	1	..	..
Slade, Aaron	..	1	..	..	1	3	1	..	..	1	..
Smead, John	..	..	3	..	1	..	..	2	..	1	..
Smith, Asa	2	2	1	..	1	2	1	..	..	1	..
Smith, Hezekiah	2	2	..	..	1	2	1	..	..	1	..
Smith, Isaiah Jr.	2	..	..	1	..	..	..	..	1	..	..
Smith, Joel	1	1	..	..	1	2	1	..	..	1	..
Spaulding, Levi	1	..	..	1	..	1	..	..	1	..	..
Squiers, David	3	..	..	1	..	2	..	..	1	..	..
Stacey, John	2	..	..	1	..	..	..	1	..	..	..
Stafford, Samuel	..	2	..	..	1	1	..	..	1	..	..
Stanliff, Josiah	1	..	1	..	1	3	..	1	..	1	..
Stanliff, Solomon	2	..	..	1	..	..	..	..	1	..	..
Stark, Jedidiah	1	..	..	1	..	2	..	1	1	..	..
Stark, William	..	..	..	1	..	2	..	..	1	..	..
Stow, David	2	..	..	1	..	3	2	..	1	..	..
Sumner, Daniel	2	1	..	..	1	..	..	..	1	1	..
Sumner, Daniel Jr.	2	..	..	1	..	3	1	..	1	..	..
Sumner, Joel	..	1	..	1	..	3	1	..	1	..	..
Sumner, Jotham	1	..	..	1	..	..	..	1	..	..	..
Swain, Joseph	3	1	..	..	1	2	2	..	1	..	..
Taggart, John	2	..	..	1	..	2	..	..	1	1	..
Taggart, Thomas	..	..	1	..	2	1	1	1	..	2	..
Thomas, Benjamin	..	2	1	..	1	..	..	2	..	1	..
Thomas, Weston	2	..	..	1	..	..	..	..	1	..	..
Thomas, William	3	1	3	1	..	3	1	2	1	..	..
Thompson, Widow M.	3	2	2	..	..	2	..	..	1	..	..
Tucker, James	2	..	1	1	..	3	..	..	1	..	..
Tucker, Joseph	1	2	..	1	1	1	..	1	..	1	..
HALIFAX—con.											
Underwood, Samuel	4	2	..	..	1	..	..	3	1	1	..
Weeks, Benjamin	..	1	..	1	1	..	1	..	..	1	..
Weeks, Benjamin Jr.	2	..	..	1	..	1	..	..	1	..	..
Well, Hubbell Jr.	1	..	..	1	..	2	..	..	1	..	..
Wells, Jonathan	..	1	2	..	1	..	..	1	..	1	..
Wells, Jonathan 2nd	1	..	1	1	1	2	1	1	..	1	..
Wheeler, Denison	1	..	..	1	..	1	..	..	1	..	..
Wheeler, Minor	1	..	..	1	..	1	..	..	1	..	..
Whitcomb, Samuel	2	2	..	1	..	2	..	..	1	..	..
Whipple, Abraham	..	..	..	1	..	4	..	..	1	..	..
Whipple, Joseph	..	..	..	..	1	..	..	..	..	1	..
Whitney, Eleazer	2	2	..	1	..	3	1	..	1	..	..
Wilcox, Benjamin	2	1	1	1	..	2	2	..	1	..	..
Wilcox, Jabez	1	1	..	..	1	1	1	1	1	..	..
Wilcox, Joseph	2	1	..	1	..	2	..	1	1	..	..
Wilcox, Stephen	2	1	2	..	1	2	1	1	2	..	..
Wilcox, Weeks	2	..	..	1	..	1	..	..	1	..	..
Wilcox, William	5	..	..	1	1	2	..	..	1	1	..
Winslow, Kenelm	1	1	..	..	1	..	1	4	..	1	..
Wood, Samuel	3	1	..	1	..	3	1	1	1	..	..
Woodward, Artemas	1	1	..	1	..	2	..	..	1	1	..
Woodward, Israel	..	..	1	..	1	..	..	1	1	1	..
Woodward, Joseph	1	..	1	1	..	1	..	..	1	..	..
Woodward, Samuel	3	2	..	1	..	..	1	..	1	..	..
Woodward, Timothy	4	..	..	..	1	2	2	..	1	..	..
Woodward, Titus	1	1	..	1	..	2	..	1	2	..	..
Worden, Asa	3	..	..	1	..	1	..	..	1	..	..
Worden, Elisha	..	1	1	..	1	1	..	3	..	1	..
Worden, Ichabod	3	1	..	1	..	2	1	..	1	..	..
Worden, Joseph	5	1	1	..	1	..	1	..	1	..	..
Worden, Peter	4	..	..	1	..	1	..	..	1	..	..
Worden, Sylvester	..	..	1	..	1	..	..	2	..	1	..
HINSDALE											
Aldrich, David	..	..	..	..	1	..	..	..	..	1	..
Alton, Amasa	..	..	..	1	..	4	..	..	1	..	..
Alton, Benjamin	..	..	..	..	1	..	..	..	..	1	..
Barrett, Moses	1	2	2	..	1	1	..	2	..	1	..
Bascom, Timothy	3	..	..	..	1	2	..	1	1	..	..
Belding, Samuel	..	..	1	1	..	..	..	1	..	..	..
Bishop, Benjamin	1	..	..	1	..	2	1	..	1	..	..
Bishop, Levi	1	..	..	1	..	..	..	1	..	1	..
Bishop, Samuel	1	..	..	1	..	..	1	..	..	..	..
Bridgeman, Guy	..	..	..	1	..	2	..	..	1	..	..
Bridgeman, Jesse	..	..	1	..	..	..	..	1	..	..	..
Bridgeman, John	2	1	..	1	1	..	1	1	1	1	..
Brooks, Nathaniel	..	..	1	..	1	..	1	..	..	1	..
Brooks, Samuel	1	..	..	1	..	1	..	..	1	..	..
Carver, Jonathan	..	..	..	1	..	1	1	..	1	..	..
Chamberlain, Ebenezer	1	..	1	..	2	2	2	..	..	1	..
Clark, Jabez	..	..	1	..	1	1	..	..	1	..	..
Clark, Widow R.	..	..	1	..	..	1	..	2	..	1	..
Cook, Oliver	2	1	1	..	1	1	..	1	..	1	..
Copeland, David	2	..	..	2	..	4	..	1	1	..	..
Dresser, John	2	..	..	1	..	2	..	..	1	..	..
Elmer, Benjamin	2	..	..	1	..	2	..	..	1	..	..
Elmer, Elisha	3	..	..	1	..	1	..	2	1	..	..
Elmer, Jacob	..	..	..	1	2	..	1	..	..	2	..
Elmer, Reuben	1	1	1	..	1	3	1	..	..	1	..
Fairman, John	4	1	..	..	1	1	1	..	1	..	..
Goss, Daniel	4	1	..	1	..	1	..	..	1	..	..
Goss, Oliver	..	..	..	1	..	3	..	..	1	..	..
Gould, Hosea	2	2	..	1	..	..	1	..	1	..	..
Gould, John	..	1	..	1	..	..	..	..	1	..	..
Gould, Nathaniel	..	..	1	..	1	..	1	..	1	..	..
Gould, Zenas	1	..	..	1	..	1	..	..	1	..	..
Harris, Abner	..	..	..	..	1	..	..	..	..	1	..
Harris, Stephen	2	..	1	..	..	1	..	1	..	..	..
Hawley, David	1	1	2	..	1	1	..	1	..	1	..
Houghton, Nehemiah	3	..	..	2	..	2	1	..	1	..	..
Houghton, Sylvanus	..	..	1	..	1	..	..	2	..	1	..
How, Ebenezer	2	..	..	1	..	..	..	1	..	..	..
How, Squier	..	2	2	..	1	4	1	..	1	..	..
Howe, Caleb	2	..	1	..	..	..	1	1	..	..	..
Howe, Moses	2	..	2	..	1	2	2	..	..	1	..
Hunt, Jonathan	..	3	1	..	2	..	1	3	..	1	..

WINDHAM COUNTY—Continued

NAMES OF HEADS OF FAMILIES	FREE WHITE MALES					FREE WHITE FEMALES					All other free persons except Indians not taxed
	Under 10 years of age	Of 10 and under 16	Of 16 and under 26 including heads of families	Of 26 and under 45 including heads of families	Of 45 and upwards including heads of families.	Under 10 years of age	Of 10 and under 16	Of 16 and under 26 including heads of families	Of 26 and under 45 including heads of families	Of 45 and upwards including heads of families	
HINSDALE—con.											
Johnson, Isaac	4	1	..	1	..	1	1	..	1	..	..
Johnson, John	..	..	..	..	1	..	1	..	..	1	..
Johnson, Stephen	..	..	1	1	..	3	1	..	1	..	..
Lee, Benjamin	..	1	..	..	1	..	1	2	..	1	..
Lee, David	1	..	..	1	..	1	..	..	1	..	..
Lee, Jesse	1	2	1	..	1	1	..	..	..	1	..
Linkfield, Benjamin	1	..	..	..	1	..	..	..	..	1	..
Liscom, Lemuel	1	..	..	1	..	1	..	..	1	..	..
Newell, Joshua	2	..	..	..	1	3	1	..	1	..	..
Parmenter, Reuben	2	..	..	..	1	2	1	..	..	1	..
Parsons, Andrew	2	2	..	1	..	3	..	..	1	..	..
Peeler, Alexander	..	..	..	1	..	..	..	1	..	..	..
Peeler, John	2	1	2	..	1	..	1	..	..	1	..
Peeler, John Jr.	..	..	..	1	..	1	..	..	1	..	..
Pratt, Isaac	3	1	..	1	1	1	2	..	1	1	..
Rawley, Widow	..	..	..	..	..	..	..	..	..	1	..
Ray, Abel	..	..	2	..	1	..	1	..	..	1	..
Robertson, John	1	..	..	1	..	..	1	..	1	..	..
Scott, Ebenezer	..	3	..	..	1	1	..	2	..	1	..
Smith, Barney	1	1	..	1	..	2	1	..	1	..	..
Smith, Simeon	..	..	..	..	1	..	..	..	..	1	..
Stebbins, Eliakim	2	..	1	..	1	1	..	..	..	1	..
Stebbins, Elijah	2	2	..	..	2	1	..	1	..	1	..
Stebbins, Joseph	3	..	..	1	..	1	..	..	1	..	..
Stoddard, Thomas	2	..	1	..	1	..	1	..	..	1	..
Stratton, Samuel	2	..	..	1	1	..	..	3	..	1	..
Streeter, Amos	..	1	..	1	..	3	..	..	1	..	..
Streeter, James	..	..	2	..	1	..	1	2	..	1	..
Streeter, James 2nd.	2	..	..	1	..	..	..	..	1	..	..
Streeter, Joseph	..	1	..	..	1	..	..	1	..	2	..
Streeter, Stephen	..	..	..	1	..	1	..	..	1	..	..
Sweetland, Benjamin	2	2	..	1	..	2	2	..	2	1	..
Thayer, Jerijah	1	1	..	1	..	2	1	..	1	..	..
Thayer, Zephaniah	..	..	..	..	1	..	..	..	..	1	..
Thomas, Israel	..	1	2	..	1	2	1	..	..	1	..
Tute, Widow J.	1	..	1	..	..	..	..	1	..	1	..
Wentworth, Charles	2	1	..	..	1	..	..	..	1	..	..
Wright, Abishai	2	..	..	1	..	..	..	1	..	..	..
Wright, Zadock	..	..	..	1	..	1	..	..	1	..	..
JAMAICA											
Adams, David	1	..	..	1	..	..	..	..	1	..	..
Adams, Seth	..	..	..	..	1	2	1	3	..	1	..
Baldwin, Levi	1	..	1	..	..	2	..	1	..	..	..
Berry, Samuel	1	1	..	..	1	..	..	2	..	1	..
Brown, Alexander, F.	1	..	..	1	..	3	1	..	1	..	..
Brown, James	2	..	..	1	..	2	1	..	..	1	..
Butler, John	..	..	2	1	..	..	..	..	..	1	..
Chaffin, Samuel	2	1	..	1	..	1	1	..	1	..	..
Chase, Elisha	1	..	..	1	..	1	2	1	1	..	..
Chase, Stephen	1	1	..	1	..	1	..	..	1	..	..
Clark, Henry	1	..	..	1	..	3	..	1	..	..	..
Cole, Amasa	2	1	..	1	..	..	1	..	1	..	..
Cole, Jonathan	3	..	1	1	..	2	..	1	1	1	..
Coombs, Simeon	2	1	2	1	..	4	1	..	1	..	..
Cotton, Abishai	3	..	..	1	..	..	..	..	1	..	..
Cowdin, Anger	2	..	..	1	..	..	..	..	1	..	..
Crapo, Francis	..	1	..	..	1	..	..	..	..	1	..
Crapo, Francis Jr.	..	..	1	..	..	1	..	..	1	..	..
Crapo, Jonathan	2	..	..	1	..	2	1	..	1	..	..
Cushing, Solomon	..	..	1	..	1	..	..	1	..	1	..
Daggett, Amos	..	..	1	..	1	..	..	1	..	1	..
Daniels, Joshua	..	..	1	..	1	1	2	1	1	1	..
Daniels, Zatha	2	..	..	1	..	1	..	1	..	..	..
Davidson, Nathaniel	..	..	3	..	1	..	..	..	..	1	..
Furnass, Benjamin	..	1	1	..	1	1	..	..	1	..	..
Gage, Asa	2	3	1	..	1	2	2	1	1	..	..
Gale, Jacob	..	..	1	..	..	..	..	..	..	..	..
Gale, Jonathan	..	..	1	..	1	..	..	..	..	1	..
Garfield, Abijah	..	..	1	..	..	..	..	..	..	..	..
Glezen, Benjamin	2	2	..	1	..	1	1	..	1	..	..
Glezen, Elisha	3	..	..	1	..	1	..	1	..	..	..
Glezen, Josiah	1	..	..	1	..	2	..	..	1	..	..
Goodell, Solomon	..	1	..	..	1	..	..	2	..	..	..
Grover, Solomon	..	1	..	1	..	1	1	..	1	1	..
JAMAICA—con.											
Harris, Oliver	..	..	..	1	..	2	..	..	1	..	..
Haskins, Rufus	2	..	1	..	..	..	..	..	1	..	..
Hayword, Amos	1	..	1	..	..	2	..	1	..	..	..
Hayword, Amos 2nd	1	..	..	1	..	2	..	..	1	..	..
Hayword, Benjamin	..	..	..	1	..	..	..	..	1	..	..
Hayword, Caleb	1	2	2	..	1	2	..	..	..	1	..
Hayword, Calvin	3	..	..	1	..	1	2	..	1	..	..
Hayword, Elisha	2	..	..	1	..	1	..	..	1	..	..
Hayword, George	2	..	..	1	..	1	..	..	1	..	..
Hayword, Ira	1	..	1	..	..	1	1	1	..	..	..
Hayword, Luther	..	..	1	..	..	..	..	1	..	..	..
Hayword, Marvel	1	..	..	1	..	2	..	..	1	..	..
Hayword, Nahor	..	..	..	1	..	1	..	1	..	..	..
Hayword, Nathan	1	1	..	1	..	1	2	3	2	..	..
Hayword, Nathan 2nd.	..	..	1	..	..	..	..	..	..	..	..
Hayword, Paul	1	..	2	..	1	..	..	1	..	1	..
Hayword, Seth	..	1	1	..	1	..	1	..	..	1	..
Hazeltine, Heman	1	..	..	1	..	1	..	..	1	..	..
Higgins, Ebenezer	..	..	1	..	1	..	..	..	..	1	..
Higgins, Ephraim	1	..	..	1	..	1	1	..	1	..	..
Higgins, Ichabod	4	1	..	1	..	3	1	..	1	..	..
Higgins, Zoheth	2	1	1	1	..	1	1	1	1	..	..
Holland, Joseph	1	..	..	1	..	..	..	1	..	..	..
Holt, Elijah	..	1	..	1	..	..	..	1	1	..	..
How, Abijah	..	..	1	..	..	..	..	1	..	..	..
How, John	1	..	2	..	1	1	..	2	1	1	..
Johnson, Abner	3	..	..	1	..	..	..	1	..	..	..
Johnson, Elijah	..	..	1	..	..	..	..	..	..	..	..
Kathan, Charles	1	1	..	1	..	3	..	..	1	..	..
Kellogg, Joseph	3	1	1	1	..	1	1	..	1	..	..
Linsey, Peter	1	2	..	1	..	2	1	..	1	..	..
Littlefield, Elijah	..	..	1	..	..	..	..	..	..	..	..
Livermore, Abijah	2	1	..	1	..	2	1	..	1	..	..
Livermore, Ezra	2	1	..	1	..	3	2	..	2	..	..
Livermore, Lott	..	..	..	1	..	..	..	..	..	..	..
Livermore, Silence	..	..	..	..	..	1	..	..	1	..	..
Magar, James	..	1	..	..	1	..	1	..	..	1	..
Muzzy, Benjamin	2	1	..	1	..	3	2	..	1	..	..
Parmenter, Isaac	1	1	1	1	..	2	1	1	1	..	..
Pierce, Jonas	2	1	2	..	1	2	1	..	..	1	..
Puffer, Amos	1	..	..	1	..	3	1	..	1	..	..
Ray, Abel	..	..	..	1	..	1	1	..	1	..	..
Sessions, Artemas	1	..	..	1	..	..	..	..	1	..	..
Sharpe, Abishai	..	..	1	..	..	..	..	1	..	..	..
Skinner, Zelotes	1	..	..	1	..	1	..	1	..	..	..
Smith, Jonathan	1	..	..	1	..	1	..	..	1	..	..
Snow, Paine	..	1	..	1	..	1	..	..	1	..	..
Stephens, Ebenezer	..	1	1	..	1	..	..	..	..	1	..
Stephens, Ebenezer Jr.	..	..	..	..	..	..	..	..	..	..	..
Stevens, Asa	..	..	1	..	..	..	..	..	..	..	..
Stevens, Martin	1	..	..	1	..	..	..	..	1	..	..
Stocker, Ephraim	1	..	1	1	..	2	1	..	1	..	..
Stockwell, Abraham	2	..	..	1	..	3	..	..	1	..	..
Stoddard, Gideon	..	..	..	..	1	..	..	..	..	1	..
Streeter, William	1	..	..	1	..	2	..	1	..	..	..
Taft, Oliver	1	1	..	..	1	..	1	..	..	1	..
Thayer, Israel	1	2	..	1	1	1	1	..	1	..	..
Underwood, Isaac	..	..	1	..	..	..	..	..	..	..	..
Vial, Nathaniel	7	2	..	1	..	..	1	..	1	..	..
Vial, Samuel	1	..	..	1	..	1	1	..	1	..	..
Watson, Enoch	..	..	..	1	..	..	..	..	..	..	..
Watson, John	1	..	..	1	..	1	1	..	1	..	..
Wellman, Jonathan	3	1	1	..	1	2	1	..	3	4	..
Wheaton, Royall	..	..	1	..	..	..	..	..	..	..	..
Whitney, Samuel	2	..	..	1	..	2	..	..	1	..	..
Wilder, Elias	..	..	..	1	..	1	..	..	1	..	..
Wilder, Samuel	..	..	2	..	1	..	1	1	..	1	..
Wilder, Samuel 2nd.	1	..	1	..	..	..	..	1	..	..	..
Willman, Adam	2	..	..	1	..	1	..	1	1	..	..
Wood, Thomas	1	1	1	1	..	..	2	..	1	..	..
Woodcock, Nathaniel	..	..	1	..	..	1	..	1	..	..	..
Woodcock, Reuben	1	..	..	1	..	2	..	..	1	..	..
Young, David	3	..	..	1	..	..	..	..	1	..	..

WINDHAM COUNTY—Continued

NAMES OF HEADS OF FAMILIES	FREE WHITE MALES: Under 10 years of age	FREE WHITE MALES: Of 10 and under 16	FREE WHITE MALES: Of 16 and under 26 including heads of families	FREE WHITE MALES: Of 26 and under 45 including heads of families	FREE WHITE MALES: Of 45 and upwards including heads of families	FREE WHITE FEMALES: Under 10 years of age	FREE WHITE FEMALES: Of 10 and under 16	FREE WHITE FEMALES: Of 16 and under 26 including heads of families	FREE WHITE FEMALES: Of 26 and under 45 including heads of families	FREE WHITE FEMALES: Of 45 and upwards including heads of families	All other free persons except Indians not taxed
LONDONDERRY											
Aikin, Daniel	1	..	..	1	..	..	..	1	..	..	..
Aikin, William	..	..	..	1	..	..	..	..	..	1	..
Allen, Joseph	..	2	..	..	1	..	..	1	..	1	..
Allen, Joseph Jr.	1	..	..	1	..	1	..	..	1	..	..
Arnold, Gideon	..	..	..	..	1	..	..	..	..	1	..
Arnold, Samuel	1	1	..	1	..	3	..	..	1	..	..
Arnold, William	2	..	1	1	..	2	..	..	1	..	..
Bickford, Samuel	1	..	..	1	..	2	2	..	1	..	..
Buxton, Jonathan	3	..	..	1	..	..	..	..	1	..	..
Chaffee, Jonathan	1	..	1	1	1	1	..	..	1	1	..
Chaffee, Stephen	2	1	..	1	..	1	..	1	1	..	..
Chase, Ebenezer	2	1	..	1	..	4	..	..	1	..	..
Cobb, Ebenezer	..	..	1	..	1	..	..	..	..	1	..
Cobb, Samuel	..	..	1	..	1	..	1	..	..	..	..
Coffin, David	3	1	2	..	1	1	1	1	..	1	..
Cook, Amos	1	1	..	1	..	2	1	..	1	..	..
Cook, Elisha	1	2	..	1	..	4	1	..	1	..	..
Cox, Jonathan	1	1	2	..	1	1	1	..	..	1	..
Cox, Jonathan Jr.	1	..	1	..	..	1	..	1	..	..	..
Cox, William	..	1	2	..	1	1	1	..	..	1	..
Dudley, Joseph	2	..	..	1	..	2	..	..	1	..	..
Elliot, Jonathan	2	..	..	..	1	..	1	..	..	1	..
Emmons, John	1	..	..	1	..	4	1	..	1	..	..
Fortiner, Silas	..	..	..	1	..	1	..	..	1	..	..
Fox, Jonathan	1	1	..	1	..	3	..	..	1	..	..
Gilson, Jason	2	..	..	1	..	..	..	..	1	..	..
Hayward, Samuel	2	..	..	1	..	3	2	..	1	..	..
Hodges, Emerson	2	..	..	1	..	1	..	..	1	..	..
Hopkins, Thomas	..	..	1	..	..	..	..	1	..	..	..
Horton, Peckham	..	1	..	1	..	..	..	..	1	..	..
Horton, Richmond	..	..	2	..	..	..	..	1	..	..	..
How, Benjamin	2	1	..	1	..	1	..	..	1	..	..
How, Nehemiah	1	..	..	..	1	2	3	1	1	..	..
How, Willard	2	1	..	1	..	1	..	..	1	..	..
Hughs, George	2	..	..	1	..	..	..	1	..	1	..
Jacobs, John	..	..	..	1	..	..	..	..	1	..	..
Larkin, Patrick	1	2	1	..	1	1	..	..	..	1	..
Mittemer, John	3	..	..	1	..	1	..	..	2	..	..
Oaks, Jonathan	2	..	..	1	..	2	..	..	1	..	..
Oaks, Thomas	1	..	..	1	..	1	..	..	1	..	..
Ortison, Josiah	2	1	1	..	1	1	..	2	..	1	..
Patterson, Ebenezer	2	1	1	..	1	..	1	1	..	1	..
Patterson, James	2	..	..	1	..	..	..	1	..	..	..
Patterson, Jonathan	..	1	..	..	1	..	..	..	1	..	..
Patterson, Moses	1	..	..	1	..	1	..	..	1	..	..
Reed, Barney	3	..	..	1	..	1	..	..	1	..	..
Stacy, Biram	2	..	..	1	..	..	..	1	..	..	..
Terril, Widow	1	..	1	..	..	..	..	..	..	1	..
Thayer, Rufus	2	1	..	1	..	1	..	..	1	..	..
Thompson, David	..	..	..	1	..	..	..	1	..	..	..
Thompson, Samuel	1	..	1	..	1	1	2	..	..	1	..
Thompson, Samuel Jr.	1	..	1	..	..	1	..	1	..	..	..
Wakefield, Ebenezer	1	2	..	..	1	..	2	..	1	..	..
Wakefield, Jonathan	..	2	..	1	..	..	1	..	..	1	..
Warner, Jonathan	..	..	..	1	..	2	..	1	..	..	..
Warner, Joshua	2	1	..	..	1	1	..	..	..	1	..
Warner, Nathan	..	..	..	1	..	1	..	1	..	..	..
Weatherspoon, Abraham	..	..	1	..	1	..	1	..	..	1	..
Wheeler, Royal P.	..	..	..	1	..	4	..	..	1	..	..
Whitmore, Noah	1	..	2	..	1	2	3	..	1	..	..
MARLBORO											
Adams, Abner	..	..	..	..	1	..	..	..	..	1	..
Adams, Bildad	2	1	1	1	..	3	..	1	1	..	..
Adams, Freegrace	4	..	..	1	1	4	1	..	4	1	..
Adams, Joel	1	1	1	..	1	..	1	1	..	1	..
Adams, Oliver	1	1	..	1	..	2	1	..	1	..	..
Adams, Simeon	1	..	..	1	1	1	1	..	1	1	..
Adams, Thomas	2	2	..	1	..	1	1	..	1	..	..
Allen, Salmon	3	3	..	1	..	1	1	2	1	..	..
Ames, Luther	2	..	1	1	..	1	..	..	2	..	..
Ayers, Joseph	1	3	2	..	1	2	..	2	..	1	..
MARLBORO—con.											
Ball, Samuel	1	2	2	1	1	1	1	..	1	1	..
Barrett, Levi	..	..	1	1	..	..	1	..	1	..	..
Bartlett, David	1	..	1	..	..	..	..	1	..	..	..
Bartlett, John	1	..	1	1	1	1	..	1	..	1	..
Bartlett, John 2nd.	1	2	..	1	..	1	3	..	1	..	..
Bartlett, Joseph	2	1	..	..	1	2	1	1	..	1	..
Bartlett, Zerajah	1	2	..	..	1	..	2	2	..	1	..
Bellows, Charles	2	3	2	..	1	..	..	..	1	..	..
Bemas, Samuel	1	..	..	1	..	2	..	..	2	1	..
Bishop, Sylvester	2	..	1	1	1	..	1	1	1	..	..
Briant, Jacob	..	1	2	1	1	..	..	2	..	..	..
Briant, Joseph	2	1	..	1	..	1	1	1	1	..	..
Britton, Josiah	1	..	..	1	..	..	..	..	1	..	..
Britton, Nathan	..	..	..	1	..	3	..	1	..	..	..
Brooks, Lemuel	..	1	1	..	1	..	1	1	..	1	..
Brown, Lyman	3	..	..	1	1	2	..	..	1	1	..
Chandler, Hiel	1	..	..	1	..	..	..	..	1	..	..
Chandler, Jonathan	3	1	1	..	1	2	2	..	1	..	..
Charter, James	1	3	..	..	1	2	1	1	..	..	..
Childs, Josiah D.	2	..	1	1	..	1	..	..	1	..	..
Church, Joseph	1	1	..	..	1	..	1	1	..	1	..
Church, Moses	..	1	1	..	1	..	..	1	..	1	..
Clark, John	..	1	..	..	1	1	..	..	..	1	..
Clark, Nathan	..	..	..	1	..	5	1	..	1	..	..
Cobleigh, Lemuel	..	2	..	1	..	2	..	..	1	..	..
Coughlan, Richard	..	1	2	..	1	3	2	..	..	1	..
Cresey, Moses	2	..	..	1	..	1	1	..	1	..	..
Cutler, James	1	..	2	..	1	2	..	2	..	1	..
Cutler, Josiah	2	3	..	1	..	3	1	..	1	..	..
Day, Arabert	1	..	1	..	..	1	..	..	1	..	..
Day, Sarah	..	1	..	..	..	1	1	..	..	1	..
Dean, Archelus	1	..	..	1	..	1	..	..	1	..	..
Erwin, John	..	..	2	..	1	..	1	2	..	1	..
Fisher, Nehemiah	3	..	..	1	..	4	2	..	1	..	..
Gilbert, Samuel	2	..	..	1	..	3	1	..	1	..	..
Gilbert, Solomon	2	..	..	1	..	..	..	..	1	..	..
Gilbert, William	1	1	1	..	1	1	..	1	..	1	..
Gilbert, William Jr.	..	..	..	1	..	..	..	1	..	..	..
Gore, Samuel	1	..	1	1	..	..	1	..	1	1	..
Harris, Abner	3	..	..	1	..	1	..	1	..	..	..
Hibbard, Dan	1	2	1	..	1	1	..	1	1	1	..
Higley, Daniel	..	2	1	..	1	..	..	2	..	2	..
Higley, Elijah	..	1	2	..	1	1	..	1	..	2	..
Higley, Jordan	1	..	..	1	..	3	..	1	..	..	..
Higley, Orange	..	..	..	1	..	..	..	..	1	..	..
Holladay, Daniel	..	..	1	..	1	..	..	1	..	1	..
Holladay, Daniel Jr.	3	2	..	1	..	1	1	..	1	..	..
Holladay, Eli	2	2	..	1	..	..	1	..	1	..	..
Holladay, Nathan	..	..	..	1	..	1	..	1	..	..	..
Houghton, Nahum	..	3	..	1	..	4	..	1	1	..	..
Howard, Jonathan	1	1	1	..	1	..	1	2	..	1	..
Howe, Rufus	3	..	..	1	..	..	..	..	1	..	..
Ingraham, Jonathan	1	1	3	..	2	2	1	..	..	2	..
Jacobs, Nathan	2	1	1	1	..	2	1	..	1	..	..
Jacobs, Stephen	2	1	..	1	..	1	1	..	1	..	..
Jenks, Boomer	3	2	2	..	1	2	2	..	1	..	..
Jones, Aaron	2	..	..	1	..	..	..	..	1	..	..
Jones, Simeon	..	..	..	1	..	2	..	..	1	..	..
Kelsey, Seymour	..	1	..	..	1	4	1	..	1	..	..
King, Ichabod	..	1	2	..	1	4	..	1	1	..	..
Knight, Benjamin	..	1	2	..	1	..	..	2	..	1	..
Knight, Daniel	..	2	..	..	1	..	1	..	..	1	..
Knight, Joseph	1	..	..	1	..	1	..	..	1	..	..
Lamb, Joel	1	..	..	1	..	4	2	..	1	..	..
Lawrance, Edmund	3	..	..	1	..	..	..	1	..	..	..
Livermore, Jonas	2	..	1	..	1	2	..	1	..	1	..
Lyman, Gershom C.	1	1	1	..	1	..	1	2	..	1	..
Lynde, Frederick	..	..	1	..	..	2	..	1	..	..	..
Mather, Erastus	1	2	..	1	..	2	..	2	1	..	..
Mather, Phinehas	3	2	3	..	1	2	..	1	..	1	..
Mather, Timothy Jr.	4	1	2	1	1	1	1	1	1	1	..
May, Amos	2	..	1	..	..	..	..	1	..	..	..
McLane, ———	1	1	..	..	1	1	1	1	..	1	..
Miles, Joseph	1	..	1	1	..	1	..	..	1	..	..
Miller, Abraham	..	..	1	1	..	1	1	1	1	..	..
Miller, David	..	..	1	..	1	1	..	1	..	1	..

WINDHAM COUNTY—Continued

NAMES OF HEADS OF FAMILIES	FREE WHITE MALES: Under 10 years of age	FREE WHITE MALES: Of 10 and under 16	FREE WHITE MALES: Of 16 and under 26 including heads of families	FREE WHITE MALES: Of 26 and under 45 including heads of families	FREE WHITE MALES: Of 45 and upwards including heads of families	FREE WHITE FEMALES: Under 10 years of age	FREE WHITE FEMALES: Of 10 and under 16	FREE WHITE FEMALES: Of 16 and under 26 including heads of families	FREE WHITE FEMALES: Of 26 and under 45 including heads of families	FREE WHITE FEMALES: Of 45 and upwards including heads of families	All other free persons except Indians not taxed
MARLBORO—con.											
Miller, David Jr.	..	..	2	1	..	3	2	1	1	..	..
Miller, Seth	2	..	1	1	..	2	..	1	1	..	..
Miller, Thaddeus	3	1	..	1	..	2	3	..	2	..	..
Moore, Samuel	..	1	2	..	1	1	..	2	..	1	..
Needham, Nehemiah	..	..	1	..	1	..	..	..	..	1	..
Needham, Nehemiah Jr.	1	..	..	1	..	2	..	..	1	..	..
Newton, Cotton	2	..	..	1	..	..	1	..	1	..	..
Norcross, Samuel	..	1	..	..	1	1	1	1	..	1	..
Olds, Benjamin	..	..	1	..	1	..	..	..	..	1	..
Olds, Benjamin Jr.	2	1	1	1	..	2	..	1	1	..	..
Olds, Joseph	4	..	..	1	..	..	..	2	..	..	..
Olds, Thaddeus	2	1	1	1	..	..	1	1	..	..	..
Otis, Araunah	1	..	..	1	..	4	2	..	1	..	..
Otis, Stephen	..	..	..	..	1	..	..	..	..	1	..
Otis, Stephen Jr.	..	..	1	1	..	2	..	..	1	..	..
Packard, Josiah	2	1	..	1	..	2	2	..	1	..	..
Parks, Josiah	..	..	1	..	..	..	..	1	..	1	..
Parmenter, Joel	2	..	..	1	..	1	..	..	1	..	..
Peck, Elijah	1	..	2	..	1	..	..	1	..	1	..
Percival, Stephen	..	..	..	1	..	..	..	..	1	..	..
Phelps, Timothy	1	1	2	..	1	..	1	1	..	1	..
Phillips, Enos	..	1	..	1	..	..	1	1	..	..	..
Phillips, John	4	..	..	1	..	1	..	1	..	..	..
Phillips, Oliver	1	1	3	..	1	..	..	1	..	1	..
Phillips, Perez	2	..	..	1	..	2	..	..	1	..	..
Powers, Josiah	2	..	..	1	..	..	..	..	1	..	..
Pratt, Alpheus	..	..	..	..	1	..	..	..	..	1	..
Pratt, Alvin	3	1	..	..	1	..	1	..	1	..	..
Pratt, Amos	2	..	1	..	1	2	1	..	1	..	..
Pratt, Emerson	2	..	..	1	..	3	..	..	1	..	..
Pratt, Isaac	..	1	..	1	1	..	..	1	1	..	..
Pratt, Orland	2	1	1	1	..	..	..	2	..	..	..
Pratt, Samuel	..	..	1	..	1	..	..	..	1	..	..
Pratt, Stephen	..	..	1	..	1	..	..	..	1	..	..
Prouty, Amos	2	1	..	1	..	..	1	..	1	..	..
Prouty, Reuben	2	..	..	1	..	1	..	..	1	..	..
Rice, Adonijah	2	..	..	1	..	..	..	..	1	..	..
Rockwell, ———	..	..	..	1	..	2	1	..	1	..	..
Sawtell, Levi	..	1	..	1	..	4	..	..	1	..	..
Shepardson, Seth	4	..	..	1	..	..	1	..	1	..	..
Shumway, Lewis	1	..	1	..	..	1	..	1	..	..	..
Slade, Aaron Jr.	2	..	..	1	..	..	..	..	1	..	..
Smith, Isaiah	..	..	2	..	1	..	1	..	..	1	..
Smith, John	..	1	1	1	..	3	1	..	1	..	..
Smith, Jonah	..	1	1	..	1	..	2	..	1	..	..
Smith, Jonathan	1	..	..	1	..	..	..	..	1	..	..
Smith, Joshua	2	..	..	1	..	2	1	..	1	..	..
Smith, Zoath	..	2	..	..	1	..	..	..	..	1	..
Snow, Daniel	2	1	..	1	..	1	1	..	..	..	..
Sprague, Nehemiah	..	..	..	..	1	3	2	3	..	1	..
Stockwell, Arad	..	1	..	1	..	..	..	1	..	..	..
Stratton, Nehemiah	5	..	..	1	..	..	1	..	1	..	..
Strong, John S.	1	..	1	1	..	1	..	1	..	..	..
Tamblin, Timothy	3	1	..	1	..	2	3	1	1	..	..
Thayer, Eseck	2	1	..	1	..	1	1	..	1	..	..
Tucker, Daniel	..	..	..	1	..	3	..	1	..	..	..
Underwood, Jonathan	2	2	1	..	1	1	2	1	..	1	..
Underwood, Thaddeus	2	1	..	1	..	2	1	..	1	1	..
Verry, Francis	3	..	..	1	..	..	..	..	1	..	..
Wallace, Ebenezer	1	1	..	1	..	2	..	..	1	..	..
Warden, Elijah	1	..	..	1	..	1	..	..	1	..	..
Warren, Dan	1	1	1	1	..	1	..	..	1	..	..
Warren, Jonathan	2	..	1	..	1	..	1	2	1	1	..
Warren, Phinehas	..	..	..	1	..	..	..	..	1	..	..
Watkins, Seth	..	..	..	1	..	1	..	1	..	..	..
Weeks, David	1	..	..	1	..	..	..	1	..	..	..
Whitney, Guilford	1	..	..	1	..	3	..	..	1	..	..
Whitney, Jonas	3	..	2	1	1	..	2	3	..	3	..
Whitney, Luther	1	..	1	..	..	..	..	..	1	..	..
Whitney, Moses	5	..	..	1	..	..	..	..	1	..	..
Whitney, Nathaniel	1	..	2	..	1	1	3	1	..	1	..
Whitney, Samuel	..	..	1	..	1	..	1	1	..	1	..
Whitney, Samuel Jr.	2	1	..	1	..	2	..	..	1	..	..
Winchester, Asa	1	1	..	1	..	2	..	..	1	..	..
Winchester, Joseph	..	2	..	1	..	2	..	..	1	..	..
Winchester, Luther	1	1	..	1	1	1	..	1	1	..	..
Worden, James	..	..	..	1	..	1	..	..	1	..	..
NEWFANE											
Aldrich, Moses	2	1	..	1	..	2	..	1	2	..	..
Aldrich, William	1	..	..	1	..	1	..	1	1	..	..
Allen, Amos	1	1	1	1	..	2	..	..	1	..	..
Allen, Ebenezer	..	1	..	1	..	1	..	1	1	..	..
Baker, Thomas	2	..	..	1	..	..	..	1	..	..	..
Balcom, Henry	..	..	..	..	1	..	..	..	..	..	..
Balcom, Isaac	1	1	..	..	1	..	1	1	..	1	..
Bartlett, William	2	..	1	1	..	1	..	1	1	..	..
Betterley, Thomas	2	1	..	..	1	2	2	..	..	1	..
Betterley, Thomas Jr.	..	..	..	1	..	1	..	..	1	..	..
Blake, James	2	2	..	1	..	2	1	..	1	..	..
Bond, Aaron	3	..	..	..	1	1	2	..	1	..	..
Boyden, Hezekiah	..	1	..	..	1	..	..	3	..	1	..
Boyden, Hezekiah Jr.	2	..	..	1	..	1	..	..	1	..	..
Boyden, William	1	..	..	1	..	1	..	1	..	..	..
Bradley, John	4	2	..	1	..	1	..	..	1	..	..
Brooks, Ephraim	1	..	..	1	..	2	..	..	1	..	..
Brown, Alexander	2	..	..	1	..	1	..	..	1	..	..
Bruce, Artimas	..	..	..	..	1	..	1	..	..	2	..
Bruce, Asa	1	..	..	..	1	2	2	1	1	..	..
Bruce, Elijah	1	1	3	1	..	3	2	..	1	..	..
Bruce, Ephraim	2	1	..	1	..	1	1	..	1	..	..
Bullard, Abel	3	2	..	1	..	..	..	1	1	..	..
Butler, Simeon	2	1	..	1	..	2	..	..	1	..	..
Chamberlin, Nathaniel	..	1	2	..	..	1	..	2	..	..	..
Coates, Benjamin	1	..	1	..	1	..	..	1	..	1	..
Cook, Jonas	1	1	..	..	1	2	1	2	..	1	..
Cook, Robert	..	1	1	..	1	..	..	3	..	1	..
Crosby, Reuben	2	..	2	..	..	..	..	1	..	..	..
Cushing, Warren	1	..	..	1	..	2	..	..	1	..	..
Darren, Ethan	..	2	2	..	1	..	1	1	..	1	..
Davis, Joshua	3	..	..	..	1	2	1	1	1	..	..
Dewey, Silvester	2	..	..	1	..	3	1	..	1	..	..
Dyar, Joseph	..	..	..	..	1	..	..	..	..	1	..
Eager, Ward	..	3	..	..	1	1	..	3	1	..	..
Eastman, James	1	1	..	..	1	3	2	..	1	..	..
Ellis, Joseph	1	..	1	2	..	..	1	1	..	..	..
Elmer, Elijah	1	1	2	..	1	2	2	1	..	1	..
Fisher, Daniel	1	1	..	..	1	..	..	..	1	..	..
Fisher, Daniel Jr.	1	..	1	..	..	1	..	2	..	..	..
Fisher, Simon	1	..	2	..	..	..	..	2	..	..	..
Fisk, Nathan	..	..	..	..	2	..	..	..	..	2	..
Flint, Benjamin	2	..	1	..	1	..	1	1	..	1	..
Forbes, Theodore	..	1	..	1	3	2	..	1	..	1	..
Fuller, Ephraim	..	3	..	1	..	3	..	..	1	..	..
Gamble, James	3	1	..	1	..	..	..	..	1	..	..
Gates, Silas	1	..	2	1	..	2	2	1	1	..	..
Glezen, Adonijah	1	..	1	..	..	..	..	1	..	..	..
Glezen, Phinehas	1	..	1	..	..	..	..	1	..	..	..
Goodenow, Isaac	..	..	..	..	1	..	..	..	..	1	..
Goodenow, Isaac Jr.	..	..	..	..	1	..	..	1	..	1	..
Goodenow, John	..	..	..	1	..	..	..	..	..	..	..
Goodenow, Oliver	2	..	1	..	..	..	..	1	..	..	..
Green, Thomas	..	..	..	..	1	..	..	..	..	1	..
Grimes, Andrew	2	2	1	..	1	..	..	..	..	1	..
Guillo, Abel	2	..	..	1	..	1	..	..	1	1	..
Hall, Aaron	1	..	1	1	..	1	..	..	1	..	..
Hall, Ephraim	1	1	..	1	..	3	..	..	1	..	..
Hall, Jonathan	..	1	2	1	..	3	1	..	1	..	..
Hall, Joseph	..	..	..	..	1	..	..	2	..	1	..
Hall, Silas	2	..	1	..	..	..	..	1	..	..	..
Harris, John	2	..	..	1	..	1	..	..	1	..	..
Higgins, Nathaniel	3	..	1	1	..	1	..	..	1	..	..
Higgins, Thomas	..	..	..	..	1	..	..	..	..	1	..
Hildreth, Timothy	..	..	..	1	..	..	..	..	..	..	..
Hodgkins, Aaron	..	..	1	..	1	..	1	2	..	1	..
Holbrook, Asa	1	..	..	1	..	1	..	..	1	..	..
Holden, Josiah	..	2	1	..	1	..	2	1	1	..	..
Holland, Ephraim	1	1	1	..	1	..	..	1	..	1	..
Holland, Jonah	3	2	1	1	..	1	1	..	1	..	..
Holland, Joseph	1	1	1	..	1	1	2	..	..	1	..
Holland, Paul	2	..	1	1	..	2	..	..	1	1	..
Holland, Samuel	1	..	1	..	..	2	..	1	..	..	..
Houghton, Solomon	2	2	..	1	..	1	1	1	1	..	..
How, Peter	1	1	1	1	..	3	..	1	1	..	..
How, Salmon	..	..	..	1	..	1	2	..	1	..	..
Hoyt, Jason	3	..	..	1	..	..	..	1	..	..	..
Jackson, Jonathan	3	..	..	1	..	1	1	..	1	..	..
Jackson, Nathaniel	..	..	..	1	..	2	..	..	1	..	..

WINDHAM COUNTY—Continued

NAMES OF HEADS OF FAMILIES	FREE WHITE MALES: Under 10 years of age	FREE WHITE MALES: Of 10 and under 16	FREE WHITE MALES: Of 16 and under 26 including heads of families	FREE WHITE MALES: Of 26 and under 45 including heads of families	FREE WHITE MALES: Of 45 and upwards including heads of families	FREE WHITE FEMALES: Under 10 years of age	FREE WHITE FEMALES: Of 10 and under 16	FREE WHITE FEMALES: Of 16 and under 26 including heads of families	FREE WHITE FEMALES: Of 26 and under 45 including heads of families	FREE WHITE FEMALES: Of 45 and upwards including heads of families	All other free persons except Indians not taxed
NEWFANE—con.											
Keyes, Ashley	2	..	..	1	..	1	1	..	1	..	..
Kimball, Asahel	2	1	2	1	..	3	..	1	1	..	..
King, Ezra	3	2	..	1	..	2	..	..	1	..	..
Kinny, John	..	..	3	6	..	..	..	1	1	..	..
Kinny, Moses	1	3	1	..	1	1	1	2	..	1	..
Knowlton, Ezekiel	..	..	..	1	..	..	..	..	..	..	..
Knowlton, Luke	1	1	2	..	2	1	1	2	1	..	..
Knowlton, Luke Jr.	..	..	2	..	..	1	..	2	..	..	..
Knowlton, Nathan	2	2	1	1	..	3	..	1	1	..	..
Knowlton, Widow Sophia	2	..	2	..	..	..	2	..	1	..	..
Lamb, James	..	..	2	..	1	..	..	1	1	..	..
Lamb, Phinehas	2	1	..	..	1	3	2	1	1	..	..
Laughton, Jacob	5	..	..	1	..	1	1	..	1	..	..
Laughton, James	1	..	..	1	..	1	..	1	..	..	..
Laughton, John	..	1	..	..	1	..	..	1	..	1	..
Marsh, Eber	1	..	1	..	..	..	..	1	..	..	..
Marsh, Jesse	..	..	..	1	..	2	..	..	1	..	..
Marsh, Samuel	1	1	1	1	..	1	1	1	1	..	..
Marsh, Zebediah	..	1	1	..	1	..	..	..	..	1	..
McMaster, Jonathan	..	1	..	..	1	2	2	1	..	1	..
Merrifield, Aaron	1	1	2	..	1	..	1	2	..	1	..
Merrifield, Jedidiah	1	..	..	1	..	2	1	..	1	..	..
Morse, Amharst	..	..	..	1	..	..	..	1	1	..	1
Morse, Amharst 2nd	..	..	1	..	..	..	..	1	..	..	..
Morse, Ebenezer	..	1	..	..	2	3	2	..	2	1	..
Morse, Ebenezer 2nd	..	..	1	..	..	..	..	..	..	..	..
Morse, Jacob	..	2	..	..	1	..	1	2	1	1	..
Morse, John	..	2	1	..	1	..	..	1	..	2	..
Morse, John Jr.	1	..	..	1	..	..	..	1	..	..	..
Morse, Joshua	1	..	2	..	1	1	2	..	1	1	..
Morse, Joshua 2nd	1	..	1	1	..	1	..	1	..	..	..
Nelson, Nehemiah	..	1	1	..	1	3	2	..	1	..	..
Newton, Calvin	2	1	..	1	..	2	1	..	1	..	..
Newton, Marshall	1	1	1	1	..	1	1	..	2	..	..
Newton, Samuel	1	2	1	1	..	1	1	..	1	..	..
Ober, Ebenezer	..	..	..	..	1	..	1	1	..	1	..
Osgood, Christopher	2	..	..	1	..	1	..	..	1	..	..
Park, Jonathan	1	..	2	..	1	2	..	2	1	1	..
Perham, Leonard	3	..	..	1	..	1	..	1	1	..	..
Perry, Amos	..	1	..	1	..	3	..	1	..	..	..
Perry, Daniel	..	..	1	..	1	..	1	..	..	1	..
Perry, Isaac	1	..	..	1	..	2	..	..	1	..	..
Perry, Joseph	3	..	..	1	..	1	1	..	1	..	..
Phillips, Lurana	..	..	..	..	..	..	1	..	1	..	..
Phillips, Paine	1	..	..	1	..	2	..	..	..	1	..
Pomeroy, Chester	..	1	1	1	1	2	1	..	1	..	..
Pomeroy, Phinehas A.	1	..	..	1	..	..	..	1	..	..	..
Rand, Richard	..	1	1	..	1	1	1	1	..	1	..
Richardson, James	..	..	1	..	..	..	..	1	..	..	..
Robinson, Jonathan	1	1	2	..	1	3	..	1	1	..	..
Rockwood, Samuel	4	..	..	1	..	2	..	..	1	2	..
Rutter, Phillip	1	1	1	..	1	..	..	2	..	1	..
Savage, Joseph	1	..	..	1	..	1	..	1	..	..	..
Sherwin, Francis	2	..	..	1	..	1	..	..	2	..	..
Sherwin, Silvanus	2	1	..	1	..	..	1	..	1	..	..
Sikes, Simeon	1	1	..	1	..	1	1	1	..	..	..
Smith, Phinehas	..	..	..	..	1	2	1	..	1	..	..
Smith, Phinehas Jr.	..	..	..	1	..	2	..	1	..	..	..
Stearns, Abigail Widow	..	..	..	..	..	..	..	2	..	1	..
Stedman, Nathaniel	..	..	1	..	1	1	2	4	..	1	..
Stevens, Israel	2	..	..	1	..	1	..	..	1	..	..
Stevens, Jacob	2	..	..	1	1	..	..	..	..	1	..
Stevens, Jacob Jr.	2	..	..	1	..	1	..	..	1	..	..
Stevens, Lemuel	..	..	..	..	1	..	..	..	..	..	..
Stone, Nathan	2	1	..	1	..	2	..	1	1	..	..
Stowers, John	1	..	..	..	1	1	1	1	..	1	..
Stratton, Daniel	..	..	1	..	..	..	..	1	..	..	..
Taylor, Daniel	3	1	1	1	..	..	1	..	2	..	..
Taylor, Hezekiah Rev.	..	1	2	..	1	..	1	1	1	1	..
Touchett, Philip	..	..	..	1	..	..	..	..	1	..	..
Ward, Nahum	1	..	..	1	..	1	..	..	1	..	..
Warren, Zenas	1	1	..	..	1	3	1	1	..	1	..
Wheeler, Darius	2	1	..	2	..	2	..	2	2	..	..
Wheeler, Thomas	2	1	1	1	..	..	1	1	1	1	..
Whitcomb, Jonathan	2	1	1	1	..	2	1	..	1	..	..
Whiting, Adam	1	..	..	..	1	2	1	1	..	1	..
Wilder, Ephraim	3	..	..	1	..	..	..	..	1	..	..
Wilder, Tilly	1	1	..	..	1	1	1	3	..	1	..
William, H. William	..	..	1	1	..	..	..	..	..	..	..
Wiswall, Ebenezer	1	..	..	1	..	2	..	..	1	..	..
Woods, Cyrus	1	..	..	1	..	..	..	1	..	..	..
Woods, Jonas	1	..	..	1	..	2	..	..	1	..	..
Woods, Solomon	..	1	1	..	1	..	1	2	..	1	..
PUTNEY											
Adams, Samuel	3	1	1	..	1	3	1	..	..	1	..
Alexander, Philip	..	..	2	1	..	4	2	1	1	..	..
Allen, Lewis	2	1	..	1	..	2	2	..	1	..	..
Aplin, Thomas	1	1	1	..	1	..	..	1	..	1	..
Attwood, Prince	..	..	..	..	..	..	..	..	..	..	9
Bachelor, John M.	..	..	2	..	..	..	..	2	..	..	..
Bacon, Abner	3	..	..	1	..	..	..	1	1	..	..
Bacon, William	..	..	..	1	..	3	..	1	..	..	..
Bangs, Nathaniel	2	..	..	1	..	..	..	..	1	..	..
Beckwith, Daniel	1	1	..	..	1	2	1	..	..	1	..
Bennett, John	1	1	..	1	..	4	..	..	1	..	..
Bennett, Joseph	1	..	..	..	1	..	1	1	..	1	..
Bennett, Samuel	..	..	..	..	1	..	..	..	..	1	..
Bennett, Samuel Jr.	2	1	..	1	..	3	1	1	1	..	..
Biglow, Levi	..	..	2	1	..	..	..	..	1	..	..
Bishop, Oliver	1	..	1	..	1	..	2	1	..	1	..
Black, James	1	1	..	1	..	2	..	..	1	..	..
Blood, Oliver	..	..	..	1	..	1	..	1	..	..	..
Blood, Robert	1	1	1	..	1	..	1	1	..	1	..
Bowen, John	1	..	2	1	1	..	1	..	1	..	..
Briggs, Abial	..	1	1	..	1	..	..	1	..	1	..
Briggs, Hezekiah	..	..	1	..	1	..	..	1	..	1	..
Brown, Daniel	..	1	2	..	1	1	1	..	..	1	..
Brown, John	1	..	..	1	..	1	1	..	1	..	..
Bruce, Joseph	1	1	1	1	..	1	2	..	1	..	..
Bugbee, Alpheus	1	1	..	1	..	1	..	1	1	..	..
Burdet, Jacob	2	..	..	1	..	1	..	..	1	..	..
Burr, Ephraim	1	..	..	1	1	3	..	..	1	..	..
Butler, Luther	1	..	..	1	..	1	..	..	1	..	..
Campbell, Alexander	1	..	..	1	..	2	..	..	1	..	..
Campbell, James	..	1	1	..	1	1	..	..	1	..	..
Campbell, John	1	2	..	..	1	2	2	1	..	1	..
Campbell, Thomas	2	..	..	..	1	..	..	1	..	1	..
Carey, Seth	1	3	1	..	1	1	..	..	..	1	..
Carr, Moses	1	2	..	..	1	1	1	..	..	1	..
Chandler, Daniel	1	..	..	..	1	2	1	1	..	1	..
Chandler, John	3	1	1	..	1	1	1	..	..	1	..
Cheney, Asahel	2	2	1	1	..	1	..	..	1	..	..
Cheney, Russell	..	..	2	..	..	..	..	1	..	..	..
Church, Thomas	1	..	1	..	..	1	..	..	1	..	..
Churchell, Benjamin	1	..	..	1	..	..	..	1	..	..	..
Clay, Ephraim	1	1	1	..	1	2	2	2	..	1	..
Clay, James	1	1	1	..	1	2	3	2	1	..	..
Cobb, Richard	1	..	3	..	1	2	..	1	..	1	..
Coflin, William	2	..	..	1	..	2	..	..	1	..	..
Coombs, Medad	..	..	1	1	..	3	1	..	1	..	..
Crawford, James	..	..	..	..	1	1	..	..	..	1	..
Crawford, Theophilas	1	1	2	1	..	2	..	2	1	..	..
Cudworth, Charles	..	1	1	..	1	1	1	..	..	1	..
Cudworth, Charles Jr.	3	1	..	1	..	..	1	..	1	..	2
Cudworth, Samuel	1	..	..	1	..	1	..	..	1	..	..
Cushing, Joseph	3	3	..	1	1	..	..	1	1	1	..
Cushing, Widow	1	1	2	..	..	1	1	1	..	1	..
Cutler, Pearley	2	..	..	1	..	3	2	1	1	..	..
Davis, Daniel	1	1	..	1	..	..	1	..	1	..	..
Denio, Harrison G.	..	..	..	1	..	1	..	1	..	..	..
Dickenson, Abraham	1	..	1	1	..	1	1	2	1	..	..
Dickenson, Job	..	..	..	1	..	..	..	1	..	..	..
Down, John	..	2	1	..	1	4	..	1	..	1	..
Fairbank, Samuel	1	..	1	..	..	..	..	1	..	..	..
Fairbank, Silas	..	..	1	..	1	..	..	1	..	1	..
Fisher, Abiel	2	1	1	..	1	..	..	1	1	..	..
Fitch, James	..	..	3	5	1	..	..	1	..	1	..
Foster, David	1	1	..	1	..	3	3	..	1	..	..
Fuller, Abiah	1	1	2	..	1	..	1	..	..	1	..
Fuller, Samuel	..	1	..	..	1	..	2	1	..	1	..
Fullerton, Edward	2	..	..	1	..	1	..	..	1	..	..
Gates, David	..	1	1	..	1	..	1	1	..	1	..
Gates, Oldham	2	1	..	1	..	3	2	..	1	..	..
Gilbert, Moses	4	..	1	..	1	1	1	..	..	1	..
Gillson, Oliver	1	..	1	..	..	..	..	1	..	..	..
Glezen, Ebenezer	1	1	..	..	1	1	3	..	2	..	1

WINDHAM COUNTY—Continued

NAMES OF HEADS OF FAMILIES	FREE WHITE MALES: Under 10 years of age	FREE WHITE MALES: Of 10 and under 16	FREE WHITE MALES: Of 16 and under 26 including heads of families	FREE WHITE MALES: Of 26 and under 45 including heads of families	FREE WHITE MALES: Of 45 and upwards including heads of families.	FREE WHITE FEMALES: Under 10 years of age	FREE WHITE FEMALES: Of 10 and under 16	FREE WHITE FEMALES: Of 16 and under 26 including heads of families	FREE WHITE FEMALES: Of 26 and under 45 including heads of families	FREE WHITE FEMALES: Of 45 and upwards including heads of families	All other free persons except Indians not taxed
PUTNEY—con.											
Glezen, Moses	..	..	1	..	1	..	..	1	..	1	..
Glezen, Reuben	2	..	..	1	..	..	..	..	1	..	..
Goodhue, Joseph	..	2	..	1	..	3	2	1	1	..	..
Goodhue, Josiah	3	1	..	1	..	1	2	1	1	..	..
Goodwin, John	1	..	1	1	..	..	1	1	1	..	..
Goodwin, Mathew	..	..	..	1	..	1	..	1	..	..	..
Graham, William	4	..	..	1	..	..	..	..	1	..	..
Griffin, John	1	2	..	..	1	1	..	3	..	1	..
Hale, James	..	..	2	..	1	..	..	1	..	1	..
Hall, Ephraim	..	..	1	..	1	..	1	..	1	1	..
Harding, Caleb	..	..	..	1	..	3	..	..	1	..	..
Harding, Daniel	1	1	..	1	..	2	..	1	..	..	..
Hill, ———	3	..	..	1	..	1	..	..	1	..	..
Houghton, Aaron	3	1	..	1	1	2	..	1	1	2	..
Houghton, Elijah	1	..	..	1	..	3	1	..	1	..	..
Hubbard, Abel	..	2	..	1	..	4	1	1	1	..	..
Hubbard, Silas	1	1	..	1	..	3	..	1	1	..	..
Hubbard, Theodore	2	..	..	1	..	..	..	..	1	..	..
Hudson, John	..	1	1	1	1	1	..	..	1	1	..
Hunt, Joel	1	..	1	2	..	2	1	..	1	..	..
Huntley, Joseph	1	1	..	1	..	..	..	1	1	..	..
Huntley, Moses	2	..	..	1	..	2	2	..	1	..	..
Hutchins, Widow	..	..	1	..	..	..	..	1	..	1	..
Hyde, Joshua	1	1	1	..	1	2	2	..	1	1	..
Jay, Amos	..	2	..	1	..	3	..	..	1	..	..
Jay, David	2	2	..	1	1	1	1	1	1	..	..
Jay, Joseph	1	..	1	..	1	1	1	1	1	..	..
Jay, Moses	..	1	4	..	1	1	..	1	..	1	..
Jay, Obadiah	2	1	1	1	..	1	..	..	1	..	..
Jewett, Daniel	..	1	3	..	1	1	1	2	..	1	..
Jewett, William	2	..	..	1	..	1	..	..	1	..	..
Johnson, Elisha	..	1	..	..	1	..	1	1	..	1	..
Johnson, Harmon	2	..	1	..	1	2	3	1	..	1	..
Johnson, Jonah	3	2	1	1	..	1	1	..	1	..	..
Kasson, Joseph	..	1	2	..	1	2	2	1	..	1	..
Keyes, Asa	2	..	..	1	..	2	..	..	1	..	..
Keys, Daniel	..	..	..	..	1	..	..	..	..	1	..
Keys, Israel	1	3	1	..	1	..	2	..	1	..	..
Keys, Jonas	1	..	1	1	..	1	2	..	1	..	..
Keys, William	3	..	..	1	..	1	..	..	1	..	..
Lacklin, Jonathan	2	1	..	..	1	3	..	1	1	..	..
Leach, Jacob	1	..	..	1	..	..	..	1	..	..	..
Leavitt, David	..	..	..	1	..	..	..	..	..	..	..
Lincoln, Elkanah	..	..	2	..	..	1	..	1	..	..	..
Lord, Benjamin	..	..	4	1	..	3	..	2	1	..	..
Lord, Reuben	..	..	..	1	..	3	..	..	2	1	..
Lord, Samuel	2	1	..	1	..	2	..	..	1	..	..
Lowell, Jacob	2	..	..	2	1	3	1	..	1	1	..
Lowell, Stephen	3	..	..	..	1	1	..	2	..	1	..
Martin, Aaron	..	..	1	..	1	..	1	..	..	1	..
Martin, Daniel	..	..	1	..	1	1	..	1	..	1	..
Martin, Robert	1	1	..	..	1	3	1	..	..	1	..
McWaine, Andrew	..	1	..	2	1	..	1	1	..	1	..
McWaine, William	..	1	2	..	1	1	1	2	..	1	..
Metcalf, George	..	..	..	1	..	2	..	..	1	1	..
Metcalf, Joseph	..	..	..	1	..	..	..	..	..	..	..
Miles, Abner	1	1	1	..	1	1	1	2	..	1	..
Miles, Jonas	2	..	..	1	..	1	..	..	1	..	..
Millett, Thomas W.	1	..	..	1	..	2	..	1	..	..	..
Minot, Samuel	..	1	3	..	1	2	1	1	..	1	..
Moore, Abijah	..	..	..	1	..	1	1	..	1	..	..
Moore, Gardner	1	3	1	1	..	2	..	3	1	..	..
Moore, Gideon	2	1	..	..	1	2	1	..	1	..	..
Moore, Newell	1	1	1	1	..	..	1	..	1	..	..
Moore, Paul	2	..	..	1	..	2	2	..	1	..	..
Moore, Rufus	1	..	..	..	1	..	..	..	1	..	..
Moore, Willard	3	..	..	1	..	1	1	..	1	..	1
Moore, William	1	..	..	..	1	1	2	..	1	..	..
Moore, William	1	1	1	..	1	1	..	1	1	..	..
Morey, Augustus	1	1	..	1	..	3	..	..	1	..	..
Nelson, Thomas	1	1	1	1	..	2	1	1	..	1	..
Nichols, Eleazer	3	..	..	1	1	2	..	1	2	1	..
Ormsby, Christopher	..	1	3	..	1	2	1	1	..	1	..
Palmer, Isaac	..	2	..	1	..	..	..	1	1	..	..
Palmer, Roswell	..	..	..	..	..	..	..	..	..	..	..
Parker, Roswell	3	..	1	1	..	1	2	..	1	1	..
Parker, Samuel D.	1	1	1	1	1	5	1	1	1	1	..
Parmenter, Jacob	..	1	..	..	1	..	..	1	..	1	..
Perry, Moses	1	3	1	..	1	3	..	2	1	..	..
PUTNEY—con.											
Perry, William	..	2	..	..	1	2	..	..	..	1	..
Perry, William Jr.	1	1	..	1	..	3	2	2	1	..	..
Pierce, Ephraim	1	..	1	..	1	..	1	..	..	1	..
Pierce, Ezekiel	2	3	1	..	1	..	..	2	1	..	..
Pierce, Henry	..	..	..	1	..	3	..	1	..	..	..
Pierce, Jonathan	2	1	..	..	1	..	1	2	1	..	..
Pierce, Joseph	3	2	5	..	1	1	..	1	..	1	..
Pierce, Joseph Jr.	2	..	..	1	..	1	..	..	1	..	..
Pierce, Roswell	1	..	..	1	..	2	1	..	1	..	..
Pierce, Rufus	..	..	..	1	..	5	..	1	1	..	..
Powers, Jonas	1	1	..	..	1	..	..	2	1	..	..
Prouty, Stephen	2	..	..	1	..	1	..	..	1	..	..
Reed, John	1	1	1	1	..	3	1	..	1	..	..
Reed, Timothy Jr.	1	..	1	1	..	2	..	1	1	..	..
Remmington, Reverend	..	..	..	1	..	1	..	1	1	..	1
Reynolds, Benjamin	2	..	..	1	..	2	1	..	1	..	..
Reynolds, Grindell	..	..	..	..	1	..	..	1	..	1	..
Reynolds, Nathaniel	2	..	..	1	..	2	..	..	1	1	..
Richardson, Salmon	1	..	..	1	..	1	..	..	1	..	..
Ridaway, David	1	..	..	1	..	1	1	..	1	..	..
Ridaway, Jonathan	2	..	..	1	..	3	1	..	1	..	..
Ridaway, Timothy	..	..	..	..	1	..	..	..	..	1	..
Ridaway, Timothy Jr.	1	1	..	1	..	2	2	..	1	..	..
Ridaway, Wilmet	2	1	..	..	1	1	..	2	..	1	..
Roberts, John	2	..	1	1	1	..	..	..	1	1	..
Ryan, Charles	..	..	..	1	1	3	..	1	3	1	..
Sabin, Noah	1	..	2	..	2	2	1	3	..	2	..
Sargeant, Samuel	2	..	..	..	1	3	3	2	1	..	..
Shaw, Abraham	..	..	..	1	..	2	..	..	1	..	..
Shaw, John	..	..	..	..	1	..	..	..	..	1	..
Shawell, Augustus	1	..	2	..	..	1	1	1	1	1	..
Skinner, Britton	1	..	..	1	..	1	..	..	1	..	..
Skinner, Samuel	..	..	..	1	1	2	..	..	1	..	..
Smith, Elijah	2	..	..	1	1	1	2	..	1	..	..
Smith, James	2	1	..	1	..	2	..	1	1	..	..
Smith, John	..	..	1	..	1	1	..	1	..	1	..
Smith, Joseph	1	3	3	..	1	3	..	1	1	..	..
Snow, John	..	..	..	1	..	2	..	..	2	1	..
Snow, Widow	1	1	1	..	..	3	..	..	..	1	..
Spaulding, Beniah	1	1	1	1	..	3	..	1	1	..	..
Steel, James	1	1	..	..	1	..	1	2	..	1	..
Stevenson, William	1	..	..	..	1	..	..	1	1	..	..
Sturtevant, Cornelius	2	..	..	1	..	1	..	..	1	..	..
Talbut, John	..	..	..	1	..	2	..	..	1	..	..
Thurber, Barnabas	..	..	..	..	1	..	..	..	..	1	..
Timothy, Reed	..	1	2	..	1	..	..	1	..	1	..
Townshend, John	1	1	3	..	1	..	1	3	1	1	..
Townshend, Nathaniel	1	..	..	1	..	2	..	..	1	..	..
Townshend, Richard	..	..	1	..	1	..	..	1	..	1	..
Turner, Thomas	..	1	..	..	1	..	1	..	..	1	..
Twiss, Benjamin	..	..	..	1	1	..	..	..	1	1	..
Twiss, Jonathan	..	..	2	..	1	2	..	1	..	1	..
Underwood, Joseph	2	1	1	1	..	1	..	1	1	..	..
Underwood, Russel	1	..	..	..	..	4	..	..	1	..	..
Upham, William	1	..	..	1	..	1	..	..	1	..	..
Ware, George	1	1	1	..	1	1	2	2	1	..	..
Warner, Luther	..	..	1	1	..	1	..	..	1	..	..
Washburn, Asa	2	1	1	..	1	2	1	2	1	..	..
Wheat, Samuel	..	2	1	..	1	1	1	1	..	1	..
White, Jonah	2	1	1	1	1	..	1	..	1	2	..
Whitney, ———	1	..	1	..	..	1	..	1	..	..	..
Whitney, Eliphalet	..	1	..	1	..	3	..	2	..	1	..
Whitney, Eliphaz	..	1	..	1	..	3	2	..	1	..	..
Wilder, David	..	..	..	1	..	..	..	..	1	..	..
Wilder, John	..	2	..	..	1	1	..	..	..	1	..
Willson, Alexander	..	..	1	..	1	..	..	2	..	1	..
Willson, David	..	..	..	..	..	..	..	..	..	..	..
Willson, David	..	..	1	..	1	..	1	1	1	2	..
Willson, David 3rd	1	..	..	1	..	2	..	..	1	..	..
Willson, Ezekiel	..	1	2	..	1	..	..	1	..	1	..
Willson, Jeremiah	1	1	2	..	1	1	1	..	..	1	..
Willson, John	2	1	1	1	1	..	..	1	1	1	..
Willson, Levi	1	..	..	1	..	2	..	..	1	..	..
Willson, Lucas	..	..	1	..	1	1	..	2	..	1	..
Willson, Lucas Jr.	1	..	..	1	..	3	2	..	1	..	..
Willson, Luke	..	..	1	..	1	2	1	1	..	1	..
Willson, Reuben	..	..	..	1	..	2	..	..	1	..	..
Winslow, Joseph	1	1	..	1	..	1	..	1	1	..	..
Winslow, Peleg	..	..	2	..	1	..	1	..	..	1	..
Winslow, Peleg 2nd	1	..	..	1	..	2	..	1	1	..	..
Wright, Ebenezer	1	1	1	..	1	..	1	1	1	..	..
Wright, Ebenezer Jr.	..	..	1	..	..	..	1	..	..	..	..

WINDHAM COUNTY—Continued

NAMES OF HEADS OF FAMILIES	FREE WHITE MALES: Under 10 years of age	FREE WHITE MALES: Of 10 and under 16	FREE WHITE MALES: Of 16 and under 26 including heads of families	FREE WHITE MALES: Of 26 and under 45 including heads of families	FREE WHITE MALES: Of 45 and upwards including heads of families.	FREE WHITE FEMALES: Under 10 years of age	FREE WHITE FEMALES: Of 10 and under 16	FREE WHITE FEMALES: Of 16 and under 26 including heads of families	FREE WHITE FEMALES: Of 26 and under 45 including heads of families	FREE WHITE FEMALES: Of 45 and upwards including heads of families	All other free persons except Indians not taxed
ROCKINGHAM											
Abbee, Hezekiah	..	..	..	1	..	..	..	2	1	..	..
Abbee, John	3	1	..	1	..	2	..	..	1	..	..
Adams, Joseph	3	..	..	1	..	1	..	..	1	..	..
Adams, Joseph	3	..	1	..	1	1	..	1	1	..	..
Adams, Joseph	3	1	..	1	..	1	..	..	1	..	..
Adams, Luther	1	..	..	1	..	3	1	..	1	..	..
Adams, Philip	..	1	..	..	1	..	1	..	..	1	..
Adams, Samuel	..	2	..	1	..	1	1	1	1	..	..
Albee, Ebenezer	..	1	1	..	1	..	..	..	..	1	..
Albee, Ebenezer Jr.	4	..	..	1	..	1	..	..	1	..	..
Aldrich, Artemas	1	..	..	1	..	..	..	..	1	..	..
Aldrich, Benoni	..	..	..	..	..	..	..	..	..	..	..
Aldrich, Widow	..	..	..	..	..	..	1	1	..	1	..
Aldrich, William	1	..	..	1	..	1	..	..	1	..	..
Amory, Samuel	2	1	2	..	1	2	1	2	..	2	..
Atkinson, Thomas	1	..	2	..	1	..	1	1	..	1	..
Ayres, Elihu	1	1	..	..	1	1	2	1	..	1	..
Bancraft, ———	2	..	2	..	1	1	3	..	1	..	..
Bancraft, James Jr.	1	..	1	..	..	..	..	1	..	..	..
Barrett, Joel	..	..	..	1	..	1	1	..	1	..	..
Barron, Jonathan	1	..	1	1	..	2	1	1	1	..	..
Bellows, Elijah	..	..	1	..	..	..	1	..	..	..	..
Bennett, Nathaniel	..	..	2	..	..	..	..	..	..	1	..
Benton, Jacob	..	..	..	1	1	..	..	..	..	1	..
Berry, Jonathan	..	..	1	1	1	..	..	..	..	1	..
Berry, Jonathan Jr.	1	..	..	1	..	1	..	..	1	..	..
Bixby, Daniel	2	2	1	1	..	2	..	..	1	..	..
Bixby, Ephraim	1	..	1	..	1	1	1	1	1	..	..
Blanchard, Jonathan	..	3	..	1	..	2	..	1	1	..	..
Boles, Jonathan	..	..	3	..	1	..	..	1	..	1	..
Boles, Jonathan Jr.	2	..	..	1	..	1	..	..	1	..	..
Boyenton, Abraham	2	..	2	1	..	..	..	..	1	..	..
Boyenton, Jonathan	2	1	..	1	..	2	1	..	1	..	..
Boyenton, Rchard	5	..	..	1	..	1	..	..	1	..	..
Bradshaw, George	1	1	..	1	..	2	..	..	1	..	..
Burk, Esmon	1	1	1	1	3	..	..	1	..	..	..
Burr, Labin	..	..	1	1	..	1	..	1	..	..	..
Burr, Samuel	2	..	..	..	1	1	2	..	..	1	..
Burt, Jonathan	..	2	2	..	1	..	..	..	..	1	..
Caldwell, George	3	..	..	1	..	..	..	..	1	..	..
Campbell, Alexander	2	2	..	1	..	2	..	1	1	1	..
Campbell, David	3	..	1	1	..	..	2	..	1	..	..
Chamberlin, Calvin	1	..	1	..	..	..	1	1	..	..	..
Chamberlin, Edmund	..	..	2	..	1	..	..	1	..	1	..
Chamberlin, Eli	1	..	..	1	..	4	..	..	1	..	..
Chamberlin, Joel	1	1	1	1	..	..	..	1	1	..	..
Chamberlin, Widow	1	1	..	..	..	2	..	2	1	..	..
Clark, Calvin	..	1	..	..	1	2	1	1	..	1	..
Clark, Hezekiah W.	..	1	1	1	..	..	2	..	1	..	..
Clark, Nathaniel	1	1	2	..	1	2	1	2	..	1	..
Clark, Rogers	1	..	..	1	..	2	..	1	..	..	..
Clark, Timothy	2	1	2	..	1	..	..	1	2	..	..
Clark, Timothy, Jr.	2	..	..	1	..	1	..	1	..	..	..
Closson, Ichabod	3	1	..	1	..	2	..	1	1	..	..
Closson, Roswell	..	..	..	1	..	..	..	..	..	..	..
Closson, Timothy	..	..	..	..	1	..	..	..	..	2	..
Closson, Wilber	1	2	..	..	1	..	..	1	..	1	..
Cochrin, John	1	..	1	1	..	2	..	..	1	..	..
Conde, George	2	1	..	1	..	1	1	..	1	..	..
Conklin, Widow	1	..	..	..	..	..	..	..	1	..	..
Coolidge, Elisha	..	..	..	1	..	2	..	1	1	1	..
Cooper, John	1	..	1	..	..	..	..	1	1	..	..
Corliss, Samuel	1	3	..	..	1	1	..	..	..	1	..
Cox, Jonathan	..	1	..	1	..	..	1	..	..	..	..
Craine, Josiah	2	..	..	1	..	..	..	..	1	..	..
Crow, Elias	2	3	2	..	1	1	2	1	1	..	..
Cushing, Noah	3	2	..	..	1	1	1	1	..	1	..
Cutler, Samuel	1	1	4	1	1	2	2	..	3	..	..
Darling, Timothy	..	..	..	1	..	..	1	1	1	..	..
Davidson, James	1	..	..	1	..	1	..	..	1	..	..
Davis, Benjamin	1	..	1	..	1	..	..	1	..	1	..
Davis, Henry	1	3	..	1	..	3	..	1	..	1	..
Davis, Nathaniel	..	..	..	..	1	1	..	..	..	1	..
Davis, Nathaniel Jr.	2	1	..	1	..	3	2	1	1	..	..
Davis, Philip	..	2	1	1	..	3	..	..	1	..	..
Derby, Edward	1	..	..	1	1	1	..	..	1	1	..
Drewry, Joseph	2	..	1	..	..	..	..	1	..	..	..
Drewry, Josiah	1	..	..	1	..	1	..	..	1	..	..
Dunbar, Daniel	1	1	..	1	..	1	..	..	1	..	..
Dunn, James	2	..	..	..	1	2	1	..	1	..	..
Easterbrooks, Abraham	..	1	..	..	1	..	..	2	..	1	..
Eastman, Samuel	2	1	..	1	..	..	1	..	1	..	..
Ellis, John	1	2	3	..	1	1	3	..	1	..	..
ROCKINGHAM—con.											
Elsworth, Elijah	..	1	1	1	..	..	1	2	1	..	..
Evans, Eli	..	1	3	..	1	..	2	1	..	1	..
Evans, Gilbert	..	..	1	..	..	..	..	..	..	..	..
Evans, Peter	1	1	1	2	1	1	1	1	1	1	..
Farley, Jesse	..	1	1	2	..	1	..	1	..	..	..
Felt, Eliphalet	2	..	2	..	1	1	2	..	1	..	..
Ferrand, Daniel	1	..	1	1	..	4	..	2	1	..	..
Finney, Samuel	1	1	..	..	1	1	..	..	..	1	..
Fisher, Enoch	3	1	1	1	..	1	1	1	1	..	..
Fisk, Jonathan	1	2	3	1	..	..	1	..	1	..	..
Frost, Abraham	1	..	..	1	..	1	..	..	1	1	..
Fuller, Ebenezer	1	..	..	..	1	1	..	..	..	1	..
Fuller, John	..	..	1	..	1	..	..	..	..	1	..
Garfield, Enoch	1	..	..	1	..	1	..	..	1	..	..
Gillmore, James	..	..	..	1	..	..	..	..	1	..	..
Gillmore, Jonathan	..	1	1	..	1	..	..	1	..	1	..
Gillsen, Joseph	..	1	1	..	1	..	..	..	..	1	..
Glezen, Isaac	1	..	..	1	..	1	..	1	1	..	..
Goodell, Abishai	..	..	1	..	..	..	..	1	..	..	..
Goodell, Elijah	..	1	2	..	2	..	1	..	1	..	..
Goven, Benjamin	4	..	..	1	..	..	..	..	1	..	..
Gowen, Levi	..	..	..	1	..	1	..	..	1	..	..
Hagar, Joseph	..	1	..	1	..	..	..	..	1	..	..
Haimes, Stephen	1	..	..	..	1	..	..	1	..	1	..
Hale, Joshua	..	1	..	2	..	2	..	1	2	..	..
Hapgood, Solomon	2	1	1	1	..	1	..	1	1	..	..
Harwood, Widow	..	..	1	..	..	..	..	1	..	1	..
Hazeltine, Jonas	2	1	..	..	1	2	1	..	1	..	..
Hazeltine, Richard	2	1	..	1	..	3	..	..	1	..	..
Hazeltine, William	..	2	..	..	1	2	1	..	1	..	..
Henderson, Andrew	..	..	..	1	..	1	..	..	1	..	..
Hitchcock, Widow	..	..	..	..	..	..	..	..	..	3	..
Holden, Isaac	1	2	1	..	1	2	1	1	..	1	..
Hooker, Riverius	..	3	3	..	1	2	1	2	1	..	..
Hooker, Ruel	3	1	1	1	..	2	1	..	1	1	..
House, Job	..	1	1	..	1	2	3	..	1	..	..
Hull, Matthew	3	1	..	..	1	1	2	..	1	..	..
Jewell, Solomon	1	..	..	1	..	..	..	1	..	..	..
Johnson, Isaac	4	2	..	..	1	1	1	..	1	..	..
Johnson, Joshua	..	..	1	..	1	1	..	1	..	1	..
Johnson, Robert A.	3	..	..	1	..	2	1	..	1	..	..
Keith, Grindell	3	1	..	1	..	1	1	..	1	..	..
Kendall, Eleazer	..	..	..	..	1	..	1	..	..	1	..
Kendall, Eleazer	2	1	..	..	1	1	1	..	..	1	..
Knight, Elijah	..	..	1	1	..	..	1	..	1	..	..
Knight, Joel	..	..	..	1	1	3	..	..	1	1	..
Lake, Henry	3	1	3	1	..	1	..	1	1	..	..
Leach, Jonathan	1	..	1	..	..	1	..	..	1	..	..
Lock, Abraham	1	2	..	..	1	..	..	1	..	1	..
Lock, Daniel	..	..	1	..	..	..	..	1	..	..	..
Lock, Ebenezer	2	1	1	1	1	3	1	..	1	1	..
Lovell, Ebenezer	2	..	1	1	..	1	..	..	2	..	..
Lovell, Elijah	2	2	1	..	1	2	1	1	1	..	..
Lovell, John	3	2	4	..	1	1	..	4	1	..	..
Lovell, Oliver	..	2	..	..	1	..	1	2	..	1	..
Lovell, Timothy	..	1	1	..	1	..	..	..	..	1	..
Macafee, James	1	..	1	1	..	2	..	1	1	..	..
Marsh, James	..	..	1	..	..	3	..	1	..	..	..
Marsh, Joseph	3	..	..	1	1	1	..	2	..	..	..
Marsh, Moses	..	1	..	..	1	..	1	1	..	1	..
Martin, Nathan	1	1	..	1	..	4	..	..	1	..	..
Mason, Daniel	..	1	..	1	..	..	..	..	1	..	..
Mather, John	1	1	1	..	1	1	2	1	1	..	..
McGalvin, Ebenezer	..	1	2	1	..	1	..	2	1	..	..
McNiel, Widow	..	..	1	..	..	..	..	1	..	1	..
Meads, Edward	1	..	..	1	..	2	..	..	1	..	..
Metcalf, Samuel	2	1	1	..	1	1	1	1	1	..	..
Miller, Mather	1	..	1	1	..	..	1	1	..	..	..
Miller, Samuel	3	1	..	1	1	2	1	2	1	1	..
Minard, Ichabod	..	1	..	1	..	1	..	1	..	..	..
Minard, Isaac	1	..	1	..	..	1	..	..	1	..	..
Minard, William	..	1	1	..	1	..	..	..	..	1	..
Minard, William Jr.	..	..	..	1	..	2	..	1	..	..	..
Morgan, Quartus	1	..	1	1	..	1	..	1	1	..	..
Morrison, Jonathan	1	..	..	1	..	4	1	1	..	1	..
Newton, Nehemiah	..	..	1	..	1	..	..	..	3	1	..
Newton, Stephen	3	..	..	1	..	2	..	..	1	..	..
Nourse, Peter	..	1	2	1	1	..	1	1	1	1	..

WINDHAM COUNTY—Continued

NAMES OF HEADS OF FAMILIES	FREE WHITE MALES					FREE WHITE FEMALES					
	Under 10 years of age	Of 10 and under 16	Of 16 and under 26 including heads of families	Of 26 and under 45 including heads of families	Of 45 and upwards including heads of families.	Under 10 years of age	Of 10 and under 16	Of 16 and under 26 including heads of families	Of 26 and under 45 including heads of families	Of 45 and upwards including heads of families	All other free persons except Indians not taxed
ROCKINGHAM—con.											
Oakes, David	3	..	1	1	..	1	..	..	1	..	..
Ober, Samuel	2	1	2	..	1	..	..	2	..	1	..
Olcut, Elias	1	1	..	1	..	..	..	2	..	1	..
Orr, Hugh	..	2	..	..	1	..	1	3	..	1	..
Page, William	..	1	9	..	1	1	1	2	2	..	2
Paine, ———	..	..	..	..	..	..	..	..	..	..	..
Paine, Ephraim	2	..	..	1	..	3	1	..	1	..	..
Park, Moses	..	..	..	1	..	2	..	..	1	..	..
Parker, John	3	2	..	..	1	1	1	..	1	..	..
Parker, Leonard	1	..	1	1	..	3	..	..	1	..	..
Parker, Lucy Widow	1	..	..	..	..	..	1	..	1	..	..
Pattridge, David	1	..	..	1	..	3	1	..	1	..	..
Pease, Chester	..	..	..	1	..	..	..	..	..	1	..
Perry, Simeon	2	1	..	..	1	..	..	..	1	..	..
Petty, Solomon	3	..	..	1	..	..	..	..	1	..	..
Pierce, Levi	3	..	..	1	..	1	..	..	1	..	..
Pike, David	..	..	..	..	1	..	..	..	1	..	..
Powers, Timothy	..	..	1	..	1	..	..	1	..	1	..
Proctor, Nathan	..	1	1	..	1	1	..	1	..	1	..
Pulsifer, David	..	..	1	..	..	..	..	1	..	..	..
Pulsifer, David	3	..	1	..	1	..	2	2	..	1	..
Pulsifer, Ebenezer	1	1	..	1	..	3	1	1	1	..	..
Pulsifer, Jonathan	1	3	1	..	1	1	..	1	..	1	..
Reed, Elijah	4	1	..	1	..	2	1	..	1	..	..
Reed, Frederick	..	2	1	..	1	3	..	1	1	..	..
Reed, Isaac	1	..	1	..	1	2	2	2	..	1	..
Reed, Matthew	..	..	..	..	1	2	1	3	..	1	..
Remmington, Samuel	..	..	..	1	..	..	..	1	..	..	..
Rice, Hezekiah	..	..	..	..	1	1	..	1	..	1	..
Richardson, Daniel	1	..	1	..	..	..	..	1	..	..	..
Richardson, Jotham	1	..	..	1	..	..	2	..	1	..	..
Ripley, Epaphras	..	..	1	..	1	3	2	1	1	..	..
Ross, Jonathan	2	..	1	1	..	..	..	1	..	..	..
Roundy, Jonathan	..	1	..	..	1	..	..	..	1	..	..
Roundy, Uriah	1	1	2	1	..	5	1	..	1	..	..
Sabin, Levi	3	..	2	1	..	2	1	..	1	1	..
Sanderson, David	..	..	..	..	1	..	..	..	..	..	..
Sanderson, Widow	2	1	..	..	..	..	1	..	..	1	..
Sargeant, Peletiah	..	..	..	1	..	2	..	1	..	..	..
Searl, Abijah	3	2	..	..	1	1	1	..	1	..	..
Shields, Daniel	2	..	..	1	..	1	..	..	1	..	..
Shipman, Abraham	2	..	3	..	1	2	1	1	..	1	..
Simonds, Thomas	..	..	..	..	1	..	..	..	..	..	..
Simonds, William	..	..	..	1	1	3	..	2	..	1	..
Smalley. David	1	..	1	..	..	..	..	1	..	..	..
Smalley, Jonathan	3	..	..	1	..	..	..	..	1	..	..
Smith, Jediah	2	..	1	..	1	1	..	1	..	1	..
Stanley, David	..	1	..	..	1	..	..	..	..	1	..
Stanley, Elijah	3	..	..	1	..	1	..	..	1	..	..
Stearns, James	2	..	..	1	..	1	1	1	..	..	..
Stearns, John	3	..	..	1	..	..	1	..	1	..	..
Stearns, William	1	..	..	..	1	..	..	..	..	1	..
Stearns, William Jr.	1	2	..	1	..	..	1	..	1	..	..
Stoddard, Isaiah	2	1	..	1	..	..	1	..	1	..	..
Stowell, Asa	3	..	..	1	..	1	..	..	1	..	..
Stowell, John	..	..	1	..	..	1	..	..	1	..	..
Stowell, Stephen	1	..	1	..	..	1	..	1	..	..	..
Taylor, Samuel	..	1	1	1	1	..	1	1	..	1	..
Taylor, Samuel Jr.	..	..	1	..	..	..	..	1	..	..	..
Thayer, Simeon	4	..	1	1	..	1	..	1	..	..	..
Thayer, William	1	1	..	1	..	2	..	..	1	..	..
Towzer, Peter	2	..	..	1	..	..	1	..	..	1	..
Waight, Jonathan	1	..	1	..	1	..	..	1	..	1	..
Walker, James	2	1	..	..	1	1	1	1	1	2	..
Weaver, Daniel	2	2	1	..	1	1	2	1	..	1	..
Webb, Calvin	2	1	1	1	..	1	1	2	..	1	..
Webb, Charles	2	2	3	..	1	..	..	..	1	..	..
Webb, Jehiel	1	..	1	..	1	1	1	1	1	..	..
Webb, Jehiel Jr.	1	..	1	..	..	1	..	1	..	..	..
Webb, Joshua	..	..	..	1	1	..	..	..	2	1	..
Webb, Joshua R.	1	1	..	1	..	..	..	1	..	..	..
Webb, Luther	1	..	..	1	..	3	..	..	1	..	..
Wells, David	1	1	..	..	1	1	..	..	..	1	..
Weston, Nathan	..	1	2	1	1	..	..	1	..	1	..
Wheeler, Annaniah	2	..	1	..	..	..	..	1	..	..	..
Wheelock, Abner	..	..	..	1	..	3	..	..	1	1	..
Wheelock, Jonathan	3	1	..	1	..	1	1	..	1	..	..
Wheelock, Solomon	3	..	..	1	..	1	..	1	..	..	..
White, Abel	3	1	..	..	1	..	3	2	1	1	..
White, Abijah	3	1	..	..	1	..	2	..	1	1	..
Whiting, Jonathan	1	1	1	..	1	1	1	1	1	1	..
Whiting, Samuel Rev.	1	1	..	..	1	..	1	1	..	1	..
Whitney, Asa	2	..	..	1	..	1	..	..	1	..	..
Whitney, Ezra	3	2	..	1	1	..	1	..	1	..	..
Wiles, Robert	2	..	1	1	..	1	..	1	..	..	..
Willard, Oliver	..	1	1	..	1	..	..	2	..	1	..
Williams, Benjamin	3	..	1	1	1	..	1	3	1	..	..
Williams, Charles	..	..	1	1	..	..	..	..	1	..	..
Wing, John	1	..	..	1	..	1	..	..	1	..	..
Wing, Thomas	6	1	..	1	..	..	..	..	1	..	..
Wing, Widow	..	..	1	..	..	..	1	2	..	1	..
Wolf, John G. S.	1	2	1	1	..	1	1	1	1	1	..
Wood, David Jr.	2	..	1	2	..	1	..	..	1	..	..
Wood, Widow	..	..	..	..	..	..	..	1	..	1	..
Woods, Barnabas	2	1	2	..	1	..	..	..	1	..	..
Woods, William	2	1	..	..	1	3	1	1	1	1	..
Woolley, Nathan	1	..	2	1	..	2	1	..	1	..	..
Woolley, Samuel	1	..	1	..	1	..	1	..	..	..	..
Wright, Moses Jr.	1	..	..	1	1	2	1	1	..	..	..
Wright, Nathan	1	1	..	..	1	..	..	2	..	..	..
Wright, Solomon	2	1	..	..	1	..	2	..	..	1	..
Wyman, Asa	2	1	1	..	2	1	..	1	..	..	..
Wyman, John	2	1	..	1	..	2	2	1	1	..	..
SOMERSET											
Albee, William	2	..	..	1	..	1	..	..	1	..	..
Allen, Robert	..	..	..	1	..	2	..	..	1	..	..
Badcock, David	..	..	..	1	..	2	1	..	1	..	..
Balcom, Caleb	..	..	1	..	..	..	..	1	..	..	..
Balcom, Isaac	1	..	..	1	..	1	..	1	..	..	..
Balcom, Micah	1	..	1	..	1	..	..	1	..	1	..
Crosby, Silas	..	..	1	..	1	..	..	..	..	1	..
Hodges, Ephraim	3	..	1	1	..	..	2	1	..	1	..
Kempton, Oliver	2	..	..	..	1	..	..	..	1	..	..
Lawton, Joshua	..	..	..	1	..	2	..	1	..	..	..
Lawton, William	..	..	3	..	1	..	..	..	..	1	..
Palmer, James	2	1	..	1	..	3	..	..	1	..	..
Palmer, Zurishaddi	2	..	2	..	1	..	..	..	1	1	..
Parmelee, John	1	1	1	..	1	2	1	2	..	1	..
Rice, Daniel	2	2	1	1	..	2	1	..	1	1	..
Sawtell, Benjamin	..	1	2	..	1	2	..	3	1	..	..
Sawtell, Enoch	..	..	..	..	1	..	..	..	..	..	..
Sawtell, Enoch Jr.	..	..	..	1	..	..	..	..	..	1	..
Sawtell, Richard	1	..	..	1	..	2	..	..	1	..	..
Sutton, Joseph	..	..	1	..	..	..	..	..	..	..	..
Waste, Bezeliel	..	..	1	..	1	..	1	1	..	1	..
Waste, Ebenezer	1	..	..	1	..	..	..	..	1	..	..
Wellman, Jacob	4	1	..	1	..	1	..	..	1	1	..
Wellman, Silas	3	..	1	1	..	2	1	..	1	..	..
STRATTON											
Allen, Jacob	3	1	..	1	..	2	1	..	1	..	..
Bachelor, Calvin	..	..	1	..	..	..	1	..	..	..	..
Bachelor, Jacob	2	2	1	..	1	2	..	..	1	..	..
Balcom, Isaac	1	..	1	..	..	1	..	1	..	..	..
Bartlett, Richard	..	..	..	1	..	..	..	..	1	1	..
Bayley, Benjamin	1	1	..	1	..	4	1	..	1	..	..
Bills, Ebenezer	2	..	..	1	..	3	2	..	1	..	..
Bixby, Samson	2	2	..	1	..	1	..	..	1	..	..
Blodgett, Samuel	..	2	..	..	1	..	1	..	..	1	..
Blodgett, Samuel Jr.	2	..	..	1	..	2	..	..	1	..	..
Boutell, Samuel	..	..	..	1	..	3	..	..	1	..	..
Boutell, William	3	..	..	1	..	1	2	..	1	..	..
Cook, David	..	1	1	1	..	1	..	2	1	..	..
Davis, Simon	1	..	..	1	..	2	..	..	1	..	..
Easterbrooks, Ezra	1	..	..	1	..	2	..	..	1	..	..
French, Jacob	1	..	1	1	..	1	1	..	1	..	..
Garfield, Eliakim	..	..	2	..	1	..	..	1	1	1	..
Garfield, Nathaniel	1	..	..	1	..	1	1	..	1	..	..
Gibbs, Edmund	1	..	..	1	..	3	..	..	1	..	..
Glezen, John	3	..	..	1	..	2	1	..	1	..	..
Glezen, Samuel	1	..	..	1	..	4	1	..	1	..	..

WINDHAM COUNTY—Continued

NAMES OF HEADS OF FAMILIES	FREE WHITE MALES: Under 10 years of age	FREE WHITE MALES: Of 10 and under 16	FREE WHITE MALES: Of 16 and under 26 including heads of families	FREE WHITE MALES: Of 26 and under 45 including heads of families	FREE WHITE MALES: Of 45 and upwards including heads of families	FREE WHITE FEMALES: Under 10 years of age	FREE WHITE FEMALES: Of 10 and under 16	FREE WHITE FEMALES: Of 16 and under 26 including heads of families	FREE WHITE FEMALES: Of 26 and under 45 including heads of families	FREE WHITE FEMALES: Of 45 and upwards including heads of families	All other free persons except Indians not taxed
STRATTON—con.											
Goodale, Jacob	..	1	..	..	1	..	..	1	..	1	..
Grant, James	..	..	..	1	..	..	..	..	..	..	..
Greenwood, Jonathan	..	..	..	1	..	1	..	..	1	..	..
Hale, Jacob	..	..	..	1	..	1	..	1	..	..	..
Hale, Levi	2	..	..	1	..	..	..	..	1	..	..
Hill, John	..	2	1	..	1	..	..	1	..	1	..
Hill, Thomas	..	1	2	..	1	..	..	1	..	1	..
Holman, John	..	1	..	1	..	1	1	..	1	..	..
Kidder, Abel	2	..	..	1	..	2	..	..	1	..	..
Kidder, Francis	..	..	..	..	1	..	..	..	..	1	..
Lothrop, Thomas	2	..	..	1	..	2	..	..	1	..	..
Man, Billy	..	..	1	1	..	..	1	..	1	..	..
Marble, Samuel	..	..	..	1	..	..	..	..	1	..	..
Marble, Samuel Jr.	..	..	..	1	..	..	..	..	1	..	..
Moulton, Nathaniel	2	1	..	1	..	1	..	..	1	..	..
Phillips, Asa	2	1	..	1	..	1	..	..	1	..	..
Pike, Jotham	..	..	1	..	..	..	..	..	..	..	..
Pike, William	..	..	1	..	..	..	..	1	..	1	..
Pratt, Asa	..	..	1	..	..	..	..	..	..	..	..
Pratt, Stephen	1	..	1	..	1	2	..	1	..	1	..
Randall, James	1	2	2	..	1	1	1	..	..	1	..
Raymore, Jonathan	1	..	..	1	..	4	..	..	1	..	..
Robbins, Levi	1	..	1	..	..	..	..	1	..	..	..
Sigourny, Anthony	2	1	1	..	1	1	..	1	..	1	..
Sprague, Hasa F.	2	..	..	1	..	2	..	..	1	..	..
Stoddard, David	..	..	..	1	..	..	..	..	..	..	..
Thurston, James	..	..	1	..	1	2	1	..	1	1	..
Wait, John	4	1	1	..	1	..	1	..	1	..	..
Woodcock, Elias	..	..	..	1	..	1	..	..	1	..	..
Woodward, Jonas	3	..	..	1	..	2	..	..	1	..	..
TOWNSHEND											
Adams, Abraham	1	..	..	1	..	1	..	1	..	..	..
Albee, Aaron	2	1	..	1	..	2	..	1	1	..	..
Allen, Cornelius	..	..	1	..	..	1	..	1	..	..	..
Allen, Elijah	..	..	1	..	..	..	..	1	..	..	..
Allen, Johnson Josiah	2	2	..	..	1	..	..	1	..	1	..
Allen, Samuel	1	..	..	1	..	1	..	..	1	..	..
Ames, John	..	1	..	1	..	4	..	..	1	..	..
Ames, Katherine Widow	..	1	1	..	..	..	..	..	..	1	..
Ames, Lemuel	1	..	..	1	..	2	..	..	1	..	..
Ames, Lydia	..	..	..	..	..	1	..	1	..	..	..
Atherton, Betsey	..	..	..	..	..	..	..	1	..	1	..
Atherton, Peter	3	2	..	1	..	1	..	..	1	..	..
Austin, Asa	..	1	1	1	..	3	1	..	1	..	..
Austin, George	4	..	..	1	..	1	..	..	1	..	..
Ayers, Levi	2	..	..	1	..	..	..	..	1	..	..
Bailey, Richard	2	2	..	1	..	1	2	..	1	..	..
Bailey, Samuel	2	..	..	1	..	1	1	..	1	..	..
Ball, Silas	..	1	..	1	..	1	..	..	1	..	..
Barber, Benjamin N.	..	..	..	1	..	1	1	..	1	..	..
Barber, Daniel M.	..	..	1	..	..	..	..	..	..	..	..
Barber, Thomas Jr.	1	..	..	1	..	..	..	..	1	..	..
Barnard, Alpha	..	..	..	1	..	..	..	..	..	..	..
Barnard, Joshua	..	..	..	..	1	..	..	..	..	..	..
Barnard, Silas	1	..	..	1	..	1	..	..	1	..	..
Barnard, Stephen	..	..	1	..	..	..	..	..	..	..	..
Barnes, Thomas	..	1	1	..	1	2	2	1	1	..	..
Belknap, Joseph	..	1	..	1	..	..	..	..	1	..	..
Black, John	..	1	..	..	1	..	..	..	..	1	..
Brigham, Ebenezer	2	1	1	1	..	2	1	1	1	1	..
Burbey, David	1	..	..	1	..	2	..	..	1	1	..
Burbey, Jonathan	2	..	..	1	..	..	..	..	1	..	..
Burbey, Thomas	..	..	1	..	..	..	..	..	..	..	..
Burt, Ebenezer	..	..	..	..	1	1	1	1	..	1	..
Burt, John	..	..	1	..	..	..	..	..	..	..	..
Chase, Betsey	2	..	..	..	..	..	..	..	1	..	..
Chase, Bezaleel	..	..	..	1	..	..	..	..	..	..	..
Chase, Enoch	1	..	..	1	..	3	..	..	1	..	..
Chase, Henry	..	2	..	..	1	..	2	..	..	1	..
Chase, Lemuel	2	..	..	1	..	1	..	..	1	..	..
Chase, Phebe	3	..	..	..	..	1	..	..	1	..	..
Church, Nathaniel	..	..	1	..	1	..	1	1	..	1	..
Clayton, Eunice	..	..	..	..	..	..	..	1	..	..	..
Clayton, Moses	1	1	..	1	..	1	..	..	1	..	..
TOWNSHEND—con.											
Cobleigh, Dan	..	1	1	..	1	..	..	1	1	1	..
Cook, Jerusha	1	..	..	..	..	..	..	..	1	..	..
Crosier, Alexander	1	..	..	1	..	1	..	..	1	..	..
Cutler, Jonathan	3	3	..	1	..	..	..	..	1	..	..
Davis, Hammond	2	..	..	1	..	2	..	..	1	..	..
Davis, Thomas	..	..	..	1	..	..	..	..	..	..	..
Doolittle, Amzi	..	1	1	..	1	..	..	1	..	1	..
Doolittle, Amzi Jr.	1	..	..	1	..	..	..	..	1	..	..
Doolittle, Origin	..	..	..	1	..	1	..	..	1	..	..
Doolittle, Roswell	..	..	1	..	..	..	..	..	..	..	..
Drake, Paul	1	..	..	1	..	3	..	..	1	..	..
Duncan, Ebenezer	..	..	1	..	..	..	..	..	..	..	..
Duncan, Seth	..	1	1	1	..	1	2	1	1	..	..
Dunton, Joseph	1	2	1	..	1	1	..	..	..	1	..
Dyar, Eliza Widow	..	1	..	..	..	..	..	3	..	1	..
Dyar, John	..	..	..	1	1	..	1	1	..	1	..
Dyar, John 2nd	..	..	1	..	..	..	..	..	..	..	..
Dyar, Joseph	1	..	1	..	..	..	..	1	..	..	..
Ewings, Calvin	2	2	..	1	..	4	1	1	1	..	..
Fessenden, John	1	..	..	1	..	2	..	..	1	..	..
Fessenden, Samuel	1	..	..	1	..	..	..	..	1	..	..
Fish, Caleb	1	1	..	1	..	..	..	..	1	1	..
Fish, Jacob	..	..	2	1	..	1	1	..	1	..	..
Fish, John	..	..	..	..	1	..	..	..	1	1	..
Fish, Ward	1	..	..	1	..	..	..	1	..	..	..
Fletcher, Samuel	1	..	..	..	1	..	2	..	..	1	..
Fletcher, Squire Hazeltine	2	..	1	..	..	1	..	1	..	..	..
Franklin, James	1	..	..	1	..	1	..	..	1	..	..
Franklin, John	..	..	1	..	..	..	..	..	..	..	..
Frost, Bezaliel	1	1	..	..	1	1	1	..	..	1	..
Gray, Amos	1	1	..	1	..	3	1	..	1	..	..
Gray, James	..	1	..	1	..	1	..	..	1	..	..
Gray, Jesse	1	1	..	1	..	..	..	..	1	..	..
Gray, Jonas	..	..	..	..	1	..	..	..	..	1	..
Gray, Jonas Jr.	1	..	1	1	..	3	..	..	1	..	..
Gray, Joseph	1	2	..	1	..	2	1	..	1	..	..
Gray, Matthew	4	..	..	1	..	1	..	..	1	..	..
Green, John	..	..	..	1	..	..	..	..	..	..	..
Green, Nathaniel	1	..	..	1	..	..	..	1	..	..	..
Grimes, James	3	..	..	1	..	1	1	..	1	..	..
Harris, Ebenezer	2	1	..	..	1	1	2	1	..	1	..
Hart, Elisha	1	..	..	1	..	1	..	..	1	..	..
Hart, Isaac H.	1	2	1	..	1	1	..	1	..	1	..
Hayward, Eli	..	1	..	..	1	..	..	1	..	1	..
Hayward, Henry	..	..	1	..	..	..	..	..	..	..	..
Hayward, Levi	1	..	1	..	1	1	1	..	..	1	..
Hazeltine, Asa	..	1	1	..	1	4	1	..	..	1	..
Hazeltine, Asa Jr.	..	..	1	..	..	..	..	1	..	..	..
Hazeltine, Elisha	..	..	..	1	..	..	..	..	..	..	..
Hazeltine, Jane Widow	..	..	..	..	..	..	..	..	..	1	..
Hazeltine, John	1	..	..	..	1	..	..	..	..	1	..
Hazeltine, John 2nd	1	..	..	1	..	..	2	..	1	..	..
Hazeltine, John 3rd	..	1	..	1	..	3	..	..	1	..	..
Hazeltine, Paul	1	..	2	..	1	..	..	..	..	1	..
Hazeltine, Peter	..	1	..	..	1	..	..	1	..	1	..
Hazeltine, Simeon	..	..	1	..	..	..	..	..	..	..	..
Hinds, Susanna	..	..	..	..	..	1	..	..	..	1	..
Hodge, Joseph	..	..	..	1	..	1	..	..	1	..	..
Holbrook, Abner	..	..	..	1	..	1	..	..	1	..	..
Holbrook, Alfred	..	..	..	1	..	4	..	..	1	..	..
Holbrook, Amos	..	2	1	..	1	1	..	..	1	..	..
Holbrook, Arad	..	..	..	1	..	1	..	1	..	..	..
Holbrook, Asa	..	..	..	..	1	..	..	..	..	1	..
Holbrook, Eli	1	1	1	..	1	..	1	..	..	1	..
Holbrook, Ezra	2	..	1	..	1	..	1	1	..	1	..
Holbrook, Jared	..	..	1	..	..	..	..	..	..	..	..
Holbrook, Lymon	..	..	1	1	..	2	1	..	..	1	..
Holbrook, Ruth Widow	..	..	..	..	..	..	..	..	..	1	..
Holbrook, Sarah Widow	..	..	..	..	..	..	..	..	1	..	..
Holbrook, Thomas	1	1	..	1	..	2	1	..	1	..	..
Holmes, Thomas	..	..	..	..	1	1	..	..	1	..	..
Hosley, Asa	1	..	..	1	..	1	..	1	..	..	..
How, Benjamin	..	..	2	..	1	..	2	..	..	2	..
How, Benjamin Jr.	3	..	..	1	..	1	..	..	1	..	..
How, Deborah	..	..	..	..	..	..	..	..	..	1	..
How, John Jr.	2	2	..	1	..	2	..	..	1	..	..
How, John W.	..	..	1	..	..	..	..	..	..	..	..
How, Milow	2	..	..	1	..	..	..	..	1	..	..
How, Rogers	..	..	1	..	..	..	..	1	..	..	..
Jennison, Robert	1	1	..	1	..	2	..	..	1	..	..
Jewett, Joseph M.	2	..	..	1	..	3	1	..	1	..	..

WINDHAM COUNTY—Continued

NAMES OF HEADS OF FAMILIES	FREE WHITE MALES: Under 10 years of age	FREE WHITE MALES: Of 10 and under 16	FREE WHITE MALES: Of 16 and under 26 including heads of families	FREE WHITE MALES: Of 26 and under 45 including heads of families	FREE WHITE MALES: Of 45 and upwards including heads of families	FREE WHITE FEMALES: Under 10 years of age	FREE WHITE FEMALES: Of 10 and under 16	FREE WHITE FEMALES: Of 16 and under 26 including heads of families	FREE WHITE FEMALES: Of 26 and under 45 including heads of families	FREE WHITE FEMALES: Of 45 and upwards including heads of families	All other free persons except Indians not taxed
TOWNSHEND—con.											
Johnson, Michael	2	2	1	..	1	..	1	1	..	1	..
Johnson, William	..	..	..	..	1	..	..	..	..	1	..
Johnson, William Jr.	2	..	..	1	..	1	..	..	1	..	..
Kidder, David	2	..	..	1	..	1	..	1	..	..	..
Kimball, Charles	..	1	..	1	..	4	..	..	1	..	..
Kimball, Ebenezer	..	1	2	..	1	1	..	1	..	1	..
King, Thomas F.	1	..	..	1	..	2	..	..	1	..	..
Kingsbury, Samuel	..	..	..	1	..	2	..	..	1	..	..
Knight, Eliza	1	..	..	..	..	1	..	1	..	..	..
Knight, Eliza Widow	..	..	..	..	..	..	..	..	..	1	..
Lamb, Isaac	..	..	1	..	..	1	..	1	..	..	..
Lamb, James	..	..	..	..	1	..	..	1	..	1	..
Lee, Joel	1	2	..	1	..	1	..	..	1	..	..
Livingston, Benjamin	..	1	1	..	1	..	1	1	..	1	..
Livingston, James	1	1	1	..	..	..	..	..	1	..	..
Livingston, Matthew	1	..	..	1	..	2	..	1	..	..	..
Lovering, Samuel	1	..	..	1	..	..	..	..	1	..	..
Low, John	1	..	1	..	..	..	..	1	..	..	..
Low, Joseph	..	..	1	..	..	..	..	..	..	..	..
Low, Thomas	..	1	1	..	1	3	1	..	1	..	..
Lowell, Solomon	1	..	..	1	..	3	..	..	1	1	..
Marsh, Eber	1	..	..	1	..	..	..	..	1	..	..
Mason, Anthony	1	..	..	1	..	3	..	..	1	..	..
Morse, John	2	..	..	1	..	1	..	..	1	..	..
Murdock, Benjamin	1	..	1	1	..	1	1	..	1	..	..
Murdock, Benjamin Jr.	1	..	..	1	..	2	..	..	1	..	..
Murdock, Jesse	1	..	..	1	..	1	..	..	1	..	..
Murdock, Samuel	1	..	..	1	..	2	..	..	1	..	..
Murdock, Thaddeus	..	..	..	1	..	..	..	..	..	..	..
Negus, Jonas	..	..	..	1	..	..	..	..	..	..	..
Newell, Hiram	1	..	..	1	..	4	1	..	1	..	..
Nichols, Reuben	..	..	..	1	..	..	..	..	..	..	..
Oaks, Seth	..	..	..	..	1	..	..	1	..	1	..
Ober, Asa	..	..	1	..	..	..	..	..	..	..	..
Ober, Ebenezer	..	..	..	..	1	..	..	..	..	..	..
Ober, Ezra	2	..	..	1	..	3	1	..	1	..	..
Parkhurst, Samuel	..	3	1	..	1	..	..	..	1	..	..
Perry, Nancy	..	..	..	..	..	..	..	1	..	..	..
Prentice, Elijah	..	..	1	..	..	..	..	..	..	..	..
Prentice, Joseph	..	..	..	1	..	..	..	3	..	..	..
Puffer, Richard	1	..	..	1	..	2	2	..	1	..	..
Putnam, John	3	1	..	1	..	1	..	..	1	..	..
Ransom, Ezekiel	1	..	1	1	..	3	..	2	1	..	..
Rawson, Bailey	2	..	..	1	..	2	1	..	1	..	..
Rawson, Gardner	1	..	..	1	..	4	..	..	1	..	..
Rawson, Stephen	..	..	..	..	1	1	2	2	..	1	..
Ray, Reuben	1	1	..	1	..	1	1	..	1	1	..
Reed, Evans	1	..	..	1	..	1	..	..	1	..	..
Reed, Thomas	1	..	1	..	1	1	..	2	..	1	..
Reed, Thomas Jr.	..	..	..	1	..	1	..	..	1	..	..
Robinson, Elijah	1	2	2	..	1	..	1	..	..	1	..
Rounds, Isaiah	1	..	..	1	..	2	..	..	1	..	..
Scott, Robert	4	..	..	1	..	..	1	..	1	..	..
Sellen, Sally	..	..	1	..	..	1	1	..	..	1	..
Shattuck, Jonathan	..	2	1	..	..	1	..	..	..	1	..
Shattuck, Jonathan Jr.	1	..	..	1	..	1	..	..	1	..	..
Smith, David	..	1	1	1	..	1	..	1	1	..	..
Snow, Joseph	1	1	1	1	..	1	2	..	1	..	..
Squires, Charles	1	..	..	1	..	2	1	..	1	..	..
Stevenson, Robert	..	..	..	1	..	..	..	..	..	..	..
Stockwell, Daniel	2	..	..	1	..	2	..	..	1	..	..
Street, Benjamin	..	..	..	1	..	..	..	..	..	..	..
Sumner, Benjamin	..	..	2	..	1	1	1	..	..	1	..
Sumner, Edward	..	..	..	..	1	..	..	..	..	..	..
Sumner, Thomas	5	2	..	1	..	..	2	..	1	..	..
Taft, Aaron	1	1	..	..	1	..	..	2	..	1	..
Taft, Amariah	..	1	..	..	1	..	..	2	..	1	..
Taft, Amariah Jr.	..	..	1	..	..	..	..	..	..	..	..
Taft, Ebenezer	1	1	..	..	1	1	..	1	..	1	..
Taft, Elisha	..	..	1	..	..	..	..	..	..	..	..
Taft, Israel	2	..	..	1	..	2	..	..	1	..	..
Taft, Willard	1	1	..	1	..	1	..	..	1	..	..
Taft, William	2	..	1	1	..	1	2	1	1	..	..
Thomas, Gardner	1	1	..	1	..	1	..	1	1	..	..
Thomas, Washington	..	..	1	..	..	..	..	..	..	..	..
Thwing, Nathaniel	3	2	..	1	..	2	..	..	1	..	..
Tinkham, Tyler	..	..	..	1	..	..	..	..	1	..	..
Tourtellot, Abraham	2	1	..	1	..	2	1	..	1	..	..
TOWNSHEND—con.											
Tyler, Joseph	..	1	..	..	1	1	1	1	..	1	..
Tyler, Joseph Jr.	..	..	..	1	..	..	..	..	..	..	..
Tyler, Timothy	..	..	..	1	..	..	..	..	1	..	..
Waldron, Benjamin	1	..	..	1	..	..	..	..	1	..	..
Waldron, James	..	..	..	..	1	..	..	..	..	1	..
Walker, Jeshuron	3	1	1	..	1	1	1	1	..	1	..
Warren, Jonas Jr.	..	..	..	1	..	..	..	..	..	..	..
Waterous, Joseph	1	..	1	1	..	1	1	..	1	..	..
Wheeler, Daniel	..	..	..	1	..	..	..	..	..	..	..
Wheelock, Caleb	..	2	2	..	1	..	..	..	..	1	..
Wheelock, Ephraim	1	..	..	1	..	..	..	1	1	..	..
Whelock, Winslow	..	..	1	..	..	..	..	1	..	..	..
Whipple, John	2	2	1	1	..	1	1	1	1	..	..
Whitcomb, Benjamin	..	..	1	..	..	..	..	..	..	..	..
Whitcomb, Jonas	1	..	..	1	..	2	..	..	1	..	..
White, Edward	2	2	..	..	1	..	2	..	..	1	..
Wilcot, Jonathan	1	..	..	1	..	3	2	..	1	..	..
Wilder, Aaron	..	..	..	..	1	..	..	..	..	1	..
Wilder, Joseph	2	1	..	1	..	2	2	..	1	..	..
Wilder, Tilly	..	..	..	..	1	..	..	..	..	1	..
Wilkinson, Elijah	1	..	..	1	..	..	..	1	1	1	..
Wilkinson, Oliver	2	..	..	1	..	2	..	..	1	..	..
Wiswall, Livi	2	..	..	1	..	1	1	..	1	..	..
Wiswall, Samuel	..	..	..	1	..	..	..	..	1	..	..
Wiswall, Samuel Jr.	1	2	..	1	..	1	1	3	1	..	..
Wood, John	..	2	1	..	1	2	..	..	1	1	..
Wood, Joshua	..	..	..	..	1	..	..	..	..	1	..
Wood, Joshua Jr.	2	1	..	1	..	..	..	1	1	..	..
Wood, Nathan	..	..	2	..	1	..	..	2	..	1	..
Wood, Thomas	..	1	1	..	1	2	..	..	..	1	..
Woodard, Joel	..	..	..	1	..	..	..	..	1	..	..
Woodard, Jonathan	1	..	..	1	..	2	..	..	1	..	..
Woodard, Nathaniel	..	1	..	1	..	3	..	..	1	..	..
Woodburn, Thomas	..	..	..	1	..	..	..	..	..	..	..
WARDSBORO NORTH DISTRICT											
Albee, Amariah	..	..	1	..	..	..	..	1	..	..	..
Albee, Artemas	1	..	..	1	..	1	..	1	..	..	..
Albee, Barzillai	..	..	..	..	1	..	..	..	..	..	..
Allen, George	..	..	1	..	..	..	..	..	..	..	..
Allen, Ithamar	1	..	1	..	1	1	1	2	..	1	..
Allen, Silvester	1	2	2	..	1	2	..	1	..	1	..
Allen, William	1	..	..	1	..	2	..	..	1	..	..
Barber, Zachariah	1	..	1	1	..	..	..	..	1	1	..
Beals, John	..	..	..	1	..	..	..	1	1	..	..
Bills, Gardner	2	..	..	1	..	..	..	..	1	..	..
Blashfield, James R.	2	..	..	1	..	2	..	..	1	..	..
Bond, Phinehas	2	..	..	1	..	2	..	..	1	..	..
Bradley, Jonathan	1	1	..	1	..	1	2	..	1	..	..
Bradley, William	..	..	..	..	1	..	..	..	..	1	..
Braley, Lemuel	3	3	..	1	..	2	..	..	1	..	..
Brayman, Ezekiel	1	1	..	1	..	3	..	..	1	..	..
Brown, Josiah	..	1	..	..	1	..	..	1	..	1	..
Brown, Silas	1	..	..	1	..	2	..	..	1	..	..
Bryant, Lemuel	..	1	1	..	1	..	1	..	1	..	..
Bullard, David	1	1	..	1	..	4	..	..	1	..	..
Butterfield, Zatter	..	..	..	1	..	..	..	..	..	..	..
Chamberlin, Jacob	..	..	..	..	1	1	2	3	..	1	..
Chapin, Samuel	..	..	1	..	1	..	1	..	..	1	..
Chapin, Zadock	2	..	1	1	..	3	..	..	1	..	..
Choate, Stephen	..	1	..	1	..	1	1	..	1	..	..
Cleaveland, Joseph	..	1	..	..	1	..	..	..	1	1	..
Cleaveland, Peter	..	..	1	..	..	1	..	1	..	..	..
Colvin, Ephraim	4	1	..	1	..	..	..	..	1	..	..
Corbin, Stephen	1	1	..	1	..	1	1	..	1	..	..
Crossett, John	1	2	..	..	1	1	..	..	..	1	..
Crowningshield, Richard	1	..	..	1	..	2	2	..	1	..	..
Cudworth, Samuel	..	..	..	..	..	..	..	..	..	..	..
Cutler, Caleb	2	1	..	1	..	1	..	1	..	..	..
Davis, Paul	3	2	1	1	..	2	1	..	1	..	..
Davis, Samuel	3	..	2	..	1	1	2	1	1	1	..
Dexter, Jonathan	1	1	..	1	..	3	..	..	..	..	..
Dix, Joseph	..	1	1	..	1	2	1	2	..	1	..
Draper, Aaron	..	..	..	1	..	2	3	..	1	..	..
Eaton, ———	..	..	..	..	..	..	..	..	..	..	..
Fairbank, Pearley	2	2	1	1	..	..	..	1	1	..	..
Fay, Asa	2	..	3	..	1	2	1	..	1	..	..
Fisher, Simeon	1	..	1	..	1	..	1	1	..	1	..
Fitts, Nathaniel	3	..	..	..	1	..	..	..	1	1	..

WINDHAM COUNTY—Continued

NAMES OF HEADS OF FAMILIES	FREE WHITE MALES: Under 10 years of age	FREE WHITE MALES: Of 10 and under 16	FREE WHITE MALES: Of 16 and under 26 including heads of families	FREE WHITE MALES: Of 26 and under 45 including heads of families	FREE WHITE MALES: Of 45 and upwards including heads of families	FREE WHITE FEMALES: Under 10 years of age	FREE WHITE FEMALES: Of 10 and under 16	FREE WHITE FEMALES: Of 16 and under 26 including heads of families	FREE WHITE FEMALES: Of 26 and under 45 including heads of families	FREE WHITE FEMALES: Of 45 and upwards including heads of families	All other free persons except Indians not taxed
WARDSBORO NORTH DISTRICT—con.											
Glezen, Bezale R.	2	2	2	..	1	..	1	1	..	1	..
Gould, Nathaniel	1	2	..	1	..	1	..	..	1	..	..
Hall, Joseph	..	..	..	1	..	2	..	..	1	..	..
Hammond, Hindsdell	2	2	..	1	..	3	1	..	1	..	..
Hammond, Samuel	..	..	2	..	1	2	..	..	..	1	..
Hammond, Simeon	..	1	..	1	..	..	..	..	1	..	..
Harris, Daniel	2	..	..	1	..	1	1	..	1	..	..
Harvey, Rufus	2	..	..	1	..	2	..	..	1	..	..
Haskins, Jacob	..	..	..	..	1	3	..	..	1	..	..
Hastings, Francis	1	..	..	1	..	1	..	..	1	..	..
Hastings, Silvanus	..	..	..	1	..	1	..	1	..	..	..
Hayward, Dependence	..	..	1	1	1	2	..	2	..	1	..
Hazeltine, Daniel	3	1	..	1	..	2	..	..	1	..	..
Hiscock, Samuel	1	2	..	..	1	..	..	..	..	1	..
Holbrook, Abner	1	1	1	1	..	1	..	1	1	1	..
Holbrook, Elijah	1	1	..	1	..	..	3	3	..	1	..
Holbrook, Miriam Widow	..	1	1	..	..	..	1	2	..	1	..
Holden, Sartell	1	2	..	..	1	1	1	..	..	1	..
Hunt, Richard	..	2	2	..	1	2	1	..	1	1	..
Jewett, Thomas	2	1	..	1	..	3	..	..	1	..	..
Johnson, David	2	..	..	1	..	..	..	1	1	..	..
Johnson, Nehemiah	..	..	..	..	1	..	..	..	..	1	..
Johnson, Timothy	2	1	..	1	..	2	..	..	1	..	..
Johnson, Ziba	..	..	..	1	..	..	..	..	..	..	..
Jones, Aaron	2	3	1	1	..	4	..	..	1	1	..
Jones, Asa	..	2	..	1	..	3	1	..	1	..	..
Jones, Elias	..	..	1	1	..	1	1	..	1	..	..
Jones, John	..	..	4	1	1	..	..	1	..	1	..
Jones, Jonathan Jr.	..	..	..	1	..	2	..	..	1	..	..
Jones, Levi	1	..	..	1	..	1	..	..	1	..	..
Kellogg, Josiah	..	..	..	..	..	..	..	..	..	..	..
Kelly, James	1	..	..	1	..	2	..	..	1	..	..
Kelly, Samuel	..	2	..	1	..	1	1	..	1	1	..
Kelly, William	1	..	3	..	1	..	1	1	..	1	..
Kenny, Samuel	1	..	..	..	1	1	..	..	..	1	..
Kidder, Ezra	1	..	..	1	..	1	..	1	..	..	..
Kidder, Jedediah	2	1	..	1	..	2	..	..	1	..	..
Kidder, Nathaniel	2	..	..	1	..	4	..	..	1	..	..
Kidder, Richard	1	..	..	1	..	2	..	..	1	..	..
Kidder, Samuel	1	2	..	1	..	3	..	..	1	..	..
Kilburn, Dan	2	..	..	1	..	2	1	..	1	..	..
Knoulton, Miles	4	..	..	1	..	..	1	..	1	..	..
Knoulton, Widow Olive	3	..	..	..	..	2	..	..	1	..	..
Knoulton, William	..	..	1	..	..	1	..	..	1	..	..
Legg, Levi	..	..	1	1	..	..	2	2	1	..	..
Martin, Abraham	2	..	..	1	..	2	..	..	1	..	..
Martin, Matthew	..	1	..	..	1	..	..	1	..	1	..
Morse, Henry	1	..	..	1	..	2	..	..	1	..	..
Morse, Joseph	1	1	2	..	1	..	..	1	1	1	..
Newel, David	..	..	..	1	..	2	..	..	1	..	..
Newel, Jared	1	1	..	1	..	3	..	..	1	..	..
Newel, Livi	1	..	1	1	..	..	1	..	1	..	..
Newel, Phillip	..	1	..	..	1	..	..	..	1	1	..
Newel, Rufus	2	1	..	1	..	..	..	..	1	..	..
Perry, Eli	2	..	..	1	..	2	2	..	1	..	..
Perry, Stephen	1	1	..	1	..	4	1	..	1	..	..
Philips, John	..	..	1	..	..	..	..	..	..	..	..
Philips, Joseph	..	..	..	..	1	..	..	..	..	1	..
Philips, Joseph Jr.	2	1	..	1	..	2	..	..	1	..	..
Philips, Samuel	1	..	..	1	..	2	..	..	1	..	..
Plimpton, Abner	..	..	1	..	1	..	..	1	..	1	..
Plimpton, Abner Jr.	1	..	..	1	..	..	..	..	1	..	..
Plimpton, Amos	..	..	..	1	..	1	..	..	1	..	..
Plimpton, William	2	..	..	1	..	2	..	..	1	..	..
Ramsdell, Farrington	2	..	..	1	..	..	..	..	1	..	..
Ramsdell, John	..	..	2	..	1	..	..	2	..	1	..
Rand, Luke S.	2	..	1	1	..	1	..	..	1	..	..
Rand, Thomas D.	1	..	..	1	..	..	..	1	..	..	..
Rawson, Samuel	1	..	..	1	..	1	..	1	..	..	..
Read, Daniel	2	1	1	1	..	1	..	1	1	..	..
Rice, Ephraim	2	..	..	..	1	2	2	..	1	..	..
Rice, John	2	..	1	1	..	2	1	..	1	..	..
Robbins, Aquilla	1	2	2	..	1	2	..	..	1	..	..
Shepherdson, Amos	..	3	2	1	1	..	..	2	..	1	..
Sherman, Noah	3	1	..	1	..	2	1	1	1	..	..
Simpson, Thomas	2	1	..	1	..	2	2	..	1	..	..
Smith, David	2	1	..	1	..	3	1	1	1	..	..
Smith, John	..	..	1	..	1	..	..	..	1	1	..
Smith, John 2nd	..	2	..	..	1	..	1	..	..	1	..
Smith, Lewis	3	1	1	1	..	1	1	1	..	1	..
Sprague, Jason	..	..	2	..	..	1	..	..	1	..	..
Stacy, John	1	..	..	1	1	2	..	..	1	1	..
Stimson, William	..	..	..	1	..	1	..	1	..	..	..
Taylor, Ebenezer	1	..	1	..	..	1	..	1	..	..	..
Tobey, Job	1	2	..	1	..	3	..	..	1	..	..
Tufts, James Rev.	..	..	..	1	..	..	..	..	..	..	..
Turner, Amasa	..	..	..	1	..	..	..	..	..	..	..
Twichell, Joseph	4	..	..	1	..	..	..	..	1	..	..
Underwood, Asa	..	1	..	1	..	1	..	1	..	2	..
Underwood, Joseph	1	1	..	1	..	..	..	..	..	1	..
Vinten, Ebenezer	1	..	..	1	..	1	..	..	1	..	..
Waight, Silas	2	1	..	1	1	1	..	..	1	..	..
Waight, Thaddeus	1	..	..	..	1	1	..	1	1	..	..
Wakefield, Ebenezer	..	..	1	..	..	1	..	1	..	..	..
Wakefield, Timothy	4	1	..	1	..	2	1	..	1	..	..
Walker, Edward	1	2	1	..	1	1	..	..	1	1	..
Warren, Noah	1	..	..	1	..	2	..	..	1	..	..
Warren, Stephen	1	2	..	..	1	..	1	..	..	1	..
Wheeler, Paul	..	..	..	1	..	..	..	..	..	..	..
Wheelock, Asa	1	1	1	1	..	2	..	..	1	..	..
White, Joseph	..	1	..	..	1	..	..	2	1	1	..
Whitney, John	3	2	..	1	..	2	..	1	1	..	..
Wilder, Abel	..	..	..	..	1	..	..	..	..	1	..
Wilder, Joseph	1	..	..	1	..	3	..	..	1	..	..
Willard, Oliver	2	1	1	1	..	1	1	1	1	..	..
Woodcock, Asahel	..	..	..	1	..	..	..	..	1	..	..
Woodcock, Elkanah	..	..	1	..	1	..	..	..	1	1	..
WARDSBORO SOUTH DISTRICT											
Adams, Abner	..	..	..	1	..	..	..	1	..	..	..
Aldrich, Ebenezer	1	..	..	1	..	2	..	..	1	..	..
Alexander, Daniel	..	..	1	..	..	2	..	..	1	..	..
Alexander, William	1	..	..	1	..	1	..	..	1	..	..
Baldwin, Daniel	..	..	1	..	1	..	..	1	..	1	..
Baldwin, Elijah	2	1	1	1	..	2	..	1	1	..	..
Baldwin, Phillip T.	1	..	..	1	..	2	..	..	1	..	..
Ballou, Stephen	..	..	..	1	..	4	..	1	..	..	..
Baxter, Asa	1	..	..	1	..	2	..	..	1	..	..
Baxter, Nathan	..	..	..	..	1	2	..	2	..	1	..
Bixbee, Darius	2	1	..	1	..	1	1	..	1	..	..
Black, George	2	..	..	1	..	2	1	..	1	..	..
Briggs, Joseph	2	1	1	1	..	1	1	..	1	..	..
Bugbee, William	..	..	1	..	..	..	..	..	..	..	..
Burr, David	1	..	..	1	..	..	1	1	..	..	..
Carpenter, Barlow	..	2	..	..	1	..	..	1	..	1	..
Carpenter, Oliver	1	1	..	..	1	1	1	..	1	..	..
Chamberlin, Joseph	4	3	..	1	..	..	..	..	1	..	..
Cheney, Ebenezer	1	..	..	1	..	2	2	..	1	..	..
Cheney, Enoch	..	..	1	1	..	2	..	..	1	..	..
Chittinden, Reuben	3	1	..	1	..	1	1	..	1	..	..
Clark, Samuel	..	..	..	1	..	..	..	1	..	..	..
Cobb, Nathan	3	1	..	1	..	..	1	..	1	..	..
Crawford, Samuel	1	..	..	1	..	3	..	..	1	..	..
Culver, Aaron	..	..	..	1	..	..	..	1	..	..	..
Culver, Nathan	..	..	..	..	1	..	..	2	..	1	..
Dean, Nathan	..	..	1	..	..	..	..	1	..	..	..
Dean, Reuben	..	1	..	1	..	1	..	..	1	..	..
Dexter, David	2	3	1	1	..	..	..	1	1	..	..
Eames, Gershom	..	..	1	1	..	..	..	..	1	..	..
Eames, Simpson	..	..	1	1	..	..	..	..	1	..	..
Eaton, Abiel	3	..	..	1	..	..	..	1	..	1	..
Ellis, Gamaliel	..	..	1	..	1	..	..	1	1	..	..
Fay, Nehemiah	..	..	..	1	..	1	..	..	1	..	..
Fitch, John	3	..	..	1	1	..	..	..	1	1	..
Fitch, Lemuel	..	..	..	..	1	..	..	1	..	1	..
Fitch, Patten	..	..	1	..	..	1	..	1	..	..	..
Gillett, Timothy	..	..	1	..	1	..	..	2	1	..	..
Goreham, Eli	..	..	2	..	..	..	..	2	1	..	..
Gould, Enos	..	1	..	1	..	..	..	2	..	..	..
Gould, John	1	..	1	..	1	..	..	1	..	1	..
Gragg, William	1	2	1	1	1	1	..	1	..	1	..
Hall, William	4	1	1	..	1	1	1	..	1	..	..
Haskins, William	2	..	..	1	..	2	1	..	1	..	..

WINDHAM COUNTY—Continued

NAMES OF HEADS OF FAMILIES	FREE WHITE MALES					FREE WHITE FEMALES					
	Under 10 years of age	Of 10 and under 16	Of 16 and under 26 including heads of families	Of 26 and under 45 including heads of families	Of 45 and upwards including heads of families.	Under 10 years of age	Of 10 and under 16	Of 16 and under 26 including heads of families	Of 26 and under 45 including heads of families	Of 45 and upwards including heads of families	All other free persons except Indians not taxed
WARDSBORO SOUTH DISTRICT—con.											
Hathaway, Edward	..	..	..	1	..	2	..	1	1	..	..
Hathaway, Zephaniah	2	..	..	1	..	2	..	..	1	..	..
Hayward, John	1	..	1	1	..	1	1	..	1	..	..
Hayward, John 2nd	1	..	..	1	..	2	..	..	1	..	..
Hazeltine, Abner	..	..	..	..	1	..	..	..	..	1	..
Hill, Israel	..	1	..	1	..	3	..	1	1	..	..
Hill, Samuel	1	..	..	1	..	3	1	..	1	..	..
Hodges, Abiathar	1	..	..	1	..	..	1	..	1	..	..
How, Gardiner	5	1	..	1	..	..	..	..	1	..	..
Johnson, Constant	1	..	..	1	..	..	..	..	1	..	..
Johnson, David	1	..	..	..	1	..	..	..	..	1	..
Johnson, Joab	2	..	..	1	..	4	..	..	1	..	..
Johnson, Lemuel	1	..	..	1	..	1	..	..	1	..	..
Johnson, Luther	1	1	..	1	..	3	1	1	1	..	..
Johnson, Silas	2	..	..	1	..	2	1	..	1	..	..
Johnson, Zebediah	4	..	..	1	..	2	..	..	1	..	..
Jones, Abraham	..	..	1	..	1	..	..	2	..	1	..
Jones, Abraham 2nd	..	..	..	1	..	..	..	..	1	..	..
Jones, Bezeliel	..	..	1	..	1	..	..	..	1	1	..
Jones, Eleazer	1	..	..	1	..	2	..	..	1	..	..
Jones, Solomon	1	..	1	..	..	..	..	1	..	..	..
Jones, Whitney	2	..	..	1	..	2	..	..	1	..	..
Kemp, John	..	..	..	1	..	3	1	..	1	..	..
Kemp. Oliver	1	..	..	1	..	3	1	..	1	..	..
Kendall, Joshua	3	..	..	1	..	..	1	2	1	..	..
Knapp, Cyrus	4	..	..	1	..	1	..	..	1	..	..
Lazdell, Isaac	1	1	2	..	1	..	1	1	..	1	..
Lee, John	3	..	..	1	..	3	1	..	1	..	..
Lee, Washington	..	..	1	..	..	..	..	..	..	..	..
Littlefield, Amasa	..	..	..	1	..	..	..	..	..	..	..
Marsh, Abijah	2	..	..	1	..	1	2	..	1	..	..
Marsh, Ebenezer	1	..	..	1	..	..	..	1	..	..	..
Marsh, Jesse	2	1	..	1	..	3	..	..	1	..	..
McDaniels, Thomas	..	2	1	..	1	2	1	1	..	1	..
Moore, Abraham	..	..	1	..	..	3	..	1	..	..	..
Moses, Royall	..	..	1	..	..	..	..	1	..	..	..
Oaks, Silvanus	1	2	..	..	1	1	..	..	..	1	..
Osgood, Lemuel	..	2	..	..	1	..	..	1	..	1	..
Perry, Abner	..	2	2	1	..	..	1	1	1	..	..
Phillips, Asa	..	1	..	1	..	2	..	..	1	..	..
Randall, Thomas	1	..	..	1	..	4	..	..	1	..	..
Rice, David	..	..	1	1	..	..	..	1	..	..	..
Rice, Perez	..	1	1	1	..	..	..	..	1	..	..
Russell, Oliver	1	..	1	..	..	1	..	..	1	..	..
Sears, Ebenezer	1	1	..	..	1	3	1	1	1	..	..
Sears, William	2	..	..	1	..	3	1	..	1	..	..
Sherman, Nathan	4	..	..	1	..	1	..	..	1	..	..
Simonds, Abel	1	..	..	1	..	2	..	..	1	..	..
Sparks, Ebenezer	4	2	1	1	..	..	..	1	1	..	..
Staples, Jacob	2	1	1	..	1	2	1	..	1	..	..
Stearns, Elijah	3	..	..	1	..	..	..	..	1	..	..
Stearns, Eliphaz	..	..	2	..	1	..	..	2	1	1	..
Stearns, Nathaniel	1	1	..	..	1	2	..	1	1	..	..
Strickland, William	1	..	..	1	..	2	3	..	1	..	..
Taft, Samuel	1	..	1	..	..	..	1	1	..	..	..
Thompson, Jonathan	1	..	..	1	..	3	..	..	1	..	..
Ward, David	..	..	1	..	1	..	..	..	..	1	..
Wells, Jonathan	2	..	..	1	1	2	..	..	1	1	..
Western, James	2	3	..	..	1	..	..	..	1	..	..
Wheeler, James	1	1	1	1	..	2	1	..	1	..	..
Wheeler, Josiah	3	..	..	1	..	1	..	..	1	..	..
White, Henry	..	..	1	..	..	..	..	..	1	..	..
White, Joseph	..	..	..	1	..	..	..	..	1	..	..
Wislow, Elisha	..	..	1	..	..	..	..	..	..	..	..
Wood, Timothy	2	1	2	..	1	..	1	..	1	..	..
Woods, Aaron	..	..	..	1	..	..	..	1	..	1	..
Woods, Phinehas	1	..	..	1	..	..	..	..	1	..	..
Works, Joseph	..	..	..	1	..	3	..	..	1	..	..
Wright, Silas	1	1	1	..	1	1	..	1	1	..	1
WESTMINSTER											
Abbot, David	..	..	..	..	1	..	1	..	..	1	..
Albee, Jacob	..	..	2	2	1	1	1	1	2	1	..
Aldrich, Simeon	1	..	1	..	..	1	1	1	..	..	..
Archer, Widow	1	1	..	..	..	..	..	..	..	1	..
Arnold, Seth	1	2	..	..	1	3	..	..	1	..	..
Arvin, Joseph	1	1	1	..	1	..	..	3	1	1	..
Attwater, Reuben	..	1	1	1	..	1	..	..	1	..	1
WESTMINSTER—con.											
Averell, Asa	..	1	1	..	1	..	..	3	..	1	..
Averell, John	..	..	3	..	1	..	2	..	..	1	..
Averell, Obed	1	1	..	1	..	4	1	..	1	..	..
Averell, Thomas	1	1	1	..	1	2	1	2	..	1	..
Avery, Samuel	..	..	3	..	1	..	2	1	..	1	1
Baldwin, Thomas	2	1	2	..	1	2	2	..	1	..	..
Baldwin, Thomas	2	1	1	1	..	2	2	..	1	..	..
Ball, Jene	1	..	..	1	..	1	..	..	1	..	..
Ballou, Eliel	1	..	..	1	..	2	..	..	1	..	..
Bartlett, Moses	..	..	1	..	1	..	..	1	..	1	..
Bates, Jabez	1	..	2	..	1	..	..	..	3	..	..
Bayley, Samuel	2	..	..	1	..	..	2	..	1	..	..
Beamos, John	..	..	1	..	1	..	3	..	..	1	..
Beckwith, Bethial	..	..	..	1	..	..	2	..	1	..	..
Berry, Elisha	1	1	..	1	..	4	..	..	1	..	..
Blackman, Charles	1	1	..	1	..	..	1	..	1	..	..
Bowls, John	..	..	..	1	..	2	..	1	..	..	..
Bradley, Stephen R.	1	1	4	..	1	3	..	2	2	..	..
Bradley, Thaddeus	2	1	..	1	..	..	2	..	1	..	..
Brailey, John	..	1	2	..	1	..	..	1	..	1	..
Braley, John	1	..	..	2	..	1	..	..	1	..	..
Briggs, Amasa	..	..	..	1	..	..	..	..	1	..	..
Briggs, Nathaniel	4	1	..	1	..	..	..	..	1	..	..
Briggs, Silas	..	..	1	..	1	..	..	..	..	1	..
Brown, Barron	1	1	..	..	1	1	1	1	..	1	..
Bullock, Nathaniel	2	..	..	1	..	1	..	..	1	..	..
Bundy, Abel	1	..	..	1	..	1	..	1	..	..	..
Bundy, James	..	..	1	..	1	..	..	1	..	1	..
Burk, Eli	1	..	..	1	..	1	..	..	1	..	..
Burk, Elijah	1	..	..	1	..	1	..	1	..	..	..
Burk, Jesse	..	1	..	1	1	..	..	..	..	1	..
Burk, Jesse Jr.	1	..	..	1	..	..	..	..	1	..	..
Burk, Silas	1	1	2	..	1	..	1	1	..	1	..
Burk, Simeon	..	..	..	1	..	1	..	..	1	..	..
Burt, Benjamin	..	..	..	..	1	..	..	..	..	1	..
Burt, Leonard	3	..	..	1	..	1	..	..	..	..	..
Campbell, Edward R.	1	2	..	2	..	1	1	..	1	..	1
Carpenter, Abel	1	1	3	..	1	2	..	4	..	2	..
Carpenter, Abuel	2	2	2	..	1	1	..	3	..	1	..
Chaffe, William Jr.	1	..	1	..	..	1	..	1	..	..	..
Chaffee, Atherton	1	..	2	1	..	1	..	..	1	..	..
Chaffee, Otis	3	2	..	1	..	1	1	..	1	..	..
Chaffee, Squire	..	..	..	1	..	5	..	..	1	..	..
Chamberlin, Calvin	1	..	..	1	..	1	..	1	..	..	..
Chitman, Samuel	4	..	1	1	..	..	..	..	1	..	..
Clapp, William	..	..	1	..	1	..	..	..	..	1	..
Clark, Abraham	..	..	..	1	..	..	..	1	..	..	..
Clark, Barnabas	..	1	1	..	1	..	..	1	..	1	..
Clark, Daniel	1	..	..	1	..	..	..	..	1	..	..
Clark, Joshua	1	..	1	..	..	..	..	1	..	..	..
Clark, Perez	3	..	..	1	..	1	..	1	..	..	..
Clark, Scotto	1	..	1	..	1	..	2	..	..	1	..
Clark, Seth	1	2	2	..	1	..	1	..	..	1	..
Codding, Francis	..	..	..	1	..	..	..	..	1	..	..
Cole, Aaron	1	..	..	1	..	1	1	..	1	..	..
Cole, Samuel	..	..	..	2	..	..	..	1	..	..	..
Cone, Ezra T.	..	..	..	1	..	..	..	..	1	..	..
Cone, Joshua	5	..	..	1	..	1	1	..	1	..	..
Cone, Samuel	1	2	..	..	1	..	1	..	..	1	..
Cone, Thomas	5	2	..	1	..	1	..	..	1	..	..
Cone, William	2	1	..	1	..	3	..	..	1	..	..
Cotton, Charles	..	..	..	..	1	..	..	..	..	1	..
Cotton, Charles Jr.	1	..	..	1	..	1	1	..	1	..	..
Craige, Thomas	1	1	..	1	..	2	..	1	1	..	..
Crawford, Robert	..	..	..	..	1	..	..	..	..	1	..
Crook, James	1	..	..	1	..	..	..	..	1	..	..
Crook, Robert	..	..	2	..	1	1	1	3	..	1	..
Crook, William	..	..	1	..	1	..	..	..	..	1	..
Crowel, Livi	2	1	..	1	..	2	..	..	1	..	..
Cutler, William B.	..	..	..	1	..	..	..	1	..	..	..
Davenport, William	2	..	..	1	..	3	..	..	1	..	..
Davis, Kitterridge	1	3	1	1	..	3	1	1	1	..	..
Demming, Josiah	..	..	1	..	..	..	..	..	..	..	..
Dickerson, Azariah	..	..	2	..	1	..	..	..	..	1	..
Dickerson, Job	..	..	1	..	1	2	2	1	..	1	..
Dile, James	..	..	..	1	..	..	..	..	..	..	..
Dunham, Calvin	2	..	..	1	..	1	..	..	1	..	..
Eaton, Asa	..	1	2	..	1	1	..	1	..	1	..
Eaton, Maverick	1	1	..	..	1	2	..	..	1	..	..
Edgel, Ephraim	1	..	..	1	..	3	..	..	1	..	..
Edgel, Widow	..	1	1	..	..	..	..	2	..	1	..
Emerson, Reuben Rev.	..	..	..	..	1	..	1	..	1	..	..
Enos, Joseph	..	..	1	..	..	..	..	..	..	..	..

WINDHAM COUNTY—Continued

NAMES OF HEADS OF FAMILIES	FREE WHITE MALES					FREE WHITE FEMALES					
	Under 10 years of age	Of 10 and under 16	Of 16 and under 26 including heads of families	Of 26 and under 45 including heads of families	Of 45 and upwards including heads of families.	Under 10 years of age	Of 10 and under 16	Of 16 and under 26 including heads of families	Of 26 and under 45 including heads of families	Of 45 and upwards including heads of families.	All other free persons except Indians not taxed
WESTMINSTER—con.											
Fairbank, Ephraim	2	..	3	..	1	2	2	1	1	..	..
Fairbrother, Richard	3	1	..	1	..	..	1	..	1	..	..
Farewell, Samuel	3	..	..	1	..	..	..	..	1	1	..
Fuller, Caleb	1	1	..	1	..	3	..	..	1	2	..
Garnsey, Amos	2	1	..	1	..	2	..	..	1	..	..
Garnsey, Oliver	..	2	..	..	1	1	1	1	..	1	..
Gerry, Benjamin	..	1	..	1	..	2	..	..	1	..	..
Gerry, Edward	..	1	..	..	1	..	..	..	..	1	..
Gerry, Edward Jr.	..	..	..	..	1	..	..	..	..	..	..
Gerry, John	1	..	..	1	..	..	1	..	1	..	..
Gibbs, Nathaniel	..	..	..	..	1	..	..	2	..	1	..
Gibbs, Rufus	2	..	..	1	..	..	1	..	1	..	..
Gilbert, David	..	..	..	..	1	..	..	1	1	1	..
Gilson, Jacob	..	1	1	..	1	1	2	1	..	1	..
Gilson, Michal	1	..	..	..	1	..	..	..	..	2	..
Gilson, Zachariah	..	..	1	..	1	1	..	2	..	2	..
Goodell, Abiel	..	1	2	..	1	..	1	..	..	1	..
Goodell, Abner	..	..	1	..	..	..	..	..	..	..	..
Goodell, Amos	1	..	1	1	..	1	..	1	1	..	..
Goodell, Asahel	2	..	..	1	..	3	2	..	1	1	..
Goodell, Edward	1	2	1	..	1	..	..	3	..	1	..
Goodell, Elias	..	..	..	..	1	..	1	..	..	1	..
Goodell, Levi	1	..	..	1	..	1	..	1	..	..	..
Goodell, Moses	..	1	2	..	1	..	..	1	..	2	..
Goodhue, Eleazer	1	..	1	1	..	3	..	1	1	..	..
Goodrich, Alpheus	..	..	1	..	..	..	..	1	..	..	..
Goodrich, Benjamin	1	1	1	..	1	2	1	..	1	..	..
Goreham, Isaac	1	..	1	..	..	..	..	1	..	..	..
Goreham, Matthias	1	2	1	..	1	..	1	1	..	1	..
Gould, Aaron	..	..	..	1	..	..	..	..	1	..	..
Gould, Jonathan	2	..	..	..	1	1	..	..	1	1	..
Gould, Jonathan	2	..	..	1	..	3	..	..	1	..	..
Gould, Nathaniel	..	1	2	..	1	..	..	1	..	1	..
Gould, Seth	1	..	..	1	..	2	1	1	1	..	..
Grout, John	4	1	..	1	..	1	2	..	1	..	..
Hadley, Peter	..	..	1	..	1	1	..	1	1	..	..
Hall, Atherton	..	..	1	..	1	..	2	2	..	1	..
Hall, Atherton Jr.	1	..	..	1	..	1	..	..	1	..	..
Hall, Lott	..	2	1	..	1	1	1	..	1	..	..
Hall, Peter	3	..	..	1	..	..	..	1	..	..	..
Hall, Zachius	1	3	..	..	1	..	..	..	..	1	..
Hallet, Gideon	2	..	1	1	..	..	..	..	1	..	..
Hamlin, Joseph	1	..	1	..	1	..	..	2	1	1	..
Hamlin, Joseph Jr.	..	..	..	1	..	2	..	..	1	..	..
Hammond, Simpson	3	2	1	..	1	..	1	3	..	1	..
Harlow, Eleazer	..	1	1	1	1	..	2	1	1	1	..
Harlow, Levi	1	..	..	1	..	2	..	1	..	..	..
Hatch, Isaiah	1	1	..	..	1	..	..	..	..	1	..
Heaton, David	..	1	1	..	1	..	..	..	..	1	..
Hickman, John F.	1	1	..	1	..	..	..	1	1	..	..
Hitchcock, Aaron	1	1	..	1	..	1	1	..	1	..	..
Hitchcock, Eldad	..	3	..	..	1	1	..	2	..	1	..
Hitchcock, Elisha	3	2	3	..	1	1	1	1	1	..	..
Hitchcock, Heli	1	2	..	..	1	2	1	..	1	..	..
Hitchcock, Zaddock	..	..	..	1	..	3	..	..	1	..	..
Hodgskins, John	1	..	..	1	..	2	..	..	1	..	..
Holden, Abraham	1	..	..	1	..	3	..	..	1	..	..
Holden, Charles	..	1	1	..	1	3	..	1	1	..	..
Holden, Francis	3	2	1	..	1	1	2	1	1	..	..
Holden, John	1	..	..	1	..	1	..	..	1	..	..
Holden, Nathan	..	..	1	..	..	2	..	1	..	1	..
Holden, Stephen	..	..	2	..	1	..	2	3	..	1	..
Holton, Joel	..	1	2	2	1	1	1	1	..	1	..
Holton, Widow	..	1	1	1	..	..	..	1	..	1	..
Holton, William	1	..	..	1	..	3	..	..	1	..	..
Hooker, Azel	1	2	..	..	1	..	2	..	..	1	..
Houghton, Jonathan	2	1	1	1	..	3	1	1	1	..	..
Howard, Theophiles	3	1	1	1	..	2	1	..	1	..	..
Ide, Ichabod	1	1	1	1	..	1	1	1	1	..	..
Ide, Israel	3	1	1	1	..	2	2	2	1	..	..
Ide, James	..	2	1	1	..	3	1	..	1	..	..
Ide, Jesse	1	..	1	1	..	1	2	..	1	1	..
Johnson, Thomas	3	1	..	1	..	1	..	..	1	..	..
Kittenridge, Nathaniel	..	..	..	..	1	..	..	..	..	..	..
Kittenridge, Nathaniel Jr.	1	3	1	1	..	..	1	..	1	..	..
Lane, Jonathan	1	..	..	1	..	..	..	..	..	..	..
Lippingwell, Reuben	..	..	..	..	1	..	..	..	..	1	..
Lippingwell, Reuben Jr.	1	1	..	1	..	1	1	..	1	..	..
Locke, John Jr.	1	..	..	1	..	3	..	..	1	..	..
Lovejoy, Benjamin	..	..	1	..	1	..	1	1	..	1	..
WESTMINSTER—con.											
Lovejoy, John	..	..	1	1	..	..	..	..	1	..	..
Lovejoy, Joseph	..	..	1	..	..	1	..	1	..	..	..
Lovejoy, Samuel	..	..	1	1	..	1	..	1	1	..	..
Mann, Samuel	1	..	1	..	..	2	..	1	..	..	..
Martin, ———	..	..	..	..	1	..	..	..	2	1	..
Martin, William	1	..	3	..	1	5	3	2	1	..	..
Mason, Isaac	2	..	..	1	..	2	1	..	1	1	..
Mason, Samuel	1	..	..	1	..	2	..	1	..	..	..
Mather, William	1	..	1	..	..	..	..	1	..	..	..
May, Eleazer	1	..	..	1	..	1	..	2	..	..	1
McKinnister, Paul	2	..	..	1	..	1	1	..	1	..	..
McNiel, Nehemiah	1	..	..	1	..	..	..	2	1	..	..
Miller, John	..	..	..	..	1	..	..	..	..	1	..
Miller, Robert	2	2	..	..	1	2	2	1	1	..	..
Miller, Veniah	4	1	..	1	..	1	1	..	1	..	..
Morse, Amos	2	2	..	1	..	..	1	..	1	..	..
Morse, John	..	1	2	..	1	..	1	..	1	..	..
Moultrip, Hezekiah	1	..	1	..	..	..	..	1	..	..	..
Moultrip, Stephen	2	..	..	1	..	2	..	1	..	1	..
Newton, Alexander	..	..	..	..	1	..	..	..	..	..	..
Newton, Daniel	..	1	1	..	1	..	..	1	..	1	..
Newton, Hubbard	3	..	..	1	..	3	..	..	1	1	..
Norcrass, Noah	..	..	..	1	..	3	..	1	1	..	..
Norman, Thomas	2	..	2	..	1	..	1	1	1	..	..
Norton, Cyrus	1	..	..	1	..	2	..	..	1	..	..
Norton, John	..	1	2	..	1	..	..	3	1	1	..
Norton, John Jr.	2	..	..	1	..	..	1	..	1	..	..
Nutting, Abraham	2	..	1	1	..	..	..	..	1	..	..
Page, Widow	1	..	..	..	..	3	..	..	1	..	..
Paine, Jabez	..	..	1	1	..	..	..	1	1	..	..
Paine, Miller	..	..	1	..	1	1	2	1	..	2	..
Parker, Obediah	2	..	1	1	..	2	..	..	1	..	..
Parker, Silvester	1	1	..	1	..	..	1	1	..	..	..
Parmenter, Joseph	1	1	..	..	1	3	1	2	1	..	..
Parsons, Benjamin	1	1	..	..	1	3	1	1	1	..	..
Paul, John	2	..	4	..	1	2	2	..	1	..	..
Peck, Ariel	1	1	..	1	..	..	..	1	1	..	..
Peck, Levi	1	2	..	1	..	1	..	..	1	..	..
Penniman, Jabez	1	2	..	1	..	1	..	1	2	..	..
Perkins, Nehemiah	3	..	..	1	..	1	1	..	1	..	..
Perry, Jabez	..	1	..	..	1	..	..	1	..	1	..
Perry, John	1	..	..	1	..	..	..	..	1	..	..
Perry, Nusun	..	..	1	..	..	..	..	1	..	1	..
Perry, William	1	..	..	1	..	..	..	..	1	..	..
Pettingill, Asa	2	..	..	1	..	..	..	..	1	..	..
Petty, Aaron	..	..	..	1	..	..	..	..	..	..	..
Phillips, Zebulon	2	3	1	1	..	2	..	1	1	..	..
Phippen, Attwater	2	1	1	1	..	3	1	..	1	..	..
Phippen, Joseph	2	..	3	..	1	2	4	..	1	1	..
Phippen, Samuel	2	1	..	..	2	2	1	..	1	..	..
Pierce, Charles	1	2	..	1	..	1	..	1	1	..	..
Pierce, John	2	..	1	1	..	2	..	2	..	..	..
Pierce, Reuben	2	..	1	1	..	2	..	1	1	..	..
Pigsley, Paul	1	3	..	1	..	2	..	1	1	..	..
Powers, Asa	5	..	..	1	..	..	..	..	1	..	..
Powers, Asa	4	1	..	1	..	..	..	..	1	..	..
Powers, Manassah	2	1	..	..	1	3	1	2	1	..	..
Powers, Nathaniel	..	..	..	1	..	1	..	1	..	..	..
Powers, Stephen	..	..	1	..	..	2	..	1	..	2	..
Pratt, Samuel	3	2	1	1	..	2	1	..	1	..	..
Priest, John	..	1	..	..	1	..	1	1	..	1	..
Priest, Levi	..	..	..	1	..	2	..	1	..	..	..
Rand, Robert	2	1	..	1	1	2	3	2	1	..	..
Ranny, Benjamin	1	1	..	1	..	2	..	1	1	..	..
Ranny, Elijah	..	..	..	..	1	1	..	..	..	1	..
Ranny, Elijah Jr.	2	..	1	1	..	..	1	1	1	..	..
Ranny, Ephraim	..	..	..	..	2	..	..	1	..	1	..
Ranny, Ephraim Jr.	2	1	1	..	1	..	1	..	1	..	..
Ranny, Ephraim 3rd	..	..	1	..	..	..	..	1	..	..	..
Ranny, Joel	1	1	..	1	..	..	..	..	1	..	..
Ranny, Joseph	..	..	2	..	..	..	..	1	..	..	..
Ranny, Phebe Widow	1	..	..	..	..	..	..	..	1	..	..
Ranny, William	1	1	1	..	2	2	1	1	1	..	..
Reed, James	1	..	..	1	..	2	..	1	..	..	..
Reed, John	1	1	..	1	..	..	..	..	1	1	..
Reed, Peter	1	..	..	1	..	4	1	..	1	..	..
Reed, Seth	1	2	1	2	..	..	..	1	..	1	..
Rice, Charles	..	1	..	1	..	..	1	1	1	..	..
Richards, Mark	..	..	1	1	..	..	3	3	..	1	1
Richardson, Daniel	..	1	..	1	..	1	1	1	..	..	..
Richardson, James	1	1	..	..	1	1	1	1	1	1	..
Richardson, Jonathan	..	..	..	1	..	2	..	..	1	..	..
Richardson, Nathaniel	1	..	1	..	..	1	..	1	..	..	..

WINDHAM COUNTY—Continued

NAMES OF HEADS OF FAMILIES	FREE WHITE MALES: Under 10 years of age	FREE WHITE MALES: Of 10 and under 16	FREE WHITE MALES: Of 16 and under 26 including heads of families	FREE WHITE MALES: Of 26 and under 45 including heads of families	FREE WHITE MALES: Of 45 and upwards including heads of families	FREE WHITE FEMALES: Under 10 years of age	FREE WHITE FEMALES: Of 10 and under 16	FREE WHITE FEMALES: Of 16 and under 26 including heads of families	FREE WHITE FEMALES: Of 26 and under 45 including heads of families	FREE WHITE FEMALES: Of 45 and upwards including heads of families	All other free persons except Indians not taxed
WESTMINSTER—con.											
Robinson, Nathaniel	..	..	..	..	1	1	..	..	..	1	..
Robinson, Noah	1	1	2	1	..	1	..	1	1	1	..
Robinson, Reuben	..	2	1	..	1	1	1	2	1	..	..
Robinson, Titus	..	..	..	..	1	..	1	..	..	1	..
Sage, Silvester Rev.	..	..	..	1	..	2	..	..	1	..	1
Sanderson, Hezekiah	..	2	..	..	1	..	1	..	1	1	..
Sawtell, Benjamin	..	3	..	1	..	5	..	..	1	1	..
Sessions, John	..	1	..	1	1	..	..	..	1	1	..
Shipman, Abraham	1	1	1	..	1	..	..	1	..	1	..
Shipman, Abraham Jr.	3	..	..	1	..	..	..	..	1	..	..
Shipman, Edmund	..	1	..	..	1	..	..	1	..	1	..
Shipman, William	3	..	..	1	..	2	..	..	1	..	..
Sickley, John	..	..	1	..	..	..	..	1	..	..	..
Skuylor, Thomas W.	..	..	..	..	..	..	..	..	..	..	5
Smith, Benjamin	..	..	1	..	..	..	..	..	..	..	..
Smith, Benjamin	..	1	3	..	2	1	2	..	1	..	..
Smith, Darius	..	..	1	..	..	..	..	1	..	..	..
Smith, Nathaniel	..	..	1	..	..	..	..	..	..	..	..
Soper, Amasa	..	1	..	..	1	..	..	2	..	1	..
Soper, Charles	..	..	1	..	..	..	..	1	..	..	..
Spencer, Ephraim	..	2	..	..	1	..	1	1	1	..	..
Spencer, Ephraim Jr.	1	..	..	1	..	..	..	1	..	..	..
Spooner, Alfred	..	..	1	..	..	..	..	..	..	..	..
Spooner, Eliakim	..	1	1	..	1	..	..	2	..	1	..
Steward, John L.	..	..	..	..	1	..	..	..	..	1	..
Stiles, David	..	1	..	1	1	1	1	1	..	1	..
Stoddard, Ezra	1	..	1	..	..	1	..	1	..	..	..
Stoddard, John	1	1	..	1	..	2	1	1	1	..	..
Stoddard, Joshua	..	..	1	..	1	1	..	1	..	2	..
Stoddard, Joshua Jr.	2	1	1	1	..	2	..	1	..	..	..
Stone, Benjamin	1	..	..	1	..	..	1	..	..	1	..
Thomas, Joseph	2	..	..	1	1	2	1	..	1	1	..
Titcomb, Moses	..	1	..	..	1	..	..	..	..	1	..
Totman, John	2	..	..	1	..	1	..	..	1	..	..
Totman, Thomas	..	..	1	..	..	..	..	..	..	1	..
Tower, Benjamin	3	1	..	1	..	2	1	1	1	..	..
Tower, Benjamin T.	1	..	1	..	..	..	1	..	1	..	..
Tower, Linde	2	..	..	1	..	2	..	..	1	..	..
Tutthill, John	..	1	3	..	1	..	1	..	..	1	..
Tutthill, Samuel	3	..	..	1	..	3	..	..	1	..	..
Upham, James	2	1	..	1	..	..	..	..	1	..	1
Wales, Aaron	2	..	2	1	..	1	..	1	1	..	..
Wales, Samuel	1	1	..	1	..	2	..	..	1	..	..
Wall, Patrick	..	..	1	..	1	..	..	..	1	1	..
Warner, Gideon	..	..	..	1	..	..	1	1	..	..	..
Washburn, Amasa	..	1	..	1	..	3	..	..	1	..	..
Washburn, Asahel	1	..	..	1	..	2	..	..	1	..	..
Washburn, Joseph	..	..	1	..	1	..	..	..	..	1	..
Washburn, Nathaniel W.	1	..	1	..	..	..	..	..	1	..	..
Whitney, Benjamin	1	2	1	..	1	1	..	1	..	1	..
Wilber, ———	..	..	1	..	1	2	..	1	..	..	..
Wilder, Levi	1	..	..	1	..	1	..	1	..	..	..
Wilder, William	..	..	..	..	1	..	..	1	..	1	..
Wilder, William Jr.	..	..	..	..	1	..	..	1	..	1	..
Willard, Billy	1	1	..	..	1	1	1	1	1	..	..
Willard, Joseph	1	1	..	..	1	1	1	1	1	..	..
Willard, Lynde	1	2	..	1	..	2	..	1	..	1	..
Willcox, Ephraim	..	..	3	..	1	..	..	..	1	1	..
Willcox, Jonathan	1	..	1	1	..	3	2	..	1	..	..
Willcox, Waitstill	3	..	..	1	..	..	1	..	1	..	..
Wills, David	2	1	..	1	..	1	..	..	..	..	..
Witt, Thomas	2	..	2	1	..	3	..	..	2	..	..
Witt, Wainwright	1	1	2	..	..	1	..	2	..	..	..
Woolley, Augustus	..	1	..	1	..	4	..	..	1	..	..
Woolley, Nathan	..	..	1	..	1	1	1	..	..	1	..
Wright, Asaph	..	..	..	1	..	..	..	..	1	..	..
Wright, Azariah	..	..	..	..	1	..	..	..	..	..	..
Wright, Azariah Jr.	1	..	..	1	..	3	..	..	1	..	..
Wright, Caleb	1	..	..	1	..	2	..	..	1	..	..
Wright, Elihu	..	..	1	..	..	1	..	1	..	..	..
Wright, Joseph	..	..	..	1	..	2	..	..	1	..	..
Wright, Medad	..	1	3	1	1	..	..	2	1	1	..
Wright, Rufus	..	..	..	1	..	..	..	..	..	..	..
Wright, Salmon	1	..	..	1	..	1	..	1	..	..	..
Wyman, Widow	..	..	..	..	..	..	..	1	..	1	..
WHITINGHAM											
Aldrich, James	1	..	..	1	..	2	..	..	1	..	..
Allen, John	2	..	..	1	..	2	..	..	1	..	..
Angel, John B.	..	..	2	1	..	2	..	1	..	..	..
Atherton, Asahel	..	1	1	..	1	1	1	..	..	1	..
WHITINGHAM—con.											
Bartlett, Widow E.	..	1	1	..	..	..	..	..	..	1	..
Beebee, Guy	..	1	..	1	..	2	..	..	1	..	..
Bemis, Edmund	2	2	1	..	1	1	1	1	..	1	..
Blanchard, Elisha	3	1	1	..	1	2	..	1	..	1	..
Blodget, Benjamin	..	1	..	1	1	..	..	2	2	1	..
Blodget, John	..	..	..	1	..	1	..	1	..	..	..
Blodget, Reuben	..	..	..	1	..	1	..	..	1	..	..
Blodget, Thomas	..	..	..	..	1	..	1	..	1	1	..
Bratton, Robert	..	..	..	2	1	..	..	..	1	1	..
Briggs, Jesse	1	..	1	..	1	..	..	..	..	1	..
Briggs, Otis	1	..	1	..	..	..	..	..	1	..	..
Brooks, Thaddeus	1	1	2	1	..	..	..	..	1	..	..
Brown, Amos	..	..	..	1	..	..	..	..	..	..	..
Brown, Asa	3	1	1	1	..	..	1	..	1	..	..
Brown, John	1	..	1	1	..	1	..	..	1	..	..
Brown, Jonas	1	..	..	1	..	2	..	..	1	..	..
Brown, Joseph	2	..	..	1	..	2	..	..	1	..	..
Brown, Josiah	2	..	..	1	..	..	..	..	1	..	..
Brown, Reuben	1	..	..	1	..	..	..	..	1	..	..
Bullock, Joel	1	..	..	1	..	..	..	1	..	..	..
Bullock, Widow D.	1	..	2	..	..	1	..	..	..	1	..
Carley, Jonathan	3	1	..	1	1	1	..	..	1	1	..
Carnigie, Andrew	..	1	1	1	..	..	1	..	1	..	..
Carpenter, Samuel	..	..	1	..	..	..	..	1	..	..	..
Chase, Abraham	2	..	..	1	..	..	..	..	1	..	..
Chase, Isaac	1	..	..	1	..	1	..	1	..	..	..
Clark, William	1	1	1	..	1	..	..	1	..	1	..
Coleman, Joseph	..	..	..	..	1	..	..	..	..	..	..
Coleman, Joshua	1	2	1	..	1	..	1	2	1	..	..
Conant, Levi	..	2	..	1	..	2	1	..	1	..	..
Cook, Benjamin	1	..	1	..	1	..	..	..	..	1	..
Cooley, Asa	1	..	..	1	..	3	..	..	1	..	..
Cooley, Barns	..	2	..	..	1	1	..	..	1	..	..
Cooley, John	1	..	..	1	..	1	..	..	1	..	..
Corbett, John	1	..	..	1	..	2	..	..	1	..	..
Corbett, Moses	1	..	..	1	..	2	..	..	1	..	..
Curtis, Asa	1	..	..	1	..	..	1	1	..	..	..
Curtis, Moses	..	1	..	1	..	..	1	..	1	..	..
Curtis, Samuel	1	..	1	..	1	1	1	2	..	1	..
Dalrymple, Andrew	..	2	..	..	1	..	..	..	..	1	..
Dalrymple, John S.	1	1	1	..	1	..	1	..	..	1	..
Davis, John	1	..	..	1	..	3	..	..	1	..	..
Davis, Nathaniel	3	2	..	1	..	2	3	..	1	..	..
Day, Samuel	..	1	2	..	1	1	2	1	..	1	..
Dix, Jonathan	3	1	1	..	1	2	1	..	1	..	..
Easton, Bildad	..	..	2	1	..	..	1	1	..	1	..
Emes, David	4	..	..	1	..	2	..	..	1	..	..
Emes, Walter	1	..	..	1	..	2	..	..	1	..	..
Fairbank, Asa	1	..	1	..	..	..	..	1	..	..	..
Fairbank, Jonathan	1	..	..	1	..	3	..	..	1	..	..
Folton, Robert	..	..	..	1	..	..	..	1	..	..	..
Foster, Jabez	..	2	2	..	1	..	..	..	..	1	..
Fuller, Abner	2	..	..	1	..	2	..	..	1	..	..
Fuller, Calvin	2	..	..	..	1	3	2	..	1	..	..
Fuller, Isaac	2	..	4	..	1	..	1	..	..	1	..
Fuller, William 1st	..	1	..	..	1	..	..	..	..	1	..
Fuller, William 2nd	2	2	..	1	..	1	1	..	1	..	..
Gains, James	..	1	1	..	1	..	..	3	..	1	..
Gates, Jonathan	2	2	1	..	1	2	..	..	..	1	..
Gault, Alexander	1	..	..	1	..	3	1	..	1	..	..
Glass, James	1	1	1	..	1	1	1	1	..	1	..
Glass, Rufus	3	..	..	1	..	..	..	..	2	..	..
Goodenough, Benjamin	..	..	2	..	1	1	..	..	..	1	..
Goodenough, Luke	1	..	..	1	..	2	..	..	1	..	..
Grant, Isaac	2	1	..	1	..	1	..	..	1	..	..
Green, Daniel	..	..	..	1	..	2	..	1	..	..	..
Green, Ira	..	1	..	..	1	..	..	..	..	1	..
Green, Nathan	3	1	..	..	1	2	2	1	1	..	..
Griffin, Viets	1	..	..	1	..	2	..	1	..	..	..
Guild, Nathaniel	3	..	..	1	..	..	..	..	1	..	..
Gustin, Daniel W.	2	..	..	1	..	3	..	..	1	..	..
Hall, Baxter	3	2	2	1	..	1	..	1	1	..	..
Hammond, Joseph	..	1	..	1	..	1	..	..	2	..	..
Higgins, Solomon	1	1	..	1	..	3	1	..	1	..	..
Hill, Moses	2	..	..	1	..	3	..	..	1	1	..
Hosley, David	1	1	4	..	1	1	1	..	..	1	..
Howard, John	..	..	1	..	..	1	..	1	..	..	..
Hull, Jesse	1	1	..	1	..	..	..	1	..	..	..
Jackson, Jones	..	2	..	..	1	..	..	..	..	1	..
Jewell, Benjamin	2	..	..	1	..	2	..	..	1	..	..
Jones, Giles	2	1	..	1	..	2	..	..	1	..	..

WINDHAM COUNTY—Continued

NAMES OF HEADS OF FAMILIES	FREE WHITE MALES					FREE WHITE FEMALES					All other free persons except Indians not taxed
	Under 10 years of age	Of 10 and under 16	Of 16 and under 26 including heads of families	Of 26 and under 45 including heads of families	Of 45 and upwards including heads of families.	Under 10 years of age	Of 10 and under 16	Of 16 and under 26 including heads of families	Of 26 and under 45 including heads of families	Of 45 and upwards including heads of families	
WHITINGHAM—con.											
Lake, Abner	2	..	..	1	..	2	..	..	1	..	..
Lamb, David	..	..	..	..	1	..	..	1	..	1	..
Lamb, Enos	1	..	..	1	..	2	..	..	1	..	..
Lamphere, Chandler	1	..	..	1	..	2	..	..	1	..	..
Lamphere, Reuben	..	..	..	1	..	..	..	..	1	1	..
Lee, Samuel	..	..	..	..	1	1	..	..	..	1	..
Lee, Samuel Jr.	1	..	..	1	..	..	..	1	..	..	..
Long, David	2	..	1	..	..	..	..	1	..	..	..
Lovett, Samuel	..	..	..	..	1	..	..	1	..	1	..
Lyon, Joseph	1	..	..	1	1	2	..	1	..	..	..
Marley, Moses	..	..	..	1	..	3	..	..	1	..	..
McKnight, John	1	..	..	1	..	1	..	..	1	1	..
Moore, Rufus	3	1	..	1	..	..	1	..	1	..	..
Moseley, Joseph	..	2	..	1	..	2	..	1	1	..	..
Moseley, Samuel	..	..	1	..	..	..	..	..	..	1	..
Murdock, Caleb	1	..	..	1	..	..	1	..	1	..	..
Murdock, Hezekiah	1	..	1	..	..	..	..	1	..	..	..
Nelson, John	..	..	1	..	1	1	..	1	1	..	..
Newell, Joshua	1	..	..	1	..	3	..	1	..	..	..
Nye, Jonathan	..	..	1	..	1	1	..	..	..	1	..
Nye, Jonathan Jr.	2	..	..	1	..	1	..	..	1	..	..
Olden, Joseph	1	1	..	1	..	3	..	..	1	..	..
Parker, Samuel	1	1	..	1	..	..	1	..	1	..	..
Peck, Nathaniel	2	..	..	1	..	1	1	..	1	..	..
Pelton, Nathan	2	..	..	1	..	3	..	..	1	..	..
Pike, Elijah	2	..	..	1	..	2	..	..	1	..	..
Pike, Leonard	2	2	4	..	1	3	2	..	..	1	..
Porter, Francis	3	1	1	..	1	..	..	1	1	..	..
Prentiss, Ashur	1	..	1	..	1	3	..	..	..	1	..
Presson, James	..	..	1	..	..	..	..	1	..	..	..
Presson, Samuel	..	..	..	1	..	2	..	..	1	..	..
Putnam, Levi	2	..	..	1	..	3	..	..	2	..	..
Putnam, Stephen	3	..	..	1	..	..	1	..	1	..	..
Ransom, Jonathan	..	..	1	..	1	..	..	..	..	1	..
Ransom, Jonathan Jr.	1	..	1	1	..	1	2	..	1	..	..
Read, James	1	2	1	..	1	1	1	..	..	1	..
Read, Oliver	..	..	1	..	..	..	..	1	..	..	..
Rider, Caleb	..	..	2	..	1	1	1	1	..	1	..
Robbins, William	..	..	..	1	..	1	..	..	1	..	..
Roberts, James	1	2	1	..	1	..	2	1	1	..	..
Rugg, Hannah	1	..	..	..	..	1	..	1	1	..	..
Sellon, Samuel	3	..	..	1	..	1	1	..	1	..	..
Shumway, Amasa	1	1	1	..	1	..	2	1	1	..	..
Shumway, Levi	2	1	2	..	1	1	..	1	..	1	..
Smith, James	1	1	..	1	..	1	1	..	1	..	..
Stafford, Obadiah	2	..	..	1	..	2	..	..	1	..	..
Stafford, Thomas	3	..	..	1	..	..	..	..	1	..	..
Stockwell, Jonathan	1	1	..	1	..	1	..	..	1	..	..
Stockwell, Thomas	1	..	1	..	..	1	..	1	..	..	..
Stone, Ambrose	1	..	..	1	..	3	..	..	1	..	..
Stone, William	1	..	..	1	..	2	..	..	1	..	..
Streeter, Jacob	1	1	..	..	1	1	1	..	1	..	..
Streeter, James	2	1	..	1	..	2	1	..	1	..	..
Sumner, Ephraim	..	..	1	..	..	..	..	1	..	..	..
Sumner, Levi	1	..	..	1	..	1	..	1	..	..	..
Taft, Marvin	..	..	..	1	..	1	..	1	..	..	..
Tainter, Stephen	1	2	..	1	..	..	..	..	1	..	..
Tottingham, David	..	..	..	1	..	..	..	..	1	..	..
Tyler, Jeremiah	2	2	..	1	..	2	1	..	1	..	..
Vickory, Merrifield	3	1	..	1	..	..	..	..	1	..	..
Walcut, Joseph	2	..	..	1	..	1	..	..	1	..	..
Webster, Giles	2	1	..	1	..	2	1	..	1	..	..
Weeks, Henry	..	..	1	..	1	1	2	1	..	..	..
Wheeler, Deliverance	1	1	1	..	1	1	3	..	..	1	..
Wheeler, Deliverance Jr.	2	..	..	1	..	1	..	..	1	..	..
Wheeler, Zachariah	2	..	1	..	..	1	..	..	1	..	..
Wilcox, Jonathan	..	..	1	1	..	1	..	2	..	..	..
Wild, Parker	..	..	1	..	..	..	..	1	..	..	..
Winslow, Edward	1	1	..	1	..	2	..	..	1	..	..
WILMINGTON											
Alvord, Ashur	1	..	..	1	1	1	1	..	1	1	..
Alvord, Seth	1	1	..	1	..	1	1	..	1	..	..
Arms, Phinehas	4	..	1	..	1	1	1	..	1	..	..
Austin, Daniel	..	..	..	3	1	..	..	1	1	1	..
Averill, Benjamin	1	..	..	1	..	..	..	..	..	..	..
Averill, James	..	..	..	..	1	..	..	1	..	1	..
Axtell, Silas	1	1	..	..	1	2	1	1	..	1	..

NAMES OF HEADS OF FAMILIES	FREE WHITE MALES					FREE WHITE FEMALES					All other free persons except Indians not taxed
	Under 10 years of age	Of 10 and under 16	Of 16 and under 26 including heads of families	Of 26 and under 45 including heads of families	Of 45 and upwards including heads of families.	Under 10 years of age	Of 10 and under 16	Of 16 and under 26 including heads of families	Of 26 and under 45 including heads of families	Of 45 and upwards including heads of families	
WILMINGTON—con.											
Ball, Lemuel	2	..	..	1	..	3	..	..	1	..	..
Ball, Noah	2	1	1	1	..	..	1	1	..	1	..
Bangs, Adnah	..	..	..	..	2	..	..	..	..	2	..
Barrows, Ephraim	2	1	..	..	2	3	1	1	..	1	..
Bassett, Jedidiah	2	1	..	..	1	3	..	..	..	1	..
Bent, Thomas	..	..	..	..	1	1	..	..	..	1	..
Bills, Aaron	1	1	..	1	..	..	..	..	1	..	..
Bills, Calvin	..	..	1	1	1	1	1	..	1	1	..
Birchard, Roger	2	..	..	1	..	3	..	..	1	1	..
Boyd, Abraham	1	..	3	1	1	1	1	..	..	1	..
Boyd, David	1	1	1	..	1	1	1	1	..	1	..
Brakenridge, George	3	..	..	1	..	..	..	..	1	..	..
Brimhall, Gideon	2	1	..	1	..	2	1	..	1	..	..
Buell, Samuel	1	..	1	..	1	..	1	..	..	1	..
Buell, Widow S.	2	1	..	..	..	1	..	..	1	..	..
Castle, Timothy	..	1	1	..	1	..	..	1	..	1	..
Chandler, Henry 2nd	1	2	..	1	..	1	1	1	1	..	..
Chandler, Simeon	1	1	..	1	2	2	1	2	1	..	..
Childs, John	2	1	..	1	..	3	1	..	1	..	..
Clark, Henry	2	..	..	1	..	..	..	..	1	..	..
Cook, Edward	1	2	1	1	..	..	..	2	1	1	..
Corse, James	3	1	1	..	1	1	1	1	1	..	..
Corse, Rufus	4	2	..	1	..	2	1	1	1	1	..
Corse, Rufus	2	..	..	1	..	3	..	..	1	..	..
Crosby, Eli	1	..	..	1	..	1	..	..	1	..	..
Crosman, Frederick	2	..	..	1	..	..	1	..	1	..	..
Cummings, Reuben	2	..	1	..	1	..	..	..	..	1	..
Cushman, Barnabas	2	2	..	..	1	1	..	2	..	1	..
Cutting, Daniel	1	..	..	1	..	1	1	..	1	..	..
Davis, David	..	..	1	..	1	..	1	..	..	1	..
Davis, John	1	..	..	1	..	1	..	..	1	..	..
Davis, Samuel	4	..	..	1	..	1	..	..	1	..	..
Dickinson, George	1	..	1	1	..	..	1	1	1	..	..
Dix, Leonard	..	..	1	..	..	..	..	1	..	..	..
Dix, Ozias	4	..	2	..	1	..	1	2	..	1	..
Doty, Ellis	..	1	..	1	..	4	1	..	1	..	..
Dwight, Alpheus	2	1	..	1	..	1	..	..	1	..	..
Easton, Elijah	1	1	1	1	..	2	..	..	2	1	..
Easton, Joel	4	..	..	1	..	1	..	..	1	..	..
Easton, Oliver	3	..	..	1	..	..	..	1	..	..	..
Farryl, John	2	1	..	1	..	..	..	..	1	..	..
Fitch, Jesse	1	1	..	..	1	..	1	1	..	1	..
Flagg, John	2	..	..	2	1	1	..	..	1	1	..
Flagg, Jonathan	2	..	1	..	..	1	..	1	..	..	..
Flagg, Josiah	..	1	..	1	..	2	..	..	1	..	..
Flagg, Timothy	..	..	1	..	..	1	..	1	..	..	..
Forbes, John	3	..	..	1	..	..	..	1	..	..	..
Foster, Nathan	..	2	1	..	1	..	..	2	..	1	..
Foster, Theophilus	2	..	1	..	1	1	..	2	..	1	..
Fox, Amos	..	1	..	..	2	1	1	1	..	1	..
Fox, Amos Jr.	2	..	..	1	..	1	..	..	1	..	..
Fox, Thomas	..	..	..	1	..	1	..	1	..	..	..
Freeman, John	1	..	..	1	..	1	..	..	1	..	..
Freeman, Watson	2	..	..	1	1	2	..	..	1	1	..
Gillett, Timothy	..	..	1	..	..	..	..	1	..	..	..
Griswold, Jared	..	..	..	1	..	3	1	..	1	..	..
Hall, Jarius	1	1	..	1	..	..	..	2	..	..	..
Hamilton, Silas	..	1	1	..	1	..	..	2	..	1	..
Haskell, Andrew	4	1	..	..	1	1	..	1	1	..	..
Haskell, Samuel	..	..	..	1	..	1	..	1	..	..	..
Haskell, Thomas	1	2	..	1	1	1	..	1	1	1	..
Haskins, David	..	..	1	..	..	1	..	1	..	..	..
Haskins, Jonathan.	1	1	..	1	..	1	1	1	..	1	..
Hastings, Jonathan	1	1	1	..	1	3	1	..	1	..	..
Hawes, Jabez	..	..	..	..	1	..	..	1	..	1	..
Haynes, Abijah	1	..	..	1	..	1	..	..	1	..	..
Haynes, Abraham	1	..	..	1	..	1	..	..	1	..	..
Haynes, Jones	1	2	..	1	..	2	1	1	1	..	..
Hill, Zilphah	1	..	..	..	..	1	..	1	..	..	..
Hubbard, Chester	..	..	..	1	..	1	..	..	1	..	..
Hubbard, Moses	4	2	..	1	..	2	1	..	1	..	..
Hubbard, Stephen	2	1	1	1	1	2	..	..	1	1	..
Hudson, Joshua	1	..	1	1	..	2	..	..	1	..	..
Hudson, Nathan	..	..	..	..	1	1	..	2	..	1	..
Hunter, Robert	1	1	1	..	1	2	2	2	..	1	..
Johnson, Jonathan	2	..	..	1	..	2	2	..	1	..	..
Keep, Seth	..	..	..	1	..	1	..	..	1	..	..
King, Cushing	1	1	..	1	..	3	..	..	1	..	..

WINDHAM COUNTY—Continued

NAMES OF HEADS OF FAMILIES	FREE WHITE MALES: Under 10 years of age	FREE WHITE MALES: Of 10 and under 16	FREE WHITE MALES: Of 16 and under 26 including heads of families	FREE WHITE MALES: Of 26 and under 45 including heads of families	FREE WHITE MALES: Of 45 and upwards including heads of families	FREE WHITE FEMALES: Under 10 years of age	FREE WHITE FEMALES: Of 10 and under 16	FREE WHITE FEMALES: Of 16 and under 26 including heads of families	FREE WHITE FEMALES: Of 26 and under 45 including heads of families	FREE WHITE FEMALES: Of 45 and upwards including heads of families	All other free persons except Indians not taxed
WILMINGTON—con.											
Lamb, Jonathan	2	1	..	1	..	3	1	..	1	..	..
Lawton, Israel	2	..	..	1	..	4	2	..	1	..	..
Lilly, Asa	..	..	2	..	..	..	..	1	..	..	..
Lincoln, Apollos	..	..	..	1	1	1	..	1	..	1	..
Lincoln, David	1	1	..	1	..	1	..	..	1	1	..
Lincoln, Jonah	1	1	..	1	..	1	1	..	1	..	..
Lincoln, Perez	1	..	..	1	..	1	..	1	..	..	..
Livermore, Daniel	..	1	1	..	1	..	..	2	..	1	..
Livermore, Edmund	1	..	..	1	..	..	..	..	1	..	..
Livermore, Samuel	1	..	..	1	..	1	..	1	..	..	..
Lock, Josiah	1	..	1	..	1	..	..	1	..	1	..
Long, Mathew	1	..	2	1	..	4	1	..	1	..	..
Lothrop, Luther	..	..	..	1	..	1	..	1	..	..	..
Marks, John	..	..	..	..	1	..	..	..	..	..	..
Marks, Joseph	2	..	1	..	1	2	2	1	1	1	..
May, David	..	..	1	..	1	..	..	2	..	1	..
May, Samuel	3	..	..	1	..	2	..	..	1	..	..
McMaster, Isaac	1	..	..	1	..	..	..	..	..	..	..
Metcalf, Benjamin	2	1	..	1	..	1	1	..	1	1	..
Miller, James	..	..	..	1	..	3	..	..	1	..	..
Millins, Ezra	1	..	..	1	..	2	..	..	1	..	..
Montague, Seth	3	..	..	1	1	1	1	..	1	1	..
Moore, Jonas	2	1	..	1	..	1	..	..	1	..	..
Moore, Jonathan	..	..	..	1	1	1	1	..	1	1	..
Moore, Judah	2	1	1	..	1	3	..	2	1	..	..
Morgan, Benjamin	2	..	..	1	1	2	1	..	1	..	..
Morgan, Oliver	..	..	..	1	1	3	..	..	1	1	..
Morris, John	..	1	..	1	..	1	..	..	1	..	..
Mory, John	2	1	..	1	..	4	2	..	1	..	..
Mudge, Ezra	1	..	..	..	1	..	3	..	..	1	..
Nash, Simeon	5	1	2	..	1	1	1	..	..	1	..
Nettleton, George	1	..	..	..	1	..	..	..	..	1	..
Nettleton, Roswell	..	..	..	1	..	1	..	1	..	..	..
Nye, Joseph	..	..	..	..	1	..	..	..	..	1	..
Packard, Joseph	2	..	..	1	..	1	..	..	2	..	..
Packard, Levi	..	..	1	1	..	5	1	1	1	..	..
Parmele, Gilbert	3	..	..	1	..	2	..	2	1	..	..
Parmele, James	1	1	..	..	1	3	1	..	..	1	..
Parmele, Widow T.	..	..	..	..	..	..	..	1	..	1	..
Petty, Samuel	..	1	1	..	1	..	1	2	..	1	..
Petty, Silas	..	..	..	1	..	2	..	..	1	..	..
Ray, Zelotas	3	..	..	1	..	..	..	..	1	..	..
Rowlandson, Sylvester	3	..	..	1	..	..	..	..	1	..	..
Smith, James	2	..	..	1	..	4	1	..	1	..	..
Smith, Medad	3	1	1	1	2	1	1	..	1	..	..
Spencer, Thomas	..	..	..	2	1	..	..	1	..	..	..
Stacey, Abel	..	..	..	1	..	2	..	..	1	..	..
Stevens, Israel	..	..	2	..	1	..	1	..	..	1	..
Studson, Anthony	..	..	..	1	..	5	..	..	1	..	..
Swan, Samuel	1	..	..	1	..	2	..	..	1	..	..
Swift, Chipman	..	..	1	..	1	1	1	2	..	1	..
Swift, Jesse	3	1	1	..	2	3	1	2	1	1	..
Taylor, David	3	2	2	1	1	..	..	..	..	1	..
Thomas, Nathaniel	..	..	..	1	..	..	..	1	..	..	..
Thompson, Samuel	..	1	..	1	..	..	..	..	1	..	..
Thompson, Samuel 2nd	1	..	..	1	..	2	2	..	1	..	..
Titus, Ephraim	..	..	1	..	1	..	..	1	..	1	..
Titus, William	2	..	..	1	..	1	..	..	1	..	..
Tower, Reuben	3	..	..	1	..	..	..	1	..	..	..
Tyler, Moses	..	..	..	1	..	4	..	..	1	..	..
Tyler, Stephen	3	..	..	1	1	1	..	..	..	1	..
Waiste, Eli	1	1	1	..	1	..	1	1	..	1	..
Ware, Asaph	2	..	1	..	1	2	..	1	1	..	..
Ware, Meletiah	..	1	2	..	..	..	..	1	..	1	..
West, Widow	1	..	1	..	..	..	..	1	..	2	..
Wetherell, Lot	1	1	..	..	1	..	..	1	..	1	..
Whitney, Levi	..	..	1	..	..	..	..	1	..	..	..
Wilder, Oliver	3	1	1	..	1	..	1	1	..	1	..
Williams, William	..	..	..	1	..	2	1	..	1	1	..
Wing, Bani	3	1	..	1	..	1	1	..	1	..	..
Winslow, David	..	1	..	..	1	..	1	..	1	..	..
Winslow, Enoch	1	..	1	..	..	2	..	1	..	..	..
Winslow, Tisdale	1	..	..	..	1	1	..	1	..	1	..
Witt, Jonathan	4	1	..	1	..	1	..	..	1	..	..
Wright, Lodowick	1	..	..	1	2	3	1	..	1	1	..
WINDHAM											
Abbot, Lemuel	2	1	..	1	..	..	..	1	..	..	..
Abbot, Peter	2	1	..	1	..	2	..	..	1	..	..
Aikin, Edward	..	..	..	..	1	..	..	..	..	1	..
WINDHAM—con.											
Aikin, James	..	..	..	1	..	..	..	..	..	..	..
Aikin, John	4	..	..	1	..	..	1	..	1	..	..
Aikin, Nathaniel	2	1	2	..	1	1	..	2	..	1	..
Aikin, Peter	1	..	..	1	..	1	..	1	1	..	..
Ayres, Samuel	..	..	1	..	1	1	..	1	..	1	..
Babbit, Daniel	3	..	..	..	1	2	..	..	1	..	..
Barrett, Calvin	1	..	..	1	..	1	..	..	1	..	..
Bemas, Zacheus	..	..	..	1	..	3	..	..	1	..	..
Bolster, Baruch	3	..	..	1	..	1	..	..	1	..	..
Brintnell, Jonathan	2	1	..	1	..	1	1	..	1	..	..
Burnap, John	3	..	..	1	..	2	..	..	1	..	..
Burnap, Thomas	2	1	1	1	..	1	1	..	1	..	..
Butterfield, Jonas	1	1	..	1	..	3	..	..	1	..	..
Cobb, Daniel	2	1	2	..	1	..	1	..	..	1	..
Cobb, David	..	..	1	1	..	..	1	..	..	1	..
Colton, Oliver	3	1	..	1	..	2	..	..	1	..	..
Covey, Joseph	..	..	1	..	..	..	..	..	..	..	..
Cummins, Ebenezer	1	..	1	1	..	3	..	..	..	..	..
Davis, Samuel	..	1	1	..	1	..	1	1	..	1	..
Dodge, Isaac	..	..	1	..	..	1	..	1	..	..	..
Dodge, Judah	1	..	..	1	..	2	1	..	1	..	..
Dudley, John	2	..	1	1	..	..	..	1	1	..	..
Emery, Amos	1	..	1	..	..	..	..	1	..	..	..
Eveleth, David	3	..	..	1	..	..	..	..	..	..	..
Farnum, Benjamin	1	..	1	1	..	1	..	1	..	..	..
Farr, Abraham	1	..	1	1	..	3	1	..	1	..	..
Fay, Reuben	1	..	1	..	..	1	..	1	..	..	..
Gould, John	3	1	..	1	..	1	1	..	1	..	..
Hamilton, John	..	..	1	..	..	1	..	1	..	..	..
Hazeltine, Turner	..	..	..	1	..	1	..	..	1	..	..
Hewett, Ephraim	..	1	..	1	..	..	1	..	1	..	..
Hopkins, John	..	..	..	..	1	1	..	..	1	..	..
Johnson, Timothy	1	1	1	..	1	2	1	..	..	1	..
Kimball, Moses	1	2	1	1	..	1	1	..	1	..	..
Leonard, Moses	..	..	1	..	..	..	..	..	..	..	..
Mack, Archebald	1	2	..	..	1	1	2	..	1	..	..
Mack, James	3	..	..	1	..	1	2	..	1	..	..
Mack, John	..	..	..	..	1	..	..	..	1	..	..
McCormick, Archebald	1	..	..	1	..	1	1	..	1	..	..
McCormick, James	1	1	..	1	1	..	..	..	1	1	..
McMurphey, George	..	1	..	..	1	..	1	2	..	1	..
McMurphey, George Jr.	1	..	..	1	..	1	..	1	..	..	..
Mills, John	..	..	..	..	1	..	..	..	..	1	..
Osgood, Asahel	1	..	..	1	..	2	..	1	..	..	..
Parson, George	..	..	1	..	1	..	1	..	..	1	..
Parson, Jonathan	3	..	..	1	..	1	2	..	1	..	..
Parson, Joseph	1	1	..	1	..	2	1	..	1	..	..
Perry, Jonathan	..	..	..	1	..	..	..	..	..	..	..
Pierce, Benjamin	2	..	1	1	..	2	1	..	1	..	..
Pierce, Nehemiah	1	1	..	1	..	1	1	..	1	..	..
Reed, Aaron	..	..	..	2	1	1	..	..	1	1	..
Rhoads, Ebenezer	2	..	..	1	..	2	..	..	1	..	..
Rugg, John	2	1	..	1	..	3	1	..	1	..	..
Scott, John	..	..	2	..	1	..	..	1	..	1	..
Sherwin, Jonathan	2	..	..	1	..	1	..	..	1	..	..
Sherwin, Timothy	..	..	..	1	..	1	..	..	1	..	..
Smith, James	..	2	..	..	1	1	1	1	..	1	..
Smith, Simeon	..	..	..	1	..	2	..	..	1	..	..
Stearns, James	..	..	..	1	..	1	..	..	1	..	..
Stevens, Martin	..	1	..	..	1	2	1	1	..	1	..
Steward, William	1	1	..	..	1	..	1	1	..	1	..
Stone, David	2	..	1	..	..	2	..	..	1	..	..
Stowell, Luther	1	..	..	1	..	1	..	1	..	..	..
Taggert, Patrick	..	1	1	1	..	4	2	..	1	..	..
Titus, Asa	1	..	..	1	..	1	..	1	..	..	..
Watkins, John	1	..	2	..	1	..	..	2	..	1	..
Weeks, Nathan	..	..	1	..	..	..	..	..	..	..	..
Weeks, Samuel	1	1	..	1	..	2	1	1	1	..	..
Wheeler, Jeremiah	1	..	1	1	..	1	2	1	1	..	..
Whitman, Abiel	2	1	..	1	..	2	1	..	1	..	..
Williams, Jonathan	..	..	..	1	..	..	1	..	1	..	..
Wilson, Peter	1	..	2	..	1	1	2	..	..	1	..
Woodburn, John	..	1	2	..	1	..	..	2	1	1	..
Woodcock, John	..	..	1	..	..	1	..	1	..	..	..
Wylles, Lemuel	..	..	..	1	..	..	..	..	..	..	..
Wyman, Nathan	1	..	1	..	..	..	..	1	..	..	..

WINDSOR COUNTY

NAMES OF HEADS OF FAMILIES	Free white males: Under 10 years of age	Free white males: Of 10 and under 16	Free white males: Of 16 and under 26 including heads of families	Free white males: Of 26 and under 45 including heads of families	Free white males: Of 45 and upwards including heads of families.	Free white females: Under 10 years of age	Free white females: Of 10 and under 16	Free white females: Of 16 and under 26 including heads of families	Free white females: Of 26 and under 45 including heads of families	Free white females: Of 45 and upwards including heads of families	All other free persons except Indians not taxed
ANDOVER											
Abbot, Joseph	1	2	..	1	..	3	..	..	1	..	..
Abel, John Jr.	..	..	2	1	..	1	1	..	1	..	..
Adams, Jonas	1	1	..	1	..	3	1	1	1	..	..
Adams, Luther	1	..	..	1	..	2	..	..	1	..	..
Adams, Samuel	..	..	1	1	..	6	..	..	1	..	..
Adams, Thomas	1	..	1	..	..	..	..	1	..	..	..
Allen, Abijah	1	2	1	..	1	..	..	2	..	1	..
Allen, Isaac	2	..	..	1	..	..	1	1	..	..	..
Andrews, John	2	1	1	1	1	1	..	1	1	..	..
Andrews, Nathan	..	..	1	..	..	1	..	1	..	..	..
Austin, David	2	..	..	1	..	3	..	..	1	..	..
Bachelor, David	1	..	1	..	..	..	..	1	..	..	..
Bailey, David	1	..	..	1	..	2	..	1	..	..	..
Bailey, Nathaniel	2	..	..	1	..	1	..	..	1	..	..
Balch, Hart	3	3	..	..	1	1	..	..	..	1	..
Balch, Joel	1	..	1	..	..	2	..	2	..	..	..
Baldwin, Benjamin	1	1	..	1	..	1	..	1	..	..	..
Baldwin, Jesse	3	2	..	1	..	1	..	1	1	..	..
Barton, Amos	1	..	..	1	..	3	..	..	1	..	..
Barton, Jeremiah	2	..	..	1	..	2	2	..	1	..	..
Barton, Rufus	1	..	1	..	1	1	..	..	1	..	..
Blanchard, John	2	..	..	1	..	2	..	..	1	..	..
Brown, Samuel	..	1	1	..	1	..	1	1	1	1	..
Bullard, Joseph	1	..	..	1	..	1	..	1	..	..	..
Bullard, Samuel	2	2	..	..	1	..	..	1	..	1	..
Burton, David	2	1	1	1	..	3	2	..	1	..	..
Burton, John	2	..	..	1	..	2	..	..	1	..	..
Burton, Polley	..	..	..	..	..	1	..	..	1	..	..
Burton, Samuel	1	..	..	1	..	3	..	1	1	..	..
Butler, John	1	..	1	..	..	..	..	1	..	1	..
Butterfield, Eleazer	1	1	..	1	..	1	1	1	1	..	..
Chamberlain, Asa	1	..	..	1	1	..	1	..	1	1	..
Chamberlain, John	1	..	..	1	..	..	2	..	..	..	..
Chamberlain, Samuel	..	..	..	1	..	..	..	..	1	..	..
Chubbuck, Elijah	2	..	..	1	..	2	2	..	1	..	..
Chubbuck, Simon	1	..	..	1	..	1	..	..	1	..	..
Clark, Samuel	..	..	..	1	..	..	..	..	1	..	..
Cox, Edward	1	2	..	1	..	3	1	..	1	..	..
Cram, Humphrey	..	..	..	1	..	..	..	..	1	..	..
Cram, Jonathan	2	..	..	1	..	1	1	..	1	..	..
Cram, Joseph	1	..	..	..	1	..	..	1	..	1	..
Croggin, Benjamin	3	..	1	..	..	1	..	1	..	..	..
Cummings, Ebenezer	4	..	..	1	..	1	2	..	1	..	..
Darling, Caleb	2	..	..	..	1	..	..	..	..	1	..
Dickenson, David	1	..	..	1	..	2	..	1	1	..	..
Dodge, Joseph	1	..	..	..	1	2	1	1	..	1	..
Dodge, Joseph	1	..	..	1	..	1	..	1	..	..	..
Dodge, Moses	..	..	1	..	..	1	..	1	..	..	..
Dodge, Thomas	..	..	2	..	..	..	..	1	..	..	..
Drury, Daniel	2	..	..	1	..	2	1	..	1	..	..
Drury, Ezra	1	..	..	1	..	..	..	..	1	..	..
Dudley, Jonathan	..	1	..	1	..	..	..	1	..	..	..
Dudley, Peter	1	..	..	1	..	1	..	1	..	1	..
Farrar, Oliver	1	..	2	1	..	2	1	1	..	..	..
Felt, Abner	1	2	1	1	..	4	1	..	1	1	..
Fidder, James	..	..	..	..	1	..	..	1	..	..	..
Fish, Ebenezer	2	..	..	1	..	1	..	..	1	..	..
Foster, Jonathan	2	..	1	..	..	1	..	1	..	..	..
French, David	..	1	1	1	..	2	..	1	1	..	..
French, John	2	1	1	1	..	1	1	..	1	..	..
French, Reuben	2	1	..	1	..	..	..	1	..	..	..
French, Thomas	3	1	1	1	..	3	2	..	1	..	..
Fuller, Joseph	..	..	..	1	..	3	..	..	1	..	..
Fuller, William	2	..	..	1	..	2	..	..	1	..	..
Gassett, Darius	2	..	1	1	..	1	..	1	..	..	..
Gilmore, Asa	2	..	1	..	..	1	..	1	..	..	..
Greele, Nathaniel	1	4	2	1	1	1	..	2	2	1	..
Gutherson, Abner	1	..	..	1	..	1	..	..	1	..	..
Hale, Simon	2	..	..	1	..	2	..	..	1	..	..
Hall, Henry	..	2	..	1	..	1	1	1	1	..	..
Hazeltine, David	..	2	1	1	..	..	3	..	1	..	..
Hazeltine, Follingsbe	3	..	..	1	..	1	..	..	1	..	..
Hazeltine, Nathan	..	..	..	..	1	..	..	..	..	1	..
Holt, Oliver	..	..	1	..	1	..	..	1	..	1	..
Howard, Antipas	3	..	..	1	..	1	..	..	1	..	..
Howard, Antipas 2nd	1	..	..	1	..	1	..	1	..	..	..
Howard, David	..	1	1	..	1	1	..	1	1	..	..
Howard, Joseph	2	..	..	1	..	1	..	..	1	..	..
Howard, Joseph	2	..	1	1	..	..	2	..	1	..	..
Howard, Samuel	3	..	..	1	..	2	1	..	1	..	..
ANDOVER—con.											
Howard, Solomon	5	1	..	..	1	..	..	..	1	..	..
Howard, William	1	..	..	1	..	3	..	..	1	..	..
Hutchinson, Ebenezer	..	..	..	1	..	2	..	..	1	..	..
Ingols, Edmond	1	2	..	1	..	2	..	..	1	..	..
Jaqueth, Joshua	..	1	..	1	..	2	1	1	1	..	..
Jewett, Jeremiah	1	..	..	1	..	..	..	..	1	..	..
Johnson, James	2	1	..	1	..	2	..	..	1	..	..
Keyes, Aaron	1	..	..	1	..	3	..	..	1	..	..
Keyes, Erastus	1	..	1	..	..	1	..	1	..	..	..
Kezar, Nathaniel	..	..	..	..	1	..	..	..	..	1	..
Kimball, Isaac	2	..	1	1	..	1	1	..	1	..	..
Lamson, Daniel	2	..	..	1	..	2	..	..	1	..	..
Lancy, Zacheus	..	..	2	..	..	..	..	1	..	..	..
Lawrence, Samuel	1	..	1	..	..	1	..	1	..	..	..
Lunor, Willard	1	..	..	1	..	3	1	..	1	..	..
Manning, Benjamin	1	..	..	1	..	1	..	1	..	..	..
Manning, Joel	3	..	..	1	..	1	..	..	2	1	..
Manning, Samuel	1	1	..	1	..	3	..	1	1	..	..
Mansur, John	1	..	..	1	..	2	1	..	1	..	..
Marsh, John	3	1	..	1	..	2	..	..	1	..	..
Marshal, Jonathan	2	2	..	1	..	1	1	1	1	..	..
Martin, Christopher	2	1	1	1	..	1	1	..	1	..	..
McIntire, Caleb	..	1	1	1	..	1	..	1	1	..	..
McNeal, John	..	1	..	1	..	2	..	1	1	..	..
Miller, Samuel	..	1	1	..	1	..	..	..	1	..	..
Murphy, John M.	..	..	..	..	1	..	..	..	1	..	..
Parker, James	..	1	..	1	..	1	1	..	1	..	..
Parker, Phinehas	2	..	2	1	..	3	..	..	1	..	..
Parkhurst, Isaac	2	..	..	1	..	..	..	..	1	..	..
Parkhurst, Jesse	2	..	..	1	..	..	2	1	1	..	..
Peabody, Isaac	..	..	1	..	1	..	..	2	..	2	..
Pease, Augustus	4	1	..	1	..	1	3	..	1	..	..
Pease, Elijah	1	..	1	1	..	2	..	2	..	..	..
Pease, Ezekiel	..	..	..	..	1	..	..	2	..	1	..
Pease, Ezekiel Jr.	..	1	1	1	..	1	..	..	1	..	..
Pease, Gideon	1	1	1	..	1	2	2	..	1	..	..
Pease, Obadiah	2	..	..	1	..	2	..	..	1	..	..
Peters, Cyrus	..	..	..	1	..	1	..	1	..	..	..
Pettingill, John	1	..	1	..	..	..	..	1	..	..	..
Pettingill, Samuel	2	1	..	1	..	2	1	2	1	..	..
Pierce, Benjamin	3	1	..	1	..	1	2	..	1	..	..
Piper, Amasa	2	2	1	1	..	2	..	..	1	..	..
Piper, Thomas	2	..	..	1	..	3	1	..	1	..	..
Putnam, Archelaus	..	..	1	..	..	..	2	..	..	..	..
Putnam, Jacob	1	..	..	1	..	2	..	..	1	..	..
Putnam, Jonathan	3	..	..	1	..	1	..	..	1	..	..
Putnam, Peter	1	..	..	1	..	1	..	..	1	..	..
Richardson, Joseph	..	..	..	..	1	..	2	1	..	1	..
Richardson, Josiah	3	1	..	1	..	1	1	..	1	..	..
Richardson, Nathan	1	..	1	..	..	..	..	1	..	..	..
Rowell, Moses	2	..	..	2	..	3	..	..	1	..	..
Rowell, Polly	2	..	..	..	..	1	..	..	1	..	..
Rowell, Richard	1	..	..	1	..	..	..	1	..	..	..
Shelden, Jacob	2	..	..	1	..	1	..	..	1	..	..
Simonds, Edward	1	..	..	1	..	1	..	1	..	..	..
Simons, Alvin	3	..	..	1	..	2	..	..	2	1	..
Simons, Dan	6	1	..	1	..	..	..	..	1	..	..
Smith, Frederick	..	..	..	1	..	2	..	1	..	..	..
Smith, Samuel	3	..	..	1	..	2	1	..	1	..	..
Smith, William	4	1	..	1	..	..	..	..	1	..	..
Somes, Isaac	1	..	1	..	..	..	..	1	..	..	..
Southworth, Solomon	..	2	..	1	..	4	..	1	1	..	..
Spafford, David	..	..	..	..	1	..	..	..	..	1	..
Spafford, David Jr.	..	1	..	1	..	5	..	..	1	..	..
Spafford, Eliphalet	1	..	1	..	..	1	..	1	..	..	..
Spafford, Jesse	1	..	..	1	..	1	..	..	1	..	..
Stevens, William	..	1	1	..	1	2	1	1	..	1	..
Stickney, Moody	..	1	..	1	..	..	..	..	1	..	..
Stors, Abner	1	2	2	..	1	2	1	1	1	..	..
Stors, David	..	..	1	..	..	1	..	1	..	..	..
Swallow, Joel	..	..	..	1	..	2	..	1	..	..	..
Town, Aaron	2	..	..	1	..	2	1	..	1	..	..
Towns, Joseph	3	..	1	..	..	..	..	1	..	..	..
Twitchell, Luther	..	..	..	1	..	1	..	..	1	..	..
Twitchell, Sawing	1	..	..	1	..	1	..	1	..	..	..
Twitchell, Stephen	..	1	..	1	..	3	..	3	1	..	..

WINDSOR COUNTY—Continued

NAMES OF HEADS OF FAMILIES	FREE WHITE MALES					FREE WHITE FEMALES					All other free persons except Indians not taxed
	Under 10 years of age	Of 10 and under 16	Of 16 and under 26 including heads of families	Of 26 and under 45 including heads of families	Of 45 and upwards including heads of families.	Under 10 years of age	Of 10 and under 16	Of 16 and under 26 including heads of families	Of 26 and under 45 including heads of families	Of 45 and upwards including heads of families.	
ANDOVER—con.											
Wait, John	1	2	..	1	..	3	1	..	1	..	..
Walker, Samson	1	1	1	..	1	..	1	1	..	1	..
Warner, Joshua	2	..	..	1	..	1	..	..	1	..	..
Warner, Moses	..	1	1	..	1	..	1	2	..	1	..
Warner, Moses Jr.	1	..	..	..	1	..	..	..	1	..	..
Warner, William	..	..	..	..	1	..	..	1	..	..	..
White, Jacob	1	2	..	1	..	1	1	..	1	..	..
Whitman, John	1	1	..	..	1	..	..	..	..	1	..
Whitman, John Jr.	1	1	..	..	1	..	..	..	..	1	..
Whitney, Richard	1	..	..	1	..	1	..	..	1	..	..
Wilkins, Stephen	2	..	1	..	..	..	..	1	..	..	..
Willington, Samuel	3	1	..	1	..	2	1	..	1	..	..
Winship, John	1	..	..	1	..	2	..	..	1	..	..
Winship, Josiah	..	..	..	1	..	..	..	..	1	..	..
BALTIMORE											
Atherton, Joseph	1	1	..	1	..	2	..	1	1	..	..
Bemis, Amos	3	1	..	1	..	1	1	..	1	..	..
Bemis, Reuben	2	..	..	1	..	1	..	..	1	1	..
Boynton, Jonathan	..	..	..	1	..	2	..	..	1	..	..
Bruce, Benjamin	1	..	..	..	1	2	2	..	1	1	..
Burnham, Francis	1	1	..	2	..	2	1	..	1	..	..
Burnham, Jonathan	2	2	1	1	..	3	..	1	1	..	..
Chamberlain, Isaac	..	..	..	..	1	..	..	..	..	1	..
Cheney, Waldo	2	..	1	..	1	1	2	2	..	1	..
Curtis, John B.	1	..	..	1	..	2	..	..	1	..	..
Davis, Levi	3	..	..	1	..	1	..	1	1	..	..
Griswold, Mathew	2	..	2	1	..	1	..	..	1	..	..
Harris, Luke	3	..	..	1	..	..	1	..	1	..	..
Hastings, Samuel	2	..	..	1	..	2	2	..	1	..	..
Hildrith, Elijah	1	..	1	..	..	..	..	1	..	..	..
Hildrith, Joseph	1	..	..	1	..	1	..	..	1	..	..
Houghton, Seth	3	2	1	..	1	3	1	..	..	1	..
Martin, Ephraim	1	..	1	..	1	..	2	..	..	1	..
Martin, Joshua Jr.	..	1	2	..	2	2	1	..	1	..	..
Martin, Joshua 3rd	1	..	..	1	..	1	..	1	..	..	..
Piper, Noah	1	2	1	..	1	1	2	1	..	1	..
Redfield, Ezra	3	..	..	1	..	1	..	1	..	1	..
Robinson, Stephen	2	..	..	1	..	1	..	..	1	..	..
Rugg, Elijah	1	..	..	1	..	1	..	..	1	..	..
Smith, Daniel	3	..	..	1	..	..	..	..	1	..	..
Woodbury, John	..	..	1	..	..	..	..	1	..	..	..
Woodbury, Jonathan	2	..	..	1	..	1	..	1	1	..	..
BARNARD											
Akin, Elijah	2	..	..	1	..	1	1	..	1	..	..
Akins, James	1	..	..	..	1	4	..	..	1	..	..
Akins, Solomon	2	..	..	1	..	1	1	..	1	..	..
Akins, Solomon	1	1	1	1	..	2	1	..	1	..	..
Ashley, Jonathan	2	1	1	1	..	1	1	..	1	..	..
Avery, Joseph	..	..	..	1	..	2	1	..	1	..	..
Babbit, Abel	..	..	..	..	1	1	..	..	..	1	..
Babbit, Abel Jr.	2	..	..	1	..	2	..	..	1	..	..
Babbit, Simeon	..	..	3	..	..	..	..	1	..	..	..
Ballard, Daniel	1	2	1	..	1	..	..	1	1	..	..
Barlow, Aaron	..	1	1	..	1	1	..	..	1	..	..
Barlow, Benjamin	2	..	2	1	..	2	..	..	1	..	..
Barlow, Joseph	4	..	..	1	..	2	1	..	1	..	..
Barlow, Joseph	2	..	..	1	..	..	2	..	1	..	..
Barlow, Lemuel	..	..	4	..	..	..	..	1	..	..	..
Barlow, Moses	..	1	1	1	1	..	..	1	..	1	..
Barlow, Nathaniel	1	1	..	1	1	..	1	1	..	..	..
Barows, John	..	..	..	1	..	..	..	..	..	..	..
Beldon, James	3	..	..	1	..	1	2	..	1	..	..
Bicknell, Amos	4	1	..	1	..	2	..	..	1	..	..
Bicknell, John S.	..	1	1	..	..	1	..	1	..	1	..
Billins, Gideon	1	..	..	1	..	2	1	..	1	..	..
Blackmore, Solomon	1	..	..	1	..	..	..	..	1	..	..
Blackmore, William	..	..	..	..	1	..	..	3	..	1	..
Bowman, Ebenezer	1	1	1	..	..	2	1	..	1	..	..
Bowman, John	1	..	..	1	..	..	..	..	1	..	..
Bowman, Joseph	..	1	1	1	1	..	..	3	..	1	..
Bowman, Nathan	1	..	1	..	1	1	..	..	1	..	..
Bowman, Nathan Jr.	..	..	..	1	..	1	..	..	1	..	..
BARNARD—con.											
Briggs, Ephraim	..	1	2	1	..	1	1	..	1	..	..
Brigham, Asa	2	..	..	1	..	..	1	..	1	..	..
Brown, Matthew	2	1	2	..	1	..	..	..	..	1	..
Burrows, Elijah	..	1	1	1	..	..	1	..	1	..	..
Burrows, Elijah Jr.	2	..	1	..	..	..	..	1	..	..	..
Byrum, James	..	2	1	1	..	..	2	..	1	..	..
Carver, Rodolphus	..	..	1	..	1	..	..	2	..	1	..
Carver, Thomas	1	..	3	..	..	1	..	..	..	..	..
Cawdry, Timothy	1	..	..	1	..	3	..	..	1	..	..
Chamberlin, John	1	..	1	..	1	1	..	1	..	1	..
Chamberlin, Joseph	1	..	..	1	..	2	..	1	1	..	..
Chamberlin, Joseph	1	1	1	..	1	2	1	..	..	1	..
Chamberlin, Levi	4	..	..	1	..	2	..	..	1	..	..
Chamberlin, William	2	2	4	..	1	..	1	5	..	1	..
Cheedle, William	1	1	..	..	1	..	..	..	..	1	..
Child, William	1	..	..	1	..	5	..	..	1	..	..
Clapp, Benjamin	2	..	..	1	1	3	2	4	1	..	..
Clapp, George	1	..	..	1	..	3	..	1	..	..	..
Clark, David	2	..	..	1	..	3	1	..	1	..	..
Cole, James	2	..	..	..	1	2	2	..	1	..	..
Cooledge, Moses	2	..	..	1	..	..	..	..	1	..	..
Cox, Benjamin	3	..	..	1	..	1	1	..	1	..	..
Cox, George	1	..	..	1	..	3	..	1	1	..	..
Crowell, Sheferick	2	..	..	2	..	2	2	..	1	..	..
Culver, Wrotham	5	1	..	1	..	..	..	..	1	..	..
Cummins, John	3	2	..	..	1	..	1	..	1	..	..
Danforth, Isaac	3	..	1	1	..	1	1	1	1	..	..
Davenport, Abel	1	1	..	1	..	2	..	..	1	..	..
Davis, Francis.	2	2	1	1	1	2	..	..	1	1	..
Davis, Moses	..	..	..	..	1	..	..	..	..	1	..
Davis, Moses Jr.	2	1	..	1	..	4	..	..	1	..	..
Dean, Seth	..	3	1	1	1	..	..	..	1	..	..
Deen, Robert	2	2	..	1	..	2	1	..	1	..	..
Dexter, Clark	1	..	..	1	..	1	..	1	..	..	..
Dimock, Joseph	4	..	..	1	..	1	..	..	1	..	..
Dudley, Levi	1	..	1	..	..	2	..	1	..	..	..
Eastman, Benjamin	..	2	..	..	1	4	..	1	1	..	..
Eastman, David	..	..	..	1	..	3	..	1	..	..	..
Eastman, Timothy	..	..	..	..	1	..	1	..	1	..	..
Eastman, Timothy Jr.	1	..	1	..	..	..	..	1	..	..	..
Eaton, Zebina	1	..	..	1	..	2	..	..	1	..	..
Ellis, John	2	1	..	1	..	2	1	..	1	..	..
Ellis, Joseph	1	..	..	1	..	1	1	..	1	..	..
Ellis, Paul	1	..	..	1	..	1	..	2	..	..	..
Ellis, Stephen	3	..	..	1	..	1	..	1	1	..	..
English, Joel	1	1	..	1	..	2	..	..	1	..	..
Fairbank, Calvin	2	3	2	..	1	1	..	1	..	1	..
Fairbank, Luther	3	..	2	..	1	1	2	1	1	1	..
Fay, Aaron	4	2	..	1	..	..	1	..	1	..	..
Fay, Eliakim	1	..	..	1	..	4	1	..	1	..	..
Fay, Moses	3	..	..	1	..	2	..	1	..	..	..
Fisk, John	2	2	1	..	1	3	1	..	1	..	..
Fisk, Jonathan	1	..	..	1	..	..	..	1	1	1	..
Foster, Jacob	..	..	..	..	1	..	..	..	..	1	..
Foster, John	1	1	1	1	..	3	2	1	1	..	..
Foster, John	..	1	4	1	1	..	1	..	..	2	..
Foster, Joseph	..	..	..	..	1	..	..	..	..	..	..
Foster, Joseph	3	1	..	1	..	1	2	..	1	..	..
Foster, Joseph	1	1	1	1	..	..	1	1	1	..	..
Foster, Peter	3	..	..	1	1	1	1	..	1	..	..
Foster, Samuel	..	..	1	..	..	..	..	1	..	..	..
Freeman, Elisha	4	..	..	1	..	1	1	..	1	..	..
Freeman, Joshua	..	..	..	1	..	2	..	..	1	..	..
Freeman, Thomas	..	..	..	..	1	..	..	..	..	1	..
Freeman, Thomas Jr.	3	..	..	1	..	2	1	..	1	..	..
Freeman, William	..	..	1	1	..	..	1	..	1	..	..
French, Roger	3	..	..	1	..	1	..	..	1	..	1
Fuller, Thomas	2	2	..	1	..	3	1	..	1	..	..
Gamboll, John	2	..	..	1	..	2	..	..	1	..	..
Gates, Simon	1	..	1	..	..	..	..	1	..	..	..
Graves, Isaac	1	..	1	..	..	1	..	1	..	..	..
Gray, Samuel	1	..	..	1	..	..	..	..	1	..	..
Gray, Thomas	2	..	..	1	..	1	..	..	1	..	..
Green, Beriah	1	..	..	..	1	..	2	..	..	1	..
Green, Elijah	2	..	..	1	..	1	..	..	1	..	..
Green, Frederick	2	..	..	1	..	2	..	..	1	..	..
Haridan, John	2	..	..	1	..	4	..	1	..	..	..
Haskell, Perrin	2	2	..	1	..	1	1	1	1	..	..
Hathaway, Ichabod	2	2	2	..	1	2	..	..	1	..	..
Houghton, Israel H.	4	1	..	1	..	2	..	..	1	..	..
How, William	1	..	..	1	..	2	..	1	1	..	..

WINDSOR COUNTY—Continued

NAMES OF HEADS OF FAMILIES	FREE WHITE MALES					FREE WHITE FEMALES					All other free persons except Indians not taxed
	Under 10 years of age	Of 10 and under 16	Of 16 and under 26 including heads of families	Of 26 and under 45 including heads of families	Of 45 and upwards including heads of families.	Under 10 years of age	Of 10 and under 16	Of 16 and under 26 including heads of families	Of 26 and under 45 including heads of families	Of 45 and upwards including heads of families	
BARNARD—con.											
Howard, Simeon	2	1	..	1	..	..	1	..	1	..	..
Hudson, Ezra	..	..	..	..	1	..	..	1	..	1	..
Hunter, Hezekiah	2	..	..	1	..	..	..	..	1	..	..
Jaquith, Daniel	3	..	2	1	..	..	..	..	1	..	..
Johnson, Hezekiah	2	1	..	1	..	1	..	..	1	..	1
Jones, John	2	1	..	1	..	1	..	..	1	..	..
Jones, John	..	1	..	..	1	..	..	..	..	1	..
Keith, Caleb	2	..	3	..	1	1	1	1	1	..	..
Kinne, Jesse	..	..	1	..	1	1	1	..	..	1	..
Lawton, Jacob	..	1	2	..	1	2	1	1	..	1	..
Luce, David	2	1	..	1	..	2	..	..	1	..	..
Luce, Jonathan	3	1	..	1	..	..	1	..	1	..	..
Lurvey, Moses	..	1	..	1	..	1	1	1	..	1	..
Lurvey, Peter	2	1	..	1	..	3	1	1	..	1	..
Mackintosh, William	..	..	1	1	1	..	..	3	2	1	..
Mason, Clement	..	..	..	..	1	..	..	..	1	1	..
McCormick, Daniel	..	..	..	1	..	..	1	1	..	..	..
Merrill, John	2	2	..	..	1	2	2	..	..	1	..
Mirack, Eleazer	..	..	..	1	..	1	2	..	1	1	..
Newton, Gideon	..	1	1	1	..	3	1	..	1	..	..
Newton, John	..	1	1	..	1	2	1	1	..	1	..
Newton, Timothy	1	1	2	..	1	3	..	..	1	..	..
Nott, John	1	..	1	1	..	1	..	..	1	..	..
Nott, Thadeus	3	..	..	1	..	2	..	..	1	..	..
Olcott, William	2	1	..	1	..	..	1	..	1	..	..
Page, Asa	3	1	..	..	1	..	2	..	1	1	..
Page, George	4	1	..	1	..	2	1	1	1	..	..
Page, Nathaniel	..	1	1	..	1	1	1	..	..	1	..
Parmeter, Nathan	2	2	..	1	..	3	..	2	1	..	..
Perkins, Abner	1	1	1	1	1	1	2	..	1	..	..
Perkins, John	1	..	..	1	..	1	..	1	..	..	..
Perkins, John	2	3	1	..	1	1	..	1	..	1	..
Perkins, William	..	..	2	..	1	..	2	..	1	..	..
Pierce, David	2	3	..	1	..	3	1	..	1	..	..
Reed, Job	1	1	..	1	..	4	1	..	1	..	..
Richmond, Amasiah	..	1	..	1	1	..	..	2	..	1	..
Richmond, Amasiah Jr.	2	1	1	1	..	2	2	2	1	..	..
Richmond, Ebenezer	..	..	2	1	1	1	..	..	1	1	..
Richmond, Gilbert	..	..	1	..	..	..	..	..	..	..	..
Richmond, Hathaway	..	..	1	..	..	..	..	1	..	..	..
Richmond, Job	..	..	..	1	..	..	..	1	..	..	..
Richmond, Lemuel	..	..	1	1	1	..	..	..	..	1	..
Richmond, Nathaniel	3	..	..	1	..	1	1	1	1	..	..
Richmond, Paul	1	..	..	1	..	1	..	1	..	1	..
Rider, Moses	..	1	..	..	1	..	..	1	..	1	..
Rider, Oliver	1	..	..	1	..	..	..	1	..	..	..
Sabin, Ebenezer	..	1	..	1	1	1	..	2	1	..	..
Sharp, Daniel	1	2	..	..	1	3	2	1	1	1	..
Southgate, Stewart	..	..	..	1	1	2	1	1	..	1	..
Spooner, Charles	1	..	..	1	..	..	..	..	1	1	..
Stebbins, Benjamin	1	1	2	..	1	1	2	1	..	1	..
Stebbins, John	1	..	..	1	..	1	..	..	1	..	..
Stevens, Andrew	..	..	..	..	1	..	..	1	..	1	..
Stevens, Andrew Jr.	2	1	..	1	..	4	..	..	1	..	..
Stevens, Lemuel	1	..	..	1	..	2	..	..	1	..	..
Steward, John	2	..	..	1	..	1	1	..	1	..	..
Stewart, Samuel	2	..	1	1	..	4	..	1	1	..	..
Swift, Charles	2	..	1	..	..	1	..	1	..	..	..
Swift, Heman	2	..	..	1	..	2	1	..	1	..	..
Swift, Joseph	1	..	1	1	..	2	..	..	1	..	..
Swift, Lemuel	..	..	..	..	1	..	..	..	1	..	..
Swift, Levi	2	1	1	1	..	..	..	1	1	..	..
Swift, Thomas	..	1	2	2	..	2	2	2	..	1	..
Topliff, Samuel	2	1	..	1	1	..	..	..	1	..	..
Townsend, George	2	..	..	1	..	2	1	..	1	..	..
Troop, Billins	2	..	..	1	..	..	..	1	1	..	..
Tucker, Robert	3	1	..	1	..	..	..	..	1	..	..
Tupper, Ellis	1	..	..	1	..	2	..	1	1	..	..
Tuppers, Israel	3	1	..	1	..	2	..	..	1	..	..
Wilber, Benjamin	2	1	2	..	1	1	1	1	..	1	..
Wing, Benjamin	3	1	..	2	..	..	1	..	1	..	..
Winslow, Hezekiah	1	..	..	1	..	2	..	1	..	..	..
Wood, Paul	3	..	..	1	..	1	..	..	1	..	..
Woods, Silas	1	..	..	1	..	1	..	..	1	..	..
Wright, Nathaniel	..	1	1	..	1	..	2	1	..	1	..
Wright, Thomas M.	1	..	..	..	1	..	1	2	..	2	..
UNCERTAIN NAMES											
Brannork (?), Levi	..	..	..	1	..	5	..	..	1	..	..
Burn (?), Moses	2	..	..	1	..	1	..	1	..	..	..
BETHEL											
Abbot, John	2	..	..	1	..	2	..	..	1	..	..
Anesworth, Daniel	..	1	1	1	..	3	1	..	1	..	..
Anesworth, Wyman	..	1	1	1	..	2	1	..	1	..	..
Babbit, Joel	..	1	..	..	1	..	..	..	1	..	..
Bachelor, Benjamin	3	2	1	..	1	1	1	..	..	1	..
Balch, Abner	..	..	2	..	..	..	..	1	..	..	..
Barns, Joseph	..	..	..	1	..	..	..	..	1	..	..
Belding, John	2	..	1	2	..	1	..	..	1	..	..
Billins, Israel	..	..	1	..	..	..	..	1	..	..	..
Bliss, Levi	..	..	1	..	1	..	..	..	..	1	..
Bowen, Joseph	2	..	..	1	..	2	..	..	1	..	..
Brooks, Reuben	2	..	..	1	..	2	..	..	1	..	..
Brooks, Simeon	3	2	..	1	..	2	..	..	1	..	..
Brown, Briant	4	..	..	1	..	..	..	..	1	1	..
Buckman, Isaiah	..	..	..	1	1	..	..	..	1	1	..
Buckman, Isaiah Jr.	2	..	..	1	..	2	..	..	1	..	..
Buckman, Ruth	..	..	..	..	..	2	1	..	1	..	..
Burbank, Eleazer	1	1	..	1	..	2	1	..	1	..	..
Burbank, Isaac	1	..	..	1	..	3	..	..	1	..	..
Burbank, William	1	..	..	1	..	2	..	..	1	..	..
Burnett, Jonathan	3	1	..	..	1	3	3	..	1	..	..
Burrows, David	..	2	..	1	2	4	3	..	1	1	..
Chaplin, William	1	..	1	..	1	1	..	..	..	1	..
Chapman, Chester	4	..	..	1	..	2	1	..	1	..	..
Chase, Simeon	1	1	..	1	..	..	1	..	1	..	..
Clark, Benjamin	3	1	1	1	..	1	1	1	1	..	..
Cleaveland, Stephen	..	1	..	1	..	3	1	..	1	..	..
Copeland, David	..	2	..	..	1	..	..	2	..	1	..
Copeland, Joseph	3	..	..	1	..	1	..	1	..	..	..
Cotten, Bibye L.	..	1	1	2	..	2	..	1	1	..	..
Crane, Amos	2	..	..	1	..	2	..	..	..	1	..
Crane, Benjamin	..	..	..	..	1	..	..	..	1	1	..
Crane, John	2	..	2	1	..	1	1	..	2	1	..
Crane, Ruth	2	..	..	..	..	..	..	2	1	..	..
Cummins, Reuben	1	..	1	1	..	1	..	1	1	..	..
Curtiss, William	2	..	1	..	1	2	2	..	1	..	..
Davis, Nathan	3	2	..	1	..	1	1	..	1	..	..
Davis, Nathan	2	..	1	..	..	..	..	1	..	..	..
Dean, James	1	..	..	1	..	2	..	..	1	..	..
Dean, Zachariah	..	..	..	..	1	..	..	1	..	1	..
Deans, Lemuel	1	2	1	1	..	2	1	1	1	..	..
Deans, Zacheus	..	..	..	..	1	..	..	1	..	1	..
Dike, Daniel	1	..	..	1	..	..	..	..	..	..	..
Dunham, Thomas	..	..	..	..	1	..	..	..	..	1	..
Dunham, William	..	1	..	..	1	2	..	..	..	1	..
Durfee, James	1	1	1	1	..	1	1	1	1	..	..
Durkee, Henry	..	..	..	1	..	2	..	1	..	..	..
Eddy, John	1	..	..	..	1	1	1	..	1	..	..
Eddy, Jonah	1	..	1	1	..	..	2	..	..	1	..
Edson, Samuel L.	3	1	..	1	..	..	..	1	..	..	..
Fenley, John	..	2	..	..	1	..	..	..	1	..	..
Fisher, Timothy	1	..	1	..	..	1	..	1	..	..	..
Flynn, Michael	3	1	2	..	1	..	1	..	1	..	..
Fowler, Elisha	2	..	..	..	1	2	2	1	..	1	..
Gates, James	..	..	..	..	1	3	2	..	..	1	..
Gates, Jeremiah	1	..	1	..	..	..	..	..	1	..	..
Gibbs, Lemuel	2	..	..	1	..	1	..	1	1	..	..
Goodale, Ebenezer	..	1	..	..	1	..	..	1	..	1	..
Gould, Asa	1	2	..	..	1	3	..	..	1	..	..
Green, Amasa	..	2	1	1	..	4	1	1	1	1	..
Grover, Amasa	..	..	..	..	1	..	..	..	..	1	..
Grover, Luther	1	..	..	1	..	1	..	1	1	..	..
Hall, Jesse	..	..	..	1	..	3	..	..	1	..	..
Hall, Samuel	1	..	1	..	..	..	..	1	..	..	..
Hamblin, Josiah	..	..	..	..	1	..	..	..	..	1	..
Hamblin, Josiah Jr.	..	..	1	..	..	..	..	1	..	..	..
Hawley, John	..	..	..	..	1	..	..	1	..	1	..
Hibbard, Dolly	..	..	..	..	..	1	..	..	1	..	..
Hinshaw, Isaac	..	..	..	1	..	4	2	..	1	1	..

WINDSOR COUNTY—Continued

NAMES OF HEADS OF FAMILIES	FREE WHITE MALES					FREE WHITE FEMALES					All other free persons except Indians not taxed
	Under 10 years of age	Of 10 and under 16	Of 16 and under 26 including heads of families	Of 26 and under 45 including heads of families	Of 45 and upwards including heads of families.	Under 10 years of age	Of 10 and under 16	Of 16 and under 26 including heads of families	Of 26 and under 45 including heads of families	Of 45 and upwards including heads of families	
BETHEL—con.											
Hunt, Benjamin	1	..	..	1	..	1	..	..	1	..	..
Huntington, David	1	3	2	..	1	..	..	1	..	1	..
Huntington, James	3	1	1	1	..	1	1	1	1	..	..
Jeffison, Ezekiel	..	..	1	..	1	2	..	1	..	1	..
Kellogg, Martin	..	..	2	1	..	3	1	..	1	..	..
Kenne, John	2	1	1	1	..	..	1	..	1	..	..
Kenny, Daniel	2	1	..	..	1	3	1	..	1	..	..
Lathrop, Asa	2	..	..	1	..	1	..	..	1	..	..
Lathrop, Daniel	2	..	..	1	..	2	..	..	1	..	..
Lathrop, John	..	..	..	..	1	..	..	..	..	1	..
Lathrop, John Jr.	2	..	..	1	..	..	..	..	1	..	..
Lincoln, Hezekiah	2	1	..	..	1	..	..	1	..	1	..
Lylie, Benjamin	1	1	..	1	..	1	..	..	1	..	..
Lylie, David	..	3	3	..	1	2	..	2	1	1	..
Lylie, Joshua	1	1	..	1	..	1	..	..	1	..	..
Markas, Samuel	..	..	1	..	1	..	1	1	..	1	..
Marsh, Joel	..	1	3	2	1	..	..	..	2	1	..
Martin, Rufus	..	..	..	1	..	3	..	..	1	..	..
McKinster, Paul	..	1	..	..	1	..	..	1	..	1	..
McKinster, Salmon	1	..	1	1	..	2	..	1	1	..	..
Mills, Joseph	..	..	..	1	..	2	..	1	..	..	..
Mills, Roswell	2	..	..	1	..	..	..	1	..	..	..
Moodey, John	1	1	..	1	..	4	2	..	1	..	..
Morse, Jeremiah	1	1	..	1	..	2	1	..	1	..	..
Neff, Rufus	1	..	..	1	..	1	..	1	..	..	..
Niff, Benjamin	3	..	1	..	..	..	..	1	..	..	..
Noble, Nehemiah	4	2	1	..	1	..	1	..	..	1	..
Owen, Andrew	1	..	..	1	..	2	..	..	1	..	..
Owen, Sylvanus	1	1	..	..	1	1	..	..	1	..	..
Parish, John	1	..	..	1	..	1	..	..	1	..	..
Parish, Nehemiah	3	..	..	1	..	..	2	..	1	1	..
Park, Samuel	1	1	..	..	1	2	1	2	..	1	..
Parker, Tille	2	..	..	1	..	2	..	1	1	1	..
Peck, Daniel	3	..	..	1	..	..	..	1	..	..	..
Peckham, Pardon	..	1	..	1	..	3	1	..	1	..	..
Peckham, Phillip	..	..	..	1	..	..	1	..	1	..	..
Putnam, Anthony	2	..	..	1	..	1	..	..	1	..	..
Putnam, Ebenezer	..	..	1	..	1	..	..	1	..	1	..
Putnam, Ezra	3	..	1	..	1	..	1	2	..	1	..
Putnam, Joshua	2	..	1	..	..	2	..	..	1	..	..
Putnam, Thomas	2	2	..	..	1	..	1	..	..	1	..
Randall, Leonard	1	..	1	..	..	..	..	1	..	..	..
Rider, Samuel	1	..	1	..	..	1	..	1	..	..	..
Robinson, Eleazer	..	1	..	..	1	..	..	1	..	1	..
Rodgers, Jeduthan	..	..	1	..	1	..	..	..	1	..	..
Sandborn, Samuel	1	..	..	1	..	1	..	1	..	..	..
Sanford, Seth	2	..	1	1	..	2	..	..	1	..	..
Smith, Benjamin	4	..	2	..	1	1	3	1	1	..	..
Smith, George	2	1	..	..	1	..	1	..	1	..	..
Smith, Moses	1	1	..	1	..	2	1	..	1	..	..
Smith, Simeon	..	..	..	1	1	1	..	..	..	1	..
Smith, Willard	1	1	3	2	1	..	..	2	..	1	..
Snow, John	..	..	1	..	..	..	..	1	..	..	..
Southend, William	2	1	1	..	1	1	..	1	1	..	..
Stone, David	..	1	..	..	1	1	..	2	..	1	..
Stone, Nathan	1	1	..	1	..	2	1	..	1	..	..
Strong, Barnabas	4	..	..	1	..	1	..	..	1	..	..
Strong, Benajah	..	..	1	..	1	..	..	1	..	1	..
Strong, Benajah Jr.	..	1	..	1	..	2	..	..	1	..	..
Teny, David	2	..	..	1	..	..	..	..	1	..	..
Teny, Ephraim	..	2	..	1	..	2	2	1	1	..	..
Teny, John	..	1	..	..	1	1	1	1	..	1	..
Tinne, Reuben	1	1	..	1	..	1	2	..	1	..	..
Townsend, John	..	..	..	1	..	2	..	2	1	..	..
Troop, Nathaniel	1	1	1	1	..	1	..	2	1	..	..
Walcott, Jabez	1	..	..	1	..	1	1	..	1	..	..
Walker, Asaph	..	..	1	1	..	..	..	..	1	..	..
Wallis, John	2	..	1	..	1	2	3	1	1	..	..
Wallis, Joseph	2	2	1	1	..	1	..	2	..	..	..
Whitingham, Joseph	1	1	..	1	..	2	1	1	1	..	..
Whitney, Nathan	2	1	1	1	..	1	1	..	1	..	..
Willard, Jonathan	..	1	1	..	1	..	1	..	..	1	..
Williams, Josiah	..	1	..	1	..	2	1	..	..	1	..
Wilson, Samuel	2	..	..	1	..	2	..	..	1	..	..
Wood, Joseph	1	..	..	1	..	3	..	..	1	..	..
Woodbury, Daniel	..	..	1	..	..	..	..	..	..	1	..
Woodbury, Peter	2	3	1	1	..	..	1	1	1	..	..
Wright, George	..	1	..	..	1	..	..	..	..	1	..
UNCERTAIN NAMES											
Downer (?), Daniel	1	3	1	..	1	1	1	..	1	..	..
Tolenson (?), Josiah	..	..	..	..	1	..	..	..	..	1	..
BRIDGEWATER											
Atwood, Ebenezer	1	..	..	1	..	1	..	..	1	..	..
Avery, Nathan	2	1	1	..	1	2	1	2	..	1	..
Ayres, Thomas	3	..	..	1	..	1	..	1	..	..	..
Badcock, Samuel	2	..	..	1	..	1	..	..	1	..	..
Barrows, Samuel	3	..	..	1	..	1	..	..	1	..	..
Bassett, Howard	1	..	..	..	1	..	..	..	..	1	..
Bassett, Zachariah	1	1	..	..	1	..	..	..	1	1	..
Bosworth, Toory	1	..	..	1	..	2	..	1	..	..	..
Boyce, George	1	1	1	..	1	2	1	3	1	..	..
Brannock, Consider	..	..	..	..	1	..	..	..	..	1	..
Bunn, Mathew	2	..	..	1	..	3	..	1	..	..	..
Burns, Hamlleton	..	..	..	1	..	..	..	..	1	..	..
Burnson, Joseph	3	..	..	1	..	..	..	1	1	..	..
Burnson, Moses	2	..	..	1	..	..	..	1	..	1	..
Clark, Isaac	..	..	..	1	..	2	..	..	1	..	..
Cleaveland, William	..	1	..	..	1	..	..	..	1	..	..
Cobb, Nathan	..	..	2	..	1	1	1	..	..	..	..
Cobb, Nathaniel	1	..	..	1	..	2	1	1	..	..	..
Dammon, Jedediah	..	..	..	1	1	1	..	..	1	..	..
Denison, Samuel	..	1	..	..	1	..	1	..	..	1	..
Dimock, Joseph	..	..	..	..	1	..	..	..	..	1	..
Dimock, Joseph Jr.	..	..	..	1	..	1	..	1	..	..	..
Fish, Benjamin	..	..	1	..	1	2	2	1	1	1	..
Fish, Benjamin Jr.	..	..	..	1	..	1	..	..	1	..	..
Fish, George	1	..	1	..	..	..	..	1	..	..	..
Fletcher, James	2	2	1	..	1	1	2	..	1	..	..
Freman, Isaiah	3	..	..	1	..	..	..	..	1	..	..
French, Aaron	..	..	..	..	1	..	1	..	..	1	..
French, Ephraim C.	1	..	..	1	..	1	3	..	1	..	..
French, Ezekiel	3	..	..	1	..	1	..	..	1	..	..
French, Ezra	1	..	1	..	..	..	..	1	..	..	..
French, Joseph	2	1	..	1	..	2	..	..	1	..	..
Gibbs, Ebenezer	4	..	..	1	..	..	..	..	1	..	..
Gibbs, Josiah	3	1	..	1	..	2	1	..	1	..	..
Gibbs, Stephen	2	..	..	..	1	1	2	..	1	..	..
Gillet, Elisha	2	..	..	1	..	2	..	..	1	..	..
Green, Asa	3	2	..	1	..	2	1	..	1	..	..
Green, Benjamin	..	..	..	..	1	..	..	..	..	1	..
Greggs, Ephraim	1	..	1	..	1	1	..	..	..	1	..
Grow, William	1	2	1	..	1	1	..	1	..	1	..
Hacket, Henry	1	..	..	1	..	2	2	..	1	..	..
Hammond, Phillip	1	1	..	1	..	2	..	..	1	..	..
Harris, John	..	..	..	1	..	2	..	1	..	1	..
Harris, Samuel	..	..	..	1	..	..	..	..	1	..	..
Hawkins, James	2	1	1	1	..	2	..	1	1	..	..
Hawkins, John	..	..	..	1	1	1	1	..	..	1	..
Hawkins, Joseph	3	1	..	2	..	2	2	1	1	..	..
Hawkins, Samuel	..	1	..	1	1	1	..	..	1	..	..
Hoisington, Billina	2	1	..	1	..	3	..	..	1	..	..
Hoisington, Bliss	1	..	..	1	..	3	1	1	..	1	..
Hoisington, Isaac	3	1	..	1	..	2	1	1	1	..	..
Hoisington, John	2	..	..	1	..	4	1	..	1	..	..
Johnson, Freeman	..	..	1	..	..	2	..	1	..	..	..
Jones, Ariel	..	..	..	1	..	..	1	..	..	1	..
Jones, Ariel Jr.	1	..	..	1	..	2	..	..	1	..	..
Jones, Samuel	3	..	..	1	..	1	..	..	1	1	..
Lamb, Aaron	..	..	1	..	..	..	..	1	..	..	..
Lamb, Thomas	4	..	..	1	..	2	1	..	1	..	..
Lamb, Willard	..	..	..	1	..	1	..	..	1	..	..
Maxham, David	2	..	..	1	..	1	..	..	1	..	..
Maxham, Isaac	..	..	..	1	..	2	..	1	..	..	..
Mendall, Amos	3	..	..	1	..	..	3	1	1	..	..
Miller, Nathaniel	1	1	1	1	..	1	..	..	1	..	..
Montague, Selah	3	1	1	1	..	..	2	..	1	..	..
Nolton, Stephen	..	2	1	..	1	..	1	1	..	1	..

WINDSOR COUNTY—Continued

NAMES OF HEADS OF FAMILIES	FREE WHITE MALES					FREE WHITE FEMALES					All other free persons except Indians not taxed
	Under 10 years of age	Of 10 and under 16	Of 16 and under 26 including heads of families	Of 26 and under 45 including heads of families	Of 45 and upwards including heads of families.	Under 10 years of age	Of 10 and under 16	Of 16 and under 26 including heads of families	Of 26 and under 45 including heads of families	Of 45 and upwards including heads of families.	
BRIDGEWATER—con.											
Osgood, Isaac	1	..	1	1	..	..	..	..	1	..	..
Palmer, Jacob	1	..	..	1	..	4	..	..	1	..	..
Palmer, Robert	1	..	..	1	..	4	..	..	1	..	..
Perkins, Benjamin	..	..	..	1	..	3	2	..	1	..	..
Perkins, Cyrus	1	..	..	1	..	4	2	..	1	..	..
Perkins, Joseph	1	..	1	1	..	2	1	..	1	..	..
Phillips, Asa	1	..	..	..	1	3	..	..	..	1	..
Pierce, Joseph	..	..	..	..	1	..	..	..	..	1	..
Pierce, Joseph Jr.	..	..	..	1	..	2	..	..	1	..	..
Pierce, William	1	1	..	1	..	4	1	..	1	..	..
Pollard, James	4	2	..	..	1	1	..	..	1	..	..
Powers, Abraham	..	..	..	..	1	..	..	1	..	1	..
Powers, Abraham Jr.	1	1	..	1	..	3	..	..	1	..	..
Powers, Thomas	2	..	..	1	..	1	..	..	1	..	..
Pratt, John	2	1	..	1	..	3	..	..	1	..	..
Pratt, John	..	..	1	..	..	..	..	1	..	..	..
Pratt, Jonathan	4	1	..	..	1	..	1	1	1	..	..
Pratt, Nathan	..	..	1	..	1	..	..	1	..	1	..
Ripley, Samuel	..	1	1	..	1	..	..	2	1	..	..
Sanders, Phinehas	1	1	3	..	1	2	2	1	1	..	..
Shaw, Benoni	2	2	..	1	..	3	..	..	1	..	..
Shaw, Elkanah	..	..	..	1	..	..	..	..	1	..	..
Shaw, Isaiah	5	1	..	..	1	..	2	..	1	..	..
Shaw, James	..	1	..	..	1	..	..	..	..	1	..
Shaw, Job	1	1	1	2	..	3	1	..	2	..	..
Shirtlieff, Levi	1	..	..	1	..	1	..	..	1	..	..
Simmons, Hope	..	..	..	..	..	1	2	1	..	..	..
Simmons, Reul	..	..	..	1	..	1	..	1	..	..	..
Slayton, Joseph	..	..	..	1	..	1	..	..	1	..	..
Smith, Elisha	..	..	..	1	..	..	..	1	..	..	..
Southgate, James	2	1	1	2	..	2	..	1	1	..	..
Southgate, Richard	..	..	..	..	1	..	..	..	..	1	..
Southgate, Richard Jr.	1	..	1	1	..	..	..	2	..	..	..
Southgate, Thomas	2	..	..	1	..	1	..	..	1	..	..
Strong, Elijah	..	..	..	1	..	2	..	..	1	..	..
Strong, John	..	..	..	..	1	..	3	..	..	1	..
Thomas, Levi	3	..	..	1	..	..	..	..	1	1	..
Thomas, Zebulon	2	2	1	..	1	..	..	1	..	1	..
Thompson, Abel	..	..	..	1	..	..	..	..	1	..	..
Thompson, Barnabas	2	..	..	1	..	1	..	..	1	..	..
Thompson, David	2	..	..	1	..	1	..	..	1	..	..
Thompson, Noah	1	2	1	..	1	..	..	2	..	1	..
Thompson, Noah Jr.	1	..	..	1	..	..	..	1	..	..	..
Topliff, James	1	1	2	1	..	2	1	1	1	..	..
Tracy, Abel	3	..	..	1	..	1	..	..	1	1	..
Vaughan, Caleb	..	..	1	..	..	..	..	1	..	..	..
Vaughan, Joseph	2	1	..	..	1	1	..	2	1	..	..
Vaughan, Samuel	2	..	..	1	..	1	..	..	1	..	..
Vose, Thomas	3	..	1	1	..	2	..	1	1	..	..
Walker, Elijah	1	1	..	1	..	4	1	..	1	..	..
Walker, James	4	..	..	1	..	1	..	..	1	..	..
Walker, John	1	1	..	1	..	3	1	..	1	..	..
Washburn, James	2	..	..	1	..	2	..	..	1	..	..
Whitcomb, Charles	..	..	..	1	..	2	1	..	1	..	..
White, David	4	..	..	1	..	..	..	..	2	..	..
White, Jonathan	3	..	..	1	..	1	..	..	1	..	..
White, Sylvanus	1	1	..	1	..	1	1	..	1	..	..
White, William	2	..	..	1	..	..	..	..	1	..	..
Williams, Phinehas	1	1	..	1	..	1	..	..	1	..	..
Wilson, Daniel	1	..	1	..	..	1	..	1	..	..	..
Windslow, William	1	..	..	1	..	..	..	..	1	..	..
Winslow, Canellan	1	..	..	..	1	..	..	..	..	1	..
Winslow, John	1	..	..	..	1	..	1	..	..	1	..
Winslow, Thomas	..	..	1	..	..	..	..	1	..	..	..
Woodbury, Joshua	2	..	..	1	..	2	1	1	1	..	..
Woodward, Phebe	1	..	..	1	..	..	..	..	1	2	..
Woodward, Stephen	..	1	1	1	1	..	2	2	..	1	..
UNCERTAIN NAMES											
Barvin (?), Isaac	..	..	..	1	..	3	..	1	..	..	..
Lewis (?), Elisha	2	..	..	1	..	..	..	..	1	..	..
Lewis (?), Nathan	..	..	1	..	..	..	..	..	..	2	..
CAVENDISH											
Adams, Benjamin	1	1	1	..	1	1	1	1	..	1	..
Adams, Timothy	3	2	..	1	..	3	1	..	1	..	..
Allen, John W.	..	..	2	..	..	..	..	1	..	..	..
Ames, Samuel	..	..	..	..	1	..	..	..	..	1	..
Atherton, Jonathan	1	2	..	1	..	..	1	1	1	..	..

NAMES OF HEADS OF FAMILIES	FREE WHITE MALES					FREE WHITE FEMALES					All other free persons except Indians not taxed
	Under 10 years of age	Of 10 and under 16	Of 16 and under 26 including heads of families	Of 26 and under 45 including heads of families	Of 45 and upwards including heads of families.	Under 10 years of age	Of 10 and under 16	Of 16 and under 26 including heads of families	Of 26 and under 45 including heads of families	Of 45 and upwards including heads of families.	
CAVENDISH—con.											
Baker, Nathaniel	..	..	..	1	..	..	..	..	1	..	..
Baldwin, Abel	2	..	..	1	1	2	..	1	1	1	..
Baldwin, Isaac	3	1	1	1	..	2	1	..	1	..	..
Baldwin, Joseph	..	1	2	1	..	..	1	..	1	..	..
Baldwin, Thomas	2	..	..	1	..	1	..	..	1	..	..
Boynton, Nathan	..	..	1	1	..	1	..	..	1	..	..
Boynton, Nathan	2	..	..	1	..	2	..	..	2	..	..
Brown, Eleazer	1	..	..	1	1	1	..	..	1	1	..
Brown, John	1	1	..	1	..	1	..	..	1	..	..
Brown, Roger	2	..	..	1	..	1	..	..	1	..	1
Butterfield, Charles	1	1	..	1	..	1	2	..	1	..	..
Chamberlain, Joseph	..	..	..	1	..	2	..	..	1	..	..
Chaplin, William	..	..	..	..	1	..	..	..	..	1	..
Chapman, Eliphalet	..	..	2	..	1	1	1	1	..	1	..
Chapman, Jonathan	..	..	1	..	..	..	..	1	..	1	..
Chapman, Reuben	4	2	..	1	..	1	1	..	1	..	..
Chubb, David	3	1	..	1	1	1	1	..	1	1	..
Clark, Ephraim	..	..	..	1	..	2	..	..	1	..	..
Clark, Reuben	1	..	1	..	1	..	2	..	..	1	..
Coffin, John	..	..	..	..	1	..	..	1	..	2	..
Coffin, Lake	..	..	..	..	1	1	..	..	1	..	..
Coffin, William	1	..	1	..	1	..	..	1	..	..	..
Conant, Nathan	1	..	..	1	..	1	..	..	1	..	..
Conway, Daniel	1	..	..	1	..	1	..	1	..	..	..
Conway, Peter	..	..	1	..	..	..	..	1	..	..	..
Davis, Joel	..	2	..	..	1	..	..	..	1	..	..
Davis, John	..	..	1	..	..	..	..	1	..	..	..
Davis, Robert	..	..	1	..	..	1	..	1	..	..	..
Day, Elkanah	4	1	..	1	..	1	..	..	1	..	..
Dix, Samuel	..	1	..	1	..	2	2	..	1	..	..
Dodge, John	..	..	..	1	..	4	2	..	1	..	..
Dutton, Salmon	..	1	1	2	1	..	..	1	1	1	..
Dwinnell, Israel	2	..	..	1	..	2	1	..	1	..	..
Eaton, Enoch	..	..	..	..	1	..	2	..	..	1	..
Eaton, Frazier	..	..	1	..	..	..	..	1	..	..	..
Eaton, Kimball	..	..	..	1	..	2	..	..	1	..	..
Falls, John	..	..	..	..	..	..	..	..	..	..	5
Fassett, Pearly	..	..	..	1	..	..	..	..	1	..	..
Felt, William	2	..	1	1	..	..	..	2	..	..	..
Fletcher, Asaph	4	1	3	..	1	..	1	3	..	1	..
French, Daniel	..	1	..	1	..	2	..	..	1	..	..
French, Josiah	2	..	..	1	..	1	..	..	1	..	..
Fullam, Sewell	1	..	..	1	..	..	..	1	1	..	..
Fullum, Ebenezer	1	..	..	1	..	3	..	..	1	..	..
Fullum, Timothy	..	..	..	..	1	..	..	1	..	1	..
Gary, Seth	1	1	..	1	..	..	1	1	1	..	..
Gerrald, Gamaliel	..	1	..	..	1	1	1	..	1	..	..
Gilbert, Isaac	1	..	..	1	..	2	..	..	1	1	..
Gilbert, Jonas	1	..	..	1	..	2	..	..	1	..	..
Gorden, James	2	2	..	1	..	..	..	..	1	..	..
Grant, Henry	1	2	..	1	..	2	1	..	1	..	..
Green, Nehemiah	..	..	3	..	1	..	2	..	..	2	..
Haggett, Jesse	2	..	..	1	..	2	1	..	1	..	..
Hall, James	..	..	1	..	1	..	1	..	..	1	..
Hardy, John	3	..	..	1	..	2	2	..	1	..	..
Hardy, Samson	2	..	1	1	1	2	3	..	1	1	..
Holt, William	2	..	..	1	..	1	1	..	1	..	..
Huston, Caleb	2	..	..	1	..	2	1	..	1	..	..
Huston, Samuel	3	..	..	1	..	1	..	..	1	..	..
Huston, Vernum	..	1	1	..	..	1	..	1	..	..	..
Hutchinson, Rufus	..	..	1	..	..	..	..	1	..	..	..
Hutchinson, Samuel	..	1	..	..	1	..	..	..	1	1	..
Hutchinson, Samuel Jr.	3	1	..	1	..	..	1	..	1	..	..
Jackman, Abner	..	..	1	..	1	..	1	..	..	1	..
Kendall, Thomas	3	..	..	1	..	..	..	..	1	..	..
Kendall, William	..	..	..	..	1	1	..	..	..	1	..
Knapp, Joshua	1	..	..	1	..	..	..	..	1	..	..
Knox, Sylvanus	2	1	2	1	..	..	..	..	1	..	..
Lincoln, Lemuel	2	2	..	1	..	1	1	..	1	1	..
Lock, Amos	..	..	1	2	..	..	..	1	..	..	..
Lovel, Michael	..	..	..	1	..	4	..	..	1	..	..
Lovel, Randal	2	1	..	1	..	..	2	..	1	..	..
Lynde, Benjamin	1	1	1	..	1	1	..	..	..	1	..
Manning, Levi	2	..	..	1	..	2	..	..	1	..	..
Mason, Daniel	2	1	..	1	..	..	..	1	..	..	..
McCoy, Thomas	1	..	..	1	..	1	..	1	..	..	..
Murdock, Robert	..	..	..	1	..	..	..	..	1	..	..

WINDSOR COUNTY—Continued

NAMES OF HEADS OF FAMILIES	FREE WHITE MALES					FREE WHITE FEMALES					All other free persons except Indians not taxed
	Under 10 years of age	Of 10 and under 16	Of 16 and under 26 including heads of families	Of 26 and under 45 including heads of families	Of 45 and upwards including heads of families.	Under 10 years of age	Of 10 and under 16	Of 16 and under 26 including heads of families	Of 26 and under 45 including heads of families	Of 45 and upwards including heads of families	
CAVENDISH—con.											
Nutting, Elijah	2	..	..	1	..	2	1	..	1	..	..
Nutting, John	..	..	..	..	1	..	..	2	..	1	..
Nutting, John Jr.	..	..	..	1	..	..	..	..	1	..	..
Page, Joseph	2	1	..	1	..	2	..	..	1	..	..
Parker, Aaron	..	1	1	1	1	..	1	..	..	1	..
Parker, Aaron Jr.	1	..	..	1	..	1	..	..	1	..	..
Parker, Abel	1	..	..	1	..	..	..	..	1	..	..
Parker, Joshua	2	..	..	1	..	1	..	..	1	..	..
Parker, Juna	..	1	1	..	1	..	1	..	1	..	..
Parker, Leonard	..	1	..	..	2	1	1	1	..	1	..
Parker, Thomas	2	..	..	1	..	3	..	..	1	..	..
Peck, Daniel	1	..	..	1	..	3	1	..	1	..	..
Peck, John	3	..	..	1	..	1	..	..	1	..	..
Pierce, Amos	2	..	..	1	..	1	..	..	1	..	..
Proctor, Leonard	..	2	1	1	1	..	1	2	..	1	..
Proctor, Leonard Jr.	2	..	..	1	..	2	..	..	1	..	..
Proctor, Thomas	..	..	1	..	..	1	..	1	..	..	..
Proctor, Timothy	2	1	..	1	..	1	1	1	1	..	..
Rand, William	..	..	..	1	..	1	..	..	1	1	..
Roberts, Daniel	3	1	1	..	1	2	1	..	..	1	..
Ross, Daniel	2	1	1	1	..	2	..	2	..	1	..
Russell, John	2	1	..	..	1	1	1	1	..	2	..
Russell, Noadiah	3	1	1	..	1	2	1	..	..	2	..
Scott, Thomas	4	3	..	1	..	2	2	1	1	..	..
Searls, David	1	1	..	1	..	4	1	..	1	..	..
Shaw, Bizalul	4	2	..	1	..	2	..	..	1	..	..
Skinner, Laban	1	..	..	1	..	2	..	..	1	..	..
Smith, James	2	..	1	1	..	1	..	..	1	..	..
Smith, Thaddeus	2	..	..	1	..	3	..	..	1	..	..
Snow, Robert	2	..	..	1	..	1	1	..	1	..	..
Spaulding, Benjamin	1	2	..	1	..	..	1	..	1	..	..
Spaulding, Jesse	3	3	..	..	1	2	..	1	1	1	..
Spaulding, Jesse	..	..	1	..	..	1	..	1	..	..	..
Spaulding, John	2	..	..	1	..	2	..	..	1	..	..
Spaulding, Joseph	2	1	..	1	..	1	..	..	1	..	..
Spaulding, Willard	2	2	..	1	..	3	2	..	1	..	..
Spaulding, William	..	1	1	..	1	1	..	1	..	1	..
Spaulding, William	2	..	1	1	..	3	..	..	1	..	..
Spaulding, Zedekiah	1	..	1	..	..	1	..	1	..	..	..
Spear, Samuel	2	1	..	1	..	1	1	..	1	..	..
Sprague, Nathan	1	2	..	1	..	3	1	..	1	..	..
Stevens, Levi	1	1	..	1	..	1	..	..	1	..	..
Stiles, Jacob	..	1	..	..	1	..	..	2	..	1	..
Stone, Timothy	2	1	4	1	..	1	1	1	1	..	..
Swift, William	2	..	..	1	..	2	..	..	1	..	..
Tarble, Edmond	..	1	1	..	..	..	..	1	..	..	..
Tarble, Whitcomb	2	2	..	1	..	2	..	..	1	1	..
Taylor, Amos	..	..	..	..	1	..	..	..	..	1	..
Taylor, Edmund	..	2	..	1	1	2	..	..	..	1	..
Taylor, Edmund Jr.	..	..	1	..	..	..	..	..	1	..	..
Taylor, William	..	..	1	..	..	1	..	..	1	..	..
Tilden, Joshua	..	1	..	..	1	..	1	..	..	1	..
Tilden, Renington	..	..	1	..	..	1	..	..	1	..	..
Town, Francis	1	1	..	1	..	1	..	..	1	1	..
Tuttle, Jedediah	1	1	..	1	..	2	1	..	1	..	..
Upton, Robert	..	2	..	1	..	4	1	..	1	..	..
Walker, Elijah	2	..	..	1	..	..	..	..	1	..	..
Walker, Elijah 2nd	1	..	..	1	1	2	..	..	1	1	..
Ward, Calvin	1	..	..	1	..	3	..	..	1	..	..
Wheeler, Asa	1	..	1	..	1	1	..	..	1	..	..
Wheelock, John	2	1	..	1	..	..	..	..	1	..	..
Wheelock, John	1	..	..	2	..	1	..	1	..	1	..
Wheelock, Jonathan	2	1	..	..	1	..	..	..	..	1	..
Wheelock, Joseph	2	..	..	1	..	2	..	..	1	..	..
White, Obadiah	3	..	..	1	..	..	..	..	1	..	..
White, Samuel	1	1	2	..	1	1	..	2	..	1	..
White, Thomas	3	..	..	1	..	..	..	..	1	..	..
Wilder, Amherst	..	1	..	1	..	2	..	..	1	..	..
Wilkins, Ezra	..	..	..	1	..	1	..	1	..	..	..
Wilkins, Joseph	1	2	..	1	1	2	2	2	..	1	..
Wright, John	1	..	..	1	..	..	..	..	1	..	..
Wyman, Samuel	..	1	..	..	2	1	1	1	..	1	..
Wyman, Samuel Jr.	..	..	1	..	..	..	..	1	..	..	..
Young, Joseph	..	..	1	..	1	..	1	2	..	1	..
CHESTER											
Abbot, Daniel	1	..	..	1	..	3	..	..	1	..	..
Adams, Archelaus	..	..	..	1	..	3	..	..	1	..	..
Alverson, Simeon	..	1	1	..	1	..	..	..	2	..	..

NAMES OF HEADS OF FAMILIES	FREE WHITE MALES					FREE WHITE FEMALES					All other free persons except Indians not taxed
	Under 10 years of age	Of 10 and under 16	Of 16 and under 26 including heads of families	Of 26 and under 45 including heads of families	Of 45 and upwards including heads of families.	Under 10 years of age	Of 10 and under 16	Of 16 and under 26 including heads of families	Of 26 and under 45 including heads of families	Of 45 and upwards including heads of families	
CHESTER—con.											
Armington, William	..	..	1	..	..	..	1	..	..	..	..
Arnold, Ebenezer	2	1	..	1	..	3	2	..	1	..	..
Arnold, Uriah	..	..	..	1	..	1	..	..	..	1	..
Atwood, Anthony	1	..	..	1	..	2	..	..	1	..	..
Atwood, Jeremiah	3	..	..	1	..	..	1	..	2	..	..
Atwood, Oliver	3	..	1	1	..	3	1	1	1	..	..
Atwood, Rufus	1	..	1	1	..	..	..	1	..	2	..
Axtell, Samuel	..	..	..	1	..	3	..	..	1	..	..
Baker, Stephen	1	..	..	1	..	3	..	..	1	..	..
Bakke, Pomp	..	..	..	..	..	..	..	..	..	..	4
Barney, Martin	2	..	..	1	..	3	2	..	1	..	..
Barton, Caleb	..	..	..	1	..	..	..	1	..	..	..
Barton, Jabez	1	..	3	..	..	..	..	1	..	..	..
Barton, Joseph	..	1	..	1	..	1	..	1	1	..	..
Bates, Moses	3	..	..	1	..	1	1	..	1	..	..
Beeman, Joshua	3	..	..	1	..	2	..	..	1	..	..
Boker, Seth	..	..	1	..	..	2	..	1	..	..	..
Bowker, John	..	..	1	..	..	1	..	1	..	..	..
Bowtell, John	2	2	..	1	..	..	1	..	1	..	..
Bowtell, Kendall	2	..	..	2	..	2	..	..	1	..	..
Boyden, Jonathan	..	1	..	1	..	1	..	..	1	..	..
Bradford, Andrew	2	..	..	1	..	1	..	..	1	..	..
Brattle, Richard	..	..	..	..	..	..	..	..	..	..	3
Briant, Edmund	2	..	..	1	..	2	1	..	1	..	..
Bridges, Benjamin	2	..	..	1	..	..	..	..	1	..	..
Briggs, Randall	2	..	1	2	..	1	..	..	2	1	..
Brooks, Jonathan	..	..	1	..	..	1	..	1	..	..	..
Brooks, Nathaniel	1	..	..	1	..	2	..	..	1	..	..
Brooks, Solomon	..	..	..	1	..	2	..	..	1	..	..
Brown, Augustus	1	..	1	..	..	1	1	..	1	..	..
Buckland, Timothy	4	..	..	1	..	..	..	..	1	..	..
Bullard, Nathan	3	..	..	1	..	1	1	..	1	..	..
Burges, James	..	..	..	..	1	2	1	..	1	..	..
Burt, Gorden	..	..	..	..	1	4	1	..	1	..	..
Burt, John	2	..	..	1	..	..	..	..	1	..	..
Campbell, Robert	2	1	..	1	..	2	1	..	..	1	..
Carpenter, Knight	2	1	..	1	..	2	..	..	1	..	..
Carpenter, William	2	..	1	1	..	2	..	..	1	..	..
Caryll, Benjamin	1	2	3	1	..	3	1	1	1	..	..
Caryll, Isaac	3	..	..	1	..	1	1	..	1	..	1
Caryll, Jonathan	..	2	..	2	2	..	1	1	..	2	..
Caryll, Thomas	2	..	2	..	1	1	..	1	..	1	..
Case, Samuel	1	..	..	1	..	4	..	..	1	..	..
Chandler, Henry	2	..	..	1	..	1	..	..	1	..	..
Chandler, Mix Bela	2	..	..	1	..	3	..	..	1	..	..
Chandler, Thomas Lord	1	..	..	1	..	2	..	1	1	..	..
Chandler, Willard	3	1	..	1	..	1	1	1	1	..	..
Chase, Joshua	1	1	..	..	1	1	1	..	..	1	..
Church, Joshua Jr.	2	1	..	1	..	..	..	..	1	..	..
Church, Nathan	1	..	1	..	..	..	..	1	..	..	..
Church, Silas	4	..	..	1	..	..	..	..	1	..	..
Clark, Aaron	..	..	1	..	..	..	..	1	..	..	..
Clark, Ephraim	..	1	..	..	1	..	..	1	..	..	..
Clark, John	1	..	1	..	..	1	..	1	..	..	..
Clark, Joshua	1	..	..	1	..	2	..	..	1	..	..
Clark, Oliver	1	..	1	..	..	..	..	1	..	..	..
Clark, Samuel	2	..	..	1	..	2	..	..	1	..	..
Clay, Timothy	2	1	..	1	..	2	..	..	1	..	..
Colburn, Ezekiel	..	3	1	..	1	2	..	1	1	..	..
Coleman, Solomon	1	1	1	1	..	1	2	2	1	..	..
Cook, Ebenezer	..	..	..	1	..	1	..	..	1	..	..
Cook, Joshua	2	..	..	1	..	1	1	..	1	..	..
Crawford, William	2	2	..	1	..	3	..	1	1	1	..
Cummings, William	2	..	..	1	..	2	..	..	1	..	..
Dana, Josiah	1	1	..	1	..	1	1	..	1	..	..
David, John	1	..	..	1	..	..	..	1	2	..	..
Davis, Daniel	3	1	..	1	..	2	..	..	2	1	..
Dean, Darius	2	..	..	2	..	2	..	..	1	..	..
Dean, Samuel	3	..	..	1	..	1	2	..	1	..	..
Duncan, Abel	2	2	..	..	1	1	1	1	..	2	..
Dutton, Benjamin	2	..	..	1	..	1	..	..	1	..	..
Dutton, Stephen	1	1	..	1	..	2	1	3	1	1	..
Dyer, Stephen	..	..	1	..	1	..	1	1	..	1	..
Earll, Artemus	1	2	..	1	..	3	..	..	1	..	..
Earll, Ashbel	..	..	..	1	..	2	..	1	..	..	..
Earll, David	..	2	1	..	1	1	..	1	..	1	..
Earll, Eseck	1	..	2	..	1	..	..	..	..	1	..
Earll, Frederick	4	..	..	1	..	1	..	..	2	..	..
Earll, George	2	..	1	1	1	2	..	..	1	1	..
Earll, Robert	2	..	..	1	..	..	..	1	..	..	..
Eaton, Abraham	..	..	..	1	..	..	1	1	..	..	..
Edson, Abel	..	..	..	..	1	1	..	..	..	1	..
Edson, Rufus	..	1	2	1	..	4	1	..	1	..	..

WINDSOR COUNTY—Continued

NAMES OF HEADS OF FAMILIES	FREE WHITE MALES					FREE WHITE FEMALES					
	Under 10 years of age	Of 10 and under 16	Of 16 and under 26 including heads of families	Of 26 and under 45 including heads of families	Of 45 and upwards including heads of families	Under 10 years of age	Of 10 and under 16	Of 16 and under 26 including heads of families	Of 26 and under 45 including heads of families	Of 45 and upwards including heads of families	All other free persons except Indians not taxed
CHESTER—con.											
Ellis, Edward	3	..	..	1	..	1	..	..	1	..	..
Ellis, John	..	..	1	..	1	..	..	..	..	1	..
Ellis, John Jr.	1	..	..	1	..	3	..	..	1	..	..
Ellis, William	..	..	..	1	..	3	..	..	1	..	..
Field, Abner	3	1	..	1	..	..	..	..	2	..	..
Field, Charles	1	..	..	1	..	1	..	..	1	..	..
Field, Elijah	1	..	..	1	..	1	..	..	1	..	..
Field, James	1	1	2	..	1	2	1	1	..	1	..
Field, Pardon	2	2	..	1	..	1	1	2	1	1	..
Field, Rebecca	1	..	1	..	..	..	..	..	1	..	..
Fish, Ebenezer	..	1	3	2	..	..	..	1	1	..	..
Fish, Jonathan	2	..	..	1	..	2	..	..	1	..	..
Fisher, Jesse	4	..	..	1	..	..	..	..	1	..	..
Fletcher, Daniel	2	2	..	1	..	2	2	..	1	..	..
French, John	..	..	..	..	1	..	..	..	..	1	..
Fuller, Bishop	..	..	..	1	..	1	..	..	1	..	..
Fuller, Francis	1	..	..	1	..	1	..	..	1	..	..
Fuller, George	..	1	..	1	..	2	..	..	2	..	..
Fuller, Johnson	3	..	..	1	..	2	1	..	1	..	..
Fullerton, Thomas S.	..	1	..	2	..	1	..	2	..	..	..
Furlong, Hampshire	..	..	..	..	..	..	..	..	..	..	2
Gibson, Gabriel	..	..	..	1	..	..	..	..	1	..	..
Gibson, Hannah	2	2	..	..	1	..	..	1	..	..	..
Gilkey, William	..	1	..	2	1	1	..	2	..	..	..
Gleason, Job	3	..	..	..	1	4	2	..	..	1	..
Gould, Jedediah	1	..	1	..	1	1	1	..	..	1	..
Gould, John	..	..	..	1	..	3	..	..	1	..	..
Gould, Otis	1	..	..	1	..	..	1	1	1	..	..
Gowing, March	..	..	1	..	..	..	..	1	..	..	..
Gowing, Nathaniel	..	..	..	..	1	1	..	..	1	1	..
Graham, John	2	1	..	..	1	3	2	..	..	1	..
Graham, Robert Jr.	2	..	1	..	..	1	..	1	..	..	..
Graves, William	4	..	1	1	..	1	..	..	1	1	..
Green, Jonathan	..	1	..	1	..	3	3	..	1	..	..
Guile, Nathan	3	1	..	1	..	3	1	..	..	..	..
Hale, Josiah	..	..	..	1	..	..	3	..	1	..	..
Hall, Richard	1	..	..	1	..	1	..	1	1	..	..
Harvey, Marshall	1	1	..	1	..	2	..	..	1	..	..
Hawks, John	..	..	..	1	..	1	..	..	1	..	..
Heald, Amos	..	1	3	1	..	1	..	1	1	..	..
Heald, Daniel	..	..	1	..	1	..	..	1	..	1	..
Heath, Daniel	1	..	..	1	..	3	..	..	1	..	..
Heath, Samuel	1	..	..	1	..	1	..	..	1	..	..
Heath, Simon	..	..	..	1	..	2	..	..	1	..	..
Hewlet, Joseph	1	2	2	..	1	..	1	1	..	1	..
Hildrith, Joel	..	..	1	..	..	1	..	1	..	..	..
Hoar, Hezekiah	1	..	1	1	..	..	..	..	1	..	..
Hoar, Joseph	1	..	..	1	..	3	..	..	1	..	..
Hoar, William	3	2	..	..	1	..	..	2	1	..	..
Hodgeman, Nathan	1	1	..	1	..	2	2	..	1	..	..
Hoit, Francis	..	1	..	..	1	..	..	..	..	1	..
Holbrook, Silas	1	..	..	1	..	3	..	..	1	..	..
Holden, Aaron	3	..	1	..	1	2	..	..	1	..	..
Holden, John	1	..	..	1	..	1	1	..	1	..	..
Holden, Joseph	1	1	..	..	1	1	1	..	..	1	..
Holton, Joshua	1	1	2	..	1	..	1	1	..	1	..
Hopkins, James	..	1	1	..	1	..	2	1	1	..	..
Horton, Adonijah	1	1	2	..	1	3	1	2	..	1	..
Horton, John	1	..	..	1	..	..	..	1	..	..	..
Hosmer, Amos	..	1	..	1	..	3	..	..	1	..	..
Hosmer, William	3	2	..	1	..	1	..	1	1	..	..
Hubbard, Lucius	..	..	1	2	..	2	1	..	1	..	..
Hutchins, Simon	2	1	..	1	..	3	1	..	1	..	..
Ingraham, Ephraim	2	2	..	1	..	2	..	..	1	..	..
Jacob, Eli	3	1	..	1	..	..	1	..	1	..	..
Jacob, John	3	..	..	1	..	1	2	..	1	..	..
Jacob, Samuel	2	..	..	1	..	3	..	..	1	..	..
Johnson, Asa	1	..	..	1	..	1	..	..	1	..	..
Johnson, Dareas	..	..	..	..	..	..	1	1	..	1	..
Johnson, Edward	..	1	..	1	..	1	..	1	..	1	..
Johnson, Hezekiah	1	..	..	1	..	2	1	..	1	..	..
Johnson, John	..	..	..	..	1	..	1	..	..	1	..
Johnson, John Jr.	3	..	..	1	..	..	..	..	1	..	..
Johnson, John 3rd	2	..	..	1	..	1	..	..	1	..	..
Johnson, Willard	1	..	..	1	..	4	1	1	1	..	..
Johnson, William	1	..	..	1	..	1	..	..	1	..	..
Kelly, John Smith	..	..	..	1	..	..	..	..	1	..	..
Kendall, Jonathan Jr.	1	..	..	1	..	..	1	..	1	..	..
Kibling, John	..	1	3	1	..	2	2	..	1	..	..
Killam, Joab	..	..	..	..	..	..	..	..	..	..	3
Kimball, Thomas	..	..	2	2	1	..	1	2	1	..	..
Kindall, Jonathan	..	..	2	..	1	..	1	1	2	1	..
CHESTER—con.											
King, Richard	..	..	1	..	..	..	..	1	..	..	..
Kingsbury, Nathan	..	..	1	..	..	..	..	1	..	..	..
Lake, Jonathan	4	3	..	1	..	..	1	..	1	..	..
Larabee, Thomas	1	1	..	1	..	1	..	..	1	..	..
Leland, Aaron	..	1	..	1	..	..	..	1	..	..	..
Leland, Asa	2	..	..	1	..	1	..	..	1	..	..
Leland, Caleb	3	..	..	1	..	1	1	..	1	..	..
Leland, Elijah	1	..	1	..	..	1	..	1	..	..	..
Leland, Joshua	1	1	..	1	..	4	1	..	1	..	..
Leland, Thomas	2	..	1	..	1	3	2	..	..	1	..
Littlefield, Levi	2	..	..	1	..	2	..	..	1	..	..
Lord, Nathaniel	1	..	..	..	1	..	..	1	..	1	..
Mann, Charles	..	..	1	..	1	..	1	..	1	..	..
Mann, Samuel	1	..	..	1	..	2	..	..	1	..	..
Mann, Willard	2	1	1	1	..	4	2	..	1	..	..
Marsh, Moses	3	1	1	2	..	1	1	1	1	..	1
Marshall, Elijah	2	1	..	1	..	1	..	..	1	..	..
McCuller, William	1	1	..	1	..	2	2	..	1	..	..
Miller, Consider	..	..	..	..	1	3	..	..	1	..	..
Miller, James	..	..	..	1	..	..	..	..	1	..	..
Miller, John	1	..	..	1	..	..	..	..	2	..	..
Millins, Daniel	1	..	..	1	..	2	..	..	1	..	..
Mitchel, Thomas	2	2	1	..	1	2	..	..	1	..	..
Morris, Uriah	..	1	1	..	1	..	2	1	..	1	..
Muzzy, Benjamin	2	..	..	1	..	3	1	..	1	..	..
Muzzy, Nathaniel	..	..	..	1	1	..	1	..	1	1	..
Olcott, Timothy	..	1	2	1	1	1	1	3	..	1	..
Onion, Ichabod	1	..	3	3	..	1	..	..	2	..	..
Page, John	1	..	1	..	..	1	..	..	1	..	..
Paine, Charles	2	1	..	1	..	..	..	..	1	..	..
Parker, Elijah	2	1	1	1	..	2	..	1	..	..	..
Parker, Timothy	..	..	..	..	1	..	..	..	..	1	..
Parks, Thaddeus	2	..	1	1	1	1	2	..	1	1	..
Parsons, Solomon	..	..	..	1	..	2	..	..	1	..	..
Perkins, Rufus	4	3	..	..	1	2	..	2	1	..	..
Perry, Daniel	4	..	..	1	..	..	..	..	1	..	..
Pierce, Joseph	1	1	..	1	..	2	1	1	1	..	..
Pierce, Simon	1	1	..	1	..	1	2	..	1	..	..
Polly, Ebenezer	..	..	..	..	1	..	1	..	..	1	..
Polly, John	1	..	..	2	..	1	2	1	1	..	..
Prentice, Samuel	..	..	..	..	1	..	..	..	..	1	..
Putnam, Artemus	1	1	..	1	..	3	2	3	1	..	..
Putnam, Jesse	..	..	..	1	..	1	..	..	1	..	..
Putnam, John	..	..	1	..	1	1	1	2	..	1	..
Putnam, Robert	1	..	1	..	..	..	..	1	..	..	..
Ralph, Edward	..	..	..	1	..	4	..	..	1	..	..
Ralph, Thomas	3	..	..	1	..	1	..	..	1	..	..
Ranny, Waitstill	1	1	..	1	..	3	1	..	1	..	..
Reed, George	2	..	..	1	..	1	..	1	..	..	..
Reed, James	1	1	..	1	..	1	1	1	1	..	..
Reed, Joseph	..	..	..	1	..	3	..	..	1	..	..
Rice, Ezekiel	..	1	..	1	..	1	..	..	1	..	..
Rice, Jason	1	1	..	1	..	3	..	..	1	..	..
Richardson, Leonard	..	..	..	1	..	..	1	..	1	..	..
Robins, Nathan	3	2	..	1	..	1	1	..	1	..	..
Robinson, Peter	..	1	..	2	..	..	..	1	..	1	..
Rogers, James	2	1	..	1	..	1	1	1	1	..	..
Rounds, Jeremiah	..	1	..	1	1	1	..	..	..	1	..
Rounds, Oliver	2	3	1	1	..	1	..	..	1	..	..
Roundy, Ralp	1	..	..	1	..	2	..	2	..	..	..
Sargeants, Amos	4	1	1	..	1	..	2	..	1	1	..
Sargeants, Jabez	..	1	2	..	1	..	1	2	..	1	..
Sawtell, Michael	1	..	..	1	..	..	..	..	1	..	..
Sawyer, Joseph	1	1	1	1	1	..	..	2	..	1	..
Seagraves	3	..	..	1	..	1	..	..	1	..	..
Sergeant, Ezra	..	1	2	..	1	..	1	1	..	1	..
Sherwen, Daniel	2	1	1	1	..	1	1	..	1	..	..
Smith, Benjamin	..	..	..	1	..	1	..	2	..	..	..
Smith, Nathaniel	2	..	..	1	..	2	..	..	1	..	..
Smith, Nicholas	1	..	..	1	1	1	..	1	..	..	..
Smith, Thomas	3	..	..	1	..	..	..	..	1	..	..
Smith, William	1	..	..	1	..	3	..	..	1	..	..
Snell, Elisha	2	2	..	..	1	1	1	..	..	1	..
Snell, Solomon	1	2	2	..	1	2	1	2	..	1	..
Snow, Joseph	..	..	..	1	..	1	..	..	1	..	..
Spaulding, Abel	1	..	..	1	..	4	..	..	1	..	..
Steadman, David	2	2	1	..	1	..	1	1	1	..	..
Stearns, Isaac	2	1	..	1	..	..	..	..	1	..	..
Stevens, William	1	1	..	1	1	2	..	..	1	3	..
Stone, Joel	1	..	..	1	..	1	..	2	..	..	..

WINDSOR COUNTY—Continued

NAMES OF HEADS OF FAMILIES	FREE WHITE MALES: Under 10 years of age	FREE WHITE MALES: Of 10 and under 16	FREE WHITE MALES: Of 16 and under 26 including heads of families	FREE WHITE MALES: Of 26 and under 45 including heads of families	FREE WHITE MALES: Of 45 and upwards including heads of families	FREE WHITE FEMALES: Under 10 years of age	FREE WHITE FEMALES: Of 10 and under 16	FREE WHITE FEMALES: Of 16 and under 26 including heads of families	FREE WHITE FEMALES: Of 26 and under 45 including heads of families	FREE WHITE FEMALES: Of 45 and upwards including heads of families	All other free persons except Indians not taxed
CHESTER—con.											
Stone, John Jr.	1	1	1	..	2	2	1	1	..	1	..
Stone, Nathaniel	3	..	..	1	..	..	1	..	1	..	..
Stukeby, William	3	..	..	1	..	3	1	..	1	..	..
Sumner, Rachel	..	1	2	..	..	..	..	..	..	1	..
Sweet, John	..	..	..	..	1	1	1	..	..	1	..
Tarble, Isaac	3	2	..	1	..	..	..	..	1	..	..
Tarble, Jonathan	..	1	1	1	..	3	2	..	1	..	..
Tarble, Nathaniel	..	..	2	..	1	..	1	..	..	1	..
Tarble, Reuben	2	1	..	..	1	2	2	2	1	..	..
Taylor, Benjamin	2	2	1	1	..	1	1	1	1	..	..
Taylor, John	1	..	1	..	1	..	..	1	..	..	..
Taylor, Samuel	2	..	2	1	..	1	1	1	1	..	..
Taylor, William	1	..	2	..	..	1	..	2	..	1	..
Thomas, William	1	..	3	..	1	1	2	..	..	1	..
Thomson, Richard	2	..	1	..	2	..	2	..	..	2	..
Thomson, William Jr.	1	..	..	1	..	..	..	1	..	..	..
Toby, Paul	2	..	..	1	..	2	1	..	1	..	..
Trask, Polley	..	..	..	..	..	..	..	2	..	1	..
Turner, Joshua	2	2	..	..	1	2	2	..	..	2	..
Vicory, Thomas	1	..	..	1	..	1	..	..	1	..	..
Wallace, John	2	1	..	1	..	2	1	..	1	..	..
Ward, Elisha	2	..	..	..	1	..	2	2	..	1	..
Ward, Peggy	..	1	..	..	..	..	..	..	1	2	..
Ward, Richard	1	..	3	..	..	1	..	2	..	..	..
Warren, Thomas	..	..	3	..	1	..	..	1	1	..	..
Watkins, Elias	3	2	1	1	1	2	2	..	1	..	..
White, Edward	..	..	..	..	1	..	..	..	..	1	..
Whiting, Cotton	2	..	..	1	..	..	2	1	1	..	..
Whiting, Nathan	2	..	..	1	..	1	..	1	1	..	..
Whitman, George	2	..	..	1	..	2	..	..	1	..	..
Whitman, Joseph Jr.	1	..	1	..	..	..	..	1	..	..	..
Whitmore, Joseph	..	2	..	..	1	1	..	1	..	1	..
Willard, Jonathan	1	2	..	..	1	2	1	..	1	..	..
Williams, Anthony	1	..	..	1	..	1	..	..	1	..	..
Williams, Othniel	3	1	..	1	..	2	1	2	1	..	..
Willson, Joseph	..	..	1	..	1	..	..	1	..	..	..
Wilson, Daniel	2	..	..	1	..	4	..	..	1	..	..
Wilson, Joseph Jr.	1	1	..	1	..	3	1	..	1	..	..
Wilson, Solomon	1	1	..	1	..	1	..	..	1	..	..
Wing, Asa	..	..	1	1	1	3	..	..	1	1	..
Winn, Caleb	1	1	..	..	1	1	1	1	..	2	..
Winn, James	..	..	1	..	..	1	..	1	..	..	..
Winn, Jonathan	..	..	..	1	..	2	1	..	1	..	..
Winn, Joseph	..	..	..	..	1	..	1	..	..	1	..
Witherill, Nathaniel	2	1	..	1	..	3	3	..	1	..	..
Woods, William	4	2	..	1	1	..	1	..	1	1	..
Wyman, Samuel	1	1	..	..	1	1	..	..	1	..	..
HARTFORD											
Austin, Abiatha	1	..	1	1	..	..	1	1	..	1	..
Baldwin, Rufus	..	..	..	1	1	..	..	..	..	1	..
Banon, Abel	..	1	..	1	..	..	1	..	..	1	..
Bartholemew, Luther	3	1	..	1	..	..	2	..	1	..	..
Bartholemew, Noah	..	..	2	..	1	..	..	..	..	1	..
Bealey, John	2	2	2	..	1	4	..	1	..	1	..
Bemas, Simon	2	..	..	1	..	1	..	1	..	..	..
Bemas, Stephen	2	..	1	..	..	..	..	1	..	..	..
Bennett, John	..	1	..	..	1	1	1	2	..	2	..
Bennett, Jonathan	1	..	2	1	1	..	..	..	..	1	..
Bill, Benajah	1	..	..	1	..	..	1	1	..	..	..
Bill, Eliphalet	1	1	..	..	1	1	1	1	..	1	..
Billins, Joel	..	..	..	1	..	2	..	1	..	..	..
Bingham, Asahel	..	1	..	1	..	..	1	..	1	..	..
Bingham, Elias	..	..	1	1	..	..	..	1	..	1	..
Bliss, David	..	..	1	..	1	..	..	..	..	1	..
Bliss, David Jr.	1	..	1	1	..	2	..	..	1	..	..
Bowin, Nathaniel	1	..	..	1	..	..	..	..	1	..	..
Bramble, Abel	3	1	..	1	..	2	..	1	1	..	..
Bramble, William	..	..	2	..	1	..	..	2	..	1	..
Bramble, William Jr.	..	..	..	1	..	..	..	1	1	..	..
Brink, Ellick	2	..	..	1	..	1	..	..	1	..	..
Brooks, Elam	..	1	1	1	..	..	1	..	..	1	..
Brown, Benjamin	2	1	..	1	..	3	2	..	1	..	..
Brown, Joseph	..	..	2	..	..	..	..	1	..	..	..
Bugbee, Benjamin	..	1	1	1	..	1	2	..	1	..	..
Bugbee, Nathaniel	..	..	1	1	..	1	1	2	1	..	..
Burch, Benjamin	..	1	1	..	1	..	..	1	..	1	..
Burch, Eddy	2	1	1	1	..	3	1	1	1	..	..
Burch, James	..	..	3	..	1	1	1	..	..	1	..
Burch, Mehitabel	..	1	..	1	..	..	..	1	1	..	..
Burch, William	2	1	13	1	..	2	..	2	1	..	..
HARTFORD—con.											
Cady, Remnels	1	2	..	1	..	1	..	..	1	1	..
Cane, John	1	..	..	1	..	..	..	1	1	..	..
Case, Zebulon	..	..	..	1	..	..	..	1	..	..	..
Chapman, Elias	..	1	1	..	1	2	..	1	1	1	..
Chapman, Erastus	1	2	1	1	3	..	1	1	1	..	..
Chapman, Junia	2	1	1	1	..	1	1	..	1	..	..
Clafford, Jacob	1	..	..	..	1	..	1	..	1	..	..
Clark, John	1	1	2	..	1	..	..	3	..	1	..
Clark, Mitchell	1	1	4	1	1	..	1	1	..	2	..
Clark, Paul	3	2	..	1	..	1	1	..	..	..	..
Closson, Alford	2	..	..	1	..	1	..	..	1	..	..
Coats, Thomas	1	2	1	1	..	1	1	1	1	..	..
Colburn, Abia	2	..	..	1	..	1	..	1	1	..	..
Colburn, David Jr.	2	..	1	1	1	2	..	2	1	..	..
Colburn, Laland	1	..	..	1	..	..	..	..	1	..	..
Cole, John	3	2	1	..	1	3	..	1	1	..	..
Cooley, Horace	2	..	2	1	..	..	..	..	1	..	..
Cummins, Joseph	1	..	..	1	..	1	..	..	1	..	..
Dean, Nathan Jr.	1	..	1	..	..	1	..	..	1	..	..
Demmon, William	3	1	..	1	1	2	1	..	1	1	..
Dewey, Joshua	1	..	2	..	1	..	1	1	..	1	..
Dilleno, Hibbard	2	..	1	..	..	..	..	..	1	..	..
Dilleno, Jonathan	..	..	..	..	1	..	..	..	..	1	..
Dilleno, Zebulon	3	..	..	1	..	1	..	..	1	..	..
Dimock, Joab	3	..	1	..	..	..	..	1	..	..	..
Dimock, Phillip	..	1	1	..	1	..	1	..	..	1	..
Dommon, Dorcas	1	1	3	..	..	2	1	1	..	1	..
Dunham, George	..	..	..	..	1	..	..	..	..	..	..
Dunham, Gershum	..	1	..	1	3	..	..	1	..	..	..
Dutton, Asahel	1	..	1	2	..	2	1	..	1	..	..
Dutton, Daniel B.	2	..	1	..	..	..	..	1	..	..	..
Dutton, Jesse	2	..	1	1	..	4	1	1	1	..	..
Dutton, John	..	..	2	..	1	..	..	..	..	1	..
Dutton, Nathaniel	..	..	1	3	..	1	3	2	..	..	1
Eaton, Brigham	..	1	..	..	1	3	3	1	1	..	..
Elmer, John	..	..	1	..	1	..	..	2	..	..	..
Estabrook, Porter	2	..	1	1	..	..	1	1	1	..	..
Fairman, Chester	1	..	..	1	..	1	..	1	..	..	..
Farr, Abijah	2	..	..	1	..	..	..	..	1	..	..
Fuller, Jonathan	2	1	2	1	..	1	1	..	1	..	..
Fuller, Seth	1	2	1	1	4	..	1	1	..	..	..
Gibs, Harvey	..	..	..	1	..	3	..	..	1	..	..
Gilbert, James	..	..	..	1	..	1	..	1	..	..	..
Gillet, Billa	2	1	..	2	..	1	..	1	1	..	..
Gillet, Israel	1	..	3	..	1	1	1	1	1	1	..
Gillet, John	..	1	2	..	1	..	2	1	..	1	..
Gillet, Roger	1	1	1	1	..	2	1	..	1	..	..
Gould, George	2	..	..	1	..	1	1	..	1	..	..
Gross, Thomas	2	..	..	1	..	..	..	1	..	..	..
Gross, Thomas	2	4	3	1	..	..	1	3	..	2	..
Hadlock, John	1	..	1	..	1	..	1	..	..	1	..
Hagar, Lemuel	2	..	..	1	..	2	..	..	1	..	..
Hall, Jacob	3	1	..	..	1	2	1	..	1	..	..
Hall, John	..	..	..	1	..	..	..	..	..	..	..
Hazen, Asa	3	2	1	..	1	1	..	2	1	1	..
Hazen, Daniel	3	1	2	1	..	1	1	1	2	..	..
Hazen, Hezekiah	2	2	1	1	..	2	1	..	1	..	..
Hazen, Mary	..	2	1	..	..	2	1	..	..	1	..
Hazen, Phillemon	2	1	1	1	..	1	..	1	1	..	..
Hazen, Reuben	1	..	..	1	..	2	..	..	1	..	..
Hazen, Solomon	4	1	1	1	..	..	1	..	1	1	..
Hazen, Thomas	2	..	2	1	..	1	2	1	1	..	..
Holbrook, Thomas	1	2	..	1	..	3	..	..	1	..	..
How, David	..	..	..	1	..	..	..	1	..	1	..
How, Robert	..	..	1	..	..	..	..	2	..	..	..
How, Stewart	..	1	..	1	..	2	1	..	1	..	..
Hoyt, Benjamin	2	1	..	..	1	1	..	..	1	..	..
Hunter, John	..	1	..	1	..	1	..	..	1	..	..
Hutchinson, Zenus	4	..	..	1	..	2	..	..	1	..	..
Ingals, Jonathan	1	..	1	..	1	..	..	..	2	1	..
Ingals, Samuel	2	..	..	1	..	2	..	..	1	..	..
Ingram, Friend	3	..	..	1	..	..	..	1	1	..	..
Ingram, Jeremiah	..	..	..	..	1	1	..	1	..	1	..
Ingram, Simeon	..	..	1	..	..	..	..	1	..	..	..
Janes, David	..	..	..	..	1	..	..	..	..	1	..
Johnson, William	..	..	1	..	1	..	..	..	..	1	..
King, Asahel	2	1	..	1	..	2	1	..	1	..	..
King, Daniel	5	1	..	1	..	..	2	..	1	..	..
King, Hopkins	..	1	..	..	1	..	..	1	..	1	..

WINDSOR COUNTY—Continued

NAMES OF HEADS OF FAMILIES	FREE WHITE MALES: Under 10 years of age	FREE WHITE MALES: Of 10 and under 16	FREE WHITE MALES: Of 16 and under 26 including heads of families	FREE WHITE MALES: Of 26 and under 45 including heads of families	FREE WHITE MALES: Of 45 and upwards including heads of families	FREE WHITE FEMALES: Under 10 years of age	FREE WHITE FEMALES: Of 10 and under 16	FREE WHITE FEMALES: Of 16 and under 26 including heads of families	FREE WHITE FEMALES: Of 26 and under 45 including heads of families	FREE WHITE FEMALES: Of 45 and upwards including heads of families	All other free persons except Indians not taxed
HARTFORD—con.											
Laurence, Elias	..	..	..	1	1	2	..	..	1	1	..
Leavitt, Freegrace	1	..	3	1	..	3	1	1	1	..	..
Loomis, Warren	1	..	..	..	1	1	..	..	1	..	..
Lyman, Elias	3	..	3	1	..	2	1	..	1	..	..
Marsh, Abel	..	..	..	..	1	..	..	..	..	1	..
Marsh, Abraham	2	..	..	1	..	3	..	..	1	..	..
Marsh, Daniel	3	1	..	1	..	2	1	2	1	..	..
Marsh, Eliphalet	..	..	1	..	1	..	1	3	..	1	..
Marsh, Elisha	1	..	..	1	1	..	1	..	..	1	..
Marsh, Elisha Jr.	5	1	..	1	..	..	1	1	..	..	..
Marsh, Joel	2	..	..	1	..	2	..	1	1	..	..
Marsh, Joseph	..	..	..	..	1	..	..	..	..	1	..
Marsh, Joseph Jr.	..	2	1	1	..	1	2	..	1	..	1
Marsh, Millo	2	1	1	2	..	1	..	1	1	..	..
Marsh, Roger	..	1	..	1	..	..	..	1	..	..	..
Merrill, Eliakim S.	1	1	..	1	..	..	1	..	..	1	..
Miller, Nathaniel	1	..	..	..	1	..	..	1	..	1	..
Miller, Peter	1	1	..	1	..	1	1	..	2	..	..
Mitchell, Cinthia	1	..	..	..	..	1	..	..	1	..	..
Newell, Oliver	2	3	4	..	1	1	1	..	..	1	1
Newell, Samuel	..	2	1	..	1	..	..	2	..	1	..
Newell, Samuel Jr.	2	1	1	1	..	3	..	2	..	..	..
Newton, David	4	1	5	..	1	1	2	2	1	..	..
Newton, Sheldon	2	1	..	1	..	..	..	..	1	..	..
Noble, Shadrack	2	2	..	..	1	..	..	1	..	1	..
Paddock, John	2	2	1	..	1	1	..	1	..	2	..
Parker, Ephraim	1	..	..	1	..	1	..	..	1	..	..
Pease, Christopher	1	1	..	..	1	2	1	2	..	1	..
Pease, Samuel	..	2	..	..	1	..	1	4	1	1	..
Phelps, Cadwell	1	..	..	1	..	1	..	..	1	..	..
Pigsley, Asa	1	..	..	1	..	2	..	1	1	..	..
Pigsley, Benjamin	2	..	..	..	1	..	1	..	1	..	..
Pigsley, William	1	..	2	..	2	1	1	..	1	..	..
Pinneo, Charles	4	..	..	2	..	..	..	..	1	..	..
Pitkin, Paul	..	2	..	1	..	3	2	..	1	..	..
Porter, Elliah	2	1	..	1	..	2	1	1	1	..	..
Porter, Sarah	..	..	..	..	..	..	..	..	..	1	..
Porter, Violute	..	..	..	..	..	2	..	1	..	..	..
Porter, William	2	..	2	..	1	..	..	1	1	..	..
Powars, William	4	..	1	..	1	1	1	6	1	1	..
Powel, Luther	..	1	..	1	..	3	..	..	..	..	..
Powel, Rowland	..	..	..	..	1	..	..	..	..	1	..
Pratt, Lewis	..	..	1	1	..	..	..	1	..	..	..
Ransom, Daniel	1	2	2	1	..	..	1	1	1	..	..
Ransom, Matthew	2	3	..	..	1	2	1	..	..	1	..
Rasey, Joseph	..	2	..	..	1	..	1	..	..	1	..
Raymond, Liberty	1	1	1	1	..	..	..	1	..	..	..
Richards, Joel	1	1	..	1	..	2	..	1	1	..	..
Richardson, Amos	2	1	..	..	1	3	..	..	1	..	..
Richardson, Frederick	2	..	1	..	..	..	..	1	..	..	..
Richardson, John	1	2	..	1	..	..	..	1	1	..	..
Richardson, Thomas	..	1	1	..	1	1	2	1	..	1	..
Richardson, William	..	..	..	..	1	..	2	..	..	1	..
Rider, Joshua	2	..	..	1	..	2	..	..	1	..	..
Rider, Peter	2	1	..	..	1	2	2	2	1	1	..
Rider, Polly	..	..	..	..	..	..	..	..	..	1	..
Rider, Zenas	1	1	..	2	..	2	..	..	2	..	..
Robinson, Amos	..	1	4	..	1	..	..	2	..	1	..
Robinson, William	1	1	..	1	..	3	..	..	1	..	..
Russ, Benjamin	1	1	..	2	..	1	1	..	1	1	..
Rust, Lemuel	1	1	..	1	..	2	..	..	1	..	..
Rust, Niel	2	1	..	1	..	..	1	..	1	..	..
Rust, Phinehas	1	1	..	..	1	..	..	1	..	1	..
Savage, Francis	1	1	1	2	..	4	..	1	1	..	..
Savage, Seth	1	1	2	1	..	1	1	..	1	..	..
Savage, Thomas	1	..	1	1	..	2	2	..	1	..	..
Scott, Luther	3	1	..	1	..	2	..	..	1	..	..
Shalliss, Francis	..	..	2	1	1	..	2	..	..	1	..
Shattuck, Ephraim	2	..	..	1	..	..	..	1	..	..	..
Smith, Asa	2	3	..	1	..	1	..	2	1	..	..
Smith, Ashbel	4	..	..	1	..	1	1	..	1	..	..
Smith, Justin	2	..	1	1	..	..	..	..	1	..	..
Smith, Sylvanus	2	3	1	..	1	2	..	..	1	..	..
Spear, Elijah	3	1	..	1	..	..	1	..	1	..	..
Sprague, Phillip	3	1	..	1	..	3	1	..	1	..	..
Strong, James	..	1	..	1	..	1	..	2	..	..	..
Strong, Jedediah	2	1	4	..	1	..	2	..	1	..	..
Strong, Solomon	1	..	1	..	1	..	..	1	..	1	..
Strong, Solomon Jr.	1	..	..	1	..	2	..	1	1	..	..
Strong, William	2	..	..	1	..	2	..	..	1	..	..
Taylor, Amasa	1	1	..	1	..	1	..	..	1	..	..
Taylor, Hezekiah	3	..	..	1	..	1	..	1	..	..	..
Tenny, Reuben	3	..	..	1	..	..	1	..	1	..	..
HARTFORD—con.											
Tilden, Asa	1	..	2	1	..	3	..	1	1	..	..
Tilden, Josiah	2	..	4	1	..	3	..	2	1	..	..
Tilden, Stephen	3	2	2	..	1	1	1	2	..	..	..
Tilden, Stephen	..	..	..	..	1	..	..	..	..	1	..
Tracy, Andrew	1	3	..	..	1	2	1	..	1	..	..
Tracy, James	3	..	1	1	1	..	..	1	1	2	..
Tracy, Joseph	3	..	..	1	..	..	1	..	1	..	..
Trimball, David	..	..	..	1	..	..	..	..	..	..	..
Turner, Isaac	2	..	..	..	1	1	2	1	..	..	..
Waldan, Walter	1	..	..	1	..	2	1	..	1	..	..
Webster, Israel	2	..	2	1	..	1	1	..	1	..	..
Webster, Samuel	..	1	1	..	1	1	1	1	..	1	..
Whitcomb, David	3	1	..	1	..	..	1	..	1	..	..
Whitney, Jonathan	3	1	..	1	..	1	1	..	1	..	..
Whitney, Nathan	..	..	..	..	1	..	1	..	..	1	..
Whitney, Peter	..	..	2	..	..	..	..	1	..	..	..
Wilson, Elias	1	1	..	2	..	3	..	..	1	..	..
Wilson, Isaac	3	1	..	..	1	..	..	..	..	1	..
Wilson, Joseph	..	..	..	..	1	..	..	..	..	..	..
Wilson, Putnam	..	..	1	..	..	1	..	2	..	..	..
Wood, Ephraim	2	..	1	1	..	2	2	..	1	1	..
Woodward, Elihu	..	1	..	..	1	..	1	1	..	1	..
Wright, Benjamin	1	..	..	..	1	..	1	..	..	1	..
Wright, David	1	1	2	..	1	..	1	..	1	1	..
Wright, Henry	..	..	1	..	..	1	..	1	..	..	..
Wright, Jonathan	1	..	..	..	1	4	3	1	1	..	..
Wright, Roger	3	..	..	1	..	1	..	..	1	..	..
UNCERTAIN NAMES											
Carvn (?), Allen	1	..	..	1	..	3	..	..	1	..	..
Pak (?), Thomas	..	..	..	1	..	..	..	1	..	1	..
Ternes (?), Timothy	..	..	1	..	..	2	..	..	1	..	..
HARTLAND											
Abbott, Samuel	..	..	..	..	1	1	..	..	1	1	..
Aldrich, Isaiah	1	1	..	..	1	..	2	1	1	..	..
Aldrich, Noah	1	..	..	1	..	..	..	..	1	..	..
Alexander, Consider	..	..	..	2	..	..	1	1	..	..	..
Alexander, Eldad	3	1	1	1	..	2	..	..	1	..	..
Alexander, Quartus	1	1	..	1	..	1	2	1	1	..	..
Allen, Ebenezer	3	2	1	1	1	2	..	2	1	1	..
Alvord, Simeon	..	1	..	..	1	..	..	..	..	1	..
Anderson, Hulda	..	..	2	..	..	..	..	1	..	1	..
Anderson, Luther	1	1	..	1	..	2	..	1	..	..	..
Ares, Peter	1	1	1	..	1	1	..	..	1	..	..
Ashley, Amos	1	..	..	1	..	1	..	..	1	..	..
Ashley, Freeman	2	2	1	..	1	..	1	..	..	1	..
Ashley, William S.	2	1	..	1	..	1	..	1	1	..	..
Avery, Sanford	..	..	1	..	1	..	..	..	..	1	..
Badger, Daniel	3	..	1	..	1	..	..	..	..	1	..
Badger, David	1	..	..	1	..	..	..	1	..	..	..
Bagley, Orlando	2	2	..	1	..	2	..	1	1	..	..
Bagley, Stephen	..	1	..	1	..	1	1	1	1	1	..
Bates, Sylvanus	..	..	1	..	..	..	..	1	..	..	..
Beann, Solomon	2	1	1	1	..	2	1	1	1	..	..
Billins, John	3	2	..	1	..	..	1	..	1	..	..
Billins, Joseph	3	2	..	1	..	2	1	1	1	..	..
Billins, Nathan	..	2	..	..	1	1	1	1	1	..	1
Bishop, Eleazer	..	..	..	..	1	1	..	2	..	1	..
Blackman, Joseph	..	..	..	1	..	3	..	..	1	..	..
Blake, William	1	..	..	1	..	1	1	..	1	..	..
Bow, Abraham	2	1	..	1	1	2	..	..	2	..	..
Briant, Amasa	2	2	1	1	..	2	1	..	1	..	..
Briant, Benjamin	..	1	1	1	1	3	2	..	1	..	..
Brick, Daniel	1	1	..	..	1	4	1	2	1	..	..
Bridge, Ebenezer	..	1	2	..	1	..	..	1	..	1	..
Britten, Joseph	..	..	..	1	..	1	..	..	4	..	..
Brown, Ebenezer	2	..	..	1	..	..	1	..	..	..	..
Brown, John	3	..	..	1	..	1	1	..	1	..	..
Buck, Ezra	1	..	2	1	..	1	..	1	..	..	..
Buck, Isaiah	..	1	..	..	1	..	..	..	..	1	..
Buck, Jonathan	1	..	..	..	1	1	..	..	..	2	..
Burbank, Joel	..	1	..	1	..	1	2	..	..	1	..
Burdick, Marey	1	..	..	..	..	1	..	..	1	..	..
Burrell, John Jr.	2	1	..	1	..	..	..	..	1	..	..
Cabbot, Martson	1	2	1	..	1	3	..	..	1	..	..
Cabot, Francis	2	..	1	..	1	4	2	..	1	..	..
Cady, Thomas H.	2	1	..	1	..	3	..	..	1	..	..
Call, Elias	1	..	..	1	..	3	..	..	1	..	..
Cambell, Alexander	1	1	4	..	1	1	1	..	1	..	..

WINDSOR COUNTY—Continued

NAMES OF HEADS OF FAMILIES	FREE WHITE MALES					FREE WHITE FEMALES					All other free persons except Indians not taxed
	Under 10 years of age	Of 10 and under 16	Of 16 and under 26 including heads of families	Of 26 and under 45 including heads of families	Of 45 and upwards including heads of families.	Under 10 years of age	Of 10 and under 16	Of 16 and under 26 including heads of families	Of 26 and under 45 including heads of families	Of 45 and upwards including heads of families	
HARTLAND—con.											
Cambell, James	1	..	1	1	..	..	..	1	..	..	..
Capin, Samuel	1	..	..	1	..	1	1	1	..	..	1
Cary, Ephraim	1	2	1	..	1	3	2	1	1	..	..
Chase, Henry	..	1	2	..	1	2	1	..	1	..	..
Chever, Samuel	1	1	1	1	..	..	..	2	..	1	..
Child, Lyman	..	2	..	1	..	3	1	1	1	..	..
Clark, Samuel	3	..	..	1	..	1	..	..	1	..	..
Cleaveland, Thomas	1	..	1	1	..	2	..	..	1	..	..
Cobb, William	2	2	..	1	..	1	2	2	1	..	..
Colstene, William	2	1	..	1	..	1	2	..	1	..	..
Combs, John	3	..	..	1	..	..	..	1	..	..	..
Cotten, Ebenezer	1	1	..	1	..	..	..	3	..	..	..
Cotten, Melvin	2	..	..	1	..	2	..	..	1	..	..
Cotten, Samuel	2	..	..	1	..	2	1	1	..	..	..
Cotten, Thomas	..	..	..	..	1	..	1	..	..	1	..
Cotten, Willard	1	2	1	1	..	3	2	1	..	1	..
Crista, Thomas	2	..	..	1	..	2	2	..	1	..	..
Crosley, Alexander	1	..	..	1	..	1	..	..	1	..	..
Currier, Aaron	..	..	2	..	1	1	1	..	..	1	..
Cushman, Holmes	2	1	1	1	..	5	..	..	1	..	..
Damon, Noah	2	..	..	1	..	1	..	..	1	..	..
Danforth, William	..	..	1	1	1	..	..	..	1	1	..
Danforth, William Jr.	1	1	..	1	..	3	1	1	1	..	..
Davis, Ephraim	4	..	1	..	..	1	..	..	1	..	..
Davison, Dan	1	..	..	..	1	..	1	..	..	1	..
Davison, Oliver	3	..	1	1	..	..	..	..	3	..	..
Denison, James	1	..	1	..	1	..	2	2	..	1	..
Denison, John	1	2	..	..	1	2	1	1	1	1	..
Denney, David	4	..	..	1	..	2	..	1	1	..	..
Dennison, George	1	1	2	1	1	..	2	..	1	..	..
Denny, Thomas	2	..	2	..	1	1	1	1	1	..	..
Densmore, John	1	1	1	1	..	..	1	1	1	..	..
Dodge, Andrew	..	..	1	..	..	1	..	1	..	..	..
Edgerton, Eliphalet	..	1	1	..	..	..	1	..	..	..	..
Ellsworth, William	4	1	..	1	..	1	..	..	1	..	..
Ely, Samuel	1	1	..	1	..	2	1	..	1	..	..
Emmens, Seth	2	..	..	1	..	2	..	..	1	..	..
Farwell, Abel	1	..	..	1	..	2	..	2	..	..	..
Finne, Job	1	..	..	1	1	1	..	..	1	1	..
Finne, Lot	1	2	..	1	..	4	1	..	1	..	..
Flowers, Elisha	..	1	..	1	1	1	..	1	..	3	..
Flowers, Hier	1	..	..	1	..	3	..	..	1	..	..
Fultum, Ellick	2	1	1	..	..	..	..	1	..	..	..
Gallup, Elisha	2	1	..	1	..	..	..	2	1	..	..
Gallup, Oliver	2	1	2	1	..	2	1	1	..	..	..
Gallup, Perus	3	..	..	1	..	2	2	..	1	..	..
Gallup, William	1	..	2	..	1	..	1	4	..	1	..
Gallup, William Jr.	2	..	..	1	..	1	1	..	1	..	..
Garvin, James	2	3	2	1	..	3	..	1	1	..	..
Gates, Zelotus	2	..	..	1	..	..	1	1	1	..	..
Gay, James	..	1	..	1	..	3	2	..	1	..	..
Gilson, Peter	1	1	..	1	..	2	1	..	1	..	..
Goff, Hezekiah	4	..	1	..	1	1	3	2	1	..	..
Goodale, Jacob	..	..	..	..	1	..	..	..	..	1	..
Goss, Hezekiah Jr.	1	..	1	..	..	..	..	1	..	..	..
Gould, Betsey	1	..	..	..	..	..	..	..	1	..	..
Green, John	1	1	..	1	..	2	..	1	1	..	..
Grow, Joseph	2	1	1	1	1	1	2	1	..	1	..
Grow, Joseph Jr.	..	1	1	..	..	1	..	1	..	..	..
Grow, Timothy	3	..	1	..	1	2	2	2	1	..	..
Hadley, Phillip	2	1	..	1	..	1	..	1	1	..	..
Hamilton, Levi	1	..	2	1	..	1	..	1	..	..	..
Hammond, James	3	1	..	1	..	..	..	..	..	1	..
Harden, John	..	..	1	..	4	..	..	1	1	..	..
Haskins, Seth	..	..	1	..	..	1	..	1	..	..	..
Hatch, Heman	..	..	1	..	1	..	1	..	..	1	..
Hatch, Thomas	1	..	1	..	..	..	..	1	..	..	..
Hathaway, Benjamin	1	1	..	1	..	3	1	..	1	..	..
Hazetine, David	2	..	1	1	..	1	..	1	1	..	..
Hendrick, Caleb	1	..	..	1	1	2	..	..	2	1	..
Higgins, Uriah	1	..	..	1	..	1	..	..	1	..	..
Higgins, Uriah	..	..	1	1	1	..	..	1	..	1	..
Hoadley, Elias	1	..	..	1	..	1	..	..	1	..	..
Hoadley, Jonathan	1	..	..	1	..	..	..	1	..	..	..
Hoadley, Thomas	..	1	..	1	..	..	..	..	1	..	..
Hoadley, Thomas Jr.	..	..	..	1	..	3	..	..	1	..	..
Hodge, Benjamin	..	..	1	..	1	1	..	1	..	..	..
Hodgman, David	3	..	1	1	..	2	..	..	1	..	..
Hodgman, Lot	3	..	1	1	..	1	1	2	1	..	..
Hodgman, Thomas	1	..	..	1	..	2	..	..	1	..	..
Hodgman, Zacheus	..	1	..	1	..	2	..	2	..	1	..
Hoffman, Joseph	..	..	2	..	..	..	..	1	..	..	..
HARTLAND—con.											
Hoffman, Simeon	2	..	1	1	..	1	..	1	..	..	..
Holbrook, Ebenezer	3	1	..	1	..	..	2	..	1	..	..
Holdrick, Thomas	..	2	1	..	1	3	..	..	1	..	..
Holmes, Absalom	1	..	..	1	..	2	..	1	1	..	..
Holt, Lemuel	..	..	..	1	..	1	..	1	..	..	..
Huntley, Moses	1	..	..	1	..	2	..	..	1	..	..
Jaquith, Benjamin	..	..	1	..	1	..	..	1	..	1	..
Jaquith, Isaac	..	1	..	1	..	..	..	..	1	..	..
Jaquith, William	..	..	..	..	1	..	..	..	..	1	..
Johnson, Asa	2	3	1	..	1	..	..	2	..	1	..
Jones, Charles	3	..	..	1	..	3	..	..	1	..	..
Keith, Asel	..	..	..	..	1	..	..	1	1	1	..
Kelly, Ebenezer	1	1	2	..	1	1	1	..	..	1	..
Kelly, Edward	1	..	..	1	..	..	..	..	1	..	..
Kendall, Amos	1	..	..	..	1	1	1	..	..	1	..
Killam, Phinehas	..	..	..	1	..	..	1	..	1	..	..
Kimball, Phinehas	..	1	..	..	1	2	1	..	..	1	..
Kimpton, Gideon	1	..	..	1	..	2	..	..	1	..	..
Lamphere, John	..	..	1	..	1	..	..	2	..	1	..
Lamphere, Robert	3	..	1	..	..	..	..	..	1	..	..
Lamphere, Roswell	2	1	..	1	..	3	1	..	1	..	..
Lamphere, Shubel	..	1	..	1	..	3	1	..	1	1	..
Lamphere, Thompson	3	..	..	1	1	2	..	1	..	1	..
Lauton, Thomas	..	1	1	..	1	..	1	1	..	1	..
Lauton, Thomas	1	..	..	1	..	1	..	1	1	..	..
Lee, Zebulon	1	..	2	1	1	1	..	2	..	1	..
Liscomb, Darius	2	..	2	..	..	3	3	..	1	..	..
Liscomb, Nehemiah	1	..	..	..	1	4	3	..	1	..	..
Liscomb, Parker	..	1	..	..	1	..	..	1	..	1	..
Livermore, William	1	2	..	1	1	..	1	1	..	1	..
Lombard, Solomon	1	..	1	..	..	..	..	1	..	..	..
Lord, Joseph	2	2	..	1	..	2	..	..	1	..	..
Lull, Asa	4	2	..	1	..	1	1	..	1	..	..
Lull, John	..	..	..	..	1	..	..	..	..	1	..
Lull, Nathan	3	..	..	1	..	3	..	..	1	..	..
Lull, Timothy	..	..	1	1	..	1	..	1	..	..	..
Lull, Titus	..	1	1	..	..	..	..	..	1	..	..
Lull, Zenus	2	2	1	1	..	3	2	..	1	..	..
Mane, Isaac	1	..	..	..	1	..	..	..	..	1	..
Mane, Stephen	2	..	..	1	..	3	..	1	..	..	..
Marble, Benjamin	2	..	..	1	..	1	..	..	1	..	..
Marey, Chester	3	..	..	1	..	1	1	..	1	..	..
Marey, Gardner	2	..	..	1	..	2	..	..	1	..	..
Marey, Joseph	2	..	1	1	..	..	..	..	1	..	..
Marey, Levi	..	..	..	1	..	2	..	..	1	..	..
Marey, William	1	..	..	1	2	..	..	1	..	..	..
Marey, Winthrop	1	..	..	1	..	2	..	..	1	..	..
Marsh, Jason	1	..	..	1	..	2	..	1	..	..	..
Marsh, John	..	..	..	..	1	..	..	..	2	..	..
Marsh, Joseph	..	..	..	..	1	..	..	..	..	1	..
Marsh, Roger	3	2	..	1	..	1	1	1	..	..	..
Marsh, Samuel	1	1	..	1	..	2	..	1	1	..	..
Matthews, Samuel	4	..	..	1	1	4	..	..	1	1	..
McCully, Alexander	1	..	..	1	..	..	..	..	1	..	..
McCully, Samuel	..	..	..	1	..	2	..	..	1	..	..
McKenzey, Joseph	1	1	1	1	1	2	..	3	..	1	..
Merrill, Isaac	..	..	..	1	..	1	1	..	1	..	..
Miller, Jonathan	1	1	1	1	1	6	1	1	1	..	..
Minor, Ephraim	1	3	1	..	1	3	1	..	1	1	..
Morgan, Isaac	..	1	1	..	1	..	2	1	..	1	..
Munsill, Daniel	2	2	..	1	1	1	..	..	1	1	..
Murray, John	2	..	..	1	..	2	..	..	1	..	..
Nichols, John	..	..	1	..	1	..	2	..	..	1	..
Nollon, Daniel	3	..	..	1	..	..	..	1	..	..	..
Paddock, William	1	4	..	..	1	1	..	2	..	1	..
Page, Benjamin	2	1	..	1	..	1	..	..	1	..	..
Page, John	..	..	1	..	..	..	..	1	..	..	..
Page, Thomas	1	1	..	1	..	4	..	..	1	..	..
Paine, Esther	..	..	1	..	..	..	1	..	..	1	..
Parker, Joseph	2	..	..	1	..	2	..	..	1	..	..
Patterson, Joseph	1	..	..	..	1	..	..	..	..	1	..
Patterson, Joseph Jr.	..	..	1	..	..	1	..	1	..	..	..
Perkins, Francis	1	..	1	1	..	3	1	1	..	..	..
Perkins, Samuel	2	1	1	..	1	1	1	..	1	..	..
Peterson, Jacob	3	1	..	1	..	..	1	..	1	..	..
Petrie, James	2	1	..	1	..	1	..	..	1	..	..
Pool, Nathaniel	..	1	..	..	1	..	..	1	1	..	..
Reed, Artemas	..	..	..	..	1	..	1	..	..	1	..
Remmington, Joseph	3	1	1	1	..	..	1	1	1	..	..
Rennels, Ebenezer	..	..	..	1	..	..	..	1	..	1	..

WINDSOR COUNTY—Continued

NAMES OF HEADS OF FAMILIES	FREE WHITE MALES: Under 10 years of age	FREE WHITE MALES: Of 10 and under 16	FREE WHITE MALES: Of 16 and under 26 including heads of families	FREE WHITE MALES: Of 26 and under 45 including heads of families	FREE WHITE MALES: Of 45 and upwards including heads of families.	FREE WHITE FEMALES: Under 10 years of age	FREE WHITE FEMALES: Of 10 and under 16	FREE WHITE FEMALES: Of 16 and under 26 including heads of families	FREE WHITE FEMALES: Of 26 and under 45 including heads of families	FREE WHITE FEMALES: Of 45 and upwards including heads of families	All other free persons except Indians not taxed
HARTLAND—con.											
Rice, Eliakim	3	1	1	1	..	..	1	1	1	..	..
Rice, Elisha	4	1	..	1	..	..	1	..	1	..	..
Rice, Gnesha	2	..	1	..	..	..	..	..	..	1	..
Richardson, Jeremiah	1	1	1	1	..	1	2	..	..	1	..
Robbins, John	..	..	..	..	1	..	1	..	..	1	..
Roberts, Eliphalet	3	2	..	1	..	2	..	..	1	..	..
Rodgers, Arthur	5	1	..	1	..	1	..	..	1	..	..
Rodgers, Jeremiah	1	..	1	..	..	1	..	1	..	..	..
Rodgers, Oliver	3	..	..	2	..	1	..	..	1	..	..
Rodgers, Paul	1	1	..	1	..	..	1	..	1	..	..
Rood, Humphrey	1	3	..	1	..	1	1	..	1	..	..
Russ, Oliver	1	1	1	1	..	..	1	1	..	1	..
Russell, Elisha E.	..	1	1	..	1	2	..	1	..	..	..
Russell, Esty	1	1	1	..	1	..	1	2	..	1	..
Rust, Matthais	..	..	..	..	1	..	..	..	..	1	..
Scott, John	1	1	1	..	1	1	1	..	1	..	..
Scott, Lemuel	2	3	1	..	1	1	..	1	..	1	..
Seargent, Isaac	..	..	1	..	1	2	1	1	..	1	..
Shattuck, Silas	..	..	1	..	1	..	..	..	..	1	..
Shattuck, Silas Jr.	..	..	..	1	..	3	..	..	1	..	..
Shaw, Ebenezer	1	..	..	1	..	..	..	1	..	..	..
Short, Daniel	..	1	2	..	1	1	..	..	..	1	..
Short, William	..	..	..	1	..	3	..	..	1	..	..
Simens, Joseph	..	2	..	..	1	1	1	..	..	1	..
Simins, Nathaniel	2	..	..	1	..	..	..	1	..	..	..
Simmens, John	2	..	..	1	..	1	1	1	..	..	..
Simmons, Simon	..	..	..	..	1	..	1	..	..	1	..
Smith, Daniel	..	..	..	1	..	1	..	1	..	..	..
Smith, Samuel	2	..	..	1	..	3	2	..	1	..	..
Spooner, Amasa	..	..	..	1	1	..	..	..	..	1	..
Spooner, Daniel	1	1	1	..	1	..	..	3	..	1	..
Spooner, Daniel Jr.	..	1	..	1	..	..	1	..	..	..	..
Stanton, James	2	2	2	1	..	2	..	..	1	..	..
Stanton, Phunehas	..	..	2	..	1	2	2	..	1	1	..
Stephens, Daniel	..	..	1	..	1	2	..	1	..	..	..
Stephens, Isaac	2	1	1	1	..	1	2	2	1	..	..
Stevens, Oliver	..	1	2	..	1	1	..	..	1	..	..
Stevens, Oliver	2	..	1	1	..	4	..	1	1	..	..
Stevens, Reuben	2	..	..	1	..	..	..	..	1	..	..
Stoddar, Daniel	2	..	..	1	..	4	..	..	1	..	..
Stowel, Elisha	..	..	..	..	1	..	1	..	..	1	..
Streeter, Isaiah	2	2	..	1	..	1	1	..	1	..	..
Strong, Ezekiel	..	2	..	1	..	4	1	..	1	..	..
Sumner, Harvey	..	..	..	1	..	..	..	1	2	1	..
Sumner, William	2	1	..	1	..	2	1	..	1	..	..
Sweeter, William	1	..	..	1	..	2	..	..	1	..	1
Taft, Artimas	..	1	3	..	1	1	1	..	1	..	..
Taft, Stephen	..	..	3	1	..	..	..	..	1	..	..
Taylor, Abigail	2	1	3	..	..	..	1	..	1	..	..
Taylor, Asa	1	1	3	..	1	1	1	..	..	2	..
Taylor, John	..	..	1	..	..	..	..	1	..	..	..
Taylor, Joseph	..	..	..	..	1	1	..	..	1	..	..
Teuxbury, Ephraim	4	..	..	1	..	..	..	..	1	..	..
Teuxbury, Isaac	..	1	1	..	1	..	1	2	..	..	..
Thair, Frederick	1	..	..	1	..	4	1	..	1	..	..
Thair, Nathan	..	..	1	..	..	..	..	2	..	..	..
Thomas, Jabez	..	..	2	..	1	..	..	..	1	..	..
Turner, Elisha	2	..	..	1	..	2	2	..	1	..	..
Tuxbury, Jacob	1	..	..	..	1	..	2	1	..	1	..
Walden, John	1	1	..	1	..	4	2	1	1	..	..
Walden, Nathaniel	1	2	1	1	..	1	1	1	1	..	..
Walker, Elnathan	1	..	..	1	..	1	..	1	..	..	..
Walker, Elnathan	1	1	..	1	1	1	1	..	1	1	..
Ward, Edward	2	3	1	1	..	2	1	1	1	..	..
Warren, Zenus	4	..	..	1	..	3	..	..	1	..	..
Webster, Laban	2	..	3	1	..	2	..	1	1	..	..
Webster, Moses	..	..	2	..	1	1	2	..	..	1	..
Webster, William	2	1	..	1	..	3	1	..	1	..	..
Weed, Jacob	..	..	1	1	..	..	..	1	..	..	..
Weed, Nathaniel	1	..	1	1	1	..	1	2	..	1	..
Weedin, Samuel	2	1	..	1	1	1	..	1	..	1	..
Whitcomb, Isaac	1	..	..	1	..	1	..	1	..	..	..
White, Thomas	1	2	1	..	1	..	..	2	..	1	..
Whitney, Eliphalet	..	1	..	1	..	1	2	1	1	..	..
Wilder, Joseph	1	1	1	..	1	2	..	1	1	..	..
Willard, Aaron	..	1	..	..	1	..	..	..	..	1	..
Willard, Aaron Jr.	..	1	1	..	..	..	..	1	..	..	..
Willard, Eli	2	1	1	1	..	1	..	..	1	..	..
Willard, James N.	..	1	1	1	1	..	..	1	..	1	..
Willard, John S.	1	..	..	1	..	3	..	..	1	..	..
Willard, Oliver	..	..	..	1	..	..	..	..	1	..	..
Willard, Oliver	..	..	1	..	1	1	..	1	..	..	..
Willard, Oliver Jr.	..	..	..	..	1	..	2	..	..	1	..
Williams, Adin	4	1	..	1	..	..	3	..	1	1	..
Williams, Allen	..	..	..	1	..	2	..	1	..	..	..
Williams, James	3	3	1	1	..	2	..	2	1	..	..
Williams, Samuel	..	1	..	1	1	..	1	1	..	1	..
Williams, Simeon	3	1	1	..	..	2	1	..	1	..	..
Winch, Jason	1	1	..	..	1	1	1	..	..	1	..
Windslow, Noah	1	..	..	1	..	4	..	..	1	1	..
Wood, Jonathan	..	1	1	..	1	..	..	..	..	1	..
Worthing, Barnard	1	1	1	..	1	1	1	..	1	..	..
Yeomans, Samuel	..	..	1	..	1	..	..	1	..	1	..
UNCERTAIN NAMES											
Pien (?), David	2	2	2	..	1	2	1	1	..	1	..
Port (?), Andrew	..	..	1	1	..	..	..	..	..	1	..
Rodgers, Phele (?)	..	..	..	..	..	..	..	..	1	1	..
LUDLOW											
Abbot, Asa	3	..	..	1	..	1	..	1	1	..	
Adams, George	..	..	..	1	..	3	1	..	1	..	..
Avery, David	1	..	1	..	1	..	..	1	..	1	..
Avery, Ebenezer	1	1	..	1	..	..	..	..	1	..	..
Bixby, Nancy	..	1	..	..	..	1	..	..	1	..	..
Bixby, Thomas	1	..	..	1	..	1	3	..	1	..	..
Briggs, Jonathan	..	..	..	1	..	..	..	..	1	..	..
Caldwell, William	..	..	..	1	..	1	..	..	1	..	..
Chamberlain, Thomas	1	..	..	1	..	1	..	..	1	..	..
Chase, Abner	..	..	..	1	..	..	1	..	1	..	..
Cooper, Timothy	..	..	..	1	..	3	..	..	1	1	..
Darby, John	1	..	1	..	..	..	..	1	..	..	..
Denison, Elisha	..	..	2	..	1	..	..	2	..	..	..
Denison, Elisha Jr.	1	..	..	1	..	1	..	..	1	1	..
Denison, Isaac	..	1	1	..	..	1	..	1	1	..	..
Dutton, Ephraim	1	..	1	1	..	2	1	..	1	..	..
Dyer, Nathaniel	1	..	..	1	..	..	..	..	1	..	..
Elsworth, Job	2	..	..	1	..	1	..	..	1	..	..
Evans, Thomas	..	..	..	..	1	..	..	1	..	1	..
Fenn, Austin	1	..	..	1	..	3	..	..	1	..	..
Finney, Willard	2	..	..	1	..	1	..	..	1	..	..
Fletcher, Jesse	4	3	..	1	..	2	1	..	1	..	..
Fletcher, Josiah	..	2	2	..	1	..	..	1	1	..	..
Gilbert, Eber	..	..	..	1	..	1	..	..	1	..	..
Goff, Samuel	3	..	..	1	..	..	..	..	1	..	..
Hale, Abel	..	1	..	1	..	1	..	..	1	..	..
Harvey, John	1	..	..	1	..	1	..	..	1	..	..
Haven, Hezekiah	1	..	..	1	..	2	2	1	1	..	..
Haven, Jedediah	..	..	..	1	1	..	1	..	1	..	..
Haven, Jedediah Jr.	1	1	..	1	..	2	..	1	..	..	..
Hemingway, Jacob	1	..	..	1	..	2	..	..	1	..	..
Hemingway, Jacob Jr.	3	1	..	1	..	..	..	..	1	..	..
Hemingway, Samuel	1	1	..	1	..	1	..	..	1	..	..
Ives, Elihu	1	..	..	1	..	1	..	..	1	..	..
Ives, Levi	2	..	..	1	..	3	1	..	1	..	..
Jewell, Abijah	..	..	2	..	..	..	..	1	..	..	..
Jones, Samuel	..	2	..	..	1	..	..	1	..	1	..
Knights, Benjamin	2	..	1	..	..	..	..	1	..	..	..
Lakin, Ebenezer	..	1	1	1	..	..	..	1	1	..	..
Lee, Seth	..	1	2	1	1	..	..	3	..	1	..
Lewis, David	3	..	..	1	..	2	..	1	1	1	..
Lyman, Solomon	1	..	..	1	..	4	1	..	1	..	..
Manning, Joseph	1	..	..	1	..	1	..	..	1	..	..
Mason, Isaac	..	1	..	1	..	..	1	..	1	..	..
Patch, Benjamin	3	1	..	1	..	..	1	1	1	..	..
Patch, Simon	..	..	..	1	..	2	..	1	1	..	..
Pelton, Freeman	1	1	..	1	..	1	2	..	1	..	..
Pettigrew, Andrew	2	..	..	1	..	1	..	..	1	..	..
Pratt, Ephraim	..	1	..	1	..	2	1	1	1	..	..
Preston, Abraham	..	1	1	..	1	..	..	2	..	2	..
Preston, Lemuel	3	..	..	1	..	1	1	..	1	..	..
Puffer, Ephraim	2	1	1	1	..	2	1	1	1	..	..

WINDSOR COUNTY—Continued

NAMES OF HEADS OF FAMILIES	Free white males: Under 10 years of age	Free white males: Of 10 and under 16	Free white males: Of 16 and under 26 including heads of families	Free white males: Of 26 and under 45 including heads of families	Free white males: Of 45 and upwards including heads of families	Free white females: Under 10 years of age	Free white females: Of 10 and under 16	Free white females: Of 16 and under 26 including heads of families	Free white females: Of 26 and under 45 including heads of families	Free white females: Of 45 and upwards including heads of families	All other free persons except Indians not taxed
LUDLOW—con.											
Reed, Peter	2	1	..	1	..	4	..	..	1	..	..
Reed, Simeon	2	2	1	..	1	2	1	2	1	..	..
Ross, Leonard	2	..	..	1	..	2	..	..	1	..	..
Ross, Thomas	1	..	..	1	..	..	..	..	1	..	..
Sargeants, Benjamin	..	..	..	1	..	2	..	..	1	..	..
Sargeants, John	1	1	1	..	1	2	1	2	..	1	..
Sargeants, John 2nd	..	..	..	1	..	2	..	..	1	..	..
Smith, Ariah	2	..	..	1	..	1	..	..	1	..	..
Spaulding, Asher	1	..	..	3	..	1	..	..	1	..	..
Spaulding, Isaac	2	1	..	1	..	3	1	..	1	..	..
Tilden, John	..	..	1	..	..	1	..	1	..	..	..
Warren, John	3	1	..	1	..	1	..	..	1	..	..
Warren, Thomas	2	..	..	1	..	1	..	..	1	..	..
Whitcomb, John	3	..	..	1	..	1	..	..	1	..	..
Whitcomb, Jonathan	1	1	..	1	..	1	1	..	1	..	..
Whitney, Oliver	1	1	1	..	1	4	1	2	..	1	1
Whitney, Orlando	2	..	..	1	..	..	..	1	..	..	..
Whitney, Widow	..	..	3	..	1	..	..	..	..	1	..
Woodward, Asa	..	..	1	..	..	1	..	1	..	..	..
Woolly, Hannah	1	..	..	..	..	2	..	..	1	..	..
Woolly, Thomas	..	..	..	..	1	..	..	..	..	1	..
NORWICH											
Allen, John	1	..	..	1	..	2	..	..	1	..	..
Allen, Jude	..	1	1	..	1	..	..	1	..	1	..
Allen, Nicholas	2	..	..	1	..	4	..	..	1	..	..
Alvord, Selah	1	..	..	1	..	1	..	..	1	..	..
Anesworth, Ezra	1	..	..	1	..	1	..	..	1	..	..
Armstrong, John	..	..	..	..	1	..	..	..	..	1	..
Armstrong, John W.	..	..	..	1	..	3	..	1	..	..	..
Avery, Charles	..	..	1	..	1	..	..	..	1	1	..
Avery, Pack	2	..	..	1	..	..	..	..	1	..	..
Badger, Jonathan	2	1	1	1	..	..	2	..	..	1	..
Baker, Gilbert	..	..	..	1	..	..	..	..	1	..	..
Baldwin, Elijah	1	1	..	..	1	..	2	..	1	..	..
Baldwin, Levi	1	1	4	..	1	..	2	..	..	1	..
Baldwin, Samuel	2	..	..	1	..	..	1	1	1	..	..
Ball, Humphrey	..	1	..	..	1	1	1	1	1	..	..
Ball, Roswell	2	..	..	1	..	2	..	..	1	..	..
Barrot, Jonathan	2	1	..	2	1	2	..	1	1	1	..
Bartlett, Elliot	2	3	..	1	..	1	1	..	1	..	..
Bartlett, Gershum	1	2	..	1	..	3	..	1	1	..	..
Bartlett, Jirus	1	..	..	1	..	1	..	..	1	..	..
Bartlett, Jonathan	1	1	..	1	..	1	..	..	1	..	..
Bartlett, Joseph	1	..	..	1	1	3	..	1	..	1	..
Bartlett, Moses	..	..	..	1	..	4	..	..	1	..	..
Bartlett, Samuel	..	1	..	..	1	1	2	3	1	..	..
Bartlett, Thomas	1	..	2	..	1	2	..	1	1	..	..
Baxter, Elihu	3	2	1	..	1	2	..	1	1	..	..
Bell, Samuel	..	..	..	..	1	..	..	..	..	1	..
Bissell, Jeremiah	..	..	..	1	1	..	1	..	..	1	..
Bissell, Jeremiah Jr.	2	..	..	1	..	1	..	..	1	..	..
Bly, James	..	..	1	1	..	1	1	..	1	..	..
Boardman, Jonas	3	1	1	..	1	3	1	..	1	..	..
Boardman, Nathaniel	..	..	..	..	1	..	..	1	..	1	..
Boardman, Nathaniel Jr.	3	..	..	1	..	2	..	..	1	..	..
Bodwell, Consider	1	..	..	1	..	..	..	1	..	..	..
Brenison, Elijah	..	..	..	..	1	..	..	..	..	1	..
Brewster, Asa	1	1	1	..	1	..	..	..	..	1	..
Brewster, Cyrus	..	..	..	..	1	..	2	..	1	..	..
Brigham, Dan J.	..	..	1	1	..	2	1	1	..	..	..
Brigham, Paul	..	..	2	..	1	..	1	1	..	2	..
Brigham, Thomas	..	1	..	1	..	3	..	..	1	..	..
Brown, Ebenezer	..	..	1	..	1	..	1	..	..	1	..
Brown, Ebenezer	1	..	2	1	..	3	1	..	1	..	1
Brown, Isaac	3	..	..	1	..	2	..	..	1	..	..
Brown, Israel	1	1	..	..	1	..	2	2	..	1	..
Brown, Joseph	..	..	..	..	1	1	..	1	1	..	..
Brown, Lemuel	3	..	..	1	1	1	2	..	1	..	..
Brown, Samuel	..	1	2	..	1	..	1	..	..	1	..
Brown, Solomon	..	..	1	..	..	1	..	1	..	..	..
Buck, Daniel	2	2	2	..	1	2	2	1	1	..	..
Burnett, Elijah	1	..	..	1	1	1	..	..	..	1	..
Burnett, John Jr.	1	2	..	..	1	1	..	..	1	..	..
Burton, Benjamin	3	1	3	..	1	2	1	1	1	..	..
Burton, Elisha	1	1	4	1	1	1	2	1	..	1	..
Burton, Henry	3	..	1	1	..	2	1	..	1	..	..
Burton, John	3	2	2	1	..	1	1	..	1	..	..
Burton, Josiah	1	..	..	..	2	..	2	..	..	1	..
Burton, Levi	2	..	..	1	..	..	..	..	1	..	..
Burton, Pierce	1	1	..	1	..	1	1	..	1	1	..
Burton, Reuben	1	..	1	1	..	..	..	1	..	..	..
NORWICH—con.											
Bush, Eleazer	2	1	1	1	..	..	1	..	1	..	..
Bush, John	2	1	1	1	..	1	..	1	1	..	..
Bush, Timothy	..	..	2	1	1	..	..	1	..	1	..
Carpenter, Simeon	1	2	..	..	1	..	1	2	..	1	..
Claud, Norman	1	..	1	1	..	1	..	1	..	1	..
Coffeer, Molten	..	..	1	..	..	1	..	1	..	..	..
Coit, Samuel	..	1	..	1	..	2	..	..	1	..	..
Colburn, Jonathan	..	..	..	1	..	..	..	..	1	..	..
Cook, Joseph	3	..	..	1	..	..	..	..	1	..	..
Cook, Samuel	1	..	..	1	..	1	..	..	1	..	..
Crary, James	3	..	..	1	..	..	..	..	1	1	..
Crary, John	1	2	..	..	1	1	1	..	2	..	..
Crary, William	..	1	..	1	..	2	..	..	1	..	..
Curtiss, Solomon	2	..	..	1	..	2	1	..	1	..	..
Cushman, Job	1	..	..	1	..	2	1	..	1	..	..
Cushman, Joseph	..	..	..	1	..	2	..	..	1	..	..
Cushman, Oliver	1	..	..	1	..	2	1	..	1	..	..
Cushman, Solomon	..	..	1	..	1	..	..	..	1	1	..
Dicke, Robert	2	1	..	..	1	3	1	..	1	..	..
Dier, Ebenezer	1	2	..	..	1	1	1	..	1	..	..
Dutten, Samuel	..	1	1	..	1	..	..	1	..	1	..
Edwards, John	..	..	..	1	..	..	2	..	1	..	..
Emmerson, Elisha	..	1	..	1	..	1	1	1	..	..	..
Emmerson, Joseph	1	1	..	1	..	..	..	1	..	..	..
Fairchild, Timothy	..	..	1	..	..	..	..	2	..	..	..
Fellows, Nathan	..	1	..	..	1	..	1	..	1	..	..
Freeman, Experience	1	1	1	1	..	1	2	..	1	..	..
Fuller, Mary	..	..	..	..	..	..	..	..	..	..	1
Gear, Abisha	1	..	..	1	..	3	..	1	..	..	..
Geer, Jesse	..	1	..	..	1	..	..	..	..	1	..
Gillet, Abel	2	..	..	1	..	1	..	..	1	..	..
Goodrich, Hezekiah	2	..	..	1	1	..	..	1	1	2	..
Goolet, Joseph	..	..	..	1	..	1	..	1	..	..	..
Gould, Francis	1	..	..	1	..	1	..	..	1	..	..
Gould, John	1	..	1	1	..	1	1	1	1	..	..
Gutteridge, Eleazer	1	1	1	..	1	2	2	..	1	..	..
Gutteridge, John	2	..	..	1	..	2	..	..	1	..	..
Hall, Isaac	1	..	..	1	..	..	..	..	1	..	..
Hall, John	..	..	1	..	..	..	..	1	..	..	..
Hall, Jonathan	..	1	..	1	..	1	..	..	1	..	..
Hammond, Titus D.	1	..	..	1	..	..	..	..	1	..	..
Hartshorn, Lampson	1	..	..	1	..	..	..	..	1	..	..
Hatch, Adrian	2	1	..	..	1	2	..	..	1	..	..
Hatch, John	3	..	2	1	1	2	1	1	1	1	..
Hatch, Joseph	1	..	2	..	1	..	..	2	..	1	..
Hatch, Oliver	1	..	2	..	..	1	..	2	..	1	..
Hawley, Lewman	3	..	1	1	..	..	..	..	1	..	..
Hedges, David	3	..	..	1	..	1	..	..	1	..	..
Hedges, Jeremiah	1	1	..	1	..	2	2	..	1	..	..
Hibbard, John	2	..	..	..	1	2	2	3	1	..	..
Hopson, Abial	..	1	1	..	..	..	2	1	1	1	..
Hopson, William	..	..	1	..	..	..	..	1	..	..	..
Horn, Benjamin	1	..	..	1	..	..	..	1	..	..	..
House, John	..	1	2	..	1	..	1	1	..	1	..
Hovey, Isaac	2	..	..	1	..	1	..	..	1	..	..
Hovey, Nathaniel	2	..	..	1	..	1	..	..	1	1	..
Howard, Moses	..	1	..	1	1	..	2	..	..	1	..
Hows, Joseph	2	2	..	..	1	1	..	1	..	1	..
Hunt, Simeon	1	1	2	..	1	..	1	1	..	1	..
Hunt, Solomon	4	1	..	..	1	1	1	1	..	1	..
Hutchinson, Jerum	1	..	..	1	..	3	1	..	1	..	..
Hutchinson, Samuel	2	2	4	..	2	3	1	3	1	1	..
Jaquis, Ebenezer	..	1	..	1	..	..	1	1	..	1	..
Jaquis, Lucy	..	1	..	..	..	1	..	..	1	..	..
Johnson, Calvin	..	2	..	..	1	..	..	1	..	1	..
Johnson, David	1	2	..	..	1	1	..	..	1	..	..
Johnson, James	..	1	..	1	..	..	1	..	1	..	..
Johnson, John	1	..	..	1	..	3	..	..	1	..	..
Johnson, Samuel	..	..	..	1	1	2	..	..	1	1	..
Johnson, William	..	2	1	..	1	1	2	1	1	..	..
Kelley, Benjamin	..	..	1	..	..	..	..	1	..	..	..
Kendrick, Thomas	1	..	..	1	..	3	..	..	1	..	..
Leavitt, Erastus	..	..	2	1	..	..	..	..	1	..	..
Lewis, Asa	2	1	..	2	..	1	2	..	1	1	..
Lewis, John	2	2	2	..	1	..	..	1	..	1	..
Lewis, Joseph	..	..	2	..	1	1	..	1	..	1	..
Lewis, Noah	1	1	..	1	..	1	..	1	..	..	..
Lewis, William	..	..	..	..	1	..	..	..	1	1	..

WINDSOR COUNTY—Continued

NAMES OF HEADS OF FAMILIES	FREE WHITE MALES: Under 10 years of age	FREE WHITE MALES: Of 10 and under 16	FREE WHITE MALES: Of 16 and under 26 including heads of families	FREE WHITE MALES: Of 26 and under 45 including heads of families	FREE WHITE MALES: Of 45 and upwards including heads of families	FREE WHITE FEMALES: Under 10 years of age	FREE WHITE FEMALES: Of 10 and under 16	FREE WHITE FEMALES: Of 16 and under 26 including heads of families	FREE WHITE FEMALES: Of 26 and under 45 including heads of families	FREE WHITE FEMALES: Of 45 and upwards including heads of families	All other free persons except Indians not taxed
NORWICH—con.											
Loomis, William	..	2	1	1	..	1	1	2	1	..	..
Lord, David	..	2	1	1	..	2	..	..	1	..	..
Lord, Jonathan	..	..	1	..	1	..	2	..	..	1	..
Lord, Joseph	4	..	..	1	..	4	1	1	..	..	..
Loveland, Joseph	2	1	3	..	1	2	2	..	..	1	..
Lyman, David	2	1	..	1	..	1	..	..	1	..	..
Lyman, James	..	..	2	1	..	..	1	..	1	..	..
Lyman, Roger	..	..	..	1	..	2	..	1	..	..	..
Marvin, Jonathan	1	..	..	1	..	1	1	..	1	..	..
McNeller, John	1	..	..	..	1	..	..	..	..	1	..
McNight, Thomas	..	..	..	1	..	..	..	..	..	1	..
Miles, John	2	..	..	1	..	3	..	..	1	..	..
Minor, Anderson	1	1	..	..	1	..	..	..	..	1	..
Morse, Gershum	2	1	1	..	1	2	1	1	1	..	..
Morse, Seth	1	2	..	1	1	2	1	..	1	1	..
Mosher, Pendon	3	..	..	1	..	2	..	1	..	..	..
Murdock, Constant	1	..	2	2	1	2	1	2	..	1	..
Neeland, Joseph	..	1	3	..	1	1	1	3	..	1	..
Newton, Baxter	1	..	..	1	..	2	..	..	1	..	..
Newton, Israel	1	..	1	1	..	4	..	1	1	..	..
Nigh, Daniel	2	1	..	1	..	1	..	..	1	..	..
Olcott, Peter	..	1	1	..	1	..	1	2	1	1	..
Olcott, Roswell	..	..	1	1	..	3	..	..	2	..	3
Parisfield, Ebenezer	1	..	..	1	1	..	..	1	..	1	..
Parisfield, Roswell	1	..	1	1	..	..	..	1	..	..	..
Parrifield, Jeremiah	3	3	..	1	..	..	..	2	1	..	..
Parsons, Moses	3	2	1	..	1	1	1	..	..	1	..
Patridge, Elias	..	1	1	1	..	..	..	1	1	..	..
Patridge, Elisha	..	..	..	1	..	..	..	1	..	..	..
Patridge, Elisha	..	1	1	..	1	1	1	1	..	1	..
Patridge, Isaac	4	2	..	2	1	1	..	2	1	..	..
Patridge, Lemuel	..	2	..	..	1	..	..	1	..	1	..
Patridge, Reuben	1	..	2	1	..	2	..	1	..	..	..
Patrill, Joseph	2	..	..	..	1	2	..	..	..	1	..
Patrill, Sarah	..	..	..	..	..	..	..	..	1	1	..
Phillips, Amos	..	..	..	2	..	..	..	..	1	..	..
Pinnick, Zela	3	1	..	1	..	1	..	..	1	..	..
Potter, Lyman	..	1	2	..	1	2	1	2	1	..	..
Rawlins, Phillip	..	..	..	..	1	..	1	..	1	..	..
Rice, Aaron	2	..	..	1	..	..	..	..	1	..	..
Rice, Isaac	1	..	3	..	1	..	1	1	..	1	..
Richards, Hannah	..	..	1	..	..	..	..	..	..	1	..
Roberts, William	..	..	1	..	..	1	..	..	1	..	..
Rodgers, William	1	..	..	1	..	..	..	1	..	..	..
Safford, Johnson	..	..	1	2	..	2	1	..	1	..	..
Sawyer, Conant B.	2	..	1	..	1	1	..	1	1	..	..
Sawyer, Jacob	..	1	1	..	1	1	..	1	1	..	..
Scale, Stephen	..	..	1	..	..	1	..	1	..	..	..
Sever, Calvin	1	2	..	1	..	3	..	..	1	..	..
Sever, Mary	..	..	..	..	..	..	..	1	1	..	..
Slafter, Edmund F.	..	..	..	1	..	1	..	1	..	..	..
Slafter, John	..	..	3	..	1	..	1	..	..	2	..
Smalley, Francis	1	1	2	..	1	..	1	2	..	1	..
Smally, Abel	..	..	1	..	..	1	..	1	..	..	..
Smith, Eleazer	1	..	1	1	..	2	..	1	..	1	..
Smith, Ephraim	1	2	1	1	1	2	1	1	..	1	..
Smith, Phillip	4	1	..	1	..	1	1	..	1	..	..
Smith, Reuben	1	..	..	1	..	1	..	..	1	..	..
Snow, Jonathan	1	1	..	1	..	1	2	..	1	..	..
Spear, John	..	..	1	..	1	..	..	1	..	1	..
Spear, Joshua	2	1	..	..	1	3	..	2	..	1	..
Stafford, John	..	..	..	1	..	..	4	..	1	..	..
Stevenson, James	2	..	1	1	..	1	1	1	1	..	..
Stiles, Peleg	2	1	..	1	..	2	1	..	1	..	..
Stimsen, Joel	4	..	2	..	1	1	2	..	..	1	..
Stowel, Asa	1	1	..	1	..	..	..	1	1	..	..
Sumner, William	2	..	..	1	..	1	..	..	1	..	..
Thatcher, Peter	1	1	2	1	..	..	..	1	1	..	..
Thomas, David	..	..	..	..	1	..	..	..	1	..	..
Tolman, Lyman	2	..	..	1	..	1	..	..	1	..	..
Tucker, Joseph	2	2	..	..	1	3	1	..	1	..	..
Turner, Samuel	1	..	1	..	..	..	..	1	..	..	..
Vincent, Joseph	..	..	2	..	1	..	2	..	..	1	..
Wade, William	..	1	..	1	..	1	..	..	1	..	..
Walker, Jason	3	..	..	1	..	..	..	..	1	..	..
Warner, Warren	2	..	..	1	..	2	..	..	1	..	..
Waterman, Ann	..	..	..	1	..	..	..	..	1	1	..
Waterman, Daniel	3	2	1	..	1	..	..	3	1	..	..
Waterman, Elijah	..	..	1	1	1	2	1	2	1	..	..
Waterman, Elisha	..	2	1	1	..	1	1	..	1	..	..
Waterman, James	..	2	1	..	1	2	2	1	1	..	..
Waterman, John	2	..	..	1	..	1	..	..	1	..	..
Waterman, Lemuel	..	1	1	1	1	..	1	1	..	1	..
West, Caleb	1	1	2	..	1	2	..	1	1	1	..
Whipple, Samuel	..	..	1	..	..	1	..	1	..	1	..
White, Eli	2	1	1	..	..	2	..	2	1	..	..
White, Elisha	1	..	..	1	..	3	1	..	1	..	..
White, Frederick	..	..	..	1	..	..	..	..	..	..	..
White, Samuel	..	..	..	..	1	..	..	..	..	1	..
White, Solomon	2	..	1	..	1	2	3	..	..	1	..
Wilder, Abel	..	1	1	..	1	3	2	2	..	1	..
Wills, Amhent	1	..	..	1	..	3	..	..	1	..	..
Wills, Jacob	2	..	..	1	1	1	..	..	1	..	..
Wilmott, Timothy	4	..	1	1	..	1	1	1	1	..	..
Woodworth, Benjamin	1	2	1	1	..	1	1	1	1	..	..
Wright, Oliver	1	1	2	..	..	1	2	..	..	1	..
Wright, Samuel	1	1	..	..	1	..	..	..	1	..	..
Yeomans, Elijah	..	1	..	..	1	..	1	..	1	..	..
Yeomans, Elijah Jr.	1	..	..	1	..	1	..	..	1	..	..
Yerangton, Ebenezer	3	1	1	..	1	2	1	..	1	..	..
PLYMOUTH											
Ashley, Francis	..	..	..	1	..	2	..	..	1	..	..
Averil, Samuel	..	..	..	1	..	2	2	2	1	..	..
Bond, Isaac	1	..	2	1	..	..	1	..	1	..	..
Boynton, Amos	..	..	..	1	1	2	..	1	1	1	..
Boynton, Amos Jr.	1	..	1	..	..	1	..	1	..	..	..
Briggs, Asa	1	2	..	..	1	..	..	1	..	1	..
Brooks, Ebenezer	1	..	1	..	..	1	..	1	..	..	..
Brown, Bowman	..	..	1	1	..	..	1	1	1	..	..
Brown, Daniel	1	..	1	..	..	..	..	1	..	..	..
Brown, Israel	..	..	1	..	..	1	..	1	..	..	..
Carlisle, William	1	3	1	1	..	1	1	..	1	..	..
Catlin, Gideon	2	..	..	1	..	..	1	..	1	..	..
Chamberlain, Benjamin	..	..	..	1	..	..	..	..	1	..	..
Cook, Samuel	2	..	..	1	..	2	..	..	2	..	..
Cooledge, John	..	1	2	1	..	1	1	1	1	..	..
Cross, Joseph	1	2	1	..	1	1	1	..	..	1	..
Cross, Joseph Jr.	..	..	1	..	..	..	..	1	..	..	..
Cross, Zachariah	..	2	2	..	1	..	2	..	..	1	..
Cutler, Silas	1	..	1	..	1	..	2	..	..	1	..
Cutler, Solomon	..	..	1	..	..	..	..	2	..	..	..
Deming, Thomas	1	..	1	1	..	1	2	1	1	..	..
Everett, Samuel	1	..	1	..	..	..	..	1	..	..	..
Farrar, Isaiah	..	..	..	1	..	1	..	..	1	..	..
Felt, Aaron	..	..	..	1	..	2	..	..	1	..	..
Felt, David	..	..	..	1	..	1	..	..	1	..	..
Foster, Daniel	1	1	1	1	..	2	1	..	1	..	..
Foster, Jonathan	2	1	..	1	..	3	1	..	1	..	..
Grover, Eleazer	..	3	..	..	1	6	1	..	..	1	..
Hawes, Nathaniel	3	..	..	1	..	..	..	..	1	..	..
Henzey, Henry	1	2	1	1	..	3	1	1	1	..	..
Holden, Benjamin	1	..	..	1	..	2	..	..	1	..	..
Hosley, William	..	..	1	..	1	1	..	..	..	1	..
Jones, Nathan	..	..	1	..	1	..	..	..	..	1	..
Jones, Nathan Jr.	2	1	..	1	..	2	1	..	1	..	..
Kelsey, Nathan	..	1	1	..	1	1	..	..	1	..	..
Kemp, John	1	..	1	..	1	1	1	1	..	1	..
Kemp, Reuben	..	..	1	..	..	..	..	1	..	..	..
Kendall, Josiah	1	..	..	1	..	..	1	..	1	..	..
Kimball, Amos	1	..	1	1	..	..	3	..	1	..	..
Lamson, James	1	..	..	1	..	..	..	..	1	..	..
Lynde, Samuel	..	2	3	..	1	..	1	2	..	1	..
Marey, Daniel	2	1	..	1	..	1	..	..	1	..	..
Marey, Wait	2	..	1	1	..	1	..	1	..	1	..
Moore, Ephraim	..	3	..	1	..	1	1	..	1	..	..
Morgan, Henry	..	1	1	..	1	1	1	..	..	1	..
Morgan, Richard	1	..	1	1	..	2	1	..	1	..	..
Morgan, Solomon	1	..	1	..	..	1	..	1	..	..	..
Mudge, John	..	..	1	..	1	..	..	..	..	1	..
Mudge, John Jr.	1	..	1	..	..	1	..	1	..	..	..
Mudge, Martin	2	..	..	1	..	1	..	..	1	..	..

WINDSOR COUNTY—Continued

NAMES OF HEADS OF FAMILIES	FREE WHITE MALES: Under 10 years of age	FREE WHITE MALES: Of 10 and under 16	FREE WHITE MALES: Of 16 and under 26 including heads of families	FREE WHITE MALES: Of 26 and under 45 including heads of families	FREE WHITE MALES: Of 45 and upwards including heads of families.	FREE WHITE FEMALES: Under 10 years of age	FREE WHITE FEMALES: Of 10 and under 16	FREE WHITE FEMALES: Of 16 and under 26 including heads of families	FREE WHITE FEMALES: Of 26 and under 45 including heads of families	FREE WHITE FEMALES: Of 45 and upwards including heads of families	All other free persons except Indians not taxed
PLYMOUTH—con.											
Page, Polly	..	..	2	..	..	..	..	..	..	1	..
Peters, John	..	..	..	1	..	..	..	1	..	..	..
Placeway, William	..	..	..	1	..	3	..	..	1	1	..
Pollard, James	1	..	..	1	..	..	1	..	1	..	..
Pollard, Moses	2	..	2	2	..	1	..	..	1	..	..
Pratt, Asa	3	1	..	1	..	..	1	2	1	..	..
Priest, Moses	1	..	..	1	1	1	..	..	1	..	..
Rhodes, Eleazer	2	..	..	1	1	2	..	..	1	..	..
Rice, Luke	2	..	..	1	..	3	..	1	1	..	..
Robinson, Zelotes	1	..	..	1	..	2	..	..	1	..	..
Sawyer, Elias	..	..	1	..	..	1	..	1	..	..	..
Sawyer, Lemuel	1	2	..	1	..	..	1	..	1	..	..
Sawyer, Paul	..	1	..	1	..	1	..	..	1	..	..
Sawyer, Thomas	2	2	3	..	1	1	2	1	..	1	..
Shead, Amos	..	1	..	1	..	..	1	1	1	..	..
Slack, Oliver	1	..	..	1	..	1	..	..	1	..	..
Slack, William	1	2	1	..	1	..	1	..	..	1	..
Slaughter, Silas	..	..	1	..	..	1	..	1	..	..	..
Slaughter, Stephen	1	1	2	..	1	2	1	1	..	1	..
Smead, Simon	1	..	1	..	1	..	..	1	..	..	..
Snow, Caleb	2	..	..	1	..	1	..	..	1	..	..
Snow, Elijah	3	..	..	1	..	..	2	..	1	..	..
Sole, Charles	..	1	..	1	..	..	..	..	1	..	..
Spaulding, Asa	1	..	..	1	..	2	..	..	2	..	..
Taylor, John	4	..	..	1	..	1	..	..	1	..	..
Tozer, Charles	1	..	1	1	..	..	..	1	1	..	..
Warner, Levi	3	..	..	1	..	2	..	..	1	..	..
Wheeler, Asa	2	2	..	1	..	1	1	..	1	..	..
Wheeler, Joel	2	2	..	1	..	1	..	1	1	..	..
Whitney, Elisha	..	..	..	1	..	2	1	1	1	..	..
Wilder, Benjamin	..	..	1	..	..	..	..	1	..	..	..
Wilder, Jacob	1	1	1	..	1	2	2	..	..	1	..
Wilder, Jacob 2nd	..	..	1	..	..	..	..	1	..	..	..
Wilder, Jotham	..	..	..	1	..	1	..	..	1	..	..
Williams, Elias	1	..	..	1	..	2	..	..	1	..	..
Willis, James	1	2	..	..	1	..	..	..	..	1	..
Woods, Amasa	..	..	..	1	..	..	..	1	..	..	..
POMFRET											
Abbot, Jeremiah	..	..	..	1	..	2	..	..	1	..	..
Abbot, Samuel	..	1	..	..	1	..	1	..	..	1	..
Allen, Elnathan	2	2	..	..	1	..	..	1	..	1	..
Badcock, Josiah	..	1	1	..	1	2	..	1	1	..	..
Bennett, Ebenezer	..	..	..	1	..	1	..	..	1	..	..
Bishop, James	1	1	1	..	1	..	1	1	1	..	..
Boynton, Andrew	1	..	..	..	1	..	..	..	..	1	..
Brennen, Joseph	2	1	..	1	..	2	..	..	1	1	..
Brounen, Robert	2	..	..	1	..	4	1	1	1	..	..
Bugbee, Abial	1	..	3	..	..	1	..	1	..	..	..
Bugbee, Abiel	1	1	2	1	1	..	1	1	..	1	..
Bugbee, Elisha	3	..	..	1	..	1	..	1	..	..	..
Bullard, Asa	..	..	..	..	1	..	..	..	..	1	..
Bullard, Reuben	..	1	..	1	..	3	..	..	1	1	..
Burnham, Fredrick	2	1	..	..	1	1	1	..	..	1	..
Burnham, James	2	2	2	..	1	1	..	1	..	1	..
Chamberlin, Samuel	1	..	2	..	1	..	..	1	..	1	..
Chandler, Josiah	2	..	..	1	..	1	1	..	1	..	..
Cheedle, Asa	1	2	..	1	..	4	..	..	1	..	..
Cheedle, Asa	1	..	..	2	..	..	..	1	..	..	..
Cheedle, John	..	..	1	..	1	..	2	2	..	1	..
Child, Abijah	..	..	5	..	1	1	..	2	..	1	..
Child, Jacob	..	..	3	..	..	..	..	2	..	..	..
Churchell, Ichabod	1	..	1	..	1	..	1	1	..	1	..
Claflin, Elijah	1	..	..	1	..	..	..	..	1	..	..
Cleaveland, Hosmore	3	..	..	1	..	1	..	..	1	..	..
Conant, Jeremiah	2	2	1	1	..	1	1	2	1	..	..
Crooker, Josiah	1	..	1	..	..	..	1	1	..	..	..
Dana, Isaac	3	1	2	2	..	1	1	1	1	..	..
Dana, John W.	1	2	3	1	1	..	1	3	..	1	..
Dana, Jonathan	..	1	2	..	1	1	..	2	1	..	..
Dana, Putnam	..	1	2	1	..	1	1	2	..	..	..
Darling, John	4	1	..	1	..	2	2	..	1	..	..
Darling, William	..	1	..	..	1	1	1	..	..	1	..
Davis, Eliphalet	3	..	..	1	..	..	..	1	..	..	..
Dean, Nathan	..	..	..	..	1	..	1	1	..	1	..
Dexter, John	1	2	3	..	1	1	1	1	1	..	..
Doton, Isaac	3	..	..	1	..	2	..	..	1	..	..
Doton, John	..	..	1	..	1	1	..	..	1	..	..
Drew, Ezra	..	1	1	..	1	3	1	1	..	1	..
POMFRET—con.											
Durkee, Andrew	3	1	..	1	..	1	..	..	1	..	..
Durkee, Bart	..	1	1	1	1	..	..	1	..	1	..
Durkee, Ransom	2	1	1	1	..	2	3	..	1	..	..
Edson, Josiah	1	..	..	1	..	2	..	..	1	..	..
Evans, Richard	..	..	..	..	1	..	1	..	1	..	..
Finley, John	..	..	..	..	1	1	..	..	1	1	..
Finno, Joseph	..	1	1	1	..	..	..	..	1	..	..
Finno, Nabby	..	1	1	..	..	1	..	..	1	..	..
Fletcher, Edmund	..	1	..	1	..	..	..	1	..	..	..
Frazier, Alkins	..	..	1	..	..	2	..	1	..	..	..
Frazier, John	..	..	..	..	1	..	..	1	1	1	..
Freeman, Clark	..	..	1	1	..	1	..	..	1	..	..
Freeman, Samuel	1	..	..	..	1	1	..	..	1	..	..
Gibbans, Fitch	..	..	..	..	1	..	..	..	..	1	..
Gipson, John	..	..	2	..	1	2	1	1	..	1	..
Goph, Oliver	3	2	1	..	1	2	1	1	1	..	..
Gould, Benjamin	..	2	..	..	1	1	..	1	..	1	..
Gould, Benjamin	..	1	..	1	..	2	..	1	1	..	..
Griswold, Jehiel	1	..	1	..	1	..	..	1	..	1	..
Haden, Henry	2	..	1	..	..	1	..	1	..	..	..
Hall, Liberty	..	..	1	..	..	1	..	1	..	..	..
Hall, Wyllys	..	..	..	..	1	..	..	..	..	1	..
Hardin, Timothy	..	2	2	..	1	..	1	4	1	..	..
Hawkins, Dexter	2	..	..	1	..	2	..	..	1	..	..
Hewet, Stephen	..	2	..	2	1	1	1	1	1	1	..
Hodges, Asa	..	1	..	1	..	..	..	..	1	..	..
Hodges, Seth	2	..	..	..	1	1	3	..	1	..	..
Homes, William	1	..	..	2	..	3	..	..	1	..	..
Hooper, Cyrus	1	..	1	1	..	2	1	..	1	1	..
Hopsin, John	1	1	..	1	..	1	..	1	..	..	..
Howard, Abel	2	..	..	1	..	2	..	1	1	..	..
Howard, Adam	5	..	1	..	1	..	2	..	1	..	..
Howard, Leonard	1	..	..	1	..	..	..	..	1	..	..
Hoyt, Jonathan	4	..	1	1	..	1	..	..	1	..	..
Humphry, Thomas	2	..	..	2	..	1	..	..	1	..	..
Hunt, Increase	..	2	1	..	1	..	..	1	..	1	..
Hutchinson, Aaron	..	..	..	2	1	..	..	..	1	1	..
Jones, William	2	..	..	1	..	2	3	..	1	..	..
Kemp, Joel	..	1	..	1	..	..	..	..	..	1	..
Kemp, Nehemiah	..	..	..	1	..	2	..	1	..	..	..
Lake, Eli	1	..	1	1	..	4	3	..	1	..	..
Lamb, John	1	..	..	..	1	..	1	1	..	1	..
Lamb, Samuel	..	..	..	2	1	..	1	..	..	1	..
Lamfere, Thomas	3	..	..	1	..	3	..	..	1	..	..
Lamphere, Abijah	..	..	1	..	1	..	..	..	..	1	..
Lasell, Joshua	2	1	..	1	..	3	1	..	1	..	..
Lasell, Zenas	..	1	..	1	..	4	2	..	1	..	..
Leonard, Enoch	1	1	..	1	..	3	..	..	1	..	..
Leonard, Marius	1	..	..	1	..	..	..	..	1	..	..
Leonard, Oppir	..	..	..	1	..	2	..	1	..	..	..
Leonard, Roland	1	2	..	..	1	2	..	..	1	1	..
Leonard, Solomon	..	..	..	..	1	..	..	..	..	1	..
Lovell, John	2	3	..	..	1	1	..	1	..	1	..
Mann, Benjamin	..	1	..	..	1	1	..	1	..	1	..
Mason, Marshall	2	..	..	1	..	1	..	1	..	..	..
Miller, John	1	1	1	..	1	1	2	1	1	..	..
Mires, Dennis N.	..	..	..	1	..	..	..	..	1	1	..
Morris, Asa	1	..	1	1	..	..	..	1	1	..	..
Morris, Wyman	1	..	1	1	..	..	1	..	1	1	..
Morse, Abia	1	2	..	1	..	1	..	..	1	..	..
Newton, Isaac	3	1	..	1	..	1	1	..	1	..	..
Paddock, Zenus	1	..	3	..	1	..	..	1	1	1	..
Paine, Asa	2	2	..	..	1	..	..	1	..	1	..
Peak, Ephraim	..	1	1	..	1	..	1	2	..	..	..
Perkins, Joel	5	..	..	1	..	1	..	..	1	..	..
Perrin, Abel	..	1	1	..	1	..	2	1	1	..	..
Perrin, Epaphrus	..	..	1	..	..	..	..	1	..	..	..
Perrin, John	..	..	1	..	1	1	..	1	1	..	..
Perrin, Mary	2	..	3	..	1	1	2	..	1	..	..
Perry, Joseph	1	..	..	1	..	2	..	..	1	..	..
Perry, Robert	1	1	2	1	1	..	1	1	..	1	..
Perry, William	1	..	..	..	1	1	..	..	..	1	..
Phillip, John	..	..	..	..	1	..	1	..	1	..	..
Porter, Samuel	..	1	..	1	..	3	..	..	1	..	..
Pratt, Benjamin	1	1	..	1	..	1	..	..	1	..	..
Pratt, Jeremiah	1	..	..	..	1	..	1	2	..	1	..
Pratt, John	..	..	..	..	1	..	..	..	..	..	1

WINDSOR COUNTY—Continued

NAMES OF HEADS OF FAMILIES	FREE WHITE MALES: Under 10 years of age	FREE WHITE MALES: Of 10 and under 16	FREE WHITE MALES: Of 16 and under 26 including heads of families	FREE WHITE MALES: Of 26 and under 45 including heads of families	FREE WHITE MALES: Of 45 and upwards including heads of families	FREE WHITE FEMALES: Under 10 years of age	FREE WHITE FEMALES: Of 10 and under 16	FREE WHITE FEMALES: Of 16 and under 26 including heads of families	FREE WHITE FEMALES: Of 26 and under 45 including heads of families	FREE WHITE FEMALES: Of 45 and upwards including heads of families	All other free persons except Indians not taxed
POMFRET—con.											
Pratt, Levi	..	1	..	..	1	2	2	..	..	1	..
Pratt, Martin	1	..	..	1	..	3	..	..	1	..	..
Pratt, Nehemiah	3	..	1	1	..	1	..	1	..	..	..
Pratt, Rufus	..	..	..	1	..	..	..	1	..	..	..
Ralph, James	2	..	..	1	..	3	..	..	1	..	..
Rawlinson, William	..	..	1	..	..	..	..	1	..	..	..
Raymond, James	..	..	..	..	1	..	..	..	..	1	..
Raymond, James Jr.	3	..	..	1	..	1	1	..	1	..	..
Raymond, Phinehas	5	..	..	1	..	..	..	..	1	..	..
Reed, Joshua	..	2	4	..	1	..	..	2	..	1	..
Reed, Levi	..	..	..	1	..	..	..	..	1	..	..
Richards, Nathan	..	..	..	..	1	..	..	..	..	1	..
Ruggles, Nathaniel	1	..	1	..	1	..	1	..	..	1	..
Runnell, Jonathan	..	1	..	1	..	..	1	..	1	1	..
Seargent, Edward	..	..	1	..	..	1	..	1	..	..	..
Seargent, Jacob	1	..	1	..	..	2	..	..	1	..	..
Sessions, Elizabeth	2	..	2	..	..	1	1	2	..	1	..
Sessions, Simeon	..	..	..	..	1	..	..	1	..	1	..
Simons, Nathaniel	2	..	1	1	..	..	..	1	..	..	..
Skinner, Benjamin	1	1	..	..	1	1	1	..	1	..	..
Smith, Aaron	2	..	..	1	..	2	..	..	1	..	..
Smith, Abisha	2	1	3	..	1	1	..	1	..	1	..
Smith, Christopher	..	1	..	..	1	..	1	..	1	1	..
Smith, Lawden	..	..	1	1	..	1	..	1	..	..	..
Snow, Bela	..	..	2	..	..	..	..	..	1	..	..
Snow, Samuel	2	2	1	..	1	..	1	..	1	..	..
Snow, Samuel Jr.	1	..	1	..	..	..	..	..	1	..	..
Spear, Joseph	1	..	..	1	..	3	..	..	1	..	..
Streeter, Enoch	3	1	..	1	..	2	1	..	1	..	..
Thomas, Abial	1	..	..	1	..	1	..	1	..	..	..
Thomas, Job	..	1	..	..	1	..	..	1	..	1	..
Thompson, Benjamin	3	2	1	..	1	..	1	1	1	..	..
Tinkam, Nathan	..	..	..	..	1	..	..	..	..	1	..
Tinkham, Isaiah	2	..	1	1	..	3	..	1	1	..	..
Troop, John	..	..	2	..	1	..	..	..	..	1	..
Tuttle, Daniel	..	..	1	..	..	1	..	1	..	..	..
Tuttle, John	..	..	..	..	1	1	3	1	1	..	..
Tuttle, William	..	..	1	..	..	2	..	1	..	..	..
Udall, Oliver	1	..	2	..	..	..	..	1	..	..	..
Vales, Abraham	..	1	2	..	1	..	1	1	..	1	..
Vales, Augustus	1	..	..	1	..	1	..	1	..	..	..
Vales, Eliphalet	1	1	1	..	1	1	1	..	..	1	..
Vales, Thomas	..	..	1	..	1	..	..	2	1	1	..
Vales, Thomas Jr.	2	1	..	1	..	1	1	..	1	..	..
Vaughan, Daniel	2	..	..	1	..	2	..	..	1	..	..
Wadsworth, Samuel	..	..	..	1	..	1	..	..	1	..	..
Ware, Frederick	3	..	..	1	..	2	2	..	1	..	..
Warren, Josiah	3	2	2	..	1	2	1	1	1	..	..
Washburn, Barnabas	..	2	..	1	..	4	1	1	1	..	..
Washburn, Nathaniel	3	1	..	1	..	1	..	..	1	..	..
Waters, William	1	..	1	..	..	..	..	1	..	..	..
Watkins, John	1	1	3	..	1	1	..	..	..	1	..
West, Elisha	1	..	1	..	1	1	1	2	..	1	..
Whore, Elijah	..	..	..	1	1	..	..	..	2	1	..
Whore, John	2	2	..	1	..	2	..	..	1	..	..
Williamson, Nathan	3	..	..	1	..	3	..	..	1	..	..
Williamson, Ransom	1	..	1	1	1	..	..	2	..	..	..
Wilson, James	3	..	..	1	..	1	..	..	1	..	..
Wilson, William	..	..	..	..	1	..	..	..	..	1	..
Winslow, Ebenezer	2	1	2	1	..	2	1	1	1	..	..
Winslow, Samuel	..	1	..	..	1	..	..	..	..	1	..
Wolf, Charles D.	..	1	3	1	..	..	1	..	1	..	..
Wright, David	2	1	..	..	1	2	..	..	1	..	..
Yates, Uzziel	..	3	..	1	1	5	..	1	1	1	..
READING											
Acley, Joseph	..	..	1	..	1	..	..	1	..	1	..
Allen, John	1	..	1	..	1	2	1	..	1	..	..
Amsdell, Abel	1	2	1	1	..	2	1	..	1	..	..
Atwood, Joshua	1	..	..	1	..	1	..	..	1	..	..
Atwood, Luke	1	1	..	1	..	..	..	..	1	..	..
Austin, Josiah	..	1	..	..	1	..	..	..	..	1	..
Bailey, Levi	2	..	1	1	..	2	..	1	1	..	..
Barker, Hannah	2	1	..	..	1	2	2	..	..	1	..
Bellows, James	..	1	1	..	1	1	1	..	..	1	..
Bellows, John	3	2	..	1	..	1	1	..	1	..	..
Benjamin, Jonas	..	..	1	..	1	..	..	..	..	1	..
Bevens, Edward	..	1	..	..	1	..	..	..	..	1	..
READING—con.											
Bigelow, Elisha	1	1	1	..	1	1	..	2	..	1	..
Bigelow, Elisha Jr.	1	..	2	..	..	..	..	1	..	..	..
Bigelow, Noah	1	..	..	1	..	2	1	..	1	..	..
Bixby, Jacob	1	..	..	..	1	1	..	1	..	1	..
Bixby, Jacob Jr.	..	..	1	..	..	..	..	1	..	..	..
Bixby, John	..	1	..	1	..	..	..	..	1	..	..
Bixby, Lovejoy	2	..	..	1	..	1	..	..	1	..	..
Briant, Jabez	..	..	2	..	1	..	..	1	..	1	..
Briant, James	..	..	1	..	..	..	..	1	..	..	..
Brooks, Samuel	1	1	..	1	..	3	..	..	1	..	..
Brown, Benjamin	1	..	..	1	..	1	..	..	1	..	..
Brown, Daniel	3	..	..	..	1	1	..	..	..	1	..
Brown, Isaac	2	1	..	1	..	1	..	..	1	..	..
Brown, Thomas	..	1	..	..	1	..	..	..	1	1	..
Brown, Thomas Jr.	2	..	..	1	..	3	..	..	1	..	..
Bruce, John	1	..	..	1	..	1	..	..	1	..	..
Buck, Benjamin	1	..	..	1	..	2	..	..	1	..	..
Buck, Benoni	3	..	..	1	..	..	..	1	1	..	..
Buck, Samuel	2	1	1	1	1	1	1	..	1	..	..
Burdue, Aaron	..	..	..	..	..	..	..	..	..	..	3
Burdue, Silas	..	..	..	..	..	..	..	..	..	..	2
Burnham, David	2	..	..	1	..	..	1	2	1	..	..
Butterfield, Stephen	..	3	..	..	1	1	..	1	..	1	..
Cady, Barekiah	..	..	2	..	1	..	..	2	1	..	..
Cady, John	..	..	..	..	1	..	..	..	..	1	..
Cady, Jonathan	1	..	..	1	..	1	..	..	1	..	..
Cady, Nedebiah	..	1	..	..	1	3	..	1	1	..	..
Cady, Timothy	1	..	..	1	..	1	1	..	1	..	..
Carlton, Asa	3	..	1	1	..	3	..	1	1	..	..
Carlton, Henry	1	1	..	1	1	..	..	..	1	..	..
Carlton, John	1	..	..	1	1	..	..	1	..	..	..
Chandler, Ebenezer	1	1	2	..	1	3	1	..	..	1	..
Chandler, Isaac	3	1	1	1	..	..	2	..	1	..	..
Chandler, Jonathan	1	1	..	1	..	2	1	..	1	..	..
Chaplin, Moses	1	2	1	1	..	2	1	..	1	..	..
Clark, Benjamin	..	1	..	1	..	..	..	..	1	..	..
Clark, Benjamin 2nd	..	..	1	..	..	..	..	1	..	..	..
Clark, Enan	..	..	..	..	1	..	..	..	..	1	..
Clark, George	..	2	2	..	1	1	2	..	..	1	..
Clark, Thomas	..	1	..	..	1	..	..	1	1	..	..
Clark, William	2	..	..	1	..	..	..	..	1	..	..
Conant, Eunice	..	..	2	1	..	..	..	..	1	1	..
Conant, Israel	..	..	..	1	..	..	..	..	1	..	..
Cowdrey, William	..	..	..	1	1	..	..	..	..	1	..
Currier, James	2	..	..	1	..	3	..	..	1	..	..
Darby, Peter	1	..	..	1	..	1	..	..	1	..	..
Dary, Alpheus	3	..	..	1	..	1	1	..	1	..	..
Davis, Cornelius	2	..	..	1	..	1	..	..	1	..	..
Davis, Eliakim	..	..	1	..	..	1	..	1	..	..	..
Davis, Ezekiel	..	..	1	..	1	..	..	..	..	1	..
Davis, Ezekiel 2nd	2	..	..	1	..	1	..	..	1	..	..
Davis, John	..	..	..	..	1	..	1	..	1	..	..
Davis, Oliver	..	..	..	1	..	1	..	..	1	..	..
Davis, Thomas	..	..	..	1	..	1	..	..	1	..	..
Dix, Samuel	1	..	..	1	..	2	2	..	1	..	..
Dix, Whitney	1	..	..	1	..	1	..	..	1	..	..
Dudley, Samuel	3	..	..	1	..	2	..	..	1	..	..
Dustin, Stephen	1	..	..	1	..	2	..	..	1	..	..
Dutton, Thomas	..	..	..	1	..	1	..	..	1	..	..
Ellis, Timothy	2	1	..	..	1	2	..	..	..	1	..
Emmerson, John	2	..	..	1	..	..	..	..	1	..	..
Estabrooks, Jonathan	..	2	..	..	1	3	1	1	..	1	..
Fay, Ezra	..	1	..	1	..	3	..	..	1	..	..
Fay, Moses	..	..	..	1	..	2	..	..	2	..	..
Fay, Noadiah	2	..	..	1	..	..	..	..	1	..	..
Fay, Thomas	3	1	..	1	..	2	..	1	1	..	..
Felch, Nathan	1	1	..	1	..	1	..	1	1	..	..
Foster, George	3	..	..	1	..	..	..	..	1	..	..
French, Jonathan	3	..	..	1	..	3	1	..	1	..	..
Gardner, George	..	..	1	..	..	..	..	1	..	..	..
Gilson, Daniel	4	3	..	1	..	..	..	..	1	..	..
Godard, Aaron	1	..	..	1	..	1	..	1	..	..	..
Godard, John	1	..	1	..	..	..	..	1	..	..	..
Godard, William	..	1	..	1	..	1	..	..	1	..	..
Gowing, Jonathan	2	2	..	1	..	1	..	..	1	..	..
Graham, Robert	2	..	..	1	..	1	..	..	1	..	..
Granby, Robert	1	1	..	1	..	2	1	..	1	..	..
Grandy, Samuel	4	3	..	1	..	..	..	..	1	..	..
Hale, John	..	1	1	..	1	..	2	1	..	1	..
Hammond, Fance	..	..	1	..	1	..	..	..	..	1	..
Hapgood, David	2	1	1	1	..	1	2	..	1	..	..

WINDSOR COUNTY—Continued

NAMES OF HEADS OF FAMILIES	FREE WHITE MALES: Under 10 years of age	FREE WHITE MALES: Of 10 and under 16	FREE WHITE MALES: Of 16 and under 26 including heads of families	FREE WHITE MALES: Of 26 and under 45 including heads of families	FREE WHITE MALES: Of 45 and upwards including heads of families	FREE WHITE FEMALES: Under 10 years of age	FREE WHITE FEMALES: Of 10 and under 16	FREE WHITE FEMALES: Of 16 and under 26 including heads of families	FREE WHITE FEMALES: Of 26 and under 45 including heads of families	FREE WHITE FEMALES: Of 45 and upwards including heads of families	All other free persons except Indians not taxed
READING—con.											
Harrison, Elihu	..	..	1	..	..	..	..	1	..	..	..
Hatch, Nathan	1	3	..	1	..	2	1	..	1	..	..
Hathan, Benjamin	4	2	..	1	1	..	2	..	..	1	1
Hawkins, William	..	1	..	..	1	..	..	..	..	1	..
Hawkins, William L.	2	..	..	1	..	..	..	1	..	..	..
Hay, Hannah	..	..	..	1	..	..	..	..	2	..	..
Hendrick, Jabez	1	..	..	1	..	..	..	1	..	..	..
Herrick, Abigail	1	2	..	..	..	2	2	..	1	..	..
Hewlet, John	2	1	1	1	..	2	..	..	1	..	..
Hibbard, Nathan	..	..	..	1	..	1	..	..	1	..	..
Hitchcock, Paul	..	..	..	..	1	..	..	..	..	1	..
Holmes, Israel	..	..	..	1	..	..	..	..	2	2	..
Holmes, Oliver	1	..	..	1	..	1	..	1	..	..	..
How, Simon	..	1	..	1	..	..	1	1	1	..	..
Howard, William	..	3	2	..	1	1	..	2	..	1	..
Hubbard, Elijah	1	..	..	1	..	4	..	..	1	..	..
Hubbard, Ephraim	..	1	..	1	..	3	2	..	1	..	..
Hutchinson, Samuel	..	1	1	..	1	1	1	..	..	1	..
Jones, Elias	..	2	..	1	..	5	..	2	1	..	..
Jones, Jonathan	2	1	..	..	1	1	2	..	..	1	..
Jones, Samuel	..	..	1	..	..	..	..	1	..	..	..
Judd, Enoch	..	1	..	..	1	..	1	..	..	1	..
Kenney, Amos	..	1	..	..	1	..	..	1	..	1	..
Kenney, Josiah	2	1	..	1	..	1	2	..	1	..	..
Kenney, Jotham	..	..	1	..	..	1	..	1	..	..	..
Keyes, Solomon	1	2	..	..	1	3	2	..	..	1	..
Kile, William	4	1	..	1	..	1	..	..	1	..	..
Kimball, Isaac	3	..	..	1	..	1	1	..	1	..	..
Lewis, Thomas	1	1	1	..	1	3	..	1	..	1	..
Marey, Woodbury	1	..	2	1	..	..	..	..	1	..	..
Marks, Adonijah	1	..	..	1	..	2	1	..	1	..	..
Marks, Elijah	..	..	..	..	1	..	..	..	1	1	..
Marks, Hezekiah	1	..	..	1	..	1	..	..	1	..	..
Morrill, Timothy	..	..	..	2	..	..	..	1	..	2	..
Morse, Alpheus	3	..	1	..	1	..	1	1	..	1	..
Morse, Jonathan	..	..	..	1	..	4	3	..	1	..	..
Newton, Jason	2	..	..	1	..	2	..	..	1	..	..
Newton, Samuel	2	1	..	1	1	1	..	..	1	1	..
Nichols, Thomas	1	1	..	1	..	3	..	..	1	..	..
Nutting, Jacob	2	..	..	..	1	1	..	..	1	..	..
Orcutt, Elisha	..	..	..	1	..	1	..	..	1	..	..
Page, John	..	..	2	..	1	..	..	..	..	1	..
Parker, Asa	1	..	..	1	..	1	..	..	1	..	..
Parker, Reuben	..	..	..	..	1	..	1	2	..	1	..
Parker, Reuben Jr.	1	..	..	1	..	..	..	..	1	..	..
Parsons, John	..	1	..	1	..	2	..	..	1	..	..
Parsons, Samuel	..	1	1	1	..	3	..	..	1	..	..
Peabody, Daniel	..	..	..	1	..	2	1	..	1	..	..
Perkins, John	1	..	..	1	..	1	..	..	1	..	..
Pope, Mitchel	3	1	..	1	..	2	..	..	1	..	..
Pope, Simeon	1	3	1	1	..	3	..	..	1	..	..
Pratt, Luther	..	..	..	1	..	..	..	..	1	..	..
Pratt, Nathaniel	..	..	3	..	1	2	1	2	..	1	..
Putnam, Archelaus	1	..	..	1	..	3	..	..	1	..	..
Ralph, Jonathan	..	1	1	..	..	2	1	1	..	..	..
Rhodes, Samuel	2	2	1	..	1	..	..	..	2	..	..
Rice, Abiah	..	1	1	1	..	1	..	..	1	..	..
Rice, Abner	1	..	..	1	1	1	..	..	1	1	..
Rice, John	..	..	..	1	..	4	..	..	1	..	..
Rice, Stephen	2	1	..	1	..	3	..	..	1	..	..
Robinson, Ebenezer	3	..	1	1	..	1	..	1	1	..	..
Robinson, James	..	2	..	1	..	5	..	..	1	..	..
Root, Rufus	..	..	..	1	..	3	1	..	1	..	..
Ruggles, Thomas	2	..	..	1	..	2	..	..	1	..	..
Rumrill, Simon	2	..	..	1	..	..	..	..	1	..	..
Sabins, Eldad	1	..	..	1	..	..	..	..	1	..	..
Sawyer, Benjamin	2	1	..	1	..	1	1	..	1	1	..
Sawyer, Cornelius	2	2	1	1	..	1	..	..	1	..	..
Sawyer, John	..	2	2	..	1	..	..	..	..	1	..
Shead, Jonathan	3	..	..	1	..	..	..	1	1	..	..
Sherwin, Jonathan	..	..	..	1	..	2	..	1	..	..	..
Sherwin, Nathan	3	1	..	1	..	..	1	..	1	..	..
Sherwin, Samuel	..	..	1	..	1	1	..	2	..	1	..
Shurtliff, Joel	1	..	..	1	..	3	..	..	1	1	..
Smith, Jason	2	1	..	1	..	2	1	..	1	..	..
Spear, Moses	2	1	1	1	1	..	..	..	1	..	..
Stanley, Joseph	1	1	..	1	..	..	..	2	1	..	..
Stearns, Daniel	..	..	..	1	..	1	..	..	1	..	..
Stearns, Paul	..	..	1	..	..	..	..	1	..	..	..
Stone, Daniel	1	1	1	..	1	1	1	2	..	1	..
Stone, David	..	..	1	..	..	..	..	1	..	..	..
Stone, Zenas	1	..	..	1	..	1	..	..	1	..	..
Swain, John F.	..	1	2	1	..	..	..	1	..	..	..
Swain, Nathaniel	2	1	..	1	..	1	..	..	1	..	..
Thomson, Seth	..	..	..	1	..	..	1	1	1	..	..
Townshend, Aaron	1	..	..	1	..	..	..	..	1	..	..
Townshend, Thomas	..	1	1	..	1	..	..	..	1	1	..
Warner, Frederick	1	1	2	1	..	..	..	2	1	..	..
Washburn, Caleb	..	..	..	..	1	..	..	1	..	1	..
Washburn, Israel	1	..	..	1	..	1	..	..	1	..	..
Waterman, Robert	2	1	..	1	..	1	..	..	1	..	..
Watkins, Amasa	4	..	..	1	..	1	..	..	1	..	..
Webster, Jonathan	1	3	..	..	1	..	..	..	1	..	..
Weld, Ebenezer	..	..	2	1	..	2	..	..	1	..	..
Weld, John	..	1	..	1	..	..	..	1	..	1	..
Weld, Thomas	5	..	..	1	..	..	..	..	1	1	..
Wetherby, Daniel	1	2	1	1	..	2	1	..	1	..	..
Wilkins, Cyrus	3	..	..	1	..	1	..	..	1	..	..
Wilkins, Darius	3	..	..	1	..	1	..	..	1	..	..
Wilkins, Ezra	..	..	..	1	..	1	..	..	1	..	..
Wilkins, Samuel	1	..	..	1	..	2	..	..	1	..	..
Willey, John	..	..	..	2	..	2	..	1	..	..	..
Witherill, Simeon	4	2	1	..	1	..	..	..	1	..	..
Wrist, Samuel	2	2	..	..	1	1	1	1	..	1	..
Wyman, Jedutham	2	..	1	..	1	1	2	..	..	1	..
ROCHESTER											
Alexander, Seth	1	..	..	1	..	1	..	..	1	..	..
Austin, David	..	..	1	1	..	3	1	1	1	..	..
Austin, John	1	2	2	..	1	2	2	..	1	..	..
Austin, Phinehas	..	..	..	1	..	..	1	..	..	..	..
Bayley, Thomas C.	2	2	..	1	..	2	3	..	1	..	..
Bliss, Elijah	..	1	..	1	..	1	1	..	1	..	..
Brown, Amos	..	1	2	..	1	..	..	1	..	1	..
Chandler, Joseph	4	..	1	..	1	2	..	..	1	..	..
Chandler, Nathan	4	..	..	1	..	2	..	1	1	..	..
Claflin, Robert	2	..	..	1	..	2	..	..	1	..	..
Cooper, Nathan	..	..	..	1	..	1	..	1	..	..	..
Currier, Ammi	1	..	..	1	..	3	..	..	1	..	..
Currier, Thomas	..	..	1	1	..	4	..	1	..	1	..
Eaton, David	..	..	1	..	..	1	..	1	..	..	..
Eaton, Simeon	1	1	..	1	..	1	..	..	1	1	..
Emmerson, Daniel	..	..	1	..	1	..	1	2	..	1	..
Emmerson, Enoch	4	..	3	1	..	2	..	1	1	..	..
Emmerson, John	1	..	..	1	..	4	..	..	1	..	..
Fay, Daniel	2	2	..	..	1	1	1	..	1	..	..
Flanders, Moses	4	..	..	1	..	..	..	..	1	..	..
Flanders, Thomas	..	..	..	..	1	1	..	..	..	1	..
Fletcher, Abel	..	..	..	1	..	..	..	..	1	..	..
Foster, Reuben	2	..	..	1	..	1	..	1	..	..	..
French, Charles	..	..	..	1	..	..	..	..	1	..	..
Goodenough, Caleb	2	..	..	1	..	2	..	..	1	..	..
Hall, Robert	..	..	..	1	..	1	..	..	..	1	..
Handy, Samuel	2	1	..	..	1	2	1	1	..	1	..
Heath, Robert	2	..	..	1	1	..	..	..	..	1	..
Hubbard, Elisha	2	4	1	..	1	2	2	..	..	1	..
Jeppison, Ichabod	3	..	..	1	..	1	..	..	1	..	..
Jeppison, Joseph	1	2	..	..	1	1	2	3	1	..	..
Jewet, Jonathan	2	..	..	1	..	1	..	1	..	..	..
Juggins, James	..	1	..	..	1	1	1	1	1	..	..
Keney, Simeon	..	..	..	1	..	2	..	1	1	..	..
Lard, Richard	4	1	..	1	..	1	..	..	1	..	..
Lard, Stephen	2	..	..	1	..	..	..	..	1	..	..
Lillie, Joseph	2	1	..	..	1	1	1	..	1	..	..
Marsh, Clark	2	1	1	1	..	3	1	..	1	..	..
Martin, Ebenezer	2	..	1	..	..	2	..	..	1	..	..
Martin, Samuel	1	..	..	1	..	2	1	..	1	..	..
Martin, Thomas	1	..	..	1	..	1	..	..	1	..	..
Mason, Oliver	..	..	..	1	..	1	..	1	..	..	..
McCallum, William	2	..	1	..	..	..	..	1	..	..	..
McWain, Silas	1	..	..	1	..	3	..	..	1	..	..
Morgan, Ebenezer	..	..	..	1	..	1	..	1	1	..	..

WINDSOR COUNTY—Continued

NAMES OF HEADS OF FAMILIES	FREE WHITE MALES					FREE WHITE FEMALES					All other free persons except Indians not taxed
	Under 10 years of age	Of 10 and under 16	Of 16 and under 26 including heads of families	Of 26 and under 45 including heads of families	Of 45 and upwards including heads of families.	Under 10 years of age	Of 10 and under 16	Of 16 and under 26 including heads of families	Of 26 and under 45 including heads of families	Of 45 and upwards including heads of families	
ROCHESTER—con.											
Morgan, Enos	..	..	1	..	1	..	..	1	..	1	..
Morgan, Timothy	..	..	..	..	1	..	..	..	..	1	..
Morgan, Timothy Jr.	2	..	..	1	..	..	..	1	..	..	..
Morse, Ebenezer	2	2	..	1	..	1	..	..	1	1	..
Morse, Eliphalet	..	1	1	1	..	..	..	1	1	..	..
Mosher, Aaron	2	..	..	..	1	..	1	..	..	1	..
Newton, David	1	..	..	1	..	..	..	..	1	..	..
Night, Abel	2	..	..	1	..	2	..	..	2	..	..
Packard, Allen	3	..	1	..	..	1	..	1	..	..	..
Patridge, Lewis	1	..	1	..	..	..	..	1	..	..	..
Patridge, Stephen	2	1	1	..	1	..	1	3	..	1	..
Pirde, Joseph	..	..	..	2	..	..	..	1	1	..	..
Powers, John	1	1	3	..	1	..	..	..	2	1	..
Putnam, Isaac	4	..	..	1	..	2	..	..	1	..	..
Ransom, John	..	..	1	..	1	..	1	1	..	1	..
Ransom, Stephen	..	..	1	..	..	..	..	1	..	..	..
Richardson, Lemuel	3	..	1	1	..	..	..	..	1	..	..
Root, Amos	1	1	1	1	..	3	..	..	1	..	..
Root, Eliakim	..	..	..	..	1	..	..	..	..	1	..
Root, Jeremiah	..	..	..	1	..	..	..	..	1	..	..
Root, Lemuel	2	..	..	1	..	..	..	..	1	..	..
Russ, Nathaniel	2	..	..	1	..	1	..	..	1	..	..
Sampson, Phillemon	1	..	1	2	..	1	..	1	1	..	..
Sangor, John	..	..	1	..	1	..	..	1	..	2	..
Shaw, Daniel	2	1	2	..	1	2	1	1	..	1	..
Sheldon, Cephas	..	..	1	..	1	..	2	1	1	..	..
Simmons, Jeremiah	1	..	1	..	..	1	..	1	..	..	..
Sparhawk, Ebenezer	1	1	1	1	..	..	..	1	..	..	..
Sparhawk, Henry	1	..	1	1	..	2	..	1	..	..	..
Stacey, William	1	..	..	1	..	2	..	..	1	..	..
Stockwell, Jeremiah	2	..	..	1	..	..	..	..	1	..	..
Swan, Ebenezer	1	..	1	..	..	1	..	1	..	..	..
Trask, Retin	2	1	..	..	1	2	1	..	1	..	..
Tupper, Silas	4	..	..	1	..	2	..	..	1	..	..
Warren, David	4	..	..	1	..	1	..	..	1	..	..
Washburn, Silas	1	..	..	1	..	1	..	..	1	..	..
Whipple, Moses	..	1	..	1	..	4	1	..	1	..	..
Whitcomb, John	3	1	..	1	..	2	..	..	1	..	..
Wiley, Robert	1	..	..	1	..	4	..	..	1	..	..
Wing, Nathaniel	2	..	..	1	..	2	..	..	2	..	..
UNCERTAIN NAMES											
Gamza (?), Eldad	3	..	..	1	..	1	..	..	1	..	..
Hall (?), Sand (?)	3	..	1	..	..	..	1	..	1	..	..
(?), Stephen	2	..	..	1	..	2	..	..	1	..	..
ROYALTON											
Allen, Silas	1	1	2	1	1	1	..	3	..	2	..
Allen, Whiting	..	..	1	..	..	..	..	1	..	..	..
Anderson, Robert	1	1	..	1	..	2	..	..	1	..	..
Anderson, Thomas	3	..	..	1	..	2	..	..	1	..	..
Anderson, Willard	3	..	..	1	..	1	..	..	1	..	..
Anesworth, Thomas	1	1	..	1	..	7	..	..	1	..	..
Arinn, William	..	1	..	..	1	..	..	..	..	1	..
Ashcraft, Daniel	..	..	..	1	..	1	..	..	1	..	..
Ayres, Joel	3	..	1	..	..	..	..	1	..	..	..
Back, Lyman	2	1	..	1	..	..	2	..	1	..	..
Backus, Stephen	2	1	..	1	..	1	1	1	1	..	..
Bacon, Jerub	..	1	..	..	1	..	2	..	..	1	..
Bacon, Thomas	1	..	..	..	2	..	..	..	..	2	..
Baker, Hezekiah	1	..	..	..	1	..	1	..	..	1	..
Baker, Hezekiah	1	..	1	..	1	..	1	1	..	1	..
Bannister, Artemas	3	..	..	1	..	1	2	..	1	..	..
Bannister, Timothy	4	1	..	1	..	3	1	1	1	..	..
Bartholomew, Elisha	2	..	1	1	..	1	..	..	2	..	..
Benjamin, Ezra	..	..	..	1	..	2	..	..	1	..	..
Bickford, Denison	..	..	..	1	..	1	..	..	1	..	..
Bigglow, Elipheus	3	..	..	2	..	3	..	..	1	..	..
Bilding, James	3	..	..	1	..	3	..	..	1	..	..
Bill, Samuel	..	..	1	..	..	..	..	1	..	..	..
Billins, John	1	2	1	1	2	2	1	3	..	2	..
Bingham, Thomas	1	2	3	..	1	..	2	1	..	1	..
Bliss, Thomas	..	..	1	..	..	..	..	1	..	..	..
Bloyes, Reuben	2	..	..	1	..	1	1	..	1	..	..
Bowen, David	2	..	..	1	..	3	1	..	1	..	..
Bowen, Jabez	2	..	..	1	..	3	..	..	1	..	..
ROYALTON—con.											
Bowen, Jonathan	3	..	..	1	..	1	..	..	1	..	..
Bowman, Joseph	4	2	3	..	1	2	1	..	1	..	..
Brink, James	3	..	..	1	..	1	..	..	1	..	..
Buchland, Alexander	..	1	..	1	..	4	1	..	1	..	..
Bucklin, Ashbel	3	..	..	1	..	2	..	..	1	..	..
Burbank, Abijah	..	..	1	..	1	..	..	2	..	1	..
Burbank, Abijah Jr.	3	..	..	1	..	1	1	1	1	..	..
Burbank, Henry	3	1	..	1	..	..	..	..	1	..	..
Burbank, Silas	..	..	..	1	..	4	..	..	1	..	..
Burk, Isaac	4	1	..	..	1	1	..	..	1	..	..
Burk, John	..	1	..	1	..	..	2	..	1	..	..
Burrows, Abner	2	..	..	1	..	1	1	1	..	..	..
Burrows, Benjamin	2	..	1	..	..	..	..	1	..	..	..
Burrows, Jonathan	..	1	..	..	1	..	1	..	1	..	..
Burrows, Josiah	2	1	1	..	1	1	1	1	..	1	..
Cay, Jonathan	1	..	1	1	1	..	..	1	..	1	..
Chafee, Water	..	..	2	..	..	..	..	1	..	..	..
Chase, Simeon	2	..	..	1	..	..	..	..	1	..	..
Child, David	..	..	1	..	..	1	..	1	..	..	..
Child, Simeon	..	..	..	1	..	1	..	1	..	..	..
Church, Ebenezer	..	1	1	1	1	1	1	1	..	2	..
Clapp, Daniel	..	1	..	..	1	1	..	1	1	..	..
Clapp, Samuel	..	3	..	..	1	..	1	1	..	1	..
Cleaveland, Chester	3	..	..	1	..	..	..	1	..	..	..
Cleaveland, Samuel	..	..	..	..	1	..	..	..	..	1	..
Cleaveland, Squier	2	1	..	1	..	3	..	..	1	..	..
Cole, Benjamin	3	1	..	1	..	2	..	..	1	..	..
Corban, Elijah	4	..	..	1	..	2	..	..	1	..	..
Crandle, Gideon	2	2	..	1	..	4	1	..	1	..	..
Crista, John	2	..	..	1	..	2	..	1	..	..	..
Curby, Joseph	..	..	..	1	..	4	2	..	1	..	..
Curtiss, Samuel	2	1	..	1	..	1	1	..	1	..	..
Curtiss, Zalead	4	..	..	1	..	..	..	2	..	..	..
Day, Benjamin	..	1	1	..	1	..	..	1	..	1	..
Day, Benjamin Jr.	5	2	..	..	1	..	1	1	1	..	..
Day, Sylvester	2	..	..	1	..	1	..	1	..	..	..
Denison, Benjamin A.	..	..	..	1	..	..	..	..	..	..	..
Dewey, Apollos	3	2	1	1	..	1	1	..	1	..	..
Dewey, Darius	2	1	..	1	..	2	1	..	1	..	..
Dewey, David	..	1	..	1	..	1	..	1	..	..	..
Dewey, Ebenezer	..	..	1	..	1	..	1	..	..	1	..
Dewey, Ebenezer Jr.	3	1	..	1	..	1	..	..	1	..	..
Dewey, Rodolphus	1	..	..	1	..	3	..	..	1	..	..
Dickinson, Joseph	2	..	..	..	1	2	1	1	1	..	..
Dunham, Ebenezer	2	..	..	1	..	1	2	..	1	..	..
Dunham, Jesse	3	..	2	1	..	1	2	..	1	..	..
Durfee, Benjamin	..	..	..	..	1	..	1	..	..	1	..
Durfee, Nathan	..	..	..	1	..	..	..	1	..	..	..
Durkee, Susa	2	1	..	..	..	1	..	1	1	..	..
Durkee, Timothy	3	..	..	1	..	2	2	..	1	..	..
Dutton, Amasa	2	2	2	..	1	1	..	..	1	1	..
Dutton, Benjamin	2	..	..	1	..	..	..	..	1	..	..
Dutton, Joseph	1	1	..	1	..	1	3	..	1	..	..
Dutton, Samuel	3	..	..	1	..	2	..	..	1	..	..
Emmerson, Benjamin	1	..	1	..	..	1	1	1	1	..	..
Evans, Cotton	1	1	..	..	1	2	..	2	..	1	..
Fay, Jonas	1	..	..	1	..	2	..	1	..	..	..
Fish, Jacob	1	..	..	1	..	..	..	1	..	..	..
Flint, John	4	..	1	..	1	1	..	1	1	..	..
Flyn, Richard	..	..	1	..	1	3	1	..	1	..	..
Fox, Jacob	..	..	..	1	..	1	..	..	1	..	..
Freeman, Stephen	2	..	..	1	..	2	..	..	1	..	..
Gilbert, Daniel	..	..	1	..	1	4	..	3	1	..	..
Gipson, Samuel	1	..	..	1	..	1	..	1	..	..	..
Goderd, Samuel	2	..	..	1	..	1	..	1	1	..	..
Goodale, Cornelius	..	..	..	1	..	..	..	..	1	..	..
Grans, John	..	1	..	1	..	2	..	1	..	..	..
Grans, John	2	..	..	1	..	..	..	..	1	..	..
Green, Cyrell	1	..	..	1	..	1	..	..	1	..	..
Hall, Storrs	..	..	..	..	1	3	1	..	..	1	..
Havens, Daniel	..	..	1	..	1	..	1	1	1	1	..
Havens, Joseph	..	..	1	..	1	4	2	..	..	1	..
Havens, Robert	..	..	..	..	1	..	..	..	..	1	..
Hibbard, Abigail	1	..	2	..	..	2	2	2	1	..	..
Hibbard, James	..	..	..	..	1	..	..	..	..	1	..
Hibbard, Jerusha	..	..	..	..	..	1	1	..	1	..	..
Hibbard, John	..	..	..	..	1	..	..	..	..	1	..
Hicks, Asahel	1	..	..	1	..	1	..	..	1	..	..
Hicks, Jacob	..	1	..	1	..	1	1	..	1	..	..
Hide, Amasa	..	1	2	1	..	3	1	..	1	..	..
How, Samuel	2	1	1	1	..	1	..	..	1	..	..

WINDSOR COUNTY—Continued

NAMES OF HEADS OF FAMILIES	FREE WHITE MALES: Under 10 years of age	FREE WHITE MALES: Of 10 and under 16	FREE WHITE MALES: Of 16 and under 26 including heads of families	FREE WHITE MALES: Of 26 and under 45 including heads of families	FREE WHITE MALES: Of 45 and upwards including heads of families.	FREE WHITE FEMALES: Under 10 years of age	FREE WHITE FEMALES: Of 10 and under 16	FREE WHITE FEMALES: Of 16 and under 26 including heads of families	FREE WHITE FEMALES: Of 26 and under 45 including heads of families	FREE WHITE FEMALES: Of 45 and upwards including heads of families	All other free persons except Indians not taxed
ROYALTON—con.											
How, Squire	2	..	1	..	1	..	2	3	..	1	..
How, Theodore	3	3	1	..	1	1	1	..	..	1	..
Howard, Phillip	2	..	..	1	..	..	..	1	..	..	..
Hows, Nathan	..	..	1	..	..	..	..	1	..	..	..
Hows, William	3	1	..	..	1	2	..	..	1	..	..
Huntington, Jacob	1	..	..	1	..	2	..	..	1	..	..
Huntington, James	..	1	1	1	1	..	..	1	..	1	..
Hutchinson, John	..	1	..	..	1	1	1	1	1	1	..
Kent, Elisha	2	1	..	1	1	3	1	1	2	1	..
Kimball, John	1	..	1	..	1	..	..	..	..	1	..
Kimball, Nathan	..	..	..	1	..	3	..	1	..	..	..
Lamb, John	1	..	3	..	..	2	..	1	..	..	..
Lamphere, George	2	3	1	1	..	1	..	1	1	..	..
Larabee, James	1	..	..	1	1	1	..	1	..	..	..
Lathrop, Simon	1	..	..	1	..	1	..	1	..	..	..
Leavitt, Nehemiah	..	..	1	1	..	..	..	1	..	..	..
Lindley, Isaiah	..	..	..	1	..	..	1	..	..	2	..
Lyman, Asa	2	..	..	1	..	2	1	..	1	..	..
Lyman, Dam	1	..	..	1	..	2	1	..	1	..	..
Lyman, Eliphalet	3	..	..	1	..	1	..	..	1	..	..
Lyman, Ezekiel	..	..	..	..	1	..	..	..	..	1	..
Lyman, Jabez	1	..	1	..	..	..	..	1	..	..	..
Lyman, Samuel	2	1	..	1	..	3	1	..	1	..	..
Lyman, William	..	..	..	1	..	3	..	..	1	..	..
Lyon, Isaiah	1	..	1	1	..	2	..	1	..	..	..
Lyon, Zebulon	2	1	1	..	1	1	1	1	..	1	..
Maynard, David	..	..	1	..	..	1	..	1	..	..	..
McKinston, Alexander	..	..	..	1	..	3	..	1	1	..	..
Metcaff, Samuel	3	..	..	1	1	2	..	..	1	1	..
Miles, Ephraim	1	1	1	1	..	1	..	1	1	..	..
Morgan, Benjamin	1	1	2	..	1	..	..	1	..	1	..
Morgan, Isaac	1	..	..	..	1	..	..	2	..	2	..
Morse, Nathaniel	1	..	..	..	2	..	..	1	..	2	..
Newton, Ebenezer	1	..	1	..	..	..	..	1	..	..	..
Packard, Benjamin	1	3	..	1	..	1	..	..	1	..	..
Page, Nathan	2	2	..	1	..	2	1	..	1	..	..
Page, Pierce	4	..	..	1	..	2	..	..	1	..	..
Park, John	..	..	2	..	1	..	..	..	..	1	..
Park, John Jr.	1	1	..	1	..	..	..	1	..	..	..
Parker, Levi	3	1	..	1	..	1	1	..	1	..	..
Parkhurst, Benjamin	3	..	..	..	1	2	2	..	..	1	..
Parkhurst, Ebenezer	3	..	..	1	..	2	..	..	1	..	..
Parkhurst, Jabez	2	1	..	1	..	1	2	2	1	..	..
Parkhurst, Joseph	1	1	..	..	1	4	2	1	1	..	..
Parkhurst, Kelle	1	..	..	..	1	..	..	..	..	1	..
Parks, Daniel	..	..	..	1	..	..	..	..	..	..	..
Paul, Kiles	3	2	..	..	1	2	..	2	..	1	..
Perkins, Elisha	3	1	1	..	1	2	1	..	1	..	..
Perrin, Asa	2	2	..	1	..	3	1	..	1	..	..
Perrin, Greenfield	2	..	..	1	1	2	..	2	..	1	..
Perrin, Nathaniel	3	..	..	1	..	3	1	..	1	..	..
Pierce, Bester	2	..	..	1	..	1	..	1	..	..	..
Pierce, Elisha	1	..	..	1	..	..	..	1	..	..	..
Pierce, Isaac	..	1	1	..	..	1	..	1	..	..	..
Pierce, Jedediah	..	..	..	..	1	..	1	2	..	1	..
Pierce, Joseph	2	..	..	1	..	3	..	..	1	..	..
Pierce, Nathaniel	..	..	..	..	1	..	..	..	..	1	..
Pierce, Willard	1	2	..	1	..	3	1	1	2	..	..
Pierce, Willard	1	2	..	1	..	3	..	..	1	..	..
Pierce, William	..	..	..	1	..	2	..	1	..	..	..
Pinne, Isaac	3	2	..	1	..	2	1	1	1	..	..
Reed, Nathaniel	3	1	1	1	..	2	..	1	1	1	..
Rex, Joseph	2	1	..	1	..	..	1	..	1	..	..
Richardson, Godfree	3	1	..	1	..	1	1	1	1	..	..
Richardson, Harper	..	1	..	1	..	2	..	..	1	..	..
Riggs, James	2	..	..	1	..	3	..	..	1	..	..
Rix, Daniel	2	..	1	..	1	1	1	1	1	1	..
Rix, Daniel	2	1	..	1	..	2	1	..	1	..	..
Rix, Daniel Jr.	..	..	1	..	..	2	..	1	..	..	..
Robinson, Amos	2	..	1	1	..	..	1	..	1	..	..
Root, John	4	..	..	1	..	1	1	..	1	..	..
Ross, Lemuel	1	3	..	1	..	4	..	1	1	..	..
Rugg, Cephas	2	1	..	..	1	1	1	..	1	..	..
Rugg, David	..	..	..	1	..	..	..	..	1	..	..
Rust, Jeremiah	1	..	..	1	..	1	1	..	1	..	..
Rust, Matthias	1	..	..	1	..	2	..	..	1	..	..
Safford, Jacob	3	..	..	1	..	..	1	..	1	..	..
Safford, Joseph	1	..	..	1	..	..	1	..	..	..	..
Searl, John	..	1	..	1	..	2	..	..	1	1	..
Sever, Comfort	..	2	1	..	1	1	1	1	..	1	..
ROYALTON—con.											
Shepherd, Thomas	1	..	..	1	..	1	..	1	..	..	..
Shepherd, Timothy	3	..	..	1	..	1	..	1	1	..	..
Shipman, John	2	..	..	1	..	..	..	1	..	..	..
Skellinger, Abraham	1	1	1	..	1	1	1	..	..	1	..
Skellinger, Joel	2	..	..	1	..	1	..	..	1	..	..
Skinner, Harvey	2	..	1	1	..	1	..	..	1	..	..
Skinner, Isaac	6	..	1	1	..	1	1	..	1	..	..
Skinner, Luther	2	..	..	1	..	4	1	..	1	..	..
Smith, Jacob	..	..	2	1	..	1	..	1	..	..	1
Soran, Thomas	2	..	..	1	..	1	..	1	..	..	..
Stevens, Abel	1	1	1	1	1	..	1	1	1	1	..
Stevens, Elias	2	..	3	1	..	1	3	..	1	1	..
Stevens, Elkanah	1	1	1	1	..	3	..	..	1	1	..
Stoors, John	3	..	..	1	..	..	1	..	1	..	..
Sumner, Daniel	1	..	..	..	1	5	..	..	1	..	..
Taylor, Elnathan	..	..	..	..	1	2	..	..	..	1	..
Terry, Daniel	..	..	..	1	..	..	..	1	..	1	..
Thompson, Bethiah	1	..	..	1	..	1	..	..	1	..	..
Thompson, Isaiah	1	..	..	1	..	1	..	..	1	..	..
Triskett, Experience	..	..	..	1	..	1	..	..	..	1	..
Triskett, Jeremiah	..	..	3	..	1	..	1	2	..	1	..
Tucker, Lucy A.	3	1	..	..	..	..	1	..	1	..	..
Tuller, Daniel	..	..	1	..	1	1	..	1	..	1	..
Tuller, Martin	..	..	..	..	1	1	3	1	..	..	..
Turner, Daniel	..	..	1	..	..	1	1	1	..	..	..
Vale, Lorre	2	..	..	..	..	1	..	1	..	..	..
Walden, Zachariah	3	..	..	1	..	1	..	..	1	..	..
Waller, David	2	..	..	2	..	2	..	..	1	..	..
Waller, John C.	1	..	4	3	..	1	..	1	1	..	..
Waller, Joseph	3	..	..	1	..	..	2	..	1	..	..
Wallridge, Isaac	1	..	2	..	1	..	1	..	..	1	..
Warner, John	3	..	..	1	2	2	..	..	1	..	..
Waterman, Abraham	1	2	2	1	..	2	..	1	..	1	..
Waterman, Abraham	..	..	..	..	1	..	..	1	..	1	..
Waterman, Dexter	3	..	..	1	..	..	..	..	1	..	..
Waterman, Gideon	4	..	..	1	..	..	..	..	1	..	..
Waterman, William	..	..	1	1	..	1	..	..	1	..	..
Wheeler, Jonas	..	..	1	..	..	1	..	1	..	..	..
Wheeler, Josiah	..	..	..	..	..	..	..	..	..	..	..
Wheeler, Piter	2	2	..	1	..	1	..	..	1	..	..
Williams, Silas	..	1	3	..	1	1	1	..	..	1	1
Wills, Sylvanus	2	2	1	1	..	1	1	..	1	..	..
Woodbury, Jonathan	1	..	..	1	..	3	..	..	1	..	..
Woodward, Ebenezer	..	1	1	..	1	..	1	1	..	1	..
Woodward, Ebenezer Jr.	..	1	..	1	..	1	..	..	1	..	..
Woodworth, Ellick	1	..	..	1	..	..	..	1	..	..	..
UNCERTAIN NAMES											
Bedern (?), Aaron	3	1	..	1	..	..	..	..	1	..	..
Tandey (?), Roswell	1	..	1	1	..	3	..	1	..	..	..
SHARON											
Alvord, Henry	..	..	1	..	..	3	..	..	1	..	..
Ames, David	1	1	..	1	..	1	1	..	1	..	..
Ballard, Shirebiah	..	..	1	..	1	..	..	1	..	1	..
Barnard, Dan	1	1	..	1	..	2	1	..	1	..	..
Bass, Cuff	..	..	..	..	..	..	..	..	..	..	8
Bass, Jared	2	..	..	1	..	1	..	..	1	..	..
Bassett, Eli	1	..	..	1	..	..	..	1	..	..	..
Bassett, Jared	..	2	2	..	1	1	1	1	..	1	..
Bede, John	2	..	..	1	..	1	..	..	1	..	..
Bingham, Thomas	3	..	1	1	..	..	1	..	1	..	..
Bissell, Ammi	3	1	1	1	..	1	..	1	..	..	..
Blanchard, John	1	..	1	..	..	1	..	1	..	..	..
Blanchard, Reuben	2	2	1	..	1	1	1	1	..	1	..
Boynton, John	..	..	1	..	..	..	..	1	..	..	..
Bradford, John	3	1	..	1	..	1	2	..	1	..	..
Brigham, Erastus	1	..	..	1	..	1	..	..	1	..	..
Brown, Jacob	2	1	1	..	1	2	1	..	..	1	..
Brown, Thomas	3	3	..	1	..	2	..	3	1	..	..
Buel, Abel	2	..	1	..	1	1	2	..	1	..	..
Burnson, Samuel	1	..	..	1	..	1	..	..	1	..	..
Burrows, John	1	..	1	1	..	3	1	..	1	..	..
Carpenter, Allen	..	1	..	..	1	1	1	..	1	..	..
Carpenter, Asa	2	..	..	..	1	2	..	..	..	1	..
Carpenter, Cephas	1	..	..	1	..	3	..	..	1	..	..
Carpenter, Ebenezer	2	..	..	1	..	1	..	..	1	..	..
Carpenter, James	..	1	1	1	1	..	1	1	..	1	..
Carpenter, James Jr.	3	2	..	1	..	2	..	..	..	2	..

WINDSOR COUNTY—Continued

NAMES OF HEADS OF FAMILIES	FREE WHITE MALES					FREE WHITE FEMALES					All other free persons except Indians not taxed
	Under 10 years of age	Of 10 and under 16	Of 16 and under 26 including heads of families	Of 26 and under 45 including heads of families	Of 45 and upwards including heads of families.	Under 10 years of age	Of 10 and under 16	Of 16 and under 26 including heads of families	Of 26 and under 45 including heads of families	Of 45 and upwards including heads of families	
SHARON—con.											
Carpenter, Saxton	1	..	..	1	..	..	..	..	2	..	..
Chase, Enoch	1	..	..	1	..	2	..	..	1	..	..
Child, Artimus	2	..	..	1	..	..	..	1	..	..	..
Child, Daniel	..	..	1	..	..	..	..	1	..	..	..
Child, David	3	2	1	1	..	2	1	..	1	..	..
Child, Elias	..	..	1	..	..	..	..	1	..	..	..
Child, Elijah	..	..	..	1	1	..	..	2	..	1	..
Clark, Ebenezer	4	..	..	..	1	1	2	1	..	..	..
Clark, Nathaniel	2	1	..	1	..	1	1	1	..	..	..
Cleaveland, John	..	..	..	..	1	3	..	..	1	..	..
Dana, George	1	1	1	1	..	1	1	1	..	..	..
Danner, Andrew	..	..	..	..	1	..	..	1	..	1	..
Danner, George	2	..	..	1	..	..	..	1	..	..	..
Danner, Jason	2	1	3	1	..	..	1	..	..	1	..
Danner, John	..	..	1	1	..	2	..	..	1	..	..
Darby, Jesse	3	1	..	1	..	2	..	..	1	..	..
Davis, Asahel	..	..	..	..	1	..	1	1	..	1	..
Davis, James	1	1	4	..	1	..	..	..	1	..	..
Davis, Samuel	..	..	1	1	..	1	..	1	..	..	..
Day, Orin	2	1	..	1	..	2	1	..	1	..	..
Densmore, Abraham	..	3	2	..	1	1	..	1	..	1	..
Doubleday, Amos	..	..	..	1	..	1	..	..	1	..	..
Doubleday, Jacob	1	..	..	1	..	1	..	..	..	..	..
Doubleday, Jesse	2	..	..	..	1	3	1	..	1	..	..
Doubleday, Joel	1	..	..	1	..	1	..	..	1	..	..
Doubleday, Joseph	..	..	..	..	1	..	..	..	..	1	..
Eldridge, Squire	2	..	..	1	..	1	..	..	1	..	..
Evans, Abner	3	..	..	1	..	..	..	..	1	..	..
Evans, Laban	..	..	1	..	..	..	..	1	..	..	..
Ferrguson, Archibald	3	..	..	1	..	..	..	..	1	..	..
Field, John M.	2	..	..	2	..	1	..	..	1	1	..
Flowers, Apollos	1	2	1	1	..	2	..	1	..	1	..
Foster, Jacob	3	1	..	..	1	1	1	..	1	..	..
Foster, Sarah	..	..	..	..	..	..	1	..	1	..	..
Foster, Stephen	1	1	3	..	1	..	1	1	..	1	..
Foster, Stephen Jr.	3	..	..	1	..	1	..	..	1	..	..
Freeman, Samuel Jr.	1	..	2	..	..	1	..	1	..	..	..
Frink, Willard	3	..	..	1	..	1	..	..	1	..	..
Fuller, Wit	3	..	..	1	1	1	1	..	1	..	..
Gallup, Joseph	..	2	..	..	1	2	..	1	..	..	..
Gilman, Joel	1	..	1	..	..	..	..	1	..	..	..
Goodspeed, Elisha	..	1	1	..	1	3	1	1	1	..	..
Grimes, Zephaniah	..	..	..	1	..	..	..	..	1	..	..
Grover, Thomas	2	..	..	1	..	1	..	..	1	..	..
Hand, Lamphere	..	1	..	1	..	..	..	1	..	1	..
Handy, Michael	4	..	..	1	..	..	..	..	1	..	..
Harrington, Larkin	1	..	1	..	..	..	..	1	..	..	..
Harrington, Matthew	..	..	..	..	1	..	1	1	..	1	..
Harrington, Stephen	3	..	..	1	..	2	1	..	1	..	..
Hatch, Isaac	3	..	..	1	..	2	..	..	1	..	..
Hayes, Phillemon	2	..	..	2	1	..	..	2	..	..	1
Hayes, Uriah	1	..	1	..	..	..	..	1	..	..	..
Heath. Phillip	1	..	..	1	..	4	..	..	1	..	..
Heut, Seth	1	1	..	1	..	2	1	..	1	..	..
Hews, Pearley	..	2	..	..	1	1	1	1	..	..	..
Hill, Ichabod	..	..	1	..	1	..	..	..	..	1	..
Hill, Moses	1	..	..	1	..	..	..	..	1	..	..
Hitchcock, Nathaniel	1	..	..	1	..	1	1	1	1	..	..
Holland, Richard	1	..	1	..	..	..	..	..	1	..	..
Holt, Abiel	4	..	..	1	..	1	2	..	1	..	..
Holt, Isaac	1	1	..	1	..	1	..	..	1	..	..
How, James	1	..	..	1	..	1	..	..	1	..	..
How, John	2	..	..	1	..	3	..	..	1	..	..
How, Jonathan	1	..	1	..	1	..	1	..	..	1	..
How, Simeon	1	..	..	1	..	..	..	..	1	..	..
How, Simeon	..	1	1	..	1	2	1	1	..	1	..
Howard, Amos	1	..	1	..	1	1	..	1	..	1	..
Humphrey, Leonard	5	..	..	1	..	2	..	..	1	..	..
Hunter, Larkin	..	1	..	..	1	1	..	..	2	..	..
Huntley, Ezra	1	..	..	1	..	1	..	1	..	..	..
Hutchinson, Eleazer	1	..	..	1	..	..	..	..	1	..	..
Hutchinson, John	..	..	..	1	..	1	1	..	1	..	..
Johnson, Daniel	..	2	1	..	1	..	..	1	..	1	..
Johnson, Elkanah	..	..	..	1	..	..	..	..	1	..	..
Keith, Israel	..	1	..	..	1	..	2	..	..	1	..
Keith, Israel Jr.	1	..	..	1	..	..	..	1	..	..	..
Keith, Jephthal	..	..	..	1	..	..	..	..	..	..	..
Kibbee, Reuben	1	..	..	1	..	..	..	..	1	..	..
Kimball, Richard	..	..	..	1	..	..	..	1	1	..	..
Kimball, Richard Jr.	..	1	2	2	..	2	2	..	1	..	..
SHARON—con.											
Ladd, Ashbell	1	1	1	1	..	..	2	1	..	1	..
Ladd, Frederick	2	1	..	1	..	1	..	..	1	..	..
Ladd, Roger	..	..	..	1	..	3	..	..	1	..	..
Ladd, Samuel	1	..	1	..	1	..	1	2	1	..	..
Lamphere, Samuel	..	..	..	1	..	..	..	..	1	..	..
Latham, Isaac	3	..	..	1	..	1	..	..	1	..	..
Lee, Frederick	2	1	..	..	1	1	2	..	1	..	..
Leonard, Daniel	1	2	1	..	1	2	1	..	1	..	..
Leonard, Nabby	2	..	..	..	..	1	2	..	..	1	..
Loomis, Charles	..	..	..	1	..	2	..	..	1	..	..
Loomis, Jonah	..	2	..	..	1	2	..	..	1	..	..
Lovejoy, Daniel	1	..	1	1	..	3	1	2	1	..	..
Lovejoy, John	2	..	..	1	..	..	1	..	1	..	..
Lovejoy, Nehemiah	2	1	..	1	..	..	..	1	1	..	..
Lovejoy, Oliver	1	..	..	1	..	..	..	..	1	..	..
Lovejoy, William	..	..	..	..	1	..	..	..	..	1	..
Marsh, Elias	1	..	..	1	..	2	..	..	1	..	..
Marsh, James	..	..	3	..	1	..	..	1	1	..	..
Marsh, Joel	1	2	1	..	1	1	..	1	..	1	..
May, Elisha	2	1	..	1	..	1	1	..	1	..	..
Miller, James	3	..	..	1	..	2	2	..	1	1	..
Morehouse, David	3	1	..	1	..	3	1	..	1	..	..
Morrill, Joseph	1	..	1	..	..	..	..	1	..	..	..
Morse, Anthony	2	2	3	..	1	2	1	1	..	1	..
Morse, Benjamin	2	..	..	1	..	2	..	..	1	..	..
Morse, David	2	1	3	1	..	2	1	1	1	1	..
Morse, David	1	..	1	..	..	2	..	1	..	..	..
Morse, Elijah M.	..	1	..	1	..	3	..	..	1	..	..
Mosher, Heber	2	..	1	..	1	2	..	2	..	1	..
Mosher, Nicholas	..	..	..	1	1	..	1	..	..	1	..
Mosher, Rodman	3	..	..	1	..	1	..	..	1	..	..
Mosher, Thomas	1	2	..	1	..	1	1	..	1	..	..
Mullen, John M.	2	..	..	1	..	3	..	..	1	..	..
Noble, Israel	1	..	..	1	..	2	..	..	1	..	..
Norton, Ira	..	..	1	..	..	..	..	1	..	..	..
Odiorn, William	1	..	..	1	..	..	..	1	..	..	..
Page, John	1	..	..	1	..	2	1	..	1	..	..
Page, Samuel	2	..	..	1	..	2	..	..	1	..	..
Parker, Amos	2	1	1	1	..	..	2	1	1	..	..
Parker, James	2	1	..	1	..	2	1	..	1	..	..
Parker, Nathan	3	..	..	1	..	1	..	..	1	..	..
Parkhurst, Abel	1	..	1	..	..	..	..	1	..	..	..
Parkhurst, Anne	1	2	..	..	..	3	1	1	1	..	..
Parkhurst, Ebenezer	..	3	1	..	1	1	..	4	..	1	..
Parkhurst, George	3	2	..	..	2	1	1	..	1	1	..
Parkhurst, Jared	2	..	..	1	..	1	..	..	1	1	..
Parkhurst, Noah	4	1	1	1	..	2	1	..	1	..	..
Parkhurst, Phinehas	..	..	1	1	..	..	..	..	1	..	..
Parkhurst, Reuben	3	1	..	..	1	1	..	..	1	1	..
Parkhurst, Roswell	..	..	1	..	..	..	..	1	..	..	..
Parrifield, Ebenezer	..	..	1	1	..	..	..	1	..	..	..
Parrifield, Stephen	2	1	3	1	..	1	2	1	1	..	..
Paul, James	3	..	1	..	..	1	..	1	..	..	..
Pigsley, John	1	..	2	..	1	4	2	..	1	..	..
Riply, Nehemiah H.	3	..	..	1	..	1	..	..	1	..	..
Russ, Amasa	2	..	..	1	..	..	2	..	1	..	..
Scale, James	1	..	..	1	..	2	..	..	1	..	..
Seeken, Aaron	2	..	..	1	..	1	..	1	..	..	..
Seeken, John	3	..	1	..	..	..	..	1	..	..	..
Shepard, Isaac	1	..	..	1	..	..	..	1	..	..	..
Shepard, Moses	1	..	..	..	1	..	..	2	..	1	..
Shepherd, Samuel	2	..	..	1	..	1	..	1	..	..	..
Shepherd, Samuel		1	..	1	..	..	..	..	1	..	..
Shepherd, Squire	..	1	1	..	1	..	..	1	..	1	..
Shepherd, Titus	1	..	..	1	..	..	1	..	..	..	..
Sherman, Enoch	..	..	1	..	..	..	..	..	..	1	..
Simens, Joshua	2	..	..	1	..	3	..	..	1	..	..
Smith, Moses	3	..	1	1	..	2	..	..	1	..	..
Spaulding, Asahel	1	2	1	..	1	2	1	..	1	..	..
Spaulding, Reuben	2	2	..	1	..	1	1	..	1	1	..
Spear, Ebenezer	..	..	1	..	1	1	1	..	..	1	..
Spear, Edward	..	1	..	..	1	1	2	..	..	1	..
Sterling, Shepherd	..	..	..	1	..	1	..	..	1	..	..
Vales, Nathaniel	..	1	..	1	..	4	1	..	1	..	..
Vincent, Timothy	..	1	..	..	1	2	1	1	1	..	..
Walker, Thadeus	2	..	..	1	..	3	..	..	1	..	..
Wallridge, John	1	1	3	..	1	..	3	2	..	..	..
Wallridge, Josiah	..	..	..	1	..	1	..	..	1	..	..
Wallridge, Roger	1	..	..	1	..	2	..	..	1	..	..

WINDSOR COUNTY—Continued

NAMES OF HEADS OF FAMILIES	FREE WHITE MALES					FREE WHITE FEMALES					
	Under 10 years of age	Of 10 and under 16	Of 16 and under 26 including heads of families	Of 26 and under 45 including heads of families	Of 45 and upwards including heads of families.	Under 10 years of age	Of 10 and under 16	Of 16 and under 26 including heads of families	Of 26 and under 45 including heads of families	Of 45 and upwards including heads of families	All other free persons except Indians not taxed
SHARON—con.											
Wallridge, William	2	..	..	1	..	..	..	..	1	..	..
Wedge, Ezra	..	..	1	..	..	1	..	..	1	..	..
Wheeler, Isaac	..	..	..	..	1	..	..	..	..	1	..
Wheeler, Nathaniel	2	..	..	1	..	2	..	..	1	..	..
White, Lemuel	2	..	..	1	..	..	..	..	1	..	..
Wile, James	2	..	..	1	..	..	..	1	..	..	..
Williams, Ebenezer	..	..	1	..	1	..	1	..	1	..	..
Wilson, John	..	..	..	1	..	3	..	..	..	1	..
Winslow, William	1	..	..	1	..	1	..	1	..	..	..
UNCERTAIN NAMES											
Runn (?), Jotham	1	..	..	1	..	2	2	..	1	..	..
Runn (?), Zenas	1	..	..	1	..	2	..	..	1	..	..
Twishee (?), John	..	..	1	..	1	..	..	1	..	1	..
SPRINGFIELD											
Adams, Eli	2	..	1	1	..	..	2	..	1	..	..
Adams, Jonathan	5	..	..	1	..	1	..	1	1	..	..
Aldrich, Benjamin	..	..	1	..	1	2	1	..	1	..	..
Ayer, David	2	..	..	1	..	1	..	..	1	..	..
Babcock, Lemuel	2	..	..	1	..	1	..	..	1	..	..
Bailey, William	2	1	..	2	..	..	..	..	1	..	..
Ball, Daniel	2	2	..	1	..	4	..	..	1	..	..
Barnard, Jenison	2	1	4	1	1	..	..	2	..	1	..
Barns, Benjamin	..	..	..	1	..	2	1	..	1	..	..
Barrett, John	..	1	..	..	1	1	..	..	1	1	1
Barrett, Thomas	1	1	..	2	..	2	..	..	1	..	..
Bascom, Elisha	..	..	1	..	1	..	..	..	1	..	..
Bates, Levi	1	..	2	..	1	..	1	..	..	1	..
Bates, Phinehas	2	..	..	1	..	2	1	..	1	..	..
Bates, Polly	..	..	..	..	..	1	1	..	1	..	..
Bates, Theophillus	1	..	1	1	..	2	2	..	1	..	..
Bel, Abigail	..	..	..	..	..	..	..	..	..	1	..
Bellows, Ezra	4	1	..	..	1	..	1	..	1	..	..
Bemis, John	3	..	2	..	1	1	1	1	1	..	..
Bemis, Silas	3	1	..	1	..	2	2	..	1	..	..
Bingham, Horatio	3	..	..	1	..	2	..	..	1	..	..
Bingham, Reuben	..	..	..	..	1	..	..	..	..	1	..
Bisbee, Abner	..	2	2	..	1	..	..	1	..	1	..
Bisbee, Abner Jr.	1	..	..	1	..	1	..	..	1	..	..
Bixby, Adonijah	3	1	..	..	1	3	2	..	..	1	..
Blodget, Asa	3	..	..	1	..	1	..	..	1	..	..
Bourn, Newcob	..	1	1	..	1	..	1	..	..	1	..
Bowker, Benjamin	1	..	..	1	..	3	..	..	1	..	..
Bowker, Elisha	2	..	..	1	..	2	..	..	1	..	..
Boynton, David	..	1	..	1	..	3	..	..	1	..	..
Bradford, Ephraim	..	..	1	..	..	..	..	1	..	1	..
Bradford, Samuel	..	2	..	..	1	..	..	..	..	1	..
Bradford, Simeon	1	..	..	1	..	..	..	1	1	..	..
Bragg, Alexander	..	..	1	..	..	1	..	1	..	..	..
Bragg, Nicholas	..	..	..	..	1	..	..	..	..	1	..
Bragg, Nicholas Jr.	..	..	2	1	..	4	3	1	1	..	..
Bragg, William	1	1	..	1	..	1	..	..	1	..	..
Britton, Benjamin	..	..	..	2	..	1	..	1	..	..	..
Britton, Jotham	..	..	..	1	..	1	..	..	1	..	..
Brown, Abel	3	2	..	1	..	1	..	..	1	..	..
Brown, Benjamin	2	..	..	1	..	1	..	..	1	..	..
Brown, Daniel	..	..	1	1	..	2	..	..	1	..	..
Brown, Elisha	2	2	1	..	1	..	1	1	..	1	..
Brown, Simeon	3	..	..	1	..	2	..	1	1	..	..
Brownell, Joseph	1	..	..	1	..	2	..	..	1	..	..
Buck, Samuel	..	2	..	..	1	1	1	..	..	1	..
Burge, Nathaniel	2	2	1	1	..	1	..	..	1	..	..
Burr, Jonathan	1	..	..	..	1	..	..	2	..	1	..
Caldwell, Nathan	3	..	..	1	..	2	..	..	1	..	..
Carr, John	2	1	..	1	..	1	..	1	1	..	..
Cass, Sarah	2	..	..	..	..	..	1	1	2	..	..
Chaplin, David	1	..	1	..	1	..	..	..	1	..	..
Chase, Moses	1	2	..	1	..	1	..	1	1	..	..
Church, Daniel	1	..	..	1	..	2	..	..	1	..	..
Cobb, Samuel	..	2	2	..	1	2	..	2	..	1	..
Cook, Ezekiel	1	..	..	1	..	2	..	..	1	..	..
Cook, Thomas	..	..	2	..	..	..	1	..	..	1	..
Corlew, Edward	1	1	..	1	..	3	..	..	1	..	..
Corlew, Thomas	1	1	..	..	1	..	1	..	..	1	..
Cummings, James	..	..	..	1	..	1	..	1	..	..	..
Cummings, Joseph	..	..	..	..	1	..	..	..	1	1	..
Cutler, Loammi	3	..	..	1	..	2	1	..	1	..	..
Daggett, John	3	..	..	1	..	1	..	..	1	..	..
Daman, Daniel	..	..	..	..	1	..	..	1	..	1	..
Daman, Daniel Jr.	1	..	1	1	..	3	..	1	..	..	..
SPRINGFIELD—con.											
Daman, Dimmick	1	1	..	1	..	2	..	..	1	..	..
Daman, Elisha	4	..	..	1	..	1	..	..	1	..	..
Daman, John	1	..	1	..	..	1	..	1	..	..	..
Daman, Noah	1	..	1	1	..	..	..	1	..	..	..
Daman, Samuel	1	2	1	..	1	2	1	..	..	1	..
Daman, Samuel Jr.	1	..	..	1	..	..	1	..	..	..	..
Dana, Thomas	..	..	1	..	..	..	..	1	..	..	..
Davis, Cyrus	..	1	1	..	1	3	2	..	1	..	..
Davis, Isaac	..	..	1	..	..	1	..	..	1	..	..
Davis, John	2	..	..	1	..	1	..	..	1	..	..
Davis, Joshua	..	1	2	..	..	1	..	1	..	1	..
Dike, Samuel	..	1	..	1	..	2	..	1	1	..	..
Draper, Asa	4	1	..	1	..	1	2	..	1	1	..
Drury, Caleb	4	..	..	1	..	1	..	1	1	..	..
Dunlap, John	1	..	..	1	..	2	..	..	1	..	..
Durant, Joseph	2	..	..	2	..	2	..	..	1	..	..
Edson, Daniel	..	1	..	..	1	1	2	..	..	1	..
Ellis, Isaac	1	1	1	1	..	4	2	1	1	..	..
Ellis, Joseph	..	1	..	..	1	..	..	..	..	1	..
Ellis, Ziba	1	..	1	..	..	1	..	1	..	1	..
Evans, Asher	1	2	1	..	1	3	2	1	1	1	..
Evans, Asher Jr.	4	..	..	1	..	2	..	..	1	..	..
Fairbanks, Oliver	2	1	1	..	1	2	1	2	..	1	..
Field, Daniel	2	1	1	..	1	4	2	2	..	1	..
Field, Luther	1	1	..	1	..	2	1	..	1	..	..
Fisher, Sylvester	1	..	1	..	..	..	..	1	..	..	..
Fletcher, David	3	..	1	1	..	..	..	1	..	..	..
Fletcher, Paul	..	..	..	1	..	1	..	1	..	..	..
Fletcher, Peter	..	..	1	1	1	..	..	2	..	2	..
French, Jacob	..	..	1	..	1	..	..	1	..	1	..
French, John	2	..	..	1	..	2	..	..	1	..	..
Gannett, Amos	1	..	..	..	..	1	1	..	1	..	..
Gannett, Molley	1	..	..	..	..	..	1	1	1	..	..
Gaylord, Margaret	..	..	4	..	..	..	..	..	..	2	..
Gilkey, William	2	1	..	1	..	1	1	..	1	..	..
Gill, Amos	3	..	..	1	..	1	..	..	1	..	..
Gill, John	1	1	1	2	..	1	2	2	1	..	..
Gill, Whitford	..	..	1	..	..	..	..	..	..	1	..
Gilson, Jonas	1	..	1	..	..	1	..	1	..	..	..
Glynn, James	3	1	..	1	1	..	..	..	1	1	..
Goodenough, Timothy	3	..	..	1	..	1	..	..	1	..	..
Goodenow, Abel	1	1	..	1	..	2	..	..	1	..	..
Goodenow, Timothy	..	1	..	1	..	1	2	..	1	..	..
Goodman, William	2	..	..	1	..	3	1	..	1	..	..
Goodnow, Israel	..	..	1	..	1	1	..	..	..	1	..
Gould, Daniel	..	1	..	1	..	2	1	..	1	..	..
Gould, John	1	..	..	1	..	3	..	1	..	..	..
Graves, Daniel	..	..	..	..	1	1	2	..	..	1	..
Graves, Daniel Jr.	1	..	1	..	..	..	..	1	..	..	..
Graves, Phinehas	1	..	..	1	..	2	1	..	1	..	..
Graves, Selah	3	..	..	1	..	..	..	..	1	..	..
Green, Thomas	..	..	..	2	..	4	..	..	1	..	..
Griswould, Daniel	2	2	..	1	..	3	2	1	1	..	..
Griswould, Francis	..	..	1	..	..	1	..	1	..	..	..
Griswould, John	1	..	..	1	..	1	..	1	..	..	..
Hall, James	..	..	1	..	1	..	..	2	..	1	..
Hall, James 2nd	4	1	..	1	1	..	1	..	1	1	..
Hall, Nathan	..	1	1	..	1	..	1	1	..	1	..
Hall, Nathan Jr.	2	..	1	..	..	1	..	1	..	..	..
Harlow, Levi	3	1	2	..	1	1	1	1	..	1	..
Harlow, Levi Jr.	..	..	..	1	..	2	..	..	1	..	..
Hartwell, Timothy	..	2	..	1	1	2	2	..	1	..	..
Haskins, Eli	..	1	..	1	..	3	..	..	1	..	..
Haskins, Samuel	..	2	2	1	..	1	1	..	..	1	..
Hatch, Lemuel	..	1	1	..	..	3	..	..	1	1	..
Hayford, Thomas	..	1	1	1	..	..	..	1	1	..	..
Henry, James	1	..	1	..	..	4	..	1	..	..	..
Herrick, Samuel	2	..	..	1	..	1	..	..	1	..	..
Hill, Eseek	2	..	1	..	..	..	..	1	..	..	..
Hodgeman, Joseph	2	1	..	..	1	2	1	..	1	..	..
Holden, Nathaniel	..	2	2	..	2	3	1	..	1	1	..
Holt, Asa	..	..	..	..	1	1	1	1	..	1	..
Holt, Jabez	..	1	..	..	1	..	1	..	1	..	..
Holt, Smith	2	..	..	1	..	2	1	..	1	..	..
Houghton, Amasa	..	..	..	1	..	1	..	1	1	..	..
Houghton, Daniel	1	..	1	..	..	1	..	..	1	..	..
Houghton, James	3	..	..	1	..	1	..	..	1	..	..
House, David	2	1	..	1	..	3	..	..	1	..	..
House, Simeon	2	..	..	1	..	3	..	..	1	..	..
How, Daniel	2	..	..	1	..	1	1	..	1	..	..
How, Joseph	..	2	..	..	1	3	2	2	1	..	..
Howard, John	1	1	..	1	..	2	1	..	1	..	..
Howard, Paul	3	1	..	1	..	..	..	..	1	..	..

WINDSOR COUNTY—Continued

NAMES OF HEADS OF FAMILIES	FREE WHITE MALES					FREE WHITE FEMALES					All other free persons except Indians not taxed
	Under 10 years of age	Of 10 and under 16	Of 16 and under 26 including heads of families	Of 26 and under 45 including heads of families	Of 45 and upwards including heads of families.	Under 10 years of age	Of 10 and under 16	Of 16 and under 26 including heads of families	Of 26 and under 45 including heads of families	Of 45 and upwards including heads of families	
SPRINGFIELD—con.											
Hubbard, Calvin	1	1	1	1	..	4	2	1	2	..	..
Hubbard, Lemuel	1	..	2	..	1	1	2	..	1	1	..
Hudson, Benaiah	..	1	..	1	1	1	..	..	..	1	..
Hudson, Nathaniel	..	..	1	..	..	..	..	1	..	..	..
Huey, Henry	..	..	..	1	1	..	..	2	..	..	..
Jenkins, John	2	..	..	1	..	1	..	..	1	..	..
Jenkins, Samuel	..	..	1	..	..	1	..	1	..	..	..
Jenkins, Zephaniah	..	..	..	1	..	..	..	1	..	1	..
Jones, Joseph	..	..	1	..	1	..	..	..	..	1	..
Kemp, Jason	..	..	..	..	1	..	..	..	..	..	..
King, Lillius	..	..	1	..	..	..	..	..	..	3	..
Kirk, William	3	1	..	1	..	3	..	..	1	..	..
Knapp, Gladden	3	1	..	1	..	2	1	..	1	..	..
Knapp, Nathaniel	1	1	3	1	2	..	1	..	1	1	..
Latham, Simeon	2	..	..	1	..	1	2	..	1	..	..
Lee, Richard	..	..	1	..	..	2	..	1	..	..	..
Lincoln, Micah	..	..	..	1	..	..	..	1	..	..	..
Litchfield, James	1	..	..	1	..	2	..	..	1	..	..
Litchfield, Josiah	2	..	..	1	..	1	..	..	1	..	..
Lockwood, Abraham 2nd	..	2	..	1	..	4	..	..	1	..	..
Lockwood, Amos	3	..	1	1	..	1	..	1	1	..	..
Lockwood, Asa	2	1	..	1	..	1	..	..	1	..	..
Lockwood, Benoni	2	3	..	1	..	3	1	..	1	..	..
Lockwood, David	1	..	..	1	..	3	..	..	1	..	..
Lockwood, Henry	2	1	..	1	..	2	..	..	1	..	..
Lockwood, Jacob	..	..	..	..	1	..	..	..	..	1	..
Lockwood, Jacob 2nd	5	1	3	1	..	1	1	1	1	1	..
Lockwood, Joseph	1	..	..	1	..	2	2	1	1	..	..
Lockwood, William	..	..	1	..	1	2	..	1	..	1	..
Lockwood, William	..	1	..	..	1	..	1	..	1	2	..
Loveman, Elizer	..	..	..	1	..	..	..	..	1	..	..
Lynde, Eliot	1	..	..	1	..	..	1	..	..	..	..
Lyon, Jesse	2	..	..	1	..	2	..	..	1	..	..
Marble, Thomas	..	..	..	1	..	..	1	..	1	..	..
Mark, John	2	1	..	..	1	1	..	..	1	..	..
Mason, Anne	2	..	..	..	..	..	..	..	1	1	..
Maynard, John	1	..	..	1	..	1	..	..	1	..	..
McAllaster, Francis	..	..	1	..	..	..	1	2	..	..	..
McCrea, William	2	2	..	1	..	2	1	..	1	..	..
McDonald, John	2	2	..	..	1	2	..	..	..	1	..
McElroy, James	2	..	..	1	..	..	..	1	..	..	..
McElroy, Robert	3	..	..	1	..	..	..	1	..	1	..
McRobert, John	..	1	..	1	..	4	..	..	1	..	..
McRobert, William	2	1	..	1	..	..	..	..	1	..	..
Morris, Lewis R.	1	1	4	1	1	1	2	2	1	1	1
Newell, Zenus	2	..	..	2	1	3	..	1	1	..	1
Newton, Elijah	2	..	2	..	1	2	1	..	1	..	..
Nichols, David	1	2	1	1	..	1	1	1	..	1	..
Nichols, Levi	..	2	2	..	1	..	1	1	2	1	..
Norse, Frances	..	..	..	1	..	2	..	..	1	..	..
Norse, Peter	..	..	1	..	..	..	..	..	..	..	..
Nott, John	1	..	..	1	1	1	..	..	..	1	..
Nye, George	2	1	1	1	..	1	..	..	1	1	..
Oakes, David	..	..	..	..	1	1	..	1	..	1	..
Olney, Abraham	..	1	..	..	1	..	1	..	1	1	..
Olney, Benjamin	3	..	..	1	..	2	..	..	1	..	..
Olney, William	2	..	..	1	..	2	1	..	1	..	..
Parker, Amos	1	..	..	2	..	3	1	..	1	1	..
Parker, Ezra	..	2	1	1	..	2	1	..	1	..	..
Parker, Isaac	..	..	6	..	1	..	2	3	..	1	..
Parker, Jeremiah	..	1	1	..	2	1	2	..	..	1	..
Parker, Jeremiah Jr.	..	..	..	1	..	2	..	1	..	..	..
Parker, Silas	2	2	..	1	..	1	..	..	1	..	..
Parker, Stephen	..	..	..	1	..	3	..	1	..	..	..
Parks, David	1	1	..	1	..	3	..	1	1	..	..
Parmeter, Oliver	1	1	..	1	..	..	..	..	1	..	..
Perry, Joseph	..	1	1	..	1	1	1	1	..	1	..
Petty, John	..	1	2	..	1	1	..	..	1	1	..
Phillips, Levi	1	1	2	..	1	..	1	1	..	2	..
Phillips, William	1	..	1	..	..	1	..	1	..	..	..
Pierce, Flavia	2	..	..	..	..	..	1	..	2	1	..
Pierce, Joseph	..	1	1	..	1	..	1	1	..	1	..
Pierce, Matthew	1	1	..	..	1	1	3	1	..	1	..
Pierce, Oliver	3	..	..	1	..	1	..	..	1	..	..
Pierce, William	..	2	..	1	..	3	1	..	1	..	..
Place, Jesse	2	..	..	1	..	1	..	1	1	..	..
Powers, Asahel	3	1	..	1	..	2	1	2	1	..	..
Price, William	..	..	..	1	1	..	..	..	..	1	..
Putnam, Thomas	..	3	..	1	..	3	..	..	1	..	..
SPRINGFIELD—con.											
Randal, James	..	1	1	1	..	5	1	..	1	..	..
Randal, John	1	..	..	1	..	..	..	..	1	..	..
Randall, Amos	2	1	2	..	1	1	..	..	..	1	..
Randall, Amos Jr.	..	..	1	..	..	2	..	1	..	..	..
Randall, Elisha	2	..	..	1	..	3	1	..	1	..	..
Randall, Lettice	..	..	1	..	..	3	..	..	1	..	..
Randall, Simeon	1	1	..	1	..	4	1	..	1	1	..
Ransted, Rufus	1	..	..	1	..	3	..	..	2	..	..
Robins, John	2	..	1	..	1	..	1	..	..	1	..
Robinson, Daniel	..	..	1	..	..	2	..	1	..	..	..
Robinson, Isaiah	1	1	..	..	1	..	2	..	..	1	..
Rogers, Chester	1	1	..	1	..	2	1	..	1	..	..
Roys, Silas	3	2	..	1	..	1	..	..	1	..	..
Safford, Daniel	1	..	1	1	1	2	1	1	1	1	..
Safford, Philip	..	1	1	..	1	..	1	..	..	1	..
Sanderson, Eli	1	2	..	1	..	3	..	..	1	..	..
Sartwell, Elijah	2	..	..	1	..	1	..	2	1	1	..
Sartwell, Hale	2	..	..	1	..	1	..	..	1	..	..
Sartwell, Oliver	..	1	2	..	1	..	..	2	..	1	..
Sartwell, Reuben	..	1	..	1	..	1	1	..	1	..	..
Sartwell, Solomon	..	1	..	..	1	..	1	1	..	1	..
Scofield, Thomas	1	2	1	..	1	2	..	..	1	1	..
Scofield, Thomas Jr.	2	..	..	1	..	1	..	1	..	..	..
Scott, Samuel	..	..	..	..	1	..	..	..	1	..	..
Sedgewick, Gad	..	..	..	1	1	5	..	..	1	1	..
Selden, Joseph	..	..	1	..	..	3	..	1	1	..	..
Seymour, David	2	1	2	2	..	1	..	1	..	..	1
Shattuck, Samuel	..	2	1	..	1	3	..	1	1	..	..
Shead, Ebenezer	2	..	1	..	..	1	..	..	1	..	..
Shead, James	..	..	..	1	..	4	..	..	1	..	..
Shead, Solomon	..	..	..	1	1	..	..	..	1	1	..
Shead, Zackiah	..	..	1	..	1	..	..	1	..	..	..
Shurtliff, John	..	..	1	..	1	2	..	2	..	1	..
Smith, Allen	2	..	..	1	..	1	..	..	1	..	..
Smith, Isaac	..	1	1	..	1	..	1	..	1	1	..
Smith, Jonathan	2	..	..	1	..	1	..	..	1	..	..
Smith, Samuel	1	..	1	..	..	1	..	1	..	..	..
Smith, Thomas	2	..	..	1	..	..	..	..	1	..	..
Snow, Benjamin	1	..	1	..	1	..	1	..	..	1	..
Spencer, Aaron	1	1	2	1	..	1	1	..	1	..	..
Spencer, Amos	3	..	..	1	..	..	..	..	1	1	..
Spencer, Jonas	..	1	..	1	..	..	1	..	1	..	..
Spencer, Nehemiah	2	..	..	1	..	2	..	..	1	..	..
Spencer, Simeon	..	..	..	..	1	..	..	..	..	1	..
Spencer, Simeon Jr.	1	..	1	1	..	..	1	..	1	..	..
Spencer, Taylor	1	1	1	..	1	..	1	1	..	1	..
Spencer, Taylor Jr.	..	..	..	1	..	1	..	1	..	..	..
Spooner, Benjamin	2	..	..	1	..	1	1	1	..	..	..
Stafford, Stukeley	..	1	..	1	..	5	3	..	1	..	..
Stafford, Thomas	1	..	1	..	1	..	3	1	..	1	..
Stevens, Simon	..	1	3	..	1	..	1	..	1	..	..
Stevens, Simon Jr.	2	..	..	1	..	1	..	..	1	..	..
Stevens, Solomon	..	..	..	..	1	..	1	..	1	..	..
Steward, Amherst	..	..	..	1	..	..	..	1	..	..	..
Stimson, David	2	..	..	1	..	2	..	..	1	..	..
Stocker, Elijah	..	1	..	1	..	4	..	..	1	..	..
Stoddard, Elijah	..	..	2	..	1	..	1	1	..	1	..
Stoddard, Thomas	1	1	..	1	..	3	1	..	1	..	..
Stow, Amos	2	..	1	1	..	1	..	..	1	..	..
Swan, William	1	..	..	1	..	..	..	1	..	..	..
Talbert, Joseph	1	..	..	1	1	1	..	1	..	1	..
Taylor, Jonas	1	1	3	..	1	3	3	1	..	1	..
Temple, Frederick	1	1	..	..	1	1	1	1	..	1	..
Thomson, John	1	..	..	1	..	1	..	1	..	..	..
Tower, Isaac	1	..	2	..	1	3	3	1	1	..	..
Twiss, Jonathan	..	..	1	..	..	..	..	..	2	..	..
Underwood, James	1	..	..	1	..	2	..	1	..	..	..
Wait, John	1	..	..	1	..	2	..	..	1	..	..
Walker, Billings	1	..	1	1	..	1	..	1	..	1	..
Walker, Gideon	..	..	..	2	..	..	..	1	..	..	..
Walker, John W.	1	..	..	1	..	4	..	..	1	..	..
Ward, Elias	1	..	..	1	..	..	..	..	1	..	..
Ward, Jabez	..	..	1	..	1	..	..	..	..	1	..
Ward, Jedediah	..	1	..	1	..	2	..	..	1	..	..
Ward, Nathan	..	1	2	..	2	1	2	..	1	..	..
Ward, Silas	..	..	2	..	1	..	1	..	..	..	..
Weaver, William	2	..	..	1	..	3	..	..	1	..	..
Westcott, Charles	1	..	..	1	1	2	..	..	1	..	..
Weston, Reuben	..	1	1	1	..	..	2	..	..	1	..
Whitcomb, Jacob	1	..	..	1	..	2	..	..	1	..	..
Whitcomb, Perez	..	..	..	1	..	1	1	1	..	..	..
White, John	2	..	..	..	1	2	1	..	..	1	..
White, Jotham	1	..	1	..	2	2	..	..	..	1	..

WINDSOR COUNTY—Continued

NAMES OF HEADS OF FAMILIES	FREE WHITE MALES: Under 10 years of age	Of 10 and under 16	Of 16 and under 26 including heads of families	Of 26 and under 45 including heads of families	Of 45 and upwards including heads of families.	FREE WHITE FEMALES: Under 10 years of age	Of 10 and under 16	Of 16 and under 26 including heads of families	Of 26 and under 45 including heads of families	Of 45 and upwards including heads of families	All other free persons except Indians not taxed
SPRINGFIELD—con.											
Whitman, Darius	..	2	..	1	..	3	1	..	1	..	..
Whitney, Abner	1	1	1	..	1	3	1	1	..	1	..
Whitney, Benjamin	1	..	..	1	..	1	..	..	1	..	..
Whitney, Cyrus	1	..	..	1	..	1	..	..	1	..	..
Whitney, John	..	..	1	..	..	1	..	1	..	..	..
Whitney, Lemuel	..	2	1	..	1	..	1	1	..	1	..
Williams, John	..	1	1	..	1	..	..	..	1	..	..
Williams, Jonathan	4	..	1	1	..	..	1	1	1	..	..
Williams, Nicholas	1	2	1	..	1	..	..	..	1	..	..
Williams, Timothy	..	1	..	1	..	..	..	..	1	1	..
Willis, Millitiah	3	..	..	1	..	2	2	..	1	..	..
Willson, Samuel	..	..	..	1	..	2	..	1	..	..	..
Wilson, Deliverance	..	1	1	..	1	..	1	2	..	1	..
Wood, Jason	..	..	1	1	..	5	2	..	1	..	..
Wood, Jonathan B.	3	..	..	1	..	3	..	1	..	..	..
Woodward, Samuel	..	1	..	..	1	3	..	..	1	..	..
UNCERTAIN NAME											
Cary, Theodore (?) F. (?)	3	..	..	1	..	1	..	..	1	..	..
STOCKBRIDGE											
Abbot, Daniel	3	1	..	1	..	1	1	..	1	..	..
Abbot, Nathan	..	1	..	..	1	3	2	1	..	1	..
Allen, John	..	1	..	..	1	2	1	..	1	..	..
Barr, James	2	..	..	1	..	2	1	..	1	..	..
Bridge, Oren	1	..	..	1	..	..	..	1	..	..	..
Brown, Asa	..	..	2	..	..	..	..	1	..	..	..
Bullard, Alpheus	..	..	1	..	..	..	..	1	..	..	..
Bullard, Benjamin	1	..	..	1	..	..	..	1	..	..	..
Bullard, Jonathan	3	..	1	1	..	1	2	..	1	..	..
Chamberlain, Amos	1	1	..	1	..	..	..	..	1	..	..
Chamberlain, Isaac	1	..	..	1	..	2	..	..	1	..	..
Chamberlain, Jed	..	..	..	1	1	..	..	2	..	1	..
Chamberlain, Jed Jr.	..	1	1	1	..	..	..	1	1	..	..
Chamberlain, Josiah	2	2	..	1	..	1	..	..	1	..	..
Chamberlain, Thomas	..	..	..	1	..	..	..	..	1	..	..
Cleaveland, Chester	1	..	..	1	..	1	2	..	1	..	..
Cleaveland, Joseph	2	..	..	1	..	..	2	..	1	..	..
Cleaveland, William	2	..	1	1	..	1	1	..	1	..	..
Dileno, Obadiah	1	..	1	..	..	..	..	1	..	..	..
Durkee, John	1	2	..	1	..	1	2	..	1	..	..
Durkee, Joseph	..	..	..	..	2	..	1	..	..	1	..
Durkee, Joseph Jr.	..	..	1	..	..	..	..	1	..	..	..
Everet, Phinehas	..	..	..	1	..	2	..	1	..	1	..
Fletcher, Jonathan	3	..	..	1	..	..	..	1	..	..	..
Gay, Daniel	1	1	..	1	..	1	..	..	1	..	..
Gay, Jere	2	1	..	1	..	..	..	1	..	..	..
Gilbert, Arunna	..	..	1	..	..	..	..	..	1	..	..
Gilbert, Asa Jr.	..	..	1	..	..	..	..	1	..	..	..
Gowing, Thomas	1	..	..	1	..	2	..	..	1	..	..
Green, Benjamin	1	..	..	1	..	3	..	1	..	..	..
Green, Reuben	2	..	..	1	..	..	..	..	1	..	..
Green, William	2	1	..	1	..	1	..	2	1	..	..
Green, William 2nd	..	..	..	1	..	..	..	1	..	..	..
Haden, Alpheus	..	..	..	1	..	1	..	..	1	..	..
Haden, Uriah	..	2	..	..	1	1	..	..	1	..	..
Haden, Uriah Jr.	3	..	..	1	..	1	..	..	1	..	..
Haper, George	..	1	1	..	1	..	1	..	..	1	..
Hixon, Elkanah	..	..	..	..	1	..	..	1	..	..	..
Holland, Reuben	2	2	..	1	..	2	..	1	1	..	..
Holt, Erastus	..	..	1	..	..	..	..	1	..	..	..
Johnson, David	..	1	1	..	1	3	1	..	1	..	..
Keyes, Elias	..	1	4	1	..	..	1	1	1	..	..
Knoulton, Jacob	..	..	1	..	..	..	..	1	..	..	..
Lothrop, Moses	..	..	1	..	..	1	..	1	..	..	..
Loveren, Daniel	1	..	..	3	..	..	..	..	1	..	..
Lyon, Robert	..	..	..	1	..	1	..	..	1	..	..
Lyon, Roswell	..	..	..	1	..	3	..	..	1	..	..
Lyon, Rufus	..	..	..	1	..	..	1	..	1	..	..
Medcalf, Zilpha	1	..	1	..	..	..	2	..	3	1	..
Notham, Joel	1	3	..	1	..	..	..	..	..	1	..
Ormsby, Ebenezer	..	1	1	..	1	..	1	..	..	1	..
STOCKBRIDGE—con.											
Packard, Joseph	2	..	..	1	..	..	..	..	1	..	..
Packard, Robert	3	..	1	..	1	..	1	1	1	..	..
Parish, Jere	2	1	..	1	..	1	1	..	1	..	..
Parmeter, Isiah	1	..	..	1	1	..	..	..	..	1	..
Parmeter, Isiah Jr.	1	..	1	..	..	..	..	1	..	..	..
Parmeter, Samuel	..	..	..	1	..	..	..	..	..	1	..
Parmeter, Thomas	1	1	2	..	1	..	1	1	2	..	..
Pettice, Nathaniel	1	1	2	..	1	2	..	..	1	..	..
Powers, Luke	1	..	..	2	..	1	..	..	1	..	..
Ranny, Daniel	..	..	2	1	..	1	2	..	1	..	..
Rogers, Ebenezer	1	..	1	..	..	..	..	1	..	..	..
Rogers, Stephen	3	..	1	..	..	1	..	1	..	..	..
Sanderson, John	1	1	..	1	..	1	1	..	1	..	..
Shaw, Andrew	..	..	..	1	..	1	..	1	..	..	..
Sprout, Zebedes	..	..	2	..	1	..	..	3	..	1	..
Swan, Joseph	1	..	..	1	..	2	..	1	..	..	..
Sylvester, Samuel	3	..	..	1	..	1	1	..	1	..	..
Thayer, Windson	1	..	1	..	..	..	..	1	..	..	..
Thurber, Francis	..	..	..	1	..	..	..	..	1	..	..
Twitchel, Ephraim	1	1	..	1	..	1	..	..	1	..	..
Webber, Norman	3	..	1	1	..	1	..	1	..	..	..
Whitcomb, Asa	..	1	..	..	1	..	..	..	..	1	..
Whitcomb, Branch	2	..	..	1	..	4	..	..	1	..	..
Whitcomb, Justice	..	..	..	1	..	..	..	1	..	..	..
Whitcomb, Lot	1	..	1	..	..	1	..	1	..	..	..
Whitcomb, Lydia	..	1	1	..	..	..	1	..	1	..	..
Whitcomb, Nathaniel	2	..	..	1	..	1	..	..	1	..	..
Whitcomb, Paul	1	1	..	1	..	1	1	1	..	..	..
Whitcomb, Philodes	..	..	1	..	..	2	..	1	..	..	..
Willey, Asa	3	2	..	1	..	..	..	..	1	..	..
Woods, Stephen	..	..	1	..	..	1	..	..	1	..	..
Woods, Sylvanus	2	..	..	1	..	1	..	..	1	..	..
Woodward, Ezekiel	..	..	..	1	..	3	..	..	1	..	..
WETHERSFIELD											
Adams, Bridgett	..	1	..	..	..	..	..	..	..	1	..
Aldrich, Joshua	..	..	..	1	..	..	..	..	1	..	..
Allen, Jonathan	1	..	..	1	..	2	..	..	1	..	..
Alliston, James	1	1	2	1	..	..	1	1	1	..	..
Armstrong, James	5	..	..	1	..	1	..	..	1	..	..
Babcock, Daniel	..	1	2	1	..	..	1	..	1	..	..
Baker, John	1	1	1	1	..	2	2	..	1	..	..
Ball, Amos	..	..	1	..	..	..	..	1	..	1	..
Barrett, William	1	1	..	1	..	1	..	..	1	..	..
Beckley, Zebedee	3	..	..	1	1	..	..	..	1	1	..
Belnapp, Joseph	..	2	1	..	1	3	..	3	..	2	..
Belnapp, Zedekiah	1	..	1	1	..	..	3	1	1	..	..
Bennett, John	1	1	1	..	1	4	3	..	..	1	..
Bidwell, Isaac	1	2	2	..	1	2	2	..	..	1	..
Bidwell, Joseph	..	..	1	..	..	1	..	1	..	..	..
Bigelow, Silas	4	..	..	1	..	..	..	..	1	..	..
Blakeley, Hannah	..	1	1	..	..	..	..	1	..	1	..
Blakeley, Josiah	2	2	..	1	..	2	..	..	1	..	..
Blakeley, Zopher	..	..	..	1	..	..	..	..	1	..	..
Blie, Eber	3	..	..	1	..	1	..	..	1	..	..
Bowman, Benjamin	..	..	1	..	..	1	..	1	..	..	..
Bowman, Thadeus	..	1	..	..	1	..	..	2	..	1	..
Bowman, Thadeus Jr.	1	1	..	1	..	3	1	..	1	..	..
Boynton, Banan	..	..	..	1	..	..	..	..	1	..	..
Boynton, Ephraim	3	1	..	1	..	2	2	1	1	..	..
Boynton, Jewet	..	1	1	1	..	2	1	..	1	..	..
Boynton, John	2	1	2	1	1	..	1	3	..	1	..
Boynton, John Jr.	..	..	..	1	..	3	..	..	1	..	..
Boynton, Steward	1	1	..	1	..	2	1	..	1	..	..
Bradish, Daniel	3	1	..	1	..	1	1	..	1	1	..
Briant, Martin	4	..	..	1	..	1	..	..	1	..	..
Briant, William	..	..	..	..	1	..	..	..	..	1	..
Brigham, Jacob	3	..	1	1	..	..	..	..	1	..	..
Brown, Stephen	3	..	..	1	..	2	..	..	1	..	..
Burlingame, Israel	..	1	1	..	1	..	..	..	..	1	..
Burlingame, John	1	1	..	1	..	2	..	1	1	..	..
Cady, Elijah	..	..	..	..	1	..	..	..	..	1	..
Cady, Jonathan	2	..	..	1	..	..	..	..	1	..	..
Cady, Noah	3	1	..	1	..	3	1	..	1	..	..
Carrier, Isaac	..	..	..	1	1	..	..	1	..	1	..
Carter, Asa	1	..	1	1	..	2	2	2	..	..	..
Cary, Richard	3	1	..	1	..	2	1	..	1	..	..
Chamberlin, Alva	3	..	..	1	..	..	1	1	..	..	..
Chamberlin Oliver	..	..	1	..	1	..	..	1	..	1	..
Chamberlin, Oliver Jr.	1	..	..	1	..	3	1	..	1	..	..

WINDSOR COUNTY—Continued

NAMES OF HEADS OF FAMILIES	FREE WHITE MALES: Under 10 years of age	Of 10 and under 16	Of 16 and under 26 including heads of families	Of 26 and under 45 including heads of families	Of 45 and upwards including heads of families	FREE WHITE FEMALES: Under 10 years of age	Of 10 and under 16	Of 16 and under 26 including heads of families	Of 26 and under 45 including heads of families	Of 45 and upwards including heads of families	All other free persons except Indians not taxed
WETHERSFIELD—con.											
Chamberlin, Wyatt	1	..	..	1	..	3	1	..	1	..	..
Chapin, Gideon	1	2	..	..	1	1	..	1	1	..	..
Chase, John	1	..	..	1	..	3	..	1	..	..	..
Chilson, Daniel	..	..	1	..	..	1	..	1	..	..	..
Chilson, Waters	2	1	..	..	1	2	2	2	..	1	..
Chittenden, James	..	1	..	1	..	3	1	..	1	..	..
Chittenden, James	1	1	..	1	..	2	1	..	1	..	..
Clark, Gersham	..	1	1	..	1	2	2	..	1	..	..
Cobb, Samuel Jr.	1	..	..	1	..	..	..	..	1	..	..
Cole, Amos	..	..	1	1	1	..	..	..	..	1	..
Cook, Daniel	..	1	1	1	..	1	1	..	1	..	..
Cook, Oliver	..	..	..	1	..	2	..	1	1	..	..
Cook, Reuben	1	1	..	1	4	..	..	..	1	..	..
Crain, Joel	2	..	..	1	..	..	..	1	..	..	..
Craine, Hezekiah	1	..	..	1	..	1	1	1	1	..	..
Crogue, William	1	1	..	1	..	3	1	..	1	..	..
Culver, Andrew	..	1	2	..	1	..	1	..	2	1	..
Culver, Phelologus	1	..	..	1	..	1	..	..	1	..	..
Cushman, Ambrose	1	..	1	1	1	..	1	1	..	1	..
Cutting, Jonas	4	3	1	1	..	3	..	1	1	..	..
Dart, Daniel	..	..	..	1	..	1	..	3	..	..	..
Dart, Joshua	1	..	..	..	1	..	..	..	..	1	..
Dart, Josiah	2	..	1	1	..	1	1	1	1	..	..
Dean, Christopher	..	..	1	1	..	2	..	1	..	..	..
Dean, Cushman	..	..	1	..	..	..	..	1	..	..	..
Dean, Lemuel	2	..	1	..	..	1	..	2	..	..	..
Dean, William	1	..	2	..	1	1	1	1	..	2	..
Demerry, Silas	2	..	..	1	..	1	..	1	1	..	..
Dewolf, Elias	3	3	..	..	1	1	1	1	2	..	..
Dickins, John	2	..	..	1	..	1	..	..	1	..	..
Dickins, Martin	1	1	..	1	..	2	2	..	1	..	..
Dickins, Oliver	..	..	..	..	1	..	..	..	..	1	..
Dickinson, Asahel	..	..	..	1	..	2	..	..	1	..	..
Dix, Benjamin	2	1	..	1	..	2	2	..	1	..	..
Downer, Abraham	..	..	1	..	1	..	..	3	..	1	..
Downer, Gayland	2	2	..	1	..	1	..	..	1	..	..
Downs, Edward	..	..	..	1	..	1	..	1	..	..	..
Dunphy, Thomas	..	..	1	..	1	..	1	1	..	1	..
Dwoll, James	..	1	1	..	1	1	..	..	1	..	..
Eager, Abraham	2	..	..	1	..	3	1	..	1	..	..
Eddy, Allen	2	..	..	1	..	2	..	..	1	..	..
Eddy, Isaac	1	..	1	..	..	1	..	1	..	..	..
Eddy, Newbury	..	..	1	..	1	1	..	..	..	2	..
Farr, Samuel	2	..	..	1	..	3	1	..	1	..	..
Farrington, Henry	..	..	..	..	1	..	1	..	1	..	..
Fassett, Jesse	1	1	..	..	1	1	..	1	..	1	..
Fellows, Verney	2	1	..	1	..	..	1	1	1	..	..
Field, Levi	1	..	..	1	..	2	1	..	1	..	..
Filley, Elnathan	3	1	..	..	1	..	1	1	1	..	..
Fisher, Josiah	..	2	1	..	1	3	1	1	..	1	..
Foster, Thomas	3	..	..	1	..	..	..	..	1	..	..
France, Christopher	2	1	..	..	1	1	..	..	1	..	..
French, Jacob	1	..	..	1	..	1	..	1	1	..	..
Frost, Aaron	1	..	..	1	..	3	..	..	1	..	..
Gilbert, Elisha	2	1	1	1	..	3	1	..	1	..	..
Gitchell, Jacob	..	1	..	..	1	2	..	1	..	1	..
Glazier, Ebenezer	2	2	1	..	1	..	..	..	..	1	..
Glazur, Aaron	..	1	..	..	1	..	2	..	1	..	..
Golden, Israel	..	..	..	1	..	..	..	..	1	..	..
Goodrich, Joshua	1	..	..	1	..	2	..	..	1	..	..
Goodwin, Davis	..	..	1	..	1	..	1	..	..	1	..
Grout, Asa	..	1	1	..	1	1	2	1	1	..	..
Grout, Demell	4	..	..	1	..	1	..	..	1	..	..
Grout, Elihu	2	1	..	1	..	2	2	1	1	..	..
Grout, Helkiah	2	2	..	1	..	1	1	1	1	..	..
Grout, Oliver	2	..	..	1	..	2	..	1	1	..	..
Grout, Orlando	..	..	..	1	..	1	..	2	..	1	..
Grout, Roy	2	..	1	1	..	..	..	1	1	..	..
Grout, Seth	1	1	..	1	..	2	1	..	1	..	..
Hadlock, John	1	1	..	..	2	..	..	..	..	2	..
Hadlock, Thomas	..	2	..	1	..	..	..	..	2	..	..
Hall, Aaron	2	..	2	1	..	..	..	..	2	..	..
Hall, Elijah	..	..	..	1	..	1	..	..	1	..	..
Hall, James	3	..	..	1	..	1	1	..	1	..	..
Harrington, Aaron	2	..	..	1	..	2	..	..	1	..	..
Haskell, Gideon	..	..	..	1	1	3	..	..	1	1	..
Haskell, Jacob	2	..	..	1	..	4	1	..	1	..	..
Haskell, John	1	..	1	1	..	3	1	..	1	..	..
Haskell, Perez	1	1	..	1	..	2	..	..	1	1	..
Haskell, Roger	3	1	..	1	..	..	..	..	1	..	..
Hatch, Ebenezer	2	..	1	1	..	3	..	1	..	..	..
Hatch, John	..	1	..	1	..	1	2	..	1	1	..

NAMES OF HEADS OF FAMILIES	FREE WHITE MALES: Under 10 years of age	Of 10 and under 16	Of 16 and under 26 including heads of families	Of 26 and under 45 including heads of families	Of 45 and upwards including heads of families	FREE WHITE FEMALES: Under 10 years of age	Of 10 and under 16	Of 16 and under 26 including heads of families	Of 26 and under 45 including heads of families	Of 45 and upwards including heads of families	All other free persons except Indians not taxed
WETHERSFIELD—con.											
Hatch, Josiah	3	1	1	1	..	1	2	..	1	..	..
Hewlet, Amos	1	..	1	..	..	1	..	1	..	..	..
Hicks, Levi	3	..	1	..	1	2	1	..	1	..	..
Hicks, Lydia	..	..	..	..	..	1	1	..	1	..	..
Hill, Richard	..	..	..	..	..	..	..	..	..	..	3
Hill, Simeon	2	1	..	1	..	..	2	..	1	..	..
Holmes, Roswell	..	1	..	1	..	..	..	2	..	1	..
Holton, Joshua	2	..	..	1	..	..	..	1	..	..	..
Howard, David	4	2	1	..	1	1	..	1	..	1	..
Hubbard, George	3	..	1	1	..	..	1	2	1	..	..
Hubbard, Joseph	..	1	2	1	1	1	2	2	1	..	..
Humphrey, Daniel	..	..	..	1	..	1	..	..	1	..	..
Hutchins, Jedediah	1	1	1	..	..	2	..	1	..	..	..
Hutchins, Sewel	2	..	..	1	..	2	..	..	1	..	..
Hutchins, Thomas	2	1	2	..	1	1	2	3	..	1	..
Jackman, Abner	3	2	..	1	..	2	2	1	..	1	..
Jackman, Josiah	..	..	..	1	..	4	..	..	1	..	..
Jackson, Marvil	..	1	..	1	..	1	..	..	1	..	..
Jeneson, John	4	..	..	1	..	..	1	..	..	1	..
Johnson, Jeremiah	1	1	..	1	..	3	1	..	1	1	..
Johnson, John	..	..	1	..	..	..	..	1	..	..	..
Johnson, Uriah	1	..	..	1	..	2	..	..	1	..	..
Joslin, Joseph	2	1	2	..	1	2	2	1	..	1	..
Judd, Hawkins	2	..	..	1	..	2	..	..	1	..	..
Kanow, John	1	..	..	1	..	2	1	..	1	..	..
Kidder, Oliver	..	1	2	..	1	..	1	2	..	1	..
Kidder, Oliver Jr.	1	..	..	1	..	3	..	..	1	..	..
Kidder, Thomas	2	1	2	..	1	1	1	2	..	1	..
Kimball, Daniel	3	..	1	1	..	..	1	..	1	..	..
Kingsbury, Dathan	..	1	1	1	..	..	..	..	1	..	..
Lane, Gersham	2	1	..	1	..	1	1	1	1	..	..
Larabee, William	..	3	..	..	1	5	1	..	1	..	..
Lawrence, Prescott	1	1	1	..	..	2	1	..	..	1	..
Lewis, Jabez	3	..	..	1	..	..	..	..	1	..	..
Lewis, Jabis	..	..	..	..	1	1	..	..	..	1	..
Lewis, Samuel	1	..	..	1	..	3	..	..	1	..	..
Litchfield, Caleb	2	1	..	1	..	3	..	..	1	..	..
Little, Fortimes	..	..	..	..	..	..	..	..	..	..	7
Loveland, Eleazer	..	..	..	1	..	..	..	..	1	..	..
Lyman, Gideon	2	2	1	1	..	2	2	..	1	..	..
Marsh, John	3	..	..	1	..	1	..	..	1	..	..
Mason, Levi	..	1	4	..	1	1	1	1	..	1	..
Matthews, Jacob	..	..	..	1	..	..	2	..	1	..	..
Matthews, Jesse	..	..	1	..	1	..	..	..	..	1	..
McCuen, Malcum	2	..	..	1	..	1	..	..	1	..	..
Morey, Samuel	..	1	1	..	1	1	1	2	..	1	..
Morgan, Joshua	..	..	..	..	1	..	1	..	..	1	..
Morgan, Joshua Jr.	2	2	..	1	..	1	..	..	1	..	..
Morgan, Samuel	2	2	..	1	..	1	..	1	1	..	..
Mosely, Samuel	1	2	..	1	..	3	..	1	1	..	..
Newell, Foster	..	..	1	..	..	..	..	1	1	..	..
Newell, John	..	..	..	..	1	..	..	1	..	1	..
Newell, Josiah	1	..	..	1	..	1	..	..	1	..	..
Newton, Edward	1	..	1	..	1	..	..	..	1	..	..
Newton, Edward Jr.	..	2	..	1	..	3	..	..	1	..	..
Newton, Hannaniah	..	1	..	3	..	1	1	1	1	..	..
Newton, James	..	1	1	..	..	2	..	1	..	..	..
Newton, Samuel	1	2	2	..	1	3	..	1	1	1	..
Nichols, Luke	..	2	3	1	..	..	..	1	..	1	..
Nichols, William	..	1	..	1	..	1	1	..	1	..	..
Norton, Joseph	..	..	..	..	1	..	..	1	..	1	..
Norton, Lot	1	..	..	2	..	1	..	1	1	..	..
Nutting, Abel	4	1	..	1	..	1	2	1	1	..	..
Nutting, John	1	..	..	1	..	1	..	1	..	..	..
Ordway, Nehemiah	1	..	2	..	1	1	..	..	1	..	..
Parker, Isaac	3	1	..	1	..	..	1	..	1	..	..
Parker, Isaac 2nd	1	1	..	2	..	4	1	2	1	..	..
Parker, Pearl	..	..	..	1	..	..	..	1	1	..	..
Parkhurst, David	..	..	..	1	..	3	..	..	1	..	..
Parkhurst, Jonathan	2	..	..	1	..	3	..	..	1	..	..
Parkhurst, Silas	2	..	1	..	..	..	..	1	..	..	..
Pettigrew, William	2	1	..	1	..	..	1	1	..	1	..
Phelps, Bishop	2	..	..	1	..	2	..	..	1	..	..
Pierce, Oliver	3	..	..	1	..	2	..	..	1	..	..
Pirkins, Jacob	..	..	..	1	..	..	..	..	1	..	..
Plant, Eli	1	..	1	1	..	2	2	..	1	..	..
Potwine, George	1	2	..	1	..	3	2	..	1	..	..
Prentice, Solomon	..	..	2	..	..	..	..	1	..	..	..
Prentice, Thomas	2	2	..	1	..	2	1	1	1	1	..
Proctor, Isaac	1	1	..	..	1	4	2	2	..	1	..
Prouty, Burpee	1	..	1	1	..	3	..	..	1	..	..

WINDSOR COUNTY—Continued

NAMES OF HEADS OF FAMILIES	Free white males: Under 10 years of age	Free white males: Of 10 and under 16	Free white males: Of 16 and under 26 including heads of families	Free white males: Of 26 and under 45 including heads of families	Free white males: Of 45 and upwards including heads of families	Free white females: Under 10 years of age	Free white females: Of 10 and under 16	Free white females: Of 16 and under 26 including heads of families	Free white females: Of 26 and under 45 including heads of families	Free white females: Of 45 and upwards including heads of families	All other free persons except Indians not taxed
WETHERSFIELD—con.											
Reed, Benjamin	..	..	..	1	..	3	1	..	1	..	..
Reed, Stephen	3	2	1	..	1	1	..	2	..	1	..
Reed, Thomas	2	..	..	1	..	3	1	..	1	..	..
Rice, Isaac	1	2	1	1	..	2	1	..	1	1	..
Rice, Jacob	3	1	..	1	..	..	1	..	1	..	..
Richards, Janna	2	..	..	1	..	..	..	..	1	..	..
Richards, Joseph	..	1	..	1	..	2	..	..	1	..	..
Richards, Thomas	1	1	..	3	..	2	..	1	1	..	..
Roberts, Joseph	4	..	1	1	..	1	..	..	1	..	..
Robinson, Benjamin	1	..	1	..	1	..	1	2	..	1	..
Robinson, Charles	..	1	..	1	..	3	1	..	1	..	..
Robinson, Elijah	..	..	1	..	1	..	..	1	..	1	..
Robinson, Elijah Jr.	1	..	1	..	..	1	..	1	..	..	..
Robinson, Jasper	2	..	..	1	..	..	..	..	1	..	..
Robinson, Peter	2	2	..	1	..	1	2	1	1	..	..
Ross, Timothy	1	..	..	1	..	..	..	..	1	..	..
Rumrill, Simeon	2	..	..	1	..	..	..	..	1	..	..
Sanders, Charles	3	1	..	1	..	..	..	..	1	..	..
Sears, Silas	2	2	1	1	..	2	..	..	1	..	..
Sherman, David	2	..	..	1	..	1	..	..	1	..	..
Sherman, Leveritt	1	..	2	..	1	..	1	1	..	1	..
Sherman, Samuel	2	1	1	1	..	..	1	..	1	..	..
Smith, Abraham	1	..	..	1	..	..	1	1	1	..	..
Smith, Squire	3	..	..	1	..	1	..	..	1	..	..
Spafford, Eliphalet	2	..	..	1	..	1	2	..	..	1	1
Spafford, Eliphalet Jr.	2	..	1	..	..	..	..	1	..	..	..
Spafford, Joseph	1	1	1	1	1	3	..	1	1	1	..
Spencer, Luther	..	1	..	1	..	4	1	..	1	..	..
Squires, John	..	2	1	1	..	2	..	..	1	..	..
Steel, Chase	..	..	..	..	1	..	..	1	..	1	..
Steel, Samuel	1	..	1	1	..	3	3	1	1	..	..
Steel, Stephen	4	1	1	2	..	1	..	1	2	..	..
Stevens, John	..	2	3	1	..	1	..	..	1	..	..
Stone, Asa	3	..	..	1	..	1	..	..	1	..	..
Stone, Gregory	1	1	1	..	..	..	..	1	..	..	..
Stoughton, Nathaniel	3	2	..	..	1	1	..	2	1	..	..
Stoughton, Nathaniel Jr.	1	..	1	..	..	..	..	1	..	..	..
Streeter, Johnson	3	1	1	1	..	2	1	1	1	..	..
Strow, Reuben	3	1	1	1	..	1	..	..	1	..	..
Taylor, David	2	1	2	1	..	2	1	..	1	..	..
Tenney, Nathan	2	..	..	1	..	..	..	..	1	..	..
Thomas, Zebel	4	2	..	..	1	..	1	1	1	..	..
Thomson, Isaac	2	..	..	1	..	1	..	..	1	..	..
Thomson, Seth	..	..	2	..	1	..	..	1	2	1	..
Toles, Benjamin	..	1	1	..	..	1	..	1	..	..	..
Toles, Clark	1	1	1	1	..	2	..	1	1	..	..
Toles, Henry	..	1	..	..	1	..	..	..	..	1	..
Toles, Henry Jr.	2	1	..	1	..	3	..	..	1	..	..
Toles, John	2	2	1	1	..	1	..	..	1	..	..
Toles, Philemon	..	..	1	..	..	..	..	1	..	..	..
Town, Jacob	..	1	..	1	..	1	..	..	1	..	..
Tuttle, Ezra	1	1	..	1	..	3	1	..	1	..	..
Tuttle, John	1	..	1	1	..	2	..	..	1	..	..
Upham, Asa	..	..	..	..	1	..	..	1	..	1	..
Upham, Asa Jr.	1	..	..	1	..	2	..	..	1	..	..
Upham, Caleb.✓	..	..	1	..	..	..	..	1	..	..	..
Upham, Ezekial	2	1	..	2	..	..	..	..	1	..	..
Upham, Joshua ✓	..	..	1	1	..	2	..	..	1	..	..
Upham, William ✓	..	..	1	..	1	..	..	..	..	1	..
Wallace, Jonathan	..	..	1	..	2	..	1	..	..	1	1
Ward, Samuel	3	2	..	1	..	..	1	..	1	..	..
Warner, Benjamin	..	1	2	1	..	2	..	1	1	..	..
Warren, John	3	1	..	1	..	1	..	1	1	..	..
Wetherbe, Charles	2	..	..	1	..	2	..	..	1	..	..
Wetherbe, David	..	1	1	..	..	..	..	1	..	1	..
Wetherbe, Oliver	2	..	..	1	..	2	..	..	1	..	..
Wheelor, Nathan	1	..	..	1	..	1	..	..	1	..	..
Wheelor, Nathan	1	..	..	1	..	1	..	..	2	1	..
Whipple, Jonathan	..	1	1	1	..	3	..	..	1	..	..
Whipple, Oliver	2	..	1	1	..	2	..	..	1	..	..
White, John	1	..	1	..	1	..	1	..	..	1	..
Whitman, Jehiel	3	..	..	1	..	1	3	..	1	..	..
Whitmore, Ebenezer	..	1	1	..	1	1	2	2	..	1	..
Williams, John	..	2	4	..	1	..	..	3	..	1	..
Wood, Josiah	1	..	..	1	..	2	..	..	1	..	..
Worcester, Benjamin	..	2	1	..	1	1	..	..	..	1	..
Wright, John	1	..	..	1	..	1	..	..	1	..	..
Wye, Jonathan	..	1	2	1	..	1	1	1	1	1	..
Young, Ichabod	1	1	2	..	1	1	1	2	1	..	..
UNCERTAIN NAME											
Maren (?), Samuel	5	..	..	1	..	1	..	..	1	..	..

NAMES OF HEADS OF FAMILIES	Free white males: Under 10 years of age	Free white males: Of 10 and under 16	Free white males: Of 16 and under 26 including heads of families	Free white males: Of 26 and under 45 including heads of families	Free white males: Of 45 and upwards including heads of families	Free white females: Under 10 years of age	Free white females: Of 10 and under 16	Free white females: Of 16 and under 26 including heads of families	Free white females: Of 26 and under 45 including heads of families	Free white females: Of 45 and upwards including heads of families	All other free persons except Indians not taxed
WINDSOR											
Adams, Abel	..	..	4	..	1	..	..	2	..	1	..
Adams, Isaac	2	..	..	1	..	2	1	..	1	..	..
Akin, Israel	4	2	..	..	1	..	1	..	1	..	..
Andrews, Peter	..	..	..	..	..	..	..	..	..	..	4
Bailey, Joshua	..	..	2	..	1	..	1	2	..	..	..
Bailey, Joshua	2	..	..	1	..	4	1	..	1	..	..
Banister, Lazerus	3	2	1	..	1	2	1	2	1	..	..
Banister, Silas	4	1	1	..	1	2	..	3	..	1	..
Barrett, Nathan	..	..	..	1	..	1	..	..	1	..	..
Barrett, Oliver	..	..	1	..	1	3	1	1	..	1	..
Barrett, Oliver 2nd	4	1	..	1	..	1	1	1	1	..	..
Baston, Joseph	2	..	..	..	1	..	..	2	..	..	..
Beach, Elihu	2	1	..	1	..	1	..	..	1	..	..
Belding, Merey	1	..	..	..	..	..	..	..	..	1	..
Benjamin, Asher	1	..	5	1	..	1	1	1	1	..	..
Billings, Joseph	3	1	..	1	..	1	..	..	1	..	..
Bishop, Levi	2	1	1	1	2	2	1	..	..	..	..
Black, Peter	..	..	..	..	..	..	..	..	..	..	9
Blanchard, Daniel	..	..	..	1	..	4	..	..	1	..	..
Blood, Abel	..	..	..	..	1	3	..	..	2	1	..
Blood, John	3	1	..	1	..	..	..	2	1	..	..
Blood, Robert	2	..	..	1	..	..	..	..	1	..	..
Blood, Sewell	3	2	..	1	..	1	..	..	1	..	..
Bogley, Thomas	2	2	..	1	..	2	2	..	1	..	..
Bradley, William	..	..	..	1	..	..	1	..	1	..	..
Brown, Briant	..	..	2	..	..	..	1	..	..	1	..
Brown, John	..	..	..	..	1	..	..	..	..	1	..
Buck, Simeon	..	1	..	1	..	..	..	1	..	..	..
Bugbe, Daniel	1	1	1	1	1	3	..	..	1	..	..
Bugbe, Samuel	3	1	..	1	..	1	..	..	1	..	..
Burk, Solomon	2	1	3	..	1	..	..	2	..	1	..
Burnham, Ebenezer	4	2	..	1	..	..	2	1	1	..	..
Burnham, Seymour	..	..	..	1	..	2	..	1	..	..	..
Burt, David	3	..	..	1	..	3	..	..	1	..	..
Burt, Jonathan	..	..	2	..	1	..	2	1	..	1	..
Burt, Jonathan Jr.	1	..	..	1	..	..	1	1	..	..	..
Burt, Reuben	..	..	1	..	..	..	..	1	..	..	..
Cady, Benjamin	1	..	1	..	1	..	1	2	..	1	..
Cady, James	..	..	2	..	..	..	..	..	..	1	..
Cady, Manassa	2	1	..	1	..	3	2	..	1	..	..
Cady, Pearley	2	1	..	1	..	2	2	..	1	..	..
Cady, Robert	1	..	..	1	..	3	..	..	1	..	..
Cady, Stephen	..	1	..	..	1	5	2	2	..	1	..
Cady, Thomas	..	..	..	1	..	3	..	..	1	..	..
Cady, William	2	..	..	1	..	1	..	2	..	..	..
Capon, John	..	1	..	..	1	..	1	..	..	1	..
Capon, John Jr.	1	..	..	1	..	1	..	..	1	..	..
Capon, Phillip	1	..	..	1	..	3	..	..	1	..	..
Capon, Samuel	1	..	..	1	..	2	..	..	1	..	..
Carlton, Abraham	..	..	..	1	..	4	..	..	1	..	..
Chapin, Calvin	2	1	1	..	1	1	1	1	1	1	..
Choat, Jacob	..	..	1	..	..	1	..	1	..	..	..
Clark, Enan	..	..	1	..	..	..	..	1	..	..	..
Clemmons, Jesse	3	..	..	1	..	1	..	..	1	..	..
Colburn, Nathan	1	1	1	..	1	1	..	1	1	..	..
Conant, Clark	2	..	1	1	1	..	1	1	1	1	..
Conant, Stephen	1	3	7	2	..	2	1	1	2	..	..
Cooledge, Nathan	1	1	2	1	..	1	1	1	1	1	..
Craw, Jonathan	2	1	1	..	1	2	1	..	1	..	..
Cummings, Benjamin	..	1	1	1	..	1	1	1	1	..	..
Cummings, Jerath	..	1	4	..	1	1	3	2	..	1	..
Cummings, Leonard	2	..	..	1	..	..	..	..	1	..	..
Currier, Peter	..	1	..	1	..	1	2	..	1	..	..
Currier, Samuel	..	..	..	..	1	..	..	..	..	1	1
Curtis, Zebina	5	1	2	2	..	2	1	3	1	1	..
Dake, Benjamin	3	1	1	..	1	1	..	..	..	1	..
Davis, Jonathan	3	..	..	1	..	2	..	..	1	..	..
Davis, Leonard	..	..	..	1	..	1	..	1	..	..	..
Dean, Reuben	1	..	..	..	1	..	..	1	..	1	..
Dean, Willard	..	..	1	1	2	1	1	2	..	2	..
Doolittle, Edward	2	..	..	1	..	1	..	..	1	1	..
Dunahue, James	..	1	..	..	1	3	2	..	..	1	..
Eastman, Polly	..	1	..	..	..	..	..	..	1	..	..
Edmond, Abijah	2	1	1	1	..	1	..	..	1	..	..
Edward, Joseph	..	1	1	..	1	2	..	..	..	1	..
Eli, Joel	..	..	..	..	1	..	..	..	..	1	..
Emmerson, William	1	1	1	1	..	5	1	..	1	..	..
Ely, Aaron	..	..	2	..	1	1	..	2	..	1	..
Ely, Abisha	2	..	..	1	..	3	..	..	1	..	..
Ely, Joel	..	..	..	1	1	..	..	..	1	1	..
Fairbanks, Joshua	2	..	..	1	..	3	1	..	1	..	..
Farmer, John	..	..	..	1	..	..	1	..	..	1	..
Fisk, Nathan	1	1	..	1	..	4	1	..	1	..	..

WINDSOR COUNTY—Continued

NAMES OF HEADS OF FAMILIES	FREE WHITE MALES: Under 10 years of age	FREE WHITE MALES: Of 10 and under 16	FREE WHITE MALES: Of 16 and under 26 including heads of families	FREE WHITE MALES: Of 26 and under 45 including heads of families	FREE WHITE MALES: Of 45 and upwards including heads of families.	FREE WHITE FEMALES: Under 10 years of age	FREE WHITE FEMALES: Of 10 and under 16	FREE WHITE FEMALES: Of 16 and under 26 including heads of families	FREE WHITE FEMALES: Of 26 and under 45 including heads of families	FREE WHITE FEMALES: Of 45 and upwards including heads of families	All other free persons except Indians not taxed
WINDSOR—con.											
Fling, Lemuel	2	2	1	1	..	1	1	..	1	..	..
Fling, Theophilus	2	..	2	1	..	1	..	..	1	..	..
Forbes, Abner	1	..	2	1	..	..	..	3	..	..	..
Gates, Abraham	2	..	..	1	..	1	..	1	1	..	..
Gates, Amos	2	..	..	1	..	..	..	..	1	..	..
Gates, Reuben	..	..	..	1	..	1	..	1	..	..	..
Gill, John	..	1	..	..	1	..	..	1	1	..	..
Gould, Ebenezer	2	..	..	..	1	1	1	1	..	1	..
Gould, Peggy	..	1	..	..	..	2	..	1	1	..	..
Gragg, John	2	2	..	..	1	3	1	1	..	1	..
Grandy, Robert	..	..	..	..	1	..	..	..	..	1	..
Green, Benjamin	..	..	..	..	1	..	1	1	..	1	..
Green, Isaac	1	2	..	1	..	3	1	2	1	..	..
Green, Josiah	..	..	1	..	..	..	..	1	..	..	..
Hale, Abigail	2	..	..	..	..	..	2	..	1	..	..
Hale, Benjamin	3	1	1	1	..	1	..	1	2	..	1
Hale, David	1	1	2	..	1	..	1	1	..	1	..
Hale, Nathan	1	..	1	1	..	1	..	..	2	..	..
Hale, Silas	1	..	..	1	..	1	2	..	..	..	..
Hall, Bela	..	..	2	1	..	1	1	..	1	..	..
Hall, Jonathan	1	..	1	1	..	2	1	..	1	..	..
Hammond, Jabez	1	..	..	1	..	2	..	1	1	..	..
Hastings, Stephen	3	..	..	1	..	2	..	..	1	..	..
Hawley, Josiah	1	1	1	..	1	1	1	1	..	1	..
Hayes, Allen	..	2	2	1	..	1	1	1	..	..	..
Hedge, Samuel	5	..	2	1	..	1	1	..	1	..	..
Hedge, Solomon	..	..	2	..	1	1	1	1	..	1	..
Hemmingway, Phinehas	1	..	2	..	1	..	..	1	..	1	..
Herrick, Henry	1	..	..	1	..	2	..	..	1	..	..
Hewlet, Thomas	..	..	..	1	..	1	..	..	1	..	..
Hinkley, Jerod	1	1	..	1	..	1	..	..	1	..	..
Hoadley, Thomas	3	..	..	1	..	3	..	..	1	..	..
Hoit, John	..	..	1	1	..	2	..	1	1	..	..
Holden, Eli	..	..	1	..	..	..	..	1	..	..	..
Holden, Jesse	..	..	1	..	..	1	..	1	..	..	..
Horsington, Aaron	..	..	..	1	..	2	..	..	1	1	..
Horsington, Abisha	..	1	..	1	..	4	1	..	1	..	..
Horsington, Elias	3	2	1	1	..	1	..	..	1	..	..
Horsington, Orange	1	..	..	1	..	1	..	1	1	..	..
Horton, Zenas	..	..	..	1	..	..	..	..	1	..	..
Hosmer, John	1	1	..	..	1	1	1	1	1	..	..
Hosmer, Reuben	..	..	1	..	..	2	..	1	..	..	..
Hosmer, Reuben	1	..	..	1	..	1	..	..	1	..	..
Houghton, Darias	2	1	2	..	4	..	..	1	1	..	..
Hubbard, Eldad	1	1	..	1	2	1	1	..	1	1	..
Hubbard, Elnathan	..	1	..	..	1	..	..	..	1	1	..
Hubbard, Jonathan H.	..	..	1	1	..	..	1	1	..	..	1
Hubbard, Luther	1	..	..	1	..	..	..	..	1	..	..
Hubbard, Watts	2	1	1	..	1	2	1	1	..	1	..
Hudson, Abijah	1	..	..	1	..	1	..	..	1	..	..
Hunter, Jabez	3	..	..	1	..	..	..	..	1	..	..
Hunter, Thomas	2	1	..	1	1	..	1	1	1	..	..
Hunter, William	1	1	..	..	1	2	2	..	..	1	..
Hurd, Abijah	2	..	1	..	1	..	3	2	..	1	..
Jacob, Stephen	..	..	1	3	..	1	..	2	2	..	2
Jewett, Jesse	1	..	1	..	..	..	..	1	..	..	..
Johonnet, William	..	1	1	1	..	..	..	..	1	..	..
Jones, Perez	1	..	1	1	..	2	1	..	2	..	1
Keath, Asahel	2	..	..	1	..	2	..	..	1	..	..
Kelly, Edward	1	..	..	1	..	..	..	..	1	..	..
Kendall, Amos	..	..	..	..	1	..	..	..	..	1	..
Kendall, Reuben	..	2	1	..	1	..	..	1	..	1	..
Kendall, Reuben Jr.	2	..	..	1	..	2	1	..	1	..	..
Langdon, Ebenezer	..	..	1	..	1	..	..	1	..	1	..
Langdon, Ebenezer Jr.	..	..	2	..	..	..	..	1	..	..	..
Langdon, Gad	1	..	..	1	..	..	..	..	1	..	..
Langdon, Jeremiah	..	..	..	1	..	..	1	..	1	..	..
Langworthy, James	3	3	3	..	1	3	1	3	..	1	..
Langworthy, Stephen	1	..	1	..	..	..	..	1	..	..	..
Leavens, Penuel	..	..	1	..	..	..	..	1	..	..	..
Leavens, Rufus	..	..	..	1	..	1	..	..	1	..	..
Leonard, Nathaniel	3	..	..	2	..	1	1	1	2	1	..
Leveritt, John	2	1	..	2	..	2	1	1	..	..	..
Leveritt, Thomas	3	..	..	1	..	1	..	1	1	..	..
Leveritt, William	..	1	..	1	..	2	..	..	2	1	1
Lovejoy, Samuel	..	1	..	1	..	1	..	..	1	..	..
Lull, Jacob	1	..	..	1	..	..	..	1	..	..	..
Lull, Joel	1	1	..	1	..	1	..	..	1	..	..
Lumbard, David	3	2	1	1	..	..	..	..	1	..	..
Lumbard, John	3	1	..	1	2	1	1	..	..	2	..
Lumbard, Solomon	..	..	1	..	1	5	1	..	1	1	..
WINDSOR—con.											
Magrah, Edward	..	..	1	..	..	..	..	1	..	..	..
Marey, Alvin	1	..	..	1	..	1	1	1	1	..	..
Marey, Jonathan	1	2	..	..	1	..	..	1	..	1	..
Marey, Joseph	1	..	1	1	..	..	..	..	1	..	..
Marey, Samuel	2	..	..	1	..	1	..	..	1	..	..
Marey, Stephen	1	..	..	1	..	2	..	..	1	..	..
McAllaster, Reuben	1	..	..	1	..	3	2	1	1	..	..
Meacham, Elisha	..	1	..	1	..	..	1	..	1	..	..
Mills, Nathan	1	..	1	1	..	1	..	1	..	..	..
Moore, Asa	..	..	1	..	..	..	..	1	..	..	..
Moore, John	2	1	1	..	1	..	2	1	..	1	..
Morrison, David	2	1	..	1	..	2	2	..	1	..	..
Morrison, Robert	..	2	..	..	1	..	..	3	..	1	..
Newman, Jonathan	1	..	..	1	..	3	..	..	1	..	..
Nichols, Josiah	1	..	..	..	1	2	..	..	1	..	..
Orvis, David	1	2	..	..	1	..	1	1	..	1	..
Paine, Amasa	1	..	4	1	..	2	..	1	3	..	..
Parker, Henry	2	..	..	1	..	..	..	2	..	1	..
Parker, Joseph	2	1	..	1	..	3	2	..	1	..	..
Parker, Nehemiah	..	..	..	1	..	1	..	1	..	..	..
Parker, Stephen	2	..	..	1	..	..	..	..	1	..	..
Parmale, Ambrose	..	..	..	2	..	..	..	..	1	..	..
Parmeter, Jesse	4	..	..	1	..	..	1	..	..	..	..
Parmeter, Joseph	..	1	1	..	1	..	1	1	..	1	..
Partrick, Benoni	5	1	..	..	1	1	1	2	..	1	..
Partrick, Matthew	2	1	..	1	1	3	1	..	1	1	..
Partrick, Samuel	1	..	2	2	2	2	2	1	1	..	1
Patterson, William	..	1	..	..	1	..	..	..	1	..	..
Persons, Ezekiel	2	..	2	1	..	3	..	..	2	..	..
Persons, Joseph	2	..	1	..	1	2	2	..	1	..	..
Persons, Samuel	..	..	..	..	1	..	..	..	..	1	..
Persons, William	..	..	..	..	1	..	..	..	..	1	..
Persons, William Jr.	3	1	1	1	..	..	1	..	1	..	..
Pike, Ebenezer	2	1	..	1	..	1	..	..	1	..	..
Pope, Simeon	2	1	1	..	1	2	2	..	..	1	..
Porter, David	1	..	..	1	..	1	1	1	1	1	..
Porter, William	2	2	1	..	1	2	1	1	..	1	..
Prescott, Nathan	1	..	..	1	..	2	..	..	1	..	..
Proctor, Israel	1	..	2	..	..	..	..	2	..	..	..
Putnam, Jonathan	1	..	1	..	1	..	2	..	..	1	..
Reed, Jonathan	2	..	..	..	1	..	1	1	..	1	..
Robinson, Silas	3	1	..	1	..	1	..	1	1	..	..
Root, Rufus	..	1	..	1	..	1	1	..	1	..	..
Root, Samuel	..	1	1	..	1	..	..	..	1	..	..
Rowe, John	1	1	2	..	1	2	2	..	..	1	..
Rowe, Joseph	2	..	1	1	..	1	..	1	1	..	..
Rowe, Thomas	2	..	..	1	..	..	..	..	1	..	..
Ruggles, Samuel	..	..	1	..	1	..	..	3	..	1	..
Rumrill, Henry	..	..	..	1	..	..	..	..	..	1	..
Rumrill, Luther	..	..	1	..	..	..	..	1	..	..	..
Rumrill, Simeon	1	..	..	..	1	..	..	..	1	..	..
Russell, Asa	..	1	..	..	1	2	1	1	1	..	..
Russell, Asa	..	1	1	1	..	1	2	1	1	..	..
Russell, Daniel	5	..	..	1	..	..	..	..	1	..	..
Russell, John	4	2	..	1	..	..	1	..	1	..	..
Russell, Reuben	1	..	1	..	1	3	2	..	..	1	..
Russell, Samuel	1	..	1	..	..	2	..	1	..	..	..
Sabin, Seth	..	1	2	..	1	1	..	..	..	1	..
Savage, Cypron	..	..	1	..	..	..	1	..	1	..	..
Savage, Elias	2	1	..	1	..	1	1	..	1	..	..
Savage, Nathan	..	1	..	..	1	..	2	..	1	..	..
Savage, Nathan	..	1	..	..	1	1	1	..	..	1	..
Savage, Samuel	..	1	1	..	1	..	2	..	..	1	..
Savage, Stephen	..	..	3	1	..	3	..	1	1	..	..
Sawing, Jerum	..	..	..	1	..	..	..	..	1	..	..
Sawing, Munning	4	..	..	1	..	1	1	..	1	..	..
Sawing, Samuel	..	..	1	..	..	..	..	1	..	..	..
Sawing, Samuel	..	..	1	..	1	..	..	1	..	1	..
Sergeant, Moses	1	..	1	..	1	1	1	..	1	..	..
Severance, Ebenezer	2	..	..	1	..	2	..	..	1	..	..
Shaw, Stephen	2	2	..	1	..	4	..	..	1	..	..
Shead, Samuel	1	..	2	..	..	1	..	..	1	..	..
Shelden, Daniel	1	1	..	2	..	..	..	..	1	..	..
Shuttleworth, Samuel	1	..	2	..	1	..	..	1	..	1	1
Slack, Jesse	3	1	1	1	..	1	2	..	1	..	..
Slaughton, Thomas	1	1	1	..	..	..	..	1	..	..	..
Smeed, Asa	1	1	..	..	1	..	..	2	..	1	..
Smeed, Elihu	..	..	..	..	1	..	..	1	1	..	..
Smeed, Joel	..	..	..	..	1	..	..	1	1	..	..
Smeed, John	..	1	2	..	1	1	..	2	..	1	..
Smeed, John 3rd	1	..	..	1	..	1	..	..	1	..	..
Smeed, Zacherich	..	1	..	1	..	..	..	1	..	..	..

WINDSOR COUNTY—Continued

NAMES OF HEADS OF FAMILIES	FREE WHITE MALES: Under 10 years of age	FREE WHITE MALES: Of 10 and under 16	FREE WHITE MALES: Of 16 and under 26 including heads of families	FREE WHITE MALES: Of 26 and under 45 including heads of families	FREE WHITE MALES: Of 45 and upwards including heads of families.	FREE WHITE FEMALES: Under 10 years of age	FREE WHITE FEMALES: Of 10 and under 16	FREE WHITE FEMALES: Of 16 and under 26 including heads of families	FREE WHITE FEMALES: Of 26 and under 45 including heads of families	FREE WHITE FEMALES: Of 45 and upwards including heads of families	All other free persons except Indians not taxed
WINDSOR—con.											
Smith, Asahel	2	1	..	1	..	1	1	1	1	..	..
Smith, Edward	..	..	..	..	1	..	..	..	..	1	..
Smith, Elijah	1	..	..	1	..	3	..	..	1	..	..
Smith, Hart	..	..	1	1	..	1	..	2	1	..	..
Smith, John	2	..	1	1	..	1	..	..	1	..	..
Smith, Reuben	..	..	..	1	..	..	..	2	1	1	..
Smith, Samuel	1	..	1	1	..	2	..	1	1	..	..
Smith, Samuel	2	..	..	1	..	3	..	1	1	..	..
Smith, Steel	..	..	1	..	1	..	..	1	..	1	..
Spafford, John	1	..	..	1	..	4	..	1	1	..	..
Spaulding, Andrew	1	2	..	1	1	1	1	..	1	..	..
Spear, Elijah	1	..	..	1	..	..	..	..	1	..	..
Spooner, Alden	..	1	3	1	..	3	3	..	1	..	1
Standley, Asahel	..	..	..	1	..	..	..	1	..	..	..
Stearns, Abijah	1	..	..	1	..	1	..	..	1	..	..
Stearns, Thomas	..	..	..	1	..	2	..	1	1	..	..
Steel, James	2	2	..	1	..	4	..	..	1	..	..
Stocking, Joseph	..	..	1	1	..	1	..	1	1	..	..
Stoel, Jacob	..	..	..	..	1	..	1	..	..	1	..
Stoel, Jacob Jr.	3	..	..	1	..	..	..	..	1	..	..
Stoel, Joel	2	..	..	1	..	3	..	..	1	..	..
Stone, Caleb	..	1	1	..	2	..	..	2	..	..	..
Stone, Ephraim	..	..	1	..	1	..	2	1	..	1	..
Stone, Samuel	1	1	2	1	1	4	2	1	1	1	..
Story, Zachariah	..	2	2	..	1	1	1	2	..	1	..
Stow, Caleb	1	..	..	1	..	1	..	..	1	..	..
Stow, George	..	..	1	..	1	..	..	2	..	1	..
Stow, George	3	1	..	1	..	1	..	..	1	..	..
Stow, Samuel	1	..	2	1	..	1	..	1	..	..	..
Stricklin, Samuel	1	..	1	..	..	1	..	1	..	..	..
Swallow, Nahum	1	..	1	1	..	2	..	..	1	..	..
Swindleton, Abigail	..	..	..	..	..	..	2	1	1	..	..
Tabor, Joseph	..	..	..	1	..	3	..	..	1	..	..
Taylor, Abigail	..	..	..	..	..	..	..	2	..	1	..
Taylor, Abraham	2	2	1	1	..	3	..	..	1	..	..
Taylor, Leonard	1	1	..	1	..	2	1	1	1	..	..
Taylor, Simeon	2	1	1	..	1	2	1	..	1	..	..
Temple, Nicanor	1	..	..	1	..	2	..	1	..	1	..
Thomson, Hezekiah Jr.	..	2	..	..	1	..	..	1	..	1	..
Thomson, Joseph	2	..	..	1	..	1	1	2	1	..	..
Tinkham, Amos	4	3	..	1	..	1	1	1	1	..	..
Tinkham, Seth	1	1	1	1	..	3	1	1	..	1	..
Tooley, Josiah	3	2	..	..	1	2	..	1	1	..	..
Towns, Benjamin	2	..	..	1	..	..	..	..	1	..	..
Towns, Edward	1	..	..	1	1	2	..	1	1	..	..
Towns, Stephen	..	..	1	..	..	1	..	1	..	..	..
Townshend, Asa	1	..	1	..	..	1	..	1	1	..	..
Trask, Nahum	..	..	1	1	..	2	..	2	1	..	..
Trowbridge, Daniel	1	..	..	1	..	2	..	..	1	..	..
Trussell, Benjamin	..	..	..	1	..	2	..	..	1	2	..
Trussell, Isaac	..	..	1	..	..	..	..	1	..	..	..
Tuttle, Isaac	1	1	..	1	..	1	..	..	1	..	..
Verney, Ebenezer	..	..	..	1	..	1	..	..	1	..	..
Wait, Joseph	3	..	..	3	..	..	..	..	1	..	..
Wait, Marshal	1	..	1	1	..	1	..	..	1	..	..
Wait, Richard	..	1	2	..	2	1	1	1	..	2	..
Wakfield, Joseph	2	1	1	..	1	1	2	..	..	1	..
Wardner, Jacob	3	..	1	..	1	3	..	..	..	1	..
Waters, Alexander	1	..	..	1	..	1	..	..	1	..	..
Waters, Sylvanus	..	1	2	2	..	1	..	1	1	1	..
Wells, Thomas	2	..	..	1	..	2	2	1	1	..	..
West, Gershom	1	..	2	..	1	1	1	1	..	..	..
Wheelor, Josiah	3	..	..	1	..	1	..	..	1	..	..
Whitcomb, Scoter	4	..	..	1	..	1	1	..	1	..	..
Whitcomb, Scotway	..	..	..	..	1	..	..	..	..	1	..
Whitcomb, Zenas	2	1	..	1	..	1	..	..	1	..	..
White, Archebald	..	..	1	..	1	2	2	1	1	..	..
White, Samuel	2	..	..	2	..	1	..	..	1	..	..
White, William	1	2	..	..	1	1	2	..	1	..	..
Whittier, David	3	..	1	1	..	2	1	..	1	..	..
Whitney, Joseph	1	..	..	1	..	3	..	..	1	..	..
Wilk, Benoni	..	..	1	..	..	..	..	1	1	..	..
Wilkins, Uriah	1	1	2	..	1	..	1	..	..	1	..
Willard, Ed	1	1	1	1	..	1	..	3	1	..	..
Willard, Oliver	2	2	..	1	..	2	1	..	1	..	..
Willis, Jonathan	3	..	..	1	..	2	2	..	1	..	..
Willis, Joseph	1	2	..	1	..	3	..	1	..	..	..
Williston, Caleb	1	..	..	1	..	1	..	..	1	..	..
Wilson, Ammi	..	2	1	..	1	..	..	1	1	..	..
Wilson, Joshua	2	1	..	..	1	..	..	..	..	..	..
Wilson, Samuel	2	..	..	1	..	2	..	..	1	..	..
Wilson, Thomas	1	1	2	..	1	..	..	..	2	1	..
Wilson, William	1	1	..	..	1	2	..	..	1	1	..
Wood, Daniel	4	..	..	1	1	..	2	2	1	1	..
Woodruff, David	1	..	1	1	..	3	..	..	1	..	..
Woodruff, Joseph	1	..	2	..	1	4	..	3	..	1	..
Woodworth, Roger	..	1	..	..	1	2	..	..	1	..	..
Worcester, Asa	..	..	1	..	1	..	..	..	..	1	..
Worcester, Asa Jr.	1	..	..	1	..	1	..	..	1	..	..
Worcester, Elijah	..	..	..	1	..	1	..	..	1	..	..
Wyman, Samuel	1	..	..	1	..	2	..	..	1	..	..
WOODSTOCK											
Adams, Jacob	1	1	1	1	1	2	1	1	..	1	..
Allen, Benjamin	1	..	..	1	..	2	..	1	..	..	..
Allen, Ephraim Jr.	1	..	..	1	..	..	..	1	..	..	..
Allen, Francis	1	..	1	..	..	..	..	1	..	..	..
Alvord, Stephen	..	1	..	1	1	2	..	3	1	1	..
Atwood, Rebeka	..	..	..	..	..	..	1	..	..	1	..
Backer, Thomas	1	..	..	1	..	1	..	1	..	..	..
Barnett, Moses	2	1	1	1	..	2	1	..	1	..	..
Barns, Joseph	1	..	..	1	..	..	..	1	..	..	..
Barritt, Joseph	2	2	1	..	1	2	..	1	..	1	..
Barrows, Samuel	1	..	..	..	1	1	..	..	1	1	..
Bayley, David	2	..	2	..	1	1	1	1	..	1	..
Bayley, Elijah	1	..	..	..	1	..	..	2	..	1	..
Bayley, Elijah Jr.	..	..	..	1	..	..	..	1	..	..	..
Bayley, Elijah 2nd	2	..	..	1	..	..	..	1	..	..	..
Bayliss, Nicholas	1	..	..	1	..	..	..	1	..	..	..
Benjamin, Jonas	1	3	..	1	..	4	..	..	1	..	..
Benjamin, Jonathan	..	1	2	1	..	3	2	..	1	..	..
Bennett, Arthur	1	2	..	1	..	1	..	..	1	..	..
Bennett, Jabez	2	1	..	..	1	1	1	1	..	1	..
Bennett, Joseph	2	1	4	1	..	..	..	1	1	..	..
Bennett, Samuel	..	..	..	1	..	..	..	..	1	..	..
Bennett, Terah	2	..	1	1	..	1	..	..	1	..	..
Bennett, William	2	..	1	1	..	2	..	..	1	..	..
Besse, Anthony	..	2	1	..	2	..	..	1	..	2	..
Besse, Moses	..	1	..	..	1	..	..	2	..	..	..
Besse, Nehemiah	..	1	1	..	1	2	1	1	1	..	..
Bibbins, Jacob	..	1	..	..	1	..	..	..	..	1	..
Bishop, Isaac	1	..	..	1	..	..	..	1	..	..	..
Blossom, Ebenezer	..	1	2	..	1	..	1	1	..	1	..
Blossom, Joseph	..	..	1	..	..	1	..	1	..	..	..
Bradley, Moses	4	..	..	1	..	1	..	..	1	..	..
Brewster, Ephraim	..	..	..	..	1	..	..	1	..	1	..
Brewster, Seth	..	..	..	1	..	..	..	1	..	..	..
Briant, Solomon	..	..	1	..	..	2	..	1	..	..	..
Briggs, Samuel	1	1	..	..	1	..	1	..	1	..	..
Brown, Thomas	2	..	1	1	..	..	..	1	..	1	..
Bugbee, Abel	1	..	2		1	1	1	1	..	1	..
Bugbee, Reuben	..	..	1	..	..	..	..	1	..	..	..
Bugbee, Walter	1	1	..	1	..	1	..	..	1	..	..
Burk, Ebed	1	1	..	1	..	3	..	..	1	..	..
Burtch, Benjamin	1	..	1	..	1	3	1	..	..	1	..
Call, John M.	3	2	..	1		..	..	..	..	1	..
Carpenter, Rufus	..	1	..	..	1	..	1	..	..	1	..
Castle, Jedediah	..	..	..	..	1	1	1	..	1	..	..
Chandler, Zebulon	1	..	..	1	..	1	1	1	1	..	..
Church, Edward	..	2	1	..	1	..	1	..	1	..	..
Churchell, Ichabod	2	1	1	..	1	..	..	4	..	..	..
Churchell, Joseph	1	1	2	2	1	1	..	1	1	1	..
Clark, Josiah	2	2	1	..	1	..	1	..	..	1	..
Cleaveland, Edward	2	..	1	..	1	..	1	..	..	1	..
Cobb, Elias	4	..	..	1	..	2	..	..	1	..	..
Cobb, Ephraim	1	..	1	..	..	1	..	1	..	..	..
Cobb, Gershum	..	..	..	1	..	2	..	..	1	..	..
Cobb, James	..	1	1	..	1	..	..	2	..	1	..
Cobb, Patien	3	..	..	..	..	2	..	..	1	..	..
Cobb, Prince	..	..	1	1	..	3	2	..	1	..	..
Cobb, Solomon	..	..	..	1	..	2	..	..	1	..	..
Cobb, Thomas	..	..	1	..	1	..	..	1	..	1	..
Cone, Oliver	2	..	..	1	..	2	1	..	1	..	..
Cook, Nathan	..	..	1	..	1	..	..	..	..	1	..
Cottle, Jabez	..	2	1	..	1	..	1	2	..	1	..
Cottle, John	1	..	..	1	..	1	2	3	1	..	..
Covel, James	4	2	1	1	..	1	..	..	1	1	..
Cox, Daniel	4	1	..	1	..	2	..	..	1	..	..
Cox, John	1	..	..	1	..	1	..	..	1	..	..
Cox, Timothy	2	..	2	1	..	3	2	..	1	..	..
Crooker, Jonathan	..	1	..	..	1	..	1	..	..	1	..
Crooker, Jonathan Jr.	1	..	..	1	..	1	..	..	1	..	..
Crooker, Noah	2	1	..	1	..	3	..	..	1	..	..
Damon, Samuel	1	1	2	1	..	3	2	2	1	2	..
Darbs, Elmer	2	..	..	1	..	..	..	1	..	..	..
Darbs, Shadrack	..	..	1	1	..	..	..	1	..	..	..
Darling, John	1	2	1	1	..	..	1	1	1	..	..

WINDSOR COUNTY—Continued

WOODSTOCK—con.

NAMES OF HEADS OF FAMILIES	FREE WHITE MALES: Under 10 years of age	FREE WHITE MALES: Of 10 and under 16	FREE WHITE MALES: Of 16 and under 26 including heads of families	FREE WHITE MALES: Of 26 and under 45 including heads of families	FREE WHITE MALES: Of 45 and upwards including heads of families	FREE WHITE FEMALES: Under 10 years of age	FREE WHITE FEMALES: Of 10 and under 16	FREE WHITE FEMALES: Of 16 and under 26 including heads of families	FREE WHITE FEMALES: Of 26 and under 45 including heads of families	FREE WHITE FEMALES: Of 45 and upwards including heads of families	All other free persons except Indians not taxed
Darling, Joseph	..	..	1	1	1	..	..	2	..	1	..
Darling, Joseph	1	1	..	1	..	5	..	..	1	..	..
Darling, Seth	3	1	..	1	..	1	1	..	1	..	..
Davis, Sampson	..	1	..	1	..	1	..	1	1	..	..
Davis, Simon	..	..	..	..	1	..	..	..	..	1	..
Day, Deborah	..	..	1	..	..	2	..	..	1	..	..
Deen, Stephen	2	1	..	1	..	1	1	..	1	..	..
Dellano, Stephen	1	2	2	..	1	1	1	1	..	1	..
Dexter, Luen	3	..	..	..	1	1	2	3	1	..	..
Dike, Calvin	2	1	..	1	..	2	2	..	1	..	..
Dike, Ebenezer	2	..	1	..	1	3	2	1	1	..	..
Dike, Reuben	1	..	1	..	..	..	..	..	1	..	..
Dilleno, Amasa	1	..	..	..	1	1	1	4	..	..	..
Dilleno, James	1	..	1	1	..	2	..	1	1	..	..
Dimock, William	1	..	1	1	..	1	..	2	..	..	..
Doubleday, Ashbel	1	..	..	..	1	..	..	1	..	1	..
Drew, William	2	..	..	1	..	1	..	1	..	..	..
Dunham, Anson	1	..	..	1	..	1	..	..	1	..	..
Dunham, Josiah	1	..	1	..	1	1	1	..	..	1	..
Dunham, Simeon	..	..	1	..	1	..	1	3	..	1	..
Eddy, Isaac	..	1	1	..	..	2	..	..	1	..	..
Eddy, Mary	..	..	1	..	..	1	2	..	1	..	..
Edson, Sylvester	..	1	1	1	..	3	2	..	1	..	..
Edward, Jonathan	..	..	..	1	..	3	1	1	..	..	..
Ellis, Charles	..	..	..	..	1	..	..	..	..	1	..
Ellis, Charles Jr.	2	..	..	1	..	1	..	..	1	..	..
Ellis, Ephraim	4	1	..	1	..	1	..	..	1	..	..
Ellis, Samuel	2	1	..	1	..	1	..	..	1	1	..
Ellis, Thomas	1	1	1	1	..	..	1	2	1	1	..
Ellis, William	2	1	..	1	..	3	1	1	1	..	..
Ellis, Zacheus	2	..	1	1	..	1	..	..	2	..	..
Emmens, Abel	2	..	..	..	1	1	..	1	..	1	..
Emmerson, James	3	1	2	..	1	2	1	1	1	1	..
Emmerson, Kendall	1	1	2	..	1	2	..	..	..	1	..
Emmerson, Kendall Jr.	..	..	1	..	..	2	..	1	..	..	..
Emmins, Benjamin	..	1	3	..	1	..	..	3	..	1	..
Emmons, Solomon	3	..	..	1	..	3	..	..	1	..	..
Estabrook, Thomas	1	1	..	1	..	3	..	..	1	..	..
Farnam, Duglass	1	..	2	..	..	..	..	1	..	..	..
Farnsworth, Abial	1	..	..	1	..	..	1	1	..	..	..
Farnsworth, Abijah	2	..	..	1	..	1	..	..	1	..	..
Farnsworth, Jonathan	2	..	1	..	1	2	1	1	1	..	..
Farnsworth, Stephen	3	1	..	1	..	1	2	1	..	1	..
Field, Elijah	4	2	1	1	..	..	1	2	1	..	..
Field, Hezekiah	..	..	..	..	1	..	..	..	..	1	..
Fitch, Ebenezer	1	2	1	2	..	1	1	..	1	..	..
Fletcher, Nathan	2	..	2	2	1	..	..	1	..	1	..
Fowl, Nathaniel	..	..	..	1	..	1	1	..	1	..	..
French, Gideon	..	..	1	..	1	..	..	..	..	1	..
Fuller, Consider	..	2	1	..	1	2	1	1	1	..	..
Fuller, Samuel	2	..	..	1	..	..	1	..	1	..	..
Fuller, William	..	..	2	..	1	..	..	1	..	..	..
Gallup, Joseph A.	1	..	..	1	..	1	1	..	1	..	..
Gilbert, Jacob	2	1	1	..	1	1	2	..	1	..	..
Green, Backos	1	..	1	..	1	..	2	..	..	1	..
Hackett, Zebede	2	1	..	1	..	2	1	..	1	..	..
Hammond, John	..	..	..	..	1	5	2	2	1	..	..
Hammond, Nathaniel	4	2	..	1	..	1	..	..	..	1	..
Handy, Barnard	3	..	1	1	..	..	..	1	1	..	..
Harlow, Elijah	1	..	2	1	..	2	..	..	1	1	..
Harlow, Lemuel	1	..	..	..	1	1	..	1	..	1	..
Harvey, Edmund	1	1	1	..	1	3	..	1	..	1	..
Harwood, James	..	..	..	..	1	..	1	..	..	1	..
Hayes, John	1	1	1	..	1	..	1	..	..	1	..
Hendrick, Francis	1	..	..	1	..	1	..	..	1	..	..
Hendrick, Hadley	2	1	1	1	..	1	1	1	1	1	..
Hill, Robert	2	..	..	1	..	3	2	..	1	..	..
Hoisington, Asahel	..	..	1	..	1	..	..	..	..	1	..
Hoisington, Ozaias	..	..	1	1	..	1	..	2	..	..	..
Holt, Jacob	1	1	1	1	..	1	..	1	1	..	..
Holt, Jonathan	..	..	1	..	..	..	..	1	..	..	..
Holt, Uriah	..	..	..	..	1	..	..	..	..	1	..
Hoten, Plutark	1	..	..	1	..	1	..	..	1	..	..
Houghton, Israel	1	..	..	..	1	..	1	..	..	1	..
Howland, Benjamin	1	..	..	1	..	..	2	..	1	..	..
Howland, Nathan	..	..	..	..	1	..	..	..	..	1	..
Howland, Seth	2	..	..	1	..	3	..	..	1	..	..
Hurlbut, John	..	..	1	..	1	..	1	1	..	1	..
Kendall, Abraham	1	2	..	..	1	1	1	..	..	..	..
Kendall, David	..	..	..	1	..	1	1	..	..	1	..
Kendall, Isaac	1	1	1	1	1	1	1	..	1	..	..
King, Jabez	..	..	..	..	1	..	..	..	..	1	..

WOODSTOCK—con.

NAMES OF HEADS OF FAMILIES	FREE WHITE MALES: Under 10 years of age	FREE WHITE MALES: Of 10 and under 16	FREE WHITE MALES: Of 16 and under 26 including heads of families	FREE WHITE MALES: Of 26 and under 45 including heads of families	FREE WHITE MALES: Of 45 and upwards including heads of families	FREE WHITE FEMALES: Under 10 years of age	FREE WHITE FEMALES: Of 10 and under 16	FREE WHITE FEMALES: Of 16 and under 26 including heads of families	FREE WHITE FEMALES: Of 26 and under 45 including heads of families	FREE WHITE FEMALES: Of 45 and upwards including heads of families	All other free persons except Indians not taxed
King, Jabez Jr.	3	..	..	1	..	2	..	1	1	..	..
Kingsbury, Billa G.	1	..	1	..	..	1	..	1	..	..	..
Kingsbury, Jonathan	1	1	1	..	1	..	..	2	..	1	..
Knox, Timothy	1	..	..	..	1	1	1	1	..	1	..
Ladd, Nathaniel	..	2	1	..	1	3	..	1	..	1	..
Lake, George	..	2	1	..	1	1	..	2	..	1	..
Lamb, Josiah	1	..	1	1	..	..	..	1	..	..	..
Lamphere, Luke	3	2	1	1	..	1	1	..	1	..	..
Logan, Joseph	3	..	..	1	..	1	..	1	..	..	..
Lord, Elisha	2	..	..	1	..	2	2	..	1	..	..
Lord, William M.	1	..	2	1	..	3	..	1	..	..	..
Lucas, Consider	2	..	..	1	..	3	..	..	1	..	..
Mack, Benjamin	..	..	2	1	..	3	3	1	..	..	..
Mack, John	1	..	..	1	..	..	..	..	1	..	..
Maner, Henry	..	1	3	1	..	1	..	1	..	..	..
Marsh, Charles	2	1	..	1	..	2	1	1	1	..	..
Marsh, Daniel	1	..	..	1	..	3	3	..	1	..	..
Marsh, Nehemiah	..	..	..	2	1	..	..	..	1	1	..
Marsh, Royal	2	..	..	1	..	2	2	..	1	..	..
Martin, Duty	1	1	..	1	..	2	..	..	1	..	..
Mash, David	2	1	..	1	..	..	1	..	1	..	..
Matthews, Ethu	2	1	..	1	..	..	1	..	1	..	..
Matthews, Jonas	..	1	1	..	1	..	1	..	1	..	..
Mayo, Judah	1	..	1	..	1	1	..	1	1	1	..
McCally, William	2	..	1	..	1	1	2	1	1	..	..
McKinzey, John	..	..	1	1	..	1	..	..	1	..	..
Meacham, Eleazer	..	..	..	..	1	..	..	1	..	1	..
Meacham, Frederick	..	1	..	1	..	..	1	..	2	..	..
Miller, Caleb	..	..	1	1	..	..	..	1	..	..	..
Mills, John	2	..	..	1	..	2	..	1	1	..	..
Morton, Sylvanus	..	..	2	..	1	..	..	2	..	1	..
Murdock, James	..	..	..	..	1	..	..	..	..	1	..
Murdock, Lemuel	2	1	..	1	..	4	1	..	1	..	..
Muxam, Gideon	4	..	..	1	..	1	..	..	1	..	..
Nichols, James	..	..	1	..	1	..	..	2	..	1	..
Niles, Daniel	..	1	..	..	1	..	..	..	..	2	..
Paddock, Appollas	2	..	..	1	..	..	..	..	1	..	..
Paddock, Gaius	1	..	..	1	..	3	2	..	1	..	..
Paddock, Stephen	3	..	1	1	..	..	..	..	1	1	..
Palmer, Ezekiel	2	1	1	1	..	1	2	1	..	1	..
Palmer, Gershum	1	..	2	..	1	..	1	..	..	1	..
Parker, Eleazer	1	1	..	..	1	4	1	2	..	1	..
Parker, Hincher	..	1	1	..	1	1	1	..	..	..	..
Parker, Jonathan	2	..	1	..	..	..	..	1	..	..	..
Pease, Luther	2	..	..	1	..	1	..	1	..	..	..
Peck, Samuel	3	..	..	1	..	..	..	..	1	..	..
Perkins, Daniel	1	2	1	1	..	3	1	..	1	..	..
Perkins, Elisha	1	1	..	1	..	..	1	..	1	..	..
Perkins, Nathan	1	1	..	1	..	3	1	1	1	..	..
Perkins, William	..	1	..	..	1	..	..	..	..	1	..
Perkins, William	1	1	1	..	1	4	..	..	1	..	..
Perry, Daniel	..	..	..	..	1	..	1	1	..	1	..
Perry, Ezra	3	2	..	1	..	2	..	..	1	..	..
Perry, Hicks G.	..	..	..	1	..	2	..	1	..	..	..
Perry, Joseph	3	..	1	1	..	1	..	..	2	..	..
Phelps, Winslow	..	1	1	..	1	1	1	..	..	1	..
Phillips, Shadrack	1	..	1	..	..	1	..	1	..	..	..
Pollard, John	2	..	..	1	..	3	..	1	1	..	..
Powers, Amasa	2	2	1	..	1	2	..	1	1	..	..
Powers, Andrew	..	..	..	..	1	..	..	..	..	1	..
Powers, John	1	1	..	1	..	..	..	1	..	..	..
Powers, Stephen	1	..	..	1	..	..	..	..	1	..	..
Powers, Stephen Jr.	6	..	..	1	..	..	..	..	1	..	..
Pratt, Joseph	1	1	2	..	1	2	..	1	..	1	..
Pratt, Silas	4	..	..	1	..	1	2	1	1	..	..
Prior, Clothin	..	..	..	..	1	..	..	1	..	1	..
Prior, Jeremiah	..	..	1	..	..	1	..	1	..	..	..
Ralph, Daniel	..	1	2	..	1	1	..	3	..	1	..
Ralph, Phinehas	..	..	..	1	..	4	..	1	..	..	..
Randall, Aaron	1	..	..	1	..	3	..	..	1	..	..
Randall, James	1	..	1	..	..	..	..	1	..	..	..
Randall, Mica	..	..	..	..	1	..	..	..	..	1	..
Randall, Nathaniel	2	..	2	..	1	1	..	..	..	1	..
Ransom, Amasa	..	..	..	1	..	4	..	1	..	..	..
Ransom, Elisha	..	1	..	..	1	..	..	1	1	1	..
Ransom, Elisha	2	..	..	1	..	1	..	1	1	..	..
Ransom, John	1	1	..	1	..	..	1	..	1	..	..
Ransom, Lynd	1	..	..	1	..	2	1	..	1	..	..
Ransom, Richard	..	..	2	..	1	..	..	..	..	1	..
Ransom, Richard Jr.	3	..	1	1	..	..	..	1	1	..	..
Raymond, George	1	..	..	1	..	1	..	1	..	..	..
Raymond, James	3	..	..	1	..	1	1	..	1	..	..

WINDSOR COUNTY—Continued

NAMES OF HEADS OF FAMILIES	FREE WHITE MALES					FREE WHITE FEMALES					All other free persons except Indians not taxed
	Under 10 years of age	Of 10 and under 16	Of 16 and under 26 including heads of families	Of 26 and under 45 including heads of families	Of 45 and upwards including heads of families.	Under 10 years of age	Of 10 and under 16	Of 16 and under 26 including heads of families	Of 26 and under 45 including heads of families	Of 45 and upwards including heads of families	
WOODSTOCK—con.											
Raymond, John	2	1	..	1	..	5	2	..	1	..	..
Raymond, Samuel	..	..	1	..	1	..	1	2	1	..	..
Raymond, Sylvanus	..	3	..	..	1	..	1	..	1	..	..
Raymond, William	..	1	1	..	1	..	..	1	..	1	..
Rice, Elisha	2	..	3	2	..	1	1	1	..	..	..
Rice, Phillip	3	1	..	1	..	..	1	..	1	..	..
Rice, Stephen	1	..	..	1	..	3	..	1	1	..	..
Rice, William	2	..	..	1	..	2	..	..	1	..	..
Richardson, Israel	2	2	2	1	..	1	..	..	1	1	..
Richardson, Jason	2	2	..	4	..	..	2	..	1	..	..
Richardson, Lysander	2	..	..	1	..	2	2	..	1	..	..
Ripley, Joseph	1	..	..	..	1	1	1	1	..	1	..
Russ, Nathan	3	2	1	..	1	..	1	1	..	2	..
Safford, Chillis	3	..	..	1	..	2	..	..	1	..	..
Safford, Jesse	1	1	1	..	1	2	1	..	1	1	..
Sampson, George	2	..	..	1	..	2	2	..	1	..	..
Sampson, Phillemon	..	..	..	1	..	2	1	..	1	..	..
Sanders, Benjamin	..	..	1	1	..	2	..	..	1	..	..
Sanders, John	2	2	1	..	1	..	1	..	..	1	..
Sanderson, Benjamin	1	..	..	..	1	..	..	1	..	1	..
Sanderson, Beriah	3	..	..	1	..	1	..	..	1	..	..
Saul, John	1	1	..	..	1	..	1	1	..	..	..
Shaw, James	..	..	..	..	1	..	..	..	..	1	..
Shaw, Lemuel	..	..	..	1	..	..	..	..	..	..	..
Shirtlief, William	1	1	..	1	..	..	..	..	1	..	..
Simmons, Beza	1	..	1	..	..	..	..	1	..	..	..
Simmons, David	4	1	..	1	..	2	..	..	1	..	..
Simmons, George	2	..	..	..	1	..	1	..	..	1	..
Slayton, James	3	1	..	1	..	1	1	..	1	..	..
Slayton, Samuel	2	1	2	..	1	3	3	..	1	..	..
Smith, Andrew	1	1	..	..	1	..	1	..	..	1	..
Smith, Benjamin	..	2	..	..	1	2	..	..	1	..	..
Smith, Beriah	..	1	..	..	1	..	..	..	..	1	..
Smith, Elijah	..	..	1	..	..	..	..	1	..	..	..
Smith, Nathaniel	4	..	3	1	..	..	..	..	1	..	..
Smith, Richard	1	1	..	..	1	1	1	..	..	1	..
Smith, Rufus	1	..	1	..	..	..	1	1	..	..	..
Smith, William Jr.	1	..	..	1	..	4	..	..	1	..	..
Spooner, Gardner	1	1	2	..	1	1	2	..	1	2	..
Sterling, Elijah	1	..	1	..	..	..	..	1	..	..	..
Sterling, Joseph	..	..	..	..	1	1	..	..	..	1	..
Sterling, Seth	1	1	..	1	..	..	1	..	..	1	..
Strong, John	..	..	..	..	1	..	..	..	..	1	..
Sturtevant, George	2	..	..	1	..	..	..	1	..	..	..
Sturtevant, Job	4	..	1	1	..	..	1	..	1	..	..
Stutson, Nathan	1	1	..	1	..	3	1	..	1	..	..
Stutson, Winslow	1	..	..	1	..	1	1	1	..	..	..
Swan, Benjamin	..	1	1	1	..	1	..	..	1	..	..
Sylvester, Era	3	..	..	1	..	1	1	..	1	..	..
Taylor, Elisha	1	..	3	4	..	3	..	2	1	..	..
Taylor, Silas	1	..	..	1	..	..	1	..	1	..	..
WOODSTOCK—con											
Thomas, Andrew	1	1	1	1	..	2	1	..	1	1	..
Thomas, Barzilla	..	1	..	1	..	1	..	1	1	..	..
Thomas, Charles	..	..	..	..	1	..	..	..	..	1	..
Thomas, David	..	1	..	..	1	1	1	..	..	2	..
Thomas, Elias	1	3	2	..	1	2	2	1	1	1	..
Thomas, Gardner	..	..	..	1	..	1	..	1	..	..	..
Thomas, George	..	..	2	..	1	3	2	..	1	..	..
Thomas, Jonathan	1	..	..	1	..	2	1	..	1	..	..
Thomas, Nathan	..	..	..	1	..	1	..	1	..	..	..
Thomas, Noah	4	..	..	1	..	3	..	..	1	..	..
Thomas, Phinehas	..	..	1	..	1	1	1	..	..	1	..
Thompson, Elias	..	..	..	1	..	2	..	..	1	..	..
Tilden, Caleb	..	..	1	..	1	..	..	1	1	1	..
Tilson, Luther	3	..	..	1	..	1	..	..	1	..	..
Triboo, Molly	..	1	..	..	..	1	..	1	..	1	..
Tucker, Alfred	2	1	..	1	..	1	1	..	1	..	..
Turner, Adam	2	1	..	1	..	2	2	..	1	..	..
Tyler, Enos	2	..	..	1	..	1	..	..	1	..	..
Warren, Samuel	..	1	..	..	1	1	3	2	..	1	..
Washburn, Seth	1	2	..	1	..	1	..	..	..	1	..
Watkins, Nathan	..	..	..	..	1	..	2	..	..	1	..
West, Thomas	3	1	..	1	..	..	1	..	1	..	..
White, Charles	3	1	..	1	..	2	..	..	1	..	..
White, Francis	2	..	..	1	..	3	3	..	1	..	..
Wilder, Jacob	2	..	..	1	..	2	..	1	..	..	..
Willard, Silas	1	1	3	..	..	1	..	1	..	..	..
Williams, Jesse	3	1	..	..	2	1	1	..	1	1	..
Williams, Oliver	4	1	..	1	..	..	1	1	1	..	..
Williams, Phinehas	..	1	1	..	1	..	..	1	1	1	..
Williams, Roger	..	..	1	1	..	1	..	..	1	..	..
Winslow, Samuel	1	..	..	1	..	1	..	..	1	..	..
Winslow, Timothy	2	1	..	1	..	2	..	..	1	..	..
Wood, Benjamin	3	..	1	1	..	2	..	..	1	..	..
Wood, Caleb	..	2	1	..	1	1	..	1	..	1	..
Wood, Caleb	1	..	..	1	..	2	..	..	1	..	..
Wood, Eleazer	2	1	..	1	..	2	1	..	1	..	..
Wood, Ezra	2	1	1	1	..	2	..	..	1	..	..
Wood, John	1	..	..	1	..	3	..	..	1	..	..
Wood, Joseph	4	..	..	3	..	1	..	..	1	..	..
Wood, Joshua	2	1	..	1	..	2	1	..	1	..	..
Wood, Nathan	..	..	..	..	1	..	..	..	1	1	..
Wood, Nathaniel	1	1	1	..	1	..	1	1	..	1	..
Wood, Seth	2	..	..	1	..	1	..	1	..	..	..
Wood, William	1	1	2	1	..	1	..	1	1	..	..
Wood, William Jr.	2	..	1	..	..	1	..	1	..	..	..
Wyllys, William	1	1	1	..	1	..	..	2	..	1	..
UNCERTAIN NAMES											
Ninellet (?), Joseph	2	..	..	1	..	1	..	..	1	..	..
Rockwell (?), John	1	..	..	1	1	1	..	1	2	..	..

INDEX

www.ingramcontent.com/pod-product-compliance
Lightning Source LLC
Chambersburg PA
CBHW051425290326
41932CB00048B/3190

* 9 7 8 0 8 0 6 3 0 5 0 3 5 *